ENCYCLOPEDIA OF THE

ENLIGHTENMENT

Editorial Board

ENCYCLOPEDIA
OF THE
Enlightenment

ALAN CHARLES KORS

Editor in Chief

VOLUME 3
Mably–Ruysch

OXFORD
UNIVERSITY PRESS
2003

OXFORD

UNIVERSITY PRESS

Oxford   New York

Auckland   Bangkok   Buenos Aires   Cape Town   Chennai
Dar es Salaam   Delhi   Hong Kong   Istanbul   Karachi   Kolkata
Kuala Lumpur   Madrid   Melbourne   Mexico City   Mumbai   Nairobi
São Paulo   Shanghai   Singapore   Taipei   Tokyo   Toronto

Copyright © 2003 by Oxford University Press, Inc.

Published by Oxford University Press, Inc.
198 Madison Avenue, New York, New York 10016
www.oup.com

Oxford is a registered trademark of Oxford University Press

Library of Congress Cataloging-in-Publication Data

Encyclopedia of the Enlightenment / Alan Charles Kors, editor in chief.
v. cm.
Includes bibliographical references and index.
Contents: v. 1. Abbadie–Enlightenment Studies—v. 2. Enthusiasm–Lyceums and Museums
—v. 3. Mably–Ruysch—v. 4. Sade–Zoology. Index.
ISBN 0-19-510430-7 (set: alk. paper)
ISBN 0-19-510431-5 (v. 1: alk. paper)
ISBN 0-19-510432-3 (v. 2: alk. paper)
ISBN 0-19-510433-1 (v. 3: alk. paper)
ISBN 0-19-510434-X (v. 4: alk. paper)
1. Enlightenment—Encyclopedias. 2. Enlightenment—United
States—Encyclopedias. 3. Philosophy—Encyclopedias. 4.
Europe—Intellectual life—18th century. 5. United States—Intellectual
life—18th century. I. Kors, Alan Charles.
B802. E53 2003
940.2′5—dc21
2002003766

1 3 5 7 9 8 6 4 2
Printed in the United States of America
on acid-free paper

Common Abbreviations Used in This Work

AD	*anno Domini*, in the year of the Lord
A.M.	*artium magister*, Master of Arts
b.	born
BC	before Christ
BCE	before the common era (= BC)
c.	*circa*, about, approximately
CE	common era (= AD)
cf.	*confer*, compare
d.	died
diss.	dissertation
ed.	editor (pl., eds), edition
f.	and following (pl., ff.)
fl.	*floruit*, flourished
l.	line (pl., ll.)
n.	note
n.d.	no date
no.	number
n.p.	no place
n.s.	new series
p.	page (pl., pp.)
pt.	part
r.	reigned
rev.	revised
ser.	series
supp.	supplement
vol.	volume (pl., vols.)

ENCYCLOPEDIA OF THE

ENLIGHTENMENT

M

MABLY, GABRIEL BONNOT DE (1709–1785), French historian, moralist, and political writer.

Mably's works exerted a wide influence on political thought in eighteenth-century France, but little is known about his life. He was born in the Dauphiné in southeastern France to a recently ennobled family, his father having obtained the position of *secrétaire du roi* in the *parlement* (sovereign court) of Grenoble. His younger brother, Étienne Bonnot de Condillac, became one of the French Enlightenment's leading sensationalist philosophers. Mably, like Condillac, was educated for a vocation in the Roman Catholic Church. He attended the Jesuit Collège de la Marche in Lyon and then the Jesuit seminary of Saint-Sulpice. In 1735, Mably received his subdeaconate; like many other eighteenth-century men of letters, he became an *abbé commendataire*, but he was never ordained a priest and soon abandoned the church, moving to Paris to pursue a career in politics and letters. There Mably profited from his family's old ties with Cardinal Tencin, whose sister, Mme. de Tencin, ran a prominent salon attended by such early Enlightenment luminaries as Montesquieu, Fontenelle, Duclos, and Saint-Pierre. Invited to join this circle with his brother, Condillac, Mably became secretary to Cardinal Tencin when the latter was appointed minister of state in 1742.

By this time, Mably had already published his *Parallèle des romains et des français, par rapport au gouvernement* (Comparison of the Romans and the French, in Respect to Government, 1740), which enjoyed considerable critical success. In this first of his major works, he compared the similar longterm historical trajectories of the Roman and French states; he found notable differences, which he explained much to the advantage of the French monarchy. Whereas Rome had collapsed under imperial tyranny, the French state had emerged triumphant from medieval chaos under a strong king, who, though unbound by any constitution, still respected the rights of his people. With its citizens enjoying liberty and the material benefits of modern civilization, France and its absolute monarchy, in Mably's view, seemed institutionally structured to escape the forces of instability and decline that had condemned the republics of antiquity to extinction. Mably's second major work, *Le droit public de l'Europe, fondé sur les traités* (The Public Law of Europe, Based on Treaties, 1746), was a direct result of his work for Cardinal Tencin. Having read diplomatic dispatches and drafted diplomatic memoranda for several years, Mably put his knowledge to good use in publishing and commenting on Europe's most important treaties since that of Westphalia in 1648. Enjoying international acclaim, *Le droit public*, like the *Parallèle*, reflected strong pro-Bourbon sentiments that might have been held by any of the Bourbon monarchy's dutiful servants.

For reasons that remain unclear, Mably's career suddenly changed course. In 1747, he resigned as Tencin's secretary over Tencin's decision to annul a Protestant marriage. Choosing a frugal independence over comfort and security, Mably severed all direct ties to the state and subsisted for the rest of his life principally on a family pension, rent from a minor ecclesiastical office, and later an ecclesiastical pension. This upheaval was accompanied by an equally dramatic shift in his ideas. Mably returned to the topics of his earlier publications, but only to recant many of his previously expressed views. Abandoning the royalism that had underpinned his focus on the optimal conditions for maintaining political stability, Mably joined other Enlightenment publicists who were reconsidering the optimal conditions for maintaining liberty under the law. Like many of these publicists, Mably leaned to deism and embraced natural law as the foundation of political virtue; however, he was never a member of the Enlightenment's inner circle, he did not contribute to the *Encyclopédie*, and he maintained strained or distant relationships with most of the philosophes. He particularly loathed the ideas of Voltaire, and he even came into conflict with Rousseau, despite the close resemblance in their views.

Scholars of the mature Mably have characterized him variously—from a Catholic conservative to a utopian socialist—but his most recent and persuasive interpreters contend that he was essentially a republican. His radical ideas were elaborated in a large number of works written over more than three decades; the most notable are *Entretiens de Phocion, sur le rapport de la morale avec la politique* (Conversations of Phocion, on the Relationship of Morality and Politics, 1763), *Observations sur l'histoire de France* (1765), *Observations sur l'histoire de la Grèce* (1766),

Doutes proposées aux philosophes économistes (Doubts Addressed to Economic Philosophers, 1767), *Observations sur le gouvernement et les loix des États-Unis d'Amérique* (1783), and *Des droits et des devoirs du citoyen* (Rights and Duties of the Citizen, 1789). Like many of his contemporaries, Mably came to view the French monarchy as dangerously inclined toward "despotism." He condemned the pursuit of wealth as a threat to political virtue and imagined that, in an ideal republic, wealth would be equitably shared. Partly for this reason, he attacked the ideas of the Physiocrats, who championed what he saw as a "legal despotism" built on private property. Yet Mably retained enough of his early royalism to reject the thesis of Montesquieu, Le Paige, and the French *parlements* that the authority of French monarchs had always been limited by a historical "constitution," and he strenuously opposed the claims of the nobility to be the exclusive representatives of the nation. Drawing inspiration from the republics of antiquity, he asserted that it was the consent of all citizens, not custom, that was the basis of political authority. He vacillated, however, on the desirability of a "mixed government" composed of countervailing branches. During the late 1750s, Mably drafted a prescient revolutionary scenario of a process whereby the French nation might gain its freedom: *parlement* and aristocratic resistance to royal despotism would lead to the calling of a permanent and more democratic Estates-General.

Ironically, the closer France approached 1789, the more pessimistic Mably grew regarding the chances of this or any other scenario of liberation. In particular, the Maupeou coup of 1771–1774, during which the monarchy dissolved the *parlements*, soured his hopes for a "controlled revolution," and he came to believe that the moment for any decisive reform of the state had passed. In his last years, Mably engaged in controversies over the fate of Poland and the future of the new American republic. His influence on French politics was to peak after his death. Mably was among the most frequently cited authorities in the pamphleteering campaigns of 1787–1789, and during the French Revolution he was virtually canonized, only to lose influence rapidly thereafter. Insofar as he may be accounted one of the Enlightenment's fellow-travelers, Mably represented one of the most critical links between the age of *lumières* and the age of Revolution.

[*See also* French Revolution.]

BIBLIOGRAPHY

Baker, Keith Michael. "A Script for the French Revolution: The Political Consciousness of the Abbé Mably." *Eighteenth-Century Studies* 14 (1980–1981), 235–263. Reprinted in revised form in Baker, *Inventing the French Revolution: Essays on French Political Culture in the Eighteenth Century*, pp. 86–106. Cambridge, 1990. Focuses on Mably's forecast of 1789.

Furet, François, and Mona Ozouf. "Two Historical Legitimations of Eighteenth-Century French Society: Mably and Boulainvilliers." In *François Furet, In the Workshop of History*, pp. 125–139. Chicago, 1984. Juxtaposes Mably and the "constitutionalist" tradition as represented by Boulainvilliers.

Galliani, Renato. "Quelques aspects de la fortune de Mably au XXme siècle." In *Transactions of the Third International Congress on the Enlightenment (II)*, Studies on Voltaire and the Eighteenth Century 88, pp. 549–565. Oxford, 1972. Useful overview of Mably interpretation, which comes down on the side of Mably as a radical.

Harpaz, Ephraim. "Mably et la postérité." *Revue des sciences humaines* 74 (1954), 25–40.

Harpaz, Ephraim. "Mably et ses contemporains." *Revue des sciences humaines* 82 (1955), 351–366.

Harpaz, Ephraim. "Le social de Mably." *Revue d'histoire économique et sociale* 34 (1956), 411–425. These articles focus on Mably's relationship to the Enlightenment, stressing the similarity of his views to those of the philosophes.

Procacci, Giuliano. "L'Abate Mably nell'Illuminismo." *Rivista storica italiana* 63 (1951), 21–44. Presents Mably as a Catholic conservative.

Stiffoni, Giovanni. *Utopia ragione in G. Bonnot de Mably*. Lecce, 1975. A general account that emphasizes the role of utopianism in Mably's thought, despite his willingness to bow to the demands of realism.

Thamer, Hans-Ulrich. *Revolution und Reaktion in der französischen Sozialkritik des 18. Jahrhunderts: Linguet, Mably, Babeuf*. Frankfurt am Main, 1973. Stresses the utopian socialism of Mably.

Schleich, Thomas. *Aufklärung und Revolution: Die Wirkungsgeschichte Gabriel Bonnot de Mablys in Frankreich (1740–1914)*. Stuttgart, 1981. Emphasizes the anti-Enlightenment aspects of Mably's work and argues that Mably's radicalism was a Revolutionary fabrication.

Wright, Johnson Kent. *A Classical Republican in Eighteenth-Century France: The Political Thought of Mably*. Stanford, Calif., 1997. The most convincing general study, underlining Mably's debt to the republican tradition.

THOMAS E. KAISER

MACLEAN, RUTGER

MACLEAN, RUTGER (1742–1816), Swedish country squire, agrarian reformer, and politician.

Perhaps no single person living in the eighteenth century has left more enduring traces on the Sweden of today than Baron Maclean. To be sure, he was not successful in his role as a politician. King Gustav III of Sweden had him arrested in 1789 when, in the parliament, he played too important a role in the aristocratic opposition. Maclean fared no better in the eyes of Gustav IV Adolf, who suspected him of harboring Jacobin sympathies and considered him *persona non grata* in Stockholm during his reign.

Yet Maclean, exiled to the Scanian manor Svaneholm in southern Sweden, paved the way for Enlightenment ideals and modernization as did few other Swedes.

Maclean had his greatest influence as an agrarian reformer, a role he undertook in 1783, partly under the spell of the French Physiocrats (who believed that the economic basis of wealth was land and free trade) and, even more so, of the English and Danish model farms. He was of rare directness and determination. He had the surveyor's map redesigned for the five parishes pertaining to Svaneholm and abolished all day-work obligations. The result was a consolidated model farm at Svaneholm, surrounded by seventy-three rectilinear leasehold farms—40 acres each, with a house and a kitchen garden in the middle—which were obligated by contract to follow a detailed program of cultivation, including crop rotation. Baron Maclean's departure from then-prevailing farming practices was by no means welcomed by his subordinate farmers, and many left his land. His project was initially in danger, but in the end he could boast a fourfold productivity on his domains.

His impressive production resulted in the *Enskifte* of 1803, an enclosure ordinance that, although at first only in force in Scania, soon became epochal in Swedish agrarian history. From that point, any landowner could demand to withdraw from his village community and have his holdings concentrated. Many villages were shattered, and previously common land was made private territory, which led to a more intensive cultivation of already extensively farmed areas, especially in the southern part of Sweden. The ordinance of 1803 was followed by the ordinances of 1807 and of 1827, both adapted to the rugged topography of the northern parts of Sweden. Maclean was also a pioneer in both having his farmers examined by a physician and in building schools for the peasantry. Together with other like-minded noblemen, he even paid a schoolmaster to go abroad in order to catch up with the latest pedagogical theories.

Maclean was a practical man. His literary interest was scant, but he was well read in pedagogy, political economy, and politics. He closely followed the events of the French Revolution of 1789 by reading otherwise prohibited publications from the French National Assembly. His passion, however, was rational householding; in fact, he wrote a book on that topic, *Lärobok i landtbruket* (On Farming), published posthumously in 1845.

[*See also* Agriculture and Animal Husbandry; Physiocracy; *and* Scandinavia.]

BIBLIOGRAPHY

Nyström, Per. "Maclean." In *Historia och biografi: Artiklar och essäer 1933–1989*, edited by Per Nyström, pp. 58–74. Lund, Sweden, 1989. Perceptive essay, originally published in 1942.

Waller, Sture M. *Maclean och 1809—10 års riksdag.* Lund, Sweden, 1953. The most documented study to date.

JAKOB CHRISTENSSON

MACPHERSON, JAMES (1736–1796), Scottish folklorist, poet, and historian.

A Gaelic-speaking Highlander born in Ruthven, Invernessshire, Scotland, Macpherson studied from 1753 to 1755 at Aberdeen (at both King's and Marischal colleges), where he almost certainly came under the influence of the classical scholar Thomas Blackwell. The latter's ideas about the nature of early poetry and Homeric epic led Macpherson to draw parallels with the literary patrimony of the Scottish Gaels, a predominantly oral culture increasingly threatened with extinction after the defeat of the Jacobites at Culloden in 1746. He seems to have begun collecting ballads and oral tales from the mid-1750s on.

At the instigation of the dramatist John Home, to whom he had been supplied with an introduction by the historian and philosopher Adam Ferguson, Macpherson produced a "translation" of a piece that later became part of the *Fragments of Ancient Poetry Collected in the Highlands of Scotland, and Translated from the Gaelic or Erse Language*. It was published in Edinburgh in 1760, with an anonymous preface by Hugh Blair, soon to become the first professor of rhetoric and belles lettres at the University of Edinburgh. Blair, together with a coterie of other Presbyterian clergymen affiliated with the Moderate party in the Church of Scotland—John Home, Adam Ferguson, William Robertson, and Alexander Carlyle—was energetic in his promotion of the Ossianic project (Ossian was the name of a legendary Gaelic poet-warrior) and was instrumental in raising money to send Macpherson on a prospecting trip to the Highlands and Western islands in order to rescue from oblivion the last remnants of ancient Gaelic epic poetry. Macpherson obliged with the epics *Fingal* (1761–1762) and *Temora* (1763), published together in London in 1765 as *The Works of Ossian*, accompanied by an extremely influential *Critical Dissertation* on the poems, from the pen of Hugh Blair.

Ossian thus emerged as very much a product of the Scottish Enlightenment, promoted in no small part to establish a respectable Scottish literary pedigree in the eyes of the skeptical English. It was, however, by no means totally fraudulent. Macpherson was an effective collector who obtained from oral and some manuscript sources (notably the sixteenth-century *Book of the Dean of Lismore*) a wealth of ballads, some of them attributed to the legendary bard Ossian (Oisìn; Oisean), concerning the third-century exploits of Fingal (Finn mac Cumaill, father of Oisìn) and his band of warriors, the *fian* (or *fianna*). Though he set his epics in Ireland, Macpherson adapted and distorted the traditional material, which formed part of a literary culture common to both Ireland and Gaelic-speaking Scotland, by making Fingal a Caledonian king. He took features of the authentic ballads—such as the geriatric Ossian's lachrymose laments for a vanished world or the quixotic magnanimity of the Fingalians—and selectively exaggerated them, in the process ruthlessly ridding the poetry of any rudeness or ribaldry that might have offended his own polished age. Genuinely primitive elements remained, however. The resulting mixture of old and new, with its masterly evocation of a wild and savage landscape, innovative combination of genres in a diction that hovered between verse and prose, sustained exploration of the melancholy pleasures of "the joy of grief," and not least, Macpherson's own considerable poetic gifts, made *Ossian* a seminal influence on the age of sensibility and Romanticism in Britain, Europe, and beyond.

Apart from an extensively revised edition of *Ossian* and a translation of the *Iliad* (into Ossianic measured prose), both published in 1773, Macpherson's subsequent publications were all political or historical; the latter usually served to glorify the Celts, and the former the Tory government. He ended his life as a member of Parliament and a wealthy man.

[*See also* Romanticism; Scotland; *and* Translation.]

BIBLIOGRAPHY

WORKS BY MACPHERSON
The Poems of Ossian and Related Works. Edited by Howard Gaskill with introduction by Fiona Stafford. Edinburgh, 1996. The only available modern edition, based on the *Works* of 1765. Includes the *Fragments of Ancient Poetry*, Blair's *Dissertation*, and variant readings from the editions of 1761–1763 and 1773.

WORKS ABOUT MACPHERSON
DeGategno, Paul J. *James Macpherson.* Boston, 1989. Useful comprehensive biography, including Macpherson's political career, and introduction to his literary work.
Gaskill, Howard, ed. *Ossian Revisited.* Edinburgh, 1991. Compilation of essays by scholars from various disciplines (includes contributions on Jefferson, Ferguson, and Hume).
Sher, Richard B. *Church and University in the Scottish Enlightenment: The Moderate Literati of Edinburgh.* Edinburgh, 1985. See especially chapter 6 for an excellent account of the involvement of Blair, Ferguson, and other Enlightenment figures in the promotion of the Ossianic project.
Stafford, Fiona. *The Sublime Savage: James Macpherson and the Poems of Ossian.* Edinburgh, 1988. Excellent account of Macpherson's early life and literary treatment of the Ossianic poetry.
Stafford, Fiona, and Howard Gaskill. *From Gaelic to Romantic: Ossianic Translations.* Amsterdam, 1998. Compilation of essays by scholars from various disciplines (includes contributions on Sterne and Mackenzie).

HOWARD GASKILL

MADISON, JAMES (1751–1836), American statesman, writer, and fourth president of the United States (1809–1817).

Long honored as the "Father of the Constitution" for his role at the Federal Convention of 1787, Madison is also regarded as the most thoughtful and creative constitutional theorist of his generation. This reputation owes much to his celebrated contributions to the *Federalist*, the set of essays that he wrote with Alexander Hamilton and John Jay in support of the Constitution. Two of these essays, the Tenth and Fifty-first, are widely viewed as paradigmatic statements of the general theory of the Constitution. However, Madison's political career during nearly half a century is interesting as well for the way in which it combined deep reflection about constitutional principles with the exigencies of public life.

Early Political Career. The eldest son of the largest landowner in Orange County, Virginia, Madison had been well educated at the College of New Jersey (now Princeton University), but when the Revolutionary War erupted in 1775, he still lacked a vocation. He quickly found one in politics, serving first as a delegate to the provincial convention and then as a member of the state council, where he first came into contact with Thomas Jefferson. In 1780, he joined the Virginia delegation to the Continental Congress, where he served until the fall of 1783, and where he grew concerned with the weakness of national government under the Articles of Confederation. Returning to Virginia, he entered the state legislature, where he pursued two principal goals: enacting the proposed revision of the statutory code that Jefferson had prepared in the late 1770s, and supporting measures to strengthen the national government. In the latter capacity, he played a critical role in the political maneuvers leading to the Federal Convention of 1787; he then set himself the task of shaping its agenda.

Madison's first political commitment was to the principle of religious liberty and the separation of church and state. As a member of the provincial convention of 1776, he secured an amendment to the celebrated Virginia Declaration of Rights, altering the article that originally promised "the fullest toleration in the exercise of religion" to include the broader affirmation that "all men are equally entitled to the free exercise of religion, according to the dictates of conscience." A decade later, as a Virginia legislator, he led the opposition to a proposed bill to provide public support for all Christian ministers, drafting a "Memorial and Remonstrance against Religious Assessments" which treated the measure as a potential legislative infringement on popular rights equivalent to Parliament's assaults on American liberty before 1776. Upon the defeat of this measure, Madison secured the passage in 1786 of the Statute for Religious Freedom, which Jefferson had drafted in the late 1770s; this effectively disestablished religion in Virginia.

Madison's commitment to the rights of conscience illuminates a critical dimension of his constitutional theory. At a time when most Americans still thought that the basic problem of rights was to protect the people as a whole against the danger of arbitrary government, Madison regarded rights in essentially liberal terms. In a republican government, the problem of protecting rights would take a different form than in the monarchical regimes of Europe. The new challenge was to find ways to protect minorities and individuals against the misrule of popular majorities acting through government, and especially through the representative assemblies that dominated government under the original state constitutions drafted since 1776.

Madison came to this conclusion from his observations of legislative politics in the mid-1780s. He opposed paper money legislation, which he viewed as a danger to property because the depreciation of this currency would injure the rights of creditors. Recognizing that the impetus for paper money came from the electorate, he worried about the danger of popular influence on the decisions of government. He was also troubled by the impulsiveness with which his fellow lawmakers acted.

Constitutional Theorist. These concerns, in turn, enabled Madison to reexamine the basic premises underlying the Articles of Confederation, which assumed that the state governments would faithfully implement the recommendations of the Continental Congress. During his service in Congress, Madison had watched as the states failed to comply with many of these measures; as a Virginia legislator, he realized that representatives and voters were unlikely to think seriously about the national interest when it clashed with local concerns. The same political factors that led states to enact unjust legislation also explained their failure to support the national government.

As a constitutional reformer, Madison was thus concerned with two distinct problems—republican government within the states, and the weakness of American federalism—but it was his genius to trace both to common causes. At the state level, he favored mechanisms to improve the quality of legislation and to enable the weaker branches of the executive and judiciary to withstand the "encroachments" of the legislature. Reform of the federal system appeared more difficult. All amendments to the Confederation required unanimous approval by the thirteen state legislatures. Equally important, any attempt to reconstitute the existing Continental Congress as a national government formed on republican lines risked contradicting the conventional wisdom that republics could safely exist only in geographically compact and socially homogeneous societies.

While contemplating the problem of federalism, Madison undertook a systematic course of reading in history and public law. (His papers include his reading notes on "Ancient & Modern Confederacies.") Scholars have also concluded that Madison drew critical inspiration from David Hume's essay on the "Idea of a Perfect Commonwealth." That Madison read widely, deeply, and critically is evident, yet his judgments about political action rested on more than his reading: they combined lessons drawn from both personal experience and the observation of events with reflections on history and the science of politics. In the months preceding the 1787 convention, Madison drew on all these sources to fashion a comprehensive agenda of reform.

That agenda began with the recognition that any federal system based on the voluntary compliance of the states with federal decisions was doomed to failure. It followed that the existing unicameral Congress had to be replaced by a conventional government capable of enacting, executing, and adjudicating its own laws, and this in turn meant creating three independent departments of government. Here Madison applied lessons drawn from the state constitutions to the new task of designing national institutions. His own preferred reforms included establishing a genuinely senatorial upper house to serve as a check on impulsive legislation; creating a joint executive-judicial council of revision with a limited negative on national legislation; and diminishing the residual sovereignty of the states by subjecting their legislation to congressional veto. Madison's key ideas were incorporated in the Virginia Plan, which provided the foundation for the convention's deliberations. In fact, the convention diluted or rejected many of the proposals that Madison supported most strongly. He adamantly opposed the idea of an equal state representation in either house of the new Congress, but the Senate was organized on just that basis. Madison preferred any other mode of electing the Senate to the one his colleagues chose when they made the state legislatures its electors. The congressional veto on state laws and the council of revision were also rejected. Nonetheless, the completed Constitution can still be seen as the product of Madison's efforts to reconcile the basic principles of republican government with the need to establish an effective national government. Without his preparatory labors, it is difficult to imagine how the convention would have taken the course it did, nor would we know nearly as much about its deliberations had Madison not kept extensive daily notes of its debates.

Madison's reputation as a constitutional theorist is also due to his role as author of twenty-nine of the eighty-five essays of *The Federalist*. His first contribution, *Federalist* 10, is also his most influential. Here Madison rejected the conventional view that republics must rely on the self-denying virtue of their citizens. All citizens act in self-interested ways, Madison argued, and naturally prefer their own interests and passions to a broad consideration of the true public good. The smaller the society, the easier it is for these interests to coalesce in "factious" ways, injuring the rights of minorities while ignoring the general good. In an extended national republic, however, it is more difficult for such harmful majorities to form; liberty therefore can remain more secure, and it is more likely that a superior class of legislators will emerge to deliberate on the general good.

Madison's later essays are concerned primarily with the division of powers between the union and the states, the separation of powers, and representation. In *Federalist* 39–46, Madison argued that the new Constitution would not "consolidate" all effective authority in the national government; instead, it created a complicated system in which particular powers of sovereignty were effectively vested in the union, while the states would retain ample authority and political influence. In *Federalist* 47–51, Madison attacked the familiar doctrine, associated with Montesquieu, that required a rigid separation of the powers of government into three insular departments. He argued instead that the real challenge of separation was to give the weaker branches, the executive and the judiciary, adequate defenses against the "impetuous vortex" of the legislature—especially the popularly elected lower house—and that this justified the various defenses that the Constitution had provided, especially its attempt to link the Senate with the executive. Finally, in the essays ending with *Federalist* 63, Madison looked more closely at the nature of representation in the new Congress.

Even though these essays probably had little effect on public opinion, Madison used many of the same arguments as he led the campaign for ratification of the Constitution in Virginia. To secure a majority in the Virginia convention, he acquiesced in the decision to recommend amendments to be considered by the new Congress. As a candidate for election to the House of Representatives, he publicly affirmed his willingness to support the adoption of amendments declaring essential rights. Once elected, he drafted a suitable set of amendments and then prevailed on his reluctant colleagues in the First Congress to take up the subject. Privately, Madison believed that bills of rights were mere "parchment barriers" that would do little to protect liberty; but he thought that the adoption of amendments would reconcile many opponents of the Constitution to the new government.

His Career during the Republic. Madison's active political career lasted another three decades following the adoption of the Constitution. It was dominated by two developments that were closely linked: the rise of organized partisan politics in the United States, and American responses to the European crisis provoked by the wars of the French Revolution and Napoleon. As a member of the House of Representatives (1789–1797), Madison joined with Secretary of State Jefferson in opposing both the domestic and foreign policies associated with Secretary of the Treasury Alexander Hamilton, which they regarded as both wrong in themselves and constitutionally suspect. Both men believed that Hamilton's policies were designed to consolidate power both in the national government and in the executive; both were suspicious of the preferences that those policies showed toward the commercial and financial interests of northern states rather than the agrarian interests of the South. Both also believed that the national interest required a neutrality that favored France rather than Britain, which they viewed as a predatory

power anxious to maintain the United States as an economic if not a political colony.

For Madison, these developments involved a reconsideration of key concerns of the 1780s. In organizing the Democratic-Republican Party to oppose Hamilton and his Federalist allies, Madison acted on the belief that organized political factions might have a necessary role to play in the conduct of republican politics, notwithstanding the concern with faction he had voiced in *Federalist* 10. Moreover, when the Democratic-Republican Party initially failed to gain control of the government, Madison and Jefferson turned to the state legislatures of Virginia and Kentucky to mobilize opposition to the Federalist administration of President John Adams during the crisis over the Quasi-War with France in 1798–1799. Here, too, Madison seemed to move away from the suspicion of state-based politics on which he had acted in the previous decade.

His Contribution. These developments raise important questions about Madison's intellectual consistency, but those questions in turn overlook the most striking feature of his approach to politics and political ideas alike. Madison was deeply empirical in his approach to both, and he was prepared to modify his ideas in response to the new evidence that political experience afforded. Yet during the long retirement of twenty years that followed his tenure as secretary of state (1801–1809) and president (1809–1817), Madison's extensive writings illustrate a deeper level of consistency on his basic concepts of republican government and constitutionalism. Above all, he resisted reducing the complexities of American federalism to the simplistic formulas of national or state sovereignty. Until his death in 1836, the last of the great revolutionary leaders insisted that the American system could be understood and maintained only by close and reasoned attention to its complex structure.

[*See also* American Revolution; Articles of Confederation; Constitution of the United States; Federalist, The; Federalists and Anti-Federalists; Political Philosophy; Republicanism; *and* Toleration.]

BIBLIOGRAPHY

Adair, Douglass. "'That Politics May Be Reduced to a Science': David Hume, James Madison, and the Tenth Federalist." In *Fame and the Founding Fathers: Essays by Douglass Adair*, edited by Trevor Colbourn, pp. 93–106. New York, 1974. Influential essay suggesting key intellectual link between Hume and Madison.

Banning, Lance. *The Sacred Fire of Liberty: James Madison and the Founding of the Federal Republic*. Ithaca, N.Y., and London, 1995. Distinguishes Madison's commitment to federalism from the nationalism of other Federalists while emphasizing underlying continuities in his constitutional thinking.

Hobson, Charles. "The Negative on State Laws: James Madison, the Constitution, and the Crisis of Republican Government." *William and Mary Quarterly* 36 (1979), 215–235. Calls attention to the critical role that the negative on state laws played in Madison's original thinking about the problem of federalism.

Ketcham, Ralph. *James Madison: A Biography*. Charlottesville, Va., 1971. Best one-volume biography.

McCoy, Drew. *The Last of the Fathers: James Madison and the Republic Legacy*. New York and Cambridge, 1989. Moving portrait of the again conservative statesman during his long retirement.

Rakove, Jack N. *James Madison and the Creation of the American Republic*. 2d ed. New York, 2001. Best short biography.

Rakove, Jack N. *Original Meanings: Politics and Ideas in the Making of the Constitution*. New York, 1996. Consistently emphasizes Madison's role in shaping the Constitution and in pioneering its public defense and early interpretation.

Zvesper, John. "The Madisonian Systems." *Western Political Quarterly* 37 (1984), 236–256. Thoughtful assessment of the relation between the constitutional founder of the 1780s and the party leader of the 1790s.

JACK N. RAKOVE

MAINE DE BIRAN, pseudonym of François-Pierre Gontier de Biran (1766–1824), French philosopher.

The son of a doctor, Gontier de Biran was destined for a military career in the ancien régime and participated in the defense of the royal palace of Versailles against the revolutionaries in 1789. In 1792, he was obliged to take refuge in the Dordogne. A liberal monarchist anxious to make up for the chaos of the Terror, he pursued a career in administration and politics. Under the Restoration, he was elected a deputy (1809) and named a member of the conseil d'état (1816).

This subprefect from Bergerac was no "professional" philosopher. His very life was a philosophical experience, more in the spiritual realm than in that of reason. Its inner meaning was both revealed and concealed in his never-completed work, which, François Azouvi writes, is marked by unity of method no matter how different the points of view. Biran invented of a new way of philosophizing, the "philosophical journal," to explore the "underground tunnels of the soul" and reflect inner life (Fessard). He based his psychology, or "subjective science," on introspection. His correspondence with André Ampère (1805–1819) is helpful in pinning down the genesis of his notion of self (an unknowable "substance") as it relates to the category of causality. Through the innermost feeling of intentional effort, the actual self is grasped as a "free cause." This is the "primitive fact" (in d'Alembert's expression) the discovery of the principle of an authentic philosophy of existence that is identified with "that of force or of causality itself."

Following the philosophers of the Enlightenment—in particular his friends, the Ideologues Georges Cabanis and Antoine Destutt de Tracy (who in 1802 had the Institut award him a prize for his *Mémoire sur l'habitude* [Report on Habit])—Biran remained attentive to Locke's empiricism and demonstrated his hostility toward the a priori systems of traditional metaphysician. Like David Hume, he wanted to construct a "science of man." Death prevented his completion of the *Nouveaux essais d'anthropologie* (New Essays in Anthropology), in which he distinguished "first life" (the sphere of organic sensitivity and affects) from the "second life," belonging specifically to humans and initiating motor activity. The work deals with the relationship between the self and its body, which resists the self in "homogeneous terms." The union of soul and body is a *sui generis* occurrence. There is no "pure subject." Biran's *Cogito* would prove extremely interesting to later phenomenologists.

Le journal intime (Intimate journal), posthumously published, shows Biran to have been extremely sensitive, an illustration of Rousseau's theory of "sensory morality." The fits and starts of self obliged this "parishioner of the vicar of Savoy" (Gouhier) to believe in the existence of the soul beyond its manifestations—the theory of the power of a "hyperorganic self." The necessary condition of the science of the complete man is the assertion of this "third life that only Christianity knows so well," set free from corporal burdens—a state of beatitude that must be attributed to grace, passivity of a different order than organic passivity—a view not too far from Fénelon's doctrine of "passivity" and "disappropriation." In any case, Biran took a long route from Condillac's sensualism to reach the point where he would assert, "Religion alone resolves the problems posed by philosophy."

[*See also* Condillac, Étienne Bonnot de; Fénelon, François-Armand de Salignac de La Mothe; Mysticism; Philosophy; Rousseau, Jean-Jacques; *and* Soul.]

BIBLIOGRAPHY

WORKS BY MAINE DE BIRAN
Oeuvres. 13 vols. Paris, 1984–1994.

WORKS ABOUT MAINE DE BIRAN
Azouvi, François. *Maine de Biran et la science de l'homme*. Paris, 1995.
Baertschi, Bernard. *L'ontologie de Maine de Biran*. Fribourg, 1982.
Fessard, Gaston. *La méthode de réflexion chez Maine de Biran*. Paris, 1948.
Gouhier, Henri. *Les conversions de Maine de Biran*. Paris, 1947.
Henry, Michel. *Philosophie et phénoménologie du corps*. Paris, 1965.

DENISE LEDUC-FAYETTE
Translated from French by Betsy Wing

MAISTRE, JOSEPH DE (1753–1821), French writer, theocrat, and Freemason.

At the crossroads of Illuminism and counter-revolutionary Catholic thought, Maistre conceived of a new form of sociability that was opposed to natural law and that was invoked during the nineteenth century by many conflicting political circles. He reasoned simultaneously from the position of a man of the Enlightenment and a conservative in political and religious matters. He took his inspiration from Edmund Burke (1729–1797), whose *Reflections on the Revolution in France* (1790) had been so extremely successful.

Maistre's family was in the service of the king of Piedmont-Savoy (the kingdom stretching along the French and Italian slopes of the Alps), and his father had been ennobled as senator (the senate being both a court of justice and a political body like the parlement de Paris). After becoming a doctor of law in 1772, the younger Maistre entered the senate in 1774 at Chambéry (Savoy), there he became a Freemason, joining a lodge where Christian esotericism was in favor. A number of its members, among them the young "Josephus a Floribus" himself, as Maistre was known, belonged to brotherhoods of penitents (associations of lay Catholics dedicated to spiritual devotion and a degree of asceticism). He later joined in the attempt to develop the mystical and visionary Masonic "Strict Templar Observance." In 1782, he sent a dissertation to the duke of Brunswick, patron of the Masonic organization and future commander of the Prussian army that intervened in France in 1792, with the aim of organizing the European masonic assembly of Wilhelmsbad in the German duchy of Hesse. However, this undertaking of a knightly Masonry based on the continuity of an initiation inherited from the Middle Ages seemed irrational to him, and he was not convinced by the secret information conveyed by members of the higher degree and thought his masters "miserly with proofs."

The French Revolution stirred dread, loathing, and general doubt concerning Maistre's prior convictions. Chased first from Chambéry and then from the capital of Piedmont, Turin, by invading French troops, in 1802 he was named ambassador to Russia by the king of Piedmont-Savoy and remained in Saint Petersburg until 1817, when the tsar demanded his recall. Maistre lived for a time in Paris and died in Turin in 1821. The Catholics suspected him of Illuminism, the sovereigns distrusted him for his Enlightenment ideas, and the revolutionaries were wary of his conservatism and nostalgia for the ancien régime.

If the French Revolution had revealed something of the age in Maistre's thought, the way that he developed this remained original and relatively independent of the circles of émigrés that he frequented in the Russian court. He began to reflect in depth about the causes of the widespread collapse of a world that he had thought capable of reform. This was clear in the first written statement that he sent to the king, filled with the ideas of the French *parlementaires*, who challenged the very foundations of sovereignty. From his reading of Edmund Burke, he took the notion of history's essential role in God's plan, which condemned the revolutionary vision of political power, but he did not share Burke's views on the relationship between the people and the

sovereign. Burke's notions were influenced by the British example of the removal of the Catholic Stuarts from power, as well as by the *contrat social* (The Social Contract) by Jean-Jacques Rousseau (1712–1778), the French philosopher of sentiment. Maistre was, rather, the heir of the Catholic concept of tradition. From his experience with Freemasonry he further retained the idea of an institution where the union of groups of people and contact among churches would become possible through a superior exercise of intellect: an aristocracy of the mind.

Les considérations sur la France (1797) laid out the path for a return to an ideal monarchy, freed from abuses and reorganized in conformity with the divine eternal plan. The direction given history by the Revolution would be reversed and God would triumph over Satan. The sufferings of the populace thus became a purifying ordeal whose meaning would soon be luminously clear, because there could be no world without God, nor any state that found its purpose in itself. The aim of the state was to retain for society its immanent divine transcendence; therein lay the happiness of the populace. Since France had been the first affected, it had the mission of setting the example of political salvation for the rest of Europe.

These reversals of the course of history were produced against all logic and were beyond the grasp of rational philosophy; they were the visible sign of the presence of divine providence in the minds of the people who retained, like a sort of primitive knowledge, the sense of an original fall and their duty to make atonement. If this dimension were taken into account, it would be possible to reach a true understanding of the functioning of societies.

Du pape (Concerning the pope) was published in Lyon in 1819; in it Maistre analyzed the powers of the papacy, which seemed to him best suited to stand in the way of modern ideas and the best guarantee against political crises. His historical argument compared the various Christian churches with the Jansenist and Gallican movements—the former being the austere Catholic community of Port-Royal in France, which had developed the theme of predestination and the latter a portion of the French Catholic church demanding autonomy from Roman rule. He concluded in favor of the popes, who were the educators of kings, preservers of knowledge, and tutors of Europe. It was positions of this sort that contributed to his disfavor with the tsar who, in 1815, had been unable to make the Congress of Vienna (reorganizing Europe after Napoleon's defeat) accept his own vision of a holy alliance of sovereigns based on eschatological prophetism and who had found himself blocked by the politics of the Austrian Empire.

This prophetic dimension was developed by Maistre in his posthumously published major work, *Les soirées de Saint-Pétersbourg* (Evenings in Saint Petersburg, 1821).

The work is composed of a series of eleven conversations between a French émigré and a Russian senator who do not see eye to eye; to clarify the present situation, he reviewed the intellectual origins of modernity from Port-Royal's *La grammaire générale* (General Grammar), which had raised the question of the metaphysics of language, to the theses of John Locke (1632–1704), the philosopher of the Enlightenment. Along the way, Maistre proved that the accusation directed at the Freemasons was wrong: they were not, in fact, responsible for the revolutionary events. He did this by making a distinction between the specific Bavarian Illuminists (an openly subversive society that dissolved in 1785) and the mystical tradition of Freemasonry, which had inherited ancient traditions of interpretation rooted in gnosis (the theory concerning access to supreme knowledge that accompanied the first centuries of Christianity) and in certain of the Church Fathers. The "lofty speculations" of these Freemasons from "the educated class" were more necessary than ever in order to decipher signs that were invisible to the prevailing materialism, "for we must make ourselves ready for a huge event in the divine order, towards which we are proceeding faster and faster.... There are formidable oracles informing us that the time has come." (11th conversation). The historical analysis of the evolution of society allowed Maistre to conclude that several of the prophecies contained in the book of Revelation pertained to the nineteenth century.

This ultimate reversal of history was not an "opposite revolution, but the opposite of a revolution," a return to order within the unity of reason and faith; it lent itself to explanation in an intellectual system, opening the way for modern political reflection but causing the rejection of those in power. In Italy, the return to order inspired by the Austrians closed the door to liberalism; the French monarchy, for its part, refused the services of this Ideologue who rejected the compromises of the Charte, the royalist constitution that Louis XVIII had to accept in order to exercise power. The Church of France kept silent on the subject of a book that risked reopening old wounds, and the popes finally refused to engage in debate against the secular powers with which they were dealing. It was not until the second half of the nineteenth century, with Pope Pius IX, that the doctrine of papal infallibility succeeded and became official doctrine (1871).

As the "prophet of the past and historian of the future" Maistre contributed to transmitting the notions of the Illuminati of the century of the Enlightenment into the esotericism of the nineteenth century. Simultaneously and perhaps paradoxically, the political ideas of Alexis de Tocqueville (1805–1859) in *La démocratie en Amérique* (Democracy in America, 1835) and his successors on the nature of democracy and its long-term consequences on

both sides of the Atlantic, are also very much indebted to Maistre's thought.

[*See also* Burke, Edmund; Counter-Enlightenment; Freemasonry; French Revolution, *subentries on* Debates about Causes *and* Iconography; Illuminati; *and* Political Philosophy.]

BIBLIOGRAPHY

WORKS BY MAISTRE

Oeuvres completes. 14 vols. Lyon, 1884–1887; repr. Hildesheim, 1984.

St Petersburg Dialogues, or, Conversations on the Temporal Government of Providence. Edited by Richard A. Lebrun. Montreal and London, 1993. Translation of *Les soirées de Saint-Pétersbourg* (1821); includes bibliography and index.

Against Rousseau: "On the State of Nature" and "On the Sovereignty of the People." Edited by Richard A. Lebrun. Montreal and London, 1996. Critical translation of *De l'état de nature* and *De la souveraineté du people*; includes bibliographical references and index.

WORKS ABOUT MAISTRE

Lafage, Franck. *Le comte Joseph de Maistre (1753–1821), itinéraire intellectuel d'un théologien de la politique.* Paris and Montreal, 1998. Contains a copious bibliography and a chronology.

Lebrun, Richard Allen. *Joseph de Maistre: An Intellectual Militant.* Kingston and Montreal, 1988.

Lebrun, Richard Allen, ed. and trans. *Maistre Studies.* Lanham, Md., 1988. Selections from *Revue des études Maistriennes* nos. 1–11. Includes bibliography and index.

Triomphe, Robert. *Joseph de Maistre: Étude sur la vie et sur la doctrine d'un matérialiste mystique.* Geneva, 1968.

Viatte, Auguste. *Les sources occultes du romantisme: Illuminisme, théosophie.* Paris, 1935; rev. ed., 1979.

JEAN-PIERRE LAURANT
Translated from French by Betsy Wing

MALEBRANCHE, NICOLAS (1638–1715), French theologian and philosopher.

The most important of Descartes's disciples in the second half of the seventeenth century. Malebranche was a Catholic priest, and his philosophy had deep religious motivations. His unusual theocentric doctrines made him the object of Enlightenment criticism, and even of ridicule. Nonetheless, because of the central role that Malebranche, a faithful Cartesian, gave to the intellect in the pursuit of truth and knowledge, and because of his commitment to mechanistic explanations in natural science, his attack on skepticism, and his emphasis on the importance of reason in the avoidance of cognitive and moral error and in the attainment of happiness, his thought foreshadowed significant themes of Enlightenment rationalism.

Malebranche was born in Paris. In 1654, after a childhood schooling at home, he entered the Collège de la Marche, from which he graduated two years later as a master of arts. The education he received there, heavily laden with Aristotelianism, left Malebranche dissatisfied. After studying theology for three years at the Sorbonne—a Scholastic curriculum with which he was equally discontented—and rejecting the offer of a canonry at Nôtre-Dame de Paris, Malebranche entered the Oratory in 1660. He was ordained on 14 September 1664.

His four years in the Oratory proved to be of great intellectual consequence for Malebranche, particularly with respect to his philosophical and theological development. The order had been founded in 1611 by Cardinal Bérulle, who had a deep veneration for Saint Augustine and who was also a good friend of Descartes (although the Oratory was, on the whole, firmly anti-Cartesian). While studying biblical criticism, ecclesiastical history, and Hebrew, Malebranche, like the other Oratorians, immersed himself in the writings of Augustine. He certainly knew of the doctrines of Descartes through certain professors of the order who considered themselves adherents of this new philosophy, but he did not actually read any of Descartes's works until 1664, when he happened upon a copy of *De l'homme* (Treatise on Man) in a bookstall. The event was life-changing: Malebranche's early biographer, Yves-Marie André, who knew him well, tells us that the joy of becoming acquainted with so many discoveries "caused him such palpitations of the heart that the had to stop reading in

order to recover his breath." Malebranche devoted the next ten years of his life to studying mathematics and philosophy, especially of the Cartesian variety. He was particularly taken with Descartes's critique of the Aristotelian philosophy that he had earlier found so stultifying and sterile.

Those years of study culminated in the publication in 1674–1675 of *De la recherche de la vérité* (The Search after Truth), Malebranche's most important work and a philosophical masterpiece in its own right. It represents a grand synthesis of the systems of Malebranche's two intellectual and spiritual mentors, Augustine and Descartes. It is a wide-ranging treatise that deals with questions of knowledge, metaphysics, physics, sense physiology, methodology, and philosophical theology. Malebranche's stated goal in the *Search* was to investigate the sources of human error and to direct us toward the clear and distinct perception of truth: truth about ourselves, about the world around us, and about God. He was ultimately concerned to demonstrate the essential and fundamentally active role of God in every aspect—material, cognitive, and moral—of the world he has created. This becomes particularly clear when one considers the three main doctrines to which Malebranche owes his reputation: occasionalism, vision in God, and his particular theodicy.

According to the "doctrine of occasional causes," as Leibniz labeled it, all finite created entities are absolutely devoid of causal efficacy. God is the only true causal agent. Bodies do not cause effects in other bodies or in minds, and minds do not cause effects in bodies or even within themselves. God is directly, immediately, and solely responsible for bringing about all phenomena. When a needle pricks the skin, the physical event is merely an occasion for God to cause the relevant mental state, pain; a volition in the soul to raise an arm or to think of something is only an occasion for God to cause the arm to rise or the idea to be present to the mind; and the impact of one billiard ball on another is an occasion for God to move the second ball. In all three contexts—mind-body, body-body, and mind alone—God's ubiquitous causal activity proceeds in accordance with certain general laws, and (except in the case of miracles) God acts only when the requisite material or psychic conditions obtain. Despite its prima facie counter-intuitiveness, occasionalism should be seen not as a bizarre attempt to replace science with theology, but rather, at least in part, as an effort to provide metaphysical foundations for mechanistic explanations—that is, explanations framed solely in terms of matter and motion—in physics, and especially to account for the dynamic features (and not just the kinetic behavior) of natural bodies.

The doctrine of vision in God demonstrates how we as knowers are as cognitively dependent on the divine understanding as bodies in motion are ontologically

Nicolas Malebranche. Engraving by Étienne Lépicié. (New York Public Library, Astor, Lenox, and Tilden Foundations.)

dependent on the divine will. Malebranche agreed with Descartes and other philosophers that ideas, or immaterial representations present to the mind, play an essential role in knowledge and perception, but he insisted that the human soul is "not a light unto itself." Thus, whereas Descartes's ideas are mental entities, or modifications of the soul, Malebranche argued that the ideas that function in human cognition are in God: they just are the essences and eternal archetypes that exist in the divine understanding. As such, they are eternal and independent of finite minds, and our access to them makes possible the clear and distinct apprehension of objective, necessary truth. Malebranche presented vision in God as the correct Augustinian view, albeit modified in the light of Descartes's epistemological distinction between understanding (via clear and distinct concepts) and sensation. The theory explains our knowledge both of universals and of mathematical and moral principles, as well as the conceptual element that, he argued, necessarily informs our perceptual acquaintance with the world. And like Descartes's theory of ideas—in which God guarantees our rational faculties—Malebranche's doctrine was at least partly motivated by anti-skepticism, since divine ideas cannot fail to reveal either eternal truths or the essences of things in the world created by God.

Finally, Malebranche, in his theodicy—the explanation of how God's wisdom, goodness, justice, and power are to be reconciled with the apparent imperfections and evils in the world—claimed that God could have created a more perfect world, free from all the defects and sins that plague this one, but that this would have involved greater complexity in the divine ways. God must act in the manner most in accord with his supremely perfect and simple nature; therefore, he always acts in the simplest way possible, and only by means of lawlike general volitions, never by "particular" or ad hoc volitions. This means, however that although on any particular occasion God could intervene and forestall an apparent evil that is about to occur by the ordinary course of the laws of nature (for example, a drought), he will not do so because this would compromise the simplicity of his *modi operandi*. Similarly, neither will he intervene to prevent a person who is about to sin. As Malebranche put it, "God acts only by a general will [*volonté générale*]." The perfection or goodness of the world per se is thus relativized to the simplicity of the laws of that world (or, which is the same thing, to the generality of the divine volitions that, on the occasionalist view, govern it). Taken together, the laws and the phenomena of the world form a whole that is most worthy of God's nature—in fact, the best combination possible. This account explains God's manner of operation, not just in the natural world of body and mind-body union but also in the moral world of beings endowed with freedom who depend upon grace for their everlasting happiness.

The abbé Simon Foucher (1644–1697), canon of the Sainte Chappelle of Dijon and a devotée of skeptical philosophy, was the first in a long line of critics of Malebranche's doctrines. The Jansenist theologian and Cartesian philosopher Antoine Arnauld (1612–1694) was undoubtedly the harshest, the most acute, and the most dogged. Arnauld approved of the *Search* upon first reading it, but when he later learned of Malebranche's views on grace and divine providence—only sketchily presented in the *Search* but more fully expounded in the *Traité de la nature et de la grace* (Treatise on Nature and Grace) in 1680—he embarked on a detailed critique of the major elements of the Oratorian's system. Arnauld's *Des vraies et des fausses idées* (On True and False Ideas, 1683) and Malebranche's reply, *Réponse du Père Malebranche au livre des vraies et des fausses idées* (1684), were only the opening salvos of what would be a long and often bitter public battle on both philosophical and theological matters. Although Arnauld succeeded in having the *Treatise* put on the church's Index of Prohibited Books in 1690 (the *Search* was added in 1709), their exchanges—public and private—continued until Arnauld's death. The Malebranche-Arnauld debate was one of the great intellectual events of the seventeenth century, and it attracted the attention of many, including Leibniz, Locke, and Newton.

After the publication of the *Search*, Malebranche turned to a "justification" of the Catholic religion and morality, presented in suitably Malebranchian terms, published as the *Conversations chrétiennes* in 1677. This was followed in 1683 by the *Méditations chrétiennes et métaphysiques*, which consists of dialogues in which "The Word" explains and defends Malebranche's system. That same year, Malebranche also published his *Traité de morale*, in which he undertook a rigorous demonstration of a true Christian ethics. There is, he insists throughout this and other works, an objective, universal, and rational order of values and moral imperatives. It is constituted by the "Order" in the divine intellect, and it is accessible to human reason because of our union with that understanding.

By the mid-1680s, Malebranche's reputation as the most important, if highly unorthodox, representative of the Cartesian philosophy was secure. He was corresponding with thinkers such as Leibniz, who criticized the Cartesian account of the laws of motion (as well as Malebranche's occasionalism), and the physicist Pierre-Sylvain Régis, who defended a more orthodox brand of Cartesianism and engaged Malebranche in a debate over some points of natural philosophy and over the nature of ideas.

Malebranche had many admirers, and at least an equal number of detractors, throughout Europe in the late seventeenth and early eighteenth centuries. His critics, of whom

Locke and Leibniz were only the most prominent, had little patience with what they saw as the deus ex machina at the heart of his system. If the Enlightenment stood for anything, it was the independence of human reason from divine authority and its mundane representatives; in this respect, Malebranche seemed to be an obstacle to philosophical, scientific, and political progress. Locke accused him of excessive "enthusiasm" with his doctrine of vision in God, while Leibniz thought that occasionalism reduced nature to a system of continuous miracles.

Malebranche did, however, have many disciples in Great Britain and on the European continent. Sometimes this was as a result of direct influence; in other cases, it came through his Oratorian followers, such as Bernard Lamy. In Britain, the philosophers George Berkeley and David Hume were, despite their critiques of Malebranche's views, deeply indebted to his analysis of causation and, in the case of Berkeley, to his understanding of the relationship between God and creation.

Malebranche had a significant impact on the French Enlightenment. His ideas received a wide and thorough hearing in the Republic of Letters, thanks initially to the efforts of Pierre Bayle and, later, of the Encyclopédistes, some of whom (such as Diderot) shared his distrust of "particularism." Jean-Jacques Rousseau was clearly familiar with Malebranche's doctrines, and there are evident traces of Malebranchian thought in the writings of Montesquieu, who had been a student at the Oratory. Although intended by Malebranche primarily as a theodicean and not a political strategy, his doctrine of God's general volitions, in particular, was highly important for the development of the notion of the General Will in eighteenth-century political thought.

[*See also* André, Yves-Marie; Arnauld, Antoine; Berkeley, George; Cartesianism; Leibniz, Gottfried Wilhelm von; Philosophy; Rationalism; *and* Roman Catholicism.]

BIBLIOGRAPHY

WORKS BY MALEBRANCHE

Oeuvres complètes de Malebranche. General editor, André Robinet. 20 vols. Paris, 1958–1967.

The Search after Truth. Translated by Thomas M. Lennon and Paul J. Olscamp. Cambridge, 1997.

Dialogues on Metaphysics and Religion. Edited by Nicholas Jolley, translated by David Scott. Cambridge, 1997.

Treatise on Nature and Grace. Translated by Patrick Riley. Oxford, 1992.

WORKS ABOUT MALEBRANCHE

Alquié, Ferdinand. *Le cartésianisme de Malebranche*. Paris, 1974. An examination of what Malebranche inherited from orthodox Cartesianism and what he modified or rejected.

André, Yves. *La vie du R. P. Malebranche, prêtre de l'Oratoire, avec l'histoire de ses ouvrages*. Paris, 1886; repr., Geneva, 1970. Written in the first half of the eighteenth century, but still the standard source on Malebranche's life.

Brown, Stuart, ed. *Nicolas Malebranche: His Philosophical Critics and Successors*. Assen, Neth., 1991. A collection of essays on Malebranche, his influence, and his contemporary and later critics.

Church, Ralph W. *A Study in the Philosophy of Malebranche*. London, 1931. A valuable general study of Malebranche's philosophy.

Easton, Patricia, Thomas M. Lennon, and Gregor Sebba. *Bibliographia Malebranchiana: A Critical Guide to the Malebranche Literature, 1638–1988*. Edwardsville, Ill., 1991. A comprehensive bibliography covering both Malebranche and his friends and critics.

Gueroult, Martial. *Malebranche*. 3 vols. Paris, 1955. An exhaustive and masterful study of Malebranche's system.

Jolley, Nicholas. *The Light of the Soul: Theories of Ideas in Leibniz, Malebranche, and Descartes*. Oxford, 1990. Examines Malebranche's theory of ideas, especially in comparison to Descartes's and Leibniz's accounts.

McCracken, Charles. *Malebranche and British Philosophy*. Oxford, 1983. Looks at the way Malebranche's philosophy was variously assimilated and criticised in early modern British philosophy; chapters on Locke, Berkeley, and Hume.

Nadler, Steven. *Malebranche and Ideas*. New York, 1992. An analysis of Malebranche's theory of ideas and doctrine of the vision in God.

Nadler, Steven, ed. *The Cambridge Companion to Malebranche*. Cambridge, 2000. A collection of essays on various aspects of Malebranche's philosophical system.

Radner, Daisie. *Malebranche: A Study of a Cartesian System*. Assen, Neth., 1978. A useful general and analytical presentation of Malebranche's doctrines.

Riley, Patrick. *The General Will before Rousseau*. Princeton, N.J., 1986. Malebranche's influence on the political thought of Rousseau and other Enlightenment figures.

Robinet, André. *Système et existence dans l'oeuvre de Malebranche*. Paris, 1965. One of the most important studies of Malebranche's philosophy, with emphasis on its development.

Schmaltz, Tad. *Malebranche's Theory of the Soul: A Cartesian Interpretation*. Oxford, 1996. An analytical study of Malebranche's doctrine of the soul in a Cartesian context.

Walton, Craig. *De la recherche du bien: A Study of Malebranche's Science of Ethics*. The Hague, 1972. An analysis of Malebranche's moral philosophy, concentrating on his account of virtue and duty.

Watson, Richard A. *The Downfall of Cartesianism*. The Hague, 1966. A study of the polemic between Malebranche and Foucher and its epistemological and ontological ramifications; a seminal work.

STEVEN M. NADLER

MALESHERBES, CHRÉTIEN-GUILLAUME DE LAMOIGNON DE

(1721–1794), French administrator, royal minister, and Louis XVI's lawyer during the Revolution.

Born into an important noble family of jurists who served in the parlement of Paris, Malesherbes was the son of Lamoignon de Blancmesnil, the chancellor of France from 1750 to 1768. Equally distinguished was his education as he attended the preeminent college of Louis-le-Grand in Paris. Most specialists in the period consider Malesherbes to have been a staunch defender of the Enlightenment and progressive ideals, in opposition to the king. They tend to ignore or indicate as exceptional his apparently contradictory role as the counsel to the monarch in 1792–1793, yet there is continuity in all

Malesherbes. Marble bust by Jean-Antoine Houdon (1741–1828). (Musée du Louvre, Paris/Giraudon/Art Resource, NY.)

Malesherbes's activities if one views him, as did his contemporaries, as a moderate philosophe.

Malesherbes is best known as the director of the Librairie from 1750 to 1763, a position in which he oversaw the domestic book and periodical trade. The main instrument of this agency, which housed the office of censorship, was the *privilège*, a formal right to publish and to receive a copyright. Publications that attacked personal reputations, the king, or morality were forbidden to appear, as were seditious works. Malesherbes took a liberal approach by permitting deviations from this doctrine. He made significant use of the "permission," which greatly lowered the standards and allowed the circulation of problematic notions. It was under this relaxed regime that Malesherbes protected, as long as he could, the *Encyclopédie* and Rousseau's *Émile*. Furthermore, he penned tracts throughout the prerevolutionary period that encouraged the free circulation of ideas. One should, however, not mistake his liberality for license; in particular, he would not tolerate critiques of monarchy. These strictly enforced limits usually protected the king from direct criticism.

In his role as head of the Librairie, Malesherbes was tireless and thoughtful. He believed that administrators ought to propose regulations that could be enforced.

Furthermore, he resisted influence-peddling. The archives contain many cases in which he opposed pressure from courtiers and even other ministers who sought to evade the policies that his office enforced. The rules were complex, but Malesherbes believed they should be maintained. These files show a model "enlightened" government at work. Malesherbes twice more assumed administrative roles, first alongside Turgot (1775–1776) and later, in 1787, as the Revolution approached. Then he worked on reform projects, and he believed none more important than improving first the plight of Protestants, then that of the Jews. Although he was unsuccessful in his effort to grant Protestants complete freedom of worship, he was deeply involved in the edicts of 17 November 1788 that granted civil equality. He left office before completing the work on rights for the Jews.

Outside the royal administration, as the head of the *cour des aides* (a customs court), Malesherbes encouraged judicial autonomy and resistance to monarchal supremacy. His defense of the courts' prerogatives allowed development of an enlightened position. Regulating customs, the *cour des aides* also had the right, as did the parlements, to register laws and to remonstrate when the justices objected to a law. Though far less important than their fellow magistrates, the judges of the *cour des aides* sometimes clashed with the monarch. Inheriting the post from his father, Malesherbes occupied the presidency from 1750 to 1775; in this role, he developed the view that the monarch must serve the country rather than direct it for his own benefit.

Two of Malesherbes's most important principles aimed at limiting royal power. As his biographer George Kelly has noted, Malesherbes sought to support the rule of law and oppose "attacks against the fundamental security of the person; arbitrary assaults on property, including offices." By criticizing practices frequently utilized by the centralizing monarch, Malesherbes dramatized his desire to constrict royal authority. Furthermore, more than fifteen years before the Revolution, Malesherbes advocated calling the Estates-General as a body that could block "despotic" acts better than the courts. Although the magistracy had, in fact, proved a substantial obstacle, the Estates-General promised even greater security. The courts could hinder edicts, but the Estates possessed final authority in the area of taxation. Because the Estates represented the nation, Malesherbes was clearly edging away from a simple defense of judicial prerogative toward a position more in line with the beliefs of the philosophes.

Despite Malesherbes's courage in opposing what he saw as royal usurpations of power, he remained extremely careful not to attack monarchy directly. He sought to lessen the sting of his criticism by consistently making monarchy central to his political plans for France. Working with Turgot in the ministry, Malesherbes supported an increase in centralization, though here enlightened progress remained part of his goal. Even in his most famous remonstrance (6 May 1775), which opposed new royal exactions on the public, he repeatedly blamed the ministers or others rather than the king himself. While noting that evil policies had prevailed, Malesherbes explained that "the combined interest of the ministers and all the powerful persons almost always prevails over that of the king and the people." Although contemporaries clearly understood that Malesherbes was using a customary exemption of the king while still launching an attack, he went further than other jurists had recently done to place the blame on others.

In sum, Malesherbes navigated between the philosophes and his abiding attachment to the monarchy. Most illustrative of his pro-Enlightenment stand was his view of the limits of the king's power. In fact, Malesherbes's reliance on the Estates-General as a useful institution reveals that his desire to constrain the monarch could in no way be construed as a narrow defense of the privileges of the judiciary. Instead, his embrace of the Estates showed that his goal was preserving rights in the face of a powerful government. His radicalism remained limited by his persistent unwillingness to abandon monarchy, or to make its existence entirely dependent on service to the country. Indeed, it was this last position that led him to defend Louis XVI during the Terror. Malesherbes did not reject reform; rather, he was demonstrating his loyalty to his former leader. This involvement with the king, along with more overtly antirevolutionary activities of his family, led to his arrest and execution on 22 April 1794.

[*See also* Censorship; France; French Revolution; Print Culture; *and* Publishing.]

BIBLIOGRAPHY

Baker, Keith Michael, ed. *The Old Regime and the French Revolution*. Chicago, 1987.

Grosclaude, Pierre. *Malesherbes témoin et interprète de son temps*. Paris, 1961. Deeply researched and thoughtful, this book presents a comprehensive view of Malesherbes, emphasizing the complexities of his viewpoints.

Jordan, David P. *The King's Trial: The French Revolution vs. Louis XVI*. Berkeley, 1979. This interesting study provides a sympathetic treatment of Malesherbes.

Kelly, George Armstrong. *Victims, Authority, and Terror: The Parallel Deaths of d'Orléans, Custine, Bailly, and Malesherbes*. Chapel Hill, N.C., 1982. The most thorough work on Malesherbes in English, this is a perceptive biography.

JACK R. CENSER

MALTHUS, THOMAS ROBERT (1766–1834), English political economist and demographer.

Malthus earned bachelor's (1788) and master's (1791) degrees at Cambridge University and was elected to a fellowship at Jesus College, Cambridge, in 1793. He was ordained as a minister of the Church of England in 1789. In 1805, he was appointed professor of history and political economy at the East India College at Haileybury, near Hertford, a position he held until his death. Among his numerous books, pamphlets, and articles, the best known are *An Essay on the Principle of Population* (1798, with subsequent editions in 1803, 1806, 1807, 1817, 1826) and *Principles of Political Economy* (1820, with a posthumous edition, with many alterations, in 1836).

The *Essay on Population* argued that population has a natural tendency to increase faster than the food supply, and must always therefore be restrained by various checks, classified by Malthus as either positive or preventive. The positive checks are those that increase the death rate—such as wars, famines, diseases, hunger, and infanticide. The preventive checks are those that reduce the birth rate—such as abortion, prostitution, contraception, and "prudential restraint," that is, postponement of marriage until there are sufficient prospects of supporting the expected number of children. The only check that Malthus approved of was prudential restraint—or preferably, "moral restraint," by which he meant prudential restraint combined with sexual abstinence before

Thomas Malthus. Engraving by M. Fornier after a portrait by John Linnell. (Bibliothèque Nationale, Paris/Giraudon/Art Resource, NY.)

marriage. He recognized that all the checks involved vice and/or misery. Even moral restraint can cause misery. This pessimistic view of human progress was particularly evident in the first edition of the *Essay on Population*. In later editions, however, a tone of cautious optimism began to appear, as he expressed the hope that with proper education the practice of prudential restraint might become more widespread. In his *Principles of Political Economy* he argued that, given the right balance between demand-side and supply-side forces, considerable economic progress might be achieved.

Thus, although Malthus rejected the extreme optimism of William Godwin and Jean-Antoine-Nicolas de Caritat Condorcet, he shared the Enlightenment belief in the possibility of progress, but he rejected the extreme optimism of Godwin and Condorcet. He cautiously argued that, even though we do not know where the limits to progress might lie, there must nevertheless be limits, and he stressed that the social, political, economic, and moral difficulties of progress should not be underestimated. He believed, or at least hoped, that the coming advances would extend to all classes of society, but he did not predict or advocate an egalitarian, classless society. He argued strongly in support of a landed aristocracy as the best safeguard of English liberties and privileges, but he advocated a wider (though not too wide) distribution of landed property. He welcomed the extension of the franchise in the Reform Act of 1832. He believed that a strong middle class would not only enhance social stability but would also generate the effective demand necessary for economic growth. His attachment to bourgeois values, typical of the Enlightenment, did not exclude a genuine concern for the welfare of the lower classes.

There can be no doubt of the influence of the Scottish Enlightenment on Malthus—particularly through Adam Smith—but the influence of the French Enlightenment is less direct and less obvious. His father, Daniel Malthus, was a friend and correspondent of Rousseau, and it is possible that Rousseau's pedagogical ideas influenced the unorthodox early education chosen by Daniel for his son, in the homes of private tutors and at the Dissenting Academy at Warrington. Malthus's library, inherited from his father, contained works by Jean-Jacques Rousseau, Jean Le Rond d'Alembert, François-René de Chateaubriand, Pierre-Paul-François Le Mercier de la Rivière, Montesquieu, and Voltaire, and his own publications include references to Condorcet, Mirabeau, Montesquieu, and Voltaire; however, it remains unclear how much they influenced him and how much his views developed independently.

In moral philosophy, Malthus was a utilitarian, or consequentialist. He regarded "the principle of utility" as "the great foundation of morals" (1989a, II, 104; later changed to "the great criterion of moral rules"). Unlike the antireligious and anticlerical attitudes of some writers of the Enlightenment, however, his utilitarianism was not presented as an alternative to Christianity. He remained throughout his life a sincere and devout minister of religion. His utilitarianism did not involve a rejection of a philosophy of natural law; he saw natural law, utility, and revelation as three different ways of arriving at the same truths. His religious convictions were not narrow or bigoted but were imbued with the spirit of religious toleration characteristic of the Enlightenment. He was a forceful advocate of the emancipation of Irish Catholics.

Malthus agreed with those Enlightenment authors who believed that a providential and benevolent order guides human destiny. The last two chapters of the first edition of his *Essay on Population* (1798) show clearly his view that the tension between population and food—far from being a blasphemous indictment of divine providence, as some critics alleged—was an essential part of the divine plan to lead us to social progress and the "growth of mind" (Malthus, 1986, vol. 1, p. 128). These last two theological chapters were omitted from later editions of the *Essay*, but there is no evidence that the omission represented a recantation. With Adam Smith and the Physiocrats, Malthus believed that a providential harmony exists between the economic interests of individuals and of society; however, like Adam Smith's, his laissez-faire individualism was of the pragmatic, not dogmatic, variety. He insisted on the need for exceptions and limitations to all the principles of political economy.

Malthus was also closely aligned with the spirit of the Enlightenment in his views on the role of passions and emotions in human affairs. He described our natural human passions as "the materials of all our pleasures, as well as of all our pains; of all our happiness, as well as of all our misery; of all our virtues, as well as of all our vices. It must therefore be regulation and direction that are wanted, not diminution or extinction" (Malthus, 1989a, vol. 2, p. 92). He also shared in the cult of sensibility and the pursuit of the sublime that are said to have been characteristics of the Enlightenment. His diary of a holiday in the Lake District (undated, but probably written in 1795, when he was twenty-nine) shows him as a devotee of the cult of the picturesque, assiduously consulting his guidebooks in the search for the most sublime views and prospects, and enhancing his visual pleasure with readings from James Thomson's poem *The Seasons*.

This early attachment to the cult of sensibility appears to have given way in later years to a cult of moderation, with an increasing emphasis on balance and proportion in human affairs. Malthus maintained that the factors determining economic growth—such as saving, consumption, and distribution—should be combined in optimal proportions; more generally, he believed that "It is not, however, in political economy alone that so much depends upon proportions, but throughout the whole range of nature and art" (1989b, vol. 2, pp. 269, 453). This pursuit of the golden mean was apparently reflected in his personal life, which according to contemporary sources was characterized by a spirit of moderation, symmetry and order.

[*See also* Economic Thought; Moral Philosophy; Natural Law; Passion; Progress; *and* Utopianism.]

BIBLIOGRAPHY

Dupâquier, J., A. Fauve-Chamoux, and E. Grebenik, eds. *Malthus Past and Present*. London, 1983. Selected papers from an international conference held in Paris, May 1980.

Hollander, Samuel. *The Economics of Thomas Robert Malthus*. Toronto, 1997. A detailed analysis of Malthus's economics.

James, Patricia. *Population Malthus: His Life and Times*. London, 1979. The most comprehensive and authoritative biography.

Jesus College (University of Cambridge). *The Malthus Library Catalogue*. New York, 1983. The library that belonged to Malthus, with later additions.

Malthus, Thomas R. *An Essay on the Principle of Population*. Edited by Patricia James. 2 vols. Cambridge, 1989. A variorum edition showing the changes that were made by Malthus in successive editions from the second (1803) to the sixth (1826).

Malthus, Thomas R. *Malthus: The Unpublished Papers in the Collection of Kanto Gakuen University*. Edited by John Pullen and Trevor Hughes Parry. Vol. 1. Cambridge, 1997. A collection of recently discovered letters to and from Malthus; a forthcoming second volume will contain sermons, diaries, and lecture notes.

Malthus, Thomas R. *Principles of Political Economy*. Edited by John Pullen. 2 vols. Cambridge, 1989. A variorum edition showing the differences between the first edition (1820) and the second posthumous edition (1836).

Malthus, Thomas R. *The Works of Thomas Robert Malthus*. Edited by E. A. Wrigley and David Souden. 8 vols. London, 1986.

Winch, Donald. *Malthus*. Oxford, 1987. An intellectual history in the *Past Masters* series, presenting Malthus's ideas on population in their social and political context.

JOHN PULLEN

MAN. *See* Human Nature.

MANDEVILLE, BERNARD (1670–1733), English moralist, satirist, physician and social philosopher.

Of Dutch birth and education, Mandeville attended the University of Leiden, earning his medical degree in 1691. In the 1690s, he emigrated to England, where he mastered the language, married, practiced medicine, translated some of La Fontaine's fables, and composed satiric verse. In his first book, *The Virgin Unmask'd* (1709), a maiden aunt and her nubile niece debate the risks and benefits of marriage. In his medical "treatise" (1711), actually a series of entertaining dialogues between patient and physician, Mandeville reveals his empirical approach to treating the "hypochondriack and hysterick" disorders. His thirty-two numbers of *The Female Tatler* (1709–1710) deal with his ideas on honor, morality, dueling, self-love, patriotism, military service, the family, and the passions. These topics are developed more fully in his masterpiece, *The Fable of the Bees* (part 1, 1714–1723; part 2, 1728), and in *An Enquiry into the Origin of Honour and the Usefulness of Christianity in War* (1732). The prose essays and dialogues comprising *The Fable of the Bees* grew out of his poem "The Grumbling Hive" (1705). In that work, a prosperous hive quickly suffers great losses in wealth and power after its morals are purified by a miraculous removal of all vices and crimes. The moral of this fable is that advanced societies cultivating luxury consumption cannot hope to eliminate the vices of mankind. The ambiguous subtitle of his *Fable of the Bees*—"private vices, public benefits"—led many to conclude erroneously that he approved of vice. He somewhat softened the stark implications of his subtitle by remarking that "Private Vices by the dextrous Management of a skilful Politician may be turn'd into Publick Benefits." Usually his examples of "benefits" resulting from vices involve the growing consumption of luxury goods and services, and the consequent increase in the circulation of money.

Following Hobbes, La Rochefoucauld, and some Augustinian writers, Mandeville regarded human beings as fundamentally egoistic creatures, proud of their reason but slaves to their selfish passions. On this basis he ridiculed Lord Shaftesbury's sentimental benevolist ethic with its doctrines of the "moral sense" and the innate goodness of mankind. He outraged many by remarking that "the Moral Virtues are the Political Offspring which Flattery begot upon Pride." His later alternative to this myth of the invention of morality by wily politicians is a naturalistic conjectural history (in *Fable*, 2) of the slow growth of language and society from untamed savagery to modern civility or politeness, bypassing the traditional account of the origins of language and society in the book of Genesis.

Mandeville's economic thought includes unconventional defenses of luxury consumption and the utility of the division of labor, analyses of the human passions in buying and selling, an emphasis on the importance of a favorable balance of trade, and mixed views on free trade (laissez-faire) versus state supervision (mercantilism), doctrines that were later transmuted or refined by Adam Smith. Rebutting supporters of the popular Charity Schools, Mandeville argued that a nation's wealth consists chiefly in possessing not money or land, but a large underclass of poor, uneducated laborers.

By insisting on a rigorous conception of virtue that excluded all taint of self-interest, Mandeville artificially narrowed the range of truly virtuous actions while expanding the empire of vice. This enabled him to unmask the hypocrisy or self-deception of many who thought they were virtuous but could not meet his difficult standard. He satirized the "man of honor" as a bully who tramples the commandments of Christian morality. Following his great countrymen Erasmus and Grotius, Mandeville attacked religious hypocrisy and supported sincere "inward religion," but he never revealed the contents of his personal faith, if he had any. Although in *Free Thoughts* (1720) he claimed to be an adherent of the Church of England, his clerical critics—notably William Law, Francis Hutcheson, Joseph Butler, and George Berkeley—viewed him as a dangerous unbeliever.

Mandeville supported the court Whigs in his later career by recommending moderation and peace in the political sphere, and he likewise supported a limited religious toleration for most sects, along the lines of Locke and Bayle, but excluding Roman Catholics and Jacobites. Surveying examples of religious cruelty over the centuries, he blamed the clergy for instigating wars and abetting religious persecution. Like Erasmus, he detested war and satirized soldiers, but he also recognized that the "aggrandized" modern state required standing armies for defense and conquest. Though appearing to accept the moral tenets of Christianity and even its "mysteries," he exhibited no sense of sin and no anxiety over the fate of his soul. His general cheerfulness reflects a neo-Epicurean and utilitarian commitment to the rational pursuit of happiness. He never advocated sweeping revolutionary reforms, although he did suggest some social reforms, such as revising the procedures at the Tyburn executions in order to curb unruly mobs and to emphasize the gravity of those occasions. The most extreme instance in his career as a reforming "projector" appeared in his ironic recommendations for legalizing prostitution, ostensibly to protect the chastity of British wives and virgins. This project, he argued, would not only generate economic benefits for the nation but would also ensure better control of venereal diseases.

Among French Enlightenment authors who reacted to Mandeville's thoughts on man and society, the most notable are Voltaire, Montesquieu, Rousseau, Diderot, d'Alembert, and perhaps La Mettrie. In England, Samuel Johnson ran counter to the usual condemnations of this "man-devil" when he admitted to Boswell that he had learned much from reading Mandeville. In the Scottish Enlightenment, Francis Hutcheson, David Hume, and Adam Smith disapproved of the immorality or "licentiousness" of his system, yet various Mandevillean ideas (e.g., the benefits of advanced commercial society) appear in their writings. Hume, Smith, Dugald Stewart, Lord Kames, and especially Adam Ferguson all employed the notion, clearly visible in Mandeville, that arts and institutions are often unintended consequences of human action—products not of individual genius but of the slow accretion of the knowledge and practices of ordinary men. Eighteenth-century German estimates of Mandeville's writings were often negative, the opinions of clerics who called him an atheist or *Freydenker*, but Kant, the towering mind in the German Enlightenment, classed him with thinkers such as Montaigne, Epicurus, and Hutcheson.

[*See also* Deism; Free Trade; Human Nature; Luxury; Medicine, *subentry on* Theories of Medicine; Moral Philosophy; Netherlands; Passion; *and* Political Philosophy.]

BIBLIOGRAPHY

Carrive, Paulette. *La philosophie des passions chez Bernard Mandeville*. Lille and Paris, 1983. A detailed study of his life, works, and influence, by the most accomplished Mandeville scholar in France.

Cook, Richard I. *Bernard Mandeville*. New York, 1974. A short, reliable survey, especially good on the *Modest Defence of Publick Stews*.

Goldsmith, M. M. *Private Vices, Public Benefits: Bernard Mandeville's Social and Political Thought*. Cambridge, 1985. Valuable analysis of Mandeville's politics, with strong emphasis on the importance of his *Female Tatler* essays.

Gunn, J. A. W. *Beyond Liberty and Property: The Process of Self-Recognition in Eighteenth-Century Political Thought*. Kingston, Ont., and Montreal, 1983. Contains a strong chapter on the interrelations of Mandeville's economic thought and his Whig politics, with new facts on the contemporary reception of his *Fable*.

Hirschman, Albert O. *The Passions and the Interests: Political Arguments for Capitalism before Its Triumph*. Princeton, N.J., 1977. Groundbreaking analysis of the transition from the language of the passions to that of interests, with salient remarks on Mandeville's place in this continuum.

Horne, Thomas A. *The Social Thought of Bernard Mandeville: Virtue and Commerce in Early Eighteenth-Century England*. New York, 1978. An overview of Mandeville's two spheres of argument, with good insights into his French sources.

Hundert, E. J. *The Enlightenment's* Fable: *Bernard Mandeville and the Discovery of Society*. Cambridge, 1994. The most ambitious recent study of Mandeville's thought, emphasizing his contributions to the "science of socialized man" in varied contexts.

Jack, Malcolm. *Corruption and Progress: The Eighteenth-Century Debate*. New York, 1989. Fine review of the development of this extensive debate, featuring Mandeville, Rousseau, and Adam Ferguson.

Monro, Hector. *The Ambivalence of Bernard Mandeville*. Oxford, 1975. Still one of the best general expositions of Mandeville's thought and its cultural contexts.

Primer, Irwin, ed. *Mandeville Studies: New Explorations in the Art and Thought of Dr. Bernard Mandeville, 1670–1733*. The Hague, 1975. Essays on Mandeville's sources, ideas and influence, with analyses of his contributions to literary genres and to the religious and political controversies of his time.

Schneider, Louis. *Paradox and Society: The Work of Bernard Mandeville*. New Brunswick, N.J., 1987. Able survey of Mandeville's thought, with special attention to his role as a forerunner of sociology, in particular of functionalist analysis.

Scribano, Maria E. *Natura umana e società competitiva: Studio su Mandeville*. Milan, 1980. The best modern Italian survey of Mandeville's social, economic and religious thought, with commendable attention to his French sources and contexts.

Speck, W. A. "Bernard Mandeville and the Middlesex Grand Jury." *Eighteenth-Century Studies* 11 (1978), 362–374. An important piece of historical detective work, explaining the factors leading to the presentment of *The Fable of the Bees* by the Grand Jury of Middlesex in 1723.

Stafford, J. Martin, ed. *Private Vices, Publick Benefits? The Contemporary Reception of Bernard Mandeville*. Solihull, U.K., 1997. An unprecedented and very useful collection including almost all the important attacks on Mandeville in Britain, together with his response to Berkeley, in the decade after 1723.

IRWIN PRIMER

MANNERS. *See* Sociability.

MAPPING. The term *mapping* best describes both the theory and practices of mapmaking and survey during the Enlightenment, as well as the period's figurative sense of how to locate the peoples of the world. This combination of metaphor on the one hand and mathematical accuracy and scientific representation on the other makes *mapping* historically more apt in the context of the Enlightenment than *cartography*, a term that was not used until 1839, and then only to signify the professionalization of mapmaking by specialists. Although the idea of mapping as a metaphor appeared throughout the Enlightenment—in their prefatory *Discours*, for example, Diderot and d'Alembert referred to their monumental *Encyclopédie* as a "map of the world"—the term is most widely understood in the second sense above, in association with the advance of geographical knowledge about Earth and with its representation in graphical and textual form.

Nevertheless, maps do not straightforwardly depict the real world. Most cartographic historians now recognize two broad and basically conflicting assumptions underlying our interpretations of how maps function (see the cited works by Burnett, Edney, Harley, and Jacob). The first assumes a direct structural relationship between the map and the territory the map depicts—the map as a mirror of the world—and thus is concerned more with notions of accuracy and map-world correspondence. The second assumes that maps never can represent the world mimetically: indeed, far from mirroring the world, maps actively constitute it. Thus, the map is less a document of spatial

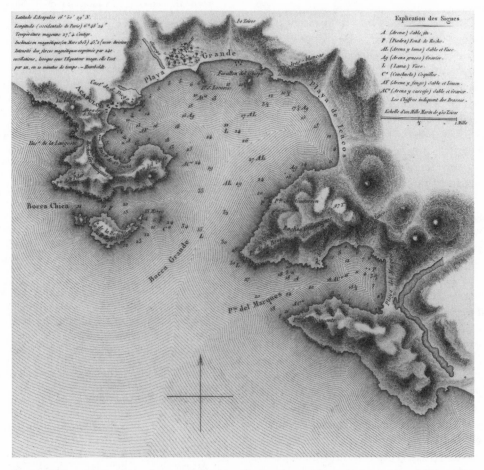

Humboldt's Atlas. Plan of Acapulco, New Spain, from Alexander von Humboldt, *Atlas géographique et physique du royaume de la Nouvelle-Espagne* (Paris, 1811). (Geography and Map Division, Library of Congress.)

accuracy and more an ideological artifact and symbol of political power. The emphasis given by most contemporaries to mapping projects in the Enlightenment was to mapping as an accurate representation of Earth's surface. The ideological and political context of such mapping, however understood as an expression of European imperial power, has been the subject of attention by modern historians of Enlightenment mapping.

By the mid-seventeenth century in Europe, there were three principal modes of mapping: maritime charting, small-scale mapping of the world and its regions (properly understood as "chorography"), and large-scale land survey. Four interrelated groups of practitioners were connected with mapmaking: mariners, mathematical and descriptive geographers, commercial publishers, and land measurers. From about 1660, argues Matthew Edney, the increasing involvement of many European nations in surveying their territories at home and overseas saw the emergence of a further group of military and state surveyors. For Edney, this group in particular drew together earlier modes of mapping into a more unified mathematical cosmography, mapping as a state enterprise undertaken via standard practices and aiming at a commonly recognizable form.

Terrestrial state survey in the early Enlightenment initially reflected concerns to locate property and thus to generate revenue from property taxes. This cadastral mapping was followed by surveys for other administrative and military purposes. The French state was the most active in this regard. Geodesists and astronomers were employed through the Académie Royale des Sciences in the first Cassini Survey (1680–1744), which helped to provide a mathematical grid of the French nation. This work was supplemented by the activities of road and bridge engineers, and most notably by the second national topographical survey of France under the control of César-François Cassini de Thury between 1747 and 1789.

The Cassini surveys of France prompted comparable undertakings in Denmark (1757–1805) and in Würtemberg (1793–1828). Surveys of the Italian and German states begun under French occupation during the Revolutionary and Napoleonic wars (1794–1815) were continued after 1815. For Britain, military imperatives underlay the mapping of the Highlands of Scotland between 1747 and 1755, following the Jacobite Rebellion of 1745, and the mapping of Bengal from 1765 to 1771. Military engineers also surveyed the Habsburg lands (1763–1787), Prussia (1767–1787), and Saxony (1780–1825).

Throughout Europe especially, but also in Enlightenment North America, mapping was likewise undertaken of individual estates, national coastlines, and expanding cities and towns. This reflects not just Enlightenment faith in the map as an instrument of improvement and utility, but also the growing social status and professionalization of the surveyor and the networks of social patronage on which many were dependent. Mapping had close connections, too, with the authority of the painterly eye in later Enlightenment aesthetic traditions: surveying was a matter of visual as well as mathematical authority. It is clear, too, that mapping was directed at a public interested, for example, in understanding the circumstances of military campaigns, the locations of current events or—as Martin Brückner has shown of the early United States—the emerging shape of the nation. Mapping, at home or abroad, was a distinctively social process with its own aristocracy and division of labor. It was also always political. Anne Marie Claire Godlewska has shown how the findings of Napoleonic survey of Egypt, in its written text but especially in its maps, sought to extend a style of geographical representation that aimed to render Egypt French and to give greater importance to Egypt's historical geography over its contemporary configuration. Mapping and its textual and visual accompaniments were a monument to geographical knowledge and also to favored concepts, power, and ambition.

Both within one's own national space and in overseas territories, then, mapping sought to reduce the complexities of the Enlightenment world to a rational order, and the map, as a product of geographical as well as of political inquiry, had close links with many eighteenth-century descriptive geographies. Yet we should not think of mapping as a straightforward process or exclusively technical practice, nor as the simple overlayering of European ideas on an uninscribed or unoccupied space. As Edney has shown in regard to the mapping of British India, the mapmakers certainly sought a visual rhetoric of empirical accuracy; however, it was often hindered by unreliable instruments and by the very nature it sought to depict—lines of sight were blocked by trees, by the dust of moving soldiers, and by native artifacts. Even in the context of precise triangulation, the "lie of the land" between measured locations was often sketched in by eye.

Daniel Clayton, for example, has charted in detail the background to George Vancouver's mapping of Vancouver Island, the processes of surveying, and the different interpretations by modern historians of the significance of these events. Vancouver's cartography, Clayton argues, allows us to understand the transition more generally in the Enlightenment between moments of contact and the causes of conflict between native peoples and European imperial nations. Vancouver used naming practices to make the island British, and he adopted surveying practices that made the island recognizably European. The map thus brought together, in an eminently transportable form, the local circumstances of mappers and natives and the global reach of the British Admiralty, European traders, and the European geographical imagination.

Such Enlightenment mapping was not, however, a simple translation of the real world into a standard and portable form of knowledge easily read by persons elsewhere. Michael Bravo has shown that the encounter between native peoples and the French geographer and navigator Jean-François de Galaup, comte de Lapérouse, in the Gulf of Tartary in Pacific Russia in 1787 was not just a moment of contact. Rather, it was a process of what Bravo has termed "ethnographic navigation," which hinged on bridging the problem of incommensurability—the gap between European visitors who wanted to know if Sakhalin was a peninsula or an island (and who would then add such new geographical knowledge to the world map), and a culture for whom the concept *map* and the idea of mapping were simply foreign. In the Pacific, in British India, and in Australia, no less than in northern Canada and in Gaelic Scotland, the processes of Enlightenment mapping were in several ways reliant on native peoples as guides, interpreters, and suppliers, but indigenous toponyms, knowledge, and the peoples themselves were usually excluded from the resulting maps.

By the late eighteenth century, the growing institutionalization and professionalization of mapping practices were apparent in Britain in the formation in 1791 of the Trigonometrical Survey, later the Ordnance Survey. Comparable bodies were delayed in France by the revolutionary state of the nation. By the same period, new graphical techniques of cartographic representation were being established and more widely adopted. In the early nineteenth century, the German naturalist scientist and geographer Alexander von Humboldt was the first person to use extensively and systematically the techniques of isoline cartography, in which lines are used to connect points of equal value, and thus to extrapolate geographical variations in a measured natural feature (such as isotherms for temperature). Humboldt's use of maps in these ways was part of a concern for what Michael Dettelbach has called a "global physics," and for a new form of explanatory and integrative earth science. Together with institutional changes, technical advances, and greater professionalization of mapping practitioners, such work signaled new beginnings for the cartographic sciences.

[*See also* Geography.]

BIBLIOGRAPHY

Bravo, Michael. "Ethnographic Navigation and the Geographical Gift." In *Geography and Enlightenment*, edited by David Livingstone and Charles Withers, pp. 199–235. Chicago, 1999.

Brückner, Martin. "Lessons in Geography: Maps, Spellers, and Other Grammars of Nationalism in the Early Republic." *American Quarterly* 51 (1999), 311–343.

Burnett, D. Graham. "The History of Cartography and the History of Science." *Isis* 90 (1999), 775–780.

Clayton, Daniel. *Islands of Truth: The Imperial Fashioning of Vancouver Island*. Vancouver, B.C., 2000. Chaps. 11–13 discuss the nature of George Vancouver's mapping of the island and relationships between mapping, commerce, native peoples, and imperialism in the late Enlightenment.

Dettelbach, Michael. "Global Physics and Aesthetic Empire: Humboldt's Physical Portrait of the Tropics." In *Visions of Empire: Voyages, Botany and Representations of Nature*, edited by David Philip Miller and Peter Hanns Reill, pp. 258–292. Cambridge and New York, 1996.

Edney, Matthew. "Cartography without 'Progress': Reinterpreting the Nature and Historical Development of Mapmaking." *Cartographica* 30 (1993), 54–68. A review article on the interpretations of map history.

Edney, Matthew. "Mathematical Cosmography and the Social Ideology of British Cartography, 1780–1820." *Imago Mundi* 46 (1994), 101–116.

Edney, Matthew. *Mapping an Empire: The Geographical Construction of British India, 1765–1843*. Chicago, 1997. The first three chapters offer a summary of the ideologies of mapmaking and the practices of cartographic representation in the second half of the eighteenth century.

Edney, Matthew. "Cartography: Disciplinary History." In *Sciences of the Earth: An Encyclopedia of Events, People, and Phenomena*, vol. 1, edited by Gregory Good, pp. 81–85. London and New York, 1998.

Edney, Matthew. "Reconsidering Enlightenment Geography and Map Making: Reconnaissance, Mapping, Archive." In *Geography and Enlightenment*, edited by David Livingstone and Charles Withers, pp. 165–198. Chicago, 1999.

Godlewska, Anne Marie Claire. *The Napoleonic Survey of Egypt: A Masterpiece of Cartographic Compilation and Early Nineteenth-Century Fieldwork*. (Cartographica Monographs 38–39.) Toronto, 1988.

Godlewska, Anne Marie Claire. "Map, Text, and Image: The Mentality of Enlightened Conquerors: A New Look at the *Description de l'Égypte*." *Transactions of the Institute of British Geographers* 20 (1995), 5–28.

Godlewska, Anne Marie Claire. *Geography Unbound: French Geographic Science from Cassini to Humboldt*. Chicago, 1999. Mapmaking is shown to be a central element of French geographical traditions and an important means to the promotion of French national identity.

Harley, Brian. "The Map and the Development of the History of Cartography." In *The History of Cartography*, vol. 1, *Cartography in Prehistoric, Ancient, and Medieval Europe and the Mediterranean*, edited by Brian Harley and David Woodward, pp. 1–42. Chicago, 1987. A valuable essay on the nature and interpretation of maps as introduction to the first volume of a major series of edited texts by cartographic historians.

Harley, Brian. "Maps, Knowledge, and Power." In *The Iconography of Landscape: Essays on the Symbolic Representation, Design and Use of Past Environments*, edited by Denis Cosgrove and Stephen Daniels, pp. 277–312. Cambridge, 1988.

Jacob, Christian. *L'empire des cartes: Approche théorique de la cartographie à travers l'histoire*. Paris, 1992.

Livingstone, David, and Withers, Charles, eds. *Geography and Enlightenment*. Chicago, 1999. An edited collection of essays on the nature of geography and geographical knowledge in the Enlightenment: see particularly chaps. 5–8 under the thematic heading "Mappings."

CHARLES W. J. WITHERS

MARCHAND, PROSPER (1678–1756), French Huguenot refugee, bookseller, bibliographer, and journalist in the Netherlands.

Born in Saint-Germain-en-Laye, Marchand was admitted as a bookseller in 1698 in Paris, where he published numerous works, including sales catalogs published in collaboration with Gabriel Martin. With Martin, he devised the organizational system of the Parisian booksellers, which was used throughout the eighteenth century in booksellers' catalogs. Having converted to Protestantism, Marchand sought refuge in the Netherlands in 1709 in the company of the engravers Étienne and Bernard Picart. He established a shop in The Hague and later in Amsterdam, returning finally to The Hague in 1712, having given up the book trade. He was engaged by the booksellers Fritsch and Böhm and supervised their edition of the works of Pierre Bayle, including the third edition of the *Dictionnaire historique*, which appeared in 1720.

Marchand was well placed to become a recognized intermediary between Huguenots throughout Europe and the Dutch booksellers. As his correspondence attests, he advised writers and publishers, mediated between them, directed and proofread numerous editions, and ensured that they were reviewed in journals. A prolific journalist, he was one of the main editors of the influential *Journal Littéraire* (The Hague, 1713–1722, 1729–1732), and then of the *Journal Historique de la République des Lettres* (Leiden, 1732–1733). He wrote many articles and reviews for the *Bibliothèque Britannique*, the *Bibliothèque Germanique*, the *Journal Littéraire d'Allemagne, de la Suisse, et de Nord*, the *Nouvelle Bibliothèque*, and the *Bibliothèque Française*; he also wrote for the *Epilogueur Moderne, Historique, Galant et Moral* of Jean Rousset de Missy.

Among Marchand's own publications, the most famous are the *Histoire des origines et des premiers progrès de l'imprimerie* (History of the Origins and Early Progress of Printing, The Hague, 1740), a history of printing, and the *Dictionnaire historique ou mémoires critiques et littéraires concernant la vie et les ouvrages de divers personnages, distingués particulièrement dans la République des Lettres* (Historical Dictionary, or Critical and Literary Memoires Concerning the Life and Works of Many Persons Particularly Distinguished in the Republic of Letters, The Hague, 1758–1759), a biographical compendium intended as a supplement to the *Dictionnaire* of Bayle. Marchand considered himself a loyal follower of Bayle, although he was far from sharing Bayle's genius. He was a meticulous bibliographer who noted with great precision the sources he used and what books had been published; he began several bibliographical works that he never finished. For him, the quality of history depended on the quality of sources that could be verified. That was one of the reasons for his strong opposition to Voltaire, which culminated in his *Observations occasionnelles sur le Siècle de Louis XIV du sieur de Voltaire* (Occasional Observations on Voltaire's "Age of Louis XIV"), published in 1753 with La Beaumelle.

Marchand was a *libertin érudit* ("freethinker") and belonged to the Chevaliers de la Jubilation, a small libertine circle that delighted in salacious poems, daring satires against the king of France, and the pleasures of the flesh and good wine, but also in philosophical discussion. He was deeply interested in Freemasonry (his friends Jean Rousset de Missy and Justinus de Beyer were Masons), although he never joined a lodge. He was also a convinced Calvinist, although he leaned toward an outspoken anticlerical skepticism that made no distinction between Rome and Geneva. In fact, Marchand's true church was the Republic of Letters.

[*See also* Bayle, Pierre; Journals, Newspapers, and Gazettes, *subentry on* The Netherlands; Print Culture; *and* Publishing.]

BIBLIOGRAPHY

Berkvens-Stevelinck, C., with A. Nieuweboer. *Catalogue des manuscrits de la collection Marchand* (Codices manuscripti XXVI). Leiden, Netherlands, 1988.

Berkvens-Stevelinck, C. *Prosper Marchand et l'histoire du livre: Quelques aspects de l'érudition bibliographique dans la première moitié du XVIIIème siècle, particulièrement en Hollande*. Bruges, Belgium, 1978.

Berkvens-Stevelinck, C. *Prosper Marchand, la vie et l'oeuvre (1688–1756)*. Leiden, Netherlands, 1987.

CHRISTIANE BERKVENS-STEVELINCK
Translated from French by Susan Romanosky and Ruth Whelan

MARIVAUX, PIERRE CARLET DE CHAMBLAIN DE (1688–1763), French novelist, essayist, and playwright.

Born in Paris, Marivaux spent his youth in the provinces, where his father was a minor bureaucrat. He returned to Paris at the age of twenty-two to study the law, a respectable goal for a connected, intelligent, but not too wealthy young man. Little verifiable biographical data exists for him, which may account for the low profile that he and his work have maintained in the mainstream history of French letters.

In 1712, Marivaux wrote a play, a proto-melodrama, *Le père prudent et équitable* (A Father, Prudent and Just), but for the next decade, he wrote long prose romances and pastiches, experimenting with the new prose format, the novel. Among those works were *Pharsamon ou le Don Quichotte moderne* (Pharsamon or the Modern Don Quixote, 1713); *Les effets surprenants de la sympathie* (The Surprising Effects of Affection, 1713–1714; which could be the title of most of his novelistic and dramatic works); and *L'Iliade travestie* (A Travesty of the "Iliad," 1716). These works had only modest success, but they reveal

Marivaux. Portrait by Louis-Michel Van Loo. (Châteaux de Versailles et de Trianon, Versailles, France/Réunion des Musées Nationaux/Art Resource, NY.)

a complex imagination, as well as an early fascination with the way language reveals personal psychology and the way personal style organizes social exchange. In 1717, Marivaux married a relatively wealthy woman, then invested much of her dowry in John Law's bank, which would fail catastrophically in 1720. As a consequence, he had to write for his living, and he did so in three genres: the journalistic essay (à la the British *Tatler* essays by Addison and Steele), the stage comedy, and the novel. During the 1720s and the 1730s, he wrote three miscellaneous prose collections, some thirty plays (only one of which, *Annibal* [*Hannibal*; 1720] was a tragedy), and two long but unfinished novels. Today, he is known primarily for his comedies; after an absence of many decades, his plays have been returned to the repertories of provincial, Parisian, and international companies. His novels and essays are still available, but they are mostly read in schools and universities.

Journals. To understand Marivaux's originality as an important transitional voice in the early French Enlightenment's definition of sociability, the best place to start is with what he called his "journals": *Le spectateur français* (The French Spectator, 1721–1724), *L'indigent philosophe* (The Indigent Philosopher, 1727), and *Le cabinet du philosophe* (The Philosopher's Study, 1734). These

works (comprising essays, apologues, and stories) have in common his attempt to explain the need for a new and viable ethics of sociability, with its requisite codes, sought by an anxious, yet impatiently mobile class of intellectuals, nouveaux riches, and urban sophisticates. Writing in the venerable *moraliste* tradition, Marivaux offered a secular ethics for an emerging public, still apprehensive about the possible return of the sectarian divisiveness of the sixteenth century and the seventeenth but eager to loosen the strictures of aristocratic, especially court, etiquette. His plays reflected the way this new public defined, experimented with, and eventually adopted the beliefs and codes of etiquette that would distinguish it from the rigid social hierarchies of the seventeenth century.

Plays. Marivaux had been influenced by several important historical and cultural phenomena: the liberal regency of the duc d'Orléans (1715–1723); the advent and fall of John Law's banking and investment bubbles (1716–1720); the resurgence of the Quarrel of the Ancients and Moderns (1714–1715); and the competition between the Comédie Italienne and the Comédie Française, the official dramatic troupe of the Crown. The Comédie Italienne preserved the traditions of the earlier Italian commedia dell'arte, which had emphasized the free, often pantomimic, play of the body, as well as the play of language. Of his twenty-nine comedies, fully nineteen (ten of his first fifteen) were performed by the Comédie Italienne. Marivaux's genius lay in marrying their agile, physical, and spontaneous performing style with a more fluid, more ambiguous theatrical discourse.

Marivaux's plays are as much about language and its slipperiness as they are about affection. His masterpieces include five that are still produced with regularity: *La surprise de l'amour* (The Surprise of Love, 1722); *La double inconstance* (Two Infidelities, 1723); *Le jeu de l'amour et du hasard* (The Play between Love and Chance, 1730); *Les serments indiscrets* (Rash Promises, 1732); and *Les fausses confidences* (False Secrets, 1737). These plays show how love surprises all. We try to combat desire with language, but our very words reveal our desire, and so we turn back to language to help manage the chaos that threatens our heretofore safe world. His major plays end as love has been (verbally) admitted; they are more about flirting than about sex.

For most of his publishing career, Marivaux was criticized for being too "metaphysical," because of his preoccupation with the psychology of sentiment and because of his idiosyncratic prose style. Given the term *marivaudage*, this disparaged style combined neologisms with subtle adjustments to affective vocabulary, which then emphasized nuance and ambiguity in dialogue. The term is still used dismissively in French for unclear verbiage, yet it was his imaginative attempt to show the psychological complexity of emotional conversation.

Novels. While making his reputation in the theater, with both the French and Italian troupes, Marivaux also wrote two experimental novels, both about young people who have to survive and succeed in a world that demands transparent identities. One is an orphan (*La vie de Marianne* [The Life of Marianne, 1731–1741]), the other, a peasant (*Le paysan parvenu* [The Peasant Who Made It, 1735–1736]), two social types marked by their lack of connection to the hierarchy that dominated power and possibility in Paris. Their merits include, instead, intelligence, the astute ability to manipulate others, and natural virtue. Both succeed, making it on merit and connections, rather than on genealogy or inherited tradition. They are quite modern protagonists.

After being elected to the Académie Française in 1743, over the candidacy of none other than Voltaire (who never forgave him for his "metaphysics" or his success), Marivaux essentially retired. He wrote but a few occasional pieces and seems to have enjoyed the last two decades of his life as a respected figure in the Parisian literary establishment. Marivaux had much in common with the Age of the Enlightenment: he believed in meritorious social advancement; had faith in the cognitive value of feeling; trusted the good judgment of the man and woman of modern tastes; thought the imagination an important avenue to individual values; and believed that a need existed for a secular ethics, to attract and aid those for whom the demands of orthodoxy were proving tiresome.

[*See also* Literary Genres; Novel; *and* Theater.]

BIBLIOGRAPHY

WORKS BY MARIVAUX

Marivaux, Pierre Carlet de Chamblain de. *Journaux et oeuvres de jeunesse*. Edited by Frédéric Deloffre and Michel Gilot. Paris, 1969.

Marivaux, Pierre Carlet de Chamblain de. *Oeuvres de jeunesse*. Edited by Frédéric Deloffre. Paris, 1972.

Marivaux, Pierre Carlet de Chamblain de. *Le paysan parvenu*. Edited by F. Deloffre. Paris, 1959.

Marivaux, Pierre Carlet de Chamblain de. *Théâtre complet*. 2 vols. Edited by F. Deloffre. Paris, 1968.

Marivaux, Pierre Carlet de Chamblain de. *La vie de Marianne*. Edited by F. Deloffre. Paris, 1957.

WORKS ABOUT MARIVAUX

Coulet, Henri. *Marivaux romancier*. Paris, 1975. An excellent study that places Marivaux's work within the novelistic traditions of early modern France.

Coulet, Henri, and Michel Gilot. *Marivaux: Un humanisme expérimental*. Paris, 1973. A thematic analysis of the subtle social ethics in all of Marivaux's work.

Deloffre, Frédéric. *Une préciosité nouvelle: Marivaux et le marivaudage*. Paris, 1955; 2d rev. ed., 1967. The most important book on Marivaux's style, language, and vocabulary, and on seventeenth- and eighteenth-century social linguistics.

Gossmann, Lionel. "Literature and Society in the Early Eighteenth Century: The Case of Marivaux." *Modern Language Notes* 82 (May 1967), 306–333. A subtle analysis of Marivaux and his social context.

Greene, E. J. H. *Marivaux*. Toronto, 1965. Still the best introduction to Marivaux and his work in English.

Haac, Oscar. *Marivaux*. New York, 1973. Another quite adequate introduction in English to Marivaux's career.

Rosbottom, Ronald C. *Marivaux's Novels: Theme and Function in Early Eighteenth-Century Narrative*. London, 1974. On Marivaux's narrative fiction.

RONALD C. ROSBOTTOM

MARMONTEL, JEAN-FRANÇOIS (1723–1799), French writer.

Though very lowborn, Marmontel finished life having known considerable social and literary success, as is evident from his election as a member (1763) and later as the perpetual secretary (1783) of the Académie Française, and from his appointment as royal historiographer (1772). His career as a man of letters was solidly founded on an uncommon ability to give his cultured, sophisticated audience in the capital precisely what it wanted. His pen took him in numerous directions: light verse, libretti, literary and aesthetic theory, high poetry, translations, journalism, short stories, and novels. His links with the Enlightenment are defined by his short stories and novels.

In his early career, Marmontel was considered one of the "philosophical" party. His exceptionally popular *Contes moraux* (1755–1765) were an important conduit through which reassuring visions of the Enlightenment were communicated not only to polite society but indeed to the literate artisans and peasants of France, Germany, Switzerland, Poland, Russia, Hungary, Romania, the Baltic states, and North America. There was little in his early career, however, that gave proof of a fierce commitment to Enlightenment values. In the *Contes moraux*, he did broach a certain number of contemporary problems, but in a way that was so discreet and uncontroversial that it has prompted the judgment that his *philosophie* was *parée de rubans* ("adorned with ribbons"). A turning point came in 1765, when, believing himself to be dying, Marmontel resolved to reveal his hand and to leave a record of his growing concern for the well-being of a France that had just emerged vastly diminished from the Seven Years' War under the inept guidance of a cynical, ruling elite. He resolved, therefore, under the guise of a work about the late Roman Empire (the choice of an equally decadent period was deliberate) to produce *Bélisaire* (1767), a didactic, patriotic work of sixteen short chapters that secured him even greater international fame.

In this work, Belisarius (Marmontel) indicates to Justinian (Louis XV) the politico-moral means of regaining the confidence and esteem of the nation, which he had increasingly alienated. Rarely could an adept of the Enlightenment have given clearer proof of his

Jean-François Marmontel. Engraving by Augustin de Saint-Aubin (1736–1807) after a portrait by Charles-Nicolas Cochin the Younger (1715–1790). (Lauros-Giraudon/Art Resource, NY.)

commitment to the cause. Outraged, however, by the severe public censure that the Sorbonne made of his fifteenth chapter (which argues for religious toleration), Marmontel wrote *Les Incas*, in which he demonstrated that religious fanaticism, which negated all the values of the Enlightenment, corrupted everything with which it came into contact.

Les Incas (composed from 1767 to 1771, but published only in 1777) reiterated the philosophy, outrage, and lapidary political maxims of *Bélisaire*. The message of this novel is nonetheless more complex than that of its predecessor. Marmontel's further mission (this period also saw the abbé Raynal's *Histoire philosophique des deux Indes*) was to engage in a sustained and not too discreet meditation on the colonization of the modern world by the unscrupulous European powers. Like Raynal (whose brutal ideological frankness Marmontel lacked), he channeled his anger toward the congregation of the philosophical faithful in the hope that the moral indignation of decent men, sufficiently awakened, would be equal to the task of countering complex politico-economic interests that clearly were growing stronger in a rapidly expanding world.

In *Bélisaire* and *Les Incas* (which the scholar Jean Fabre called "important works" because they were engines of war in the service of suffering humanity), Marmontel was obviously seeking to popularize a very particular kind of socio-political community, an ideal city, a moral utopia. Yet Marmontel, at the center of the philosophical party in the Academy, a true champion of *bienfaisance* and *régénération* who should have been as ardent as his confrères Condorcet, La Harpe, Bailly, or Chamfort for the fashioning of a new France in 1788–1789, was among the very first (long before the fall of the Bastille) to demonstrate a growing attachment to "counter-revolutionary" positions.

His alleged "palinode" has attracted some unfavorable comments. The *Grand dictionnaire universel*, usually a solid source of enlightenment, is fairly typical in suggesting that in growing old he foreswore his *encyclopédiste* doctrines and became religious. Marmontel did not really part company with the Enlightenment in 1788–1789. For him, what injected an unwelcome new factor into the Enlightenment equation was the vigorous assertion of the natural civic equality of man. In the fraught world of 1788–1789, desperately trying to redefine itself, the immediate, unsupervised, and untutored access gained by every man and woman to political influence struck Marmontel as the defeat of rationalism and good sense, and ultimately of humanitarian endeavor. The view of the Revolution that emerges from his profoundly revealing *Mémoires* (1793–1796) is that of a tragic *dérapage*. The philosophe Marmontel honestly saw the salvation of France in 1788–1789, and at least for the immediate future, in the shape of a hierarchical society subservient to genuine, equitable monarchical paternalism ordered by enlightened and Philanthropic philosophy. He wished for a world of personal human generosity within a patriarchal regime of social and moral protection. That was compatible, for him, with working to bring the nation "up to the level of its Constitution." Marmontel did renounce the Revolution, but he did not renounce the Enlightenment. He was convinced that it was the former that had betrayed the ends and the means of the latter. Between 1792 and 1799, withdrawn from society, he devoted his time to educating his young sons, a microcosmic version of that other, equally noble macrocosmic task of regeneration to which he would, in other happier circumstances, have devoted himself with courage and all due sense of obligation.

[*See also* French Revolution; Raynal, Guillaume-Thomas; *and* Toleration.]

BIBLIOGRAPHY

WORKS BY MARMONTEL
Marmontel, Jean-François. *Bélisaire*. Edited by Robert Granderoute. Paris, 1994. Contains an excellent introduction.

Marmontel, Jean-François. *Mémoires*. Edited by John Renwick. 2 vols. Clermont-Ferrand, 1972. The 60-page introduction deals with composition, style, Marmontel's reaction to that other autobiographer Jean-Jacques Rousseau, and to the Revolution, but above all with the mentality of the author as it can be glimpsed in his text.

WORKS ABOUT MARMONTEL

Ehrard, Jean, ed. *De l'Encyclopédie à la Contre-Révolution: Jean-François Marmontel (1723–1799)*. Clermont-Ferrand, France, 1970. This collection of nineteen articles devoted to various aspects of Marmontel's career is, though becoming dated because of subsequent scholarship, still very useful.

Lenel, S. *Un homme de lettres au XVIIIe siècle: Marmontel*. Paris, 1902; repr. Geneva, Switzerland, 1970. The only full-length study, reasonably solid though very dated.

Renwick, John. *La destinée posthume de Jean-François Marmontel (1723–1799): Bibliographie critique*. Clermont-Ferrand, France, 1972. A compilation and critical reading of practically everything written on Marmontel up to 1972.

Renwick, John. *Marmontel, Voltaire and the* Bélisaire *affair: Studies on Voltaire and the Eighteenth Century* 121 (1974). A study of the reasons behind the composition of *Bélisaire*, and a reconstruction of the (by then) long-forgotten confrontation to which it gave rise (1767–1768) between philosophes and reactionaries.

JOHN RENWICK

MARSHALL, JOHN (1755–1835), American statesman, biographer of Washington, and third chief justice of the United States (1801–1835).

Marshall was an American original: a judge who was a founding statesman. He has been called "the great chief justice" and as "the expounder of the Constitution," he was the founder of American constitutional law. His judicial opinions helped work into American custom the framers' Montesquieuan plan for balanced government, as well as the common law and law of nations associated with reformers such as William Blackstone and Emeric de Vattel.

Marshall was of that generation of hardy Virginia statesmen who fought for independence and then for a national government. To his suffering and soldiering "with brave men from different states" he attributed much of his "devotion to the union, and to a government competent to its preservation." At the Virginia Ratifying Convention, he vigorously defended the proposed Constitution as adequately democratic and as desirable for its independent judiciary. Then, while prominent at the Richmond bar, he became the leading defender in anti-Federalist Virginia of the Washington administration's policies, especially the Jay Treaty (1795) of conciliation with Great Britain. He was one of President John Adams's emissaries to conciliate France (1797); there, he led the way in publicizing the Directory's contemptuous slights and thus in countering at home the immense appeal of French democracy and and its advocates, the Jeffersonian republicans. Marshall certainly believed in modern popular sovereignty—he thought the rights of self-government "the most precious rights"—but he disavowed the "wild and enthusiastic democracy" of his youth and distrusted the French revolutionaries as "visionary," violent, and imperialist. He became a moderate Federalist with a classical republican's concern with virtue. Marshall admired Cicero's *De officiis* and wrote a *Life of George Washington* to set forth his hero's character and politics.

After Marshall had distinguished himself in the House of Representatives (1799–1800), Adams appointed him Secretary of State in May 1800, and then, in January 1801, as chief justice. This was a lame-duck appointment, made after the Jeffersonian landslide in the political branches. The Federalist Marshall faced the most dangerous situation ever to confront a new chief justice. Nevertheless, he managed to turn a rather discredited Supreme Court into the authoritative voice of a semi-sacred fundamental law, a semi-political eminence that the Court has since maintained. He avoided every appearance of partisanship, instituted one opinion for the court in place of individual opinions delivered seriatim, discouraged dissents, and appointed a reporter of opinions. He remained chief for thirty-four years, the longest tenure ever. He authored nearly half of all the opinions for his court, including all opinions during his first five years and almost all the constitutional judgments during the whole period. He was a master of the law's words, the framers' intent, and the enlightened theories on which they drew. He was master not least of the Blackstonean art of finding enlightened principles in familiar customs. *Marbury v. Madison* (1803) affirmed the primacy of the fundamental political law and of its interpretation by judges, not legislatures. *McCulloch v. Maryland* (1819) protected great federal powers from rival powers of the states. *Gibbons v. Ogden* (1824) fostered a national market by reading an implicit "right to trade" into minor exercises of Congress's power "to regulate." Cases such as *Fletcher v. Peck* (1810) secured rights under contract, even protecting rights of private corporations from changes in public charters. Still, whatever Marshall's efforts on behalf of effective government and free society, by the end of his life he could see divisions on the Supreme Court and the rise of Jacksonian democracy and Southern nullification. He feared for the future of his country and its constitutional democracy.

[See also Constitution of the United States; Republicanism, *subentry on* The United States; *and* Washington, George.]

BIBLIOGRAPHY

Faulkner, Robert. *The Jurisprudence of John Marshall*. Princeton, N.J., 1968; Westport, Conn., 1980. Marshall's constitutional and political views.

Hobson, Charles. *The Great Chief Justice*. Lawrence, Kans., 1996. A good biography focusing on Marshall as judge, by the editor of *The Papers of John Marshall*.

Marshall, John. *An Autobiographical Sketch*. Edited by John Stokes Adams. Ann Arbor, Mich., 1937. A long letter recounting Marshall's life and opinions up to becoming chief justice, in his own words.

Marshall, John. *Life of George Washington*. Edited by Robert Faulkner and Paul Carrese. Indianapolis, 2000. Marshall on Washington, the war of revolution, and the politics of founding, in a new edition of the final one-volume version.

Smith, Jean Edward. *John Marshall, Definer of a Nation*. New York, 1996. A good biography, with many new details as to the life, career, and times.

ROBERT K. FAULKNER

MASON, GEORGE (1725–1792), American farmer and statesman.

The eldest son of a prosperous Virginia tobacco planter, Mason was nine years old when his father drowned in a boating accident. Thrust into early maturity, Mason quickly learned the lessons taught by his Scottish tutors. He developed into a shrewd businessman, shipping crops to England from a private wharf on the Potomac. Unlike many planters, whose expenses often outran their income, Mason accumulated wealth as he continued to read the classics and built up a sizable library. An advantageous marriage, along with his business acumen, enabled him to amass a comfortable fortune and to build (1755–1758) an elegant home that he named Gunston Hall, an architectural gem that still stands.

When the Stamp Act crisis erupted in 1765, Mason and his neighbor, George Washington, were soon on the resistance stage, urging a boycott of British goods. After the Stamp Act was repealed, Mason warned, "Such another Experiment as the Stamp-Act wou'd produce a general Revolt in America."

Parliament was unmoved. After the 1773 Boston Port Bill was enacted, Mason took the lead among northern Virginians ready to boycott British goods. He then wrote the Fairfax Resolves (1774), which called for the colonies to cease the importation of British products, asked Parliament to decree an end to the slave trade, and denounced recusants as enemies of the people. When Washington left the Virginia House of Burgesses to serve in the Continental Army, Mason replaced him; he soon became a dominant figure in the rebellious body that met in the spring of 1776 as the Virginia Convention. Assigned to committees charged with preparing a constitution and bill of rights, Mason took over the work almost single-handedly. His draft of the Virginia Declaration of Rights, the first such document to deal with a citizen's rights, called for a free press, free speech, and "the free exercise of religion." Mason's draft also expressed the idea that all men were due their right "to life, liberty, and the pursuing and obtaining of happiness and safety." Other states soon enacted their own versions of Mason's pronouncements, and Thomas Jefferson borrowed some of its wording for his draft of the Declaration of Independence.

Mason avoided service in the Continental Congress but was a key figure on the Virginia Committee of Safety, which maintained civilian responsibilities during the war for independence. Vexed with gout and the trials of a widower rearing nine children, he avoided service in the Virginia legislature, but he did accept a place on the Virginia delegation to the Federal Convention in 1787. There, he spoke 134 times and was responsible for the ban on taxing interstate commerce and for the impeachment clause "for high crimes and misdemeanors." He opposed ratification of the Constitution, however, citing the fact that it lacked a bill of rights. He joined Patrick Henry in opposing Virginia's ratification, but he accepted defeat without bitterness. Jefferson—who once characterized Mason as a citizen "of the first order of greatness"—last visited Mason shortly before the patrician died in October 1792.

[*See also* American Revolution *and* Constitution of the United States.]

BIBLIOGRAPHY
Miller, Helen Hill. *George Mason: Gentleman Revolutionary*. Chapel Hill, N.C., 1975.

Rutland, Robert A. *George Mason: Reluctant Statesman*. Baton Rouge, La., 1997.

Rutland, Robert A., ed. *The Papers of George Mason*. 3 vols. Chapel Hill, N.C., 1970.

ROBERT ALLEN RUTLAND

MATERIALISM.
In philosophy, materialism is the assertion that all natural phenomena can be explained entirely in terms of matter, without recourse to any sort of immaterial prime mover or intelligent structuring principle; this implies the denial of final causes. In the seventeenth and eighteenth centuries, however, materialism could coexist with a type of deism that posited a creator who had endowed matter with its inherent motive force. This was primarily because the main concern of materialists, particularly in the early Enlightenment, was the human being; all human faculties, intellectual as well as physical, it was claimed, could be explained in material terms without the need for an immaterial or immortal soul. Debates thus tended to center on the question of the existence of the soul, and therefore of what, if anything, distinguishes humans from animals. The seventeenth-century debate over animal soul held serious implications for humans, because, as Pierre Bayle pointed out in his *Dictionary* article "Rorarius," to admit a type of sensitive soul in animals endangered the specificity of the human soul; and the Cartesian solution of soulless material animal-machines, while it seemed to provide a solution, could be extended to humans, despite the problems this involved.

Types of Materialism. In fact, a purely material conception of human beings could take several different forms.

The definition of a materialist given in the *Encyclopédie* in 1765, for example, indicates a diversity of forms of materialism and considers it as more or less the equivalent of Spinozism, the deformation of Spinoza's philosophy that was current in the eighteenth century. In fact, the roots of Enlightenment materialism are much more varied than used to be supposed. The longstanding interpretation saw two separate strands, one drawing on Cartesianism and the other on Lockean sensualism as transmitted by Condillac, but it is now accepted that it was indebted to a wider range of traditions, although an isolated thinker like the village priest Jean Meslier could develop a materialism derived essentially from the Cartesian philosophy of Father Nicolas Malebranche. The ancient tradition of materialism, especially Epicureanism, was important, particularly as transmitted by the French priest Pierre Gassendi, and as it influenced the "mechanical" philosophy in England; indeed, attacks on materialism in late seventeenth century England were directed mainly against Epicureanism. John Locke's hypothesis that God might have added thought to matter was also invoked, notably by Voltaire and by others who attempted to combine a materialistic conception of humans with belief in a divine creator. The Leibnizian dynamic conception of matter probably also played a role. In addition, whatever the philosophical inspiration, the results of recent scientific experimentation and physiological study were frequently used to support a materialistic conception of humans, as were discoveries such as that of the regenerative powers of the freshwater polyp, made by the Swiss naturalist Abraham Tremblay in 1742. There was also a specifically British tradition that drew on the current of the Christian mortalists whose ideas were revived in the seventeenth century, in particular by the work *Man's Mortality* (1644), attributed to the Leveller Richard Overton, as well as by John Milton and in Thomas Hobbes's *Leviathan* (despite the fact that Hobbes was generally condemned as an atheist). Though they claimed to be Christians and affirmed the existence of God, the mortalists' concern was to deny the existence of an immortal soul and of any life after death before the general resurrection at the Last Judgment, for they believed that this was the true Christian doctrine, corrupted by the Roman Catholic Church under the influence of paganism. The debate on these opinions at the turn of the century revolved around the works of the English doctor William Coward, which were condemned by the House of Commons in 1703. In the later part of the century, the materialism of the leading Unitarian scientist and political thinker, Joseph Priestley, continued this Christian mortalist tradition, mainly in his *Disquisitions Relating to Matter and Spirit* (1777).

Main Issues. Whatever the nature of materialism or the inspiration for it, it discussed certain fundamental questions that had to be solved by those who were attempting to provide a convincing material explanation for vital phenomena. These questions concerned, above all, the nature and status of matter and its properties, and whether there was a soul; the latter issue could be subdivided into the question of whether one posits a material soul or denies any soul and explains thought by a particular organization of matter. The second alternative implies a study of the relationship between sensitivity and intelligence and of the functioning of the brain. There was also the issue of free will or determinism, which in turn posed the question of the foundation of morality.

The fundamental question obviously involved the nature of matter. How can matter explain all the workings of the human being, in particular the intellectual functions? Materialism in general rejected the Cartesian doctrine of the dualism of matter and spirit, but diverse solutions of this question were proposed. The Irish-born freethinker John Toland affirmed in his work *Letters to Serena* (1704) that matter always possesses the capacity to move; he distinguished this motion from local movement from place to place, in order to claim that matter is sufficient to explain all phenomena. He did not, however, exclude the possibility that this movement might have been communicated by God at the Creation. Later, in his *Pantheisticon* (1720), Toland still posited materialism but unusually combined it with a pantheistic conception of the soul of the world. It is not surprising that the most outspoken champion of materialism, Julien Offray de La Mettrie, began his first philosophical work with this question. *L'histoire naturelle de l'âme* (Natural History of the Soul, 1745) opens with a discussion of matter and its properties in which the author rejects the Cartesian definition, but the only conclusion he can reach is that matter as it is observed in organized bodies always possesses a certain number of properties, including the faculty to move and to feel. He abandons any further attempt to understand the nature of matter as such, admitting his ignorance and preferring to stick to a discussion of organized matter, to show experimentally that it possesses these qualities. Thus, *L'homme machine* (Man a Machine, 1747) provides a series of examples of experiments on animals intended to show that the smallest parts of organized matter, the "fibers," possess the capacity to react and to move, even when separated from the whole body of the animal.

The same questions are at the heart of the philosophe Denis Diderot's discussion of materialism, particularly in the central work, *Le rêve de d'Alembert* (D'Alembert's Dream), which remained unpublished during his lifetime. It begins with the nature of matter; rejecting Descartes's dualism, Diderot affirmed that, as a consequence of motive power in matter, it is capable of feeling and can therefore explain all intellectual as well as physical capacities. This question had already been touched on in Diderot's *Pensées sur l'interprétation de la nature* (Thoughts on the Interpretation of Nature, 1753), in which he insisted on the energy of the living molecule; however, like La Mettrie, Diderot hesitated to ascribe the faculty of feeling to the smallest parts of matter, or molecules, and could not decide whether it is not rather the result of a particular organization of matter. Despite his study of chemistry, Diderot, like La Mettrie, came to no very clear conclusion concerning the nature of matter. In the discussion of nature and matter that opens *Le système de la Nature* (The System of Nature), d'Holbach followed Toland in insisting on the motion inherent in all matter and explained feeling by the union of insensitive molecules to form bodies, according to the laws of nature.

On this crucial question of the nature of matter, Priestley provided an original answer. He refused the usual definition of matter as a solid, impenetrable substance, possessing merely a *vis inertiae*, and proposed a new conception of matter with which the faculties of feeling and thinking are not incompatible. He demonstrated that the smallest particles of matter, or atoms, possess a power of attraction and, drawing on experiments on electricity and light, he showed that matter is not impenetrable, but that its resistance can be explained by its power of repulsion. He adopted the Croatian scientist Father Boscovich's definition of matter as composed only of physical points with space between them. Priestley's matter is thus defined simply in terms of its powers of attraction and repulsion. His aim was to show that there is nothing to oppose the "thinking matter" hypothesis.

Unresolved Questions. Thus, the initial basic question about the nature of matter led to a certain number of unresolved problems that could hardly be solved at the time. The unambiguous statement that matter was enough to explain all phenomena left hanging several questions, because there was no clear explanation as to how this could come about. There were also difficulties concerning the transitions from inert to feeling matter and from sensation to thought. The first issue tended to be left unresolved. Likewise, the question of the relationship between sensitivity and intelligence was problematic. Perhaps under the influence of the French scientist P. M. L. Moreau de Maupertuis, Diderot seems at times tempted to believe that to say that molecules can feel is the same thing as saying that they can think; for La Mettrie, this would apparently run the risk of, as he says, spiritualizing matter rather than materializing the soul, and would thus be inacceptable. But more frequently for Diderot, intelligence is the result of memory and the comparison of sense-impressions in the brain rather than a faculty of all matter. Apart from Toland, there was little pantheism

in Enlightenment materialism, most of which can more properly be described as "vitalistic" materialism.

The essential question, therefore, concerns the workings of the brain, because it seemed clear that it is in this particular organization of matter that intelligence is located. But this brought thinkers up against the question of the soul, for it was obvious that the denial of an immaterial and immortal soul was at the heart of a material view of humans. One of the important themes of clandestine philosophical treatises in French, dating mainly from the early eighteenth century but circulated throughout the century, was the soul; indeed, one of the most famous of them is called *L'âme matérielle* (The Material Soul). Early in the century, there were essentially two ways of denying the immortal soul. One was to try to show how thought could be the result of a particular organization of matter in the brain; this became the most fertile strand of reflection. There were others who posited the existence of a material soul made up of a very subtle type of matter, like fire or light; this theory, part of the Epicurean tradition, was taken particularly from Italian Renaissance works. One version of this theory, expounded by the French doctor Guillaume Lamy in a famous passage in his sixth *Discours anatomique* (1675), was inserted into several other works, notably the most notorious and widely distributed of the clandestine antireligious treatises, *L'esprit de Spinosa* (The Mind of Spinosa) or *Traité des trois imposteurs* (Treatise on the Three Impostors).

Materialists increasingly tried to look at the structure and functioning of the nerves and the brain in order to explain the production of thought. The claim that it is a particular structure of matter in the brain that produces thought is present in Toland's *Letters to Serena*, as well as in William Coward's works from the same period (*Second Thoughts Concerning Human Soul*, 1702, and *The Grand Essay*, 1704). These authors, like later ones, refer to the analysis of the functioning of the brain contained in the writings on the structure of the brain by the influential seventeenth-century Oxford physiologist Thomas Willis. The attempt to show how the nerves and the brain could produce thought is made particularly in La Mettrie's *Histoire naturelle de l'âme*, which discusses the functioning of the different nerves and the role of the brain as *sensorium commune*. Retaining the Cartesian model of brain traces brought by the animal spirits through the nerves by means of the impact of spherical globules on one another, La Mettrie claimed that the seat of the soul, situated in the nerve-endings in the brain, cannot be in a single spot; he therefore concluded that different parts of the brain are responsible for different sensations, and that the *sensorium commune* is spread over the whole brain. His *L'homme machine* (1747), however, presents a much more dynamic view of the brain, emphasizing its creative power, the imagination, and the internal senses. Diderot, particularly in *Le rêve de d'Alembert*, similarly attempted to account for the production of intelligence by the brain, but he could do so only in very general terms, again by the use of metaphors. Here we see an attempt to provide a material explanation of humans, but one that is not simply reductionist; the brain is seen as creative and dynamic, with its own energy, and not merely the sum of its parts or a mere receiver of external stimuli. It was obviously impossible to go any further at the time, in view of the state of scientific knowledge, but these intuitions are very important for future thought.

Helvétius and an Alternate View. A very different model is found in the writings of Claude-Adrien Helvétius, for whom it was external sensation that was fundamental, and for whom all thought could be reduced to sensation, a position opposed by Diderot. Helvétius considered that humans are all endowed with the same organization, and that the differences among them come from experience and education. Questions about how the brain produces intelligence and how to account for human creativity and originality are therefore of little importance. This type of materialism is concerned essentially with external factors and how they shape ideas and behavior, rather than with the internal functioning of the material "machine." Helvétius was therefore concerned much more with the organization and development of societies and the environmental and educational factors influencing them, thus prolonging the discussion inaugurated by Montesquieu on the influence of climate and developed in Buffon's monumental *Histoire naturelle*, published from 1749 on. It is this type of materialism that was later criticized by the French materialist doctor Pierre-Jean-Georges Cabanis during the Revolutionary period as being insufficient because of its lack of medical knowledge; he himself attempted to provide a material explanation of human intelligence, without acknowledging his debt to earlier materialists who had shared his preoccupations.

Consequences of Materialism. The question of the factors determining behavior raises the issue of the consequences of eighteenth-century materialism. The first is related to determinism and liberty. As was very early pointed out, to claim that humans' intellect is determined by either their physical organization or their experiences is to deny free will. The denial of human liberty, associated with the names of Spinoza and Hobbes, was a frequent theme in eighteenth-century irreligious writings, which were often influenced as well by the works of the English freethinker Anthony Collins. La Mettrie increasingly affirmed humans' lack of liberty and total dependence on physical functions. This was the main understanding of Spinozism in the period, as can be seen in clandestine works like *L'esprit de Spinosa* or *L'examen de la religion*, and also in Diderot's *Jacques le fataliste et son maître* (Jacques the Fatalist and His Master, 1778–1780). In *L'anti-Sénèque* (1748–1751), La Mettrie affirmed that one cannot criticize humans for following their impulses, however criminal; one can only try to understand them and have compassion for them, as a doctor. An even more extreme determinism in many ways is present in d'Holbach's *Système de la Nature* (1770), which comes very close to reintroducing a sort of finalism in nature, subject to immutable laws; this is very different from La Mettrie's physical determinism, more influenced by Epicureanism in the seventeenth-century *libertin* tradition. In the question of determinism and liberty, the position of Diderot is particularly interesting, since he was more concerned than other materialists to preserve human liberty as far as possible. There is no doubt that for Diderot, too, humans are part of nature and subject to its laws; they are therefore determined by their physical workings. However, Diderot wishes to ensure a certain liberty, founded in the creativity of the brain and the human capacity to organize itself and act on the brain. For him, there is no general system of fatality or mechanical plan of nature of which humans are part—they are, like the rest of nature, subordinate to its laws—but the multiplicity of nature's causes means that that the single necessary cause, on which Diderot insists and which constitutes the individual's being, does not exclude a form of liberty. The cause of human actions is within the individual; it is the physical organization and the result of the interaction between this organization and the evolving self that results from the activity of the material brain. It is not an external fatalism preordained by nature, as seems to be much more the case for d'Holbach.

The question of freedom was also discussed at length in England by Priestley, who proclaimed his "philosophical doctrine of necessity." He explained that if we accept that humans are purely material beings, then we cannot deny that they are mechanical beings, subject to certain laws. Thus, any argument in favor of materialism is an argument in favor of necessity, as he insisted in a famous debate with his fellow Unitarian thinker Richard Price. Priestley referred to Thomas Hobbes as the first to understand this doctrine of philosophical necessity, which for him did not contradict liberty, defined as the possibility to do what we want. For Priestley, this does not mean that humans are not responsible for their decisions or that they cannot be punished or rewarded. On the contrary, because the doctrine of philosophical necessity denies God's direct influence on human mind, it reaffirms human responsibility and free will.

The importance accorded by Priestley to divine judgment (after the resurrection of the body) was totally opposed to the preoccupations of the atheistic French materialists. For the latter, the consequences of determinism in the field of ethics presented serious problems. If there is nothing in the universe but matter, no presiding God or universal plan, then good and evil do not exist in absolute terms but are created by society and taught by education; and because human actions are determined by physical causes, it is difficult to consider humans responsible for their behavior. The Spinozistic theme of the nonexistence of moral values in nature is found in several clandestine works from the early century, including two of the most important ones, *L'esprit de Spinosa* and *L'examen de la religion*, a deistic anti-Christian work. Among the materialists, it was above all La Mettrie who emphasized this question in a particularly scandalous manner, notably in *L'anti-Sénèque*, where he dealt with the moral implications of his materialism. For La Mettrie, the remorse felt for crimes, far from being the result of an innate natural law, simply comes from education and conditioning in childhood. Since remorse is useless to society and merely makes people suffer needlessly, we should try to free people from it, instead of condemning them for following the dictates of nature. Those who commit crimes must be condemned by the laws for the good of society, but morally, they cannot be criticized, because they are not free to act otherwise. This amoral stance, in which La Mettrie placed himself in the role of a medical observer, was naturally calculated to shock his contemporaries, particularly as he referred to Hobbes to justify his position.

For that reason, Diderot and d'Holbach, whose materialism was closest to that of La Mettrie, attacked him violently and rejected any connection with his thought; however, at times Diderot had come very close to a position similar to that of La Mettrie, particularly in his *Letter to Landois* (1756). Similar ideas are expressed in the *Encyclopédie* article "Liberté." Diderot preferred the thesis that humans are modifiable and can be improved, which made punishments and rewards valuable in encouraging useful actions and discouraging harmful ones. A basis for morality can be found in the similar organization of humans and in their agreement on the nature of useful or harmful actions. D'Holbach, in *Le système de la nature*, also attempted, while basing moral values in the needs of society, to show that they are universally valid. He claimed that the distinction between good and evil is founded on relationships existing between humans in society. Social behavior is reinforced by the actions of the government, by education, law, and so on. For Helvétius, humans are determined by their physical sensitivity, so human needs and interests lead them to be sociable, and this can be reinforced by good laws and moral education.

Assessment. Despite these attempts to reconcile materialism and morality, the argument most frequently used by the defenders of organized religion against materialists was that their philosophy undermined the moral basis of society, a criticism that seemed to be confirmed by the works of La Mettrie, however much others distanced themselves from him. The fact that, during the Revolution, the marquis de Sade claimed to base his thought on the writings of materialistic thinkers such as La Mettrie or d'Holbach did nothing for their reputations. But although it was the object of violent attack and in its most open atheistic form it remained very much a minority position, materialism had more influence on Enlightenment thought than might be imagined; aspects of it can be found in several thinkers, including deists like Voltaire. At the end of the century, the French Idéologues, in particular Cabanis, followed in the same tradition, although they did not openly claim to do so, and their social and anthropological thought was strongly marked by it. The attempt to provide a purely material understanding of humans, seen as a part of nature like other animals, also had a clear effect on the development of physical anthropology in the late eighteenth century, and on the view that physical organization influences mental capacity, which led to the classification of humans according to skull shapes. Phrenology, which was elaborated in the Revolutionary period, was a related development. In the early nineteenth century, materialism was at the basis of the thought of socialists like Robert Owen.

Materialism should therefore be seen as a much more diverse and multifaceted phenomenon than many scholars have claimed, in part because of their emphasis on its more open campaigning form embodied in *Le système de la Nature*. When its diverse manifestations are taken into account, it can be seen to represent not so much a body of doctrine as a complex of tendencies, questions, and attempted solutions put forward by thinkers who generally refused metaphysical systems. Its attempt to provide a natural history of man exercised an undoubted influence over many fields of enlightened thought, making it relevant to most of the central questions of the Enlightenment.

[*See also* Atheism; Cartesianism; Clandestine Literature; Diderot, Denis; Empiricism; Epicurianism; Epistemology; Helvétius, Claude-Adrien; La Mettrie, Julien Offray de; Moral Philosophy; Pantheism; Philosophy; Priestley, Joseph; Spontaneous Generation; *and* Vitalism.]

BIBLIOGRAPHY

Bloch, Olivier, ed. *Le matérialisme du XVIIIe siècle et la littérature clandestine*. Paris, 1982. An important collection of papers presented at a conference in Paris in 1980, discussing many aspects of Enlightenment materialism.
Bloch, Olivier, ed. *Le matérialisme des Lumières*. Special issue of *Dix-huitième Siècle* 24 (1992). A wide-ranging collection of essays which also looks at thinkers other than those generally classified as materialists.

Bloch, Olivier. *Matière à histoires*. Paris, 1997. Contains several important articles on various aspects of seventeenth- and eighteenth-century materialism.

Ehrard, Jean. *L'idée de nature en France dans la première moitié du XVIIIe siècle*. Paris, 1963. An exhaustive work on the various conceptions of nature in early Enlightenment France, which helps to understand the place of materialism in the thought of the period.

Lange, Friedrich A. *History of Materialism and Criticism of Its Present Importance*. Translated by E. C. Thomas. 3 vols. London, 1879–1881. English translation of *Geschichte des Materialismus* (1866), a classic work which has still not been replaced.

Rosenfield, Leonora C. *From Beast-Machine to Man-Machine: The Theme of Animal Soul in French Letters from Descartes to La Mettrie*. New York, 1941. A partial but useful discussion of an important aspect of materialistic thought.

Salaün, Franck. *L'ordre des moeurs: Essai sur la place du matérialisme dans la société française du XVIIIe siècle (1734–1784)*. Paris, 1996. A survey of some of the main themes of French materialism and the debate it engendered.

Spink, John S. *French Free Thought from Gassendi to Voltaire*. London, 1960. Contains much on materialism in France in the late seventeenth and early eighteenth centuries.

Staum, Martin S. *Cabanis: Enlightenment and Medical Philosophy in the French Revolution*. Princeton, N.J., 1980. Includes much on Cabanis's relationship to earlier materialists and shows the further development of Enlightenment materialism.

Thomson, Ann. *Materialism and Society in the Mid-Eighteenth Century: La Mettrie's "Discours préliminaire."* Geneva, Switzerland, 1981. Discusses La Mettrie's relation to other materialists and the problems of reconciling materialism and morality.

Wade, Ira O. *The Clandestine Organization and Diffusion of Philosophic Ideas in France from 1700 to 1750*. Princeton, N.J., 1938; repr., New York, 1967. A groundbreaking study of French clandestine philosophical works, many of which helped to disseminate materialistic ideas.

Yolton, John W. *Thinking Matter: Materialism in Eighteenth Century Britain*. Oxford, 1983. A useful survey which looks mainly at the fortunes of Locke's hypothesis.

Yolton, John W. *Locke and French Materialism*. Oxford, 1991. Deals with the discussion of Locke's hypothesis in France by disciples and opponents, mainly in the first half of the eighteenth century.

ANN THOMSON

MATHEMATICS.

The practice of mathematics was transformed during the long Enlightenment not only by the development of new theories, but by the social rise of mathematics from a specialized activity whose practitioners were employed by monarchs of various kinds to a profession with most leaders holding professorships or analogous positions in state-supported organizations. The dominating branches of mathematics throughout are the calculus and mechanics, both developing in competing forms; geometry and algebra continued to occupy a steady place, while probability theory and mathematical statistics emerged as rather new topics. The effect of the French Revolution was more fundamental than in many other disciplines, because mathematics was given great prominence in the revision of the educational structure in France, then the leading mathematical country, a change that led to partial imitation elsewhere.

The Calculi, Fluxional and Differential. A major development of the middle third of the seventeenth century was the introduction of the calculus by Isaac Newton (1643–1727) starting in the 1660s and then by Gottfried Wilhelm von Leibniz (1646–1716) a decade later. Each theory greatly extended the known means of determining the tangent to a curve and the area under it relative to some axis system, for it also gave means of finding the rate at which variable quantities changed in value, also the rate at which the change itself changed, and so on indefinitely. The paradigm example was dynamics, where the rate of change of location was velocity, with its own change as acceleration, and so on. Further, the relationships could be reversed: from acceleration to velocity to location. But while the scopes of the theories were the same, the means of achieving them were fundamentally different.

Newton imagined a variable quantity x "flowing" with respect to (some abstractly conceived) time t at a rate given by its first "fluxion" "$\dot{x}$," which itself changed at the rate of the second fluxion "$\ddot{x}$"; reversing, $\dot{x}$ was the "fluent" of $\ddot{x}$, and x of $\dot{x}$, so that the fluxion of the fluent of x was x itself (Whiteside, 1961, ch. 11). Such a function was conceived as the limiting value of the ratio of finite differences in values of x and of t as each increment approached zero, but the underlying theory of limits was very unclear.

By contrast, Leibniz explicitly avoided limits: the variable x (line, force, time, whatever) was increased by an infinitesimally small "differential" increment dx, of the same kind as x, and itself susceptible to second-order increase ddx, and so on to higher orders. Reversing, x was the differential of an infinitely large variable "$\int x$," with "$\int$" suggested by the Latin word "*summa*"; then came the second-order infinitely large variable $\int\int x$, again and so on. Inversion took the form $d\int x = \int dx = x$. The basic notions of the calculus were defined as follows: the rate of change of variable y with respect to variable x was given by the ratio $dy \div dx$, written "dy/dx"; its own change was given by $ddy \div (dx)^2$, written "d^2y/dx^2," and so on. Further, the region between the curve representing y as a function of the (horizontal) x axis was taken to be a collection of infinitesimally thin neighboring strips y high and dx wide, like sliced bread, so that its area was the sum of their products: "$\int y\, dx$" (Bos, 1974). Phenomena were usually expressed by "differential equations," that is, literally equations relating differentials.

The introduction of these calculi was one of the greatest innovations in the entire history of mathematics. Their initial advance was hindered by the slowness of their publication (Leibniz took a decade, Newton nearly forty years), though manuscripts circulated in the interim. They came to supplant infinitesimal geometry, which Christiaan Huygens nevertheless continued to use until his death in 1695.

Each tradition gained good recruits. The Leibnizians were led by a remarkable collection of Swiss guards at Basel: the brothers Jakob and Johann Bernoulli, Johann's son Daniel, and also Leonhard Euler (1707–1783) from down the road. The first textbook was the *Analyse des infiniment petits* (1696) by the marquis de l'Hôpital, with Johann Bernoulli's hand often on the Lordship's pen. In Paris, the Academy of Sciences furthered the Leibnizian cause, with Pierre Varignon very effective on its behalf.

In Britain, the Royal Society of London was the main forum for the Newtonian cause. Sadly, in the 1700s the ageing Newton decided that he had been plagiarized, despite lack of credible evidence (least of all Leibniz's calculus itself), so he arranged an international "tribunal," under the auspices of the Society itself, to conclude in his favor. Thus the natural separation of the two traditions by geography was accentuated into a feud, British fluxions versus Continental differentials. The Newtonians were a respectable second until the 1740s, after which British contributions fell away markedly, and almost all the best work was Continental until the 1810s.

A favored procedure in each tradition was to render a variable (y, say) as a series of powers of variable x:

$$y = a + bx + cx^2 + \ldots \text{ to infinity,} \qquad (1)$$

where the constant coefficients $a, b, c, \ldots$ could be determined. The most general form of (1) used the calculus (in either tradition) to determine them; Colin Maclaurin named this form after Brook Taylor, as it is still known, but in fact Newton, Leibniz and Johann Bernoulli had known it earlier. Taylor's own version, in 1715, is significant for a different reason: it was a special case of a series involving finitely separated data, such as came from readings taken by engineers, astronomers, and navigators. Curves to be fitted through such data, and other kinds of approximative analysis, constituted a major part of numerical mathematics of the time, complementing the use of continuous variables in the calculus.

In each tradition the enormous success rested upon shaky foundations: incoherent limit theory, or mysterious infinitesimals. George Berkeley made perceptive fun of this irony in *The Analyst* (1734), in a *tu quoque* argument against critics of Christianity. He also proposed as solution that equal and opposite errors were committed in formulating the theory; but it works only for special functions, and in his treatment he rather muddled the two traditions. Nevertheless, his attack provoked new attention to basic concepts, especially by Maclaurin.

Mechanics and Energy. A major event was the publication in 1687 of Newton's *Philosophiae naturalis principia mathematica*, based upon a law asserting that between any

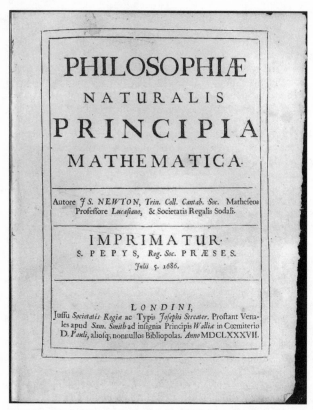

Mathematical Treatise. Title page of Isaac Newton's *Principia Mathematica* (1687). (The Pierpont Morgan Library/Art Resource, NY.)

two particles an attractive force obtained along the joining straight line, proportional to the product of their masses and to the inverse square of the measure of their separation. Upon this mysterious assumption he put forward three laws:

1. Bodies remain at rest or moving with uniform velocity if left alone. Here he highlighted two kinds of equilibrium, which later became called "static" and "dynamic" respectively.

2. Increments of impulse applied to a body caused incremental increases in its momentum (mass × velocity). This law became known as force = mass × acceleration, and Newton himself used it thus sometimes. It is striking, however, and regularly forgotten, that he cast it in this more general form.

3. To any action there is an equal and opposite reaction. An important case was the effect of centripetal forces, such as acting from a point toward a center of force like the sun, acting opposite in direction to centrifugal forces, well recognized by predecessors such as René Descartes and Huygens.

Upon these principles, and in fact a few others taken for granted, Newton built up an impressive treatment of both celestial and terrestrial motion; the ability to treat both topics by the same means is especially striking. Book 1 laid out basic properties of orbits and paths in vacuo; Book 2 handled various cases of resistant media; and Book 3, on "the system of the world," dealt specifically with the planets, the moon, and comets. Newton had new revised editions of his book published in 1713 and 1726.

Newton studied both principles and consequences, allowing much more precise predictions than before to be tested against observation. In Britain, the full bundle of Newton's laws were adopted, but on the Continent the inverse-square law was treated much more skeptically (Guicciardini, 1999). One point of advance everywhere was to cast Newton's theory into calculus form. Newton himself had not done this, using it at most only to help solve some special problems. The form of the calculus used depended, as usual, upon geography.

A particularly important area for mathematics was planetary mechanics, which carefully studied the size and shape of the heavenly bodies. Newton's expectation that the earth was flattened at the poles, instead of elongated as was thought by the French astronomers, was corroborated (though only qualitatively) by an expedition to Lapland in the 1740s (Greenberg, 1995). Again, the precession of the poles (that is, their very slow circular rotation) could be explained in terms of the slightly but significantly different distances from the sun of its various parts. Other phenomena, however, caused difficulties; in particular, the many motions of the moon resisted analysis to a great extent, and the "three-body-problem" of determining the actions between sun, moon, and earth seemed to be insoluble in general, although special cases could be handled (Gautier, 1817).

The other main alternative approach to mechanics was to consider the energy of body or system, which Leibniz called "vis viva" and used to elaborate a vortex theory of planetary motion more mathematically than had Descartes. Ironically, a charge of plagiarism from Newton here would have been in order (Bertoloni Meli, 1993), although Leibniz's theory was quite different. Here conservation of "vis viva" was stressed, though not always clearly; in particular, if energy was lost, where did it go? Engineers had worked intuitively with energy notions for centuries; a major author was the Frenchman Bernard Forest de Belidor (1697–1761), with a general survey of *La science des ingénieurs* (1729) followed by two volumes of *Architecture hydraulique* (1737–1739), which were reprinted and translated extensively.

A third approach to mechanics was proffered by Jean Le Rond d'Alembert (1717–1783), initially in his *Traité de dynamique* (1743). Suspicious of the notion of force, he took Newton's second law to define it and replaced it with a principle still named after him. Distinguishing the free motions under gravity of bodies in a system from those occurring under constraints and interactions with other bodies there, he claimed, rather unclearly, that the latter collection of forces was in static equilibrium (Fraser, 1985). Using the calculus in the Leibnizian form, he nevertheless tried to raise the status of limit theory. He advocated these and related positions in the *Encyclopédie*.

The Phenomenon of Euler. From his late teens in the mid-1720s until his death in 1783, Euler maintained a steady flow of papers, textbooks, and treatises on all branches of mathematics. The prolificity continued after his death, with the Saint Petersburg Academy publishing him posthumously for nearly half a century. He had been a member there from 1727 to 1741, and then again for the last seventeen years of his life. The intervening twenty-five years were passed at the Berlin Academy.

Had he not been a mathematician, Euler would be generally acknowledged as one of the greatest intellects of the eighteenth century (Euler, 1983). The edition of his collected works started to be published in 1911, and a few of the seventy-two planned quarto volumes are still not done; further, the dozen large tomes of correspondence and manuscripts began their appearance only in 1975. His major achievements were many.

In the calculus, Euler modified the Leibnizian form by introducing the notion of the "differential coefficient" (his term), in which the ratio $dy \div dx$ was defined with dx taking a constant (infinitesimal) value (1755); this move systematically clarified the relationship between independent variables and those dependent upon them. The use of several such variables together had been another major advance, made with d'Alembert in the mid-1740s: "partial" differential equations involving functions of them could express a far wider range of physical phenomena than the "ordinary" ones, since both time and at least one spatial variable could be taken. A spectacular start was made with a dispute between these two about the general solution to the motion of the vibrating string (Truesdell, 1960, pt. 2). Very soon many other phenomena were formulated this way, and the formation and solution of such equations has been a major branch of mathematics ever since.

In astronomy, Newton's second law asserted that each planet was "perturbed" off its basic orbit set by its attraction to the sun and by the actions upon it of other planets. The expressions were quite easy to formulate, but impossibly hard to handle until in 1747 Euler realized that they could be cast into the form of an infinite series of sine and cosine functions (Wilson, 1980); this uniformization has remained as a basic technique. He also transformed the utility of the second law itself by realizing that it could be applied in any direction, not just special ones like along or perpendicular to a path (1752); an immediate application led him to the equations named after him for the rotation of a solid body about a point. On rotation in general, he realized that the general equations of "angular momentum" (our term) needed to express it could not be obtained directly from Newton's laws (1775), a feature that is still frequently not understood (Truesdell, 1968, ch. 5). In technology, he wrote important books on ballistics (1745) and on the construction and steerage of ships (1749, 1773).

The study of phenomena involving continuous media also needed more than Newton's laws. Euler initiated the modern theory of two major cases: elasticity theory, where he successfully expressed the equilibrium and motion of lines and surfaces (1770s); and hydrodynamics, where he introduced the notion of pressure when formulating the differential equations (1757). Earlier he showed that the motion of tides should be analyzed by working from the horizontal component of motion of the body of water (1742).

Lagrange. Euler's normal way of working was geometrical, even if diagrams were not explicitly drawn: functions construed as curves or surfaces, differential rectangles or cuboids of matter formed through which a phenomenon was occurring, and so on. Partly under influence from d'Alembert, the next major figure challenged this approach by raising the status of algebra. This was the Italian Luigi de la Grange Tournier (1736–1813), who became known as Joseph-Louis Lagrange when he began to publish in French. When just out of his teens he helped form the Academy in his home town of Turin, but he moved in 1766 to Berlin for twenty-one years, succeeding Euler there.

More concerned with rigor than was usual for his time, Lagrange tried as much as possible to cast theories in algebraic form, in order to avoid the danger in geometric approaches of assuming conditions special to the configurations used. Wishing to avoid both limits and infinitesimals in the calculus, he proposed in 1772 that, from algebraic manipulations alone, the power series expansion (1) could be found for any function from the base value 0 for any value of x, and that Euler's differential coefficients could be defined formally in terms of the coefficients $a, b, c, \ldots$; he renamed them "derived functions," from which came the later standard name "derivative." Integration was effected by working backward up the series, from c to b, and so on.

Lagrange also algebraized a part of the calculus that Euler came to call "the calculus of variations." The differential dx was understood to be an increment of a variable along its traverse; however, from early on the calculus had been used to tackle problems asking which of a spectrum of neighboring curves satisfied some optimizing condition. For example, for the path followed by a particle falling under gravity from a given point A to a given lower one B in least time, the straight line AB was not the answer. Work by the elder Bernoullis, Euler, and others

had continued this kind of research, but Lagrange greatly extended the techniques involved by letting any point on a curve vary slightly to produce a new neighboring curve. Giving this operation the special symbol "δ," he algebraised the theory by assuming that $\delta d = d\delta$.

In celestial mechanics, Lagrange made an important change. By Newton's second law the perturbations of a planet could be large enough to send it out of orbit and/or to cause a small inclination to the ecliptic plane. Neither Newton nor Euler was worried, however, believing that God would choose to prevent such an occurrence and thereby show His presence. However, Lagrange wanted to prove stability from Newton's laws and the assumption that the planets orbited in the same direction around the sun. Drawing upon Euler's trigonometric series expansion, he brilliantly transformed the equations of motion of the planets under the second law into an antisymmetric form which greatly aided possibilities of solution. This theory was of major importance in the (later) development of linear algebra.

In his algebrized mechanics, a basic principle for Lagrange was that of "least action," which Euler and others had advocated in the 1740s without, however, always using it (Pulte, 1989); it claimed that in equilibrium a dynamical system satisfied the equation $\delta \int A \, dx = 0$, where action A was a given function of the bodies in the system. Another principle, of "virtual velocities," gave sufficient conditions for equilibrium; finding a proof of it became a major task for followers (Lindt, 1904).

From his principles Lagrange obtained some basic equations that are named after him; from these, both Newton's laws and energy equations followed deductively. By 1782, he had a book ready, which came out in 1788 under the title *Méchanique analitique*. While impressive in its range, it showed its power best when reproving results already found, often by some geometric approach; it was also rather confined to equilibrate situations.

Carnot and Laplace. On this latter point Lagrange had already been challenged by Lazare Carnot (1753–1823). An engineer by profession (the politics largely came later), he realized that mechanics must be able to deal with cases of disequilibrium, such as water hitting the blade of a waterwheel; so he took up the energy tradition. In his *Essai sur les machines en général* (1783) he proposed that its loss on impact went into force × distance, a general notion that became known as "work" in the 1820s when his successors extended his insights (Scott, 1970, bk. 2). Meanwhile, engineering mechanics received a substantial presentation in the two large volumes of *Nouvelle architecture hydraulique* (1790–1796) by Gaspard Riche de Prony (1755–1843).

Another ambitious new figure emerged in the 1770s: Pierre-Simon Laplace (1749–1827). Adopting and adapting the work of Euler, d'Alembert, and Lagrange, he contributed to all aspects of the calculus and many of mechanics, where he specialized in the celestial branch. He wrote major papers on the three-body problem and the consonance in the motions of Jupiter and Saturn, and found some important new methods of solving differential equations. The latter included a problem that Newton had launched in the *Principia*: the attraction of a spheroidal body to an external point lying on one axis according to the inverse-square law. Also using geometrical methods, Maclaurin had extended the results to any such point; now with the partial differential calculus available, Laplace expressed the problem in terms of an equation that still bears his name. He then found solutions using functions which in the nineteenth century were also called after him but now bear the name "Legendre functions" after the contributions made by Adrien-Marie Legendre (1752–1833) in a rather unlovely rivalry.

One consequence of the algebraic leanings of both Lagrange and Laplace was the rethinking of the differential calculus as concerned with operating upon a function to produce its derived function: for $f(x)$ Lagrange wrote the latter as "$f'(x)$," with the prime denoting differentiation, a notation that has remained standard although his theory was later abandoned. Similarly, the sign "dy/dx," which with Leibniz denoted the ratio $dy \div dx$, was reread as the operation $(d/dx)y$, and a new algebra of these operations began to be developed: iteration rendered as powers, integration treated as the inverse power, and so on. Lagrange and especially Laplace were somewhat apprehensive of this tendency; nevertheless, in the new century it gained various adherents, and played an important role in the introduction of new algebras into mathematics.

Probability Theory. Laplace also put life into probability theory, which had developed much more fitfully. The first major figure of the century was Jakob Bernoulli; his posthumous *Ars conjectandi* (1713) brought a new level to the mathematicization of chance, especially a theorem that became known as the weak law of large numbers, which related the theoretical probability of a given event with the frequency of its occurrence in a long series of trials. He also solved various problems involving games of chance. A later prominent contributor was Abraham de Moivre (1667–1754), a Huguenot refugee in England who hoped to raise probability theory to Newtonian status; to this end he had produced various theorems on the distributions of large collections of data (Schneider, 1968).

The next stages were also taken by the French, but at home: d'Alembert in the *Encyclopédie* and also the marquis de Condorcet (1743–1794) encouraged the topic for its utility in social contexts, such as assessing population through demography and rationally calculating the probability that judges would come to the correct decision

without having to force confessions (Daston, 1988). Probability theory was the branch of mathematics upon which Enlightenment views made the most impact. Progress, however, was not serene: Daniel Bernoulli had raised the "Saint Petersburg paradox" about gambling (1713), which troubled the foundations of probability theory. Around 1760 he also joined with d'Alembert in disputing the statistical analysis of the benefits to health of inoculation against smallpox.

Other growing areas of interest included mortality and demography, "political arithmetic" in English, and "Staatistik," to coin the word in its German original form, where data on the population, activities, economy, and weather of a state would be recorded (the smallness of most of the German states made such enterprises relatively feasible). At this stage the word "statistics" carried only the sense of data gathering, though theory was beginning to form, with Euler making important starts.

In 1764, a significant and controversial contribution was made in England by Thomas Bayes with his friend Richard Price: a theorem (proved via the fluxional calculus) about estimating the probability of the next event given its previous occurrences. Price worked for an insurance company, an enterprise that stimulated probability theory and actuarial science, especially in Britain, whose ever growing maritime and commercial Empire motivated such study.

Soon afterward Laplace derived similar theorems, apparently independently, and also came to various others following Moivre. Problems in astronomy and topography were among his motivations: given that observations and measurements were inexact, how can we calculate the "most probable" value of a parameter from them? One refinement was the notion that we call "weighted means," in which different levels of accuracy would be admitted. In much of this work distribution functions began to be used, and the methods of the calculus applied to them.

Among other concerns, various ways were considered of assessing sets of data in terms of some sort of average value; in England, Thomas Simpson made valuable contributions for various special kinds of distribution. The theory of the spread of data was less well developed, though the polymath Ruggiero Boscovich advocated it in 1760, working with the sum of the absolute deviations of data from their mean m (that is, ignoring whether a datum was greater or less than m).

Geometry. While geometrical approaches were prominent, the subject of geometry advanced less spectacularly. In Euclidean geometry, some worry continued over the need and form of the axiom stating that only one line parallel to a given line could be drawn though a given point not on it. In particular, the Italian mathematician Girolamo Saccheri (1697–1733) published an argument in his final year trying to obtain a contradiction from any other assumption; it was a good effort, but not conclusive. Some interest was historical: in Scotland, Robert Simson devoted his career to a most unusual enterprise, though in line with the Enlightenment veneration of antiquity, of publishing editions of Greek mathematicians and reconstructing lost works; the principal beneficiaries were Apollonios (1735, 1749) and Euclid (1756). In addition to various editions of Euclid, Legendre published an *Elémens de géométrie* in 1794, of which many editions and some translations appeared for decades.

Concerning links with algebra, the status of analytic and coordinate geometry was heightened by the second volume of Euler's *Introductio ad analysin infinitorum* (1748), which succeeded one on functions and series. Map-making continued to attract attention, especially with the methods of the calculus; in 1772 the Alsatian Jean-Henri Lambert beautifully outlined the basic criteria for the preparation of both maps (for land, where area and lengths could be well represented) and charts (for waters, where good representation of angles was the prime need). Euler worked on this topic, and may have lost the sight in his second eye following his endeavors.

The geometry of curves and surfaces was also enhanced by use of the calculus; a significant figure was the Frenchman Gaspard Monge (1746–1818). However, he gave much more prominence to his generalization of theories of perspective into "descriptive geometry," where a three-dimensional object was projected onto planes upon which the analysis of size and shape could be executed. This was not the artistic geometry of the past; he was teaching at the École du Génie at Mézières, and the aims included the determination of the trajectory of a projectile fired at a high angle, the design of cannons, stone-cutting, and carpentry.

Algebra and Number Theory. Mathematicians outside Britain had more or less tolerated the use of negative numbers and usually realized that zero was not nothing (Pycior, 1997). Complex numbers were also found unavoidable in the theory of equations, although their manipulation could cause trouble; in particular, Euler made an influential blunder in a textbook on algebra (1769), asserting that

$$\sqrt{(-2)} \times \sqrt{(-3)} = \sqrt{6} \text{ instead of } \sqrt{(-2)} \times \sqrt{(-3)} = -\sqrt{6}. \tag{2}$$

A major context for such numbers was in the solution of polynomial equations. Since the mid-sixteenth century it had been known that all equations up to the fourth power in the unknown could be solved by the four algebraic operations together with taking roots; but the quintic was proving troublesome. Indeed, in 1772, Lagrange showed that solution by such means was unlikely, since the special equations constructible from the roots of a polynomial was

of still higher degree for the quintic instead of a lower one as in the other cases. The Italian mathematician Paolo Ruffini devoted many years to justifying Lagrange's view (more or less); however, he did not show that some other means could not deliver the roots by the standard operations.

One application of algebra was to number theory, which excited a tiny though distinguished clientele. For some decades Euler was the only significant practitioner. One conjecture was posed to him by a colleague, Christian Goldbach: to show that any prime number could be expressed as the sum of two even ones: he failed to find either proof or counter-example, but so has everyone else since. Later workers included Lagrange and Legendre, with nice theorems such as being able to express every integer as the sum of at most four squared integers. Among other results, Fermat's last so-called theorem, that the relationship

$$x^n + y^n = z^n, \text{ where } xyz \neq 0, \tag{3}$$

had no solutions by integers if $n > 2$, was proved for some low values of n.

Most of this work has become known as "algebraic" theory because it involved arithmetical and algebraic properties of integers. In the 1730s with his so-called "zeta function," Euler had innovated the "analytic" theory, which invoked the methods of the calculus to pose and solve problems.

Effects of the French Revolution. The early 1780s marked an accidental but important change in mathematical activity. D'Alembert, Euler, and Daniel Bernoulli died, and the mantle fell upon Laplace and Legendre, and especially upon Lagrange, in Berlin but in Paris from 1787. The French Revolution benefited mathematics to a remarkable degree. All universities were abolished in 1793, but within a year the École Polytechnique was founded; in its definitive form from 1799 it gave a two-year engineering course in many techniques (hence the name), especially mathematical ones (Fourcy, 1828). Founder professors included Lagrange, whose approach to the calculus was widely publicized in *Théorie des fonctions analytiques* (1797); Monge, with lots of *Géométrie descriptive* (1795); and Prony, whose lectures *Mécanique philosophique* (1800) followed *encyclopédiste* principles, such as using synoptic tables to classify different kinds of engineering activity. Laplace, not a teacher there, nevertheless worked his influence (often against Monge) on the governing council that he had established himself. In 1799 he also published the first two volumes of his *Traité de mécanique céleste*, which for a long time was to be the standard reference work in celestial and planetary mechanics; two more volumes followed, in 1802 and 1805.

At the École Polytechnique, Lagrange had been succeeded as professor in 1799 by Sylvestre-François Lacroix

(1765–1843), a protégé of Condorcet who became the leading textbook writer of his day. A suite of eight volumes was available from the early 1800s as a *Cours complet*, and the individual books were frequently reprinted and revised and sometimes translated. They rivaled a series of books by Étienne Bézout, which had been very popular since the 1760s. Lacroix also produced a vast *Traité* on the calculus, covering functions, series, differential equations, and numerical mathematics: its three volumes (1797–1800) were to be surpassed only by the second edition (1814–1819).

Also deeply interested in the history of mathematics, Lacroix contributed to the major writing of this time: the general *Histoire des mathématiques* written by the administrator Jean-Étienne Montucla (1725–1799). In his first edition (1758), Montucla had come up to fairly modern times; at the time of his death he had just published the first two of a four-volume revision, which was completed by the astronomer Jerome Lalande with Lacroix's help (1799–1802). A landmark in its subject, at three thousand pages, it was conceived on an unprecedented scale.

The École Polytechnique professors also advanced numerical mathematics at this time. Lagrange found in 1795 a simple "interpolation formula" for fitting a curve defined by a polynomial through a set of data. Engineers of all kinds required ever more elaborate sets of tables of logarithms, and to serve their needs Prony directed through the 1790s a gigantic project in Paris to prepare vast tables of values of various basic functions to many places of decimals; however, economic arithmetic intervened, for they were too expensive to publish.

A more successful and international enterprise of the decade was the decimal reform of weights and measures (Bugge, 1969). After an extensive triangulation project in which the astronomer Joseph Delambre (1749–1822) was prominent, the meter was defined as 1/10,000th of the (mis-)calculated longitudinal quadrant of the earth. The gram system was also introduced; but also a centesimal division of the quadrant of the circle into 400 degrees, and of hours (ten in a day) into centuries of minutes, which did not endure.

One of the junior staff members at the École Polytechnique was Joseph Fourier (1768–1830), who left to join Bonaparte's expedition to Egypt in 1798. Upon his return in 1801 he was appointed prefect of the *département* centered at Grenoble; yet he found time to pursue research on the then novel mathematical topic of the diffusion of heat in bodies. The first main outcome was a huge manuscript presented before the Institut de France in 1807; the reception was cool, from Lagrange on mathematical grounds, and from Laplace because Fourier's model did not conform to his own program of the time to express all physical phenomena in terms of molecular interaction. Nevertheless, Fourier won an Institut prize on the topic in 1811, though full acceptance of his work waited until the 1820s. He launched mathematical physics with this first major treatment of a topic outside mechanics; it was soon joined by substantial theories in optics, electricity, and magnetism and their own interaction in electromagnetism. Further, his methods of solving the differential equation for heat used series and integrals still named after him, which posed major questions for the calculus.

Graduates of the École Polytechnique would normally continue with three more years of specialized work at already existent schools (the original *grandes écoles*) such as the civil École des Ponts et Chaussées in Paris (directed by Prony), or the École du Genie et d'Artillerie formed at Metz in Lorraine in 1802 as a fusion of the school at Mézières and one at Chalons-sur-Marne. In these and other institutions many branches of mathematics were not only extensively taught but also greatly advanced, especially by the *polytechniciens*: from the first year until the late 1810s, the École Polytechnique unintentionally produced a continuous string of graduates who became major figures in their own right, often quite quickly (Grattan-Guinness, 1990). Thus the French dominance was maintained until the 1820s.

One of the first graduates, Louis Poinsot (1777–1855), made a notable contribution to mechanics in his first publication, *Élémens de statique* (1803) by closing an extraordinary oversight in statics. Take two forces at a point P; then their resultant is specified by the diagonal through P of the parallelogram which the forces define. However, this theorem breaks down when the forces are equal in value, opposite in direction, and not coincident. Although long known, only Poinsot understood that this "couple" (his term) of forces had to be studied for a full theory of static equilibrium to be produced. Among colleagues was a nonfriend Siméon-Dénis Poisson (1781–1840), who devoted his entire career (which was passed at the École Polytechnique) to elaborating the traditions established by Lagrange and Laplace in the calculus, mechanics, and probability theory. An early major effort, made in collaboration with the aged Lagrange, extended the theorem on the stability of the planetary system; soon afterward he produced an influential two-volume *Traité de mécanique* (1811), treating many topics but not the couple.

Gauss. Other countries reacted to the prominence of France, sometimes by imitation. The École Polytechnique served as the model for the restructuring of the United States Military Academy at West Point, and engineering schools were partly founded or remodeled elsewhere along École Polytechnique lines. Many of the French textbooks, treatises, and papers were widely read, and several translated into other languages; Lagrange's *Fonctions analytiques* and Laplace's *Mécanique céleste* were especially influential. Various reforms took place in Britain: the last one, eventually with the greatest impact, took place at Cambridge, where in the mid-1810s undergraduates Charles Babbage and John Herschel led a conversion from Newtonian principles to Euler's and Lagrange's continental calculi in the Analytical Society, the adjective alluding to Lagrange-style algebras.

Apart from all this was as great a mathematician as any: Carl Friedrich Gauss (1777–1855), a graduate of Göttingen University and soon director of the observatory there. A prodigy in mathematics, he was much slower at publishing his results, several of the best not at all. However, in the 1810s, he became involved in a controversy with Legendre and Laplace over priority and generality over the least squares criterion for fitting lines through a collection of data (instead of Boscovich's absolute deviation criterion, which was much harder to manipulate algebraically). His most prestigious early publication lay, however, in a different area: the book *Disquisitiones arithmeticae* (1801), where he raised algebraic number theory to a new level of mathematical sophistication in the concepts introduced and the methods of proof used. Not only did it leave Legendre's *Essai* way behind; it was translated into French, in 1807. Like Fourier, his various contributions were to help usher in a fresh phase in the development of mathematics.

The focus of this survey has naturally fallen upon Europe; its mathematics were transported elsewhere in the world, including the Far East. As usual, Euclid was served up plentifully, and some modern works were also translated. In Japan a tradition in numerical mathematics continued, often linked to astronomy and calendar; but in addition, a delightful indigenous tradition of "temple geometry" developed there, posing and solving problems about touching circles inscribed within other circles or quadrilaterals (Rothman and Fukagawa, 1998).

[*See also* Academies; Alembert, Jean Le Rond d'; Ancient Greece; Astronomy; Berkeley, George; Condorcet, Jean-Antoine-Nicolas de Caritat; Education; Electricity and Magnetism; French Revolution; Kant, Immanuel; Language Theories; Leibniz, Gottfried Wilhelm von; Medicine, *subentry on* Theories of Medicine; Meteorology; Musschenbroek, Petrus van; Natural Philosophy and Science; Newton, Isaac; Nieuwentijt, Bernard; Optics; Physics; Pneumatics; Royal Society of London; Saint Petersburg Academy; *and* Weights and Measures.]

BIBLIOGRAPHY

Bertoloni Meli, Domenico. *Equivalence and Priority: Newton versus Leibniz.* Oxford, 1993. On the relationship between their early mechanics.

Bos, Henk. "Differentials, Higher-Order Differentials and the Derivative in the Leibnizian Calculus." *Archive for History of Exact Sciences* 14 (1974), 1–90.

Bügge, Thomas. *Science in France in the Revolutionary Era.* Edited and translated by M. P. Crosland. Cambridge, 1969. Edition of excellent Danish original (Copenhagen, 1800) about the weights and measures conference.

Cannon, John, and Dostrovsky, Sylvia. *The Evolution of Dynamics: Vibration Theory from 1687 to 1742.* Heidelberg, Germany, 1981. On the theory of acoustics.

Chabert, Jean-Luc, et al. *From the Pebble to the Microchip.* Heidelberg, Germany, 1999. French original 1994. Fine review of numerical mathematics in general; the Enlightenment period *passim*.

Daston, Lorraine. *Classical Probability in the Enlightenment.* Princeton, N.J., 1988.

Engelsmann, Steven. *Families of Curves and the Origin of Partial Differentiation.* Amsterdam, 1984.

Euler, Leonhard. *Opera omnia.* 4 series in progress. Basel, 1911–. Substantial editorial commentaries in some volumes.

Leonhard Euler: Beiträge zu Leben und Werk. Basel, 1983. Wide review by many authors, and large bibliography.

Fourcy-Gaudain, Ambroise Louis. *Histoire de l'École Polytechnique.* Paris, 1828; repr., Paris, 1987. Still a major source, by the founder librarian.

Frängsmyr, Tore, John Heilbron, and Robin Rider, eds. *The Quantifying Spirit in the 18th Century.* Berkeley and Los Angeles, 1990. Includes links between mathematics and physics.

Fraser, Craig. "D'Alembert's Principle: The Original Formulation and Application." *Centaurus* 28 (1985), 33–61, 145–159.

Gautier, Alfred. *Essai historique sur le problème des trois corps, ou dissertation sur la théorie des mouvemens da la lune et des planètes, abstraction faite de leur figure.* Paris, 1817.

Gillispie, Charles. *Pierre Simon Laplace.* Princeton, N.J., 1998. Biography, with contributions from Robert Fox and I. Grattan-Guinness.

Gillispie, Charles. *Science and Polity in France at the End of the Old Regime.* Princeton, N.J., 1980. On the institutional aspects.

Goldstine, Hermann. *A History of the Calculus of Variations from the 16th through the 19th Century.* New York, 1980.

Grattan-Guinness, I. *Convolutions in French Mathematics, 1800–1840: From the Calculus and Mechanics to Mathematical Analysis and Mathematical Physics,* 3 vols. Basel and Berlin, 1900. Much information from about 1770 onward.

Grattan-Guinness, I. "The Varieties of Mechanics by 1800." *Historia mathematica* 17 (1990), 313–338. With extensive secondary bibliography.

Grattan-Guinness, I., ed. "Mathematics in the 18th Century." In *Storia della scienza,* vol. 5, sect. 4, pp. 357–539. Rome, 2002.

Greenberg, John. *The Problem of the Earth's Shape from Newton to Clairaut.* Cambridge, 1995. Important also on the emergence of the calculus of several variables.

Guicciardini, Niccolò. *The Development of Newtonian Calculus in Britain 1700–1800.* Cambridge, 1989.

Guicciardini, Niccolò. *Reading the Principia: The Debate on Newton's Mathematical Methods for Natural Philosophy from 1687 to 1736.* Cambridge, 1999.

Hankins, Thomas. *Jean d'Alembert: Science and the Enlightenment.* Oxford, 1970.

Jouguet, E. *Lectures de mécanique: La mécanique enseignée par les auteurs originaux.* Vol. 2. Paris, 1909. Vol. 1 (1908) covers the seventeenth century.

Lindt, Richard. "Das Prinzip der virtuellen Geschwindigkeiten." *Abhandlungen zur Geschichte der Mathematik* 18 (1904), 145–195.

Maltese, Giulio. *La storia de "F = ma."* Florence, 1992.

Newton, Isaac. *The Mathematical Papers*, 8 vols. Cambridge, 1967–1981. With substantial notes by the editor, D. T. Whiteside.

Pulte, Helmut. *Das Prinzip der kleinsten Wirkung und die Kraftkonzeptionen der rationellen Mechanik*. Stuttgart, 1989.

Pycior, Helena. *Symbols, Impossible Numbers, and Geometrical Entanglements*. New York, 1997. On British algebra with and after Newton.

Rothman, Tony, and Hidetoshi, Fukagawa. "Japanese Temple Geometry." *Scientific American* (May 1998), 85–91.

Schneider, Ivo. "Der Mathematiker Abraham de Moivre." *Archive for History of Exact Sciences* 5 (1968), 177–317.

Scott, Wilson Leonard. *The Conflict between Atomism and Conservation Theory, 1644 to 1860*. London and New York, 1970.

Taton, René, ed. *Enseignement et diffusion des sciences en France au XVIII siècle*. Paris, 1964. Reprinted 1986. Institutional history.

Todhunter, Isaac. *A History of the Mathematical Theories of Attraction and Figure of the Earth from the Time of Newton to That of Laplace*. 2 vols. London, 1873; repr., New York, 1962.

Truesdell, Clifford. *The Rational Mechanics of Flexible or Elastic Bodies, 1638–1788*. Zurich, 1960. (as Euler *Operaomnia*, ser. 2, vol. 11, pt. 2).

Truesdell, Clifford. *Essays in the History of Mechanics*. Berlin, 1968.

Whiteside, Derek Thomas. "Patterns of Mathematical Thought in the Later Seventeenth Century." *Archive for History of Exact Sciences* 1 (1961), 179–388. On infinitesimal geometry and early Newtonian calculus.

Wilson, Curtis Alan. "Perturbation and Solar Tables from Lacaille to Delambre: The Rapprochement of Observation and Theory." *Archive for History of Exact Sciences* 22 (1980), 53–304. Other major articles by this author here, in 1985 and 1987.

IVOR GRATTAN-GUINNESS

MATHER, COTTON (1663–1728), American minister.

Scion of New England's leading clerical family and a polymath, Mather engaged the new learning through the mind-set of a devout Puritan. While shepherding the region's largest congregation, he became a one-man encyclopedist, publishing 388 titles (as well as completing numerous unprinted manuscripts) ranging from sermons and religious polemics to history, philosophy, ethics, medicine, and science. The size of this output, coupled with his intellectual habits (enthusiastic rather than systematic), voracious curiosity, attentiveness to the political niceties of being a Dissenter within an empire governed by Anglicans, and desire to win distinction from England's learned elite resulted in a corpus filled with inconsistencies that make interpreting his relationship to the Enlightenment difficult.

Mather's overtures toward natural religion and his unequivocal interest in scientific observation do suggest affinities with eighteenth-century English rationalism. His campaigns for Protestant unity and assertions that Christianity could be reduced to a few essential headings intimate a genial ecumenism distrustful of dogmatism. His exhortations to manifest one's religion by joining moral reform societies and committing oneself to always doing good seemingly evince an Arminian valuation of pious duty over spiritual regeneration as the hallmarks of true faith. His belief that increasing human knowledge through studying nature would glorify God allied him with natural theologians. His championing of inoculation to combat smallpox and authorship of significant medical works rightly enshrine him as a pioneer in public health. He wrote the first American treatise on what might be called general science and posted eighty-two papers to the Royal Academy of Science, which contributions earned him the coveted election as a fellow. Viewed in isolation, these activities mark Mather as a supernatural rationalist, a convert to the argument from design as proof of God's existence, and a kind of American Latitudinarian.

He was none of these things. His tolerationism issued primarily from concerns to keep Anglo-American Dissenting Protestantism vital in the face of increasing imperial control and Anglican resurgence, especially in the colonies, rather than from a fundamental commitment to ecumenism. His personal piety, not always exhibited in his publications, featured angelic visitations, deeply ascetic devotional regimens, repeated self-examinations, protracted meditation, occasionally ecstatic experiences, and, increasingly as he aged, millennial speculation, all of which evidence a spiritual intensity unusual even among Puritans and utterly foreign to eighteenth-century Arminianism's moral *politesse* and disdain for enthusiasm. Deeply troubled by natural theology's implications of a mechanistic universe, Mather always maintained that God is not bound by eternal principles and can burst into the created world according to his will; confuting biblical criticism, he maintained the absolute veracity of the Scripture's witness. Although a talented spectator of natural phenomena, he neither utilized the experimental method to develop knowledge nor (despite profound linguistic skills) familiarized himself with mathematics, the lingua franca of scientific communication, remaining, as a result, epistemologically wedded to the supremacy of revelation. In the end, Mather's appetite to assimilate the new learning subserved the orthodox reformed Protestant project to celebrate and worship the majestic triune God.

[*See also* Dwight, Timothy; Edwards, Jonathan; Great Awakening, *subentries on* First Great Awakening *and* Second Great Awakening; Hopkins, Samuel; Johnson, Samuel; Mayhew, Jonathan; *and* Winthrop, John.]

BIBLIOGRAPHY

Lovelace, Richard. *The American Pietism of Cotton Mather: Origins of American Evangelicalism*. Grand Rapids, Mich., 1979.

Middlekauff, Robert. *The Mathers: Three Generations of Puritan Intellectuals, 1596–1728*. New York, 1971. Chapters 11–19 provide a comprehensive view of Mather's thought.

Silverman, Kenneth. *The Life and Times of Cotton Mather*. New York, 1984. A sympathetic portrait of the man and his works.

Winship, Michael P. *Seers of God: Puritan Providentialism in the Restoration and Early Enlightenment*. Baltimore, 1996. Chapters 4–7 situate Mather's thought in the context of Enlightenment rationalism and imperial politics.

CHARLES L. COHEN

MAUPERTUIS, PIERRE-LOUIS MOREAU DE

(1698–1759), French philosopher and scientist.

Maupertuis became a member of the Paris Academy of Sciences, at the early age of twenty-five, in 1723, and in 1743, he was elected to the Académie Française; in 1741, he was elected to the refounded Berlin Academy of Sciences, serving as its first president from 1745 to 1753. He published papers and books on mathematics, mechanics, music, geography, astronomy, cosmology, and philosophy.

Maupertuis began his studies with Cartesian philosophy and music and soon extended them to the natural sciences. A visit to London in 1728 converted him to Newtonianism. After returning to France, he propagated Newton's ideas. Maupertuis called for expeditions to verify the Newtonian view of the shape of the Earth by measurements. In 1736, he led one such expedition; the data he collected in Lapland confirmed Newton's prediction, and Maupertuis became famous. (Today, however, his measurements of meridians are not regarded as completely convincing.)

Maupertuis was at the start a pure empiricist, believing that perception is the only origin of knowledge and that there is no absolute certainty, even in mathematics. Regarding the solid bodies in his philosophy of nature, he laid down a hierarchy of properties that descended from such universal qualities as extension and impenetrability, to restricted properties such as mobility, and finally to particularities such as form and color. The question of how to classify Newton's "gravity" in this scheme was problematic, and Maupertuis eventually created his own metaphysical system, which he regarded as superior to that of Newton. For example, he extended his concept of matter to include consciousness. In the end, Maupertuis, once Newton's prophet, became his opponent.

In mechanics, from 1740 on Maupertuis published papers on the laws of rest and movement, in which he also compared laws from different branches of physics. These investigations culminated in his famous principle of action that explained all changes in nature: In all the changes that take place in the universe, the action is the least action that is possible ("La quantité d'action ... est la plus petite qu'il soit possible"). Moreover, Maupertuis regarded his principle as a proof of the existence of God, and God as a strictly economical creator. However, Maupertuis gave only a rather vague version of the principle, not making use of the new techniques of infinitesimal mathematics. In a more mathematical form, the principle was later clarified and extended by Leonhard Euler, Rowan Hamilton, Carl Gustav Jacobi, and others. Formally, it is used in quantum mechanics and biology to this day, though without Maupertuis's anthropomorphic interpretation. Above all, the universal philosophical claims of the principle embroiled Maupertuis in one of the most famous controversies of the century: the *affaire Koenig*, in which his opponents included the malicious Voltaire, and which finally ruined Maupertuis's career.

Maupertuis also contributed to biology, where he anticipated the concept of mutation. He postulated the existence of hereditary particles ("genes"), and—like Gregor Mendel a century later—he constructed mathematically an epigenetic theory of heredity that opposed the traditional theory of preformation. Furthermore, according to his principle, he proposed a calculus of pleasure and pain to manage a good life.

As a person, Maupertuis was a problematic and petty man, always trying to attract attention and rather proud of his superior intelligence, and therefore easy to offend and thus involved in numerous controversies. As a philosopher and as a scientist, however, he represents a powerful and highly original thinker in the French spirit, well informed on the science of his time.

[*See also* Newtonianism *and* Physics.]

BIBLIOGRAPHY

Beeson, David. *Maupertuis: An Intellectual Biography*. Oxford, 1992. With an extensive bibliography and information on the Nachlass.

Brunet, Pierre. *Maupertuis: Étude biographique*. Paris, 1929.

Glass, Bentley. "Maupertuis, Pioneer of Genetics and Evolution." In *Forerunners of Darwin, 1745–1859*, edited by B. Glass, et al. Baltimore, 1959.

Hecht, Hartmut, ed. *P.-L. M. de Maupertuis: Eine Bilanz nach 300 Jahren*. Berlin, 1999.

Maupertuis, Pierre-Louis Moreau de. *Oeuvres de Maupertuis*. 4 vols. Lyon, 1756; repr., Hildesheim and New York, 1974.

RÜDIGER THIELE

MAURISTS. *See* Benedictines of Saint-Maur.

MAYANS Y SISCAR, GREGORIO (1699–1781),

Spanish historian, literary critic, and educational reformer.

Mayans was the leading light in the Valencian contribution to the Spanish Enlightenment, and the heir to an earlier generation of Valencian writers and thinkers who were in touch with the new intellectual currents outside Spain. Born in Valencia into a family that had opposed Philip V in the War of the Spanish Succession, Mayans became a professor of law at the university there and an advocate of the reform of the study of law. For seven years he was also employed in the Royal Library. However, Mayans's desire to apply the critical historical method of Mabillon to the study of Spanish history prompted doubts about his patriotism, and prevented his obtaining the post of official historian of the Indies. This conservative atmosphere, one unsympathetic to Mayans's ideas and aspirations led him to retire in 1740. He dedicated himself henceforth to studying, writing, and publishing.

Mayans is most important as the heir and successor of the so-called *novatores*, a group of Spanish thinkers and writers who, at the end of the seventeenth century, sought greater contacts with modern science and new ideas. Among his most important activities in this respect was his reissue of some key works of this school, including Tomas Vicente Tosca's *Compendium philosophicum* (Philosophical Compendium), which owed a great deal to both Descartes and Gassendi and was originally published in 1721 and reprinted under Mayans's direction in 1754. Mayans's major contribution to the Enlightenment in Spain, however, was undoubtedly his insistence on a critical approach to the study of the past. This attitude led to his confrontation with the Augustinian Enrique Flórez, author of *España sagrada* (Sacred Spain), which sought to purge religious history of unfounded legends, but which Mayans, in his *Censura de historias fabulosas* (Critique of Fabulous Histories, 1742), still deemed too indulgent toward pious and patriotic myths. Mayans also applied this rigorous method to literary analysis, in effect founding the critical history of the Spanish language and its literature, notably in *Orígenes de la lengua española* (Origins of the Spanish Language) and *Vida de Cervantes* (*Life of Michael de Cervantes Saavedra*, Eng. trans., 1738) (both 1737). These works also reflected Mayans's great respect for the achievement of Spanish writers of the sixteenth and seventeenth centuries; he coined the now widely used name, "the Golden Age," to refer to this era in the history of Spanish arts and letters, and he edited a number of classic Spanish texts of that period. Indeed, Mayans saw himself as, in many respects, the heir of the sixteenth-century humanists, as expressed in his writing the *Vida de Fray Luis de León* (Life of Fray Luis de León, 1761). Above all, he saw himself as a successor of the Erasmians, who were also critical and reformist in their religious attitudes. This identification was given expression in Mayans's last great undertaking, an edition of the works of the great sixteenth-century Spanish humanist Juan Luis Vives, published as *Opera omnia* (1782–1790). Mayans also continued to interest himself in education, preparing a scheme for reforms in the way Spanish universities functioned (1767). His published works helped to ensure that, despite his Valencian home, Mayans's influence extended far beyond the confines of Valencia in eighteenth-century Spain.

[*See also* Language Theories *and* Spain.]

BIBLIOGRAPHY

Artola, Miguel, ed. *Enciclopedia de historia de España*, vol. 4: *Diccionario biográfico*. Madrid, 1991. A good brief biography.

Ward, Philip. *The Oxford Companion to Spanish Literature*. Oxford, 1978. An extremely brief, but informative entry.

CHRISTOPHER STORRS

MAYHEW, JONATHAN (1720–1766), Congregational minister and outspoken religious and political liberal.

From his ordination as pastor of Boston's West Congregational Church in 1747 until his untimely death in 1766, Mayhew's views received sustained attention in local newspapers, but his fame was not confined to Boston or even to New England. His was one of the few American names well known in England at the time of the Stamp Act crisis in 1765.

Mayhew was from the fifth generation of a family that ministered to the Indians on Martha's Vineyard, an island south of Cape Cod. The missionary Mayhews had encountered difficulty in explaining the fine points of Calvinism to their numerous Indian converts. Thus Jonathan Mayhew brought to his ministry a theological heritage that was practical rather than orthodox. He used his pulpit and writings to attack the doctrine of the Trinity as an illogical corruption of the Holy Scriptures. In a controversial sermon published in 1755, he declared that there was only one God and that Christ's role was as a mediator between man and "the *only* living and true GOD." His views became so prominent that nineteenth-century Unitarians would claim him as a founder of their faith.

Mayhew's greatest vehemence was reserved for the Church of England doctrine that subjects of the king owed their monarch unlimited submission and nonresistance. Mayhew's most famous sermon on this subject was published in 1750 on the anniversary of the execution of Charles I, an occasion observed by some Anglican churches near Boston as a holy day of remorse. This sermon, *A Discourse Concerning Unlimited Submission and Non-Resistance to the Higher Powers*, stated bluntly that "when Iniquity comes to thus be established by a Law, it cannot be any iniquity to transgress that law by which it is established. On the contrary, it is a sin not to transgress it." Resistance to the tyranny of Charles I was not a rebellion, but a "most righteous and glorious stand, made in defense of the natural and legal rights of the people, against the unnatural and illegal encroachments of arbitrary power." In thus justifying rebellion against an evil king, Mayhew provided a catechism of revolution that combined the political thought of such writers as John Locke with the moral duty of Christians. This sermon was reprinted several times before the American Revolution and was long remembered by John Adams and others as one of the first public declarations of American rights. Mayhew's reputation reached England and led Thomas Hollis, a philanthropist, to begin stocking the library of

Harvard College with the tomes of radical Whig political theory.

In this vein of thought, Mayhew's fiery sermon in 1765 justifying resistance to the Stamp Act led royal officials in Boston to charge him with provoking riots. Among Mayhew's other causes was an attack on the supposed plan of Church of England officials to appoint a bishop for the American colonies. His language was typical: "Bishops have commonly been the most useful...*instruments*...in establishing a tyranny over the bodies and souls of men." Even the Archbishop of Canterbury could not ignore this voice from Boston.

Mayhew was not a systematic thinker. He drew ideas from any source that suited his purpose, but in so doing he left his mark on American history and became one of the most quoted voices at the beginning of the American Revolution.

BIBLIOGRAPHY
Akers, Charles W. *Called Unto Liberty: A Life of Jonathan Mayhew, 1720–1766.* Cambridge, Mass., 1964.

CHARLES W. AKERS

MECHANICAL ARTS. *See* Technology.

MEDICINE. [*This entry contains four subentries:* Theories of Medicine, Practice of Medicine, Medicine and Physiology, *and* Anatomy and Surgery.]

Theories of Medicine

During the Enlightenment, theories of medicine were many, diverse, and controversial. Nevertheless, underlying most of them was an assumption, often explicit, that medicine (physic) should be learned and practiced through a *system*; a term that had at least two related meanings. Pedagogically, a systematic approach to medicine typically required learning it by progressing through natural philosophy (including chemistry), then through subjects particular to medicine, such as anatomy and materia medica, then through the Theory of Medicine, and finally by studying the Practice of Medicine (a course of lectures, not a practical course). System also meant a rational theory of medicine based on natural science, which explained, in general, the cause and progress of diseases; thus it served as a guide to management in particular cases. In short, to learn by system was to learn a system. In this matter, Enlightenment physicians confirmed the tradition established in Europe's medieval universities, when the system (in both senses) of the ancient Greek physician Galen (c. 130–200 CE) was adopted. The details of Galenic medicine had long been abandoned, and during the Enlightenment no one system replaced it. System-making (which during the nineteenth century became a term of opprobrium) was thus at the core of Europe's eighteenth-century orthodox medicine. Teachers declared that medicine could only be learned and practiced by system. Some denounced those of their rivals; others, such as William Cullen (1712–1790), professor at Edinburgh University, told students that if they did not care for one system they must adopt another as a practical, heuristic device that organizes information to guide their inquiries and to make rational practice possible.

All Enlightenment systems show their debt to the Scientific Revolution, notably to the theory of the French philosopher René Descartes (1596–1650), that the body was a machine. Equally significant was the work of British physicist Isaac Newton (1642–1727), because a number of physicians aspired to be "Newtons of medicine," creating systems that explained health and disease by a single force (akin to *gravity*, the force described by Newton in physics, 1664–1666). Early in the Enlightenment, Newton's theory was the inspiration for various efforts to incorporate the details of his mechanics and dynamics into accounts of health and disease. One such was by Archibald Pitcairne (1652–1713), a practitioner in Edinburgh and, in 1692, professor of medicine at the University of Leiden, the Netherlands. Pitcairne, who was acquainted with Newton, denounced the qualitative explanation of bodily events and expressed the necessity of stating corporeal laws in terms of the mathematics of particles. Like so many early Enlightenment thinkers, Pitcairne laid great stress on the circulatory system. This is scarcely surprising, since it celebrated the British physician William Harvey's 1628 discovery and was thus a putative progress in medicine. In addition, the motion of the blood seemed to be the body's dynamic activity that was then most likely to lend itself to mathematical analysis. Similar projects were espoused in England by James Keill (1673–1719) and John Freind (1675–1728).

Notable Systems. Perhaps the most celebrated system of this period was that of Hermann Boerhaave (1668–1738), who taught medicine at the University of Leiden in the early 1700s. His fame and immense success as a teacher followed from his provision of an eclectic system that was deemed modern, complete, and clinically practical. Its modernity lay both in its praise of mechanics as the basis of medicine and its claim that life consisted in the dynamic, lawlike interaction of the body's fibers and circulating fluids. There was, however, no attempt in Boerhaave's system to formulate these laws in precise terms, as Pitcairne and others had done; instead, such phenomena as temperature were explained qualitatively, by the flow of particles through resistant channels. The modernity of Boerhaave's system also lay in his espousal of chemistry and the introduction of the most recent chemical explanations into physiology and pathology. The completeness of his system was rooted in his detailed attention, in his course on the Institutes of Medicine, to explanations of how air, diet, and exercise, as accessory causes of health and disease (traditionally the six non-naturals), might conspire with a constitutional problem (the proximate cause) to produce a pathological effect (the secondary cause). This, coupled with a knowledge of the appearance and progress of actual diseases (gleaned from the greatest medical authorities since antiquity), taught in the course on the Practice of Physic, equipped a practitioner with the skills to manage individual cases. Eighteenth-century university teaching incorporated little in the way of instruction about specific causes and specific therapies, a medicine appropriate to large populations. The most successful Enlightenment medical systems were constructed from the best modern science and the soundest traditional clinical knowledge, which taught practitioners to minister to individual sickness among a small and wealthy clientele. Boerhaave's system was widely admired and was exported, for example, to Vienna by Gerhard van Swieten (1700–1772), prefect of Austria's imperial library, who devoted some thirty years to commenting on Boerhaave's work.

The varieties of meanings that modern science might have in medicine were well brought out by the system of Friedrich Hoffmann (1660–1742) of the University of Halle. Whereas Boerhaave drew heavily on the prestige of circulation theory, Hoffmann stressed the centrality of the nervous system in normal and abnormal activity. Also at the University of Halle, one of the century's most famous chemists, Georg Stahl (1660–1734), constructed a system to overcome Cartesian dualism, which was based on the soul having a role in corporeal affairs (animism). Stahl claimed that disease was a disruption of the soul's normal regulation of the body's ongoing mechanical activities. The soul, stimulated adversely by abnormal environmental conditions, generated inappropriate motions within the body. Stahl's animism signalled the first sign of retreat from the programmatic and substantive allegiance to reductionism in medical theory. After 1750, this retreat was accelerated as medical teachers built their systems on what were then variously called vital properties and forces.

A key figure in this development was the Swiss physician Albrecht von Haller (1708–1777) who, in his much cited work of 1752, claimed that on the basis of numerous experiments, he had discovered that the muscles possessed the property of irritability and the nerves that of sensibility. Haller had been a devoted pupil of Boerhaave and, in many ways, his system was a refinement of his teacher's; it was updated by prodigious reading and experimental work. Nonetheless, the effect of the adoption of Haller's findings into other systems was to shift the emphasis from the body's fluids (humoralism) to its solids (solidism). To some extent, French medicine stood aloof from northern European change, but there too the move to vitalism occurred. The most famous French systematist of the 1700s was Théophile de Bordeu (1722–1776), founder of the vitalistic school of Montpellier. In Bordeu's system, each separate part of the body had a *vita propria* (its own "vital principle").

In the late 1700s, the most famous teacher of a medical system was William Cullen. After the foundation of the medical school at Edinburgh University in 1726, the first professors were all devoted disciples of Boerhaave. Robert Whytt, appointed to a chair in 1746, used Boerhaavian ideas but shifted attention to the nervous system and its vital, regulative properties. Cullen, whose first appointment at the school was in 1756 and who taught there until 1789, effected a new synthesis that drew from the work of both Hoffmann and Haller, while retaining aspects of Boerhaave. The basis of vitality for Cullen was the excitability of the nervous system and the attendant powers of irritability it generated in the muscles. Life, for Cullen, was a forced state, and excitability was dependent on environmental stimulation. In turn, excessive or insufficient stimulation, by multifarious pathways, could result in disease. In his more speculative moments, Cullen suggested that the source of the nervous system's excitability might be the aetherial fluid that was the basis of light and electricity. A suggestion that brought accusations of materialism—on the grounds that Cullen linked excitability to sensibility and, by way of Lockean psychology—linked sensibility to mind (then regarded as the soul). One feature of Cullen's system had not been significantly present in any of its predecessors: an explicit nosology, that is, a classification of disease. During the 1700s, the theory of nosology postulated that by classifying diseases by their essential symptoms, the juxtaposition of similar disorders might reveal similar causes and, therefore, possibly similar treatments. The social significance of nosology is that physicians incorporated into their systems an interest in the common properties that might be exhibited in a diseased population, rather than its unique features in an individual. This idea was given weight by Cullen's students, most of whom did not become physicians in genteel society but in the British army and navy, among the population of burgeoning industrial towns, or in the colonies, where they might treat slaves as well as masters and townsfolk.

The most notorious medical system of the late eighteenth century, Brunonianism, was spawned by an outsider to the establishment; it gained favor among students and radicals, never finding support in a British university. It was the system of John Brown (1735–1788), an erstwhile pupil of Cullen, who failed to get preferment and fell out with his mentor. Brown claimed to have built an entirely new system (although the disciples of Cullen portrayed it as a ludicrous parody of their master's work), in which he deemed excitability to be the ultimate cause of life and dependent on stimulation; diseases were simply measurable changes in excitability. Nosology, declared Brown, was a fraud and a retreat into empiricism, from which he had rescued medicine by discovering the simple quantitative law that underlay health and disease, just as Newton's Law of Gravitation underlay planetary and terrestrial motion. His claim to be the medical Newton was quite explicit. Brunonianism created some chaos in Edinburgh for a time, because it was perceived, correctly, as an attack on the privileged control of teaching and practice. Its political dimensions and possibilities were also evident in the works of others who, although they did not profess to be Brunonians, expressed sympathy for the system's creator and drew on it for their own enterprises. Erasmus Darwin (1731–1802), for example, although not the devisor of an entire medical system, constructed an overarching evolutionary theory of nature that was based on principles not far from those used by Brown. Brunonianism took deepest root in Germany and, to a lesser extent, in France and Italy. In Germany, its dualist principle (the poles of excitability) appealed to the cultivators of *Naturphilosophie*. In Germany, also, its potential political uses became manifest; riots broke out between supporters and opponents of the system.

By the end of the eighteenth century, the new United States of America had its own medical system. There, Benjamin Rush (1745–1813) of Pennsylvania, a graduate M.D. from Edinburgh University in 1768, practiced and taught medicine in Philadelphia. He had been a signer of the Declaration of Independence and, from 1799 to 1813, Treasurer of the U.S. Mint. Although an admirer of Cullen, he radically modified his theories, reducing all diseases to a single pathological cause. Although similar to Brown's system, the two men could not have been more different. Brown was a heavy-drinking, opium-addicted Jacobite, whose system specified the use of brandy in large doses. Rush was a high-minded reformer, and he employed his system to explain the evil effects of such spirits on the mind.

The End of System-making. With Brown and Rush, system-making more or less came to a close. Ironically, one of the men credited with its downfall, Xavier Bichat (1771–1802), might well have created, had he lived long enough, yet another vast rational structure. Bichat was drawn to the doctrine of the Montpellier vitalists and aspired to be the "Newton of physiology." As it was, his tissue theory was central to the sceptical clinico-pathologic method of the Paris school which, to some extent, renounced system-making and proclaimed itself to be building medicine anew on empirical lines. Similar

developments were taking place elsewhere and, by about 1820, a second Scientific Revolution would end eighteenth-century system-building, just as the first Scientific Revolution had made it possible.

[*See also* Botany; Chemistry; Electricity and Magnetism; Hospitals; Inoculation and Vaccination; Midwifery; Natural Philosophy and Science; *and* Vitalism.]

BIBLIOGRAPHY

Brunonianism in Britain and Europe, edited by W. F. Bynum and Roy Porter. Supplement 8 of *History of Medicine*, 1988.

Jewson, N. D. "Medical Knowledge and the Patronage System in 18th-Century England." *Sociology* 8 (1974), 369–385. A much cited paper that first suggested eighteenth-century medical thought to be a product of the patronage system. Still challenging, even if flawed in detail.

King, Lester S. *The Medical World of the Eighteenth Century*. New York, 1958; 1971. Very presentist and judgmental but thorough and still the only survey.

King, Lester S. *The Philosophy of Medicine*. Cambridge, Mass., 1978.

Lawrence, Christopher. "Disciplining Disease: Scurvy, the Navy and Imperial Expansion, 1750–1825." In *Visions of Empire*, edited by D. Miller and P. Reill, pp. 80–106. Cambridge, 1996. For nosology and Brunonianism in the British Royal Navy.

Lindeboom, G. A. *Hermann Boerhaave: The Man and His Work*. London, 1968.

Risse, Guenter B. "Medicine in the Age of Enlightenment." In *Medicine in Society: Historical Essays*, edited by Andrew Wear, pp. 149–195. Cambridge, 1992.

Schofield, Robert E. *Mechanism and Materialism: British Natural Philosophy in an Age of Reason*. Princeton, N.J., 1970.

Thomson, John. *An Account of the Life, Lectures, and Writings of William Cullen M.D.* 2 vols. Edinburgh, 1859. Reprinted in 1997 with a new Introduction by Mike Barfoot. The "classic" biography, unsurpassed.

Warner, John Harley. *Against the Spirit of System: The French Impulse in Nineteenth-Century American Medicine*. Princeton, N.J., 1998.

CHRISTOPHER LAWRENCE

Practice of Medicine

A general marketplace of medical practice existed throughout Europe early in the Enlightenment. The occupational practices of physicians, surgeons, apothecaries, and barbers were often separated by quite fluid boundaries. Generalizing about the type of medical care most often received is complicated by unauthorized healers—including self-appointed midwives, bone-setters, oculists, herbalists, mystics, and a variety of quacks. Period works, including Daniel Turner's *The Modern Quack, or Medicinal Impostor* (London, 1718) and P. Coltheart's *The Quacks Unmask'd* (London, 1727), provide illuminating details about those who, without any legitimate authority, regularly advertised and offered medical services. At a time when Europeans expressed an increasing interest in the exotic, a wide range of alternative medical practices gained popular appeal and support.

Within orthodox medical practice, a reform measure was advocated to stabilize what was envisioned

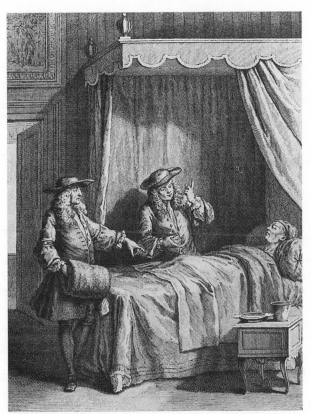

Medical Practitioners. The two doctors, Tant-Pis (Too Bad) and Tant-Mieux (So Much the Better). Engraving by Charles Nicolas Cochin after a drawing by J.-B. Oudry for an edition of Jean La Fontaine's *Fables* published in 1772. (Giraudon/Art Resource.)

as a crumbling infrastructure of medical practice. In the 1690s, Fellows of London's Royal College of Physicians, in ways similar to comparable groups elsewhere in Europe, divided over their recognition as to who represented acceptably qualified, expert practitioners. As Harold J. Cook observed (*The Decline of the Old Medical Regime in Stuart London*, Ithaca, 1986), the College of Physicians, after years of debate, established a new medical agenda that recognized licensed surgeons, and notably apothecaries, as legitimate medical care providers. Like other social projectors, many physicians envisioned their new agenda as fulfilling a moral, cultural, and economic obligation to provide a sufficient number of able practitioners to maintain the health and, thereby, the strength, of a rapidly enlarging urban population.

By expanding the types of medical practices recognized, this new agenda condoned more liberal, empirical forms of practice than had previously been sanctioned. Although the ensuing increase in competition within the marketplace of practice met both the physicians' new agenda and the public's need of available practitioners, it also created an environment in which the control of quack practice became increasingly difficult.

Efforts to standardize and police medical practice were most pronounced in German-speaking Europe. Vienna's Johann Peter Frank's elaborately detailed, rationalized, and bureaucratized *System einer vollständigen medicinischen Polizey* (System of a Complete Medical Policy, vols. 1–4, Mannheim, 1779–1788; vols. 5–6, Tübingen, 1812–1827) provided a comprehensive "womb to tomb" prevention-driven, public-health policy to be implemented by and operated under the auspices of the government. Frank's *System* reflected the cameralist government's support of a healthy productive citizenry, which abided by the rule of an absolutist monarch—Enlightenment ideals that prevailed throughout his region of Europe.

Theory. Theoretical writings of an iatromechanical sort predominated in the prolific output of medical guides issued during the early Enlightenment. Most of those theories were formulated in light of the mechanical philosophy that derived mainly from Isaac Newton (but also from Galileo and René Descartes), which explained diseases—consumption, jaundice, and fevers—in terms of forces, powers, and causes, as adopted from Newtonian natural philosophy. In essence, they promoted theoretically informed medical practices. Physicians who abhorred theoretically derived practice frequently turned to authors who advocated a practice based on the work of the ancient Greek physician Hippocrates, notably Thomas Sydenham and Hermann Boerhaave. Their writings reinforced the ancient art of observing the patient's natural surroundings and natural temperaments, whereby a better understanding of the whole patient would be gained. "I dare say," as one Hippocratic physician of the Enlightenment quipped, "the Patient will be equally thankful for his Cure, though [the physician] should be sometimes at a loss for the Modus, or Mechanism, by which the Disease . . .was produced" (Daniel Turner, *Syphilis: A Practical Dissertation on the Venereal Disease*, London, 1732). A mid-Enlightenment Hippocratic revival ensued that focused physicians' attention on individual patients, seen as having a right to be treated holistically, rather than as members of a class of similarly diseased individuals.

Medical Reform. Considerable reform within the medical practice of the late Enlightenment, in areas including hygiene, hospital care, and public health, conformed with more expansive efforts to improve social conditions, particularly within the cities. For example, foundling hospitals were developed to provide better care for the increasing number of abandoned children; they proved effective in saving many orphans' lives and in providing them with skills to better serve expanding industrial needs. Other new specialist hospitals throughout Europe, both in the cities and the provinces, were designated as caretaking institutions for specific diseases, including syphilis, smallpox, and insanity. Although designed as religious or charitable institutions, their organization and further expansion were often guided by economic and political incentives.

Another area of Enlightenment medical reform centered around childbirth. For centuries, women had dominated the care for and delivery of pregnant women. Male physicians and, particularly, surgeons were resorted to only on an emergency basis. This began to change when more formalized training of midwives began: notable innovators included François Mauriceau (1637–1709) in France; James Douglas (1675–1742), William Smellie (1697–1763), and William Hunter (1718–1783), three Scots who taught in London; and Lorenz Heister (1683–1758) in Germany. All taught many students and published significant works in the field. The chief result of these innovative programs was an escalation in the number of "man-midwives" (Fr., *accoucheurs*). The increasing presence of male practitioners in and subsequent dominance over midwifery troubled traditional female midwives. One such practitioner, Elizabeth Nihell, charged, in her *Treatise on the Art of Midwifery* (London, 1760), that female practitioners actually delivered safer care to their parturient patients; man-midwives' regular use of forceps was unwarranted, and women claimed to be less threatened by female midwives attending their vulnerable, exposed bodies. Despite objections, the authority that male practitioners garnered shifted the paradigm of childbirth practice so that attendance by male midwives became common and applauded by the medical profession.

Therapeutic Advances. Smallpox plagued Enlightenment Europe, with mortality rates approaching 50 percent. No one was immune. Mary, queen of England, contracted it in 1694, and France's Louis XV succumbed to it in 1774. The thousands who survived were often hideously scarred. That affected them not only physically and psychologically but also socially, because these scars considerably reduced marriageability. In 1717, Lady Mary Wortley Montagu, wife of the British ambassador to Constantinople, reported that severe attacks of smallpox in Turkey had been prevented by inoculations: "The smallpox, so fatal, and so general amongst us, is here entirely harmless, by the invention of engrafting." Every autumn, an "old woman comes with a nut-shell full of the matter of the best sort of small-pox, ... rips open [a vein] ... and puts into the vein, as much [smallpox] matter as can lie upon the head of her needle" (Mary Wortley Montagu, *Letters*, London, 1763). After her return to Britain in 1722, Montagu had her own children inoculated. Britain's George I, acting under the advice of the physicians Sir Hans Sloane (1660–1753) and Richard Mead (1673–1754), offered freedom to incarcerated criminals who submitted to testing the efficacy of inoculation. Caroline, princess of Wales, expressed interest in having her children inoculated, but

first wanted the method tested on fifty charity children. Those inoculated exhibited a mild infection, but it was not fatal and did not scar; they appeared to be immune from contracting smallpox. The English country physician Edward Jenner (1749–1823) modified the method that Montagu had described through a process labeled *vaccination* (in *An Inquiry into the Causes and Effects of the Variolae Vaccinae*, London, 1798). In 1798, Jenner introduced a milder form of the related disease, cowpox, into uninfected patients. Montagu's and Jenner's efforts shifted the emphasis from treating to preventing smallpox on a global scale; the saving of life was great, and vaccination was one of the few therapeutic advances made in the 1700s.

Many patients continued to search for healers who promised cures that conventional medicine did not provide. Physicians commonly used harsh, strong medicines in their heroic efforts to treat complaints. Unsatisfied with the results, many patients embraced new ideas, ranging from electrical therapy to the power of hypnotic suggestion. Some of these new practices focused simply on improved hygiene and preventive measures, whereas others were promoted as cures for disease. Often, healers advocated a combination of therapeutic approaches to produce a healthier mind and body. One noted healer, Franz Anton Mesmer, considered that the natural movements associated with gravity and the tides—both active areas of discussion then among natural philosophers—resulted from a fluid that permeated the universe and, with its vital force, infused both matter and spirit. He envisioned similar fluids flowing throughout the body and employed magnets in an effort to remove any bodily barriers that, by disrupting the flow, caused pain or nervous disorders. Later, he held fashionable group sessions in ornately furnished Parisian treatment rooms, where patients were gathered around a central tub filled with "magnetized water." Patients grabbed iron rods protruding from the sides of the tub, placing them near their diseased body part. During the treatment, many patients were reputedly cured though a convulsive fit, whereas others were healed while mesmerized into a hypnotic trance.

Water became a common component of many curative protocols. Hydrotherapy (or balneotherapy), such as that delivered in England's fashionable spa-towns, including Bath, Harrogate, and Tunbridge Wells, employed water both to combat specific illnesses and to enhance natural vitality in patients. Innovative entrepreneurs drew their medical inspirations from an array of sources, ranging from ancient Hippocratic environmentalist ideas to those of the Lichfield physician John Floyer, who advocated cold baths. Celia Fiennes's travel journal is noted for its comparative account of spas throughout England, and Bath's Beau Nash created a career around the conspicuous consumption of water. Cold-water cures, *sitz* baths, and mineral springs at Plombières, Spa, Aix-la-Chapelle, and Forges-les-Eaux in France, and Baden in Switzerland all became popular medical resorts for the enlightened upper classes.

Disease Prevention. Military and naval practice also changed as water provided the basis of another form of disease prevention during the Enlightenment. Scurvy had caused numerous sailors' deaths aboard both commercial and military vessels. English naval physician James Lind related his findings of the diagnosis and treatment of this threat to national defense in his *Treatise of the Scurvy* (Edinburgh, 1753); he concluded that an unbalanced diet was chiefly responsible for this sickness and that fresh fruit had been observed to quell the problem. In the 1770s, Captain James Cook expanded Lind's findings, noting additional foods that he found to be successful in preventing scurvy during his three colonialist Pacific voyages. In 1795, Britain's navy declared citrus juice an obligatory preventative agent to be carried aboard all official vessels. As knowledge of anatomy improved, and as surgeons and physicians were better trained, they became concerned with sanitation and prevention, as can be seen in the careers of Sir John Pringle and Sir Gilbert Blaine.

Many religious healers then viewed disease as "a portal through which man acquired eternal salvation." Yet some clerics, like Britain's John Wesley, recognized it as a clerical duty to care for both the physical and the spiritual well-being of his patients. Wesley provided the lay public with a manual, *Primitive Physick* (London, 1747), designed to be neither "too dear for poor men to buy" nor "too hard for plain men to understand." His prescriptions—like those commonly used in contemporaneous domestic, self-help manuals—contained "only safe and cheap and easy" ingredients, so that any literate individual could compound useful medicines for his or her own use. Similar medical advice written for the lay public also flourished in late Enlightenment secular writings. Most notable are the multiple editions and translations of Simon André Tissot's *Avis au peuple sur sa santé* (Lausanne, 1761) and William Buchan's *Domestic Medicine* (Edinburgh, 1769). Both exemplify the Enlightenment's goal of popularizing information to enhance public knowledge and "know-how."

Diagnostic Techniques. Enlightenment medical practice also changed with the introduction of new diagnostic techniques. Specific techniques were devised to ascertain the healthiness of the lungs at a time when tuberculosis was killing many in Europe. One diagnostic innovator who gained renown for his clinical practice in Paris, Jean-Nicolas Corvisart, credited his successful diagnostics to Viennese physician Leopold Auenbrugger's *Inventum Novum* (Vienna, 1761), a work he translated and supplemented with his own case studies (*Nouveau méthode pour reconnaître les internales de la poitrine*, Paris,

1808). Auenbrugger had emphasized the importance of percussion, a technique based on the systematic tapping of the practitioner's fingers over the patient's body to determine the density of underlying structures. During an age when information about the condition of an individual's internal physiology and pathology was largely inaccessible, this technique, when perfected, became heralded for revealing particular insights into respiratory function. Corvisart's pupil, René-Théophile-Hyacinthe Laennec (1781–1826), expanded the usefulness of percussion with his development of an auscultation tube that clarified and amplified natural lung and heart sounds considerably more than the weak, diffuse, and partially inaudible sounds that were artificially produced by percussion alone. Laennec described his clinical success at localizing and differentially diagnosing pulmonary diseases through his invention, the stethoscope, in his *Traité de l'auscultation médiate* (Paris, 1819).

[*See also* Botany; Cameralism; Chemistry; Electricity and Magnetism; Hospitals; Inoculation and Vaccination; Insanity; Midwifery; *and* Natural Philosophy and Science.]

BIBLIOGRAPHY

Bell, Whitfield J., Jr. *The Colonial Physicians and Other Essays*. New York, 1975. Useful biographical essays on central figures in early American medicine.

Bynum, W. F. "Health, Disease and Medical Care." In *The Ferment of Knowledge: Studies in the Historiography of Eighteenth-Century Science*, edited by G. S. Rousseau and Roy Porter, pp. 211–253. Cambridge, 1980.

Bynum, W. F., and Roy Porter, eds. *Medical Fringe and Medical Orthodoxy, 1750–1850*. London, 1987. Essays that distinguish fringe from more traditional practices in England and France.

Cunningham, Andrew, and Roger French, eds. *The Medical Enlightenment of the Eighteenth Century*. Cambridge, 1990. Essays that provide valuable insight into Enlightenment medicine in England, Scotland, Germany, France, and America.

Darnton, Robert. *Mesmerism and the End of the Enlightenment in France*. Cambridge, 1968. An exemplary microhistory, using Mesmer's practice as a lens to examine French Revolutionary culture.

Duden, Barbara. *The Woman beneath the Skin: A Doctor's Patients in Eighteenth-Century Germany*. Translation by Thomas Dunlap. Cambridge, 1991. English translation of *Geschichte unter der Haut: Ein Eisenacher Artz und seine Patientinnen um 1730* (first published in 1987). An analysis of Johannes Storch's notebooks of twenty years of medical practice in Saxony, regarding what female patients disclosed about their bodies.

Forster, Robert, and Orest Ranum, eds. *Medicine and Society in France: Selections from the* Annales: Economies, Sociétés, Civilisations. Translated by Elborg Forster and Patricia M. Ranum. Baltimore, 1980. A broad cultural overview of medical practice, hospital systems, folk medicine, and childbirth during the French Enlightenment.

Foucault, Michel. *The Birth of the Clinic: An Archaeology of Medical Perception*. Translated by A. M. Sheridan Smith. New York, 1973. Translation of *Naissance de la clinique: Une archéologie du regard médical* (first published in 1963). A special focus on the physician's perception, or "gaze," resulting from the interactions of space, language, and death, which identified the Paris clinic.

Jewson, N. D. "Medical Knowledge and the Patronage System in Eighteenth-Century England." *Sociology* 8 (1974), 369–385.

Porter, Roy. *Health for Sale: Quackery in England, 1660–1850*. Manchester, 1989. A valuable work that shifts the paradigm from "quacks" as deceivers of the public into providers. Consumers deemed them integral to the commercialized marketplace of medical practice in Enlightenment England.

Porter, Roy, ed. *Patients and Practitioners: Lay Perceptions of Medicine in Pre-industrial Society*. Cambridge, 1985. Essays that incorporate views of religion, childbirth, and the popularization of medical "know-how" in Enlightenment England and Germany.

Porter, Roy, ed. *The Popularization of Medicine, 1650–1850*. London, 1992. Essays that focus on the corpus of lay medical writings and the dispersion of medical and surgical "know-how" in Enlightenment England, France, Spain, and Hungary.

Porter, Roy, ed. *Medicine in the Enlightenment*. Amsterdam, 1995. Essays that examine a wide range of influences on Enlightenment medical practices in England, France, and Germany.

Riley, James C. *The Eighteenth-Century Campaign to Avoid Disease*. Basingstoke, U.K., 1987. A focus on the measures taken to reduce the contact between humans and the vectors believed to be responsible for spreading disease in Enlightenment Europe.

Wilson, Adrian. *The Making of Man-Midwifery: Childbirth in England, 1660–1770*. Cambridge, 1995. Lucid exploration of the shift from a women-only ritual to a man-dominated practice.

Wilson, Philip K. *Surgery, Skin and Syphilis: Daniel Turner's London (1667–1741)*. Amsterdam, 1999. Special focus on the skin's role as a physical and professional boundary between medical and surgical practice.

PHILIP K. WILSON

Medicine and Physiology

A mechanistic program in physiology dominated medicine in the first half of the eighteenth century, but by mid-century its failure to provide experimentally verifiable mechanistic structural explanations of the basic functions of animal life, such as muscular motion, nutrition, and growth, was apparent to many. Unwilling to accept animist accounts—such as that developed by Georg Stahl (c. 1660–1734), professor of medicine and chemistry at the University of Halle—many Enlightenment physiologists developed vitalist theories, which explained life processes through "sensibility" conceived as a universal property of living matter. They sought to break down the dualism between the psychic and the physical that lay behind the mechanist physiology initiated by René Descartes (1596–1650) and adopted by Oxford physiologists such as Robert Hooke (1635–1703) and Robert Boyle (1627–1691) in the seventeenth century. This article focuses on the background and outcome of the important work on muscular physiology undertaken by two leading experimental medical physiologists at midcentury: Robert Whytt (1714–1766) and Albrecht von Haller (1708–1777).

The most influential physiologist in the first half of the eighteenth century in Europe was Hermann Boerhaave, professor of medicine at the University of Leiden. In his widely circulated *Academical Lectures on the Institutes of Medicine* (published posthumously by his student Albrecht

von Haller in 1739–1744), Boerhaave adopted a form of Cartesian dualism, maintaining that mind and body are entirely different kinds of substances, that the body itself operates according to the same mechanical laws as the rest of the universe, and that the basic functions of life occur independently of the mind or soul. According to Boerhaave, the essential properties of the soul are thought or consciousness, while the essential properties of bodily substances are extension and the power of resistance. Although his overall scheme was Cartesian, in describing the laws governing the body Boerhaave turned to Newtonian matter theory. The body is "an Assemblage of small elastic Solids, by whose conjoined and regular actions, Life and Health are produced." He identified "elasticity" as a universal principle of Nature, like the power of gravitation by which planets are attracted to each other. Elsewhere, he described life as an interaction between the solid and fluid parts of the body: the elastic solids, which constitute the "vessels" of the body, react to the expansion caused by the fluids that flow into them and thereby produce motion. Even though Boerhaave held that the automatic motions that give life to the body operate entirely without any influence of the soul or mind, he believed that the nervous system is still involved in their production. He presented an elaborate mechanical hypothesis explaining how the flow of blood into the auricles of the heart makes them expand and cut off the flow of "nervous fluid" from the cardiac nerve to the ventricles, so that the auricles in turn become "paralytic" and fill up with blood. The source of the nervous fluid is the cerebellum, which operates entirely separately from the higher brain (medulla), the physical seat of the voluntary motions of the body as well as of the senses and memory. Corresponding to this anatomical distinction between two different centers of the central nervous system, Boerhaave postulated a functional distinction between unconscious automatic motions, such as those of the heart, and motions such as excretion, which require an "uneasy sensation." The latter are conscious and are normally voluntary.

The physiology of Georg Stahl published in his *Theoria medica vera* (1706) was in stark contrast to the mechanism of Boerhaave. Stahl held that life functions cannot exist without the influence of a rational soul or mind. It is true that the body is a machine, but it is not one that can operate automatically. For him, a machine is an instrument that requires a mind to coordinate its actions and give them purpose. Taken in themselves, the physical and chemical processes of an organism are unstable and constantly subject to forces of corruption. Stahl noted, for example, that when blood is taken from a living organism it quickly coagulates and ceases to have the characteristics of life that it has as part of a living organism. The living organism requires an intelligent immaterial soul to coordinate the parts of matter and make them operate to perform a certain function. Stahl held that the soul understands, albeit without consciousness, the structure of the body organs and the functions they are suited to perform. He ascribed to this intelligent soul the task of directing the vital motions of the body, including nutrition, the circulation of the blood, secretion and excretion, regeneration of tissue, and so on. In so doing, the soul operates with a kind of will, but one independent of the will that directs voluntary movements. It is the soul's failure of will or its ignorance—or both—that results in disease or even in the death of the organism. Stahl's "holistic" conception of the person appealed to practicing physicians and their patients; it was adopted by George Cheyne (1671–1743), the most popular medical writer in early eighteenth century Britain, in his book *The English Malady* (1733).

A far more systematic and experimental criticism of physiological mechanism was developed by the Scottish physiologist Robert Whytt, professor of the Institutes of Medicine at Edinburgh University from 1747 to 1766. In his *Essay on the Vital and Other Involuntary Motions of Animals* (1751), Whytt systematically criticized mechanistic hypotheses put forward by Boerhaave and others, showing that they were purely hypothetical and did not account for the phenomena they were supposed to explain. He gave eight arguments based on anatomical and physiological evidence to demonstrate that the mechanism Boerhaave postulated for the motion of the heart simply would not work. Whytt experimented on muscles both *in vivo* and *in vitro*, showing that they do not operate according to the mechanical, chemical, and electrical hypotheses that his contemporaries had offered to explain. By careful experimentation, he located the source of reflex action in the spinal marrow, and he established that such automatic responses of the body do not require any connection with the cerebellum, as Boerhaave thought. Having rejected mechanist and materialist models to explain the motion of muscles, Whytt argued that they are caused by "feeling," which pervades the nerves of the muscles and is retained in them even after they are removed from the rest of the body. He rejected Boerhaave's distinction between purely automatic responses and those that arise from an "uneasy sensation," arguing that all bodily motions arise from the latter principle. Noting that muscles react to a stimulus in a manner that indicates that they are trying to remove an irritant, Whytt argued that their motions are best explained by an immaterial "sentient Principle." He maintained that this principle provided a far simpler explanation of the vital motions of the body than the complex mechanisms put forward by his predecessors. This sentient principle had the further explanatory advantage that it made intelligible the manner in which muscles react. For Whytt, it is one and the same soul that accounts for both the vital motions of the body and the higher conscious functions; however, it operates very differently in these different operations. He stressed that, in producing the vital motions of the body, the soul does not act with any kind of intelligence or will; rather, its operations are as fully determined as those of any purely mechanical system. Nevertheless, Whytt insisted that the vital soul is immaterial, and that his physiological theory provided a defense for medicine from charges of "scepticism and irreligion."

A very different criticism of Boerhaave's physiology was given by his former student Albrecht von Haller, professor of anatomy, botany, and surgery at the University of Göttingen. Haller accepted the Cartesian mind–body dualism of Boerhaave and argued that the vital motions of the body operate without the soul. However, he rejected Boerhaave's theory that the motions of muscles require nervous energy from the central nervous system. Like Whytt, Haller criticized Boerhaave's account of the motions of the heart: he argued that they derive from an unknown mechanical force that lies "concealed in the very structure of the heart itself." More generally, all muscles of the body possess this internal force, or "irritability." Haller refused to speculate on its nature, insisting only that it has its source in some "arrangement of the particles" making up the "animal gluten" of the muscles. Thus, he affirmed the mechanical nature of the force while refusing to speculate on its specific character. In a famous paper entitled "A Dissertation on the Sensible and Irritable Parts of Animals" (1753), Haller defined a "sensible" part of the body as one that "occasions evident signs of pain and disquiet in the animal," and an "irritable" part as one that contracts when stimulated. He described numerous gruesome experiments in which he tested various tissues of 190 living animals in order to discover which were irritable and which sensible. He argued, against Whytt, that the most irritable parts of animals (such as the muscles of the heart) are not sensible, and that the most sensible (such as the nerves themselves) are not irritable. Further, the "irritability of the muscle fibers," especially when they are entirely removed from the body, shows that their basic action is totally "independent of the nerves." Haller rejected Whytt's claim that a life soul underlay all bodily motions, and he reestablished on a firmer foundation the mechanistic dualism of Boerhaave. He wrote, in opposition to Whytt, that "the soul is a being which is conscious of itself, and represents to itself the body to which it belongs." The soul cannot, as Whytt maintained, operate unconsciously in any part of the body, and it is not responsible for its vital motions. There is no such thing as sensibility or uneasy sensation apart from that of which one is aware. For Haller, unlike Whytt, it is consciousness, not merely life, that requires the existence of an immaterial soul.

The physiological discoveries of both Haller and Whytt were used by writers of the French Enlightenment to dispose of the belief in an immaterial soul, whether its essence was considered to be thought (as maintained by Descartes, Boerhaave, and Haller) or life (as maintained by Stahl and Whytt). Julien Offray de La Mettrie, like Haller a student of Boerhaave, became one of the most outspoken materialists of the Enlightenment. In *L'homme machine* (1748), La Mettrie adopted Haller's notion of irritability in order to argue that self-movement in the body of living beings derives merely from the organization of lifeless matter, and that there is no need for any immaterial soul of either kind in man. La Mettrie regarded Haller's experiments as opening up the possibility for a universal mechanism that could explain both the highest human functions and the basic processes of life.

Whytt's views of sensibility as the essential property of living matter gained widespread acceptance among vitalist physiologists in France in the second half of the eighteenth century. They did not, however, share his opinion that sensibility derives from an immaterial soul. Most physicians of the Montpellier school, who identified sensibility as the essential property of living matter, denied that it resulted from an immaterial soul. Henri Fouquet (1727–1806), who wrote the article "Sensibilité" in the *Encyclopédie*, postulated a sensible soul that was diffused throughout the body; however, he identified this sensible soul as a dynamic material substance, in the manner of seventeenth-century writers of the Epicurean tradition such as Thomas Willis (1621–1675) and Pierre Gassendi (1592–1655). In this he was followed by Denis Diderot's friend, the famous physiologist Theophile de Bordeu (1722–1776). The idea of sensibility as the basic principle of life was also central to the biological and metaphysical speculations of Diderot, who postulated a continuity between organic and inorganic forms and regarded all matter as containing a latent life force.

The arguments of Whytt and von Haller and their vitalist successors dominated discussions of physiology until the 1780s. By then, research on heat, animal heat, combustion, and respiration had led to new approaches to physiology. In the mid-1780s, Antoine-Laurent Lavoisier (1743–1794) related these interests to a new chemistry of living things. He changed the course of future debates after 1790, but the Enlightenment was preoccupied by the ideas of Boerhaave, Stahl, Whytt, Haller, and their vitalist successors.

[*See also* Boerhaave, Hermann; Botany; Chemistry; Diderot, Denis; Haller, Albrecht von; La Mettrie, Julien Offray de; Lavoisier, Antoine-Laurent; Life Sciences; Materialism; Natural Philosophy and Science; Physico-Theology; Rush, Benjamin; *and* Zoology.]

BIBLIOGRAPHY

Duchesneau, François. *La physiologie des Lumières*. The Hague, 1982.

Duchesneau, François. "Stahl and Leibniz on Soul and Body." In *Psyche and Soma: Physicians and Metaphysicians on the Mind-Body Problem from Antiquity to Enlightenment*, edited by John P. Wright and Paul Potter, pp. 217–235. Oxford, 2000.

Fearing, Franklin. *Reflex Action: A Study in the History of Physiological Psychology*. Cambridge, Mass., 1930. A classical study of the origins of this key physiological concept.

French, R. K. *Robert Whytt, The Soul, and Medicine*. London, 1969.

Hall, Thomas. *History of General Physiology*. 2 vols. Chicago, 1969. See especially chapters 26, 27, 32, 33, and 34. An excellent account of physiological theories of the Enlightenment in their historical context.

Hankins, Thomas. *Science and the Enlightenment*. Cambridge, 1983. See chapter 5. A concise and insightful account of life sciences in the Enlightenment.

Holmes, Frederic Lawrence. *Lavoisier and the Chemistry of Life: An Exploration of Scientific Creativity*. Madison, Wis., 1985.

Mendelsohn, Everett. *Heat and Life: The Development of the Theory of Animal Heat*. Cambridge, Mass., 1964. This study shows the transition from the physical analogies used to explain animal heat in the mid-seventeenth century to the applications of the new science of chemistry in the late eighteenth century.

Rey, Roselyne. "Psyche, Soma and the Vitalist Philosophy of Medicine." In *Psyche and Soma*, edited by John P. Wright and Paul Potter, pp. 255–266. Oxford, 2000.

Rey, Roselyne. *Naissance et développement du vitalisme en France, de la deuxième moitié du XVIIIe siècle à la fin du Premier Empire*. Oxford, 1999.

Roger, Jacques. *Les sciences de la vie dans la pensée française du XVIIIe siècle*. Paris, 1963.

Temkin, Owsei. "Albrecht von Haller, 'A dissertation on the sensible and irritable parts of animals'." *Bulletin of the History of Medicine* 4 (1936), 651–699. This reprint of a contemporary English translation of Haller's famous paper is prefaced with a commentary by Temkin, putting the concept of irritability into historical context.

Wright, John P. "Metaphysics and Physiology: Mind, Body and the Animal Economy in Eighteenth-Century Scotland." In *Studies in the Philosophy of the Scottish Enlightenment*, edited by M. A. Stewart, pp. 251–301. Oxford, 1990.

JOHN P. WRIGHT

Anatomy and Surgery

Enlightenment anatomists developed skill at both uncovering natural form within human bodies and creating artistic representations of their findings.

Anatomical Representations. A wide array of artistic expressions appeared in Enlightenment anatomists' displays of human form. The Amsterdam anatomist Frederik Ruysch (1638–1731) preserved dissected specimens, positioning them as lifelike objects for his anatomical cabinet of curiosities. His specimens and their influence upon illustrators such as Jean-Jacques Scheuchzer represented a combination of moralizing monstrosity, whimsical artform, and realistic anatomy. Italian anatomical artists gained renown for exacting highly accurate, life-size wax replicas or simulacras of humans in various states of dissected disembodiment. Felice Fontana of

Rovereto (1720–1805) offered students over fifteen hundred wax models, some of which were manipulable with removable body parts, thereby allowing prolonged investigation into naturally concealed spaces. Giovanni Antonio Galli developed an extensive museum of wax obstetrical sculptures prepared by Bologna's Anna Morandi Manzolini, together with her husband, Giovanni. Albrecht von Haller, at Göttingen and Bern, emphasized a comparative study in *Elementa Physiologia Corporis Humani* (Lausanne, 1757–1766) of anatomical specimens to better distinguish normal from abnormal structure. Leiden's Bernhard Albinus (1697–1770) furthered comparative study by establishing images he deemed representative of a universal or geometrically average form. His student, Pieter Camper (1722–1789), developed proportional comparative morphologies in *Dissertation physique* (Utrecht, 1791) by superimposing human and animal anatomies and conceptualizing a visual evolution from animal to human form.

Other anatomical representations focused on particular bodily organ systems or parts. The Toulouse printmaker Jacques Gamelin vividly represented the growing Enlightenment interest in osteology and myology in *Nouveau recueil d'osteologie et de myologie* (New Collection of Osteology and Myology, Toulouse, 1779). Jacques Gautier Dagoty applied and improved upon his teacher Jacques-Christophe Le Blon's invention of the colored mezzotint such that flesh and muscle were easily distinguishable in the naturally pigmented illustrations of his *Anatomie de la tête* (Anatomy of the Head, Paris, 1748). William Cheselden's *Anatomy of the Humane Body* (London, 1713) gained renown for its accurately proportioned anatomical figures drawn from a camera obscura, and notoriety for its author's plagiarism of the Dutch anatomist Govard Bidloo's anatomical plates (1685). Jan van Rymsdyk's illustrations for William Hunter's *Anatomy of the Human Gravid Uterus* (Birmingham, 1774) featured detailed images of different stages of fetal development and complications set within butchered female bodies, unlike the more conventional and somewhat erotic anatomies of pregnancy in William Smellie's *Sett of Anatomical Tables* (London, 1754) and Charles Nicholas Jenty's *Demonstrations of a Pregnant Uterus* (London, 1757). William Hunter created a lasting controversy by "shifting visual priorities" so that the viewer could "no longer identify effortlessly with the fetal body and encounter the female body as peripheral" (Newman).

By mid-Enlightenment, many asserted that knowledge was not only derived from reason, but that it could also be gained via imagination and feeling. Anatomical representations began to focus upon displays of the nervous system, conforming with the growing Enlightenment awareness of sensitivity. Natural philosophical discourse over the interrelatedness of body, mind, and sensation often centered around particular artistic interpretations of nerve pathways. The subsequent interest exclusively focusing on the mind and sensation provoked what the medical historian Roy Porter described as the body's "aetherialization into invisibility."

Dissection and Treatment. In the eighteenth century, dissection became increasingly incorporated into the training of surgeons. Surgeons used human cadavers to gain experiential insight into the arrangement and layering of structures beyond that gleaned from anatomical atlases. Many also used them to practice their surgical technique. Dissection gradually led some healers, particularly iatro-mechanists, to adopt a "soulless" view of the human body. The human body, according to the French physician Julien Offray de La Mettrie's *L'homme machine* (Man a Machine, Leiden, 1748), was a machine wound by its own springs. This growing man-machine image stemmed primarily from the work of the French philosopher René Descartes (1596–1650). La Mettrie had depicted humans as dynamic, physiologically functioning machines. Blood circulated, food was digested, and humans reproduced via purely mechanical means. The body was composed of material parts that worked together according to mechanical, physical laws. According to some Enlightenment accounts, God acted as the engineer behind this great terrestrial machine. The question remained, however, as to whether God could intervene at any stage of malfunction or whether humans functioned entirely by a predetermined course or by free will. Healers who intervened with God's work in order to fix the broken machine were frequently called atheists.

Procuring human specimens for anatomical dissection was difficult and impeded the training of surgeons. Although Edinburgh had three generations of talented professors of anatomy named Alexander Monro (I, II, and III), its lasting, popular anatomical image is tied to the notorious practice of body snatching. Alexander Monro I was accused of this in 1725 as were many other teachers of anatomy in Britain and on the Continent until the nineteenth century. To alleviate further public outcry over grave robbing, which reached its peak with the case of Robert Knox about 1829, the British Parliament in 1832 passed the Anatomy Act, which assured from then on a plentiful supply of pauper corpses for dissection; elsewhere the timing was much the same. This meant that for much of the eighteenth century, anatomical instruction depended on the wax models noted above and upon the preserved preparations of specimens which, in Edinburgh, were owned by the Monros and assured their continuance in office. This was often the case elsewhere in universities and in private academies such as William Hunter's famous school in London.

Enlightenment surgeons treated a different domain of disease than physicians. Physicians regularly attended patients suffering from internal disorders such as fevers, gout, consumption, asthma, rheumatism, and palsies. Their armamentarium consisted primarily of internally administered medicines. Alternatively, surgical texts described treatments for externally manifest disorders. Surgeons were instructed how to incise and dress tumors, set fractured limbs and dislocated joints, repair fistulae, amputate limbs, and cut for bladder stones. Additionally, they frequently applied topical medications. More noticeably than for practicing physicians, the skin provided the basis for the mechanical handicraft of surgery.

Like surgical texts, Enlightenment domestic manuals such as *Aristotle's Family Physician* proffered remedies for treating boils, burns, corns, and piles, together with suggesting remedies for removing moles, freckles, and the pits on the faces of smallpox victims. Readers were, however, urged to limit the range of disorders they attempted to treat, leaving the most severe situations for a surgeon's care. Contemporary accounts suggest that patients only sought surgeons as a last resort, after all other treatments had failed.

Bladder stones were among the most common disorders whose treatment surgeons undertook and described. Descriptive accounts throughout Europe abound praising particular methods for "curing the stone," either by extirpation or dissolution. The lithotomists Johann Jacob Rau, François Tolet, Claude Nicolas le Cat, Jean Baseilhac, John Douglas, and William Cheselden each gained renown for a particular method of cutting for the stone. Public clamor over and personal experience with this surgery inspired the composer Marin Marais to set this operation to music in his 1725 *Tableau de l'opération de la taille* (Tableau of the Operation of the Stone).

Numerous advertisements and public testimonials supporting nonsurgical dissolution of the stone suggests that the public did not share the surgeons' enthusiasm for the knife. Contemporaneous with geologists' investigations of terrestrial petrifaction, inquiries into the composition of human stones flourished. Perhaps the most celebrated challenge to surgeons was Joanna Stephens's medicinal "cure." After a year-long experiment, Stephens persuaded Britain's Parliament to pay her £5,000 for divulging her secret stone-dissolving remedy. Controversy over her revealed "cure" provoked decades of experimentation, indicating that consumer culture demanded successful alternatives to surgery.

As syphilis was frequently diagnosed by its external appearance, this disorder frequently fell within the realm of surgical care. French "venerologists" including François Chicoyneau, Jean-Louis Petit, Augustin Belloste, Vincent Brest, Pierre Desault, and especially Jean Astruc (1684–1766), gained international renown for special curative treatments. Such treatments typically involved variations of either mercury salivation (promoting excessive production of saliva) or fumigation (smoking a patient over fumes). Accustomed to manually administering long, labor-intensive treatments, surgeons routinely attended "foule" (venereally diseased) patients for weeks.

French surgery was admired throughout Europe for its improvements in both surgical instruments and technique. Jean-Louis Petit's (1674–1750) screw tourniquet was widely copied, as were Dominique Anel's (1779–1830) ligation of aneurysms, Hugues Ravaton's double-flap amputation, and Jacques Daviel's (1696–1762) cataract operation. France also gained renown for its institution of the clinic. The success of the Paris clinic stemmed from the opportunity to view the signs of disease upon a clustered group of patients suffering similar maladies and, subsequently, to observe the internal anatomical pathology of these patients at autopsy. Following the initiative laid out by the Bolognese physician Giovanni Battista Mogagni's *De sedibus et causis morborum* (On the Seats and Causes of Death, Venice, 1761), Paris clinic practitioners correlated autopsy findings with particular signs and symptoms that the patient had experienced while living. Although earlier, smaller models of clinical experience existed in Enlightenment Leiden, Vienna, and Edinburgh, the Paris clinic epitomized an established observational medical practice founded upon correlative pathological anatomy.

The time-honored tradition of surgical apprenticeship also declined during the Enlightenment as more surgeons attended university classes and medical schools. They also increasingly followed that with service as military and naval or hospital surgeons, in effect prolonging their training. In hospital settings, surgeons could see a greater variety of diseases and conditions requiring treatment. They could also see operations that daring surgeons and brave patients, who usually had nothing to lose, were willing to try, operations that are often astonishing in their complexity. One does not typically think of eighteenth-century surgeons removing tumors from the throat, slicing away cancerous breasts, or cutting for bladder stones, but many performed such procedures with considerable success. They were more often to be found attending accident victims, setting bones, and applying bandages. Hospitals of all kinds played a pivotal role in formulating, questioning, verifying, and disseminating surgical knowledge. As these changes came, the status of surgeons rose and their recruitment was more often from the genteel ranks of society than had been the case earlier. Many came to be regarded as genteel because of their charitable services in hospitals and elsewhere. By the end of the century a genteel surgeon in Britain often had a larger income than a physician. By 1800, surgeons in most of Europe were usually recognized as professional men and not as mere artisans working with their hands.

[*See also* Clubs and Societies; Haller, Albrecht von; Hospitals; Inoculation and Vaccination; La Mettrie, Julien Offray de; Medicine, *subentry on* Practice of Medicine; Midwifery; Ruysch, Frederik; Sensibility; Smollett, Tobias; *and* Universities.]

BIBLIOGRAPHY

Ackerknecht, Erwin H. *Medicine at the Paris Hospital, 1794–1848.* Baltimore, 1967.

Ars Obstetrica Bononiensis: Catalogo ed Inventario del Museo Obstetrico Giovan Antonio Galli. Bologna, 1988. An extensively illustrated catalog of this famous Enlightenment obstetrical museum.

Choulant, Ludwig. *History and Bibliography of Anatomic Illustration.* Translated by Mortimer Frank. New York, 1945. English translation of *Geschichte und Bibliographie der anatomischen Abbildung,* first published in 1852. An analysis of the art and craftsmanship behind the anatomical illustrations as well as graphic and plastic artforms in early modern and Enlightenment Europe.

Foucault, Michel. *The Birth of the Clinic: An Archaeology of Medical Perception.* Translated by A. M. Sheridan Smith. New York, 1973. English translation of *Naissance de la clinique: Une archéologie du regard médical,* first published in 1963. A special focus upon the physician's perception, or "gaze," resulting from the interactions of space, language, and death which identified the Paris clinic.

Gelfand, Toby. *Professionalizing Modern Medicine: Paris Surgeons and Medical Science and Institutions in the Eighteenth Century.* Westport, Conn., 1980. An examination of the professionalization and related academic institutionalization of Paris surgery set within the sociopolitical climate of pre- and postrevolutionary France.

Haslam, Fiona. *From Hogarth to Rowlandson: Medicine in Art in Eighteenth-Century Britain.* Liverpool, 1996. An illustrated overview placing Enlightenment England's medical art within its social and political context.

Lawrence, Susan. *Charitable Knowledge: Hospital Pupils and Practitioners in Eighteenth-Century London.* Cambridge, 1996. A revisionist history focusing on the ways in which hospitals provided a network of relationships among people, institutions, and knowledge critical to health care delivery.

Le Cere Anatomiche bolognesi del settecento. Bologna, 1981. An extensively illustrated catalog of this renowned Enlightenment anatomical collection in Bologna.

Merians, Linda E., ed. *The Secret Malady: Venereal Disease in Eighteenth-Century Britain and France.* Lexington, Ky., 1996. An edited collection of essays focusing on the causes and consequences, the diagnosis and treatments, and the literary and artistic representations of venereal disease in Enlightenment Britain and France.

Newman, Karen. *Fetal Positions: Individualism, Science, Visuality.* Stanford, Calif., 1996.

Nicolson, Malcolm. "Giovanni Battista Morgagni and Eighteenth-century Physical Examination." In *Medical Theory, Surgical Practice: Studies in the History of Surgery,* edited by Christopher Lawrence, pp. 101–134. London, 1992. An account, based in Enlightenment Padua, demonstrating how Morgagni's insights reshaped the formulation of medical and surgical knowledge.

Porter, Roy. "Bodies of Thought: Thoughts about the Body in Eighteenth-Century England." In *Interpretation and Cultural History,* edited by Joan H. Pittock and Andrew Wear, pp. 82–108. New York, 1992.

Richardson, Ruth. *Death, Dissection, and the Destitute.* London, 1987. An in-depth analysis of the early nineteenth-century medico-legal debate over the ownership of the body.

Risse, Guenter B. *Hospital Life in Enlightenment Scotland: Care and Teaching at the Royal Infirmary of Edinburgh.* Cambridge, 1986. A case study of Enlightenment hospital diagnosis and treatment drawn from primary sources.

Roberts, K. B., and J. D. W. Thompson. *The Fabric of the Body: European Traditions of Anatomical Illustration.* Oxford, 1992.

Stafford, Barbara Maria. *Body Criticism: Imaging the Unseen in Enlightenment Art and Medicine.* Cambridge, 1991. An art-filled multidisciplinary investigation into Enlightenment art and surgical technology whereby the unseen, below-the-surface body components became visualized.

Todd, Dennis. *Imagining Monsters: Miscreations of the Self in Eighteenth-Century England.* Chicago, 1995. An extensive analysis of Mary Toft's 1726 hoax in which she deceived anatomists, surgeons, and physicians into believing that she had given birth to seventeen rabbits.

Vila, Anne C. *Enlightenment and Pathology: Sensibility in the Literature and Medicine of Eighteenth-Century France.* Baltimore, 1998.

Viseltear, Arthur. "Joanna Stephens and the Eighteenth-Century Lithontriptics: A Misplaced Chapter in the History of Therapeutics." *Bulletin of the History of Medicine* 42 (1968), 199–220.

Wilson, Philip. *Surgery, Skin, and Syphilis: Daniel Turner's London (1667–1741).* Amsterdam, 1999. A biographical approach illuminating commonplace Enlightenment London surgical practice.

PHILIP K. WILSON

MEIJER, LODEWIJK (1638–1681), Dutch theologian.

Although Meijer obtained a degree in medicine, he was mainly active in literary circles, being one of the founders of a literary society, *Nil volentibus arduum,* and procuring new editions of a Dutch dictionary. He became friends with Spinoza and edited the geometrical adaptation of Descartes's *Principia* (1662) and probably also *Opera posthuma* (1677). His main work, however, was *Philosophia S. Scripturae interpres* (1666; Dutch translation by Meijer as *De philosophie uytleghster der H. Schrifture,* 1667).

The *Philosophia* is based on a theory of language, according to which a word never directly refers to a thing but only to the concept of a thing as it exists in the mind of an author. This means that we can never recover the "true meaning" of a text, unless we can interrogate the author. As a result, strict interpretation is impossible. According to Meijer, the only exception is Scripture. We know that Scripture contains the truth and nothing but the truth, so if we know the truth we also know the true meaning of Scripture. Now, according to Meijer, Descartes had taught us how to know the truth with certainty. Accordingly, we can know the true meaning of Scripture by applying Cartesian philosophy to it. Meijer admitted that some texts remain impenetrable, however much they are scrutinized in the light of philosophical knowledge. Consequently, the interpretation of such texts was open-ended. After all, the

Holy Spirit must have foreseen this problem, which means that the resulting plurality of meaning was intentional.

That the book was designed as a provocation becomes clear in the epilogue, in which Meijer deals with an obvious objection: If we can interpret Scripture only to the extent that we know the truth, we do not need Scripture in order to know the truth. According to Meijer, however, the identification of meaning (interpretation) should be separated from that of truth (philosophy). We identify a meaning on the basis of an idea that we already have but that idea does not have to be adequate. Even if it is adequate, identifying the true meaning is not enough to know the truth. For example, however much we understand the phrase "God is omnipresent," we know that God is omnipresent only by reflecting on our ideas. Interpretation never produces knowledge; at best it incites us to reflect on our ideas. Obviously, the whole point of Meijer's argument is that theology is impossible. First, because we can interpret a text with "authority" only by using an instrument that has as much "authority" as the text, so we always fall back on the certitude of philosophy; second, interpretation does not yield knowledge, so the notion of revealed knowledge, which is knowledge obtained by interpreting a text, is impossible. *Philosophia S. Scripturae interpres* was an immediate source of controversy, provoking more than twenty reactions within a year after publication.

[*See also* Bible; Cartesianism; *and* Netherlands.]

BIBLIOGRAPHY

Bordoli, Roberto. *Razione e Scrittura tra Descartes e Spinoza*. Milan, 1996.

Harmsen, A. J. E. "Onderwys in de toneel-poëzy." Ph.D. diss., Amsterdam University, 1989.

Iofrida, Manlio. "Linguaggio e verità in Lodewijk Meyer." In *L'hérésie spinoziste / The Spinozistic Heresy*, edited by Paolo Cristofolini. Amsterdam, 1995.

Meijer, Lodewijk. *Philosophia S. Scripturae interpres*. Amsterdam, 1666; Dutch translation, Amsterdam 1667; French translation, *La philosophie interprète de l'Écriture sainte*, by Pierre-François Moreau and Jacqueline Lagrée. Paris, 1988.

Scribano, M. E. *Da Descartes a Spinoza*. Milan, 1988.

Steenbakkers, P. "Spinoza's Ethica from Manuscript to Print." Ph.D. diss., Groningen University, 1994.

Thijssen-Schoute, C. Louise. "Lodewijk Meyer en diens verhouding tot Descartes en Spinoza." In *Uit de Republiek der Letteren*, pp. 173–194. The Hague, 1964.

Thijssen-Schoute, C. Louise. *Nederlands Cartesianisme*. Amsterdam, 1954; repr., Utrecht, 1989.

THEO VERBEEK

MEISTER, HENRI (1744–1826), Swiss man of letters and journalist.

The son of a Protestant minister, Jakob Heinrich Meister studied theology in Zurich and was ordained in 1763 at the age of nineteen. He then spent some time in Geneva, where he met Paul-Claude Moultou, Jean-Jacques Rousseau's loyal friend, and visited Voltaire and Rousseau. In 1766 he left for Paris as private tutor to the son of Mme. de Vermenoux. In 1767 Meister briefly returned to Zurich, publishing *De l'origine des principes religieux* (1768), in which he affirmed the universality of religious principles while underlining the role of the imagination. As a result of this publication, he was suspended as minister and deprived of his civic rights (he was rehabilitated in 1772). Meister returned to Paris, where he remained until 1792 before emigrating to England. At the end of 1793 he settled for good in Zurich, from where he made several trips to Paris (1795, 1801, 1804, 1806).

Meister had arrived in Paris in 1766 with a letter of introduction to the German man of letters Friedrich Melchior Grimm, through whom he met Louise d'Épinay and Denis Diderot. He became a frequent guest in Suzanne Necker's salon. It was the publication of *De l'origine des principes religieux* that assured his admittance into the circle of the *encyclopédistes*. Voltaire was enthusiastic about the work, and Meister himself later said that his persecution by the Zurich authorities made him into one of the martyrs of the new philosophy.

In March 1773 Grimm put Meister in charge of his manuscript journal, the *Correspondance littéraire*, first on a provisional basis, then permanently from 1775. A conscious vehicle of the French Enlightenment, the *Correspondance littéraire*, which Grimm had started in 1753 and which was then at the height of its success, reported on the literary and cultural events of the French capital and was distributed twice monthly to some fifteen princes and crowned heads of northern Europe.

The journal contained critical articles, but also original works published in serial form, in particular those of Diderot, by this time a close friend of Meister. The subscribers to the correspondence, and the entourage of the subscribers, were thus familiar with Diderot's works long before they were published. We know that Johann Wolfgang von Goethe and Johann Gottfried Herder, for example, were among these early readers who had access to *Jacques le fataliste* (1778–1780), *La religieuse* (1780–1782) and *Le rêve de d'Alembert* (1782), among others. In November 1786, Meister published his famous panegyric *A la mémoire de M. Diderot*, better known as *Aux mânes de Diderot*, a text that was to set the pattern for later interpretations of Diderot's personality.

After his return to Zurich and until 1813, Meister continued to dispatch his manuscript journal to a diminishing number of subscribers, still reporting, mostly from secondary sources, on the literary events of the French capital. Meister also published his own works in more than thirty volumes, including moral essays, short stories, poetry, translations, and a novel.

After the Revolution, Meister distanced himself from the French philosophes, whose influence he by then considered unhealthy. He had, however, as literary correspondent, acted as an important mediator and a purveyor of the French Enlightenment, particularly to the courts of Northern Europe.

[*See also* Correspondents and Correspondence; Grimm, Friedrich Melchior; *and* Switzerland.]

BIBLIOGRAPHY

Meister's papers and personal library are housed at the Fondation Paul Reinhart, in Winterthur, Switzerland.

Grubenmann, Yvonne de Athayde. *Un cosmopolite suisse: Jacques-Henri Meister (1774–1826)*. Geneva, 1954.

Kölving, Ulla, and Jeanne Carriat. "Inventaire de la Correspondance littéraire de Grimm et Meister." *Studies on Voltaire and the Eighteenth Century* (1984), 225–227.

Moog-Grünewald, Maria. *Jacob Heinrich Meister und die "Correspondance littéraire": Ein Beitrag zur Aufklärung in Europa*. Berlin and New York, 1989.

Tourneux, Maurice, ed. *Correspondance littéraire, philosophique et critique par Grimm, Diderot, Raynal, Meister, etc., revue sur les textes originaux comprenant outre ce qui a été publié à diverses époques les fragments supprimés en 1813 par la censure, les parties inédites conservées à la bibliothèque ducale de Gotha et à l'Arsenal à Paris*. Paris, 1877–1882. 16 vols. This edition is out of date and will be replaced by a new critical edition, in preparation.

ULLA KÖLVING

MEN AND WOMEN OF LETTERS. Women were as vital to the Enlightenment Republic of Letters as were men, but the roles played by women and men were generally different. Gender relations were theorized in the ongoing debates known as the *Querelle des femmes* and were practiced in various activities, from reading, writing, and conversing to competing for academic prizes and chairs.

Gender Relations. Since its beginnings in the Renaissance, the *Querelle des femmes* had focused on the question of female virtue: women were either excoriated as agents of the Devil, the daughters of Eve, and the embodiment of Original Sin, or they were defended by writers who catalogued the virtues of female saints and other "women worthies." In the seventeenth century, the focus changed from virtue to reason. Cartesians argued for the equality of men and women on the basis of their shared capacity to reason, while neo-Platonists maintained that the two sexes were fundamentally different but fully complementary, each necessary to the other, and both necessary to society and the progress of civilization. In the eighteenth century, men of letters tended to embrace complementarity in gender relations while continuing to champion women's ability to reason. Even as they proclaimed women's value, they defined a different and limited role for women in society, the family, and the Republic of Letters.

The primary gender division within the Republic of Letters was between writers and readers. Women were often figured as the implied readers of Enlightenment texts, from the marquise in Fontenelle's *Entretiens sur la pluralité des mondes* (Conversations on the Plurality of Worlds, 1686) to Mme. de Puisieux in Diderot's *Lettre sur les aveugles* (Letter on the Blind, 1749) and the German princess to whom Euler addressed his *Lettres à une princesse d'allemagne sur divers sujets de physique ed de philosophie* (Letters on Different Subjects in Natural Philosophy, 1768). The female reader was presented as intelligent but ignorant, the embodiment of natural reason or common sense. Either by asking intelligent questions or by responding honestly to those posed by the author's male persona, these characters demonstrated both the simplicity and the truth of the scientific concepts being laid out and the capacity of the universal reader to grasp them. At the same time, the gendering of the positions of teacher and pupil, master and ignoramus, reinforced specific gender roles. By figuring women as readers of their texts, male writers both welcomed women into the Republic of Letters as reasoning beings and established their role within it as different from and subordinate to that of men.

Genres. Women were also the designated readers of the novel, a literary form pioneered by women in the seventeenth century that came to prominence in the eighteenth. The epistolary novel, in particular, targeted a female readership that would identify with its naive heroine. Beginning with Samuel Richardson's *Pamela* (1740) and *Clarissa* (1748), the central theme of the letter-novel was a young woman's struggle to maintain her virtue in the eternal tug-of-war between duty and desire. When Jean-Jacques Rousseau wrote *Julie* (1761) and subtitled it *La nouvelle Héloïse*, he merged pedagogy and the novel by putting his letter-writing heroine in the position of the pupil and giving his authorial persona the role of the tutor who seduces her: this was tutor and pupil, writer and reader, with a gendered erotic charge. In a companion work, *Émile* (1762), Rousseau set out fundamentally different educational programs for Émile and for Sophie, the girl he would marry. For Rousseau, complementarity meant that women's role was to make men happy. Louise d'Épinay challenged Rousseau's gendered pedagogy in *Les conversations d'Émilie* (Conversations of Émilie, 1777), as did Mary Wollstonecraft in *The Vindications of the Rights of Woman* (1792), often considered the first statement of modern feminism.

Letter-writing was considered a feminine art in the eighteenth century because it seemed to be natural and was not intended to reach a public through print, or to make a name for the women who excelled at it. When male writers such as Richardson and Rousseau wrote epistolary

discourse. Women were brought into the Enlightenment as readers, but, unlike men, they were discouraged from taking the step from reading to (published) writing, from passive to active citizens of the Republic. They were excluded from royal academies and masonic lodges, and in the salons of Paris they were admired for their ability to orchestrate male discourse. Nevertheless, as men of letters touted the mixed-gender sociability of Paris as a sign of civilization, English bluestockings found their own voices in a tea-table sociability in which they encouraged one another to write and publish. Women contributed to the Enlightenment in many ways, but always within constraints established by increasingly unequal power relations within a Republic of Letters in which their male counterparts fought for power, prestige, and literary immortality.

[*See also* Republic of Letters *and* Salons.]

BIBLIOGRAPHY

Chartier, Roger. "The Man of Letters." In *Enlightenment Portraits*, edited by Michel Vovelle and translated by Lydia G. Cochrane, pp. 142–189. Chicago, 1997. Women figure in this excellent but concise treatment primarily as *salonnières*.

Duby, Georges, and Michelle Perrot, eds. *A History of Women*, vol. 3, *Renaissance and Enlightenment Paradoxes*. Edited by Natalie Zemon Davis and Arlette Farge; translated by Arthur Goldhammer. Cambridge, Mass., 1993. Useful though rather uneven, this includes some short selections of primary texts in translation.

Gelbart, Nina Rattner. *Feminine and Opposition Journalism in Old Regime France: Le Journal des Dames*. Berkeley, Calif., 1987.

Goldsmith, Elizabeth C., and Dena Goodman, eds. *Going Public: Women and Publishing in Early Modern France*. Ithaca, N.Y., 1995.

Goodman, Dena. *The Republic of Letters: A Cultural History of the French Enlightenment*. Ithaca, N.Y., 1994. Feminist interpretation with major emphasis on role of salons and *salonnières*.

Harth, Erica. *Cartesian Women: Versions and Subversions of Rational Discourse in the Old Regime*. Ithaca, N.Y., 1992.

Hufton, Olwen. *The Prospect before Her: A History of Women in Western Europe, 1500–1800*. London, 1995; New York, 1996. Good chapter with extensive bibliography on women of letters within magisterial but highly readable survey.

Jensen, Katharine Ann. *Writing Love: Letters, Women, and the Novel in France, 1605–1776*. Carbondale, Ill., 1995.

Keener, Frederick M., and Susan E. Lorsch, eds. *Eighteenth-Century Women and the Arts*. New York, 1988. Wide-ranging collection of essays treating women's contributions to Enlightenment in general and poetry, the novel, and the fine arts across Europe.

Lanser, Susan Sniader. *Fictions of Authority: Women Writers and Narrative Voice*. Ithaca, N.Y., 1992.

Myers, Sylvia Harcstark. *The Blue Stocking Circle: Women, Friendship and the Life of the Mind in Eighteenth-Century England*. Oxford, 1990.

Shevelow, Kathryn. *Women and Print Culture: The Construction of Femininity in the Early Periodical*. London, 1990.

Spencer, Samia I. *French Women and the Age of Enlightenment*. Bloomington, Ind., 1984. Comprehensive but not entirely reliable collection of essays on topics from law to literature.

Steinbrügge, Lieselotte. *The Moral Sex: Woman's Nature in the French Enlightenment*. Translated by Pamela E. Selwyn. New York, 1992. Excellent compact analysis of Enlightenment views of women.

DENA GOODMAN

MENDELSSOHN, MOSES (1729–1786), philosopher and writer, a central figure of the Berlin Enlightenment and of the Jewish revival known as the Haskalah.

Born to a poor but learned Jewish family in Dessau, Mendelssohn came to Berlin in 1743 entirely untaught in secular culture, but by the time he began his lifelong friendship with Gotthold Ephraim Lessing in 1754, he was well oriented in contemporary philosophy. Mendelssohn worked in the orbit of Christian Wolff's philosophy but was always an independent thinker. When he came of age intellectually, German philosophers were investigating two areas that Wolff himself had failed to develop: aesthetics and theology. It was in these areas that Mendelssohn was to make his mark.

Mendelssohn and the Berlin Enlightenment. Mendelssohn's philosophical works gained him a reputation throughout Europe as the "Socrates of Berlin." In a philosophical tradition known for tedious comprehensiveness, his works were lively and lucid. This achievement was all the more remarkable because Mendelssohn had acquired German in late adolescence after growing up with Yiddish and Hebrew. His reputation was further enhanced by his being an *animateur des idées*: as an essayist and reviewer, he was at the forefront in many areas of thought and helped introduce ideas that others then developed.

Moses Mendelssohn. (New York Public Library, Astor, Lenox, and Tilden Foundations.)

Wolff had treated aesthetics as a lesser form of knowledge, but the next generation of Wolffian philosophers (Bodmer, Breitinger, and Baumgarten) elaborated a theory of aesthetic cognition and thus helped to create, and to name, the field of aesthetics. All Mendelssohn's philosophical works were grounded in Wolffian metaphysics, but his early works were at the border of metaphysics and aesthetics.

In his first work, *Philosophische Gespräche* (Philosophical Dialogues, 1755), Mendelssohn established his adherence to the Leibnizian-Wolffian notion of pre-established harmony, as well as to the idea of this world as the "best of all possible worlds." Mendelssohn also attempted to rehabilitate Spinoza's thought, seeing him as a "sacrifice for human reason" who, lost in the chasm between Descartes and Leibniz, nonetheless prefigured many of Leibniz's key ideas.

In the *Briefe über die Empfindungen* (Letters on the Sensations, 1755) and other essays, Mendelssohn, who was influenced by Shaftesbury, liberated aesthetics from metaphysics through a psychological turn: "Every rule of beauty is simultaneously a discovery in psychology." He argued that beauty derives not from the perfection of the object being represented, but from the harmony of all parts of the representation itself ("a perfect sensuous representation"). Art, thus, is created by introducing a beauty not present in nature. In consequence, art also possesses its own laws: "The stage has its own morality"—for example, the suicide that in life is morally reprehensible is aesthetically commendable on stage.

In his essays, reviews, and conversations, Mendelssohn influenced many of the major strands of aesthetic thinking in Germany, including Lessing's notions of drama and the relationship between poetry and the plastic arts, Schiller's ideas on art's role in human development, and Kant's conceptions of the disinterestedness of beauty and the existence of a third faculty for aesthetic judgment.

Two major metaphysical works secured Mendelssohn's reputation. In *Abhandlung über die Evidenz in den metaphysischen Wissenschaften* (Treatise on Evidence in the Metaphysical Sciences, 1763), which won first prize in the competition of Berlin's Royal Academy of the Sciences (Kant won second prize), he asserted that philosophy provides the same level of certainty as mathematics, but with less "perspicuity" (*Fasslichkeit*), because philosophy deals with qualities (in contrast, mathematics treats quantities) and also has to be applied to reality. For the existence of God, he offered a priori proofs as well as the "argument from design" (or physicotheology) common to the German Enlightenment. He also formulated an ethical principle grounded in the individual's free choice of the central Wolffian category of perfection: "Make your internal and external condition and that of your fellow human being, in the proper proportion, as perfect as you can."

Mendelssohn's *Phädon* (1767), both a translation and reworking of Plato's dialogue, appeared in numerous languages and won him a European reputation. He argued that the soul, as a simple created substance, is imperishable since it can be destroyed only by an act of God. Because of man's divinely ordained vocation to pursue perfection, the soul is also immortal, retaining consciousness and memory.

In 1771, Mendelssohn was elected to the Academy of Sciences, though King Frederick II exercised a pocket veto. A Berlin landmark, he received numerous visitors in his home and at the silk factory where he was employed (he rose from bookkeeper to manager and then to partner, and was a recognized expert on silk production, consulted by the Prussian government). He corresponded with scholars throughout Europe. He was immortalized in the character of Nathan in Lessing's play *Nathan der Weise* (Nathan the Wise, 1779).

Mendelssohn and the Haskalah. As a central figure of the Haskalah, Mendelssohn was honored with the saying first used by Johann Jacob Rabe in 1761. "From Moses [Maimonides] unto Moses [Mendelssohn] there was none like Moses," recognizing his stature as the leading Jewish thinker of his day. Mendelssohn published Hebrew works throughout his career. He also produced the most important and enduring work of the Berlin Haskalah, a German translation of the Pentateuch (printed in Hebrew letters) with a Hebrew introduction and commentary (*The Book of the Path of Peace*, 1779–1783).

Mendelssohn participated in the early Haskalah effort (1720–1770) to revive neglected aspects of the textual heritage of central European Jewry. He used Wolffian categories and terminology to update and rearticulate the traditions of philosophy and Biblical exegesis in Hebrew. In two issues of the first journal in modern Hebrew, *Kohelet Musar* (1758?), he created Hebrew equivalents for Wolffian categories in order to discuss central theological issues. In a commentary on Maimonides's philosophical primer (*Biur Milot ha-Higayon*, 1760–1761), he made a systematic effort to update the lexicon of philosophy in Hebrew and to replace Aristotelian concepts with Wolffian ones. In addition, he defended the study of logic as a pious pursuit necessary for correct belief. He continued this effort in a Hebrew treatise on the immortality of the soul (*Sefer ha-Nefesh*, 1769). In a commentary on Ecclesiastes (*Biur Megilat Kohelet*, 1770), Mendelssohn defended the medieval Jewish tradition of simultaneous levels of exegesis by arguing that they were inherent in language usage and were in keeping with reason. He also used Wolffian categories to discuss immortality and providence. He allayed potential anxieties about skeptical or heretical opinions in the text by attributing them to notional interlocutors.

In 1769–1770, the Swiss chiliast (millennarian theologian) Johann Caspar Lavater publicly challenged Mendelssohn to justify his beliefs or convert to Christianity. Mendelssohn deflected Lavater's challenge with a plea for toleration, but he suffered a nervous debility as a result of the strain.

Mendelssohn then devoted himself to biblical translation and commentary. In 1783, he published a German translation of Psalms, which he conceived as a contribution to natural religion and aesthetics (the "sublime") for a general audience. His exegetical efforts culminated in a German translation of the Pentateuch (*Sefer Netivot ha-Shalom*, 1779–1783), accompanied by a Hebrew introduction and commentary (he wrote the commentary to the first lection of Genesis and to Exodus, and commissioned and edited the others). In the introduction, he used the oral nature of the Hebrew language as a means to defend the authenticity of the Hebrew text of the Bible, as established by the Masoretes (traditional textual commentators). In the commentary, he offered a digest of the medieval tradition of plain or literal exegesis as well as making systematic use of the Masoretic accents as a guide to interpretation. Throughout the work, Mendelssohn took a historical approach, recognizing the impact of time and place on ancient Israel, yet he consistently resisted the sort of historicist interpretation, propounded by Johann Gottfried Eichhorn and other scholars, that either questioned the authenticity and unity of the Pentateuch text or qualified the validity of the revelation at Sinai. Mendelssohn hoped that his translation and commentary would lead Jews without sufficient knowledge of Hebrew back to the original text.

Mendelssohn's fame ineluctably made him a spokesman for the Jews, an activity that began in the late 1760s and resulted in the publication of a compendium of Jewish law for use in German courts (*Ritualgesetze der Juden*, 1778) and an introduction to a translation of a seventeenth-century plea for the readmission of the Jews to England (*Rettung der Juden*, 1782), in which he publicly advocated "civic acceptance" for the first time. He called for an end to the prejudice that impeded the Jews ("Our hands are tied and we are rebuked for not using them") and cited Holland as a model of economic and civic freedom.

This work elicited a serious challenge by an anonymous writer that forced Mendelssohn to write *Jerusalem, oder ueber religioese Macht und Judentum* (Jerusalem, or On Religious Power and Judaism, 1783), in which he delineated a state and a Judaism that rendered emancipation of the Jews possible. Mendelssohn understood the state in the optimistic terms of Wolffian natural rights theory: the social contract allows mankind to fulfill its innate need for benevolence. He also used ecclesiastical natural rights theory ("collegialism") to advocate strict separation of church and state and an end to all religious coercion.

Mendelssohn proposed a famous definition of Judaism as a "divine legislation" that drew on the heteronomous tradition in medieval Jewish thought: the law, revealed publicly to the entire nation at Sinai, and transparent to the divine legislator but not to its human recipients, prescribes not beliefs but symbolic actions that remind those who perform them of eternal truths. Thus, Judaism claims no monopoly on truth and could be constituted as a voluntary society without powers of coercion.

Pantheism Controversy. As a result of Friedrich Heinrich Jacobi's claim that Lessing had professed Spinozism, Mendelssohn became involved in the so-called pantheism conflict (*Pantheismusstreit*), in which he attempted to defend Lessing's reputation and his own understanding of his lifelong friend. Although the controversy involved miscommunications, blunders, and even some acts of bad faith, it turned essentially on whether Lessing subscribed to a fatalistic pantheism or, as Mendelssohn claimed, to the sort of "refined pantheism" Mendelssohn had discussed in *Philosophical Dialogues* (1755), in which the world is created by God's thoughts but is not in God, because space is not a real attribute of God. Mendelssohn's last work was devoted to this controversy. In the *Morgenstunden* (1785), he attempted to defend Lessing, offered an extended proof for God's existence—including the ontological argument—and reiterated his understanding of Spinoza.

Conclusion. Mendelssohn should not be dismissed, as used to be the case, as a mere "popular philosopher." Rather, he was one of the most original of the Wolffian philosophers. His reputation suffered to the extent that other eighteenth-century philosophy prior to the "all-destroying Kant" (Mendelssohn's phrase) was discredited. Although he was celebrated by many as the "patron saint" of the German Jewish subculture, he was vilified by others as the false prophet of Jewish assimilation. Perhaps his achievements in the world of the German Enlightenment and the Haskalah are rendered more comprehensible if he is seen as the preeminent Jewish representative of a religious enlightenment whose major figures, such as Siegmund Jacob Baumgarten, William Warburton, and Lodovico Muratori, were also engaged in both religious and secular pursuits.

[*See also* Aufklärung; Haskalah; Judaism; Pantheism; *and* Wolff, Christian.]

BIBLIOGRAPHY

Albrecht, Michael. "Moses Mendelssohn: Ein Forschungsbericht." *Deutsche Vierteljahrsschrift für Literaturwissenschaft u. Geistesgeschichte* 57 (1983), 64–166.

Albrecht, Michael, Eva Engel, and Norbert Hinske, eds. *Moses Mendelssohn und die Kreise seiner Wirksamkeit*. Tübingen, 1994.

Altmann, Alexander. *Moses Mendelssohn: A Biographical Study.* Tuscaloosa, Ala., 1973. The definitive biography.

Altmann, Alexander. "Moses Mendelssohn as the Archetypal German Jew." In *The Jewish Response to German Culture,* edited by Jehuda Reinharz and Walter Schatzberg, pp. 17–31. Hanover, N.H., 1985. Seminal reflection on Mendelssohn's role for German Jewry.

Arkush, Allan. *Moses Mendelssohn and the Enlightenment.* Albany, N.Y., 1994. A Straussian reading of Mendelssohn.

Breuer, Edward. *The Limits of Enlightenment: Jews, Germans and the Eighteenth-Century Study of Scripture.* Cambridge, Mass., 1996. A re-evaluation of Mendelssohn's biblical exegesis.

Feiner, Shmuel. "Mendelssohn and 'Mendelssohn's Disciples': A Re-examination." *Leo Baeck Institute Yearbook* 40 (1995), 133–167. Reinterpretation of Mendelssohn's role in the Haskalah.

Gilon, Meir. *Kohelet Musar le-Mendelssohn al Reka Tekufato.* Jerusalem, 1979. Detailed study of Mendelssohn's first Hebrew publication.

Mendelssohn, Moses. *Gesammelte Schriften: Jubilaeumsausgabe.* 27 vols. in 36. Stuttgart, 1971–.

Mendelssohn, Moses. *Jerusalem, or On Religious Power and Judaism.* Translated by Allan Arkush. Hanover, N.H., 1983. The authoritative translation.

Mendelssohn, Moses. *Moses Mendelssohn: Philosophical Writings.* Translated and edited by Daniel O. Dahlstrom. Cambridge, 1997. Translation of key philosophical works.

Segreff, Klaus Werner. *Moses Mendelssohn und die Aufklärungsaesthetik im 18. Jahrhundert.* Bonn, 1984. Mendelssohn's place in aesthetic thought.

Sorkin, David. *Moses Mendelssohn and the Religious Enlightenment.* Berkeley, 1996. A reinterpretation emphasizing the Hebrew works.

Sorkin, David. "The Mendelssohn Myth and Its Method." *New German Critique* (1999), 7–28. The Germanification of Mendelssohn.

DAVID SORKIN

MERCANTILISM. The idea that a mercantile system governed the economic policies and practices of early modern Europe was first conceived in the Enlightenment. This idea took hold mainly because of one man, Adam Smith, who devoted a section of his famous book, *The Wealth of Nations* (1776), to "the Principle of the Commercial or Mercantile System." The word *mercantilism* for essentially the same concept came into use a century later, first in German writings as *Merkantilismus,* but soon after in English and French forms.

Principles. The content of mercantilism has been a matter of dispute; some historians have even doubted the usefulness of the term. Few, however, would deny that there were certain principles that may be deemed essential ingredients.

First, mercantilists aimed at benefiting the realm, or the state—unlike medieval economic writers, who commonly had all Christendom in view, or Enlightenment writers whose outlook tended toward universalism.

Second, foreign trade was of elevated importance. It was a rather small sector of any country's economy, but its rate of growth in this period was tremendous. Since newly risen mercantile cities obviously promoted agricultural prosperity in surrounding areas, foreign trade could be perceived as a form of economic growth not bounded by constraints of land and population. The sudden rise of Holland and the amazing growth of London were the most impressive indicators. Yet the growing popularity of exotic goods from East and West in the seventeenth century—sugar, tea, coffee, tobacco, and comfortable cotton clothing—raised the question of whether their importation might be ruinously expensive.

Third, heavy emphasis was placed on the development and increase of manufacturing to provide employment and amplify export earnings. Manufactured goods generally earned more than "rude commodities" such as timber or agricultural products.

A fourth mercantilist principle rose to prominence in the early decades of the seventeenth century: the balance of trade. There were two ways of approaching the issue. One was to focus on bilateral balances: if imports from a country cost more than was earned by exports to it, the result was a "losing trade" that drained away precious metals. Whether this actually occurred was sometimes not easy to ascertain, but lack of proper statistics did not restrain the fervor of the arguments. The alternative approach was to pay attention only to the realm's overall balance. Proponents of this approach did not deny that there were "losing trades," but they argued that some of those should be allowed to continue because, often by circuitous transactions, they were ultimately profitable. It was an important line of argument, as we will see.

Fifth, there was the goal of preserving and increasing the realm's stock of gold and silver (bullion, specie, precious metals, coin, "treasure," or "money"). Since a stock of bullion could not be preserved by prohibiting its export (a futile method, as experience had shown), the only answer lay in providing a continual influx through a favorable overall balance of trade. Everyone at the time agreed that a scarcity of precious metals was one of the worst things that could befall a country. Portugal and Spain were exceptions because they had direct access to gold and silver mines in their overseas empires.

Finally, it was assumed that government intervention in (but not government control of) economic life was required. Barriers and tariffs for defending domestic manufacturing from foreign competition were commonplace, as were measures for increasing manufactured exports. Maritime powers confined the trade of their overseas colonies and favored national over foreign shipping. Such measures were aimed at fuller employment, prosperity, and national security. To the question of whether mercantilism was concerned mainly with prosperity or power, the answer is "Both." As practically all writers recognized, the prosperity of any early modern European country was vulnerable without power to protect it.

Were these principles deluded or intelligent? Adam Smith gave the mercantile system a name in order to exhibit the folly of its doctrines, and under the influence of classical economic theory (to which Smith gave birth), the consensus has been that mercantilism was indeed deluded. An alternative, less familiar approach situates mercantilist ideas within the political, commercial, and monetary conditions of the early modern era and holds that the economic writers of the time understood their situation far better than has been commonly supposed. This article pursues the second approach, focusing on three key topics and two countries, England and France. (A comprehensive view of the subject that encompasses all European countries may be found in Charles Wilson's chapter in *The Cambridge Economic History of Europe*, vol. 4.)

Treasure and Trade Balances. The belief that countries must try to maintain a stock of treasure and that trade policy should be directed toward accumulating precious metals lay at the core of mercantilist thought. According to the economic historian Eli Heckscher, this belief was irrational—an idée fixe inherited from the medieval past and not in any way a response to contemporary economic circumstances. The most common mode of critique ignores his emphasis on origins of the "bullionist fallacy," however. Instead, its absurdities are exposed by reference to modern economics. For instance, steady accumulation of precious metals was a recipe for price inflation, and the excuse that bullion shortages endangered the currency vanished when paper money was introduced.

Ridicule of bullionism is prominent in modern commentaries on mercantilism. No doubt there was a mindless popular fixation on bullion from which some statesmen were apparently not exempt. Yet, as modern economic thought stands on the writings of economists, mercantilist thought should be judged by what the economic writers of the time wrote. Most of them were merchants, or conversant with merchants. Often writing in times of economic crisis, they were struggling to understand, with an inadequate vocabulary, the phenomenon of elaborated market relations, which had suddenly risen to great importance. Sustained analysis and intellectual exchange were uncommon, so the fabric of thought must be pieced together.

The writers clearly stated their reasons for believing a stock of gold and silver to be vital to the realm. Precious metals were an indispensable support for the currency, based as it was on the coinage; scarcity meant monetary depression; and widespread resort to barter was one of the worst things that could befall an economy. As for paper currency, the writers well knew how speedily a serious commercial disruption or political crisis could destroy it; in any case, its use for everyday transactions was quite limited, even in the eighteenth century. The writers also gave political reasons: the near futility of tax collection in the absence of hard money, and the utility of a stock of treasure as a cushion in emergencies such as dearth of food, outbreak of war, or violent disruption of trade. Finally, since there was a constant and well-known tendency for coin and bullion to drain out of a country in those days, mercantilists could no more be expected to focus on superabundance as a problem than people living in arid climates can be expected to focus on the problem of excessive rainfall.

On occasion, a kingdom did have "plenty of money," and, according to Thomas Mun (1571–1641), everyone recognized that the consequence was price inflation. Mun went on to observe, however, that this situation never lasted. Although it was "a very hard lesson for some great landed men to learn," he continued, "when wee have gained some store of mony by trade, wee lose it again by not trading with our mony." In short, good policy involved the use of treasure for driving profitable trade. The argument is to be found chiefly in chapter 4 of Mun's *England's Treasure by Foreign Trade*, the most influential mercantilist tract ever written.

Mun began to write down his ideas in the early 1620s, when he was asked to participate on committees commissioned by the Privy Council for inquiring into why England was mired in depression and bullion was leaving the realm. He was a director of the East India Company. Since the public mind was fixated on the drainage of bullion, he faced a perplexing problem. The company exported a lot of bullion: its purchases of spices, silks, and cotton textiles cost far more than could be gained by selling English goods in Asia, and the balance had to be made up with gold and silver. Nonetheless, the trade was exceedingly profitable. Mun reasoned that bullion sent forth for purposes of profitable trading always came back, however circuitously, in greater abundance—as he put it, "with a Duck in the mouth." Exporting treasure for this purpose was not only harmless; it was beneficial, and often essential. Mun recognized the many advantages of retaining a stock of bullion for public emergencies, but he was making an argument that treasure ought to be used positively, as trading capital (a term he clearly needed).

Mun's treatise was probably written in the mid-1620s and was widely circulated in that decade (though not printed until 1664, after which it was translated into other languages). Because he addressed the prevailing concern about treasure and was much engaged in refuting experts who claimed that exchange rates rather than trade balances were the problem, his argument that treasure functioned as wealth-creating trading capital has frequently been overlooked.

No statistical backing for the argument was available, and Mun was open to the charge that his reasoning was biased by his situation as an East India Company director. In the treatise, he said that he learned the lessons about employing treasure in foreign trade from his earlier experience as a merchant in Italy. Was there, in fact, any substance to his argument? Perhaps the only way to approach the question is to observe what merchants of the time actually did. The economic historian Charles Wilson undertook such a study and found that, during the mercantilist era, English merchants regularly used—and were allowed by government to use—treasure as trading capital, not just in the East India trade but also in the Baltic. Further, he found that they often used it elsewhere, in locations where the mechanisms of international exchange were flawed or when those mechanisms were disrupted, as they frequently were. The concern for an ever-replenished supply of bullion was understandable, Wilson concluded: mercantilists "were right to assume that a nation which neglected the bullion problem did so at its peril."

Industry and the State. Mercantilists in all countries emphasized industry. In both England and France, measures affecting industry were commonplace, but there was a vast difference in the level of enforcement. In England, an internal bureaucracy capable of supervising industrial regulation did not exist, and the will to create one was weakened by the public's deep suspicion of royal motives. Under Elizabeth I and James I, the crown granted private industrial monopolies, ostensibly to bring good order to particular industries, but most of these appeared to be erected for the purpose of rewarding courtiers, who could then sell licenses to break them. As the seventeenth century progressed, older forms of industrial regulation based on guilds were undermined by industry's spread to regions where means of enforcement were nonexistent. Little could be done to prevent this.

Wool cloth dominated the English industrial scene, and its export was vital. Depressed sales generated fearful distress and unrest. The real priority of English policy was avoiding these social disturbances, which explains the stress on exchange rates and access to foreign markets. Parliamentary acts were routinely aimed at promoting both domestic and external sales of cloth, but quality was the responsibility of manufacturers and merchants. As time passed, English tracts dealing with industry focused increasingly on wages and employment for the poor.

French industrial policy, instituted by Jean-Baptiste Colbert (1619–1683), was of a different character. Its main impulses had been prominent in French economic thought a half-century or more earlier. A key assumption was that France, thanks to its variety of climates and soils, was capable of economic self-sufficiency. As the Assembly of Notables confidently declared in 1583, the country was of "such plenty" that it could "do without all its neighbors and none of them [could] do without it." France had no

gold or silver mines, though, and the currency suffered. The bullion France acquired was carried away by foreign merchants. These ideas were part of the elemental patriotism of Barthélemy de Laffemas (1545–1611), who rose from humble origins to become Henry IV's advisor on commercial policy. His pamphlets enunciated a vigorous mercantilism. To stem the outflow of bullion, he recommended a total ban on imported manufactures along with strong measures for rehabilitating and enlarging French industry. His contemporary, Antoine de Monchrétien (1575–1621), made proposals in the same vein.

As Louis XIV's loyal servant, Colbert accepted the goal of strengthening and consolidating the French monarchy, but he was convinced that economic foundations were essential. Preventing bullion outflow was a dominant element in Colbert's thinking, but he knew that prohibitions or high duties on foreign manufactured goods would not work. French industry had been seriously damaged by internal strife during the preceding century, and the state had to help restore it. Uneven quality (textiles were the prime category) hampered French sales in export markets. Colbert's famous rules of 1669 laid down standards, created an inspectorate, and used guild supervision where applicable. It is incorrect to suppose that the regulations were ill-contrived; officials were expected to learn the details from the manufacturers themselves, and in due course, the guaranteed standards of quality often gave advantage to French goods. It was not Colbert's intention that the regulatory regime should continue for long, but it became embedded, and by 1750 it was widely regarded as a nuisance. In France, mercantilism has often been termed *colbertism*, with industrial regulation particularly in mind.

Trade, Shipping, Colonies, and Power. By 1750, colonial trade was a prominent element of the mercantile system. Its systematization began about 1650. The English system was essentially defined by acts of navigation and trade passed between 1651 and 1673. Practically all goods imported by the colonists had to be shipped from the mother country—undoubtedly a tight restriction, but in practice not onerous because English goods were generally preferred and competitively priced. Certain "enumerated" goods—the list included major plantation products such as sugar and tobacco—were required to be sent first to England. British colonies were forbidden to trade with foreign colonies. (Nevertheless, a good deal of this was tolerated, especially clandestine trading between British North America and Spanish America, which was permitted because the former desperately needed silver for coinage and purchase of British manufactured goods.)

From beginning to end, however, navigation (that is, shipping) was at least equally important. In contrast with the regulations concerning commodities, many of which were loosely enforced or modified, the navigation restrictions (especially those regarding colonial traffic) were tightly enforced and strictly maintained. The underlying reason was a concern for naval power, vital for protection of trade and, in the case of England, for defense of the realm. Everyone in the age of sail understood that without access to a body of trained mariners sustained by a merchant marine, a navy was bound to be inferior, regardless of how many warships were built.

Meaningful systematizing of French overseas trade began under Colbert. In 1664, he strove mightily to mobilize investment for a French East India Company. He then created a French West India Company, to which he awarded monopoly power. In both instances, the object was to supplant the Dutch, whose merchants controlled the trade of France's West Indian islands. Colbert himself fully shared his royal master's antagonism toward Holland, and he regarded trade as a variety of war. Since the Dutch seemed to command every aspect of French trade, Colbert expected them to retaliate. The great navy that France built under his guidance was intended to counter the Dutch.

The East India project failed, a wasted investment. The West India Company was beset with problems, and Colbert canceled its monopoly in 1674, by which time French merchants and shipowners were in a position to carry on independently. Louis XIV's eagerness to reap revenue constrained the development of French colonial trade, but later, under lessened burdens, French sugar and coffee production grew enormously, and French re-exportation of colonial products to other parts of Europe generated great wealth. This commerce was vulnerable, however. While the British navy grew stronger, the French navy was allowed to decay, and its restoration, begun about 1730, was fitful and slow. Because seaborne commerce abetted a state's financial power, which was a primary factor in war and diplomacy, the French monarchy could not afford to ignore it.

It has traditionally been alleged that mercantilists looked on the world's trade as a "fixed cake." On the contrary, everyone saw global trade as a dynamic and growing sphere. The fervent trade contentions of the mercantilist era arose from awareness of expanding opportunities, and from fear that a rival would acquire naval and financial dominance.

Mercantilism and the Enlightenment. In France during the 1750s, a need to understand, emulate, and counter British economic success became an important theme of public discourse. Britain's growing economy and its naval, commercial, and financial prowess were suddenly visible and seemed to present a serious challenge to France's dominance in Europe. These concerns fueled an emerging popular patriotism. The traditional mercantilist concern for national power was never entirely absent from economic writings of the French Enlightenment.

The same decade witnessed the blossoming of the philosophical Enlightenment, and French economic writings reflected a new approach. The ground was partly prepared by English writers such as Nicholas Barbon (d. 1698) and Sir Dudley North (1641–1691), who had probed the issue of prices in a framework that highlighted supply and demand. In France, Richard Cantillon (1680?–1734), an Irish-born London merchant who became a Paris banker, wrote a systematic treatise that also tried to account for market pricing; in it, he divided society into producers and consumers. There were other indications of a growing tendency to view economic relations as both social and "natural," and most likely to flourish if left alone. Pierre de Boisguilbert (1646–1714) had argued in 1695 that French economic growth would come naturally if only the burdens and barriers imposed by the state were removed.

François Quesnay (1694–1774), writing in the early 1750s, approached economic relations in a scientific, analytical mode. His objection to mercantilism was that it emphasized the wrong economic sectors: it encouraged the state to favor commerce and manufacturing, both of which by his analysis were "sterile," contributing nothing to economic growth. The true source of capital accumulation (a term not available to him) was agriculture, but French agriculture needed to develop large-scale operations under market incentives, a conclusion he drew from observing English agriculture. Quesnay's program would have been radically transformative, a probability that he preferred not to address. The problem of how to reconcile an aggressively capitalistic agrarian system with ancien régime laws and social privileges became even more pronounced when he teamed up with the marquis de Mirabeau (1715–1789), who hoped to restore the influence of the territorial aristocracy. For all the abstraction of Quesnay's economic analysis and Mirabeau's belief that he was a friend of mankind, their "plan of Physiocracy" (as it was called) presupposed a strong monarchy. Quesnay, a physician at Versailles, maintained that his plan would increase royal revenue.

Thus, in regard to the power of the state, the French Enlightenment's antimercantilism was hesitant. Still, the sense that colbertism was seriously constricting was widespread. Even members of the bureau of commerce began to question whether manufacturing regulation was any longer desirable. For a time, deregulation of grain marketing was attempted, though it could not be sustained.

The truly radical rejection of mercantilism came from Scotland. The political economy of the Scottish Enlightenment, like the French, was built on fundamental ideas about human conduct, but it accented a stage theory of

Smith's *Wealth of Nations*. Title page of the first edition of *The Wealth of Nations* by Adam Smith (London, 1776). [For a portrait of Smith, see the article "Smith, Adam."] (Rare Books and Special Collections Division, Library of Congress.)

societal development. The "age of commerce" was dawning, and none of the old thinking was of any use, actually it was worse than useless. The whole framework of the mercantile system was seen to be a massive hindrance to the adoption of new principles that would enable civilized humankind to enjoy the full benefits of the new age.

In advancing this project, Adam Smith (1723–1790) was by far the dominant figure. As Donald Winch has

observed, his "mercantile system" was a "negative polemical construction" combining doctrine and practice—an "anti-type" serving as an "inverted mirror-image of his own system." Smith lumped all mercantilist writings together without regard to when or why they were written. When he commented that "the title of Mun's book, England's Treasure in [*sic*] Foreign Trade, became a fundamental maxim in the political economy, not of England only, but of all other commercial countries," his substitution of "in" for "by" constituted a significant distortion. As for the book's content, Smith submerged it in the genre, which he dismissed wholesale. He admitted that "the best English writers on commerce, set out with observing, that the wealth of a country consists, not in its gold and silver only, but in its lands, houses, and consumable goods of all different kinds," but then he said that in "the course of their reasonings" they forgot this and fell into supposing "that all wealth consists in gold and silver, and that to multiply those metals is the great object of national industry and commerce." The "best writers" were thus placed in the grip of the "popular notion that wealth consists in money"—no mercantilist ever wrote this (*Wealth of Nations*, IV, chap. 1). Smith's friend, David Hume (1711–1776), writing essays aimed at refuting the importance of precious metals (1752), sometimes carried his arguments to erroneous extremes, but they were always directed against the belief that precious metals performed vital functions in respect to money supply, interest rates, and trade, not against a careless confusion of specie and wealth.

Smith had ample respect for the cunning of mercantilist writers when they were fashioning public-interest arguments for measures that would benefit private interests. He portrayed statesmen as either politically weak or gullible. How could Colbert "notwithstanding his great abilities" have fallen into so many regulatory temptations? He was "imposed upon by the sophistry of merchants and manufacturers" (*Wealth of Nations* IV, chap. 2).

A sweeping instance was Smith's proposition that the whole British North American empire was foisted on the public by "shopkeepers"; that is, it had been created and maintained "for the sole purpose of raising up a people of customers" as a captive market for English producers and sellers. But shopkeepers, he reasoned, would not have been foolish enough to spend their own money on so extravagant a scheme; instead, a "nation of shopkeepers" had persuaded statesmen to do it (*Wealth of Nations*, IV, chap. 7, pt. 3). In this way, Smith reduced the rationale for the empire to just one aspect of the laws of trade and navigation.

At one point, Smith did recognize that Britain's national defense depended "very much upon the number of its sailors and shipping," and he added the oft-quoted remark that, because defense was more important than opulence, the navigation acts were "perhaps, the wisest of all the commercial regulations of England" (*Wealth of Nations*, IV, chap. 2). The remark was purely an aside, however. His scheme of economic analysis excluded such considerations, and he never admitted that the colonial empire played any role in the magnitude of the British merchant marine.

The *Wealth of Nations* is by no means a dry economic treatise. There is wit, and it is easy to sense the passion in Smith's detestation of the empire. He was certain that it was the sole cause of recent costly wars (IV chap. 8). From this it was but a short step to the supposition that wars were generally motivated by national and imperial economic rivalries of the sort that mercantilism promoted. Free trade, therefore, promised much more than enhanced prosperity: it would remove a prime cause of war. The Enlightenment vision of the possibility of universal peace is embedded in the *Wealth of Nations*.

Adam Smith pilloried mercantilism's fallacies, but mostly he feared the power of group interests inspired by mercantilist ideas to manipulate national concerns. The individually based "system of natural liberty" on which his hopes for the future rested could not stand up to such strong political forces. Smith had no wish to understand mercantilism in its historical and political contexts. Having achieved a profound new understanding of economics, he aimed to rid the civilized world of those contexts.

[*See also* Commerce and Trade; Economic Thought; Free Trade; *and* Physiocracy.]

BIBLIOGRAPHY

PRIMARY WORKS

McCulloch, J. R. *Early English Tracts on Commerce*. Cambridge, 1954. A reissue of McCulloch's *A Select Collection of Early English Tracts on Commerce, from the Originals of Mun, Roberts, North, and Others* (London, 1856), reprinting eight tracts issued from 1621 to 1701, including the whole of Thomas Mun's *England's Treasure by Foreign Trade*.

Smith, Adam. *An Inquiry into the Nature and Causes of The Wealth of Nations*. London, 1776. Among modern editions the most useful is that published as volumes 2 and 3 of *The Glasgow Edition of the Works and Correspondence of Adam Smith*, edited by R. H. Campbell and A. S. Skinner (Oxford, 1976), which contains an important introduction and numerous cross-references; a majestic work that encompasses social, political, and cultural topics, arguably the most influential book on economics ever written and the fountainhead of all subsequent attacks on mercantilism.

OTHER WORKS

Ames, Glenn J. *Colbert, Mercantilism, and the French Quest for Asian Trade*. DeKalb, Ill., 1996. A detailed study of the creation of Colbert's East India company and its operational failure.

Appleby, Joyce Oldham. *Economic Thought and Ideology in Seventeenth-Century England*. Princeton, N.J., 1978. Explores with penetrating intelligence the struggle of English economic writers to understand the operation and significance of the emergent market forces.

Baugh, Daniel A. "Maritime Strength and Atlantic Commerce: The Uses of 'a Grand Marine Empire'." In *An Imperial State at War: Britain from 1689 to 1815*, edited by Lawrence Stone, pp. 185–223. London, 1994. On the motivation, evolution, and realities of enforcement of British policy under the navigation acts.

Cole, Charles Woolsey. *French Mercantilist Doctrines before Colbert*. New York, 1931; repr., New York, 1969. An uncomplicated, brief introduction.

Cole, Charles Woolsey. *Colbert and a Century of French Mercantilism*. 2 vols. New York, 1939; repr., Hamden, Conn., 1964.

Although parts have been superseded by more recent studies, this remains a valuable comprehensive work; Colbert's program occupies three-quarters of the book, and the opening chapters address its antecedents.

Coleman, D. C., ed. *Revisions in Mercantilism*. London, 1969. Reprints eight articles by recognized authors; the collection with Coleman's introduction provides a guide to many of the disputes about mercantilism.

Coleman, D. C., and A. H. John, eds. *Trade, Government and Economy in Pre-industrial England*. London, 1976. Contains four articles relevant to mercantilism; Coleman's looks at the English debate over whether specie would be lost by the proposed Anglo-French Trade Treaty of 1713.

Dziembowski, Edmond. *Un nouveau patriotisme français, 1750–1770: La France face à la puissance anglaise à l'époque de la guerre de Sept Ans*. Oxford, 1998. A pioneering study of the relevant publications, chiefly of the 1750s, with particular attention to the language used, the role of the public, the precise historical timing of French reactions to British power, and the ultimate significance of this wave of Anglophobia.

Fourquet, François. *Richesse et puissance: Une généalogie de la valeur (XVIe–XVIIIe siècle)*. Paris, 1989. Explores selected themes in French and British economic thought from the Middle Ages to Adam Smith against a background of social and ideological influences.

Fox-Genovese, Elizabeth. *The Origins of Physiocracy: Economic Revolution and Social Order in Eighteenth-Century France*. Ithaca, N.Y., 1976. An insightful approach to Quesnay and Mirabeau that places their ideas in the social and political contexts of the Old Regime.

Gomes, Leonard. *Foreign Trade and the National Economy: Mercantilist and Classical Perspectives*. London and New York, 1988. The early chapters offer a discerning, fair-minded analysis of the merits and flaws of mercantilist ideas about foreign trade, with special attention to Thomas Mun.

Heckscher, Eli F. *Mercantilism*. 2 vols. 2d ed. London, 1955. Translated from the German edition and revised by the author; the major study of the subject, though a very large portion is devoted to internal regulation of industry; Heckscher's criticism of mercantilism follows the path marked out by Adam Smith.

Heckscher, Eli F. "Multilateralism, Baltic Trade, and the Mercantilists." *Economic History Review*, 2d ser., 3 (1950–1951), 219–228. A response to Charles Wilson's article of 1949, cited below.

Mims, Steward L. *Colbert's West India Policy*. New Haven, Conn., 1912; repr., New York, 1977. The background and outcome of the policy, to about 1680; still the best treatment.

Minard, Philippe. *La fortune du colbertisme: État et industrie dans la France des Lumières*. Paris, 1998. An insightful history of industrial regulation from its institution by Colbert to the end of the Old Regime; addresses the reasons why it was instituted, how it operated in practice, and why it came to be criticized.

Pares, Richard. *War and Trade in the West Indies, 1739–1763*. Oxford, 1936; repr., London, 1963. A brilliant study of the problems of carrying on overseas commerce in wartime toward the end of the mercantilist era; especially helpful with respect to France.

Schaeper, Thomas J. *The French Council of Commerce, 1700–1715*. Columbus, Ohio, 1983. The realities of the regulatory regime are examined in the general context of French wartime policy; addresses trade as well as industry.

Supple, Barry E. *Commercial Crisis and Change in England, 1600–1642*. Cambridge, 1959. The historical background of English economic thought and policy carefully researched and considered; Supple argues convincingly that monetary manipulations occurring in England's cloth export markets were a prime cause of the 1620s depression; the closing portions deal directly with mercantilism.

Suviranta, Bruno. *The Theory of the Balance of Trade in England: A Study in Mercantilism*. Helsinki, 1923; repr., New York, 1967. A little-known study of the economic ideas of the seventeenth-century English writers, but one of the first to accord them intellectual respect.

Viner, Jacob. "Economic Thought: Mercantilist Thought." In *International Encyclopedia of the Social Sciences*, vol. 4, pp. 435–443. New York, 1968. Viner was most interested in mercantilist doctrines and did not look closely at the historical conditions in which they arose; this essay employs an interpretive framework based on modern economics.

Wilson, Charles H. "Treasure and Trade Balances: The Mercantilist Problem." *Economic History Review*, 2d ser., 2 (1949–1950), 152–161; and "Treasure and Trade Balances: Further Evidence." *Economic History Review*, 2d ser., 4 (1951–1952), 231–242. The first article argues, in support of Thomas Mun, that bullion was often necessary for conducting foreign trade in the mercantilist era; the second answers Heckscher 1950–1951.

Wilson, Charles H., and E. E. Rich, eds. *The Cambridge Economic History of Europe*, vol. 4, *The Economy of Expanding Europe in the Sixteenth and Seventeenth Centuries*. Cambridge, 1967. Chapter 8, "Trade, Society, and the State," pp. 487–575, by Wilson, is an authoritative survey of mercantilist ideas throughout Europe.

Winch, Donald. "Adam Smith: Scottish Moral Philosopher as Political Economist." In *Adam Smith: International Perspectives*, edited by Hiroshi Mizuta and Chuhei Sugiyama, pp. 85–111. Basingstoke and London, 1993. A sagacious essay that shows how Smith's philosophical perspective shaped the character and style of his attack on the mercantile system.

DANIEL A. BAUGH

MERIT. *See* Moral Philosophy *and* Sociability.

MERKEN, LUCRETIA WILHELMINA VAN (1721–1789), Dutch poet.

Merken was considered by her contemporaries as the great lady of literature, and not without reason. At the age of twenty-four, she made her debut with a classical tragedy, *Artemines*—the first Dutch woman to write a serious play without a male collaborator. Seven more tragedies followed, most of them based on historical events. *Jacob Simonszoon de Rijk* (1772) was selected to inaugurate the new Amsterdam City Theater in 1774; its protagonist was one of the heroes of the Dutch War of Independence against Spain. The Eighty Years' War also inspired her next play, the much-applauded *Beleg der Stadt Leyden* (Siege of the City of Leiden), which debuted in 1774 in commemoration of the siege and relief of Leiden two hundred years earlier.

Merken ventured into the most respected of classical genres, the epic, with *David* (1767, on the biblical Jewish king) and *Germanicus* (1779, on the Roman conqueror of the Germans), the latter inspired by Voltaire's *Henriade*. Both works were greatly admired, and the lengthy *Germanicus* was translated into French. (Merken sent a copy of the translation to George Washington, who, as the conqueror of the English, was extremely popular in Holland; unfortunately, Washington did not read French.) Some critics, though, disliked the subject because the alleged ancestors of the Dutch, the Batavians, had been a Germanic tribe.

Merken also wrote several long didactic poems, notably *Het nut der tegenspoeden* (The Profit of Tribulations, 1762), and much occasional poetry, and she made a number of contributions to a new version of the psalm-book. All her works evidence her wide reading in literature and history, her outstanding command of the conventions of classical poetry and poetic language, and her deep, resigned trust in God.

The reserved, distinguished Merken, who in 1768 married the rich merchant and poet Pieter van Winter, kept aloof from public life and literary circles, but many female writers of her own generation and of the next declared that her example had given them inspiration and confidence to publish. However, Merken represented the older, moribund tradition of fixed literary forms, conventional language, and polished versification. In that regard, she was the opposite of Elisabeth Wolff-Bekker, seventeen years her junior, who in 1777, in a vain attempt to gain Merken's friendship, wrote to her, "You are the greatest female poet of the country"; Wolff-Bekker, however, would reject poetic conventions and artificiality and would participate passionately in religious, social, and political debates. While Wolff-Bekker and her contemporary Aagje Deken continued to attract new generations of readers, Merken sank into oblivion from which specialist studies did not succeed in rescuing her. Recently, scholars in women's studies have cast new light on the role of Merken and other forgotten female writers in literary history.

[*See also* Deken, Aagje; Drama; Men and Women of Letters; Netherlands; Poetry; *and* Theater.]

BIBLIOGRAPHY

Bosch Reitz, S. C. "An Unpublished Correspondence of George Washington." *Journal of American History* 24 (1930), 48–58.
Meijer Drees, Marijke. "'Grootste dichteresse onzes lands': Lucretia Wilhelmina van Merken, Amsterdam 21 augustus 1721–Leiden 24 oktober 1789." In *Met en zonder lauwerkrans. Schrijvende vrouwen uit de vroegmoderne tijd 1550-1850: van Anna Bijns tot Elise van Calcar*, edited by Riet Schenkeveld-van der Dussen et al., pp. 572–579. Amsterdam, 1997.
Smit, W. A. P. *Kalliope in de Nederlanden: Het Renaissancistisch-klassicistische epos van 1550 tot 1850*. Groningen, Netherlands, 1983. See vol. 2, pp. 601–620, 757–774.

JOOST KLOEK

MESLIER, JEAN (1664–1729), French priest.

Meslier spent all his life in the Ardennes region of northeastern France. After studying at the seminary in the town of Reims, in Champagne, he became priest in the village of Etrépigny in 1689; he remained there until his death. Although he was reprimanded in 1716 for preaching against the nobility, like some other priests in the region, his life seems to have been generally uneventful, and he apparently fulfilled his duties as parish priest conscientiously. Shortly before dying, however, he deposited with the local legal authorities three manuscript copies of a very long *Mémoire* of more than three hundred folios, together with a letter addressed to the neighboring village priests, affirming that he did not believe in the teachings of the church, or indeed in any religion, and that he was an atheist.

Despite the fact that these three copies were immediately consigned to a private library and later to that of a monastery, before entering the Bibliothèque Nationale at the time of the French Revolution, the existence of the manuscript soon became known, and copies of the work as well as extracts from it began to circulate in the 1730s. Also circulated, at least by the end of the century, were copies of Meslier's critical annotations in the margins of a copy of the French theologian Fénelon's *Démonstration de l'existence de Dieu* (1718). The atheistic village priest of Etrépigny thus became a reference for enlightened freethinkers and enemies of organized religion, and there were several spurious attributions of other works to him in the later part of the century, in particular d'Holbach's *Le bon sens du curé Meslier* (1772). Voltaire showed particular interest in this antireligious priest and, in 1762, published an extract from his work that omits all the most radical elements, in particular the atheism and social criticism, and which turns Meslier into a Voltairean-type deist.

In fact, Meslier's rather rambling and repetitive but hard-hitting work constitutes one of the most radical eighteenth-century attacks on the whole religious and political structure of society. His life as village priest in a rural community in a particularly poor part of France, during a period marked by a series of famines as well as by the horrors of war, which particularly affected this frontier region, had aroused in him a sense of violent outrage at the injustice he witnessed and the sufferings of the ordinary people he lived with. His reaction, kept secret until his death, was a violent denunciation of the system, based on a communistic vision of society. He denounced the behavior of the rich and powerful as well as that of the clergy, the social inequality based on huge differences in property-ownership, and the trappings of absolutism. This denunciation led him to advocate a society without private property, based on complete equality and on common property-holding in self-governing village communities under the rule of elders.

This vision of a just society was based on a rejection of the social order, and in particular, of the church and the religion it defended, which Meslier saw as propping up the existing system of inequality. Here he did not simply denounce the corruption of the church and the behavior of its representatives; he developed an atheistic and materialistic philosophy that radically opposed Christian teachings. It was based on a denial of the existence of a god and expounded a monistic view of a world composed solely of uncreated, self-moving matter. The movements of this matter and the modifications occurring in the brain account for all human feelings, thoughts, and knowledge. Although this philosophy contained elements of Epicureanism, its inspiration was essentially Cartesian, despite its refusal of dualism. In fact, the main influence on Meslier was his reading of the French priest and philosopher Nicolas Malebranche, whose *De la recherche de la vérité* (1674–1675) he often quoted. He seems to have known few of the classical materialistic texts and instead elaborated his philosophy, in isolation, on the basis of Cartesian physiology, and in opposition to its dualism and to works of theology. In his rural isolation, he could not be aware of developments in physiology that could support his arguments, or of other irreligious treatises.

Meslier's influence on Enlightenment thought, especially on the French materialists who followed him, is difficult to ascertain. His name was known, and copies of his work or extracts from it circulated in manuscript form; the case of a poor village priest in revolt against the church could not fail to capture the imagination of the freethinkers of the age, but clear traces of any real knowledge or influence of his arguments are rare. Manuscript copies of his entire *Mémoire* were very expensive, and thus reserved for only a few rich people. He appears to have had little impact on materialists like Julien Offray de La Mettrie—who was, however, one of the first to refer to him specifically—or Denis Diderot; and in the later part of the century, the works that circulated under his name gave a deformed picture of his beliefs. Meslier thus appears present as a name, as a curious story, and as one of the list of famous anti-Christian thinkers, and the actual content of his work appears to have been little known. The true extent of his revolt, in particular of his radical social criticism, became familiar only much later.

[*See also* Atheism; Materialism; *and* Voltaire.]

BIBLIOGRAPHY

Meslier, Jean. *Oeuvres complètes*. Jean Deprun, Roland Desné and Albert Soboul, eds. 3 vols. Paris, 1970–1973. In addition to the annotated text, this edition contains substantial introductions discussing Meslier's social and philosophical thought.

Morehouse, Andrew R. *Voltaire and Jean Meslier*. New Haven, Conn., 1936. Although in some ways out-of date, provides a useful introduction to Meslier's ideas.

Spink, John S. *French Free Thought from Gassendi to Voltaire*. London, 1960. Contains much on Meslier's work and its circulation.

Wade, Ira O. *The Clandestine Organization and Diffusion of Philosophic Ideas in France from 1700 to 1750*. Princeton, N.J., 1938; repr., New York, 1967. Despite being partly superseded, still useful on the circulation of Meslier's work.

ANN THOMSON

MESMER, FRANZ ANTON (1734–1815), physician, psychic healer, and proponent of animal magnetism.

Mesmer was born in the area of Iznang, Germany, near Lake Constance. At age nine he began his studies at a nearby monastery and later continued at the Jesuit University in Dillingen. He entered the University of Vienna to study medicine; he was a nontraditional medical student, abhorring the use of purging and bleeding to effect cures. Influenced by the works of Paracelsus (1493–1541) and of the English physician Richard Mead (1673–1754), Mesmer began to study the purported effects of planets and magnets on the human body. His thesis, *De Planetarum Influxu* (On the Influence of the Planets), drew heavily on Mead's works, possibly to the point of plagiarism.

Following graduation, Mesmer entered the practice of medicine. He married a wealthy widow, Maria Anna von Bosch, and he entertained famous personages, including the Mozart family and the empress of Austria. Mesmer courted Maximilian Hell, the originator of the use of magnets in treating medical problems, and himself began treating patients by that method. He sought to demonstrate to other physicians examples of his unique healing process, but all refused his overtures. His final rejection, dismissal from the Academy of Physicians, came as a result of problems with his treatment of the blind pianist Maria von Paradis. Leaving Vienna, Mesmer went to Paris to continue his work.

Mesmer's arrival in Paris was preceded by his reputation, both good and bad. He established a medical practice treating both rich and poor for a variety of complaints by using what he termed "animal magnetism," which he defined as the ability of a person to produce in another person the same effects as those produced by a magnet. He would later conclude that physical magnets were no longer necessary to effect his cures. Mesmer's techniques included placing groups of patients together, holding hands, and immersing their extremities in a tub—the *baquet*—of "magnetized" water. Word of Mesmer's treatment and theory soon reached King Louis XVI, who ordered two commissions to study animal magnetism. One was composed of members from the Faculty of Medicine in Paris and from the Academy of Sciences, and the other was drawn from Paris's Royal Society of Medicine. Benjamin Franklin, minister plenipotentiary to France and an academician, headed one of the commissions. Following months of debate and some demonstrations of animal magnetism, both commissions reported to the King that this was a dangerous technique and should be banned.

Mesmer, disgraced, departed for his home in Vienna. Following a brief stay in Vienna, where he was not allowed to practice, Mesmer retired to Meersburg, Germany, where he died of a cerebral hemorrhage while being treated with animal magnetism techniques by one of his associates.

Mesmer scholars will reach their individual conclusions regarding the validity of his work, but there can be little doubt of his place in medical and scientific history. Animal magnetism, or mesmerism, became an element of faith healing. Individuals in a hypnotic "trance" are still referred to as being "mesmerized." According to some historians, mesmerism was an early, elementary form of hypnotism or psychotherapy.

[*See also* Academies *and* Medicine.]

BIBLIOGRAPHY

Gauld, Alan. *A History of Hypnotism*. Cambridge, Mass., 1992. Contains an analysis of Mesmer as a pioneer in the field of hypnotism.

Pattie, Frank A. *Mesmer and Animal Magnetism*. Hamilton, N.Y., 1994. A thoroughly documented history, covering Mesmer's life and his impact on society, reaching the conclusion that he was a charlatan.

ROBERT B. CRAIG

METEOROLOGY. Meteorological theory, methods, and practice underwent major changes during the eighteenth century. As a body of theoretical knowledge, meteorology ceased to be a theory of "meteors" (that is, substances of the sublunary region, as defined in Aristotle's *Meteorologica*) and became a chemical philosophy of the atmosphere. Beginning as place-centered and curiosity-driven qualitative reporting during the first half of the century, the discipline grew into an analytical and a largely quantitative study of the large-scale meteorological processes. As a public and even political topic, the weather was widely discussed among prophets, preachers, wits, and the general populace until the end of the century, and beyond. Its relation to diseases also interested physicians.

Theorists of the seventeenth and early eighteenth centuries—for instance, Pierre Gassendi (1592–1655), John Woodward (1665–1728), Thomas Robinson (d. 1719), and John Pointer (1668–1754)—held that meteorological phenomena originated in the processes of rising, explosion, and alteration of nitro-sulfurous exhalations of subterranean origin. Support for this "exhalation" view was textual and experimental (Robert Boyle, 1627–1691; William Derham, 1657–1735; Joseph Wasse, 1672–1738), but evidence based on sense perception (especially olfactory) was predominant. During the 1740s, researches on electrical origins of lightning by J. H. Winkler (1703–1770) and Benjamin Franklin (1706–1790) challenged the exhalation view. In the next two decades, electricity emerged

as the preferred explanation for other "meteors": earthquakes (Stephen Hales, 1677–1761), the aurora borealis (John Canton, 1718–1772), rain (Giovanni Beccaria, 1716–1781), and fireballs (Charles Blagden, 1748–1820). The exhalation theory was further attacked by John Pringle (1707–1782), whose criticism of the atmospheric explanation of meteoric stones opened a debate about the possibility of their extraterrestrial origin.

The eventual rejection of exhalation views and a far-reaching reshaping of meteorological subject matter came with experimental researches on the chemistry of gases, thermometry, barometry, and hygrometry. Landmark studies include Daniel Fahrenheit's (1686–1736) early research on freezing, William Cullen's (1710–1790) on vaporization, Joseph Black's (1728–1799) on latent heat during the 1750s, and Joseph Priestley's (1733–1804) analyses of atmospheric air (1772). Jean André Deluc's (1727–1817) idea that water might be a union of water and heat, and the study of mountain weather by Horace Benedict de Saussure (1740–1799) brought pneumatic chemistry to bear on meteorology to the extent that a late Enlightenment naturalist such as George Adams (1750–1795) could describe the atmosphere as a global chemical laboratory in his Lectures on Natural Experimental Philosophy (1794).

Simultaneous with these developments was a shift in methods of observation. Before the 1770s, most published observations remained descriptive and qualitative, the first-person narratives about unusual or extreme weather. This was partly because the exhalation model favored an analysis of individual (especially unusual) meteors, and partly because meteorological reportage supported regional geography that stressed the natural (and cultural) specificity of locality. Characteristic of this approach were the English clergymen William Borlase (1695–1772) and his correspondents around midcentury. Two developments challenged this emphasis on the local and descriptive. First, maritime exploration and commerce stimulated interest in large-scale meteorological processes, but their full-scale investigation would not commence until the nineteenth century. Isolated attempts did appear, however: Edmund Halley (1656–1742) drew up a wind chart in 1686; William Dampier (1651–1715) surveyed the world's winds in 1697; William Derham investigated the causes of the Great Storm of 1703; and John Hadley (1682–1744) studied the dynamics of the trade winds in 1735.

Second, the growing popularity of meteorological instruments (especially the barometer), led more naturalists to reject circumstantial narratives as inferior to quantification, standardization, and coordination. Proposals, not always realized, for routine instrumental measurements and consistent weather diaries were made by Robert Hooke (1635–1702) in 1663, Woodward in 1696,

Georg Hamberger (1662–1716) in 1701, Johann Kanold (1679–1729) around 1717, James Jurin (1684–1750) in 1723, Isaac Greenwood (1702–1745) in 1727, and Roger Pickering (d. 1755) in 1741. Petrus van Musschenbroek (1692–1761) in Holland organized an informal group of weather observers in the 1730s. In German lands, local "patriotic" societies invited the compilation of weather registers for the promotion of economy and agriculture. In Mannheim, the Meteorological Society of the Palatinate (1780–1792), founded under the auspices of the elector Karl Theodore and led by J. J. Hemmer, cooperated with more than thirty European individuals and societies.

In France, in the wake of a cattle plague of the early 1770s, Anne-Robert-Jacques Turgot (1727–1781) and Felix Vicq d'Azyr (1748–1794) founded a Commission for Epidemics to coordinate the medico-meteorological work of provincial physicians by distributing question-naires with weather queries, perhaps the first example of state-sponsored weather observation. The Commis-sion, which became the Société Royale de Medicine in 1778, encouraged the empirical study of the relationship between the seasons and epidemics, planning a medical map of France. Such projects followed neo-Hippocratic ideas of a "natural history of diseases" in which ail-ments corresponded to, or were caused by, changes in season, weather, or place of residence. Promoted by Thomas Sydenham (1624–1689) and Hermann Boerhaave (1668–1738), Hippocratic meteorology found expression in the works of Francis Clifton (d. 1736), John Arbuthnot (1667–1735), John Lining (1708–1760), John Huxham (1692–1768), John Rutty (1698–1775) and many others.

Beginning in the 1760s, encouraged by the grow-ing number of instrumental observations, Tobias Mayer (1723–1762), Johann Lambert (1728–1777), and Richard Kirwan (1733–1812) derived "climatological" relations between average temperatures and geographic latitudes and concerned themselves with the prospect of seasonal forecasts. Similar questions were debated in agrometeo-rological literature, influenced by the French *agronomes* H.-K. Duhamel du Monceau (1710–1782) and the marquis de Mirabeau, as well as by the revival of Virgil's *Georgics*. Linnaeus's disciples in Sweden, agricultural improvers in England, and members of German economic soci-eties circulated "naturalist calendars" with information on weather and vegetation. While deterministic weather prediction was considered a chimera, a discovery of cycles of weather and "prognostication" from signs became a priority in works by John Mills (1770), Allen Hall (1788), and the numerous British and continental forecasting "manuals" that used the folk tradition of "weather signs."

[*See also* Astronomy; Commerce and Trade; *and* Natural Philosophy and Science.]

BIBLIOGRAPHY

Feldman, Theodore S. "Late Enlightenment Meteorology." In *The Quantifying Spirit in the 18th Century*, edited by Tore Frangsmyr, John L. Heilbron, and Robin E. Rider, pp. 143–178. Berkeley, 1990.

Goodison, Nicholas. *English Barometers, 1680–1800: A History of Domestic Barometers and Their Makers and Retailers*. London, 1969. An extensive and well illustrated survey of the production of and market for barometers.

Jankovic, Vladimir. *Reading the Skies: A Cultural History of English Weather, 1650–1820*. Chicago, 2000. Centers on social, religious, and geographical dimensions of eighteenth-century meteorology.

Riley, James. *The Eighteenth-Century Campaign to Avoid Disease*. New York, 1986. A reliable discussion on medical meteorology.

Rusnock, Andrea, ed. *The Correspondence of James Jurin (1684–1750)*. Amsterdam, 1996. An excellent source of information on meteoro-logical networks.

VLADIMIR JANKOVIC

METHODISM. *See* Enthusiasm *and* Wesley, John.

MIDDLE AGES. *See* Tradition.

MIDWIFERY. Enlightened midwifery implies a chal-lenge to old ways of practice and the discarding of tradi-tional ideas and techniques of delivery in favor of a more progressive and scientific approach. Yet for midwifery, the eighteenth century was a period of both continuity and change. It was marked by a shift from faith to rea-son, in which traditional practices gave way to experiment and creativity, and tales and custom to experience-based knowledge; but these changes were partial and varied greatly among countries and locales, being most marked in major towns and cities. For mothers, once safely deliv-ered, the lying-in remained a time of ritual and celebration shared with other women, but pregnancy and childbirth were dreaded, and justly so: many women and children failed to survive the confinement. The involvement of governments, chiefly through local initiatives, grew con-siderably, but midwives remained closely allied with the church, particularly because of their authority to carry out emergency baptisms and through the ceremony of churching.

Recent scholarship has challenged the notion that mid-wifery during the eighteenth century was carried out chiefly by unskilled crones. The existence of a close link between witches and midwives has also been challenged. Yet the period was not a golden age for midwives, either. Babies born during the Enlightenment were more likely to be delivered by a midwife, but the role and influ-ence of the man-midwife or accoucheur was increasing. Midwifery remained an important female occupation, for many women a source of income and authority, though standards and the scale of practice varied enormously.

Most midwives were trained by apprenticeship with an experienced midwife, but by the eighteenth century many urban midwives in Europe received some form of training provided by a town council or local college of surgeons or obstetricians. Some also had access to midwifery texts and witnessed dissections, and a very small number wrote books intended to improve the skills of their colleagues. In Spain, efforts to reform midwifery practice were linked closely to Enlightenment notions of education; in Denmark, the training of midwives was spurred by reform and mercantilist concerns. Governments expressed anxiety about the loss of infant life, and the training of midwives was often depicted as part of the response to fears of population decline. Britain and colonial America lagged behind in formal midwife training and regulation. In Britain, midwives were still licensed by bishops, though many found licenses too costly and troublesome to obtain.

Some outstanding midwives practiced during the Enlightenment: Sarah Stone and Elizabeth Nihell in England, Elizabeth Phillips and Martha Ballard in North America, Justine Siegemund in Germany, Luisa Rosado in Spain, Teresa Ployant in Italy, Catharina Schrader in the Netherlands, and Mme. Du Coudray in France. Sarah Stone has been portrayed as an exemplar of enlightened midwifery. She was trained by her mother, a renowned midwife, in the late seventeenth century, and she practiced in Somerset and Bristol until around 1737, at the peak of her career delivering more than three hundred babies a year. She had a good understanding of anatomy, was dexterous in her work—supporting the use of forceps in cases of real need—and stressed the importance of knowledge in her book, the *Complete Practice of Midwifery* (1737).

Mme. Du Coudray was sent out by the king of France, Louis XV, in 1759 on a unique mission to teach midwifery to the nation's midwives. She traveled around provincial France with her entourage, demonstrating with an obstetrical mannequin. As she traversed France for three decades, Du Coudray was often critical of the barbaric practices of country midwives that led to the loss of babies and mothers for France.

Vrouw Schrader, too, attacked her fellow midwives as being "torturers" and "know-nothings," as she accomplished a total of 3,060 deliveries during some forty years in practice in Friesland in the north of the Netherlands, between 1693 and 1745. Schrader became a local expert who was called to attend at difficult cases. She was a busy manipulator, intervening actively in the labor process, usually manually, and becoming particularly adept in podalic version, turning the baby to deliver it feet first. She became a woman of considerable repute and wealth. Though skilled and creative in her work, Schrader still clung to traditional beliefs, particularly that maternal imagination and actions could influence the unborn child.

Most midwives fell somewhat short of the impressive skills—obstetrical, learned, and political—of women such as Stone, Du Coudray, and Schrader, practicing their art quietly in their localities. Often women of mature years who had themselves borne children, midwives could be well paid for their work, and they built up a clientele based largely on reputation and repeat custom. Midwives were also called on as court witnesses in cases of domestic violence, rape, infanticide, abortion, and fornication, and they were urged by the local authorities, who employed them to deliver the poor and to persuade mothers to name the fathers of bastard children. For some midwives, however, standards of practice remained low and their reputations poor.

The Enlightenment saw an increasing role for male obstetrical practitioners, particularly in Britain and America, where failure to tighten up the practices of midwives in the towns offered more scope to medical men. In their textbooks, obstetric practitioners such as William Smellie, William Hunter, Jean Louis Baudeloque, and Hendrick van Deventer described female anatomy, the parturition process, and preternatural births and recommended techniques to improve the outcome for mother and baby. Perhaps the most visually stunning of these texts is William Hunter's *Anatomy of the Gravid Uterus* (1774), which combines remarkable artistry with detailed anatomy encompassing the Enlightenment belief that seeing is knowing. The most formidable of the instruments of the Enlightenment accoucheur were the obstetric forceps, which enabled a living child to be delivered in cases where the mother was unable to give birth naturally, but the vectis and fillet were also in wide usage. Many versions of the forceps were developed during the seventeenth and eighteenth centuries, but their use caused great controversy among men-midwives. William Hunter derided their use, declaring that "it was a thousand pities that they were ever invented for where they save one they murder twenty." Techniques of cesarean section were elaborated during this period, but the procedure was rarely carried out. Some men-midwives advocated it as a means of delivering women with a badly deformed pelvis, but others condemned what was a gruesome and usually deadly operation.

During the eighteenth century, lying-in hospitals were established throughout Europe, intended to deliver poor, often unmarried women free of cost, and to provide pupil men-midwives and midwives access to large numbers of deliveries. London established four such charities in the mid-eighteenth century. Embodying ideals of philanthropy and the aim of improving the health of poor women, many lying-in hospitals became important centers of learning. They were also notorious for their outbreaks of childbed or puerperal fever, which could sweep through maternity wards, causing many deaths.

Until the eighteenth century, the work of obstetrical doctors was confined largely to emergency deliveries, but during this period they became more interested in general midwifery work. The aristocratic and middle classes were the first to seek the attendance of men-midwives, and obstetrics was seen increasingly as a doorway into fashionable general practice. Obstetrics became an increasingly important component of the curricula of medical schools and universities, and a number of eminent men-midwives set up private schools to teach midwifery. William Smellie set up a school in London in the 1740s to teach male pupils. Smellie developed his own popular design of obstetric forceps, published his *Treatise on the Theory and Practice of Midwifery* (1752), and together with his pupils he delivered more than one thousand poor women within ten years. He incurred the wrath of the prominent London midwife Elizabeth Nihell, who had trained at the Paris Hôtel-Dieu and who in her *Professed Midwife: A Man-Midwife or a Midwife? A Treatise on the Art of Midwifery* (1760) mocked male midwives and their instruments, particularly Smellie with his "delicate fist of a great horse-godmother of a he-midwife." Some midwives and doctors cooperated with each other, but diatribes between midwives and men-midwives and their supporters, each accusing the other of bad practice, became part and parcel of late-eighteenth-century midwifery. The period saw a slow but sustained drift toward the male practitioner and a growth in his practice, earnings, and authority.

[*See also* Medicine *and* Natural Philosophy and Science.]

BIBLIOGRAPHY

Bynum, W. F., and Roy Porter, eds. *William Hunter and the Eighteenth-Century Medical World.* Cambridge, 1985.

Donegan, Jane B. *Women & Men Midwives: Medicine, Morality and Misogyny in Early America.* Westport, Conn., 1978.

Gelbart, Nina Rattner. *The King's Midwife: A History and Mystery of Madame du Coudray.* Berkeley, 1998.

Grundy, Isobel. "Sarah Stone: Enlightenment Midwife." In *Medicine in the Enlightenment,* edited by Roy Porter, pp. 128–144. Amsterdam, 1995.

Marland, Hilary. *"Mother and Child Were Saved": The Memoirs (1693–1740) of the Frisian Midwife Catharina Schrader.* Amsterdam, 1987.

Marland, Hilary, ed. *The Art of Midwifery: Early Modern Midwives in Europe.* London, 1993.

Ulrich, Laurel Thatcher. *A Midwife's Tale: The Life of Martha Ballard, Based on Her Diary, 1785–1812.* New York, 1990.

Wilson, Adrian. "The Ceremony of Childbirth and its Implications." In *Women as Mothers in Pre-Industrial England,* edited by Valerie Fildes, pp. 68–107. London, 1990.

Wilson, Adrian. *The Making of Man-Midwifery: Childbirth in England, 1660–1770.* London, 1995.

HILARY MARLAND

MILAN. The northern Italian territory of the Milanese, as the duchy of Milan or Lombardy is known in Italy, passed during the War of the Spanish Succession (1701–1713/1714) from the Spanish to the Austrian Habsburgs, who retained it—apart from brief periods of foreign conquest and occupation—until the unification of Italy during 1859–1861. Around 1750, the Milanese extended over eight thousand square kilometers and had a population of about one million. About one-tenth of this number lived in the capital, Milan, the biggest, wealthiest, and most important city in Lombardy. Economically, the Milanese was rich; its wealth derived from its prosperous agriculture, as was noted by the English agronomist and traveler, Arthur Young, in the 1780s. Politically, the Milanese was very loosely controlled from Vienna. The government of Lombardy was the preserve of an oligarchic nobility that dominated the key institutions of the Milanese, including the Senate, the Congregazione dello Stato, the financial magistracies, and the city of Milan. Between the end of the War of the Austrian Succession (1740–1748) and the Seven Years' War (1756–1763), Empress Maria Theresa and her ministers sought to maximize Milan's contribution to and integration within the larger monarchy. This involved administrative and tax reforms which reduced but did not end the independence of the Milanese and its ruling oligarchy.

Inevitably, this elite played a leading role in the Milanese Enlightenment and its institutions, including the Accademia dei Filosofi (founded in 1733) and the Accademia dei Trasformati (1743). It also provided an audience for Milan's first literary journal, the *Raccolta milanese,* which appeared in 1756–1757. The salons of contessa Borromeo and duchessa Serbelloni in Milan were important mediators of a wider (in particular French) culture. Later, the elite would play a key role in the improving Patriotic Society of Milan (founded in 1776).

Accademia dei Pugni and *Il Caffè.* The Milanese Enlightenment, however, was associated above all with those who gathered in the 1760s around Pietro Verri (1728–1797), another scion of the Milanese ruling oligarchy. This group made up the so-called Accademia dei Pugni, a deliberately informal gathering that met in Verri's home; its name reflected its combative reformist stance. It included Verri's younger brother Alessandro, Cesare Beccaria, Alfonso Longo, Giuseppe Visconti di Saliceto, Luigi Lambertenghi, Pietro Secco-Comneno, Gian Battista Biff, Gian Rinaldo Carli, and Paolo Frisi. Many of these individuals were in touch with, and associated themselves with, the French Enlightenment. Pietro Verri, who in 1760–1761 immersed himself in the works of Montesquieu, Voltaire, Rousseau, and Helvétius, openly expressed his admiration of their work.

Between 1762 and 1764, Verri and his associates expounded their reform program in *Il Caffé*, a radical journal published at Brescia to evade the Lombard censorship. In some respects, the project was a Milanese version of the French *Encyclopédie*, though on a much smaller scale and modeled on the English *Spectator*. The targets of *Il Caffé* included popular ignorance and superstition, idle clergy and nobles, corrupt tax farmers, backward agriculture, and even the defects of the Italian language. The group also produced other works typical of the Enlightenment, including Pietro Verri's *Discorso* (or *Meditazioni*) *sulla felicità* (Discourse on Happiness, 1763), which has been seen as a manifesto of the Milanese Enlightenment. Verri focused particularly on political economy, but the most famous, influential, and enduring contribution of the Milanese group to the European Enlightenment was Beccaria's work on penal reform, *Dei delitti e delle pene* (Crimes and Punishments, 1764).

Many of these reformers entered government service. Carli and Verri, for example, were appointed to the Supreme Economic Council, set up in 1765 to direct the economic and financial policy of the Milanese. They were thus able to put some of their reforming ideas into practice. The Milanese Enlightenment was linked to a regime in Vienna that, to ensure the survival of the Austrian Habsburg Monarchy, was even more determined toward reform after the Seven Years' War than in the 1740s and 1750s. For some historians, Lombardy was a testing ground for enlightened reform, which was then extended to the rest of the monarchy. It is clear that, between 1763 and 1789, the Milanese experienced wide-ranging and increasingly radical reforms.

Religious and Economic Reform. This spirit of reform extended to the church, which was not surprising in view of the great wealth and power of the Milanese clergy, achieved largely during the Counter-Reformation. Reform of the church was the particular responsibility of the Giunta Economale (1765). The jurisdiction of both the pope and the local ecclesiastical authorities and their role in censorship and education were restricted. Efforts to limit the wealth of the church and the number of clergy and to put them to more productive use led to the suppression of a number of monasteries and convents. Education measures included reform of the University of Pavia and of the so-called Palatine Schools.

Economic reform was also a priority. Count Kaunitz was the Austrian State Chancellor with primary responsibility for the Milanese after 1757. Reflecting changing attitudes elsewhere in Europe, Kaunitz was increasingly disillusioned with the traditional system for controlling the food supply—the *annona*—especially following the harvest failures and famine of the 1760s, and he moved to dismantle it. At the same time, however, he sought to stimulate the economy of the Milanese, hoping in this way to improve the government's tax revenues. This same fiscal concern also inspired the abolition of the farming of the taxes (partial in 1765, with the establishment of the so-called mixed farm, and complete in 1770). Henceforth, tax collection was in the hands of the state.

These measures were not entirely successful, and it was only in the reign of Joseph II (1780–1790), who visited Milan in 1769 and again in 1784 and 1785, that reform became truly radical. Thus, in 1781, all religious orders that did not maintain schools or hospitals were suppressed, and the regular and secular clergy were subjected to closer government supervision. A "general seminary" was set up at Pavia (one of twelve founded throughout the Austrian Habsburg monarchy) to train the future clergy of the Milanese, thus reducing their need to study abroad. In 1784—after efforts in this direction in the 1760s had been blocked by the Senate of Milan—torture was at last abolished and the death penalty restricted. More strikingly, in 1786 Joseph overhauled the government of the Milanese at the expense of the traditional elite. The Senate and the Congregazione dello Stato were abolished, and the autonomy of the various regions and cities was ended. The Milanese was divided into eight new districts, each the responsibility of an intendant appointed by the government. A more bureaucratic, centralized ruling council in Milan became responsible to Vienna for the administration of the province.

Inevitably, these radical measures provoked opposition across a wide spectrum, including conservative opposition to Joseph's attack on traditional power structures and religious life. This proved powerful enough—particularly given the absence of alternative economic, social, and political forces in the Milanese—to force Joseph II and his brother and successor, Leopold II (1790–1792), to make concessions. The opposition also included some, such as Pietro Verri, who saw Joseph II as abusing his authority to create a despotism rather than to effect enlightened reform. Paradoxically, such men began to defend some of their own earlier targets in the Milanese as local bastions against centralizing despotism, and they moved in the direction of liberalism. They welcomed the French Revolution, which at first seemed to be realizing their own new ideals; however, the further progress of the Revolution and French military occupation of the Milanese (1796–1799), associated as it was with Jacobin measures, were a great disappointment. In addition, French occupation provoked a popular anti-Jacobin reaction that revealed just how limited was the hold of radical, enlightened attitudes on the vast majority of the population of the Milanese.

[*See also* Beccaria, Cesare; Salons, *subentry on* Italy; Verri, Alessandro; *and* Verri, Pietro.]

BIBLIOGRAPHY

Capra, Carlo. "Il Settecento." In *Il Ducato di Milano dal 1535 al 1796*, pp. 151–617, edited by Domenico Sella and Carlo Capra, vol. 11 of *Storia d'Italia*, Turin, 1984. The best general survey of the Milanese in the eighteenth century.

Carpanetto, Dino, and Giuseppe Ricuperati. *Italy in the Age of Reason, 1685–1789*. London, 1987. Makes available in English much of the work of Capra, Venturi, and others.

Grab, Alexander. "Enlightened Despotism and State Building: The Case of Austrian Lombardy." *Austrian History Yearbook* 20 (1984), 43–72. Good broad survey.

Grab, Alexander. "The Politics of Subsistence: The Liberalisation of Grain Commerce in Austrian Lombardy under Enlightened Despotism." *Journal of Modern History* 57 (1985), 185–210. Focused study of one specific area of reform.

Limoli, Donald A. "Pietro Verri: A Lombard Reformer under Enlightened Absolutism and the French Revolution." *Journal of Central European Affairs* 18 (1958), 254–280. Useful study of one key figure, his career, and the evolution of his thinking.

Roberts, John. "Lombardy." In *The European Nobility in the XVIII Century*, pp. 60–82, edited by A. Goodwin. London, 1953. Invaluable study of the Milanese elite.

Venturi, Franco. *Settecento Riformatore*, vol. 1, *Da Muratori a Beccaria, 1730–1764*. Turin, 1968. Chapter 9, "La Milano del 'Caffe,'" is a very useful analysis of Milanese at midcentury, and of Verri's circle and its output.

Venturi, Franco. *Settecento Riformatore*, vol. 5, *L'Italia dei Lumi (1764–1790), pt. 1, La rivoluzione di Corsica; Le grandi carestie degli anni sessanta; La Lombardiax delle riforme*. Turin, 1987. Typically, most useful for its analysis of contemporary texts.

Woolf, S. J. *A History of Italy, 1700–1860*. London, 1979. Useful general survey.

CHRISTOPHER STORRS

MILLAR, JOHN (1735–1801), Scottish political philosopher and professor of civil law at the University of Glasgow (1761–1801).

Millar, the son of a Presbyterian minister, was a successful law student at the University of Glasgow. Through Lord Kames's patronage, he was appointed Regius Professor of Civil Law there in 1761, succeeding Adam Smith. In his lectures, he followed the example of Smith's *Lectures on Jurisprudence* by acknowledging the influence of economic factors on the development of society, but he gave more scope to the political dimension of legal studies. He was known to have a marked Foxite Whig bias, which showed in his early approval of the French Revolution and his permanent attachment to Charles James Fox's cause. Above all, he was famous for his extensive legal knowledge and his lively teaching, which attracted numerous students to his classes, even from abroad.

In 1771, Millar published a social history of mankind entitled *Observations Concerning the Distinction of Ranks in Society*, which was much enlarged in 1779 under the title *The Origin of the Distinction of Ranks; or, An Inquiry into the Circumstances which Give Rise to Influence and Authority in the Different Members of Society*. The first chapter contains a long, detailed historical account of the condition of women, showing a profound interest in cultural variety. The second chapter is devoted to a study of the evolution of paternal authority. In the third and fourth chapters, Millar deals with the various forms of political authority linked to the different stages of social and economic advancement, identifiable mainly by the prevailing modes of subsistence. The political consequences of the progress of arts, manufactures, and trade are then studied more specifically in a chapter in which Millar describes the emergence of political liberty. The final chapter describes the condition of servants and slaves and vigorously advocates the abolition of slavery. The topics chosen by Millar clearly demonstrate his debt to French and Scottish Enlightenment figures like Montesquieu, David Hume, Adam Smith, and Adam Ferguson, but the profusion of historical and pre-anthropological documents quoted—from the *Bible* to the most recent travel accounts—shows a universal curiosity and holistic approach to human issues, shared with the compilers of the *Encyclopédie*. In fact, Diderot made use of Millar's history of the condition of women in one of his contributions to Raynal's *Histoire philosophique* (1780).

Millar's failing health, and his political disillusionment, prevented him from completing his next work, partly published in 1787 as *An Historical View of the English Government* and reissued in a much enlarged posthumous edition in 1803. It offers a Whig account of the British constitution and can be seen as an imperfect pendant to Hume's *History of Great-Britain*, questioning the extent of the royal prerogative and emphasizing the adverse effects of the division of labor. It is sometimes called the first English constitutional history. Some anonymous Whig pamphlets, such as the *Letters of Crito* (1796) and, less probably, the *Letters of Sidney*, have occasionally been attributed to Millar's late production.

[*See also* Education, *subentry on* Reform and Experiments; Home, Henry; Hume, David; Moral Philosophy; Political Philosophy; Scotland; Smith, Adam; *and* Tradition.]

BIBLIOGRAPHY

Lehmann, William Christian. *John Millar of Glasgow 1735–1801*. Cambridge, 1960; repr., New York, 1979. Contains an edition of *The Origin of the Distinction of Ranks* (with many references omitted) and a very full biography.

Millar, John. *An Historical View of the English Government*. 4 vols. London, 1803. First complete edition.

Millar, John (attributed to). *"Letters of Crito" e "Letters of Sidney."* Milan, 1984. With a commentary by Vincenzo Merolle on these attributions.

Millar, John. *The Origin of the Distinction of Ranks*. Edinburgh and London, 1806; repr., Bristol, 1990. Contains a full biography written by Millar's nephew.

MICHEL FAURE

MILLENARIANISM. Millenarianism (also known as *millennialism* and *chiliasm*) is the belief in a future millennium, a thousand-year period of Christ's rule on earth with his saints, sometimes seen as being advanced by the violent overthrow of existing ungodly rulers.

Millenarianism has long and deep roots in the Christian tradition. In Matthew 24, Jesus reveals to his disciples the characteristics of the time of his return: false prophets, wars and rumors of war, nation rising against nation, famine, plague, earthquakes, the darkening of the sun and moon, stars falling from heaven, and an undefined "sign of the Son of man in heaven." When this appears, "they shall see the Son of man coming in the clouds of heaven with power and great glory." A trumpet will sound, and angels will "gather together His elect from the four winds, from one end of heaven to the other." The Revelation of Saint John the Divine gives further details. He speaks of a "beast" who rules over mankind for forty-two months, and is granted "great authority" by Satan. At a certain time, the kings of the world gather at "a place called in the Hebrew tongue Armageddon," followed by natural disasters and the appearance of Jesus Christ on a white horse. Christ defeats the beast and the false prophet in battle, casting them "alive into a lake of fire burning with brimstone," with Satan thrown into a bottomless pit for a thousand years. It is during this millennium that Christ rules on earth with those martyred by the beast. After the end of the thousand years, Satan is released for a final battle, again defeated, this time forever, to join the beast and false prophet in the lake of fire. Jesus then sets up "a great white throne" for the Last Judgment of all human beings who ever lived, as "a new heaven and a new earth" descend from above, "for the first heaven and the first earth were passed away."

To this basic scenario was added further evidence from Daniel 7, a vision of "four great beasts," thought to represent the rise and fall of four successive world-empires, to be followed by the fifth millenarian kingdom. The identity of these empires has changed with the times, but the last generally included the Roman Empire and the Catholic Church.

Although there was support in the early Church for millenarian ideas, even by orthodox writers, both Origen (third century AD) and Augustine (fifth century AD) rejected detailed messianic speculation, initiating a decline in such concerns. Joachim of Fiore (c. 1132–1202), a Calabrian monk, devoted himself to millenarian studies, however, and created a prophetic system and chronology that to a great extent are still prevalent today.

During the Reformation, millenarianism was taken up by the Anabaptists, the Bohemian and Moravian Brethren, and other radical groups, and was seen as another aspect of God's constant intervention in human affairs. Two

schools of thought developed: the premillennialists (who argued that Christ would return before the onset of his thousand-year rule) and the postmillennialists (who believed that the improvement of conditions on earth would prepare the way for the Second Coming, which would be more obviously apocalyptic). Millenarianism was especially popular among Protestants, partly because of the necessity of close scriptural study and partly because of its usefulness as an explanation of why God allowed the Roman Catholic Church to exist for so many centuries, and why he condoned the very real mundane tribulations of early modern Europe.

The three major early modern millenarian theorists were all Protestants. The first was Thomas Brightman (1562–1607), a Cambridge-educated minister with Presbyterian tendencies who championed the postmillennialist interpretation. The second was a German, Johannes Alsted (1588–1638), whose view was premillennialist. Joseph Mede (1586–1668) also believed that the Second Coming would occur before the thousand-year rule, and promoted this concept while remaining within the Anglican Church. He turned millenarian study into a vastly more complicated system of textual analysis by introducing the idea of "synchronism," the notion that the events described in the book of Revelation are meant to be seen as taking place at the same time, like split-screen images.

Millenarianism was especially influential in seventeenth-century England. The comparative freedom of the press in the 1640s allowed the publication in English of the works of Brightman, Alsted, and Mede. A group of radical millenarians known as the Fifth Monarchy Men appeared in England and rose against both Oliver Cromwell's regime (1657) and that of the newly restored King Charles II (1661). Even among the less violently inclined, the perception was that scientific knowledge was being expanded at the same time that the prophetic books were being unsealed. If it were true (from an analogy with the biblical account of Creation) that the world would last only six thousand years, then perhaps the postmillennialists were right that they were living in the millennium before the Second Coming. These ideas did not die even in England with the Restoration, but having been moderated by the scholarly studies of men such as Mede, millenarianism was a philosophy that did not necessarily lead to rebellion against existing political structures. At the same time, groups like the Camisards ("the French Prophets") were both strongly millenarian and aggressively revolutionary.

The French Revolution was clearly an event on a millenarian scale. In overthrowing their king, the greatest of the Roman Catholic kingdoms had withdrawn its support for the pope, seen as a man of sin. Joseph Priestley (1733–1804) believed that the time was ripe for the return of Christ "in the clouds, so as to be seen by all," prefigured by the conversion of the Jews to Christianity ("of which there are no symptoms at present") and the fall of the Turkish empire. Richard Brothers (1757–1824), formerly an English naval lieutenant, wrote to George III in 1792 revealing that God commanded him to inform the king and the House of Commons that the time had come for the fulfillment of Daniel 7. A year later, Brothers was calling himself the Nephew of the Almighty on the grounds that his surname took its origin from the fact that he was descended from King David through Jesus' brother James. By 1795 he was in an insane asylum in Islington, but he garnered a significant following. Another millenarian group active at the same time followed Joanna Southcott (1750–1814), who claimed to be the "woman clothed with the sun" of Revelation 12.

The distance between Joachim of Fiore in the twelfth century and Joanna Southcott seven hundred years later can be measured in many different ways, but in some respects they are similar, in that both were driven to comb the Bible in search of divine clues about the course of history and the time of its prophetic conclusion, which is the essence of millenarianism.

[*See also* French Revolution; Priestley, Joseph; Revealed Religion; *and* Roman Catholicism.]

BIBLIOGRAPHY

Christianson, P. *Reformers and Babylon*. Toronto, 1978.
Clouse, R. G. "The Rebirth of Millenarianism." In *Puritans, the Millennium and the Future of Israel*, edited by P. Toon, pp. 42–65. Cambridge and London, 1970. An excellent and detailed survey of seventeenth-century millenarian theory.
Cohn, N. *The Pursuit of the Millennium*. 2d ed. London, 1970. A classic book, emphasizing the Middle Ages and a sociological interpretation of millenarianism.
Firth, K. R. *The Apocalyptic Tradition in Reformation Britain*. Oxford, 1979.
Harrison, J. F. C. *The Second Coming: Popular Millenarianism, 1780–1850*. London, 1979. A good source for Richard Brothers and Joanna Southcott.
Katz, D. S. and R. H. Popkin. *Messianic Revolution: Radical Religious Politics to the End of the Second Millennium*. New York, 1999. A general survey of millenarianism from Joachim of Fiore to American fundamentalism and Waco.
Knox, R. A. *Enthusiasm: A Chapter in the History of Religion with Special Reference to the XVII and XVIII Centuries*. Oxford, 1950. A classic book.
McGinn, B. *Visions of the End: Apocalyptic Traditions in the Middle Ages*. New York, 1979.
Reeves, M. E. *The Influence of Prophecy in the Later Middle Ages*. Oxford, 1969. A standard treatment.
Tuveson, E. L. *Millennium and Utopia*. Berkeley and Los Angeles, 1949.

DAVID S. KATZ

MILLER, SAMUEL (1769–1850), American Presbyterian minister and professor.

Miller was a leading proponent in the United States of a cautious and conservative appropriation of the Enlightenment. A native of Delaware, he was educated at the University of Pennsylvania and studied theology with Charles Nisbet, the first president of Dickinson College. Ordained to the Presbyterian ministry in 1793, Miller served several churches in New York City. He quickly became a major figure in his denomination, was elected moderator of its governing body in 1806, and played an important role in the creation of Princeton Theological Seminary in 1812. He was appointed as the second professor at the seminary in 1813 and taught ecclesiastical history and church government there until ill health forced his retirement in 1849.

As a pastor in New York, Miller established himself as a man of letters deeply engaged with the Enlightenment. He was a member of the Friendly Society, a group of intellectuals who gathered to read the works of writers such as Condorcet, Volney, Mary Wollstonecraft, and William Godwin. In 1803, Miller published his magnum opus in two volumes. *A Brief Retrospect of the Eighteenth Century*, styled by some as one of the first intellectual histories written by an American, is largely derivative, but it covers developments in the world of ideas with a breadth suggestive of the French *encyclopédistes*. It surveys work in geology, medicine, agriculture, geography, the fine arts, philosophy, and literature.

Miller's stance toward the new learning was ambivalent. On the one hand, he rejoiced that knowledge had advanced to a degree that previous generations "would have anticipated with astonishment, or pronounced altogether impossible"; on the other, he remained skeptical of notions of unlimited progress and of human perfectibility. Although human learning might attain great things, "extravagant expectations" would fail. Moreover, advances in knowledge would come by "patient inquiry, by faithful observation" and not "by fanciful speculation, by the dreams of hypothesis, by vain boasting, or by waging war against Nature's God!" (*Brief Retrospect*, vol. 2, pp. 440, 441, 442.) Miller endorsed Enlightenment to the extent that it was cautious, avoided skepticism, eschewed theorizing in favor of inductive research, and placed its findings within a theistic framework. His views reflected the influence of the Baconian ideal and of the Scottish common sense philosophy then becoming nearly ubiquitous among American philosophers, theologians, and moralists. Miller, in short, was a conspicuous representative of an increasingly influential movement that acknowledged the achievements of the Enlightenment while simultaneously repudiating its radical implications and seeking to incorporate it within a Christian worldview.

After *A Brief Retrospect*, Miller's major published works dealt with ecclesiastical topics. For example, he wrote against the office of bishop in *Concerning the Constitution and Orders of the Christian Ministry* (1807). In such works as *Letters on Clerical Manners and Habits* (1827), *Letters to Presbyterians* (first published as a series of articles in 1831), and *Essay on the Warrant, Nature, and Duties of the Office of Ruling Elder in the Presbyterian Church* (1831), he showed increasing concern for correct doctrine and proper polity—a preoccupation reflecting intramural Presbyterian debates in which Miller was engaged, and which would split the denomination in 1837. Yet despite the narrowing compass of his work, Miller did not entirely abandon the urbanity and breadth of interests that had characterized *A Brief Retrospect*. Among other topics, he wrote in his later career on slavery, the masonic movement, and temperance.

[*See also* Men and Women of Letters.]

BIBLIOGRAPHY

Chinard, Gilbert. "A Landmark in American Intellectual History: Samuel Miller's *A Brief Retrospect of the Eighteenth Century*." *Princeton University Library Chronicle* 14 (1953), 53–71.

Lane, Belden C. "Presbyterian Republicanism: Miller and the Eldership as an Answer to Lay-Clerical Tensions." *Journal of Presbyterian History* 56 (1978), 311–324.

Loetscher, Lefferts A. *Facing the Enlightenment and Pietism: Archibald Alexander and the Founding of Princeton Theological Seminary*. Westport, Conn., 1983.

May, Henry F. *The Enlightenment in America*. New York, 1976.

Miller, Samuel. *The Life of Samuel Miller*. Philadelphia, 1869. Still the fullest biographical treatment, by the subject's son.

Schorsch, Anita. "Samuel Miller, Renaissance Man: His Legacy of 'True Taste.'" *Journal of Presbyterian History* 66 (1988), 71–88.

Stephens, Bruce M. "Watchmen on the Walls of Zion: Samuel Miller and the Christian Ministry." *Journal of Presbyterian History* 56 (1978), 296–309.

JAMES H. MOORHEAD

MIRANDA, FRANCISCO (1750–1816), Venezuelan revolutionary.

Born in Caracas to a prosperous merchant family, Miranda enjoyed many of the privileges afforded the sons of wealthier Latin American families. However, his family never attained a position of high social status, a fact that no doubt influenced the young Miranda and would shape both his outlook and some of the choices he would make later in life.

Miranda's father, Sebastián de Miranda y Ravelo, a native of Spain, had emigrated from the Canary Islands as a young man, striking out for the New World in search of financial opportunities. His success enabled him to marry the daughter of an established creole family. The status of Miranda's family, however, was complicated by the traditions and mores of Caracas society.

The eighteenth century was a time of gradual social change and increasing discontent, particularly among the colonial elite. This was particularly true among affluent creole families, American-born whites of Spanish descent, who had been residents of the colony for generations. They regarded themselves as its social elite, frequently adopting aristocratic airs toward newly arrived *peninsulares*. While many recent Spanish immigrants tended to be merchants and working professionals, the landed creole elite derived their wealth from enormous land grants awarded by the Spanish crown in return for early exploration and colonization efforts. Having lived in the region for successive generations, the creoles had begun to identify themselves not as Spaniards, but as natives of their own regions. An increasing sense of pride in their homelands led creoles to question the distant authority of the crown.

Under Charles III, the Spanish crown seized on the Enlightenment ideas of greater rationalization of administration, centralization of authority, economic reforms through the establishment of monopolistic companies and increased taxation, and a greater emphasis on the collection of demographic, geographic, and botanical information. In addition, the Spanish crown now insisted that the highest military, government, civil, and religious positions be reserved for peninsulares, Spanish-born colonists. The creoles chafed at these new restrictions on their access to administrative power and wealth. This attempt to tighten control on the colonies, coinciding as it did with a nascent sense of nationalism, served only to alienate further the increasingly dissatisfied elite. As the eighteenth century wore on, the creoles and merchant *peninsulares* began to form an uneasy alliance, realizing that their interests would be better served by achieving greater control over economic and political power.

In Caracas, the young Miranda found his own road to advancement blocked due to official restrictions of the royal administration, as well as lingering social divisions. Like many of his social class, Miranda had received a classical education at the Academy of Santa Rosa in Caracas, followed by enrollment in the Royal and Pontifical University of Caracas. Miranda's education clearly stimulated his great curiosity and endowed him with a lifelong interest in books. Nevertheless, rather more of a dilettante than an intellectual, he left the university before completing his degree. Shortly afterward, his father became embroiled in a petty dispute over social privileges pertaining to his military service in Spain, an occurrence that further revealed the determination of the creole aristocracy to guard its rights and privileges. Unable to secure a position in the local military, in 1771, Miranda embarked for Cádiz, Spain, where he purchased a commission in the army. It would be more than thirty years before he returned to Venezuela.

Before joining the military, Miranda traveled in Spain, continuing his studies and collecting books for what eventually became an impressive private library. Among the items he purchased were works by the English satirist Alexander Pope and the Scottish essayist David Hume, an essay on government by John Locke, as well as historical works about the New World by Bartolomé de Las Casas, the famous Dominican who had condemned Spanish mistreatment of the Indians in the Americas, and Abbé Guillaume Raynal, who criticized European colonization of the Americas in his *Histoire philosophique*. The avid reader also acquired works by Rousseau and Voltaire. As an officer, Miranda fought in North Africa, and when Spain joined its Bourbon ally France in support of the American colonial revolution against Britain, Miranda took part in battles in the Caribbean, rising to the rank of colonel. Apparently too outspoken for the military lifestyle, he found himself involved in disputes over what he regarded as questionable practices and poor leadership in the Spanish army. Finally, accused of a misuse of funds and threatened with imprisonment, Miranda fled to the United States.

When Miranda arrived in 1783, the newly liberated colonies had recently signed a preliminary treaty of peace with England. During his nearly two years in the United States, Miranda traveled extensively, visiting each of the thirteen states. A man of enormous charm and an excellent conversationalist, he met an impressive number of statesmen and influential individuals, among them Samuel Adams, Tom Paine, Alexander Hamilton, Henry Knox, and the presidents of Yale and Harvard. He attended sessions of the Massachusetts and New Hampshire legislatures and visited numerous battlefields of the Revolutionary War, carefully noting their strategic merits. During that time, he also began to formulate a plan for the liberation of Spanish America, discussing his ideas with some of those he met. Miranda developed a mixed opinion of the young United States, admiring the religious tolerance and relative social equality (at least among white men), while deploring what he viewed as the ignorance of some elected officials leading him to question the ability of common citizens to rule themselves. In Miranda's view, the government of the United States was successful in so far as it followed the British example.

Wishing to further extend his knowledge of the world, and especially to evaluate different forms of government, Miranda embarked for England in 1785. While there he made an unsuccessful attempt to settle his dispute with the Spanish military, and then set off on a tour of the Continent. His travels took him through Prussia, Austria, Italy, and Greece where, as in the United States, he visited battlefields, libraries, and museums, and met with many illustrious figures. In Russia, he charmed Catherine the Great and spent two years at her court attempting in leisurely fashion to win her patronage for his liberation plan. Ultimately, she granted him a thousand rubles and the support of the Russian embassies.

Returning to England in 1789, Miranda made earnest efforts to obtain international aid for overthrowing Spanish control of its American colonies. Realizing that poorly developed methods of communication and transportation would hamper unified action across such a vast territory, and recognizing the strength of the Spanish navy, Miranda desired a strong ally with vessels, funds, and soldiers to spare. During the next several years he sought to take advantage of shifting alliances among France, England, and Spain, seeking an opportune moment to convince one of the former to join his revolutionary plan. Desiring both to win French support and to observe firsthand the momentous events occurring in the country, Miranda joined the revolutionary forces as a general. With Robespierre's rise to power, however, Miranda fell out of favor and was jailed for nearly three years. On his release, he returned to England where he continued to lobby for support, while he drafted proposals outlining his military strategy and describing the constitutional monarchy he believed would best suit the needs of a liberated Spanish America.

Long an admirer of the British system of government, he favored a bicameral legislature featuring an elected and an appointed house. Borrowing from Amerindian traditions, he proposed that the two executive officers be called Incas; one would administer from the capital city, while the other would travel throughout the empire. During times of national emergency, the Incas could relinquish power to an appointed dictator for a temporary one-year term. Customs duties would be reduced to a flat rate and oppressive tributes exacted from the Indians by the crown would be discontinued. Further, whites, Indians, and free blacks were to be treated equally under the law. Local power would rest in the cabildos, which would increase their membership to include Indian and black representatives. Although Roman Catholicism would remain the national religion, he advocated separation of church and state, religious toleration, and abolition of the Inquisition.

Finally, in 1805, frustrated by a lack of official British commitment to his cause, and thinking to take advantage of the dispute between Spain and the United States over the Florida boundary, Miranda sailed for New York. Meetings with President Thomas Jefferson and Secretary of State James Madison failed to yield official U.S. support, but Miranda did succeed in winning private help from a shipowner and a wealthy New York merchant. With their help, Miranda gathered arms and supplies and enlisted men, usually under false or exaggerated pretexts. The *Leander* sailed to Santo Domingo, where two smaller ships and a handful of men joined their meager expedition. By this time, the Spanish forces had become aware of his intentions and easily squelched the attack when the vessels sailed into Puerto Cabello in Venezuela. Miranda and some of his men escaped in the *Leander*, later mounting a second expedition that landed at Coro. Unable to secure support from English forces in the Caribbean and failing to rally the townspeople, Miranda was again defeated and returned to England.

Yet not all Venezuelans were indifferent to the cause of independence. Revolutionary rumblings grew louder in the early nineteenth century, increasing when France invaded Spain, forced Ferdinand's abdication, and placed Napolean's brother on the throne. In 1810, a provisional junta was formed in Caracas, which denied the authority of the Regency. Revolution was underway.

In England, Miranda met Simón Bolívar and Andrés Bello, who had been sent to petition the English government to recognize their cause. With their backing, Miranda returned to Caracas. As a member of the Sociedad Patriótica, Miranda shared his military and political experiences, debating issues and helping to determine policies. In particular, Miranda urged that Venezuela formally declare its independence, which it did in July 1811. Miranda had been absent from Venezuela for many years, however—while some welcomed his return and acknowledged his long commitment to independence, others distrusted him, seeing his outlook and loyalties as more European than Spanish American. Some viewed with alarm his involvement in the French Revolution, fearing the ultimately radical nature of that struggle, particularly in light of the recent slave rebellion in Saint Domingue (present-day Haiti).

Nor did Miranda always agree with the decisions of his countrymen. To his dismay, his proposal for a constitutional monarchy was rejected. Instead the Constitution of 1811 established a federal republic headed by three chief executive magistrates to be chosen by indirect election. Members of the Senate would be elected by the provincial legislatures, while the members of the House of Representatives would be chosen by the electors. Although the *fueros*, or special privileges of the clergy, were abolished, Roman Catholicism was declared to be the national and sole religion of the people. The constitution guaranteed freedom of expression and of the press, and abolished the slave trade. Although the constitution granted citizens the rights of liberty and equality, slaves were not emancipated and restrictions on voting rights in effect guaranteed that political power would remain in the hands of the white upper classes.

Meanwhile royalist forces continued to oppose the new government. When a massive earthquake shook the country in March 1812, revolutionary forces were devastated and many citizens, interpreting the disaster as a sign of God's anger, renounced the independence movement. In an attempt to regain control and stability, the Venezuelan Congress named Miranda commander in chief, granting him dictatorial authority. The royalists kept up their attacks and Miranda was unable to defeat their forces. On 25 July 1812, Miranda capitulated to Domingo de Monteverde with the understanding that no harm would come to the revolutionaries or their property. Despite Miranda's explanation of wanting to save patriot lives, many, including Bolívar, saw his capitulation as treasonous. Miranda attempted to flee to England, but with Bolívar's help, the Spanish captured him. He was imprisoned in Cádiz, Spain, where he died in 1816.

Whatever his failings as a military and political leader, Miranda was a precursor of Spanish American independence. For most of his adult life, he maintained a vision of an independent Spanish America. His nearly single-minded pursuit of this goal brought the cause of Spanish American liberation to the attention of many of the foremost statesmen and women of his day. Although he did not live to see his dream of independence truly become a reality, Miranda was among the actors who were pivotal to setting the revolutionary process in motion.

[*See also* Bolívar, Simón; Latin America; *and* Spain.]

BIBLIOGRAPHY

Egea, Antonio. *El pensamiento filosófico y politico de Francisco de Miranda*. Caracas, 1983. A discussion of the philosophical and political ideas that were particularly influential in shaping Miranda's outlook and worldview.

Harvey, Robert. *Liberators: Latin America's Struggle for Independence, 1810–1830*. Woodstock, N.Y., 2000. Engaging account written in a journalistic style focuses on seven key figures, Miranda among them, of Latin American liberation.

Los Libros de Miranda. Caracas, 1979. Includes two essays, "Los libros de Miranda" by Arturo Uslar Pietri and "Advertencia bibliográfica" by Pedro Grases, as well as facsimile reproductions of a London bookdealer's catalogs (1828 and 1833) from the sale of Miranda's private library. Lists more than 3,000 volumes.

Lynch, John, ed. *Latin American Revolutions, 1808–1826: Old and New World Origins*. Norman, Okla., and London, 1994. Series of topically organized essays by leading scholars examines causes of revolution in colonial Spanish American and Brazil. Although discussion of Miranda is brief, work provides an excellent interpretation of the complex social, economic, and political structures of the time.

Miranda, Francisco de. *Colombeia*. 13 vols. Preface by J. L. Salcedo-Bastardo. Introduction, bibliography, prologue, and notes by Josefina Rodríguez de Alonso. Caracas, 1978. Edition of the Archive of General Francisco de Miranda (24 vols., 1929–1950), which includes documents and correspondence pertaining to Miranda's family, education, and travels.

Robertson, William Spence. *The Life of Miranda*. 2 vols. New York, 1929, 1969. The first detailed biography of Miranda based on his personal archives. Quotes broadly from Miranda's journals and letters providing the reader some insight into Miranda's perspective and his immediate impressions during his travels.

Thorning, Joseph F. *Miranda: World Citizen*. Gainsville, Fla., 1952. A lively biography of Miranda. Written in the spirit of the post–World War II era, the book tends to emphasize Miranda's democratic ideals, beliefs in human equality, and the search for order and stability without autocracy. Includes bibliographical essay.

Whitaker, Arthur P., ed. *Latin America and the Enlightenment*. New York, 1942. A classic work containing six essays on the impact of the Enlightenment on Spanish America and Brazil. Indicates the prominence of French influences, and discusses the spread of ideas in the New World and their reception by various social groups, as well as the influence of the Enlightenment on the Spanish crown.

KATHERINE D. MCCANN

MOEURS. *See* Sociability.

MONEY. *See* Economic Thought.

MONINO, JOSE, conde de Floridablanca (1728–1808), Spanish diplomat and administrator.

Monino, a native of the city of Murcia in eastern Spain, studied law; as a practicing lawyer, he acquired a number of influential clients, including the duke of Alba, at one time president of the Council of Castile. This helped to smooth the way for Monino's own entry in 1766 into the Council as one of its *fiscales*, or lawyers, for criminal matters. Among his earliest tasks in this post was the investigation of the so-called Esquilache riots in Madrid earlier that year. Monino, a staunch defender of royal jurisdiction against the pretensions of the Roman Catholic Church, firmly supported the expulsion of the Jesuits that followed (1767). Following the provincial riots of 1766 and the government's request that its intendants report on the state of agriculture, Monino (and Pedro Rodríguez Campomanes) wrote a commentary that favored reform and was published in 1771. Thereafter, he was appointed to the Spanish embassy in Rome, in part to secure the suppression of the Jesuits.

Monino's success in that effort (1773) was rewarded by Charles III with his promotion as count of Floridablanca. These successes also helped secure Floridablanca's appointment (1777) as secretary of state, an office he held for fifteen years. In this post, Floridablanca sought to reassert Spanish power against England—most notably, in the unsuccessful siege of Gibraltar (1782) and the recovery of Florida (1783)—while at the same time maintaining Spain's independence from France, as well as good relations with Portugal, Rome, Naples, and Parma. At home, he continued to encourage agricultural improvement, for example by establishing public credit institutions (*montes pios*) to help small farmers to borrow necessary funds. It was Floridablanca who initially allowed the import of the French *Encyclopédie méthodique* (1783), but he was later obliged to ban it and to arrange the publication of an effective response, by Juan Pablo Forner, defending Spain against severe criticisms in that publication.

As de facto chief minister, Floridablanca faced the opposition of the so-called Aragonese party, led by the count of Aranda, a confrontation which in part reflected different political and constitutional positions and programs. Aranda and his supporters favored a greater role for the old councils, while Floridablanca favored the superiority of the new secretaries of state. Toward the end of his period of office, in 1787, Charles III created—at Floridablanca's suggestion—the Junta de Estado, an attempt to ensure greater coordination between the secretariats of state. A program of action for the new body envisaged reform of Spain's diocesan system, improved education of the clergy, and an improvement in the quality of the Inquisition and its officials, in the hope that these institutions could better, or even enlighten, the mass of the population. However, the outbreak of the French Revolution and fear of seditious ideas imported from France led Floridablanca to abandon his progressive credentials and gradually to restrict the press, partly in alliance with the Inquisition. This did not prevent his enemies from engineering his dismissal in 1792, which was followed by the reversal of some of his recent measures. Floridablanca was briefly imprisoned in Pamplona and later, again briefly, returned to the national political stage as president of the Junta Suprema Central, established following the revolt against the Napoleonic regime in 1808.

[*See also* Jesuits, *subentry on* Role in Politics; *and* Spain.]

BIBLIOGRAPHY

Artola, Miguel, ed. *Enciclopedia de historia de España*, vol. 4: *Diccionario biográfico*. Madrid, 1991. The best brief study of this key figure.

Herr, Richard. *The Eighteenth Century Revolution in Spain*. Princeton, N.J., 1958. A good English language account of contemporary Spain and of Floridablanca.

Lynch, John. *Bourbon Spain, 1700–1808*. Oxford, 1989. A general survey with useful details of Floridablanca and his work.

CHRISTOPHER STORRS

MONTAGU, ELIZABETH (1720–1800), English author and bluestocking.

Elizabeth Montagu was born on 2 October, at York, to Matthew and Elizabeth Drake Robinson. She grew up in Kent with eight siblings on an estate inherited and managed by her mother, who was reputedly a student of Bashua Makin. Although Mrs. Robinson's practicality and financial astuteness were mirrored in her daughter, the extroverted Elizabeth was temperamentally more akin to her father, a gregarious wit and accomplished painter. A precocious child whose education was encouraged by her step-grandfather, the Cambridge scholar and librarian Dr. Conyers Middleton, Elizabeth was befriended in 1732 by the first of her many correspondents, Lady Margaret Harley. Following Lady Margaret's marriage in 1734 to the second duke of Portland, Elizabeth periodically visited Bulstrode, the Portland estate, whose convivial environment possibly inspired the salon that Elizabeth later established.

On 5 August 1742, Elizabeth married Edward Montagu, grandson of the earl of Sandwich and member of Parliament for Huntingdon. Almost thirty years her senior, he was a scholarly man with a sizable fortune. Elizabeth's intelligence, beauty, and vivacity apparently compensated for her relatively modest dowry. The Montagu's only child, a son, was born 11 May 1743, but he died of convulsions in August of 1744. As her husband retreated into more solitary pursuits, Elizabeth sought solace in the informal socializing of the town of Tunbridge Wells, where she began cultivating a network of friendships and relationships unrestricted by class, age, or gender. By 1750, her Mayfair residence in London, on Hill Street, had become the daytime meeting place for a small group of men and women who shared her interest in rational entertainment. The heterosocial composition, informality, and decorous moral tone of the gatherings distinguished them from many contemporaneous French salons. Eschewing both the political discourse common to male clubs and the dancing and card games typical of mixed company, the coterie focused on literary topics selected by their hostess, whose circular seating arrangement epitomized "Enlightenment domesticity"—a philosophy that minimized competitiveness and emphasized, irrespective of class and gender, friendship and piety that were grounded in reason. Typical of the English Enlightenment, a preoccupation with propriety, with rectitude, and with the reconciliation of reason and religion served to engage many of the participants, who were popularly known as *bluestockings*. The sobriquet initially embraced witty and learned people of both sexes, but by 1800, it was usually applied, often derogatorily, to female savants. Montagu's circle included such luminaries as Samuel Johnson, David Garrick, Sir Joshua Reynolds, Sir George Lyttleton, Elizabeth Carter, Hannah More, and Fanny Burney.

Widowed in 1775, Montagu inherited the bulk of her husband's estate, farms, and collieries (coal production), worth £7,000 per year. Her enlightened administration of those properties, valued at £10,000 per year at her death, situate this bluestocking in the agricultural revolution and proto-Industrial Revolution. Her inheritance financed numerous acts of benevolence (schools for miners' children; an annual May Day dinner for London chimney sweeps; and annuities for family, friends, and needy literati) and a new residence at Portman Square in London, where she hosted as many as seven hundred guests. Such ostentation made her vulnerable to the growing backlash against learned ladies. The woman once complimented by Samuel Johnson for her exceptional intelligence was lampooned by Richard Cumberland in 1786 as a pretentious Vanessa (an allusion to Jonathan

Swift's mock-epic prodigy in his *Cadmus and Vanessa*): even her beneficence was criticized as vainglorious. Almost blind, Montagu died on 25 August 1800.

Montagu's publications consist of three essays in Lyttleton's *Dialogues of the Dead* (1760) and the *Essay on the Writings and Genius of Shakespeare* (1769), a rejoinder to Voltaire's critique of the bard. Samuel Johnson's dismissive judgment of that piece has been sustained by later scholars. Montagu's written legacy is found instead in her voluminous correspondence, which provides a window into the age of English Enlightenment.

[*See also* Feminist Theory; London; *and* Salons, *subentry on* England.]

BIBLIOGRAPHY

WORKS BY MONTAGU
Elizabeth Montagu: The Queen of the Blue-stockings: Her Correspondence from 1720–1761. 2 vols. Edited by Emily J. Climenson. London, 1906.
An Essay on the Writings and Genius of Shakespeare, Compared with the Greek and French Dramatic Poets, with Some Remarks upon the Misrepresentations of Mons. de Voltaire. London, 1769.
Mrs. Montagu, "Queen of the Blues": Her Letters and Friendships from 1762 to 1800. ed. 2 vols. Edited by Reginald Blunt. London, n.d.

WORKS ABOUT MONTAGU
Beckett, J. V. "Elizabeth Montagu: Bluestocking Turned Landlady." *Huntington Library Quarterly* 49 (Spring 1986), 149–164.
Bodek, Evelyn Gordon. "Salonières and Bluestockings: Educated Obsolescence and Germinating Feminism." *Feminist Studies* 3 (1976), 185–199.
Brown, Irene. "Domesticity, Feminism, and Friendship: Female Aristocratic Culture and Marriage in England, 1660–1760." *Journal of Family History* 7 (Winter 1982), 406–424.
Larson, Edith Sedgwick. "A Measure of Power: The Personal Charity of Elizabeth Montagu." In *Studies in Eighteenth-Century Culture*, vol. 16. Edited by O. M. Brack. Madison, Wis., 1986.
Myers, Sylvia Harcstark. *The Bluestocking Circle: Women, Friendship, and the Life of the Mind in Eighteenth-Century England.* Oxford, 1990.
Ross, Ian. "A Bluestocking over the Border: Mrs. Elizabeth Montagu's Aesthetic Adventures in Scotland, 1766." *Huntington Library Quarterly* 28 (May 1965), 213–233.

CARLA H. HAY

MONTAGU, MARY WORTLEY

MONTAGU, MARY WORTLEY (1689–1762), English woman of letters.

Born Lady Mary Pierrepont, Montagu was an avid reader who taught herself Latin as a young girl. She met Edward Wortley Montagu, a Whig member of Parliament and a friend of Steele and Addison, who also loved literature, and the two corresponded. Despite her father's opposition, the couple married secretly in August 1712. Her marriage soon disappointed the young woman, but she decided to devote herself to promoting her husband's career. The Whigs were victorious in the elections of 1715, and Edward Wortley Montagu was elected a member of Parliament.

In London, Lady Mary met many famous writers, including the abbé Conti, Joseph Addison, and Alexander Pope. In 1715, she contracted smallpox, which spoiled her beauty but not her charm, and left her with an interest in finding its cure.

Edward Wortley Montagu became ambassador to the Ottoman Court in 1716. Lady Mary left with him and her son for Constantinople, satisfying a deep desire to travel. The letters she wrote to her sister Frances, later published as *Letters from the East*, are an invaluable record of conditions in eastern Europe and the customs of the Turks at the beginning of the eighteenth century. In Turkey, she discovered the medical use of inoculation against smallpox and did not hesitate to use it for her children.

On her return to London, Montagu was celebrated. She re-entered high society and promoted the idea of inoculation at court. In 1722 the couple bought a home in Twickenham, where Pope also lived. The friendship between Montagu and Pope strengthened before eventually collapsing in a literary quarrel around 1730. From December 1737 to March 1738, she published the *Nonsense of Commonsense*, a weekly paper that replied to the journal of the Tory opposition, *Common Sense*. Her essays gave early and vigorous expression to feminist ideas.

In 1736, Montagu met Francesco Algarotti, author of *Newtonianismo per le dame* (Newtonianism for Ladies, 1737), and fell in love with him. She followed him to Europe, using her health as a pretext. Thereafter, she lived in several cities—Genoa, Geneva, and Avignon—from which she wrote to Algarotti, who kept his distance. Her passionate letters to him, written in French, reflect the influence of the *Lettres portugaises* (1669) of Gabriel-Joseph Guilleragues.

In 1747, Montagu moved to the castle of Gottolengo with the unscrupulous count Ugolino Palazzi, who became her companion. She still corresponded frequently with her husband and with her daughter, Lady Bute. In 1756, she left Gottolengo for Padua and Venice, where she renewed her friendship with Algarotti. In 1761, after her husband's death in England, she left Italy and returned to London, where she died.

Lady Mary Montagu was a notable figure in the literary and intellectual movements of her time, even though her literary output was not large. It includes poems, a play, some journalism, and a short epistolary novel as well as the letters. Her daughter destroyed her personal journals. The last, however, earned her a place in literary history. She was careful to edit her travel letters from Turkey before confiding them to a friend. They eventually appeared in several editions and were welcomed by the greatest writers of the time. Voltaire, in a review in the *Gazette littéraire* (4 April 1764), called them "letters for all nations" and, praising her audacity, described Lady Mary as "the English woman with the greatest mind and the greatest strength of spirit." He counted her among the few women who were free from prejudice, and in his *Lettres philosophiques* (1734) he lauded her for promoting inoculation. Her truthful spirit, biting irony, and acerbic style even led him to rank her above the two great French female epistolary writers, Mme. de Sévigné and Mme. de Maintenon.

[*See also* Addison, Joseph; Astell, Mary; Authorship; Conti, Antonio; Feminist Theory; Inoculation and Vaccination; Journals, Newspapers, and Gazettes, *subentry on* Great Britain; Medicine, *subentry on* Practice of Medicine; Men and Women of Letters; *and* Pope, Alexander.]

BIBLIOGRAPHY

WORKS BY MONTAGU

The Complete Letters of Lady Mary Wortley Montagu. Edited by Robert Halsband. Oxford, 1965–1967. The standard edition of her correspondence.

Embassy to Constantinople: The Travels of Lady Mary Wortley Montagu. Edited by Christopher Pick. London, 1988. Letters describing her Turkish journey, illustrated with contemporary prints.

Essays and Poems and Simplicity, a Comedy. Edited by Robert Halsband and I. Grundy. Oxford, 1993.

WORKS ABOUT MONTAGU

Halsband, Robert. *The Life of Lady Mary Wortley Motagu*. Oxford, 1956. The standard life.

Halsband, Robert. "Lady Mary Wortley Montagu as Letter-Writer." *Publications of the Modern Language Association* 30 (1965), 1555–1563. Presents the epistolary writings of Montagu and certain aspects of their reception.

Haroche-Bouzinac, Geneviève. "'I thought the first duty was truth,' Lady Mary Wortley Montagu." In *La lettre et la politique*. Paris, 1996. On the moral view of politics in Montagu's European letters.

Lew, Joseph. "Lady Mary's Portable Seraglio." *Eighteenth Century Studies* 24 (1991), 432–450. Montagu's experience in the East.

Moulin, A.-M., and R. Chuvin. *L'Islam au péril des femmes: Une anglaise en Turquie au XVIIIᵉ siècle*. Paris, 1981. Well-documented introduction to Montagu's trip to Turkey.

GENEVIÈVE HAROCHE-BOUZINAC

Translated from French by Susan Romanosky

MONTESQUIEU, CHARLES-LOUIS DE SECONDAT,

baron de La Brède et de (1689–1755), French writer and political philosopher.

Montesquieu was one of France's most influential Enlightenment authors. His work spans a broad array of literary forms and topics, but he is most widely known for *Lettres persanes* (The Persian Letters, 1721) and *L'esprit des lois* (The Spirit of Laws, 1748). His writing resonates with the values of human freedom, moderation, and toleration, while demonstrating a realist and detailed attentiveness to the complexity of rules, customs, physical forces, and human motivations that shape social and political life.

Life. Born at the chateau of La Brède, south of Bordeaux in the Guyenne region of France, Montesquieu came into a family with a long history of service to the kingdom. In noble tradition, a village beggar was named as his godfather in order to remind him of his obligations to the poor. He received formal education from the Oratoriens at the Collège de Juilly in Meaux and at the faculty of law of the University of Bordeaux. On graduation, he made his way to Paris, where he acquired more practical knowledge of the judicial system through legal observation and met various intellectuals, including Pierre Desmolets and Nicolas Fréret, who encouraged his broad interests and helped to shape the course of his future work. His provincial origins remained of importance to him, however, and he kept his Gascon accent all his life.

After the death of his father in 1713, Montesquieu returned to La Brède to manage the family estates, including extensive vineyards, and to begin a career in law at the *parlement* of Bordeaux. Starting out as a councillor, he then inherited the office of *président à mortier* and the title of baron de Montesquieu from his uncle. For twelve years, he worked almost exclusively as a magistrate for the criminal court (*la Tournelle*), a position that not only furthered his understanding of the law and its application

Montesquieu. Portrait (c. 1728) after an original by Jacques-Antoine Dassier. (Châteaux de Versailles et de Trianon, Versailles, France/Réunion des Musées Nationaux/Art Resource, NY.)

but also presented him with a rich tableau of the foibles of humanity. He married Jeanne Lartigue, a practicing Calvinist, with whom he would have three children. In 1716, he joined the Academy of Bordeaux; he became its director for the year in 1718.

It was also during these years that Montesquieu began his first serious writings, including his "Memoir on the Problem of Public Debt." In 1721, *Lettres persanes* was published anonymously by the Amsterdam publisher Desbordes. It sold prodigiously, with at least ten editions in the first year. On the surface, it can be read as a spirited satire of French society from 1711 to 1720 from the point of view of two Persian travellers, Usbek and Rica. However, through the account of the difficulties arising in Usbek's harem during his absence, as well as allusions to the Persian court itself, the work also provides a structure for the comparison and contrast of competing forms of domination and rule and the practices of dissimulation, self-deception, and cruelty they can engender. The concluding letter, in the form of a suicide note addressed to Usbek from one of his unfaithful wives, serves as an eloquent and spirited call for freedom from domestic tyranny as well as an indictment against despotism in all its forms.

Montesquieu's authorship of this work was soon made known, and this helped him gain entry to the literary salons of Paris. He made frequent trips to the capital, making contacts in courtly circles and frequenting the salons of Anne-Thérèse de Lambert and Marie de Vichy-Chamrond, marquise du Deffand as well as the Club de l'Entresol, also attended by well-known political economists such as Jean-Baptiste Boyer, marquis d'Argens and Charles-Irénée Castel, Abbé de Saint-Pierre. Montesquieu wrote several pieces in the late 1720s for presentation and discussion in these forums; his growing renown led to his election to the Académie Française in 1727.

Montesquieu was still not satisfied with his career, so he decided to sell his judicial office and to pursue his ambitions in other ways. He embarked on a three-year journey around Europe, during which he conducted numerous interviews on a wide variety of matters. In Rome he met Fouquet, a French Jesuit who had spent thirty years as a missionary in China, and they had many discussions about the Far East. In Venice he encountered Claude-Alexandre Bonneval, who had disgraced himself in both the French and Austrian armies (and who became an officer in the Turkish army), and John Law, a famous Scottish economist who had caused the financial ruin of many in France. The most significant portion of his travels was his stay in England, where he was a regular visitor to the debates of the House of Commons and became acquainted with many of England's elite. During his stay, he was elected a member of the Royal Society and was inducted into the Freemasons. Though few papers remain from his stay in England, it is widely thought that it was one of the most formative experiences of his intellectual development.

On return from his travels, Montesquieu embarked on a life devoted to the managing of his estates and to writing, interspersed with regular trips to Paris. In 1734, he published his *Considérations sur les causes de la grandeur des Romains et de leur décadence* (Considerations on the Causes of the Greatness of the Romans and of Their Decline), in which he attacked the notion of providential history (associated in his day with the writings of the seventeenth-century bishop Jacques Bénigne Bossuet) and began to develop a theory of general causes, both physical and moral, that could serve more adequately for long-term historical explanation. He shared a fascination with the politics of ancient Rome with many contemporaries, but he went against the dominant fashion of praising imperial Rome as a glorious precursor and model for contemporary monarchy. Instead, Montesquieu expressed a nostalgic admiration for the Roman republic and saw the imperial designs of successive emperors as ultimately destructive of the regime itself. His engagement with the lessons of Roman history remained a defining feature of his later work.

The following years were devoted to the preparation and writing of his major work, *L'esprit des lois*, published by Barillot in Geneva in 1748. Hume, a correspondent of Montesquieu's, praised the work as "the best system of political knowledge that, perhaps, has ever yet been communicated to the world." His objective was no less than to provide a comprehensive understanding of the diversity of positive laws, morals, and manners that govern human conduct. The immensity of the task was not without its costs: Montesquieu's eyesight grew progressively worse. Nearby blind from cataracts by the end of his project, he was obliged to dictate large portions of the manuscript. The work was, in general, well received in intellectual circles, though Montesquieu fought vigorously in subsequent years to defend it against ecclesiastical criticism and censure. In 1750, he published his *Défense de l'esprit des lois* (Defense of the Spirit of Laws) to rebut charges that he espoused Spinozism and that he was a deist. Although *L'esprit des lois* was ultimately censored by the Vatican in 1751 and placed on the Index of Forbidden Books, the chancellor of France did permit the printing and sale of the work in Paris.

One of Montesquieu's last works was the *Mémoire sur la Constitution* (Memoir on the Constitution). Addressed to the king, it stood as a defense of religious toleration in the context of the ongoing persecution of Jansenists and continued disputes within the Gallican church. He also began to write his *Essai sur le goût* (An Essay on Taste,

1785) for the *Encyclopédie*. Shortly before his death, he penned with characteristic stoic dignity: "There are two matters left for me to attend to: one, to know how to be ill; and the other, to know how to die." He died in Paris in February 1755, having received Catholic rites, and was buried in the Ste. Geneviève chapel of Saint-Sulpice.

Major Themes. There are three important aspects of Montesquieu's work: his deep intellectual curiosity and extensive scholarship, which worked toward a comprehensive understanding of the diversity of social and political affairs; his strong criticism of all forms of tyranny, including incipient forms he saw within France itself; and his interest in political and social arrangements, including those of England, that promoted political moderation and freedom.

The major objective of Montesquieu's key work, *L'esprit des lois*, was to provide a framework whereby the myriad laws, customs, and morals that shaped human behavior could be better understood. As he states in the Preface, "I began by examining humanity and I believed that, amidst the diversity of laws and mores, they were not led by their fancies alone." His focus was the principles, or the spirit, that informed the various ways in which humans organized their collective lives. The uncovering of these principles involved a systematic exploration of how various factors—including constitutional structure, popular customs, climate, commerce, and population—affect the life of communities. Notes from interviews and from the reading of travel accounts and histories gathered throughout his lifetime provided the material from which he developed his conclusions. In this respect, his work marked a departure from the traditional method of modern natural law theory exemplified by the work of Grotius and Pufendorf, who based their understanding of the principles of human society on an analysis of the fundamental commonalities in the nature and needs of human beings rather than on comparison and contrast of human beings in differing social contexts. In drawing from a wide variety of sources, Montesquieu sought to be all-encompassing, while remaining nonformulaic, so as to be able to account for a wide variety of human practices and the "nuances of things."

At the beginning of the work, Montesquieu divided regimes into three types: the republic, monarchy, and despotism. Each is distinguished by its nature—that is, the locus of the sovereign power—and its principle, the set of human passions that gives life to the regime. A republic is defined as a regime in which all or some sector of the people have sovereign power, animated by the principle of virtue or love of the republic. A monarchy is a regime in which one person governs by fixed and established laws, animated by the principle of honor; a despotism is a regime ruled by one person without law and is animated by the principle of fear. Montesquieu first showed how various factors such as education, criminal punishment, and the condition of women relate to these regime types; he went on to show how other factors such as climate, size, and commerce affect the laws. At the end of thirty-one books, he had provided a wide-ranging account of the diversity of social practice in the world, with reference to a vast range of travel and historical accounts.

His discussion of physical causes, particularly of climate, has been controversial since the publication of *L'esprit des lois*. Some have expressed concern that his ideas imply a form of determinism. Others recognized that Montesquieu held that moral causes, including laws themselves, are of greater weight and importance; they argued that, according to Montesquieu, climate is only one factor among a myriad that may help to shape the nature of collective life.

Another factor discussed by Montesquieu, which has received more recent scholarly attention, is that of commerce. Montesquieu noted the potentially peaceful effects of commerce, independently of physical causes, and its central role in the civilizing process ("Commerce corrupts pure morals…and polishes and softens barbarous morals" [XX, 1]). He saw great potential in the advent of modern commerce to transform modern European politics.

For some commentators, including the sociologist Émile Durkheim, Montesquieu's concern for empirical grounding, along with his general theory of moral and physical causes, makes his work a precursor to the discipline of sociology. Montesquieu does share a concern for comprehensive social explanation, but others recognize that one cannot ascribe to him any intent to treat social facts as things in a neutral way, because his judgments on the undesirability of certain forms of community and social practice are evident throughout his work. Instead, some recognize his work as his own unique, multifaceted adaptation of the comparative method, explored also in his earlier work, *Lettres persanes*, and evident in political theory since the work of Aristotle.

In broader terms, the main significance of Montesquieu's methodological approach is that it served to shift political thinking away from the seventeenth-century legalist tradition of social contract theory (identified with Hugo Grotius, Thomas Hobbes, and Samuel Pufendorf) and the moralist tradition of individualism (identified with La Rochefoucauld), both of which were identified at the time as bolstering established structures of absolutist rule. His methodological approach was thus intricately tied to a second major theme of his writing: his concern to demonstrate the evils of an excessive concentration of political power.

Montesquieu's indictment of despotism was based on his understanding of the effects of the concentration of power. By fostering a climate of fear, a despotic regime undermines associational life and a basic sense of sociality and solidarity that grounds human community. Citizens lose their potential for autonomous development and become, as Montesquieu stated, like beasts who only obey a creature who wills (I, 6). It is as if the portrayal of misery and ensuing chaos in the harem of *Lettres persanes* was offered as a general model of a despotic political regime in *L'esprit des lois*.

Montesquieu often identified this type of regime with the Orient, including the Ottoman Empire and Persia, as well as with the military governments of ancient Rome. Some, however, have questioned his portrayal as an inaccurate portrait of the complexity of power relations within those regimes and have discussed what polemical purposes Montesquieu had for his seeming caricature of despotism.

One answer is that Montesquieu's depiction served as a portrait of the latent possibilities within the absolutist tendencies of the French monarchy. Voltaire had praised the rule of Louis XIV the Sun King, and was, in general, an advocate of absolutist rule; in contrast, Montesquieu was critical of the means by which Louis XIV had stifled legitimate political opposition and centered the political life of France on his own person. In *Lettres persanes*, Montesquieu had harshly criticized and satirized Louis XIV's policies including the Revocation of the Edict of Nantes in 1685. He also recognized the weakened status of the French *parlements* in the face of growing central state power. This is bolstered by Montesquieu's remark in *L'esprit des lois* that monarchies have a tendency to degenerate into despotism, just as rivers flow into the sea (VIII, 17).

From this perspective, Montesquieu has been read as an apologist for various factions of the aristocratic reaction after the death of Louis XIV in 1715, whether among the feudal nobility of the sword, the nobility of the robe, or the local *parlements* themselves. Others see in his denunciation of despotism a more modernist agenda of promoting within France political freedoms of various constitutional forms. Putting aside the question of his contemporary political engagements, it is clear that, fundamentally, Montesquieu harbored a strong humanist concern for the universally debilitative effects of tyrannical rule.

It is through his strong denunciation of despotism that Montesquieu has become best known as a theorist of political freedom. In books XI and XII of *L'esprit des lois*, he drew the distinction between political liberty and civil liberty. Although he clearly shared sympathies with the civic humanist tradition in his concern for the quality of common life and his advocacy of political freedom, he did not share the civic humanist position of attributing political and civil freedom to all republican regimes. His reading of ancient history and his knowledge of the Dutch and Venetian republics in his day led him to acknowledge how forms of popular and aristocratic rule could work in corrupt ways. Instead, Montesquieu judged that liberty is to be found in moderate governments where power is not abused. Moderation, furthermore, can be attributed both to republican and monarchical forms, under the right circumstances. For Montesquieu, political liberty is not identified with self-rule but refers to a relation of fearlessness or security that citizens have with their own government, and civil liberty refers to how citizens can be protected justly from encroachments by one another. For both, the law is not only central but constitutive, insofar as it creates the climate in which security is assured. "In a state, that is, in a society where there are laws, liberty can consist only in having the power to do what one should want to do and in no way being constrained to do what one should not want to do" (XI, 3).

In book XI, 6, a chapter that received much attention during debates concerning the drafting of the U.S. constitution and was published autonomously at the end of the eighteenth century, Montesquieu provided his abstract analysis of the working of the English constitution. Some earlier scholars derived from this reading the doctrine of the separation of powers, but subsequent scholars have clearly demonstrated the more subtle analysis of Montesquieu, who recognized constitutional features requiring the sharing of legislative and executive powers among the two houses of Parliament and the crown. Some writers refer, more accurately, to Montesquieu's doctrine of a "balance of power." Key components of this chapter are Montesquieu's analytical division of government power into legislative, executive, and judicial—for the first time in the history of political ideas—and his notion that a concentration of all power in the hands of any one of these would be detrimental to political liberty. This division of powers, however, functions effectively only in the context of social divisions that give the crown and both legislative houses allegiances to competing class constituencies in order to sustain competition. Thus, for many scholars, the full meaning of this most famous chapter of Montesquieu's work must be discerned by reading it in conjunction with his analysis of "party" (that is, prepolitical party) competition in book XIX, 27.

It is crucial to recognize that Montesquieu did not believe that propitious constitutional mechanics (for it is ironic to speak of design when the British constitution was the dominant reference) was sufficient to guarantee liberty. Political liberty may enhance a sense of personal security, but it does not always protect a citizen from arbitrary judgment. For this reason, Montesquieu recognized the higher significance to liberty of criminal laws

and punishments, the workings of which he noted to be the most important object of human knowledge (VI, 2). The most important argument running through his study of criminal laws is the need for moderation. He called on rulers not to regulate certain behaviors by law if they could be modified through moral suasion, custom, or religion, and not to apply harsh punishments for crimes if lesser ones could be just as effective. In addition, he provided a strong defense for the rule of law and advocated maxims to guide magistrates more effectively in prescribing punishments. In its implications, his work provided some justification for a process of legal consolidation that had been occurring in France since the fifteenth century, but as a means to restrain the very system of absolutism that had initiated this process.

The main significance of Montesquieu as a political theorist may be his success in recognizing the embeddedness of state institutions in a wide web of human practices, such as religion, commerce, customs, and morals. Political effectiveness depends on the state's ability to recognize and work with the complexity of human associational life, and this in turn requires political moderation.

Montesquieu and the Enlightenment. In his eulogy of Montesquieu, Jean Le Rond d'Alembert called him the "legislator of nations." This is true insofar as his work evoked strong resonances in the writing of influential thinkers throughout Enlightenment Europe and America.

The publication of *L'esprit des lois* gave rise to multiple debates within France. The book was hailed as a work of genius, though this praise was accompanied by criticism. Though participating in a tradition of Anglophilia inaugurated by Voltaire and his *Lettres philosophiques*, Montesquieu often found himself at odds with his fellow philosophes. Voltaire and Helvétius considered Montesquieu to be largely an apologist for his noble class. Condorcet criticized him for focusing only on political explanation while ignoring the deeper issues concerning the justice of laws and the framework by which this could be judged.

Nevertheless, the influence of Montesquieu is evident throughout the work of the later philosophes; in numerous citations or appropriations of his theories of government in various articles of the *Encyclopédie* by writers such as Louis Jaucourt, d'Alembert, and Denis Diderot; in endorsements of his denunciations of slavery, the Inquisition, or the harshness of punishments; or in building on his theory of ancient republican government, as did Rousseau in *Du contrat social*. By the time of the Revolution, Montesquieu was regarded with a certain ambivalence—hailed as a critic of absolutism and a defender of Enlightenment values, but suspect for anachronistic political allegiances. During the Revolution, his work was most popular in years III and IV (1795–1796), when the idealism of the early Revolutionary period had given way to more pragmatic concerns of reconciling government efficiency and liberty. In the post-Revolutionary period, his work was carried on in several traditions, including the nascent Continental liberal tradition of Benjamin Constant and Alexis de Tocqueville, the radical tradition of Proudhon, and the Europeanist tradition advanced considerably by Claude-Henri de Rouvroy, comte de Saint Simon.

The versatility of Montesquieu's ideas is also evident in the numerous ways in which his theories were propagated outside France. His constitutional discussions were perhaps best known in the Anglo-American world; in America, his work was used as a resource for arguments by both Federalists and Antifederalists. Some argued that his portrayal of the Lycean Federation was a clear justification of the possibility of republicanism on a larger scale in modern times, while others held that Montesquieu saw republicanism as a definite anachronism. His reputation as a constitutional thinker reached Denmark, where various thinkers struggled with the implications of Montesquieu's analysis for their own recent move to absolutist rule, and to Russia, where his work inspired Catherine the Great in her drafting of the *Nakaz*.

Some of Montesquieu's writing resonates in the work of those thinkers who sought an alternative to a theory of natural right in politics. His theory of commerce was a common reference for Scottish Enlightenment writers such as Ferguson and Smith, and it became instrumental in the development of new theories of civil society. Edmund Burke saw Montesquieu as a political genius and drew on his work to develop his understanding of the importance of custom, history, and tradition in collective life. Even William Godwin, while embarking on writing *Political Justice* as a means to refute the role he felt Montesquieu gave to climate in restricting human possibilities, praised Montesquieu for his understanding of humanity's social nature.

There has recently been a renewed interest in Montesquieu's work as that of a broadly liberal thinker willing to deal with political reality in all its complexity. His cosmopolitanism, his advocacy of moderation, his rejection of uniform political solutions, and his dogged defense of human freedom lend his work particular import in the present era.

[*See also* Ancient Rome; Aristocracy; Federalists and Antifederalists; Natural Law; Parlements; Political Philosophy; *and* Republicanism.]

BIBLIOGRAPHY

Courtney, C. P. "Montesquieu and the problem of 'la diversité.'" In *Enlightenment Essays in Memory of Robert Shackleton*, edited by G. Barber and C. P. Courtney, pp. 61–81. Oxford, 1988. Considers Montesquieu's work in the light of modern natural law theory.

Cox, Iris. "Montesquieu and the History of French Law." In *Studies on Voltaire and the Eighteenth Century*. Oxford, 1983. A close study of the long-neglected historical books of *L'esprit des lois*.

Ehrard, Jean. *L'esprit des mots*. Geneva, 1998. The dean of Montesquieu scholarship offers insightful essays on a variety of aspects of Montesquieu's life, work, and influence.

Hulliung, Mark. *Montesquieu and the Old Regime*. Berkeley, 1976. A valuable study of Montesquieu's work in context, portraying him as a radical reformer.

Keohane, Nannerl. *Philosophy and the State in France*. Princeton, N.J., 1980. Keohane places particular emphasis on Montesquieu's sympathies for the Roman republic.

Kingston, Rebecca. *Montesquieu and the Parlement of Bordeaux*. Geneva, 1996. A study of Montesquieu's work in the context of his twelve-year career as a criminal court judge.

Larrère, Catherine. "Montesquieu." In *Dictionnaire de philosophie politique*, edited by P. Raynaud and S. Rials, pp. 399–407. Paris, 1996. A good overview of the evolution of Montesquieu scholarship.

Montesquieu. *Oeuvres complètes*. 2 vols. Edited by R. Caillois. Paris, 1949. The best edition of Montesquieu's works in French, though a better and more complete version is being edited by members of the Société Montesquieu in conjunction with the Voltaire Foundation of Oxford.

Montesquieu. *Selected Political Writings*. Edited by Melvin Richter. Indianapolis, 1990. A good selection of writings in translation, with an insightful introductory essay.

Montesquieu. *The Spirit of the Laws*. Edited by A. Cohler et al. Cambridge, 1989.

Pangle, Thomas. *Montesquieu's Philosophy of Liberalism*. Chicago, 1973. Argues that Montesquieu is a modern in the tradition of Hobbes.

Postigliola, Albert, and Maria Palumbo, eds. *L'Europe de Montesquieu*. Naples, 1995. An interesting and valuable collection of essays on the idea of Europe in Montesquieu and on the dissemination of Montesquieu's ideas in a broad European context.

Shackleton, Robert. *Montesquieu: A Critical Biography*. Oxford, 1961. Still a good source of information about Montesquieu's life and works.

Shklar, Judith. *Montesquieu*. Oxford, 1987. One of the better and briefer introductions to Montesquieu's works.

REBECCA E. KINGSTON

MORAL PHILOSOPHY. Moral philosophy, also known as ethics, is not just the study of the moral rules that regulate how human beings live with one another. Since antiquity it has been one of the most important disciplines of philosophy. Indeed, the Stoics subdivided the entire subject of philosophy into logic, physics, and ethics. However, moral philosophy is more than just analysis and discussion of moral rules and moral concepts—it is also a critique and discussion of their validity, correctness, or appropriateness. In other words, moral philosophy is not merely a descriptive but a prescriptive enterprise.

One of the central questions of moral philosophy concerns the meaning of the terms "good" and "bad." What criteria should be used to determine whether an act is praise- or blameworthy? What makes an act moral or immoral? Usually this question has close connections with questions of what makes for a good or happy life and how moral actions are connected with human fulfillment. There have been various answers given to this question in the history of human thought, and we unhesitatingly employ such terms as "Buddhist ethics," "Christian ethics," "ancient ethics," or the "ethics of modernity." The history of moral philosophy is part of the history of philosophy and therefore subject to the same periodizations as philosophy itself.

It would be an oversimplification to say that there is one distinctive version of the moral philosophy of the Enlightenment—in fact, there are several. Even if these versions have definite "family resemblances," they vary greatly in their foundations, their arguments, their central outlook, and their import. This suggests that it is better to discuss the various versions of the moral philosophy of the Enlightenment in their national and linguistic contexts rather than trying to superimpose categories on them—such as rationalism, intuitionism, sentimentalism, utilitarianism, naturalism, virtue, and Kantian ethics—that must be largely anachronistic. This article will concentrate on Great Britain, France, and Germany, the three most important centers of Enlightenment thought, beginning with an overview of the immediate prehistory of moral philosophy and concluding with a short discussion of the common threads or family resemblances among the different moral positions taken during the Enlightenment in Europe.

Early Modern Precedents. During the sixteenth and seventeenth centuries, Europe underwent a great number of deep and far-reaching changes. After the rediscovery of the original works of ancient philosophers in the fifteenth century, some of the ancient schools such as Platonism, skepticism, and Stoicism became attractive alternatives to more traditional scholastic philosophy. Renaissance humanism and the Reformation had not only brought new ideas but also new questions. The same holds for the "discovery" of America in 1492 and the so-called Copernican revolution.

Modern moral philosophy is often said to have begun with Thomas Hobbes (1588–1679), who, at least partially as a result of the turbulent times in which he lived, thought that the preservation of life was the most important consideration in practical philosophy. Based on a thoroughgoing materialism and egoism, he developed a social contract theory of ethics, in which such terms as good and bad express only personal preferences and just and unjust are merely social constructs. While he thus tried to free moral philosophy entirely from revealed theology and the Christian view of nature and to provide it with a foundation in the laws of psychology and biology, he completely undermined the objective status of moral judgments. Pierre Gassendi (1592–1655), who like Hobbes advocated a form of materialism, argued

that an Epicurean moral philosophy was compatible with Christianity and that pleasure and self-love did not contradict its basic tenets. Others, such as René Descartes and Baruch de Spinoza (1632–1677), turned to Stoic models. Pierre Bayle (1646–1706) opted for skepticism. Samuel Pufendorf (1632–1794), following the lead of Hugo Grotius (1583–1645), tried to develop further the concept of natural law by transforming the Aristotelian and Thomistic conceptions of nature and teleology into something that could be integrated with the concepts of nature and human nature as developed by modern science. Still others reacted sharply to what they viewed as Hobbes's attack on morality and tried to show that morality was objective and not merely conventional. The most important among these were the so-called Cambridge Platonists, especially Benjamin Whichcote (1609–1683), Ralph Cudworth (1617–1688), and Henry More (1614–1687). According to them, moral principles are self-evident truths—for this reason they are also called intuitionists. Insofar as the Enlightenment is the continuation of early modern philosophy—all the early attempts of doing justice to both scientific and moral concerns—the moral philosophy of the Enlightenment consists in further development of these early answers.

British Arguments. From a contemporary perspective, British moral philosophers contributed perhaps the most to the discussion of moral issues—at least during the first two-thirds of the eighteenth century and thus during the period of the early Enlightenment. During the last third, it was the Germans, and especially Immanuel Kant (1724–1804), who determined the agenda for the future of this philosophical discipline.

John Locke (1632–1704) is the best starting point for an account of moral philosophy in the Enlightenment. He is sometimes regarded as one of the most important precursors of utilitarianism, since he not only claimed, like the Cambridge Platonist, that we could reach mathematical certainty in moral matters but also argued, like Hobbes, that pleasure is the ultimate goal of human action. Good is "what has an aptness to produce pleasure in us." The third earl of Shaftesbury (1671–1713), a student of Locke who was also influenced by Cambridge Platonism, argued in his *Inquiry Concerning Virtue or Merit* (1699) that moral obligation can be traced back to benevolent affections, such as love, pity, and sympathy. These affections are as natural as the selfish ones that Hobbes had identified (envy, greed, and self-preservation). Furthermore, the two are not necessarily contradictory to one another and the proper balance between them is necessary for public and private good. He also claimed that human beings possess a moral sense that leads them to pursue the public good.

Samuel Clarke (1675–1729) followed the lead of the Cambridge Platonists and argued that natural religion determines what we ought to do through the necessary and eternal relations of fitness. The "original obligations of morality" can be deduced from "the necessary and eternal reason and proportion of things." Our duties and obligations (to God, ourselves, and others) thus precede any consideration of personal advantages and disadvantages or reward and punishment. They also precede any contract. Indeed, they can be apprehended and should be followed by all intelligent beings. Plato's theory of anamnesis is essentially correct not just in matters geometrical, but also in matters of right and wrong. Indeed, contradiction in action and in thinking amount to the same mistake. The rules of equity demand the same consistency as the rules of thinking. Accordingly, Clarke rejected any kind of voluntarism. Hobbes and others, who denied the eternal and natural difference of good and evil, mistook difficulties in determining what in a particular case may be right or wrong with the difficulty of determining right and wrong themselves. In the former there may be some latitude, but in the latter there cannot be any.

Bernard Mandeville (1670–1733), by contrast, argued that morality contradicted human nature, which he understood in terms close to those of Hobbes: People seek only their own interests and especially their own power. Morality is artificial. It is "contrary to the impulse of nature" because it prescribes that we should strive not just to help others but also to subdue our own passions and be rational. Mandeville argues, as did some of the early Greek sophists, that human beings are at first persuaded by politicians to control their appetites and their lust for immediate enjoyment. This then becomes second nature or at least pretense. Even when people follow their own passions, however, they unwittingly bring about the general good, as if there were a hidden hand that turns private vices into public benefits. In any case, there is neither a natural nor a divine reason why morality and happiness should coincide. This would lead almost necessarily to hypocrisy.

Francis Hutcheson (1694–1746) argued against both Clarke and Mandeville. Following Locke, he tried to show that moral approval presupposes a special moral sense. Since moral approval is the most important moral experience, morality cannot be based on reason. Indeed, reason is nothing but the "power of finding out true propositions." It neither moves us to action nor can serve as a means of justifying moral ends. Both are functions of our moral sentiments. At the same time, these moral sentiments show that morality cannot be reduced to egoistic considerations. While the moral sense may be in some individuals "exceedingly weakened, and the selfish passions grown strong," it is part of our nature and provides us with benevolent motives. While Hutcheson also believed that it is possible to develop a felicific calculus or a universal rule by which we can "compute the morality of any actions with all their circumstances," he did not make utility the basic principle of morality. Morality was for him ultimately based on sentiment or feeling. This does not have to mean, however, that Hutcheson's theory is a kind of emotivism. Moral perceptions are not mere affective experiences. The moral sense can be construed as a cognitive sense, like the sense of sight, for instance. Therefore, his moral-sense theory is sometimes argued to amount to a kind of moral realism (see Norton, 1982).

Though Hutcheson argued that egoism is wrong as a moral theory, he also held that there need be no contradiction between self-interest and morality and that self-love is as necessary for the greater good as benevolence. This idea was pursued even further by Joseph Butler (1692–1752), who remained in many ways closer to Clarke than to Hutcheson, while arguing just as much against the theories of human nature as propounded by Hobbes and Mandeville. Butler did not argue against abstract relations or natural law and insisted that moral principles are ultimately rational or that they are precepts whose reason we see. According to him, we are not just motivated by the two principles of benevolence and self-love, but also by a third principle, the principle of reflection that has greater authority than any particular impulse. We are creatures who reflect on our own natures. And the principle of reflection allows us to distinguish between our actions and to approve and disapprove of them. "This principle in man, by which he approves or disapproves his heart, temper and actions, is conscience." While Butler thus discusses morality as it is based on the "inward frame of man," he thinks that this inward frame (or the three principles) shows that we "were made for society, and to promote the happiness of it" and that our nature corresponds to nature itself and thus also to the will of God. Thus every person is through his "make, constitution, or nature" in "the strictest and most proper sense a law to himself"—and that means that he is subject to a universal law of nature that is prior to all will, even that of God.

David Hume (1711–1776) pursued further the moral-sense theory of Shaftesbury and especially Hutcheson by trying to clarify not just the relationship between the utilitarian and the sentimentalist aspects in it but also the relation between feeling and understanding in moral judgments. In doing so, he also tried to free the discussion of morals from any religious intrusions. Morality should have nothing to do with religion. Religion and morality are not only not incompatible with one another, but religion leads necessarily to hypocrisy and thus to a frame of mind incompatible with true morality. Like Hutcheson, he argued against rationalism by insisting that reason allows us to establish truth and to judge matters of fact, whereas moral judgments are based on sentiment. Though some of the virtues, such as justice, are based on the utility they have either for the individual or for the public and therefore depend on rational assessment of the consequences, all are ultimately based on the appreciation of moral ends. He answered the question of why utility pleases us by pointing toward sympathy and fellow feeling. We cannot help but feel good when someone exhibits some of the virtues and bad if someone has vices. We feel in such cases the pleasing sentiment of approbation or the unpleasing sentiment of disapprobation. However, these feelings or sentiments are to be trusted only when they are felt by a disinterested observer, who knows precisely what has happened in a certain case or who has the relevant information about an actor. Hume's moral sentimentalism involves reflection at several levels. It is not to be identified with a simple form of emotivism. Furthermore, though nature is supposed to have made the moral sense universal in the human species, this does not mean that there cannot be different moral ideas in different societies and in different periods. Education, climate, and other external circumstances can have various influences on the moral sense and thus also on our moral concepts and principles.

These ideas were developed even further by Hume's friend Adam Smith (1723–1790), who used the phrase "impartial spectator" for the disinterested observer and impartial enquirer whom Hume also described. However, Smith's spectator is more an expression of our own dual nature. The spectator is not so much a device by which to judge the behavior of others as one by which to judge ourselves. We always see ourselves as others would see us. Human beings are mirrors to one another and we can know our moral character only insofar as we imagine how we might look to others.

One of the most important critics of sentimentalism was Thomas Reid (1710–1796), who argued that morality is not based on feeling but on self-evident principles or truths. Though these principles do not form a system or a geometric order, they are like axioms that formulate not only the general and substantive conditions of morality but also allow us to settle conflicts that may arise when different virtues are pursued. Ethics elucidates "the structure of our moral powers." Reid's view was in some ways close to that of Richard Price (1723–1791), who was indebted to Cudworth and Clarke and thought that our moral concepts are based on "the intuition of truth or immediate discernment of the nature of things by the understanding." Sentiment, feeling, or emotion, which plays such a large role in the thought of the moral-sense school, also has a place in morals, but only one of secondary importance. Feeling may accompany intuition, but it should not be confused with it. Like Reid, he claimed

that the moral worth of an agent depends on the intentions behind an act.

Apart from these rationalistic or intuitionist answers to sentimentalism, there are also developments of utilitarian elements in the thought of Hutcheson, Hume, and others that lead to a new, antireligious conception of ethics. Most important among those who advocated utilitarianism in the eighteenth century was Jeremy Bentham (1748–1832), for whom the question concerning the moral worth of any action could be determined only by considering "the tendency, which it appears to have to augment or diminish the happiness of the party whose interest is in question." While this form of utilitarianism may be said to go hand in hand with a kind of radical enlightenment, it also points beyond the ideals of the Enlightenment and belongs more to the nineteenth century.

French Voices. In France, there was a lack of concern for intricate discussions of the fundamental principles of morals. For the French philosophers, the discussion of moral issues was closely bound up with materialism and what Smith called the "licentious system." Rejecting any attempt at a religious foundation of morality, most of them were interested in showing that egoism and self-interest did not preclude interest in the well-being of our fellow creatures. Though there are great differences between such thinkers as Julien Offray de La Mettrie (1709–1751), Claude-Adrien Helvétius (1715–1771), Paul-Henri Thiry d'Holbach (1723–1789), Denis Diderot (1713–1784), Jean Le Rond d'Alembert (1717–1783), and Voltaire (François-Marie Arouet, 1694–1778), they remain ultimately within the framework of the ideas of Hobbes and Mandeville. They were following the lead of British "egoists," and they cannot be said to have contributed anything really original to the discussion of the principles of morality. They were writing to advance the enlightenment of humanity and thus to make a practical contribution to our cultural advancement, and as such they were eclectics who took what they considered best from wherever they could find it. It should not come as a surprise, then, that they also made use of ideas from Shaftesbury, Hutcheson, and Hume. This does not mean, however, that any of them made an original and decisive contribution to what we have called the foundations of morality debate. They left things more or less as they found them. If there was an exception, it was Jean-Jacques Rousseau (1712–1778). In his *Discours sur l'origine et les fondements de l'inégalité parmi les hommes* (Discourse on the Origin of Inequality, 1755), he challenged many of the central notions of the ideas of his fellow Enlightenment thinkers. His central idea of a "state of nature" in which "original man" was innocent and characterized by "a feeling of pity," freedom, and perfectibility as opposed to the artificial and harmful "civil state" and corrupting "society," was meant to subvert the project of those who hoped to better the world by "enlightenment." It also was an original contribution to the discussion of moral philosophy. In a letter to the editor of the *Edinburgh Review* in 1756, Adam Smith argued that Rousseau is "English philosophy...transported into France." And he compared Rousseau's *Discours* favorably to Mandeville's *Fable of the Bees*, which, he claimed, gave rise to Rousseau's work. In "Mr. Rousseau...the principles of the English author are softened, improved, and embellished, and stript of all that tendency to corruption and licentiousness which has disgraced them in their original author." In other words, from the perspective of one of the best moral philosophers, it appeared that there was nothing new here either. Though turned on its head, softened, improved, and embellished, it was still the "licentious system."

Perhaps this was too harsh a judgment. If Rousseau was right that man "in his savage...and...in his civilized state, differ so essentially in their passions and inclinations," then any attempt to found morality on "natural and original principles" would be far more complicated than Hume and Smith had ever believed. Neither the language nor the moral feelings of civilized men would be reliable guides to those natural and original feelings. Of course, it would only be a difficulty if Rousseau were right about the state of nature and the state of civil society, and it is at the very least doubtful that this could be shown empirically. However that may be, Rousseau's theory was most fundamentally a form of naturalism. He insisted that moral issues needed to be discussed in terms of human nature and the principles operative at different stages of its development. This was not fundamentally at odds with Hume's view. If Rousseau's view was the "licentious system," softened, improved, and embellished, then why was that of Hume any different?

German Reservations. Until the second part of the eighteenth century, the discussion of the foundations of morality had played no important role in Germany. Philosophers seem to have had less interest in the analysis of morality and a greater concern with fostering a certain kind of morality. This is especially clear in Germany, where the discussion of every philosophical subject was largely defined by the opposition between the followers of Christian Wolff, also called the Leibniz-Wolffian school, and the Pietists, a religious movement within the Protestant churches, which favored a "religion of the heart" very much opposed to intellectualism and at times characterized by an emotionalism that bordered on mysticism. Until the beginning of the eighteenth century, the philosophy taught at German universities was Aristotelianism. It was attacked by the adherents of Pietism, which was, at least in part, a protest movement against the orthodoxy within the Protestant churches. Pietists emphasized the importance of independent Bible study, personal devotion, the priesthood of the laity, and a practical faith issuing in acts of charity. Its most important source of inspiration was Philipp Jakob Spener's *Pia desideria* (Pious Desires, 1675), whose subtitle read "heartfelt desire for the improvement of the true evangelical Church that is approved by God, together with some Christian suggestions, designed to lead towards it." Another important proponent of this view was August Hermann Francke (1663–1727). The Pietists rejected not just Aristotelianism, but all of philosophy because it could only be the result of reason corrupted by the Fall. Whatever merits their view may have had, philosophical sophistication was not one of them. And their presence in the philosophical debate in Germany during much of the first half of the eighteenth century was—at least in part—responsible for its mediocrity.

The best philosophers among those closely affiliated with Pietism were Christian Thomasius (1655–1728) and Christian August Crusius (1715–1775). Thomasius was more interested in practical issues than in theoretical problems about basic principles, and his views changed repeatedly. He began as an adherent of Pufendorf, then adopted a position that contained a heavy dose of utilitarianism, only to abandon it in favor of Pietism. During his pietistic period he emphasized love and the corruption of reason by an evil will, but during his last years, disillusioned with Pietism, he returned to a more worldly view. One would look in vain for a consistent answer to Smith's question "Wherein does virtue consist?" Propriety, prudence, and benevolence (or "reasonable love," as he would have put it) would all have been good answers for Thomasius. If he had been asked which of our faculties is responsible for virtue, and if he had been given the choice among self-love, sentiment, or reason, he would have rejected all of them, and answered that it was the will, and the will alone. Crusius was, if anything, even more skeptical about reason than Thomasius. He adopted a Lutheran position on morality, in which everything became a question of how our will, which was corrupted by the Fall, can become good. Not surprisingly, he considered the concept of freedom of the will as the most central concept of morality. And virtue was for him nothing but "the agreement of the moral condition of a mind with the divine laws." Crusius's main work in ethics, *Anweisung vernünftig zu Leben* (Instructions for Living Rationally, 1744), was characterized by the view that ethics is not founded on reason, but on God's will. A moral act cannot be done in order to obtain happiness. It must have been done to fulfill the duties imposed on us by God. We must follow our conscience. The only true foundation of morality consists in divine laws or in God's choices, which are inscrutable to us. This was theology, not philosophy.

Wolff and his followers, who found themselves constantly criticized and attacked by the Pietists, dominated the philosophical discussion between 1720 and 1750. They pursued ethics as *philosophia practica universalis methodo mathematica conscripta*, that is, as a universal practical philosophy drawn up following the mathematical method. It was, in effect, a form of neo-Stoicism. Its basic principle was: Act so as to make you and the condition of yourself and others more perfect; do not act so as to make them less perfect. Every rational person can know this principle and therefore is in no need of another law. Through reason every man is "a law unto himself." Thus the faculty by which "virtue is recommended to us" is reason. Wolff appears to have viewed this feature of his moral philosophy as properly basic, and thus did not provide any arguments for this view. So, for him virtue consisted of some sort of propriety and the principle of approbation was nothing but reason. There are many interesting aspects to Wolffian thought and although it is important for understanding the further philosophical development in Germany, it did not present any new ideas about the foundations of morality. Like the young Thomasius, Wolff was interested in furthering the cause of Enlightenment and educating people to think for themselves and better themselves. While the discussion "concerning the nature and origin of our moral sentiments" continued in Britain even after Hume's subtle contribution to it, the really significant new developments took place in Germany. The Germans were not really talking to such philosophers as Smith and Hume at all, however. They tried to solve problems inherent in the philosophical position then prevalent in Germany, namely the so-called Leibniz-Wolffian philosophy.

Not long after the middle of the eighteenth century, Leibniz-Wolffian philosophy rapidly declined in influence. German philosophers began to take a closer look at British authors. A new generation of philosophers discovered that the works of Locke, Shaftesbury, Hutcheson, Hume, and Smith were full of problems that needed solution and observations that needed explanation. Most of these problems seemed to concern the role of sensation in theoretical, moral, and aesthetic contexts. The task at hand was conceived by most—at least at first—as one of incorporating British "observations" in a comprehensive theory. Moses Mendelssohn (1729–1786) noted in a review of Edmund Burke's *A Philosophical Enquiry into the Origin of Our Ideas of the Sublime and Beautiful* that the British neighbors had made significant discoveries in the theory of human sensations and passions. He claimed that they preceded the Germans with philosophical observations of nature, and that the Germans followed them with "rational inferences." He believed that, "if it were to go on like this, namely that our neighbors observe and

we explain, we may hope that we will achieve in time a complete theory of sensation." What was needed, he thought, was a universal theory of thinking and sensation, and such a theory would cover sensation and thinking in theoretical, aesthetic, and moral contexts. In it British "observations" and German (read Wolffian) "explanations" would be happily married. Mendelssohn had definite ideas about the general approach to be followed. It had to be shown that the phenomena observed by British philosophers and traced by them to a special sense were really rational. Thus it is wrong, he argued, to speak of a special "moral sense." Though both may appear to be independent faculties of the mind, they must be reduced to reason. This reduction to reason may appear difficult in the case of moral judgments, since our moral judgments "as they present themselves in the soul are completely different from the effects of distinct rational principles," but that does not mean that they cannot be analyzed into rational and distinct principles. Our moral sentiments are "phenomena which are related to rational principles in the same way as the colors are related to the angles of refraction of light. They are apparently of completely different nature, yet they are basically one and the same." Moral phenomena are phenomena in the Leibnizian sense, but they are also "phenomena bene fundata," because they are ultimately founded in something rational. It was precisely this task that defined one of the central concerns of German moral philosophers during the second half of the eighteenth century, namely to show how "moral sense" could be reduced to "rational principles."

Johann August Eberhard (1739–1809) followed Mendelssohn closely. His attempt to show that sensation can be reduced to something rational is perhaps typical. Starting from the observation that "most recent speculative philosophy" is best characterized "by its discoveries in the theory of sensation" and that these discoveries are often found in the writings of British philosophers, he claimed to develop the theory itself that fits them. Hutcheson and others had gone only "half way" in their explanation. His first step in this was to prove that sensation and thinking are united in what he calls "the original basic power" of the soul. Using one of the commonplaces of Wolffian psychology, he asserted without further argument that this basic power can only be "the striving to have representations." Accordingly, sensation and thinking consist of the same "basic stuff," namely representations. It's just that thinking consists of clear and distinct representations or ideas, whereas sensations are confused representations. Given these (relatively large) assumptions, it follows that moral judgments are ultimately also rational. Now, if there are those who "have transformed a kind of feeling into criteria of the truth and the good, they have given our faculty of sensation a reputation that it should not have." While Eberhard did not mean to deny that we can speak of a moral sense, he did think it was important to be clear on precisely what this means. Feeling is "a depository of all clear judgments which are kept in the soul by consideration or conscious abstraction, so that they may express themselves in all cases with a rapidity that is characteristic of sensation." He does not doubt that there is a moral sense in this meaning, while he chides Hutcheson, Hume, and others for claiming that there is an independent and separate moral sense.

Many other German philosophers followed the same approach. Though they were not all as confident as Mendelssohn and Eberhard that the moral sense could actually be so easily reduced to rational principles, most seem to have thought that it was possible in principle. Johann Georg Heinrich Feder (1740–1821) characterized the moral sense as a human capacity "of very mixed relations" that could be analyzed as an effect of "education and our own reason, that is, as concepts and principles resulting from experience and thinking." Jurisprudence, religion, political laws, considerations of utility, all play a role. Finally, and most importantly, however, it is sympathy that is the cause of our approval of the good. We do not have to postulate a special sense in order to account for our moral approval and disapproval. Though we usually are not aware of these multiple causes of our moral convictions, we can become aware of them. And "insofar as we commonly and not always quite properly . . . call 'sense' or 'feeling' any species of knowledge of whose origin in other representations we are unconscious, and especially when it is connected with emotions and passions, we can say that man has a moral feeling or a moral sense in this meaning." This does not mean, however, that it is an independent sense. It may very well be a consequence "of the merging of several sensations and representations which themselves are of such a kind that they cannot be called a moral sense." In this way many other Germans were able to accept most everything said by Shaftesbury, Hutcheson, Hume, and Smith about the nature of moral phenomena without having to renounce all of the basic tenets of Wolffian morality. Some of them went further in the direction of Hume than others. Feder, for instance, was in many ways closer to Hume and Smith. Indeed, he admitted that "in the first development and ordering of [his] concepts," Hume's second *Enquiry* was more important to him than any other book, and that he had learned a great deal from Smith's account of sympathy. As an eclectic with a definite German background, however, he not only wanted to hold on to the Wolffian account of virtue as perfection, but he also was confident that there was ultimately no incompatibility between reason and sentiment.

Immanuel Kant (1724–1804) followed at first a very similar approach as did his German contemporaries. In his "prize essay," entitled *Untersuchung über die Deutlichkeit der Grundsätze der natürlichen Theologie und Moral* (An Inquiry into the Distinctness of the Fundamental Principles of Natural Theology and Morals) of 1764, he endorsed the distinction between "the faculty of conceiving the truth" and that of "sensing the good" (or feeling)—arguing that the two must not be confused—but he also pointed out that Hutcheson and others had "under the name of moral 'feeling' . . . provided some excellent observations" relevant for the discussion of the fundamental principles of morals. Accepting the view of the moral-sense school that good "is never found in a thing by itself but always in the relation to a feeling being" and that there are "simple sensations of the good," which give rise to "indemonstrable material principles of obligation," he tried to account rationally for this feeling. However, in the last section of this essay he observed that the highest degree of philosophical evidence in morals cannot be obtained, since the "supreme principles of obligation must first be defined with more certainty. Furthermore, it still remains to be settled whether it is simply the cognitive faculty or whether it is feeling . . . which decides the basic principles of practical philosophy."

The way Kant ultimately answered the question concerning the ultimate foundation of morality was very different from that of any of his predecessors. Indeed, his *Grundlegung zur Metaphysik der Sitten* (Groundwork of the Metaphysics of Morals, 1785) and *Kritik der practischen Vernunft* (Critique of Practical Reason, 1788) changed the discussion of the foundations of morals forever. Kant's mature work in ethics represents a radical break with both the Wolffian and the moral-sense tradition.

This break is evidenced by four fundamental aspects of Kant's "metaphysics of morals." First, it is "a complete abandonment of any form of eudaemonism" (Ross, 1954, 92). For Kant, morality per se has nothing to do with happiness or pleasure. Any view that sees morality as intimately or essentially connected with happiness—be it our own or that of others—is not just wrong for him but a perversion of true morality. Second, morality is not in any sense founded upon natural principles. Morality is not a natural phenomenon, as Hume had argued, for instance. Third, and more positively, morality has its foundation in rational and absolutely a priori principles of reason. Indeed, Kant argues that the "fundamental principles" of morality "must originate entirely a priori." They result from reason itself, and they are "supported by nothing in either heaven or earth." This insistence on the a priori and rational character of morals is closely connected to a fourth and most fundamental point in which he breaks with the tradition. According to Kant, we are morally autonomous. "Autonomy" is for him another word for freedom. To be moral or autonomous means not to submit to nature, but to assert our rationality. Indeed, we freely legislate moral laws. Morality has to do with mastering our will, or, as he would say, with transforming our will into a "good will."

The most fundamental concept of Kant's ethical theory is duty, not virtue. Virtue is nothing but the result of acts done from duty. It is not sufficient for an action to have moral worth if we act merely in accordance with duty. We must act from the realization that it is our duty. The criterion of such dutiful acts is his well-known categorical imperative, which states that we should act in such a way that the maxim of our action can become a universal law (of nature), that we should never treat ourselves or other rational beings simply as a means, and that we should look at ourselves as legislating moral laws for all rational beings. Morality is not a question of what is given to us in nature. Ultimately it is not an object of empirical inquiry, as Hutcheson and Hume had believed. It is an ideal that we need to realize.

Kant argued that all philosophers before him have not sufficiently appreciated the autonomous nature of morality, and that they therefore have based morality on "heteronomous principles," which for him is just another way of saying that they were wrong. In a highly revealing passage in *Foundations* he classifies all possible principles of morality from the assumed principle of heteronomy. They appear to exhaust all the principles of morality that have been advanced before him, and they are all characterized by a failure to recognize the fundamental importance of autonomy for the foundations of the metaphysics of morals. They are either empirical or rational. In the empirical category, he differentiates further between principles that are based on self-regarding considerations or are concerned with happiness and principles that are based on a moral sense. In so far as both these positions are empirical, he rejects them equally. Yet he finds it necessary to point out that the moral feeling "is nearer to morality and its dignity." The rational principles also fall into two different camps for him, namely the theological concept "which derives morality from a most perfect divine will" and the ontological concept of perfection as a possible result of our moral actions. The ontological concept of perfection seems better to him than the theological concept. Indeed, it appears that Kant has rank-ordered these principles in accordance with his view of morality and dignity. Egoism is the lowest form of a moral principle in this scheme; the altruistic moral sense is better, but both are less perfect than the two rational principles. The theological concept is better, according to Kant, than either of the empirical principles. The ontological concept of perfection is the best of all

of them, however. The philosopher closest to Kant in his rejection of any form of naturalism is Plato, and there are many passages (especially in reflections that were not published during Kant's lifetime) that suggest that Plato was not only viewed by Kant as closest to his own view, but that he also helped him in formulating it.

Still, Kant's emphasis on the absolute autonomy of the moral agent and the corresponding glorification of "freedom" is revolutionary. It undoubtedly would have struck earlier eighteenth-century philosophers as blasphemous, overly enthusiastic, or even dangerous. Hume would have rejected it as not being based on "a true delineation or description of human nature." Kant certainly would have understood such objections. He would have tried to explain to such objectors that what he was after was an "ideal," something to be believed in, not something that already existed or that could easily be achieved. I doubt whether he would have succeeded in convincing them that such an idealistic foundation of morality was possible, but it is a fact that he had a profound effect on the members of the younger generation whose view of the world and philosophy was formed more by the developments connected with the American and French revolutions and who themselves craved freedom from oppressive authority. While many of the older generation saw Kant's attempt at a foundation of the metaphysics of morals (and indeed his entire philosophy) as a form of skepticism, the younger generation found its effects liberating. Thus Moses Mendelssohn felt it wise to ignore, at least in public, the works of the "all-crushing" Kant, while Karl Leonhard Reinhold, whose *Briefe über die kantische Philosophie* (Letters on Kantian Philosophy, 1786–1787) were instrumental in popularizing the Kantian view, celebrated Kant's moral philosophy and its consequences for religion. Whether Kant's moral philosophy is the pinnacle of the Enlightenment or whether it represents the end of the Enlightenment is a hotly debated issue. One thing is certain, however—it is highly relevant whenever the Enlightenment is discussed.

Concluding Remarks and Influence. While the ideals and the moral conceptions developed during the period that we now call the Enlightenment are increasingly under attack, they still determine not just the philosophical discussion but also everyday moral discussions. Notions such as "impartiality," "objectivity," "universality," and "autonomy" remain important. Butler, Hume, Smith, Rousseau, and Kant still loom large—as they should. The nineteenth and twentieth centuries cannot be understood without the ideas developed in the period of the Enlightenment. While some of our contemporaries are willing to blame the Enlightenment for all or most of the sins of modernity, others still view the Enlightenment as an unfinished task.

I for one believe that we have not yet learned enough from the moral philosophy of the Enlightenment.

[*See also* Human Nature; Natural Sentiment; Passion; Philosophes; Philosophy; Pietism; Secularization; Utilitarianism; *and* Virtue.]

BIBLIOGRAPHY

Berman, Marshall. *The Politics of Authenticity: Radical Individualism and the Emergence of Modern Society*. New York, 1970.

Carey, John. *Pagan Virtue: An Essay on Ethics*. Oxford, 1990.

Gay, Peter. *The Enlightenment: An Interpretation*. 2 vols. London, 1967–1970.

Goldmann, Lucien. *The Philosophy of the Enlightenment*. Cambridge, Mass., 1973.

Griswold, Charles L., Jr. *Adam Smith and the Virtues of Enlightenment*. Cambridge, 1999.

Macintyre, A. *After Virtue*. London, 1981.

Norton, David Fate. *David Hume: Common-Sense Moralist and Sceptical Metaphysician*. Princeton, N.J., 1982.

Raphael, D. D., ed. *British Moralists, 1650–1800*. 2 vols. Oxford, 1969.

Ross, Sir David. *Kant's Ethical Theory: A Commentary on the* Grundlegung zur Metaphysik der Sitten. Oxford, 1954.

Schneewind, J. B. *The Invention of Autonomy*. Cambridge, 1998.

MANFRED KUEHN

MORAL SENSE. *See* Moral Philosophy.

MORELLET, ANDRÉ (1727–1819), French thinker and reformer.

Morellet's long career is important because it illustrates the complex interaction between Enlightenment liberalism and French Revolutionary ideology. The relationship between the Enlightenment and the Revolution is a classic historical topic, but it is not one that lends itself to the classic method of historical writing—narration. Because most of the philosophes died before 1789, the historian is forced to construct ideal-type images of the Enlightenment and Revolution and to posit abstract connections between the two. Morellet is the rare case of a philosophe who not only lived into the Revolutionary era but who managed to survive its persecution of the old intellectual elite. His memoirs and other writings from the post-1789 period are vehemently antirevolutionary, even antidemocratic. They thus suggest, in many ways, that the Enlightenment and French Revolution were antithetical to each other. Yet a critical perspective on Morellet's career also permits one to see that his liberal ideas constituted a part of the Revolutionary ideology that he came to oppose. In this context, the most revealing feature of his post-Revolutionary development is the fact that he did not simply defend his pre-Revolutionary ideas; rather, he modified the ideas he had propounded before 1789 so as to avert their most radical implications. In doing so, he formulated a new political outlook, a new liberalism that negated both the Enlightenment and the Revolution.

Born in Lyon, Morellet studied for the priesthood and was licensed by the Sorbonne in 1752. It was in the Sorbonne's library that he discovered the works of Locke and Voltaire. As his reading took a secular turn, he began to imagine the possibility of heaven on earth: "[I was] firmly convinced that this world would develop inexorably, through the progress of enlightenment and virtue, into a sanctuary of peace and perfect happiness" (*Mémoires*, 51–52). After leaving the Sorbonne, Morellet became an energetic reformer. Through brochures, books, and translations, he promoted religious toleration, the abolition of torture, freedom of the press, and freedom of trade. Morellet was not a profound thinker but he was an effective purveyor of liberal ideals.

Although the substance of his reformist tracts varied, Morellet framed them all in the same way. He consistently appealed to an imaginary "public," which he idealized as a repository of good judgment. In other words, he was optimistic that through the free circulation of critical ideas, a wise "public opinion" would emerge and would force the government to adopt the very policies he advocated. Morellet discussed more explicitly than other philosophes the process by which a rational public opinion comes into being.

The relevant work is his *Réflexions sur les avantages de la liberté d'ècrire et d'imprimer sur les matières de l'administration* (Reflections on the Benefits of the Freedom of Writing and Publishing on Administrative Matters, 1775). Morellet had written this in 1764 in response to the law of silence of 28 March of the same year, but was not able to publish it until the ministry of Turgot, a great believer in freedom of the press. The law of silence had prohibited subjects from publishing any criticism of the government's financial policies. Grievances were to be channeled to the monarch privately through petitions and administrative reports. There was to be no independent circuit of political communication. Morellet took advantage of Turgot's liberal ministry to contend that the monarch cannot govern effectively without the general intelligence of all his subjects. Most of the petitions the king received from members of the bureaucracy were poorly reasoned, according to Morellet, because the authors did not have to face the test of public criticism. At the same time, the king ignored many useful ideas simply because they originated in the minds of individuals who had no access to the ruler and no right to publicize their views. Morellet thus anticipated that printing and public discussion would generate a more responsible and intelligent political culture.

Morellet achieved prestige and prosperity in the 1780s. His induction into the Académie Française in 1785 was the high point of his career. In 1788, as the Estates General prepared to convene, Morellet was enthusiastic about the prospects of reform, but after the Estates General transformed itself into the National Assembly and began to dismantle the corporate structure of the Old Regime, he turned against the Revolution. From this time onward, his writings illustrate the evolution of an Enlightenment liberal concerned with the defects of absolute monarchy into a post-Revolutionary liberal concerned with the defects of democracy.

In August 1789, he published a pamphlet against the National Assembly's decision to abolish clerical benefices. The question directly concerned Morellet because he had himself acquired a benefice in the village of Thimert. In 1790, he came to the conclusion that radical journalists were inciting popular acts of violence by slandering the wealthy. In a pamphlet defending nobles and large property owners, he suggested that the government should block the publication of writings that attacked innocent people. This contradicted his earlier philosophy: He was now saying that one had a right to publish only the truth; before the Revolution he had argued that publicity was sufficient to guarantee that the outcome of any public debate would be the truth.

In August 1793, the assembly, now called the National Convention, abolished the Académie. Morellet secretly stored its archives in his home. During the Terror of 1793–1794, when all priests and aristocrats were suspected of being counterrevolutionaries, he lived in fear. He was denounced by the woman who washed his clothes on 15 July 1794. His neighborhood Revolutionary committee declared that he was not a threat, but the episode intensified Morellet's disenchantment with the ideal of public deliberation. He now realized that free communication could create a culture of denunciation where slander rather than truth won the day.

In his memoirs, Morellet confessed that under the absolute monarchy he had been too confident about the benefits of open communication. He even suggested that the truth often should be kept secret. In this way, Morellet reflected not only on the French Revolution but also on his own former idealism. In the Old Regime, he had been more concerned with breaking down the barriers to freedom and publicity than with theorizing about the necessary restrictions on freedom. The violence and licentious language of the Revolution attuned him to the need to regulate not only the power of governmental elites but also the range of action of ordinary citizens.

Morellet never succeeded in developing a new and coherent set of philosophical ideals, but he left behind some ambitious manuscripts that indicate the direction of his thought. He came to regard private property as the essential basis of a civilized society. This entailed redefining the individual as an owner of things—in contrast to eighteenth-century liberalism that emphasized sociability, or the communicative interaction among individuals. The right to participate in government belongs exclusively to proprietors. Morellet developed these ideas in an unpublished treatise on property that he started in 1790 but never completed. Here he observed that democracy is the enemy of property because "it naturally tends to move toward equality through the plundering of property owners."

Morellet also left behind an unfinished history of the French Revolution that he seems to have begun writing in 1793. While portraying "the horrors of the Revolution," He engages in the comparative study of political and legal institutions. A highly interesting section compares the malfunctioning of Revolutionary tribunals to the successful jury system in England. A tendency to idealize England and to urge the French to copy the English model is characteristic of his post-Revolutionary thought. Morellet's career thus reveals how French liberalism, through its interaction with the problems posed by the French Revolution, became hostile to popular sovereignty and partisan to England. With the exception of Tocqueville, who admired America more than England, French liberals of the nineteenth century followed this pattern.

[*See also* Economic Thought *and* French Revolution.]

BIBLIOGRAPHY

WORKS BY MORELLET
Mémoires. Paris, 1988.
Réflexions sur les avantages de la liberté d'écrire et d'imprimer sur les matières de l'administration. London, 1775.
Traité de la propriété. Edited by Eugenio Di Rienzo. Florence, 1990.

WORKS ABOUT MORELLET
Merrick, Jeffrey, and Dorothy Medlin, eds. *André Morellet (1727–1819) in the Republic of Letters and the French Revolution*. New York, 1995. Contains a catalog of Morellet's writings and a bibliography of secondary literature. This volume also contains extracts from Morellet's projected history of the French Revolution.

DANIEL GORDON

MORITZ, KARL PHILIPP (1756–1793), German novelist, teacher, journalist, and philologist.

Moritz was born in Hameln, the son of a regimental musician. The family was poor, and Johann Gottlieb was a devout disciple of Herr von Fleischbein, a religious separatist who espoused an extreme form of Quietism, influenced by the teachings of the seventeenth-century French mystic Jeanne-Marie de la Motte Guyon.

Our knowledge of Moritz's youth comes mostly from his autobiographical novel *Anton Reiser*, which appeared in four parts from 1785 to 1790. As a young boy, he went to school to learn to read and even acquire some Latin, but in 1768 he was dispatched to Brunswick to work for the hatter Lobenstein, described in *Anton Reiser* as a "dreamy-eyed" and "intolerant" follower of Fleischbein. *Anton Reiser* continually engages not just with the facts of Moritz's life but also with mood, vision, and art. As Moritz did, Anton begins quite young to feel the call of the theater, which was flourishing in Germany at this time. Anton obtains a position with the Speich Troupe but is forced to resign at the University of Erfurt's behest.

In the early 1780s, after briefly studying at the university in Wittenberg, Moritz turned to teaching, first in Potsdam and then in Berlin. His pedagogy was decidedly unorthodox, and he traveled often, neglecting his duties. It is clear in retrospect that he was not simply a charlatan, although this possibility must often have occurred even to those who entertained no malice toward him. The figure in Berlin who made the deepest impression on Moritz was probably Moses Mendelssohn, who intervened more than once to help Moritz out of his recurrent depressions. In 1782, Moritz traveled to England, already acquainted with English literature, especially Shakespeare. He found London, in comparison with Berlin, to be a city of freedom and social release, of political emancipation and egalitarianism; he was impressed by the patriotic feelings of the citizenry and amazed by their open contempt for the monarchy. His travels in England included a visit to Oxford and to Castleton Hole. He described the trip in *Reisen eines Deutschen in England* (Travels of a German in England); the second edition was translated into English and published as the work of "Charles P. Moritz, a literary gentleman of Berlin."

Besides *Anton Reiser*, Moritz is best known for his journal, the *Magazine zur Erfahrungsseelenkunde*, which he published for ten years (1783–1793). It was an attempt to shed light into some of the murkiest corners of eighteenth-century life, especially the area of personality disorder and psychoses. Karl Fredrick Pockels (1759–1814) and Solomon Maimon (1744–1800) worked with Moritz on the project, Pockels during Moritz's absences in Italy and Maimon for the last three and a half years of Moritz's life. By 1876, Moritz's interest had shifted to Italy, and he resigned his post as a teacher and set off for that country, where he remained for two years.

Moritz came to Rome in late October 1786. He met Goethe at the Café Greco on November 17 and they strolled to the Villa Pamphilia. A few days later, on an outing to Fiumicino, Moritz broke his arm and was laid up for several months, an occurrence that helped to cement his friendship with Goethe, who served as Moritz's amanuensis, writing letters on his behalf. Moritz was "crawling around" again (Goethe said) in February, but they then parted for several months until Goethe returned to Rome in June. He was considerably influenced by Moritz's *Versuch einer Deutschen Prosodie* (Attempt at a German Prosody, 1786), and particularly by *Über die bildende Nachahmung des Schönen* (On the Artistic Imitation of the Beautiful, 1788), a richly problematical working out of a variety of insights in the light of Goethe's passionate concern with classical art.

Moritz eventually arrived in Weimar in December 1788. He was entertained by such people as Frau von Stein and Caroline Herder, and Goethe soon joined the company. The intellectuals of the Weimar Court Circle, otiose, gossipy, and intellectually incestuous, seem to have made their visitor the sensation of the winter season. They were dazzled by the impromptu discussions Moritz led on practical criticism. He returned in grand style to Berlin in February 1789, in the company of the duke of Weimar. He soon established himself as a literary personality of considerable importance and as a lecturer and professor attached to the Prussian Academy of Sciences. He died in Berlin of tuberculosis.

The permanence of Moritz's literary reputation rests essentially on *Anton Reiser*, the only one of his works—except perhaps *Reisen eines Deutschen in England* (A German's Travels in England)—that is reprinted with any regularity today. He stands revealed as a second-rate intellect, but an intriguing and original one. The remorseless depiction of paranoia in his autobiographical novel is hardly equaled in the literature of the period; the examination of claustrophobic aggression and inferiority complex is as revealing as it is new for its day. It is a quasi-fictional analogue of the *Magazine*, both marking the beginning of an empirical psychology. Moritz assumes the persona of the superior narrator who is sometimes a candid observer and analyst. Two less substantial full-length novels—*Andreas Hartknopf: Eine Allegorie* (1784) and *Andreas Hartknopfs Predigerjahre* (1789)—can be regarded essentially as a complement to *Anton Reiser*. Both are satirical and show masonic influence; they were published anonymously and convey mystification and a certain egregious whimsy.

In *Reisen*, a Romantic view of the world emerges in the description of the cave at Castleton and the discovery of a Kingdom of the Earth beneath, and Moritz's influence on the German Romantic movement was considerable. He played a part in the German Classical movement too, through his friendship with Goethe and the aesthetic theory of the *Nachahmung*.

Moritz was a born anti-Establishment man who struggled all his life to belong to the Establishment, and here he had a certain success. He sought hard, though in vain, for a stable philosophy of life that transcended the Enlightenment.

[*See also* Aesthetics; Novel; *and* Romanticism.]

BIBLIOGRAPHY

Boulby, Mark. *Karl Philipp Moritz: At the Fringe of Genius.* Toronto, 1979. A well-contextualized and broad-ranging intellectual biography.

Catholy, Eckehard. *Karl Philipp Moritz.* Tübingen, 1962.

Eybisch, Hugo. *Anton Reiser: Untersuchungen zur Lebensgeschichte von K. Ph. Moritz und zur Kritik seiner Autobiographie.* Leipzig, 1909. A careful reconstruction of Moritz's life and its relationship to his novel.

La Vopa, Anthony J. *Grace, Talent, and Merit: Poor Students, Clerical Careers, and Professional Ideology in Eighteenth-Century Germany.* Cambridge, 1988. Includes analysis of the social psychology of *Anton Reiser.*

Minder, Robert. *Glaube, Skepsis und Rationalismus: Dargestellt aufgrund der autobiographischen Schriften von Karl Philipp Moritz.* N.P., 1936. Uses the case of Moritz for an insightful exploration of the affinities between eighteenth-century piety and Enlightenment subjectivity.

MARK BOULBY

MOSER, CARL FRIEDRICH VON (1723–1798), German statesman and man of letters.

Moser's association with the German Enlightenment is not so much the result of an original contribution to philosophical debates, nor can it be explained in terms of allegiance to the tenets of Enlightenment thinking. It is more the result of his special contribution to the political development of his society. As a civil servant and writer, he exerted an influence on political and intellectual affairs of the old Holy Roman Empire, representing a policy of reform that corresponded closely to the concepts of the Enlightenment. He expounded on the maxims of politics that worked in the best interests of one's fellow human beings, while appealing to the better nature of his readers to act unselfishly for the survival of the "fatherland," which lay in shambles after the devastation of the Seven Years' War.

Moser's values and moral inclination were shaped by his upbringing. Born in Stuttgart, the son of Johann Jacob Moser, a famous legal authority, he learned early to appreciate the virtues of the old constitution and German legal system. He criticized despotic governance and the arbitrary behavior of princes, which led to his father's downfall, as a departure from existing legal principles as well as a breach of the contract that rulers had sworn to abide by on entering their office. He did not expect a revolution to improve the political conditions of the day, instead firmly placing his hopes on a reform that would validate the spirit of the old constitution.

Moser achieved a remarkable political career at a time when Germany was fragmented into numerous territories and principalities. His early success during difficult negotiations between rival princes drew attention to his judicial astuteness and diplomatic skills. In 1767, he was called by kaiser Joseph II to the Reichshofrat (court council). In 1772, he became president of all the Landescollegien (regional governing bodies) and chancellor of the duchy of Hessen-Darmstadt, a position comparable to prime minister. The duke demonstrated little interest in the running of government, and so Moser gained great authority.

According to his contemporaries, he considered himself to be a co-regent or vice-regent, and justifiably so. He used the power granted through his position to implement an enlightened political program. Fundamental reforms in administration were undertaken to promote the common good. One of the commissions set up at Moser's initiation in 1777 was awarded the task of "making the various labors of our worthy industrious subjects more productive, their taxes lighter, their whole lives more joyful; to help make the sky appear bluer with more reason to be proud of their fatherland and to be content within themselves and to live in gratitude to their Princes." His measures were intended to improve the economy in both towns and country, to help credit institutions, to provide the population with food, and to promote trade, education, and culture in the broadest sense. Moser pursued a line of politics that—seen in the context of his era—sought to reform the existing political system from within. He sought to effect positive change in political and social circumstances by introducing enlightened reform policies gradually. A revolutionary upheaval would have led to the destruction of a world of which Moser basically approved in its fundamental beliefs, history, and possibilities for development.

After ten years, Moser was ousted from his office in disgrace for high-handedness and disloyalty. Thus, he experienced at first hand the disturbingly fragile nature of this political system, which could easily sway toward arbitrary rulership at any time. His reflections on experiences of this kind formed the subject of his writings: the battle against every form of tyranny was his central theme. He confronted the lack of interest displayed by some monarchs and officials in their approach to their duties, contrasting this with the example of a responsible and devoted prince backed by a reliable councilor. He denounced some royal courts for corruption and profligacy, and criticized the ignorance and subservience of the masses, placing the blame for this on both secular and clerical authorities.

Moser developed his political theory in a series of writings in the 1750s and 1760s: *Der Herr und der Diener* (Lord and Servant, 1759), *Beherzigungen* (Important Points, 1761) *Von dem deutschen Nationalgeist* (On the German National Spirit, 1765), *Patriotische Briefe* (Patriotic Letters, 1767), and *Reliquien* (Relics, 1766). These publications stem from the period prior to his term as minister of Hessen-Darmstadt. After being dismissed from office in 1782, he took up his literary work again, but in a minor vein. He turned his attention to the journals *Patriotisches Archiv für Deutschland* (1784–1790), *Neues Patriotisches Archiv* (1792–1794), and *Politische Wahrheiten* (2 volumes, 1796).

Closer reading of Moser's writings leads to the question of whether his works can be classified as literature of the Enlightenment. Although there was no alteration in his strong political impetus and intentions to motivate political involvement, his style, line of argument, form of communication, and choice of topics point in some respects to other traditions. His language, rich in biblical allusions and with a persuasive narrative style, reminds the reader of his Pietistic background. Moser originated from the Württemberg branch of pragmatic Pietism, a movement that sought to lead people, out of Christian conviction, from deviation back to the path of salvation—a model Moser transferred to the state. The reader is brought face to face with the desolate situation of the fatherland, described in vivid scenes, stirring laments, and forceful imagery. The state of the country is deplorable, corrupt, desperate; the political, social and moral conditions of the fatherland as well as its people are depraved. Moser appeals to the reader to comprehend the urgent situation of the Empire and to join forces in changing things for the better.

The moral and didactic intent of these writings is not unknown in Enlightenment literature; however, Moser's persuasive and suggestive diction may overpower the reader and therefore hinder independent thought. Does Moser's moral argumentation, which defines the relationship between the self and the world in a certain way, aim to encourage and strengthen the autonomy of the individual? A detailed analysis of his figurative language shows clearly that his plea to the reader in moral terms is meant to arouse a willingness to act, defined in turn by the juridical grounding of political goals. Moser probably chose this form of rhetoric in order to reach a particular audience: the monarchs and councilors, the princes and civil servants. He knew their mentality and behavior from his own experience and thus also knew that it would not be easy to gain their support for his political ideas. This accounts for his style of appellation.

All of Moser's writings, even the journals, were addressed to this comparatively narrow audience. Other journals during this time typically encouraged readers to send in opinions and critical comments to be published in later issues, but this feature is missing from Moser's writings. In his journals, we find an author writing in order to instruct. By presenting exemplary behavior, he encourages readers to model their lives and actions accordingly.

Critics expressing doubt as to Moser's place in the German Enlightenment tend to overlook the impact he was to have. The liberal movement in the 1840s claimed Moser as a forerunner. According to Robert von Mohl, himself a significant man of letters, it was Moser who helped Germans to cast off their "doglike submissiveness" and thereby to pave the way for the establishment of a government based on a constitutional legal system.

[*See also* Aufklärung *and* Enlightened Despotism.]

BIBLIOGRAPHY
Becher, Ursula A. J. "Moralische, juristische und politische Argumentationsstrategien bei Friedrich Carl von Moser." In *Aufklärung als Politisierung-Politisierung der Aufklärung*, edited by Ulrich Herrmann and Hans Erich Bödeker, pp. 178–195. Hamburg, 1987.
Stirken, Angela. *Der Herr und der Diener: Friedrich Carl von Moser und das Beamtenwesen seiner Zeit*. Bonn, 1984. Includes a list of Moser's publications.

URSULA A. J. BECHER

MOSHEIM, JOHANN LORENZ (1693–1755), German scholar and scientific historian of religion.

Mosheim was the main founder of modern scientific church history and a cofounder of Göttingen University. As a professor at Helmstedt, Mosheim exercised a powerful conservative influence on the ecclesiastical adaptation of Enlightenment themes in Protestant Germany and the English-speaking countries (Moeller, 1998; Oyer, 1994). His important work *Institutionum Historiae Ecclesiasticae Antiquae et Recentioris Libri Quatuor . . .* (Introduction to Ancient and Modern Church History, 1755) saw numerous versions and translations, including English and American editions. His care with sources and his moderate, reasonable tone made his work well-received by rationalists, including Thomas Jefferson.

Mosheim's career in its local context emerges as an effort to mobilize scholarly, juridical, and practical aspects of ecclesiastical culture on behalf of an antiabsolutist tradition indigenous to the Welf territories (Moeller, 1987). His work on the ancient Christian church and his presentation of the sweep of church history remain his most enduring contributions. Although Mosheim did not break with the standard schematic presentation of topics by century, his work prepared the way for the presentation according to internally consistent "epochs" by his prolific student, Johann Matthias Schröckh. (Stöve, 1989, 544; Meinhold, 1967) Mosheim also adopted forward-looking approaches in taking account of streams of ideas in and relativizing confessional clichés. His overall approach has been well summarized by Gernot Wiessner:

Mosheim stands as the founder of the so-called pragmatic church history. In it the metaphysical dualism of ecclesiastical historiography (in which the history of the church is interpreted by the struggle of the godly with the antigodly) is overcome by a human-centered approach. . . . With regard to method Mosheim aimed at freedom of the researcher from dogmatic presuppositions, at a rigorous closeness to the historical sources, at a deliberate criticism of sources, and at a description of the human causes for historical phenomena.

(Wiessner, 1997, 210)

Current work on Mosheim as historian has shifted emphasis from the superficially innovative in his work to elements of long-term continuity. Peter Hanns Reill (1975) sets Mosheim and other Enlightenment historians within a chain of continuity stretching back to Leibniz and ahead to the historicism of Ranke and Meinecke. Stroup (1984) argues that a major theme underlying and unifying Mosheim's work and aims is that of restraining extreme aspects of absolutist-oriented secularization of the institutional church and its clergy.

With regard to theology, earlier scholars are now implicitly criticized for characterizing Mosheim and other theologians of his period as "transitional," "early Enlightenment," or "early rationalist," thus virtually conceding they cannot find a common denominator within Protestant theology in its early moves away from strict orthodoxy. Locating that core will certainly become more difficult as researchers begin to take full account of the fact that Mosheim (however conservative he wanted to be) assigned a greater place to human efforts in salvation than had prior Lutheran tradition as a whole, and certainly far more than had Luther himself, whose whole Reformation grew from a passionate opposition to recognizing any human contribution to justification. This particular passion was lacking in both radical and conservative theologians of the Protestant Enlightenment. Here, as in other ways, Mosheim ultimately stands as a product of his age, not least in his willingness to downplay even the emphasis on the communication of properties in Christology, hitherto the key to Luther's metaphysics and view of salvation.

[*See also* Aufklärung; Germany; Reformed Churches, *subentry on* Lutheranism; *and* Revealed Religion.]

BIBLIOGRAPHY

Mager, Inge. "Mosheim, Johann Lorenz v." In *Lexikon für Theologie und Kirche*, vol. 7, p. 495. Freiburg, 1998.

Meijering, Eginhard Peter. "Mosheim on the Philosophy of the Church Fathers." *Nederlands Archief voor Kerkgeschiedenis* 56 (1975), 367–383.

Meijering, Eginhard Peter. *Die Geschichte der christlichen Theologie im Urteil Johann Lorenz von Mosheims*. Amsterdam, 1995.

Meinhold, Peter. *Geschichte der kirchlichen Historiographie*. vol. 2. Freiburg, 1967.

Meusel, Johann Georg. *Lexikon der vom Jahr 1750 bis 1800 verstorbenen teutschen Schriftsteller*. Leipzig, 1809. The contemporary retrospective bibliography of Mosheim's works appears in vol. 9, pp. 347–364.

Moeller, Bernd. "Johann Lorenz von Mosheim und die Gründung der Göttinger Universität." In *Theologie in Göttingen: Eine Vorlesungsreihe*, edited by Bernd Moeller. (Göttinger Universitätsschriften, series A, vol. 1.) Göttingen, 1987. An important study.

Moeller, Bernd. "Mosheim, Johann Lorenz von." In *Deutsche Biographische Enzyklopädie*, edited by Walther Killy and Rudolf Vierhaus, vol. 7, p. 230. Munich, 1998.

Mosheim, Johann Lorenz von. *Die Macht der Lehre Jesu über die Macht des Todes annotiert und mit einem Nachwort sowie einem Beitrag über Mosheims Predigten*. Edited by Johann Anselm Steiger. (Doctrina et Pietas, Abteilung II, Varia, Band 1.) Stuttgart-Bad Cannstatt, 1998.

Mulsow, Martin, ed. *Johann Lorenz von Mosheim (1693–1755): Theologie im Spannungsfeld von Philosophie, Philologie und Geschichte*. (Wolfenbütteler Forschungen, 77.) Wiesbaden, 1997.

Oyer, John S. "Mosheim, Johann Lorenz von." In *Theologische Realenzyklopädie*, vol. 23, pp. 365–367. Berlin, 1994. A key article.

Pelikan, Jaroslav. *From Luther to Kierkegaard: A Study in the History of Theology*. St. Louis, 1950.

Reill, Peter Hanns. *The German Enlightenment and the Rise of Historicism*. Berkeley, 1975. Vital background.

Stöve, Eckehart. "Kirchengeschichtsschreibung." In *Theologische Realenzyklopädie*, vol. 18, pp. 534–560. Berlin, 1989.

Stroup, John. *The Struggle for Identity in the Clerical Estate: Northwest German Protestant Opposition to Absolutist Policy in the Eighteenth Century*. (Studies in the History of Christian Thought, 33.) Leiden, 1984.

Stroup, John. "Protestant Church Historians in the German Enlightenment." In *Aufklärung und Geschichte: Studien zur deutschen Geschichtswissenschaft im 18. Jahrhundert*, edited by Hans Erich Bödeker et al., pp. 169–192. Göttingen, 1986.

Wiessner, Gernot. "Mosheim, Johann Lorenz v." In *Neue deutsche Biographie*, vol. 18, pp. 210–211. Berlin, 1997. Essential for this article's approach.

JOHN STROUP

MOZART, WOLFGANG AMADEUS (1756–1791), Austrian composer.

There is no other eighteenth-century composer whose life and works appear to be more enmeshed with the Enlightenment than Mozart. Most conspicuously, a number of critical ideological themes of Enlightenment thought were given explicit expression in operatic texts he set (above all in *Le nozze di Figaro* and *Die Zauberflöte*): criticism of aristocratic privileges and abuses, sympathetic portraits of bourgeois and female characters, tropes of exoticism, and vaguely deistic and even pantheistic sentiments. Aside from such overt expressions of Enlightenment topoi, Mozart's music itself seems to radiate an aesthetic of clarity, sentiment, and rationality that resonates with Enlightenment ideals.

Mozart's engagement with the Enlightenment can, first of all, be measured in concrete social terms. After touring as a child keyboard prodigy he traveled widely throughout his short life and came into contact with leading intellectual figures sympathetic to many Enlightenment reforms in Germany, France, and Italy. In 1778, for example, Mozart traveled to Paris in order to explore the possibility of securing an opera commission or perhaps a court appointment as composer; he lodged for three months with baron Grimm and Mme. d'Épinay, the former an old acquaintance of Mozart's father, Leopold. Though Mozart's career ambitions in Paris were disappointed, some historians have argued that his encounter with Grimm and his circle exposed the young composer to many progressive ideas on drama and opera then being discussed by the philosophes.

Mozart's final decade in Vienna (1781–1791) was full of lively encounters with leading representatives of the Austrian Enlightenment, including Joseph von Sonnenfels, Gottfried van Swieten, and Ignaz von Born. Although

Wolfgang Amadeus Mozart. Anonymous portrait. (Accademia Rossini, Bologna, Italy/Giraudon/Art Resource, NY.)

the extent to which Mozart himself was widely read in Enlightenment literature is debated by scholars, there seems little doubt that he was fully sympathetic to the social and ecclesiastical reforms of Joseph II.

Certainly the most compelling evidence of Mozart's connection to Enlightenment ideas—although it has been exaggerated by some scholars—was his involvement with Freemasonry. Long an enthusiastic admirer of the masons (he had written, as early as 1773, incidental music for a play with unambiguous masonic overtones, *Thomas, König in Ägypten*), he joined a small Viennese lodge, Zur Wohltätigkeit, in December 1784, advancing quickly to the rank of Master Mason the following year. Mozart was a dedicated member, not only attending numerous meetings but also composing a large number of musical works for performance during formal masonic ceremonies. After Joseph II ordered the dissolution of several lodges in 1785, including Zur Wohltätigkeit, Mozart joined one of the remaining lodges, Zur Neugekrönten Hoffnung, although he at one point evidently thought about founding his own lodge, which was to be given the very Rousseauian name of the Grotto. While few of the masonic works Mozart wrote that have survived are of high quality (an exception is the "Masonic Funeral Music," K. 477, composed

in 1785), there is little question that he identified fully with the masonic ideals of fraternity, equality, and deism. There is no evidence, however, to suggest that he was a member of a more radical sect of Freemasonry, the Order of Illuminati, although he was well acquainted with a number of its members and certainly sympathized with its strong anticlerical bias.

We are fortunate that a large part of Mozart's voluminous (and in places, riotously bawdy) correspondence has survived to convey a fuller picture of his personality and views. In his many letters to his family, Mozart often railed against aristocratic ignorance and clerical hypocrisy and offered general affirmations of human dignity and justice. His own poor treatment while employed by the archbishop of Salzburg left Mozart with deep bitterness and resentment towards class privileges, as well as a fierce desire to establish himself as a free and independent composer—a wish he was finally able to fulfill on his move to Vienna in 1781. Although he never ceased his efforts to secure royal patronage (as late as 1787, he attained appointment by Joseph II as the official court chamber composer), he was ever adamant about the need to protect his integrity as an artist.

Mozart's deep-seated convictions regarding social justice found their most concrete expression in his setting of Beaumarchais's celebrated and controversial play, *Le mariage de Figaro*, which he completed in 1786 in collaboration with his new Italian librettist, Lorenzo Da Ponte, who toned down some of the most inflammatory passages. Through an unprecedented integration of music and dramatic action, Mozart was able to present the radically subversive tale of the clever valet Figaro and his intrigues against the abusive and egoistic Count Almaviva, as well as sympathetic portraits of his heroines, Suzanna and the Countess, all drawn with unprecedented emotional depth and psychological complexity.

Mozart's social views are also perhaps in evidence in his devotion to—and identification with—the broader public, of whom he was ever mindful when composing. In many of his letters, he reiterated the importance of public approbation for his compositions. It was the "silent applause" of his listeners, he wrote in one of his last letters to his wife, that meant the most to him (letter dated 7 October 1791). He never pandered to audiences by diluting the quality of his music, yet in the genres of music that he developed for public performance—the symphony and, above all, the piano concerto—he was keen that even nonspecialists would gain satisfaction from the most sophisticated of his creations. Indeed, one of the hallmarks of Mozart's mature style is the seeming effortlessness with which he mixed "high" and "low" styles of music, "learned" techniques of counterpoint integrated within more popular, *galant*-inspired musical idioms.

As critics since E. T. A. Hoffman have noted, there is a more troubling, darker side to Mozart's music that belies the received picture of the ever-mirthful child genius effortlessly pouring out prodigious quantities of music radiating warmth, optimism, and classical order. Though often difficult to explicate empirically, there are moments in his music that unexpectedly turn to more somber moods and chromatic darkness. Even in his operas, his heroes and heroines face disconcerting reversals and troubling moral ambiguities. It is possible to attribute these shadows to Mozart's increasingly precarious financial problems after 1786, or perhaps, as Maynard Solomon has suggested, to the unresolved tensions after his father's death in 1787; however it might also be possible to hear them as a reflection of the dialectical undercurrents and hesitancy straining the Enlightenment as it approached the final, calamitous decade of the century.

[*See also* Austria; Freemasonry; Music; *and* Opera.]

BIBLIOGRAPHY

Anderson, Emily, ed. and trans. *The Letters of Mozart and His Family.* 3 vols. London, 1938; 3d ed., 1985.

Elias, Norbert. *Mozart: Portrait of a Genius.* Translated by Edmund Jephcott. Berkeley, 1993.

Gay, Peter. *Mozart.* New York, 1999.

Heartz, Daniel. *Mozart's Operas.* Berkeley, 1990. An indispensable collection of essays by the leading scholar of Mozart's operas.

Knepler, George. *Wolfgang Amadé Mozart.* Translated by J. Bradford Robinson. Cambridge, 1997. Knepler is a noted Marxist musicologist keen to rehabilitate Mozart as a radical thinker fully engaged with contemporaneous political and philosophical thought.

Schuler, Heinz. *Mozart und die Freimaurerei: Daten, Fakten, Biographien.* Wilhelmshaven, 1992.

Solomon, Maynard. *Mozart: A Life.* New York, 1995. A penetrating, exhaustive, and at times speculative psychological study of Mozart and his troubled relationship with his father.

Till, Nicholas. *Mozart and the Enlightenment: Truth, Virtue, and Beauty in Mozart's Operas.* London, 1992. A close reading of Mozart's last three operas as emblems of Enlightenment thought, although Till's readings often become tendentious.

THOMAS CHRISTENSEN

MURATORI, LODOVICO ANTONIO (1672–1750), Italian civil reformer and historian.

Born at Vignola, near Modena, from a family of small farmers, Muratori was schooled in grammar and the humanities by the Jesuits. He also studied law at the local university, but his true mentor was Benedetto Bacchini, a great and learned scholar associated with the Parisian Benedictines of Saint Maur, from whom he learned Greek and philology. After further study, at the Ambrosian Library in Milan, Muratori returned to Modena in 1700 as librarian to the Este family. Under the pseudonym Lamindo Pritanio he proposed in 1703 a great Italian Academy to attract important scholars and to renew interest in the sciences and scholarship in general. Muratori sought to involve all Italian states in this project. The Academy was initially conceived as an institution under the protection of the pope, but gradually Venice emerged as an alternative and more secular center. During the difficult years of the War of the Spanish Succession, Muratori helped shape intellectual reform with his important work *Riflessioni sopra il buon gusto* (1708–1715). Good taste was not only an aesthetic and literary reference, but also a cultural strategy that comprised reason, experience and a well-regulated and antisuperstitious faith. Two important encounters influenced him greatly: his participation in the jurisdictional controversies against Rome (Comacchio), and his relationship with Leibniz. In 1717, Muratori edited the first volume of *Antichità estensi ed italiane* (1717). He was developing his main scholarly project, a collection of Italian chronicles from 500 to 1500, *Rerum Italicarum Scriptores* (1723–1738). This work in twenty-seven volumes in folio was the true starting point for an erudite exploration of the Middle Ages, deepened in the critical dissertations of *Antiquitates Italicae Medii Aevi* (1738–1742). Muratori also wrote *Annali d'Italia* (1744–1749), the first history of Italy (from the beginnings of the Christian age to 1749) since Niccolò Machiavelli, Francesco Guicciardini, and Carlo Sigonio, offering an interesting model of "civil history" in which the true values of the civil society were pacifism, public happiness, progress, and reason. As a philosopher and intellectual reformer, he touched on many fields, including Roman jurisprudence, which he criticized in calling for a true modernization of the legal system, and public health, which he addressed in his efforts to foster a better connection between medical science, civil, and religious authorities in the fight against plague. He synthetized his proposals in his last work, *Della pubblica felicità* (1749) which can be considered a great handbook for the reforms proposed from the point of view of enlightened Catholicism. In this work, the aging scholar expressed his hope for a long period of peace for Italy and Europe. Princes, he believed, had to build public happiness as their first duty, had to ensure not only good ministers, but also public instruction, economic development, an effective system of justice, a well-regulated religious devotion, and a new open connection between civil ethics and politics. Muratori is certainly the most important intellectual voice of enlightened Catholicism. Not only as a scholar, but also as a civil reformer, Muratori had a reputation throughout Europe, above all in the Austrian Empire, Spain, and France, all countries in which his work on public happiness was known directly or in translation. His attempt to reconcile faith and reason, to reevaluate progress and experience, to build civil history on scholarship, and to outline a clear path for reforms were all rooted in the Italian Enlightenment, which in turn reflected the ideas that were transforming European culture.

[*See also* Italy; Men and Women of Letters; *and* Roman Catholicism.]

BIBLIOGRAPHY

Bertelli, Sergio. *Erudizione e storia in Ludovico Antonio Muratori*. Naples, 1960. Still the best work on Muratori.

De Martino, Giulio. *Muratori filosofo: Ragione filosofica e coscienza storica in Lodovico Antonio Muratori*. Naples, 1996. Correct, but largely a compilation.

Ferrone, Vincenzo. *The Intellectual Roots of the Italian Enlightenment: Newtonian Science, Religion and Politic in the Early Eighteenth Century*. Princeton, N.J., 1995.

La fortuna di Ludovico Antonio Muratori. Florence, 1975.

Ludovico Antonio Muratori e la cultura contemporanea. Florence, 1975.

Ludovico Antonio Muratori storiografo. Florence, 1975.

Muratori, Lodovico Antonio. *Opere*. Edited by Giorgio Falco-Fiorenzo Forti. Milan-Naples, 1965. Vol. 2 is a rich and clever anthological choice with a complete bibliography.

Ricuperati, Dino Carpanetto-Giuseppe. *Italy in the Age of Reason*. London, 1987.

Venturi, Franco. *Settecento riformatore: Da Muratori a Beccaria*. Turin, 1969.

GIUSEPPE RICUPERATI

MURRAY, JUDITH SARGENT (1751–1820), American writer.

More than one hundred essays, three plays, a novella, and quantities of verse constitute Judith Sargent Murray's literary legacy. Until recently, however, Murray was best known for her connection with the spread of Universalism in the United States. In 1778, Murray was among the small group in Gloucester, Massachusetts, that founded the first Universalist church in America. Her first and last literary efforts emerged from her religious commitments. She initially found her way into print with a Universalist catechism for children. Her final literary effort involved completing and editing two important books in the history of Universalism: the sermons and letters (1812–1813) and the autobiography (1816) of John Murray, her second husband and a key figure in American Universalism. Murray, however, wrote mostly of secular concerns for secular audiences, driven by her convictions about the needs of the fledgling United States and her desire to achieve fame and financial security through her pen.

Of greatest interest to readers today are Murray's writings on issues concerning women. Her two periodical essays on women, "Desultory Thoughts upon the Utility of Encouraging a Degree of Self-Complacency, Especially in Female Bosoms" (1784) and "On the Equality of the Sexes" (1790), established her as an insightful advocate of expanded educational and vocational opportunities for women. The moral and intellectual equality of the sexes is a central tenet in her *magnum opus*, *The Gleaner* (1798), a collection of one hundred serial essays, some of which had appeared in the *Massachusetts Magazine* between 1792 and 1794. To them, Murray added an introduction and conclusion that revealed "the Gleaner" to be a woman.

As the Gleaner, Murray used a male persona to write, without apology or explanation, about the many subjects that interested her: contemporary politics, manners, philosophy, religion, history, and literature. Interspersed among these authoritative essays are episodes from the Gleaner's family life, in which "he" reports the activities and conversations of his fictive female relatives, including his wife's extensive program for educating their daughter. The resulting domestic novella, with its traditionally female concerns, stands alongside the Gleaner's considered opinions on topics more typical of the male eighteenth-century essayist. Through this careful interweaving of male and female voices, and of conventionally male and female realms of inquiry, Murray underlined her advocacy for women with a subtle exploration of the relationships among gender, intellect, and authority.

The Gleaner is also a digest of Murray's other belletristic endeavors. Throughout her life, she contributed verse to Boston periodicals, and each Gleaner essay begins with several lines of original poetry. Murray hoped to make money in the early 1790s by writing for the theater. Two of her plays, *The Medium, or Virtue Triumphant*, and *The Traveller Returned* (both of which had brief and unsuccessful runs at the Federal Street Theatre in Boston) were printed in full in *The Gleaner*. Though it failed to bring Murray the acclaim she sought, *The Gleaner* is an unparalleled resource for modern readers seeking to understand how the intellectual ideals of the Enlightenment were interpreted by a middle-class American woman of letters.

[*See also* Men and Women of Letters.]

BIBLIOGRAPHY

Harris, Sharon M., ed. *Selected Writings of Judith Sargent Murray*. New York, 1995.

Murray, Judith Sargent. *The Gleaner*. Schenectady, N.Y., 1992. Poorly edited but complete modern edition of the 1798 *The Gleaner: A Miscellaneous Production*, originally published in three volumes in Boston by I. Thomas and E. T. Andrews.

KIRSTIN R. WILCOX

MUSEUMS. *See* Lyceums and Museums.

MUSIC. Music was of critical import to the Enlightenment. It was, first and foremost, a potent medium through which a multitude of ideas—and ideals—could be conveyed effectively to a wider public in a provocative opera libretto, a sentimental ballad, a risqué political song, or a rousing revolutionary cantata. But music was far more than a sonorous vehicle for the transmission of texts. It was itself a challenging subject for philosophical analysis: an affective art to explain aesthetically; an opaque language system to decode semiotically; an acoustical phenomenon to analyze mechanistically; and a marker of ethnic cultures to study comparatively and historically. Music was, in short, a magnet toward which almost the full range of Enlightenment intellectual concerns could be drawn. In this essay, I will discuss four areas in which music intersected in particularly resonant ways with Enlightenment ideas: aesthetics, culture, science, and social practice. (This article does not attempt to survey the engagement of individual composers of the eighteenth century with Enlightenment ideas nor to speculate as to how these ideas may have been reflected in their music. See however, individual entries on Mozart and Rameau.)

Musical Aesthetics. Enlightenment views on musical aesthetics were particularly rich and varied. To an unprecedented degree, music became a central concern of philosophical aesthetics in the eighteenth century. Indeed, it was through speculations concerning musical expression and meaning that some of the most radical changes in Enlightenment aesthetic thought were carried out.

The particular challenge music posed for eighteenth-century critics lay in resolving a number of tensions in music's accepted classification as a mimetic art. Although imitative theories of music possessed a long pedigree traceable to Aristotle, it was in the seventeenth and early eighteenth centuries—a period musicologists typically (if problematically) have designated as "Baroque"—that an aesthetics of musical mimesis was most thoroughly developed. Catalyzed by Descartes's study *Les passions de l'âme* (The Passions of the Soul, 1649) and subsequently developed by French critics such as Jean-Baptiste du Bos (*Réflexions critiques sur la poésie et sur la peinture* [Critical Reflections on Poetry and Painting, 1719]) and Charles Batteux (*Les beaux-arts réduits à un même principe* [The Fine Arts Reduced to a Single Principle, 1746]), mimetic aesthetics held that music, like painting or poetry, was an imitative art capable of capturing and portraying a gamut of human passions, or "affections." A given musical composition, ideally, would sustain a single emotional affect with which a listener could identify and empathize, becoming in essence a kind of portrait of a passion.

In Baroque music theory, there were a number of specific musical means by which affections could be represented. German writers, in particular, were industrious in itemizing the various affects or qualities associated with given keys, modes, melodic "figures," and rhythmic gestures. In this regard, music theorists often drew comparisons with rhetoric, which also taught how given affections might be aroused and sustained by a skilled orator using specific figures of speech, topics, and modes of delivery. On this basis, the prolific German music theorist Johann Mattheson specifically called musical composition

a "sonorous discourse" (*Klangrede*). As d'Alembert put it in his Preliminary Discourse to the *Encyclopédie*, music is "a kind of discourse, or even language, through which the different sentiments of the soul, or rather its different passions, are expressed."

Still, the correlation between music and affect was not a transparent one. This is why so many writers in the eighteenth century insisted that music needed the aid of a poetic text in order to define its affective aims. By the same token, instrumental music was often deprecated by eighteenth-century critics as "noise" and "meaningless babble." Bernard Fontenelle captured the perplexity of many of his contemporaries concerning instrumental music when he famously asked, "Sonate, que me veux-tu?" ("Sonata, what do you want from me?"). An instrumental sonata or keyboard fugue might be entertaining to the ear and an amusing diversion for the player, but without the semantic clarity of vocal music, it could never rise to the same aesthetic status.

To be sure, there were more mathematical conceptions of music that offered potential counternarratives to music's accepted classification as a mimetic art, emphasizing the structurally autonomous nature of its material and form. In fact, the notion of musical beauty lying in pure *harmonia*—sounding elements judiciously proportioned in quantifiable ratios—had a long neo-Platonic pedigree. Yet despite some sympathetic echoes in the later eighteenth century (particularly in the writings of Shaftesbury, Diderot, and Herder), no one developed the idea of musical formalism systematically, or at least to any degree that would threaten the overwhelming prestige and acceptance of mimetic theory. Nor would they have wanted to, since there was one genre of music in which the overwhelming mimetic power of music was most keenly to be felt: the opera. In opera, the affective meaning of music was made clear by the text, or—in the case of incidental instrumental or dance music—by the dramatic context. In particular, the Italian *opera seria*, the most dominant genre of opera throughout the eighteenth century outside France, could be divided into various stock types of arias and ensemble numbers depending on the affection to be depicted (arias of love, rage, lament, etc.).

The many musical pamphlet wars that raged throughout the eighteenth century concerning the respective merits of French and Italian opera were spurred by mimetic questions: Which language and music was best suited for conveying affections? What dramaturgical norms were most effective for moving the passions? For a conservative critic like Rousseau, French opera proved distinctly inferior in this regard because of the unsonorous and guttural nature of the French language, as well as the overly rationalized harmonic accompaniment preferred by French composers such as Rameau.

In Rousseau's view, the key to musical expressivity lay in melody. In a series of chapters in the posthumously published *Essai sur l'origine des langues* (Essay on the Origin of Languages), he proposed that melody was the quintessential language of human passions. Before the advent of spoken language, Rousseau argued, early man communicated by verbal utterances that constituted a kind of primitive melody. By conforming to the natural inflections (or "accents") of the human voice, melody was able to express the passions better than any other musical parameter. Thus, music that adhered most closely to these origins—like the melodies of Italian opera—was for Rousseau the most expressive. In contrast, music that veered from its origins through the use of learned conceits such as counterpoint and harmony, like that composed by Rameau, was deemed cold and sterile, incapable of arousing any passions.

The musical ideals Rousseau advocated in both his critical writings and his own attempts at composition found resonance at midcentury in a growing public taste for lighter, more lyrical musical textures, such as those found in the songs of Italian *opera buffa*. Such a style—often labeled by music historians as *galant*—avoided the contrapuntal complexity and harmonic elaboration associated with high Baroque music, and also the virtuosic passage-work and vocal displays typical of the *da capo* arias of Italian *opera seria*. Instead, the musical texture tended toward a reduced bass–soprano polarity, lyrical and typically symmetrical melodic lines supported by a simplified harmonic syntax punctuated by regular cadential articulations. If the simplest of such galant genres (sentimental songs, minuets and polonaises for keyboard, etc.) ultimately could not sustain intense compositional development, many of the *galant* stylistic ideals—simplicity, lyricism, order—were considered essential for music to be truly expressive, and they provided a key foundation for the mature "classical style" of Haydn and Mozart. (From this perspective, then, the mid-eighteenth century does not constitute the stylistic boundary line traditionally depicted by music historians in which the Olympian pinnacles of "Baroque" and "Classical" styles loom at either end. Rather, the galant ideal becomes a defining and unifying feature of eighteenth-century music, one in which Italian opera can be seen as a stylistic suture binding the century together.)

The emphasis of midcentury music critics on expressivity and sensibility suggests that the focus of aesthetic debate was moving in a more psychological direction. Critics were becoming less concerned with music's ability to *portray* emotions than with its capacity to *express* them. This naturally led to an increased subjectivization of the musical experience that proved resistant to the rationalized semiotics of classical mimetic theory. After midcentury, a number of critics, particularly in England, began to adopt a more empirically grounded approach to musical aesthetics that concerned the sentient responses that music could provoke. For James Harris, music did not literally imitate the affections as much as provoke them "by a sort of natural sympathy" (*Three Treatises Concerning Art*, 1744). Daniel Webb attributed this uncanny power of music to its ability physically to stimulate nerves and humors in the body (*Observations on the Correspondence between Poetry and Music*, 1769). For Adam Smith, however, it was the combination of sensual and intellectual pleasure that was most characteristic of musical listening (*Of the Imitative Arts*, 1795). In Germany, Johann Sulzer disseminated elements of English empirical aesthetics in his *Encyclopedia of the Fine Arts*, while in France, writers such as André Morellet and Michel de Chabanon penned influential essays in which the sentient element of musical cognition was more thoroughly explored.

Still, the gradual evolution toward a more sensationalist aesthetics of music led to a number of troubling moral concerns that seem to lurk just below the surface of many musical writings in the latter half of the eighteenth century. As an art that stimulated sensuous pleasure more viscerally than any other, music seemed most to elude rational control. Even as it was growing in popularity with musicians, instrumental music continued to be viewed with suspicion by some critics as a potentially dangerous force capable of arousing volatile, violent, and even erotic emotions. Among the styles of instrumental writing that enjoyed brief but intense surges of popularity during the third quarter of the century were a "sentimental" (*Empfindsam*) school of keyboard composition cultivated in Northern Germany by composers such as Carl Philip Emanuel Bach, characterized by dramatic contrasts of texture, tonalities, and dynamics, and a "Sturm und Drang" repertoire of orchestral allegros from central Europe, by composers such as Haydn, Mozart, Johann Vanhall, and Carl Ditters von Dittersdorf, which is characterized by driving rhythms, angular themes, and an almost exclusive use of the minor mode.

Consequently, few Enlightenment music critics were willing to abandon mimetic theories of music altogether, nor to dispute the aesthetic superiority of texted music over instrumental music. Even Kant relegated music to an inferior position in the hierarchy of the arts as ephemeral stimulation, a mere play of tonal sensations. The final steps toward an aesthetic of true musical autonomy would be taken by the first generation of German Romantic critics early in the nineteenth century, who can be seen in part as revitalizing aspects of the venerable neo-Platonic aesthetics of musical *harmonia*. Thus, if music moved in the course of Enlightenment aesthetics from an art of imitation to one of expression, it was still an expression tethered to the ideal of mimetic theory.

Music and Culture. In addition to being a subject of intense aesthetic debate, music also became an object of cultural study in the Enlightenment. Scholars in the eighteenth century were beginning to discover a deeper historical dimension to music. Before this, the musical equivalent of the Battle of the Ancients and Moderns was carried on in rather abstract terms because so little music from earlier periods was known, and none from ancient Greece. Not until the latter half of the eighteenth century do we find the first systematic studies of music history published (John Hawkins and Charles Burney in England, Charles Henri de Blainville and Pierre Jean Burrette in France, G. B. Martini in Italy, and Martin Gerbert and Johann Forkel in Germany). At the same time, historically distinct musical repertoires were being uncovered, published, and performed. Specific concert series were founded—such as the "Concerts of Ancient Music" in London (1776), the "Concerts de la Loge Olympique" in Paris (1780), and the "Gesellschaft der Associerten Cavaliere" in Vienna (1778)—that offered venues for the performance of "classical" compositions to a wider public (particularly the music of Handel, arguably the first historical composer to be widely "canonized"). Although Johann Sebastian Bach was little known in the later eighteenth century, a few connoisseurs active in Berlin, Vienna, and London preserved and cultivated his music in private performance. In Bologna, Martini delved even further back in history by supervising regular performances of Renaissance vocal works.

The Enlightenment's recognition that music possessed a deeper historical dimension was complemented by a growing awareness of its ethnic diversity, made known through travel reports and scholarly studies. To be sure, there was a long tradition of employing exotic settings and stock ethnic characters in opera librettos and ballet scenes, and composers had long parodied certain ethnic styles (e.g., "Gypsy" music in Haydn, or "Turkish" music in Mozart). Little by little, however, a more sophisticated understanding of the differing tonal systems, instruments, and performing practices of non-Western musical cultures was being gained. The study of the Jesuit missionary Joseph Amiot on Chinese music and music theory, published in 1779, was exemplary in this regard. The *Encyclopédie*, too, offered remarkably insightful discussions of Indian and Arabic music, along with some transcriptions that are still of value to ethnomusicologists.

As awareness of music's value as a distinct cultural marker deepened through the eighteenth century, much speculation was devoted to the particular national characters of European music. The differences between Italian and French music constituted a long-running debate, but it must be kept in mind that, in the early stages of this debate, such characteristics, however defined, were rarely culturally essentialized. Even though Italian and French music constituted particular vernacular styles and genres, these were generally available to any sophisticated composer for emulation. This stylistic cosmopolitanism also permitted composers such as François Couperin, Johann Joachim Quantz, and Christoph Willibald Gluck to advocate a "mixed taste" in musical composition, drawing from the best features of all national musics.

Not until the latter half of the century, after Rousseau had so strongly tied music to his theory of language, did national styles in music begin to be interpreted more organically. The Piccinni–Gluck debate in the 1770s reflected these changes in attitude in its speculations as to whether the German Gluck was able to write an authentic Italian opera. It was primarily in Germany, though—especially after the wider dissemination of Herder's writings—that the most pronounced nationalistic, and even racial, consciousness entered critical writings on the definition and nature of German music. Mozart, despite his enthusiasm for and complete absorption of Italian compositional models, proudly considered himself a German composer, and he was eager to help establish and promote such indigenous dramatic genres as the *Singspiel*. By the end of the century, the music historian Johann Nikolaus Forkel could write the first biography of Johann Sebastian Bach, celebrating him in unabashed nationalist terms as a native genius unique to the German peoples.

Music as Science. If music was widely accepted by Enlightenment thinkers as a language of sentiment, it was also a language that was uniquely susceptible to scientific analysis. As a phenomenon whose physical properties can be precisely quantified using the ratios of vibrational frequencies, music invited empirical investigation by natural scientists throughout the seventeenth and eighteenth centuries. Descartes, for example, used music in one of his earliest essays to test his nascent rationalist method (*Compendium musica*, c. 1618). Indeed, music became one of the favored subjects of research in the early decades of the scientific revolution. Galileo, Bacon, Mersenne, Huyghens, Hooke, and Newton all wrote on the mathematical basis of musical consonance and tuning (traditionally called "harmonics"). At the same time, acoustical problems of music stimulated fruitful research into areas of rational mechanics and the calculus that continued through the eighteenth century in the work of Taylor, Euler, d'Alembert, the Bernoullis, and Lagrange.

Arguably, however, the scientific approach to music most characteristic of Enlightenment thought was not that of the natural philosopher but the attempts of numerous music theorists to explain the language of tonal music as a rationalized, universal grammar, akin to the efforts of

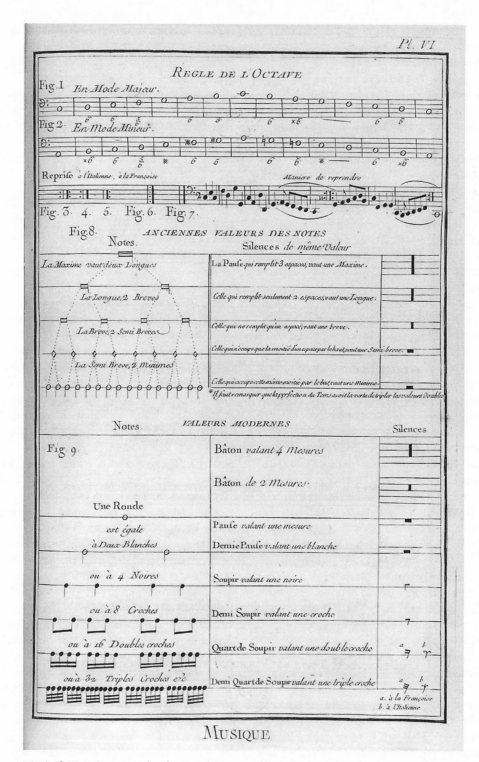

Musical Notation. Sample of musical notation from the *Encyclopédie*. (New York Public Library, Astor, Lenox, and Tilden Foundations.)

Port-Royale on language. By the end of the seventeenth century, the system of Western harmonic tonality was being consolidated among European musicians. In this tonal system, one key and one tonic note act as a central reference point to which all other keys and notes are subordinated. All harmonies and dissonances are controlled through an efficient and rationalized syntax of chordal progressions.

Jean-Philippe Rameau (1683–1764) was the first to analyze systematically the grammar of harmonic tonality, in his important *Traité de l'harmonie* (Treatise on Harmony, 1722). Rameau figures prominently in the history of French opera in the eighteenth century, but in his day he was as renowned for his work in music theory, for which he was widely dubbed the "Newton of harmony." Through careful empirical analysis of the musical practice of his contemporaries, he formulated a few principles to account for the vocabulary and grammar of all tonal music. These principles are contained in his theory of the *basse fondamentale* ("fundamental bass"), which he presented as a kind of synthetic regulator of musical harmony. Essentially, it consisted of a series of chord fundamentals—or "roots"—that are displayed below the continuo-bass of any composition and by which normative patterns of harmonic motion may be observed. More important, Rameau found the consonant intervals that comprise most of the harmonic vocabulary of tonal music as well as the syntax of root motion in the fundamental bass to originate in an apparently universal and natural source: the resonating partials ("overtone series") of any periodically vibrating body (*corps sonore*). On this basis, Rameau argued for the primacy of harmony over melody in his arguments with Rousseau. Since harmony is found to be generated by nature, Rameau claimed, it has to be ontologically prior to melody.

Although the details of Rameau's harmonic theory are rather involved, his basic claim is easy to understand: music has a natural origin in the *corps sonore* from which the vocabulary and grammar of tonal music may be deduced in a methodical manner. Much as Newton was celebrated for having unified Galileo's kinematics of free fall and inclined planes with Kepler's three laws of planetary orbit, Rameau was able to offer a theory that brilliantly synthesized precepts of seventeenth-century "canonics" (the science of mathematical interval measurements) with the practical pedagogy of Baroque basso-continuo practice. Rameau was hailed by the *encyclopédistes* for his work in music theory, and despite their subsequent and often acrimonious disputes, Rousseau, Diderot, and d'Alembert each would help Rameau to develop and disseminate his musical theory.

Though undoubtedly the most "philosophical" music theorist of the eighteenth century, Rameau was not the only one to attempt a scientific analysis of musical practice. The Italian violin virtuoso and composer Giuseppe Tartini (1692–1770), for example, wrote a number of theoretical treatises in which he proposed an alternative source for musical harmony to Rameau's *corps sonore*—the "difference" tones that resulted when certain intervals were strongly bowed on the violin (Tartini called them "third sounds"). Rousseau became an enthusiastic convert to

Tartini's theory after his break with Rameau, since the theory of difference tones seemed to support more strongly his views as to the priority of melody over harmony. Scientists such as Daniel Bernoulli, Giodano Riccati, and Ernst Chladni, however, strongly criticized musicians such as Rameau and Tartini for seeking musical principles in acoustical phenomena, arguing that harmony was more a convention of cultural taste than a dictate of nature.

The parameter of melody so highly valued in *galant* aesthetics was the subject of a major treatise by the German music theorist Heinrich Koch (1749–1816). He analyzed melodic composition as a series of modular phrases and periods that could be manipulated and concatenated in various configurations, following a series of "mechanical rules" (*Versuch einer Anleitung zur Composition* [Attempt at an Introduction to Compositioin, 1782–1793]). Koch also presented a general rhetorical model of compositional process (adapted from Sulzer) in which the composer would work through three stages of invention: plan, realization, and elaboration.

Finally, in the musical subject that arguably received the most "scientific" attention in the eighteenth century, problems of tuning and temperament were addressed in countless publications. It is significant, however, that most keyboardists of the time used some approximation of equal temperament rather than employing the often intricate "meantone" tuning systems proposed by scientists and amateurs with little musical experience. Equal temperament is a perfect example of the Enlightenment's ideal of reason and rejection of dogmaticism, a compromise between the musician's desire for pure sonorities and the keyboardist's need for a playable chromatic gamut.

Music as Social Practice. Beyond the intellectual and cultural issues posed by music in the context of Enlightenment thought, it is also possible to see music as a practice that reflects deeper social changes manifest in the eighteenth century that are now considered fundamental to an understanding of the time. In perhaps the most conspicuous change, music in the eighteenth century was becoming a commercialized profession. Over the course of the century, it moved from being a product of largely royal or aristocratic patronage to one that was increasingly dependent on public patronage. Emblematic of these differences are the careers of Johann Sebastian Bach (1685–1750) and Wolfgang Amadeus Mozart (1756–1791). Bach, throughout his life, was employed by various ecclesiastic, aristocratic, or municipal authorities; Mozart, however, resigned his appointment with the Salzburg archbishop in 1781 to move to Vienna and earn his living in the "free market" as an opera composer, performer, and teacher. There, he was able in a short time to draw lucrative commissions, royalties, and performance fees (contrary to the myth of Mozart as an impoverished, neglected artist). Mozart's entrepreneurship was hardly unique; cities throughout Europe in the second half of the eighteenth century were filled with itinerant musicians, especially of Italian or Bohemian origin, seeking their own fortunes. Aristocratic and royal patronage continued to be vital to musical life, but many composers clearly were writing music with a broader public in mind. Haydn was only reflecting a deeper shift in attitude when he conveyed to his publisher his wish that henceforth "I should dedicate my compositions directly to the public."

To this end, the rise of the public concert must be considered one of the most significant changes in the way music was performed and heard. Although there were certainly precedents, it was in the eighteenth century that musical performances in a large number of opera houses, salons, masonic lodges, and concert halls were opened up to a paying public throughout Europe. Subscription concerts became commonplace in larger urban areas, and even public gardens were opened up for frequent musical entertainments.

To supply these public concert programs with music, new genres of instrumental music were cultivated, including the concert symphony and the instrumental concerto. The symphony, which originated as a short, three-part overture that prefaced Italian operas, eventually was detached and performed as an autonomous concert piece. The concerto originated in the seventeenth century as a more intimate chamber work for aristocratic entertainment and only later developed into a public showcase for a virtuosic soloist.

Parallel to the vigorous growth of musical performance within the emerging public sphere, there was a robust culture of public criticism. Journals and newspapers regularly carried increasingly expansive reviews of musical performances and publications. At the same time, journals specializing exclusively in musical topics appeared in growing numbers through the century—particularly in German-speaking lands—offering reviews and discussions of aesthetic or theoretical matters. Earliest among these were the short-lived journals of Johann Mattheson (*Critica Musica*, 1722–1723, 1725) and Johann Scheibe (*Critischer Musicus*, 1737–1740). More enduring were J. A. Hiller's *Wöchentliche Nachrichten und Anmerkungen die Musik betreffend* (1766–1770), J. Fr. Reichardt's *Musikalischen Kunstmagazin* (1782–1791), and Carl Friedrich Cramer's *Magazin der Musik* (1783–1789). Also of note were the *Journal de musique* in Paris (1764–1768) and the *Review of New Musical Publications* in London (1784).

The cultivation of music in the public sphere was complemented by its growth in the intimate domestic sphere. Through the popularity of instruments like the harpsichord and clavichord (and after about 1770, the improved forte-piano), music became a favorite pastime in small bourgeois households, prompting increased demand for lighter chamber pieces accessible to amateur performers. The popularity at midcentury of the simple *galant* genres must be attributed to the tastes and values of this new consumer class of amateur musicians. Composers churned out countless collections of sentimental songs, simple keyboard dances, and variations on popular operatic tunes throughout the later eighteenth century. More demanding genres like the instrumental sonata and string quartet were played by more accomplished performers. The string quartet was an ideal emblem of the new bourgeois sociability; in Goethe's famous quip, it represented a gathering of four equal individuals engaged in reasoned conversation.

To satisfy the growing demand of consumers for music to play, music publishing houses sprang up throughout Europe. In Germany, Johann Gottlob Breitkopf established his firm's dominance after 1756 by pioneering a new technology of movable type that vastly decreased the cost of publishing. Elsewhere in Europe, important music publishing houses were established: John Walsh (1695) and Robert Bremner (1754) in London, Burchard Hummel (1756) in Amsterdam, and the Artaria family (1778) in Vienna. French music publishing was more tightly controlled than elsewhere on the Continent. Still, after Foucault in 1713 broke the monopoly of music publishing held through royal decree by Ballard, about eighty music publishing houses were established in Paris before the Revolution. The extension of copyright publishing laws to music—first granted in England in 1710—also aided the growth of the music publishing business. At the same time, publishers served a lucrative market for didactic literature from which amateur musicians could learn to read music, play an instrument, and master the rudiments of music theory.

[*See also* Aesthetics; Bourgeoisie; Concert; Criticism; Handel, Georg Frideric; Herder, Johann Gottfried; Mozart, Wolfgang Amadeus; Opera; Publishing; Rameau, Jean-Philippe; Sensibility; Sturm und Drang; *and* Virtuosi.]

BIBLIOGRAPHY

Baker, Nancy Kovaleff, and Thomas Christensen. *Aesthetics and the Art of Musical Composition in the German Enlightenment*. Cambridge, 1995. An annotated translation of selected writings by Johann Sulzer and Heinrich Koch.

Cannone, Belinda. *Philosophies de la musique, 1752–1789*. Paris, 1990. A general review of well-known aesthetic issues, useful for its comprehensive annotated bibliography of primary sources.

Christensen, Thomas. *Rameau and Musical Thought in the Enlightenment*. Cambridge, 1993.

Didier, Béatrice. *La musique des Lumières*. Paris, 1985. A provocative, if at times desultory, study, with thorough discussion of musical topics in the *Encyclopédie*.

Fubini, Enrico. *Music and Culture in Eighteenth-Century Europe: A Source Book*. Chicago, 1994. A useful anthology of critical writings on music, especially strong on the many opera polemics.

Lester, Joel. *Compositional Theory in the Eighteenth Century*. Cambridge, Mass., 1992. A highly technical but comprehensive survey of music theory in the eighteenth century.

Lipmann, Edward. *A History of Western Musical Aesthetics*. Lincoln, Neb., 1992. A good historical survey, particularly strong on the eighteenth century.

Neubauer, John. *The Emancipation of Music from Language: Departure from Mimesis in Eighteenth-Century Aesthetics*. New Haven, Conn., 1986. A useful survey of music-aesthetic thought, although heavily teleological in bias.

Rosen, Charles. *The Classical Style: Haydn, Mozart, Beethoven*. New York, 1972. A canonical study of the music of the Viennese classicists, although with little overt reference to broader Enlightenment themes.

Schroeder, David P. *Haydn and the Enlightenment: The Late Symphonies and Their Audience*. Oxford, 1990.

Thomas, Downing. *Music and the Origins of Language: Theories from the French Enlightenment*. Cambridge, 1995. Especially valuable for its discussion of Rousseau.

Verba, Cynthia. *Music and the French Enlightenment: Reconstruction of a Dialogue, 1750–1764*. Oxford, 1993. Lucid presentation of the musical views of Diderot, Rousseau, and d'Alembert, particularly in regard to aesthetic issues.

THOMAS CHRISTENSEN

MUSSCHENBROEK, PETRUS VAN (1692–1761), Dutch physicist.

Born in Leiden of a well-known family of instrument-makers, Petrus was the son of Johan Joosten van Musschenbroek, who made scientific instruments such as air pumps, microscopes, and telescopes in his workshop in Leiden. His brother Jan had an internationally famous workshop in the same city. As a youth, Petrus studied medicine at the University of Leiden, where he attended the lectures of Hermann Boerhaave, Wolferd Senguerd, and Willem Jacob 'sGravesande. He received his doctorate in medicine in 1715. He practiced medicine in his native city from 1716 to 1719, and, in 1717, went on a study tour to London, where he met Isaac Newton and the circle of English Newtonians and attended the lectures in experimental physics given by John Theophilus Desaguliers. In 1719, van Musschenbroek became professor of mathematics and philosophy, and in 1720 of medicine, in Duisburg. From 1723 to 1740, he held the chair of mathematics and philosophy at the University of Utrecht, and also the chair of astronomy from 1732. In 1723, he delivered his important *Oratio de certa methodo philosophiae experimentalis* (Discourse on the Most Certain Method for the Natural Sciences), in which he defended the empirical-mathematical method of Newton. In 1730, he delivered a celebrated *Oratio de methodo instituendi experimenta physica* (Discourse on the Method for Performing Physical Experiments).

Van Musschenbroek was nominated in 1740 to the chair of mathematics and philosophy at the University of Leiden. In 1743, he succeeded the Newtonian physicist and philosopher 'sGravesande in the teaching of experimental physics, but by this time he was more interested in speculative philosophy.

The time van Musschenbroek spent at Utrecht, where he reformed the teaching of science in accordance with Newtonian principles, was his most productive from the point of view of publication. He published a concise textbook, the *Epitome elementorum physico-mathematicorum, conscripta in usus academicos* (1726), and six more elaborate versions, the last of which, the *Introductio ad philosophiam naturalem* (1762) appeared posthumously in two volumes and remained a standard work for a long time. Some of these versions were translated into English, French, German, and Swedish, and van Musschenbroek also prepared a Dutch edition (1736) especially intended for the layperson who could not read Latin. An English edition was published in 1744 as *The Elements of Natural Philosophy, Chiefly Intended for the Use of Students in Universities*. During his Utrecht period, van Musschenbroek published essays on magnetism and capillarity (1729), which he explained in terms of attractive and repulsive forces. He also did investigations on the strength of materials and made systematic meteorological observations. He became known for his invention of the pyrometer, an apparatus for determining the thermal expansion of metals, which he described in 1731; his name is also associated with the invention of the Leyden jar in 1746.

Van Musschenbroek was an accurate and careful experimentalist who continually advocated the study of the natural sciences according to Newtonian method. He was convinced that knowledge about bodies and their qualities could be obtained only by observation and experiment; the data collected must serve as a foundation from which we reach conclusions by means of logic and mathematics. All natural phenomena should then be explained by these mathematically formulated natural laws.

Van Musschenbroek's Newtonianism was shot through with strong Baconian tendencies. His study of the natural sciences was fundamentally empirical, and he emphasized strongly our dependence on the careful accumulation of data. He rejected any hypotheses that, in the manner of the Cartesians, were derived a priori and not from controlled experiment. He carried on a fierce polemic against Cartesian natural philosophy, especially in his early textbooks. However, not unlike that of Descartes, whose scientific rationalism had a religious basis, van Musschenbroek's scientific empiricism was also based on religious presuppositions. He was convinced that things cannot be known by a priori reasoning because they are as God freely has willed them.

Together with Boerhaave and 'sGravesande, van Musschenbroek played an important part in the dissemination of Newtonianism throughout the Continent. He is remembered chiefly as an inspiring university teacher and as an author of influential textbooks on physics, which he continually revised and brought up to date. His lectures were attended by large numbers of students from all over Europe. Van Musschenbroek, together with 'sGravesande, was largely responsible for the growing popular interest in natural sciences in the Dutch Republic during the second quarter of the eighteenth century.

[*See also* Boerhaave, Hermann; Gravesande, Willem-Jacob 's-; Medicine; Natural Philosophy and Science; Netherlands; Newton, Isaac; Scientific Instruments; *and* Universities.]

BIBLIOGRAPHY

Clercq, Peter de. *At the Sign of the Oriental Lamp: The Musschenbroek Workshop in Leiden, 1660–1750*. Rotterdam, 1997.
Pater, Cornelis de. "Petrus van Musschenbroek (1692–1761), a Dutch Newtonian." *Janus* 54 (1977), 77–87.
Pater, Cornelis de. *Petrus van Musschenbroek (1692–1761), een Newtoniaans natuuronderzoeker*. Utrecht, 1979. A full-length scientific biography with a full bibliography, in Dutch with English summary.
Pater, Cornelis de. "The Textbooks of 's-Gravesande and van Musschenbroek." In *Italian Scientists in the Low Countries in the XVIIth and XVIIIth Centuries*, edited by Cesare S. Maffioli and Lodewijk C. Palm, pp. 231–241. Amsterdam, 1989.
Ruestow, Edward G. *Physics at Seventeenth- and Eighteenth-Century Leiden: Philosophy and the New Science in the University*. The Hague, 1973. Chapter 8 is on Petrus van Musschenbroek.
Struik, Dirk Jan. "Musschenbroek, Petrus van." In *Dictionary of Scientific Biography*, edited by Charles Coulston Gillispie, vol. 9, pp. 594–597. New York, 1974.

H. A. M. SNELDERS

MYSTICISM. On 12 March 1699 Pope Innocent XII condemned twenty-three propositions of Fénelon's *L'explication des maximes des saints* (Explanation of the Maxims of the Saints) in his papal brief *Cum alias*. This act, bringing to a conclusion the long theological elaboration in Catholicism of the problem of pure love, a disinterested love without hope for reward or dread of punishment, would be decisive for the history of mysticism in the eighteenth century. It was the final touch, following the condemnation of Molinos's propositions in Rome in 1687, after numerous spiritual works (by Marie d'Agreda, Pietro Matteo Petrucci, François Malaval, Juan Falconi, Benedict Canfield, Jean de Bernières Luvigny, Jean-Joseph Surin, and others) had been put on the Index of forbidden books and measures had been taken against Mme. Guyon in France.

Fénelon, the archbishop of Cambrai, submitted in all sincerity to the condemnation. Taking as his model the figure of the crucified one "abandoned by his Father" who yet obeys him with perfectly selfless love, he stopped writing on mysticism and developed instead, in opposition to the Jansenists, a Christology based on the perfect submission of devout believers to the authority of the church.

Fénelon's small spiritual works, extracts from letters, or meditations that various booksellers continued to publish would even be corrected with the expression "pure love" easily replaced by "perfect love." Despite his victory over Fénelon, bishop Jacques-Benigne Bossuet, Fénelon's most powerful and unyielding critic, did not lay down his weapons and in 1702 did not fail to raise suspicions that the archbishop of Cambrai was clandestinely circulating mystical texts (Fénelon, *Correspondance*, ed. J. Orcibal, vol. 1, Paris, 1972, p. 220). In Rome, caution notwithstanding, prosecutions continued even if these did not lead to any spectacular measures; for example, in July 1704, the priest Léonard noted: "Nine or ten of the most important mystics such as Tauer, Blosius and others whose names I don't know have been turned over to the Holy Offices; it is believed they will be condemned." (Paris, Bibliothèque Nationale, ms. Fr. 19208, fo 270vo).

As in Rome, Church censure in France vigilantly refused publication for books that were too assertively mystical, less for reasons of orthodoxy than because mystical texts appeared to the censors to draw upon a "not very enlightened piety," promoting "superstitions," "illusions," and "visions." Throughout the century, mysticism will remain the object, within the Christian denominations, of a prejudice on the part of the educated and enlightened, and refutations of the Quietists continue to be published almost ceaselessly, such as the *Crisis Theologica* (1719) by the Jesuit C. A. Casnedi, which was directed against the mystics condemned in 1717 by the Portuguese Inquisition. From this perspective one can see parallels between the reactions of the Catholic church toward mysticism and those of orthodoxy within the evangelical church toward Pietism.

One way of defending the mystics, already attempted by Fénelon and Mme. Guyon, was to demonstrate how their works and doctrine formed part of a long and sound tradition—one thoroughly approved and quite remote from all the errors attributed to them. This was achieved in an extremely scholarly fashion by the discalced Carmelite Honoré de Sainte-Marie in his thick two-volume work, *Tradition des pères et des auteurs ecclésiastiques sur la contemplation* (Tradition of the Fathers and Ecclesiastical Writers Concerning Contemplation, 1708). The danger of this, however, was to weaken what constituted the activity of this doctrine and of these experiences by reducing them to the level of ordinary Christian spirituality.

Another defense lay in the publication of the great mystical works of the sixteenth and seventeenth centuries: those of Saint Teresa, Saint John of the Cross (canonized in 1726), Saint Francis of Sales (in an edition "corrected" by Père Brignon), and Surin (this edition "corrected" by Père Fellon) were published frequently. These, however, often appeared in editions expurgated to eliminate not just anything that seemed stylistically or conceptually archaic but also anything potentially disturbing to the suspicious representatives of orthodoxy. Fénelon's spiritual works were also republished during the eighteenth century, and in German translation were an influence in Pietist circles. Mme. Guyon's works were published even before the author's death, thanks to the Protestant Pierre Poiret (1646–1719), who had also produced numerous editions of both old and modern mystical texts (among others the famous *Theologia Germanica* [Germanic Theology]). Later, thanks to the pastor of Lausanne, Jean-Philippe Dutoit-Membrini (1721–1793), who had experienced a deeply moving spiritual "conversion" in 1752, Mme. Guyon's works were republished at the end of the eighteenth century and included especially her *Lettres chrétiennes et spirituelles* (Christian and Spiritual Letters, 1767–1768). Meanwhile these texts had been translated into German and it was thanks to them that Lutheran Pietism became the heir not only of the medieval mystical tradition but also of assimilated modern catholic mysticism. Moreover English translations guaranteed that Guyon's form of mysticism would be successful in Anglican and Methodist communities in Great Britain and the United States. Most modern mystical works thus were able to be known and influential right up to the beginning of the nineteenth century, although more in non-Catholic Christian denominations than in Catholicism.

The less than favorable conditions created simultaneously by rationalism, libertinism, and the theological opposition to mysticism did not, however, prevent the mystical trend from having numerous forms of expression. In Catholicism its presence was maintained particularly inside the convents, which is why not much is known about it still. The manuscripts, spiritual correspondences, and collections of meditations found today in many libraries or many archives, either public or in convents, bear better witness to its continuing presence in a more or less underground fashion than do printed texts that underwent rather strict censorship. We do know something about several mystical nuns: in Italy the experiences of the Capuchin saint Veronica Giuliani (1660–1727), the Carmelite saint Teresa Margherita Redi (1747–1770), and other nuns are in the tradition of earlier centuries with all its excesses of penitence, ecstasy, or surrender to pure love. In Swabia, Crescence de Kaufbeuren, a Franciscan, roused the suspicions of Rome with her theologically bold visions and prompted the letter *Sollicitudini Nostrae* by Benedict XIV in 1745; she was, nonetheless, beatified in 1900. In Spain, despite criticism from those who were more "enlightened," despite the refutations of mysticism published throughout the eighteenth century that assimilated it into the condemned Quietism, and despite

theologians' challenges to so-called "acquired" contemplation (they even wanted to ban the writings of Saint John of the Cross), there were important treatises published on mystical theology. Among these was *Cursus Theologiae Mystico-Scholasticae* (Textbook of Mystico-Scholastic Theology, 1720–1740) by the Carmelite Joseph du Saint-Esprit.

The Society of Jesus provides a good example of this permanent mystical current in the eighteenth century under intellectual and theological circumstances rather unfavorable to this type of spirituality. At the time of the quarrel over "pure love," the Jesuits were as a whole closer to Fénelon than to Bossuet. The Jesuit journal, the *Mémoires de Trévoux*, otherwise distinguished by its clear rationalism and suspicion of "fanaticism," would maintain this extremely qualified attitude, to the point that it more than once incurred the accusation of Quietism from the Jansenists. Mystical theology, however, seemed to the Jesuits to be "neither a science nor an art," as Father Ménestrier wrote in 1704. Consequently, Jesuits who continued the spiritual tradition of Fathers Lallemant, Surin, or Jean Rigoleuc would remain practically unknown until the recent publication of their manuscripts. There are documents, nonetheless, attesting to the fact that Jesuit spirituals of the previous century, Surin or François Guilloré, were still being recommended by Jesuits in the eighteenth century.

Several books also, much criticized at the time by their enemies, prove that the mystical tradition had a persistent appeal for certain Jesuits. Examples in France would be Jean Pichon's *Esprit de Jésus-Christ et de l'église sur la fréquente communion* (The Mind of Jesus Christ and the Church concerning Frequent Communion, 1745), and in Italy Giovanni Battista Scaramelli's *Direttorio mistico* (Mystical Guide, 1754). It is above all in the works of the Jesuits Claude Judde (1661–1735), Claude-François Milley (1668–1720), and especially Jean de Caussade (1675–1751), however, some of which were not published until recently, that we discover the influence of the great seventeenth century authors, Saint François de Sales, Surin, or Fénelon. In the only one of his texts published in the eighteenth century, *Instructions spirituelles en forme de dialogues sur les divers états d'oraison suivant la doctrine de M. Bossuet* (Spiritual Instructions in Dialogue on Various States of Prayer According to the Teaching of Bossuet, 1741), Caussade attempted to rehabilitate with Bossuet's name a spirituality distinguished by the mysticism of pure love. It is only through the recent publication of his letters and other spiritual works, all of which were written as guides for nuns, that we have learned the extent of this influence. The writings of these Jesuits, in fact, especially those by Milley and Caussade, were intended for nuns and not supposed to leave the walls of the convents. They trace, therefore, a hidden history of spirituality useful in explaining the resurgence of mysticism in a totally different context, that of the French Revolution and the romantic spiritual renewal through the writings of Jean-Nicolas Grou (1731–1803) and Pierre-Joseph Picot de Clorivière (1735–1820). The suppression of the Society of Jesus occurred right at the beginning of this mystical renaissance, not only in France but also in Bavaria and in Spain.

Alongside its permanent presence hidden away in convents, mysticism—in a distorted fashion but one accessible to all the faithful—had an effect on devotion. The most important example is that of devotion to the Sacred Heart, perhaps the greatest creation of Roman Catholic piety in modern times. Certainly devotion to the heart of Christ-made-man had many traditional aspects and went back to the Middle Ages. It was starting with the visions from 1673 to 1675 of a nun of the Visitation order from Paray-le-Monial, Marguerite-Marie Alacoque, however, that it spread throughout the entire Roman Catholic world, in Latin as well as Germanic countries and as far as Spanish and Portuguese America. The mysticism of Marguerite-Marie was, however, interpreted in the eighteenth century with an emotional and affective sense that was rather far-removed from the volontarism of the earlier sense of devotion to the heart of Christ. The political orientation, the warning of punishment threatening society if amends were not made to a transgressed, almighty God, were still there in the background, but they were dominated by the manifestation of an exalted sensitivity in search of emotional rewards at the very moment when disbelief and the enlightenment were putting staunch believers on the defensive. This was, perhaps, a misinterpretation of the meaning of Marguerite-Marie's message, but the shift of mysticism in the direction of emotional devotion is evidence of a genuine transformation of spirituality.

Another shift away from the great mysticism of the seventeenth century can be seen in the evolution of Jansenism from one century to the next. The Jansenists did, of course, display extreme hostility to the mystical tendencies of certain Jesuits and denounced devotion to the Sacred Heart and Jean-Joseph Languet de Gergy's *La vie de la venerable Mère Marguerite-Marie* (Life of the Venerable Mother Marguerite-Marie, 1729). However, persecutions, and the development in the work of Jean-Joseph Duguet and Jacques-Vincent Bidal d'Asfeld of a figurist and apocalyptic exegesis, transformed their theocentric spirituality. Distinguished during the period of Saint-Cyran and Pascal by the influence of Saint Teresa of Avila and Saint Francis de Sales, it turned into a search for signs: Physical phenomena, paroxysms of suffering, and the witness of bodily convulsions were an attempt to ward

off by their excess the essential absence that had been the object of mysticism in the previous century. These intense forms, attaining barbaric and cruel heights, were certainly a manifestation of mysticism, just as in a different way the work of the marquis de Sade was very explicitly its reverse image.

By these diverse ways, mysticism would survive the condemnations of the end of the seventeenth century and reemerge with the beginning of romanticism in the works of Joseph de Maistre, who had read Fénelon and Mme. Guyon, as well as in those of Louis-Claude de Saint-Martin and of Anne-Sophie Swetchine, and in Joseph von Görres's great synthesis. Survival, however, came at the cost of striking transformations and of slipping toward an illuminism and esotericism.

[*See also* Clorivière, Picot de; Duguet, Jacques-Joseph; Fénelon, François-Armand de Salignac de La Mothe; Guyon, Jeanne-Marie Bouvier de La Motte; Jansenism; Jesuits, *subentry on* Jesuits and Jansenists; Revealed Religion; *and* Roman Catholicism.]

BIBLIOGRAPHY

Boespflug, François. *Dieu dans l'art:* Sollicitudini Nostrae *de Benoît XVI (1745) et l'affaire Crescence de Kaufbeuren.* Paris, 1984.

Cherel, Albert. *Fénelon au XVIIIème siècle en France (1715–1820).* Paris, 1917; repr., Geneva, 1970.

Chevallier, Marjolaine. *Pierre Poiret, 1646–1719: Du protestantisme à la mystique.* Geneva, 1994.

Cruz Moliner, José de la. "Espagne, du 18ème siècle au 20ème siècle." In *Dictionnaire de spiritualité.* Paris, 1937–1995. Vol. 4, col. 1178–1183.

Gusdorf, G. *Dieu, la nature, l'homme au siècle des lumières.* Paris, 1976.

Gusdorf, G. *Naissance de la conscience romantique au siècle des lumières.* Paris, 1976.

Le Brun, Jacques. "Censure préventive et littérature religieuse en France au début du XVIIIème siècle." *Revue d'Histoire de l'Église de France* (1975), 201–225.

Le Brun, Jacques. "Entre la mystique et la morale." In *Les Jesuites, Dix-huitième Siècle* 8 (1976), 43–66.

Le Brun, Jacques. "Résurgences au dix-huitième siècle de la question du pur amour." In *Studies on Voltaire and the Eighteenth Century.* Vol. 265. Oxford, 1989, pp. 1242–1245.

Prandi, Alfonso. "Italie, au 18ème siècle." In *Dictionnaire de spiritualité.* Paris, 1937–1995. Vol. 7, pt. 1, col. 2258–2266.

Petrocchi, Massimo. *Storia della spiritualità italiana.* Vol. 3. Rome, 1979.

Rayez, André. "Dutoit (Jean-Philippe)." In *Dictionnaire de spiritualité.* Paris, 1937–1995. Vol. 3, col. 1849–1853.

Schrader, Hans-Jürgen. "Madame Guyon, le piétisme et la littérature de langue allemande." In *Madame Guyon: Rencontres autour de la vie et l'œuvre.* Grenoble, 1997, pp. 83–129.

Ward, Patricia. "Madame Guyon et l'influence quiétiste aux États-Unis." In *Madame Guyon: Rencontres autour de la vie et l'œuvre.* Grenoble, 1997, pp. 131–143.

JACQUES LE BRUN
Translated from French by Betsy Wing

MYTH. *See* Aesthetics *and* Tradition.

N

NAIGEON, JACQUES-ANDRÉ (1738–1810), French philosopher and man of letters.

Naigeon's life before he met Denis Diderot (1713–1784) and Paul-Henri Thiry d'Holbach (1723–1789) in the mid-1760s is almost completely unknown. According to Diderot, who made Naigeon his literary executor, he had been an artist "before becoming a philosopher." Diderot introduced Naigeon into d'Holbach's philosophical salon, where he became the baron's close collaborator, working on the editing, translation, and publication of a large number of anti-Christian and atheistic works.

In 1781, the publisher Charles Joseph Panckouke chose Naigeon to edit the three volumes on "Philosophy" for the ambitious *Encyclopédie méthodique*. These became his *Philosophie ancienne et moderne*, an idiosyncratic critical and atheistic history of philosophy, published in three volumes between 1791 and 1794. After d'Holbach's death in 1789, Naigeon edited the works of a great diversity of celebrated authors, including Jean-Jacques Rousseau and Diderot.

Naigeon initially greeted the French Revolution with enthusiasm, but he turned against it over its persecution of the Roman Catholic Church and its promulgation of the deistic Cult of the Supreme Being. He was an atheist who favored the disestablishment of the Catholic Church, but with religious toleration, freedom of opinion and publication, and no revolutionary religious creed. He articulated these ideas forcefully in his *Addresse à l'Assemblée Nationale sur la liberté des opinions* (Address to the National Assembly on Liberty of Thought and Expression, 1790). In 1793, in the *Philosophie ancienne et moderne*, he called the Revolution's deism even more intolerant than the Catholicism against which the philosophes had fought.

As the Revolution progressed, Naigeon withdrew from active life, devoting himself to scholarly editing, book collecting, and the oversight of Diderot's manuscripts. Napoleon named him to the Institut National, but Naigeon's reputation as an atheist made him too controversial a figure for higher honors.

Naigeon was a serious and original atheistic philosopher. He was more interested in the life sciences than was d'Holbach, and more interested in epistemology and logic than was Diderot. He shared with both, however, a sense that atheism was a way of limiting and directing the claims of human knowledge to material beings and their behaviors—matter in motion—knowledge that alone would enhance the "coexistence" of man and nature. He saw belief in God as the fundamental barrier to human progress, closing off our search for useful natural knowledge and denying the primacy of the quest to ease unnecessary human suffering. He argued that there was only one natural, physical reality, and that it was empirically and logically absurd to divide phenomena into natural and supernatural, or material and spiritual. He also believed that religion of any form was a great aid to political tyranny. Nonetheless, Naigeon concluded pessimistically that the need for religious belief was "inherent in human nature," given human fear and weakness, and that, sadly, the tyranny of those who abused superstition for personal gain would be the historical norm.

Posterity generally has seen Naigeon as a minor thinker who happened to oversee the publication of Diderot's posthumous works. In fact, his commentaries on Diderot's thought are a treasury both of insight into Diderot and of the exposition of Naigeon's own original philosophy, and he was a major materialist and atheistic voice of the late Enlightenment.

[*See also* Atheism; Diderot, Denis; Holbach, Paul-Henri Thiry d'; Materialism; *and* Panckoucke, Charles Joseph.]

BIBLIOGRAPHY

Brummer, R. *Studien zur französischen Aufklärungsliteratur im Anschluss an J. A. Naigeon.* Breslau, 1932. The first serious scholarly effort to sort out Naigeon's contributions to the literature and thought of the Enlightenment.

Kors, Alan Charles. "The Atheism of d'Holbach and Naigeon." In *Atheism from the Reformation to the Enlightenment*, edited by Michael Hunter and David Wooton, pp. 273–300. Oxford, 1992. Study of the sources of and influences on Naigeon's atheistic philosophy, and of the similarities and divergences of Naigeon's and d'Holbach's thought.

Kors, Alan Charles. *D'Holbach's Coterie: An Enlightenment in Paris.* Princeton, N.J., 1976. Study of the milieu in which Naigeon flourished, with discussion of Naigeon's thought and his place in the Enlightenment, Old Regime, and French Revolution.

Naigeon, Jacques-André. *Mémoires historiques et philosophiques sur la vie et les ouvrages de D. Diderot.* Paris, 1821.

Naigeon, Jacques-André. *Philosophie ancienne et moderne.* 3 vols. Paris, 1791–1794. In his remarkable memoirs on Diderot and in his notes to his history of philosophy, Naigeon reveals much about his own life as a philosophe.

ALAN CHARLES KORS

NAPLES. The Kingdom of Naples and Sicily formed part of the Spanish monarchy in the sixteenth and seventeenth centuries. In 1707, Naples passed by conquest, during the War of the Spanish Succession, from Spanish Bourbon rule to Austrian Habsburg dominion under Emperor Charles VI, who ruled his new possession from Vienna through successive viceroys. Sicily was given in 1713 to the duke of Savoy, who was later (1720) obliged to surrender it to Charles VI. Charles proposed reforms to enhance the resources, authority, and jurisdiction of the government in Naples at the expense of the power and privileges of the Roman Catholic Church and the feudal barons. In support of these efforts, he could draw on the vibrant intellectual life of the kingdom, represented by Giambattista Vico (1668–1744), author of the *Scienza nuova* (1725), and Pietro Giannone (1676–1748), whose *Istoria civile del regno di Napoli* (1723) typified the historical and jurisdictional concerns of the early Neapolitan Enlightenment. Charles VI's reforming efforts failed, however, in large part because of the entrenched power of his opponents. Putting a period to the Austrian Habsburg failure was the conquest of Naples and Sicily by Spanish forces in 1734. They now became an independent kingdom ruled by a resident monarch, the first in centuries: Carlo di Borbone, son of the Bourbon king Philip V of Spain and Isabel Farnese.

Reform. The years after 1734 saw a wide range of reform initiatives, in which Carlo was ably supported by a number of ministers, chief among whom was the Tuscan Bernardo Tanucci (1698–1782). Reform efforts included a renewed attack on the extent and abuses of feudal jurisdictions (1738) and measures to stimulate trade, including the creation of a supreme magistrature for commerce and greater toleration for Jews (1740). The conclusion in 1741 of a concordat with the papacy reduced the fiscal and other immunities of the clergy and paved the way for the first revision of the tax register since 1669, as well as for the abolition of the tribunal of the Inquisition in Naples. As in earlier years, however, these measures faced powerful opposition. Opponents of reform gained ground after Naples's costly and disastrous participation in the War of the Austrian Succession. This, and an outbreak of plague at Messina (1743), obliged Carlo to retreat: in 1746, the supreme magistrature for trade was suppressed and the recent toleration of the Jews repealed.

The initiative for enlightened reform now passed from the government into private hands, as Neapolitan thinkers and writers became more concerned with economic issues. Naples had remained to some extent immune—even hostile—to English and French currents traditionally associated with the Enlightenment. Around 1730, however, Celestino Galiani, Bartolomeo Intieri, Nicola Cirillo, and other intellectuals effectively constituted an academy at Naples, which subscribed to the ideas of John Locke. Ferdinando Galiani (1728–1787) translated Locke's writings on financial subjects; he anonymously published *Della moneta* (1751), a contribution to the contemporary debate about money which amply reflected such Enlightenment concerns as utility and happiness. (Subsequently, as Neapolitan minister at Paris, Galiani was an intimate of d'Holbach and Diderot.) More importantly, Bartolomeo Intieri played a leading part in the establishment, at the University of Naples in 1754, of the first European chair in "trade and mechanics," whose first incumbent was Antonio Genovesi (1712–1769).

In 1758, Carlo di Borbone left Naples for Spain, where he succeeded his half-brother, Ferdinand VI, as King Charles III. His young son, Ferdinand, remained as king in Naples, with Tanucci as regent. Tanucci continued the reforms along regalist and jurisdictionalist lines, expelling the Jesuits from Naples in 1767 as part of the Bourbon attack on the Society of Jesus. The most important event in these years was the famine of 1764, which devastated Naples because of the kingdom's backward economy and inefficient system of provision. As many as 200,000 people may have died from hunger and disease in the kingdom as a whole, including 40,000 in the capital. Inevitably, Neapolitan writers and officials became even more preoccupied with issues of food production and supply, and with removing obstacles to the effective operation of the economy. In 1776, Galiani published *Dialogue sur le commerce des blés* (Dialogue on the Grain Trade), both an attack on the French Physiocrats and a contribution to discussion of this vital issue in Naples.

Probably the most important expression of the Neapolitan Enlightenment's new focus on economics, however, was the work of Antonio Genovesi. He distilled his lectures at the University of Naples in *Delle lezioni di commercio o sia di economia civile* (Lectures on Commerce or on Civic Economy, 1765–1767), a powerful and widely translated argument for free trade which engaged broad Enlightenment themes and dealt critically with many of Naples's institutions. It had a powerful influence on the next generation of Neapolitan writers and thinkers, many of whom were Genovesi's pupils.

One of them, Giuseppe Maria Galanti, published *Elogio di Genovesi* (Eulogy of Genovesi, 1772) and founded his own publishing house to promote the Enlightenment. Galanti's combination of geography and history to chart and explain the decline of Naples found expression in his *Nuova Descrizione storica e geografica dell'Italia* (New Historical and Geographical Description of Italy, 1782) and his *Descrizione dello stato antico ed attuale del Contado del Molise* (Description of the Former and Present Statoe of the Country of Molise, 1782). Some of Genovesi's pupils were associated with the periodical *Scelta miscellanea* (1783–1784) which was published by Galanti. They included Francesco Antonio Grimaldi, whose *Riflessioni sopra la disuguaglianza tra gli uomini* (Reflections on Inequality among Men, 1779–1780) was a contribution to the late Enlightenment concern with equality and inequality, and Francesco Maria Pagano (1748–1799), whose *Saggi politici* (Political Essays, 1783), drawing on Vico, Locke, and others, urged reform as the only solution to Naples's economic and social ills.

These men—some of whom were associated with the expanding masonic network in Naples—had high hopes following Tanucci's dismissal in 1776. His fall, owing in part to his opposition to Freemasonry, had been engineered by King Ferdinand's queen, Maria Carolina. With her favorite, Sir John Acton, she seemed keen to embark on more radical reforms, offering the prospect of a fruitful collaboration between enlightened reformers and the monarchy. This view was articulated by Gaetano Filangieri (1752–1788) in *La scienza della legislazione* (1780–1783), a wide-ranging work also read in the United States and Revolutionary France, whose vision of "philosophy in the service of government" proved influential among the reforming elite. Jurists, economists, and philosophers—Filangieri himself, Galanti, Grimaldi, and many others—entered government service and introduced a range of reforms. These again focused on the specific problems of Naples, in particular the devastating Calabrian earthquake of 1783. Their measures included the suppression of some feudal jurisdictions, the distribution of communal lands, educational reform, and the creation of the Academy of Sciences (1780). Serious efforts were also made to extend reform to Sicily during the viceroyalty (1781–1786) of Domenico, marchese di Caracciolo (1715–1789), who as Neapolitan minister in London and Paris had come to know and admire both England and France. He suppressed the Inquisition, restricted feudal and other privileges and power, and sought to restrain the excesses of popular religion. After his return to Naples in 1786, Caracciolo helped coordinate the larger state reform program.

Reform Obstructed. Once again, the entrenched forces of traditionalism and opposition to reform were powerful obstacles. In addition, Ferdinand and Maria Carolina were not truly committed to the enlightened, radical reform sought by many of their collaborators, especially after 1789. Frustration drove some younger reformers to desperate measures. In 1794, the exposure and severe repression of an extensive antigovernment plot, which involved both Freemasons and Jacobins, effectively ended all possibility of dialogue between reformers and the monarchy. It was the regimes of Joseph Bonaparte and Joachim Murat, between 1806 and the restoration of the Bourbon monarchy in Naples in 1815, that first effectively tackled the problems identified earlier by the Neapolitan Enlightenment.

[*See also* Filangieri, Gaetano; Galiani, Ferdinando; Genovesi, Antonio; Giannone, Pietro; Italy; Salons, *subentry* on Italy; *and* Vico, Giambattista.]

BIBLIOGRAPHY

Acton, Harold. *The Bourbons of Naples, 1734–1825.* London, 1956, 1974, 1998. Out of date but still probably the best narrative account in English.

Carpanetto, Dino, and Giuseppe Ricuperati. *Italy in the Age of Reason, 1685–1789.* London, 1987. Makes available in English much of the work of Venturi and others.

Imbruglia, Girolamo, ed. *Naples in the Eighteenth Century: The Birth and Death of a Nation State.* Cambridge, 2000. An edited collection of essays by leading Italian scholars, focusing on the failed Neapolitan experiment in Enlightenment statebuilding.

Mack Smith, Dennis. *A History of Sicily: Modern Sicily after 1713.* London, 1969. Useful for Caracciolo's period in Sicily.

Marino, John. *Pastoral Economics in the Kingdom of Naples.* Baltimore, 1988. A focused study of one key aspect of the Neapolitan economy, with useful material on the Enlightenment attitude and eighteenth-century reform.

Robertson, John. "Enlightenment and Revolution: Naples 1799." *Transactions of the Royal Historical Society* 6th ser., 10 (2000), 17–44. Invaluable brief survey of the Neapolitan Enlightenment and the origins of the Revolution of 1799, drawing on recent scholarship in Italian.

Venturi, Franco. "The Position of Galiani between the Encyclopedists and the Physiocrats" and "The Enlightenment in Southern Italy." In his *Italy and the Enlightenment: Studies in a Cosmopolitan Century,* edited by Stuart J. Woolf, pp. 180–197, 198–224. London, 1972. Translation of work by a key interpreter of the Neapolitan Enlightenment.

Woolf, Stuart J. *A History of Italy, 1700–1860.* London, 1979. Useful general survey.

CHRISTOPHER STORRS

NATIONAL CHURCHES. The century of the Reformation marked the splintering of Christianity and ratified the emergence of political Europe. In the countries that adopted Protestantism, the constitution of national churches was a driving force behind both the formation of cultural identities and the construction of the nations themselves. Martin Luther appealed to the German nation; Elizabeth I embodied England's new values as distinguished from those of Philip II of Spain and the papacy. What was the status of this relation between, indeed this interweaving of, religion and politics, church and state, during the century of Enlightenment?

In Protestant lands, the equivalence was no longer as clear as before. Diversity was the rule, and the more or less forced coexistence of church and state often led to

Anglican Archbishop. Thomas Herring, archbishop of Canterbury from 1747 to 1757, portrait by William Hogarth (1697–1764). (Tate Gallery, London/Art Resource, NY.)

a slow but inexorable process of secularization. The Holy Roman Empire remained a mosaic of states, principalities, and cities that were divided, after the Treaties of Westphalia (1648), between Catholics, Lutherans, and Calvinists. In the eighteenth century, the confrontation between (Protestant) Prussia and (Catholic) Austria was not at all a war of religion. Switzerland was a confederation grouping Catholic and Protestant cantons. In Sweden, as in the Protestant countries of northern Europe, Lutheran orthodoxy was maintained but no longer had the vigor of its heroic period of vigorous expansion (1648–1721). Within the United Provinces, the Reform (Calvinist) religion was the only official one, to be sure, but it did not achieve the status of a state religion. The situation in Great Britain was even more complex. The act of union between England and Scotland (1707) preserved two distinct established churches: in England the Anglican Church, which maintained its bishops, and in Scotland the Presbyterian (Calvinist) Church, generally known as the Kirk of Scotland. Over and beyond this fundamental difference, however, both countries had their marginal dissidents: Presbyterians, Independents, Baptists, and Quakers in England, Anglicans in Scotland. Ireland presents a still more complicated picture. It was an island, and a separate

country; it did not become part of the United Kingdom until 1800. The Protestant ascendancy guaranteed quite extensive rights to the Protestant minority, to the detriment of Catholics, who made up 85 percent of the population.

England. Owing to the influence it exercised on the Enlightenment, England warrants special attention. After two revolutions in the seventeenth century, England experienced a relative openness, a freedom of tone in religious and politico-religious debates that drew the admiration of the French philosophes. This state of affairs cannot be separated from the legacy of the Glorious Revolution of 1688. While the Bill of Rights established the monarchy on new foundations that limited the prerogatives of the Crown, the Act of Toleration legalized the existence of minority Protestant churches on the fringes of established Anglicanism. This text reaffirmed the necessity of adhering to the doctrines of the Trinity and of the divine inspiration of the Bible, two points that would be undermined by the partisans of natural religion.

Two great figures mark the beginning of the Enlightenment. As early as 1695, John Locke published (anonymously) *The Reasonableness of Christianity as Delivered in the Scriptures*, a synthesis of philosophical rationalism and the Christian faith. In 1696, John Toland's *Christianity Not Mysterious* produced a major scandal. If, to quote Voltaire, an Englishman of the Enlightenment went "to heaven by the path he pleased," that path could nevertheless be strewn with pitfalls. The national church was no longer at the heart of the construction of the nation; the construction of a philosophical model relied, in contrast, on the dialectics of the majority and the minority, Anglicanism and dissent.

The minority, the Dissenters, played a role that was simultaneously central and marginal to the politico-religious phenomena. At the beginning of the century, they represented between 5 and 10 percent of the population of certain counties of the south, the southwest, the northwest, and the southern Midlands. By 1773, no more than one county in four had concentrations above 5 percent. The numerical decline of the Dissenters is indisputable, but their fate constituted a major political issue: their alliance with the Whigs was one of the chief components of the system. The Test Act and the Corporation Act excluded them, in theory, from all official functions. In 1727, the first of a series of indemnity acts was passed; these acts tempered the most discriminatory measures against the Dissenters, without abolishing them entirely. In 1736, a proposal to abandon such discriminatory measures was rejected in the House of Commons by a vote of 251 to 123.

In the face of this upsurge of diversity, even within Protestantism itself, the Anglican clergy was on the defensive. In 1736, Bishop William Warburton (1698–1779) felt the need to defend the necessary complementarity of political power and religious authority in *The Alliance between Church and State*, a treatise advocating the status quo. The official clergy had not seen the end of its troubles, however, for a second form of dissent arose in the form of Methodism, which broke with the prevailing religious rationalism. Methodism was originally a Pietist movement within Anglicanism appealing to the social categories that had been neglected by the Anglican clergy. The Anglicans were in fact obliged to respect age-old parish divisions that did not coincide with the leading zones of the industrial revolution, the northeast, the northern Midlands, and Yorkshire. Lay preachers set out to conquer these mission territories. George Whitefield (1714–1770) and especially John Wesley (1703–1791) organized the movement that, in the case of the Methodists, was to break away from the Anglican Church at the end of the century.

Welcome or not, diversity and tolerance came into Protestant churches along with the Enlightenment. In America, even the Puritan myth of the foundation of a New Jerusalem was challenged. Church-state relations changed to the extent that the political state tolerated a plurality of churches and confessions.

The Catholic World. Within the Catholic world, this dialectic took on new relevance. The various sovereigns had more and more difficulty accepting Roman claims to supranational authority. The suppression of the Jesuits was a good index of national desires for independence. The affair began in Portugal in the reign of Joseph I, under the influence of his minister, the marques de Pombal. The treaty of 1750 between Spain and Portugal conferred on Portugal the task of reducing the number of Jesuits in Paraguay; the revolt of the Guarani Indians (1754–1756) was interpreted as a Jesuit plot. As early as 1759, Pombal expelled the order from Portugal: the Jesuits were shipped to Rome, and the kingdom of Portugal seized their possessions. Under the combined influence of the Jansenists and the philosophes, France followed suit: the suppression of the order was confirmed by Louis XV in 1764. The Bourbon monarchies got caught up in the spiral, as did Joseph II in Austria. For Pombal in Portugal, Choiseul in France, Campomanes in Spain, Tanucci in Naples, and Du Tillot in Parma, it was a matter of freeing states from the influence of a church judged to be far too involved in secular affairs. They conducted a veritable war of attrition, and Pope Clement XIV finally gave in to them in 1773, when he promulgated the bull *Dominus ac Redemptor*, which dissolved the Jesuit order. It was paradoxically in the Protestant Prussia of Frederick II and within the Orthodox Russian empire of Catherine II that the Jesuits found refuge and waited for better times, whereas Lorenzo Ricci, the last general of the Society of Jesus, died in 1775 in the Castel Sant'Angelo prison. The papacy gave in to the demands of the secular monarchies, and the Jesuits were made

convenient scapegoats. How did the national churches behave during this conflict at the top? In Germany, Austria, and France, the protest movements ran deep.

In the Holy Roman Empire, Catholicism was highly dependent on Rome. The Curia intervened frequently; papal nuncios played an important role. Pontifical infringements on the authority of the bishops had been denounced for a long time. The ideas of Johann Nikolaus von Hontheim (1701–1790), suffragan bishop of Trier, known by the pseudonym Justinus Febronius, were all the rage. In his masterwork *De Statu Ecclesiae et Legitima Protestate Romani Pontificis* (On the State of the Church and the Legitimate Power of the Roman Pontiff, 1763), he represented the bishops as successors of the apostles rather than as simple functionaries acting on behalf of an all-powerful pope. In 1769, church authorities signed the Gravamina of Koblenz, which challenged in particular the interventions of the Holy See in episcopal elections. In 1786, the prince-bishops set forth a veritable program of resistance; in defending the autonomy of episcopal power, they demanded the suppression of nunciatures. The Curia negotiated and drew closer to the states; the opposition front splintered. It was finally the French occupation during the French Revolutionary Wars and the policy of secularization that put an end to the debate in 1803.

In the hereditary lands of the Habsburgs, the empress Maria Theresa and later her son Joseph II led the resistance of the national church, even moving out ahead of the ecclesiastical reformers at times. The church seemed to be a state within the state, and even the very devout empress sought to limit its influence over society. She wanted to apply the vast ecclesiastical revenues to the support of parishes and to the better training of priests. For the state, it was a matter of controlling the property of the ecclesiastical institutions and reducing the number of nonworking days arising from the many religious holidays. Joseph II followed similar policies, but gave them a new inflection.

At first glance, Josephinism seems to have been simply a matter of applying reason of state to ecclesiastical affairs. Joseph II, however, was profoundly marked by Enlightenment rationalism. He took an authoritarian approach to remodeling church-state relations, drawing inspiration from Febronianism and Jansenism. As supreme protector of the church in Austria, Joseph II intended to limit the church's role strictly to moral instruction of the faithful and dispensation of the sacraments. No decree of the Holy See could be published without the authorization of the sovereign. Bishops could no longer contact the pope directly. The property of hundreds of suppressed convents was transferred to a state fund intended to support the church. Ecclesiastical libraries were closed. All this was sometimes carried out quite brutally.

The emperor, however, also created new dioceses for the benefit of new population concentrations, and he sought to impose a more enlightened religion by limiting processions, pilgrimages, and ecclesiastical pomp and ceremony. Theology was henceforth taught in state institutions, entrusted to a corps of teachers subject to the emperor's ideas. Joseph II granted freedom of worship to the Protestants and the Orthodox by an edict of toleration on 13 October 1781. Although Joseph II restored civil rights to minorities, Catholicism still remained the dominant religion, and the official registry of vital statistics was maintained by Catholic clergy. The situation of the Jews also improved: they were authorized to practice manual trades and to attend universities, and they were no longer required to wear special clothing.

The Gallican Church in France. Joseph II's reforms gave rise to anxieties and protests in Austria, but they found favorable echos in Habsburg Tuscany, where his brother Leopold reigned, and also—especially—in France, where the Jansenists celebrated the Austrian emperor as the model of a patriot king. Jansenism lay behind most of the national church-building enterprises, which kept their distance from Rome to varying degrees. The way the situation evolved in France is at the heart of the historical problematic that allows us to understand the relations between the political and the religious aspects of eighteenth-century Catholicism, just as the situation in England is the key to understanding the relations between churches and the state in Protestant culture.

Gallicanism was not a new phenomenon, but in the eighteenth century its association with Jansenism gave it a second wind that had a major critical impact. The well-known formula "the liberties of the Gallican church" was created during the great schism in the fourteenth and fifteenth centuries. The sacred text of Gallicanism remained the Pragmatic Sanction of Bourges (1438), which called for regular meetings of councils and declared the superiority of a general council over the pope. The Concordat of Bologna (1516) abrogated that foundational text, but the parlement and an important segment of the clergy became its most ardent supporters. The Pragmatic Sanction was an ideal reference point: it advocated a return to the ancient practice of election of bishops, limited Rome's interventions, and provided a doctrinal basis for conciliarism. The French kings were not very fond of that monument of Gallicanism, but they did not hesitate to brandish it like a red flag when relations with the pope became strained. Louis XIV found himself in something like this state of mind in 1682 when he came in conflict with Innocent XI. Royal Gallicanism was starting to fade by 1693, however, except for a brief episode in 1716 during the regency. It is even possible to affirm that it was henceforth in spite of the king that the Gallican declaration of 1682 continued to be the object of instruction in faculties of theology.

The bull *Unigenitus* of 1713, which condemned Jansenism once again, linked it definitively to Gallicanism in the ninety-first of the propositions it censured: "Even the fear of unjust excommunication must never stand in the way of doing one's duty. One never leaves the church, even when it seems that one has been banished by the wickedness of men, when one is attached to God, to Jesus Christ, and to the church itself, by charity." To condemn this proposition as *Unigenitus* did was to assert that the authority of "men" is infallible, and that of Rome in particular. According to the Gallicans, however, history was full of counterexamples, and the Holy See had sometimes acted without discernment with respect to sovereigns, some of whom had even been excommunicated without reason. If the spirit of the bull was observed, the king was dependent on the pope, because the pope could free the king's subjects from obedience and thus ultimately distribute crowns as he pleased. Commenting on the consequences of the bull, canon law specialists Gabriel Nicolas Maultrot and Claude Mey wrote in 1753: "The whole kingdom is in a state of astonishment, so to speak, upon discovering that it is ultramontanist." The movement of appeal against the bull was led by the Jansenists, to be sure, but the Gallicans joined forces with them readily.

This convergence was further reinforced in 1728, when Benedict XIII inserted a liturgy of Saint Gregory VII into the breviary. Paris revived the medieval quarrels between the papacy and the Holy Roman Empire, and French Jansenists and Gallicans organized the defense of the emperor Henry IV. When a judicial ruling imposed the bull as a law of the state in 1730, a Jansenist member of the parlement, the abbé Pucelle, declared that he was "too faithful a subject of the king to concede that he should be stripped of his rights and declared a vassal of the pope." Defenders of the king in spite of themselves, the Gallicans also tended to become reluctant defenders of the bishops. The episcopacy was gradually taken in hand, and the Jansenists were progressively excluded and replaced by colleagues favorable to the bull, or constitution, *Unigenitus*—"bullists" or "constitutionaries," to use the polemical vocabulary of the times. The magistrates of the parlement of Paris did not hesitate to limit episcopal prerogatives at that time: "The ministers of the church are accountable to the king, and, in cases of abuse, to the court under his authority, for the exercise of the jurisdiction that they hold from the king and even for all that might, in the exercise of the power that they hold directly from God, injure public tranquillity or the laws and maxims of the kingdom."

Magistrates, lawyers, priests, and laymen became spokespersons over time for a Gallicanism that shared much with the so-called Richerist theses. In the beginning of the seventeenth century, Edmond Richer had defended the idea that the church was an aristocratic and not monarchical body: "Jesus Christ conferred the keys, that is, ecclesiastical jurisdiction, in common and undivided, on the entire priesthood, which was represented by the apostles and the seventy-two disciples." His eighteenth-century partisans asserted that the power of the keys indeed belonged to the body of the church, but they enlarged this body quite remarkably by claiming that while bishops are successors of the twelve apostles and priests are successors of the seventy-two disciples, there is no fundamental difference between them. Many thinkers went on to defend a totally democratic conception of the church that granted a fundamental place to lay members: the mass in French, a renovated liturgy, encouragement for everyone to read the Bible—these were the changes advocated by the group of innovators who identified with the heroic times of the primitive Church, the era of apostles and martyrs. From democracy in the church, some moved on to the notion of democracy in the state.

Such theses, whose revolutionary potential could not be ignored, still remained relatively marginal under the Regency, when they were first formulated. However, Gallicanism and Richerism met during this period without converging. The scandal of the *billets de confession* (certificates of confession), around the middle of the century, considerably reinforced these diffuse tendencies. While Jansenism was gradually losing its impetus, the archbishop of Paris, Christophe de Beaumont, decided to require of the faithful on their deathbeds that they produce a certificate of confession signed by a priest who had accepted *Unigenitus*. Otherwise, the last rites were denied the dying person, who then might not be buried in consecrated ground. This extreme measure was highly unpopular. The chroniclers all said the same thing: Paris had become Jansenist overnight. Protesters formed funeral processions to accompany the bodies of those rejected by the clergy. The parlement intended to conscript priests so they would fulfill their functions; it claimed to be defending "religion, state, and crown" against an attempt at schism. The parlement openly placed the clergy at the service of the state and the nation. In 1752, it even proposed to put the archbishop on trial. The written remonstrances of the parlement were hugely successful; those published in 1753, long and full of quotes in Latin, sold 200,000 copies. Gallico-Jansenism helped shape the opposition to the monarchy, which now found itself associated with Roman despotism. Similar views appeared in the arguments against the Jesuits, who were denounced as spies in the service of a foreign power, slaves in the pay of an absolute and despotic authority.

In the final decades of the Old Regime, conflicts between the Roman and Gallican tendencies could be found in all the major quarrels that agitated French society, but they were diluted, so to speak, within new problems. It was in this way that the Jansenists played a significant role in the struggle for civic tolerance with respect to Protestants, while the mainstream church mistrusted the effects of that good will and mobilized its forces to oppose it. The example of Joseph II, hailed by the Jansenist press, was greeted with considerable approval. Beyond the Jansenist influence, however, a vast movement of defense of the lower clergy against the episcopacy was also developing in the years that preceded the revolution. The poor priests, who had access to minimal resources, stood up to the powerful dignitaries and beneficiaries of a church accused of having lost its evangelical values. Whereas monks were more and more unpopular and bishops viewed with suspicion, parish priests benefited from an undeniable undercurrent of sympathy; their charity was celebrated, and "the good priest" was a topos of the sentimental and right-thinking literature of the late Enlightenment.

The French Revolution and After. As they developed in resistance to the influence of Rome, did the churches that were based on national values tend to challenge monarchical values? Josephinism clearly offers the inverse schema: in Austria as in Tuscany, with the famous Synod of Pistoia in 1786, the authorities set the pace. The only real schism recorded in the eighteenth century came from the United Provinces, that is, from a country with a Protestant majority where the Catholics were simply tolerated. The suspension of the Bishop of Utrecht by Rome provoked exasperation on the part of his diocesans; in 1723 a French missionary, Dominique Varlet, bishop of Babylon, moved to Holland and confirmed the schism by proceeding to consecrate four archbishops. The Church of Utrecht survived in the eighteenth century thanks to French refugees; the synod of Utrecht of 1763 allowed them to regroup. In the Austrian Low Countries, on the contrary, hostility to the measures of Joseph II brought the dissidents together, to such an extent that the French Jansenists, profoundly hostile to "the revolution of the Belgians," saw it as a maneuver of the ex-Jesuits.

The religious policies of the French Revolution completely altered the perception of these problems and upset the roles of the various actors. In the beginning, hostility to the church was not on the revolutionary agenda. On the contrary, the church was closely associated with the state in patriotic celebrations. However, especially under the pressure of economic factors, the Church of France was rapidly and thoroughly restructured. The Constituents acted in the tradition of royal Gallicanism or of Josephinism. Ecclesiastical geography was constructed according to a logical order: the number of dioceses was reduced and their dimensions equalized; parishes were also remodeled, and many ecclesiastical benefices were eliminated. Members of religious orders became special targets. The Revolution's monastic commission acted vigorously; its leader, Étienne-Charles de Loménie de Brienne, acquired the nickname "antimonk." The Constituent Assembly went further in opposing religious vows.

The Civil Constitution of the Clergy, decreed on 12 July 1790, was even more radical. The return to ecclesiastical elections, a much-vaunted practice of the primitive church, raised the most profound problems. Starting from the principle that everyone was Catholic, even if the minority religions had a right to exist, all electors were called upon to take a stand on religious affairs. Bishops were thus elected by the electors of their departments, parish priests by those of the district, potentially by non-Catholics. The clergy of the majority religion became a body of ecclesiastical functionaries. A parish priest asked his bishop for permission to exercise spiritual authority, the bishop asked his metropolitan, and the latter asked the pope, but only "as testimony to the unity of faith and communion." The break with Rome might have looked inevitable, but—and this is worth emphasizing—at the time, it did not seem to be taken for granted: the Holy See was very slow to announce its decision, and in the meantime Louis XVI thought he could accept the Civil Constitution of the Clergy. However radical it may be, the text of the Constitution did not come down on the side of the Richerists; to be sure, it offered guarantees to parish priests and vicars, and it suppressed chapters, but it denied the right of the lower clergy to participate in the government of the church through the intermediary of the synods.

On 27 November 1790, the Constituent Assembly demanded an oath of fidelity from the clergy. The cleavages between the constitutional clergy (who took the oath) and the refractory clergy (who refused it) deepened, and the Revolution evolved toward increased anticlericalism. In 1797, when the first national council, focused on the reconstruction of the church, was held, the Gallican and Richerist principles were defended, but this was unquestionably their swan song. The Revolution failed in its attempt to create a national religion.

In 1801, Napoleon Bonaparte and Pius VII negotiated a concordat that put an end to the revolutionary divisions. The supreme authority of the pope over bishops and of bishops over parish priests was forcefully reaffirmed. Ecclesiastical geography was disrupted once again, but this time with Rome's consent. Elections were eliminated. Overall, the refractory clergy was preferred to the constitutional clergy. This was not the end of Gallicanism, but a return to state Gallicanism. Bishops were named by the head of state according to "the forms established with respect to France before the change of government," a highly euphemistic formula that refers to the Concordat of Bologna. Consular and then imperial Gallicanism followed in the footsteps of royal Gallicanism. When the concordat was published in April 1802, seventy-seven organic articles accompanied it; these had not been negotiated with Rome, and they reinforced the Gallican tonality of the whole. In the case of a potential conflict, the Council of State was called to play the role that the parlement played under the Old Regime. Prior authorization by the government was indispensable for pontifical acts to be published and for legates to exercise their functions. Every council, even at the diocesan level, had to depend on the government. Bishops had to take an oath of fidelity to the regime, and they could not go to Rome without permission. Professors in seminaries had to teach the declaration of 1682. The circle was complete.

Destinies of the National Churches. The national churches of the eighteenth century had differing destinies. Within Protestantism, the religious dimension tended to play a less important role in the organization of the state. Even where there was only one official church, plurality and toleration—however relative these values may have been—led to a secularization of society. Religion permeated cultures and mentalities and inspired the functioning of the state, but it was no longer coextensive with the state.

In Catholic countries, the evolution is still more difficult to grasp. The national churches could play a role in reinforcing the state; a distancing from Rome was often the occasion for internal reforms and for taking into account a certain number of Enlightenment values. The revolt of the Low Countries against Joseph II, and especially the anticlerical developments of the French Revolution, sounded the tocsin for these new tendencies. Napoleon confined the pope to a spiritual function even as he restored his authority over the Church of France. The latter, in exchange, had to celebrate the imperial cult. Despite some crises, this balance of power was to remain in place for a century.

[*See also* Austria; England; Enlightened Despotism; France; French Revolution; Jansenism; Josephinism; Netherlands; Reformed Churches; Roman Catholicism; Scandinavia; Toleration; and Ultramontanism.]

BIBLIOGRAPHY

Beales, Derek. *Joseph II in the Shadow of Maria-Theresa (1741–1780)*. Cambridge, 1987.

Cottret, Bernard. *Le Christ des Lumières*. Paris, 1990.

Delumeau, Jean, and Monique Cottret. *Le catholicisme entre Luther et Voltaire*. Paris, 1996.

François, Étienne. *Protestants et catholiques en Allemagne: Identités et pluralisme, Augsbourg (1648–1806)*. Paris, 1993.

Gres-Gayer, Jacques. *Paris-Cantorbéry (1717–1720): Le dossier d'un premier oecuménisme*. Paris, 1989.

Hersche, Peter. *Der Spätjansenismus in Oesterreich*. Vienna, 1977.

Mandrou, Robert. *L'Europe absolutiste: Raison et raison d'état*. Paris, 1977.

Martimort, Aimé-Georges. *Le gallicanisme de Bossuet*. Paris, 1953.

Martimort, Aimé-Georges. *Le gallicanisme*. Paris, 1973.

Mayeur, Jean-Marie, Charles Pietri, Luce Pietri, André Vauchez, and Marc Venard. *Histoire du christianisme.* Vol. 9, *L'âge de raison,* and vol. 10, *Les défis de la modernité.* Paris, 1997.

Sykes, Norman. *Church and State in the Eighteenth Century.* Cambridge, 1934.

MONIQUE COTTRET

Translated from French by Catherine Porter

NATIVE AMERICANS. European exploration and settlement of the Americas played a crucial role in Enlightenment thought by prodding Europe's political philosophers, social theorists, and scientists to think about the sudden rise of diversity now apparent in the world around them. In coming to terms with the existence of Native Americans and the questions of difference and similarity that their existence raised, Europeans responded in opposing ways. They became endlessly curious, but they simultaneously reduced Native Americans to stock types against which Europe's social and political institutions could be constructively juxtaposed.

Native American. Iroquois warrior with tomahawk and ball-club. Drawing (1787) by J. Grasset de St.-Sauveur. (The Granger Collection, New York.)

Enlightenment curiosity was an open-ended search for all knowledge about the natural world. Details about Native American physical features and cultural practices crossed the Atlantic along with tobacco, opossums, and other American oddities. Collecting objects and information was for many natural historians a goal in itself, but for others it served as the basis for comparative analyses of the world's people. Taxonomies provided one means to make the physical world comprehensible, such as in the 1740 edition of *Systema Naturae,* in which Swedish naturalist Carolus Linneaus grouped the world's people into four categories—white Europeans, red Americans, dark-skinned Asians, and black Africans. For other early modern Europeans, the big question about Native Americans was that of origins, because the vast oceans separating the New World from the Old turned biblical truths into question marks. Two popular options were either to think of Indians as one of the lost tribes of Israel or to accept a more radical proposition of separate creations (polygenesis).

Despite the wealth of information demonstrating great diversity within the Americas, the most enduring conception of America's peoples divided them into two simplified stereotypes, often called "noble savage" and "brutal savage." Beginning with Christopher Columbus's 1492 landing in the Caribbean, Europeans cast Native Americans as either good or bad, but always inferior to Europeans' own sense of themselves as Christian and civilized people. Columbus described encountering two kinds of indigenous people. The Taino on the island of Hispaniola were naked (or nearly so), naïve, timid, childlike, innocent, and generous. Reminiscent of Edenic innocents before the Fall, the Taino were unspoiled people who could easily be converted to Christianity. The Taino's neighbors, the Caribs, appeared from hearsay to be the opposite sort of people: vicious cannibals. With Spanish colonization of the Americas, this dichotomous view of American Indians became more entrenched. A formal debate on whether Indians could be converted or should be enslaved took place in Spain in the mid-sixteenth century. Juan Ginés de Sepúlveda drew upon the sensationalist pseudoethnographies of early exploration to make the case for Native savagery and mental incapacity, the moral basis upon which enslavement could proceed. His opponent, Bartolomé de Las Casas, argued for the inherent rationality and equality of Native Americans, but he also asserted that they had no religion of their own and therefore could learn to become Christian.

These images of Native Americans circulated throughout Europe in the sixteenth century and influenced how European writers and philosophers conceived of human nature. Of these, one of the most influential was Michel de Montaigne, who produced several essays that used the Americas as the basis for self-reflection. Ruminating on a visiting entourage of Tupinamba Indians from Brazil (whom he may or may not have met in person), Montaigne foreshadowed what would become a common role for the noble savage in European literary circles: the noble savage as social critic. The title of Montaigne's essay "Of Cannibals" (1580) evokes the essence of the brutal savage, but the essay itself conveys more ambivalence. Montaigne's litany of supposed Native American insufficiencies—no literature, no laws, no political or social hierarchies, no ambition, no words for deceit or greed—may have stripped Native Americans of the attributes Europeans linked to civilized society, but it also bordered on a romantic primitivism that made Native American life appear almost enviable. Living by natural law alone seemingly freed Indians from social striving and political authority and allowed them to lead lives of carefree pleasure.

In constructing the image of the savage, whether noble or brutal, Europeans made analogies of Indians as living examples of ancient peoples. Artists capturing the New World on paper gave Indians the bodies of Greek and Roman statues. Writers compared Indians to Greeks and Romans, too, but also to wild men found in folklore, to the "barbarian" tribes absorbed by the expansion of Rome and Christianity, to Turks and Arabs, and to peoples just recently invaded or conquered. (English writers often compared Indians to the Irish.)

However, by the late eighteenth century, the American noble savage had formed an identity all its own as a starting point for defining republican virtue. The political philosophers John Locke and Jean-Jacques Rousseau, who speculated on the origins of government, drew upon the noble-savage model to characterize human behavior in a state of nature. Rousseau, writing in France in the mid-1700s, is often mistakenly cited as the sole progenitor of the noble-savage idea, but scores of literary precedents had promoted the belief that Europe's ancient ancestors and contemporary American Indians lived simpler lives in which no man ruled over another. By presuming that Indians most closely captured humanity's original state and by imagining that they lived lives as individuals free from the constraints of tyrannical power and inherited social status, the founding philosophers of republican political thought criticized the power of absolute monarchs as artificial and heralded the republican revolutions of later generations.

Romantic stereotyping did not translate into protections or rights for real Indians but instead worked against them in contests for power and in courts of law. Noble savages, so it was said, had no property, no government, no laws. Whether cast as brutal or noble, in the eyes of European colonizers Indians had no legitimate claim to the lands they occupied. Moreover, the association of Indians with a primitive past led to colonial policies that made Christianization and other efforts at cultural assimilation appear as humanitarian reforms and not as assaults on civil liberties.

[*See also* Colonialism; Human Nature; Jesuits, *subentry on* Role as Missionaries and Explorers; Lafitau, Joseph-François; Lahontan, Louis-Armand de Lom D'Arce, baron de; Locke, John; Republicanism; Rousseau, Jean-Jacques; *and* Scientific Expeditions.]

BIBLIOGRAPHY

Berkhofer, Robert F., Jr. *The White Man's Indian: Images of the American Indian from Columbus to the Present*. New York, 1978. Traces the impact of the noble and brutal savage stereotypes on culture and federal policy in the United States.

Dickason, Olive Patricia. *The Myth of the Savage and the Beginnings of French Colonialism in the Americas*. Edmonton, Alberta, 1984. A good account of how sixteenth-century Europeans interpreted Native Americans in light of preexisting expectations.

Hamlin, William M. *The Image of America in Montaigne, Spenser, and Shakespeare: Renaissance Ethnography and Literary Reflection*. New York, 1995. Gives more background information and context than the specificity of the title suggests.

Hodgen, Margaret T. *Early Anthropology in the Sixteenth and Seventeenth Centuries*. Philadelphia, 1964. A little outdated in some details but still a thorough study of how knowledge of the Americas changed European ideas about cultural difference.

Pagden, Anthony. *European Encounters with the New World: From Renaissance to Romanticism*. New Haven, Conn., 1993. The best overview of Enlightenment thinking about Native Americans.

Sheehan, Bernard W. *Seeds of Extinction: Jeffersonian Philanthropy and the American Indian*. Chapel Hill, N.C., 1973. Examines how eighteenth-century natural historians set the stage for U.S. Indian policies.

NANCY SHOEMAKER

NATURAL HISTORY. Natural history is the scientific discipline that systematically studies natural materials (animals, plants, minerals) by naming, describing, classifying, and attempting to uncover their overall order. As a scientific discipline, natural history emerged during the eighteenth century and reinforced Enlightenment ideals with both its secular and its rationalistic orientation. Even those naturalists who explicitly described natural objects as God's creations exhibited a method of investigation that stressed careful empirical observation and physical explanation and avoided direct theological conceptions. Two naturalists set models that came to dominate the modern subject of natural history: Carolus Linnaeus and Georges-Louis Leclerc de Buffon.

Linnaeus and His System of Classification. The Swedish naturalist Linnaeus (1707–1778), like many naturalists of the 1700s, received his intellectual training in medicine. Universities then did not have degrees in natural history, but medical education provided knowledge of anatomy, physiology, and medical botany. Early in his career, Linnaeus demonstrated a serious interest in naming and classifying natural objects. His interests

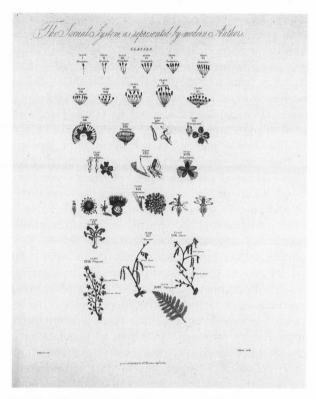

Linnaean Classification. Plate showing twenty-four classes of plants from Robert John Thornton, *A New Illustration of the Sexual System of Linnaeus* (1807). (Prints and Photographs Division, Library of Congress.)

reflected the time. Europeans then colonizing Africa, the New World, the Pacific Islands, and Asia had, since the seventeenth century, encountered thousands of new animals, plants, and minerals. Naturalists eagerly sought specimens, both to document the diversity of the Creation and to discover valuable natural products. Governments, merchant houses, scientific bodies, and individual entrepreneurs encouraged the enterprise, with the result that botanical gardens, menageries, and natural history collections greatly expanded their holdings.

Linnaeus participated in one expedition, to Lapland, where he collected plants, animals, and minerals for the Swedish Royal Society of Science. The majority of his career was centered around natural history collections, first in the Netherlands and then in Uppsala, Sweden. Linnaeus attempted to bring order to the expanding subject of natural history. Like others attempting to name and classify the wealth of new information, he found himself frustrated both by the lack of standardized procedures for naming and by the enormous confusion that resulted from misidentifications (some earlier naturalists had given different species names to the male and the female forms of the same animal). One of his earliest publications, *Systema naturae* (The System of Nature, 1735), outlined

a general system of classification for plants, animals, and minerals. Of particular importance, the *Systema naturae* contained a system of classification for plants based on the reproductive organs. This widely adopted hierarchical system arranged all known plants into twenty-four classes, according to the number and relative position of their stamens (male parts). The classes had sixty-five orders, primarily based on the number and position of the pistils (female parts). Using other characteristics, Linnaeus further divided the orders into genera (sing., genus) and species. His system had a simplicity and relative ease of application that attracted many followers.

Linnaeus did not claim that the sexual system reflected any "real" order in nature; rather, it supplied a key to classification that permitted easy and quick identification of plants, and it allowed naturalists to organize a vast quantity of material. He believed that a "natural" system of classification could be constructed—one based on the actual order of nature and utilizing many characteristics of plants rather than just the sexual. Linnaeus worked on such a system for the rest of his life. At his death, however, it remained incomplete. The "artificial" system that he had supplied, nonetheless, was valued by naturalists and amateurs alike, and it was quickly adopted throughout most of the scientific world.

Equally important was the new set of rules that Linnaeus proposed for naming and identifying plants and animals. Botany, in particular, suffered from considerable confusion in nomenclature. Before Linnaeus's reforms, the scientific names of plants consisted of two parts: a word (or phrase) that denoted a group of plants and a list of characteristics that distinguished the plant from similar ones. No single agreed upon list of names existed and, consequently, naturalists used a variety of characteristics to name the same plant. A plant, therefore, possessed many names, given by many authors in many languages during the centuries. Linnaeus proposed a change: plant names should be like human names, a single name that was common to all the species in a genus, and a specific name that distinguished the species from others in its genus. He also suggested rules of nomenclature: that names of genera should have Greek or Latin roots only, should not consist of compounds, and should not commemorate saints or individuals unconnected with science. Linnaeus's proposals gained wide acceptance, partly because he solved a pressing issue, but mostly because he also provided a complete list of all the known species of plants, using his new system in his *Species plantarum* (1753). To this day, it is still the starting point for botanical nomenclature. Likewise, the names he gave to animals in his earlier *Systema naturae* provided a baseline for zoological nomenclature.

Naming and classifying constitute Linnaeus's most valuable activities but, in addition, he envisioned the natural world in a particular manner that influenced later generations. He believed that nature displayed a balanced and harmonious order. Plants and animals occupied particular places in, and helped to maintain, a network of life. Carnivores, for example, daily destroyed animals that, if unchecked, would reproduce so quickly as to outstrip their sources of food; the reciprocal relationship of predator and prey linked each in an overall harmonious system. The idea of a balance of nature became a powerful metaphor, and it contributed to later studies of plant and animal interactions.

After Linnaeus's death, a wealthy young Englishman with an avid interest in natural history, James Edward Smith (1759–1828), purchased the Linnaeus library and collections. These later became the prized possessions of the Linnean Society of London (founded in 1788), the prototype for many natural history societies that also bore Linnaeus's name. Yet the Linnean Society of London was not the first to have used his name; ironically, that honor goes to the Société Linnéenne de Paris (1787). Although a number of important French naturalists valued the contributions of Linnaeus, and a number of French Linnean societies were founded, in France his influence was overshadowed by his great rival, Georges-Louis Leclerc, comte de Buffon (1707–1788).

Buffon and His Study of Nature's Diversity. Buffon's work in natural history played a vital role in the Enlightenment. By education and early scientific interests, he was somewhat atypical of the new naturalists of the eighteenth century. Buffon studied law, as was appropriate for the son of a recently made member of the *noblesse de robe*, and his first scientific work addressed mathematical and physical problems associated with Newtonian science. Like other figures of the French Enlightenment, Buffon contributed to spreading the new English philosophy in France. He translated Isaac Newton's (1642–1726) work on the calculus into French, and he conceived of his own scientific work as part of a larger intellectual movement. The Newtonian science that he helped to popularize was an integral part of the philosophes' program to secularize European society. Nature, to Buffon, could be described and understood in terms of natural law, rather than by means of the theological myths that had been invented by ignorant and superstitious people of earlier times.

Buffon did not limit his early scientific interests to the physical sciences. On his estate in Burgundy, he concerned himself with problems of forestry, and in 1735 he translated a classic of English writing on physiology, Stephen Hales's *Vegetable Staticks* (1727). His major interest in natural history, however, dated from his appointment in 1739 as intendant of the royal gardens and the natural history collection. Charged with the task of providing a catalog of the royal collection, Buffon embarked on an ambitious project of writing a complete natural history of all the animals, plants, and minerals on Earth. His approach differed considerably from that of Linnaeus. Unlike his contemporary to the north, Buffon had little interest in lists or arranged relationships of plants and

The Jardin du Roi. Buffon was intendant of the Jardin du Roi, Paris. Engraving by J.-B. Hilaire, eighteenth century. (Bibliothèque Nationale de France, Paris.)

animals. Perhaps reflecting his Newtonian background, as well as his scant acquaintance with the existing morass of botanical classification and nomenclature, Buffon aspired to uncover nature's order by revealing its underlying laws of operation and by documenting its diversity. In 1749, he began publishing a sweeping survey of the natural world that ran to thirty-six volumes by his death in 1788. His *Histoire naturelle, générale et particulière*, an encyclopedia of nature, originally promised descriptions of each type of plant, animal, and mineral. Buffon lived to complete the volumes on humans, quadrupeds, birds, and minerals, in addition to a general theory on the origin and composition of Earth (a team of specialists then completed the remaining topics for the two decades after his death). General essays throughout the volumes discussed methodology, the geographic distribution of life, the order of nature, and the general characteristics of living organisms.

Buffon's *Histoire naturelle*, along with Linnaeus's *Systema naturae*, stands as one of the major achievements of Enlightenment natural history. If Linnaeus organized all the known natural objects into a classification system that permitted easy identification and standardized nomenclature, Buffon provided their detailed descriptions and attempted to discern nature's underlying order. In the first fifteen volumes of the *Histoire naturelle*, where Buffon discussed all the known quadrupeds, he included anatomical descriptions of the internal and external characteristics of the animals (based on specimens in the royal collection), and he summarized the current knowledge of their distribution, environments, breeding habits, life stages, varieties, and behavior. He also cataloged the various names given to the animals through the ages by other naturalists. Further, each volume contained engravings illustrating the descriptions.

Biological forces to explain animal life.
Buffon's boldness of thought led him to speculate on a wide range of topics, from cosmology to the nature of generation. Few of his readers accepted his entire vision, but many of his general ideas had a lasting impact. Of particular importance was his belief in the existence of biological forces that account for properties unique to living beings. He did not conceive of them as mysterious forces, occult properties, or the like; rather, he described them as analogous to natural physical forces, such as gravity. Buffon referred to these biological forces to explain organization, growth, development, and reproduction in animals. In an important synthesizing leap, he related his ideas of biological forces to classification, thereby creating a natural system of classification based on descent. Buffon held that each animal possessed an "internal molding force" (*moule intérieur*) that determined its form and guided its functioning. The expression of the internal molding force, however, could be influenced by the environment. This influence allowed Buffon to explain individual differences among specimens of the same species. More importantly, he thought that it explained the close affinity of certain different species: they were the descendants of a common stem. The horse, zebra, and ass, for example, had all come from a primitive horse, just as the dog, wolf, and fox might be variations of a common ancestor. The alleged hybridization within these natural "families," Buffon contended, provided evidence of their shared internal molding force.

Buffon believed that to understand the appearance of modern animals, it was necessary to understand their past history, their patterns of distribution, and the history of the surface of Earth. A temporal dimension had to be part of any understanding of natural history, and that observation of external and internal characteristics had to be supplemented with studies of Earth's history, fossils, environmental history, and distribution. Only after such studies could meaningful classifications be constructed (i.e., not artificial ones like that of Linnaeus). According to Buffon, the real quest in natural history was not in ordering, but in discovering the order. Linnaeus, of course, agreed with Buffon that the ultimate goal in natural history remained the uncovering of the order in nature (for Linnaeus, God's order), but Linnaeus held that artificial systems had considerable value as interim measures. In fact, an intense debate took place in the late eighteenth century over the relative merits of artificial and natural systems. The proliferation of systems made it difficult to judge which position was in the ascendancy, however, because many of the systems consisted of hybrid efforts that employed natural criteria for some levels of classification and artificial criteria for other levels.

Natural laws.
Buffon's encyclopedia supplied a secular conception of natural history. He designed his interpretation in the style of the philosophes—a clear presentation, in French, based on accurate information that was understandable to the average educated reader. His articles described the wonders of nature, and his essays uncovered its order. Of great importance, his work broke with the Christian tradition that had informed European nature writing since the 1500s; more accurately, he transformed it. Like other philosophes, Buffon believed in an all-pervasive design in nature. He did not envision the design as the handiwork of a personal Christian God, whose truths could be discovered in both scripture and the book of nature. Instead, Buffon reified nature into the creative power that was responsible for the harmony, balance, and fullness of creation. His reinterpretation did not simply stand natural theology on its head by providing a materialistic account of accepted opinions, but it provided a new vision of the living world. He argued that, like the physical world, the living world followed discoverable

natural laws. He described nature as an end in itself, not as a reflection of a higher reality; no Christian Creator or biblical story of Creation constituted part of his vision. He described the animals that currently existed, how and why they had changed in time, and how fossils had been formed, all without reference to scripture or to the direct action of a deity. Instead, Buffon relied on a set of basic forces, analogous to Newton's theory of gravitation and laws of motion.

Buffon's secular vision of nature provided an attractive alternative to the Bible's first book, Genesis, because his natural history provided a historical account of the development of Earth and its products. He described without reference to scripture how Earth was formed, including its plants, animals, and minerals. His readers could trace the history of Earth from its early molten state to its present stage of development, and they could learn the reasons for the observed distribution of living forms on its surface. His bold attempt incurred the wrath of the theologians of the Sorbonne at the University of Paris, but his political connections at court, and his own restraint, kept him from having his work banned or from being imprisoned. In his lifetime, Buffon attained a considerable reputation. He belonged to both the Académie Royale des Sciences and the Académie Française; from his position as intendant of the Jardin du Roi (Royal Garden) in Paris, where he also maintained a weekly salon, he ruled the world of natural history. Louis XV had a statue of Buffon, by Augustin Pajou (1730–1809), erected in the Royal Garden; Catherine II, empress of Russia, commissioned a bust of him, by the French sculptor and portraitist Jean-Antoine Houdon (1741–1828), which still sits in the Hermitage Museum in Saint Petersburg.

When Buffon died in 1788 the popular press in France and England noted that the fourth and last lamp of the Enlightenment had gone out (the other three they considered to have been Montesquieu, Voltaire, and Rousseau). For his contemporaries, Buffon had provided a secular *Genesis*, a natural history that gave the appearance of being grounded on an extensive scientific foundation and on a broad observational base. The first volume of his *Histoire naturelle* appeared one year after Montesquieu's *L'esprit des lois* (1748) and two years before Denis Diderot and Jean Le Rond d'Alembert began publishing their monumental *Encyclopédie, ou Dictionnaire raisonné des sciences, des arts et des métiers* (1751–1765). Buffon's *Histoire naturelle* appeared at a critical period in Enlightenment thought. His contemporaries regarded it as the essential encyclopedia of the natural world, one that complemented the more general *Encyclopédie*.

Collections and Collecting. Linnaeus and Buffon established a tradition of natural history that expanded and became a scientific discipline by the late 1700s in Europe and its colonies. Linnaeus valued classifying and naming, whereas Buffon stressed detailed description and the broad outlines of the order in nature. Their works were the result of the sizable collections that they had labored to construct. The Jardin du Roi in Paris contained the world's largest collection of quadrupeds, birds, insects, and minerals, and it had an impressive botanical garden, with some six thousand living plants and a study collection of some twenty-five thousand pressed plants. Linnaeus's personal collection contained 19,000 sheets of pressed plants, 3,200 insects, and 2,500 mineral specimens by the time of his death.

Buffon and Linnaeus had encouraged travelers to collect, and each established a worldwide network of correspondents to enlarge their collections. Toward the turn of the nineteenth century, information in natural history expanded impressively. In part, the expansion of natural history resulted from the stimulus given by Linnaeus's systematics and Buffon's encyclopedia, both of which inspired many attempts at describing and listing a locale's animals, plants, and minerals. These studies of regional flora and fauna, mostly European, built on earlier attempts to survey local geographic areas. Notable new surveys included the following: Gilbert White, *The Natural History of Selborne* (1789); Philippe Picot de Lapeyrouse, *Tables méthodiques des mammifères et des oiseaux observés dans le departement de Haute-Garonne* (1799), Johann Matthaeus Bechstein, *Gemeinnützige Naturgeschichte Deutschlands nach allen drey Reichen* (1789–1795), and Sven Nilsson, *Skandinavisk Fauna* (1824–1828).

Europeans had long valued exotic specimens, and the fashionable *cabinets d'histoire naturelle* of the seventeenth and eighteenth century proudly displayed seashells, stuffed birds, and minerals from distant lands. European explorers, colonial officials, traveling naturalists, and employees of commercial houses supplied an eager audience in the late eighteenth century and the early nineteenth, with specimens of interesting or new species. The Jardin du Roi, reorganized into a public museum after the French Revolution of 1789 and renamed the Muséum d'Histoire Naturelle in 1793, established a program to train young traveling naturalists in collecting, preserving, labeling, and classifying specimens. Professors at the Muséum encouraged young naturalists to explore areas poorly represented in their collections, such as West Africa, the Cape of Good Hope, Madagascar, India, Australia, and South America. The French were not alone in this, and naturalists from Britain, Germany, the Austro-Hungarian Empire, and the Netherlands scoured the remote corners of the colonial world for exotic specimens, with impressive results. Private collectors often financed expeditions. For example, the Dutch amateur Jacob Temminck (1748–1822) financed François Levaillant's (1753–1824) important trip to South Africa of 1781 to 1784, which resulted in one of the most significant publications on African birds in the century; the German collector Count Johann Centurius von Hoffmansegg (1766–1849) sent Friedrich Wilhelm Sieber (born 1789) to South America in the early nineteenth century, where he collected in the lower Amazon region for eleven years. Some men of means traveled themselves, and among the best known was Alexander Philip Maximilian, prince of Wied-Neuwied (1782–1867), who explored and collected in Brazil in the early nineteenth century.

Although numerous private collectors either mounted expeditions for themselves or supplied the funds to do so for individual naturalists, governments provided the largest means of support. The Paris Muséum set a model that was followed by the Dutch who established a Natuurkundige Commissie to explore the East Indies, and that inspired the royal courts of Berlin and Vienna to send naturalists to enrich their collections. The greatest sources of specimens came from the large-scale expeditions that governments sent out to explore vast areas. Britain's Captain James Cook's (1728–1779) three voyages to the South Pacific, the Antarctic, and the Arctic from 1768 to 1779, although known for their astronomical and geographical dimensions, brought back enormous numbers of specimens (even if Cook and numerous members of the expeditions did not make it back alive). Nicolas Baudin (1754–1804) led a French voyage to Australia from 1800 to 1804, to return with one of the most impressive natural history collections of the period.

There were also other sources of specimens. The large trading companies, for example, the Dutch East India Company and the British East India Company, devoted efforts to find indigenous plants and animals for potential commercial use, and they supported collecting on a large scale. The British East India Company even had a museum in London that was open to the public. Enough demand existed that commercial agencies of natural history came into existence. The two most important of the eighteenth century were Leadbeater's, a natural history and taxidermy business located near the British Museum in London, and the Maison Verreaux in Paris.

The flood of new specimens that poured into Europe made possible a new sort of natural history collection. Amateur collections, some quite large and impressive, stored and displayed natural history materials along with antiquities, books, and coins. When Margaret Cavendish Bentinck, duchess dowager of Portland, died, her Portland Museum took thirty-eight days to sell by auction. Visitors to foreign lands considered natural history collections among the great sights; in fact, a well-known guide to Paris, published in 1787, listed forty-five natural history cabinets worthy of a visit. Letters of introduction, or personal acquaintance, gained one access to the collections, and a few were open to the public for a fee.

The 1793 reorganization of the Jardin du Roi in Paris as a professional national museum exhibited the new specimens that for decades had been enlarging its collections. That set the model for the next hundred years. The museums that followed, worldwide, provided professional opportunities for naturalists to study collections and publish their findings.

Physiology. Natural history emerged with a focus on naming, classifying, and searching for the order of plants and animals within nature. Naturalists also conducted research on related topics, particularly in physiology. The close tie of natural history and medicine reinforced the naturalists' intrinsic physiological interests, especially their researches in nutrition, respiration, and reproduction. The effect of the seventeenth century's mechanical philosophy, which envisioned the animal body as a material or organic mechanism, inspired naturalists to examine the chemical and mechanical functioning of the body. The French scientist René-Antoine Ferchault de Réaumur (1683–1757) performed a set of classic experiments on the digestion of birds, which he published in 1752. His countrymen Antoine-Laurent Lavoisier (1743–1794) and Pierre-Simon de Laplace (1749–1827) published in 1783 studies that used an ice calorimeter to measure the amount of heat given off in both respiration and combustion. Their experiments demonstrated that the amount of heat produced in both processes was proportional to the amount of a specific gas (carbon dioxide) given off, which suggested that the organic function of respiration was chemically the same as that of combustion.

During the Enlightenment, reproduction (generation) was the major topic of concern in physiology. For the earlier savants of the 1600s, who espoused the mechanical philosophy, explaining reproduction represented a major scientific challenge. Their use of the clockwork analogy in understanding the functioning of the animal body seemed to flounder when confronted with the phenomenon of generation: clocks display elaborate functions, but they do not reproduce. The invention of the microscope, and its use in observing what were understood to be eggs in the ovaries of animals, led naturalists in the 1600s to propose a theory of "preformation"—that all embryos were "preformed" in the ovaries. The theory accorded well with philosophical attempts to reconcile science and religion, by denying creative agency to nature. Early Christian theologians had written of God as having created "seeds" that emerged in time; more importantly, the preformation theory depended on a divine Creator who, in his infinite wisdom, created all generations at the beginning of life. According to proponents, Eve had carried all the future generations in the Garden of Eden, as did the first female agents of all sexually reproducing organisms. Preformation accorded well with the mechanical philosophy, because the process of generation and development could be explained as an unfolding of preexisting mechanisms. By the early 1700s, the theory was generally accepted; the observation of parthenogenesis in the aphid (an insect) by the Swiss naturalist Charles Bonnet (1720–1793) provided alleged empirical evidence for such views.

Newtonian science, however, which stressed the existence of "forces" in nature that operated on brute matter, suggested to some Enlightenment naturalists an alternative to the widely held preformation theory. Instead of relying on encapsulation and unfolding, which strained the imagination in the cases of single organisms that produced vast quantities of potential offspring (e.g., fish, oysters, oak trees), naturalists suggested that a force, or a set of forces, might account for the process of reproduction and development. Building on speculations in Newton's *Opticks* (1704), the German naturalists Johann Friedrich Blumenbach (1752–1840) and Casper Wolff (1733–1794) and the French naturalists Buffon and Pierre-Louis Moreau de Maupertuis (1698–1759) soon proposed theories of generation that rested on the existence of such forces. Called "epigenetic," these theories ultimately replaced preformation by the end of the 1700s. In 1749, Buffon described his theory of epigenesis, along with a set of supporting observations made with the microscope, in the second volume of his *Histoire naturelle*. There, he proposed that an internal molding force, analogous to Newton's gravitational force, determined the form and the functioning of an organism, and that its expression could be influenced by the environment. Although controversial, Buffon's version of epigenesis attained popularity and acceptance, mostly because of its inclusion in his widely read natural history. Epigenesis provided an important link in the Enlightenment's approach to replace or secularize the Christian world view. Where preformation had depended on a Creator who designed the human generations, as well as those of the other species, Buffon's epigenesis supplied a natural explanation for this basic life function.

Legacy. As a modern scientific discipline, natural history emerged in the eighteenth century. In its search for a secular and rational order, its goals coincided with those of the Enlightenment. Although much of the work by Enlightenment naturalists consisted of detailed classifications and nomenclatures, they also conceived of natural history as a subject that had a temporal dimension. For some, like Buffon, natural history became a substitute for earlier Christian theological conceptions of nature. Whatever their philosophical commitments, Enlightenment naturalists did realize the incompleteness of their knowledge of the natural world, and they stressed the importance of continued efforts. The modern biological and medical sciences emerged from their tradition, and today the naturalist tradition continues to expand its efforts to document, order, and understand the natural world.

[*See also* Buffon, Georges-Louis Leclerc de; Lavoisier, Antoine-Laurent; Linnaeus, Carolus; Lyceums and Museums; Maupertuis, Pierre-Louis Moreau de; Natural Philosophy and Science; Scientific Instruments; *and* Spontaneous Generation.]

BIBLIOGRAPHY
Allen, David Elliston. *The Naturalist in Britain: A Social History.* London, 1976. An engaging and valuable social history of natural history.
Baker, Daniel. *Explorers and Discoverers of the World.* Detroit, Mich., 1993. Contains a survey of all the major expeditions of the period.
Blunt, Wilfrid. *The Compleat Naturalist: A Life of Linnaeus.* New York, 1971. A useful study that sets Linnaeus's life into a broader social context.
Browne, Janet. *The Secular Ark: Studies in the History of Biogeography.* New Haven, Conn., 1983. Contains a useful discussion of early ideas on the distribution of plants and animals.
Coats, Alice. *The Plant Hunters.* New York, 1969. A broad survey of the worldwide search for plants.
Farber, Paul Lawrence. *Discovering Birds. The Emergence of Ornithology as a Scientific Discipline: 1760–1850.* Baltimore, 1996. A case study of the emergence of natural history as a scientific discipline.
Farber, Paul Lawrence. *The Naturalist Tradition: From Linnaeus to E. O. Wilson.* Baltimore, 2001. A general survey of the naturalist tradition, starting in the Enlightenment.
Frängsmyr, Tore. *Linnaeus: The Man and His Work.* Berkeley, Calif., 1983. Essays on Linnaeus's life and work.
Holmes, Frederic Lawrence. *Lavoisier and the Chemistry of Life.* Madison, Wis., 1985. A detailed account of Lavoiser's experiments.
Jardine, N., J. A. Secord, and E. C. Spary, eds. *Cultures of Natural History.* Cambridge, 1996. Essays on many aspects of the history of natural history.
Larson, James L. *Interpreting Nature: The Science of Living Form from Linnaeus to Kant.* Baltimore, 1994. A general treatment of eighteenth-century developments in the life sciences.
Larson, James L. *Reason and Experience: The Representation of Natural Order in the Work of Carl von Linné.* Berkeley, Calif., 1971. A careful study of Linnaeus's classification.
Roe, Shirley. *Matter, Life, and Generation: Eighteenth-Century Embryology and the Haller-Wolff Debate.* Cambridge, 1981. Discussion of the debates on epigenesis and preformation.
Roger, Jacques. *Buffon.* Ithaca, N.Y., 1997. A full biography that discusses both Buffon's science and as well as its place in eighteenth-century France.
Roger, Jacques. *The Life Sciences in Eighteenth-Century French Thought.* Stanford, Calif., 1997. A major study of the life sciences during the Enlightenment, and the most complete discussion of eighteenth-century theories of generation.
Torlais, Jean. *Réaumur: Un esprit encyclopédique en dehors de "L'Encyclopédie."* Paris, 1936. A detailed study of Réaumur's science that includes a discussion of his work on digestion.

PAUL LAWRENCE FARBER

NATURAL LAW. The term *natural law* refers less to a single doctrine or discipline than to a genre of thought. At the core of this genre lies the conception of a moral law that is natural in two senses: as a law given in man's moral nature; and as a law that is accessible by means of natural knowledge as opposed to revealed (or biblical) knowledge. Natural law is thus distinguished from positive or voluntary law—that is, law given in the proclamations of a particular lawmaker—whether the legislator is God (divine positive law) or the civil sovereign (civil law). As such, natural law has been used to set moral criteria against which civil law might be judged and sovereign states held to account.

Before the Enlightenment. The theme of a natural moral law, accessible to reason and establishing universal criteria for assessing positive law and politics, recurs throughout the history of European thought from Greek and Roman antiquity to the present day. This continuity is more apparent than real, however; man's moral nature, the rational faculty through which natural law is known, and that law's relation to the state's civil law have been subject to the most diverse constructions, depending on the religious and political circumstances of particular historical periods. The Greek philosopher Aristotle (b. 384 BCE) provided a key element of natural law thought through his doctrine that all substances or natures contain a purposive law of development (*telos*), although he limited the realization or perfection of man's "rational and sociable nature" to political life in the city-state (*polis*). Stoic philosophers such as Cicero and Seneca, however, situated human nature in the cosmos, all parts of which strive to preserve themselves in accordance with a universal law. This linkage between natural law and the desire for self-preservation would be recovered in the Renaissance and would play a key role in Enlightenment natural law.

The most formidable doctrine of natural law prior to the Enlightenment, however, was that developed by the theologian Thomas Aquinas (1224–1274). Aquinas married Aristotle's conception of purposive natures to Christian metaphysics and theology, giving rise to a form of natural law suited to the teachings of Roman Catholic universities and seminaries (and hence called scholasticism). Thomist natural law is a branch of theology dedicated to defending the moral supremacy of the church by deriving the law from principles accessible only through Catholic metaphysics. As such, it may be characterized in terms of its metaphysical foundations and its suprapolitical scope.

In his *Summa Theologiae* (Summary of Theology, 1265), Aquinas grounded natural law in God's *eternal law*, the law through which divine reason imprints creatures with their purposive natures. As the bearer of such a nature, humans must obey the eternal law, but because their nature, like God's, is rational, they can also have natural access to this supernatural law. This takes place through human intuitive knowledge of the principles of *natural law*. As humans' natural mode of "participating" in eternal law, natural law differs both from *divine positive law* (the biblical commandments) and from *human law*, which, as the application of natural law to particular circumstances, lacks the certainty of natural law. As a result of its moral and rational superiority to human law, Thomist natural law assumes a suprapolitical character, allowing Aquinas to declare that "we can only accept the saying that *the ruler's will is law*, on the proviso that the ruler's will is ruled by reason; otherwise a ruler's will is more like lawlessness."

After the Reformation, under circumstances of confessional conflict and religious war, the metaphysical and suprapolitical character of Thomist natural law turned it into a powerful weapon against non-Catholic rulers and states. Under the assumption that the "reason" required to make the ruler's will into a just law was in fact determined by the metaphysics of Catholic natural law, Protestant rulers could be deposed as heretics incapable of fulfilling the true ends of natural law. In the attack on England's Protestant King James I (1566–1625), launched in his *Defensio Fidei Catholicae et Apostolicae* (Defense of the Catholic and Apostolic Faith, 1612), the Spanish Jesuit theologian Francisco Suárez thus argued that natural law justified the pope in authorizing the overthrow or assassination of heretical kings.

Early Enlightenment Natural Law. Enlightenment natural law—which developed between 1670 and 1770 by such writers as John Locke and Richard Cumberland in England, Samuel Pufendorf, Christian Thomasius and Christian Wolff in Germany, the exiled French Huguenot Jean Barbeyrac, and the Swiss law professor Jean-Jaques Burlamaqui—was in large part a reaction to Thomist scholasticism and the so-called second scholastic of the later sixteenth century. Richard Tuck has thus characterized this "modern" natural law as the "anti-scholastic Enlightenment." Drawing on and reacting to the English political philosopher Thomas Hobbes (1588–1679) and the Dutch humanist jurist Hugo Grotius (1583–1645), early Enlightenment writers sought to shift the center of gravity of natural law from theology to politics and jurisprudence, with a view to adapting it to the secular scope and territorial limits of the sovereign state.

Grotius is plausibly seen as taking important steps in this direction in his *De Jure Belli ac Pacis* (Law of War and Peace, 1625). Here he sketched a nonmetaphysical conception of law in terms of the maintenance of social order, arguing that, although the law of nature might not be founded in the exigency of man's natural unruliness, it "nevertheless has the reinforcement of expediency." Yet, somewhat inconsistently, Grotius also maintained the scholastic doctrine that natural law is grounded in rational insight into an act's conformity with man's rational and sociable nature, and hence into the act's objective goodness or evil. In his *Leviathan* (1651), Hobbes launched a far more uncompromising attack on the metaphysical grounds of natural law, arguing that its rules are ultimately grounded in the self-interested desire of individuals for their physical survival. However, in reducing natural law to prudential rules whose consistency and effectiveness are entirely dependent on their enforcement by the sovereign, Hobbes almost obliterated the distinction between natural and civil law, leaving little of the tradition standing.

The most complete elaboration of an antischolastic natural law was provided by the German political jurist Samuel Pufendorf (1632–1694) in his massive *De Jure Naturae et Gentium* (Law of Nature and Nations, 1672) and its widely translated and disseminated digest, *De Officio Hominis et Civis* (On the Duties of Man and Citizen, 1673). Pufendorf honored Grotius as the founder of an enlightened natural law but was critical of his "scholastic" attempt to provide an objective deduction of the law from man's nature as a rational and sociable being. Pufendorf was also a careful and respectful reader of Hobbes, from whom he learned much, while remaining critical of the Englishman's attempt (as he saw it) to reduce the natural law to individual self-interest and to collapse it into the sovereign's positive law. Pufendorf's objective was not to marginalize natural law but rather to transform it from within. He sought to retain its core function of providing a moral basis for civil law and the state, while rescaling this rationale to suit the system of secular territorial states whose architecture had been provided by the treaty that ended the wars of religion, the Treaty of Westphalia (1648). These were the circumstances in which Pufendorf focused his critical powers on the metaphysical foundations and suprapolitical scope of scholastic natural law, with devastating effect.

Pufendorf drew on the Lutheran conception of the primacy of God's will over his reason ("voluntarism"), together with the associated doctrine of fallen man's radical incapacity to participate in divine reason. This allowed him to argue that there could be no rational moral law binding on both God and man from which objective moral principles might be derived for natural law. Pufendorf therefore refused to treat natural law as a branch of eternal law, insisting that while the latter was the proper concern of a moral theology dedicated to salvation, natural law was an independent discipline oriented solely to human conduct in civil life. The paradoxical result of this theologically grounded attack on the metaphysical basis of scholasticism was, in fact, the secularization of natural law thought. Now people had to view human nature not as bearing the purposive imprint of a transcendent reason whose principles they could intuit, but as an "empirical"

phenomenon whose moral character could be gathered only through observation. This secularization of the object and method of natural law allowed Pufendorf to advance the doctrine that moral duties and rights do not flow from a single substantial moral nature—scholasticism's rational and social being—but are instead attached to a plurality of "imposed," or instituted, "moral entities." The most important of these entities are the moral personae, the statuses or roles people occupy when acting in particular capacities. Pufendorf regards these as "imposed" on humans' physical nature with the express purpose of governing their conduct in accordance with the ends of civilized existence.

With this architecture in place, Pufendorf was able to provide a new construction of natural law. If we begin not with the intuition of rational nature shared with God but with the empirical observation of man in his natural condition (the "state of nature")—the contents of which Pufendorf in fact drew from Stoic sources—then we discover creatures whose weakness means that they require mutual assistance in order to survive, but whose mutual viciousness threatens their existence. All natural law, therefore, is grounded in the fact that "in order to be safe, it is necessary for [man] to be sociable; that is to join forces with men like himself and so conduct himself towards them that they are not given even a plausible excuse for harming him, but rather become willing to preserve and promote his advantages." Pufendorf thus enunciated the rule of a natural law that is secular in the sense of being governed by the cultivation of worldly sociability and social peace. The distinguishing feature of Pufendorf's derivation of natural law from the observation of man's natural condition is that he was the first to treat this condition as an imposed status (*status naturalis*) rather than as given in man's rational or physical nature. Unlike Grotius, Pufendorf viewed sociability not as a principle imprinted in man's rational nature, but as a kind of comportment to be cultivated in accordance with pragmatic rules. Unlike Hobbes, however, he viewed these rules not as the expression of a self-interested desire for physical self-preservation, but as a means of cultivating the sociable persona whose imposition on man's physical nature transforms its preservation into the shared duty of maintaining civil peace.

Pufendorf's antimetaphysical treatment of duties and rights also plays a key role in his attack on the suprapolitical character of scholastic natural law. Some of the sociable duties—to God, to oneself, and to others—arise from the human natural condition (state of nature) that results from divine imposition. Other duties—those associated with property, language, family life, and the state—are the adventitious product of human agreement, instituted through a series of pacts or contracts by which men impose on themselves a variety of moral personae and their associated duties. This allowed Pufendorf to view the sovereignty pact ("social contract") and the creation of the state not as the natural expression of man's purposive need to perfect his rational and sociable being, but as the artificial means by which men institute a new moral persona—the "composite moral person" of the sovereign—for the specific and limited purpose of mutual self-defense. By treating duties and rights as attached to locally instituted personae, Pufendorf broke with the scholastic conception of sovereignty as arising from the contractual delegation of rights already possessed by individuals or communities in their natural condition—and hence, as something that could be reclaimed should the sovereign fail to honor these "natural rights."

Later Enlightenment Natural Law. In restricting the natural law to the purpose of social peace, and in establishing the civil sovereign as the sole bearer of the supreme rights and powers needed to achieve this purpose, Pufendorf realized the Enlightenment aim of providing politics with a moral basis suited to a system of sovereign territorial states. Translated into all the major European languages and used as a textbook in Protestant universities, Pufendorf's shorter *De Officio Hominis et Civis* (On the Duties of Man and Citizen) ensured the wide dissemination of his version of the antischolastic Enlightenment. In Germany, it was above all the political jurist and cultural reformer Christian Thomasius (1655–1728) who was responsible for disseminating Pufendorf's program, developing his own natural law doctrines, and mounting public campaigns for religious toleration and against witchcraft trials on the basis of Pufendorf's separation of state from society.

Despite his importance, however, Pufendorf should not be regarded as the founder of a uniform tradition of Enlightenment natural law. In treating the right of supreme political power as something created by the pact itself, rather than as something transferred from a domain of natural right, Pufendorf radically detached sovereignty from God and the people, its two traditional sources. If this immunized the post-Westphalian territorial state against the delegitimating power of Roman Catholic natural law, then it also separated Pufendorf's "absolute" conception of the state from the "liberal" conception advanced by the English political philosopher John Locke (1632–1704), in which the state remains beholden to natural rights invested in a sovereign people. Pufendorf's enlightened absolutism was not illiberal, however, and even less was it "totalitarian," for it too imposed strict limits on the exercise of state power. Whereas Locke derived such limits from the natural rights to life, liberty, and property that citizens brought with them into the state, Pufendorf built them into the structure of the state itself. As an artificial person constructed solely for the purposes of security, Pufendorf's state had no right to intervene in other (commercial, familial, religious) associations, unless they threatened social peace, which was something that only the state could decide.

In translating and commenting on Pufendorf for the refugee Huguenots—French Protestants driven into exile by religious persecution—Jean Barbeyrac (1694–1744) developed a version of natural law that mediated between the positions of Pufendorf and Locke. Having experienced the oppressive power of a religious state, Barbeyrac was keen to spread Pufendorf's secularized construction of a state restricted to the ends of security. At the same time, however, Barbeyrac was unwilling to grant the secular state too much power, which led him to endorse Locke's conception of natural rights and to treat the state as the bearer of a delegated sovereignty originating in the people.

By the middle of the eighteenth century, these versions of natural law had been joined by that of the German metaphysical philosopher Christian Wolff (1679–1754). Drawing on the metaphysics of Gottfried Wilhelm Leibniz (1646–1716), but also incorporating Thomistic themes, Wolff elaborated a Protestant version of scholastic natural law, once again treating the law as grounded in self-evident perfective principles to which humans have access by virtue of the rational nature they share with God. Wolff is often seen as carrying the torch of Enlightenment natural law down to the time of Immanuel Kant, whom some regard as having terminated the tradition by banishing the concept of human nature from the foundations of morality. In fact, the several versions of Enlightenment natural law passed unreconciled into the nineteenth century, as did their great enemy, Thomistic natural law.

[*See also* Enlightened Despotism; Locke, John; Natural Rights; Political Philosophy; Pufendorf, Samuel; *and* Wolff, Christian.]

BIBLIOGRAPHY

PRIMARY SOURCES

Aquinas, Thomas. *Summa Theologiae*. The full translation runs to sixty volumes; English readers seeking points of entry can begin with *Summa Theologiae: A Concise Translation*, translated by Timothy McDermott. Allen, Tex., 1989.

Grotius, Hugo. *The Law of War and Peace*. Translated by Francis W. Kelsey. Oxford, 1925.

Hobbes, Thomas. *Leviathan*. Cambridge, 1991.

Pufendorf, Samuel. *The Law of Nature and of Nations in Eight Books*. Translated by C. H. Oldfather and W. A. Oldfather. Oxford, 1934.

Pufendorf, Samuel. *On the Duty of Man and Citizen According to Natural Law*. Translated by Michael Silverthorne. Cambridge, 1991.

Suárez, Francisco. *Selections from Three Works*. Translated by G. Williams. Oxford, 1944.

SECONDARY SOURCES

Brown, B. F. "Natural Law." In *New Catholic Encyclopedia*, vol. 10, pp. 251–256. New York, 1967. A useful short history of natural law written from the perspective of Catholic scholasticism.

Haakonssen, Knud. "Christian Thomasius." In *The Routledge Encyclopedia of Philosophy*, edited by E. Craig, vol. 10, pp. 376b–380b. London, 1997. An excellent short account of Thomasius's theory of natural law in the context of his life and work.

Haakonssen, Knud. *Natural Law and Moral Philosophy: From Grotius to the Scottish Enlightenment*. Cambridge, 1996. A comprehensive account of the natural law tradition in the context of the history of moral philosophy.

Hochstrasser, T. J. *Natural Law Theories in the Early Enlightenment*. Cambridge, 2000. A valuable account of how the early Enlightenment natural jurists viewed their break with the tradition of scholastic natural law.

Hunter, Ian. *Rival Enlightenments: Civil and Metaphysical Philosophy in Early Modern Germany*. Cambridge, 2001. Discusses Pufendorf's and Thomasius's natural law doctrines in terms of the development of an antimetaphysical civil philosophy.

Seidler, Michael. "Introductory Essay." In *Samuel Pufendorf's "On the Natural State of Men,"* edited and translated by Michael Seidler, pp. 1–69. New York, 1990. A perceptive introduction to Pufendorf's central concerns and a detailed account of his use of the state of nature doctrine.

Skinner, Quentin. *Foundations of Modern Political Thought*. 2 vols. Cambridge, 1978. Vol. 2 contains a fundamental discussion of Catholic and Protestant natural law doctrines from the perspective of their roles in the formation of modern political theory.

Tierney, Brian. *The Idea of Natural Rights: Studies on Natural Rights, Natural Law and Church Law, 1150–1625*. Atlanta, 1997. Sympathetic history of Roman Catholic natural rights doctrines.

Tuck, Richard. "The 'Modern' Theory of Natural Law." In *The Languages of Political Theory in Early-Modern Europe*, edited by Anthony Pagden, pp. 99–122. Cambridge, 1987. An influential article calling for renewed attention to "modern" natural law characterized as the "anti-scholastic Enlightenment."

Tully, James. *An Approach to Political Philosophy: Locke in Contexts*. Cambridge, 1993. Contains fundamental discussions of Locke's natural law and political philosophy in relation to both the Thomist and Protestant traditions.

Tully, James. "Editor's Introduction." In *Samuel Pufendorf: On the Duty of Man and Citizen According to Natural Law*, pp. xiv–xl. Cambridge, 1991. Excellent short account of Pufendorf's natural law doctrine in the context of the post-Westphalian system of territorial states.

IAN HUNTER

NATURAL PHILOSOPHY AND SCIENCE.

Many philosophes appealed to the natural science of the eighteenth century to support their pedagogical, political, economic, and religious views; a few of them helped in its popularization both individually, like Voltaire, and collectively, like the encyclopedists; and a very few, like Jean Le Rond d'Alembert, Benjamin Franklin, and Pierre-Louis Moreau de Maupertuis, made substantive contributions to it. This article describes representative portions of natural knowledge that the philosophes used or increased, and representative institutions that they furthered.

The years 1700 to 1770 saw the dissemination of the Newtonian world system and a multiplication of learned societies; the popularization of natural knowledge through books, lectures, entertainments, and encyclopedias; the experimental investigation of life processes; and the application of the new learning to undermine established institutions. The period after 1770 witnessed political revolutions powered in part by the rhetoric of natural knowledge; an Industrial Revolution that produced, in England, the beginnings of a society propelled by steam and steel; a revolution that took chemistry from a collection of recipes to a system of science, and physics from a qualitative to a quantitative description of nature; a broadening and synthesizing of what are now called earth and biological sciences; the effective application of knowledge gained by systematic and sustained experiment to practical problems; and a rapid increase in the number and quality of instruments and journals for procuring and distributing natural science.

Promising Engagements (to 1740). In 1720, Jacques Cassini, son of the astronomer Gian Domenico Cassini and his heir as leader of the royal observatory in Paris, published the family's conclusions about the size and shape of the earth. The result of fifty years of intermittent fieldwork, *De la grandeur et figure de la terre* disclosed that the earth's equatorial diameter falls short of the distance from pole to pole. The earth was elongated along the polar axis. The disclosure surprised Isaac Newton, who had proved that the earth looks like a pumpkin in his *Principia mathematica philosophiae naturalis* (1687). Leading members of the Académie Royale des Sciences of Paris, who held to Cartesian natural philosophy, accepted the polar elongation because it contradicted an important consequence of Newton's theories of gravity and motion. The resolution of the controversy by expeditions sent to Lapland (led by Pierre-Louis Moreau de Maupertuis [1698–1759]) and to the equator (led by Charles-Marie de La Condamine [1701–1774]) in the 1730s by the Paris Academy established Newton as the sage of the age. Meanwhile Voltaire, the loudest anglophile philosophe, had composed his praise of English institutions, popularized Newton in France in *Elémens de la philosophie de Newton* (1738), and celebrated the measurements of the earth that flattened the poles and the Cassinis.

In 1715, a Dutch lawyer good at mathematics, in England on a diplomatic mission, met Newton and other fellows of the Royal Society of London (the English rival to the Paris Academy). Having become a fellow himself, Willem J. 'sGravesande returned to Holland to be named professor of mathematics at the University of Leiden. He developed a course on Newtonian physics illustrated by experiments, *Physices elementa mathematica, experimentis confirmata, sive Introductio ad philosophiam newtonianam* (2 vols., 1720–1721), that served as a standard text up to the midcentury. With his colleague in medicine and chemistry Hermann Boerhaave, his instrument maker Jan van Musschenbroek, and his successor Petrus van Musschenbroek, 'sGravesande made Leiden the European center for the study, and beachhead for the dissemination, of natural philosophy during the first half of the eighteenth century. Accordingly, Voltaire brought his *Elémens* to "the man whose name begins with an apostrophe" for critical prepublication review.

A site for Enlightenment. The Paris Academy began life in the 1660s as a bureau of experts to advise the crown on technical matters. A restructuring in 1699 brought Bernard Le Bovier de Fontenelle, a favorite of the salons and the author of perhaps the first best-seller in popular science, *Entretiens sur la pluralité des mondes* (1686), as its permanent secretary. Fontenelle invented two literary genres that would draw the academy's work within the grasp of the ordinary citizen of the Republic of Letters: the *histoire*, or annals of the year's advances in natural knowledge made by members of the academy; and the *éloge*, or panegyric on the scientific contributions, academic virtues, and noble character of a deceased member. The annual *histoire* prefaced a collection of *mémoires* that, by statute, the academicians had to write and read to one another during the year. The *éloges* provided role models for cultivators of natural knowledge during the Enlightenment and a shining face for science before the general public.

In 1716, the academy underwent a new organization into classes and ranks. No one attached to a religious order could belong. The fifty or so academicians exercised their influence not only through their publications and their correspondence, but also through prizes they offered for essays on set subjects. Savants throughout Europe competed. The prize competition was an emblem of the academic mind: the advancement of knowledge in critical areas through the mobilization of the natural abilities of men capable of more than they believed possible.

The Royal Society of London, which also dates from the 1660s, was not a governmental bureau. Rather than salaried members it had dues-paying fellows. The need for a large membership able to afford the fees explains the readiness with which gentlemen with any claim to science, like 'sGravesande, were elected. In 1700, the membership stood at 150, in 1720, 195, in 1740, 300. In keeping with its poverty, the society gave few prizes. Its chief publication, its *Philosophical Transactions*, carried reviews, correspondence from nonmembers as well as from fellows, relatively little mathematics, and, in the early days, tales of monsters and mermaids. The Paris *mémoires* transmitted only reports of original work done by members of the academy and sought rather than eschewed mathematics.

Newton became president of the Royal Society in 1703, four years after Fontenelle took over the Paris Academy, and remained its virtual dictator until his death at seventy-five in 1727. Newton used the Society not only to perfect parts of his world system but also to fight his battles. Through Society members, he wrangled with Leibniz over priority in the invention of calculus, and, hiding behind the Reverend Samuel Clarke, over the role of God in the world system.

The Royal Society and the Paris Academy exemplify the two types of learned companies that led the eighteenth century's quest for knowledge. Only monarchs could ape the Paris model. The Berlin Academy, established in 1700 on the nagging of Leibniz, was underfunded and underproductive until its reorganization by the philosophes' king, Frederick the Great, in 1744. Peter the Great created the St. Petersburg Academy in 1725 to help Europeanize Russia. He chose its members with the advice of Leibniz's synthesizer, Christian Wolff. Thus, until around 1740, St. Petersburg and Berlin tended to be Wolffian in natural philosophy, Paris Cartesian, and London Newtonian.

Academies of the London type multiplied after 1740. Before then, only three noteworthy examples came into being. The Kungliga Vetenskapsakademien in Stockholm, founded in 1739 at the urging of people who, like Carolus Linnaeus, were familiar with natural philosophy as practiced in Leiden and London, emphasized experimental physics, natural history, and "economics," that is, husbandry, agriculture, mining, and forestry. The Bordeaux Academy, founded in 1712 by the parliamentary aristocracy to which Montesquieu's family belonged, emphasized natural history in its early years, experimental physics around the midcentury, and technology, agriculture, and commerce toward its end. It thus stayed close to the changing interests of the doctors, lawyers, military men, and landholders who made up its membership.

The Accademia delle Scienze dell'Istituto di Bologna (1714) brought something new. The gift of a Bolognese senator, the institute had as the nucleus of its academy of sciences a group of professors who had organized themselves during the 1690s into a social-intellectual group of a type frequently met with in seventeenth-century Italy. Professors at the University of Bologna made use of the academy's collections and, later in the century, owing to the beneficence of Pope Benedict XIV, of a fund to buy out teaching time. That was a rare arrangement. According to a distinction frequently made in the eighteenth century, academicians sought new knowledge whereas professors only taught the old; research and teaching did not mix. Academies, observatories, and botanical gardens, not universities, were the principal places for the advancement of natural science during the eighteenth century.

High roads to Enlightenment. The philosophes liked to say that unfettered healthy minds like theirs could follow and assent to any properly presented truthful argument. Proper presentation meant reduction to clear and distinct elements and their step-by-step integration. In this way,

Descartes had replaced Aristotelian philosophy with a solider, starker structure: Where established learning populated the world with uncountable independent essences, Descartes made do with matter and the perceiving mind. The properties of matter were simply extension, shape, and mobility. One bit of matter could act on another only by pushing, and since no space void of matter could exist, every motion had to involve a closed loop, or vortex.

The Cartesian natural philosopher, therefore, filled the world with specially shaped particles in vortical motion: a great *tourbillon* (vortex) carries the planets around the sun; a lesser maelstrom centered on the earth rotates the moon and causes gravity and the tides; little whirlpools bring iron to lodestones and chaff to electrics. What else but matter in motion accounts for the reflex actions of animals and the physiology of life? Since God could achieve the same effect with different shapes and motions of matter, the details of the machinery of the universe could be found only by experiment, which also, in the form of demonstrations, could be used to confirm and illustrate the principles accessible to pure thought. Several dexterous Cartesian philosophers made a living showing experiments. The most important and popular of them, and also the last, was the abbé Jean-Antoine Nollet. A member of the Paris Academy, preceptor to the royal family, instructor of military engineers, favorite of learned ladies, and supplier of instruments to Voltaire, Nollet adhered in a general way to Cartesian natural philosophy even as he taught the principles of universal gravity.

"I left France full and found England empty." Thus Voltaire, in his *Lettres philosophiques* (1734), put the difference between the Newtonian philosophy informing the Royal Society and the plenary Cartesian cosmos. Voltaire referred to Newton's demonstration that the celestial spaces cannot be filled with resisting media like vortices. To move in a manner entirely consistent with Newton's principles and with observation, the planets needed only to gravitate toward the sun while striving to leave the solar system along a tangent to their orbit. Without the material vortex, however, what provided the tendency toward the center? In his *Principia* Newton generally avoided that question—*hypotheses non fingo* ("I feign no hypotheses"), but he did hint at possible causes of gravity both in the *Principia* and in the famous "Queries" that he appended, in increasing numbers, to successive editions of his *Opticks* (1704, 1706, 1717, 1721). He offered a choice among a hail of particles from remote space, the action of a springy resistanceless ether, and the direct intervention of God, "to discourse of whom from the appearances of things does certainly belong to natural philosophy" (*Principia*, 1713).

The problem of finding God's place in his creation preoccupied Newton as did fear of asserting more than he knew. He gave the creator the task of keeping the planets from slowing down under their mutual gravitational tugs, and he formulated his insights—about gravity, chemical processes, and the subtle elastic ether responsible for electricity, optical phenomena, sensation, and the motion of animals—as hints and queries. The Dutch Newtonians got around these problems by understanding gravity and other "attractions" in a purely operational sense, as the mutual accession of bodies. Later Newtonians threw away the scruples that had weighed upon Newton, spoke unabashedly of actions at a distance, and invoked springy weightless ethers with the same rococo abandon as Cartesians multiplied the shapes and motions of material particles.

Leibniz favored a physics in Descartes's style set on the golden pillars of logical consistency and intuitive sufficiency. Not even God could create a contradiction in terms. Nor, according to Leibniz, could he create without a sufficient reason. The creator could make only the best things, as many of them as possible—a doctrine popularized and ridiculed by Voltaire in *Candide* (1759). Wolff deployed the principle of sufficient reason as Descartes had wielded the touchstone of clear and distinct ideas, and to much the same effect: Matter acts only by contact; the world runs by pushing. Wolff's textbooks on mathematics and physics, which emphasized experiments, helped to protect German speakers from English ideas until the middle of the century.

The contract of the first natural philosopher engaged by the St. Petersburg Academy required that he teach physics according to Wolff's principles. His successor won a prize from the Berlin Academy in 1728 for an effort to save the *tourbillons*. Wolffianism was by no means synonymous with reaction, however. The marquise du Châtelet, despite her mastery of Newton's *Principia* and intimacy with Voltaire, announced suddenly in 1740 that no philosophy but Leibniz's could satisfy her.

High Tide (1740–1770). In 1751, a pamphlet appeared in London that offered a new theory of electrical action and a hare-brained scheme for conducting lightning harmlessly into the ground. The scheme attracted the director of the Jardin du Roi, Georges-Louis Leclerc, later comte de Buffon, who had studied in London and translated Newton. If successful, the experiment would be important and might also undercut Nollet, France's reigning electrician and the protégé of Buffon's arch-rival, the conservative exemplary academician René de Réaumur. Buffon hired an old soldier to test the electricity of lightning. A priest attended, to witness the affair and administer last rites if the spark exceeded expectations. The complete success of the experiment made a celebrity of its author, a colonial printer named Benjamin Franklin. Eventually, most of the electricians of Europe accepted Franklin's theories and installed his conductors. His contributions to natural philosophy made the reputation he later exploited when enlisting French ministers in the American cause. The homespun cosmopolitan philosopher, who, in the words of Turgot, "snatched the lightning from the sky and the scepter from the tyrant's hand," was the embodiment of Enlightenment, a harmonious blend of the natural and reasonable, the active and contemplative, and the simple and profound.

The first two fat volumes of Diderot's *Encyclopédie* appeared in the same year as Franklin's slim *Experiments and Observations on Electricity*. It promoted science and Enlightenment in three main ways besides cataloging natural knowledge. First, its emphasis on the need and opportunity for rationalization of the trades and manufactures—pictured in its magnificent plates (derivative to some extent from a survey Réaumur had conducted for the Paris Academy)—forced home the utilitarian value of natural science. Second, the *Encyclopédie* communicated that the application of science, in the sense of a coherent, unprejudiced synthesis of elements found in nature, did not stop at the arts; politics, economics, psychology, education, all could be improved by the same methods that had enabled Newton to deduce the world system and Franklin to tame lightning. Third, the *Encyclopédie* insinuated that truth and science together made a whole and, also, a weapon against religion and other superstitions. To be sure, one man could not oversee it all. Diderot, who had no special scientific training, took on the mechanical arts and bits of qualitative sciences like psychology and chemistry, whereas d'Alembert, an important authority on Newtonian mechanics, a member of the Paris Academy and the Royal Society, oversaw the mathematical sciences and general physics, and, in his *Discours préliminaire*, showed how everything fit together.

The philosophes' academy. The academic movement reached its pinnacle in the middle years of the century. Kings and princes created new versions on the Paris model at Berlin (1744), Göttingen (1751), Munich (1758), and Turin (1759); lesser patrons ushered in societies elsewhere; provincial academies multiplied in France; "economic and patriotic societies" concerned with promoting the best practices of the domestic arts and sciences sprang up in their dozens in Germany. The French crown chartered a Société Royale d'Agriculture (1761) and the English an economic and patriotic society, the Royal Society of Arts (1754). Fellows of the Royal Society became more concerned with useful inventions. A group of them resident around Birmingham established a club they called the Lunar Society in 1766, and made substantial improvements in pottery manufacture (Josiah Wedgwood), steam power (Matthew Boulton and James Watt), and other technologies.

The Berlin Academy revived almost immediately on the accession of the friend of the philosophes, Frederick II, in 1740. He made sure that his academy spoke French and offered prizes, the first of which, on the winds, went to d'Alembert. He installed as president Maupertuis, formerly the leader of the Newtonians in the Paris Academy and the measurer of the telltale degree of the meridian that had disconfirmed the Cassinis.

To head the mathematical class, Frederick acquired Leonhard Euler from the St. Petersburg Academy. Euler applied his combination of Newton's mechanical principles and Leibniz's calculus to everything that moved, from sailing ships and windmills to moons and planets. At Berlin, among many grander things, he calculated the minuscule alteration of the earth's axis occasioned by the pulls of Jupiter and Saturn. This slow motion joined others discovered by James Bradley, a fellow of the Royal Society who became the astronomer royal of England in 1742: the aberration (an annual apparent rotation of stars in very tiny circles) and the nutation (a small rise and dip of the earth's axis). All three phenomena found straightforward explanations in Newton's universe. They rendered the Catholic Church's condemnation of Copernican theory, which made little enough sense in Galileo's time, altogether absurd. In 1757, Benedict XIV, strengthened by these academic findings, removed the general proscription against Copernican texts from the Index of Prohibited Books.

The Societät (later Akademie) der Wissenchaften at Göttingen made another bowl for the mixing of English and Continental ideas. The University of Göttingen, founded in 1737 by the Hanoverian dynasty in England, was enriched in 1751 with a Royal Society and an observatory to provide time and facilities for a few of its professors. Albrecht von Haller, a native of Bern and a student of Boerhaave, became the first professor of anatomy and medicine at the university, the founder of its botanical garden, and an architect of the society. Irritability, as displayed by muscle tissue, was his trademark, the object of his pioneering work at Göttingen, and the keynote of his responses to his critics. A Zwinglian in religion, a do-gooder in civic affairs, a practical technologist, and, through his textbooks on physiology, an influential teacher, Haller acted many of the parts of a man of the Enlightenment without being one. Someone closer to the mark, Haller's colleague Johann Tobias Mayer, had made himself a cartographer and astronomer by private study of Wolff's textbooks on mathematics. Developing mathematical prowess often gave upward mobility during the eighteenth century. Called to Göttingen in 1750 to teach his specialties and head the observatory, he soon laid the golden egg expected of him, his lunar method of finding longitude. For this he was awarded, posthumously, three thousand pounds from the fund disposed of by the British Admiralty for a satisfactory solution to the technical problem of the age. After 1770, Georg Christoph Lichtenberg, an expert on Hogarth's art as well as on experimental physics, was the chief representative of natural knowledge at Göttingen and, through his textbooks, the most influential teacher of physical science in Protestant Germany for a generation.

The people's physics. The experiments illustrating the natural philosophies of Descartes, Leibniz, Wolff, and Newton differed only in the explanations accompanying them. Before 1740, the demonstrators emphasized the principles of mechanics and hydrostatics and showed geography and astronomy on globes and armillaries. These subjects represented only a small fraction of the phenomena belonging to "physics" in the large sense in which the seventeenth century had used it. Experimental physics dealt only with the general phenomena of the inorganic world, exclusive of chemistry. This limitation arose from two exigencies: The natural philosophies of the time did not extend to plausible accounts of chemical and vital processes; and experimental demonstrations before audiences had to be dependable, reproducible, striking, and easily visible. Instrument makers and the public that attended the demonstrations, therefore, had as much or more influence on the content of experimental physics as did the philosophers who wrote about it. Between 1740 and 1770, physics became identified with experimental natural philosophy, and the public, as consumers of books and demonstrations, helped to reshape the body of natural knowledge during the high Enlightenment.

In 1746, Musschenbroek reported a new experiment to Réaumur: "I would not do it again for the entire kingdom of France." Nollet tried the experiment, which amounted to electrifying a jar half filled with water as a condenser and discharging it through his body. He received a smart shock. In a celebrated demonstration, he propagated the shock though a string of insulated monks. The Leiden jar evidently had the qualities required for a successful physics demonstration: It was inexpensive, portable, and enjoyable by many simultaneously. A serious example, the "thunder house," used a spark from a Leiden jar to show the destructive power of lightning and the preservative action of Franklin's conductors.

Even before he had news of the Leiden experiment, Franklin had worked out a new concept of electrical action modeled on a primitive moral calculus he had invented as a young man. The young moralist had supposed that for every unit of pleasure (or pain) a person experiences, an answering unit of pain (or pleasure) is reserved for him; we must undergo many ups and downs before returning, in death, to insensibility. The mature electrician taught that all bodies have a natural quantity of a self-repulsive

electrical fluid that makes them neutral (they show no signs of electricity). Electrification occurs when one body gains a surplus of electricity at the expense of another, which suffers an equal deficit. The analogy between pleasure, pain, and insensibility, on the one hand, and positive electricity, negative electricity, and neutrality, on the other, is so obvious that Franklin did not bother to mention it.

The theory of plus and minus electricity made a revolution in physics. Before Franklin, electricians had ascribed electrical action and repulsion to a material emanation from electrified bodies. Franklin's theory of the Leiden experiment required the positive charge inside the bottle to repel the electrical fluid from the outside surface. The theory was refined and quantified by several electricians, among whom Johan Carl Wilcke of the Stockholm Academy and Franz Ulrich Theodor Aepinus of the St. Petersburg Academy made the decisive contributions. More speculative applications of Franklin's concept of plus and minus charge occurred in meteorology (cloud formation), geophysics (earthquakes), and physiology (the operation of nerves and muscles).

Nature's profusion. The teeming life in every drop of water revealed by Antoni van Leeuwenhoek's microscopes, and reported by him to the Royal Society beginning in the 1670s, indicated that even the prolific flora and fauna of America occupied but a small niche in nature. Calculating from information provided by Boerhaave, Musschenbroek reckoned the number of plant species at 13,000 (*Oratio de sapientia divina*, 1744). He allowed each of them five insects, making around 72,500 species in the animal kingdom as a whole, or, better, 145,000, since every animal served as food for another, or, to be safe, 290,000, since so little of the earth had been explored. "How manifold are thy works, O Lord!" And how great a headache for encyclopedists.

Abraham Trembley, an inquisitive tutor from Geneva, gave them another. In 1740, having turned his microscope on ditch water, he spied a vegetable, or perhaps an animal, which he cut into pieces. They regenerated into replicas of the original. The fullness of nature had obliterated the secure division between plants and animals. To get hold of it all, Linnaeus, who published his sexology of plants in Holland in the 1730s under the patronage of Boerhaave and others, grouped God's creatures into classes and orders in accordance with the number of stamens, pistils, teeth, toes, nipples, and so on, they possessed. A refinement of 1753 introduced the binomial designator locating each species in its genus. The system allowed for ready classification and reference but suffered from two disabilities. The arithmetic of Linnaeus's system did not always place in the same higher groupings the species that obviously went together; and the superficiality of

Linnaeus's demarcators put off naturalists who delighted in details of anatomy and behavior. Buffon may stand for the first set of objectors, and Réaumur, whose six stout volumes of *Mémoires pour servir à l'histoire des insectes* (1736–1742) dwelt upon bees, ants, clothes' moths, lice, locusts, and other little animals that live with humans, for the second.

With little previous experience as a naturalist, Buffon depended on books, associates (especially Louis Daubenton, a painstaking anatomist), and literary élan to create his famous *Histoire naturelle* (15 volumes, 1749–1767). It opens with a sweeping account of the earth from its creation in a collision of a comet with the sun through the appearance of seas and mountains down to the arrival of man. Buffon assigned seventy-five thousand years to this pageant, over ten times the span allowed by literal exegetes, for which he won the condemnation of the theological faculty of the Sorbonne. Of Réaumur's plodding *Mémoires*, he observed that a fly should not occupy a greater place in the mind of a naturalist than it does in nature; of Linnaeus's classifications, that a scheme that placed man, monkeys, and sloths in the same box proved its own absurdity. Buffon discussed animals in the order of their usefulness to human beings, much as Réaumur had dealt with insects; his account of the horse and its kindred (the donkey, mule, zebra), illustrated with Daubenton's comparative anatomies, was a particularly happy example of his method. His eloquence, emphasis on utility, and descriptions of animal habits and habitats won him both a large following among nonexperts and his own party among philosophers. As in experimental physics, the public to which the philosophes appealed helped to redefine the character and divisions of natural knowledge.

One of the crowd of nonspecialists who appreciated Buffon was Diderot, who had the leisure to read the first three volumes of *Histoire naturelle* while in prison in 1749. He later borrowed much from Buffon for the *Encyclopédie* and recruited Daubenton to write many of the articles on natural history. Diderot did not seek contributors from Réaumur's camp. "What would posterity think of us if we passed on to it only . . . an immense history of microscopic animals: great objects for great geniuses; small objects for small ones." Thus, in his *Pensées sur l'interpretation de la nature* (1754), did Diderot fix the distance between the science of the philosophes and the knowledge of the naturalists.

The disbeliever's religion. In the article "Genève," d'Alembert compared the gentle and enlightened local religion, Calvinism, to the superstitious practices of French Catholicism, and ended with the highest compliment he could give to any organized religion: "respect for Jesus Christ and the scriptures are perhaps the only thing that distinguishes the Christianity of Geneva from pure deism."

Like much else in the repertoire of the philosophes, the program of stripping religion to respect for a creator, and theology to propositions attainable by reason, had its origin and partial realization in English natural philosophy.

Newton again provided the exemplar. In his private but lofty unorthodox thoughts, God figured as the playground of gravitational forces and Jesus as a great but not a divine teacher. Newton's biblical criticism and ancient chronology disclosed a mind at once devout and critical, obedient to sacred scripture as he interpreted it, but not to established religion. Some of Newton's disciples worked his theories into a physicotheology. Clarke proved God's existence as if he were a proposition in geometry and discussed his capacities as revealed by Newtonian cosmology. William Derham, like Clarke an Anglican minister and fellow of the Royal Society, gave the operation of universal law as an illustration of the Almighty's designs. Voltaire marveled at the grand design—as revealed by Newton.

The gravitational theory made a cold frame for a warm appreciation of the work of the creator, but here too science had an answer. The extravagant profusion and perfect adjustment of nature provided the rational mind with all the evidence it needed to revere a creator and reject religion. Just as the ascendency of experimental demonstrations reduced the coverage of physics, so attention to the machinery of life narrowed the operations of the soul. Descartes had reduced animals to automatons. Matter alone might itself act the part of the vegetable and animal souls of traditional philosophy. And perhaps also of the rational soul? John Locke could find nothing definitive against the proposition. The supposititious continuity of the chain of being from man to polyp and polyp through the plant kingdom argued that matter alone, properly organized, could perform many, maybe all, the functions of the soul. Another doctor trained by Boerhaave, Julien Offray de La Mettrie, published a scandalous work, *L'homme machine* (1747), that pushed the argument to its logical conclusion: Humans like other animals should be regarded as automatons. Forced to flee France, La Mettrie found refuge with Frederick II, who made him an academician. Buffon put forward a similar view less aggressively: Taking a hint from Leibniz's *Monadologie* (1714, second edition 1721), he pictured living beings as an assemblage of animate particles. Buffon and Maupertuis, among others, thus hoped to explode the then dominant doctrine of preformation, which taught that descendants exist preformed in their parents, like an endless set of nesting dolls.

Antireligion derived further comfort from a major nondiscovery. The pullulation of "insects" in decaying organic matter suggested the spontaneous creation of life. Not so cried Lazzaro Spallanzani, priest and ovist, classicist, mathematician, and natural historian, indeed, a polymath, a graduate of Bologna and a professor at Pavia.

Spallanzani showed that solutions of decaying matter boiled and hermetically sealed did not breed insects. This demonstration convinced pious naturalists such as Haller and the Genevan Charles Bonnet, who had bettered his countryman Trembley's finding of polyps with the discovery of parthenogenesis. It did not convince Buffon or Diderot. Other encyclopedists too dipped their toes in this materialistic quicksand, or, as happened with baron d'Holbach, sank in completely.

Electricity provided a valuable tool for those who would peer into life with the equipment of natural philosophy. The involuntary movements stimulated by the Leiden shock suggested that an electrical fluid filled the nerves and stimulated the irritability of the muscles. The brain needed only to act as a condenser, like the peculiar organ that Henry Cavendish, the most brilliant fellow of the Royal Society since Newton, and others had found in electric fish. Following upon the ideas of Haller understood electrically, Luigi Galvani began, around 1770, an investigation that culminated in the mid-1780s in the discovery of "animal electricity," a fluid similar to, but not identical with, ordinary electricity. The new electricity, stored in the muscles as if in a Leiden jar, activated them when discharged through the nerves. Galvani, a man of exemplary and even painful piety, would have been shocked by the fictional conclusion of his discoveries in the spark that gave life to Frankenstein's monster.

Outcomes: Revolutionary, Recondite, and Romantic (1770–1815).

Revolutionary. In June 1799, an international committee of experts, convened to review the measurements and calculations that underlay the meter, liter, and kilogram, formally, though belatedly, presented the new units to the people. The project, started by the Paris Academy, responded to complaints about the abusive old system of weights and measures. However, citizens not fully instructed in natural knowledge reasoned that the academy should perish with other elite corporations of the age of kings; it fell with the regime it served.

One of the five commissioners for the metric project was Antoine-Laurent Lavoisier. An encyclopedist at heart, he had a head for figures, the energy to undertake an inventory of the natural resources of France, and the desire to improve agriculture and manufacture. He also, improbably, combined the characters of a revolutionary and a tax-farmer. The one made his reputation throughout Europe; the other cost him his head during the Terror.

Lavoisier gave chemistry a new set of principles, and a logical, coherent, and expandable language. The key to his revolution was the discovery by others that "air" comes in chemically different kinds. During the early 1770s, Watt, Cavendish, and Lavoisier independently made the scarcely credible discovery that two of these gases, one necessary to support combustion and the other highly inflammable, united to form the great enemy of fire, water. Pneumatic experiments soon replaced electrical demonstrations in the public lecturer's bag of best tricks. Natural philosophers armed with eudiometers—instruments developed to test the oxygen content of air—visited prisons, hospitals, mines, and swamps to measure, if not improve, air quality. Technologists substituted hydrogen for the hot air used in the first *montgolfières* (hot-air balloons), reached great heights, and promised unprecedented improvements in communications and the art of war.

Cavendish (the discoverer of the flammable constituent) and Joseph Priestley (the discoverer of the combustive principle) supposed that the gases were compounds incorporating "phlogiston," a hypothetical weightless or levitating principle that gave metallic properties to metals and, by escaping from bodies, caused their combustion. Lavoisier took the two gases to be elementary and called them hydrogen and oxygen, respectively; he insisted that combustion, and the slow burning sustained by respiration, implied combination with oxygen, not emission of phlogiston. Several of Lavoisier's French colleagues accepted his bold new chemistry and helped him to develop a terminology to secure his revolution. The new names, such as "nitrous oxide," resembled Linnaeus's binomials.

The *Traité élémentaire de chimie* (Elementary Treatise on Chemistry) in which Lavoisier crystallized his reforms appeared in the revolutionary year 1789. Inevitably, chemists of the old school, especially in Britain and Germany, associated the overturning of established government and religion with the brutal rejection of the pedigreed phlogiston. Resistance to Lavoisier's chemistry was also resistance to other excesses to which the overly rational, aggressively critical French mind was leading the God-fearing peoples of Europe. The Genevan who served as natural philosopher in residence to the queen of England, an exact experimenter named Jean André Deluc, was one of many men of science perceptive enough to see through the clever conspiracy that linked French politics and French chemistry. Lichtenberg, who had independently stigmatized Lavoisier and his band as a "club of Jacobins," had the same insight. The phlogistic chemists, however, succeeded no better in arresting the progress of the new chemistry than the European powers did in stopping the armies of Napoleon.

The work of the Revolution included revamping educational and research institutions and staffing them with eligible survivors of the ancien régime. The old Paris Academy, apart from a few "enemies of the people," reappeared as the First Class of the Institut de France. The Jardin du Roi became the Muséum d'Histoire Naturelle; Daubenton stayed on and was joined by Georges Cuvier and others already famous. The Ecole Polytechnique, which took students by competitive examination and nourished them on calculus and chemistry, had a staff that included Pierre-Simon de Laplace and other great mathematicians; Claude-Louis Berthollet, formerly a collaborator of Lavoisier and now the Laplace of chemistry; and Gaspardde Prony, an engineer who taught hydraulics and classified the theorems of mechanics in the style of Linnaeus. Their students emerged with more exact science than was needed to build forts and bridges. What the state lost in engineering efficiency, science gained in applied mathematicians.

Recondite. The highest-ranking French participant on the international metric commission, Laplace, presented his friend Napoleon with the first two volumes of his *Mécanique céleste* (Celestial Mechanics, 1799). Napoleon read enough to see that God did not figure in Laplace's cosmology. "Sire," he replied, "I have no need of that hypothesis." His calculations showed that, contrary to Newton, the solar system can run on its own forever. Laplace's calculations exceeded the reach of Napoleon, who considered himself a mathematician, and lay far beyond the reach of the literate who enjoyed Buffon and supported the *Encyclopédie*. Laplace and his followers subjected electricity, magnetism, heat, and optical phenomena to severe quantification. Whereas, in 1750, a retired printer in America could transform ideas about electricity entertained by European philosophers, in 1800, only an accomplished mathematician could make a substantial contribution to the higher reaches of the subject.

Charles-Augustin de Coulomb, a former military engineer and a senior member of the Paris Academy, began the rigorous mathematization of electricity and magnetism in 1785. He built a very sensitive (indeed, for unpracticed users, uncontrollable) balance with which to measure forces between droplets of the electrical fluid (or fluids, because Coulomb and most French philosophers supposed the existence of a second fluid to play the part of the negative charge in Franklin's theory). As David Hume and Immanuel Kant had made clear, however, we cannot know things as they are, we might as well make physical theory to suit our mathematical convenience. Since, as Lichtenberg observed, no experiment settled whether electricity came in one fluid or two, the choice was as indifferent as that between the spellings "deutsch" and "teusch." Coulomb's measurements indicated that droplets of the same electrical fluid repelled one another with a force of the same mathematical form as gravity's. Similar experiments secured a similar result for the austral and boreal fluids supposed to make up magnetic poles. That allowed mathematicians to bring the machinery of the gravitational theory, which they had been perfecting for a century, to bear. They soon outdistanced experimental

philosophers of the previous generation such as Priestley, Deluc, and Lichtenberg.

Romantic. A few months after the formal presentation of the meter, Alessandro Volta, Spallanzani's colleague at the progressive Austrian-run University of Pavia, put the finishing touches on his electric "pile." Two years later, "citoyen" Volta of the new Cisalpine Republic stood before the First Class of the Institut de France. Napoleon also was there. Volta showed the perpetual source of electrical current that he had been led to devise by following up Galvani's activations of dead frogs. The pile—a stack of pairs of silver and zinc disks separated by pieces of moistened cardboard—made a sensation. When scaled up, it could cause newly executed criminals to twitch and smile, and separate new elements from tightly bound compounds, giving, on the one hand, much grisly entertainment, and, on the other, sodium and potassium. Napoleon thought Volta a prince, and made him a senator.

Volta's pile reopened the study of electricity to people excluded by the severe mathematics of Laplace's school. Its pronounced chemical and physiological effects suggested ties between large domains of knowledge. That made it a preferred object of study of synthesizing nature philosophers (*Naturphilosophen*) imbued with the ideas of transcendental philosophers descended from Kant. *Naturphilosophie* emphasized the action of oppositely directed forces, like attraction and repulsion, and so made the pile, which produces and suffers different chemical effects at its different ends, as well as the magnet, emblems of truth as well as objects of study.

In his *Metaphysische Anfangsgründe der Naturwissenschaft* (Metaphysical Foundations of Natural Science, 1786), Kant had shown that the best guess philosophers could make about the nature of the noumena (the unperceived world of things in themselves) was a dynamic equilibrium between attraction and repulsion rather than (as Newton had supposed) a collection of hard, indestructible atoms. Kant's teaching about the ultimate inaccessibility of the noumena to empirical science combined with his dynamic physics to challenge some bold spirits to deduce the workings of the fundamental polar forces by pure thought. The most influential of the spirits was Friedrich Wilhelm Joseph Schelling, whose first essays on what he called "speculative physics" appeared in 1799. Schelling explained that light consists of ether (repulsive) and oxygen (attractive); electricity and magnetism, of obvious polar forces; chemical processes, of struggles between acidic and basic principles; and life, of battles between individual and environment.

Naturphilosophie's systematic, fuzzy, holistic character recommended it chiefly to romantic writers antagonistic to exact experimental science. Still, *Naturphilosophen* obtained results of singular interest and importance.

Goethe's sustained attack on Newton's optics secured insights into the perception of color; the expectation, encouraged by *Naturphilosophie*, that living creatures, despite their great diversity, had some unity of form, underwrote much comparative anatomy; and similar perceptions of unity in diversity inspired experiments with the pile that uncovered profound relations between electrical currents and magnetism.

The several emphases of late-eighteenth-century science—the encyclopedic, rational, critical, and utilitarian stream favored by the philosophes: the exact physics characterized by the Laplacian school, and the qualitative dynamics of the *Naturphilosophen*—came into harmonic equilibrium in the career of Alexander von Humboldt (1769–1859). In 1799, he embarked on a tour of South America, where he observed, measured, and recorded everything of botanical, zoological, and physical interest, which he later systematized in novel graphs and charts. He was the first to use isobars and isotherms to plot average temperatures and pressures. He established biogeography as a subject. He understood the distribution of plants and animals as an equilibrium between the opposing forces represented by temperature, pressure, rainfall, and altitude.

Humboldt's synthetic program opposed the centrifugal force of increasing specialization indicated by the formation of specialist scientific journals, the rising standards of learned societies, the increasing accuracy and complexity of instrumentation, and, not least, the beginnings (as at Pavia) of a research culture in the universities. This struggle between the polar opposites of analysis and synthesis, and of mathematics and speculation, occurred halfway through the publication of Humboldt's *Kosmos* (1845–1862), a systematic account of the universe from its origins to the creation of landscapes and life forms, an encyclopedic popularization of natural knowledge in the style of the Enlightenment.

[*See also* Agriculture and Animal Husbandry; Astronomy; Botany; Chemistry; Electricity and Magnetism; Heat; Hospitals; Inoculation and Vaccination; Life Sciences; Mathematics; Medicine; Meteorology; Midwifery; Natural History; Optics; Physics; Pneumatics; Scientific Instruments; Spontaneous Generation; Taxonomy; Weights and Measures; *and* Zoology.]

BIBLIOGRAPHY

Alder, Ken. *Engineering the Revolution: Arms and Enlightenment in France, 1763–1815.* Princeton, N.J., 1997. The rationalization of manufacture by the introduction of interchangeable parts.

Beretta, Marco. *The Enlightenment of Matter: The Definition of Chemistry from Agricola to Lavoisier.* Canton, Mass., 1993.

Clark, William, et al., eds. *The Sciences in Enlightened Europe.* Chicago, 1999. Downplays experimental natural philosophy, rejects positivism, and draws inspiration from Foucault.

Donovan, Arthur. *Antoine Lavoisier: Science, Administration and Revolution.* Cambridge, 1993.

Ferrone, Vincenzo. *The Intellectual Roots of the Italian Enlightenment: Newtonian Science, Religion and Politics in the Early Eighteenth Century.* Atlantic Highlands, N.J., 1995.

Frängsmyr, Tore, ed. *Linnaeus: The Man and His Work.* Berkeley, Calif., 1983.

Frängsmyr, Tore, et al., eds. *The Quantifying Spirit in the Eighteenth Century.* Berkeley, Calif., 1990. Traces the rationalization of natural knowledge and some natural history through mathematics.

Gillispie, Charles Coulston. *Science and Polity in France at the End of the Old Regime.* Princeton, N.J., 1980. Details the institutions serving natural knowledge and its applications.

Glass, Bentley, et al., eds. *Forerunners of Darwin.* Baltimore, 1959. Hints and anticipations of the theory of evolution, many from the eighteenth century.

Godlewska, Anne Marie Claire. *Geography Unbound: French Geographic Science from Cassini to Humboldt.* Chicago, 1999. Decline and rebuilding of geography (including cartography) and its uses.

Golinski, Jan. *Science and Public Culture: Chemistry and Enlightenment in Britain, 1760–1820.* Cambridge, 1992. Chemistry as a gentlemanly pastime, oxygen and Enlightenment, laughing gas and medicine.

Guerlac, Henry. *Essays and Papers in the History of Modern Science.* Baltimore, 1977. Mostly about Newtonianism on the Continent and the chemical revolution.

Hahn, Roger. *The Anatomy of a Scientific Institution: The Paris Academy of Sciences, 1666–1803.* Berkeley, Calif., 1971.

Hankins, Thomas. *Jean d'Alembert: Science and the Enlightenment.* Oxford, 1970. Salons and mathematics.

Heilbron, J. L. *Electricity in the 17th and 18th Centuries: A Study of Early Modern Physics.* Berkeley, Calif., 1979; New York, 1999. Includes Jesuit work, professorial finances, and learned academies.

Heilbron, J. L. *Weighing Imponderables and Other Quantitative Science Around 1800.* Berkeley, 1993. Electricity, magnetism, light, heat, and the "measure of Enlightenment" (the meter).

Laudan, Rachel. *From Mineralogy to Geology: The Foundations of a Science, 1650–1830.* Chicago, 1987.

McClellan, James E., III. *Science Reorganized: Scientific Societies in the Eighteenth Century.* New York, 1985. A typology with systematic information about founding, patronage, and organization.

Paul, Charles B. *The Eloges of the Paris Academy of Sciences (1699–1791).* Berkeley, Calif., 1980. A taxonomy.

Roger, Jacques. *Buffon.* Paris, 1989. An elegant and dependable synthesis of modern scholarship.

Rousseau, G. S., and Roy Porter, eds. *The Ferment of Knowledge: Studies in the Historiography of Eighteenth-century Science.* Cambridge, 1980. The state of knowledge around 1980.

Ruestow, Eugene. *Physics at 17th and 18th Century Leiden.* The Hague, 1973.

Schofield, Robert E. *Mechanism and Materialism: British Natural Philosophy in an Age of Reason.* Princeton, N.J., 1970.

Schofield, Robert E. *The Lunar Society of Birmingham: A Social History of Provincial Science and Industry in Eighteenth-Century England.* Oxford, 1963.

Sparry, E. C. *Utopia's Garden: French Natural History from Old Regime to Revolution.* Chicago, 2000.

J. L. HEILBRON

NATURAL RELIGION.

NATURAL RELIGION. Natural religion is defined in Chambers's *Cyclopedia* (London, 1728) as "whatever we descry to be due and meet by the meer Dictates of natural Reason; as, to love, and honour God, not to abuse his

Creatures &c." Its scope embraces not only God's existence and attributes—natural theology—but also his relation to his creation and, in particular, to human beings as rational, accountable creatures. It extends to the nature of the human soul; the existence of a state of rewards and punishments after death, the liberty of the will; and the duties that arise from God's relation to his rational creation, or ethics—insofar as these are discoverable by natural reason. If human actions are necessitated and hence not free, some Enlightenment thinkers asked, how could human beings be held accountable for them, whether in this life or in another? If God acts arbitrarily without regard to the welfare of his creation, how can he be a moral governor to whom honor and service are due? Nearly all Enlightenment thinkers addressed issues of natural religion, supportively or critically, and these constitute a pervasive framework for their thought. This must be kept in mind because contemporary treatments of their ideas commonly ignore this context.

Natural religion contrasts with revealed religion, which depends on something other than natural reason: the revelation of God's will. The medieval theologian Thomas Aquinas (1225–1274), whose thought enjoyed a revival in the seventeenth and early eighteenth centuries in Catholic France, regarded natural religion not only as consistent with revealed religion, but also as a preliminary and foundation to it if religion, even revealed, were to be claimed as rational. In his view, natural religion does not compete with revealed religion but complements faith. The contrast was also blunted by John Locke (1632–1704), who characterized reason as natural revelation, since it is equally God's gift. Correspondingly, he described revelation as natural reason, enlarged by God's communication, since it is within reason's province to determine that revelation has God as its source. To deny reason this role, he argues, can only undermine revelation.

Enlightenment thinkers differed strikingly about how much natural reason could or should attempt to establish based on different conceptions of its scope. On one metaphysical view, the truths of reason, like those of mathematics, are independent of sense experience, in contrast to those in which reason uses truths furnished by experience. A related but different contrast is between views that seek to demonstrate the existence of a necessary being—whether or not they rely on premises derived from sense experience—and those that do not. At the extreme, some claimed that reason, of whatever kind, has no place in religion, which depends entirely on faith as a gift of the Holy Spirit and, far from being supported by reason, is undermined by it. Alternatively, reason was held to show that there can be neither natural nor revealed religion, because reason undermines claims to God's existence.

At a minimum, natural religion needed a compelling argument for God's existence. Some also argued that natural reason could establish the human soul's immateriality, from which its immortality could be inferred. More ambitious was the claim that a future state in which virtue is rewarded and vice punished could be established by reason. Still more ambitiously, some argued that natural reason could establish the truth of Christianity, while others claimed that the principles and duties of ethics, which bind God as much as human beings, are discoverable by natural reason. The greater natural reason's scope, the fewer the demands on faith; for most, however, natural reason's role was not to displace faith, but to support and strengthen it.

The figure of the atheist was used to motivate natural religion. How could atheists embrace revealed religion except through natural religion? How else could the doubts that prey on believers and make them vulnerable to the atheist's beguiling arguments be put to rest? In the seventeenth and early eighteenth centuries, the atheist was, on most accounts, not only rare but usually disguised as a deist, pretending to believe in God while rejecting revelation—Christian revelation, in particular. By the end of the eighteenth century, however, the atheist was out of the closet. Anthony Collins (1676–1729) claimed the atheist was an artifact of the natural religion intended to silence him. He said of the Boyle Lectures—the great showcase for natural religion and Newtonian science in the late seventeenth and early eighteenth century, to which Richard Bentley (1662–1742), Samuel Clarke (1675–1729), and William Derham (1657–1735) contributed—that they made atheism, not otherwise a question, into one. His quip was echoed through the eighteenth century by figures as diverse as Henry Dodwell the younger (d. 1784), who cited the lectures to show the ineffectiveness of natural religion and to demonstrate that salvation has nothing to do with argument; or Benjamin Franklin (1706–1790), who confessed his exposure to them had the opposite of the intended effect, making him a skeptic, though not an atheist. Atheism, however, was a common and facile accusation. The Unitarian scientist Joseph Priestley (1733–1804), himself a materialist, noted that materialism was commonly seen to be tantamount to atheism. He argued that it is not only compatible with natural religion but offers the most plausible account of Christian revelation, once alien accretions (notably Platonism) are stripped away.

The deists, who subordinated revealed to natural religion, also used natural reason to examine and reject central Christian mysteries, such as the Trinity. They attacked them as unintelligible contrivances of priests, whose object was to impose on a gullible public in order to enhance clerical power. For them, true religion had nothing to do with such doctrines and everything to do with living a virtuous life. They threatened Christian revelation by questioning the external marks on which it depends—miracles and prophecies—and they cast doubt on the authenticity of its texts, which were becoming the objects of systematic critical examination. For deists, the supreme virtue in life and religion is not a faith opposed to reason, but the sincere attempt to discover truth through examination and the exercise of individual reason—freethinking, as it was commonly called. The Welsh deist David Williams (1738–1816)—supported by Franklin and Voltaire—and the Theophilanthropists of revolutionary France conducted experiments with forms of worship based solely on natural religion. Critics regarded their limited success as showing that, although natural religion has value in support and justification of revealed religion, it is too dry and unappealing by itself to serve the needs of religious worship.

The arguments that became staples of natural religion trace their ancestry to the Middle Ages and classical antiquity. Their structure, however, became much better understood in the Enlightenment. The discoveries of natural philosophy, or science, inspired a confidence in the power, certainty, and range of natural religion. This confidence was disarmed by a series of remarkable analyses of the limits of human reason that questioned natural religion's foundations. In Immanuel Kant's (1724–1804) image, reason stretches its wings in vain when it seeks to soar beyond the world of sense by the power of speculation alone.

Cartesianism. Descartes's *Meditationes de Prima Philosophia* (Meditations on First Philosophy, 1641) preceded the Enlightenment, but its influence extended well into the period as a seminal statement of one approach to natural religion. Descartes noted that infidels would not abandon their beliefs unless God's existence could be demonstrated by philosophical rather than theological reasoning, nor would most people prefer virtue unless the expectation of a future life were similarly supported. In making God and the soul the primary objects of his reasoning, he placed them at the foundations of all knowledge, secure against the skeptic's systematic doubt. He established the soul's distinctness by his dictum "I think, therefore I am," and then proved God's existence as a being embodying all perfections. It is natural to believe that the soul's (mind's) ideas correspond to and are caused by external material objects beyond them, but can there be certainty that this belief is not caused by some evil genius? The justification of an external world immune from skepticism lies through God, whose existence as a nondeceiver must be proved without presupposing his existence itself.

Descartes formulated two related arguments. The first starts from the idea in our minds of God as embodying all perfections, an idea he claimed to be innate. He inferred from the principle that there must be at least as much reality in the cause as in the effect that God must be the cause of this idea. The second argument claims, more directly, that since the idea of God embodies all perfections and existence is a perfection, God necessarily exists, unlike humans, who are contingent beings.

Descartes's approach was followed, with variations, by Nicolas Malebranche (1638–1715). For him, however, the existence of an external world of material objects beyond the ideas in our minds is a matter of faith, not philosophical demonstration. God is no deceiver, but neither is there a compelling proof of his creation of such a world outside revelation, since the soul (mind) cannot directly perceive material objects, given that, lacking extension, it can have no union with them. Not only do the ideas of sensible objects beyond the mind itself not originate from it; they are and can only be in God. We see all things in God, and they testify to his existence. Of God himself, however, we can have no idea, because none can represent him; we can only know him in himself.

Of Malebranche's view, Locke remarked: "Since God does all things by the most compendious ways, what need is there that God should make a Sun that we might see its Idea in him when he pleas'd to exhibit it, when this might as well be done without any real Sun at all" ("An Examination of Malebranche's Opinion of Seeing All Things in God"). This logic was adopted by George Berkeley (1685–1753), who used it to justify a philosophical idealism that recognizes only the existence of ideas and the spiritual substances that support them. In reply to those who accepted the existence of material objects independent of sensory impressions and argued that such objects are necessary as causes and support for these impressions, Berkeley said that their claim was incoherent and paved the way to skepticism and atheism, which his theory was intended to destroy. For where they posited material causes, sensory impressions point to an omnipresent and providential God: "As sure, therefore, as the sensible world really exists, so sure is there an infinite omnipresent Spirit, who contains and supports it." Unlike in Malebranche's view, God is not directly apprehended but is inferred from the commonest data of sensible experience. Nor must God's veracity be invoked, as Descartes does, to justify the existence of a material world, which makes no sense. The simplest sensory impressions establish God's existence, while the organization of ideas testifies to his goodness.

During the seventeenth century, Aristotelian-inspired scholasticism, including that of Aquinas, enjoyed a revival in Catholic France that extended into the eighteenth century, while Cartesianism appealed not just to Catholics but also to Protestants such as Issac Jaquelot (1647–1708). Aquinas's approach contrasts with Descartes's. In his celebrated "five ways," Aquinas, accepting the existence of the external world, argued to God's existence as a first mover, a first cause, and a necessary being, responsible for the order of the universe. In contrast, Descartes's account of the soul rejected Aristotelian notions for a Platonically inspired dualism. The destructive conflict between supporters of these two approaches to natural religion convinced bystanders that reason could not deliver what either party to the conflict pretended. Thus, it opened the door to an atheism that had scarcely existed outside the imaginations of the debate's protagonists.

For Kant, the ontological argument (from perfect being) is the most fundamental of all arguments for God's existence, because the others either imply that argument or retreat to it when what they show proves too weak or indeterminate. To him is owing the classic statement of its refutation: that it mistakenly treats existence as a predicate. Existence is not part of the concept of God in the way that omniscience, omnipotence, and benevolence are. To say that God exists is to say that the concept of God with these other properties is instantiated, not that its instantiation is part of the concept. Kant's attack on the Cartesian strategy is more global, however, since he also questioned its claim that certainty can be had about one's own existence prior to anything else, arguing that one's consciousness of one's existence as a thinking being is possible only against the background of a world of spatial objects outside one. Without it, it would be impossible to order one's experiences.

Design. In an unpublished letter, Samuel Clarke responded to the question of why, if God really existed, he did not make his existence more evident by challenging the question's premise: "No Miracle is (in Truth) a stricter Proof of the Being of God, than are the principal Works of Nature, which require the very same Power to effect them, as any Miracle does; & tis nothing but mere Custom & careless inattentiveness, which makes men think continued Works not to be the Effects of the great Power as *occasional* ones" (Cambridge University Library, Add. 7113). In a similar vein, Joseph Priestley remarked that, although God could have made the world without any trace of design had he wished, he did so in order to demonstrate to human intelligence unmistakable evidence of his existence and nature. As Richard Bentley represented it in the inaugural set of Boyle Lectures, atheists, unwilling to acknowledge the authority of Holy Scripture as an expression of God's will, ought to acknowledge God's existence after inspecting "the mighty volumes of visible nature and the everlasting tables of right reason; wherein, if they do not wilfully shut their eyes, they may read their own folly written by the finger of God." Those unconvinced could be so only because they were moved by appetite and passion, not by reason.

Underlying this confidence were Newton's seminal discoveries in astronomy and physics, as well as the progress of biology. Whiston remarked: "That there is a God . . . who, as at first he made the World, so does now continually govern and act on it, is so certain and so next to Mathematical Demonstration, from the Wonderful Discoveries made in Sir *Isaac Newton*'s Works." The argument, founded on observation of the natural world, not only relied on the same kind of inference as any in science but could readily be seen to be equally compelling. As Kant observed, natural religion was viewed not only as a natural consequence of scientific discovery but also as a stimulus to it, because it encouraged an expectation of order not otherwise apparent to unaided observation. Unlike the Cartesians, the champions of design were untroubled by skeptical doubts about the existence of the natural world or its order, which they viewed as needing no justification beyond sensory observation. The argument's advantage was that it seemed plainly correct to anyone of ordinary intelligence and became even more compelling as knowledge increased. Thus, Whiston claimed that a common weed in his garden contained a better argument for God's existence and attributes than all abstract metaphysics. Whether by itself or in combination with an argument for the necessity of a first cause, design was used to infer God's most salient natural and moral attributes, notably his intelligence and knowledge. It was the flagship of natural theology in the empiricist tradition.

As Whiston remarked, the argument's inference is the same as that by which "from the Contemplation of a Building, we infer a Builder; and from the Elegancy and Usefulness of each Part, we gather he was a skilful Architect; or by which from the view of a Piece of Clockwork, we conclude the being of the Clockmaker; and from the many regular Motions therein, we believe that he was a curious Artificer." If a telescope is the contrivance of a craftsman designer, it is even more evident that the eye must have been formed by a consummately skillful divine designer with a mastery of optics and a providential regard for those who possess eyes. The similarity between artifacts and nature implies a similarity in their causes, although the cause of the latter must have been immeasurably greater. To Whiston or the Scots Newtonian Colin Maclaurin (1698–1746), a page or two was more than enough to make the case convincingly; subtlety was not needed. As Robert Hurlbutt has observed, the design argument, reinvigorated by the assistance of science, "dominated religious thought for a century or more," not just in England but well beyond.

The most exhaustive presentation of the argument is William Paley's (1743–1805) *Natural Theology* (1802), which develops it over more than 500 pages. Unlike some, Paley relied almost exclusively on biological illustrations, especially the human frame and the bodies of animals. Astronomy did not strike him as "the best medium through which to prove the agency of an intelligent Creator; but that, this being proved, it shows beyond all other sciences, the magnificence of his operations." For him, reflection on the intricacy of the eye's structure was sufficient to cure atheism. That the divine craftsman is known through his effects rather than by direct observation does not weaken the inference any more than it weakens the inference to an ancient seabed from the discovery of marine fossils. A watch formed by another watch so wonderfully contrived as to produce its own successors must still be attributed to design, and likewise an animal produced by its parent. Given that nature has been contrived by thought, God must be a person; given its uniformity, God must be a unity; given its breadth, God must be powerful beyond human imagining; given the benefits of his contrivance and the fact that the pleasures of sentient creatures far exceed the strict requirements of design, God must be good—a judgment Paley made from the standpoint of utilitarianism.

The Newtonians drew the same inferences from the contrivance and beauty evident in the fabric of the heavens and from the universal mathematical laws that governed them, especially gravitational attraction. To Whiston and Clarke, the nonmechanical nature of gravitational force, penetrating the very core of matter, acts as God's finger, not explainable by the external collisions to which materialist physics was not only historically but, they believed, necessarily tied. For them, only God could cause gravity by continual intervention everywhere, demonstrating his providence in matters great and small. This view occasioned Leibniz's taunt that natural religion in England was in serious decay because its God, lacking prescience, was constantly compelled to wind his watch to keep it going. Others, like Maclaurin, argued that whether or not this was so, the wonderful movement of the planets in regular orbits from west to east, not itself accounted for by gravity, implied a divine agent. It was supposed that God, as an immaterial agent, was needed to account for motion and change in material objects, because matter was regarded as by nature inert. This supposition can be traced to Greek philosophy; while Aristotelian physics was generally rejected in the Enlightenment, this conception of matter remained deeply entrenched.

The most sustained and damaging critique of the design argument was developed by David Hume (1711–1776) in *Dialogues Concerning Natural Religion* (1759). The question of whether human reason overreaches itself in making inferences beyond human experience forms the context of his analysis. The adaptation of means to ends in a machine does not itself warrant the inference to design and a designer—only repeated experience that certain effects are produced by such causes. The greater the similarity in the effects, the safer the inference; the weaker the analogy, the more doubtful. Even were it conceded that the universe or the human frame is strikingly similar to a house or a watch, how much more could be legitimately inferred? That there is only one God, say, rather than many? That the universe was not the botched product of an apprentice? That it was created? Or that the divine craftsman was not designed by another being with better credentials for the designation of God? Can God's goodness and providence be inferred in light of the pain, disorder, and evil that pervade earthly existence? Such phenomena might be reconciled with a God known to be good on other grounds, but the inference is not warranted from experience.

Returning to the basic question, how similar is a house to the universe? Are there not other available models in the world as we know it of organized systems coming into being, such as sexual generation? Could not the universe have come into being in this way, as Hesiod imagines in his *Theogony*? Is there any advance in understanding from the supposition that the universe is the product of an immaterial, thinking architect when thought is as little understood as matter? Are experience and observation even adequate to rule out the possibility of a principle of organization inherent in matter—not in some sample chosen at random, but in the system of matter itself? Thus, Hume observed, "The beginning of motion in matter itself is as conceivable a priori as its communication from matter and intelligence."

Hume thereby challenged the widespread conviction that matter is passive and demands the action of some altogether different and distinct being even to move, and still more to be organized. A similar challenge came from John Toland (1670–1722), who used it to justify a pantheism that identifies God with the mind or soul of the universe, but not separated from it except by a distinction of reason. It would be challenged again by d'Holbach in his *Système de la nature* (The System of Nature, 1770), where it is a cornerstone of his aggressive atheism. Another challenger was Joseph Priestley, however, whose account of the created universe is also unapologetically materialist and necessitarian. Priestley argued that the design argument, which he accepted as foundational to natural religion, was compatible with his view. The disputes between materialists and dualists or between libertarians and necessitarians, he claimed, had little bearing on fundamental questions of natural religion, but where they did, materialism strongly supported Unitarianism. If Jesus was a man, he was material, like other men, and had no existence prior to his birth. Materialism ruled out prior existence because no one has any memory of it, although not resurrection, where this depends not on the reconstitution of the same body but of one with the same consciousness. Although his materialism allows for resurrection, Priestley relied on revelation for assurance that it would occur.

Cause and Revelation. When Whiston pointed to a weed as better evidence of God's existence and nature than abstract metaphysical a priori reasoning, he was reproving the most notable of the Boyle Lecturers, Samuel Clarke. Clarke accepted the argument from design, but he was not satisfied that it could establish God as a necessary being or prove other essential attributes such as God's singularity. Clarke's approach to natural religion was widely recognized to be far more significant than Whiston's reproof suggests, as Voltaire and Jean-Jacques Rousseau (1712–1778) testified. For the deist Matthew Tindal (1655–1733), Clarke's claims about the need for revelation are the ones that needed answering; for d'Holbach, his argument for God's existence, as the most solid and convincing of those available, demanded a challenge point by point. Hume was more economical, challenging Clarke on a fundamental point: the nature of causality.

Clarke, whose demonstrative argument owed much to the Cambridge Platonist Ralph Cudworth (1617–1688), was not just trying to silence atheists from premises he claimed that an atheist must accept. Cudworth was engaged in the same enterprise, although it was said of his attempt that he succeeded in making the arguments against the being of God so strong that he was not able to answer them. Clarke went further: he attempted to prove the human soul's immateriality and immortality; and to show that there must be a future state of rewards and punishments. He aimed to demonstrate the unalterable obligations of natural religion, which he took to be not just plain and self-evident but the essence of true religion. He concluded by showing the moral certainty in natural reason of a revelation from God, and indeed, the certainty of the Christian revelation—not demonstrative certainty, but enough to convince a reasonable, unprejudiced person.

Clarke's project is breathtaking because he attempted to establish so much by natural reason, embedding it in a Newtonian account of the natural world. For doctrines like God's temporal creation and Christ's divine nature, there is for him no alternative to revelation. Even so, such doctrines must be both possible and not unreasonable. Clarke's central argument for the Christian revelation is not just that miracles and prophecies support it, but that the content of its morality is the same as that sanctioned by natural religion. Clarke set significant limits through natural religion on revelation, including the orthodox

doctrine of the Trinity, should it not conform with reason. He was an Arian, believing that only a single and simple God could be self-originating and necessary. Christ and the Holy Spirit, accordingly, could be eternal, but theirs was, of necessity, a dependent being. Clarke was no Unitarian, but his natural theology, closely tied to the constraints of reason, was an inspiration to that sect. Having conceded so much to natural reason, he left relatively little to faith or revelation. For Clarke, revelation is necessary not so much because of how little reason can do, but because in man's fallen state reason is so ineffective. His view on this point has much in common with Locke's *Reasonableness of Christianity* (1695), although it is considerably more skeptical about the capacities of human reason.

Clarke's argument for God's existence incorporates the cosmological argument, embedded in Aquinas's five ways, to show that there must be a prime mover, a first and necessary cause for all else that is. However, proving just this much, far from demonstrating God's existence, is compatible with atheism, as French critics argued against Aquinas's proofs. For Clarke, the real divide between the atheist and the theist is not reached until God is shown to be intelligent, but he cannot be shown to be intelligent unless he is free and not necessitated. Clarke's God always acts for the best, but only because he freely chooses to do so.

Clarke's argument to show that a necessary being has these attributes relies on a principle evident in his proof that something must have existed from all eternity, given that something now is. Were this not so, something could have come from nothing, which is a contradiction. Whereas the argument from design established God's intelligence from the evidence of contrivance in the universe, Clarke justified the same conclusion by means of his principle of necessary being. Since human beings are intelligent, a distinct characteristic, it cannot be explained—as materialists like Thomas Hobbes (1588–1679) attempted—by the motion and figure of material bodies. From motion and figure nothing can arise but motion and figure; otherwise, something would come from nothing. Human intelligence can be produced only by a cause at least as perfect as its effect. God, then, must be intelligent to create intelligent beings.

Since intelligence cannot be a property of a divisible, material subject, it must belong to an immaterial soul distinct from the body. Otherwise, there would be as many intelligences as material parts. Clarke was unimpressed not only by Descartes's ontological proof but also by his use of extension as the distinguishing property of matter. This, he argued, opens the way for matter to be a necessary being. Clarke's God is not only intelligent but also immaterial and extended.

Clarke's proof of an immaterial soul or mind conflicts with Locke's celebrated claim that human reason cannot demonstrate the impossibility of a thinking material subject. For Locke, nothing precludes God from superadding the power of thinking to a material body. Since natural reason cannot establish with certainty either the soul's immateriality or its immortality, these claims depend on revelation. Clarke's proof was challenged by Anthony Collins, who argued that consciousness and thought could be properties of a material system even if they were not properties of its parts, just as circularity is not a property of segments of a circle, but is of circles as such. Collins also argued against Clarke's account of liberty, claiming that actions could be both necessitated and free. Such claims threatened the core of Clarke's argument for God's existence—little wonder that he charged Collins with irreligion.

The most fundamental challenge to Clarke, however, came in Hume's *Treatise of Human Nature* (1739–1740). Hume asked two questions: Is it necessary for everything that has a beginning to have a cause? And can particular causes be known of necessity to have certain effects independent of experience, notably that the cause must be at least as perfect as its effect? To both questions, he answered "No. Anything can produce anything." If so, Clarke's demonstration collapses.

Deism's Challenge to Revelation. Clarke tried to demonstrate not only atheism's incoherence but also the untenability of deism, since, on analysis, he argued, it collapses into either atheism or Christianity; there are no defensible alternatives. Critics argued that his efforts were self-defeating. By claiming too much for natural reason, he effectively undermined faith and revelation and, contrary to his intentions, opened the way to deism.

The classic defense of deism is Matthew Tindal's *Christianity as Old as the Creation* (1731), which codifies and extends positions defended by the freethinkers. The relation between natural and revealed religion is key to their outlook. Their opponents portrayed them as disguised atheists, irrationally hostile to Christianity. The freethinkers pictured themselves as champions of everyone's right to use reason to decide the meaning and to judge the evidence and truth of propositions. For them, reason is its individual use, not its use simply by an elite of theologians; freethinking is a right and duty that underlies the Reformation and Protestantism; and religion's real core is the promotion of human virtue, identifying the overriding human virtue as the love of truth, which finds expression in rational examination, whatever the conclusion. In light of the differences of opportunity and talent among individuals, the appropriate standard for judging their virtue is the determination, impartiality, and sincerity with which they pursue such examination—not simply its results. A good and just God will judge human beings by the same standard. For the freethinkers, this view justified both the toleration of religious differences and an intolerance of superstition, which they viewed—following Pierre Bayle (1647–1706)—as a greater threat than atheism.

We need not determine whether Tindal (or his colleagues) was a deist in his heart; the point here is his subordination of revealed to natural religion and his claim of the sufficiency of human reason in religion. The first claim derives from Locke, who argued that where the same truth is discovered by natural reason and revelation, there is little need for revelation. When that view was combined with reason's sufficiency—a claim Locke was far from making—the effect was to sideline revelation, since it had nothing to offer that natural religion could not better supply. Tindal's title expresses his central thesis that revealed religion is merely a republication of natural religion by different means. Revealed religion may have been more suitable to earlier times, but natural religion offers the clearer and more compelling edition of God's word.

The freethinkers were influenced by Locke's claim that assent to a proposition ought to be proportioned to the evidence for or against it. A properly understood proposition expressing a revelation evidently from God must be certainly true, but there may be uncertainty about the source and meaning of claimed revelations, which characteristically rely on human testimony. In general, testimony does not yield certainty—only varying degrees of probability. It is an object of faith, not knowledge, to which it gives way where knowledge is available. In his *Dialogues Concerning Natural Religion*, Hume observed that Locke's originality is that he "seems to have been the first Christian who ventured openly that faith was nothing but a species of reason."

From this foundation, the freethinkers attacked the celebrated distinction between matters contrary to reason and those above it, which surpass ordinary human understanding. They did not deny that there are many things human beings, individually or collectively, do not understand. What they rejected is that anyone can properly be called on to assent to the truth of mysteries such as transubstantiation and the Trinity; the proper response is to withhold assent until they can be understood and evaluated. For them, the real purpose of the mysteries is to maintain the clergy's power by keeping a bemused laity under its thumb—in the language of the period, "priestcraft."

Freethinkers contrasted the clarity and simplicity of the duties and obligations of natural religion with the obscurity of revelation. Far from serving as the foundation of morality, revelation presupposes it and cannot be grasped without it. Natural reason is more comprehensive in scope, since no finite set of rules, given in revelation, can apply to all circumstances, and there is no option but to rely on natural reason in most cases. Natural reason is needed even to make sense of the rules sanctioned by revelation, and to determine how to apply them. According to Collins, "Revelation is so far (as it stands in Fact) from being the Means and consequently from being the *necessary Means* to *ascertain Religion*, that there is a Religion antecedent to Revelation, which is necessary to be known in order to *ascertain Revelation*; and by that Religion, I mean *Natural Religion*, which is presupposed to Revelation, and is a Test by which Reveal'd Religion is to be tried, is a Bottom on which it must stand, and is a Rule to understand it by" (*A Letter to the Reverend Dr. Rogers*, London, 1727). Since natural religion yields knowledge of duty and virtue while revelation yields probabilities, Tindal concluded, "must not Faith be swallow'd up by Knowledge; and Probability by Demonstration?" By the same token, freethinkers attacked those conceptions of God, associated with the Irish archbishop William King (1650–1729), that require the subordination of human will to God's while his nature is incomprehensible to human understanding. If God's justice bears so little relation to human justice, God cannot serve as a model to be imitated or even admired. Berkeley, otherwise unsympathetic with free-thinkers, agreed; such views, he argued, were incompatible with religion. Although the deist arguments subordinating revelation to natural religion apply even if there is a revelation of God's will, they also question claims of revelation, whether in whole or in part, by emphasizing the corruption of the texts or by undermining confidence in the traditional external evidence for them: prophecy and miracles.

Bayle and the Problem of Evil. If skepticism about reason's powers was regarded by champions of natural religion as hostile to religion, it was seen as its ally by those who argued that natural and revealed religion were at odds. The most notable of these was the French Protestant theologian Pierre Bayle, who posed deep problems that, he claimed, are insoluble by human reason and can be settled only by subjecting the understanding to the obedience of faith. Salvation lies not simply in a life of virtue, but in humbling reason as a preparation for submission to a God whose mysteries test faith. The task of conversion is faith's work, which comes through grace and can only appear foolish to philosophy.

Among the most influential of Bayle's examinations was that of the problem of evil. Newtonians pointed to the heavens to establish God's benevolence; Bayle redirected the focus to human life, where the evidence of experience supports a different conclusion. A priori proofs of God's benevolence do not change the picture; a proof cannot be of much account, he argued, if it

is unable to account for experience, any more than an argument purporting to demonstrate the impossibility of motion. The evidence of experience is better explained by the theory of Manicheanism, which posits two antithetical beings—one good, but limited by the other, which is evil. For Bayle, this troubling knot is intractable to natural reason. Its solution is found in faith and revelation, which alone can convince us of Manicheanism's falsity and, against human reason, that a good God could create a universe with evil in it.

Leibniz, a defender of the ontological argument, was not convinced by Bayle's logic. Bayle showed only that the appearances of experience conflict with reason. This does not set reason against faith, but faith against probability, where reason is not defenseless. According to Leibniz, Bayle too easily abandoned confidence in reason when there was no need to do so. To concede that there are conflicts that cannot be resolved by reason is to oppose God against God. The mysteries of religion are above reason, not because human beings can have no idea of them or because they entail contradictions, but because human beings have no fully adequate idea about matters that are merely improbable. An improbability merely establishes a presumption, which can be overcome by the credibility of a witness, while God's credibility as that witness is unimpeachable.

Leibniz's response did not satisfy everyone. In *Candide* (1759), Voltaire mercilessly parodied his claim that God created the best of all possible worlds. Hume also addressed the underlying issue in his account of miracles in his *Enquiry Concerning Human Understanding* (1749). The credibility of witnesses, he argued, can only outweigh the improbability of a miracle if their falsity would be more miraculous than the miracle. If God is the witness, there is no issue; but the miracle's occurrence is known through human testimony, which is not just questionable but feeds off a disposition to credulous wonder. Of miracles and mysteries, then, there is not only no proof, but not even well-grounded probability. Even if such miracles as Christ's rising from the dead are comfortable to reason, not being inconsistent with it, they are not reasonable on an assessment of the balance of probabilities.

Reactions against Reason in Religion. The boasts of natural religion were confronted by a wide range of opponents. William Law (1686–1761), for example, argued that human reason unaided is feeble. Even if it permits us to be aware of God's perfection, it cannot judge divine reason by its puny standard. The soul's nature and its relation to the body are at bottom as mysterious to natural reason as the origin of sin and evil. Human reason depends for its proper exercise on the inspiration of revelation. The reasoning that seemingly disables revelation, were it applied to natural religion, would have the same impact and lead inevitably to atheism. Human salvation lies in accepting God's guidance as Abraham did when he prepared to sacrifice Isaac. He could not comprehend God's commands, but he had unmistakable external signs that these commands were God's. Confronted by a revelation, the human duty is to submit to a higher and more perfect order that it cannot comprehend from its own resources, and not, as the deists or Clarke claimed, to challenge it because of its conflict with human reason's perspective.

In *Christianity Not Founded on Argument* (1742), Henry Dodwell the younger argued against natural religion and the attempt to justify Christianity by reason. For him, "the Foundation of Philosophy is all Doubt and Suspicion, as the Foundation of Religion is all Acquiesence and Belief." At best, reason can lead to rational faith, subject to change in the light of further reflection and not fully convincing to the human mind. Religion and salvation demand a faith altogether different: unshakable, absolute, immediate, life-transforming, universal, and possessed of an unimpeachable source that is conveyed not by miracles but by the Holy Spirit, who delivers the faith of grace. Natural religion is so removed from religion's real point that it is positively dangerous. Dodwell's attack on reason is so extreme that it has sometimes been taken as a satire.

Natural Religion and the State. Most eighteenth-century thinkers believed that civil society requires the support of civil religion to support the virtue of citizens by the promise of a future state of rewards and punishments from a supreme lawgiver. Where a variety of religious sects existed, this argument could lead some thinkers to see the need for a universally acceptable natural religion based on natural law. Jean-Jacques Rousseau (1712–1778), for example, argued that a nonsectarian civic religion, based on a few simple principles largely derivable from natural religion, is essential to the state. For many freethinkers, support for a civic religion based on natural religion combined with a powerful anticlericalism, as well as with hostility to a church authority independent of the state.

Bayle cast doubt on such arguments by defending the possibility of a society of atheists. The claim that without a belief in God and a future state there would be no protection against monstrous actions, he argued, is at odds with experience. In the ancient world and more recently, there had been actual or reputed atheists such as Vanini and Spinoza, and others such as the Saducees and Epicurus, who, though not atheists, denied the soul's immortality or God's providence but lived exemplary lives, even prepared to undergo martyrdom for their beliefs. For that matter, many who accepted the soul's immortality and a future state of rewards and punishments do not lead estimable lives. Religious belief governs human conduct far less than generally supposed, Bayle argued, while

the motives for leading a good life do not indispensably depend on religion.

[*See also* Atheism; Bayle, Pierre; Clarke, Samuel; Collins, Anthony; Deism; Hume, David; Kant, Immanuel; Leibniz, Gottfried Wilhelm von; Locke, John; Newtonianism; Reason; Rousseau, Jean-Jacques; Theology; *and* Tindal, Matthew.]

BIBLIOGRAPHY

Bentley, Richard. *A Confutation of Atheism.* In *Works of Richard Bentley,* edited by Alexander Dyce. London, 1838; repr., New York, 1966.

Byrne, Peter. *Natural Religion and the Nature of Religion: The Legacy of Deism.* London, 1989.

Champion, Justin. *The Pillars of Priestcraft Shaken.* Cambridge, 1992. A corrective to accounts that see secularization as an early development.

Enlightenment and Dissent 16 (1997). An issue devoted to Samuel Clarke, the influences on him and the impact of his thought.

Hazard, Paul. *European Thought in the Eighteenth Century, from Montesquieu to Lessing.* Translated by J. Lewis May. New Haven, Conn., 1954. English translation of *La pensée européenne au XVIIIème siècle, de Montesquieu à Lessing,* first published in 1946.

Hurlbutt, Robert H. *Hume, Newton, and the Design Argument,* rev. ed. Lincoln, Neb., 1985. Useful survey of the argument from design.

Kors, Alan Charles. *Atheism in France, 1650–1729,* vol. 1. *The Orthodox Sources of Disbelief.* Princeton, N.J., 1990. Valuable for its account of the warfare in France between Cartesians and scholastics.

Leibniz, G. W. *Theodicy: Essays on the Goodness of God, the Freedom of Man, and the Origin of Evil.* Edited by Austin Farrar; translated by E. M. Huggard. London, 1952.

Locke, John. *The Reasonableness of Christianity.* Edited by John C. Higgins-Biddle. Oxford, 1999. Chapter 14 includes an attack on priestcraft and an account of the need for revelation.

Priestley, Joseph. *The Theological and Miscellaneous Works of Joseph Priestley.* Edited by J. T. Rutt. 25 vols. London, 1817–1831; repr., New York, 1972. See especially his *Institutes of Natural and Revealed Religion* in vol. 2, and *Disquisitions Relating to Matter and Spirit* in vol. 3.

Rivers, Isabel. *Reason, Grace, and Sentiment: A Study of the Language of Religion and Ethics in England, 1660–1780.* 2 vols. Cambridge, 1991–2000. Particularly valuable for its account of freethinkers.

Torrey, Norman L. *Voltaire and the English Deists.* New Haven, Conn., 1930.

Waring, E. Graham. *Deism and Natural Religion.* New York, 1967. Includes selections from deists as well as their opponents.

Whiston, William. *Astronomical Principles of Religion.* London, 1717; repr., Hildesheim, Germany, 1983.

Young, B. W. *Religion and Enlightenment in Eighteenth-Century England: Theological Debate from Locke to Burke.* Oxford, 1998.

JAMES DYBIKOWSKI

NATURAL RIGHTS. As astute a student of the Enlightenment as Alexis de Tocqueville observed that the thinkers of the era were so varied in the political systems they adopted "that it would be impossible to reconcile them together, and mold them all into [one] theory of government." Nonetheless, it seems fair to say that the dominant political idea of the Enlightenment was the idea of natural rights. Tocqueville himself concedes as much when he notes the concerns all these thinkers shared: "the origin of society, the natural principles of government, and the primitive rights of man." These are not, as they might appear, three separate topics, but the topic of natural rights adumbrated in its several dimensions and implications.

Natural Rights Thinking. The centrality of natural rights is clearly visible whether we consider the chief theorists and writers of the era, or whether we look to the chief monuments of the political practice of the Enlightenment. In the sphere of theory, Enlightenment or proto-Enlightenment thinkers—for example, Thomas Hobbes, Baruch de Spinoza, Samuel Pufendorf, John Locke, Thomas Jefferson, John Adams, Denis Diderot, Jean-Jacques Rousseau, Jean-Antoine-Nicolas de Caritat Condorcet, Francis Hutcheson, and Immanuel Kant—organized their political thinking around natural (or human) rights. In the sphere of practice, to look only at the most prominent—or, some would say, the most characteristic—phenomena, the two great revolutions of the Enlightenment era, we see their chief literary products, the American Declaration of Independence (1776) and the French Declaration of the Rights of Man and Citizen (1789), putting natural rights at the center. The American Declaration proclaims that "all men are endowed by their creator with certain unalienable rights," and that "governments are instituted among men in order to secure these rights." The French Declaration self-consciously echoes the American; it aims "to expound in a solemn declaration the natural, inalienable and sacred rights of man" (Prologue). The French, moreover, agreed that "the final end of every political institution is the preservation of the natural and imprescriptible rights of man" (Article 2).

One of the most striking aspects of the near-universal recourse to the language of rights during the Enlightenment, however, was the extent to which these thinkers varied in their precise conceptions of what natural rights there are, and of what grounds or validates claims of rights. Some attached or derived natural rights to or from theories of moral sense (Hutcheson), others from arguments of natural theology (Locke), and still others from the phenomenon of self-ownership (Montesquieu), or of human autonomy (Kant), or of the natural order of the passions (Hobbes). Despite their differences, there were certain typical elements of natural rights thinking that recurred for all or at least most of these writers. In order to focus primarily on these elements, it will be most convenient to consider the two best-known revolutionary documents of the era; they are not only the places where Enlightenment theory and practice most dramatically converge, but also the places where the commonalities of natural rights thinking stand forth most perspicaciously.

The doctrine of natural rights in all its various expressions fulfilled two functions simultaneously: it adumbrated a theory of natural justice, on the one hand, and a theory of political legitimacy, on the other. The unprecedented way in which the doctrine of natural rights combined these two elements was perhaps its most fateful feature, for it produced a revolution in the theory of politics of the most far-ranging sort. The question of regime, constitution, or form of government had, at least since Aristotle, been considered more or less a matter of prudence. The desirable form was understood to vary according to circumstances; thus, we seldom find, over the entire course of Western thought from the Greeks up to the Enlightenment, a rigid development of a doctrine of "the one legitimate form"—with the possible exception of divine-right theories of monarchy. This changed with the coupling of the theory of natural justice and the theory of legitimacy in natural rights philosophy. Over time, as thinkers and political actors worked out for themselves more clearly the meaning and implications of natural rights philosophy, they came increasingly to the view that only popular government—what we now loosely call democracy—could be legitimate. With that discovery, made around the time of the American Revolution, the truly unsettling and even revolutionary implications of natural rights philosophy became patently visible. This prompted the first wave of anti–natural-rights thinking, for example by Edmund Burke, Jeremy Bentham, and Joseph de Maistre.

Natural Justice. The natural rights philosophy constitutes a theory of natural justice, in the first instance, because it propounds a set of norms found in *nature*. As Jeremy Bentham rightly said, "Natural, as applied to rights, if it mean anything, is to stand in opposition to *legal*—to such rights as are acknowledged to owe their existence to government, and are consequently posterior in their date to the establishment of government." The American Declaration of Independence signals its commitment to the view that rights are pregovernmental in this sense when it affirms that men "are endowed by their creator" with these rights, which precede all government and human law, because government is said to be made in order "to secure these [already existing] rights." The French Declaration is even more straightforward: the rights are decreed "natural" and "sacred." (Some other documents of the era speak of the rights as "inherent.")

Both documents also insist that the rights are "inalienable"; that is, they cannot be given up, and moreover cannot be presumed to have been given up, or even more certainly, cannot be taken away by another. Rights can be violated, but they cannot be alienated. One retains one's right even as it is being infringed. The insistence on inalienability establishes the continuing force of the natural or prepolitical within political society.

The natural rights philosophy affirms a theory of natural justice, in the second instance, through affirming that all human beings possess *rights*. The most traditional and most common formula for justice is "Render to each his own," or "his due." The natural rights philosophy constitutes one answer to the question of what is one's own, or what is one due. A person is due respect for his rights, and his own possessions are the objects of his rights. The American Declaration lists a series of "unalienable rights"—life, liberty and pursuit of happiness—but it specifies that these are only "among" those rights with which "all men" are "endowed." The French Declaration has a similar list: "liberty, property, security and resistance to oppression" (Article 2). Despite the somewhat different formulations, these two related lists of natural rights are very similar and reveal a deep coherence.

In the first place, the substitution in the American document of the "pursuit of happiness" for "property," as in the most common, Lockean formulation ("life, liberty, and property") and as in the French list, does not imply that the Americans did not consider property a natural right. Many similar American documents contained both "property" and "pursuit of happiness," so there certainly was no widespread consensus that the two were in any way incompatible.

The first right in the American Declaration, the right to life (restated as "security" by the French) is a right to what is most one's own: one's life. Given the nature of a human life, it is difficult to see how it could be anything other than one's own, or how it could in any sense belong to others. Given the dependence (or base) of life in or on the body, the right to life must contain a right to bodily immunity (or security), the right not to have one's body seized, invaded, or controlled by others.

The right to liberty extends the right to life: not only does one possess a rightful immunity against the depredations of others on one's body, one also has a right to the use of one's body. Liberty is required, in part, as a means to securing one's right to life; more than that, human existence is such that we can take control of our bodies and invest our movements with our intentions and purposes—we can act. The natural right to liberty proclaims the prima facie rightfulness of active use of mind and body.

The right to property involves an extension of rights from the sphere of one's own life, body, and actions to the external world. It proclaims the rightful power of human beings to make the external their own in the same way they can make their bodies their own. The French announce a right of "resistance to oppression," paralleled in the American document by the "right to alter or abolish any government destructive" of the primary natural rights. In both cases, the right of resistance is a token of the inalienability of the basic rights and of the rightfulness of acting forcefully on behalf of one's rights.

These rights together amount to the affirmation of a kind of personal sovereignty, a rightful control over one's person, actions, and possessions in the service of one's intents and purposes. When seen as an integrated system of immunities and controls, the specific rights amount to a comprehensive right to the pursuit of happiness—that is, the right to pursue a self-chosen shape and way of life. Of course, this right, as well as the other more specific rights, is not absolute. The rights of specific others, as well as the public good (the genuine common needs of the community), serve as valid limitations on personal rights (see Articles 4 and 5 of the Declaration of Rights).

The natural rights philosophy as a natural moral code can be distinguished from the related notion of natural law with which it is often confused. As deployed in the natural rights doctrine, rights consist of a relationship among three parties—the rights bearer, governments, and nongovernmental others. The rights bearer possesses a right in the sense of a liberty, a morally valid power to do or to forbear. For example, to have a right, such as a right of free speech, is to have moral permission to speak freely or not, at the discretion of the rights bearer. Nongovernmental others, however, have a strict obligation toward the rights bearer. In the most typical case, this is an obligation not to interfere with the rights bearer in his or her exercise of a right. Government also has a strict obligation, but of a double sort: the obligation to act so as to secure the rights of rights bearers within its jurisdiction by supplying them protection of the laws, and the obligation not to interfere with the rights bearers' exercise of a right. Rights, then, are characterized by the pairing of permission (liberty) and strict obligation of these two sorts, inhering primarily in the two other parties to the rights relationship.

Natural law philosophy also constitutes a theory of natural morality, but here the relations are rather different. The addressee of the natural law faces a natural norm that is not a permission (liberty) but an obligation: natural law theory conceives moral norms as strict obligations grounded in nature. Natural law, thus, does not inherently involve a plurality of parties as natural rights do, because the essential relation is between each actor and the natural norm itself.

Political Legitimacy. The possession of natural rights implies several further propositions or corollaries, which together constitute a theory of political legitimacy. The first such corollary is equality. The American Declaration famously pronounced "that all men are created equal." The French Declaration, attempting to be more precise, proclaimed: "In respect of their rights men are born and remain free and equal." The Americans, it is clear, meant by *equality* what John Locke before them had meant: "the equality in which all men are, in respect of jurisdiction or dominion one over another." Equality means that no one is rightfully subject to another by nature. The French Declaration made the connection to natural rights more explicit than the Americans did, but the point of both is much the same. The comprehensive natural right of self-government, the sum of the rights, is entirely incompatible with naturally ordained subjection to another. Natural equality as natural freedom or independence is a correlate or even a derivation from the natural rights possessed by all.

A second implication of natural rights is popular sovereignty. According to the Americans, governments "derive their just powers from the consent of the governed." According to the French, "the basis of all sovereignty lies, essentially, in the nation. No corporation or individual may exercise any authority that is not expressly derived therefrom" (Article 3). Popular sovereignty follows necessarily from the primitive condition in which there is no natural authority, and in which each and every individual possesses rights of self-government, including a right to resist infringements of rights. This individual right of resistance, transferred or delegated to public authorities, must be the basis for legitimate authority.

The third corollary is popular government. This goes beyond popular sovereignty, which involves tracing all legitimate authority ultimately back to the people. Popular government requires actual rule by "the general will." In the early versions of natural rights philosophy, this third conclusion was generally not drawn. Both Locke and Montequieu, for example, found a constitution like the British one, with its hereditary monarch and House of Lords, to be perfectly legitimate under natural rights criteria, consistent with popular sovereignty if not with popular rule. The Americans in their Declaration of Independence seemed to accept the Locke-Montequieu position; they spoke of the right of a people to cast its government in any form that shall seem convenient to them. The people may ordain a limited monarchy or aristocracy, if they desire. The French Declaration, likewise, was thought to be compatible with a limited or constitutional monarchy when it was first issued (see Article 1).

Despite the openness in their Declaration of Independence, the Americans concluded at the outset of the Revolution that only popular or republican government could be legitimate. The French drew a similar conclusion, at least as regards the legislative power: "Legislation is the expression of the general will. All citizens have a right to participate in shaping it either in person, or through their representatives" (Article 6).

The original equality and personal quasi-sovereignty are eventually taken to imply as a right, or as a matter of principle, rule by the general will; they imply the rejection of rule by any body of persons not ultimately authorized by the people. The proper organization of society is no longer a prudential matter, but a correlate of the rights-bearing character of human beings. Democracy becomes, strictly speaking, a right of all peoples, whether or not they are capable of sustaining it. The original version of the natural rights philosophy had attempted to make peace with the old regimes; by the time the Enlightenment played itself out, this was no longer possible. Radical transformation of old regimes was required, and all forms but democracy lost legitimacy.

[*See also* Declaration of Independence; Declaration of the Rights of Man; *and* Political Philosophy.]

BIBLIOGRAPHY

Becker, Carl. *The Declaration of Independence*. New York, 1958. A detailed examination of the American Declaration, setting it in the context of Enlightenment thought.

Gottschalk, Louis, and Margaret Maddox. *Lafayette in the French Revolution: Through the October Days*. Chicago, 1969. An account of the drafting of the French Declaration of the Rights of Man and Citizen, bringing out the connection to the American Declaration and its chief draftsman, Thomas Jefferson.

Locke, John. *Two Treatises of Government*. Cambridge, 1967. The classic statement of modern natural rights philosophy, of great influence throughout the Enlightenment.

Rousseau, Jean-Jacques. *The Social Contract*. New York, 1978. The best-known French restatement of natural rights and social contract theory, a restatement that modified the Lockean version in important respects and contributed to the blending of natural rights and democracy.

Strauss, Leo. *Natural Right and History*. Chicago, 1954. A classic analysis of the meaning of natural rights philosophy.

Tierney, Brian. *The Idea of Natural Rights: Studies on Natural Rights, Natural Law and Church Law, 1150–1625*. Atlanta, 1997. A thorough exploration of the emergence of natural rights concepts within medieval political thinking.

Tocqueville, Alexis de. *The Old Regime and the French Revolution*. New York, 1955. A classic consideration of the role of enlightenment thinking in the coming of the French Revolution.

Tuck, Richard. *Natural Rights Theories: Their Origin and Development*. Cambridge, 1979. A wide-ranging historical search for "the origin and development" of natural rights concepts.

Zuckert, Michael P. *Natural Rights and the New Republicanism*. Princeton, N.J., 1994. An attempt to distinguish natural rights from related natural law theories and to explore the philosophic ground of natural rights.

Zuckert, Michael P. *The Natural Rights Republic*. Notre Dame, Ind., 1996. A discussion of natural rights in the context of the American founding.

MICHAEL P. ZUCKERT

NATURAL SENTIMENT. Natural sentiment is a concept expressing the view that morality is based on a sentiment, or feeling, that is the result of our natural makeup. In its strongest form natural sentiment is a component of the theory that human beings possess a moral sense or an internal feeling of what is right and wrong. This theory is often also called sentimentalism or the moral sense theory. It is closely allied with naturalism and was mainly advocated by eighteenth-century British thinkers, who had a significant influence in other European countries. There were also more minor philosophers, however, who developed a theory somewhat independent of that of their British forerunners. One of these was Johann Georg Heinrich Feder (1740–1821), a critic of Immanuel Kant, who argued in 1792 in a paper entitled "Über das moralische Gefühl" (On Moral Feeling) for a position similar to that of Adam Smith (see below).

For David Hume, one of the fundamental questions concerning the foundations of morals is whether they are "derived from reason, or from sentiment; whether we attain the knowledge of them by a chain of argument or induction, or by an immediate feeling and finer internal sense; whether, like all sound judgment of truth or falsehood, they should be the same to every rational intelligent being; or whether, like the perception of beauty and deformity, they be founded entirely on the particular fabric and constitution of the human species" (Hume, 1998, 74). This way of posing the question is significant because it shows that moral sentiment is mainly a rival to the kind of rationalism or intellectualism in ethics that could be found in Ralph Cudworth, Richard Price, and others. If morality is based on a moral sense or on a natural sentiment, then it is universal in the sense that all human beings must ultimately be able to make the same moral distinctions. However, it is not universal in the sense in which claims to truth are universal. Morality depends on human nature in a way in which truth claims do not. If human nature were to change, our moral sentiments might change as well, whereas the truth of claims about the nature of things has nothing to do with how we are made up. Indeed, if morality is based on natural sentiment, then it is plausible that there will be some variation in moral customs, just as there are variations in taste. Moral philosophy would, accordingly, be more closely related to aesthetics and history than to epistemology and metaphysics. Indeed, would necessitate a skeptical attitude about metaphysics.

Hume ultimately came to the conclusion that morals depend on some "internal sense or feeling, which nature has made universal in the whole species" (1998, 75), even if reason is absolutely necessary for paving the way for this sentiment. In the *Treatise of Human Nature* (1740), Hume goes even further and claims that "reason is, and ought to be, the slave of the passions." Nevertheless, just as in aesthetic contexts, we must cultivate our feelings, make fine distinctions, and understand precisely what is involved in a certain moral issue. For this reason, his endorsement of natural sentiment does not imply that anyone can determine equally well whether an action is right or wrong. Ultimately this is left to a disinterested spectator, who fully understands the facts relevant to a particular situation. It is in this way that the theory of moral sentiment leads to the "ideal spectator" theory of morals.

While Hume came close to formulating the ideal spectator theory in book 3 of his *Treatise of Human Nature* and his *Enquiry Concerning the Principles of Morals* (1751), it remained for Adam Smith to formulate this theory in his *Theory of Moral Sentiments* (1759). Smith's impartial spectator judges not only the behavior of others but also his own from the perspective of a spectator. For Smith, however, morality depends not so much on natural sentiment or nature as on moral education. Moral sentiments represent our second nature. We acquire them on the basis of other sentiments, passions, or emotions. Most important among these is sympathy, which for Smith means simply "feeling-with."

Moral sense or the view that natural sentiments are the foundation of morals was, however, not Hume's invention. Its conception dates back to the beginning of the eighteenth century. At first, it was not just designed to be an answer to rationalism in ethics but also to be an answer to moral egoism. The earl of Shaftesbury was the first to invoke it against Thomas Hobbes's "selfish" theory of morals, arguing that human beings were originally equipped with a moral sense that allowed them to distinguish good and evil, virtue and vice, and that this sense formed the foundation of morals. Although Shaftesbury's essays as collected in the 1711 text *Characteristicks of Men, Manners, Opinions, Times* proved to be influential, it was Francis Hutcheson who came to be seen as the real proponent of the moral sense theory of ethics. His *Inquiry into the Original of our Ideas of Beauty and Virtue* of 1725 and his *Essay on the Nature and Conduct of the Passions and Affections with Illustrations upon the Moral Sense* (1728) gave a more systematic account of this notion, which deeply influenced David Hume and Adam Smith. Hutcheson was not just arguing against Hobbes but also against Bernard Mandeville. The problem of egoism or "moral scepticism," as Hume calls it, continued to play a role in the works of Hume and Smith, but was of secondary importance compared with the problem of the foundations of morals. While the theories of Hume and Smith are perhaps better regarded as critical discussions and adaptations of the moral sense theory rather than as simple extensions of it, they did come to be seen in the eighteenth century as part of the same school.

Apart from the function of natural sentiments in the foundations of morals debate as an alternative to rationalism and in the moral skepticism debate as an alternative to egoism, the theory of natural sentiment was also meant to give an account of the nature of virtue. In that context it competed with theories that viewed virtue either as the "proper government and direction of all our affections" or as the pursuit of enlightened self-interest. According to the moral sense theorists, virtue consisted in those affections only that aim at the happiness of others, not in those that aim at our own. Accordingly, disinterested benevolence was the only motive that could stamp upon any action the character of virtue.

One of the important questions that has more recently been raised is whether a theory that makes natural sentiments the foundation of all ethical judgments does not undermine the very notion of ethical judgments by collapsing into emotivism, the theory that moral utterances amount to mere expressions of feelings and no more. William Frankena, for example, has argued that one of the great achievements of Hutcheson was that he anticipated emotivism. David Fate Norton, by contrast, has tried to show that the moral sense was for Hutcheson as well as for Hume a cognitive sense. It should be clear that it has both emotivist aspects as well as elements that point beyond mere emotivism. After all, it is conceived in analogy to the external senses, especially sight.

One of the most interesting criticisms of the moral sense theory came from Thomas Reid, who argued that the crucial question with which Humean moral philosophy needs to be concerned is "What are the qualities of mind which produce, in the disinterested observer, the feeling of approbation, or the contrary feeling?" The Humean answer to this factual question was that they are qualities of the mind "which are agreeable or useful" either to the person who has them or to his fellow human beings. However, as Reid explains, this means that morality has been reduced to the agreeable and the useful, to the *dulce* and the *utile*. There is thus no room left for any essentially moral quality, and in particular there is no longer any room for moral worth or what Reid calls, with Cicero, *honestum*. This makes Hume, in Reid's eyes, essentially an Epicurean. Pleasure remains ultimately the only end "that is good in itself, and desirable for its own sake; and virtue derives all its merit from its tendency to produce pleasure." He also notes that there is at least one difference between Hume and the Epicureans in that the latter were essentially egoists and defined virtue to be whatever is agreeable or pleasant to ourselves, while Hume allows that human beings also have "disinterested," or as we might say, altruistic affections. As a result, he must admit that Hume's system is more "disinterested" or "liberal" than that of Epicurus, but this seems to him only a difference of degree and not one of kind. Essentially Hume is a hedonist of the Epicurean persuasion. His moral philosophy is as mechanistic an account as has ever been given.

More importantly, if a theory involving natural sentiments is correct, then as Reid explicitly points out, we should no longer speak of moral judgments, for, if "what we call *moral judgment* be no real judgment, but merely a feeling, it follows, that the principles of morals, which we have been taught to consider as an immutable law to all intelligent beings, have no other foundation but an arbitrary structure and fabric in the constitution of the human mind...[then] beings of a different structure...may have different, nay opposite measures of moral good and evil" (Reid, 1965, vol. 2, 678f.). It debases our rational nature and makes us no different from the ox that "eateth grass." Furthermore, this theory makes it impossible to differentiate between the sentence "Such a man did well and worthily; his conduct is highly approvable" and the sentence "The man's conduct gave me a very agreeable feeling," but it appears that our moral experience depends precisely on our ability to make such a distinction.

While John Stuart Mill still appealed to a powerful natural sentiment as late as 1863 in *Utilitarianism*, even though admitting that it might have a basis in the social feelings of mankind, Kant argued late in the eighteenth century forcefully against any kind of natural feeling or sentiment as a foundation of ethics. Moral maxims and moral judgments must be universally valid, and sentiments of any kind cannot provide such universality. Though his position is in some way similar to that of Reid and earlier rationalists, his moral theory is an even more radical alternative to theories involving natural sentiments.

[*See also* Human Nature; Hume, David; Hutcheson, Francis; Moral Philosophy; *and* Smith, Adam.]

BIBLIOGRAPHY

Frankena, William. "Hutcheson's Moral Sense Theory." *Journal of the History of Ideas* 16 (1955), 356–375.

Griswold, Charles L., Jr. *Adam Smith and the Virtues of Enlightenment.* Cambridge, 1999.

Hume, David. *Enquiry Concerning the Principles of Morals.* Edited by Tom L. Beauchamp. Oxford, 1998.

Norton, David Fate. "Hutcheson's Moral Sense Theory Reconsidered." *Dialogue* 13 (1974), 3–23.

Norton, David Fate. *David Hume: Common-Sense Moralist and Sceptical Metaphysician.* Princeton, N.J., 1982.

Reid, Thomas. *Philosophical Works.* Edited by Sir William Hamilton. 8th ed. Edinburgh, 1895; repr., Hildesheim, Germany, 1965.

Stecker, Robert. "Thomas Reid on the Moral Sense." *The Monist* 70 (1987), 453–464.

Stewart-Robinson, J. C., and David F. Norton. "Thomas Reid on Adam Smith's Theory of Morals." *Journal of the History of Ideas* 45 (1984), 309–321.

MANFRED KUEHN

NATURAL THEOLOGY. *See* Natural Religion.

NECKER, SUZANNE (1739–1794), French-Swiss salon hostess and woman of letters.

Daughter of the pastor of the village of Crassier in the province of Vaud, Switzerland, and his wife, a child of recent Protestant refugees from France, Suzanne Curchod enjoyed a humanistic education that was unusual for a woman of her time. Her father taught her to compose Ciceronian Latin prose and schooled her in English, mathematics, physics, and religious doctrine, while also developing her "feminine" skills in music and drawing. It is not surprising that, when she moved to Lausanne in her teens, the accomplished girl dazzled its society. *La belle* Curchod was depicted as presiding, like Molière's Célimène, over attentive gatherings of male wits and as composing verbal portraits. The historian Edward Gibbon, smitten with this distinguished but poor local celebrity, was influenced by paternal disapproval to end their engagement after five years of hesitation.

The early loss of both parents left the young woman, at twenty-four, destitute of both material and emotional support. Transplanted to Paris as companion to Mme. de Vermenoux, sister-in-law to the Genevan banker Thélusson, she met Jacques Necker, Thélusson's young Genevan associate, whose marriage proposal she soon accepted.

The serious business of this intellectually and socially ambitious woman's life took flight on the union with her wealthy, politically ambitious husband. Their satisfaction in their marriage, incessantly asserted in elaborate expressions of mutual devotion, proved irritating to observers but eminently pleasing to the Neckers. In April 1766, Suzanne Necker gave birth to their only child, Anne-Louise Germaine, who was to become the noted woman of letters Germaine de Staël; her mother educated the girl "like [Rousseau's] Émile."

A pious Protestant, Suzanne Necker reacted stiffly to the racy and skeptical atmosphere of Paris, losing some of the social spontaneity of her Swiss youth. Nevertheless, she established a successful Parisian salon, buttressing her husband's rise as finance minister under Louis XVI just before the French Revolution of 1789. Having apprenticed in the salon of the accomplished Mme. Geoffrin, she extended her severe self-discipline to her salon, where ideas were exchanged in a spirit of gravity. Although Mme. Necker's guarded manners inspired xenophobic mockery from some French critics, her salon's popularity—attracting personages like Denis Diderot, Georges-Louis Leclerc de Buffon, Friedrich Melchior Grimm, and Jean-François Marmontel—confirmed her stature as a social leader. Exiled from France with Jacques Necker, she died in her native Switzerland during the Terror.

Although Jacques Necker had discouraged his wife from undertaking serious literary work, he published two collections of her *Mélanges* after her death. These aphoristic jottings illustrate the often astringent cogency of her thinking, as well as the strictures her religious beliefs imposed on her. Her "Réflexions sur le divorce" (1794), protesting the effects of the legalization of divorce in 1792, passionately decries the loosening of marital ties.

Despite her belief that a woman's life must be devoted to others, Suzanne Necker left her mark on the society around her. The most concrete of her works was the founding of a hospital for indigent patients: the still-standing Hôpital Necker in Paris.

[*See also* Education, *subentry on* Education of Women; Gibbon, Edward; Men and Women of Letters; Salons, *subentry on* France; *and* Staël, Germaine Necker de.]

BIBLIOGRAPHY

Corbaz, André. *Madame Necker, humble Vaudoise et grande dame*. Lausanne, 1945. The only modern biography of Suzanne Necker.

Goodman, Dena. *The Republic of Letters: A Cultural History of the French Enlightenment*. Ithaca, N.Y., 1994. A major reassessment of the role of salon leaders, including Necker, in the Enlightenment.

Haussonville, Gabriel Paul Othenin de Cléron, comte d'. *Le salon de Madame Necker: D'après des documents tirés des archives de Coppet*. Geneva, 1970 (reprint of 1882–1885 edition). A close examination of Suzanne Necker's life, quoting liberally from her correspondence.

Necker, Jacques, ed. *Mélanges extraits des manuscrits de Mme Necker*. 3 vols. Paris, 1798.

Necker, Jacques, ed. *Nouveaux mélanges extraits des manuscrits de Mme Necker*. 2 vols. Paris, 1801.

MADELYN GUTWIRTH

NEEDHAM, JOHN TURBERVILLE (1713–1781), English naturalist and microscopist.

Needham's observations on the generation of microscopic organisms were crucial to eighteenth-century discussions of nature. Born in London into a recusant family, he attended the English school of Douai; he was ordained a secular priest in Cambrai in 1738. He became professor of philosophy at the English school in Lisbon, where he made his first observations with a microscope. He was welcomed in Paris by the naturalist Georges-Louis Leclerc de Buffon, with whom he collaborated on microscopic experiments. Elected a fellow of the Royal Society (1747) and of the Society of Antiquaries of London (1761), he also became Buffon's correspondent for the Académie Royale des Sciences (1768). In 1768 he settled in Brussels, where, as the first director of the Royal Academy of Belgium (1773), he fostered careful laboratory science.

Needham made observations in natural history that were crucial to Enlightenment debates. His first published work, *An Account of Some Microscopical Discoveries* (London, 1745), focused on the squid, in a quest to discover creatures analogous to the famous and controversial polyps of Abraham Trembley, which had suggested the legitimacy of spontaneous generation. The question of spontaneous generation was central to the development of reproductive theory. Before the development of cell theory, naturalists debated whether new creatures were preformed from the primordia, or whether gradual differentiation occurred as the embryo developed. Mechanists favored preformation, because mechanism could not explain differentiation; vitalists, most notably Buffon, explained differentiation by hypothetical but undiscovered natural principles distinct to living things.

In 1748, at the urging of Buffon, Needham extracted fluids from the reproductive organs of animals and examined them under a microscope. The two scientists saw globules, which became, in Buffon's theory, *organic globules*. (The second volume of Buffon's *Histoire Naturelle*, 1749, relied on these experiments.) Although Buffon did not claim to see these microscopic creatures develop, Needham thought he saw creatures forming out of disorganized material. To substantiate his claim, he performed his famous "mutton gravy" experiment (1748), which corroborated his view that spermatic animalcules were formed from seminal fluid. Many attempted to refute Needham by logic or experiment. Their efforts were inconclusive until 1765, when Lorenzo Spallanzani performed the mutton gravy experiment again, but with more effective sterilization, and found no living creatures.

Needham's experiments had philosophic ramifications. His belief in animalcules formed by a vegetative force put him in the vitalist camp; for him, unlike Buffon, these developments could not occur by chance, because chance denied a role to God. Despite his own religious convictions, his experiments fostered philosophical positions, particularly materialism, that were dangerous to religion. In 1767, he retired to the English seminary in Paris to defend his science against Spallanzani's critique and to attack those who accused or congratulated him for providing the crucial evidence to support materialism. Despite such efforts, baron d'Holbach still used Needham's experiments to prove his claim that matter can think, expressed in his work of atheistic materialism, *Le Système de la nature* (1770). Needham's Enlightenment reputation remains that constructed by his philosophical adversaries, the materialists, who exploited his work in the polemical battles over the philosophical implications of investigations of living creatures.

[*See also* Buffon, Georges-Louis Leclerc de; Holbach, Paul-Henri Thiry d'; Materialism; Natural History; Natural Philosophy and Science; *and* Spontaneous Generation.]

BIBLIOGRAPHY

Buffon, Georges-Louis Leclerc, comte de. *Histoire naturelle, generale et particuliere, avec la description du cabinet du roy*. Vol. 2. Paris, 1749. Demonstrates the integration of Needham's observations into Buffon's natural history.

Farley, John. *The Spontaneous Generation Controversy from Descartes to Oparin*. Baltimore, 1997. Places Needham's work in the context of an ongoing biological debate to which he was a contributor.

Mazzolini, Renato G., and Shirley A. Roe. *Science against the Unbelievers: The Correspondence of Charles Bonnet and John Turberville Needham, 1760–1780. Studies on Voltaire and the Eighteenth Century*, vol. 243. Oxford, 1986. A modern edition of an eighteenth-century text with an extensive introduction. This correspondence indicates Needham's religious thought and his objections to the materialist use of his observations.

Needham, John Turberville. *An Account of Some New Microscopical Discoveries*. London, 1745.

Roger, Jacques. *The Life Sciences in Eighteenth-Century French Thought*. Edited by Keith R. Benson, translated by Robert Ellrich. Stanford, Calif., 1997. A thorough introduction to issues of the life sciences in the eighteenth century.

KATHLEEN WELLMAN

NEOCLASSICISM. Based on unprecedented enthusiasm for extant and recently rediscovered Greek and Roman antiquities, neoclassicism (the neoclassic style) began its steady rise to prominence in the decades after 1750, when it became the major art style of the Enlightenment. Specific and symptomatic events marked its beginnings and introduced the essential trends of its development. These include the following:

1. The publication of sensational discoveries at the ancient Roman sites of Herculaneum, Pompeii, and their environs (1748–1749; 1755–1792). The unearthed lost world, which had been covered by the volcanic ash from nearby Mount Vesuvius in 79 CE, encouraged both romanticism and archaeology.

2. Robert Wood's *The Ruins of Palmyra* (1753) and his *The Ruins of Baalbec* (1757), as well as James Stuart's and Nicholas Revett's *Antiquities of Athens* (1762–1830), motivated a growing interest in and the exploration of the extant monuments in ancient Greece.

3. The charismatic manifesto *Thoughts on the Imitation of Greek Works* (1755), by the Prussian scholar Johann Joachim Winckelmann (1717–1768), rapturously advocated emulating the forms and virtues of Greek art, to acquire its excellence and its immortality—thereby initiating a new religion of history and aesthetics, which was furthered in his *History of Ancient Art* (1764), then taken up by a host of contemporaries, including the French encyclopedist Denis Diderot.

4. In 1750, Madame de Pompadour's envoys—the architect Jacques-Germain Soufflot and the future royal superintendent of buildings, her brother, the marquis de Marigny—studied antiquities in Rome, to create a fresh, new style for her proposed chateau and for other projects, including the neoclassic temple-church Sainte-Geneviève in Paris, later called the Panthéon (1757–1790). Increasingly, both artists and their patrons followed this newly established pattern.

5. Especially important from the 1740s onward, increasing numbers of Transalpine "Goths" on the Grand

Tour—from Britain, the Germanies, Scandinavia, and eastern Europe—visited Rome, Naples, and Sicily to experience there the ruins and the remnants of classical art and culture. To embellish their villas and palaces, they bought copies of antiquities and many refurbished fragments from the Roman Campagna (countryside) or from the stores of local dealers and collectors. Such works became both models and sources of competition for artists and collectors throughout Europe.

Meanings of Neoclassicism. In broad terms, neoclassicism illustrated the interests of the Revolutionary generation then inheriting or taking power. Aspects of the style were soon practiced by almost all artists and artisans, and the style pervaded all arts and crafts, which resulted in Europe's first comprehensive modernism. Its dedicants rejected the perceived excesses of baroque and rococo styles, as reflections of the corrupt, sybaritic, effeminate, and vacuously self-indulgent values of the old order. Their clean, classic style could represent constitutional republicanism, and it could promote a natural aristocracy of talent, beauty, and virtue (as proposed by Thomas Jefferson). The style extolled the so-called masculine virtues of stoicism, effort, patriotism, fraternalism, good government, and morality—qualities ostensibly manifest in the ancient models. The neoclassic art of middle-class political and commercial nationalism replaced the art of the Roman Catholic Church, and especially the lavish missionary style of the Jesuits (Society of Jesus), whose understanding of revelation and of divine-right ethics supported elite absolutism.

Neoclassicism coexisted with other idioms, old and new; its evolution was filled with inconsistency, but it strongly evoked a trend called romanticism, which viewed antiquity as an ideal Golden Age. That image promised new life, a blank slate (John Locke's tabula rasa) from which to begin again. That sense of rejuvenation, of opportunity for self and social rediscovery, had motivated interest in ancient and classical art since the Renaissance—but the intense reassessments of the eighteenth century were unprecedented. The new archaeological scholarship led to the explorations of ethnic art and to nationalism.

The word *neoclassicism* was coined long after its flourishing, some half a century after 1815 (Napoleon's final defeat at Waterloo), when the style became, in part, a conflict-ridden symbol of the despotic French Revolution and Empire. As a sign of authority, reason, clarity, constancy, and legitimacy, however, neoclassicism remained esteemed as a conservative style that signified rational, established power, both governmental and commercial. Josiah Wedgwood (1730–1795), the British pottery industrialist, was its most successful promoter and disseminator; echoing Winckelmann's enthralled paean to the "noble simplicity and tranquil grandeur" in Greek art, Wedgwood promoted it as the "quiet and simple antique style," a polarized opposite to rococo extravagance.

The developing neoclassic arts reflected the utopian ideals of the Enlightenment—rationalism, intellect, scientific investigation; reassessments in search of origins and empirical exploration as opposed to divine revelation; the pursuit of universal laws; simplicity, clarity, and order; optimism about the accessibility of knowledge, freedom, and the perfectibility of humankind; representative government; laissez-faire enterprise, and more. The style actually illustrated or embodied the culminating phases of the age of reason, especially those of humanist enquiry. Formal, emotive, and realistic aspects of neoclassicism that were latent in its archaizing imagery steadily emerged during its evolution—especially after the American Revolution (1775–1783) among radical European and American artists, whose sublime primitivism complemented the romantic pre-Nietzschean individualism that was contained within its anonymous and seemingly simple style.

Development. Neoclassicism's early phases were most influenced by remains from imperial Rome—themselves largely of ancient neoclassic and museological origin. Such antiquities had already inspired the Renaissance and later classicisms—from Raphael to Poussin, Palladio, and Lord Burlington. They all became models for neoclassicism's first artists. Fresh discoveries in and around Rome, in Pompeii and Herculaneum, in various sites of Magna Graecia (the ancient Greek colonies), and in the Greek homeland added to the growing number of examples that illustrated the ancient arts. They also helped to intensify the pursuit of authentic sources for the new arts. Especially important were the outlined two-dimensional paintings on Greek vases (then called Etruscan, after the Etruscan lands in Italy where they were chiefly found), best known from the collection, and sumptuous publications, of the British ambassador to Naples, Sir William Hamilton (1766–1767; 1791–1795).

During Napoleon's military campaigns in Italy and elsewhere in Europe, antiquarian attentions were turned to Greek sites in the eastern Mediterranean, as well as to Bronze Age and earlier art from the civilizations of Egypt and Mesopotamia. Lord Elgin, then the British ambassador to Turkey, gathered the Parthenon sculptures from the Acropolis in Athens after 1801; they were purchased in 1816 for the British Museum in London. European national museums with core collections of tastemaking antiquities had been established before 1750. Those interests, as well as the grandiose and glamorous prints of the ruins around Rome and the Greek temple at Paestum in Southern Italy by the architect, theorist, and antiquarian Giovanni Battista Piranesi (1720–1778), helped to intensify a romantic archaeological vision among artists and collectors well into the nineteenth century.

Preference in classical narratives turned from the well-known Greco-Roman compendium of Ovid's *Metamorphoses* to the epic poems of Homer and the works of other early Greek writers, explored for their primitive vigor and authenticity. Such historicizing stimulated archaeological investigations and the imagery that celebrated national origins, real and fabricated, as with James Macpherson's "Gothic" hoax, his Homeric-style poems of Ossian (1760–1763). There were also the Gaelic-accented poems of Robert Burns and the Germanic ones of Johann Jakob von Bodmer in his gathering of the *Niebelungenlied* (1757). These literary enterprises accompanied publication of excavations, ruins, travel books, and catalogs, as well as essays, fiction, and poems of antiquarian interest, ultimately epitomized by John Keats in his *Ode to a Grecian Urn* (1819).

Early neoclassic art was influenced by prior styles and artistic traditions, and its leading artists were supported by aristocratic patronage. Even the development of a young master like Francisco Goya (1746–1828) ran a full gamut of styles that reveal his baroque and rococo training, various neoclassic inventions, and, in more numerous later works, romantic classicism, romanticism, and realism.

Neoclassicism flourished first in the very capitals of absolutism—in Rome, Paris, and London. Its seminal mover was the adventurous papal diplomat Cardinal Alessandro Albani (1692–1779), the antiquarian impresario of his age. With his noted protégé Winckelmann and others—including Bartolomeo Cavaceppi (c. 1716–1799), who helped restore his collection of antiquities for the Capitoline Museum in Rome after 1734—he completed a villa-museum, begun in 1746, that attracted persons of taste. The art was organized to progress from chaos to reason, from ancient Egypt and Greece to contemporaneous neoclassic Rome; it contained thousands of antiquities, mock ruins, and works by Rome's leading artists.

Albani championed the election of Pope Pius VI (1775–1799), who considered the Vatican's new museum of classical antiquities the jewel of his enlightened—but politically disastrous—reign. In 1797, after Napoleon Bonaparte's army conquered Italy, Vatican antiquities were taken to France's new national museum, the Louvre in Paris. Tellingly, Italian sculptor Antonio Canova's svelte neoclassic *Perseus* then temporarily replaced its classical inspiration, the *Apollo Belvedere*. The church militant, with its emphasis on religion and revelation, had given way to neoclassical cults of history, nationalism, aesthetics, and individualism—which continued as prime concerns into the present.

Architecture, Sculpture, Painting, and Applied Arts. After 1780, visionary architects like Claude-Nicolas Ledoux, Étienne-Louis Boullée, and Sir John Soane explored spare, reductive compositions, using the simple square, circle, and triangle, in acute and compressive contrasts of rustic masses with Doric and Tuscan columns, to achieve the elemental, sublime, and utopian imagery desired in neoclassic aesthetics. Their subtle sophistications, as in the gigantic cosmic sphere design of Boullée's Newton monument (1784), were the very antithesis of baroque frill. This fundamentalism recalled theories of Marc-Antoine Laugier (1753) and Sir William Chambers (1759), who traced the origins of architecture, its authentic structure, and its evolution, back to the primitive Vitruvian hut—the ancient Greek *megaron* at the core of classical temples.

The architects Robert Adam, Charles-Louis Clérisseau, and Jacques-Germain Soufflot produced ingratiating eclectic designs, based on the study of antique ruins and classicizing precursors; they created fine, light ensembles, whose idiom Thomas Jefferson and his British ally Benjamin Latrobe used in the new United States of America after 1789, as did architects and artists traveling to Russia, such as James Cameron and Giacomo Quarenghi. Town planning and garden design—variously combining parks, squares, grids, arcs, and radial courses—continued to flourish, as in the layout of Washington, D.C. Architectural copies of ancient Greek structures were built, from James "The Athenian" Stuart's reproduction of the Agora's Theseum as a temple facade in England's Hagley Park (1758) to Leo von Klenze's reconstruction of the Parthenon peristyle for his gigantic German hall of fame, walhalla, in Regensberg (1816–1842). Conservatively illustrating both survival and revival, from the outset of the neoclassic movement, architects eclectically and selectively enlisted ancient classical orders, elevations, and floor plans. That architectural syntax and vocabulary would continue as an elevated, bureaucratic style associated with bourgeois nationalism throughout Europe and in its political dependencies worldwide.

Like architects, purist neoclassic sculptors from the 1780s onward—such as Antonio Canova (the new Phidias and a favorite of popes, Napoleon, kings, and wealthy patrons) or the similarly popular English academicist John Flaxman, and their followers—created "new classics," *antico* pastiches and inventions, with long smooth simplifying contours and masses, reserved-looking classicized nudes of white marble, plaster, or ceramic bisque.

In comparison, the early pioneering work by Cavaceppi and his international coterie of restorers, copyists, portraitists, and inventors still retained elements of *barochetto* style. The brilliant work of Antoine Houdon and his classicizing rococo contemporaries in Paris similarly capitalized on surviving antiquities as models, especially in insightful and lucrative portrait busts with a Greco-Roman veneer. Casts, copies, and *antico* inventions also became significant commodities in a growing antiquarian market. Like their architect brethren, noted sculptors enjoyed sustained aristocratic, bureaucratic, and even ecclesiastic patronage.

The neoclassic artistic heritage was furthered after the Napoleonic era by the Dane Bertel Thorvaldsen, the Italian Lorenzo Bartolini, and the German Gottfried Schadow; it flourished in portrait and narrative sculpture into the twentieth century as the sanctioned imagery of academically conservative establishments.

The acme of recognition for neoclassic painting belongs to the French painter Jacques-Louis David (1748–1825), artist to the king, to the French Revolution, and to Napoleon. Initially facile in the rococo style, David only slowly absorbed, then consolidated, taste for *antico* form, narrative, and theory at the French Academy in Rome, under the directorship of his master Joseph Marie Vien (1716–1809), a founder of neoclassicism. David's *Oath of the Horatii* (1783–1784) and his *Brutus* (1789)—ironically, commissioned by Louis XVI as didactic subjects to foster patriotism and moral virtue—were prophetic harbingers of the French Revolution; David later voted for the king's execution. Artists from David's large international studio were influential throughout Europe and in the New World. His later followers, including the radically archaizing *primatifs* and the more conservatively adventuring Jean-Auguste-Dominique Ingres (1780–1867), practiced an even greater so-called Greek simplicity and softness than their master, whose politicizing historicisms they extended into exotic and esoteric art styles.

Their precursors who worked in an antiquarian and neo-Poussinesque mode had paved the way for such innovation—for example, the pioneering Scottish painter, excavator, antiquities entrepreneur, and savant Gavin Hamilton (1723–1798), whose paintings and classicist ideas were much admired by Johann Joachim Winckelmann; the Anglo-American painter Benjamin West (1738–1820); the Italian sculptor Antonio Canova; and Jacques-Louis David. Such neoclassic founders among visiting and local painters in Rome as the popular portraitist Pompeo Battoni (1708–1787), the genre painters of antiquarian conversation pieces, and the classicizing landscapist Richard Wilson, also inspired followers.

Similarly influential was the German emigré Anton Raphael Mengs (1728–1779), the academic ally and sometime mentor of Winckelmann, whom, according to Goethe, Mengs tricked with his piquant Pompeiian pastiche and fake *Zeus Kissing Ganymede* (1758–1759). In 1761, Mengs painted the large and paradigmatic antiquarian fresco *Parnassus* that crowned the Villa Albani Salon; he created the philosophical *Allegory of History* (1772) for the Vatican Museum. His art wed the old masters Raphael, Correggio, and Titian with ancient models, as

he recommended in his treatise *Thoughts on Beauty and Taste in Painting* (1762).

The radical Viennese Nazarenes, trained by neoclassical academicians in the school of Mengs and Winckelmann, used their formal and idealistic means to create a neo-Gothic style and a brotherhood of artists, which flourished in Rome after 1809. Their primitivism, akin to the primitifs' archaicizing, anticipated pre-Raphaelite interests in late Gothic and early Renaissance art after 1848. Visionary extremists in painting and graphics, like the Anglo-Swiss academician Henry Fuseli (Heinrich Füssli), the poet-limner William Blake, and the sculptor-illustrator John Flaxman, were already practicing an *antico* severity that was based on the mannerisms and outlines of ancient vase painting, Northern European Gothicism, and other exotic styles.

A romantic classicism emanated from the studio of David after 1800. It affected not only his well-known students like Antoine-Jean Gros, Anne-Louis Girodet, Pierre-Narcisse Guérin, and François Gérard, but also Théodore Géricault, who worked in a neoclassicist mode before adopting a dark expressionist and Bonapartist reportage—as would his admirer, the archromantic Eugène Delacroix (1798–1863), as well as their avant-garde followers, who challenged the reign of neoclassicism. Neoclassic art, however, kept its authority in the national academies, especially in Paris, Europe's new capital of art, through refractory directors like Ingres, the "Greek revivalist" Jean-Léon Gérôme (1824–1904), and their followers well into the twentieth century. Forays into neoclassicism by experimenting moderns—like the sculptors Antoine-Louis Barye, Adolf von Hildebrand, and Aristide Maillol, and the painters Pierre Auguste Renoir, Georgio de Chirico, and Pablo Picasso—illustrate its continued viability as an alternate style within and of modernism.

Following the lead of academic artists in France and elsewhere, craftsmen in the decorative or applied arts worked in the new classic style, informed by freshly excavated materials and published accounts or by prior inventions. Furniture, made within the tradition of rococo technical excellence, was often designed by architects who improvised on ancient models or by craftsmen and publicists like Thomas Chippendale, Duncan Phyfe, David Roentgen, Sir Thomas Hope, and Carl Friedrich Schinkel. Ceramics, based on scholarly imitation of ancient models or on invention, were well suited to industrial mass production, such as those from Wedgwood, Spode, Sèvres, and virtually all royal porcelain factories. Silver plate and trophies by Wedgwood's industrialist friend Matthew Boulton (1728–1809) similarly used long flowing lines and surfaces that were derived from classical shapes, ornaments, figures, and narrative. Eleanor Coade's successful factory (fl. 1769–1821) specialized in expensive architectural ornament made of artificial stone. Fine, small bronze and terra-cotta statuettes made by Giacomo Zoffoli, Clodion (Claude Michel), Étienne Maurice Falconet (1716–1791), and others were relatively inexpensive antiquarian copies and inventions. Neoclassicism influenced not only stucco work and painted relief or ornament but, ultimately, decorative wallpaper, textiles, costume, jewelry, coiffure, and all manner of trivia, as seen in the early 1800s fashion books by Thomas Hope.

Attractive architectural and furnishing ensembles by Robert Adam and his aides (after 1758) included classical frameworks, stucco or painted reliefs and ornaments, restored sculptures and copies, furniture, fireplace surrounds, tableware, rugs, inlaid floors, mirrors, sconces, window treatments, door handles, hinges, and so on.

Instructive in this synthesizing context is the villa at Wörlitz begun in 1769 and designed by Winckelmann's protégés in Rome, the Grand Tour anglophiles Leopold III, duke of Anhalt (1740–1817), and his architect and companion Friedrich Wilhelm von Erdmannsdorff (1736–1800). The setting at Wörlitz recalls an informal English park, echoing Stourhead, and emulating "classical" landscapes by Claude Lorraine (1600–1682) or Nicolas Poussin (1594–1665) and Lancelot "Capability" Brown's studied but informal Arcadian paths by ponds and streams, with tree-framed vistas to architectural follies that allude to Grand Tour favorites. The park and buildings, sympathetically taming and uniting mankind and nature, make an informal museological setting for encyclopedic gatherings of classic, classical, exotic, folk, and primitivist styles, which reflect all that was tasteful in the late eighteenth century. The interiors—furnished with restored antiquities, copies, casts, prints, drawings, and painted facsimiles of classicizing Italian and Germanic old masters, as well as chinoiserie, industrial revolution ironware, choice Wedgwood and Zoffoli productions, and art works that reflected, like other park structures, ethnic, Gothic, and Central European concerns—were all integrated into an iconographic program of fashionable Enlightenment interests, including freemasonry. Such patterns of collecting and display were desired norms for society and private life in Europe from the 1750s to the 1830s—and indeed, thereafter.

Related Arts and Attitudes. Like the fine arts and architecture, the performing arts—pageantry, drama, chironomia, and ballet—and manners quoted ancient models. The wooden postures of the Jesuits' baroque theater changed to gestures of classical restraint, economy, and trenchancy, which evolved into romantic histrionics. By 1800, actors used *antico* period costumes and gestures that, like the new simplified wigless hair styles, elastic poses, and kinetic display, featured a potent virile body in form-fitting dress; their poses alluded to trim classical youth and nudity. *Tableaux vivants* were created in Naples for visiting Grand Tour dignitaries, in which the former actress Lady Emma Hamilton, wife of the British ambassador, struck memorable poses that illustrated classical imagery and costume from Pompeii, among her husband's classical vase collection.

Winckelmann and others likened long smooth classical contours of white marble to clear water, youth, innocence, purity, and light—equated with Platonic and utopian ideals of the good and god—or with homoerotically tinged visions of athletic and adolescent male beauty in an aesthetic appalled by blemish or deformity. This polarization of classical clarity and dark baroque romanticism anticipated Goethe's dictum: classic, health; Gothic, disease. (One thinks also, without ambivalence, of the appeal of neoclassical clarity of form and subject in music from Christoph Willibald Gluck to Wolfgang Amadeus Mozart or the simplified penmanship encouraged by early industrial revolution steel pens.) The flattened perspectives that appeared in texts and silhouettes for Caspar Lavater's popular pseudo-science, physiognomy—a protopsychology based on ancient categories of temperament and loose anecdotal observations that were justified by contemporaneous Pietistic divining intuition and rationalized prejudice. Interest in unions of science, sentiment, trickery, experiment, and industry were amply documented by minor graphic illustrators and in paintings by Joseph Wright of Derby for members of the influential Lunar Society, which included major English industrial reformers. Their imagery both exploited and competed with classicism, continuing the quarrel of the ancients and the moderns, already found in Renaissance *paragone*.

Neoclassicism, repeated exceptions notwithstanding, has been conveniently, more than rightly, described as flavored by regional tradition and ethnic predilection: for example, a bright French, South German, and Alpine rococo sprightliness; a more weighty central Italian and Iberian baroque or *barocchetto* taste; transalpine Gothicism with British linearity tending toward transparency or the darker, more sober, northern Germanic and Scandinavian Sturm und Drang expressionism; the homey central European Biedermeier style; and the eastern European use of imported artists of reputation. Such distinctions aside, each nation's version was informed by mature Enlightenment ideals. Each maintained a learned, classicizing art academy in its capital and subsidized artists' study abroad, to foster a proven taste and style, giving legitimacy to illustrations of national interest.

Visually and politically, the antique models romantically symbolized simple beginnings, when people instinctively chose the virtues of sacrifice, patriotism, loyalty, liberty, fraternity, and equality. Those so-called virile examples might restore in the current era the mind, body, and senses to utopian states of aesthetic and ethical strength and rectitude—a way to perfect personal and social conduct. Increasingly, didactic narratives that deal with naive, even savage, beginnings were chosen as models for emulation in history painting, literature, and archaeological or art-historical research. In general, the admired, strongly male-oriented injunctions to decisiveness and action, echoing Winckelmann's hero worship, ran counter to the rococo era and style, which Delacroix would condemn as the bastard style of Madame Pompadour. Such a view occasionally gave rise to a taste for colossal, even megalomanic and overcompensatory scale and ambition.

During early-modern neoclassicism the noble savage and the antique Greek or British boxer were admired as culture heroes, as models for self-enhancing identification, romantically illustrating the essential goodness of natural man, in what might now be described as a sophisticated regression in the service of the ego. These views accompanied and motivated exploration into origins and innocence, with their preternatural powers to know, change, grow, and progress; they were contemporaneous with Europe's discovery of childhood, the nuclear family, and infant education, as celebrated in art, publications, and the colonizing of hitherto uncharted worlds and native peoples. Politically, the neoclassic art style was associated with Greek democracy and republican Rome, with rights of self-determination and individual enterprise. Winckelmann attributed the unrivaled beauty and creativity in Greek art to the freedom that he argued its people enjoyed.

Mediterranean and transalpine patronage of neoclassic art flourished through commission and subscription; some major artists, like Canova, also worked independently of immediate patronage. Initially, sponsorship was by aristocrats, but new middle-class wealth widened the arena of collectors; industrial production soon created a still greater market among clients of modest means. As patrons and protectors, the antiquarian grandees, like the members of London's Society of Dilettanti (which was founded in 1733) and national academies thrived throughout Europe, celebrating and supporting new and ancient classics.

Neoclassic Survivals and Transformations. In the decades after 1815—when nearing a century of domination—neoclassicism, by then the staid and restricted style of authority, began to wane. Adventurous young artists pursued the more emotive romanticism or more factual realism—both styles that were partly derived from their parent style, whose classical means and motifs they often reused. Invention and reportage of history and events approached both extravagant visions and minute observation (the latter eventually enhanced by photography after 1826); they embraced a new pantheistic religion of nature worship in landscape and trivial-romantic genre scenes.

Vestiges of neoclassical taste continued throughout the nineteenth century, during its academic battle of styles, when Greek revival imagery coexisted with related romantic idioms—exotic, primitivist, neo-Gothic, neo-Egyptian, orientalizing, folkloric, and even Renaissance-to-rococo revivals—chosen as relevant iconographies to clothe pragmatic contemporary structure and composition.

Today's postmodern neo-neoclassicism, derived from much-popularized art history and archaeology, variously continues such references. This is evident in the classicist sculptures of the fascist or communist totalitarianisms; the Herculaneum-based prototype for the J. Paul Getty Museum in Malibu, California (1970–1975), and in the paintings of Carlo Maria Mariani (born 1931)—each of which reflects visions of the Enlightenment.

[*See also* Academies; Ancient Greece; Ancient Rome; Classicism; Grand Tour; Pompeii and Herculaneum; Rationalism; Rococo; *and* Utopianism.]

BIBLIOGRAPHY

The Age of Neo-classicism. Catalog, Royal Academy and Victoria and Albert Museum. London, 1972. International scholars introduce some two thousand entries, informatively dealing with key examples of major and minor arts, relevant contemporary publications, and artists' biographies; also some two hundred plates.

Boime, Albert. *Art in the Age of Revolution 1750–1800.* Chicago, 1987. Sociopolitical and economic orientation toward neoclassic art; the study continues in Boime's *A Social History of Modern Art: Art in an Age of Bonapartism, 1800–1815* (Chicago, 1990).

Bowron, Edgar Peters, and Joseph J. Richel, eds. *Art in Rome in the Eighteenth Century.* Catalog, Philadelphia Museum of Art. London, 2000. Extensive scholarly introductions to cultural ambience, Arcadianism, and key figures, as well as art works, masters, and style phases in the First capital of neoclassic art. 628 pp.; 444 entries, each illustrated in color or black and white; massive bibliography; Roman chronology.

Burgess, Anthony, and Francis Haskell. *The Age of the Grand Tour.* London, 1967. Excellent introduction to and illustrations of this influential institution, with lengthy excerpts by eminent travelers from 1720 to 1820.

Diderot, Denis. *Diderot on Art.* 2 vols. Translated and edited by John Goddman. London, 1995. Observations by the encyclopaedist founder of French art criticism, who fostered ideals in art akin to those of J. J. Winckelmann, Joshua Reynolds, et al.

Eitner, Lorenz. *Neoclassicism and Romanticism, 1750–1850.* 2 vols. Englewood Cliffs, N.J., 1970. Documents on art from Winckelmann to Baudelaire, with valuable historical and biographical introductories.

Goethe, Johann Wolfgang von. *Italian Journey* [1786–1788]. Translated by W. H. Auden and Elizabeth Mayer. London, 1962. The best-known travel book and diary on Grand Tour personalities, experiences, and gossip.

Gombrich, Ernst H. *The Ideas of Progress and Their Impact on Art.* New York, 1971. Two illuminating essays on primitivism and archaizing in art, viewed mainly in the wake of Winckelmann's writings, by a doyen of art history.

Haskell, Francis, and Nicholas Penny. *Taste and the Antique: The Lure of Classical Sculpture, 1500–1900.* New Haven, Conn., 1981. An erudite overview of antiquities collecting, especially during the eighteenth century, with an illustrated catalog of ninety-five influential ancient sculptures, the histories of their provenances, and their fluctuating reputations. Extensive background bibliography.

Hawley, Henry. *Neo-Classicism, Style and Motif*. Catalog, Cleveland Museum of Arts. New York, 1964. A broad spectrum of masters and genres; 193 items, all illustrated.

Honour, Hugh. *Neo-classicism*. Harmondsworth, U.K., 1968. A thorough and reliable survey of the major and minor arts in their context of ideas and historical events. Honour's *Romanticism* (New York, 1979) continues the narrative into the nineteenth century.

Howard, Seymour. *Antiquity Restored: Essays on the Afterlife of the Antique*. Vienna, 1990. Seventeen essays on the classic, classicisms, neoclassicism, and archaizing—ancient and modern—in matters of dealing, collecting, patronage, theater, technology, calligraphy, Winckelmann's aesthetics, and the restoration, fakery, or invention of antiquarian sculpture, especially in the circle of Cavaceppi. Howard's *Art and Imago: Essays on Art as a Species of Autobiography* (London, 1997) in part further discusses these and related subjects as norms and as vehicles that reify deep-seated, psychogenic interests of artists and their constituencies.

Irwin, David. *Neoclassicism*. London, 1997. Authoritative and comprehensive survey by a leading specialist; addresses diverse fresh and canonical subjects and works; valuable sections on the commercial and international uses and afterlife of the style. Chronologies, a glossary, biographies, maps, and color illustrations.

Irwin, David, ed. *Winckelmann Writings on Art*. London, 1972. Choice selections in English translation of texts by the prophet of neoclassicism that deal with his most influential theories and descriptions. Essays discuss the origin and impact of Winckelmann's ideas; his life and reputation; his perceptions of the Antique; and his relation to Romanticism and place in the history of art.

Janson, Horst W., and Robert Rosenblum. *19th Century Art*. New York, 1984. Through half of this sumptuously illustrated volume, these authorities alternately present rich individual analyses of widely dispersed paintings and sculptures made after 1776. Extensive bibliographies of books and catalogs, primarily in English, list artists and general, national, and special subjects.

Pevsner, Nikolaus. *Academies of Art*. London and New York, 1973. The basic study on academic institutions that helped to establish and sustain the forms and ideals of Enlightment neoclassicism.

Rosenblum, Robert. *Transformations in Late Eighteenth-Century Art*. Princeton, N.J., 1967. Brilliant, pathbreaking essays, with rich annotation and illustrative expositions that deal with the major themes and images of the era: matters of definition, the virtuous example, aspects of architecture, and strivings for a tabula rasa.

Rykwert, Joseph. *The First Moderns: Architects of the Eighteenth Century*. Cambridge, Mass., and London, 1980. Detailed survey, massive bibliography.

Stafford, Barbara M. *Artful Science: Enlightenment Entertainment and the Eclipse of Visual Education*. Cambridge, Mass., and London, 1994. Like other of the author's works, an investigation into relationships between the visual arts and science, pseudo-sciences, technology, charlatans, and popular and esoteric illustrations.

Summerson, John. *The Architecture of the Eighteenth Century*. London, 1969, 1986. A renowned architectural historian's short and well-illustrated introduction to a wide range of late baroque, rococo, and neoclassic monuments in diverse building types.

SEYMOUR HOWARD

NETHERLANDS. [*This entry contains two subentries, an overview of the history of the Netherlands in the Enlightenment and a discussion of press freedom in the Netherlands.*]

An Overview

The notion that there was ever a Dutch Enlightenment is relatively new. Until recently, Dutch historiography was so preoccupied with the Golden Age of the seventeenth-century Republic that it saw in the eighteenth century only a poor reflection of former glory. More recently, however, the Dutch eighteenth century has been studied vigorously, and although there is every reason still to consider it an age of economic and political decline, an increasing awareness of its importance both in relation to its European context and to the Netherlands in the nineteenth and twentieth centuries seems to be emerging. Most experts agree that it makes sense to distinguish a very early Dutch Enlightenment that had already taken off during the 1650s (marking the beginning of the "long" Dutch Enlightenment) from the late Enlightenment, which reached its first climax during the revolutionary 1780s. At present, the most comprehensive account of the late Dutch Enlightenment in particular is supplied by Kloek and Mijnhardt (2001).

The 1650s witnessed the suspension of the political state based on the stadholderate (1650–1672), only shortly after the Treaty of Westphalia (1648) had granted the Republic international recognition as a sovereign state. Following the sudden death of the highly ambitious William II, in 1650, the States General embarked on a policy that served the interests of the regents who owed their fortunes to trade. Domestically, the States now actively opposed calls by Calvinist hard-liners for a "further Reformation" of Dutch morals. This resulted in the perpetuation of the celebrated policy of religious toleration that, its supporters argued, had been the very cause of the revolt in the first place. Dutch foreign strategy was mainly concerned with protecting and furthering the commercial interests of the nation. This period of "True Freedom," as it was also called at the time, came to an end in the summer of 1672. After the secret Pact of Dover (1671), England, France, the bishop of Munster, and the elector of Cologne jointly declared war on the Republic. Within weeks French armies had reached the city of Utrecht, threatening to invade Holland as well. Throughout the Republic, the populace erupted, demanding that William II's only son, the young William III, be called in to save the nation from the "treachery" of the States and the regents, who were thought to have willfully neglected the armed forces. In the Hague, in August 1672, the brilliant regent of Holland, Johan de Witt, together with his brother Cornelius, was lynched by an Orangist mob. However, once William III took over as the new Stadholder, he turned out to favor rather tolerant politics himself. His main objective was to curb the increasingly aggressive foreign policies of Louis XIV of France. Indeed, once William III also became king of England in 1689, he turned into a champion of the Protestant cause in western Europe. In 1702, when he died without an heir, the states of Holland again decided to suspend the stadholderate, leaving the House of Orange to content its political aspirants with supplying hereditary stadholders of Friesland and some of the eastern provinces.

By the early eighteenth century, the Republic had become a highly urbanized and remarkably literate nation. With a fairly irrelevant and steadily dwindling aristocracy, who were mainly domiciled in the northern and eastern provinces, 40 percent of its two million inhabitants lived in the cities and towns. In 1795, in the province of Holland, which housed nearly a third of the entire population, urban inhabitants exceeded 60 percent. Throughout the century these percentages did not change significantly. Although the population of Leiden and Haarlem dropped heavily during the later decades of the eighteenth century, Amsterdam, Rotterdam, and The Hague continued to prosper until the 1780s. The figures for literacy arguably testify even more to the modernity of the Dutch Republic. In 1650, 70 percent of grooms and 40 percent of brides signed their marriage certificates; in 1795 these percentages rose to 80 and 60 respectively. By the late seventeenth century, one out of every forty Dutchmen matriculated at one of the five Dutch universities that had been established since the beginnings of the revolt. By the end of the eighteenth century, the Republic had some three hundred booksellers. More than a third of these were located in Amsterdam, which had almost as many bookshops as the vastly larger Paris.

From a cultural point of view, the latter half of the seventeenth century was particularly advanced. This was mainly because the Republic was the first European nation to embrace the philosophical and scientific insights of René Descartes, who had spent some twenty years in the Republic, leaving it only in 1649, just months before his death in Stockholm. During the second half of the seventeenth century, a host of professors in philosophy, mathematics, medicine, and even theology, managed to turn Cartesianism into the philosophical norm taught in the Republic, to the obvious chagrin of many Calvinist ministers. In fact, Cartesianism turned into something of a political party opposing the efforts of the so-called "further Reformation," which was led by the Utrecht divine Gijsbert Voet, who felt that Cartesian philosophy would result in both skepticism and atheism. During the first suspension of the stadholderate, Cartesianism even inspired a number of nonacademic, republican political philosophers, who

Dutch East India Company. Wharf and shipbuilding yard of the Dutch East India Company. Engraving by J. Mulder, 1694. (Granger Collection.)

combined their pleas in favor of the sovereignty of the States with their brand of "Cartesianism."

The most important Cartesian republican was of course Baruch de Spinoza. However, his *Tractatus theologico-politicus* (1670) and *Ethica* (1677) were widely considered atheistic, and even in the "tolerant" Republic were soon forbidden. Although Spinoza never became so popular as Descartes continued to be until the early eighteenth century, quite a bit of evidence has been unearthed that points to a continuing semiclandestine tradition of Dutch Spinozism, which inspired the early, radical Enlightenment in France and Germany in particular. Unlike their foreign counterparts, however, these early Dutch Spinozists, such as the Zwolle minister Frederik van Leenhof, were often deeply religious. The kind of materialism that in France was to be associated with Spinozism was exceptional in the Netherlands, and much of the philosophical radicalism of the early Dutch Enlightenment was anticlerical rather than antireligious. The pyrrhonism rampant among the Parisian *libertins érudits* was equally rare; Dutch Cartesians and Spinozists more or less ignored the pyrrhonist challenge, and classical scholars, who continued the brilliant tradition of Dutch humanism, favored the pedagogical uses of antiquity over its skeptical inheritance.

The Impact of French Immigration. Another major factor that helped to shape the early eighteenth century scholarly and literary culture in the Netherlands was the huge influx of French immigrants following the revocation of the Edict of Nantes (1685). Within a short period of time, thousands of highly skilled and very literate French Protestants settled in the Netherlands, mainly in Holland, where they set up important publishing houses that became crucial to the distribution of enlightened thought all over Europe. Many of the most important scholarly journals of the time, including, for example Pierre Bayle's *Nouvelles de la République des Lettres* (1684), were produced and printed in Holland. In the eyes of the Dutch, this French invasion was not just an asset, and several influential Dutch authors reflected the increasing uneasiness among their contemporaries over the spreading of "French" morals.

Justus van Effen, who, during the early decades of the eighteenth century, had made a name for himself as a journalist and author who published exclusively in French, launched his *De hollandsche spectator* (1731–1735), a journal in Dutch largely devoted to the effort of defining the Dutch roots of a civil morality that should protect his compatriots from the corrupting influence of the French way of life. According to van Effen, the moral and cultural decline he perceived during the 1730s could be reversed only by a return to the moral standards that had once laid the foundations of the Republic's greatness and had been the product of reasonableness, virtue, belief in the future, and, of course, in a benevolent creator. Van Effen's concerns were voiced during the second suspension of the stadholderate (1702–1747) that started after the death of William III. During this period, the Republic was no longer able to steer an independent course in the European political arena. Fear of the French had turned into subservience to the British. Although many of the wealthier families managed to secure their fortunes by clever investment abroad, the Dutch economy became just as defensive as Dutch foreign policies had become. It was hampered by a demographic decline from the late seventeenth century and burdened by the massive interest payments on public debts accumulated as a result of the expensive political ambitions of William III and the part played by the Republic in the War of Spanish Succession (1702–1713). Moreover, a shift in economic activity from trading goods to the capital market not only hit the lower classes badly, but also affected the large middle class, leading to a dramatic increase in costs for poor relief after 1770.

In 1747, during the War of Austrian Succession and after another French invasion in the south, the stadholderate was reinstated, and the Friesian stadholder William IV became stadholder of Holland, Zeeland, Utrecht, and Overijssel. The political structure of the Republic, however, remained largely intact. William IV died in 1751 and his widow, Anne of Hanover, daughter of George II of England, took over as regent during the minority of their son, in an attempt to continue the legacy of her husband. This did not stop the Amsterdam regents from regaining their hold on Dutch policy-making. In 1780, in the wake of the American Declaration of Independence, the division between Orangists and their opponents reached a new climax, when critics of the stadholderate dragged the Republic into a disastrous war with Britain (1780–1784). By this time the Republic, whose finances had been steadily dwindling throughout the century, was facing a complete economic breakdown. This did not stop the anti-Orangists, who, during the 1780s, reorganized under the banner of so-called "Patriotism." William V's prerogatives were being dismantled step by step, and the States of Holland acted as if no stadholder was in place. In 1787, after a particularly embarrassing incident involving the arrest of the Gouda militia of Princess Wilhelmina, William V felt forced to call in the help of his brother-in-law, the king of Prussia, to stem the tide. Patriot militias were effectively taking control over much of the country. The Prussian king quickly responded by sending a 25,000 strong army, which restored the stadholderate and caused several thousand patriots to flee the Netherlands for France.

It was clear that the Republic had become defenseless, and in 1795 it was simply abolished when the French decided to invade their northern neighbors, establishing a Batavian Republic. At first, patriot radicals governed the newly established National Assembly, but by this time, their ideological direction had changed considerably. Under the influence of the French, they no longer emphasized the sovereignty of the States, but, rather, the need to erect a single state. They only ruled until 1798, however, when they in turn were toppled by moderate supporters of the French. In 1806, Napoleon installed his brother Louis as first king of Holland. This was a crucial step toward the establishment of the unitary kingdom of the Netherlands, a process that was completed in 1815.

From a political perspective, the "long" Dutch Enlightenment—which took off after the sudden demise of William II in 1650 with the triumphant ascendancy of the States of Holland as leaders of the Dutch Republic—was completed with the crowning of William I as king of the Netherlands in 1815. It will come as no surprise, then, that the very concept of a Dutch Enlightenment has baffled historians, who look for similarities with the French Enlightenment in particular. Furthermore, the fragmentary political structure of the Republic and its astonishing religious pluralism from the sixteenth century onward have led specialists to identify many different Enlightenments, once they started to investigate the specific nature of the Dutch Enlightenment. Recently, attempts have been made to identify an early, a late, a moderate, a radical, a Reformed, or a conservative Enlightenment, and so on.

Natural Philosophy and Toleration. The fact that no particular thought dominated the Dutch Enlightenment is another contributory factor to this rich diversity of interpretation. It is true that Cartesianism was very important, at least until the early eighteenth century. It even penetrated the Leiden faculty of theology, where well into the eighteenth century, the disciples of the German professor Johannes Cocceius were generally perceived as supporters of Descartes. From the 1670s however, many Leiden natural philosophers, such as Burchard de Volder, became aware of the limits of Cartesian physics, and during the 1720s Willem Jacob 'sGravesande, editor of the *Journal Littéraire*, made Newtonian natural philosophy the norm at Leiden. His international prestige was considerable, as was the fame of his younger colleague Petrus van Musschenbroek, who after having held chairs at Duisburg and Utrecht, in 1740 joined 'sGravesande at the university of Leiden.

'sGravesande was a lawyer by training, but after having spent two years in England, where he befriended Isaac Newton and became a member of the Royal Society, he was appointed to the Leiden chair of mathematics and astronomy in 1717, and immediately began to lecture on Newtonian natural philosophy. He attracted scores of foreign students, including, most famously, Voltaire. Van Musschenbroek followed 'sGravesande's example and did much to popularize physics, publishing, for example, a *Beginselen der Natuurkunde, beschreven ten dienste der landgenooten* (Principles of Physics, Described for the Benefit of My Compatriots, 1736). Later physicists such as Pieter Camper and J. H. van Swinden, however, though successful as popularizers, no longer belonged to the international avant-garde in the natural sciences. Gradually, the disadvantages of the essentially didactic purpose of the university began to make themselves felt. Poorly equipped to do original research, even Leiden and Utrecht found it increasingly difficult to keep up with the latest developments in the natural sciences.

Meanwhile, from the 1730s onward, Wolffianism, essentially based on the views of Gottfried Wilhelm von Leibniz, also met with considerable support, especially at Groningen University, among both natural and moral philosophers, who turned much of their attention to the study of natural law. Gerard Noodt, arguably the greatest lawyer of the Dutch Enlightenment, was in many ways still a Cartesian, however. His natural law rationalism coupled with his enormous erudition—steeped in the humanist tradition of classical philology—turned him into a major representative of the early Enlightenment within the Dutch academy. Noodt became something of a European celebrity after the publication, in 1706, of a forceful plea in favor of religious toleration that was based on the strict separation of civil affairs from religious matters. He relegated the latter to the individual conscience in a manner reminiscent of the earlier arguments in favor of toleration developed by Spinoza, Locke, and Bayle, whose works on the matter were incidentally all composed and published in the Dutch Republic.

Although not every "enlightened" Dutch person was prepared to go as far as Spinoza and Noodt in their defense of religious pluralism, there was general and quite natural agreement on the need to be tolerant, which was to be Dutch, as many came to feel. Despite the ferocity of some of the quarrels between Newtonians and Wolffians, there was also a widely shared common understanding of the providential nature of God's design and maintenance of the universe at large. Following the huge success of Bernard Nieuwentijt's *Het regt gebruik der wereltbeschouwingen* (The Right Use of Philosophy, 1715), specifically intended to stop the rise of Spinozism, physico-theology became a flourishing industry, which produced many dozens of learned treatises, according to which the detailed wonders of nature all testified to the benevolence of its creator.

Leiden was not only famous for its lawyers and its philosophers, Cartesian or Newtonian. Its medical reputation was also secure, and Hermann Boerhaave in particular added to its luster. Initially, he upheld Cartesian mechanism, but during his professorship at Leiden he came to endorse Baconian empiricism. His foreign visitors included Peter the Great, and one of his pupils, the Catholic Gerard van Swieten, was appointed personal physician to Empress Maria Theresa. During the 1740s, van Swieten was invited to reorganize the University of Vienna, a position he used to turn it into a bastion of the natural sciences. Quite apart from Boerhaave's professional achievements as a physician—his own research was mainly in the emerging discipline of chemistry—he was the first to launch Newtonianism at Leiden.

Dutch Cultural Societies. According to the *Encyclopédie*, Leiden was still "the first academy of Europe," and during the first half of the eighteenth century, the Netherlands was indeed much more than the printshop of European Enlightenment, in particular on account of its advanced universities. What is more, the much quoted fact that during the last quarter of the century the numbers of foreign students dropped dramatically does not necessarily imply any substantial loss of intellectual prowess. Dutch science had a structural problem, however, that increasingly undermined its development throughout the course of the century, namely, its lack of a national research academy. The Dutch Republic never had any equivalent to the Royal Society or the Académie Royale. This did not stop Christiaan Huygens from becoming the first president of the French Academy, nor did it prevent Dutch universities from keeping up with scientific developments in England and France for a long time. In the course of the eighteenth century, all sorts of scientific clubs, Masonic lodges, literary and broadly cultural societies, and reading associations sprang up all over the Republic, in an attempt to make up for the growing backwardness, or so it was perceived, of a once great Republic, now suffering acute decline.

By the end of the century, some five hundred of these societies were active. They became the framework in which the cultural elite of the time attempted to define its own enlightened self-consciousness. Research into the constitution of the Dutch reading public of the time has revealed that it largely coincided with membership of these societies. During the second half of the eighteenth century, the line of thought first expressed by Justus van Effen's *Hollandsche spectator* inspired a fierce debate in all sorts of "spectatorial" journals on the essence of citizenship. This eclipsed the classical vocabulary of political republicanism that was directed only at a regent class whose virtues had to be enhanced. Van Effen and his successors addressed all citizens, not only those in power.

It also invoked a continuous reflection on the history, the present state, and the possible future of Dutch civilization. In 1778, at Leiden, the ardent Orangist Adriaan Kluit was appointed to the first chair in Dutch history. It was only fitting that his inaugural lecture addressed the legitimacy of the Dutch Revolt. Several experts have pointed out that this eighteenth-century obsession with the glories of a national past tended to lead to a certain isolation within the European context—although it also furthered the awareness of national unity, the lack of which had always been a cause for anxiety in these not so United Provinces.

Traditionally, the literary efforts in particular of the societies that supplied Dutch enlightened discourse have suffered a bad press. In spite of the attempts of many spectatorial authors to invoke a wide variety of literary genres, their exhortations to cultivate a sober, virtuous, and reasonable lifestyle, which they presented as "Dutch," no longer makes for thrilling reading today. More often than not, their overriding concern with the necessity of turning men, women, and children into useful members of a national community borders on the tedious, to say the least. Nonetheless, the sheer volume of journals, poems, plays, and even novels involved goes to show that the significance of these texts is not primarily artistic. Even major poets such as Hieronymus van Alphen and the young Willem Bilderdijk, who did much to emphasize the need for literary quality, shared many of the pedagogical assumptions of their less-talented colleagues. The same holds for the remarkable female duo of Betje Wolff-Bekker and Aagje Deken, authors of the celebrated *Sara Burgerhart* (1782), conventionally considered to be the first original novel in the Dutch language.

As Mijnhardt has shown (1988), these societies were largely apolitical. One of the virtues high on the agenda of Dutch enlightened sociability was concord. Time and again, the unity of Dutch family life was presented as the model for the nation as a whole. As a consequence, it would be a serious mistake to regard the patriots as defending the "true" heritage of the Dutch Enlightenment. Moreover, several of the most gifted enlightened thinkers in the Republic were staunch Orangists. Apart from Elie Luzac, the political economist Isaac de Pinto should be mentioned, as well as Rijklof Michael van Goens, professor at Utrecht before being forced to give up his chair in history under Voetian pressure, and who was one of the few Dutch intellectuals who knew philosophes, such as Denis Diderot, personally. The single, truly important Dutch philosopher of the time, François Hemsterhuis was no patriot either. Hemsterhuis, though very well versed in the classics, studied mathematics with 'sGravesande, and served for several years with the corps of engineers of the States army. In 1755, after a failed attempt to

Netherlandish Landscape and Seascape. Scene near Zierikzee. Engraving by J. C. Philips after a drawing by C. Pronk, 1745. (Culver Pictures, Inc.)

get a chair at Franeker University, he became a civil servant with the Raad van State (council of state) in the Hague, where he lived for the rest of his life, amid Orangist politicians and foreign diplomats. Not unlike Luzac—the publisher of Julien Offray de La Mettrie's *L'homme machine* (1747)—Hemsterhuis detested French materialism, and sought to complete Newton's philosophy of nature with what he held to be "Socratic philosophy." This led him to aesthetics and ethics, and to the composition of a series of Platonic dialogues such as *Sophyle ou de la philosophie* (1778), *Aristée ou de la divinité* (1779), and *Simon ou des facultés de l'âme* (1787). Toward the end of his life, he became involved in the German *Pantheismusstreit* on the nature of Spinoza's "atheism." Once again, he fiercely attacked the left wing of the French Enlightenment in his *Lettre sur l'athéisme* (1787).

In the Dutch Republic of the eighteenth century, however, science and religion were rarely at loggerheads with one another, or so it would seem. The Cartesian separation of philosophy and theology—which even Spinoza subscribed to—coupled with the ubiquitous argument from design apparently remained an attractive solution for both philosopher and theologian. However, the appeal to reason—identified as being God's gift to humankind—gradually became more prominent among professional theologians and Protestant ministers as the century progressed. Whereas seventeenth-century Dutch authors had been quick to respond to foreign developments in the arts and sciences, however, latter-day eighteenth-century and early nineteenth-century Dutch people seem to become hesitant to import new ideas from abroad. This is illustrated, for instance, by the apparent lack of interest in French materialism, but also by

Johannes Kinker's failure to raise any substantial interest for the writings of the German philosopher Immanuel Kant, who had launched a "Copernican revolution" that was largely ignored by Dutch philosophers. Although it has been shown that by the early nineteenth century, Kinker had managed to rally quite a number of radical Freemasons behind his calls for a Kantian *Aufklärung*, Dutch philosophers became seriously interested in German Idealism only during the latter half of the nineteenth century.

One should bear in mind, however, that until now research into the Dutch eighteenth century has been dominated by literary and cultural historians. The history of eighteenth-century political thought has also been dealt with quite impressively, but historians of philosophy have all but ignored the Dutch eighteenth century. At the moment, there are no histories available of Dutch Newtonianism or Dutch Wolffianism, let alone of Dutch Kantianism. Serious research into the writings of Hemsterhuis has only just started. What is more, the question of the wider significance of eighteenth-century academic philosophy has hardly been addressed. This is all the more unfortunate in view of the self-assessment of many eighteenth-century Dutch people, who saw themselves as living in an eminently "philosophical" age—a remarkable self-perception in view of the absence of a professional class of Dutch philosopher. The size of the Dutch reading public simply did not allow for profitable literary careers. Even a highly productive author such as Luzac could not make a living from his literary efforts.

The most popular early nineteenth-century professors of philosophy, including Daniel Wyttenbach and Philip Willem van Heusde, went so far as to congratulate themselves on their intellectual xenophobia. It would seem that once the Republic, whose domestic history was so much at odds with the history of its surrounding neighbors, more or less fell apart during the 1780s, it saw little value in what its neighbors had to offer. Instead, it chose to reinvent its own identity by creating a national past from which a future nation was to emerge that in its insistence on reasonableness and frugality, on the need for its people to be Protestant, virtuous, and proud to be Dutch, owed more to its late-eighteenth-century Enlightenment than it cared to admit.

[See also Bayle, Pierre; Bekker, Balthasar; Boerhaave, Hermann; Calvinism; Cartesianism; Deken, Aagje; Effen, Justus van; Glorious Revolution; Leibniz, Gottfried Wilhelm von; Locke, John; Luzac, Elie; Musschenbroek, Petrus van; Newtonianism; Nieuwentijt, Bernard; Noodt, Gerard; Pinto, Isaac de; 'sGravesande, Willem Jacob; Spinoza, Baruch de; Toleration; Universities; and Wolff-Bekker, Betje.]

BIBLIOGRAPHY

Berkel, Klaas van, Albert van Helden, and Lodewijk Palm, eds. *A History of Science in the Netherlands: Survey, Themes and Reference*. Leiden, Netherlands, 1999.

Bergh, G. C. J. J. van den. *The Life and Work of Gerard Noodt (1647–1725): Dutch Legal Scholarship between Humanism and Enlightenment*. Oxford, 1988.

Berkvens-Stevelinck, C., H. Bots, P. G. Hoftijzer, and O. S. Lankhorst, eds. *Le Magasin de l'Univers: The Dutch Republic as the Centre of the European Book Trade*. Leiden, Netherlands, 1992.

Bosma, Jelle. *Woorden van een gezond verstand: De invloed van de Verlichting op de in het Nederlands uitgegeven preken van 1750 tot 1800*. Nieuwkoop, Netherlands, 1997.

Bunge, Wiep van. *From Stevin to Spinoza: An Essay on Philosophy in the Seventeenth-Century Dutch Republic*. Leiden, Netherlands, 2001.

Grijzenhout, F., W. W. Mijnhardt, and N. C. F. van Sas, eds. *Voor Vaderland en Vrijheid: De revolutie van de patriotten*. Amsterdam, 1987.

Hanou, A. J. *Sluiers van Isis: Johannes Kinker als voorvechter van de Verlichting in de vrijmetselarij en andere Nederlandse genootschappen, 1790–1845*. 2 vols. Deventer, Netherlands, 1988.

Israel, Jonathan I. *The Dutch Republic: Its Rise, Greatness, and Fall, 1477–1806*. Oxford, 1995.

Israel, Jonathan I. *Radical Enlightenment: Philosophy and the Making of Modernity, 1650–1750*. Oxford, 2001.

Jacob, Margaret C. *The Radical Enlightenment: Pantheists, Freemasons and Republicans*. London, 1981.

Jacob, Margaret C., and Wijnand W. Mijnhardt, eds. *The Dutch Republic in the Eighteenth Century: Decline, Enlightenment and Revolution*. Ithaca, N.Y., and London, 1992.

Kloek, Joost, and Wijnand Mijnhardt. *1800: Blauwdrukken voor een samenleving: Nederlandse cultuur in Europese context*. The Hague, 2001.

Mijnhardt, Wijnand W. *Tot Heil van't Menschdom: Culturele genootschappen in Nederland, 1750–1815*. Amsterdam, 1988.

Ruestow, E. G. *Physics at Seventeenth and Eighteenth-Century Leiden: Philosophy and the New Science in the University*. The Hague, 1973.

Schama, Simon. *Patriots and Liberators: Revolution in the Netherlands, 1780–1813*. New York, 1977.

Velema, Wyger R. E. *Enlightenment and Conservatism in the Dutch Republic: The Political Thought of Elie Luzac (1721–1796)*. Assen, Netherlands, 1993.

WIEP VAN BUNGE

Press Freedom in the Netherlands

In the eighteenth century, no country was free of censorship—not even the Republic of the United Provinces, although it had a reputation for freedom of the press from the beginning. For example, the Dutch gazettes were famed for their objectivity. Yet, as recent research has confirmed, this was a tempered freedom, and its cause was the particularism reigning in the Republic. The seven provinces were relatively autonomous, towns went their own way, and the city councils and magistrates put obstacles in one another's way. In some cases, where the stadholder used his authority to make the regents cooperate, the supervision of the press became stricter. Publishers in the Republic also were increasingly forced to accept self-imposed censorship for economic reasons, especially when they were working in the Dutch language. Their publications were partly funded by government patents, and their patrons and customers were members of the different religious denominations—factors that made publishers cautious. Because the Dutch language area was so small, publishers in the Republic continued to make small profits, despite the expansion in the reading public that resulted from increasing literacy in the last decades of the century. In France, Germany, and England, where readers were proportionately more numerous, publishers had larger profit margins and so had less reason for caution.

The particularism that characterized the Republic until 1795 acted as a moderating influence on censorship. Preventive censorship, which required that copy be submitted in advance of publication to a censor nominated by the secular authorities, had proven ineffective during the previous century. The repressive censorship exercised by the secular authorities, which involved banning certain publications and posting the bans in public, took a heavy toll in the eighteenth century, despite the opposition of those concerned or lack of cooperation from the appointed officers. Nonetheless, implementation of the censorship laws was well below the actual strictness of the legislation. Whole bodies of work were banned (for example, Jean Rousset de Missy's in 1749); sometimes high fines were imposed; authors were removed from public service; sentences of exile or detention were pronounced; and books were publicly burned or torn up by the hangman; but there continued to be a discrepancy between the stringency of the laws and their implementation.

Repressive censorship could be used to ban either individual titles or a certain number of books, and even to ban publications more generally. General prohibitions, often published as placards, banned material offensive to the home government and that of foreign countries or injurious to the Christian religion and sound morals; they were also directed against publications that had been printed anonymously or that were offensive to individuals or authority figures. Patent laws enabled the authorities to ban new editions that were considered to be competitive with existing ones. Publications in which judicial sentences were questioned were regularly forbidden.

The authority to ban books lay within the remit of the States General, the provincial states—especially those of Holland—and their delegated councilors, the court of Holland and the judicial authorities of the towns. The Dutch Reformed Church exercised censorship on its own behalf, based on Article 55 of the Church Order of 1619, which stated that all members of the church should present texts they wished to publish to the *visitatores librorum*. This was often ignored. For clergymen, however, church approbation could be valuable. Often the church applied to the secular authorities to ban a book, but frequently without success because the institution of *visitatores librorum* was never officially recognized by the state. Church censorship, whether in the Dutch or French Reformed churches, was applied through its various committees: the national and provincial synods, parishes, classes, and consistories. Ecclesiastical censorship was not completely powerless, though, because its influence was not negligible.

The authorities took action either on their own initiative or as the result of a complaint and were particularly attentive to the frequent complaints issuing from foreign ambassadors. When an investigation was mounted, public officials disguised as customers spied on the bookshops, and the government promised rewards in order to elicit information. Censorship was not only exercised by the state authorities but also, more drastically, by the theater of Amsterdam. The directors of the theater, who not only decided what would be played but also, after 1730, held exclusive rights on the publication of all the plays performed or to be performed in Amsterdam, kept out anything that might be offensive to the state, the church, or the citizens.

The only extant survey of censorship in the Republic as a whole is the one carried out by W. P. C. Knuttel in 1914, who listed 244 titles as being the object of government scrutiny in the eighteenth century. Ton Jongenelen's excellent study of censorship in Amsterdam from 1747 to 1794 mentioned 150 titles of forbidden publications that had not appeared on Knuttel's list. An investigation of censorship at the local level in the Republic in the eighteenth century remains to be done.

It is nonetheless possible to say that the period of democratization in 1747–1748 and the period of the Patriots in the 1780s were relatively free of censorship but were followed by renewed repression. The works of authors considered Spinozist (Frederick van Leenhof, 1706), Socinian (Johannes Stinstra, 1742), materialist (La Mettrie, 1748), or deistic or injurious to the Christian religion (Voltaire, 1764, 1765; Rousseau, 1762, 1765) were banned. Even the publications of a mystical writer could be condemned (Willem Schortinghuis, 1745), or those expressing outright antipopery (Laurens Steversloot, 1720). Freemasons also had their works banned (1736). In short, there were risks for everything that fell outside the barriers of an enlightened Protestant Christianity. Political writings were frequently banned, especially toward the end of the century—for example, the famous open letter to the people of the Netherlands by J. D. van der Capellen tot de Poll (1781), pro-Orangist publications by J. L. Le Francq van Berkhey (1783), works by antistadholder authors, or the writings of Mirabeau (1788, 1789). Issues of newspapers were also banned—for example, in Haarlem and Groningen in 1748—and these were particularly vulnerable because they had to be licensed by the government.

[*See also* Clandestine Literature; Journals, Newspapers, and Gazettes, *subentry on* The Netherlands; La Mettrie, Julien Offray de; Reformed Churches, *subentry on* Dutch Reformed Church; Rousseau, Jean-Jacques; Stinstra, Johannes; *and* Voltaire.]

BIBLIOGRAPHY

Huussen, Arend H., Jr. "Freedom of the Press and Censorship in the Netherlands, 1780–1810." In *Too Mighty to Be Free: Censorship and the Press in Britain and the Netherlands*, edited by A. C. Duke and C. A. Tamse, pp. 107–126. Zutphen, Netherlands, 1987.

Huussen, Arend H., Jr. "Censorship in the Netherlands." In *The Age of William III & Mary II: Power, Politics, and Patronage, 1688–1702: A Reference Encyclopedia and Exhibition Catalogue*, edited by Robert P. Maccubin and Martha Hamilton-Philips, pp. 347–351. Williamsburg, Va., 1989.

Huussen, Arend H., Jr. "Censuur in stad en ommelanden van Groningen 1594–1795." In *Jaarboek voor Nederlandse boekgeschiedenis*, vol. 2, pp. 13–33. Leiden, Netherlands, 1995.

Jongenelen, Ton. *Van smaad tot erger: Amsterdamse boekverboden, 1747–1794*. Amsterdam, 1998.

Knuttel, W. P. C. *Verboden boeken in de Republiek der Vereenigde Nederlanden: beredeneerde catalogus*. The Hague, 1914.

J. J. V. M. de Vet

NEW FRANCE. The conventional understanding of New France and French Canada in the eighteenth century has been one of a colonial society bound by the strictures of ancien régime France: divine right monarchy, the Roman Catholic Church, and an economic system based on mercantilism. The revolutionary ideas of the

American colonies (1776–1783) and the French Revolution (1789–1799) did little to influence the thought of *Canadiens* living in the St. Lawrence River valley.

More recent scholarship, however, has questioned the rigidity of French Canadian thought. There is evidence of an interest in science, and there are echoes of some of the philosophical writings of the Enlightenment in the official correspondence between the colony and Versailles and, in the post-mortem inventories of colonial merchants and functionaries who died at Quebec. With the appearance of the *Gazette de Québec* (1764) and the *Gazette de Montréal* (1785), reports were circulated of ideas and events from the American colonies and Europe. By the late eighteenth century, essays on discoveries in medicine and science were regular fare for colonial readers. Although many living on the St. Lawrence were illiterate, historians remind us that ideas filtered down from the literate elite to the masses through oral culture, pamphlets, broadsides, and songs.

By the 1770s, clubs such as the Société des Patriotes offered a venue for discussion of religious toleration, individual rights, and representative government. These ideas helped to shape policy in the Quebec Act of 1774 and the Constitutional Act of 1791 (see below). Although most of the people of New France and French Canada were not consumed by revolutionary fervor during the eighteenth century, their lives were touched, nonetheless, by thoughts of individual freedoms and collective decision-making.

New France originated in sixteenth- and seventeenth-century French exploration and settlement in the New World. Between 1608 and 1763, the colony offered France a strategic foothold in North America as well as a resource base for fur, fish, and timber. As the population grew, a market emerged for the products of metropolitan industry and for the exotic produce of the French West Indies. European wars between France and Britain played out in varying degrees in North America, but it was not until the Seven Years' War (1756–1763) that the French colony was seriously challenged. The battle on the Plains of Abraham in the autumn of 1759 and British victories the following summer brought an end to French rule in Canada. With the Treaty of Paris (1763), the French colony became a possession of the British empire.

Before the British conquest, the post-mortem inventories of merchants living at Quebec reveal libraries that included works by Pierre Corneille, Molière, and Michel de Montaigne. Later, during the British period, the writings of Jean Le Rond d'Alembert, Denis Diderot, Samuel Pufendorf, Montesquieu, Jean-Jacques Rousseau, and Voltaire circulated in the town of Quebec.

One can find evidence during the French regime of research in natural science and medicine by a colonial botanist, physician, and zoologist, Michel Sarrazin (1659–1734). For over thirty years, Sarrazin dispatched specimens and research notes on the flora and fauna of New France to Joseph Pitton de Tournefort, a renowned

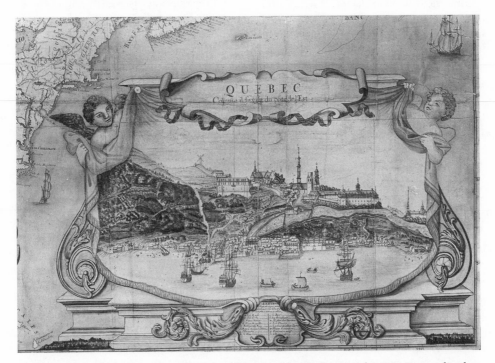

Capital of New France. View of the city of Québec, detail of a map by J.-B. Franquelin, late seventeenth or early eighteenth century. (Musée de la Marine, Paris/Giraudon/Art Resource, NY.)

professor at the Royal Academy of Science in Paris. Many of Sarrazin's findings—for instance, *Sarracenia purpurea*, a plant then thought to be effective in the treatment of smallpox—were published in the *Journal des Savants*.

Following the Treaty of Paris in 1763, British colonial administrators were faced with governing a colony of 75,000 French-speaking Roman Catholics. In the first decade of British rule, the goal was to transform *Canadiens* into English-speaking Protestants governed by English criminal and civil law. By the 1770s, expediency demanded that the Colonial Office change the Canadian constitution to accommodate these earlier settlers. The Quebec Act of 1774, although it did not grant an elected assembly, was liberal in its approach to governing a bilingual population. French civil law was confirmed, and the French language, Roman Catholic religion, and culture were accepted. Catholics were allowed to hold office. Threats to Canadian sovereignty by the American Revolution and an influx of American Loyalist settlers into the St. Lawrence region forced another constitutional change in 1791. By the Constitutional Act, the colony was divided into Upper and Lower Canada. Both Canadians and *Canadiens* were granted elected assemblies and specific rights pertaining to language, religion, and governance.

From 1764 on, colonial newspapers played a role in bringing the Enlightenment to the St. Lawrence. The *Gazette de Québec* and the *Gazette de Montréal* exposed their readers to the ideas of Benjamin Franklin, the philosophes, and the *Encyclopédie* of Diderot and d'Alembert. Essays on medicine and science included "Observations on the Nature of Sleep," "On the Natural History of the Shark," and "On the Theory of Agriculture and the Means of Fertilizing the Soils."

The newspapers also recorded the American and French revolutions. By 1789, they were reporting on a new era of liberty, equality, and fraternity marked by the storming of the Bastille, the abolition of the feudal rights of aristocrats, and the march of women on Versailles. At the Société des Patriotes Club in Montreal (membership 200), glasses were raised to Lafayette and Mirabeau, patriotic songs were sung, and pamphlets were distributed extolling Voltaire's attacks on the clergy. By 1792, however, reporting of the Revolution was more restrained as news emerged of the king's imprisonment, the September massacres, and the outbreak of war. Yet an attempt was made by some in this period to incite revolt among *Canadiens* with a dispatch of broadsheets from the United States calling for a republic and the abolition of clerical tithes. Revolutionary songs and copies of Thomas Paine's *Rights of Man* were spread throughout the province. Working French Canadians, though, never rose up to aid their former countrymen.

Nevertheless, Enlightenment thought did touch some of the people of New France and French Canada during the eighteenth century. The writings of the philosophes were found in colonial libraries and newspapers, and Canadian constitutions, after 1770, offered Canadiens religious and cultural toleration and an early form of self-government.

[*See also* Canada *and* North America.]

BIBLIOGRAPHY

Eccles, W. J. *France in America*. East Lansing, Mich., 1990. A standard work on New France and French Canada to 1783.

Greenwood, F. Murray. *Legacies of Fear: Law and Politics in Quebec in the Era of the French Revolution*. Toronto, 1993. A thoughtful treatment of the relationship of Enlightenment ideas and the shaping of colonial policy.

La Gazette de Québec/The Quebec Gazette. William Brown and Thomas Gilmore, trained in Philadelphia, founded this bilingual colonial newspaper in Québec in 1764; it is available on microfilm in many large libraries.

Lawson, Philip. *The Imperial Challenge: Quebec and Britain in the Age of the American Revolution*. Montreal and Kingston, 1989. A thorough investigation of the tensions in British colonial policy and governance of a French-Canadian, Roman Catholic population.

Wallot, Jean-Pierre. *Un Québec qui bougeait: Trame socio-politique au tournant du XIX siècle*. Quebec, 1973. A solid study of the revolutionary period and Enlightenment ideas.

Young, Kathryn A. "Crown Agent-Canadian Correspondent: Michel Sarrazin and the Académie Royale des Sciences, 1697–1734." *French Historical Studies* 18 (1993), 415–433. A concise study of the research of Michel Sarrazin and his association with the Royal Academy of Paris.

Young, Kathryn A. *Kin, Commerce, Community: Merchants in the Port of Quebec, 1717 to 1745*. New York, 1995. A socio-economic study, with an emphasis on material culture, of the merchant community in the Quebec port.

Young, Kathryn A. "'. . . sauf les perils et fortunes de la mer': Merchant Women in New France and the French Transatlantic Trade, 1713–1746." *Canadian Historical Review* 77 (1996), 388–407. An investigation of female commerce revealing a knowledge of suppliers, market, insurance, and shipping.

KATHRYN A. YOUNG

NEWTON, ISAAC (1642–1727), natural philosopher, biblical scholar, and civil servant.

Newton was born on Christmas Day 1642 into a world of ascendent Puritanism. An explosion of sectarianism, prophetic fervor, and Calvinist moral austerity sent shock waves through England during the earliest years of his life, as did the concomitant upheaval of the Civil Wars. The young lad also saw his domestic world turned upside down. His father, Isaac, an illiterate yeoman, died three months before Newton's birth at Woolsthorpe manor in Lincolnshire. Three years later Newton suffered a second loss when his mother married an elderly clergyman and moved to his parish, leaving Isaac behind. Widowed again in 1653, she returned to Woolsthorpe. In 1655, Isaac was enrolled in King's School, a grammar school in Grantham seven miles to the north. There Newton was

Isaac Newton. (Giraudon/Art Resource, NY.)

fed a diet of Latin heaped on Latin, a helping of Greek, and a pinch of Hebrew, but virtually no mathematics. At the core of his education was a solid grounding in the Word of God and the Protestant faith. Eventually he rose to the top of his class and was encouraged by the schoolmaster to prepare for university. In 1661, he arrived in Cambridge—his home for the next thirty-five years. Unsubstantiated evidence has Newton engaged to his Grantham landlord's daughter. If so, this was soon forgotten as he embarked on the life of a solitary scholar.

Early Career. Newton's mother was better off than many gentlemen, but Newton was enrolled as a lowly sizar, which entailed the performance of menial duties for the fellows and more genteel members of Trinity College, where he matriculated. Here his formal education diverged little from the medieval curriculum and concentrated on Aristotle, Plato, logic, rhetoric, religion, and chronology. Newton, however, soon began to imbibe the new mechanical philosophy of Copernicus, Galileo, Johannes Kepler, René Descartes, Thomas Hobbes, Robert Boyle, and Cambridge's own Henry More. Following their example, he took up experiments and began to carry out observations of the heavenly bodies. Rumor has it that he placed second in the B.A. examinations of 1665; the evidence of his extracurricular readings shows that he had already outstripped most of the tutors in modern learning.

In 1665, the plague descended on Cambridge and the university was closed. Newton returned to Woolsthorpe where his voyage of discovery continued. It was here, Newton said, that he saw the apple fall and received his first insight into universal gravitation, thus laying the foundation for his work in physics. Here he also completed his work on the calculus, allowing him to solve problems involving curves and rates of change of points moving along them, thereby solving elegantly a problem that had long plagued mathematicians. Here he also performed revolutionary optical experiments with refraction that demonstrated the heterogenous nature of light. Excepting a brief return to Cambridge in 1666, he spent the better part of two years at home, a period rightly described as his *anni mirabiles* and one he himself called "the prime of my age for invention."

Back at Cambridge in the spring of 1667, Newton competed successfully for a fellowship at Trinity. His position at Cambridge was now secure. He took his M.A. in 1668 and in 1669 was appointed Lucasian Professor of Mathematics. Although this new academic chair had acquired none of the prestige it enjoys today, it was a step up in rank. He delivered his first lectures on optics.

By 1671, Newton had developed the first working reflecting telescope, which was shown to the Royal Society late that year and afterward to the king himself. In 1672, Newton sent the society his revolutionary discoveries on optics, which were promptly published in the *Philosophical Transactions*, the society's journal. These included his prism experiments and his *experimentum crucis*, which demonstrated that light refracted into the various homogeneous colors of the spectrum does not further divide. Newton was rewarded with both fame and controversy. Robert Hooke, the society's curator of experiments, expressed doubts. Philosophers on the Continent who were unable to replicate the experiments attacked him. Impatient and hostile, he charged his critics with placing too much weight on philosophizing and not enough on experiment. Nor was it lost on him that his chief European opponents were Jesuits, a society the anti-Catholic Newton believed was given to cavil and dispute.

Newton had by now been attracted to the crucible of alchemy. He had taken notes on works by such "chymists" as Boyle in the mid-1660s; in 1669, he bought two furnaces, some chemicals, and the six-volume alchemical compendium *Theatrum Chemicum* (Theater of Chemistry), and began to experiment himself. Soon he became involved in secretive alchemical networks and copied out unpublished treatises passed around in these circles. The precise nature of his alchemical studies is debated, but he apparently saw in alchemy evidence of divine activity in matter that could serve as an antidote to the extreme mechanization evident in such philosophies as Cartesianism. He drank deeply of alchemy's religious symbolism and agreed with its teachings about a general *renovatio* in both matter and humanity. Some scholars now believe that Newton's concept of attraction owed much to alchemical thought.

Religious Thought. Newton's fellowship required him to seek ordination within eight years. As the deadline neared, he earnestly began to study theology, prophecy, and church history. Newton scoured the fathers of the early church, analyzed the creeds, and combed the annals of ecclesiastical history. The result was his conclusion that the doctrine of the Trinity was a pagan corruption imposed on primitive Christianity in the fourth century by Athanasius. Newton faced a dilemma: A man of conscience, he could not now take holy orders, but to express the reason why would have led to his immediate and ignominious expulsion from the university. Newton had been prepared to resign when a special dispensation came from Charles II exempting Lucasian professors from ordination. Newton was safe. Nevertheless, until his dying day he lived the dangerous life of a secret heretic, outwardly conforming to Anglicanism while inwardly denying many of its articles.

Newton looked forward to a thorough reformation that would restore primitive Christianity—a stance that signals his distance from most of his Protestant contemporaries. For more than half a century, he studied history and theology to purge Christianity of its corruptions. This research exhibited his commitment to the Renaissance commonplace that the ancients had once possessed true knowledge about God and the world. Retrieving this *prisca sapientia* was his great life's work. A massive manuscript of ecclesiastical history was but one product of this effort. He also sifted through biblical and talmudic sources to reconstruct the plan of the Jerusalem temple because he believed that it and its rituals provided a backdrop to the visions of the Book of Revelation, but also because he thought it and other ancient temples modeled a heliocentric solar system—knowledge lost in antiquity.

Newton discovered in the Scriptures that the Father alone is God. Jesus Christ, preexistent and miraculously born, was God's son but not ontologically God in any Trinitarian sense. Although Newton's Christ is not to be worshiped or invoked in prayer, he occupies an elevated position through the atonement wrought by his blood and because of his apocalyptic role at the end of time. Newton had nothing but disdain for the monks and Trinitarians whom he thought had corrupted the pure teaching of God with metaphysics and doctrinally novel terms. These same agents of false doctrine introduced the unbiblical notion of the immortality of the soul to underpin Catholic saint worship. For Newton, eternal life is granted to the faithful only after resurrection. Nor did the orthodox demonology stand before Newton's reformation. Evil spirits came to represent distempers of the mind, the Devil, human lust. Far from pointing to some incipient rationalism, his rejection of demons likely derives from the logic of his radically monotheistic belief in a God whose absolute dominion does not brook lesser rivals. In religious outlook, Newton's views resemble some elements of contemporary Non-Conformity or Dissenting thought and show strong doctrinal analogies with Judaism, pre-Nicene Christianity and contemporary biblicist anti-Trinitarian Socinianism.

Newton was not only interested in the past but in the future foretold in the Christian prophecies. In the 1670s, he wrote the first of several large prophetic treatises in which he sought to uncover the symbolism of the Books of Daniel and Revelation, along with their fulfillment in history past and future. Newton was no Deist, but rather someone who found in the exact and literal fulfillment of prophecies a powerful argument for the existence of the God of the Bible. Strongly premillenarian in eschatology, he believed in the return of Christ, the restoration of the Jews to Israel, the rebuilding of the Temple, and the coming of the Kingdom of God on Earth—for which he thought believers should pray daily. All this research was carried out in private. Not only was denial of the Trinity a punishable offense, but Newton believed that the higher truths of religion were not fit for the masses. He did, however, reveal his heresies to similarly minded friends such as John Locke, who described him as a "very valuable man not onely for his wonderful skill in Mathematicks but in divinity too and his great knowledg [*sic*] in the Scriptures where in I know few his equals." The two men also discussed biblical prophecy. In the early 1690s, Newton came close to publishing anonymously and on the Continent an anti-Trinitarian treatise through Locke. This was suppressed at the last moment and, aside from some rumors that circulated late in his life, few contemporaries knew that the great Isaac Newton was a heretic.

***De Motu* and *Principia*.** In August 1684, Edmond Halley laid before Newton a problem that he had discussed with Robert Hooke and Sir Christopher Wren. Could Newton demonstrate why a planet should move in an elliptical orbit when acted upon by a force of attraction from the sun that decreases in an inverse proportion to the square of the distance between the two bodies? Newton said he had solved the problem but he could not then find his calculations. In November, Halley received from Newton a nine-page manuscript set of calculations entitled *De Motu Corporum in Gyrum* (Concerning the Movement of Revolving Bodies). Halley immediately recognized it as nothing less than the beginnings of a new physics. It built upon Newton's study of comets in 1680 and 1682, which had convinced him that heavenly bodies meet no resistance from an ether, and that comets, like planets, travel about the sun in closed elliptical paths. *De Motu* shows that Newton had finally dropped the Cartesian doctrine of fluid vortices. *De Motu* also spurred Newton into giving a more complete answer to Halley's question. After a flurry of activity that lasted almost two years, he finished his *Philosophiae Naturalis Principia Mathematica* (Mathematical Principles of Natural Philosophy, 1687, later revised editions in 1713, 1726).

Book I lays out the foundations of Newton's system of mechanics, treating the movement of bodies without resistance and identifying gravity as the force operating on moving bodies in space. Book II tackles the problem of the motion of fluids and the movement of solid bodies through fluids. Book III demonstrates how the law of gravitation operates consistently on moving bodies throughout the universe. Included in this great book is his inverse-square law of gravitation and his now famous three laws of motion. Newton had produced a new general theory of dynamics rooted in empirical observations but set out deductively in mathematical language. It is the most revolutionary book in the history of science.

What most readers did not know was that Newton saw his magnum opus less as a book of discovery than the recovery of ancient wisdom long since lost. What is more, Newton believed his universe could only be sustained through the providence of God and that his physics confirmed the argument from design. In a 1692 letter to Richard Bentley, he acknowledged: "When I wrote my treatise about our Systeme I had an eye upon such Principles as might work with considering men for the beleife [*sic*] of a Deity & nothing can rejoyce me more than to find it usefull for that purpose." His theology was present in other ways as well. The four rules of reasoning he developed through the three editions of the work, rules often seen as emblematic of scientific induction, were modeled upon sixteen rules of prophetic interpretation he had drafted in the previous decade. He relied on induction because he believed God guaranteed simplicity in nature. In the General Scholium appended in 1713, Newton stated explicitly that discoursing about God "does certainly belong to Experimental Philosophy." This was all of a piece for a man who believed that an integral constituent of the original religion was the study of nature. For Newton there was no cognitive barrier between the study of God and the study of His creation.

For some readers the *Principia* itself seemed divine. Halley summed up the reaction when he declared in his introductory ode: "Nearer to the gods no mortal may approach." For most, the work seemed almost impossibly difficult. Impenetrability is a feature of many revolutionary works, but the difficulty with the *Principia* was intentional. Newton later confessed that he had "designedly

made his Principia abstruse" so as to sideline "little Smatterers in Mathematicks" even while he reached the "able Mathematicians." As with his heretical theology, Newton revealed his analysis only to the adepts.

The publication of the *Principia* heralded a more assertive and public phase of Newton's career. In 1687, as James II moved to introduce Catholics into the English universities, Newton defended the right of his university not to grant an M.A. degree to a Benedictine monk. In 1689, after the Glorious Revolution, he was elected a member of Parliament for Cambridge University. He thus sat in the Convocation Parliament and voted with the majority to declare the throne vacant, a necessary step to the accession of William and Mary. During this period, Newton had his first sustained contact with the upper echelons of London society. Soon the grand metropolis would become his home. Newton arrived in London in 1696 to become warden of the Royal Mint. In 1699, he became its master, a position he held until his death. In both posts he revealed a gift for administration. He spent long hours at the mint, dramatically increasing production and directing it through a major recoinage. Counterfeiters were prosecuted with the same zeal with which he wrote against doctrinal forgery; several "coiners" were sent to the gallows under his regime. In 1703, with his old foe Hooke dead, Newton was elected president of the Royal Society. Newton set out at once to restore its intellectual vitality and redirect its focus back to experiments and natural philosophy. In 1705, he was knighted to help him oust a Tory incumbent member of Parliament at Cambridge in the general election of that year. This he failed to do, but the title and honor remained.

In 1704, Newton published his *Opticks* (revised editions in 1706, 1718, 1721, and 1730). Based on his Lucasian optical lectures, a 1675 paper, and some new material, Newton had waited to release this book until the death of Hooke, who had criticized his earlier efforts in optics. Written in English and more experimental than theoretical, this book reached a great international audience and became the methodological guide of enlightened empirical scientists. Like the *Principia*, it proceeded in a geometrical fashion from definitions and axioms resting on empirical studies to deductively drawn conclusions. In its Queries, or speculative questions about nature, particularly those on ether, heat, light, and forces of attraction and repulsion, Newton set out the research programs of many into the next two generations.

Assertiveness showed in other ways. He ruled the Royal Society like an autocrat, treating it as his institution. In 1713, he appended to the second edition of the *Principia* the General Scholium, which affirmed God's continual intervening providence in nature as well as an encoded critique of Trinitarian hermeneutics. The Scholium also attacked Descartes's theory of vortices and Gottfried Wilhelm von Leibniz's cosmos, which did not require particular providence for its operation. A philosophical debate between Leibniz and the Newtonian Samuel Clarke ensued. Newton also challenged Leibniz's claim to priority in the discovery of calculus. Petty disputes continued with John Flamsteed, the Astronomer Royal, until he, like Hooke and Leibniz, succumbed to mortality.

Newton's Legacy. Newton's own end came on 20 March 1727. Anticipating his death, he evidently began to think of his image in posterity. Before his final illness he burned a number of his manuscripts. His last days were spent preparing for publication his *Chronology of the Ancient Kingdoms Amended* (1728), a work that excised four centuries from received chronologies of ancient Greece. As an incredulous Voltaire reported, Newton confessed on his deathbed that he had "never had intimacies with a woman." He also refused the sacrament. No act of irreligion, this was likely a rejection of the idolatrous, Trinitarian Church of England in whose communion he had so long uneasily remained. These were private matters, however. Newton's funeral was a very public affair conducted with pomp and ostentation. Interred at Westminster Abbey, six noblemen served as his pallbearers. Voltaire, in attendance, marveled that he had been "buried like a king who had benefitted his subjects." The monument erected over his tomb shows Newton reclining on four books representing the range of his thought: *Opticks*, *Principia*, theology, and chronology. The inscription below concludes with the doxology: "Let Mortals rejoice That there has existed such and so great an Ornament to the Human Race."

The Enlightenment conception of heavenly bodies in the Newtonian planetary system traveling unhindered through empty space guided by nothing but well-ordered laws is still dominant today. Newton seemed the perfect icon for a rational, secular age, but this image is a mirage. The materialistic version of the universe constructed by the philosophes is one from which the great man himself would have shrunk back in horror. Isaac Newton was not an Enlightenment man. Newton's firm conviction in the argument from design, his fierce opposition to skepticism and atheism, along with his fervent belief that he had recovered the lost wisdom of the ancients, and, above all, his profound piety, biblicism, and prophetic faith reveal his great distance from the Enlightenment. Even in Augustan Britain, where the Enlightenment included many with a religious orientation, his heretical thought and commitment to the *prisca sapientia* tradition remained largely hidden. Newton was known in Britain primarily through popular broadsheets, simplified textbooks, and coffeehouse demonstrations of his optics and physics. These accounts rarely focused on the faith of the man, and the great outpouring of verse commemorating his life

in the early years following his death is more deistic than Christian in tone. The Newton venerated in eighteenth-century Britain differed only by degrees from the Newton apotheosized in France. For most, Newton was a celebrated natural philosopher, a man of affairs, but not a religious thinker. Ironically, by keeping most of his theology private, Newton himself bears part of the blame for his posthumous secular legacy.

When Voltaire in his *English Letters* (1733, later published as *Lettres philosophiques*, 1734) mentioned Newton's denial of the Trinity, he believed he was demonstrating the great man's rationalism, even though Newton's *Observations on the Prophecies of Daniel, and the Apocalypse of St. John*, a text that played a minor role in the rise of Protestant fundamentalism, appeared the same year. It was easy to ignore this work or to suggest, as did Antonio Conti, that Newton was brilliant only as a natural philosopher and not as a historian and chronologist; there his failings were all too apparent. Others explained the theology away. Pierre-Simon de Laplace and Jean-Baptiste Biot publicized a story that Newton had suffered an intellectual derangement after his 1693 breakdown, after which he turned to the study of theology. The Enlightenment desacralized the Newtonian universe. This process culminated in the work of Laplace who, hailed as the "Newton of France," famously told Napoleon that in his own physics he had no need of the hypothesis of God. Only now are scholars beginning to study Newton's manuscript corpus of one million words on alchemy and four million on theology to reconstruct a holistic view of the man in which his theology and natural philosophy are seen as equally important elements of the same grand unified project, the restoration of man's original pristine knowledge of God and the world.

[*See also* Ancients and Moderns; Astronomy; Chemistry; Clarke, Samuel; Electricity and Magnetism; Empiricism; Epistemology; Fontenelle, Bernard Le Bovier de; Hales, Stephen; Leibniz, Gottfried Wilhelm von; Locke, John; Meteorology; Millenarianism; Natural Philosophy and Science; Natural Religion; Newtonianism; Optics; Physics; Rationalism; *and* Royal Society of London.]

BIBLIOGRAPHY

Dobbs, Betty Jo Teeter. *The Janus Faces of Genius: The Role of Alchemy in Newton's Thought*. Cambridge, 1991.

Fara, Patricia. *Newton: The Making of Genius*. London, 2002.

Fauvel, John, Raymond Flood, Michael Shortland, and Robin Wilson, eds. *Let Newton Be! A New Perspective on His Life and Works*. Oxford, 1988.

Force, James E., and Richard H. Popkin, eds. *The Books of Nature and Scripture: Recent Essays on Natural Philosophy, Theology, and Biblical Criticism in the Netherlands of Spinoza's Time and the British Isles of Newton's Time*. Dordrecht, Netherlands, 1994.

Force, James E., and Richard H. Popkin. *Essays on the Context, Nature, and Influence of Isaac Newton's Theology*. Dordrecht, Netherlands, 1990.

Force, James E., and Richard H. Popkin, eds. *Newton and Religion: Context, Nature, and Influence.* Dordrecht, Netherlands, 1999.

Guerlac, Henry. *Newton on the Continent.* Ithaca, N.Y., 1981.

Guicciardini, Niccolò. *Reading the* Principia: *The Debate on Newton's Mathematical Methods for Natural Philosophy from 1687 to 1736.* Cambridge, 1999.

Hahn, Roger. "Laplace and the Vanishing Role of God in the Physical Universe." In *The Analytic Spirit: Essays in the History of Science in Honor of Henry Guerlac,* edited by Harry Woolf, pp. 85–95. Ithaca, N.Y., 1981.

Iliffe, Robert. "'Is He Like Other Men?' The Meaning of the *Principia mathematica,* and the Author as Idol." In *Culture and Society in the Stuart Restoration,* edited by G. Maclean, pp. 159–176. Cambridge, 1995.

Mamiani, Maurizio. "To Twist the Meaning: Newton's *Regulae philosophandi* Revisted." In *Isaac Newton's Natural Philosophy,* edited by Jed Z. Buchwald and I. Bernard Cohen, pp. 3–14. Cambridge, Mass., 2001.

Mandelbrote, Scott. "'A Duty of the Greatest Moment': Isaac Newton and the Writing of Biblical Criticism." *The British Journal for the History of Science* 26 (1993), 281–302.

Manuel, Frank. *Isaac Newton, Historian.* Cambridge, 1963.

Manuel, Frank. *The Religion of Isaac Newton.* Oxford, 1974.

Newton, Isaac. *The Correspondence of Sir Isaac Newton.* Edited by H. W. Turnbull, J. F. Scott, A. Rupert Hall, and Laura Tilling. 7 vols. Cambridge, 1959–1977.

Newton, Isaac. *The* Principia: *Mathematical Principles of Natural Philosophy.* A new translation by I. Bernard Cohen and Anne Whitman, assisted by Julia Budenz. Berkeley, Calif., 1999.

Schaffer, Simon. "Newton's Comets and the Transformation of Astrology." In *Astrology, Science, and Society: Historical Essays,* edited by Patrick Curry, pp. 219–243. Woodbridge, U.K., 1987.

Snobelen, Stephen D. "Isaac Newton, Heretic: The Strategies of a Nicodemite." *The British Journal for the History of Science* 32 (1999), 381–419.

Stewart, Larry. *The Rise of Public Science: Rhetoric, Technology, and Natural Philosophy in Newtonian Britain, 1660–1750.* Cambridge, 1992.

Stewart, Larry. "Seeing Through the Scholium: Religion and Reading Newton in the Eighteenth Century." *History of Science* 34 (1996), 123–165.

Westfall, Richard S. *Never at Rest: A Biography of Isaac Newton.* Cambridge, 1980.

STEPHEN D. SNOBELEN

NEWTONIANISM. By 1765, according to the *Encyclopédie* of Diderot and d'Alembert, Newtonianism had already acquired five distinct meanings. During the subsequent quarter of a millennium, the word has become still further loaded with ambiguities as new interpretations of Newton's ideas have been generated. Like a religious creed, a Newtonian ideology founded in the first half of the eighteenth century has continued to consolidate, and Newtonianism has become almost synonymous with a scientific approach not only to the physical world but also to living beings and social systems. Most basically, during the Enlightenment the term *Newtonianism* signified adopting a rational, empirical approach in order to model nature and society with mathematical laws.

Despite his emphasis on the objectivity of experimental demonstration, Newton himself employed many rhetorical strategies to make his ideas convincing; similarly, *Newtonianism* was a polemical label rather than the designation of a single, coherent philosophy. Because Newton rapidly became an important figurehead, many authors claimed authority by describing themselves as Newtonians yet produced theories that differed greatly from one another. This diversity was facilitated by the inconsistencies, mistakes, and vague phrasings in Newton's own writings; many so-called Newtonians argued vehemently for one aspect of his natural philosophy while denying others.

Although very few people actually read Newton's *Philosophiae naturalis principia mathematica* (1687), its central arguments became the major theme of Newtonian ideology. Newton's coup was to introduce mathematical order and predictability to the universe. He unified the heavens and the earth by formulating a simple mathematical law that described the rotation of the Sun and the planets, as well as falling apples, and, with his laws of motion, colliding billiard balls. Because his gravitational attraction successfully described so many phenomena, it seemed possible that more elusive problems might be solved—electricity, magnetism, and chemical reactions, or even the behavior of living organisms and social groups.

Newtonianism also owed much to the *Opticks* (1704), which, belying its title, covered a wide range of topics. Here Newton spelled out his insistence on experimental research. Experimentation had become increasingly important during the seventeenth century, but Newton made his experimental approach a distinguishing feature of his philosophy. His famous rejection of hypotheses and his insistence on proof through combining reason with experimental demonstration became hallmarks of Newtonianism. Newtonianism's commitment to experiment also implied a rejection of biblical doctrine and Aristotelian philosophy. Newton had been writing with his philosophical rivals Gottfried Wilhelm von Leibniz and René Descartes in mind, and particularly during the first half of the eighteenth century, chauvinistic Newtonians emphasized that rational experimentation guaranteed the superiority of Newtonianism over the Leibnizian and Cartesian doctrines. As Newton became elevated into a cult hero, natural philosophers who eclectically combined elements from many sources—including Descartes and Leibniz—strategically pledged allegiance to Newtonianism.

The growth of Newton's international renown was intertwined with the dramatic increase in the status of natural philosophy during the eighteenth century. During his lifetime, his own rational, experimental approach became generally accepted, and his subsequent rise to fame corresponded with the development of a scientific, industrialized society. The statue of Newton in Westminster Abbey, completed in 1731, shows how his contemporaries wanted him to be celebrated. His elbow rests on four tomes, to commemorate the *Principia*, the *Opticks*, and his studies of theology and ancient chronology; below, industrious cherubs coin money, to reflect his long reign at the Mint. Less than a century later, however, his image had been retailored to fit a scientific role model. As propagandists for the new scientific disciplines converted him into a heroic father figure, they succeeded in marginalizing his many other activities, particularly his extensive alchemical research. Concerned to promote their own interests, they also burnished Newton's reputation as England's greatest scientific genius. By the end of the eighteenth century, it was almost impossible for a self-professed anti-Newtonian to be taken seriously.

Patterns of Reception. Newton first achieved prominence with his 1672 article on optics, which generated

Newtonian Treatise. Frontispiece from Isaac Newton's *Method of Fluxion and Infinite Series*. English translation by John Colson (London, 1736). (Prints and Photographs Division, Library of Congress.)

great controversy in England and abroad. In contrast, the *Principia* of 1687 was forbiddingly complex, yet it rapidly established his international reputation as a brilliant scholar. Led by David Gregory, a Scottish mathematician who taught at Edinburgh and at Oxford, a small, protective clique in Scotland and England worked hard to promote Newton's ideas. As president of the Royal Society from 1703 to 1727, Newton himself exerted patronage, supervised experiments to vindicate and develop his suggestions, and ensured that his disciples disseminated his ideas throughout Europe.

By the early eighteenth century, the experimental methodology enshrined in the *Opticks* had essentially been universally adopted. For several decades, Newton's theoretical speculations (disguised as the *Opticks'* "Quaeries") provided the basic experimental agenda for natural philosophers. Broadly speaking, British support for Newton was associated with Latitudinarian Whigs, while opposition was most marked among Tory High Church groups. Important exceptions to this general pattern existed; for instance, a small group of Scottish Jacobites and Tories were successful proponents, and such eminent English Tories as Samuel Johnson condemned speculation yet admired Newton. Debates with eminent critics such as George Berkeley and Leibniz, now famous as philosophers, were often conducted in abusive terms. At Cambridge, Newton's allies—notably Richard Bentley, Master of Trinity College—ensured that Newtonian natural philosophy became a standard part of the undergraduate curriculum. At Oxford, however—despite early lectures given by Newton's ardent supporter, John Keill—the University mostly retained an Aristotelian approach, and at midcentury it spawned the Hutchinsonian movement. This small yet vocal group (named after John Hutchinson, author of *Moses' Principia*, 1724) opposed Newton's ideas largely on religious grounds, but it was effectively silenced by the strategies of Newtonian propagandists.

Outside the universities, Bentley was also involved in the annual Boyle Lectures, many of which influentially argued that Newton's philosophy demonstrated God's benevolent design. Numerous other lecturers, authors, and translators made simplified versions of Newton's theories and experiments accessible to wide audiences, playing a vital role in establishing a Newtonian hegemony. For example, the ex-Cambridge mathematician William Whiston collated some of Newton's unpublished papers into a mathematics textbook and lectured in London on Newton's natural philosophy as well as his millenarian theology; the physician Henry Pemberton edited the influential third edition (1726) of the *Principia* and was the first to produce a general introduction combining Newton's optics, mechanics, and cosmology; and Andrew

Motte published an English translation (1729) of the *Principia* in a small, cheap format. John Desaguliers, an Oxford clergyman and entrepreneur, was particularly influential: in addition to his own research, through his lectures, books, and translations he strongly encouraged the dissemination of Newton's ideas throughout Europe, and through his engineering innovations, he demonstrated the value of Newtonian experimental philosophy for technological projects, thus bonding Newtonianism with commercial and national interests.

As in Britain, European responses were affected by religious and political attitudes. Cartesian ideas persisted in many Catholic countries, especially where educational institutions were controlled by Jesuits, who feared that Newtonian philosophy encouraged the spread of materialism and determinism. In France, this rejection was heightened by chauvinist loyalties. Thus, after his funeral *éloge* to Newton at the Académie Royale, Bernard le Bovier de Fontenelle was attacked for comparing Newton with France's intellectual hero, Descartes. English victory was symbolically assured in 1737, when a French expedition to Lapland confirmed—albeit on insecure evidence—that the theories of Newton rather than Descartes correctly predicted the exact shape of the earth. Although Jesuit resistance continued into the 1770s, influential writers successfully campaigned for French conversion to Newtonianism. Jean Le Rond d'Alembert placed forceful endorsements of Newtonianism in the *Encyclopédie*; Voltaire published a widely read, if slightly garbled, introduction to Newton's philosophy; and Émilie du Châtelet, a brilliant and independent scholar, added a lucid commentary to her 1759 translation of the *Principia*. By the end of the century, the mathematical astronomer Pierre Laplace judged it advantageous to present himself as a Newtonian, and even though his theories differed greatly from Newton's own, Laplacian determinism was often equated with Newtonianism.

In the German-speaking lands, many natural philosophers remained loyal to Leibniz. The bitter priority debate between Newton and Leibniz about the invention of calculus owed much to political antagonisms aroused by the Hanoverian succession to the English throne, and it was continued by their supporters after their deaths. At the St. Petersburg Academy, the mathematician Leonhard Euler related with relish that Leibniz's supporters had been vanquished by the Newtonians at midcentury, but here as elsewhere, so-called Newtonians blended precepts from many sources.

In contrast, during the first half of the century, Protestant Holland was a vital center for transmitting Newtonian philosophy. At Leiden University, Willem Jacob 'sGravesande's student textbook of 1720 explained Newton's philosophy through original experimental demonstrations, using wooden devices that became important teaching aides. Written in Latin, it was accessible all over Europe and was soon translated into English, thus affecting the pattern of Newtonianism in Britain. Slightly later, the experimenter Peter van Musschenbroek also published educational books on Newton in Latin; translated into French, these significantly reinforced positive attitudes toward Newtonianism in France.

Gravitational Attraction and Cosmology. Newton's universe was composed of small impenetrable particles, and although many earlier philosophers had also proposed corpuscular models, in the eighteenth century the term *Newtonianism* often referred to a mechanical, corpuscular view of nature. One novelty of Newton's system was his suggestion that God had given these particles what he called "active principles," so that they could attract—or perhaps repel—one another. The nature of attraction remained hotly contested. Critics accused Newton and his followers of merely disguising an occult force with a new name, or of attributing to ordinary matter spiritual powers that belong only to God. Throughout the century, in some hostile circles Newtonianism was inextricably linked with materialism and atheism.

Early work focused on attempting to quantify short-range forces between particles. Newton's own colleagues—notably, his experimental assistant Francis Hauksbee, the clergyman Stephen Hales, and Desaguliers—investigated corpuscular theories by experimenting on topics such as capillary action, plant growth, and the behavior of gases. However, simple corpuscular models became increasingly untenable. In 1743, Bryan Robinson, a Dublin professor of physics, published his mathematical version of Newton's speculations about an "aether" composed of small particles that could, in some ill-defined way, exhibit both attractive and repulsive behavior. Theories proliferated of aethers with various strange characteristics, especially to explain heat, light, and electricity, for which they provided a convenient but vague means of accounting for God's interaction with passive matter. Other natural philosophers—notably the radical chemist Joseph Priestley and the Jesuit Roger Boscovich—proposed models of matter in which force played a more important role. By the early nineteenth century, diverse forces and aethers had been postulated that bore scant resemblance to one another or to Newton's, but laid claims to Newtonian origins.

One of the perceived strengths of Newton's model was its ability to predict celestial phenomena. In particular, Newton and his followers wrested public authority from astrologers because his theories successfully foretold the return of comets, previously interpreted as signs of God's vengeance on the sinful. During the eighteenth century,

Newtonian astronomers repeatedly designed observational procedures to test his mathematical laws, and they developed new theories to clarify mistakes, omissions, and obscurities in Newton's own work. In addition to the expeditions corroborating the shape of the earth, other key events included confirmation of the moon's motion, the return of Halley's comet in 1759, and Laplace's mathematical demonstration of the stability of the solar system.

The image of a clockwork, mechanical universe is often associated with Newtonianism, but this metaphor had been prevalent well before the *Principia* appeared. Rapid British enthusiasm for Newton's cosmology was linked to its political and theological interpretations. In England, Newton's orderly solar system conformed to Hanoverian Whig social ideals: just as the planets revolved separately around the Sun, so too Britain's independent citizens could operate freely yet be harmoniously bonded together under the patriarchal care of a benevolent ruler. Bentley and other promoters emphasized the providential aspects of Newtonian natural philosophy, describing a universe whose stability was maintained through God's periodic intervention, possibly through comets. As Leibniz and other critics pointed out, though, such maintenance procedures implied either that supernatural miracles were occurring—an explanation that undermined rationality—or else that God was an inferior clockmaker who had not been able to initiate His universe satisfactorily, an implication that detracted from God's omnipotence.

As natural philosophers gradually accepted gravity's existence without worrying too much about its nature, Newtonianism came to imply a universe that functioned without God's constant supervision. In post-revolutionary France, where Newton's stable, predictable universe provided a metaphorical contrast with the country's political turmoil, Laplace provided a new version of Newtonian cosmology, from which—as Napoleon remarked—God had completely vanished. In this deterministic model, which was often equated with Newtonianism, the movement of tiny independent point particles is governed by the forces acting between them. Since Laplace's universe is determined by abstract, ruthless laws of nature, in principle its state can be accurately known and predicted.

Developed further in the early nineteenth century by Laplace's important research group, this brand of Newtonianism dominated physics in Germany as well as in France. Nevertheless, other Newtonian approaches were also crucially important. For instance, during the 1780s, Joseph-Louis Lagrange, Euler's French successor at Berlin, used calculus to develop Newton's ideas in a different mathematical direction, and his abstract force-based model underpinned important changes in celestial mechanics. Slightly later, Joseph Fourier also moved away from Laplacean centrally directed forces to consider phenomena such as heat conduction from a more practical perspective, an engineering approach that profoundly influenced British work on electromagnetism and other topics. By the early twentieth century, Newtonianism had altered and splintered so dramatically that, as Bertrand Russell quipped, even Newton himself "was not a strict Newtonian."

Mathematics. Because Newton was so famous, the term *Newtonianism* often acquired the broader meaning of using mathematical tools to tackle problems in natural philosophy, as advertised by the *Principia*'s programmatic title. As in other aspects of Newtonianism, far deeper transformations were occurring in mathematics than could be effected by a single individual. Traditionally, philosophers had been interested in causal, qualitative explanations of natural phenomena, while mathematicians focused on quantitative, descriptive accounts. While gentlemanly scholars concentrated on abstract topics of pure mathematics, skilled artisans—often called "mixed mathematicians"—used arithmetic and geometry to solve practical problems. During the seventeenth and eighteenth centuries, these disciplinary and social boundaries changed. Initially in France and later in Britain, mathematical techniques became central to natural philosophy, giving rise to the new field of mathematical physics; and as entrepreneurial philosophers such as Desaguliers used their learning to make money, Newtonian mathematics also became fundamental to engineering, which became an academic subject in its own right.

Newton was an enormously accomplished mathematician, but many of his manuscripts on algebra and analysis were published only posthumously and so did not play nearly such an important role in promoting Newtonian ideologies as did the more geometrical techniques appearing in the *Principia*. Before that book's publication, Newton had already developed his version of calculus, an analytical algorithm to describe changing quantities, or fluxions. However, because of his concern to establish continuity with Greek knowledge, when he addressed his public audiences he translated this language of fluxions back into geometry. Leibniz devised a related method with a different notation, and the priority row between them resonated throughout the eighteenth century. Newtonians on the Continent took advantage of Euler's powerful post-Leibnizian version of calculus to provide heavily mathematized versions of natural philosophy. In Britain, where Newtonians were swayed not only by Newton's direct example but also by the religiously based objections to infinitesimal quantities expressed by critics such as Berkeley, natural philosophers tended to spurn analytical methods.

Optics. By the time that Newton first published his *Opticks* in 1704, his earlier papers had helped to change attitudes toward the value of experimental evidence. He initially aroused international hostility by his revolutionary proposition that the Sun's white light is not homogeneous but is a mixture of the basic colors of the rainbow. As he continued to experiment, he also consolidated his enormously influential new style of research, which advocated reducing the role of hypotheses by relying on experimental and mathematical demonstrations. Consequently, debates about Newton's optics focused on experimental issues; in particular, his so-called crucial experiment, in which he refracted light through two successive prisms, became a powerful rhetorical tool for converting critics to Newtonianism.

By around 1720, most natural philosophers throughout Europe accepted the fundamental principles of Newton's color theory, and his ideas also greatly influenced artists, many of whom were interested in combining concepts of musical harmony with visual aesthetics. Newton's circular diagram showing seven primary colors provided the model for several different color systems and underpinned early techniques of color printing; still more significantly, toward the end of the century painters and natural philosophers developed his concept of color complementarity. Although many artists disagreed with the order and number of his primary colors, even his poetic critic William Blake painted Newtonian rainbows. The most outspoken of Newton's Romantic opponents was the German author Johann Wolfgang von Goethe, then renowned for his new science of vision, who vituperatively rejected Newton's chromatic theories. Deliberately incorporating the subjective experiences of observers, Goethe railed against Newtonian attempts to achieve detached objectivity and to separate the human and the physical worlds. Taken very seriously in Germany, Goethe's criticisms also influenced English thought during the early nineteenth century, most importantly through the philosophical writings of Samuel Taylor Coleridge.

Newton's color theories and experimental demonstrations became central to optics, but his theories about the nature of light were less successful. Although his arguments lacked detailed evidence and mathematical precision, Newton clung to an emission or corpuscular theory. Especially during the first half of the eighteenth century, his followers tried to answer critics by developing metaphorical models based on minute grains of sand or ballistic mathematics, but after Euler published his wave theory of light in 1746 and as aether models proliferated, simple projectile theories lost support. At the end of the century, the experimental lecturer Thomas Young developed a wave model based on vibrations carried through an all-pervasive aether. Despite this blatant overthrow of Newton's corpuscular model, Young still claimed to found his ideas on Newton's own, a good example of how powerfully Newtonian ideology was entrenched in England. In France from 1815 on, the research papers on diffraction produced by Augustin Fresnel and other physicists in Laplace's group definitively established the primacy of wave theories; like Young, many nineteenth-century scientists tried to accommodate this embarrassing conclusion within a Newtonian framework.

The Living World. Struck by Newton's success at explaining the physical universe, many scholars claimed to adopt Newtonian methods to describe the characteristics of living organisms and of human minds and societies. With varying degrees of mathematization, they explored the possibilities of establishing regular laws to bring order to the biological, psychological, and social realms.

Some of Newton's contemporaries immediately extended his work to describe the human body mechanically, and the British school of "iatromathematics" flourished during the first third of the century. Searching for the facts of life in the short-range forces between particles, Newtonian physicians such as George Cheyne (1671–1743) conceived the body as a hydraulic system filled with moving fluids whose behavior could be explained mathematically. Cheyne's most influential successor was another religious physician, David Hartley, who, developing Newton's aetherial speculations, suggested that vibrations were transmitted between the brain and the body through a nervous fluid. Hartley's psychological theories were developed by biologists and social reformers throughout Europe. Following the lead of the naturalist Georges-Louis Leclerc de Buffon, from midcentury French researchers trying to account for the mystery of life explicitly adopted Newtonian principles. Drawing close analogies between physiological, physical, and mathematical unknowable properties, they invoked ill-defined powers to describe the distinguishing features of living organisms, much as Newton had used gravity to explain the universe.

Describing himself as the Newton of the human mind, the philosopher David Hume set out "to introduce the experimental method of reasoning into moral subjects." Especially in Scotland, other moral philosophers and the political economist Adam Smith explicitly embraced Newtonian experimentalism and modeled their theories on Newton's gravitational attraction and law-governed cosmology. Henceforth, society was to be analyzed methodically and given foundations drawn from nature rather than from Aristotelian and theological texts. Although their quantitative approach was also stimulated by other developments, Newtonianism often provided a convenient rhetorical label to legitimate their work. Poems and pictures reveal how pervasively Newtonian metaphors of bonding, regularity, and illumination permeated British

Enlightenment thought. Tributes to Newtonian rationality also abounded among the many French social reformers (such as Jean-Antoine-Nicolas de Caritat Condorcet) who sought to derive lawlike models for human behavior from one or two basic characteristics. The utopian socialists Henri Saint-Simon and Charles Fourier portrayed themselves as Newton's successors, and Newtonianism continued to underpin social planning and models of human behavior during the nineteenth century.

The Cult of Newton. The grip of Newtonianism on Enlightenment activities in so many diverse areas was inextricably linked not only to the increasing legitimation of science but also to the growing cult of Newton himself. Now universally celebrated as England's greatest scientific genius, Newton has become iconic both of national achievement and of scientific creativity, even though the word *scientist* was not invented until more than a century after his death. It was during the Enlightenment period that Newton's swelling personal fame contributed to fundamental transformations in beliefs and practices that affected the whole of European and American society.

As Voltaire remarked, in 1727 Newton was given a funeral fit for a king. By then, although not yet famous in Europe, Newton was celebrated in England for his theories on gravity and optics, his long presidency of the Royal Society, his innovative regime as Master of the Mint, and his modifications of ancient chronology. Outside elite circles, however, Newton was less well known than Alexander Pope, the poet and essayist renowned for his wit and his Latin translations. In Augustan England, educated people looked back toward classical antiquity, not forward to a scientific and industrial future. In promoting Newton to endorse themselves, Newton's followers also advertised the power of what would become known as a scientific, Newtonian approach to the world.

Newton's increasing fame was boosted in many different ways. For example, lecturers demonstrated his experiments to large audiences and wrote simplified explanatory books, so that familiarity with Newtonian natural philosophy became a badge of culture. Newtonian ideals were also distributed along less obvious routes. Close colleagues constructed material glorifications, including the monument erected by his family in Westminster Abbey and the Temple of British Worthies at Stowe; such built memorials also generated further literary and artistic commemorations. To promote Cambridge as an intellectual center of excellence, the midcentury Master of Trinity College displayed several images of Newton, including the statue that prompted William Wordsworth's famous lines, "The marble index of a Mind for ever / Voyaging thro' strange seas of Thought, alone." In addition to the eulogies following Newton's death, poets such as James Thomson provided their own versions of Newtonian ideas.

This proliferation of tributes ensured that Newton became paired with Pope as an English Enlightenment hero. Important transitions occurred around the beginning of the nineteenth century, a period now often described as the second scientific revolution, when modern scientific disciplines became established. The concept of individual genius was also being consolidated as Romantic writers sought legitimation through copyright reforms. Formerly restricted to literary or artistic creativity, the meaning of *genius* gradually expanded to embrace scientific originality, and Newton became the first exemplar of a new social category: the scientific genius. For British men of science in the early nineteenth century, to declare their allegiance to Newtonianism was no mere description of their scientific principles; it signaled their patriotic confidence in the nation's intellectual superiority and their faith that scientific greatness paralleled literary or artistic fame.

[*See also* Academies; Alembert, Jean Le Rond d'; Cartesianism; Fontenelle, Bernard Le Bovier de; Franklin, Benjamin; Gravesande, Willem Jacob 's; Hales, Stephen; Hume, David; Leibniz, Gottfried Wilhelm von; Mathematics; Natural Philosophy and Science; Natural Religion; Optics; *and* Voltaire.]

BIBLIOGRAPHY

Beer, Peter, ed. *Newton and the Enlightenment.* Oxford and New York, 1978.

Cantor, Geoffrey. *Optics after Newton: Theories of Light in Britain and Ireland, 1704–1840.* Manchester, U.K., 1983.

Cantor, Geoffrey, and Michael Hodge, eds. *Conceptions of Ether: Studies in the History of Ether Theories, 1740–1900.* Cambridge, 1981. Valuable introduction and some good articles.

Dobbs, Betty Jo Teeter, and Margaret Jacob. *Newton and the Culture of Newtonianism.* Atlantic Highlands, N.J., 1995. Clear, concise introductory text for students.

Fara, Patricia. *Newton: The Making of Genius.* London, 2002. A nontechnical study of how Newton became acclaimed as a national hero and a scientific genius.

Fauvel, John, et al., eds. *Let Newton Be! A New Perspective on His Life and Works.* Oxford, 1988. A well-illustrated collection of lively yet scholarly introductory essays.

Gascoigne, John. "From Bentley to the Victorians: The Rise and Fall of British Newtonian Natural Theology." *Science in Context* 2 (1988), 219–256.

Guerlac, Henry. *Newton on the Continent.* Ithaca, 1981. A close examination of the reception of Newton's *Opticks* in France.

Guicciardini, Niccolò. *Reading the* Principia: *The Debate on Newton's Mathematical Methods for Natural Philosophy from 1687 to 1736.* Cambridge, 1999. A detailed and innovative technical analysis.

Hankins, Thomas. *Science and the Enlightenment.* Cambridge, 1985. Sound and useful introduction.

Heilbron, John. *Physics at the Royal Society during Newton's Presidency.* Berkeley and Los Angeles, 1979. Short yet informative account.

Olson, Richard. *Science Deified and Science Defied: The Historical Significance of Science in Western Culture.* Vol. 2. Berkeley, Los Angeles, and Oxford, 1990. Chapters 3–6 provide a well-written and unusual investigation of the broader implications of Newton's ideas during the Enlightenment.

Schaffer, Simon. "Newtonianism." In *Companion to the History of Modern Science*, edited by Robert Olby et al., pp. 610–625. London and New York, 1990. The best historical essay on Newtonianism as an ideology in modern science.

Stewart, Larry. *The Rise of Public Science: Rhetoric, Technology, and Natural Philosophy in Newtonian Britain, 1660–1750*. Cambridge, 1992. An excellent, detailed study exploring the technological impact of Newton's ideas on British society.

Thackray, Arnold. *Atoms and Powers: An Essay on Newtonian Matter-Theory and the Development of Chemistry*. Cambridge, Mass., 1970. A lucid and useful account of how Newton's ideas about matter were transmitted.

Yeo, Richard. "Genius, Method, and Morality: Images of Newton in Britain, 1760–1860." *Science in Context* 2 (1988), 257–284.

Yolton, John W. *Thinking Matter: Materialism in Eighteenth-Century Britain*. Oxford, 1983. A thorough discussion of theological and philosophical issues from Cudworth onwards.

PATRICIA FARA

NICOLAI, FRIEDRICH (1733–1811), German bookseller, publisher, writer, and historian.

Friedrich Nicolai attended school in Berlin and Halle an der Saale and completed an apprenticeship in a bookshop in Frankfurt an der Oder before joining his father's publishing house in 1752. In 1758 he took over management of the firm. A prolific writer whose work covers a wide range of subject areas, for several decades Nicolai was something of a cultural entrepreneur, working as a literary critic and historian. In addition, he maintained an enormous correspondence, of which eighty-nine manuscript volumes have survived.

A pugnacious and polemical Berliner with a sober, biting wit, Nicolai was rooted firmly in the principles of the Protestant, Berlin-Prussian Enlightenment, and in his literary and publishing activities he sought to ensure their ascendancy. Through his work in the societies of Enlightenment intellectuals of his time and in Freemason lodges as well as through his journals and reviews, Nicolai contributed considerably to the development of an enlightened republic of scholars.

In 1755, together with his friends Gotthold Ephraim Lessing and Moses Mendelssohn, Nicolai published *Briefe über den itzigen Zustand der schönen Wissenschaften in Deutschland* (Letters on the Current State of the Humanities in Germany) and, in 1756–1757, *Briefwechsel über das Trauerspiel* (Correspondence on Tragedy). From 1759 to 1765 the literary journal he founded with Lessing and Mendelssohn, *Briefe, die neueste Literatur betreffend* (Letters on Modern Literature), a total of twenty-four volumes, was brought out by his publishing house. The aesthetic and poetic ideals Nicolai advocated in these publications and the structure of ethical norms on which they were based were in opposition to literary developments in Germany.

In his often effective, but seldom subtle and sometimes crude, satires, Nicolai denounced fashionable aesthetic movements and styles that he considered dangerous. For example, in 1775, in a parody of Johann Wolfgang von Goethe's novel *Die Leiden des jungen Werthers* (The Sorrows of Young Werther), he excoriated Goethe for his association with the Sturm und Drang movement and that movement's cult of the genius, which he judged disastrous for society. Always a rationalist and defender of the Enlightenment ethic of responsibility, Nicolai disapproved of the elitist affectation and unbridled individualism associated with the literary avant-garde.

Nicolai was a member of both the royal Prussian and Bavarian academies of science, and as a philosophical empiricist he attacked Immanuel Kant, even though until 1781 (when Kant's *Kritik der reinen Vernunft* [Critique of Pure Reason] appeared) he had considered him a fellow spirit. Nicolai's strongest attacks, however, were directed against Kant's disciples.

Nicolai's novel in three volumes (1773–1776), *Das Leben und die Meinungen des Herrn Magisters Sebaldus Nothanker* (Life and Opinions of Master Sebaldus Nothanker), became the focus of discussion among philosophers of the Enlightenment because it dealt with the topics of church, theology, and society and was critical, as was typical of Enlightenment theology in Berlin, of both Protestant orthodoxy and Pietism.

The groundbreaking works in Nicolai's oeuvre are, however, his historically grounded three-volume topography of Berlin, *Beschreibung der Königlichen Residenzstädte Berlin und Potsdam* (Description of the Royal Capitals of Berlin and Potsdam; 3d expanded edition, 1786), and his twelve-volume *Beschreibung einer Reise durch Deutschland und die Schweiz im Jahre 1781* (Description of a Journey through Germany and Switzerland in the Year 1781), which was published from 1783 to 1796. In addition to offering polemics against the Roman Catholic Church and various contemporary cultural tendencies, this latter work in its best parts still serves as an informative historical source on demographic, economic, social, cultural, and urban history. In addition to these achievements, Nicolai published the monumental *Allgemeine deutsche Bibliothek* (General German Library) from 1765 to 1806. In the 264 volumes of this journal, 433 reviewers discussed more than 80,000 works (recent research has found the number to be lower). Nicolai was undoubtedly one of the most influential and significant representatives of the German Enlightenment and had a unique way of combining theory and practice.

[*See also* Academies, *subentry on* Germany; Berlin; Literary Genres; Print Culture; *and* Publishing.]

BIBLIOGRAPHY

Fabian, Bernhard, ed. *Friedrich Nicolai, 1733–1811: Essays zum 250. Geburtstag*. Berlin, 1983. Includes complete bibliography by M.-L. Spiekermann.

Friedrich Nicolai, Leben und Werk: Ausstellung zum 250. Geburtstag. Berlin, 1983–1984.

Habersaat, Sigrid. *Verteidigung der Aufklärung: Friedrich Nicolai in religösen und politischen Debatten.* Würzburg, Germany, 2001.

Möller, H. *Aufklärung in Preussen: Der Verleger, Publizist und Geschichtsschreiber Friedrich Nicolai.* Berlin, 1974.

Nicolai, Friedrich. *Gesammelte Schriften in Neudrucken.* Edited by B. Fabian and M.-L. Spiekermann. Hildesheim, Germany, Zurich, and New York, 1985–. Estimated to run to fifteen volumes.

Raabe, P., ed. *Friedrich Nicolai: Die Verlagswerke eines preussischen Buchhändlers.* Wolfenbüttel, Germany, 1983.

Schneider, Ute. *Friedrich Nicolais Allgemeine Deutsche Bibliothek als Integrationsmedium der Gelehrtenrepublik.* Wiesbaden, Germany, 1995.

HORST MÖLLER

NICOLE, PIERRE (1625–1695), French Jansenist philosopher and theologian.

Nicole was involved in every great intellectual conflict of seventeenth-century France, and his influence continued to be felt until the mid-eighteenth century. His life is generally divided into two periods, before and after 1679, the year in which he decided to remain in France and defend the monastery of Port-Royal, rather than joining Antoine Arnauld in permanent flight and exile. Before this, despite a few suspicions (particularly on the part of Mother Angélique de Saint-Jean), he was close to this convent of nuns and to the other men of Port-Royal, while writing his major works. Later, in spite of his constant claims of faithfulness to Augustinian principles and the cause of efficacious grace, his Jansenist friends regarded him as suspect, and some of his ambiguous choices only fueled this opinion.

Concerning the question of grace, Nicole's work displays surprising indecision. In collaboration with Arnauld, an ardent Augustinian, he claimed that his purpose was, after Pascal, to make the doctrine of efficacious grace more acceptable. He did so first in a rather Thomist formulation, and later by the assertion of a "general grace" that he defined in texts not published until after his death, but that were described, with cause, as almost Molinistic by Arnauld himself during the years 1680–1690. The exiled theologian did not cease being a friend, but these ambiguities alienated the most intransigent Port-Royalists, a fact that has continued to influence what is remembered of Pierre Nicole.

Along with Arnauld, Nicole played a fundamental role in reasserting, in opposition to the Protestants, the Roman Catholic doctrines of real presence and transubstantiation. (*La perpétuité de la foi de l'Église catholique touchant l'Eucharistie* [Enduring Faith of the Catholic Church Regarding the Eucharist], 1664 and 1669–1674). In this, one of the most sensitive areas at the time, the work also served to demonstrate the orthodoxy of the supposed movement against accusations of Calvinism. However, the

Pierre Nicole. Engraving (1765) by Charles Gaucher after a portrait by Philippe de Champagne (1602–1674). (Collection of Stephen Wagley.)

method employed, known as "prescription," was strongly criticized by a number of the movement's sympathizers who regretted that, unlike the members of the Reformed orders, the Port-Royalists had not based their work on the patristic tradition. Nicole would later defend against Pierre Jurieu the Catholic concept of the unity of the visible church.

Nicole led a battle against the mystics, and more generally against what he called "false spiritualities." As a result, he was one of the main people responsible for the "rout of the mystics" and a general ousting of the spirit of the imaginaries and visionaries from the seventeenth century. To oppose the legacy of the first Port-Royal mystic, Mother Agnès, he defended and preached recourse to thoughts and methods in a "spiritual" form of prayer; after 1695, he denounced the mystics in analyses that his enemies would judge unfeeling (*Traité de l'oraison* [Treatise on Meditative Prayer], 1679, and *Traité de la prière* [Treatise on Prayer], 1695).

The *Essais de morale* (Essays on Ethics) that made Nicole famous cannot be separated either from his fight against mystical forms of spirituality or from *La logique* (Logic, 1662), a work in whose composition, with Arnauld, he played an active part. The *Essays* are based simultaneously on the denunciation of the evil in man and, in the fight against that evil, on the assertion of "human means," on the necessity of the "good use of reason," the best being "Christian civility." With regard to political ethics, man is a "cooperator" with God, from which he derives specific duties.

Nicole's influence gradually declined. His *Essais de Morale* were published and read until the mid-eighteenth century, and he exercised an influence on Jean-Jacques Rousseau, who knew his work well. After 1750, his subjects were no longer on the agenda; his restrained style weakened his appeal; his treatises on ethics no longer corresponded to the questions being raised at the time; and his work slipped into oblivion. A new edition (following the example of Arnauld's *Oeuvres completes*) was projected at the end of the eighteenth century, but it was only partially completed and included only his major works. In the nineteenth century, only a few texts and some of his "thoughts" were published, although he continued to be read by certain moralists. The money left by his will contributed in the long run to the birth of the present-day Société et Bibliothèque de Port-Royal (Society and Library of Port-Royal), which, in return, has kept his work alive for scholars and students.

[*See also* Arnauld, Antoine; Jansenism; Moral Philosophy; Mysticism; Philosophy; *and* Roman Catholicism.]

BIBLIOGRAPHY

A bibliography will be found in the *Dictionnaire de Spiritualité* at the end of the article "Nicole (Pierre)." The following is a list of recent and important works that have given Nicole's image new life.

"Antoine Arnauld." *Chroniques de Port-Royal* 44 (1995). Contains several articles concerning Pierre Nicole.

Guion, Béatrice. *La vraie beauté et son fantôme, et autres textes d'esthétique*. Paris, 1996. A remarkable analysis of Pierre Nicole's aesthetics.

"Pierre Nicole (1625–1695)." *Chroniques de Port-Royal* 45 (1996). Proceedings of the proceedings of an important colloquium organized at Chartres, 21–23 September 1995, for the tercentennial of Nicole's death. This indispensable work is invaluable in developing most of the themes of this article.

Thirouin, Laurent. *Pierre Nicole: Traité de la Comédie et autres pieces d'un procès du théâtre*. Paris, 1998.

BERNARD CHÉDOZEAU
Translated from French by Betsy Wing

NIEUWENTIJT, BERNARD (1654–1718), Dutch physicist and theologian.

The son of a Protestant pastor, Nieuwentijt (also spelled Nieuwentyt) was born in West-Graftdijk, a little village in the north of the province of Holland. He studied medicine at the universities of Leiden and Utrecht, receiving his doctorate in medicine at Leiden in 1676. He then established a medical practice in his birthplace, and, in 1682, became physician to the nearby town of Purmerend. He was twice married: to Eva Moens in 1684, and to Elisabeth Lams in 1699. He was a member of the city council and became a burgomaster of Purmerend.

Nieuwentijt was influenced by Cartesianism in his youth. His thesis, *De obstructionibus* (On Constipation) was a typical example of Cartesian physical speculation. His later work, however, was strongly anti-Cartesian in tenor and was based on the new experimental philosophy. Nieuwentijt was one of the first Continental adherents of Newton's law of gravity. In 1695, Nieuwentijt published a fully developed system of infinitesimal methods, *Analysis infinitorum*; he spent the next five years contending with Leibniz and Johann Bernoulli on the foundation of calculus.

Nieuwentijt became celebrated in the Netherlands and abroad for his enormously successful apologetic, *Het regt gebruik der wereltbeschouwingen, ter overtuiginge van ongodisten en ongelovigen* (The Right Use of Contemplating the World, Designed to Convince Atheists and Unbelievers, 1715). An eighth edition appeared in 1759; it was translated into French and German, and into English as *The Religious Philosopher, or, The Right Use of Contemplating the Works of the Creator* (1718; 3d ed., 1730). Inspired by the work of Robert Boyle, Nieuwentijt developed in this lengthy work a way of defending the Christian religion on the basis of experimental philosophy. Using his thorough knowledge of the natural sciences of his own time, he attempted to demonstrate the existence of God from the wonders of nature, an approach known as physico-theology. He was very critical not just of Cartesian a priori speculations, but of rationalism in general. He argued that true knowledge could be obtained only by experiment, whether in physical matters or in theology and philosophy.

Nieuwentijt's second major work was published posthumously in Dutch in 1720: *Gronden van zekerheid, of de regte betoogwyse der wiskundigen, so in het denkbeeldige, als in het zakelyke* (The Foundations of Certitude, or The Right Method for Mathematics in the Imaginary as in the Real). This work is a methodical refutation of Spinoza's geometrical way of philosophical reasoning. Nieuwentijt argues that the natural sciences are totally in accordance with biblical revelation, and rejects the arguments of the Spinozists, whom he calls atheists, as untenable from a scientific point of view. In his view, the main error of such atheists is their application of the results of pure, abstract mathematics to the real world, in the place of experimental philosophy. This book was less successful than *Het regt gebruik*, which was regarded as authoritative for years both in the Netherlands and elsewhere.

[*See also* Apologetics; Cartesianism; Empiricism; Leibniz, Gottfried Wilhelm von; Natural Philosophy and Science; Netherlands; Physico-Theology; *and* Spinoza, Baruch de.]

BIBLIOGRAPHY

Beth, Evert W. "Nieuwentijt's Significance for the Philosophy of Science." *Synthese* 9 (1955), 447–453.

Freudenthal, Hans. "Nieuwentijt, Bernard." In *Dictionary of Scientific Biography*, edited by Charles Coulston Gillispie, vol. 10, pp. 120–121. New York, 1974.

Petry, Michael J. *Nieuwentijt's Criticism of Spinoza in Mededelingen vanwege het Spinozahuis*, 40. Leiden, Netherlands, 1979.

Vermij, Rienk. "Bernard Nieuwentijt and the Leibnizian Calculus." *Studia Leibnitziana* 21 (1989), 69–86.

Vermij, Rienk. "Religion and Mathematics in Seventeenth-Century Holland: The Case of Bernard Nieuwentijt." In *Science and Religion/Wissenschaft und Religion: Proceedings of the XVIIIth International Congress of History of Science at Hamburg–Munich 1–9. August 1989*, edited by Änne Bäumer and Manfred Büttner, pp. 152–157. Bochum, Germany, 1989.

H. A. M. SNELDERS

NOMINALISM. Nominalism can be understood as the denial of the existence of essences or universals. In historical terms, it amounts to the rejection of a metaphysical doctrine that originated with Plato and Aristotle and dominated Christian thought until the late Middle Ages. This doctrine, which came to be known as realism, stipulated that things that were called by the same name shared an essence that defined their fundamental natures. Accordingly, realism not only postulated the real existence of universals, but placed positive value on the general as opposed to the individual. (In Aristotelian and scholastic parlance, individual variations were mere "accidents.") Although students of the so-called problem of universals often disagree regarding whether a given thinker is a full-fledged nominalist (who believes that universal terms are mere verbal constructs or names) or a conceptualist (who occupies an intermediate position, explaining general ideas in terms of mental concepts), during the early modern period the term *nominalism* tended to signify the rejection of essences or universals, ignoring the question of whether a given writer is in fact a conceptualist. This article will follow the early modern practice, since we are less interested in technical distinctions than in the historical significance of the general antiessentialist tendency to see the world in terms of individual entities rather than universals.

Although the late medieval nominalist challenge to the doctrine of universals is associated with the fourteenth-century English philosopher William of Ockham, it has been argued that the way to Ockham's rejection of universals had been paved by Christian theology, specifically by new responses to the doctrine of the Incarnation. The adoration of God in the human person of Jesus ultimately "succeeded in overthrowing the ontological priority of the universal" (Dupré, 1993).

Like other intellectual innovations that have arisen in a religious context, however, nominalism had secular implications that soon became more conspicuous than the Christian ones. Among the trends of Enlightenment thinking that may be seen to be premised on nominalism, some—such as an intense interest in the individual subject and the textures of individual experience—had begun to take shape during the Renaissance. In the *Essays* (1580, 1588) of Michel de Montaigne, one already finds a focus on the particularities of human experience linked to an explicitly nominalistic suspicion concerning statements and philosophies that purport to offer general truths about species or classes of things. In Miguel de Cervantes's *Don Quixote* (Part 1, 1605; Part 2, 1615), one finds anticipations of the tendencies that would, during the Enlightenment proper, blossom into the novel, the literary genre that, more than any other, rejected the conception of literature as a distillation of universal truths and instead made itself the vehicle of the particulars of experience.

Among the implications of nominalism specifically associated with the scientific revolution and the new philosophical movements of the seventeenth century, one might cite not only the pervasive ridicule of scholasticism for its use of abstract terms that purported to refer to real entities that were now deemed to be imaginary, but also the new emphasis on empirical observation as the correct way to obtain knowledge of the natural world. In spite of the new methodological emphasis on observation (and experimentation), however, there was often the presumption that the observation of particulars would yield knowledge of underlying universal principles. Francis Bacon, for example, thought his inductive method would move from observation of particulars to the discovery of more and more general axioms, culminating in comprehensive explanations. Thus, nominalism on the eve of the Enlightenment may be said to operate in the realm of method, while at the same time often presupposing that a method based on particulars would yield an understanding of an orderly, hierarchically structured universe.

While the impulse to order and classify has sometimes been seen to lie at the heart of Enlightenment thought, any such impulse is often frustrated by a conspicuous strain of nominalism. Beyond the nominalism that manifests itself in psychological individualism and the rise of the novel—the new strain does not simply place value on the individual subject and his or her experiences, but treats any ordering of reality as nothing more than an arbitrary arrangement of particulars. This tendency is largely inspired by John Locke. For Locke, a complex idea, such as that of a given man or tree, is composed by an act of mind out of the simple ideas of qualities (shape, color, solidity) that are the fundamental givens of experience and the building blocks of our conceptual universe. More abstract ideas, such as those of men in general or trees in general, are similarly products of the human mind rather than features of external reality. Locke's insistence that when "we quit particulars, the generals that rest are only creatures of our own making" (*Essay*, III, iii, 11) certainly lies in the background of the claim of the French naturalist Georges Louis Leclerc, comte de Buffon that—since species and other biological classifications exist only in our imagination (whereas in nature the only things that really exist are individuals)—the more we classify the natural world, the farther we remove ourselves from reality. Denis Diderot, writing on scientific method in his *Interpretation of Nature* (1753), applied the same sort of nominalistic thinking to the explanation of the physical universe. While embracing the Baconian method that privileges the observation of particulars, Diderot lacks Bacon's confidence that the separate discoveries will be tied together by some comprehensive general explanatory axiom. This is not skeptical doubt concerning the human capacity to know; rather, it is nominalistic doubt as to whether the actual structure of reality is amenable to general explanation. The same attitude informs Diderot's approach to the great *Encyclopédie*, of which he was general editor. Echoing the nominalism of Buffon and the Lockean nominalism of the English encyclopedist Ephraim Chambers, Diderot stresses the arbitrariness of any arrangement of human knowledge. Since both Chambers and Diderot believe that the universe offers us only an infinite array of particulars, which the human imagination can combine in various ways, they declare that the arbitrary alphabetical arrangement of articles aptly represents reality, and that cross-references point to various ways in which the particulars can be combined. Thus some of the most celebrated Enlightenment demonstrations of confidence in the grand expansion of human knowledge are tethered in a kind of nominalistic diffidence.

[*See also* Buffon, Georges-Louis Leclerc de; Diderot, Denis, Empiricism; Encyclopédie; Locke, John; Natural Philosophy and Science; Novel; *and* Philosophy.]

BIBLIOGRAPHY

Aaron, Richard I. *The Theory of Universals.* 2d ed. Oxford, 1967. A classic study that includes a historical analysis, centering on Locke, Berkeley, and Hume.

Dupré, Louis. *Passage to Modernity: An Essay in the Hermeneutics of Nature and Culture.* New Haven, Conn., 1993. A synoptic essay that stresses the importance of nominalism in the development of modernity.

Kenshur, Oscar. *Open Form and the Shape of Ideas: Literary Structures as Representations of Philosophical Concepts in the Seventeenth and Eighteenth Centuries.* Lewisberg, Pa., 1986. Chapters 2 and 5 deal with the scientific and encyclopedic nominalism of Diderot, Buffon, and Chambers.

Locke, John. *An Essay Concerning Human Understanding* (1690). Edited by John Yolton. 2 vols. Revised edition, New York, 1965.

OSCAR KENSHUR

NOODT, GERARD (1647–1725), Dutch law professor.

Noodt was born in Nijmegen to a prominent merchant family. His father, a goldsmith by training, was a member and representative of the Gemeente, the commune of merchants and artisans; his mother came from the local patriciate. Prosecution and oppression formed part of his family history. The Gemeente had long played a role in local government, but from the late sixteenth century on its power was suppressed, robbing half the citizens of a voice in politics. In 1703, this caused a bloody revolt, an ominous beginning to an age ending with the French Revolution.

During the truce in the Eighty Years' War (1609–1621), Nijmegen was on the side of the grand pensionary, Oldenbarnevelt (1547–1619), and its leading families belonged to the Remonstrant Church. In 1617, Prince Maurice (1567–1625) cracked down on the Remonstrants and persecution began. Noodt's maternal grandmother was arrested for allegedly organizing Remonstrant services in her house, and her son, later to become Noodt's father, went into exile in Warsaw, returning for his marriage twenty years later. By then persecution had ceased, but he still had to join the Reformed Church in order to be eligible for public office.

Gerard went to the grammar school and short-lived university (1655–1679) at Nijmegen, where he studied philology, philosophy, mathematics, and law. His philosophy teacher was Theodoor Craanen (1620–1689), a follower of René Descartes. In 1669, Noodt took his degree in Franeker and settled down to practice law in Nijmegen; by 1671, he had been appointed law professor at the local university. Barely half a year later, however, Nijmegen was occupied and pillaged by the French; the students fled, and the professors could no longer be paid. By 1679, when Noodt took up a professorship in Franeker, Nijmegen's university ceased to exist. Thereafter, Noodt's professional advancement was rapid. In 1684 he went to Utrecht, and in 1686 to Leiden, the oldest and largest university in the Dutch Republic, where he became one of its leading lights, teaching there until his death. He acted as *rector magnificus* in the years 1698–1699 and 1705–1706.

Career in Law. Noodt, an outstanding expert in Roman law, was among those who brought international recognition to Dutch humanist jurisprudence. He was a brilliant legal historian, but as a critic sometimes rather audacious. As early as 1679, in his inaugural address at Franeker, he pleaded for the inclusion of natural law in the law curriculum, and he actually taught it himself. His treatises were often a mixture of natural law in matters of principle and Roman law in technical points. Reason was the criterion for all his interpretations. If any law seemed unreasonable, that could only be the fault of the commentators, because the law itself could never be unreasonable. Although as an academic Noodt disliked literary quarrels, he was brave enough to speak his mind on important political issues. His critical rationalism, rooted in humanist philology but reinforced by Cartesianism and natural law theory, clearly places him in the Enlightenment.

Throughout his life, Noodt studied Roman law in the humanist manner, but he was no blind admirer of antiquity. In his most controversial legal interpretation, he suggested that the classical jurist Scaevola had given an incorrect legal opinion (reported in *Digest* 2.15.14) to favor a friend. Another fierce debate was caused by Noodt's book *Julius Paulus* (1700), which treated what seemed a purely antiquarian question: At what time in ancient history was the exposing and killing of newborn children prohibited? Noodt proved that this happened only in the fourth century. As a consequence, all classical jurists—those models of humanity—as well as many Christian emperors were shown to have accepted the dire custom. In this book, moreover, he argued that not all texts in the Corpus Juris—the collection of laws and legal opinions made by order of the emperor Justinian (527–565) and regarded as binding all over Europe since the Middle Ages—were in fact meant as commands or prohibitions. Cornelis van Bijnkershoek (1673–1743), member and later president of the supreme court of Holland and Zeeland, was so upset that, nineteen years later, he was still engaged in a vigorous attack on Noodt.

Another characteristic treatise was Noodt's condemnation of the objectionable habit of bargaining between bailiffs and suspects, which caused much extortion and corruption. This practice, which had existed for ages, had worsened under the absolutist regime of King-Stadholder William III (1672–1702). In his book *Diocletianus et Maximianus* (1704), Noodt proved that Codex 2.4.18, the text generally regarded as the legal basis for the practice, did not, in fact, authorize it. Noodt still accepted the humanist belief that changing the reading of an authoritative text could change the world. It did not, of course.

Rectorial Addresses. Noodt achieved exceptional European fame with his two rectorial addresses. In the first, *De jure summi emperii et lege regia* (On the Law of Sovereignty and the *Lex Regia*, 1699), he defended, in a world of growing absolutism, the sovereignty of the people. This could hardly be welcome to the scions of William III, but it was anathema in the France of Louis XIV (1643–1715). In the second address, *De religione ab imperio jure gentium libera* (On the Freedom of Religion from Supreme Power according to the Law of Nations, 1706), he argued that, according to natural law, the sovereign has absolutely no power with regard to the religion of his subjects. Atypically, Noodt's plea in this case was not for toleration but for freedom of religion. A comparison with John Locke's *Letter on Toleration* (1685)

is revealing. Locke excluded atheists and Roman Catholics from toleration, thereby emphasizing that toleration was discretionary and relative, but Noodt maintained that freedom of religion was absolute. Not only Christians were entitled to it, said Noodt, but also Muslims and even heathens. During the French Revolution, the French politician Mirabeau (Honoré de Riqueti, 1749–1791) stressed the same point in the National Convention: toleration is a favor, freedom a right. Within a few years the two addresses, given in Latin as academic custom required, had been translated into Dutch, French, and English. They went through many impressions and editions. The address on freedom of religion was also translated into German and Swedish. Noodt's address on freedom of religion was a major contribution to the development of the legal concept of human rights.

[*See also* Natural Law; Reformed Churches, *subentry on* Dutch Reformed Church; *and* Toleration.]

BIBLIOGRAPHY

Ahsmann, Margreet. "Gerard Noodt." In *Juristen: ein biographisches Lexikon von der Antike bis zum 20. Jahrhundert*, edited by M. Stolleis. Munich, 1995.

Ahsmann, Margreet, and Robert Feenstra. *Bibliografie van hoogleraren in de rechten aan de Leidse universiteit tot 1811*. Amsterdam, 1984. Bibliography of Noodt's works, 419–480; additions in M. Ahsmann, *Bibliografie van hoogleraren in de rechten aan de Utrechts universiteit tot 1811* (Amsterdam, 1993), pp. 41f.

Bergh, Govaert C. J. J. van den. *Die holländische elegante Schule: Ein Beitrag zur Geschichte von Humanismus und Rechtswissenschaft in den Niederlanden 1500–1800*. Frankfurt, 2001.

Bergh, Govaert C. J. J. van den. *The Life and Work of Gerard Noodt (1647–1725): Dutch Legal Scholarship between Humanism and Enlightenment*. Oxford, 1988.

Israel, Jonathan I. *The Dutch Republic, Its Rise, Greatness, and Fall 1477–1806*. Oxford, 1995. See pp. 674, 962–963, 964, 1104.

GOVAERT C. J. J. VAN DEN BERGH

NORDENFLYCHT, HEDVIG CHARLOTTA (1718–1763), Swedish poet.

Nordenflycht grew up as the youngest child in a wealthy bourgeois family named Nordbohm (later raised to the nobility with the name Nordenflycht), in which the two sons received university education as a matter of course, while the three daughters were trained in traditional women's work. While a young girl she showed strong literary interests and received sporadic tutoring in languages and religion. In an autobiographical letter, she recounts that she was affected by religious uncertainty early in life and delved deeply into philosophical literature, which increased her doubts. The crisis was resolved when she met a young university graduate, later her fiancé, who introduced her to the modern university philosophy that was created by the German mathematician and philosopher Christian Wolff.

In response to the premature death of her fiancé, Nordenflycht wrote poems that expressed her sorrow. Several years later she met her future husband, the clergyman and poet Jacob Fabricius; they married in 1741 and moved to Karlskrona in the south of Sweden, where he had been appointed chaplain to the Admiralty. His death after only eight months of marriage affected Nordenflycht deeply and moved her to write a collection of poems, *Den sörjande turturduvan* (The Mournful Turtle Dove), published in 1743. These elegies strike a new note in Swedish and perhaps world literature by their unveiled subjectivity.

Philosophical Writings. For the rest of her life, until the year before her death, Nordenflycht lived in Stockholm. There she made contacts with prominent and influential people who could promote her writings, and she received a substantial allowance from the royal court. She soon wrote, almost exclusively, religious and philosophical poetry, which she published in a yearbook of her own, *Kvinnligt tankespel* (Female Play of Thoughts, 4 vols. 1744–1750). An epistle to the Danish author Ludvig Holberg reveals her effort to grapple with metaphysical problems; it is a thorough treatment of questions raised by the early Enlightenment philosophers. Is there such a thing as an immortal soul of heavenly origin? Is virtue an empty, man-made idea, or can it be ascribed an objective value? Nordenflycht said that if they had still been alive, she would have approached Isaac Newton, Gottfried Wilhelm von Leibniz, John Locke, and Pierre Bayle—since they had revealed the ignorance from which we suffer. Apparently Holberg never responded to her overture. Nordenflycht later wrote an answer herself, in which she rejected her own questions as presumptuous, but maintained the necessity of cultivating the intellect.

In 1753, Nordenflycht became a member of a literary society, Tankebyggare (Thought Builders), whose main purpose was to modernize Swedish literature, based on French classical models. Within a period of ten years, the society published the anthologies *Våra försök* (Our Essays, 1753–1756) and *Vitterhetsarbeten* (Works of Polite Literature, 1759–1762), in which some of Nordenflycht's most important works were printed. The society also introduced her to new and radical philosophical ideas. In her poem "Skaldebrev till Criton" (Epistle to Criton), she asked whether an enlarged knowledge really entails a greater virtue and happiness. In other poems from those years, Nordenflycht pointed out the difficulties that confront the Enlightened man in everyday life. At the same time, she wrote great works in the French classical tradition, such as *Pindaric* odes and even an epic. In a grand ode to Paul Petrovitch, the Russian successor to the throne, she enthusiastically depicted the ideal image of the Enlightened sovereign, who tenderly takes care of his people and peacefully works only for the public weal.

Poetry. While still in her twenties, Nordenflycht had bravely attacked the principles of male-governed society, but her greatest feminist achievement was the voluminous didactic poem "Fruntimrets försvar emot J. J. Rousseau" (The Defense of Women against J. J. Rousseau), which was published in 1762. In that work, her aim was to refute the misogynistic views that Rousseau had put forth in his *Lettre à d'Alembert sur les spectacles*, and she maintained that women can compete successfully with men in all social fields, including government and the church.

In 1762, Nordenflycht moved to a lonely country house to restore her health—both physical and financial—but died after living there for only one year. Some of her last poems are dedicated to her tragic love for a younger man. There, as in her early elegies, she gave herself up to her innermost feelings and created some of the finest poems in eighteenth-century Swedish literature.

Nordenflycht lived during the time when Sweden was recovering from the long wars of Charles XII. She was highly susceptible to the new ideas that penetrated from abroad, and she followed contemporaneous scientific developments as well as religious and philosophical debates with unflagging interest. Above all, she deserves to be remembered as an early representative of modern awareness of the self.

[*See also* Men and Women of Letters; Poetry; Rousseau, Jean-Jacques; *and* Scandinavia.]

BIBLIOGRAPHY

WORKS BY NORDENFLYCHT
Samlade skrifter, vols. 1–3. Edited by Hilma Borelius and Theodor Hjelmqvist, in the series *Svenska författare utgivna av Svenska vitterhetssamfundet*. Stockholm, 1924–1938. A scholarly edition containing all known texts.
Skrifter. Edited by Torkel Stålmarck, with an introduction by Sture Allén, in the series *Svenska klassiker utgivna av Svenska Akademien*. Stockholm, 1996. A popular but extensive edition.

WORKS ABOUT NORDENFLYCHT
Byström, Tryggve. *Studier i Hedvig Charlotta Nordenflychts biografi*. Stockholm, 1980. Presents new biographical information concerning her family and friends.
Hansson, Sven G. *Satir och kvinnokamp i Hedvig Charlotta Nordenflychts diktning*. Stockholm, 1991. Deals with her relations to the author Olof Dalin and with her feministic writings.
Kruse, John. *Hedvig Charlotta Nordenflycht. Ett skaldinne-porträtt från Sveriges rococo-tid*. Lund, 1895. An extensive and still indispensable biography.
Platen, Magnus von. "Från fru Nordenflychts sista tid." In *1700-tal. Studier i svensk litteratur*. Stockholm, 1963. Treats her love for a younger man and her impressions of the philosophe Jean Jacques Rousseau.
Stålmarck, Torkel. *Hedvig Charlotta Nordenflycht: Ett porträtt*. Stockholm, 1997. A popular biography.

TORKEL STÅLMARCK

NORTH AFRICA AND THE LEVANT. The southern and eastern shores of the Mediterranean Sea, most of which was under the direct or indirect domination of the Ottoman sultan in Istanbul, were to Enlightenment Europe a part of the world at once familiar and strange, a region with which trading and cultural contacts had never been interrupted. It had long been an object of interest to Europeans, as is attested by the large number of publications and reeditions of works on the area. There were many accounts by travelers and by those who had resided in the Middle East or North Africa, normally in European trading posts, so books on the region frequently began by acknowledging its familiarity to the European reading public. At the same time, however, it was part of an alien and hostile civilization, the embodiment of Islam, and the enemy of Christendom. Indeed, at that period the word *Turk* was synonymous with *Muslim*. This last factor obviously made it a region of particular significance for the Enlightenment. By the late seventeenth century, the fear inspired in Europe by Ottoman expansionism was on the wane; the Ottoman Empire was no longer a direct threat, and dread was gradually replaced by curiosity and later by a growing contempt. Lively curiosity can be seen in the popularity of the French Orientalist Barthélemy d'Herbelot's monumental *Bibliothèque orientale*, a comprehensive reference work on the Islamic world based on Arabic, Persian, and Turkish sources, whose aim was to provide a more objective understanding of its culture; it was published posthumously in 1697 with an introduction by the French scholar Antoine Galland, and republished several times throughout the following century.

Europe's main contacts with the Ottoman Empire during this period were in the field of trade, as the balance of trade in the Mediterranean gradually swung in favor of the Europeans. Shipping was nevertheless in constant danger of harassment by corsairs, or Barbary pirates, operating out of North African ports such as Algiers and Tripoli. For them, attacking European shipping and capturing their crews or passengers was an important source of revenue, which derived in part from the ransoming of European captives; this practice fed the European imagination with accounts of the sufferings of the Christian slaves and their supposed forced conversion to Islam, a stereotype encouraged by the churches' anti-Islamic propaganda. Several enlightened thinkers, however, accused European governments of tolerating and even encouraging the pirates through treaties made with them and tribute paid to keep the peace; these North African states were considered useful weapons in wars against their own European enemies.

Impressions of Turks. This negative aspect of the Ottoman presence in the Mediterranean helped to reinforce the deeply rooted and longstanding image of the Turks as an ignorant, barbarian, cruel people, which led writers such as the French philosophe Constantin-François de Volney to equate them with the plague, which was endemic in the Ottoman Empire. Their government was seen as the epitome of "Oriental despotism," an important category in enlightened thought, with a role in the classification of political regimes by writers such as Montesquieu in *L'esprit des lois* (1748). A similar view, which had already been given currency by the English merchant Paul Rycaut in his *History of the Present State of the Ottoman Empire* (1668), is found in an influential work on the Turkish Empire published by the baron de Tott in 1784, after several years as a military advisor at the sultan's court in Istanbul. In addition to the Imperial government, particular governments of the region—for example, that of the corsair state of Algiers, nominally a vassal of Istanbul but in fact governed by a dey chosen by the army, often after a bloody palace revolution, or the independent Moroccan Empire—were bywords for cruelty and despotism. Associated with the image of Oriental despotism and Turkish cruelty was the seraglio or harem, which simultaneously fascinated and horrified Europeans. The most famous manifestation of this fascination is Montesquieu's *Lettres persanes* (1721), in which a critique of French society put into the mouths of Persian visitors to Paris is intermingled with the description of the tyranny imposed on the wives left in their harem in Persia. Europeans' taste for exotic tales from the East had already been whetted by Galland's French translation of the *Thousand and One Nights* in 1704–1708, which inspired a large number of vaguely Eastern, more or less erotic tales, including the philosophe Denis Diderot's *Les bijoux indiscrets* (1747). The English writer Mary Wortley Montagu claimed to present a truer picture in her descriptions of Istanbul, where she spent some years with her husband, the British ambassador to the sultan. She was allowed to visit the harem and talk to the sultan's wives. In her letters, which circulated from 1724 onward, she expressed admiration for Turkish refinement, culture, and learning, providing translations of Turkish poetry and introducing into Europe the Turkish practice of inoculation against smallpox. Her accounts of sexual intrigues probably contributed to the fascination with the harem, which remained an object of titillation and horror.

As this example shows, the Near East and North Africa tended to figure in the imagination of enlightened Europeans through certain stereotypes concerning the "Turks," rather than as a group of countries, each with its own character. Despite travelers' accounts of the various countries and descriptions of their different populations, this region tended to be seen as a relatively undifferentiated whole. Travelers' accounts often gave rise to stereotypes corresponding to preconceived European categories of thought. Thus, particular interest was shown in the nomadic Bedouin of the desert, generally designated simply as *Arabs*, who were carefully distinguished from the sedentary populations of the towns and were considered to be the same people living in all the deserts from the Atlantic Ocean to Arabia. Praised for their simple lifestyle, independence, and love of liberty, and reputed to practice a type of religion that was simpler and closer to natural religion or deism, they were sometimes presented as akin to noble savages. This is how they appear, for example, in Diderot's article "Bedouins" in the *Encyclopédie*, and in the French philosophe Volney's description of Egypt and Syria (1787). Despite some attempts to understand the different populations making up the Ottoman Empire, and despite authors' claims to knowledge of the region, stereotypes were frequently substituted for true understanding.

Islam. This tendency is most evident in the other important role played by the Turkish world in Enlightenment thought as the embodiment of Islam. This was the main rival to Christianity, since it had emerged after the Christian revelation and therefore posed the greatest challenge to Christian pretensions to universal truth. Islam and its prophet had been the objects of European hostility since the Middle Ages. These attitudes never entirely disappeared, but they were somewhat abated during the Enlightenment. Curiosity about the Turks extended to their religion, which, following the revival of Arabic studies in Europe, was the object of new scholarship. The Dutchman Adrian Reland published *De religione mohammedica* (1705), in which he undertook to destroy certain anti-Islamic prejudices. The English translation of the Qur'an by the Arabic scholar George Sale in 1734 marked a turning point and a break with earlier translations, in that Sale's introduction contained a defense of the Prophet Muhammad against Christian detractors. This earned Sale a reputation as a secret Muslim convert, or at least as a freethinker. Freethinkers showed sympathy to Islam—partly as a way of attacking Christian intolerance, and partly because they portrayed it as a pure religion emphasizing the unity of God. This appealed to Unitarians, as can be seen from *The Naked Gospel* (1690) by Arthur Bury, an English clergyman who was persecuted and excommunicated as a result of this work. Henry Stubbe's *An Account of the Rise and Progress of Mahometanism*, which circulated clandestinely in manuscript form in the late seventeenth century, offered a discussion of Islam that praised its notions of God as "great and noble." It is likely that the theologian Humphrey Prideaux's attack on Islam, entitled *The True Nature of Imposture Fully Displayed in the Life of Mahomet* (1697) and directed at freethinkers, was provoked by Stubbe's work. Later, the freethinker John Toland's *Nazarenus* (1718) depicted Islam as a purer version of Christianity, close to Unitarianism. Toland had already shown an interest in Islam and its use against the church in his *Letter from an Arabian Physician to a Famous Professor* (1705 or 1706).

This use of Islam as a weapon with which to attack the church, whether from the point of view of Unitarianism or deism, is found in many works, in particular the *Vie de Mohamed* written by the French freethinker Henri de Boulainvilliers, which circulated in manuscript form before being published in London in 1730. The relative indulgence for Islam expressed in Edward Gibbon's *Decline and Fall of the Roman Empire* (1776) can be seen as a continuation of this point of view. Several clandestine philosophical treatises in French used Islam in a similar way to attack Christianity; the most notorious, the *Traité des trois imposteurs*, presents Moses, Christ, and Muhammad all as impostors. A similar ambiguity of reference to Islam can be seen in the popular multivolume, semijournalistic *Lettres juives*, written by the deist marquis d'Argens; fictional Jewish travelers in various countries are used as his voices, both to attack Turkish despotism in the Near East and North Africa and to express admiration for Islam as a tolerant religion close to deism. This ambiguity is most obvious in the writings of Voltaire, who on one hand praised Muslim toleration in contrast to Catholic persecution and introduced an old Turk as the embodiment of wisdom at the end of *Candide*, while on the other hand he wrote a play about the Prophet Muhammad that reproduces the stereotypes of Christian propaganda that claimed he was an unscrupulous and fanatical impostor; in this play, however, "Mahomet" in fact conceals an attack on the Catholic clergy. Islam could be a two-edged sword.

Anti-Ottoman Sentiment. As the century progressed, hostility toward the Turks seemed to come to the fore. It was clearly expressed in the works of Tott and Volney, who were both in the Ottoman Empire on semiofficial government missions. Denunciations of Oriental despotism, of the Turks' oppression of native populations in North Africa or elsewhere, and of the depredations of the Barbary corsairs combined in various plans for expeditions to conquer part of this declining empire. The best-selling, multivolume *Histoire philosophique et politique des établissements des Européens dans les Deux Indes*, published by Guillaume-Thomas Raynal from 1770 onward, with contributions from philosophes such as Diderot, denounced the slave trade and provided the most up-to-date information on the rest of the world; it also included an appeal for an international expedition to free North Africa from Ottoman oppression and open it up to European trade. The expedition that was finally launched was Napoleon's invasion of Egypt in 1798; although the French occupation was short-lived, the intellectuals who accompanied the expedition contributed to a better knowledge of the country and its culture, thus prolonging both enlightened curiosity and misconceptions, and preparing for the imperial attitudes of the nineteenth century.

[*See also* Deism *and* Despotism.]

BIBLIOGRAPHY

Daniel, Norman. *Islam, Europe and Empire*. Edinburgh, 1966. Contains a survey of enlightened attitudes but essentially begins with the French Revolution.

Grosrichard, Alain. *The Sultan's Court: European Fantasies of the East*. London, 1998. English translation of *Structure du sérail* (Paris, 1979), a psychoanalytical study of the role played by the harem in the European imagination, devoting much space to the Enlightenment.

Gunny, Ahmad. *Images of Islam in Eighteenth-Century Writings*. London, 1996. A detailed study especially concerned with theological questions.

Hentsch, Thierry. *Imagining the Middle East*. Montreal, 1992. Translation of *L'Orient imaginaire: La vision politique occidentale de l'Est méditerranéen* (Paris, 1988), a study of how the European image of the eastern Mediterranean emerged through political contacts and reflection; devotes much space to the Enlightenment period.

Hourani, Albert. *Islam in European Thought*. Cambridge, 1991. A collection of essays which includes a discussion of the eighteenth century.

Netton, Ian Richard. "The mysteries of Islam." In *Exoticism in the Enlightenment*, edited by G. S. Rousseau and Roy Porter, pp. 23–45. Manchester, 1990. Studies reactions to the Middle East by four representative writers.

Rodinson, Maxime. *Europe and the Mystique of Islam*. Oxford, 1988. Translation of *La fascination de l'Islam* (Paris, 1980). A survey of European attitudes toward Islam; includes a section on the Enlightenment.

Said, Edward W. *Orientalism*. London, 1978. More useful on the colonial period from the late eighteenth century on.

Thomson, Ann. *Barbary and Enlightenment: European Attitudes towards the Maghreb in the 18th Century*. Leiden, 1987. Situates writings on North Africa in the context of Enlightenment thought.

ANN THOMSON

NORTH AMERICA. Embedded in the Enlightenment in North America was a contradiction: the call for reason in the continent's pristine environment seemed to lead to a world of equality, yet the American philosophe saw himself as a natural aristocrat. Enlightened simplicity seemed to repose in the honest farmer, but enlightened manners were the province of gentlemen. Before the American Revolution, few thinkers had reason to confront this contradiction. The American philosophe could confidently assert both his own natural superiority and the virtues of the husbandman. After independence, however, these two strands pulled at each other, creating intellectual and political ferment.

Nature in the New World. We can see the elements of the contradiction between the enlightened ideal of equality and the faith in a natural elite in the American response to the European debate over the role of nature in the New World. Europeans were divided over the value of the New World. In *Candide*, Voltaire flippantly dismissed New France (French Canada) as "a few acres of snow," and Diderot and d'Alembert's *Encyclopédie* in the mid-eighteenth century referred to the natives of Canada as *sauvages* (savages). For some European writers, all North America, including the British colonies, shared in this negative stereotype. The comte de Buffon held that all living creatures in the wilderness of the New World were inferior, pointing to the fact that America had no large mammals like the elephant as evidence for this proposition. Its beardless natives lacked virility; their men, it was reported, had milk running from their breasts. The enervating effects of American extremes of weather even had a debilitating impact on Europeans who had gone to America as colonists: people were shorter and feebler, and they died earlier; women stopped bearing children at a younger age. From this perspective, it was a mistake to intrude on the pristine but backward wilderness.

Other Europeans saw the forests of British America, if not of Canada, as a realm where nature and reason might rule supreme, unfettered by the dead past. Voltaire believed that William Penn had ushered in a "golden age" and saw him as the epitome of civic virtue. Pennsylvania (which Voltaire placed to the south of Maryland) became the locus of a new world of religious toleration, fair treatment of Indians, and opportunity for all men. For philosophes like Voltaire, the simplicity of the Quakers was not contemptible but was a model for others to follow.

American writers seized on that simplicity and sanctified it as a value to be cherished even above the philosophe's vaunted antiquity. In *Letters from an American Farmer*, a Frenchman turned British colonist, J. Hector St. John de Crèvecoeur, contrasted the "musty ruins of Rome" that must "fill the mind with the most melancholy reflections" with the newness of America, where one could "contemplate the very beginnings and outlines of humane society." In the rest of the world, Crèvecoeur believed, "misguided religion, tyranny, and absurd laws everywhere depress and afflict mankind." In America, "our laws are simple and just; we are a race of cultivators; our cultivation is unrestrained; and therefore everything is prosperous and flourishing." Thomas Jefferson, sharing Crèvecoeur's vision, believed that "those who labour in the earth are the chosen people of God."

In defending the natural setting of the New World against European attacks, the Americans had the ultimate goal of making their country the embodiment of the Enlightenment. Jefferson wrote his *Notes on the State of Virginia* to refute Buffon and others who denigrated American nature. He repeatedly highlighted the beneficent effects of the American environment. When the remains of a woolly mammoth were uncovered, Jefferson rejoiced, convinced that this huge mammal demonstrated not just

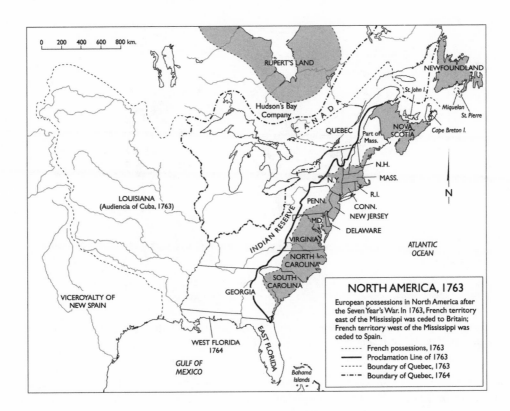

North America. Shading indicates British territory.

the equality of North American nature but its superiority; he confidently asserted that, once the entire continent was explored, living examples of this creature larger than an elephant would be found. Jefferson drew up long lists comparing the number and sizes of species in Europe and America to emphasize the positive role of nature in the American wilderness. Jefferson and similar American thinkers saw their continent as a land where nature and reason worked hand in hand and provided the best hope for the future of mankind.

Social conditions in colonial America appeared to encourage faith in the beneficent partnership of nature and reason. Many philosophes hailed the absence there of an entrenched aristocracy that hindered the rise of natural talent and the fullest expression of reason. As Crèvecoeur put it, America was "not composed, as in Europe, of great lords who possess everything and of a herd of people who have nothing." Instead, most Americans owned property and were "animated with the spirit of industry which is unfettered and unrestrained, because each person works for himself." The result was "a pleasing uniformity of decent competence." Crèvecoeur called the American a "new man," who, having left behind corrupt ancient principles, now lived in prosperity with a new mode of life and under a new government. Before 1776, however, this new man lived in British North America, where a

beneficent king of England had allowed representative forms of government to develop. Although Crèvecouer admitted to a greater equality in America that seemed to spring naturally from the air and the forest, he retained faith in hierarchy; thus, his exemplary American success story of Andrew the Hebridian depended on the assistance and guidance of an established and wealthy patron.

Colonial Elites. The Enlightenment also furnished ideals of leadership based in education and gentility. Colonial elites even designed their architecture to further these ideals, building Georgian mansions that embodied the principles of balance and order: a door at the center, with an equal number of windows on either side on the first and second floors. Inside was a center hall large enough to host guests of all social orders, with rooms for the family and friends separate and to the sides. A grand staircase led from the hall to more intimate and private spaces above. In such a house, Andrew the Hebridian might transact business with his patron without ever visiting the inner sanctum. Along with the benevolence that was the duty of a gentleman, social order and decorum were maintained.

Jefferson and other American leaders of the eighteenth century learned about the Enlightenment from books and then strove to fulfill its ideals. Colonial libraries held works by John Locke, Isaac Newton, and David Hume. American philosophes acquired their political

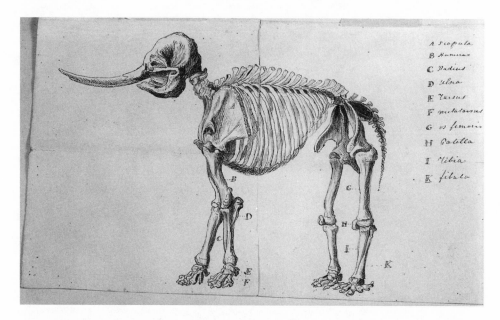

"Superiority" of North American Nature. "Working Sketch of the Mastodon," drawing by Rembrandt Peale, 1801. (American Philosophical Society.)

ideas through Algernon Sidney as well as John Trenchard and Thomas Gordon's *Cato's Letters*. They read the poetry of Alexander Pope. Exposure to French philosophe writing was more limited and usually was filtered through English commentators and translations, but the most literate colonists would have been familiar with Voltaire and the political writings of Montesquieu, which held up the English constitution as an ideal.

Eighteenth-century Americans took this book learning and applied it to the world around them. As is evident in Jefferson's effort to answer Buffon, science and the natural world were important to American intellectuals. John Bartram of Pennsylvania earned a reputation as a naturalist that won him an appointment as royal botanist. David Rittenhouse, also of Pennsylvania, gained fame for his astronomical observations and mechanical orrery. These and other Pennsylvanians organized the American Philosophical Society in the 1760s to encourage the pursuit of scientific knowledge. At Harvard College, John Winthrop's astronomical work also won him some fame. The best-known American man of science was Benjamin Franklin, whose study of electricity gained him an international reputation.

Franklin was also the outstanding spokesman for self-improvement. In the nineteenth century, his *Autobiography* would become the American exemplar of the rags-to-riches myth. Within the context of its own century, however, it should be seen as a product of the Enlightenment and an assertion of the need for practical and secular education. Franklin devoured books as a youth, organized a lending library, and helped to form a society,

the Junto, to discuss, debate, and exchange ideas—the wellspring for what would become the University of Pennsylvania. If America was to be the land where nature and reason were to rule supreme, then those endowed with natural intelligence needed to be encouraged, nurtured, and educated. For the same reason, Jefferson helped to found the University of Virginia.

The reading of the American philosophes also had an impact on religion. Before the American Revolution, all the colonies but Rhode Island and Pennsylvania had some form of religious establishment, but the number of denominations had created a de facto religious freedom in the colonies. Some Americans pushed the idea of religious freedom further, conceiving a deist God who created the universe like a clockmaker, wound it up, and then merely let it go on ticking. Franklin's religion was typical of an American philosophe. Swept into brief enthusiasm by the evangelist George Whitefield, he once emptied his pocket after a sermon, but this response was the exception; Franklin was never committed to a particular sect and had a pragmatic approach to religion. He believed in God and the immortality of the soul, but he had doubts about the divinity of Jesus, even though he admired the Christian moral system, which he believed to be the best possible.

Americans also viewed government through the teachings of the Enlightenment. Many writers before the American Revolution praised the British colonial governments and emphasized the similarities between their organization and the mystical balance of the English constitution that was the envy of the European Enlightenment.

Philosophes pointed out that the English constitution balanced different elements of society in its government, with the king representing the one (monarchy), the House of Lords the few (aristocracy), and the House of Commons the many (democracy). By the same token, each colony had a governor standing in for the king, an upper house (except in Pennsylvania) for the aristocracy, and a lower house for the democracy. This theory had even less relation to reality in America than in England, but on both sides of the Atlantic it was heralded as a triumph of rational and enlightened government.

The American Revolution. Change would disrupt this constitutional illusion. Eighteenth-century thinkers believed that if natural laws and reason ruled all things, then history, too, could be studied and men and nations plotted within a predictable scheme. History was organic: all nations ran a predetermined course from their youth, charged with vigor and enthusiasm, to their maturity, a period of judgment, intelligence, and power, to their old age, weak and senile. American philosophes, following the lead of those Europeans who held North America in high esteem, knew where they fit—America was young and vibrant. Many American political leaders joined in the American Revolution partly to prevent an acceleration of the organic development of their society. They viewed British imperial measures as an effort to corrupt the pristine youth of America and to infect it with an early decay.

Other Americans disagreed with the idea that Britain was leading the colonists down the path of corruption; these people became the Loyalists during the Revolutionary War. They argued that the revolutionaries were pursuing their own interests at the expense of the public good. Loyalists believed that the mobs and committees that propelled Americans toward independence threatened property, order, and good government, and that only a beneficent king could provide a shield to protect all of society. This stream of enlightened thought, emphasizing balance and order in society and government, was brought to Canada by exiled Tories after the Revolutionary War and led to an emphasis on "peace, order and good government" in the British North America Act (now called the Constitution Act) of 1867.

For the revolutionaries, however, the move to independence unleashed great hopes for the achievements of the new republic. Before independence, some European philosophes ridiculed American accomplishments. After it, even the former critic, the abbé Raynal, gushed with optimism, declaring that the new nation across the Atlantic might give birth to "a new Olympus, a new Arcady, a new Athens, a new Greece," and that it was in North America "that the first rays of knowledge are to shine." Jefferson, of course, agreed with this assessment. He praised the achievements of Washington in war and of Franklin and Rittenhouse in science and philosophy, and then proclaimed "in government, in oratory, in painting, in the plastic art...that America, though but a child of yesterday, has already given hopeful proofs of genius." Such hopes depended on how deeply enlightened ideas reached in society.

Rather than ushering in a new age of enlightened and benevolent leadership worthy of the Roman Senate, the American Revolution unleashed egalitarian impulses that contradicted notions of a natural aristocracy. The ferment of revolution brought a host of changes that spread Enlightenment ideas more broadly within society but simultaneously carried the seeds of a new order that spelled the demise of the Age of Reason.

It is difficult to measure the impact of the Enlightenment on all levels of American society. We can get some idea of its influence among the elite by examining their writings and looking at the books they owned. We know that some American philosophes, like Franklin and Rittenhouse, had humble origins; others, like Crevecoeur, may have started life higher in society but claimed humble circumstances in North America. All three wrote as members of the elite. Our knowledge of the ideas of the typical mechanic or farmer remains limited.

With the American Revolution, we begin to get a broader view of the reach of enlightened ideas. Thomas Paine's *Common Sense* sold hundreds of thousands of copies after publication in January 1776. Its plain language and avoidance of all learned references except to the Bible had great mass appeal, but it was also a bold testimony to the power of the Age of Reason. On almost every page, Paine referred to "nature" and "natural rights" as the test of good government. He simplified the ideas of Locke, relating the origins of society to first principles and viewing government as "the badge of lost innocence." Although some revolutionaries, like Jefferson, agreed with Paine's separation of government and society, Paine's message was not entirely comforting to American elites. Following Enlightenment teachings, this former corset-maker wanted to strip society of all anachronisms, including hereditary monarchy and nobility. Paine wrote that "one of the strongest *natural* proofs of the folly of hereditary right in kings, is, that nature disapproves it." He also asserted that, since all men are "originally equals, no *one* by *birth* could have a right to set up his own family in perpetual preference to all others for ever." His language and message were so potent that a crowd of New York mechanics destroyed a pamphlet critical of *Common Sense*, printed in April 1776. Other enlightened ideas spread through American society as well. After 1776, even deism had some mass appeal: in frontier Vermont, Ethan Allen published *Reason the Only Oracle of Man* (1784), decrying the Bible and the clergy;

and Franklin's grandson, Benjamin Franklin Bache, distributed 15,000 copies of Paine's deistic *Age of Reason* (1794) in Philadelphia in the 1790s.

The American Revolution also allowed middle-class men such as Benjamin Rush to come into prominence. Trained as a physician, Rush joined the resistance movement and was a signer of the Declaration of Independence. In the 1780s, he became more conservative, supporting a more restrictive state constitution and backing the nationalist efforts of the authors of the United States Constitution. A true American philosophe, Rush had many enthusiasms in his pursuit of Enlightenment ideals. He was a man of science who wrote extensively, if at times erroneously, on the origins of diseases such as yellow fever. He joined the American Philosophical Society and headed a medical association. He espoused a variety of reform measures for society, opposing slavery, working for prison reform, calling for the end of capital punishment, and supporting better treatment for the insane. He also strove to organize a state-run educational system to encourage the young (including women) to develop to their full potential.

Decline of the Age of Reason. Such reforms gained national attention after independence and pushed Americans in unexpected directions. For example, northern states moved toward the abolition of slavery, often through the passage of gradual emancipation laws. New York enacted its law in 1799, and then altered its provisions several times before freeing all its slaves on 4 July 1827. In other states, such as Massachusetts, where judicial decisions ended slavery, abolition occurred more quickly. Even a few southern states discussed freeing slaves, but they only passed laws that allowed a master to manumit his slaves. All states abolished the external slave trade before 1808, when the U.S. Congress made it a federal crime to import slaves from abroad.

Subscribing to the ideal that the human race, as Massachusetts clergyman Samuel Williams declared in 1775, was "capable of continual advances towards a state of perfect happiness," Americans influenced by European writers such as Cesare Beccaria began to create institutions to deal with social ills. Previously, punishment of crime had been a community responsibility that emphasized physical chastisement; the criminal was whipped, branded, or executed in a public place as an example. Now, armed with the Lockean theory of sensationalism, in which evil was not innate and all knowledge could be gained through the senses, civic thinkers could imagine the perfectibility of man. Reforming criminals and teaching them the difference between right and wrong became the focus of punishment. Buildings that had indiscriminately held criminals, debtors, lunatics, and the poor of both sexes now became specialized institutions. Gradually, even executions were moved out of the public eye.

This interest in reform led to a general demand to codify and declare the rights of man. On a pragmatic level, this call meant that states agreed to constitutional guarantees with state bills of rights during the 1770s and 1780s. The first ten amendments to the U.S. Constitution, insisted on by the Anti-Federalists, wrote into the fundamental law of the land freedom of religion, speech, assembly, right to a fair trial, and other protections that owed a great deal to the ideals of the Age of Reason.

There were limits to the extension of the rights of man, however. Remnants of established churches lasted in Connecticut and Massachusetts until well into the nineteenth century. More important, despite the appeal of deism and the emergence of Universalism, the American public remained largely Protestant and intolerant of attacks on religion. Paine's diatribe against religion in the *Age of Reason* led many to call him "godless" and diminished his reputation as an American hero. Other ingrained attitudes limited the extension of rights. Although some African Americans gained their freedom, they were denied full equality in both North and South. Adhering to the idea that only independent men could exercise enough judgment to participate fully in the political process, free blacks were disenfranchised in many states. The same concern with independent judgment lay behind the exclusion of women from politics (although a few propertied women briefly exercised the franchise in New Jersey). The early years of the republic also saw an acceleration of efforts to deprive Native Americans of their land east of the Mississippi, culminating in the policy of Indian removal in the 1830s, the infamous "Trail of Tears."

Enthusiasm for natural rights can also be seen in popular support for the French Revolution, which at least began in the spirit of the Enlightenment. Americans were excited by the prospect of exporting their revolutionary principles. When Frenchmen stormed the Bastille in 1789, many Americans believed that the dawn of a new age had come. As the promise of an enlightened government in France degenerated into the unreason of mass executions in the Reign of Terror, Americans became divided; some sustained their support for revolution and the rise of the common man, while others rejected the violence and disorder of revolutionary France. Politics in the 1790s became polarized as some Americans sang French patriotic songs and celebrated revolution around the liberty pole, while others decried "mobocracy" and the evils of faction.

The great debate of the 1790s can be seen as a contest over interpretations of the American Revolution and of contrasting visions of the Enlightenment. On one hand, Alexander Hamilton and the Federalists stressed natural order and reasonable balance. Appalled by the violence in France, they still admired the symmetry of the English constitution. They believed that the U.S. Constitution had recaptured that equilibrium without the trappings of hereditary monarchy and nobility. Hamilton wanted to go even further by pushing an activist economic program that would tie the different elements of society together through dependence on a national debt and bank. Federalists believed that the national government would become the cement that bound all Americans. A new Athens was to fulfill this ideal—a national capital laid out following enlightened principles, with monumental buildings modeled after Greek and Roman architecture.

On the other hand, Thomas Jefferson, James Madison, and the Democratic Republicans clung to the belief that the French ultimately would establish a republican form of government. They also believed that America differed from Europe because here, nature and reason had worked unfettered to create independent men. The American Revolution had released these men from their last attachments to a degenerate world of dependence, and now they could exercise their independent judgment through a democratic process and select the natural leaders of their society. Jefferson abhorred dependence on debt and a national bank, which he said would return America to the corruption represented by imperial Britain.

Jefferson's election in 1800 thus represents both the triumph of Enlightenment ideas in America and the beginning of the decline of the Age of Reason. As a tour of Jefferson's home, Monticello, reveals, few Americans better represented the ideal philosophe. He was an architect who drew inspiration from classical forms, and an inventor who sought to create practical devices. He was a skilled writer who could render the complex ideas of his age in simple but elegant prose, a thinker who pondered the world about him, and a patron of science and exploration who inspired the journey of Lewis and Clark. He strove to streamline government, putting into practice the maxim that the best government governs least. His victory also ushered into America the laissez-faire economics of Adam Smith and the Scottish Enlightenment. Government became increasingly invisible, and the individual, that human repository of reason and rights, ever more transcendent. Small government meant that the District of Columbia was not to be a new Rome; the Jeffersonians restrained the building of monuments. They also abandoned the Federalist notion that government should reflect a balance between monarchy, aristocracy, and democracy. As Republicans pursued the ideal of equality and unleashed the individual in society, the Age of Reason came to an end. In its place emerged a rough-and-tumble democracy that found its ultimate expression in the frontiersman president, Andrew Jackson. Thus, the contradiction between belief in equality and faith in enlightened "natural aristocrats"—a contradiction that

had bedeviled American enlightened thought from the beginning—was settled in favor of the former.

[*See also* American Revolution; Canada; Constitution of the United States; Franklin, Benjamin; Jefferson, Thomas; Learned Societies; *and* Paine, Thomas.]

BIBLIOGRAPHY

Appleby, Joyce. *Capitalism and a New Social Order: The Republican Vision of the 1790s*. New York, 1984. The Jeffersonians were proto-capitalists because, building on the ideas of John Locke, they believed that the individual should be freed in the marketplace to pursue their own interests.

Bailyn, Bernard. *The Origins of American Politics*. New York, 1967. The American Revolution applied the ideas of English radical thinkers who saw the liberty of the people opposed to the power of government, the imperial crisis, and the creation of a new nation.

Banning, Lance. *The Sacred Fire of Liberty: James Madison and the Founding of the Federal Republic*. Ithaca, N.Y., 1995. James Madison consistently adhered to ideas centered on the fear of the tyranny of the majority from the days of being a nationalist and leading force in developing the U.S. Constitution to his opposition to the Hamiltonian.

Commager, Henry Steele. *The Empire of Reason: How Europe Imagined and America Realized the Enlightenment*. Garden City, N.Y., 1977. Europeans may have imagined the Enlightenment, but Americans through their revolution were able to live it.

Crèvecoeur, J. Hector St. John de. *Letters from an American Farmer and Sketches of Eighteenth-Century America*. New York, 1981. Eighteenth-century writer who viewed the British colonies as the fulfillment of the Enlightenment dream of a land of nature and reason, but who saw the American Revolution as shattering that idyllic world.

Echeverria, Durand. *Mirage in the West: A History of the French Image of American Society to 1815*. Princeton, N.J., 1957. The French philosophe view of America as a land of nature and reason was a distortion of reality created by the French to fulfill their own needs to sustain a dream of a new order.

Ellis, Joseph J. *After the Revolution: Profiles of Early American Culture*. New York, 1979. American art and literature would reflect high cultural ideals and would enjoy widespread popularity.

Ferguson, Robert A. *The American Enlightenment, 1750–1820*. Cambridge, Mass., 1997. The literature created during the American Revolution, pulling on the ideas of the Enlightenment, struggled to create consensus on government and society.

Franklin, Benjamin. *The Autobiography and Other Writings*. New York, 1986. The autobiography and self-help manual of one of America's most famous founding fathers that reflected the ideal of the perfectability of mankind through personal action.

Greene, John C. *American Science in the Age of Jefferson*. Ames, Iowa, 1984. Science during the Jeffersonian era gradually constructed an institutional base and developed a uniquely American character.

Jefferson, Thomas. *The Portable Thomas Jefferson*. New York, 1975. A collection of Jefferson's major writings, including some letters and the "Notes of the State of Virginia."

McCoy, Drew. *The Elusive Republic: Political Economy in Jeffersonian America*. New York, 1980. Jeffersonian republicans believed that commerce based on agricultural production would allow the American republic to develop a sophisticated and civilized state and economy, while maintaining the virtue of the people.

May, Henry F. *The Enlightenment in America*. New York, 1976. The Enlightenment consisted of four contradictory impulses: a moderate Enlightenment based on balance; a skeptical Enlightenment that was more a style of criticism than a body of ideas; the revolutionary Enlightenment that held out the possibility of the millennium and radical change; and a didactic Enlightenment that emphasized an intelligible universe, clear moral judgement, and progress.

Meyer, Donald H. *Democratic Enlightenment*. New York, 1978. The American Enlightenment spanned the eighteenth century and, although it went through several shifts in emphasis, its essential quality was in the application of theory to the practical world, rather than in the creation of new ideas.

Paine, Thomas. *Common Sense*. New York, 1976. Famous revolutionary tract advocating independence and the end of hierarchy in America.

Wood, Gordon S. *The Radicalism of the American Revolution*. New York, 1991. The American Revolution was a radical break from the past; it began with a world committed to social distinctions, became a movement motivated by a republican ideal that sought to balance different levels of society, and ended with a democratic world committed to the ideal of equality.

PAUL A. GILJE

NOUVELLES ECCLÉSIASTIQUES. *See* Jansenism *and* Revealed Religion.

NOVEL. No other literary genre was as crucial to the age of Enlightenment as the novel.

During its formative period, the modern novel was in large part the result of massive shifts of influence back and forth across the English Channel. From 1660 to about the mid-eighteenth century, the prose fiction created both in England and in France was overwhelmingly "French": readers everywhere were reading French novels; the most widely influential trends in prose fiction originated in France. During this period, fiction produced in England generally has a very French air. Then, from roughly 1750 to the end of the long eighteenth century, the tide was reversed, and the novel became increasingly "English." At that moment, novels written in France were massively influenced by trends that originated in England. It is at this time that the novel begin to develop in other national literatures, but the mark of English fiction is always evident.

From the time that the modern novel began to take shape during the second half of the seventeenth century, the genre's subversive potential was widely recognized and exploited. Many early novelists referred to their works as "secret histories" to highlight their claim that they were revealing the underside of history, the truths about great kings and their motivations that historians had attempted to cover up. The novel's first critics were quick to attack the genre for just this reason: They contended that novelists were tricking their readers into taking their fraudulent fictions for historical fact.

The early novel was seen as subversive in many ways, first of all in generic terms. Some of its defenders contended that it had classical precedent and discussed the

works in antiquity from which it was descended. Most observers of the literary scene, however, recognized—and often criticized—the novel as a bastard form, a literary upstart without the type of classical pedigree then expected of great literature. The novel—like many of its best-known heroes, from Daniel Defoe's Robinson Crusoe (1719) to Pierre Carlet de Marivaux's "upstart" peasant Jacob (*Le paysan parvenu*, 1734–1735)—threatened the foundations of the Republic of Letters as it then functioned. The novel had no birthright, and it sought acceptance on its merits alone.

The novel was also perceived as threatening because of its association with women. No other genre has ever been so overtly associated with them, and this association was never more controversial than during the long eighteenth century. With the fledgling genre, for the first time ever, women writers played a major, often even the major role in the creation of a literary form. Novelists such as the woman often said to have authored the first modern novel, Marie-Madeleine Pioche de La Vergne, comtesse de La Fayette, Marie-Catherine Desjardins (known as Madame de Villedieu), and Mary Delarivière Manley helped popularize the secret history. From then until the end of the Enlightenment, record numbers of women writers participated in every significant moment in the genre's development. Often their contributions (Aphra Behn's *Oroonoko, or The Royal Slave* [1688] is a particularly striking example) dealt with the most controversial subject matter: the first novels to represent slavery, as well as the first novels to fictionalize the French Revolution, were authored by women. With a genre so heavily coded as female, male novelists quickly learned that they could win recognition by ventriloquizing women. Thus, major novelists—most notably, Samuel Richardson and Marivaux—became famous because their style was considered inherently feminine, because they had created what their readers considered the perfect female voice. At no other time in its history was the novel so overwhelmingly feminocentric. Novelists male and female alike celebrated, pitied, and sometimes condemned the female characters whose psychology they explored, all the while doing something that had very rarely ever been done in literature before—centering their works on women and their lives. Finally, and perhaps predictably, the novel's detractors warned ominously that it had the potential to feminize its readers, and even that it would prove a menace to society because it would weaken its (male) moral fiber.

Many of the major eighteenth-century novelists capitalized on the novel's reputation for being a subversive genre. All of them profited in different ways from its original status as somehow truer than other genres, as more real and more believable than more established literary forms. Believability was evidently what Enlightenment audiences were after, for eighteenth-century novels had previously unheard of sales. A number of them—most spectacularly, Richardson's *Clarissa, or, the History of a Young Lady* (1747–1748), Jean-Jacques Rousseau's *Julie, ou la nouvelle Héloïse* (1761), and Johann Wolfgang von Goethe's *Die Leiden des jungen Werthers* (The Sorrows of Young Werther, 1774)—became true social phenomena, publication "events" that provoked vast numbers of readers to feel a strange new bond with both author and characters, to care with an intensity that literary works had never before inspired. Readers somehow came to feel that they "knew" Richardson and Clarissa alike, both Rousseau and Julie, or that their lives would find new meaning if they were able to meet Goethe or Rousseau.

Readers in droves wrote letters to these authors, advising them on how their characters might have acted and asking advice on how to carry out their own lives. The public couldn't get enough of these books, and its obsession with them fueled the first precursors of today's media tie-ins. Sequels and dramatizations were published, as well as volumes of the favorite sayings of these beloved characters. For the first time ever, literature generated merchandise inspired by it. Women could carry fans depicting scenes from *Clarissa*; they could wear Werther jewelry and eau de Werther. There were even Clarissa playing cards—and porcelain statues of Werther were produced in China. Moreover, the audience for eighteenth-century prose fiction was not only broad but admirably targeted. The correspondences of famous authors prove that the novels of the Enlightenment had particular appeal for female and bourgeois readers, precisely those new readerships that publishers had been hoping to attract since the mid-seventeenth century, when the print industry began consciously to reach out to the period's equivalent of a mass audience.

The desire to find an audience broader and more diverse than the readership for treatises and other more traditional vehicles for the exploration of philosophical and political ideas also explains the philosophes' long and complex involvement with the novel. That involvement was launched in 1721, with Charles-Louis de Secondat Montesquieu's *Lettres persanes*. This is a classic Enlightenment fiction: Two Persian gentlemen, hoping to acquire "knowledge" and "lumières," travel to Paris. There, they circulate freely in French society. They send back to Persia letters filled with scathing accounts of political corruption, social hypocrisy, and economic scandal. Montesquieu's novel is representative of two major traditions of the eighteenth-century novel. The fiction of foreign visitors with a completely fresh perspective on European society was exploited by many novelists, notably Voltaire. Further, epistolary fiction was both the Enlightenment's favorite kind of novel and among its preferred vehicles for

social critique. Denis Diderot's graphic and violent denunciation of the abusive treatment received by young women locked away in convents by uncaring families, *La religieuse* (written 1760, published 1780–1783), for example, takes the form of extended letters written by a young nun to an enlightened protector in the hope that he will intercede on her behalf. One of the greatest of all epistolary novels, Pierre-Ambroise-François Choderlos de Laclos's *Les liaisons dangereuses* (1782), recounts the wide swath cut through a corrupt upper-class world by two of the most thoroughly corrupt characters in literature. Many subsequently saw it as a sign of the inevitability of the Revolution of 1789.

Montesquieu's truest heir was a woman. With *Lettres d'une Péruvienne* (1747), Françoise de Graffigny became the only woman writer to participate in the Enlightenment project on the philosophes' own terms. In her fiction of French society viewed through the eyes of a Peruvian woman, she often seems to be following the parameters of Montesquieu's critique. Her most scathing commentary is reserved, however, for a subject that her male counterparts left largely unexamined: The ways in which contemporary society, no matter how enlightened, continued to exclude women from participation in the public arena. Graffigny's novel is a perfect example of the "French" tradition of the letter novel, in which the story of the characters' lives and the development of their psychology always goes hand in hand with their participation in contemporary philosophical and social debates.

The Enlightenment was just as powerfully marked by a second tradition of the epistolary novel that can be seen as "English" because of the founding role played in it by Richardson's *Pamela* (1740) and *Clarissa*. The novels in this tradition testify to the powerful influence exercised by sentimentality throughout the archetypal age of reason. The protagonists of these letter novels are almost all men and women of feeling. "English" letter novels explore what Richardson termed "writing to the moment," the unfolding—almost literally moment by moment—of their characters' emotional lives; they do so in a temporal mode that aims as much as possible to erase the distinction between the time at which an action takes place and that at which it is described. Together, Richardson and Rousseau, Richardson's most famous heir, inspired a tradition of epistolary novels, the majority of which were authored by women. All these novels have a strong domestic streak: They focus on daily life and mundane objects rather than great deeds and major events, and they do so from a woman's perspective. They feature private homes and are often set in the country, a choice of setting that inspired novelists, Rousseau in particular, to celebrate natural beauty, thereby paving the way for Romanticism.

Among the finest examples of the "English" epistolary style are Marie-Jeanne de Laboras's *Lettres de Milady Juliette Catesby* (1759); Sophie von La Roche's *Geschichte des Fräuleins von Sternheim* (1771), recognized as the first novel in German literature by a woman; Frances Burney's *Evelina* (1778); and Isabelle de Charrière's *Lettres écrites de Lausanne* (1785).

"English" letter novels almost always had international appeal. All over Europe, translation was particularly rapid during the Enlightenment: These works were quickly made available, sometimes even in translations that became famous in their own right. For example, *Lettres anglaises, ou histoire de Miss Clarissa Harlowe* (1751), a translation by the abbé Antoine-François Prévost d'Exiles, a noted novelist himself, quickly took on classic status and made Richardson famous in France.

In addition, this variant of the eighteenth-century novel has a particularly strong transnational flavor, perhaps due to the backgrounds of many of its creators. Rousseau, a citizen of Geneva, for example, composed his major works in England and in France, as well as in his native country; Laboras (Madame Riccoboni) was married to an Italian and Burney (Madame d'Arblay), who lived for many years in France, to a Frenchman; the woman scholars today refer to as Isabelle de Charrière was of Dutch origin (she was born Isabella van Tuyll van Serooskerken) and composed her *oeuvre* in French while living in Switzerland. Sentimental letter novelists carried this transnational spirit into their works. *Julie*, for example, is set in Switzerland. Charrière repeatedly depicted a pan-European cast of characters who encounter each other in various Swiss cities. Riccoboni preferred English characters and settings, while Burney's heroine has complex French connections. The "English" letter novel's transnational flavor can be viewed as paying homage to the central doctrine of sentimentalism: Sympathetic individuals are destined to find each other and instantly and fully to understand each other; no national boundaries could ever hinder this communion of sensitive, sympathetic souls.

The epistolary novel was the dominant, but far from the only, form in which first-person narration reigned over the eighteenth-century novel. Memoir novels were introduced in the seventeenth century, once again by women writers: Villedieu's *Mémoires de la vie de Henriette-Sylvie de Molière* (1671) is a particularly fine example of the genre's potential. The influence of the Spanish picaresque novel is evident in this tale of the feverish social ascension of an irrepressible heroine. With her keen appraisals of those she encounters during her travels through France and the Low Countries and her eagerness to manipulate all those she meets in order to reach her goals, Sylvie announces the heroine of the century's best known French memoir novel, Marivaux's *La vie de Marianne* (1731–1737). With her frank appreciation of the power of her sexuality—which she never hesitates to use for her advancement—Villedieu's heroine looks forward to the protagonist of Defoe's celebrated memoir novel, *Moll Flanders* (1722). (Moll's lustiness may even one-up Sylvie's sexual displays.)

Memoir novels come in many very different guises. In all cases, they give a remarkably different portrait of the character describing his or her life in the first person from that found in letter novels. Fictional memoirs in general work against the foundation of sentimentalism, the idea that sentiment and the emotional life are at the core of our being. Instead, they give their readers a series of diverse portrayals of what most preoccupied the eighteenth-century hero or heroine. In perhaps the most celebrated of them all, *Robinson Crusoe*, Defoe plays off against the confessional autobiography, a major contemporary strain in nonfictional prose, particularly in Protestant countries. Rather than give readers the portrait of an individual's inner moral life, Defoe suggests that business and the work ethic play the central organizing role in the human psyche. Even when stranded on a desert island, his hero remains the ideal figure for an age of nascent capitalism. Fully an economic man, Robinson Crusoe gives an account of his life that is closer to a bookkeeper's ledger than to the re-creation of the stirrings of a human heart.

Indeed, all eighteenth-century memoir fictions frequently call attention to finance's role in the formation of character. No French hero would ever stoop to providing the actual cost of anything; all of them do, however, pay eloquent testimony to the central role played by things, and luxury goods in particular, in their lives. Characters such as Marianne and Jacob devote so much energy to their quest for the luxury goods and status symbols that would give them the appearance of noble birth that it could be argued that Marivaux is suggesting that consumerism is the measure of a man—and, even more so, of a woman. The heroes of a characteristically French form, the libertine memoir novel, are also heavily involved in the culture of appearances. As aristocrats, they do not lust for expensive objects; their possession is rather but one of the tools for seduction manipulated by the libertines. For the young men (this type of novel bears almost no trace of the feminocentrism elsewhere so overwhelmingly present) who tell their tales in memoir fictions such as Claude-Prosper Jolyot de Crébillon's *Les égarements du coeur et de l'esprit* (The Wanderings of the Heart and Spirit, 1736) and Charles Duclos's *Les Confessions du comte de**** (1741), a man's worth is evaluated by one standard alone: his capacity for sexual conquest.

Still another variant of the memoir novel presents the existence of those whose pursuit of worldly goods leads them to a life of crime. Once again, the English version of this story is both more explicit and more practical. Defoe's Moll Flanders proudly flaunts her life as a petty criminal and, in numerous finely detailed vignettes, she shows the reader the tricks of her trade. Prévost's *Histoire du Chevalier des Grieux et de Manon Lescaut* (1731) gives an upper-crust and less celebratory perspective on the criminal life. The blame, however, is laid only on the woman, as Prévost's male narrator endlessly protests that he would never have become a high-class thief had he not fallen for a mysterious femme fatale.

The first person is also present in eighteenth-century fiction in another, less easily defined category. Works in this category are often referred to as comic or self-conscious because they all offer an explicit challenge to the manner in which first-person narrative is used in other types of eighteenth-century prose fiction. In the epistolary and the memoir novel, characters speak directly to their audience; the immediacy of the contact thus established played an essential role in encouraging readers to believe that those to whom they had such direct access were somehow more real than other fictional beings. Self-conscious novels also use a first-person narrator. In these works, however, the narrator speaks directly to readers in order to force them to question the reality principle operative in other first-person novels. Wherever readers of self-conscious novels might begin to get involved in their characters' lives, the narrator intervenes to explain, for example, that he's not sure what really happened to them, or if the protagonists ever reached their destination, or to remind readers in some other fashion of the completely arbitrary nature of lives lived in the pages of a novel.

The eighteenth century's most famous comic novel was English, Laurence Sterne's vertiginously witty *Tristram Shandy* (1760–1767). *Tristram Shandy* can be seen as an extreme version of the memoir novel: Because of its narrator and its narrative structure, the reader comes away above all with a sense that character is measured by eccentricity. Sterne had his most profound impact across the Channel, with Diderot's brilliant experiments in self-conscious fiction, notably *Jacques le fataliste* (written 1771–1781, published posthumously 1796). Readers are asked to follow Diderot's narrator through so many digressions that they ultimately lose track of the allegedly basic elements of the novel's plot. In the Enlightenment's comic fictions, plot is always subordinated to narrative technique.

The hold exercised by first-person narration over the eighteenth-century novel was so powerful that the rare novels told in the third person seem almost to disappear in a sea of "I"s. In addition, third-person novels in the eighteenth century cannot be classified into a single genre, although most have some loose affiliation with travel literature. In Voltaire's *Candide* (1759), the hero's voyages and many encounters make it possible for him to acquire firsthand knowledge of a variety of philosophical systems. Donatien-Alphonse-François de Sade's *Les 120 Journées de Sodome* (*The 120 Days of Sodom*, written 1785–1789, published 1931–1935) is a radically different but equally extreme case: The libertine protagonists journey to the ends of the earth to find the absolute seclusion that will permit them to make a scientific study of sexual perversions. Indeed, the only novelist whose third-person fictions resist even this minimal classification is Henry Fielding. *Tom Jones* (1749), for example, features many of the issues that preoccupy contemporary memoir novels, notably, the secret of the protagonist's birth. Rather than giving readers access to the subjective dimensions of such issues, however, it focuses above all on their repercussions for society and the larger order it represents.

From the time of the genre's origins in the seventeenth century, authors who chose to write novels were among the first to understand our modern economy of authorship. Novelists such as Madeleine de Scudéry and Aphra Behn were some of the earliest authors who managed to free themselves either completely or nearly so from the patronage system and to make a living by selling their manuscripts directly to publishers. While in the seventeenth century few writers achieved this measure of success, in the eighteenth century many novelists lived by their pens. This new situation was made possible by the vastly increased sales potential of successful novels during the age of Enlightenment.

The size of the print runs of early fiction is only rarely known. Early in the novel's history, they were small, often 750 to 1,000 copies. Subsequently, they were often larger. The first four volumes of *Clarissa* were so successful, for example, that 3,000 copies of the first edition of the final three volumes were printed. The last three volumes did not sell out immediately, however, so they were not reprinted when a second edition was demanded. Factors such as this make it highly unlikely that we will ever determine exactly how many copies of any novel circulated. It is possible, however, to use the total number of editions of a given novel as an indicator of its sales.

In the seventeenth century, even the most acclaimed novels were rarely published in more than two or three editions. La Fayette's *La princesse de Clèves* was perhaps the most talked about novel of the seventeenth century, but it was reedited only twice between 1678, the year of its original edition, and 1715, the end of Louis XIV's reign. In the eighteenth century, highly popular novels had a vastly different publication history. The novel's sales potential was first realized in France. The century's best-selling novel by a woman writer, Graffigny's *Lettres d'une Péruvienne* (1747), went through forty-eight editions, in the first forty years of its existence alone. In France, the title of the century's greatest best-seller goes to Rousseau's *Julie* (1761): in its first forty years, *Julie* went through at least seventy editions.

In England, Richardson's novels are often called the first modern best-sellers. *Pamela*'s fifth edition was issued within a year of its original publication. Between 1747 and 1810, *Clarissa* appeared in some fifteen editions in London, Dublin, Boston, and Philadelphia. As the century progressed and the novel fell increasingly under English influence, English novels appeared in ever greater numbers of editions: Burney's *Camilla* (1796) went through twenty-six editions; Henry Mackenzie's *The Man of Feeling* (1771) forty-six; Tobias Smollett's *The Expedition of Humphry Clinker* (1771) appeared fifty-three times; Ann Radcliffe's *The Italian* (1797) went through seventy editions.

Finally, on both sides of the Channel the increased presence of circulating libraries and the beginning of a new practice, the renting of books by booksellers, meant that, in the eighteenth century, copies went farther than before. In the case of *Julie*, the demand for copies so outstripped their availability that booksellers rented it out not only by the day, but even by the hour!

The Revolution of 1789 altered the novel's history in many ways. In France, the printing of works of prose fiction radically tapered off during its bloodiest years. Some of Sade's works were among the rare novels to find their way into print: It was as if historical violence had authorized the making public of perhaps the most violent fictional universe of all time. With the almost simultaneous appearance of Radcliffe's *The Mysteries of Udolpho* (1794) and Matthew G. Lewis's *The Monk* (1795), the English novel initiated the craze for the unsettling fictions known as gothic that quickly spread all over Europe.

In the aftermath of the Revolution, the novel lost the remarkable unity so often evident in its eighteenth-century incarnation. The memoir novel and the epistolary novel briefly reappeared—Benjamin Constant de Rebeque's *Adolphe* (1816), Germaine Necker de Staël's *Delphine* (1802)—but the first person's reign over the territory of the novel was fast coming to a close. The nineteenth-century novel quickly showed its allegiance to third-person narration—consider Jane Austen, Honoré de Balzac, or Goethe's memorable contribution to the prose fiction of the new century, *Die Wahlverwandtschaften* (Congeniality, 1809).

After a few last gasps—notably Mary Shelley's *Frankenstein* (1818)—the age of the transnational novel, sentimentalism's legacy, also ended. No longer would an international cast of characters meet up in a neutral space such as Switzerland and, sensitive souls all, instantly and fully understand each other. The nineteenth-century novel is built upon a far more concentrated and more nationalistic sense of space. Austen's novels are set in a very small and a very homogeneous England. Despite the universalizing claim of his general title, *La comédie humaine*, Balzac's novelistic universe is terribly French and massively Parisian: The nineteenth-century French novel converges on Paris, the place where the young heroes who replace the heroines of eighteenth-century fiction feel that they must make their mark. This new national focus was reinforced by new practices of translation. During the long eighteenth century, the French and the English translate each others' most acclaimed novels with extraordinary rapidity: *La princesse de Clèves*, *Robinson Crusoe*, *Tom Jones*, and even *Pamela* all appeared in translation the year following their original publication. Then, in the nineteenth century the two traditions develop largely in isolation: *Le père Goriot* appeared in English twenty-six years after its original publication, *Le rouge et le noir* seventy years after its first edition, and *Wuthering Heights* appeared in French forty-five years after its original publication.

Because of this isolation, the nineteenth-century novel took on radically different shapes all over Europe. In the great age of the nation-state, the genre played a distinctly different role in each national literary tradition. In the Europe of the Enlightenment, readers of many nations shared the dreams fashioned by English and French novelists, dreams of communication without barriers—Persians can instantly become fluent in French, a young English lady is able immediately to record all her life in letters. After the Revolution, people of different cultures evidently preferred to dream their separate dreams.

[*See also* Feminist Theory; Literary Genres; Men and Women of Letters; Nominalism; *and* Publishing.]

BIBLIOGRAPHY

Alliston, April. *Virtue's Faults: Correspondences in Eighteenth-Century British and French Women's Fiction*. Cambridge, 1994.

Anderson, Benedict. *Imagined Communities: Reflections on The Origins and the Spread of Nationalism*. London, 1991. Brilliant account of print culture's role in shaping the bourgeoisie's class consciousness and of the relation between the novel and the nation-state.

Armstrong, Nancy. *Desire and Domestic Fiction*. New York, 1987. Considers the politics of fictions of domesticity.

Castle, Terry. *Masquerade and Civilization: The Carnivalesque in Eighteenth-Century English Culture and Fiction*. Stanford, Calif., 1986.

Davis, Lennard J. *Factual Fictions: The Origins of the English Novel*. New York, 1983.

DeJean, Joan. *Tender Geographies: Women and the Origins Of the Novel in France*. New York, 1991. Discusses the central role played by women novelists in the creation of the modern novel.

Denby, David. *Sentimental Narrative and the Social Order in France, 1760–1820*. Cambridge, 1994.

Doody, Margaret. *The True Story of the Novel*. New Brunswick, N.J., 1997. The longest view possible of the novel's history.

Eighteenth-Century Fiction. January–April 2000 and January–April 2001: *Reconsidering the Rise of the Novel*, edited by David Blewett, and *Transformations du genre romanesque au XVIIIᵉ siècle*, edited by English Showalter. Two special issues devoted to recent theories of the novel's development during the eighteenth century.

Gallagher, Catherine. *Nobody's Story: The Vanishing Acts of Women Writers in the Marketplace, 1670–1820*. Berkeley, Calif., 1994. An excellent introduction to the presence of English women writers in the long eighteenth century.

Hunter, J. Paul. *Before Novels: The Cultural Contexts of English Eighteenth-Century Fiction*. New York, 1990. Discusses other kinds of reading material that helped inform the English novel.

Kavanaugh, Thomas. *The Enlightenment and the Shadows of Chance: The Culture of Gambling in Eighteenth-Century France*. Baltimore, 1993. On the presence of gambling in eighteenth-century French fiction.

May, Georges. *Le Dilemme du roman au XVIIIᵉ siècle*. Paris and New Haven, Conn., 1963. The study that first attracted widespread scholarly attention to the eighteenth-century French novel.

McKeon, Michael. *The Origins of the English Novel, 1600–1740*. Baltimore, 1987. Discusses the interplay between the French and English traditions.

Miller, Nancy K. *The Heroine's Text: Readings in the French and English Novel, 1722–1782*. New York, 1980. Excellent explorations of the consequences of the novel's feminocentrism.

Moretti, Franco. *The Atlas of the European Novel, 1800–1900*. London, 1998. Wonderfully suggestive view of the effects of geography on the novel's history.

Showalter, English. *The Evolution of the French Novel (1641–1782)*. Princeton, N.J., 1972. An excellent study of French fiction in the long eighteenth century.

Warner, William. *Licensing Entertainment: The Elevation of Novel Reading in Britain, 1684–1750*. Berkeley, Calif., 1998.

Watt, Ian. *The Rise of the Novel*. London, 1957. The study that put the eighteenth-century English novel back on the scholarly map.

JOAN DEJEAN

NOVERRE, JEAN-GEORGES (1727–1810), ballet-master and publicist.

Noverre was the leading figure in the development of the *ballet d'action*, in which dance and pantomime were conjoined to form an independent theatrical art. Fired from childhood with the ambition to become a dancer, he studied under several teachers, including the celebrated Louis Dupré, and he began his career modestly on the popular stage in Paris. After an engagement in Berlin, in 1753 he became ballet-master at the Opéra-Comique, where he staged a Chinese ballet that won him his first acclaim.

An abortive engagement in London then brought Noverre into contact with the actor David Garrick, who was a major influence in leading him to apply his mind to the problems affecting theatrical dance. His *Lettres sur la danse et sur les ballets*, published in 1760, was essentially a work in the tradition of the Enlightenment, being at once a radical analysis and a practical call for the reform of many existing abuses. It was immediately hailed as the authoritative polemic in support of the *ballet d'action*, and its influence was immense.

Noverre's reputation now spread beyond the borders of France, and in 1760 he was engaged at the ducal court of Württemberg, where over the next few years he was able to put his ideas into practice without regard to expense. Foremost among his productions was *Médée et Jason*, in which the great French dancer Gaëtan-Apolline-Balthasar Vestris played Jason. Noverre's stay there ended when the duke was forced to cut down on his expenditure. By then, his fame was such that Noverre was soon engaged as court ballet-master in Vienna. His output there included a wide variety of ballets, but his appointment ended when the Empress Maria Theresa closed the court opera.

In 1776, through the intervention of the French queen, Marie-Antoinette, Noverre was appointed ballet-master at the Paris Opéra. His arrival there was not taken kindly by those who had assisted the outgoing incumbent, and he was beset with difficulties. In 1781, he gave way to pressure and resigned. *Médée et Jason* had previously been staged in Paris by Vestris, so the cause of the *ballet d'action* already had made headway before Noverre's arrival, but the ballets he produced were instrumental in laying the foundations for his successors to establish the form. Among his ballets, it was the lighter works, such as *Les petits riens* (for which Mozart composed part of the music), that were the more successful.

Noverre's career as a ballet-master closed with a series of seasons in London between 1781 and 1794. He spent his last years in France, finally settling in Saint-Germain-en-Laye, where he devoted much of his time to writing. In 1807, his *Lettres sur les arts imitateurs*, a valuable compendium of articles on a wide variety of matters concerning his art, was published. At the time of his death, he was still active, working, it was reported, on a *Dictionary of Ballet*, which does not appear to have survived.

[*See also* Ballet.]

BIBLIOGRAPHY

Chéruzel, Maurice. *Jean-Georges Noverre: Levain de la danse moderne*. Saint-Germain-en-Laye, 1994.

Guest, Ivor. *The Ballet of the Enlightenment*. London, 1950.

Krüger, Manfred. *J. G. Noverre und das "Ballet d'action."* Emsdetten, 1963.

Lynham, Deryck. *The Chevalier Noverre: Father of Modern Ballet*. London, 1950.

Randi, Elena. *Pittura vivente: Jean-Georges Noverre eil balletto d'action*. Venice, 1989.

Tugal, Pierre. *Jean-Georges Noverre, der grosse Reformator des Balletts*. Berlin, 1959.

IVOR GUEST

NOVIKOV, NIKOLAI IVANOVICH (1744–1818), leading publisher and journalist in the Russian language.

Novikov was one of the small number of individuals who can be said to have shaped the institutional fabric of the Russian Enlightenment. Born into the provincial nobility, Novikov was one of a small cohort that was able to take advantage of the humanistic education offered by the newly opened Moscow University (1755), first at its pension for noble boys, then for two years at the university. Like other young men of his background, he began his career in the guards' regiments, but he first gained prominence as a secretary to the Legislative Commission that Catherine the Great had initiated in 1767 with the goal of creating a new law code for the empire. Once the Legislative Commission disbanded, Novikov moved on to journalism, translating, editing, and ultimately publishing. During the mid-1780s he was the largest publisher in the Russian Empire.

His first editing ventures were made in the Russian language during the era of the so-called satirical journals (1769–1774); he edited several periodicals in Saint Petersburg, where he then resided. These included *Zhivopisets* (The Painter), *Pustomelia* (The Tattler), *Koshelek* (The Hair Net), *Truten'* (The Drone). After that time, he undertook the publication of historical periodicals, including *The Ancient Russian Library*, which published hundreds of previously unknown documents from state archives. These publications provide an insight into Novikov's approach to Enlightenment as a mixture of both cosmopolitanism and a positive view of Russian customs and the Russian past. At this time he also developed his critique of foppishness, which he dubbed "Voltairianism," after the French philosophe Voltaire.

Novikov moved to Moscow in 1779. There he took over the press of Moscow University. After private publishing became easier in 1783, he established two significant publishing operations, the Typographical Company and the Masonic Press. During this time, his operations accounted for close to a third of the lay titles printed in the Russian language. His presses produced hundreds of translations of contemporary European literature, history, and social thought. He relied on a wide circle of literati and students at Moscow University, gathered into circles such as the Seminar of University Pupils. The relaxed rules of censorship and the government's relative tolerance for written expression enabled Novikov to offer an exceptionally wide range of thought to Russian readers. During the 1780s, his presses translated and published nearly one hundred contemporary novels, as well as the leading works of Voltaire, Jean Le Rond d'Alembert, Jean-Jacques Rousseau, Johann Gottfried Herder, and numerous other leading Enlightenment thinkers. With the possible exception of Catherine the Great, Novikov was the central figure in integrating the Russian reading public into the debates of European letters.

Ultimately, Novikov fell afoul of the authorities, in part because of the increasingly repressive atmosphere of post-1789 Russia, but largely because of his activities as a Moscow Rosicrucian, the most mystical and impenetrable of Russian Masonic lodges. First investigated in 1782, then again in 1785, he saw his publishing enterprise severely disrupted by a nationwide raid on bookstores in 1787, which led to the confiscation of a number of the Masonic titles published under his auspices. In 1789 he lost his lease to Moscow University; by 1792 his publishing empire was gone. In that year he was arrested, imprisoned for several years, and ultimately exiled to his estate in Tikhvinskoe, where he remained until his death in 1818.

[*See also* Print Culture; Publishing; Russia; *and* Translation.]

BIBLIOGRAPHY

Jones, W. Gareth. *Nikolay Novikov: Enlightener of Russia*. Cambridge, 1984. The most extensive English-language biography of Novikov.

McArthur, Gilbert. "Catherine II and the Masonic Circle of N. I. Novikov." *Canadian Slavic Studies* 4 (1970), 529–546. A discussion of Novikov's Masonic work.

Rogger, Hans. *National Consciousness in Eighteenth-Century Russia*. Cambridge, Mass., 1960. A synthetic analysis of the role of national identity in Russian letters, with extensive commentary on Novikov.

GARY MARKER

O

OLAVIDE, PABLO DE (1725–1803), Peruvian-Spanish reformer and man of letters.

Olavide spent the first twenty-four years of his life in Lima, Peru, where he had a brilliant academic career, earning degrees in theology and in canon and civil law. He was awarded a university chair and appointed to important government positions. After being charged with fraud, in 1749 he left for Spain, where he was incarcerated (1754). Until 1766, he held no further public office.

After traveling for almost nine years in Europe, primarily in France and Italy, Olavide returned to Madrid in 1765. Between 1766 and 1776, he held various public offices. His first public charge was in Madrid, where he undertook reforms to make productive citizens of the poor and uneducated. In 1767, he was named to positions of high responsibility in Seville and Andalusia; the enlightened ministers of Charles III, Pedro Pablo Abarca, count of Aranda, and Pedro Rodríguez de Campomanes, wanted men of similar ideas to carry out a wide range of reforms. Olavide and his team of reformers attempted to apply enlightened ideology to bring about change in a variety of areas, including education, agriculture, hospices, commerce, church lands, industry, river navigation, patriotic and worker groups, and the theater. His program of colonizing new towns in the south of Spain (the Sierra Morena), which were to be models for the rest of the nation, brought him fame, but it also made him powerful enemies. In 1776, he was the object of a cruel satire titled *El siglo ilustrado* (The Enlightened Age).

As a result of his activities as a faithful executor of reforms proposed by the government of Charles III, the Inquisition prosecuted Olavide in 1776. Despite being imprisoned, he escaped from prison and succeeded in fleeing to France in 1780, where he was welcomed as a martyr in the ideological struggle against the traditionalists. Ironically, Olavide was later imprisoned in France (1794) as a foreigner whose country was at war with France. Saved from the guillotine, he returned to Spain in 1798, when Prime Minister Manuel de Godoy was courting enlightened minds and friends of Olavide were influential. He died in 1803 in Baeza.

While in France, Olavide wrote perhaps his best-known work, *El evangelio en triunfo o Historia de un filósofo desengañado* (The Evangel Triumphant, or History of a Disillusioned Philosopher, 1797–1798). It deals primarily with religious themes and is generally considered a recantation of his youthful philosophy. In the fourth volume, however, Olavide restated, with some modifications, the socio-economic ideas that had generated his program of reforms prior to his imprisonment.

Olavide's significant socioeconomic works include *Informe al Consejo sobre la ley agraria* (Report to the Council on the Agrarian Law, 1768) and *Plan de estudio para la Universidad de Sevilla* (Plan of studies for the University of Seville, 1768). His other nonfiction writings deal with a wide variety of reforms. Olavide's poetry reveals his assimilation of Enlightenment philosophy. In addition, he was an author of sentimental novels in the style of Richardson and Fielding, a composer of spiritual hymns and a musical play (*zarzuela*), and a translator of the Psalms and French plays.

Olavide played a significant role, comparable to that of Floridablanca, Aranda, Campomanes, and Jovellanos in promoting and instituting reforms based on the spirit and ideas of the Enlightenment until his prosecution by the Inquisition.

[*See also* Latin America *and* Spain.]

BIBLIOGRAPHY

Aguilar Piñal, Francisco. *La Universidad de Sevilla en el siglo XVIII: Estudio sobre la primera reforma universitaria moderna.* Seville, 1969. Explains Olavide's program of university reform.

Aguilar Piñal, Francisco. *Sevilla y el teatro en el siglo XVIII.* Oviedo, Spain, 1974. Provides information on Olavide's cultural activities.

Defourneaux, Marcelin de. *Pablo de Olavide ou l'afrancesado (1725–1803).* Paris, 1959. Portrays Olavide as greatly influenced by the French philosophes.

Perdices Blas, Luis. *Pablo de Olavide (1725–1803) el ilustrado.* Madrid, 1993. This biography emphasizes economic reforms and indicates the importance of the Spanish tradition in the intellectual formation of Olavide.

EDWARD V. COUGHLIN

OPERA. Opera was at the center of some of the largest cultural debates of the Enlightenment. Combining the sensual and nonrational powers of music with the representational strengths of the theater, the expressive attributes of language, and the projection of national character, opera in the abstract was a perfect locus for discussions of nature, freedom, imitation, verisimilitude, language, national character, and morality. The first part of this essay explores those debates. There are, however, some gaps between operatic theory and practice, both in particular and in general. The individual works we know best today (Mozart's operas being the most obvious) are only partially "explained" by the substance of the aesthetic debates, though, like most eighteenth-century operas, they rely on themes germane to the Enlightenment—the use and abuse of power, the nature of class distinction, the characteristics of the "Other," the nature of marriage, the debunking of superstition, and the meaning of the natural world. Broader musico-dramatic trends like the rise of comic opera, the increase in ensemble singing, and more flexible and varied dramatic structures, though in accord with elements of enlightened aesthetic thought, are also related only indirectly to the debates. These trends and their aesthetic implications are discussed in the second part of this essay.

Opera in Enlightenment Aesthetics. A number of important debates touching on opera arose during the eighteenth century. Probably the most famous was the series of *querelles* (debates) that raged in waves in France throughout the century. They began in 1702 with a pamphlet by François Raguenet, reignited in the 1740s and

Opera Performance. Interior of the Royal Theater, Turin, by Domenico Oliviero. (Museo Civico, Turin/Scala/Art Resource, NY.)

1750s with the contributions of Jean-Jacques Rousseau and other *encyclopédistes* (this phase was called the Querelle des Bouffons), and revived in the 1770s with the debate between the adherents of Gluck and Piccinni over Gluck's sojourn in Paris. The principal issue in the first two waves was the relative merits of Italian and French opera, and in the last, the relative merits of passion and suavity. Whether couched as a national issue or as something more "universally" aesthetic, the central question was always the relation of words to music. Questions about which medium should determine the other, which should captivate the primary attention of the listener, and which should sometimes be sacrificed in favor of the other run throughout the century. Under these questions lie broader aesthetic and moral questions about musical expression and pleasure. These debates mirror the broader musical discussion of "imitation" and "expression" and the signifying powers of textless music. Bernard le Bovier Fontenelle's famous apostrophe, *Sonate, que me veux tu?* ("Sonata, what do you want of me?") is specifically not about opera, but its resonances are ever present in the operatic debates.

François Raguenet's position, in *A Comparison between the French and Italian Music and Operas* (1702), was that Italian music (instrumental and sacred, as well as operatic) was more "bold and astonishing" than French, more musically inventive, more independently expressive, and thus more apt to illustrate the words. Jean-Laurent Lecerf de la Viéville responded, with respect to opera, in *Comparison of French and Italian Music* (1704), that Italian music was too "spicy," too unnatural, and unhealthy both morally and physically. The terms of this debate—national character, nature, music's capacity to draw attention to its own means, and a moral overlay about pleasure, remained in midcentury, but, chiefly thanks to Rousseau, questions of language also entered the fray.

Rousseau was one of the century's most important thinkers about opera. In addition to writing about opera, he also composed. His most important operatic composition is *Le devin du village* of 1752, a response to Italian comic intermezzi and a direct progenitor of *opéra-comique*. This work remained in the repertory for sixty years, an astonishing lifespan for any opera in the eighteenth century. Rousseau's writings about music span his whole professional life. His famous *Essai sur l'origine des langues* (Essay on the Origin of Languages, c. 1761) is perhaps his most important general statement about vocal music, but more pertinent to the Querelle des Bouffons are his *Letter on Italian and French Opera* (c. 1744–1745) and the subsequent *Lettre sur la musique française* (Letter on French Music, 1752–1753, 2d ed. 1754). The first letter praises French opera at the expense of Italian *opera seria*, on the basis that stories based in history (as were most *seria* libretti) were less operatically verisimilar than stories based on fables, in which the pervasive magic of the setting might justify the unnatural act of singing. Rousseau also commented that Italian music was more independently "beautiful" than French, but that, being less intimately tied to the rhythms and cadences of its language, it was pleasing rather than moving. His more famous *Letter on French Music* represented, in some respects, a remarkable change of heart. Its impetus may have been the Parisian performances by Felice Bambini's troupe of *bouffons* of Pergolesi's intermezzo *La serva padrona*, which evidently opened up new aesthetic (and political) possibilities for Rousseau and other *encyclopédistes*. Retaining the notion that language and music had to be intimately connected to render a vocal number moving and plausible, Rousseau contended that French was a fundamentally unmusical language, and thus that there could be no good French opera. He demonstrated this with a close analysis of Armide's "Enfin il est en ma puissance," from Jean-Baptiste Lully's *Armide* (1686). Jean-Philippe Rameau, the most famous living composer of French serious opera and Lully's heir in many respects, responded furiously to Rousseau's broadside, including in his response—*Observations sur notre instinct pour la musique* (Observations on Our Instinct for Music, 1754)—another analysis of the *Armide* recitative, showing how the harmonic progressions did in fact mirror the dramatic progress of the scene.

Although Rousseau's aesthetic outlook changed between the two letters, the objective generic differences between Metastasio, whom he lambasted, and his beloved Pergolesi should not be underestimated. "Unity of melody"—the complete subservience of every other element to the textually responsive contour of an inherently pleasing melody, using spare and simple harmonies and unobtrusive accompaniments—was much more readily found in comic opera. Its combination of mellifluousness and simplicity allowed three things that Rousseau especially valued: the interaction of characters, the relative subservience of singers to their roles, and a fair dose of sensual pleasure.

The French-versus-Italian aspect of the Querelle des Bouffons was in part a pretext for other political and intellectual disagreements; most of the *encyclopédistes* took the Italian side, and more conservative intellectuals defended the French, linking support of Italian opera with a penchant for dangerous freedoms. Jean Le Rond d'Alembert skewered this propensity in *On the Freedom of Music* (1759): "It is hard to believe, but it is nonetheless true that in certain people's idiom, 'bouffoniste,' 'republican,' 'frondeur,' 'atheist,'—I was about to forget 'materialist'—are so many synonymous terms." Rousseau's defense of the Italians did indeed have a political dimension. Rousseau

surely represented an anticeremonial and implicitly antiroyalist position. His preference for the small-scale and bourgeois over the grand and ceremonial, the acuter, bodily pleasures of Italian music over the tranquil, cerebral pleasures of the French, and the more text-dependent (and thus perhaps "meaningful") preeminence of melody over the more "scientific" emphasis on harmony. At the same time, the operatic qualities he valued—dramatic intensity, psychological plausibility, an immediate connection between words and music, and a good measure of pleasure—were shared by both sides. His definition of the genre in his *Dictionary of Music* (c. 1765) may not represent a personal rapprochement with Rameau, but it certainly embodies an attitude with which the greater composer could scarcely disagree: "*Opera*: A dramatic and lyric Spectacle in which one endeavours to bring together all the charms of the fine Arts in the representation of passionate action in order to arouse interest and illusion with the help of pleasant sensation."

Rousseau's last writings about the genre concerned Christoph Willibald Gluck, the great composer most associated with Rousseauian ideas about opera. Gluck consulted Rousseau about the Italian version of *Alceste* before rewriting it for the Parisian stage; although Rousseau did not withhold his criticism of the work's dramatic trajectory and uniformity of mood, he tempered it with general commentary summing up the principal problems of opera in this age. Among the most striking of these is: "Determining to what point one can make language sing and Music speak is a great and fine problem to resolve. The whole theory of Dramatic Music depends on a good solution to this problem." This statement, uniting the need for both labor and taste on the authors' part, the audience's need for both pleasure and meaning, and the implicit recognition that there may be many solutions to this great and fine problem, economically and comprehensively encapsulates the operatic issues of the age.

The final Querelle, between the Gluckists and Piccinnists in Paris in the 1770s, was both more trumped up and less vitriolic than the previous debates. Although "Italian" and "French" were still used as adjectives, they were less stable in meaning and less attached to the language of the operas than they had been earlier. Both sides agreed that passionate topics, noble sentiments, emphasis on the text, and minimal performative display were desirable, and the supporters of each composer conceded merit in the works of the other. The chief question was the extent to which "harsh" dissonances, incomplete forms, and other "rough" musical devices were appropriate to the expression of painful subjects. Gluck's supporters generally supported more radical modes of musical expression; Piccinni's tended to express more interest in refinement.

Although the French Querelles were the most celebrated operatic debates of the century, discussions and arguments went on in other countries as well. Most closely connected to the Querelles were the debates in Italy involving mainly literary men, and conducted in a framework of comparing "the ancients" (Greek tragedy or Renaissance counterpoint) with "the modern." Until the end of the century, this debate lacked the vitriolic opposition of the French Querelles, perhaps because there was less at stake politically. Chief and admirable aspects of "the ancient"—usually identified with tragedy—were simplicity and moral power, achieved through the subordination of music to poetry and the avoidance of excess, whether in the form of elaborate instrumental music or vocal display. Chief problems with the modern were the "din" of the orchestra, the senselessness of repetition and vocal virtuosity, music's tendency to dissolve the meanings of the words in a flood of purely sensual pleasure, and the corollary institutional problem of the musicians' (composers' and singers') insubordination toward the librettists. The heading of one chapter in Ludovico Muratori's *Della perfetta poesia italiana* (On Perfect Italian Poetry, 1706) summarizes these: "On the Defects that Can Be Observed in Modern Operas. Their Music, Pernicious to Morals. Criticized also by the Ancients. Poetry is the Servant of Music. The Purpose of Tragedy Cannot Be Realized by Means of These Operas. Other Defects of Poetry for the Theatre. And Various Incongruities."

Benedetto Marcello's famous satire, *Theatre à la mode* (1720), accuses the operatic enterprise of (among other things) incoherence, extravagance, singer-dominated excesses, and no care for sense or meaning. Marcello's accusations against the quality of operatic music *qua* music were stronger than those of many contemporaries (unlike them, he was a composer), but his evident desire for a well-regulated theater whose operas would convey noble moral messages, with music that would declaim the text clearly and draw little attention to performative display, was consistent with the ideas of the literati. Encapsulating this idea is Francesco Algarotti's remark from his *Saggio sopra l'opera* (Essay on Opera, 1755): "... True simplicity, which alone can imitate nature, will always be preferred to the most intricate ways of seasoning art." This directly anticipates Calzabigi's comment in the preface to his and Gluck's *Alceste* (1767): "I have deemed it my greatest task to seek the beauty of simplicity.... I have not judged any novelty estimable unless it immediately and naturally flows from the situation and the expression."

Just as the Gluckists and the Piccinnists in the final French Querelle held many aesthetic principles in common, despite being drawn to different musical qualities, so the apparently opposed defenders of the ancient and the modern in Italy held in common values, such as clarity,

truth, and expressiveness. Esteban de Arteaga, in his massive *Le rivoluzioni del teatro musicale italiano dalla sua origine fino al presente* (Revolutions of the Italian Musical Theater from Its Origin to the Present, 1785), noted: "The first and capital fault of contemporary theater music is that it has too little philosophy and too much refinement; its sole objective is to tickle the ear, not touch the heart." Vincenzo Manfredini, in the *Difesa della musica moderna e de suoi celebri esecutori* (Defense of Modern Music and Its Celebrated Performers, 1788), agreed that excessive elaboration could destroy the communicative properties of an aria, but he insisted that the formal variety in modern operas and the judicious use of the instruments and vocal passagework enhanced the expression of the text. Manfredini was almost unique in this discussion in referring to particular composers and contemporary musical devices, and in distinguishing between better and worse practitioners of the genre.

Neither England nor Germany produced France's or Italy's weight of operatic philosophy. In both countries Italian opera—both serious and comic—formed the backbone of the operatic repertory, though Italian opera's hold loosened in Germany after the 1750s. In England, the complaints against Italian opera reflected England's long suspicions of Italians; effeminacy, extravagance, and untrustworthiness were among the chief accusations. These complaints also mirrored Continental concerns about music's sensual and "meaningless" qualities when not subservient to poetry ("meaninglessness" being magnified when the language was not indigenous). Lord Chesterfield wrote in 1754: "Were what is called the poetry of Italian opera intelligible in itself, it would not be understood by one in fifty of a British audience; but I believe that even an Italian of common candor will confess, that he does not understand one word of it. It is not the intention of the thing; for should the ingenious author of the words, by mistake, put any meaning into them, he would, to a certain degree, check and cramp the genius of he composer of the music, who perhaps might think himself obliged to adapt his sounds to a sense." Ballad opera, England's most significant vernacular genre, responded to the inaccessibility of Italian opera not only linguistically, but also by using spoken dialogue and simple songs. John Gay's *The Beggar's Opera* (1728), with music arranged by J. C. Pepusch, was the most significant work in this genre.

German criticism of Italian opera was comparably focused on that genre's triviality, extravagance, and immorality, but the more important elements of German operatic aesthetics concerned the move toward a truly German opera. Important cultural figures like Johann Christoph Gottsched, Johann Adolf Scheibe, Johann Adolph Schlegel, Gotthold Ephraim Lessing, Christoph Martin Wieland, and Johann Wolfgang von Goethe contributed both to the discussion of general aesthetic issues around opera and to the articulation of an aesthetic of German opera. More specifically musical writers on opera include Johann Mattheson, Christoph Gottfried Krause, Johann Adam Hiller, and Friedrich Wilhelm Marpurg. Particularly in the second half of the century, writers on German opera were much influenced by French aesthetic theories: Charles Batteux's *Les beaux-arts reduits à un même principe* (The Fine Arts Reduced to a Single Principle, 1746) and Jean-Baptiste DuBos's *Réflexions critiques sur la poésie et sur la peinture* (Critical Reflections on Poetry and Painting, 1719) were chief among them. The basic verisimilitude of opera (in any language) was a central issue, with authors increasingly combating the idea that opera's ontological "realism" depended on its representing the world of fable. Increasingly, critics suggested that singing was no more "unnatural" than other modes of representation. Schlegel, for example, wrote in *Das Orakel: Ein Singspiel* (1747), "Opera deviates from actual nature one degree further than tragedy does; but will that which is not wondrous [i.e., based on fable] in opera therefore stop being probable?" After midcentury, with a rising interest in German-language opera, the issues most debated were the character of the language, the relation of words to music, and the relation between the inexplicable but inarguable pleasures of music and its broader significance, as well as a desire to replicate the power and high seriousness of Greek drama. Perhaps most characteristic of German thought about opera was its emphasis on the nonrational and to some extent indescribable pleasures of music. Schlegel took this as a basis for wanting to welcome whatever new genres "gave pleasure by presenting the beautiful, the good, or both," regardless of whether they fit into a predetermined system or scheme. In a similar vein, Lessing suggested that individual taste was the primary criterion by which opera should be judged, a position with clear social implications: "Whatever charms a peasant discredits no rule, for in him its driving force still operates truly genuinely" ("On the Rules of the Sciences with Respect to Pleasure; especially Poetry and Music," 1749). Lessing doubted, however, that a peasant would appreciate more sophisticated works.

Operatic Trends and Their Implications. The primary concerns of eighteenth-century operatic philosophers, then, were verisimilitude and naturalness, word–music relations, national character (including language), taste, and pleasure. The story of opera through the century as seen through its works emerges as related to these questions, but distinct. *Opera seria*, with librettos either by, or based on those by, Pietro Metastasio, was the most widely disseminated operatic genre in Europe from the early 1720s until the 1770s. It was performed not only in Italy but also in court-sponsored theaters in England, Germany, Scandinavia, and eastern Europe. Most of Metastasio's libretti were set by dozens of composers, the more popular works hundreds of times. His typical subjects came from ancient Roman, Greek, or Persian history and involved the obligations of a ruler; they often turned on a conflict between love and duty, usually resolved (in the obligatory *lieto fine*, or happy end) by the discovery that the two were compatible. The structures of Metastasian opera were clear and regular: generally, three acts with around ten scenes each, scenes being defined by the entrances and exits of characters. The vast majority of scenes began with recitative and ended with an exit aria. Arias were stanzaic, often included two strophes, and were usually set as *da capo* forms—ABA forms in which the return of A was usually ornamented by the singer.

Metastasio's verse was compact, graceful, and limpid; his capacity to represent the essence of a dramatic or psychological situation in a few mellifluous words was unparalleled. The aria-opening line *Tu me da me dividi* ("You tear my heart in two") from *L'Olimpiade*, exemplifies the sonorous yet meaningful economy of Metastasio's verse. This elegance and regularity was the result of reforms early in the eighteenth century, in which the "abuses" of late Baroque opera—the mixing of comic with serious, irregularity of form, and "immoral" content—were systematically expunged. Critics have seen the absolute well-orderedness of Metastasian opera, as well as its concentration on the obligations of absolute power, as an important representation and reinforcement of enlightened despotism. The theatrical and cultural power of the virtuosic castrato singers who played the most heroic roles can also be understood as an analogue for the nonrational and unchallengeable power of the ruler.

At the same time as Metastasian opera in its ideal form represented a completely orderly world, it also engendered its own abuses. The power of the singers was a favorite target of reformers of all stripes, as were the historical distance and social elevation of Metastasian characters. In addition, *opera seria*'s hegemony throughout Europe (except in France) in the first part of the century inevitably generated resistance. Although Metastasian opera was not the starting point for all eighteenth-century reforms (French *opéra comique* is the obvious exception), it did serve as the foil for many of the most important trends of the century. These include the reform of serious opera in Italian, the development of self-sufficient Italian-language comic opera, and the development of vernacular genres in German and English.

The French parallel to Metastasian opera was the *tragédie en musique*, of which Jean-Baptiste Lully and later Jean-Philippe Rameau were the chief practitioners. This genre (and the associated *opéra ballet*) was performed only in the royal theaters in and around Paris, because the Académie Royale de Musique held a monopoly on the works. This monopoly notwithstanding, the speechlike character of much of the vocal music and the absence of opportunities for vocal display may well have made the genre less exportable than *opera seria*, despite its greater use of spectacle in danced divertissements, choruses, and elaborate scenic devices. One of Rameau's principal contributions was to increase the amount of such spectacle, thus lessening the genre's vaunted claim to have revived classical tragedy.

In contrast to *opera seria*, the five-act plots of *tragédie en musique* were based on myth and fable. Where the orderliness of *opera seria* consisted of the regular rhythm of recitatives and arias and the careful distribution of arias and aria types (rage, love, bravura, sentiment, etc.) among the characters and singers, in the *tragédie en musique* the sense of discipline and order stemmed from careful prosody, the subordination of the singer to the text, and the elaborate and minutely planned arrangement and movement of groups of participants (soloists, chorus, dancers) on the stage. The characters of *tragédie en musique* were as distant from ordinary people as were those of *opera seria*, but the overall tone of the French genre was typically more serious, with deaths, disasters, and wrenching choices more frequent.

Both these serious genres had comic foils in their own languages. The *tragédie en musique* was regularly parodied by works performed at the Fair Theaters, later to become the Opéra-Comique and the Comédie Italienne, and later yet (1762) to merge. The works performed in the Fair Theaters, with spoken dialogue and a variable number of sung airs, incorporated characters and riffs from the *commedia dell'arte*, whose troupes had appeared in Paris since the mid-seventeenth century; they aimed both politically and culturally loaded barbs at high society. *Opera seria*—especially in Naples—often incorporated *intermezzi*, modest comic operettas interpolated between the acts of the "main" serious opera. The opportunities for parody here are obvious. By midcentury, comic opera in French and Italian (*opera buffa*) was increasingly independent of its elevated foils. Indeed, its rise in the eighteenth century is perhaps the most striking musico-dramatic achievement of the period—it is certainly the development that most directly influenced Mozart's three great collaborations with Da Ponte (*Le nozze di Figaro* [The Marriage of Figaro], *Don Giovanni*, and *Così fan tutte* [Women Are All Like That])—but it is barely discussed in the philosophical treatises of the time. Even the numerous writings extolling Pergolesi's *La serva padrona* attribute its admirable features to its national origin rather than to its genre.

The kind of *opera buffa* that most directly influenced Mozart and Da Ponte featured realistic characters from several layers of society in contemporary settings and included a strong sentimental element, drawn in part from the English and French novel. This genre, developed by Carlo Goldoni, was pitted against the works of Carlo Gozzi, which were both more fabulous and more satirical. In some ways the Goldoni-Gozzi quarrel reflected the arguments about whether verisimilitude in serious opera required or encouraged the use of mythical settings and fabulous characters; Goldoni's characters, however, clustered around the middle ranks of society (in contrast to *opera seria*'s kings, generals, and princes) and thus also reflected the Enlightenment's explicit encouragement of bourgeois values and habits. The use of sentiment in the comic genre also occasioned debate; critics raised the political question of whether a character of nonnoble birth was worthy of sympathetic treatment (Goldoni's most sentimental figures were uniformly nonaristocratic), and the aesthetic issue of how, if comedy's role was to correct small vices by ridiculing them, there was room for sympathy and sentiment. Goldoni's libretto *La buona figliuola*, most successfully set by Niccolò Piccinni (1760) and based, by way of Goldoni's own spoken-drama adaptation, on Samuel Richardson's novel *Pamela*, proved the success of sentimental comedy. The explicit class tensions evident in Mozart's and Da Ponte's *Le nozze di Figaro* are related not only to the Beaumarchais play on which the libretto is based but also to Goldonian antecedents.

The most notable musical feature of *opera buffa* was its use of ensembles, especially act-ending finales in which active plot development was carried out in complex music. By the end of the century, these ensembles and finales were being criticized (especially in Germany) as artificial and improbable, but they represented an important step in the integration of concerted music and dramatic action, and they can be seen as responding to contemporary calls for the integration of natural action and pleasure.

Opéra-comique, started by Rousseau with *Le devin du village*, also included an element of sentiment, but its settings were more pastoral than those of *opera buffa*, and it was more inclined to magic than the Italian genre. Jean-François Marmontel and Michel-Jean Sedaine were perhaps the most important librettists of *opéra-comique*, and André-Ernest-Modeste Grétry its most important composer. As with *tragédie en musique* in comparison with *opera seria*, the dramatic rhythms of *opéra-comique* were more flexible than those of *opera buffa*: airs were typically shorter and less virtuosic, and there was more opportunity for spectacle, including orchestral elaboration. Ensembles, on the other hand, were much less developed than in *opera buffa*.

The combination of sentimentalism and ordinary characters in both *opera buffa* and *opéra-comique* was connected to the calls from *encyclopédistes* and other Enlightenment thinkers for a genre of musical drama (analogous to Diderot's *drame*) that dealt with high-minded topics as they concerned ordinary people. *Opera buffa*'s increasing fusion of the serious and the comic (especially in Vienna) went some way to meet this demand, though that was not usually acknowledged by writers about opera; the introduction of grander, more didactic, or more politically salient subjects into *opéra-comique* accomplished a similar goal. There were also some attempts to bring contemporary characters and subjects into *opera seria*—for instance, Bartolomeo Benincasa's *Il disertore* (1785), based on an *opéra-comique* libretto, set by Francesco Bianchi, and equipped with a long and earnest preface.

The genre of opera most directly connected to the writings of the philosophes and to enlightened cultural thought more generally, however, was Gluckian "reform opera." The works of Niccolò Jommelli and Tommaso Traëtta began the reform movement, but Gluck's later operas were its culmination. Beginning in 1762 with *Orfeo ed Euridice*, Gluck and his librettist Ranieri Calzabigi combined the French propensity for flexible dramatic structures and the presence of chorus and dancers with a relatively unadorned (but nevertheless Italianate) vocal line in which music served the text, and singers were subordinate to their roles. The use of Greek myth as material conveyed the nobility of the subject matter; it also linked the genre with the *tragédie en musique*. The use of the Orpheus story, in particular, also reflexively signaled that the nature and power of music were at issue. The famous C-minor chorus of Furies, "Chi mai dell' Erebo," with its unrelieved dactylic rhythms, exemplifies the reformist ideals of passion and simplicity. This chorus was copied and parodied for the rest of the century and beyond. Gluck's later "reform" operas (especially *Iphigénie en Aulide*, 1774, and *Iphigénie en Tauride*, 1779) became increasingly daring in their emotional intensity, in formal flexibility, and in the integration of the chorus and dancing into the center of the work.

While Gluck, a German composer, made his career (both pre- and post-reform) as a court-sponsored composer, writing only in French and Italian, German-language opera was burgeoning, especially in middle-class venues. *Singspiel*, influenced by *opéra comique* in its subject material, its self-conscious naïveté, and its use of spoken dialogue between sung arias and ensembles, was launched in the 1760s in northern Germany by C. F. Weisse (librettist) and Johann Adam Hiller (composer). As this genre became increasingly respectable, attempts at a more elevated German musical drama were also made; chief among them were Christoph-Martin Wieland's *Alceste* (1773), responding to Gluck's opera on the same subject, and Georg Benda's *Medea* (1775) and *Ariadne auf Naxos* (1775), which responded to Rousseau's *Pygmalion* (1772), a "melodrama" that combined the spoken word with fragmentary and intense instrumental commentary on the verbal thread. (Mozart's unfinished *Zaide*, 1779–1780, includes one melodrama number.)

Comic and exotic *Singspiel*, however, had more enduring success than these attempts at German serious opera. In Vienna, although Joseph II's politically motivated attempts to make *Singspiel* the official musical genre of his Nationaltheater (founded in 1776) failed, Mozart's *Die Entführung aus dem Serail* (The Abduction from the Seraglio, 1781) being the emperor's last *Singspiel* commission, the genre eventually enjoyed tremendous success in the middle-class suburban theaters made possible by Joseph's declaration of *Schauspielfreiheit*, or permission for independent entrepreneurs to establish theaters. Mozart's and Emmanuel Schikaneder's *Die Zauberflöte* (The Magic Flute) was the crowning product of this milieu. It exemplifies *Singspiel's* absorption of many different operatic styles and habits (the Queen of the Night's *opera seria*-like ravings and Papageno's naive, "folklike" songs are the two extremes) and thus aspires to a sort of operatic universality. It also, of all the extant operas of this period, is the one most explicitly concerned with the Enlightenment itself. Prince Tamino's search for self-knowledge, his fascination with the exotic, his acceptance by a self-consciously enlightened brotherhood (representing the Freemasons), and his co-equal but protective relationship with Pamina all reflect and propagate the period's most important ideals.

[*See also* Aesthetics; Criticism; Literary Genres; Mozart, Wolfgang Amadeus; Music; Rousseau, Jean-Jacques; *and* Theater.]

BIBLIOGRAPHY

Allanbrook, Wye Jamison. *Rhythmic Gesture in Mozart: Le nozze di Figaro and Don Giovanni*. Chicago, 1983. A reading of these two Mozart operas, linking them to broader musical and gestural topics of the period.

Bauman, Thomas, ed. *German Opera, 1770–1800: A Collection of Facsimiles of Printed and Manuscript Full Scores*. New York, 1985. A collection of otherwise unpublished works, with excellent prefaces by the series editor. There is a comparable series of Italian operas, edited by Howard M. Brown.

Bauman, Thomas. *North German Opera in the Age of Goethe*. Cambridge, 1985. Scholarly treatment of both serious and comic operas, particularly strong on institutional history, intellectual context, and descriptions of the works themselves.

Charlton, David. *Grétry and the Growth of Opéra-Comique*. Cambridge, 1986. The best work available on the structures and conventions of this genre. Many discussions of individual works.

Dill, Charles. *Monstrous Opera: Rameau and the Tragic Tradition*. Princeton, N.J., 1998. A consideration of all of Rameau's operas in light of his aesthetic theories and creative habits, and in the context of eighteenth-century aesthetic debates.

Fiske, Roger. *English Theatre Music in the Eighteenth Century*. 2d ed. Oxford, 1986. The standard survey of English theatrical music, ranging from ballad operas and mostly sung works to incidental music in spoken plays.

Flaherty, Gloria. *Opera in the Development of German Critial Thought*. Princeton, N.J., 1979. A useful survey of German aesthetic and critical writing from the late seventeenth until the early nineteenth centuries; shows how opera was crucial to the growth of critical thought about drama and literature more generally.

Fubini, Enrico. *Music and Culture in Eighteenth-Century Europe: A Source Book*. Translated by Bonnie J. Blackburn. Chicago, 1994. Excerpts from the most important aesthetic writings of the whole eighteenth century, including many on opera; the introduction gives the best overview of the century's aesthetic thought available in English.

Heartz, Daniel. *Mozart's Operas*. Edited, with contributing essays, by Thomas Bauman. Berkeley, Calif., 1997. Essays on individual operas, describing their circumstantial and intellectual contexts, and providing analyses of many sections.

Howard, Patricia. *Gluck: An Eighteenth Century Portrait in Letters and Documents*. Oxford, 1995. A biography created principally from primary sources, particularly useful in showing the evolution of Gluck's interest in complete control of his work.

Hunter, Mary. *The Culture of Opera Buffa in Mozart's Vienna*. Princeton, N.J., 1999. A consideration of the poetics and social meanings of the *opere buffe* that surround Mozart's masterpieces.

Petty, Fred. *Italian Opera in London, 1760–1800*. Ann Arbor, Mich., 1980. Describes the repertory of operas performed in London during this period, but also provides a summary of English aesthetic thought on opera.

Price, Curtis A., Robert D. Hume, and Judith Milhous. *Italian Opera in Eighteenth-Century London*. Vol. 1. Oxford, 1995. Survey of the institutions and repertory, especially strong on institutional history.

Rousseau, Jean-Jacques. *Essay on the Origin of Languages and Writings Related to Music*. Translated and edited by John T. Scott. Hanover, N.H., 1998. All of Rousseau's writings on music, with the writings by others (e.g., Grimm and Rameau) that stimulated or responded to Rousseau's treatises and pamphlets; the introduction presents an overview of Rousseau's aesthetic thought.

Sadie, Stanley, ed. *The New Grove Dictionary of Opera*. 4 vols. London, 1992. An invaluable reference work with relevant essays on places (cities and countries), people (composers, librettists, singers, etc.), institutions, and individual works.

Strohm, Reinhard. *Dramma per Musica: Italian Opera Seria of the Eighteenth Century*. New Haven, Conn., 1997. A collection of

essays, mostly concentrating on early eighteenth-century figures and works.

MARY HUNTER

OPTICS. Optics was one of the most important branches of natural philosophy during the century of the Enlightenment. Isaac Newton, the second Lucasian Professor of Mathematics of Trinity College, Cambridge, opened the century with his *Opticks* (1704). The work owed much to the tradition of English experimental natural philosophy as practiced by Francis Bacon and Robert Boyle. Newton was rather skeptical of any hypothesis that was not based on a plethora of experimental evidence. Indeed, he often attacked Cartesian natural philosophy for its lack of experimental rigor.

Isaac Newton. Newton argued that white light was composed of rays of various colors, each ray possessing a different angle of refrangibility. He asserted that prisms did not alter the composition of white light; they merely separated it into its fundamental components. His famous *experimentum crucis* proved his point. He cut a small slit in a screen, which he placed over a window, allowing a small beam of light to enter a darkened room. The beam passed through a prism onto another screen, generating the spectrum. He then cut a slit in the second screen, allowing rays of one color to fall onto a second prism. Instead of changing color after the second refraction, the rays remained the same.

Such a conclusion contradicted earlier theories of light, such as those proposed by Descartes, Boyle, and Robert Hooke, all of whom argued that prisms somehow modify light, thereby producing the spectral colors. Descartes, for example, argued that the prism alters the rate of axial rotation of spherical particles comprising a beam of light. Using this mechanical model, Descartes provided the first mathematical formula for the refraction of a light beam as it travels from one material with a given density to another with a different density. He accounted for vision

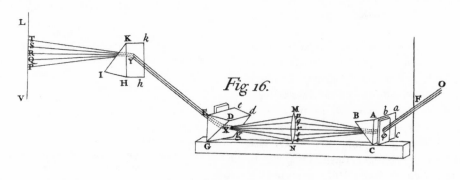

Newton's *Experimentum Crucis*. From Newton's *Opticks* (1704). (Prints and Photographs Division, Library of Congress.)

by analogy. The colors we perceive, like the impulses transmitted by a blind man's stick, result from pressure. Color was for Descartes a secondary quality, not a property of external objects but a product of our perception of them via pressure registered on the optic nerve and conveyed through it to the brain.

During the 1670s, the young Newton had not been totally averse to an undulatory theory of light, and by the publication of the first edition of *Opticks*, he did draw upon the undulatory theory in order to explain some of light's properties. With the first Latin translation, *Optice* (1706), however, Newton pondered in queries twenty and twenty-one whether all hypotheses in which light is propagated through a fluid medium are erroneous, and if rays of light are simply very small bodies. He would go on to support a projectile, particulate theory of light.

Newton's emphasis on experiment, which was exemplified by his optical work, reflected a more encompassing epistemology. He was a deeply religious man, but not an orthodox Anglican, for he rejected the Trinity. He was an ardent (yet silent) follower of Arianism, a precarious faith for a professor at the exclusively Anglican Cambridge University. His goal as a scholar was nothing less than to understand the universe and God's role in it. Such a daunting task could be achieved only by mastering a myriad of intellectual activities such as astronomy, celestial mechanics, mathematics, alchemy, history, and biblical chronology, all of which Newton actively pursued. His experimental natural philosophy, bolstered in part by his extremely powerful position as president of the Royal Society, became the prevalent scientific model of the eighteenth century. Thanks in large part to Voltaire and Francesco Algarotti, Newton's natural philosophy crossed the English channel to France and Italy, where it was a major topic of rigorous discussions and demonstrations not only in the various academies of science, but also in polite court society.

After Newton. It would, however, be a mistake to subsume the entire eighteenth century under the rubric of Newtonianism. Newton's doctrine of light and colors was fundamentally challenged by research in telescopy. He argued that refracting telescopes would always suffer from chromatic aberration, or the appearance of colored rings, which destroy the instrument's ability to resolve under high magnification. Hence, he turned his attention to reflecting telescopes, which employ a mirror to channel the incoming light rays, to study the heavens. Between 1729 and 1732, however, the London barrister Chester Moor Hall discovered that chromatic aberration could be partially overcome by combining different types of glass: a concave lens made of flint glass and a convex lens made of crown glass.

In 1746, Leonhard Euler's *Nova theoria lucis et colorum* proffered a wave theory of light that contradicted Newton's model. Euler suggested that every particle of a luminous body oscillates much like a stretched string, causing surrounding particles to vibrate. The end result is a sinusoidal, longitudinal wave of light emanating from the light source. A year later, Euler argued in his paper to the Berlin Academy of Sciences, contra Newton, that it was indeed theoretically possible to correct for chromatic aberration. Using the physiology of the eye as his model, Euler mathematically demonstrated that water placed between two concave lenses should correct chromatic aberration. Euler's paper was read with great interest by the Uppsala mathematician Samuel Klingensterna, who, in 1754, published a mathematical demonstration proving that Newton's assertion of the impossibility of constructing an achromatic refracting telescope was fallacious.

Drawing upon Chester Moor Hall's work, London's leading optician of the period, John Dollond, determined in 1757 that objects viewed through flint and crown glass prisms, with refractive powers of two to three respectively, were seen with very little chromatic aberration. Dollond reckoned that lenses could be cut from these two prisms, producing a telescope that was nearly achromatic. With those lenses, he manufactured the world's most-coveted achromatic refracting telescopes of the period. The instrument maker was awarded Britain's highest scientific honor, the Copley Medal, and membership in the Royal Society of London.

Beginning in 1761, Alexis-Claude Clairaut replicated Dollond's experiments and noted that objects seen through supposedly achromatic lenses did suffer from colored rings distorting the resolution. After determining the refractive and dispersive indices of several glass samples, Clairaut deduced theorems for pairing the glasses in order to reduce the effect of the secondary spectrum. In the 1760s, Ruggiero Giuseppe Boscovich, a Jesuit professor at Padua, attempted to design object lenses free of chromatic aberration. He was able to demonstrate a method of uniting three spectral colors by means of three media, each possessing different refractive and dispersive powers. In the 1790s, Robert Blair, a professor of astronomy at Edinburgh, developed liquid lenses (filled with various oils and hydrochloric acid) in an attempt to reduce the secondary spectrum. Chromatic aberration was to remain a problem for refracting telescopes until well into the nineteenth century.

Although geometrical optics was relatively advanced by the late eighteenth century, the practice of making achromatic lenses was not. One of the most serious problems facing opticians was the quality of the crown and (especially) flint glass. Glassmakers who could manufacture optical disks larger than four inches in diameter were highly sought after. Larger disks often suffered from such imperfections as bubbles and striae, rendering the glass unusable for optical purposes.

The most widely read text for eighteenth-century English opticians trying to cope with the limitations of the glassmakers was Robert Smith's *A Compleat System of Opticks* (1738). This work was sufficiently influential during the late eighteenth century to warrant an abridged edition for university students as late as 1778. This abridged work, which omitted the mechanical treatise of the original, hints at the extreme sundering of optical theory from practice that had emerged during the early eighteenth century, but which had become extreme in Britain by century's end, with students of natural philosophy concentrating exclusively on physical and geometrical optics, and opticians on technical optics, limited to basic algebra and the rule of sines, relevant to the construction of optical glass and instruments.

In late eighteenth- and early nineteenth-century France, the Newtonian theory of light was being actively pursued within a broader framework of mathematical physics. Pierre Simon Laplace (1749–1827), Étienne Malus (1775–1812), and Jean Biot (1774–1862) all elaborated the projectile theory of light in terms of short-range centrally directed forces between particles of matter and light, very much in line with Newtonian mechanics.

Critiques of Newton. During the first decade of the nineteenth century, Newton's theory of light and colors, however, came under attack from two very different sources: Johann Wolfgang von Goethe and Thomas Young (1773–1829). Goethe felt that optics had gone terribly wrong with the works of Newton and his followers. Echoing the sentiments expressed in Joseph Priestley's *The History and Present State of Discoveries Relating to Vision, Light, and Colours* (1772), Goethe claimed in his *Zur Farbenlehre* (On Color Theory, 1810) that the field had become too mathematical and had lost sight of the importance of the investigator in understanding nature's phenomena. He linked Newtonianism with the private knowledge within the illuminated circles of the late Enlightenment, and countered such knowledge with a more accessible epistemology, as reflected in his color demonstrations and his assault on the uniqueness of Newtonian prisms. Goethe demonstrated that the color green was not a homogeneous color with a specific angle of refraction, as Newton argued, but rather was a compound color, formed by a blue band overlapping and mixing with a yellow band. Colors, according to Goethe, arise only in the presence of the *Urphänomen* (archetypal phenomenon) of a boundary formed by the juxtaposition of black and white. Much of his *Beiträge zur Optik* (Contributions on Optics, 1791–1792) and *Zur Farbenlehre* underscored the importance of physiology and

anatomy to the perception of color, a topic on which Newton had very little to say. Goethe experimentally showed that the Newtonian spectrum was merely one in a series of spectra. His respecification of the Newtonian spectrum, along with the history that he himself provided the reader in his *Zur Farbenlehre*, offered an epistemology far more accessible than the closed circles of interpretation formulated (according to Goethe) by the Newtonians, Roman Catholics, and Illuminati.

The British physician Thomas Young also challenged Newton's optical work. He proffered experimental evidence that suggested light was indeed a wave, not a particle. During the first decade of the nineteenth century, Young drew upon the analogy of sound in order to explain the properties of light's propagation. In 1807, he published his famous two-slit experiment, revealing the interference of light. A beam of light passed through a screen with two small slits to another screen. He noticed that bands of black were flanked by bands of white on the second screen and concluded that light was traveling in waves, much like water. Where the bands were black, destructive interference had occurred; where the bands were white, constructive interference had taken place.

Largely independent of Young's work, the French military engineer Augustin Fresnel (1788–1827) published from 1815 to 1827 a number of critical papers proposing a wave theory of light, which overthrew the models of Laplace, Biot, and Malus, and which was to become the nineteenth-century model of light propagation. One of Fresnel's major contributions to the wave theory was the explanation of diffraction, or the ability of light to bend around corners. Such a phenomenon was typical of waves, not particles. Fresnel explained diffraction by means of a wave spreading from the source in such a way that, pace Christiaan Huygens's *Traité de la lumière* (Treatise on Light, 1690), each point on the wave front serves as a source of secondary waves. By taking into account the contribution of those secondary waves combined with the principles of interference discovered by Young, Fresnel could determine the intensity of light at any point on the screen. The other major contribution of Fresnel's theory was its ability to explain polarization phenomena, as discovered by Malus in 1808. His work argued for the concept of transverse vibrations in light waves, which he analyzed mathematically.

[*See also* Astronomy; Cartesianism; Epistemology; Goethe, Johann Wolfgang von; Huygens, Christiaan; Natural Philosophy and Science; Newton, Isaac; Newtonianism; Physics; Priestley, Joseph; *and* Scientific Instruments.]

BIBLIOGRAPHY
Buchwald, Jed Z. *The Rise of the Wave Theory of Light: Optical Theory and Experiment in the Early Nineteenth Century*. Chicago, 1989. The

most thorough and technical account available on French optics of the early nineteenth century.

Cantor, Geoffrey. *Optics after Newton: Theories of Light in Britain and Ireland, 1704–1840.* Manchester, U.K., 1983. The most thorough account of British optics during the eighteenth and nineteenth centuries.

Cantor, Geoffrey. "Physical Optics." In *Companion to the History of Modern Science*, edited by R. C. Olby, G. N. Cantor, J. R. R. Chandler, and M. J. S. Hodge, pp. 627–638. London, 1990.

Dobbs, Betty Jo Teeter, and Margaret C. Jacob. *Newton and the Culture of Newtonianism.* Atlantic Highlands, N.J., 1995.

Hakfoort, Casper. *Optics in the Age of Euler: Conceptions of the Nature of Light, 1700–1795.* Cambridge, 1995.

Jackson, Myles W. "A Spectrum of Belief: Goethe's 'Republic' versus Newtonian Despotism." *Social Studies of Science* (1994), 673–701.

Jackson, Myles W. *Spectrum of Belief: Joseph von Franhofer and the Craft of Precision Optics.* Cambridge, Mass., 2000. Chapter 2 is most relevant to Enlightenment optics. The work analyzes the relationship between artisanal knowledge and experimental natural philosophy.

Schaffer, Simon. "Glass Works: Newton's Prisms and the Uses of Experiment." In *Uses of Experiment: Studies in the Natural Sciences*, edited by David Gooding, Trevor Pinch, and Simon Schaffer, pp. 67–104. Cambridge, 1989. This study offers a sociohistorical account of prisms and the difficulty of replicating Newton's optical experiments.

Shapiro, Alan E. *Fits, Passions and Paroxysms: Physics, Method, and Chemistry and Newton's Theories of Colored Bodies and Fits of Easy Reflection.* Cambridge, 1993.

MYLES W. JACKSON

OPTIMISM, PHILOSOPHICAL.

What the Enlightenment came to term "optimism" was the view, derived from philosophical claims about the goodness of God, that despite apparent evils the world is as good as it can possibly be: that, in the famous phrase of the German philosopher Gottfried Wilhelm von Leibniz (1646–1716), we live in "the best among all possible worlds" (*Essais de théodicée*, 1710; Eng. trans., *Theodicy*, 1952, 128). Optimism typically took a universal perspective, frequently appealing to the great chain of being and to the plenitude of the world system. The diverting abundance of natural kinds and the orderliness of the laws of nature were offered as evidence of God's benevolence and care in constructing the world. Optimism is thus a rationalist position, one that assumes the essential comprehensibility of the divine design. It found strong reinforcement in the new science; for example, in Isaac Newton's account of an orderly, God-activated universe, and in Antoni van Leeuwenhoek's discoveries of the microscopic intricacies of animal physiology. Most eighteenth-century Christian philosophers and divines might appear to be optimists in a loose sense, since they accepted that Providence worked generally for the good of all and not particularly for the individual. Most also adhered, however, not without some contradiction, to the doctrine of the Fall: that human suffering is the price of human sin, and that our lives are times of trial in which we prove ourselves fit for God's reward or punishment in the afterlife. Strict optimistic discourse tended to ignore or downplay these beliefs, avoiding discussion of original sin. While not a wholesale denial of suffering, optimism urged the acceptance of evil as necessary in a complex universe. That said, the growing divide between epistemology and theology in the period meant that relatively few philosophers were committed to delineating an optimistic position. Moreover, optimism as a school of thought was only fully articulated in retrospect, and then only by its enemies. The chief and most influential historian of optimism was Voltaire (1694–1778), who devoted enormous energy to establishing the existence of optimism as a coherent philosophical movement and then ridiculing it mercilessly in his picaresque tale, *Candide; ou, Optimisme* (1759). It is worth noting that none of the thinkers whom Voltaire associated with optimism used the word in describing their own work.

Leibniz and His Influence. Voltaire identified and pilloried Leibniz as the father of modern optimism, not taking into account the complexity of his thought. Leibniz's "best of all possible worlds" is but one part of a synthetic philosophical system aimed at promoting harmony in all human endeavor. His optimistic ideas were expressed relatively consistently throughout his many writings; they found their most lucid expression in the late *Principes de la nature et de la grâce* (Principles of Nature and Grace, 1714), though they owed their wide dissemination in the Enlightenment to the more popular but less coherent *Theodicy* (1710). Leibniz's compelling version of the cosmological argument began with his principle of "sufficient or final reason": we must be able to give a reason for why anything exists in the world, but explanations of material cause and effect are insufficient, involving as they do an endless chain of contingencies. The only sufficient reason must then involve "a necessary being, which carries the reason for its existence within itself . . . and that final reason for things we call *God*." The world that God has created is of course imperfect; if not, the world itself would be God. However, "it follows from the supreme perfection of God that in producing the universe He chose the best possible design, in which there was the greatest variety, together with the greatest order" (*Philosophical Texts*, 1998, 262–263). Consistently casting God as a careful architect, Leibniz emphasizes the admirable efficiency of the divine plan, which is "simplest in theories and richest in phenomena" (*Philosophical Texts*, 1998, 58).

God governs the world by a very few principles, such as the laws of motion, but through the interactions of these principles he nonetheless attains a variety of effects so great that the human mind can grasp only a small fraction. Leibniz held that in making the universe,

God freely chose the best; he could have created a less perfect world, but such an action would be inconsistent with his goodness. That God has permitted evil in the world is undeniable. While we cannot in any particular case determine why God permits suffering, however, we can nonetheless confidently determine generally from the nature of God that he has good reason: "One knows that he takes care of the whole universe, whereof all the parts are connected; and one must thence infer that he has had innumerable considerations whose result made him deem it inadvisable to prevent certain evils" (*Theodicy*, 1952, 93).

Leibniz had a considerable influence on German philosophy: he found a disciple in Christian Wolff (1679–1754), and Immanuel Kant (1724–1804) entertained optimistic ideas in his earliest work. Voltaire argued in his *Dictionnaire philosophique* (1764) that optimism was rife in England, and that Leibniz had sympathizers in Anthony Ashley Cooper, third earl of Shaftesbury (1671–1713), Henry St. John Bolingbroke (1678–1751), and Alexander Pope (1688–1744). The first two of these thinkers held the position that virtue was sufficiently rewarded in this life, and that those who were truly good would find happiness on earth. It was Pope, however, who gave Leibniz's ideas their fullest and most influential English articulation in his poem *An Essay on Man* (1733–1734). Here Pope argued that the apparent evils and injustices that befall us in life are the necessary consequences of general laws working for the good of the whole, and he urged his readers to submit to God's plan:

> All Nature is but Art, unknown to thee;
> All Chance, Direction which thou canst not see;
> All Discord, Harmony not understood;
> All partial evil, universal Good:
> And spight of Pride, in erring Reason's spight,
> One truth is clear; "Whatever Is, is RIGHT.
>
> (I, 289–294)

The Attack on Optimism. Early in his career, Voltaire seemed to have held opinions that could well be called optimistic, but his subsequent reading in history and his horror at the carnage of the Lisbon earthquake (1755) made him skeptical of both human motivations and God's immediate concern for human affairs. He came to doubt that the material world was as full and as orderly as Leibniz claimed, and as for evil and suffering, they seemed too often to prevail in human life to be dismissed as unfortunate side effects of a divine program to promote the general good. Schooled by history in the baser motives of the powerful, he also became suspicious of the political implications of optimism, particularly the dangerous complacency of assuming that all is for the best. Voltaire worked out his critique of optimism in many writings: if the most influential of these was *Candide*, the most serious philosophical challenge to

optimism occurs in the *Dictionnaire philosophique* (1764). Here, under the heading "The Chain of Being," Voltaire attacks optimism's central trope. There seemed to be troublesome gaps in the chain—between man and ape, for instance, and between the highest angel and God. And what about creatures that have become extinct? Even the solar system, which Newton showed moved to the immutable laws of attraction, is highly irregular, with gross disproportions in the size and orbits of the planets. Turning directly to optimism in the entry "All Is for the Best," Voltaire denounced the idea as undermining orthodox Christianity by failing to take sufficient account of the Fall and by turning God into a cruel and powerful tyrant, intent upon his own designs and uncaring about the suffering of his subjects. Finally, he objects to the optimists' apparent callousness; Leibniz, Bolingbroke, Shaftesbury, and Pope all seem strangely oblivious to the deluge of evil that engulfs the world. It is this blindness to suffering that is the focus of the satire in *Candide*, where the philosopher Pangloss teaches the innocent Candide his doctrine that all is for the best in this, the best of all possible worlds. Structurally, *Candide* is a picaresque tale, with its protagonists wandering from encounter to encounter over much of Europe and South America. Stylistically, it is an experiment in the Rabelaisian grotesque, providing an overwhelming catalog of the varieties of human vice and suffering: murder, rape, slavery, war, disease, mutilation, prostitution—even an auto-da-fé. This litany of atrocities serves as a simple, experiential rebuttal to optimism; if there is plenitude in the world, it is a perverse plenitude of misery. Voltaire, however, repudiated not just optimism in *Candide*, but dogmatic philosophy altogether. Pangloss does not budge from his position, refusing to let the chaos of life shake his metaphysical dream. "I am a philosopher after all," Pangloss observes, "It wouldn't do for me to go back on what I said before, what with Leibniz not being able to be wrong, and pre-established harmony being the finest thing in the world" (*Candide*, 1990, 93). With its famous final injunction that we go and cultivate our gardens, *Candide* proposes simple labor as an antidote to the vanity of irrelevant philosophizing.

In England, Samuel Johnson published at about the same time his own attack on optimism in the form of an extended review of Soame Jenyns's *A Free Inquiry into the Nature and Origin of Evil* (1757), a book that offered little more than a prose paraphrase of Pope's *Essay on Man*. Like Voltaire, Johnson had doubts about the fullness of the chain of being, but he saved his driest irony for Jenyns's cheerful diminishment of human pain, as when Jenyns suggested that poverty is somehow ameliorated by ignorance, or that the anguish of illness is compensated by the joy of recovery. Johnson's response: "Life must be seen before it can be known. This author and *Pope* perhaps never saw the miseries which they imagine thus easy to be born" (Johnson, 1965, 357). Compared with Voltaire's panoramic view of the world's ills, Johnson's argument is more psychological and more influenced by the emergent discourse of moral sympathy, but the approaches of both thinkers are distinctively empirical as they ring the death knell of optimism. Whatever its integrity as a metaphysical axiom, "all is for the best" could not stand against the powerful immediate evidence of human suffering.

[*See also* Deism; Johnson, Samuel; Leibniz, Gottfried Wilhelm von; Natural Religion; Philosophy; Pope, Alexander; Rationalism; *and* Voltaire.]

BIBLIOGRAPHY

PRIMARY SOURCES

Johnson, Samuel. "Review of *A Free Inquiry into the Nature and Origin of Evil*." In *Johnson: Poetry and Prose*, edited by Mona Wilson, pp. 351–374. Cambridge, Mass., 1965.

Leibniz, Gottfried Wilhelm. *Philosophical Texts*. Edited by R. S. Woolhouse, translated by Richard Francks and R. S. Woolhouse. Oxford, 1998. The best modern English collection, carefully translated and balanced in its annotation.

Leibniz, Gottfried Wilhelm. *Theodicy*. Edited by Austin Farrer, translated by E. M. Huggard. New Haven, Conn., 1952. The work by which Leibniz was best known in the eighteenth century.

Pope, Alexander. *An Essay on Man*. Edited by Maynard Mack. Vol. 3, pt. 1 of the Twickenham edition of the poems of Alexander Pope. London, 1950.

Voltaire. *Candide and Other Stories*. Edited and translated by Roger Pearson. Oxford, 1990. A lively translation that captures much of Voltaire's irony.

Voltaire. *Philosophical Dictionary*. Edited and translated by Theodore Besterman. Harmondsworth, U.K., 1972.

SECONDARY SOURCES

Bernstein, John Andrew. "Shaftesbury's Optimism and Eighteenth-Century Thought." In *Anticipations of the Enlightenment*, edited by Alan Charles Kors and Paul J. Korshin, pp. 86–101. Philadelphia, 1987. Argues, contra Willey, that English optimists such as Shaftesbury and Pope were not enemies to the progressivism of the age.

Hudson, Nicholas. *Samuel Johnson and Eighteenth-Century Thought*. Oxford, 1988.

Mason, Haydn Trevor. *Candide: Optimism Demolished*. New York, 1992.

Vereker, Charles. *Eighteenth-Century Optimism*. Liverpool, 1967. Considers the prevalence in the period of the belief in the possibility of attaining harmony in human affairs.

Willey, Basil. *The Eighteenth-Century Background*. New York, 1940. An early and influential study, which picks up on Voltaire's political critique and labels English optimists of the eighteenth century "cosmic Tories" for their emphasis on the importance of keeping one's place in the chain of being.

PETER WALMSLEY

ORATORIANS. The primary mission of the Oratory of Jesus, founded by Pierre de Bérulle on 10 November 1611 and approved by the Holy See in 1613, was to return to favor the eminent dignity of the priestly state that led to perfection. Despite being clearly established in the lineage of the original Oratory of Saint Filippo Neri (1515–1595), and borrowing both its name and its style of teaching, the Oratory of France differed in being a centralized organization and in aspiring to make this new congregation a breeding ground for priests. Oratorians never had to take vows; their founder accepted only vows of servitude to Jesus Christ and Mary, which were not obligatory and, having only a spiritual aim, had no canonical consequences. Ordination to the priestly state, a state of holiness, resulted only from consecration to God.

The tasks initially devolving on Oratorians were "functions necessary and proper to the state of priesthood": rural missions, stations for the observance of Lent or Advent in the cities, curacies (although the number of parishes run by the Oratory always was limited because the father superior insisted on communal life), and seminaries.

Because the congregation professed obedience to local bishops, it took responsibility for the education of the youth in schools, though this was not the original intention. The constitutions of the congregation, established during the first general assembly held in August 1631, gave legislative power to general assemblies held every three years. These assemblies had certain ex officio deputies (the superior general and his direct associates) as well as elected deputies. The latter, chosen from among those who had been admitted for at least seven years and who had been priests for five, regularly elected the officers of the congregation, except for the superior general, who was elected for life.

Initially, the congregation included mostly simple residences or curacies (about fifty out of a total of seventy-three in 1630, in contrast to only seventeen schools). The map of the congregation's establishments changed during the years from 1660 to 1690, however, when the Oratorians accepted the bishops' request that they take responsibility for fifteen diocesan seminaries and eleven new schools (including those at Bavay and Thuin in Wallonia). The Oratory of France thus spread beyond the French borders into the Walloon portion of the Netherlands, where it became established very early. (The houses in the province of Malines split off and elected a *praepositus* [superior] of Flanders, who was independent of the French superior general after 1649.) During the eighteenth century, the bishops became suspicious of the congregation, and it lost eight seminaries between 1709 and 1743; however, after the expulsion of the Jesuits it got back seven schools. In 1789, it had thirty colleges, eight seminaries (including one associated with the Collège de la Trinité in Lyon and the one created in connection with the curacy of La Dalbade in Toulouse), four houses of formation where those entering spent a year training in the spirit of the congregation, two houses of study, and forty curacies.

The congregation was deeply affected by the Jansenist theological controversies raging throughout the century. In 1717–1719, 43 percent of the Oratorians signed either the first appeal by the four bishops or the second appeal by the cardinal of Noailles for an ecumenical council in opposition to the anti-Jansenist bull *Unigenitus*, pronounced on 8 September 1713 by Pope Clement XI. In 1727–1728, there was still a nucleus of 22 percent of the members of the congregation who supported the Jansenist bishop of Senez, Jean Soanen, a former Oratorian deposed by the provincial council of Embrun and exiled to La Chaise Dieu. This tells us something about the strong impact of Jansenism on the Oratory, which caused a major internal crisis. Not only do we observe a great drop in the numbers entering between 1715 and 1747, but we also see an increase in the number of associates leaving the congregation without having been ordained (as many as two-thirds of those entering during the period 1730–1749). The numbers of priests as well as their share in the congregation constantly went down: 650 were electors in the general assembly of 1714, but only 319 in 1755. In 1729, there were 907 members, two-thirds of whom were priests and a third associates; in 1782–1783, 59 percent of the total were associates. From being a congregation of priests, the Oratory became primarily a lay body. This transformation, contrary to Bérulle's initial project, first came about as a result of the bishops' refusal to ordain clerics who refused to sign Alexander VII's formulary *Regiminis Apostolici* (1655) concerning the five propositions "extracted" from Jansenius's *Augustinus*. The last superior general, Sauvé Moisset, died in 1790 and was not replaced because the congregation had not been given authorization to hold a general assembly. The Oratory of France was suppressed, like other lay congregations, by decree of the legislative assembly on 18 August 1792.

[*See also* Education, *subentry on* Pedagogical Thought and Practice; France; Jansenism; *and* Roman Catholicism.]

BIBLIOGRAPHY

Ambrieres, R. d'. *L'esprit de l'Oratoire de France au tournant du XVIIIe siècle*. Versailles, France, 1995.

Ehrard, J., ed. *Le Collège de Riom et l'enseignement oratorien en France au XVIIIe siècle*. Paris and Oxford, 1993.

Frijhoff, W., and D. Julia. "Les Oratoriens de France sous l'ancien régime: Premiers resultants d'une enquête." *Revue d'histoire de l'Église de France* 65 (1979), 225–265.

Frijhoff, W., and D. Julia. "L'Oratoire et le jansénisme: L'assemblée de 1746." In *Jansénisme et Révolution: Chroniques de Port-Royal*, edited by C. L. Maire, 39 (1990), 25–45.

Ingold, A. *Essai de bibliographie oratorienne*. Paris, 1880. *Supplément à l'essai de bibliographie oratorienne*. Paris, 1882. In the absence of any systematic bibliography of the writers of the Congregation of the Oratory, these two works remain extremely useful.

Ingold, A. *L'Oratoire et le jansénisme*. Paris, 1887.

Judge, H. G. "The Congregation of the Oratory in France in the Late Seventeenth Century." *Journal of Ecclesiastical History* 11 (1961), 46–55.

Lallemand, P. *Histoire de l'éducation dans l'ancien Oratoire de France*. Paris, 1888; repr., Geneva, 1976.

Maire, C. *De la cause de Dieu à la cause de la nation: Le jansénisme au XVIIIe siècle*. Paris, 1998. Particularly good on the theologians of the seminary of Saint-Magloire in Paris.

Perraud, A. *L'Oratoire de France aux XVIIe et XVIIIe siècles*. Paris, 1865.

DOMINIQUE JULIA
Translated from French by Betsy Wing

ORLÉANS, PHILIPPE D' (1674–1723), regent of France (1715–1723).

The duc d'Orléans was the only son of Louis XIV's younger brother, Philippe (1640–1701), and his second wife, Elisabeth-Charlotte (1652–1722), daughter of the Elector Palatine, one of the seven German princes who elected the Holy Roman Emperor. In 1692, he made an arranged marriage with Françoise-Marie (1677–1749), known as mademoiselle de Blois, his uncle's illegitimate daughter by Mme. de Montespan. A century later, his great-grandson sat in the Revolutionary Convention and voted for the death of Louis XVI. Philippe has traditionally been represented as a man no less dissolute than many other members of the colorful collateral line before and after him. He was long remembered more for his hedonism and skepticism than for his successful military career during the War of the Spanish Succession, his patronage of artists and writers, his interest in the sciences and the occult, and his support of the royal library. He befriended Fontenelle and Voltaire, but his private conduct and personal relations had less impact on the Enlightenment, in the long run, than did his public policies.

When Louis XIV died in 1715, he left his crown to his five-year-old great-grandson and divided the responsibilities of the regency between his nephew Philippe and his illegitimate son, the duc du Maine. Philippe persuaded the Parlement of Paris, the most influential of the dozen regional appeals courts in France, to disregard the late king's will and name him regent in his own right, in return for restoring the parlement's right to make remonstrances about royal edicts before registering them in its books. He initially appointed seven specialized councils, known collectively as the polysynody, to advise him about foreign and domestic affairs, but he subsequently reorganized the administration under the leadership of his former tutor, Guillaume Dubois (1656–1723). Debates about dynastic questions and concerns about aristocratic factionalism were compounded by confrontations with the parlement over financial and religious issues. The magistrates opposed a variety of edicts intended to decrease royal debts and increase royal revenues, and they criticized the ambitious efforts of the Scottish financier John Law (1671–1729) to operate a monopolistic national bank and a monopolistic commercial company. They also resisted repeated attempts to settle ongoing conflicts over the interpretation and implications of the papal bull *Unigenitus* (1713), which condemned Jansenism and divided the French clergy. In both cases, the parlement defended what it regarded as the laws of the realm and the privileges of subjects against what it described as abuses of authority, and the Regent eventually resorted to coercive measures. These episodes, documented in Montesquieu's *Lettres persanes* (Persian Letters, 1721) and in a voluminous pamphlet literature, marked the beginning of decades of disputes among the crown, the clergy, and the magistrates over the political, religious, and social traditions of the kingdom. Those disputes constituted the context in which the philosophes claimed to represent the public interest by using the faculty of reason to resolve contested questions in practical as well as abstract matters.

[*See also* France *and* Parlements.]

BIBLIOGRAPHY

Ceyssens, Lucien. "Autour de la bulle Unigenitus: Le Régent." *Bulletin de l'Institut historique belge de Rome* 57 (1987), 111–163. A thorough account of the Regent's role in the disputes about Jansenism.

Kaiser, Thomas. "Money, Despotism, and Public Opinion in Early Eighteenth-Century France: John Law and the Debate on Royal Credit." *Journal of Modern History* 63 (March 1991), 1–28. An important analysis of the impact of Law's schemes on French political culture.

Meyer, Jean. *Le Régent.* Paris, 1985. The best biography in French.

Shennan, J. H. *Philippe, Duke of Orléans: Regent of France, 1715–1723.* London, 1979. The most readable and reliable biography in any language.

JEFFREY MERRICK

OTIS, JAMES (1725–1743), American lawyer, politician, and political thinker.

James Otis Jr. was born into a prominent family in Barnstable County, Massachusetts. He graduated from Harvard College in 1743 and studied law. Rising rapidly in the profession, Otis became the colony's acting advocate general in 1757. A man of letters as well as a lawyer, Otis wrote books on Latin and Greek prosody.

In 1760 Otis abruptly resigned his position as the king's attorney. He did so shortly after Boston's merchants challenged the legality of the Writs of Assistance in court. These Writs gave broad discretion to customs agents searching for contraband. Otis held them to be illegal, and took charge of the legal case against them. Some of Otis's contemporaries charged that Otis acted for personal, not principled reasons. In early 1760 Governor Francis Bernard appointed the colony's first lieutenant governor, Thomas Hutchinson, to be the chief justice, passing over Otis's father, who had expected to be appointed.

Hutchinson would preside over the Writs case. While Otis enjoyed making Hutchinson's life difficult, Otis's actions squared with his convictions.

In court, Otis maintained that the Writs of Assistance were grants of arbitrary authority, and as such were contrary to law. He declared, "An act against the constitution is void; an act against natural equity is void; and if an act of Parliament should be made, in the very words of this petition, it would be void. The executive Courts must pass such acts into disuse." From July 1776 on, John Adams looked to Otis's argument as the starting point of the American Revolution. Hutchinson, however, ruled that the Writs were legal.

After the Writs case, Boston elected Otis to the colony's lower house. Otis soon took charge of the "country" party, in opposition to Hutchinson's "court" party. Otis and Hutchinson argued about monetary policy (Otis was a bimetalist and Hutchinson was not), about the death penalty (Otis thought it should be applied to fewer crimes), about trade policy (Otis wanted freer trade), and about wealth (Hutchinson held that vice increased with wealth; Otis disagreed). Otis also criticized plural officeholding, an implicit criticism of Hutchinson's own practice. By undermining the separations of power, Otis contended, plural officeholding threatened the rule of law.

In 1764 Parliament passed the Sugar Act and indicated that it would also pass a Stamp Act. Otis took charge of the opposition in Massachusetts. His slogan, "taxation without representation is tyranny," was soon heard throughout Anglo-America. His 1764 pamphlet, *The Rights of the British Colonies Asserted and Proved*, was popular across the colonies. Otis held that "the colonists are by the law of nature freeborn, as indeed are all men"; that men created governments to serve their legitimate purposes; and that no government may legitimately take away the rights of men. God was the only absolute sovereign. Otis understood the implications of his argument, calling slavery "a most shocking violation of the law of nature." In a subsequent pamphlet he called for universal manhood suffrage.

In 1765 Otis changed course. Some accused him of deserting the colonial cause, but it is more accurate to say he changed tactics. Otis turned away from the abstract question of the rights of men and focused on the practical problem of securing the rights of Anglo-Americans. Otis called for what became the Stamp Act Congress to unify Anglo-American opposition against taxation by Parliament, and to moderate colonial anger until an accommodation could be reached. He also called for free and equal trade in the empire, and for an equitable representation of Anglo-America in Parliament. Otis wanted to forge "a thorough beneficial union of these colonies to the realm." Few men in Britain or America took the proposal seriously, but Otis could think of no other way to make the empire both secure and free. As with his principled argument against slavery and his call for branches of government that "check and balance each other," Otis's call for a federal union would be more important in the United States after 1776 than before.

In the late 1760s Otis remained active in politics, even as he gradually lost his mental stability. The final blow to his lucidity came in late 1769 when he suffered a severe beating to the head in a fight with a British customs commissioner. In May 1783 he was struck dead by a bolt of lightning. According to tradition, this was both how he wanted and expected to die.

[*See also* American Revolution.]

BIBLIOGRAPHY

Bailyn, Bernard. *The Pamphlets of the American Revolution*. Cambridge, Mass., 1965; pp. 409–417, 546–552. The introductions to the reprints of two Otis pamphlets argues that Otis was ideologically confused and trying to reconcile irreconcilable ideas. (The pamphlets follow.)

Breen, Timothy. "Subjecthood and Citizenship: The Context of James Otis's Radical Critique of John Locke." *New England Quarterly* (1998), 378–404. An insightful study of Otis's embrace of human equality.

Brennan, Ellen E. "James Otis, Recreant and Patriot." *New England Quarterly* 12 (1939), 691–725. Argues that Otis shifted back and forth in his support for the colonial cause.

Samuelson, Richard. "The Constitutional Sanity of James Otis: Resistance Leader and Loyal Subject." *Review of Politics* 61 (1999), 493–523. Presents Otis as a politician trying to fix the British Empire.

Shaw, Peter. "James Otis." In *American Patriots and the Rituals of the Revolution*, pp. 77–108. Cambridge, Mass., 1981. A psychological study of Otis.

Shipton, Clifford K. "James Otis." In *Biographical Sketches of Those Who Attended Harvard College: In the Classes 1741–1745*, vol. 11, pp. 247–287. Boston, Mass., 1960. A solid biographical treatment of Otis.

Smith, M. H. *The Writs of Assistance Case*. Berkeley, 1978. More than one could possibly want to know about the case. Reprints the notes John Adams and Josiah Quincy took while observing the case.

Waters, John J., Jr. *The Otis Family of Provincial Massachusetts*. Chapel Hill, N.C., 1968. Sets Otis in the context of his family's development from migration to the American Revolution. Good biographical treatment.

RICHARD A. SAMUELSON

OTTOMAN EMPIRE. The Ottoman Empire, with its capital at Constantinople, the political center of the Islamic world, still occupied in the eighteenth century a large part of the Near East, the Balkans, and North Africa, but it was in decline and no longer posed a serious threat to Christian Europe, as was shown by its army's failure at Vienna in 1683 and the Treaty of Karlowitz (1699). By the middle of the century, it was clearly lagging behind Northern Europe in technology, particularly military, despite efforts to modernize its armies with the help of Europeans such as the French renegade Claude-Alexandre, count Bonneval, in the 1730s and 1740s under Mahmut I, or baron François de Tott, employed as a military adviser and mathematics teacher to the navy by Mustafa III in the 1770s. The disastrous war against the Russians between 1768 and 1774 ended in the Treaty of Küçük Kaynarca, by which the Ottomans ceded the Crimea.

The interests of the different European countries in the Empire were reflected in their strong commercial and diplomatic links, as can be seen not only in the number of Europeans resident there, but also in Ottoman missions to European capitals. In particular, the lavish visit to Paris by Mehmed Said Efendi in 1720–1721, in order to report on aspects of European civilization that could be imported to the Empire, created a fashion for things Turkish in France. While the fear inspired by the Turks had not totally disappeared, it was mixed with curiosity and a certain fascination, to which was added a growing disparagement.

This empire embodied for Europeans the alien culture of the Islamic world, to the extent that the word 'Turk" was used as an equivalent for "Muslim." At the same time, it represented the epitome of "oriental despotism," an idea popularized by Montesquieu's *L'esprit des lois* (1748), but which drew its substance from the English merchant Paul Rycaut's *History of the Present State of the Ottoman Empire* (1668), still considered by Volney over a century later as the best book on the subject. Rycaut's detailed description of the functioning of the government of the Empire insisted on the absolute nature of the sultan's power, claiming it was his whim rather than the law which was supreme and that no individual or property was secure. This work helped to instill in Europeans' minds the view of the cruelty and arbitrariness of life under the sultan, and Montesquieu used Rycaut's authority to characterize despotic power, symbolized by the Turks, as based on fear.

Voltaire protested against what he called this prejudice in his *Essai sur les mœurs* (Essay on Morals), indicating the limits on the sultan's authority, and he insisted on the Ottomans' toleration toward Christians and Jews, contrasting it with Catholic intolerance. In addition, he puts the words of wisdom at the end of *Candide* in the mouth of an old Turk and situates Candide's refuge in the suburbs of Istanbul. Nevertheless, Montesquieu's representation of the Ottoman government became the dominant one, repeated by the *Universal History* and by historians such as William Robertson (who refers to Rycaut), despite criticisms by, for example, James Porter, ambassador to the Porte from 1746 to 1762, in his *Observations on the Religion, Laws, Government and Manners of the Turks* (1768 and 1771).

The harem, symbol of this despotism, also fueled the imagination, with a large number of works exploiting

Ottoman Capital. View of Constantinople. Colored engraving, late eighteenth century. (Stapleton Collection, U.K./Bridgeman Art Library International Ltd.)

the sexual titilation connected with the seclusion of women. These works were inspired by Antoine Galland's translation of *The Thousand and One Nights* (from 1704), but also by descriptions of the Ottoman court, in particular those contained in the letters written from Istanbul by Lady Mary Wortley Montagu, the wife of the British ambassador. She was one of the few outsiders to visit the harem and meet the sultan's wives, and thus to give a more authentic picture of the court. Her letters, which began to circulate from 1724, described the refinement and riches she saw and expressed her admiration for Ottoman art and literature, which was still brilliant. But although she popularized in Europe the Turkish practice of inoculation against smallpox, her admiration remained a minority view and was denounced by writers such as Tott in the account of his experiences which he published as *Mémoires sur les Turcs et les Tartares* (1784), where he stigmatized her ignorance of the language. Tott saw the Ottomans as a scourge infecting the whole of the Mediterranean.

Increasingly, in the later part of the century, Europeans emphasized their ignorance, encouraged by what was seen as their religiously-inspired fatalism and embodied in the plague, which was endemic in the Ottoman Empire, necessitating quarantine for those who returned from there. These attitudes are already found in the marquis d'Argens's *Lettres juives* (1738 onwards), despite a desire to counter certain prejudices concerning the Turks. The abbé Raynal's *Histoire philosophique des Deux-Indes* (Philosophical History of the Two Indies, 1770–1780) is more consistently hostile, presenting the Ottoman Empire as corrupt and in decline but as imposing a fanatical and despotic government on its subject peoples, whom it has ruined. This reflects both a desire to criticize fanaticism and arbitrary government nearer to home and the

greater denigration of the Porte and its perceived contempt for arts and learning, to be found in the writings of both Tott and Volney. Volney visited the Near East in 1783–1785, and his account of the journey published in 1787 is very hostile, as are his *Considérations sur la guerre des Turcs en 1788* (Considerations on the Turkish War in 1788), which describes the decadence of the Empire and its barbarity and corruption. Even the former French consul Louis de Chénier's *Révolutions de l'empire Ottoman* (1789), which attempted to counter such hostility, admitted the Turks' fanaticism and ignorance. His belief that decline was not however inevitable was shared by Mouradja d'Ohsson's monumental *Tableau général de l'empire Othman* (1788 onwards), which attempted to counter prejudices by describing in great detail the history, laws and governing system of the Ottoman Empire, and to demonstrate that its decline was caused not by its principles but their neglect. Such attempts did not succeed in changing fundamental European perceptions, and in the following century the barbarity, ignorance and corruption of Ottoman despotism were generally agreed.

[*See also* Diplomacy; Inoculation and Vaccination; Islam; Montagu, Mary Wortley; Montesquieu, Charles-Louis de Secondat; Raynal, Guillaume-Thomas; Robertson, William; Volney, Constantin-François de Chasseboeuf; *and* Voltaire.]

BIBLIOGRAPHY

Beck, Brandon H. *From the Rising of the Sun: English Images of the Ottoman Empire to 1715*. New York, 1987. Brief survey of the background to eighteenth-century attitudes to the Ottomans.

Daniel, Norman. *Islam, Europe and Empire*. Edinburgh, 1966. The early chapters deal will attitudes to the Ottoman Empire in this period.

Grosrichard, Alain. *The Sultan's Court: European Fantasies of the East*. London, 1998. English translation of *Structure du sérail*.

Paris, Seuil, 1979. A psychoanalytical study of the role played by oriental despotism in the European imagination, devoting much space to the Enlightenment.

Hentsch, Thierry. *Imagining the Middle East*. Montreal, 1992. Translation of *L'Orient imaginaire: La vision politique occidentale de l'Est méditerranéen*. Paris, 1988. A study of how the European image of the Eastern Mediterranean emerged through political contacts and reflection. Devotes quite a lot of space to the Enlightenment period.

Naff, Thomas. "Ottoman Diplomatic Relations with Europe in the Eighteenth Century: Patterns and Trends." In *Studies in Eighteenth Century Islamic History*, edited by Thomas Naff and Roger Owen, pp. 88–107. Carbondale, Ill., 1977.

Shaw, Stanford. *History of the Ottoman Empire and Modern Turkey*, vol. 1, *Empire of the Gazis: The Rise and Decline of the Ottoman Empire, 1280–1808*. Cambridge, 1976.

Wortley Montagu, Mary. *Turkish Embassy Letters*. London, 1995.

ANN THOMSON

P–Q

PAGANISM. *See* Tradition.

PAGANO, FRANCESCO MARIO (1748–1799), Neapolitan philosopher and leader of the Neapolitan Republic of 1799.

Mario Pagano was born in the countryside of southern Italy in 1748. Law was the profession of his family, which Pagano continued, taking a degree in jurisprudence in Naples. Two authors influenced him: Giambattista Vico and Antonio Genovesi. From Vico he took the theory of savage existence as the essential moment in the formation of social institutions, which aligned him with the philosophes of the Enlightenment, with Rousseau, and with Boulanger. From Vico he also drew the belief that political and social conflict lay at the base of all societies, a theory linked to the most radical currents of modern political thought from Machiavelli to Hobbes. He knew his other master, Genovesi, personally, and learned that philosophy consists in knowing the limits within which it is possible to carry out scientific inquiry. By defining these methodological limits Genovesi recognized the social and civil conditions through which culture was produced. Hence philosophy had to have utility.

Pagano's own works reflect these interests. Among his works on jurisprudence, the principal ones are *Logica dei probabili* (The Logic of Provables), drafted in 1784 but only published posthumously under both that title and the alternative title *Teoria delle prove* (Theory of Proofs), and *Considerazioni sul processo criminale* (Considerations on Criminal Trials), published in 1787. An enthusiastic reader of Montesquieu and Beccaria, he too was convinced that by means of penal law a challenge could be mounted to existing social and political structures, if there was a strong will to reform. Until 1792–1793 this will to reform signified for him trust in the Bourbon monarchy, in the actions of an absolute and enlightened prince.

In 1783–1785 he published *Saggi politici: De' principii, progressi e decadenza delle società* (Political Essays. On the Origins, Progress, and Decadence of Societies), republished with significant changes in 1791. The *Saggi* are the great masterpiece of the late Enlightenment culture, not just of Naples, but of all Italy. They may be described as a "philosophical and political history" of the Kingdom of Naples. As philosophical history they follow Vico, but also Ferguson, Rousseau, and Boulanger, in sketching an anthropological history of humankind. Pagano ponders the earliest forms of humankind's barbaric and savage past, the societies of hunters and herders, their transformation into more stable agriculturally-based communities. He seeks to identify the rudiments of culture and society, their progress toward more cultivated forms, and finally, inevitable decadence. As a political history of the Kingdom of Naples, the *Saggi* analyzes the role of feudalism in the south of Italy, traces the ongoing role of the church there, and identifies it as one of the most profound causes of intellectual and social corruption. The central theme of the work is thus the relation between authority and liberty, politics and conflict.

In 1789, Pagano published *Ragionamento sulla libertà del commercio del pesce* (Discussion of Free Trade in Fish), in which he stated again that greater liberty would lead to the betterment of political and social conditions. In line with his theory of history, which highlighted the social value of art, he believed that the regeneration of the kingdom could be furthered through the theater, and himself composed several tragedies between 1782 and 1792: *Gli esuli tebani, Gerbino, Agamemnone, Corradino.*

Then his faith in the monarchy crumbled. The French Revolution had deep influence on Neapolitan political life, creating a dramatic split between the court—which allied itself with Austria under the influence of Queen Carolina, a sister of Marie Antoinette of France—and the elites, who chose the side of the French republic. Neapolitan intellectuals, once reformers, now became Jacobins and republicans. In 1794 a conspiracy was discovered; Pagano defended the conspirators. Under suspicion of Jacobinism himself, he was arrested in 1796. When he was freed in June 1798, Pagano went into exile. In January 1799, the Neapolitan republic was declared and Pagano was nominated to head the legislative committee. The Enlightenment intellectual took revolutionary action: As one of the principal leaders of the republic Pagano wrote the laws abolishing entailed estates and feudal duties, and oversaw the debate on the abolition of feudalism in the kingdom. He also launched the process of deciding on a new constitution and a new penal code. The republic, however, collapsed after five months, and the Bourbon reaction was severe. Pagano was condemned to death and was hanged on 29 October 1799.

His life's work marks the high point of the Italian Enlightenment. Pagano was able to incorporate into his own theoretical approach radical components that projected it beyond the confines of eighteenth-century reformism toward the new world of democratic and liberal politics. With his death, this culture vanished from civic life in the south of Italy, and it is no exaggeration to say this tragic loss was felt for a long time.

[*See also* Economic Thought; French Revolution; Genovesi, Antonio; Italy; Naples; Political Philosophy; *and* Vico, Giambattista.]

BIBLIOGRAPHY

Pagano, Mario. *Saggi politici: De' principii, progressi e decadenza delle società*. Edited by Luigi Firpo and Laura Salvetti Firpo. Naples, 1993. The text of the second, corrected, and augmented edition of 1791–1792.

Pagden, Anthony. "Francesco Mario Pagano's 'Republic of Virtue': Naples, 1799." In *The Invention of the Modern Republic*, edited by Biancamaria Fontana, pp. 139–153. Cambridge, 1994.

Venturi, Franco, ed. *Illuministi Italiani*, vol. 5, *Riformatori napoletani*. Milan and Naples, 1962. The best selection of excerpts from Pagano's works is at pp. 834–937. See as well the outstanding introductory note by Venturi, pp. 785–833.

GIROLAMO IMBRUGLIA

Translated from Italian by William McCuaig

Thomas Paine. Mezzotint engraving (1783) by James Watson after a portrait by Charles Willson Peale. [For an image of the title page of *Common Sense*, see the article "Pamphlets."] (National Portrait Gallery, Washington, D.C./Art Resource, NY.)

PAINE, THOMAS (1737–1809), American political thinker and pampleteer.

Perhaps more than any other intellectual figure of the Enlightenment, Thomas Paine and his writings sparked the bitterest public disputes about matters of public importance. Paine enjoyed a reputation, among friends and enemies alike, as an extraordinary citizen. Born on 29 January 1737, in the small English town of Thetford, Norfolk, he burst onto the stage of public life as a commoner. During the first half of his life, Paine was variously employed as a corsetmaker (his father's trade), a ship's hand, and a Methodist lay-preacher. He also worked as an exciseman, a teacher of English, and a writer who dabbled in public affairs. His first wife and child died during labor, and generally dogged by unhappiness and misfortune, he decided with the help of Benjamin Franklin to emigrate to the American colonies in late September 1774. There, on the side of the revolutionaries, he volunteered for military service with a Pennsylvania "flying" camp. He was a political adviser to George Washington, a war correspondent, and (as evidenced during 1782 by his public criticisms of the Rhode Island authorities) a proponent of federalism. He held the post of Secretary to the Committee for Foreign Affairs of the Continental Congress. Author of the best-selling tract *Common Sense* (1776), which contains the first modern use of the terms "society," "civil society," and "civilised society," and is still considered by many an intellectual cornerstone of American democracy, Paine was also widely considered the most prominent political thinker and writer during the revolutionary struggle against the British. He was twice invited to France, where he helped draft the 1793 constitution and completed a dramatic plea for secularism, *The Age of Reason* (1794). During the Reign of Terror, after having argued for abolishing the monarchy and preserving the life of Louis XVI, Paine spent nearly a year in the Luxembourg prison, where he almost died of exhaustion and narrowly escaped the guillotine. After completing several works, including *Dissertations sur les premiers principes de gouvernement* (1795), and one of the earliest pleas for citizens' income funded by an inheritance tax, *Agrarian Justice* (1796), he returned to America in the autumn of 1802. There, in old age, he and his supporters suffered much public criticism and private discrimination for his alleged atheism, his attacks on George Washington's royalist character, and his defense of Deism in a series of essays in the New York journal, *Prospect; or, View of the Moral World*. Paine died in New York in the summer of 1809 and was buried on the small farm he had owned, in nearby New Rochelle.

Through the acknowledged brilliance of his quill, Paine forged a reputation as one of the eighteenth century's chief public defenders of what came to be called republican democracy. Author of over six hundred works, including letters, he was widely considered a living symbol of the modern fight for the rights of citizens against warring states and arbitrary governments, social injustice and prejudice. Not only the message, but also the modernist style of *Common Sense*, *The Age of Reason* and the two-part *Rights of Man* (1791–1792), ensured that they became the three most widely read political tracts of the century. The sales of the first part of *Rights of Man* were breathtaking by contemporary standards. They helped widen and deepen the boundaries of the reading public. Paine himself estimated (accurately) that in Britain alone the sales of the complete edition of that work reached "between four and five hundred thousand" copies within ten years of publication—which (in an age of widespread illiteracy) made it the most widely read book of all time, in any language.

In his various works, Paine helped effect something of a revolution in political language. Encouraged by his reading of the works of Daniel Defoe, Jonathan Swift, and others, he won a wide reputation as a master of daring assertion, sly humor, and witty metaphor. His books, pamphlets, letters, essays, and poetry tried to communicate complications simply. They invented a plain style crafted to capture the attention, and secure the trust, of audiences previously accustomed to being pushed about or ignored, not being written for, talked about, and taken seriously as active citizens. "As it is my design to make those that can scarcely read understand," Paine wrote, "I shall therefore avoid every literary ornament and put it in language as plain as the alphabet."

Paine specialized in writing for audiences he knew well—self-educated artisans and ordinary folk like himself, for whom reading and being read to were exhilarating first-time experiences. He supposed that in politics words count, and that words are deeds. He further thought that liberty is connected with prose, and that power groups unfriendly to citizens' liberty normally wrap their power in pompous or meaningless phrases. Paine had no elaborate theory of language. He rarely questioned his own conceited view that his writing was "plain truth," a reflection of the world as it actually is. He counted himself among the modern believers in the originally Greek idea that what makes humans clever, language-using animals is our ability to rise above the contingencies of time and place, and to know the nature of things. Paine nevertheless thought that his contemporaries displayed a bad habit of falsely attributing universal importance to their own particular ways of life, and so displayed an alarming tendency to boss others into accepting their contingent version of the world. "Bastilles of the word" was his phrase for needlessly haughty language, and he consequently wrote as if it were the duty of the citizen, and certainly the political thinker and writer, to be on the lookout for hubris.

Paine's didacticism dovetailed with his compassion for the unjustly treated, and his contempt for haughty power-mongers. Paine so disliked arrogance and venality (as he made plain during the Silas Deane affair, the young American republic's first corruption scandal) that he championed citizens' right to tell others what they do not want to hear. He alleged that human beings could live together on earth without the superstitious belief in earthly Gods—indeed, that we live fully only in their absence. Paine has been described as an eighteenth-century critic with ultra-modernist predilections. He doubted most existing Grand Ideals—his belief in historical progress, Newtonian science, and God-given reason were contradictory exceptions—because he was convinced that they unleashed hypocrisy and deception, power hunger, and violence upon the world.

Paine's early years in England made him skeptical of the presumption that government and religious institutions are above public suspicion. On this basis, he began his public career as a journalist, a defender of government employees' right to organize into trade unions (in a 1772 pamphlet, *The Case of the Officers of Excise*), and a critic of the enslavement of Africans. Paine then laid into monarchy, which he likened to a bad play. Monarchy is "something kept behind a curtain, about which there is a great deal of bustle and fuss, and a wonderful air of seeming solemnity," he wrote. "But when, by any accident, the curtain happens to open, and the company see what it is, they burst into laughter."

Initially, Paine worked to abolish monarchy in the name of "the people" or "the nation," terms that he used interchangeably. He soon questioned the principle of popular sovereignty, notably in his first writings on the Pennsylvania constitution for the *Pennsylvania Journal* and the *Pennsylvania Packet*. He suspected that the formula of "the people" as a unified God on earth, from whom all power and wisdom emanates, was the mirror image of the old doctrine of monarchy that many republicans had fought hard to replace. The formula made him nervous, especially after witnessing, firsthand, figures as different as Robespierre and George Washington attempting, in his view, to abuse political power in the name of "the people."

To see "the people" as an invented fiction, prone to misuse by dictators speaking in the name of their subjects, was considered by many contemporaries a bold move—although perhaps not as electrifying as his thunderous attacks on organized religion. "All national institutions of churches, whether Jewish, Christian, or Turkish, appear to me no other than human inventions set up to terrify and enslave mankind, and monopolise power and profit," he wrote. Paine was not the first republican to challenge Christianity, but the way he did so, as his enemies saw, helped make skepticism about every kind of organized religion a subversive living force. Paine's point was that talk of sacred scriptures, God's designs, and the sanctity of the church was merely talk—the talk of some mortals bent on empowering themselves over others.

Paine's public attacks on dogma were not intended to push citizens into a void of confused disbelief. Life based on reason without dogmas was possible, he thought, but only insofar as individuals cultivated their own personal morality and cooperated with others as public beings. He considered individuals of all countries as potential citizens. As citizens, he argued, they were entitled to enjoy certain rights, but were also bound to honor certain duties within a worldwide framework of constitutional governments that maximized civil and political freedom and guaranteed social justice. "Where liberty is, there is my country," his good friend Benjamin Franklin once reportedly remarked to him. "Where liberty is not, there is my country," Paine quipped in reply. Citizenship for him implied the global abolition of despotism and injustice: "When it shall be said in any country in the world, 'My poor are happy; neither ignorance nor distress is to be found among them; my jails are empty of prisoners, my streets of beggars; the aged are not in want, the taxes are not oppressive; the rational world is my friend, because I am a friend of its happiness':—when these things can be said," wrote Paine, "then may that country boast of its constitution and its government."

BIBLIOGRAPHY

There are two principal collections of the 620 writings by Paine, and other materials about him: the Gimbel Collection, the American Philosophical Society Library, Philadelphia; and the John Keane Collection, Norfolk and Norwich Millennium Library, Heritage Centre, Norwich, England.

Barry, Alyce. "Thomas Paine, Privateersman." *Pennsylvania Magazine of History and Biography* 4 (1977), 451–461.

Foner, Eric. *Tom Paine and Revolutionary America*. New York, 1976.

Hayden Clark, Harry. "An Historical Interpretation of Thomas Paine's Religion." *University of California Chronicle* 35 (1933), 56–87.

Keane, John. *Tom Paine: A Political Life*. London and New York, 1995.

King, Arnold Kimsey. "Thomas Paine in America, 1774–1787." Ph.D. diss., University of Chicago, 1951.

Paine, Thomas. *Complete Writings of Thomas Paine*. 2 vols. Edited by Philip S. Foner. New York, 1945.

Vincent, Bernard. *Thomas Paine ou la religion de la liberté*. Paris, 1987.

JOHN KEANE

PAINTING. The movement toward investigation and reform that characterized eighteenth-century intellectual history can also be seen in the development of European painting and aesthetics. One of the most significant directions during the Enlightenment was a renewed emphasis on painting as a vehicle for ideas, and art as a form of knowledge. Kant's famous Enlightenment dictum "Dare to know!" could be applied to the domain of painting, as artists increasingly sought to use visual representation as a means of expressing cultural, political, and historical ideas. This pan-European movement in art found its most organized manifestation in France, where it became part of the leading discourses on painting and aesthetics, fully developed by the time of the French Revolution. However, the European movement to intellectualize art, which reached fruition in the late eighteenth century, originated decades earlier. Renaissance tenets that painting should be didactic as well as aesthetically pleasing and should serve as a vehicle for ideas, not mere sensual enjoyment, began to reemerge at the height of the Rococo period.

France and the Rococo. The aesthetics of sensual beauty characteristic of much early eighteenth-century art in Europe is exemplified in the paintings of Antoine Watteau. His celebrations of courtly leisure and love in the idyllic countryside, often tinged with melancholy and nostalgia, in such canonical *fêtes galantes* as the *Pilgrimage to Cythera* (1717), set the standard in subject, style, and composition for decades to come. His depiction of elegant, graceful figures in sumptuous dress, of delicate manners and the enjoyment of life and love among the elite in harmonious, effervescent natural settings, appealed to aristocratic taste and convention. Costume, music, dance, games, the *commedia dell'arte*, and a calm, pleasing landscape constitute essential elements of Watteau's compositional vocabulary, which depends on the aesthetic principles of unity, harmony, movement, and grace. Influenced by the palette of Rubens as well as his application of paint in free, rapid strokes, Watteau emphasized color over outline as a means of delineating form.

The early decades of the eighteenth century in France witnessed the continuation of seventeenth-century academic debates: the ancients versus the moderns, line versus color, and Poussin versus Rubens. In the works of Watteau, the "modern" came into the ascendant; color triumphed over line, and Rubens over Poussin. Roger de Piles had promulgated these "modernist" values in his *Cours de peinture par principes* (1708), which had a decisive impact on art. He stated that painting imitates nature primarily through the use of color, while sculpture depends on contour and the modeling of form. In the paintings of Watteau, color rather than contour defines form. Nature motifs prevail in these compositions, including the shell-like shapes from which the Rococo, or *rocaille*, derives its

Painting. *Pilgrimage to Cythera (Embarcadère pour Cythère)* by Jean-Antoine Watteau (1684–1721). (Musée du Louvre, Paris/Lauros-Giraudon/Art Resource, NY.)

name. These motifs can be seen in Watteau's architectural fantasies, such as the fanciful boat in the *Pilgrimage to Cythera*.

A Rococo vocabulary of forms was disseminated throughout Europe by such works as Juste-Aurèle Meissonier's *Livre d'ornéments inventés et dessinés* (1734), depicting sumptuous objects designed to adorn aristocratic residences—salt and pepper shakers and soup tureens as well as fountains and architectural motifs—based on curvilinear shapes in nature, such as shell, leaf, or flower. The *Livre d'ornéments* helped to forge the international Rococo style in Europe.

By the mid-eighteenth century, the Rococo had become established as an international court style. Various artists were commissioned to paint for monarchs and other court patrons throughout Europe. The Venetian painter Giovanni Battista Tiepolo, continuing in the grand manner of Paolo Veronese, became one of the most sought-after painters, commissioned to execute large-scale wall decorations representing historical and religious subjects. *The Marriage of Frederick Barbarosa and Beatrice of Burgundy* (Würzburg Residenz, 1752) and the *Banquet of Anthony and Cleopatra* (Palazzo Labia, Venice, 1746–1747) are among his best-known monumental works.

In France in the 1740s and 1750s, François Boucher—who was influenced by Watteau, the precepts of de Piles, and Meissonier's vocabulary of forms—emerged as the most important court painter. Boucher was a prolific history painter, most celebrated for myriad compositions representing the amatory escapades of classical gods and goddesses in an erotic and joyous style. *The Triumph of Venus* (1748) and *Diana at Her Bath* (1742) exemplify this style. Boucher also worked in other genres, such as portraiture, rustic landscape, pastoral, chinoiserie, and scenes of domestic life. He created these works primarily for aristocratic patrons, including Mme. de Pompadour, of whom he painted numerous portraits.

As a result of avid patronage, portraiture flourished in the eighteenth century, associated not only with monarchs and their courts but also, especially during the second half of the century, with middle-class patrons. Portraits of leading Enlightenment intellectual and political figures became a specialized category, as in Francisco Goya's memorable depictions of the *illustrados* and Jacques Louis David's great *Monsieur and Madame Lavoisier* (1788). Portraits of the great individuals who had contributed to a nation's military or cultural history and heritage were also popular in the latter eighteenth century as the cult of nationalism began to emerge. David's depictions of Revolutionary martyrs in the early 1790s (Lepelletier de St. Fargeau, Marat, and Bara) belong to this category.

Genre scenes emerged as a category popular with the aristocracy and middle class alike. Jean-Honoré Fragonard continued in the manner of Watteau and Boucher but specialized in representations of contemporary life in paintings that celebrated sensuality and erotic amusements, like *The Swing* (1767). Even *Corésus and Callirhoé* (1765), for which Fragonard gained admittance to the

Académie Royale de Peinture et de Sculpture as a history painter, focused on the theme of erotic love and sacrifice. One of his most important commissions was an ambitious series of four large-scale paintings, *The Progress of Love* (1771–1773), for the residence of Mme. du Barry at Louveciennes, but by the time Fragonard completed the series, the Rococo idiom in which he excelled had been overshadowed by the emergent neoclassical style, and du Barry rejected the paintings.

Genre Painting. During the same period that witnessed the triumph of the Rococo style in Europe (1730s–1750s), countercurrents in theme and style had already begun to emerge. Seventeenth-century Dutch genre painting, with its emphasis on humble interiors and moralizing, bourgeois themes, was collected by the French aristocracy and exerted a powerful impact on French art. In addition to his magnificent still-lifes, Jean Siméon Chardin specialized in genre paintings of middle-class children learning important lessons—from books, from games, or from observing correct adult behavior and values. In paintings such as *Soap Bubbles* (1734), *Saying Grace* (1740), *The Morning Toilet* (1741), *The Young Schoolmistress* (1731–1732), and *Boy with a Top* (1737–1738), Chardin emphasized perception and learning in simple images.

Denis Diderot, who helped to create the modern genre of art criticism, repeatedly emphasized the role of the imitation of nature in visual representation, but also the didactic mission of art, which should instruct as well as please. In this regard, he was generally dissatisfied with historical and mythological paintings of the period, but he held Chardin in high esteem for his brilliance in creating the illusion of nature, and he praised him for the moral content of his compositions. Similarly, Diderot lauded the moralizing narratives of another genre painter of the period, Jean-Baptiste Greuze, who specialized in moral emblems and familial narratives. Greuze's *Girl with a Dead Bird* (c. 1765) and *The Broken Pitcher* (1773) had moral lessons to teach about virtue or the consequences of its absence, but their emphasis on the erotic beauty of adolescent girls linked them to principal directions of the Rococo. In family narratives such as *The Village Betrothal* (1761) and *The Well-Beloved Mother* (1765), Greuze emphasized bourgeois sentiment and virtues. Some of these familial narratives relate to themes of the *drame bourgeois*, a new genre in French theater (created largely by Diderot) that focused on the values, comportment, and tragedies of the contemporary middle-class family.

In Great Britain, too, a number of artists were interested in depicting the values and activities of the middle class. Like Chardin, the Irish artist Joseph Wright of Derby focused on study and learning within the bourgeois familial milieu. He was particularly fascinated with the scientific instruments and experiments that were becoming accessible to a broader, more educated public. Thus, *Experiment with an Air Pump* (1768) and *Philosopher Giving a Lecture on the Orrery* (1766; see the cover of volume 1 of this encyclopedia) represent acquaintances and family members of various ages responding to this new form of scientific education, which could take place in the home.

Earlier in the century in England, William Hogarth, a moralist interested in revealing the turpitude of contemporary society, had satirized, parodied, and critiqued bourgeois and upper-class mores and manners in cycles of narrative paintings and engravings. His *Harlot's Progress* (1731), *Rake's Progress* (1733–1734), and *Marriage à la Mode* (1743) were meant to be "read" in sequence.

The Classical Revival. Hogarth published his theories of art in an influential treatise, *The Analysis of Beauty* (1753), in which he promulgated the imitation of nature in its great variety over imitation of antique sculpture, and prescribed the serpentine line of beauty and grace as the basis for conveying life and movement in art. These principles, associated with a Rococo aesthetic, would be overturned by the neoclassical reforms of the mid-eighteenth century, which sought to purge art of Rococo excess by returning to the ideal of beauty found in classical sculpture.

The classical revival and the call for reforms in painting emerged in Rome, an international center for European professional artists and amateurs in the mid-eighteenth century. In a celebrated series of engravings, *The Antiquities of Rome* (1756) and *Vedute* (1759), Giambattista Piranesi had refocused attention on the great ruins of the Roman past, especially architectural monuments still half buried. The excavation of these monuments was related to the eighteenth-century interest in reconstructing the past, part of a new perspective in history and historicism that emphasized the historian not as a mere chronicler of events but as an interpreter of the past. This new perspective characterized historical writings of the period from Voltaire to Gibbon. Meditations on the melancholy of ruins, the sad yet noble vestiges of past civilizations that had believed in their own permanence, became a major theme in painting after the mid-eighteenth century, exemplified by the Italian Giovanni Panini and the Frenchman Hubert Robert, who specialized in such paintings of ruins.

This interest in reconstructing the past was fueled by excavations at Herculaneum and Pompeii in the 1730s and 1740s. The subjects, style, and compositional structures of the rediscovered wall paintings, disseminated through engravings in publications such as *Le pitture antiche d'Ercolano* (The Ancient Paintings of Herculaneum, 1757), directly inspired the development of the neoclassical style in painting throughout Europe. Artists finally had access to the aesthetics of antique painting. Earlier in the century, Bernard de Montfaucon's large, richly illustrated folios, *L'antiquité expliquée* (Antiquity Explained, 1722), had provided artists with a dictionary of sculpted images from antiquity; the engravings of Pompeii and Herculaneum would serve as a similar artistic sourcebook. Another important influence on the neoclassical style was the four lavishly illustrated folios of the "Etruscan" vase collection of Sir William Hamilton (*Collection of Etruscan, Greek and Roman Antiquities from the Cabinet of the Honorable William Hamilton*, edited by P. F. H. d'Hancarville, 1766–1767). By the turn of the century, John Flaxman would adapt the contour style from these reproductions for his series of illustrations to Homer and Dante, which exerted a powerful influence on early nineteenth century painting.

The classical wall and vase paintings offered an alternative to the Rococo. In the wall paintings, which typically depict mythological themes, a reduced number of figures are presented on a shallow foreground plane. The format is rectilinear and stagelike; objects, furniture, architectural elements, and decorative motifs are simplified and sparse; backgrounds are minimal, and colors muted or monochromatic. These stylistic and compositional features, also present in images reproduced from vase paintings, formed the basis of the pan-European neoclassical style.

The rediscovery of antique painting converged with the publication of works by one of the most important writers on art and aesthetics of the Enlightenment: Johann Winckelmann. After publishing *Gedanken über die Nachahmung der greichischen Werke in der Malerei und Bildhauerkunst* (On the Imitation of the Painting and Sculpture of the Greeks, 1755) in Dresden, Winckelmann moved to Rome and worked as librarian for Cardinal Albani. His *Geschichte der Kunst des Altertums* (History of Ancient Art, 1764) provided the first systematic historical account of ancient Greek sculpture and promulgated ideal beauty as codified in that art as the goal for both sculptors and painters. Winckelmann's Platonic notions of ideal beauty as the embodiment of calm stasis and perfected form had an indelible impact on neoclassical aesthetics. His theories were widely discussed and debated in the late eighteenth and early nineteenth centuries and were ultimately challenged by Romantic aesthetics and a new emphasis on naturalism, movement, and modern subjects and styles.

The first generation of neoclassical painters who were profoundly influenced by Winckelmann formed part of the international community of artists living in Rome in the 1760s and 1770s. The German Anton Raphael Mengs, a friend and disciple of Winckelmann, painted large-scale works intended to represent the new ideal of antique beauty with neoclassical compositional and stylistic traits. His ceiling painting *Parnassus* (1761), executed for Cardinal Albani's villa, is an example of the lifelessness and vacuity that could result from slavish imitation of what was being promulgated as antique aesthetics. Other artists in Rome, inspired by the rediscovery of classical painting as well as by Winckelmann's theories, created more imaginative and inventive interpretations of antique themes. The Swiss painter Angelica Kauffman (e.g., in *Cleopatra Adorning the Tomb of Mark Anthony*, 1769), and Pompeo Batoni, the head of the Italian neoclassical school (*Education of Achilles*, 1746, and *Bacchus and Ariadne*, 1769–1773), offered inspired and imaginative reinterpretations of antique historical and mythological themes in an emerging neoclassical format and style they helped to create.

Of essential importance were new choices for subjects in painting based on classical literature and histories. Robert Rosenblum has reconstructed the development of the theme of the *exemplum virtutis*, which dominated much neoclassical art. Artists working in this idiom tended to choose subjects from antiquity that were moralizing and didactic, illustrating virtuous actions and ideas. Amateur classicists prescribed appropriate subjects for painting. The *Iliad* emerged as a popular source; Scottish painter Gavin Hamilton did a series of paintings based on it that were later engraved and widely disseminated, exerting a considerable impact on the neoclassical style, of which his *Achilles Mourning over Patroclus* (1763) is a prominent example. The seventeenth-century classical painter Nicolas Poussin, who had spent much of his career in Rome, enjoyed a dramatic revival, now seen as a classicist, a moralist, and a philosophical painter of ideas.

One of the most significant revivals of Poussin occurred, as might be expected, in France, where neoclassical reforms had a profound impact, culminating in the innovative paintings of Jacques-Louis David. David, like Poussin, aspired to be a philosophical painter, and thus he quickly surpassed his mentor, Joseph-Marie Vien. Vien, a leading member of the Académie Royale de Peinture et de Sculpture in the 1760s and 1770s, had popularized classical themes but had often linked them to Rococo sensuality and eroticism, as in his *Merchant of Loves* (1763), based on an engraving of a wall painting from Herculaneum.

After winning the coveted Prix de Rome, David spent several years in the Eternal City, studying antique sculpture and emulating in drawing a contour style he observed in classical reliefs. His *Oath of the Horatii* (1784–1785; see the cover of volume 4 of this encyclopedia) created a sensation at its first exhibition in Rome, and then in Paris, where it quickly became the paradigm for the entire French school. In this *exemplum virtutis* of patriotic self-sacrifice, David sought to convey meaning primarily through pantomime and gesture. He restricted the role of facial physiognomy, which had been considered the most critical expressive feature in academic doctrine since the seventeenth century. Eloquent corporal expression takes precedence over physiognomy in several subsequent paintings of the 1780s, such as the *Death of Socrates* (1787), a subject dear to the philosophes, and *The Lictors Bringing to Brutus the Bodies of His Sons* (1789), in which moral ambiguity is a principal theme. In the late 1780s, David continued his study of classical literature and myth. His interest in painting as a branch of knowledge, particularly philosophy, led him to paint *The Loves of Paris and Helen* (1787–1789) as a pendant to the *Death of Socrates*. *Paris and Helen*, a melancholy reinterpretation of an episode from the *Iliad*, launched a new direction in French painting—the psychological interpretation of mythic themes—which converged with the rise of the discipline of mythography in the late eighteenth century. David's students would focus attention on the reinterpretation of erotic mythic themes in innovative works of the 1790s, such as Anne-Louis Girodet-Trioson's *Sleep of Endymion* (1793) and François Gérard's *Psyche and Amor* (1798). David devoted the final years of his career, while exiled in Brussels (1816–1825), to a complex psychological reinterpretation of myth.

During the Revolutionary period, David served the cause by his direct involvement in politics as deputy to the Republic (1792–1794), as organizer of Revolutionary and republican festivals, pageants, and funerals, and as painter of contemporary events and personages (e.g., *The Oath of the Tennis Court*, 1791, and the icons of the Revolutionary martyrs Lepelletier de Saint Fargeau, Marat, and Bara, 1793–1794). In choosing to represent a contemporary historical event in a nonallegorical manner in *The Oath of the Tennis Court*, David departed from a basic practice of history painting as codified at the Académie Royale—that contemporary historical events of significance (meaning those that involved the king and country) should be depicted allegorically, because the proper subjects of history painting were from the more distant past (nonallegorical depictions of contemporary history would become the norm, however, during the Consulate and Empire). In choosing to paint historical iconic portraits of citizens such as Marat and Bara, rather than of the royal family or nobility, David was again challenging academic conventions. His problematic relationship with the Académie Royale led to his role in founding the Commune des Arts (1791) and ultimately in helping to abolish the Académie in 1793. His helping to democratize the arts and overturn the rigid hierarchical structure of the Académie reveals the influence of Enlightenment philosophy.

The Sublime. The association in eighteenth-century European painting of reason, science, nature, philosophy,

and the revival of classical antiquity was counterbalanced by currents that emphasized the irrational, the subjective, and the fantastic, and these led directly to the development of the Romantic "sublime." Edmund Burke, in *A Philosophical Enquiry into the Origin of Our Ideas of the Sublime and Beautiful* (1757), investigated the "passion" caused by the sublime in nature and defined categories of the sublime: terror, obscurity, power, privation, vastness, infinity, difficulty, magnificence, light and color, suddenness, cries of animals, extreme smells and tastes, and pain. Many painters who rejected the rationality of the philosophes and the neoclassical revival, with its emphasis on the *exemplum virtutis*, produced works that correspond to Burke's categories.

The Swiss artist Henry Fuseli, who studied with the philosopher Johann Jakob Bodmer in Zurich before settling in Rome and then in London, created many works that depicted extreme emotional or psychological states. His celebrated painting *The Nightmare* (1781) represents the erotic and demonic states associated with sleep and the unconscious, and the monstrous visitations that beset a young woman in her dreams. Depictions of sleep, the unconscious, and the irrational grew in popularity during the later decades of the eighteenth century. In *The Artist Moved by the Grandeur of Antique Fragments* (1778–1779; *see* Ancient Rome) Fuseli depicted the melancholy and despair of an artist overwhelmed by the enormous fragments of an antique colossus; this composition reveals negative emotional and psychological responses to ancient art. Fuseli was also the first to translate Winckelmann's writings on ancient art into English (1766), but he clearly did not share Winckelmann's view that the ideal beauty found in ancient art should be emulated by modern artists.

Many British artists, too, would subvert the rational ideals of the Enlightenment by representing subjects of the sublime. In the paintings of George Stubbs, the Enlightenment interest in the scientific investigation of nature, as seen in his superb *Anatomy of a Horse* (1766), became transformed into a meditation on the extreme states of animal psychology. This emphasis can be seen in his representations of terror and fear within sublime landscape settings, such as *Horse Frightened by a Lion* (1770). Stubbs's paintings were the forerunners of similar explorations of animal psychology and the sublime in the works of Théodore Géricault and Eugène Delacroix.

A new interest in the scientific study of nature, concurrent with the development of the picturesque garden in Europe, inspired the emergence of landscape painting as an important genre. Two principal directions developed in late-eighteenth-century landscape painting: the picturesque, which celebrated a harmonious, cultivated nature; and the sublime, which represented tempestuous nature's overpowering drama and force. Picturesque landscapes were often associated with lyrical portrayals of the homeland, while representations of sublime sites (such as the Alps) or events in nature (avalanches, storms, erupting volcanoes) resulted from a keen interest in world travel and concomitant investigations into geography and geology. In France, Claude-Joseph Vernet, whose paintings were admired by Diderot, combined the picturesque with elements of the Romantic sublime in such compositions as *Storm on the Coast* (1773). Thomas Gainsborough's picturesque landscapes of his native England, including such works as *View of Dedham* (1750–1753) and *Going to Market* (1770), prefigure John Constable, who would combine scientific observations of nature with lyrical beauty. Alexander Cozens in England and Pierre-Henride Valenciennes in France wrote treatises on landscape that established aesthetic and stylistic principles of the genre for decades to come. Developments in German landscape were dramatic; artists such as Caspar Wolfe painted images of sublime sites, such as *Alpine Landscape* (1778). These compositions served as precursors to the Romantic sublime in the landscapes of Caspar David Friedrich and J. M. W. Turner.

By the end of the eighteenth century, the Romantic sublime found one of its chief proponents in Francisco Goya. His paintings from the 1790s of the insane in the madhouse of Saragossa, and his later images of death, destruction, and despair reveal his obsession with unreason. This development could not have been predicted from his early career, when he painted compositions in the Rococo style for tapestry designs at the Spanish court. The work that seemed to express the culmination of Enlightenment thinking, and at the same time sound its death knell, was Goya's *Caprichos* (1799), a collection of strange and compelling compositions that tended to expose folly by representing fantastic images of its triumph. The Rococo dreams and fantasies of gallant or courtly love found in Watteau's *Pilgrimage to Cythera* (1717) ended in the nightmares of Goya's *Caprichos*. Goya, associated with the *illustrados* of the Spanish Enlightenment, seemed to experience acute disappointment at the failure of reason. The famous frontispiece to the *Caprichos*, "The Sleep of Reason Produces Monsters," is a problematic image on which to end the Enlightenment.

[*See also* Academies, *subentries on* France *and* Great Britain; Aesthetics; Archaeology; Classicism; David, Jacques-Louis; Diderot, Denis; Exhibitions; Gainsborough, Thomas; Grand Tour; Hamilton, William; Hogarth, William; Illustrators and Illustrations; Kauffman, Angelica Maria Catherina Anna; Neoclassicism; Peale, Charles Willson; Pompeii and Herculaneum; Rococo; Romanticism; Stuart, Gilbert; West, Benjamin; *and* Winckelmann, Johann Joachim.]

BIBLIOGRAPHY

Art in Rome in the Eighteenth Century. Edited by Edgar Peters Bowron and Joseph J. Rishel. Philadelphia, 2000. Exhibition catalog with accompanying essays. Broad coverage.

Conisbee, Philip. *Painting in Eighteenth-Century France*. Ithaca, N.Y., 1981. General overview of the subject, organized chronologically and thematically.

French Painting, 1774–1830: The Age of Revolution. Detroit and New York, 1975. Exhibition catalog with essays.

Honour, Hugh. *Neo-classicism*. Harmondsworth, U.K., 1968. Survey of neoclassicism in eighteenth-century European art.

Levey, Michael. *Painting and Sculpture in France, 1700–1789*. New Haven, Conn., 1994. A valuable handbook of major moments and monuments.

Levey, Michael. *Painting in Eighteenth-Century Venice*. 3d ed. New Haven, Conn., 1994. Historical and chronological study.

Levey, Michael. *Rococo to Revolution: Major Trends in Eighteenth-Century Painting*. New York, 1966. Major artists and works in social and political contexts.

Rosenblum, Robert. *Transformations in Late Eighteenth Century Art*. Princeton, N.J., 1967. Mid-eighteenth century to 1800 study of major directions in art in context of aesthetics and society.

Wakefield, David. *French Eighteenth-Century Painting*. London, 1984. Chronological, historical treatment of the subject in broad cultural context.

DOROTHY JOHNSON

PAMPHLETS. In the eighteenth century, the pamphlet was ubiquitous in western Europe and in the British colonies of North America. As brief, topical publications, pamphlets ranged in length from a few pages to well over one hundred; their print runs were as low as a few hundred copies or as high as several thousand. Once printed and published, they were sold at modest prices or distributed free (*gratis*). This favored form of publication offered authors a means of expressing themselves openly, anonymously, and relatively inexpensively. In countries with severe publication restrictions, individuals were able to produce illegal brochures and usually avoided detection or arrest because neither the authors nor the printers were readily identifiable. Even in locales like England, with no overt government censorship, the anonymous pamphlet allowed its author to speak boldly, with little fear of running afoul of the libel laws.

Pamphlets remained the principal polemical instrument for most of the eighteenth century. Opinion could rapidly follow events, and authors could respond quickly to the arguments of their opponents. Long pamphlet wars on specific topics were frequent. Pamphlets provided the perfect instrument for personal attacks on individuals. Known as *libelles* in France, they targeted important persons, sparing no one, including Louis XV and his mistresses, as well as Louis XVI and Marie Antoinette, his wife. The ideal medium of persuasion, pamphlets were the preferred instrument of argument in every area of eighteenth-century contestation. Authors wrote on all subjects, no matter how sensitive, in an effort to persuade the public of the truth of their particular viewpoints. Thus, pamphlets played an important role in the development of public opinion.

Distinguished authors. The literature of the Enlightenment, which had its fair share of contested issues, frequently appeared in pamphlet form. The great philosophes often wrote as pamphleteers even when their publications expanded beyond the limits of the typical pamphlet. For example, from 1757 to 1765, the character and political structure of Geneva (Switzerland), the birthplace of Jean-Jacques Rousseau and for a time the residence of Voltaire, proved to be a subject of considerable philosophic dispute and pamphlet debate. While opposing the oligarchic structure of Geneva's government, Rousseau argued for maintaining the city's ban on theaters to prevent the development of aristocratic artificiality. Defending enlightened culture, Jean Le Rond d'Alembert and Voltaire opposed the ban on theaters, but Voltaire undercut the local aristocracy by favoring political reform of the city. Another dispute, the *Querelle des Bouffons*, which was initiated in Paris in 1753, concerned the relative merits of French opera versus Italian opera. Eventually involving d'Alembert, Rousseau, Denis Diderot, and the composer Jean-Philippe Rameau, this pamphlet debate ultimately centered on the quality of Rameau's French operas. A similar *querelle* ("quarrel") emerged in the 1770s in Paris between defenders of the operas of Christoph Willibald von Gluck and the advocates of his rival Niccolò Piccinni, which resulted in the appearance of scores of philosophic pamphlets. In Italy, a considerable pamphlet war began in 1749 between enlightened writers, who attacked superstitious belief in witchcraft and magic, and Christian authors, who feared that denying the supernatural would undermine the very basis of religious truth. Voltaire, perhaps the Enlightenment's premier philosophe-pamphleteer, waged his best-known pamphlet campaign against the religious fanaticism and judicial improprieties of the Calas Affair, which involved the Parlement of Toulouse's notorious decision in 1762 to condemn and execute, on very weak evidence, Jean Calas, a Huguenot, for the murder of his son. Although Calas was executed, Voltaire's publications played an important role in persuading Louis XV to reverse the Parlement's judgment. In the end, the enterprise of the Enlightenment became the subject of a polemical debate; it was initiated by authors who attacked the entire philosophic establishment and its work.

Pamphleteers and Patrons. Most eighteenth-century pamphlets were not written by the great literary figures of the Enlightenment. Anyone with an opinion and the resources to pay for its publication could produce a pamphlet. In France, for example, pamphlets on such diverse subjects as economics, agricultural practices, relations with Great Britain, royal finances, and the private life of the king were written and published by clergy, nobility, and members of the urban middle classes. *Mémoires judiciares*, pamphletlike legal briefs of civil cases that could be legally published and circulated in huge numbers, allowed barristers to bring numerous social, moral, and even political issues before the public in the guise of discussing their cases before the courts. Important personages, lacking the talent or inclination to write their own pamphlets, could always engage writers willing to undertake the task for them. Much of the eighteenth-century political pamphlet literature in England and France was sponsored by patrons. Some of their writers were great literary figures, like Daniel Defoe, who served both Tory and Whig ministries in England in the early 1700s, but others were Grub Street hacks, hoping to acquire literary reputations while earning meager livings. Both the English and French governments employed writers to justify ministerial policies to the public. In contrast, American pamphleteers tended to be individuals—clergymen, merchants, lawyers, or planters—who wanted to express their views publicly.

Political Pamphlets. Although all pamphlets were intended to influence and shape public opinion, the overtly political pamphlets had the greatest impact on society. During the 1700s, as politics moved increasingly into the public sphere in much of western Europe and in Britain's American colonies, pamphlets provided a basic medium for political discussion. Some well-developed political newspapers and journals existed in both Britain and its American colonies, but the traditional pamphlet with its unique characteristics and potential of complete anonymity remained a vital part of all political discussion. Many of the journals were little more than periodical pamphlets.

Lively political-pamphlet debate occurred, as well, in the 1700s in Switzerland, the United Provinces (Low Countries) and the Austrian Netherlands. Perhaps most significant was the body of French pamphlet literature, which grew in both volume and intensity during that century. Such pamphlets helped transform France—where the government was committed to the maintenance of the sovereign authority of the monarch and the prevention of public discussion of matters of state—into a society in which all parties entered the public sphere and sovereign authority was ultimately transferred to the citizenry.

Eighteenth-century political pamphlets developed the language of patriotism, which, in the context of the era, implied the restoration of ancient constitutional rights that had been usurped by monarchical government. In England, this was the language of the Country Party, which expressed deep distrust of the ministry, its placemen (members of the House of Commons on the ministerial payroll), a standing army, British involvement on the European continent, modern public finance, and government bureaucracy. Country ideology, which had its origins in seventeenth-century English republicanism [*see* Republicanism], called for Parliament's reform and a return to the ancient constitution of England. The Country Party argued that the independent landowners of the kingdom, rather than the ministers, should control Parliament, thereby restoring the traditional balance between the king, the House of Lords, and the House of Commons. American colonists, some of whom fought the British attempts to tax them in the 1760s and 1770s, utilized these Country arguments in pamphlets that expressed opposition to ministerial policies. In France, patriot ideology emerged from the attempts of the Parlement of Paris to undermine royal support for *Unigenitus*, a papal bull (pronouncement) of 1713, which condemned as a heresy the Roman Catholic sect of Jansenism. In the 1750s, Jansenist barristers, writing in support of the activities of Jansenist magistrates in the Parlement, developed theories that were based on the ancient constitutional structure of France, which established firm limits on royal authority. These theories formed the ideological basis of much of the French patriot pamphlet literature of the 1770s, which attacked the despotism of Chancellor René-Nicholas de Maupeou in his attempt to destroy the Parlement of Paris and, necessarily, the French constitution. Patriots in the United Provinces (Low Countries) wrote pamphlets condemning the monarchical pretensions of the House of Orange and demanded a return to the pure republican system of the seventeenth century. Similar arguments appeared in the Austrian Netherlands in an attempt to counter the authority of the Austrian emperor, Joseph II. Only in republican Geneva (Switzerland) did opposition-pamphlet literature not posit arguments calling for the reestablishment of traditional constitutional forms.

The political debate in England became explosive during the John Wilkes affair. Wilkes had not only suffered from ministerial despotism (when arrested in 1763 for publishing a libelous attack on King George III in the *North Briton*) but had also been denied a seat in Parliament after being duly elected three times in 1769. Wilkes then became the focus of a political battle fought through pamphlets, newspapers, and popular agitation. Although this agitation did not lead to revolution, popular participation in the Wilkes affair offered a serious threat to the political practices of the kingdom.

Pamphlets in North America. After 1763, every act of the British Parliament that affected the Thirteen Colonies in America met a hostile response in American pamphlets and newspapers. Political writers, well acquainted with the Country Party's ideology, believed that Parliament under the domination of corrupt ministers was despotic and that every new law undermined the British constitution,

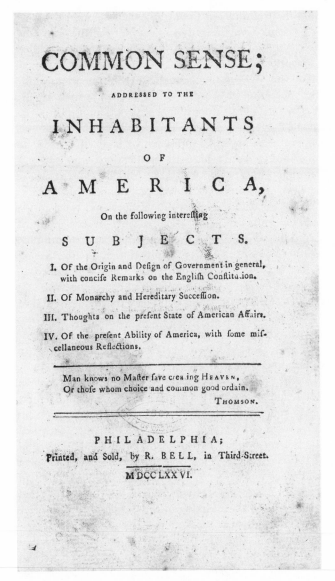

Paine's *Common Sense*. Title page of Thomas Paine's *Common Sense* (1776). [For a portrait of Paine, see the article "Paine, Thomas."] (Prints and Photographs Division, Library of Congress.)

thereby threatening liberty in America. After a decade of such warnings, the implementation in 1774 of Britain's Coercive Acts, which severely limited the authority of the colonial assembly of Massachusetts, made the despotic intentions of the ministry clear to Americans. Soon, the arguments for independence from England became increasingly compelling. In early 1776, Thomas Paine's *Common Sense*, the most startling pamphlet to appear during that crisis, helped Americans to recognize the necessity of independence from Britain; it advocated a republicanism that decisively rejected the arguments in favor of the balance of the ancient English constitution.

Still, the traditions of Country ideology remained strong as evidenced by the publications battling the proposed constitutional changes put forward by the Philadelphia convention of 1787.

On the Eve of the French Revolution. Meanwhile, the impending bankruptcy of the French monarchy, the Parlement of Paris's continued obstruction of ministerial financial reforms, and the decision to recall the Estates General (the ancient representative body of France) to solve those problems led to the publication of thousands of pamphlets in 1788 and early 1789. Initially, the debate was between the ministry, determined to control the Estates General through a reorganization that would weaken the political influence of the nobility, and the Parlement of Paris, the official voice of the Patriot Party determined to maintain the traditional constitution in the face of ministerial despotism. The debate quickly expanded to include a third element, the National Party, which sought the maintenance of the constitution through an alliance of the nobility and the third estate against the ministry. Jansenist ideology and the theories of the eighteenth-century political philosopher Montesquieu continued to inform the language of political publications. Increasingly, however, National Party pamphleteers also relied on Rousseau's concept of the general will in constructing their arguments. In January 1789, Abbé Emmanuel-Joseph Sieyès's powerful contribution to this literature, *Qu'est-ce que le Tiers État?*, provided the most original adaptation of Rousseau to the issue of the proper representation of the French nation. Nevertheless, more traditional political arguments continued to dominate both the pamphlet literature and the thinking of the public until well after the establishment of the National Assembly in June 1789.

Pamphlets had an important function during the Enlightenment era. At a time when many polities did not permit the sanctioned free expression of thought, that form of publication provided the means for writers to air issues of public concern and to expose both the hidden secrets of governments and those of prominent individuals, opening society to wider scrutiny and public influence. Such literature also provided a route for misinformation, innuendo, and slander to pass easily into the public sphere. Nevertheless, pamphlets did help disseminate enlightened thought, expand knowledge, promote understanding of a wide variety of ideological and political arguments, and increase participation in eighteenth-century public affairs.

[*See also* Civil Society; Print Culture; *and* Revolution.]

BIBLIOGRAPHY

Bailyn, Bernard. *The Ideological Origins of the American Revolution*. Cambridge, Mass., 1967. The classic analysis of American political ideology as it developed in the colonial pamphlet literature of the 1760s and 1770s.

Bell, David Avrom. *Lawyers and Citizens: The Making of a Political Elite*. Oxford, 1994. Examines the work and the publications of Parisian barristers during the political controversies of the eighteenth century.

Darnton, Robert. *The Literary Underground of the Old Regime*. Cambridge, Mass., 1982. A widely read study that reveals the character and influence of the Grub Street writers in France during the Enlightenment.

Gay, Peter. *Voltaire's Politics: The Poet as Realist*. Princeton, N.J., 1959. Contains accounts of many of Voltaire's pamphlet campaigns.

Hyland, P. B. J. "Liberty and Libel: Government and the Press during the Succession Crisis in Britain, 1712–1716." *English Historical Review* 101 (January 1986), 863–888.

Jacob, Margaret C., and Wijnand W. Mijnhardt, eds. *The Dutch Republic in the Eighteenth Century: Decline, Enlightenment, and Revolution*. Ithaca, N.Y., 1992. Provides considerable information on eighteenth-century political publications in the United Provinces.

Margerison, Kenneth. *Pamphlets and Public Opinion: The Campaign for a Union of Orders in the Early French Revolution*. West Lafayette, Ind., 1998. Examines the French political-pamphlet literature of 1787 to 1789 and the ideological suppositions contained therein.

Maza, Sarah. *Private Lives and Public Affairs: The Causes Célèbres of Prerevolutionary France*. Berkeley, Calif., 1993. An analysis of the *mémoires judiciaires*.

Peters, Marie. *Pitt and Popularity: The Patriot Minister and London Opinion during the Seven Years' War*. Oxford, 1980. Thoroughly treats the use of polemical literature in mid-1700s British politics (in the United States, called the French and Indian War).

Popkin, Jeremy. "Pamphlet Journalism at the End of the Old Regime." *Eighteenth-Century Studies* 22 (Spring 1989), 351–367. Explains the role of wealthy elites in the production of French political pamphlets.

Robbins, Caroline. *The Eighteenth-Century Commonwealthman: Studies in the Transmission, Development, and Circumstance of English Liberal Thought from the Restoration of Charles II until the War with the Thirteen Colonies*. Cambridge, Mass., 1961. Explores the ideas and publications associated with the Country party's ideology.

Van Kley, Dale. *The Religious Origins of the French Revolution: From Calvin to the Civil Constitution, 1560–1791*. New Haven, Conn., 1996. Identifies the role of Jansenism in the ideological disputes of eighteenth-century France and its relationship to the origins of the Revolution of 1789.

Venturi, Franco. *Italy and the Enlightenment: Studies in a Cosmopolitan Century*. Translated by Susan Corsi. New York, 1972. A collection of Venturi's journal articles, in English.

Verba, Cynthia. *Music and the French Enlightenment: Reconstruction of a Dialogue, 1750–1764*. Oxford, 1993. Provides an analysis of the philosophic disputes over eighteenth-century music.

Wood, Gordon. *The Creation of the American Republic, 1776–1787*. Chapel Hill, N.C., 1969. Utilizes pamphlets and other political literature in explaining the development of American republicanism.

KENNETH MARGERISON

PANCKOUCKE, CHARLES JOSEPH (1736–1798), French publisher, bookseller, creator of journals, and merchant.

Familial, cultural, and political events influenced the conception of the Enlightenment that underlay all Panckoucke's activities from 1750 to 1798. These headings correspond to the evolution of the three stages of his life.

This son of a Jansenist bookseller, who died at odds with Catholic orthodoxy, had little formal education and seems to have gleaned his early learning from his father's bookstore. In this modest but active environment, the Enlightenment was for Panckoucke at first tied to prestigious friendships, then transformed into an ideal, and then into a cause. A bookseller himself from 1757, he strengthened the business relations begun by his father with Voltaire; he became the champion of George-Louis Leclerc de Buffon against Albrecht von Haller; and he entered into a relationship with Jean-Jacques Rousseau.

Around the 1760s, the Enlightenment, in both its scientific and philosophical manifestations, took the place of Panckoucke's paternal Jansenism, as an ethos founded on the progress of the individual and on public usefulness. It was a faith that he had to make productive for the profit of the many, and it took into account neither social nor political forces, nor established religion. He acted on these convictions by publishing brochures and a periodical, and by joining a literary society in his city, Lille.

In this border province, where orthodox Roman Catholicism had just triumphed over a deeply entrenched Jansenism, the regional and national authorities worked together to stop both the publication of books judged licentious and the activities of the literary society. Panckoucke found himself in prison for a time. With neither reputation nor fortune remaining, he moved to Paris.

There, Panckoucke threw his energies into the struggle for the commercial distribution of Enlightenment ideas, which occupied the second phase of his life (1762–1788). The bookseller found fortune and social advancement in his new circle. Settled at the "Parnasse" on the Left Bank, then at the Hôtel de Thou, Panckoucke put down deep roots in the literary and scientific circles of the capital. Jean-Baptiste Suard became his brother-in-law; Jean-François Marmontel, Sébastien-Roch-Nico Chamfort, Jean-Antoine-Nicolas de Caritat Condorcet, and many academicians frequented his shop and salon. He did not remain simply an enlightened merchant, however.

Because he did not belong to any academy, masonic lodge, or church, the Enlightenment became for Panckoucke the humanistic foundation that underlay his professional activity. It was the essential source of his publications and his sales: collections of the *Mémoires de l'Académie des Sciences*; great editions of the *Histoire naturelle* of Buffon, Louis-Jean-Marie Daubenton, and Bernard-Germain-Étienne Delaville de Lacépède; reeditions in folio and quarto of the *Encyclopédie* of Diderot; and publication of the *Encyclopédie méthodique*, beginning in 1782. Panckoucke was henceforth "a merchant of ideas" who served the commercial functions of the Enlightenment by directing its talents and public opinion, forming alliances with the power structure, innovating technical and commercial processes. He collaborated closely with Voltaire to launch the *Journal de littérature* in 1774 and to guarantee the quality of his *Encyclopédie*

méthodique. He worked similarly with Buffon and the "talented careerists" Jean-François de La Harpe, Suard, Marmontel, and Jacques Mallet du Pan in order to satisfy a public he also wished to guide. With the *Mercure*, he informed the public on philosophical and literary debates; with the *Journal de Bruxelles*, he furnished the political information for which there was an ever greater demand.

The commercialization of the Enlightenment was accomplished under official protection. From 1764, Panckoucke was bookseller for the Imprimerie Royale; in 1774, he obtained authorization to compete with the *Gazette de France*; and in 1785, he obtained a monopoly for the distribution of news. Personally connected to the lieutenants of the Paris police, he managed to choose the censors of his publications and was able to sell clandestine works such as the *Oeuvres de Voltaire* printed by Cramer in Geneva, or the abbé Raynal's *Histoire des Indes*.

Bookselling was still a luxury trade, but Panckoucke wanted to make books widely accessible. He put out less expensive editions and edited important journals, which, through skillful publicity, drew subscribers away from minor competitors, as occurred with the *Mercure de France*. So that France might reap the profits of its cultural inheritance, heretofore exploited largely by foreigners, Panckoucke eliminated competing editions of the *Encyclopédie*, bought them back, and even dealt with pirates.

The results were spectacular. Panckoucke dominated the market for journals: the *Journal de Genéve*, created in 1772, had four thousand subscribers in 1778 and 8,500 in 1782; the *Mercure de France* between 1778 and 1784 laid claim to twenty thousand. He reconquered the French market from the Swiss and Dutch. The second edition of Diderot's *Encyclopédie* in folio (1768–1776) was printed in four thousand copies. The *Encyclopédie méthodique* had five thousand subscribers in 1785, and another three thousand in 1792. The editions of the *Histoire naturelle* probably had even larger runs. The benefits realized were considerable. All of France, except Brittany and Provence, knew the *Encyclopédie*, as did the elite of northern Europe and of the shores of the Mediterranean. Panckoucke could be proud of being "useful to humanity."

For this exploiter and distributor of Enlightenment literature, the Revolution was both a catastrophe and a remarkable reconversion. The Republic of Letters and its hierarchy no longer existed. The academic milieu splintered into a conservative tendency and one favorable to a new definition of the purposes of culture. Men of letters, deprived of royal patronage, sought a solution in politics, and Panckoucke saw his role as patron vanish. Intellectually, the Revolution represented a failure of the encyclopedism he had supported. Learning and knowledge were decidedly not an immobile world to be classified methodically, but a realm of perpetual change that obliged Panckoucke continuously to augment his *Encyclopédie méthodique*. This era also marked the failure of an abstract scientific academicism, which the new English economic dominance rendered void.

Panckoucke reacted in several ways. On the professional level, he criticized the despotism of the publishers' guilds, the perpetual "privileges" (licenses) that prevented provincial booksellers from expanding, and censorship. On the political level, as a purchaser of lands sold off by the revolutionaries, he was an enemy of Robespierre as well as of the counter-revolution. On the social level, he did not understand the antagonism between the bourgeoisie and the nobility, believing their interests to be common. His enlightened outlook was thus transformed into a liberalism limited by the interests of the most enterprising and the wealthiest, protected by a professional semi-corporatism and the government.

In 1791, Panckoucke presented himself for election as a deputy to the legislative assembly, but he failed. He henceforth directed his efforts toward the reorganization of the former royal press and the publication of newspapers. For him, freedom of the press was not the freedom of journalists to express their opinions, but the access of the many to books and journals. His book production became less luxurious and less closely tied to current advances in science. He created the *Moniteur universel*, which became the revolutionary assemblies' journal of record. Advertisements furnished the majority of the capital needed for the publication of his daily journals. Thus, Panckoucke greatly enlarged the reading public, and he was praised for it.

The Enlightenment, first an ideal, then a source of raw material rationally exploited, and finally the ideology of a social group that soon lost political power, at last gave way for Panckoucke to an English-style liberalism in which the state, guarantor of order and peace, became the protector of powerful employers. The Enlightenment and capitalism were thus at the root of a social and geographical diffusion of thought the consequences of which could be neither foreseen nor measured by its authors.

[*See also* Encyclopédie; Journals, Newspapers, and Gazettes, *subentry on* France; Men and Women of Letters; Print Culture; *and* Publishing.]

BIBLIOGRAPHY

Barthes, R., R. Mauzi, and J. P. Seguin. *L'Univers de l'Encyclopédie*. Paris, 1964.

Bingham, J. "Voltaire et l'*Encyclopédie méthodique*." In *Studies on Voltaire and the Eighteenth Century*, pp. 1–9. Geneva, 1958.

Estivals, R. "La production des livres dans les dernières années de l'Ancien Régime." *Actes du 90ᵉ Congrès national des Sociétés Savantes*, pp. 11–54. Nice and Paris, 1966.

Feyel, G. "L'annonce et la noucelle: La Presse d'information et son évolution sous l'Ancien Régime (1630–1788)." Diss., Paris, 1994.

Furet, François. "La Librairie du Royaume de France au XVIIIᵉ siècle." In *Livre et société dans la France du XVIIIᵉ siècle*, pp. 3–32. Paris, 1965.

Groult, M. "La systématique de l'*Encyclopédie* de Diderot et d'Alembert." Diss., Paris, 1995. Discusses how Panckoucke extended the philosophical project of Diderot's work into his *Encyclopédie méthodique*.

Tucoo-Chala, Suzanne. *Charles-Joseph Panckoucke et la Librairie française (1736–1798)*. Pau and Paris, 1977.

SUZANNE TUCOO-CHALA

Translated from French by Sylvia J. Cannizzaro

PANTHEISM. The philosophical and religious position known as pantheism has its roots, of course, in antiquity, but the word itself appears at the turn of the eighteenth century. The invention of the word *pantheist* has usually been credited to the Irish freethinker John Toland, who used it on the title page of his *Socinianism Truly Stated* in 1705; however, it would seem that he himself, in fact, took it from the Cambridge mathematician Joseph Raphson, who discussed pantheists in his *De spacio reali*, published with the second edition of his *Analysis aequationum universalis* (1697 and 1702). Raphson's text seems to indicate that the word already existed, at least in Latin, but it is difficult to confirm this in the present state of our knowledge. It is, in any case, clear that the word *pantheist*, followed rapidly by *pantheism* (used in 1709 by the Dutch theologian Jacques de La Faye in *Defensio religionis* against Toland), came into usage at the turn of the eighteenth century, which would seem to imply a greater importance of pantheistic ideas in this period. It is, however, difficult to delineate their real importance in the Enlightenment, which has led to serious disagreement on this question among scholars.

Definition. Pantheism is generally taken to be the doctrine that God and Nature are identical, or that Nature is God; from this follows the belief that the world is eternal and uncreated, and also that there is an absolute necessity of all things, or fatalism. Precise definition of the term is, however, difficult, and while pantheism is normally a form of monism, certain forms of pantheism, implying the worship of an immanent divine principle in nature, could be interpreted as dualist. In the monist systems of the eighteenth century, it is not always easy to disentangle pantheism from materialism, so that certain historians have conflated the two or have labeled much eighteenth-century materialism "pantheistic materialism." It is true that the dividing line between the two is often difficult to draw and much depends on the definition given. Hassan El Nouty insists on the religious character of pantheism and on pantheists' concentration on the idea of divinity, which lays them open to the accusation of "enthusiasm" but not to that of atheistic materialism.

For Paul Vernière, however, eighteenth-century pantheism oscillated between two interpretations of the word, depending on whether God was seen as the only reality, and the substantial unity of the world, or as simply the abstract sum of all that exists. The latter point of view, which was the dominant one for much of the century, most often took the form of a denial that the sum of what exists, namely matter, has any divine attributes, and can thus be seen as atheistic materialism rather than pantheism. Wilhelm Gottfried von Leibniz, in an exchange of letters with Toland concerning the latter's *Origines judaicae* (1709), which claimed that Moses was in fact a pantheist, clearly indicates that for him, the ancient as well as the Chinese philosophers who equate God with the material world, endow this God with intelligence despite their denial of transcendence. He does not, therefore, seem to see those pantheists as atheists (letter dated 30 April 1709).

Raphson makes a clear distinction between pantheism on the one hand and atheism and materialism on the other, and it seems useful to take his definitions as a starting point. He distinguishes, among those who have claimed that there is only one substance in the world, two types of belief: firstly, there are those, called pantheists, who maintain that this universal substance is both material and intelligent, creating everything from its own essence; and secondly, those who recognize only matter, from which everything is derived, are atheists and materialists, or what he calls "panhylists." It is interesting to note that he classes as materialists both those who, like the atomists, postulate a matter devoid of life and sensibility, and the "hylozoists" who attribute energy or life to all matter, and whom some modern scholars have classified as pantheists or pantheistic materialists. Those whom he calls pantheists range from certain ancient Greek philosophers and followers of certain oriental religions to Spinoza.

Spinozism. For it was, of course, Spinoza's philosophy (expounded in his *Ethics*, published in 1677) that was at the origin of the renewed interest in pantheism in the late seventeenth century, and to a large extent the question of pantheism in the Enlightenment is closely linked to the diverse reception of his philosophy. This reception was overwhelmingly influenced by Pierre Bayle's very long article on Spinoza in his *Dictionnaire historique et critique* (1697, 1702) that presented the Dutchman as the first thinker who had established a rigorous system of atheism; thus Spinoza's equation of God with the world is seen not as pantheism but as a denial of any God. Before attempting a refutation, Bayle links this system to that of the Greek peripatetic philosopher Strato (third century BC) on the one hand, and to the religion of the Indians and Chinese on the other; in another article, on the sixteenth-century Italian heretic Giordano Bruno, he assimilates Bruno's philosophy to Spinoza's monism. For Bayle, theories of the "soul of the world" are seen as equivalent to those which postulate an intelligent universe. As a result partly of his article on Spinoza, followed by the writings of several theologians, Spinozism tended generally, for much of the eighteenth century to be seen as a form of atheistic materialism, which is how it appears, for example, in the *Encyclopédie*. It should, however, be noted that Henri de Boulainvilliers, whose *Essai de métaphysique dans les principes de Benoît de Spinoza* (Essay on the Metaphysics Following the Principles of Baruch de Spinoza, dating from around 1712 but in general printed circulation from 1731) also contributed to diffusing a rather unfaithful version of Spinoza's philosophy, can more accurately be described as a deist.

There were, however, certain writers who presented Spinoza, often together with the others mentioned, not as atheists but as pantheists. Thus Johann Heinrich Zedler's *Dictionary*, published in German in 1740, includes, exceptionally, an article on pantheism that equates it with Spinozism. Around the same time, in the French journalist Thémiseul de Saint-Hyacinthe's *Recherches philosophiques sur la nécessité de s'assurer par soi-même de la vérité* (Philosophical Investigations into the Necessity of Establishing the Truth for Oneself, 1743), which contains presentations of the main philosophical systems, those of Strato and the Stoics are said to be pantheistic systems, like that of Spinoza, which is discussed at some length. For this author, there are four types of pantheist, namely Spinozists, Naturalists, Stoics, and Materialists, which indicates a much wider interpretation of the word than that of Raphson. A further indication of the confusion that reigned on the subject can be found in the French freethinker André-François Boureau-Deslandes's *Histoire critique de la philosophie* (Critical History of Philosophy, 1737); the author regards all these thinkers as materialists, and his brief discussion of those philosophers who are called pantheists concludes that they are in fact materialists. The general impression is that it was the presence of materialists rather than pantheists that preoccupied thinkers for much of this period; it is noticeable that there is no article on pantheists in the *Encyclopédie*. This seems to have been generally the case until the dispute over Spinoza and pantheism in Germany in the last quarter of the century, discussed below. Saint-Hyacinthe does however describe a contemporary group of pantheists, whose ideas, according to him, come from those of Strato, Democritus, and Zeno, and whose liturgy is presented in the work *Pantheisticon*. This book, first published in Latin in 1720, was by John Toland, who is central to any discussion of eighteenth-century pantheism.

Toland. As we have seen, Toland attempted to popularize the word from 1705 onward, and in his 1720 publication he claimed that there existed a widespread sect of pantheists whose liturgy he was presenting. This is also the impression given by Saint-Hyacinthe, who was in contact with Toland and his associates, although Saint-Hyacinthe clearly states that it is not at all an organized religious sect, but simply a drinking club. He does, however, refer to the role of this group in circulating in Europe the works of Giordano Bruno, often in English translation. Toland is indeed central to claims, made in particular by Margaret Jacob, that the radical Enlightenment, representing pantheistic and republican ideas, was furthered by a group of people around him and Anthony Collins, forming a clear underground current for much of the century. Their distribution of the works of Bruno is seen to be part of this concerted plan to popularize pantheistic and radical ideas, as was the publication and diffusion of the clandestine work variously known as *L'esprit de Spinosa* (The Spirit of Spinoza) or the *Traité des trois imposteurs* (Treatise on the Three Impostors). In order to see how far these assertions can be substantiated, one needs to look in more detail at the philosophy defended in these works.

What is noticeable, first, is the fact that among late-seventeenth-century and early-eighteenth-century English freethinkers it is difficult to find much trace of pantheistic ideas; Charles Blount does discuss a version of the theory of the soul of the world that comes close to sounding like a form of pantheism, as he insists that God made the world not from without but by "inoperation," like a soul in an animal (*Anima Mundi*, 1679). But he seems to preserve a type of dualism between soul and body that would tend to preclude pantheism, and scholars have tended to conclude that he did not espouse pantheism.

Toland appears to be the only person in this period who openly presents his philosophy as pantheism; but even with him, things are not so simple, and the precise definition of his philosophical beliefs is notoriously difficult. The work that sets out most clearly his philosophical views on matter and the world is *Letters to Serena*, published in 1704; here he develops arguments, ostensibly against Spinoza (who, he claims, did not go far enough) to show that motion is essential to matter and thus that matter possesses its own intrinsic force (a view described by Raphson, as we have seen, as hylozoistic). He is defending an essentially materialistic conception of humans, in which he affirms that only a particular organization of matter, in the brain, can think. This is combined with a view that could be seen as deistic, despite serious doubts as to Toland's sincerity on this subject; for at the end of the work, he criticizes the claim made by the atomists that pure chance could have created the world and continues, "And as for the infinity of matter, it only excludes what all reasonable and good men must exclude, an extended corporeal God, but not a pure spirit or immaterial being."

The criticism of the Epicurean attribution of the world to blind chance is repeated in the *Pantheisticon* in 1720, and God is here said to be simply the intelligence in the universe, which can be called the soul of the world; Toland insists, however, that this should not be taken to mean that this mind can be separated from the world except by the reason. However, in this work, as in *Letters to Serena*, thought is again said to be produced by a particular part of the brain, or in other words by a particular organization of matter. His pantheism is thus combined here also with elements that could more appropriately be defined as materialistic, which has again led certain scholars to wonder as to his true philosophical position, the precise meaning he accords to the label *pantheist*, and what was his real purpose in championing pantheists and expounding their supposed liturgy.

Toland's travels brought him into contact with many European freethinkers, particularly through Prince Eugene's court in Vienna. It was there that the exiled Italian historian Pietro Giannone read his works, whose influence can be seen in his own deistic *Triregno*, written in the early 1730s and reflecting Spinozistic monism. Toland's thought clearly also had an influence on the Italian freethinker Alberto Radicati di Passerano, who sought refuge in England in 1730. He published in London in 1732 *A Philosophical Dissertation on Death*, which caused such a great scandal that he was arrested, together with his translator Joseph Morgan and the publisher. The aim of the work is to argue for freedom of behavior and belief, based on a view of nature as purely material but endowed with power, wisdom, and perfection. Creation is simply a new modification of this matter, while death, being merely the dissolution of corporeal parts and their reorganization in another body, is not to be feared. Here again it is difficult to know whether to define this as pantheism or as materialistic atheism. The subversive nature of the work, which questioned the principles at the basis of society, was, however, clear to the authorities.

The radicalism of such writers has led to a link being made between pantheism and republicanism in the constitution of what now tends to be called the "radical Enlightenment." Margaret Jacob in particular, pointing to Toland's efforts in republishing the works of the seventeenth-century English republicans, has seen this as an integral part of the beliefs of what she presents as his network of radicals. It is certainly true that among the most radical of the English revolutionaries were people like the Ranters or the Digger Gerrard Winstanley, who expounded a type of pantheistic religion, essential to his egalitarian beliefs. As has been pointed out by several historians, however, Winstanley is far from representing the majority of seventeenth-century radicals and indeed has little in common with those republicans whose works Toland did publish, in versions that were frequently adapted for his own time. As for Toland himself, his own republicanism is that of certain Whigs of the period following the Glorious Revolution and far removed from that of the Diggers or Levellers. While it is true that heterodox ideas, and Spinozism in particular, were linked to certain republican groups in Holland at the turn of the century and after, it is difficult to postulate the existence, running through the early Enlightenment, of a coherent tradition of politically radical egalitarian republicanism espousing pantheistic, or even materialistic, ideas. Political radicalism in Britain in the later part of the century was more linked to Unitarianism and to various nonorthodox forms of Christianity, even when combined with materialism, as in Joseph Priestley. As for the situation in France, the link is likewise doubtful.

France. It is possible to find in certain Enlightenment thinkers traces of what can be called pantheism, but in general there is little evidence of a clearly defined pantheistic philosophy. *Traité des trois imposteurs*, which seems to have been originally elaborated in Holland in the late seventeenth century and then altered and augmented by various hands when it circulated clandestinely in France, is typical of much clandestine antireligious literature. It draws on a mixture of inspirations that are only partly Spinozist; God is defined as being simply Nature, or the sum of everything that exists, and to be their immanent cause, but this is combined with a presentation of the soul as a material substance, derived from the Gassendist tradition. Thus while there are undeniably pantheistic elements in the various versions of the work, the overall effect is rather atheistic, with the aim of showing that the vision of God presented by the different religions is false and that religions are simply the creations of crafty leaders.

An illustration of the problems involved in the question of pantheism and the debate about Spinoza can be found in the confrontation between Denis Diderot and the scientist Pierre-Louis Moreau de Maupertuis that occurred in the middle of the century as a result of the latter's publication in 1751, under the pseudonym Doctor Baumann, of *Dissertatio inauguralis metaphysica* (Inaugural Dissertation on Metaphysics), translated in 1754 as *Essai sur la formation des corps organisés*. Maupertuis described the smallest parts of matter, or elements, as being endowed with something like desire, aversion, or memory, which allowed him to explain reproduction as the coming together of elements from both parents to form new bodies similar to theirs. Diderot commented on Dr. Baumann's thesis in his *Pensées sur l'interprétation de la nature* (Thoughts on the Interpretation of Nature, 1753), in which he affirmed that Maupertuis's theory, pushed to the extreme, would lead to "terrible consequences," because if he affirmed that the world is an organized whole, then there is an infinite soul of the world and the world is God. Maupertuis replied in 1756, rejecting among other things Diderot's interpretation of All *(tout)* and denying that his own All corresponded to Spinoza's God. Diderot's veiled accusation of Spinozism was clearly intended to bring out the materialistic implications of Maupertuis's theory rather than to point to pantheism. When he himself later elaborated on "le Tout," it was in the context of his own materialistic philosophy, based on a conception of matter as endowed with motion and sensitivity; and his denial of any transcendent principle implied an atheistic position and a form of materialism that has been called hylozoistic.

A similar point of view was adopted by Paul-Henri Thiry d'Holbach, whose *Système de la nature* (1770) was the signal for a campaign of atheistic propaganda. This work presents a materialistic system of nature, demonstrating that all religions are political institutions. D'Holbach's discussion of matter, to which motion and sensibility are essential, draws partly on Toland's *Letters to Serena*, which d'Holbach had translated into French in 1768. In view of this, together with his presentation of nature as a sort of benign deity, who is invoked in quasi-religious terms, one might be tempted to interpret this philosophy as in fact a form of pantheism. Nevertheless, a study of the text shows that d'Holbach's main aim was to demonstrate how beliefs in deities were human constructions, and the earliest form of religious belief, which he calls pantheism (a view similar to Toland's claim that pantheism was the natural religion), is shown to be behind ancient polytheism. Despite some ambiguities of expression, the general conclusion is that this is without doubt an atheistic and materialistic system that uses elements of Spinoza's philosophy, while indicating the extent to which this philosophy is in fact incompatible with atheistic materialism. Indeed, both Paul Vernière and J. Mouteaux ("D'Holbach et Spinoza" in Bloch, 1990) consider that d'Holbach's interpretation marks a dividing line in attitudes to Spinoza, as this distinction enabled others to rediscover a pantheistic interpretation of Spinoza centered on the divinity.

Another indication of the diversity of reflections on "All" is provided by the curious and completely original metaphysical system of the Benedictine monk Léger-Marie Deschamps, who engaged in a critical debate with his materialistic contemporaries in the period following the elaboration of his system in the 1750s until his death in 1774. His voluminous works, devoted to the question of totality, were not published at the time, but exist in manuscript form; they are difficult to classify but, opposed to deism and atheism, perhaps come close to something that could be defined as pantheism. Indeed, Vernière qualifies Deschamps as a "logical pantheist." Drawing on Spinoza, but also on Plato, Malebranche or Leibniz, and the Hermetic tradition, he postulates the essential unity of reality, and distinguishes "Tout," which is pure, infinite existence, the unique necessary being without parts and equivalent to nothing, from "Le Tout," which is relative being, the finite universe, the sum of all particular existences. These two names correspond to substance seen from two contradictory points of view, namely as God the creator and God the noncreator. Deschamps opposed the philosophy of his time and in particular its materialism and he remained an isolated figure, closer perhaps, some have suggested, to Hegel.

Germany. It was, of course, in Germany at the end of the eighteenth century that pantheism came to occupy center stage with the famous *Pantheismusstreit*, which was also a debate over Spinoza's philosophy. The reactions to Spinoza in Germany were numerous from the late seventeenth century onward, although they more often took the form of refutation than defense. This is the case, for example, of Johann Georg Wachter's *Spinozismus im Jüdenthumb* (Spinozism in Judaism, 1699), which links Spinoza's philosophy to the Jewish cabala and denounces it as pantheism, seen once again as atheistic materialism; later, however, Wachter attempted to reconcile Spinoza's philosophy with Christianity. Some German Spinozistic writings, such as Friedrich Wilhelm Stosch's *Concordia rationis et fidei* (Concord of Reason and Faith, 1692), do have pantheistic overtones, but this work also combines materialistic elements drawn from a mixture of Socinian and Spinozistic influences. It is therefore difficult to speak of a clearly developed pantheistic system. The first to have openly espoused pantheism seems to have been the notorious freethinker J. C. Edelmann, who defended Spinoza in the 1740s despite combining in his philosophy notions derived from the Neoplatonic tradition; he replied to critics' accusations that he was a pantheist by equating God with totality, or "To Pan" and affirming God's immanence (*Das Evangelium St. Harenbergs*, 1747), but his stance is strongly tinged with mysticism.

Much of this early debate came to the fore in the quarrel over pantheism in the 1780s sparked off by the publication in 1785 of a letter written by Friedrich Heinrich Jacobi claiming that Gotthold Ephraim Lessing was a disciple of Spinoza and that in a private conversation shortly before his death, he had offered a résumé of his philosophy in the phrase "en kai pan" ("one and all"), or a refusal of a transcendent God. According to Jacobi, Bruno's writings are the purest expression of this pantheism in its widest sense. The philosopher Moses Mendelssohn understood this presentation of Lessing as an attack on the whole of the Enlightenment defense of reason, of which Lessing was an eminent representative, as it was equivalent to accusing him of atheism, and Mendelssohn denied vigorously that this represented his true opinion. In his *Morgenstunden* (1785), Mendelssohn presents Lessing's position as a purified form of pantheism which is no longer incompatible with religion and is summed up in the formula "all is one and one is all"; the true reality is therefore God. This position has been defined rather as panentheism. Jacobi's publication and the debate were a reflection of the "Spinozarenaissance," a reversal of attitudes toward Spinoza in the 1770s, seen, for example, in the poet Johann Wolfgang von Goethe and the philosopher Johann Gottfried von Herder, who studied Spinoza together and discussed him with Jacobi in the 1780s. Herder replied to Jacobi's publication in his *Gott, einige Gespräche* (1787), a defense of Spinoza against accusations of atheism and pantheism, which expounds a monistic philosophy of nature strongly tinged with Neoplatonic mystical overtones, in which God is All. Herder's position, like that of Goethe, which conceives of God as an immanent cause, has often, therefore, been called pantheism, although the use of this term has been criticized as their religiosity also implies transcendence, and here again the term *panentheism* has sometimes been preferred. This stance, involving worship of a divinized nature expressed in poetical language and combined with a form of transcendence, had a profound effect on Romantics such as Friedrich Wilhelm Joseph von Schelling or Samuel Taylor Coleridge (despite the latter's misgivings about pantheism), and came to permeate much nineteenth-century thinking and literature.

It is clear that this belief, which has led to a diversity of interpretations among scholars, many of whom hesitate to use the word *pantheism* to describe it, marks a break with much of enlightened thought, and if the word is understood in this way, then pantheism plays a very minor role in the eighteenth century. The prime target for attack by most defenders of orthodoxy was rather atheism, often linked to materialism, and when pantheism was denounced it was generally seen as an equivalent term. While Spinozism was an important element in much antireligious thought, Pierre Bayle's interpretation of Spinoza as an atheist prevailed for much of the century. Any attempt, therefore, to evaluate the role of pantheism in the Enlightenment comes up against the extreme difficulty of defining it satisfactorily, which is at the root of scholarly disagreement on the subject. This should incline one to caution when making claims for its importance.

[*See also* Atheism; Bayle, Pierre; Diderot, Denis; Holbach, Paul-Henri Thiry d'; Jacobi, Friedrich Heinrich; Materialism; Maupertuis, Pierre-Louis Moreau de; Mendelssohn, Moses; Natural Religion; Philosophy; Radicati di Passerano, Alberto; Romanticism; Spinoza, Baruch de; *and* Toland, John.]

BIBLIOGRAPHY

Bell, David. *Spinoza in Germany from 1670 to the Age of Goethe.* London, 1984. Deals mainly with the period after 1750 and considers that the word *pantheism* should be avoided as too vague.

Bloch, Olivier, ed. *Spinoza au XVIIIe siècle.* Paris, 1990. A useful collection of articles on different aspects of the reception of Spinoza's thought.

Brykman, Geneviève, ed. *Toland (1670–1722) et la crise de conscience européenne.* In *Revue de synthèse* 116, 2–3 (1995). A collection of articles that reflects recent research on Toland. Particularly relevant are Justin A. Champion, "John Toland: The Politics of Pantheism," pp. 259–280, and Jean Seidengart, "L'infinitisme panthéiste de John Toland et ses relations avec la pensée de Giordano Bruno," pp. 315–343.

El Nouty, Hassan. "Le panthéisme dans les lettres françaises au XVIIIe siècle." *Revue des Sciences Humaines* 100 (1960), 435–457. Dated and biased, but one of the rare studies of the subject, with useful bibliographical references.

Israel, Jonathan I. *Radical Enlightenment: Philosophy and the Making of Modernity 1650–1750.* Oxford, 2001. Spinozism is central to this detailed but rather idiosyncratic study, as is Holland, but there is little on pantheism as such.

Jacob, Margaret C. *The Radical Enlightenment: Pantheists, Freemasons and Republicans.* London, 1981. Influential study of freethinkers in the early eighteenth century whose claims for the existence of a pantheistic, republican, and masonic network have, however, been criticized by many historians.

McFarland, Thomas. *Coleridge and the Pantheist Tradition.* Oxford, 1969. Somewhat dated, but contains a review of currents of thought seen as pantheistic.

Spink, John S. *French Free Thought from Gassendi to Voltaire.* London, 1960. Contains a lot on clandestine thinking in France in the late seventeenth and early eighteenth centuries and the link between Spinozism and other currents of thought.

Sullivan, Robert E. *John Toland and the Deist Controversy.* Cambridge, Mass., 1982. Comprehensive study of Toland's life and thought, well situated in its context.

Van Bunge, Wiep, and Klever, Wim, eds. *Disguised and Overt Spinozism around 1700.* Leiden, 1996. An important collection of articles dealing with all aspects of reactions to Spinoza at the beginning of the period.

Vernière, Paul. *Spinoza et la pensée française avant le révolution.* Paris, 1954. The standard work on Spinoza's influence in France, which remains indispensable.

ANN THOMSON

PAPACY. The papacy is the title of the office held by the pope, believed by Roman Catholics to be the Vicar of Christ and head of the Universal Church on earth. The pope's other titles include Bishop of Rome, Primate of Italy, and Patriarch of the Latin Church. The office is held to originate in the commission given by Christ to Saint Peter, recorded in the Gospels of Matthew, 16:17–19, and John, 21:15–17, and transmitted by him to his successors in the See of Rome. Until 1870, the popes were also temporal rulers of the Papal State (or States of the Church), a large territory in central Italy accumulated at different times in the Middle Ages. In addition, the papacy controlled two outposts of the Papal State at Benevento and Pontecorvo

Pope Pius VI. Portrait by Pompeo Batoni (1708–1787). (Pinacoteca, Vatican Museums and Galleries, Vatican City/Scala/Art Resource, NY.)

in the Kingdom of Naples, the Comtat Venaissin in the south of France, ceded to the papacy in the thirteenth century, and the neighboring city of Avignon, bought by Clement VI in 1348.

Although he drew his authority from Christ, the pope owed his election to the cardinals, the leading dignitaries of the church, who in turn owed their status to papal nomination. The cardinals have almost always elected the popes from among their own number, and, fearful of creating a pope who might reign over them for many years, have tended to elect from among their more elderly colleagues. The average age of the eight popes elected in the eighteenth century was almost sixty-four, and some were still in office in their eighties. Clement XII was seventy-eight and already unwell when he was elected in 1730; within two years he had gone blind, and in his later years he had to conduct business from his bed. All the popes of this period were Italian (though none from Rome itself), and all but one came from prominent noble families. But not all were well-qualified for the post. Even Benedict XIV admitted that his predecessor Benedict XIII (a Dominican elected in 1724) "had not the first idea how to rule." But they were generally devout and conscientious, and some (notably Benedict XIV himself, elected in 1740) were able and learned.

As head of the Roman Catholic Church, the pope claimed jurisdiction over all Catholics in matters of the faith. Rome, therefore, served as the final authority in all disputes, and over time, the papacy had developed a large and complex system of ministries known as the Roman Curia to support its work. The upper levels of the Curia were staffed by clerics, and in particular by the cardinals. Like the popes themselves, the cardinals tended to come from Italian families of high social status. In previous centuries, the Curia had been dominated by cardinal nephews, close relatives of the popes by blood or adoption; but in 1692, Innocent XII had decreed that popes could nominate only one kinsman to the cardinalate and had limited the role of the cardinal nephew. Subsequently, although Clement XII still entrusted the conduct of business largely to his nephew, Cardinal Neri Corsini, the most significant figure in the Curia was normally the cardinal secretary of state. Other cardinals served on the many congregations that took responsibility for different aspects of church life—the supervision of bishops and regulars, for example, and the wider pastoral system of the church, the prosecution of heresy and the censorship of books. The procedures of the Curia, however, were often only poorly developed, the scope for corruption was great, and its officials were underpaid. Despite the efforts of some popes to use the curial offices more systematically, therefore, papal attempts to control the worldwide church through the Curia were often of only limited effectiveness.

The same can be said of the pope's temporal government in the Papal State. The administration of these territories had developed in much the same way as elsewhere in Europe; in the Papal State, however, the administrative structure was dominated by clerics. By the eighteenth century, the most significant figures were again the cardinal secretary of state, who dealt with foreign affairs, and the cardinal camerlengo or chamberlain, who was responsible for local administration and in particular for the government's income and expenditure. More detailed matters, such as food supply, or roads and bridges, were handled by further congregations of cardinals. The laity, and even the nobility, were thus excluded from all but purely local institutions. This did not mean, however, that they were entirely powerless, for even in the eighteenth century, these bodies retained some significant governmental and juridical autonomy—especially in the bigger papal cities such as Bologna. The work of the central government was, therefore, frequently obstructed by the survival of local traditions and privileges; and the popes' ability to control local affairs correspondingly diminished.

A further limitation on the operation of papal power in Church and state in this period was financial. The loss of territories in northern Europe to Protestantism during the Reformation had significantly reduced the popes' revenues, and they turned increasingly to the states of the church to make up the difference, and especially through indirect taxation. But this policy did little to foster the development of agriculture and industry, and the papal budget was consequently always in deficit. In the eighteenth century, the problems were exacerbated as Catholic governments also sought to stem the flow of money from their local church to Rome. The famines of 1763–1766, brought on initially by poor weather conditions, served to demonstrate the severity of the problems, and by the 1780s, contemporary estimates suggested that the value of imports into the Papal State was three times greater than the value of its exports. By then, the camerlengo's officials had become seriously alarmed at the state of papal finances, and Pius VI, elected in 1775, did try to improve the economy by abolishing tolls and encouraging local agriculture. He also made proposals for tax reforms. From 1789, however, when ecclesiastical revenues from France were blocked by the Revolutionary government, the deficit soared out of control.

Despite these problems, papal Rome remained an important cultural and intellectual center in the eighteenth century. The city was an important focus for artistic activity, and for the study and display of antiquities. The Roman colleges, run by the religious orders, retained their good reputation, and Benedict XIV and Pius VI both made efforts to reform the Sapienza, the University of Rome. Benedict XIV also sought to make better use of the city's talent by the creation of four new academies, designed to bring together scholars interested in both ecclesiastical and secular learning. And in Rome, as elsewhere, some loyal Catholics responded positively to the new ideas emerging from France. Leading figures in this "Catholic Enlightenment" called for reforms in the Church and often for a simplification of its teaching. Lodovico Antonio Muratori (1672–1750), for example, a devout secular priest who worked as archivist and librarian for the duke of Modena, published a series of influential studies in which he argued for a Christianity cleansed of superstition and unnecessary ceremonies. Cardinals Angelo Maria Quirini (1680–1755) and Domenico Passionei (1682–1761) protected Montesquieu's *L'esprit des lois* (1748) from a full condemnation by the Congregation of the Index. Benedict XIV at one point engaged in an amiable correspondence with Voltaire; and the *Dei diritti dell'uomo* (On the Rights of Man) of Nicola Spedialieri (1740–1795), first published in Assisi in 1791, sought to enlist the rights of man and even the social contract in a defense of Catholicism and papal authority.

But as Benedict XIV recognized, the most immediate intellectual threat to the papacy came not from Enlightenment ideas but from dissident tendencies within the Church itself. The most serious was Jansenism, which began with the attempt of Bishop Cornelis Jansen of Ypres (1585–1638) to revive what he saw as Saint Augustine's doctrine of grace. During several decades of theological debate and dispute, however, in which Jansenism grew in popularity in France, Italy, and Iberia as well as the Low Countries, the movement came to be associated with a much wider range of ecclesiastical and, at times, even political opinion. Further, because the Congregation of the Inquisition and the papacy repeatedly condemned the errors attributed to Jansen and his followers, support for Jansenism often took the form of hostility to the papacy's doctrinal authority. A further institutional challenge came from those such as Zeger Bernard van Espen (1646–1728), a professor of canon law at Louvain, and his pupil Johann Nikolaus von Hontheim (1701–1790), known as Febronius, an auxiliary bishop himself, who sought to elevate the authority and autonomy of the bishop in his diocese. Febronius's ideas were condemned by Clement XIII in 1764, but followers of Edmond Richer (1560–1631) extended the argument for independence to the entire clergy, while others insisted on the liberties and privileges of their national church in opposition to papal supremacy. These positions were sometimes merged. Pasquier Quesnel (1634–1719) adopted some of Richer's ideas as well as those of Jansen in a series of texts (condemned in 1708 and 1713) that suggested that authority in the Church lay with a council of all its clergy and not with the papacy alone. Toward the end of the century, Scipione de' Ricci (1741–1810), the reforming bishop of Pistoia and Prato in Tuscany, encouraged his flock to read Jansenist texts, including those of Quesnel, and presided over a celebrated diocesan synod in 1786 that repeated the earlier assertion of local ecclesiastical independence. The synod's conclusions were condemned by Pius VI in 1794.

The practical effect of many of these ideas was to attribute greater power over local church life to the state, and jurisdictional conflicts between the papacy and Catholic governments, in which rulers sought to increase their control over ecclesiastical life and discipline, became increasingly strident in this period. In virtually all states, new restrictions were imposed by governments on Church property and on the publication of papal decrees, while established clerical exemptions from taxation were abolished. Papal appointments were challenged, the role of the Church in the control of the press was reduced, and Inquisition tribunals were closed. A particularly thorough assault was launched against the monastic orders: In the Habsburg monarchy, for instance, in the 1780s, Joseph II suppressed some seven hundred contemplative houses,

calling them "unnecessary and useless." The papacy's response to these measures was eventually conciliatory: Given their own limited powers and the determination of rulers to reduce papal influence, the best the popes could hope for was a compromise. These agreements were then formulated in concordats. But although specific conflicts were thus brought to an end, the concordats always involved a surrender of significant papal powers and revenues to the state.

The weakness of the eighteenth-century papacy even in ecclesiastical matters was demonstrated in a spectacular fashion by the success of the campaign to expel and eventually suppress the Society of Jesus. Hostility to this order, formally established by Paul III in 1540, was widespread even within the Church, and the Jesuits' own doctrinal disagreement with Jansenist teaching ensured their support for papal authority in the wider conflicts of the period. Opposition to the Society thus became linked with opposition to papal supremacy, and was backed by a number of secular governments. The Marquês de Pombal was the first to take action when he expelled the Society from Portuguese territories in 1759; his lead was followed by France (1764), Spain and Naples (1767), and finally by Parma and the Knights of Malta (1768). In 1773, Clement XIV, a Franciscan elected in 1769, reluctantly submitted to political pressure from Spain and the other Bourbon states and suppressed the Society. It was not restored until 1814.

This episode served only to confirm the political impotence of the papacy. Ever since the later seventeenth century, in fact, papal influence on the international scene had been in decline, and papal territories were invaded and occupied on several occasions in the eighteenth century. But the greatest humiliation came after the French Revolution. Following a series of disputes with the papacy, the new government in France ordered Napoleon to invade the Papal States in 1796. Pius VI agreed to surrender Avignon, Bologna, Ferrara, and Ravenna to secure peace; but in 1798, the French army occupied the remaining territories of the Holy See, and Rome itself was taken in the following year. A republic was declared, and the pope exiled. Napoleon subsequently permitted the restoration of a depleted state for the pope, and signed new concordats with Pius VII, elected in 1800. But the pope's refusal to abandon his position of neutrality in the subsequent European wars provoked Napoleon to occupy the Papal States once again and in 1809 to incorporate its territory into the Kingdom of Italy. Pius VII was imprisoned.

It was only after Napoleon's defeat that the pope returned to Rome. Paradoxically, however, despite the political damage of the previous century, the experience of imprisonment and exile did much to restore the reputation and authority of the papacy. Pius VI and Pius VII, holders of the oldest and most authoritative office in Europe, could now be seen as victims of tyranny and martyrs for liberty. That new reputation helped to reestablish papal credibility in the nineteenth century.

[*See also* Benedict XIV; Clement XIV; Pius VII; *and* Revealed Religion.]

BIBLIOGRAPHY

Chadwick, Owen. *The Popes and European Revolution*. Oxford, 1981. A masterly and lively account of Roman Catholicism in the eighteenth century.

Gross, Hanns. *Rome in the Age of Enlightenment: The Post-Tridentine Syndrome and the Ancien Régime*. Cambridge, 1990. A detailed study of the economic, social, and cultural history of papal Rome in this period.

Jedin, Hubert, and John Dolan, eds. *History of the Church*. London, 1965–1981. Vol. 6: *The Church in the Age of Absolutism and Enlightenment*. English translation of *Handbuch der Kirchengeschichte*, first published in 1953.

Koeppel, Philippe, ed. *Papes et papauté au XVIIIe siècle: VIe colloque franco-italien Société Française d'Étude du XVIIIe siècle*. Paris, 1999.

Pastor, Ludwig Friedrich A., Freiherr von. *The History of the Popes, from the Close of the Middle Ages*. London, 1891–1953. Vols. 33–36. English translation of *Geschichte der Päpste seit dem Ausgang des Mittelalters*, first published in 1886–1933. Remains essential as a work of reference.

Wright, Anthony David. *The Early Modern Papacy: From the Council of Trent to the French Revolution, 1564–1789*. Harlow, U.K., 2000. The most recent overview of papal history.

N. S. DAVIDSON

PARINI, GIUSEPPE (1729–1799), Italian poet.

Born in Bosisio in Lombardy, the son of a modest dealer in silk, Parini left to study in Milan at an early age. Though obliged to enter the priesthood, his vocation was poetry; his first collection, *Alcune poesie di Ripano Eupilino* (Some Poems of Ripano Eupilino, 1752) earned him entry into the Accademia dei Trasformati, whose members were moderate innovators. His entire oeuvre, composed primarily of occasional poems, is interwoven with the history of the Grand Duchy of Lombardy, drawn from his close associations with the political elite of Milan. He became an assistant tutor to the children of the duchess Serbelloni, then professor at the Palatine School; later he participated in the republican municipal government during the revolution. Repelled by its excesses, he died celebrating the return to power of the Habsburgs.

As a poet Parini was not content to be an associate of the great; rather, setting the duties of his ecclesiastical estate to one side, he wished to exercise a sort of secular priesthood. With his *Dialogo sopra la nobiltà* (Dialogue on Nobility, 1757) he launched an offensive against the privileges of birth, and expressed satisfaction that the philosophic spirit had appeared "to reestablish good sense and reason on their throne" (*Discorso sopra la poesia* [Discourse on Poetry]). Anxious to place his art at the service

of "utility and truth" (*Discorso sopra la carità* [Discourse on Charity]), he never ceased to denounce error and prejudice and to fight as a Christian humanist (*Il bisogno* [Need]) for justice (*La laurea: La magistratura*), toleration (*L'auto da fé*) and peace (*Sopra la guerra* [On War]), all the while concerning himself with education (*L'educazione*), hygiene (*La salubrità dell'aria* [The Salubriousness of the Air]) and public health (*L'innesto del vaiolo* [Inoculation against Smallpox]).

In his major work, *Il giorno* (The Day), a sort of comico-heroic poem, Parini showed his full stature. Only the first two parts (*Il mattino* [Morning], 1763; *Il mezzogiorno* [Noon], 1765) were published during his lifetime. An eternal perfectionist, he was unable to complete *Il vespro* and *La notte* (Evening; Night). The protagonist is a "Young Lord," who has nothing better to do than to fill the void of his existence with frivolous pastimes; he is flanked by a preceptor, a sort of ironic narrative conscience, who is no more than a mask for the author. The young lord is a ladies' man who projects the image of an aristocracy entirely occupied with its worldly pleasures, thinking of nothing but itself, and offering ritual sacrifice to those two deadly genii, ennui and punctiliousness in defending noble honor. Pope's *Rape of the Lock* influences the form, as his *Essay on Man* does the content; other influences include the *Télémaque* of Fénelon, especially as regards the polemic against riches and luxury and the corresponding praise of agriculture and the laborious healthy life of the peasantry. Parini is more sympathetic with the philosophes of the first half of the century than those of the second half (Voltaire, Rousseau), whom he qualifies as "new sophists." His role as a moralist of happiness conforms totally to the ideology of enlightened Lombard reformism, the protagonists of which were the ministers and functionaries of the Austrian government.

[*See also* Italy; Milan; *and* Poetry.]

BIBLIOGRAPHY

Jonard, Norbert. *Introduzione a Parini*. Bari, Italy, 1988.
Perroud, Robert. *Giuseppe Parini: L'homme et l'oeuvre*. Lille, 1973.
Petronio, Giuseppe. *Parini e l'illuminismo lombardo*. Milan, 1961.

NORBERT JONARD

Translated from French by William McCuaig

PARIS. As much as any other single city, eighteenth-century Paris shaped the Enlightenment. The second largest metropolis in Europe after London, it had a population approaching half a million in the late seventeenth century, and perhaps seven to eight hundred thousand by 1789. The role of the city as an administrative, legal, and business center and the proximity of the royal court at Versailles made Paris the focus for the social and political elites of France. As the capital, it was also the location of the dominant cultural and political institutions of France, which gave the city a large population of lawyers, teachers, scientists, and other professionals. The literature and the sociability of the Enlightenment, however, must be seen in the context not only of institutions, but also of changes in consumer practices from the late seventeenth century on. The importance of aristocratic consumption in national politics meant that much of the wealth of France was spent in Paris, and the thriving commerce—particularly the luxury industries of the city—created a large, prosperous, and well-educated commercial middle class. The size and wealth of Paris thus produced a critical mass of intellectuals, of readers, and of consumers. Markets, networks of distribution, and habits of consumption were crucial to the intellectual and cultural production of the Enlightenment.

Paris also influenced the wider Enlightenment because of the prestige it enjoyed as the capital of the most powerful kingdom in Europe. Parisian clothes, furniture, and other luxury products were exported all over the world and were generally regarded as the height of fashion. The French language was a vital part of the education of the upper classes throughout Europe and was spoken in most European courts, and this meant that the prestige and influence of Paris were magnified. The national and international audiences for its literary and cultural production were extensive, and the latest news and intellectual fashions from the French capital were eagerly awaited throughout Europe.

Administration. Because of this wider role, local factors influencing the intellectual output of Paris had repercussions well beyond the city. Foremost among these local factors were the institutions of control: the courts, the church, and the police. The principal courts were those of the Parlement of Paris, which covered both civil and criminal matters and whose jurisdiction extended well beyond the city. The assembled magistrates also had what we would now call a legislative role, giving orders based on existing legislation. They issued decrees on matters ranging from animals in the streets to religious observance. Several times during the eighteenth century, they ordered the arrest of people held responsible for disturbing public order. The Parlement also banned books that it deemed irreligious or antimonarchical, such as Voltaire's *Lettres philosophiques* (1734). It outlawed organizations and meetings that it thought might contravene French law, repeatedly banning workers' associations and, in 1760, dissolving unregistered religious confraternities. During Louis XIV's reign, the Parlement of Paris remained very much a tool of royal policy, but after Louis's death in 1715, it increasingly tested the limits of its authority, particularly in religious and financial matters. In 1762, it took the highly contentious measure of banning the Jesuits from its jurisdiction, closing their schools and houses. Because the Jesuits were among the most formidable critics of the philosophes and were deeply involved in the education of the French elite, this action had far-reaching consequences.

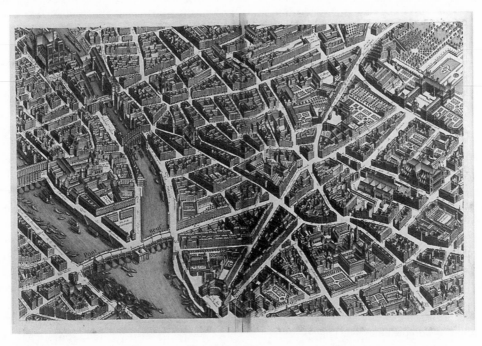

Paris. The Île de la Cité and the Latin Quarter from the Plan Turgot. From Louis Breretz, *Plans de Paris* (1739), plate 11. (Geography and Map Division, Library of Congress.)

The distinction between administration and judiciary was blurred under the Old Regime. Not only did the Parlement play an important role in legislating for the city, but individual magistrates were active in Paris politics and administration. The king's principal spokesman in the Parlement, the *procureur général,* was directly responsible for all the Paris parishes and was kept busy by the religious disputes that raged in the city up to the 1760s.

Most of the day-to-day administration of the city, after the creation of the position of lieutenant general of police in 1667, was handled by the police. While a municipality continued to exist and remained a potent symbol of urban independence, much of its former role was taken over by the police. They were responsible for executing the laws and for public order, and played a key role in areas such as food supply and public health, street lighting and maintenance, fire prevention, and regulation of the city's industry. The police also functioned as an arm of the lower-level courts of Paris, collectively known as the Châtelet. The police chief, the lieutenant general, was a royal appointee who reported both to the king and to the Parlement, but he was at the same time a magistrate of the Châtelet, judging a host of minor misdemeanors in the city's police court. Other police officials worked both for the civil and for the criminal courts, hearing witnesses and undertaking preliminary investigations. While surveillance of the Paris trades was a police role, the officials of the different trade guilds officially reported to another Châtelet magistrate. Gradually, the Châtelet courts took over from the remaining seigneurial and ecclesiastical courts of Paris, and as their jurisdiction grew, so did that of the police.

In addition, a major task for the police was the maintenance of public morality, interpreted to mean enforcing religious observance, suppressing begging, and controlling gambling and prostitution. Much effort also went into preventing any threat of rebellion. To this end, bread was subsidized, access to firearms controlled, and potentially subversive ideas and activities suppressed. The police used networks of informers to watch anyone whom its lieutenant general thought a danger to religion or to the monarchy. In the late seventeenth century, this primarily meant dissident nobles, Protestants, Jansenists, and others who might be plotting against the crown. From the late 1720s, Freemasons were also perceived to be a potential threat, and, along with the Jansenists, they were vigorously pursued until the middle of the eighteenth century. Throughout this time, both these groups were seen as far more dangerous than the philosophes.

In the second half of the eighteenth century, the preoccupations of the police gradually changed. They perceived irreligion as a greater threat than Protestants, Jews, or Jansenists, but they were no longer concerned about rebellion against the crown. They increasingly saw their role as the protection not solely of church and state but of a wider public. Thus, they began to undertake criminal investigation as a normal part of policing. They became more bureaucratic, kept more comprehensive records, and began to adopt the ideal of total surveillance within the city. Under the influence of Enlightenment thought, they increasingly came to see their role as the improvement of society. Successive lieutenant generals worked to ameliorate the Paris water supply, street cleaning, and other sanitary problems. Among other things, they established the Mont-de-Piété (a publicly run pawnbroker), created a centralized wet-nursing system to help poor families, and helped found new hospitals.

Although the police and the courts played the most important role in running the city, they had to negotiate constantly with numerous other institutions and individuals. The great nobles did not consider themselves or their servants answerable to the police, and the army largely ran its own affairs. The church enjoyed numerous privileges and exemptions. Furthermore, quite a number of areas in the city claimed special rights: the Temple was the best-known example, where officially the police could not go and where debtors therefore took refuge. The Faubourg Saint Antoine, a large area on the eastern side of the city, claimed exemption from the normal guild regulations, a privilege fiercely defended by the local abbey. The municipality, too, jealously guarded its control over the river and the ports. Particular types of activities also came under other bodies. The customs posts around the city were run by the General Farm, the agency that collected indirect taxes, and the municipality also had a keen interest in them because most of its revenue came from the tax levied on goods entering the city. There were repeated conflicts between these different jurisdictions, but, in general, the administration ran smoothly enough because it was in the hands of a small number of officials and magistrates who knew one another well and negotiated constantly.

The Church. After the institutions of government, the Roman Catholic church was the most important influence in Paris, both politically and in cultural terms. At the end of the Old Regime, Paris contained fifty-two parishes, nearly fifty hospices and hospitals, eleven chapter houses, eighty convents, thirty-eight male religious houses, and a number of other ecclesiastical establishments, including the thirteen houses attached to the university. There were about 133 free schools attached to different parishes, 316 fee-paying schools controlled by the cathedral chapter of Notre Dame, and a large number of others run by various religious orders. (A great many private schools for both boys and girls also existed, some legal and some not.) Altogether, in 1789, there were nearly five thousand nuns and monks and nearly two thousand secular clergy with positions in the city, as well as a large number of other ecclesiastics who lived there without official duties. Earlier in the century, these numbers were probably even higher.

The archbishop of Paris was a very powerful figure and a key player in the religious disputes of the period. Successive archbishops had considerable influence at court and exerted enormous influence within the Paris diocese, though they were limited by the privileges of powerful abbeys and religious orders. Archbishop Christophe de Beaumont, in office from 1746 to 1781, was particularly active in combating both Jansenism—bringing him into constant conflict with the Parlement of Paris—and the philosophes. In 1751, he condemned Claude-Adrien Helvétius's *De l'esprit;* in 1762, Jean-Jacques Rousseau's *Émile;* and in 1768, Jean-François Marmontel's *Bélisaire*.

In a broader sense, however, the church subsidized the Enlightenment in Paris. The clerical population of the city ran many of the schools and colleges responsible for the growth of an enlightened readership, among them the Jesuit collège Louis-le-Grand, where Voltaire, Anne-Robert-Jacques Turgot, and thousands of others were educated. Both the Jesuit and the Oratorian schools, in particular, were quick to add science to the curriculum, while providing the classical education that was common to the entire Enlightenment. Meanwhile, the Ursuline, Benedictine, and other teaching convents of the city provided much of the formal education for the daughters of the Parisian elite, including women like Marie de Vichy-Chamrond, marquise Du Deffand (1696–1780), who for forty years ran one of the leading Paris salons; she had been a boarder at the fashionable convent of La Madelaine de Trénelle.

Churchmen were also prominent among the Parisian intellectuals who participated on both sides of Enlightenment debates, and they included many scientists and men of letters. The abbé Jean Antoine Nollet (1700–1770) is one example: he taught at the collège de Navarre, and his experiments with electricity enthralled Parisian high society in 1753. The abbé Nicolas Baudeau (1730–1792), one of the principal physiocrats, and the former Jesuit Guillaume Raynal (1713–1796), author of the best-selling *Histoire des Deux Indes,* are other prominent examples.

Institutions of Learning. The University of Paris was also an ecclesiastical institution, a federation of a large number of colleges and three faculties (theology, law, and medicine). None of these faculties had a reputation as an enlightened institution, and they rarely figure in histories of the Enlightenment. Indeed, their contribution was in some ways a negative one. In 1725, the university was given a considerable role in surveillance of the book trade, and the Sorbonne, part of the Faculty of Theology, played a particular role in policing religious doctrine. In 1751, it censured Georges-Louis Leclerc de Buffon for implying that the Earth was far older than the biblical account suggested, and a few years later it condemned Claude-Adrien Helvétius's *De l'esprit*.

Yet the University of Paris made a much greater contribution to the Enlightenment than is generally recognized. It provided the core for a cluster of institutions of learning that contributed much to the medical and scientific dimensions of the Enlightenment. The Faculty of Medicine enjoyed an international reputation for up-to-date, high-quality teaching. Natural philosophy at the university was also strong, including among its professors important scholars such as the philosopher Pierre Sigorgne (1719–1809), a strong advocate of Newtonian physics. In 1772, the Collège Royal (later to become the Collège de France) became part of the university, which thus gained professors such as the astronomer Joseph Lalande (1732–1807) and the naturalist Louis Daubenton (1716–1799). The university also attracted large numbers of students from all over France. Charles de Montesquieu (1689–1755) and the chemist Antoine-Laurent Lavoisier (1743–1794) both studied law in Paris, and in the early 1750s the future philosophes Anne-Robert-Jacques Turgot (1727–1781) and André Morellet (1727–1819) were both at the Sorbonne, where they not only met personally but were introduced to the writings of John Locke, Pierre Bayle, and other key philosophers and scientists. While theology remained the most studied subject, with many thousands of students, more than fourteen hundred young men took law degrees between 1760 and 1790 alone, and many of them subsequently found work in Paris—in the 1760s, there was already one legal official for every eighty-five people in the city (Andrews, 1994). Although the degree was not always rigorous, it helped to provide the educated public necessary for the spread of enlightened ideas.

Paris was home to a great many other institutions of learning and culture, some sponsored by the crown and others unofficial. The Collège Royal taught mathematics, botany, surgery, pharmacy, and medicine, and for much of the eighteenth century it rivaled the university. So too did the Jardin du Roi and its associated Cabinet d'Histoire Naturelle, which taught medicine in addition to chemistry and natural history. Established by the crown in the mid-seventeenth century, by the early eighteenth it had become the model for similar schools elsewhere in France. Students could attend lectures by such major figures as the comte de Buffon, three members of the Jussieu family, the chemist Antoine Fourcroy (1755–1809), Daubenton, and a number of other ground-breaking scholars.

Academies and Learned Societies. As the national capital, Paris was also where the various royal academies were located. The Académie Française (founded 1635) was the most prestigious, providing recognition for literary

Paris Scene. Palace and gardens of the Tuileries, painting (1757) by Nicholas-Jean-Baptiste Raguenet. (Musée de la Ville de Paris, Musée Carnavelet/Giraudon/Art Resource, NY.)

achievements, though selection was dependent on patronage and connections. Voltaire's election in 1746 marked the definitive integration of part of the Enlightenment into the Old Regime elite, and many other philosophes subsequently became members. The second great academy, the Académie Royale des Sciences, was founded in 1666 and became the leading scientific institution in France, numbering among its members the naturalist René Réaumur (1683–1757), the mathematicians Jean Le Rond d'Alembert (1717–1783) and Jean-Antoine-Nicolas de Caritat Condorcet (1743–1794), and the astronomer Lalande. It was an important mechanism for disseminating a new worldview. The third great academy was the Académie des Inscriptions et Belles Lettres founded in 1663, and specializing in history and archaeology. There were also academies of painting and sculpture (1648), architecture (1671), and music (1672). The academies provided some income, but, above all, status and official recognition, both for the profession and for the individuals elected. They ran competitions, awarded prizes, and, through addresses and publications, played a central role in the dissemination of enlightened ideas.

The academies also provided a model for professional groups seeking to raise their status by obtaining royal recognition. The surgeons obtained their own royal academy in 1731, and the apothecaries an independent college of pharmacy in 1777. Both ran courses in competition with the Faculty of Medicine and had a reputation for innovation. The Société Royale de Médecine, growing out of Turgot's reforms and founded in 1778, sponsored both the new environmental medicine of the late eighteenth century and the ideal of scientific objectivity in the service of society. It provided national leadership, holding competitions, publishing approved medical work, and

developing an international network of correspondents. The Société d'Agriculture, founded in the early 1760s under the impulse of the physiocrats, played a similar role.

A lesser role was played by other public institutions that provided a living to numerous individuals, some of whom played influential roles within the Parisian Enlightenment. Antoine Augustin Parmentier (1737–1813) was one, based at the Invalides military hospital, where he conducted experiments in chemistry and agronomy. The various hospitals provided laboratories for surgeons, pharmacists, and sometimes physicians. The Royal Mint housed a chair of mineralogy. Even the Gobelins manufactory, producing tapestries and furnishings for the royal palaces, was the venue for experiments with dyes. Pensions and offices granted by the crown funded or subsidized the work of a number of scientists and writers.

Central to the Enlightenment project was the dissemination of useful knowledge. By the 1770s and 1780s, educated Parisians could attend public dissections, scientific demonstrations at the Collège de Navarre, and lectures at the School of Mines, the Jardin du Roi, and a number of other institutions. The various learned societies opened some of their sessions to the public, and reports were often published in the *Journal de Paris*, a daily news sheet founded in 1777 by a group including the chemist Antoine Alexis Cadet de Vaux (1743–1828). The Académie des Beaux Arts had run a salon in the palace of the Louvre every second year since 1737, and by the 1780s was attracting more than thirty thousand visitors from all walks of life. In a similar spirit, in 1780 Antoine Court de Gébelin (1725–1784) organized the Musée de Paris, where the respectable public could attend literary and scientific presentations. It was followed by the Musée de Monsieur of 1781, sponsored by the king's brothers and offering weekly classes in literature, history, languages, and science.

The same educational impulse underlay the many publications sponsored by the academies and societies, targeting an expanding reading public. Not only was Paris a publishing center and one of the largest markets for this output; it also offered unparalleled access to well-endowed libraries. The most important was the Bibliothèque Royale (the core of today's Bibliothèque Nationale), opened to the public in 1720. The abbey of Sainte Geneviève, several other religious houses, and a number of private collectors also allowed access to their rich libraries.

Other Cultural Institutions. Another key cultural institution was theater. Paris had three official theaters—the Opéra, the Comédie Française, and the Comédie Italienne (later Opéra Comique)—all conservative in their productions and very defensive of their privileges. The Comédie Française had a monopoly on classical drama, and every serious playwright aspired to have work presented there. The Comédie Italienne put on lighter plays containing music. While the Opéra remained very expensive, after 1760 the other theaters opened their doors to a wider public, including servants and workers. As many as thirty thousand people may have attended some of the more popular plays, including those of Voltaire and Pierre-Augustin Caron de Beaumarchais.

Popular enthusiasm for theater encouraged the vigorous growth of small private theaters, at first during the annual fairs, but, in the second half of the eighteenth century, along the northern boulevards and later in the Palais Royal. The farces produced by Jean-Baptiste Nicolet and Nicolas-Médard Audinot were enormously popular and often contained elements of barbed social commentary.

Outside the official scientific and cultural establishments, Enlightenment thought and sociability flourished in a variety of private cultural institutions. Foremost among them were the salons, one of the few areas where women could play a significant role in shaping discussion. Nevertheless, the role of the small number of famous salon women has often been exaggerated. The Parisian Enlightenment was far wider, including a great many dining clubs, café societies, literary and theatrical groups, and other regular gatherings at which men and women discussed books and current affairs, read poetry, and sang songs. The participants included many from the expanding Paris middle classes, not only lawyers, office-holders and other professionals, but also well-to-do merchants and even craftsmen and their wives and children. A similar range of groups belonged to the many lodges of Freemasons that first appeared in Paris in the 1720s. By the second half of the eighteenth century, Freemasonry had become respectable and counted thousands of adherents in the city, mostly men but also some women.

Philanthropic Institutions. In the 1780s in particular, philanthropic associations flourished in Paris, testimony to the adoption by the social elite of the city of the ideal—already celebrated in the *Encyclopédie* in the 1750s—of the enlightened man or woman readily moved by the sufferings of others. The Société Philanthropique, the Société de la Charité Maternelle, and a number of similar organizations—but also some of the Freemasons' lodges and salons like that of Mme. Helvétius (Anne-Catherine de Ligniville, 1719–1800)—were primarily concerned to help the "deserving" or "honest" poor, ideally widows, orphans, the infirm, and "respectable" people in prison for debt. They combined a genuine humanitarianism with a hostility to traditional religious charity, including the central hospital, the Hôtel Dieu, which they criticized for helping all comers and thereby encouraging laziness. This sentiment inspired the founding of separate hospices in several parishes, the first of them established at Saint Sulpice through the efforts of the finance minister Jacques Necker (1732–1804) and his wife, Suzanne Curchod (1739–1794). It also inspired the eventual reform of the Hôtel Dieu in the late 1780s.

An Enlightened Paris. In retrospect, the years around 1760 marked a turning point in Paris. The quarrels over Jansenism ended, and thereafter many aspects of enlightened thought were adopted by elements of the royal administration and by most of the Parisian elite. The new forms of sociability drew in ever larger numbers of people and provided the core of a public that was educated, affluent, and relatively independent of church and state. Literacy rates were increasing, and a consumer culture was beginning to influence even the working population of the city. Products from all around the world, the growth of tourism, and the influence of newspapers, popular literature, and theater were expanding the horizons of all Parisians. Chinese characters and noble savages paraded the stages of street theaters, and even waxworks portrayed the customs of exotic peoples. Some elements of current scientific and medical thought reached a very wide public. The memoirs of the Paris artisan Jacques Louis Ménétra show how the religious questioning of the radical Enlightenment could link up with a deep-rooted popular anticlericalism. All this was a direct result of the number and the growing social and geographical mobility of the city's inhabitants, which weakened traditional mechanisms of social control. Social change within Paris thus provided a climate propitious for the secular and the politically radical elements of late Enlightenment thought.

The political and cultural institutions of Paris helped to shape the French and even the European Enlightenment. The police and the church were sufficiently oppressive to limit what could be said and published, but the size and dynamism of Paris, the limited means of surveillance available, and the institutional rivalries within the city meant that they were never powerful enough to suppress debate entirely. In a period of rapid scientific and social change, these were ideal conditions for the growth and spread of the Enlightenment.

[*See also* Academies, *subentry on* France; Clubs and Societies; Coffeehouses and Cafes; Learned Societies; Parlements; Scholarly Associations and Publications; *and* Universities.]

BIBLIOGRAPHY

Andrews, Richard. *Law, Magistracy, and Crime in Old Regime Paris, 1735–1789*, vol. 1, *The System of Criminal Justice*. Cambridge, 1994. The General Introduction contains the best description of eighteenth-century Paris available in English.

Brockliss, L. W. B. *French Higher Education in the Seventeenth and Eighteenth Centuries: A Cultural History*. Oxford, 1987.

Brockliss, L. W. B., and Colin Jones. *The Medical World of Early Modern France*. Oxford, 1997.

Chagniot, Jean. *Nouvelle histoire de Paris: Paris au XVIIIᵉ siècle*. Paris, 1988. Largely political and institutional.

Crow, Thomas. *Painters and Public Life in Eighteenth-Century Paris*. New Haven, Conn., and London, 1985.

Garrioch, David. *The Formation of the Parisian Bourgeoisie*. Cambridge, Mass., 1996. On social change in eighteenth-century Paris.

Gelfand, Toby. *Professionalizing Modern Medicine: Paris Surgeons and Medical Science and Institutions in the Eighteenth Century*. Westport, Conn., 1980.

Goodman, Dena. *The Republic of Letters: A Cultural History of the French Enlightenment*. Ithaca, N.Y., and London, 1994. Argues for the central role of women in the salons.

Gordon, Daniel. *Citizens without Sovereignty: Equality and Sociability in French Thought, 1670–1789*. Princeton, N.J., 1994.

Isherwood, Robert. *Farce and Fantasy: Popular Entertainment in Eighteenth-Century Paris*. New York, 1986.

Kaplan, Steven. *Bread, Politics and Political Economy in the Reign of Louis XV*. 2 vols. The Hague, 1976.

Kaplow, Jeffry. *The Names of Kings: The Parisian Laboring Poor in the Eighteenth Century*. New York, 1972. A superb survey of aspects of eighteenth-century Paris, heavily influenced by Marxist history and social anthropology.

Kors, Alan. *D'Holbach's Coterie: An Enlightenment in Paris*. Princeton, N.J., 1976.

Marraud, Mathieu. *La noblesse de Paris au XVIIᵉ siècle*. Paris, 2000.

Ménétra, Jacques Louis. *Journal of My Life*. Edited by Daniel Roche. New York, 1986. English translation of *Journal de ma vie*, first published in 1982, the earliest known autobiography by a Parisian artisan.

Roche, Daniel. *The Culture of Clothing: Dress and Fashion in the Old Regime*. Cambridge, 1994. English translation of *La culture des apparences*, first published in 1989. A seminal work in the history of material culture, showing its spread among the Paris population and drawing out its wider implications.

Roche, Daniel. *The People of Paris*. Leamington Spa, U.K., 1986. English translation of *Le peuple de Paris*, first published in 1981. Deals primarily with workers and servants, with an excellent chapter on reading practices.

Sonnet, Martine. *L'éducation des filles au temps des Lumières*. Paris, 1987.

Williams, Alan. *The Police of Paris*. Baton Rouge, La., 1979. A thorough institutional study.

DAVID GARRIOCH

PARLEMENTS. Supreme courts of appeal in both civil and criminal cases, French parlements also exercised a range of extrajudicial powers, which made them a leading forum and focus of political life between the death of Louis XIV in 1715 and the French Revolution of 1789. Their magistrates also played a prominent part in cultural life, and a number of important Enlightenment figures were drawn from their ranks.

Sovereign Courts. Although parlementary judgments might be overridden by the royal council, and whole cases might be evoked for resolution by the council alone, the jurisdiction of a parlement was normally final, or sovereign. In the early Middle Ages the only parlement had been that of Paris, and it remained by far the most important, with a jurisdiction (Fr., *ressort*) covering a third of the kingdom. As the king's dominions expanded, however, newly acquired provinces were given their own parlements. The first of these was established for the province of Languedoc at Toulouse in 1437, the last for the province of Lorraine at Nancy in 1775. By then, there were thirteen: the others being (in order of establishment) Grenoble, Bordeaux, Dijon, Rouen, Aix, Rennes, Pau, Metz, Besançon, and Douai. In addition, there were sovereign councils that enjoyed comparable powers at Arras, Perpignan, Colmar, and Bastia, and there were a number of financial courts (*chambres des comptes, cours des aides, cours des monnaies*) that also exercised sovereign jurisdiction.

In addition to judging cases brought to them on appeal, parlements on their own initiative could make administrative bylaws (*arrêts de réglement*). Above all, no royal legislation came into force in a parlement's *ressort* until the court had registered it. Registration, however, might be delayed to allow protests or requests for modification to be sent to the king in the form of remonstrances. Further (iterative) remonstrances might be made if he took no notice and ordered registration by *lettres de jussion*. Ultimately, the king could enforce registration in a *lit de justice*, when he or a personal representative came to the parlement and presided at a forced transcription of the contested measures onto its registers; this was normally the last word, although parlements would increasingly denounce forced registrations as null and illegal.

Louis XIV had rendered most of those procedures obsolete, by stipulating that registration must precede remonstrances; but in 1715, in return for the Paris parlement's cooperation in annulling Louis's will, the regent, Philippe d'Orléans, restored the power of prior remonstrance. Although official private communications between magistrates and the monarch, remonstrances during the eighteenth century began to be printed and sold publicly. Accordingly, they became the main vehicle for expressing and fomenting opposition to royal policies,

Session of the Parlement of Paris. *Lit de justice* (formal appearance of the king before the parlement) marking the coming of age of Louis XV, 22 February 1723. Painting by Nicolas Lancret. (Musée du Louvre, Paris/Scala/Art Resource, NY.)

and the king increasingly felt compelled to reply to them by printing the texts of proceedings taken to override them. In extreme cases, magistrates were prepared to push opposition to the point of judicial strikes, even mass resignations. The king would reply by exiling them or transferring their sittings to uncongenial little towns far from their homes. It was difficult, however, for the government to act more effectively because of the tenure that magistrates enjoyed through ownership of their offices. Under the system of venality, generalized throughout the judiciary since the sixteenth century, offices could be bought, sold, or inherited. They could be abolished only if the king reimbursed their value to the holders. It was therefore no coincidence that the climactic confrontation between the king and the parlements, under the chancellorship of René-Nicolas de Maupeou from 1771 to 1774, was accompanied by the abolition of venality in those courts and by a scheme for the liquidation of offices.

Patterns and Themes of Opposition. From 1715 to the early 1730s, the government and the Parlement of Paris clashed repeatedly over financial issues—but, above all, over the determination of ministers to enforce the 1713 bull *Unigenitus*, a blanket condemnation of Jansenism issued by the pope at Louis XIV's request [*see* Jansenism]. The magistrates' objection to *Unigenitus* was largely jurisdictional, but a small group of Jansenists became adept at manipulating their colleagues' sense of French legal traditions—to obstruct both episcopal and governmental attempts to impose the bull as a law of church and state. Eventually the parlement's resistance was overcome, but conflict was renewed in the 1740s over attempts by a new generation of bishops to stamp out residual Jansenism by demanding confession notes from the dying, attesting acceptance of *Unigenitus*. Appeals to the parlement, on grounds of abuse of episcopal jurisdiction, brought a decade of bitter clashes, which in 1753 led to its replacement by an interim "royal chamber." By then, opposition had spread to the provincial parlements, as the cost of midcentury wars forced the king to seek additional revenues through new taxes. Claims then began to be heard that the parlements were coeval with the monarchy, and that they had the right and duty to convey to the king the grievances of his otherwise voiceless subjects. By the 1760s, some were arguing that the various courts were merely subdivisions, or classes, of a single parlement. From 1762 to 1764, most of the provincial parlements followed the lead of Paris in expelling the Jesuits (Society of Jesus) from French jurisdiction—the ultimate triumph for the judicial Jansenists. Provincial parlements began to obstruct the administration of intendants and governors and, in the late 1760s, such a clash in Brittany developed into a confrontation between Louis XV and the entire judiciary.

In 1771, advised by a new chancellor, Maupeou, the king resolved on a complete remodeling of the parlements. Exploiting divisions within each court behind their appearances of solidarity, Maupeou dismissed hundreds of more obdurate magistrates while wooing others. He abolished the venality of their offices and judicial fees and, thereby, managed to reduce the parlements to relative silence and compliance for the last three years of Louis XV's reign. There was no disguising that this was a constitutional crisis of the first magnitude, however, and these years were marked by a bitter propaganda war. While government supporters condemned the old magistracy as dangerous rebels against divinely ordained authority, self-styled patriots denounced the king and his ministers as despots, with no respect for law; some called for a meeting of the long-defunct national representative assembly, the Estates-General.

In 1774, on his accession, Louis XVI felt obliged to restore confidence by recalling the old parlements and dismissing Maupeou. Apart from a burst of hostility to the reforms of Anne-Robert-Jacques Turgot in 1776, the Paris parlement returned, chastened. Several provincial courts, however, were torn for years by internal recriminations over choices made under Maupeou, and there were further spectacular clashes with royal intendants, whose authority was increasingly denounced as despotism. In 1787, when the assembly of notables failed to endorse ministerial plans for wholesale fiscal and institutional reform and was dismissed, it called for a meeting of the Estates-General and the parlements took up that call. Despite exiles, they refused for months to transact public business. In May 1788, the Brienne-Lamoignon ministry attempted to muzzle them once again, vesting the power of registration and remonstrance in a single plenary court. The collapse of the ministry in August brought about the abandonment of those plans, along with agreement that the Estates-General would meet in 1789. Failed attempts by the parlement of Paris to preordain the form of the Estates, however, marked the beginning of a rapid political decline, in which the magistrates' claim to speak for the nation passed to its elected representatives. Before the end of 1789, the courts were put into perpetual vacation, pending their replacement the next year by a new judicial system.

A Social and Cultural Elite. Some twelve hundred magistrates of the parlements, and their families, were the core of the so-called nobility of the robe, ennobled by the offices that they or their ancestors had bought. Although looked down upon by the great nobles of the royal court at Versailles, and both envied and despised by poor provincial nobles of longer lineage, the metropolitan-robe nobility provided most of the senior personnel of government and administration throughout the seventeenth and eighteenth centuries. Outside Paris, membership of the self-styled senates represented the summit of social aspiration. Exclusive and endogamous, some provincial parlements even voted formally not to admit candidates

of recent extraction. But the social hegemony of robe nobles in provincial capitals was also based on extensive wealth, and the family networks forged before the French Revolution often resurfaced afterward at the heart of provincial notability. Such an educated legal milieu was equally a source of cultural leadership. Magistrates of the sovereign courts were prominent in the foundation and the subsequent activity of provincial academies; they occupied places of honor, even if relatively thinly represented, in other literary and philanthropic societies, as well as in Masonic lodges [*see* Freemasonry]. The parlement of Bordeaux produced Montesquieu, one of the most influential writers of the Enlightenment, and his thought was steeped in his experience on the bench; other such prominent literary and scientific figures included Charles de Brosses and Louis Bernard Guyton de Morveau (Dijon), Michel Joseph Antoine Servan (Grenoble), Louis-René de Caradeuc de La Chalotais (Rennes), Jean Pierre François Ripert de Monclar (Aix), Charles-Marguerite-Jean-Baptiste Dupaty (Bordeaux), Antoine-Louis Séguier and Jean-Baptiste Gaspard Bochard de Saron (Paris), and Chrétien-Guillaume de Lamoignon de Malesherbes (*cour des aides* of Paris).

An Ambiguous Reputation. Nevertheless the parlements and their members were seldom perceived as leaders of the Enlightenment. Magistrates who participated actively in intellectual life were always in the minority, and those who did were often viewed suspiciously by colleagues. The sovereign courts took an active part in the suppression of works considered by them as offensive to religion and morals, including at one point the *Encyclopédie* (1759) and later Pierre François Boncerf's *Les inconvénients des droits féodaux* (1776). Such action was often counterproductive: a work condemned by a parlement to be torn and burned could not have received better publicity. Although the philosophes applauded the expulsion of the Jesuits in the 1760s, they were at pains to claim the credit for themselves (as d'Alembert did in a pamphlet on the subject), in order to take it from the Jansenist magistrates, whose intolerance they feared. Voltaire, notoriously, hated the parlements cordially. He blamed the bigotry of that of Toulouse for the execution of the Protestant Jean Calas in 1762 and that of Paris for the death of the freethinking chevalier de La Barre in 1766. He thought that venality of office and judicial fees were a scandal, and he was a vocal supporter of Maupeou's reforms in 1771. Other philosophes were more hesitant. They suspected Maupeou of wishing to restore the Jesuits, and they thought his methods despotic. Denis Diderot believed that the parlements were the only realistic defenders of French liberties and that the tenure magistrates enjoyed through venality was a necessary evil. Turgot, whom the parlements were to attack so mercilessly, had reluctantly advised their recall in 1774 as a way of restoring public confidence.

In any case, it was possible to manipulate parlementary procedures to promote reform. Skillful use of printed legal briefs (which were not subject to censorship) could turn carefully chosen appeals into causes célèbres that engaged public opinion in supporting such aspirations as religious tolerance and criminal-law reform. Criminal trials could also have unpredictable consequences, as in 1786 when the prosecution of fraudsters in the diamond necklace affair cast discredit on the tastes and lifestyle of the queen and the royal court at Versailles. Meanwhile, the language of remonstrances became crucial in familiarizing the public with ideas of fundamental law, national rights, patriotism—and the presumed opposite of all these, despotism. In the 1770s and 1780s, the parlements led the call for more representative institutions (at the provincial level, at least), the limitations of their own power having been exposed by Maupeou. Until 1787, their calls for the Estates-General were more hesitant and sporadic; by the end of 1788, their identification with the "forms of 1614" for the Estates had aligned them with the forces of aristocratic conservatism. The elections of 1789 provoked resentments and jealousies among other nobles toward the magistracy, and relatively few members of the parlements were elected. Then, early in the Revolution, sporadic attempts to intervene in public affairs merely confirmed the parlements' reactionary reputation. While willingly acknowledging the part that parlements had played in preparing the Revolution of 1789, the National Assembly soon regarded them as an obstacle to its further work, and it abolished them with relief in September 1790.

[*See also* Aristocracy, *subentry on* Cultural Contributions; *and* France.]

BIBLIOGRAPHY

Bluche, François. *Les magistrats du Parlement de Paris au xviiie siècle, 1715–1771.* Paris, 1960. Classic social analysis.
Campbell, Peter Robert. *Power and Politics in Old Regime France, 1720–1745.* London, 1996. Thoughtful and wide-ranging, with relevance for the whole century.
Doyle, William. *The Parlement of Bordeaux and the End of the Old Regime, 1771–1790.* London, 1974. Combines socioeconomic analysis with political narrative.
Doyle, William. "The Parlements." In *The French Revolution and the Creation of Modern Political Culture,* vol. 1: *The Political Culture of the Old Regime,* edited by Keith Michael Baker, pp. 157–168. Oxford, 1987. A convenient overview of the power of the Parlements.
Echeverria, Durand. *The Maupeou Revolution: A Study in the History of Libertarianism. France, 1770–1774.* Baton Rouge, La., 1985. The best study of the ideological ferment aroused by the policies of Maupeou.
Félix, Joël. *Les magistrats du Parlement de Paris, 1771–1790.* Paris, 1991. More than the biographical dictionary it appears at first sight to be.
Maza, Sarah. *Private Lives and Public Affairs: The Causes Célèbres of Pre-Revolutionary France.* Berkeley, Calif., 1993. A brilliant analysis of a major cultural phenomenon.
Register, John. *Louis XV and the Parlement of Paris, 1737–1755.* Cambridge, 1995.
Stone, Bailey. *The French Parlements and the Crisis of the Old Regime.* Chapel Hill, N.C., 1986.
Swann, Julian. *Politics and the Parlement of Paris under Louis XV, 1754–1774.* Cambridge, 1995. More usefully analytical than Register (1995).
Van Kley, Dale. *The Jansenists and the Expulsion of the Jesuits from France, 1757–1765.* New Haven, Conn., 1975. A study that completely renewed its subject when it appeared.

WILLIAM DOYLE

PARTIES. *See* Political Philosophy.

PASSION. According to a psychological model widely accepted for most of the eighteenth century, the passions and affections supply the motives for all human behavior. Reason, which had held pride of place in Plato and Christian Platonism as an organ of morality capable of influencing the will, was demoted to instrumentality. The characterization of passion as the spring of action, and of reason as passion's tool, may be found in the writings of philosophers, essayists, and poets from Thomas Hobbes, La Rochefoucauld, and John Wilmot, earl of Rochester, to Bernard Le Bovier de Fontenelle, Bernard Mandeville, and Joseph Addison. Addison wrote influentially in the *Spectator* (no. 408, 1712): "The Actions of Men follow their Passions as naturally as Light does Heat, or as any other Effect flows from its Cause; Reason must be employed in adjusting the Passions, but they must ever remain the Principles of Action. . . . the Passions . . . are to the Mind as the Winds to a Ship, they only can move it, and they too often destroy it; if fair and gentle, they guide it into the Harbour, if contrary and furious, they overset it in the Waves." By the time of *An Essay on Man* (1733–1734), Alexander Pope did no more than elegantly express a common thought: "On life's grand ocean diversely we sail, / Reason the card [mariner's chart], but Passion is the gale."

David Hume pronounced in *A Treatise of Human Nature* (1739–1740), the century's most systematic analysis of the passions' role in social life, "Reason is, and ought only be, the slave of the passions, and can never pretend to any other office than to serve and obey them." A wide variety of Protestants and Jansenist Catholics might have agreed that reason is, among fallen mankind, the slave of the passions; Pierre Bayle noted that, among the pagan philosophers, Cicero had also recognized "the servitude of the soul under the empire of the passions" (*Critical and Historical Dictionary* [1697], article "Ovid," note H).

However, Hume's innovative assertion that reason *ought to be* a slave runs afoul of Protestant orthodoxy. Hume's own ethics is resolutely secular, but a belief in the benign efficacy of the passions need not be. Pope, for example, elaborated a providential theory whereby God assigns different "ruling Passions" to different individuals in order to assure a harmonious division of labor in society; some will aspire to political power, some to learning, some to wealth, and so forth.

Yet if passions were the acknowledged masters of humanity, reason retained its regulatory role: as David Fate Norton argues of Hume's moral theory, reason acts like an enlightened Greek slave to an educable Roman master. Most major British philosophers, moralists, and novelists active before the French Revolution (Francis Hutcheson, Joseph Butler, Henry Fielding, Samuel Johnson, Laurence Sterne, Adam Smith) concurred that the passions ought to be regulated by practical reason for the good of both the individual and his or her community. British writings on the passions tend to be comedic in

The Kiss. "St-Preux and Julie Embracing," illustration that Jean-Michel Moreau the Younger proposed for Jean-Jacques Rousseau's *La nouvelle Héloïse*. Rousseau rejected the illustration as too explicit. From a suite of plates for an edition of Rousseau's works printed at Brussels, 1774–1783. (Prints and Photographs Division, Library of Congress.)

the sense of showing that, when calmly and reflectively controlled, the passions may lead to happiness. The situation in France, by contrast, was more complex. Traditional erotic tragedy, which paints the passions as incorrigible, flourished in novels by the abbé Prévost, the marquise de Tencin, and Samuel Richardson (France's favorite English novelist); however, in *La nouvelle Héloïse*, Jean-Jacques Rousseau explored the extent to which eros might be rationally managed. In France, the passions thought to move the human machine—especially self-love, eros, and the love of glory—could also be analyzed without explicit regard to their moral purpose, whether in the science of man (Julien Offray de La Mettrie) or in the libertine novel (Crébillon fils, Pierre-Antoine Choderlos de Laclos).

Limiting our purview to moral philosophy, however, we find on both sides of the Channel the belief that the passions could supply the foundation for a universally shared and universally applicable morality. Jean-Jacques Rousseau, in Book IV of *Émile*, theorized the positive social roles of pity and compassion. Francis Hutcheson and Hume constructed systematic ethics on the bedrock of sympathy and the "calm desire" of benevolence. As Hutcheson first argued in his *Inquiry into the Original of Our Ideas of Beauty and Virtue* (1725)—a work indebted to the moral intuitionism of Anthony Ashley Cooper, third earl of Shaftesbury—we approve the actions of a benevolent agent through an internal moral sense in the same way that we perceive the secondary qualities of objects through our external senses (sight, taste, smell, and sound). At a fundamental level, then, the statements "I approve/I disapprove of this" mean "this is good" or "this is bad." This "emotivist" moral standard ran up against the challenge, late in the eighteenth century, of characters who naturally approved conduct alien or repugnant to most philosophes—for example, the title character of Denis Diderot's *Le neveu de Rameau* and the Tahitian Orou in his *Supplément au Voyage de Bougainville*; or, a fortiori, Dolmance in the marquis de Sade's *La philosophie dans le boudoir*.

Hutcheson maintained that the natural virtue of benevolence, supplemented by the natural religious belief in a benevolent deity, was sufficient for life in society. Subsequent moral philosophy, however, detected and sought to remedy the shortcomings of Hutcheson's position, and in so doing engaged more complexly with the motivating passions of human nature. Joseph Butler argued, in the dissertation "Of the Nature of Virtue" (appended to his *Analogy of Religion*, 1736), that general benevolence cannot account for, and may often conflict with, our duty to adhere to the general rules of justice. The rules of distributive and retributive justice, although ultimately beneficial to mankind, need not immediately contribute to the general happiness: sometimes, for example, a poor man may have to be shackled for stealing coins from the pocket of a man too rich to notice the loss.

Prompted by Butler, Hume maintained that society requires the "artificial virtue" of justice. This virtue, unlike benevolence, is not based immediately on a feeling of approval or disapproval, but rather on a rational calculation that adhering to the rules of justice ultimately serves one's self-interest. Individuals, who for Hume are driven primarily by the "avidity of acquiring goods," determine "upon the least reflection" that their passion for gain is better satisfied by adhering to the general rules necessary to civil society than "by running into the solitary and forlorn condition, which must follow upon violence and an universal license." Subsequent to their induction into civil society, individuals come to see justice not simply as a practical necessity but, through sympathy with what other individuals feel, as a moral good. We morally approve the rules of justice because we sympathetically partake of the uneasiness of those who suffer from injustice: "Thus self-interest is the original motive to the *establishment* of justice; but a sympathy with public interest is the source of the *moral approbation*, which attends that virtue."

In Hume's account, then, justice and civil society—before they are morally sanctioned through sympathy—originate in the calm passion of self-interest (or the "avidity of acquiring goods") and its prevalence against potentially destructive passions of human nature such as rapacity, anger, and lust for power. As Albert O. Hirschman has argued, this triumph of interest over less pacific passions figures in the enlightened narratives of civil society offered by Charles-Louis de Secondat Montesquieu, Johnson, Claude-Adrien Helvétius, William Robertson, Paul-Henri Thiry d'Holbach, *The Federalist*, and above all Adam Smith. The passion of self-interest becomes a virtue when it seeks its fulfillment not through rapine or any extraordinary form of domination over others, but through its own regulation by justice and positive law—and through the growing opportunities afforded in the eighteenth century by commerce and modern finance.

Indeed, the economic realities of an increasingly commercial society, along with the philosophic endorsement of commerce for its ideal ability to polish the manners and refine the passions, lie behind the rehabilitation of the passions that had been designated deadly sins in the feudal era: pride, anger, envy, sloth, avarice, gluttony, and lust. As we have seen, Enlightenment philosophers sought to vindicate "pride" (or self-love, self-interest) by showing it to be not only compatible with but causally related to sociability. (Rousseau criticized this optimistic Enlightenment assessment of self-love with his notion of *amour-propre*, introduced in his *Discours sur l'origine et les fondements de l'inégalité* [Discourse on the Origin of Inequality]; for Rousseau, the pride an individual feels in society—at least in political society as it has typically been constituted—is a corrupt passion predicated on self-comparison with others and the consequent desire to dominate others.) The vice of avarice becomes in Enlightenment philosophy the beneficial "love of gain" that lies at the very root of civil society. Gluttony, refined to an epicurism of the palate, receives its finest paean in Anthelme Brillat-Savarin's *Physiologie du goût* (Physiology of Taste, 1825), but it may also be sanctioned in the blanket approval of commercial "luxury" found in Mandeville, Hume, Voltaire, and Adam Smith. The vice of envy becomes the virtue of emulation, which is widely accorded a crucial role in the rise and progress of all arts and sciences; as Pope put it in *An Essay on Man*, "*Envy*, to which th'ignoble mind's a slave, / Is *emulation* in the learned and the brave." Although emulation received praise as the spur to achievement, retardant sloth received little criticism aside from perennial Protestant satires on the idleness of monks; Johnson included in his great *Dictionary* "abbey-lubber," defined as "a slothful loiterer in a religious house." Translated into "indolence," the one-time vice received a nod from Hume, who premised every person's need to divide his or her time among industry, pleasure, and indolence ("Of Refinement in the Arts"; cf. *Treatise* 1.4.7). For Pope, sloth refined becomes nothing less than the philosophic temperament: "See anger, zeal and fortitude supply; / Ev'n av'rice, prudence; sloth, philosophy." Little good can come of cruel or excessive anger, and the philosophers of a polite and commercial Europe had perhaps more reason to reject this vice than had those of an earlier order based on Christian zeal and military fortitude. Nevertheless, a number of figures (including Pope, Butler, Hutcheson, and Hume) held with Aristotle that anger is, in certain instances and to a proper degree, a valuable passion; the want of it, as Hume observed, "may even be a proof of weakness and imbecility." Finally, of sexual desire, Pope speaks for his age: "Lust, thro' some certain strainers well refin'd, / Is gentle love, and charms all womankind."

In sum, the Enlightenment philosopher envisioned an orderly modern world set in motion by a host of refined passions but centered on enlightened self-interest, natural benevolence, and the ability to feel with others. This vision was partially descriptive of, but largely prescriptive for, the commercially linked civil societies of the modern Atlantic world. By contrast, Enlightenment historiography tended to depict past ages as more or less driven by violent and unsettling emotions, principally those of hope and fear. The Epicurean theory that placed fear at the origin and root of religion was revived and elaborated—at least with regard to gentile religion—by Bayle, Mandeville, Fontenelle, Giambattista Vico, and Hume. The religious temperament, Hume contended in "Of Superstition and

Enthusiasm," oscillates between the poles of fear, which gives rise to superstition, and excessive hope and pride, which give rise to enthusiasm or fanaticism.

Although Enlightenment thinkers prophesied the withering away of violent or primordial passions from civil society, after 1750 they were increasingly pleased to find them in art. Vico, Condillac, and Rousseau agreed that speech arose so that humans might communicate passions, and it was thus poetic (metaphors and metonymies being the language of the passions) before becoming literal in a more developed stage of civilization. Concurrently with this conjectural history of language there arose an aesthetic preference for the passionate, oral poetry of past ages—or of the "folk"—over the urbane productions of modernity, hence the international vogue of *Ossian* and the popularity of folk ballads and Gothic imitations in Britain and Germany. The aesthetics of the sublime was fueled by this fascination with the poetic power of antiquity, and it revived the putatively antique passion of fear; Edmund Burke argued in his *Philosophical Enquiry...into the Sublime and Beautiful* (1757) that our delight in the sublime derives from "the passions of self-preservation," and that these are far stronger than the "passions of society" that underlie our response to the beautiful.

Immanuel Kant largely followed Burke in his own early treatise on the sublime and beautiful (1764), but in his mature writings of the 1780s he famously rejected the entire moral psychology of his century. For Kant, practical reason is capable of motivating behavior independently of the passions; indeed, ethical conduct occurs only when the individual acts from rational duty and not from inclination. In his uncompromising appeal to reason, Kant responded to—and so underscored the centrality of—the appeal to and of the passions in moral and literary writings of the Enlightenment.

[*See also* Human Nature *and* Moral Philosophy.]

BIBLIOGRAPHY

Calhoun, Cheshire, and Robert C. Solomon, eds. *What Is an Emotion? Classic Readings in Philosophical Psychology.* New York, 1984. The Introduction provides a good overview of philosophical writings on the passions; Part I contains excerpts from Aristotle, Descartes, Spinoza, and Hume.

Hirschman, Albert O. *The Passions and the Interests: Political Arguments for Capitalism before Its Triumph.* Princeton, N.J., 1977. A seminal study of the moral and social theory of the Enlightenment.

Hume, David. *A Treatise of Human Nature.* Edited by L. A. Selby-Bigge, revised by P. H. Nidditch. Oxford, 1978.

Hutcheson, Francis. *On the Nature and Conduct of the Passions and Affections with Illustrations on the Moral Sense.* Edited by Andrew Ward. Manchester, 1999.

Jones, Peter. *Hume's Sentiments: Their Ciceronian and French Contexts.* Edinburgh, 1982.

MacIntyre, Alasdair. *After Virtue: A Study in Moral Theory.* 2d ed. Notre Dame, Ind., 1984. Chapters 2–5 constitute an Aristotelian critique of the Enlightenment project of justifying morality; special attention is paid to Hume, Diderot, and Kant.

Mandeville, Bernard. *The Fable of the Bees: or, Private Vices, Publick Benefits.* Edited by F. B. Kaye. 2 vols. Oxford, 1924. Kaye's extensive Introduction surveys the motivational psychology of the passions as it develops from the seventeenth century to the late eighteenth in France and England.

Manuel, Frank. *The Eighteenth Century Confronts the Gods.* Cambridge, Mass., 1959. Traces the neoclassical revival of naturalistic theories of religion, with special emphasis on the Epicurean fear theory.

Meyer, Michel. *Philosophy and the Passions: Towards a History of Human Nature.* Translated by Robert F. Barsky. University Park, Pa., 2000. English translation of *Le Philosophe et les passions: Esquisse d'une histoire de la nature humaine*, first published in 1991. A critical engagement with theories of passion from Plato to Nietzsche; substantial sections are devoted to Descartes and Kant.

Norton, David Fate. *David Hume: Common-Sense Moralist, Sceptical Metaphysician.* Princeton, N.J., 1982.

Pocock, J. G. A. *The Machiavellian Moment: Florentine Political Thought and the Atlantic Republican Tradition.* Princeton, N.J., 1975. Of particular interest is Chapter 14, "The Eighteenth-Century Debate: Virtue, Passion, Commerce."

Pope, Alexander. *Poetry and Prose.* Edited by Aubrey Williams. Boston, 1969.

Potkay, Adam. *The Fate of Eloquence in the Age of Hume.* Ithaca, N.Y., 1994. Chapter 4 concerns the role of the passions in Enlightenment historiography, focusing on Hume's *Natural History of Religion*.

Potkay, Adam. *The Passion for Happiness: Samuel Johnson and David Hume.* Ithaca, N.Y., 2000.

Taylor, Charles. *Sources of the Self: The Making of the Modern Identity.* Cambridge, Mass., 1989. Chapters 8–11, 15, and 19 trace the shift in philosophy from substantive to procedural notions of reason, and the corresponding increase in attention paid to the passions.

ADAM POTKAY

PATRONAGE. The evolution of cultural patronage in the age of Enlightenment reflects the gradual erosion of the older structures of political and ecclesiastical power and the emergence of new educated elites. While traditional forms of court patronage remained conspicuous in absolutist regimes such as Spain, Russia, and some German states, new methods of what might be called "diluted" patronage emerged in those nations where the urban middle classes evinced strong interest in the possession of works of art and the control of their production—Great Britain and France being the most striking examples. The relations between patrons and artists were consequently very diverse in this transitional period. Royal and ecclesiastical patrons still considered art to be just a means of enhancing their power or influence and considered artists basically as mouth-pieces, while the "bourgeois" patrons were more attracted to the intrinsic aesthetic value of works of art, even if they also appreciated them as status symbols.

Royal and Ecclesiastical Patrons. If absolutist regimes and the Roman Catholic Church were both tempted to use the arts for purposes of self-advertisement, they did it rather differently. Monarchs were above all concerned with their self-image, and were often as eager to make a show of their personal taste as to encourage straightforward monarchist propaganda. Thus Augustus II, elector of Saxony and king of Poland, was proud of turning Dresden into a sort of architectural manifesto of the Rococo, while his son Augustus III formed there an astonishing art gallery that displayed both ancient and contemporary paintings. The model of the enlightened despot could even involve patronage of radical writers. For example, Catherine II of Russia and Frederick the Great of Prussia befriended and pensioned some of the French philosophes, and the empress even invited Denis Diderot to have the *Encyclopédie* printed in Russia.

The existence of a monarchy in a given country, however, did not necessarily mean that royalty was the most enthusiastic patron of the arts. In France, after the golden age of royal patronage under Louis XIV, his successors failed to encourage the most innovative artists with any consistency. Versailles only saw isolated embellishments such as Jacques-Ange Gabriel's Opera House and the Petit Trianon. Although Madame de Pompadour and her brother Marigny evinced a sincere interest in the arts, court favor mostly meant a few commissions for already famous painters like François Boucher, Jean-Baptiste-Siméon Chardin, and Jean-Honoré Fragonard. During the ancien régime the really influential French patrons of painting were, rather, Parisian bankers, manufacturers, and civil servants. For example, Pierre Crozat, who vied with Jean de Julienne as a patron of Antonie Watteau, consistently supported many of the greatest painters of the early eighteenth century. After the 1789 Revolution, the French government had little time to spare for the arts, and it was Napoleon Bonaparte who gave back to the state a prominent role in sponsoring monumental building, the decorative arts, and the formation of national collections.

In Britain, on the other hand, the patronage of artists was very largely the affair of the landed aristocracy, and was not purely metropolitan. Richard Boyle, third earl of Burlington, is the classic type of the eclectic and cultured landowner, who supported musicians like George Frideric Handel, and writers like Alexander Pope and John Gay, as well as architects like William Kent. The considerable demand for prestigious country houses in Britain offered many opportunities to aspiring architects and landscape gardeners, sculptors, and cabinet-makers throughout the country. The skillful combination of architectural design and landscaping is probably the most attractive achievement of such comprehensive patronage.

The artistic role played by churches was certainly more conservative than that of courts or aristocracies. On the Continent the main tendency of the Roman Catholic Church in its patronage was to make art subservient to the defense and illustration of the faith. In the early part of the century, a number of Italian cardinals such as Pietro Ottoboni in Rome had indeed tried to maintain the old tradition of individual patronage of musicians and painters by great prelates. In central Europe, particularly Austria, Bohemia, and Bavaria, however, the Roman Catholic Church sponsored the building of richly decorated late Baroque and Rococo churches and monasteries, enabling the spirit of the Counter-Reformation to survive well into the age of Enlightenment. The Dietzenhofers, the Asam brothers, and Balthasar Neumann thus designed a series of churches in which sculptures and frescoes were combined with architectural form to create spectacular ecclesiastical scenographies. In Venice, the rich Carmelite, Dominican, and Oratorian orders patronized the most famous painters of the city, such as Giovanni Battista Tiepolo and Giovanni Battista Piazzetta, who produced for them some of their best frescoes and altarpieces. Yet Rome itself, although the center of Roman Catholicism, now failed to attract the more gifted painters of the day, who often preferred to try their luck elsewhere in Europe. As for the Protestant churches of northern Europe, with their traditional hostility to religious iconography, they only sponsored a minimal program of church reconstruction.

Enlightenment patronage, however, should not be assessed in purely national or even religious terms. One of its most stimulating developments was in fact its international dimension. The widespread habit of educational travel across Europe, and particularly Italy, allowed both patrons and artists an increased knowledge of foreign schools and styles. This dual benefit was possible because on their Grand Tours the young British, German, French, and Russian noblemen were often flanked by artists expected to produce drawings of the countries visited. For example, in 1773, Fragonard discovered Italy in the wake of Bergeret de Grancourt. Three years later, John Robert Cozens followed suit, in company with Richard Payne Knight. Traveling connoisseurs thus had a good opportunity to buy foreign paintings, and to become acquainted with local brokers who could later supply them with works by famous artists. Consul Smith, an Englishman who resided some sixty years in Venice, managed to "export" Canalettos by the dozen. Thus a European network of collectors, artists, and agents was gradually formed, which powerfully contributed to the exchange of information on new styles in art and architecture. The rapid spread of neoclassicism in European architecture from the 1760s, for example, would not have been possible without the constant flow of visitors in and out of Rome. The existence of such a network, however, also offered considerable opportunities of employment to artists willing to leave their native country for long periods: some of the more distant outposts of European culture, such as Saint Petersburg or Madrid, could thus follow the latest artistic fashions. For example, the Spanish court employed expatriate painters like the Venetian Tiepolo and the German Anton Raphael Mengs for many years, while Catherine II had new palaces designed by foreign architects such as the Italian Quarenghi and the Scott Cameron.

Another novelty of eighteenth-century patronage was the increasing involvement of women. By hosting parties, or having literary assemblies on a regular basis, women of the aristocracy or upper bourgeoisie could introduce artists and writers to the elites of society, and even make and unmake reputations. It was above all in Paris that literary salons flourished throughout the century. Voltaire long enjoyed the protection of the duchesse du Maine, while the more distinctly intellectual salons of Madame Geoffrin and Mademoiselle de Lespinasse welcomed the major French philosophes and contributed to the success of their ideas.

"Bourgeois" Patrons. The emergence of a cultured and prosperous middle class in many European cities also led to the gradual formation of a new public for the fine arts as well as for music and literature. Its approach to works of art was of course very different from that of traditional patrons. Musical performances, literary works, and engravings were now viewed to some extent as consumer goods and status symbols, rather than as the natural outcome of a personal acquaintance with an artist. Indeed, the new public often had no personal knowledge of the artists themselves. Arnold Hauser (1951) adequately described this crucial shift in the position of artists when he observed that in courtly and aristocratic societies, artists' reputations depended on the standing of their patrons. However, in an age of liberalism and emerging capitalism, the freer that artists were from personal ties, and the more successful in their impersonal dealings with other people, the greater was the esteem they enjoyed.

Such a shift in the nature of patronage first meant that the transaction between the artists or writers and their new, faceless public, was bound to become largely commercialized, at least in some artistic fields. While painters and architects still mainly produced pictures or buildings for a single patron, musicians and writers and engravers now worked for a vast, anonymous public, whose financial contribution reached them mostly via commercial channels. The patron, then, had become a mere client. Consequently writers were forced to bargain with bookseller-publishers for a good price, instead of hoping for the favor of a nobleman, as Samuel Johnson unwisely did when he tried to attract Lord Chesterfield's attention to his great *Dictionary of the English Language* (1755). In many countries, writers began the long struggle to obtain the legal "copyright" that alone could secure income from their literary property. They also were forced to look for subscribers if their books were unusually expensive to produce. This new position was felt to be humiliating by some writers, such as Jonathan Swift, who regretted the practical disappearance of the patronage of writers by the great and good. Music, similarly, went public. While private musical clubs for amateur performance continued to exist, public concerts began to be organized from the 1750s in specially designed concert rooms. Paris had its "Concert Spirituel," London had its Bach-Abel concert season. Even the aristocratic opera was often financed by subscription.

As a result, the less socially exclusive enjoyment of art came to rely more on aesthetic than on personal considerations. The practical disappearance of the single aristocratic patron in music and literature implied that collective criteria of quality had to be defined to replace the patron's own pronouncements. This was increasingly done by critics, who published numerous essays on painting, architecture, sculpture, and music, and also by the academies set up in the northern countries in imitation of the older Italian and French ones. Aesthetic theory itself developed, providing reasoned arguments in favor of such or such a style. The general intellectualization of artistic production, in turn, enhanced the social status of artists and writers, who now could hope to acquire professional status in society and to ignore the subservience formerly demanded by traditional patrons.

[*See also* Aesthetics; Architecture; Aristocracy, *subentry on* Cultural Contributions; Bourgeoisie; Grand Tour; Literary and Intellectual Property; Men and Women of Letters; Painting; Print Culture; Publishing; *and* Royal Courts and Dynasties.]

BIBLIOGRAPHY

Gay, Peter. "Patrons and Publics." In *The Enlightenment: An Interpretation*, vol. 2, *The Science of Freedom*. London, 1970. A short overview of the European scene.

Haskell, Francis. *Patrons and Painters: A Study in the Relations between Italian Art and Society in the Age of the Baroque*. London, 1963. An erudite study of cosmopolitan patronage in Italy.

Hauser, Arnold. *The Social History of Art: Rococo, Classicism, and Romanticism*. London, 1962. A major survey of the transformation of the patron into a client.

Hirschfeld, P. *Mäzene, die Rolle des Auftraggebers in der Kunst*. Munich, 1968. A historical sociology of patronage through the ages.

Korshin, Paul J. "Types of Eighteenth-Century Patronage." *Eighteenth-Century Studies* 7 (1973–1974), 453–473. A useful typology of patrons in the English-speaking world.

Pomian, Krzysztof. *Collectionneurs, amateurs, et curieux, Paris, Venise, 16e–18e siècle*. Paris, 1987. A sociology of European collecting.

Solkin, David. *Painting for Money: The Visual Arts and the Public Sphere in Eighteenth-Century England*. New Haven, Conn., and London, 1993. An inspiring reassessment of the artist's place in a commercial society.

Waller, Richard. "L'homme de lettres en France et en Angleterre." *Dix-huitième Siècle* 10 (1978), 229–252. A useful comparative perspective on the writer's status.

JACQUES CARRÉ

PEALE, CHARLES WILLSON (1741–1827), artist, inventor, and naturalist.

Peale studied painting with Benjamin West in London. In 1769, he returned to his native Maryland to paint portraits of the colonial elite—including, in 1772, our only likeness of George Washington before the Revolution, Peale's first of seven life portraits. In 1776, Peale moved to Philadelphia and became active in the city's radical republican circles. He served as a captain in the city militia, fighting at Trenton and Princeton. He continued to paint during the war, providing many of our only likenesses of prominent Revolutionary figures; he was also an agent for the confiscation of Loyalist estates and served one term in the Pennsylvania Assembly. In addition, he utilized his artistic and mechanical skills to orchestrate large political demonstrations in Philadelphia, such as the Benedict Arnold ceremony of punishment (1780), and the Arch of Triumph celebration of peace (1784).

After the Revolution, Peale converted his painting gallery into a museum of "Natural Curiosities," which he developed by the 1790s into the first scientifically organized museum of natural history in the United States. From this point onward, although he never stopped painting, Peale devoted most of his creative energies to expanding and improving his museum. In 1794, he moved it to larger quarters in the hall of the American Philosophical Society, the beginning of a fruitful relationship between two of early America's most important institutions of learning and scientific research. In 1801, with the Philosophical Society's aid, Peale was able to exhume and erect the first known skeleton of an American mastodon, an important event to paleontologists in America and Europe who were eager to demonstrate the existence of extinct animals. Peale's mastodon exhibit made his museum a popular attraction as well as a respected scientific institution. At its high point during the first two decades of the nineteenth century, it was housed in the Pennsylvania State House (Independence Hall). In 1816, the peak attendance year, more than 47,000 people may have visited the museum. Peale envisioned his museum as "a world in miniature," a republican school where all people could rationally view the wonders of creation.

Although the museum occupied Peale until his death, he was a man of varied interests, representing many facets of the American Enlightenment. He was a pivotal figure in the founding of the Pennsylvania Academy of Fine Arts and an active member of the American Philosophical Society. He was an inventor who held the first U.S. patent for bridge design, and also one for a portable vapor bath. He was a co-inventor of the polygraph, a pantograph device that copied letters; although not commercially successful, the device was used for decades by two of Peale's friends, Thomas Jefferson and Benjamin Henry Latrobe, providing later scholars with thousands of legible copies of their correspondence.

At age sixty-nine, Peale "retired" to a 104-acre farm outside Philadelphia, where he experimented with new methods of plowing and farm machinery. Among his inventions during those years was a milk cart balanced like a mariner's compass to avoid spillage, and a windmill designed to withstand sudden gusts and storms. As an octogenarian, he turned his artisanal talents to dentistry, becoming one of the first in the country successfully to manufacture false teeth out of porcelain. Peale was a man of great range and diversity in his practical accomplishments, a representative figure of the American Enlightenment.

[*See also* Philadelphia.]

BIBLIOGRAPHY

Appel, Toby A. "Science, Popular Culture and Profit: Peale's Philadelphia Museum." *Journal of the Society for Bibliography of Natural History* 9 (1980), 619–634. Demonstrates the coexistence in Peale's museum of private profit, scientific research, and popular education.

Brigham, David R. *Public Culture in the Early Republic: Charles Willson Peale's Museum and Its Audience*. Washington, D.C., 1995. Argues that the museum, notwithstanding Peale's expressed ideology, was not a republican or enlightened institution because its audience underrepresented women and effectively excluded minorities and poor people.

Hart, Sidney, and David C. Ward. "The Waning of the Enlightenment Ideal: Charles Willson Peale's Philadelphia Museum, 1790–1820." *Journal of the Early Republic* 8 (1988), 389–418. An analysis of Peale's museum as an expression of the American Enlightenment.

Miller, Lillian B., and David C. Ward, eds. *New Perspectives on Charles Willson Peale*. Pittsburgh, Pa., 1991. A diversified collection of reprinted and original articles on Peale's varied interests.

Miller, Lillian B., ed. *The Collected Papers of Charles Willson Peale and His Family*. Millwood, N.Y., 1980. A comprehensive microfiche edition of Peale family documents.

Miller, Lillian B., Sidney Hart, David C. Ward, and Toby A. Appel, eds. *The Selected Papers of Charles Willson Peale and His Family*. New Haven, Conn., 1983–. A modern documentary edition covering three generations of the Peale family in America.

Sellers, Charles Coleman. *Charles Willson Peale*. New York, 1969. The standard biography, exhaustively researched and solid.

Sellers, Charles Coleman. *Mr. Peale's Museum: Charles Willson Peale and the First Popular Museum of Natural Science and Art*. New York, 1980. A comprehensive narrative of Peale's Philadelphia museum, emphasizing its republican and Enlightenment character.

Sellers, Charles Coleman. *Portraits and Miniatures by Charles Willson Peale. Transactions of the American Philosophical Society* 42, pt. 1 (1952). A complete catalog to its date of Peale's portraits and miniatures; more recent information can be found in *The Selected Papers*.

Sellers, Charles Coleman. *Charles Willson Peale with Patron and Populace: A Supplement to Portraits and Miniatures by Charles Willson Peale. Transactions of the American Philosophical Society* 59, pt. 3 (1969). A supplement to the above.

SIDNEY HART

PERFECTIBILITY. *See* Human Nature *and* Moral Philosophy.

PEOPLE, THE. In "the people," the philosophers of the Enlightenment confronted a central dilemma. Their program for a world informed by critical intellect and unencumbered by undue reverence for the past had to grapple with the fact that most of the society they observed was beyond the reach of their arguments. Indeed, the author of the article "Philosophe" in the *Encyclopédie* essentially defined *the people* as the very opposite of that enlightened ideal:

> The *philosophe* forms his principles on the basis of an infinite number of individual observations. The people adopts the principle without thinking about the observations which produced it: it believes that the maxim exists, as it were, by itself; but the *philosophe* takes the maxim right to its source; he examines its origin, he recognizes its value, and uses it only as it suits him.

The growing confidence of those who participated in the Enlightenment exacerbated this sense of separation and difference. If Enlightenment depended on literacy, learning, and leisure—qualities notably increasing among some elites—then the abysmal ignorance of those without access to *Lumières* seemed dire.

This fundamental problem generated active discussion, richest in the decades after 1750. The debate about the question of the people was fullest among the French philosophes, but it had strong echoes throughout the European continent. The people appear in several guises in this discourse: as embodiments of unreason, as producers of essential products, and as victims of neglect. Any Enlightenment program, therefore, had to mediate among those categories. The social station of the people was best defined by the French term *gens des bras*—persons defined by their laboring "arms" rather than by thinking heads. This ignorance was associated with moral incapacity, since ignorance could lead to folly and brutishness. The literature of the Enlightenment offers numerous harsh and elitist judgments along these lines. The words that came to the philosophes' minds to describe the people often conjured up images of animality and even of madness. "The people will always be composed of brutes," Voltaire jotted in a notebook; some time later, he added "The people is between man and beast."

If these judgments were the final word of the Enlightenment, then we would simply be witnessing a new form of elitism. As advocates of a culture based on leisure, education, reflection, and critical intellect, the philosophes were defining what was not they, much as the "gentleman" of the Renaissance defined the manners and morals that set him apart. This way of talking, however, was the beginning of the conversation, not the end. Enlightenment thinkers were engaged intellectuals, and with that engagement came urgent questions about utility and justice, equally compelling standards of the Enlightenment.

In the philosophes' writings, we find widespread praise of the people as the true source of the wealth of nations, without much association of this dignity to the actual agents of that labor. As Helvétius explained in *De l'esprit* (1758), because everyone can do common work, then one honors the enterprise as a whole—productive labor in the fields and the shops—but not the individual laborer. Economic reformers across Europe—French Physiocrats, Spanish economic societies, German Generalists, or Scottish economists—sounded a vigorous call for recognition of the social value and dignity of manual work.

Such respect for the laborer's enterprise had a powerful effect. In an Enlightenment program stimulated by anger over the exploitation of the world by priests and aristocrats, there was created a space for empathy and concern. If the general wealth of society was the key to its health, then governments and philosophes simply could not ignore the plight of the people. As the public debate centered increasingly on questions about the generation of prosperity, leading philosophes and reformers entered into discussions of public responsibility in matters of religious belief, education, economic justice, and equality.

Religion. The role of religion in the Enlightenment program created special tensions with regard to the people, best embodied in the moments when the same Voltaire who sought to "crush the infamous thing" of traditional religion had no qualms about celebrating the Mass before his workers on his estates. On the one hand, the philosophes were essentially unanimous in their disdain for "superstitious" religion, espousing for the most part a highly rarified deism for themselves. On the other hand, several key figures were adamantly opposed to open assault on all traditional religious forms, for fear that the people, unable to reach moral positions through reason, needed the ritual and symbolism of faith to keep them within bounds.

The discussion was carried out largely within a long intellectual tradition, dating back to classical writers such as Cicero, that proposed a double truth in matters of religion: a refined, minimalist deism for the lettered elite, and for the people, a more elaborate official religion with symbols, rituals, and creeds, especially the prospect of reward and punishment in an afterlife. Turgot, for instance, speculated in 1753 on how the church might be tamed to the uses of a stable moral order without incurring the risks of fanaticism and superstition. Accepting the ideal of pure tolerance, Turgot posited a duty on the part of the state to prevent the confusion and indifference that neutrality toward religion might create. He feared the fierce conflicts and barbarous superstitions that a people left entirely to its own devices might nurture. To counter this threat, he advocated "an education for the people which would teach it probity; which would place before its eyes a summary of its duties in a form that is clear and easy to practice." Most men, he thought, were incapable of choosing their own religion in any rational manner; the state, therefore, should present them with a clear, established example. Turgot's state church would have its subsistence guaranteed by public lands supporting a number of *curés* sufficient to spread public instruction to villages and towns. He presumed that the majority religion would probably become the state-sponsored cult, but since the basis of choice should be utility, he acknowledged that a majority religion might be unsuitable. The state, he argued, should tolerate but not protect or sponsor a religion that encouraged celibacy, defied political authority, or maintained inflexible dogmas. "Would not natural religion," he concluded, "systematized and accompanied by a cult, prove more solid by defending less terrain?"

In his most cynical moments, Voltaire despaired of any change in popular superstition, but in preparing more detailed visions of a future popular religion, he clearly desired not to allow superstition free rein, even among the people. In a noteworthy addition to the article "War" in the *Dictionnaire philosophique*, Voltaire distinguished between "natural religion," which included a "just and vengeful God," and "artificial religion," with all the vicious trappings of superstition. He advocated for the people not the idolatry of oracles, soothsayers, and priests, but a natural religion much as it had been defined in the *Encyclopédie* and (supposedly) practiced by the guardians of pure religion in ancient times. Had Voltaire been the legislator, the religion of the masses would have been the natural religion of the Stoics, early Egyptian priests, and Chinese literati. All metaphysics being subject to debate, he argued, the legislator could choose on the basis of social utility. Voltaire found the natural religion of history suitably utilitarian in that it kept a bridle on the mob while avoiding the dangers of superstition.

Helvétius, in *De l'homme* (1773), anticipated the secular social religions of the Revolutionary and later periods. He proposed a religion of public utility with no beliefs or dogmas. The basic principles of the religion would be the sanctity of property, life, and liberty. Famous legislators and benefactors of humanity would comprise its calendar of saints. The distinction between magistrate and priest would disappear, as it had in Rome. Public ceremonies would honor the classical virtues of Humanity, Pride, and Fame. Through a religion of the public good, Helvétius hoped to exploit what he found valuable in the antique pagan deities, stripping the Roman religion of its deception and double standard and bringing its spirit into the open. The magistrate would prevent any move to turn the cult of fame or the public good into dogmatic belief. Helvétius recognized that the public might insist

that temples be raised to the various virtues of the Eternal One (the public good), but he charged his magistrates with the responsibility of preventing any further disintegration toward superstition.

The Enlightenment division between philosophes and the people was thus unstable in the matter of religion. The standards of social utility and intellectual truth were in conflict, and thinkers eventually searched for mediating positions predictive of the nineteenth-century fascination with "secular religions."

Education. The question of public education raised oddly parallel dilemmas as the debate was framed in Enlightenment parlance. If religion was useful for keeping moral order, it was just possible that ignorance was essential for keeping manual laborers at their dreary tasks. Voltaire characteristically stated this position in its harshest form:

> I understand by "people" the populace which has only its hands to live by. I doubt that this order of citizens will ever have the time or capacity to educate itself; they would die of hunger before becoming philosophes. It seems to me essential that there be ignorant wretches. If you were developing an estate like me, and if you had some plows, you would indeed be of my mind. It is not the day laborer who must be educated, it is the good bourgeois, it is the city dweller; this enterprise is formidable and great enough.
>
> (Letter to Damilaville, 1 April 1766)

The Enlightenment discussion did not rest with this position. Advanced by the economic reformers and more temperate French philosophes, the idea of some form of universal instruction became increasingly part of the Enlightenment program from the 1750s on. With their earnest concern for public utility, they thought it essential to propound a certain kind of practical enlightenment for the masses, focused on the most elementary forms of literacy and numeracy for the better propagation of enlightened agriculture and elements of morality. Hence, in 1768, the abbé Nicolas Baudeau insisted that "the clearest, most obligatory, most universal instruction is the first duty of government." Such notions became standard to the Enlightenment program of reform. These thinkers did not envision a massive reading public in a political sense; they assumed that workers would barely have time to learn the rudiments of practical instruction. Still, much ink was spilled on the mechanics of national education, above all on the potential role of the church.

The Physiocrats often saw the church's structure as an opportunity and advocated adding layers of more secular instruction alongside religious instruction—a secular catechism next to the religious. Others, predictably, were less sanguine. D'Holbach urged secular power to seize church properties and convert them to the purposes of secular public instruction. Among the Parisian atheists,

Diderot proved most moderate and accommodating in his educational program. Though he regarded Russia as a young nation in which the legislator could begin on a proper footing, he still had to deal with the official piety of Catherine II. He proposed, therefore, only a modified version of French public education for Russia. His plans called for a network of schools that would serve the villages and towns, providing elementary education and moral instruction from a combined religious, moral, and political catechism. Unlike the physiocratic plans, Diderot's system would provide absolute supervision by secular authority of the content of this instruction. To avoid the economic difficulties that forced many parents to keep their children away from the French primary schools, Diderot insisted that the schools must also provide bread for the people's children.

These concerns radiated to other reaches of the Enlightenment. The 1770s saw efforts by Frederick II (despite grave doubts), Maria Theresa, Karl Frederick of Baden, Maximilian III Joseph, and other central European monarchs to require instruction for their lowliest subjects. French agronomists and their Spanish, Italian, and German counterparts usually urged minimal literacy on the part of all peasants and looked for formal institutional ways to spread new agricultural learning. The economic societies of Spain made popular instruction, in both literacy and working techniques, a central part of their program. Once demands for public instruction had reached both the land of the Basques and the regions of the papal states, no one could doubt that instruction for the people had become a central aim of the mature Enlightenment.

All agreed that such instruction was to be very basic compared to the education of the elite, and very different in form—catechetical rather than critical. Constraints of social order would limit popular instruction to rote learning of received moral wisdom and modern agricultural and mechanical knowledge. None proposed a model leading to advancement. Indeed, some thought the multiplicity of secondary schools to be a hindrance rather than a help to a prosperous nation. Instruction was there to make the people more able in their station, not to help them escape it.

Economic Justice. The philosophes inherited a traditional language in which poverty bore connotations of social and spiritual discipline. Moreover, many writers of the seventeenth and eighteenth centuries had urged that it was necessary to hold wages at or below the poverty level to force the people to work harder. The philosophes, following the suggestion of physiocratic economics, rejected "the maxims of those cruel men who insist you must reduce the people to misery to force it to work"; instead, they believed that free trade, the abolition of guilds, and

Portrait of the People. "Man of the Village, or Born for Hardship," caricature by Nicolas Guerard. (Bibliothèque Nationale, Paris/Giraudon/Art Resource, NY.)

state-sponsored education could create enough free play in the system to ensure a willing work force. Thus, the twentieth "General Maxim" of Physiocracy, written by François Quesnay, stated *"That the ease of the lower classes should not be diminished*; because they will not be able to contribute enough to the consumption of those foodstuffs which can only be consumed in the nation, thus diminishing the reproduction and revenue of the nation." No one was more eloquent on this subject than Adam Smith, addressing in the *Wealth of Nations* (1776) the question of whether the improvement of circumstances of the "lower ranks" was advantageous to society:

Servants, laborers and workmen of different kinds, make up the far greater part of every great political society. But what improves the circumstances of the greater part can never be regarded as an inconveniency to the whole. No society can surely be flourishing and happy, of which the far greater part of the members are poor and miserable. It is but equity, besides, that they who feed, clothe and lodge the whole body of the people, should have such a share of the produce of their own labor as to be themselves tolerably well fed, clothed and lodged.

(I, chap. 8)

In this spirit, philosophes often vigorously pursued certain rudimentary programs for economic justice within the control of the state. They attacked feudal burdens, and they argued against the inverted pyramid caused by the tax exemption of so much wealth. The *Encyclopédie* offered several variations on the theme of equitable tax reform. In the article "Economy (Moral and Political)," Rousseau proposed a massive program of taxation on imports, exports, and luxuries. In addition to producing revenues based on the ability to pay, these taxes would allow control of luxury consumption. In the articles "Impost" and "Tax," Louis de Jaucourt offered a more balanced reform approach based on "distributive justice" in all taxation. To avoid exploitation by tax farmers, he insisted that taxes flow directly into state coffers. A progressive capitation, with rates increasing with income, would provide the bulk of revenues. A tax on luxuries would bring additional revenues and might, he suggested elsewhere in the *Encyclopédie*, provide a fund with which to buy out manorial dues and obligations. A moderate proportionate tax on land and a modest sales tax on foodstuffs would complete the state's revenues.

In a different vein, the article "Vingtième" ("Five-percent Tax") offered a close approximation of the physiocratic proposal of a single tax on land. Echoing Mirabeau, the authors suggested that labor itself was the people's tax, and that the wealthy should bear any additional burdens in the form of monetary taxes. In this plan, all taxes would fall on landowners, whose property and revenues would be determined by cadastral survey. The proportional *vingtième* would replace all duties, including the highly lucrative but regressive duties on wine and salt.

Beyond urging the rich to take up the burden of taxation, the philosophes praised the moral rectitude of those who used their wealth to produce yet more wealth through wise management of property and production. The absentee landlord, simply pursuing rents and feudal dues, was an anathema. The alternate model that Voltaire offered was himself, an enlightened entrepreneur bringing improved agriculture and crafts to his rural estates.

Monarchs were to act in a similar way for the kingdom as a whole. In proposals to Catherine the Great, Diderot imagined himself "King Denis," an economic leader of wide vision. He sold royal domains to increase tax revenues and improve production; he drastically reformed the royal household; he reduced pensions; he gradually eliminated monastic holdings and lowered clerical revenues to those needed for social services; he streamlined the collection of taxes and eliminated most tax agents; and he eliminated privilege and shifted tax burdens onto the

rich. In other memoranda, he proposed additional duties: building roads, creating cities, and fostering the growth of a Third Estate of artisans and shopkeepers. All these goals, he claimed, rested within the reach and responsibilities of leadership.

All this presupposed a society that valued work, from both the rich and the poor. On the rich, the only sanction was the social stigma of representing wasteful luxury, of failing in moral obligation. For the poor, the philosophes had other benefits and sanctions. For the worthy poor unable to find work or burdened by disease and age, they proposed vigorous state action. Their favored proposal, anticipating the later action of revolutionaries, urged that church properties be seized by the state and used for the purposes of providing food, shelter, and work for the deserving poor. The unworthy poor—the beggars who attempted to live without producing—were the object of considerable scorn. Enlightened reformers rejected the discipline of poverty as a general policy, but they retained the sense of righteous discipline for those who scorned work in a world of forced labor on the boundary between charity and punishment.

The world the philosophes envisioned was to be rid of irresponsible kings living off their lands, absentee landlords exploiting peasants through feudal dues, grain monopolists artificially raising prices, guildsmen refusing entry to work to those capable and willing, nobility and clerics immune from taxation, and monastic orders living off permanent foundations. Wise intervention by the state against these evils, combined with wise stimulation of production through the spread of enlightened techniques, would bring whatever measure of economic justice was to be had in a world inevitably populated by many who were poor and a few who were rich.

Equality. In this way, the philosophes substituted a mitigated hierarchy of property and wealth for one of birth and privilege. This view of the world, conservative in its own way, was implicitly subversive of the many legal distinctions of a way of life based on inherited status at all levels. Significant economic inequality was viewed as inevitable, but they saw no need to compound this with civil inequality. Diderot summarized the mature Enlightenment position in his bold recommendations to Catherine the Great. The Dutch example, including its provision of prompt, free justice to all, remained vivid in his mind as he formulated his legislation for Russia. He urged many measures on Catherine, but "above all" he insisted on "laws so general that they except no one." "The universality of the law," he continued, "is one of the greatest principles of the equality of subjects. Let no one be able to strike or mistreat or seriously injure another without punishment.... Use your commission above all to establish this kind of legal equality; it is so natural, so human, that only wild beasts could resist it." Though Diderot's insistence on justice that was prompt and free as well as equal was unusual, his concern for civil equality was common among philosophes in the 1770s.

Such strong endorsement of civil equality did not in any way imply endorsement of political equality. The philosophes barely considered the possibility of giving the people political responsibility. The passions of the mob seemed real enough to these writers, to whom urban violence remained a sporadic threat. Turgot received word of the Gordon riots in England six years after the bread riots of 1774 that had helped undermine his position as controller general. The news brought despair, not anger. The riots proved, Turgot wrote to a friend, "what we already knew, that men are far from being enlightened, and what many do not know so well, that there is no greater enemy to liberty than the people." For Turgot, the riots revived a lesson of classical history: popular power destroys the hope of stability and the foundations of liberty.

D'Holbach commented at length on the prospects of popular power in his *Politique naturelle* (1773). In keeping with classical political theory, he included democracy as a possible form of government, but ancient experience proved to him that popular power had no place in a realist perspective. He discussed democracy as a natural stage in the growth of society after the rule of kings. "Sovereignty rested in the whole of society," he wrote, "but the confusion which soon followed usually turned it into merely modified anarchy." The "idol of equality" drove the people to expel its best leaders and to accept those who catered to its whims; eventually, all men of exceptional virtue or wealth felt the wrath of the people. D'Holbach discovered insupportable dangers even within the supposedly safe confines of mixed government. The people, "susceptible to frenzy, fanaticism, and passion, and usually deprived of foresight" drove such governments to precipitous acts. His judgment was absolute, and typical of fellow French philosophes and many elite Europeans:

> In a word, wherever the people possesses power, the state carries within it the principle of its destruction. Liberty degenerates into license, and anarchy follows. Furious in adversity, insolent in prosperity, proud of its power, surrounded by flatterers, a multitude knows no moderation; it is ready to receive the impressions of all those who make the effort to deceive it; barely held back by the bonds of decency, it acts without reflection or shame; it inclines toward the most shameful crimes, the most shocking excesses.
>
> (*La politique naturelle* vol. 2, 240)

Most liberal reformers proposed some variation of a senatorial order to serve, advise, and correct those in authority, thereby leavening and enlightening absolutist and corporatist authorities. Property rather than heredity

would allow access to full citizenship with its consultative and legislative powers. Turgot and Du Pont de Nemours outlined the most complete plan for creating this order in their *Mémoire sur les municipalités* (1776), proposing a hierarchy of assemblies beginning at the parish level. The unit that defined one vote would be 600 *livres* of annual landed revenue, by no means a small sum. Men would vote in proportion to their revenues; one man might cast several votes, while several might have to combine their allotments to produce one vote. These provisions effectively disfranchised almost all of those called the people. The reformers feared the tumult of large assemblies and saw a distinct probability that the money of the rich might buy the votes of the poor. With elitist logic, they therefore denied power to the corruptible poor in order to protect society from the corruption of the rich. Du Pont and Turgot estimated that in a parish of a hundred families, only five or six might actually exercise the *voix du citoyen* ("citizen's voice"). The weight of decision would then fall on the wealthy, educated few, making the assemblies much more "reasonable" than if the illiterate and uneducated had control. Not surprisingly, they associated wealth with political stability, education, and a sense of the wider public interest. In their optimism, they assumed that the uneducated and volatile people without land and without a voice could expect equitable treatment within a reformed political order. The association of property with citizenship was frequently echoed throughout the Enlightenment period and became a staple of revolutionary constitutions.

With this observation, we approach the boundaries of the period of the French Revolution. It is clear that the philosophes' views of the people did not lend themselves to any vision of radical democracy. The reformers spoke mostly from the perspective of rational reform, a largely top-down vision inspired by the reforming ministries and enlightened absolutists of France, Prussia, Russia, and Habsburg Austria.

Fundamental transformation of the political order lay outside their vision, and it was only the pressured and chaotic environment after 1788 that allowed much more rhetoric of popular will and power to emerge. The philosophes assumed a society of substantial social difference between the people and the truly enlightened, and though they could use standards of reason and equity to urge reform, they had no doubt where ultimate political authority lay. Their contribution was to recognize, sometimes cautiously and sometimes boldly, that such authority was grounded on earth and not in heaven, in the present and not in the past, and hence brought with it substantial responsibilities toward those who lived by labor.

[*See also* Democracy; Economic Thought; Education; Literacy; Philosophes; *and* Political Philosophy.]

BIBLIOGRAPHY

Armogathe, Jean-Robert, et al. *Images du peuple au XVIIIe siècle.* Paris, 1973. Excellent compendium, for the reader of French.

Baker, Keith Michael. *Inventing the French Revolution.* Cambridge, 1990. Allows one to see the transition of "the people" from a social to a political category.

Chisick, Harvey. *The Limits of Reform in the Enlightenment: Attitudes toward the Education of the Lower Classes in Eighteenth-Century France.* Princeton, N.J., 1981.

Hufton, Olwen. *The Poor of Eighteenth-Century France, 1750–1789.* Oxford, 1984. Excellent for the social and political background to the philosophes' discussions.

Payne, Harry. *The Philosophes and the People.* New Haven, Conn., 1976. The present entry summarizes the basic arguments of this book.

Payne, Harry. "Elite versus Popular Mentality in the Eighteenth Century." In *Studies in Eighteenth-Century Culture 8*, edited by Roseann Runte, pp. 3–32. Baltimore, 1979.

Roche, Daniel. *The People of Paris: An Essay in Popular Culture in the 18th Century.* Berkeley, Calif., 1984.

Sewell, William H., Jr. *A Rhetoric of Bourgeois Revolution: The Abbé Sieyes and* What Is the Third Estate? Durham, N.C., and London, 1994. Good for comparison of the philosophes' rhetoric with that which emerged in the Revolutionary cauldron.

HARRY C. PAYNE

PERRAULT, CHARLES (1628–1703), French writer and polymath.

Perrault is among the few seventeenth-century men of letters who exemplify the crucial role played by the golden age of French absolutism in setting the stage for the Enlightenment. Perrault's career had many facets, and each age has privileged the one that best fit its particular passions. Thus, the modern craze for fairies and fairy tales has meant that Perrault is known today almost exclusively as the man who (a century before Germany's Grimm brothers) first collected and gave written form to the Mother Goose tales that French nurses had passed on orally for centuries. The stories in his 1697 *Contes de ma mère l'oye* (Tales of Times Past) do much more than preserve folk culture: some inform us, as do few works published under the exceptionally tight censorship of the troubled final decades of Louis XIV's reign, of such contemporary societal crises as famines; others provide early evidence of the belief that a corrupt aristocracy might be saved by the introduction of a meritocracy.

Perrault's style is characterized above all by its bone-dry, barely perceptible irony. For his tales of ogres and cats who walk in seven-league boots, Perrault invented a key Enlightenment polemical mode that was subsequently perfected by Montesquieu and Voltaire. Perrault was the first to comprehend a lesson eighteenth-century writers understood perfectly: the overtly escapist trappings of fairy tales can camouflage social and political critique.

A Bureaucratic Career. Perrault's contemporaries probably would have considered him a propagandist for Louis XIV's relentlessly absolutist monarchy and a bureaucrat who worked tirelessly for the projects designed to promote French cultural and economic superiority that were carried out under the direction of the powerful superintendent of finances, Jean-Baptiste Colbert. Perrault and his architect brother, Claude, were leading figures in Colbert's inner circle of advisers. Charles Perrault was Colbert's right-hand man and shaped in essential ways the cultural, scientific, and commercial policy of the Sun King's reign, a policy that transformed France into a modern state. Perrault supervised every detail—from the quality of the construction to the accuracy of the bookkeeping—of the vast architectural projects that are Louis XIV's most visible legacy, including the modernized Louvre (for which Claude Perrault designed the façade), the Tuileries gardens, and Versailles.

Moderns versus Ancients. This wide-ranging cultural and practical experience served Perrault well when he fell from favor after Colbert's death in 1683 and embarked on a new life as a man of letters. He had long been a pillar of the Académie Française—he was named director in 1681—when, in 1687, he almost brought the house down upon itself by interrupting one of the august body's sessions with a lengthy proclamation of the absolute superiority of "the century of Louis XIV." According to Perrault's argument, modern science, modern military science, even and especially modern literature, all proved that the Moderns, that is, seventeenth-century Frenchmen, were superior to the Ancients, their counterparts in antiquity.

The French cultural world quickly split into two camps; adversaries engaged in heated, often acrimonious debate over such issues as whether modern (French) literature should be taught in schools alongside, or instead of, the works of classical antiquity. The controversy, known to posterity as the Quarrel between the Ancients and the Moderns, continued virtually without a check for decades in France, where Perrault was the most influential champion of the modern agenda. Nowhere are his contribution and the Quarrel's generative role for the Enlightenment more evident than in his four-volume *Parallèle des Anciens et des Modernes* (Parallel between the Ancients and the Moderns, 1688–1697). A proto-*Encyclopédie*, the *Parallèle* was the first work to treat literary, artistic, and scientific accomplishments together and as equally worthy of consideration. In it, Perrault formulated doctrines essential to eighteenth-century thought, especially the existence of progress, artistic as well as scientific, and the belief in the right to personal judgment.

The Quarrel quickly spread all over Europe; in England, for example, it became known as the Battle of the Books.

As a result, intellectuals throughout Europe began to debate for the first time in a truly public manner the importance of received ideas and standards. Aided by the simultaneous contemporary triumph of print culture in the vernacular and of newspapers, it played an essential role in the democratization of taste, in the imposition of a new definition of the writer as creator of unique works of literature, and in the formation of public opinion, a force without which the Enlightenment could not have taken place. Thus, because Perrault predicted the future of French society, arguments developed to demonstrate the wonders absolutism had made possible eventually helped to create the radically different intellectual climate in which the Enlightenment took shape.

[*See also* Académie Française *and* Aesthetics.]

BIBLIOGRAPHY

DeJean, Joan. *Ancients against Moderns: Culture Wars and the Making of a Fin de Siècle*. Chicago, 1997. A survey of Perrault's role in the Quarrel between the Ancients and the Moderns and of the Quarrel's long-term consequences.

Jauss, Hans Robert. "Aesthetische Normen und geschichtliche Reflexion in der 'Querelle des Anciens et des Modernes.'" Preface (pp. 8–64) to his edition of Perrault's *Parallèle des Anciens et des Modernes*. Munich, 1964.

JOAN DEJEAN

PHILADELPHIA. The center of the American Enlightenment and the largest American city in the mid-eighteenth century—indeed, one of the largest cities in the British Empire—Philadelphia early possessed an ambitious, prosperous, and literate population connected by ties of commerce and culture to centers of Enlightenment throughout the Atlantic world. In one sense, Philadelphia's Enlightenment was not unusual; the eighteenth century here, as elsewhere, brought, in Carl and Jessica Bridenbaugh's words, a "golden era for middle-class intellectuals." Philadelphia, however, was also at the vital center of a political revolution that was in some measure born of enlightened thought. From the American Revolution, Philadelphia's middle-class intellectuals drew a heightened sense of calling; without it, their Enlightenment might never have managed to shake off the dust of provincialism.

Early foundations for Philadelphia's Enlightenment were established by figures such as James Logan (1674–1751), who owned the first copy of Newton's *Principia* in the American colonies and built one of the best libraries of the colonial period; John Bartram (1699–1777), botanist and early organizer of the American Philosophical Society; and the central figure, Benjamin Franklin. In 1727, Franklin founded his Junto (the "Club of the Leather Aprons"), a discussion club devoted to scientific study and self-improvement, and he revived the idea of a scientific society in the early 1740s, when his ideas for experiments with electricity began to take shape. His scientific publishing, the connections he made to the Royal Society, and the introductions he provided to other Americans visiting London and Edinburgh were all important, but so was the way Franklin brought the luster of the European Enlightenment home to Philadelphia. With a hand in the establishing of the Philosophical Society, the Library Company of Philadelphia (1742), the Pennsylvania Hospital (1750), and the Academy and College of Philadelphia (1750), Franklin helped to make his city the model for other American centers of learning.

By the end of the 1760s, Philadelphia boasted a flourishing book trade, considerable literary production, two rival philosophical societies (merged as the American Philosophical Society in 1769), and the reputation of intellectual center of the colonies. Charles Thompson, patriot and scientific promoter, urged Philadelphians to recognize their city's preeminence and to "call to our assistance Men of Learning and Ingenuity from every quarter, and unite in one generous noble attempt, not only to promote the interest of our country, but to raise her to some eminence in the rank of polite and learned nations." Through such institutional support, and through the informal community of letters and polite learning (evident in places such as the literary salon of Elizabeth Graeme Ferguson), it was the Philadelphians who drew Americans in other cities into a larger web of correspondence and exchange.

In matters of philosophy, both natural and political, Philadelphians in the first half of the eighteenth century looked to London, and they coveted the approval—through publication or election to membership—of the Royal Society. Other centers assumed more importance during the late colonial and revolutionary periods. Lists of foreign members in the American Philosophical Society and the range of subjects addressed in its *Transactions* point to a growing familiarity with Paris. The scope of Philadelphia's Enlightenment broadened with the comings and goings of Philadelphians trained in European universities—Uppsala, Leiden, Aberdeen, and especially Edinburgh, the school of choice for Philadelphia's physicians (including John Morgan, John Redman, William Shippen, Adam Kuhn, Caspar Wistar, Benjamin Smith Barton, and the indefatigable revolutionary Benjamin Rush, all professors at the medical school of the College of Philadelphia, later the University of Pennsylvania). Similarly, higher education in Philadelphia was shaped by the Scottish university training of immigrants such as Francis Alison, who taught metaphysics and moral philosophy at the College of Philadelphia, and William Smith, first rector of the college. Philadelphians were made familiar with the Scottish Enlightenment in its full range and depth, including its natural philosophy, physiology, medicine, botany, history, and moral philosophy.

Even as they were anxious to secure their place in the wider republic of letters centered on Europe, Philadelphians were confident that they had the power to use enlightened ideas to accomplish things glorious and altogether new. The complex relationship between independence and Enlightenment showed in varied ways, from Alison's adopting the philosophical justification for rebellion offered by his mentor, Francis Hutcheson, to the patriotism of the scientific lecturer Ebenezer Kinnersley, who protested the Privy Council's treatment of his friend Franklin by using sparks from "electrical fire" to ignite effigies of royal officials in Philadelphia's streets. The republican passions of figures such as Benjamin Rush lent a radicalism to Philadelphia's culture of Enlightenment, and an extraordinary optimism about enlightened progress in a world swept clean by revolution. Political language focused on "the science of government" and the "republican experiment" marked the Philadelphians' conviction that the lessons of Enlightenment *were* the lessons of the Revolution.

Philadelphia's Enlightenment had also been shaped by its religious context. In the 1740s, the city became contested terrain in the controversy between opponents and proponents of Calvinist revival. The aftershocks of the Great Awakening rippled through the small Presbyterian academies surrounding the city, and through the College of Philadelphia and the nearby College of New Jersey at Princeton. Both sides sought to bend enlightened learning to their own purposes, and they pursued Christian enlightenment with an evangelical zeal that balanced confidence in progress with mistrust of reason unaided by grace. The insistence that, as Benjamin Rush argued, there could be no true enlightenment without divine intervention later worked to insulate much of Philadelphia's enlightened culture from deism on one hand, and from religious conservatism on the other. In the late eighteenth century, Philadelphia could be a congenial home for the common-sense refutation of Humean skepticism, but it was also a safe intellectual harbor for Thomas Jefferson, even when enlightened Americans elsewhere had grown weary—and wary—of Jefferson's associations with the French Revolution and his departure from Christian orthodoxy. Thus, despite what might appear to be the confines, both religious and political, of its American setting, Philadelphia's Enlightenment developed an expansive character that showed plainly the ways in which familiar enlightened ideas might be turned to fresh purpose.

[*See also* American Philosophical Society; American Revolution; Bartram, John and William; Franklin, Benjamin; North America; *and* Rush, Benjamin.]

BIBLIOGRAPHY

Bridenbaugh, Carl, and Jessica Bridenbaugh. *Rebels and Gentlemen: Philadelphia in the Age of Franklin*. New York, 1942. This "biography of a city" remains the most thorough treatment of enlightened Philadelphia's scientific, intellectual, and cultural life.

May, Henry. *The Enlightenment in America*. New York, 1976. May's sweeping account places Philadelphia's "Revolutionary Enlightenment" in a wider intellectual history of the Enlightenment in America.

Reid-Maroney, Nina. *Philadelphia's Enlightenment, 1740–1800: Kingdom of Christ, Empire of Reason*. Westport, Conn., 2001.

Wright, Esmond. *Franklin of Philadelphia*. Cambridge, Mass., 1986. An excellent biography of Franklin that clarifies his lifelong interest in placing Philadelphia at the center of "a single and beneficent empire of science and curiosity."

NINA REID-MARONEY

PHILANTHROPINISM. *See* French Revolution *and* Moral Philosophy.

PHILOSOPHES. In a France that was highly stratified by birth and title, there emerged by the middle of the eighteenth century a community of thinkers and writers of quite diverse social origins who shared attitudes favorable toward the new philosophy and critical toward arbitrary authority and the French Catholic Church. They saw themselves as part of a Republic of Letters, a phrase widely used from the seventeenth to the eighteenth centuries to describe the world of writers and educated readers. Within that Republic, in theory, authors would be judged by merit, not by birth. They also saw themselves as a unique generation in the history of humankind. In their self-image, they stood between a sad past of superstition, despotism, ignorance, and suffering and a possible future of human enlightenment. In their image of that enlightenment, humankind, free of the presumptive authority of the past, educated by experience methodically gathered and tested, and applying knowledge toward the end of reducing human suffering and increasing human well-being, would rewrite its relationship to the natural and social world. This generation embodies a remarkable moment in the history of human consciousness, seeing itself as leading Europe, and perhaps all of mankind, from a phantasmagoric past into a world that would seek to change the conditions of its being closer to the heart's desire for happiness.

The word *philosophe* was merely the French noun for "philosopher," but eighteenth-century French Enlightenment authors took the word for their own. They detached it from any sense of being a student of abstract, metaphysical philosophy as taught in the universities of Europe. Rather, it came to stand for a thinker who possessed a critical spirit informed by the intellectual revolution of

A Group of Philosophes. Among those dining at the Café Procope in Paris are Condorcet, Diderot, d'Alembert, and Voltaire (with hand raised). Anonymous engraving, eighteenth century. (Granger Collection.)

the seventeenth century, above all in its empirical and practical modes.

When Voltaire wrote back to France from a brief exile in England, his work was entitled *Letters from the English Nation* in the English-language London edition, but *Lettres philosophiques* (Philosophical Letters) in the French-language Paris edition. The work dealt only peripherally with formal philosophy in any metaphysical sense. It began with a critical, detached, irreverent, and relativistic look at diverse Christian sectarian religions. If offered a paean to religious tolerance. It provided a glowing account of the liberty and lack of arbitrary authority in both English politics and science compared to those of France. It celebrated the newest trends in English letters and culture. It interwove throughout its chapters, and concluded emphatically with, a critique of views of the human condition that assumed, fatalistically, the necessity of suffering and penance. The French Jesuit learned review, *Journal de Trévoux*, reviewing the work, denounced "a philosophe" as an insolent rebel against the political and religious foundations of his own society and its traditional authorities. By early in the century, then, critics of the existing intellectual and social order, Voltaire foremost among them, successfully had claimed the terms *philosophe* and *philosophique* as their own, and critics of the Enlightenment in France often described themselves as "antiphilosophique."

The philosophes—the philosophers of the French Enlightenment—were diverse in social and educational origin, but bright, sociable, and recognizing each other by common values, interests and opponents. They coalesced around certain institutions: cafés, salons, liberal patrons, academies; and around certain ideas. By midcentury, they had developed a sense of community with purpose. They came to consciousness of the drama of their rejection of inherited authority per se, and, in theory at least, of their commitments to empirical evidence, rational analysis, nature as the sole source of our knowledge and values, and, from their analysis of nature, a commitment to the principle of utility. By utility, they meant that the happiness of the species was the highest value, and that all things should be judged by their contribution to happiness or suffering.

Their commitment to these values, and their competition with the clergy for the role of educator of their society, leads them into a fundamental conflict with the Roman Catholic Church in France, a conflict that became one of the defining characteristics of the French Enlightenment. Struggling with the church over issues of tolerance and censorship, and offering quite different histories and analyses of their societies, the philosophes come to identify the church (and the church the philosophes) as their antithesis, their deepest foe. The philosophes rejected traditional authority and supranatural claims, and they espoused secular need as the highest value. This led the community of philosophes to see the church as the epitome of arbitrary traditional authority, antisecularism, antiutilitarianism, and through its powers (often exaggerated by the Enlightenment) of censorship, persecution, intolerance, and monopoly of most education, as the greatest barrier to the future they would bring into being. Anticlericalism was the most common denominator of the Enlightenment. Primarily deistic, the Enlightenment, where it had piety, believed that God spoke to mankind through nature and nature alone, and that the priests had usurped and falsified God's voice in sectarian religions.

The great *Encyclopédie* of Denis Diderot and Jean Le Rond d'Alembert became one of the major agencies of the organization and dissemination of the philosophes' enlightenment, such that the terms *philosophe* and *encyclopédiste* often were used interchangeably. The audacious polymath Diderot and the prudent mathematician and man of letters d'Alembert projected a vast work that would be a sanctuary of all acquired knowledge and experience, a bridge to the future, and a barrier against any new dark ages. It would link the expanding concerns of the philosophe: not simply what we know, but how we came to know it; not simply philosophy, but history, the arts, the letters, and the mechanical and technical inventions changing the human relationship to power and production.

By engaging more than 160 writers and possibly another hundred informal consultants, and drawing into its orbit and its frame of reference the expertise and scholarship of France, the *Encyclopédie* did much to solidify the sense of community among the philosophes. Its *Preliminary Discourse* (1751), written by d'Alembert, articulated the philosophes' overarching historical narrative and worldview. In this view, the seventeenth century had witnessed a rebirth of knowledge and a qualitative change in the human capacity to acquire and apply science and enlightenment. In this account, knowledge was a human power to understand the world in which we found ourselves and to alter what could, in fact, be altered.

The *Encyclopédie* provided a focus and a means of diffusion for the worldview, scholarship, polemic, and analyses of the new philosophy: its vision of the questioning of the origins and foundations of all authorities, beliefs, and institutions; of intellectual progress; of the dynamism of science, technology, and secular inquiry.

Frequently attacked and occasionally suppressed, the *Encyclopédie* drew its authors, experts, and readers into the drama of censorship. It found agents of collusion and support in the highest structures of the Old Regime, in the courts, the aristocracy, the ministries of the monarchies. Its very existence as well as its contents were corrosive upon the sacred idols and established intellectual authorities of its culture. It played a major role in establishing the self-consciousness of this movement that more and more came to call itself, in Voltaire's phrase, "the party of humanity," or "the party of reason." It presented and sought to embody criteria of truth that were not claims of special authority or revelation, but the reason and experience of all of mankind's natural lights. It offered a vision of knowledge that claimed transparency, explanations that all could judge by the evidence of the world. It offered a secular agenda of knowledge whose goal was not despotic power over conscience and creed, but, rather, utility and the happiness and self-preservation of the human race. In all these things, from the cultivation of agents of assistance near the throne to a Lockean notion of replicable knowledge supported by plain evidence, the *Encyclopédie* both helped to create and to reinforce the self-image of the philosophes. Increasingly, their self-image became the image of them held by an educated culture in which they were winning the war for public opinion.

The *Encyclopédie* formalized the self-image of the individual as philosophe in a celebrated and influential unsigned article, probably by the man of letters César-Chesneau Dumarsais. The article already had appeared as an essay in several collections, and variations on it would reappear throughout the century. (For the publishing history of this, see the work by Herbert Dieckmann cited in the bibliography.) The article simultaneously reflected, influenced, and crystallized for the *Encyclopédie*'s vast array of readers and admirers the emergent and triumphant notion of a philosophe. The true philosophe was neither a man withdrawn from the world for the purposes of reflection nor, as critics of the new philosophy would have us believe, a dogmatically antireligious thinker who looked upon his fellow creatures with "disdain." Rather, the philosophe sought "well being and a reasonable life" through awareness and understanding of the forces that acted upon him. Sometimes, he would choose to allow those forces to act freely; sometimes, he would reasonably adjust his relationship to the world. For the philosophe, action always should be preceded by reflection. The philosophe had no arrogance about the scope of his knowledge, but in a world that indeed could be dark, he carried a lantern of rational reflection. What "grace" was to "the Christian," "reason" was to the "philosophe."

The philosophe did not allow either mere tradition or prejudice to determine his principles. Rather, he sought the foundation of principles in his observations of nature, striving to know every principle's origin, real worth, and applicability (including the limits of its applicability). He always was interested in the appropriate boundaries of his knowledge, seeking to distinguish carefully and at all times among the true, the false, the doubtful, and the merely probable. Indeed, the distinctive intellectual mark of a philosophe was to know what he did not know, and to suspend judgment when appropriate.

In a world in which most individuals were content "to guess" and felt impelled to reach a conclusive judgment on all issues, the philosophe was concerned with "judging well," and with seeking the proper grounds of the various degrees of consent and belief. He did not disdain brilliance and intuition, but he preferred intellectual caution, linking his judgment to "precision, flexibility, and clarity." As part of that, the philosophe knew that he must inquire into the views of others, must understand the opinions that he rejects, and must do so with the same effort that he expends on his own ideas.

The philosophe did not cultivate these qualities for their own sake, detached from the life of his fellow creatures. Far from withdrawing from the world, which would make of him "a monster," he understood the indispensability of society to his well-being, and he cultivated "the qualities of sociability." The philosophe did not see society as enemy, alien territory, but knew that giving pleasure is itself a pleasure, and thus adapted to those who were his neighbors by accident or by conscious choice. He was an honorable, honest, and sociable man, who sought the well-being of others and wished to make himself "useful" to the world. Without condescension toward his fellow creatures, he divided his time wisely between time alone and sociable time, knowing, as a human, his common humanity with his fellow beings.

The philosophe understood his obligations to "honor" and to "probity." An enlightened mind without a devotion to "civil society" was worthless. That devotion not only made the philosophe reject isolation, but also "fanaticism" and "superstition," which were the scourges of civil society. Reflective and knowing both the principles of society and the moral order of God's creation by the lights of his reason, he was simultaneously rational and precise in his use of mind, sociable, honest, and benevolent in his social intercourse, and truthful with himself in his self-awareness. Where the Stoic ideal of the philosopher had been someone detached from the world and disdainful of humanity, the philosophe cherished his humanity, and he both partook of and delighted in the moderate pleasures and rewards of the world. If such a philosophe were king, the people would be happy indeed.

This self-portrait, self-flattery, and self-justification of the Enlightenment philosophe struck deep chords, as we may see by the fame that befell the article, the frequent republication of this essay, and the enduring force of these themes throughout the French eighteenth century. In 1765, the most celebrated philosophe of all, Voltaire, reiterated and developed similar themes in his article, "Philosophe," in the exceptionally popular and appropriately named *Dictionnaire philosophique* (Philosophical Dictionary).

For Voltaire, the term *philosophe*, correctly used, refers to those thinkers throughout all history who have devoted themselves to "wisdom" and to "truth" and have given lessons in "moral truth" in their teachings and "examples of virtue" in their lives. The mark of such "philosophes" is not that they correctly grasped a natural system of the world—it had taken centuries to know even a part of the operations of nature—but that they understood the natural ethical truths of human life. The philosophe stood in contrast to all those arrogant thinkers who declared themselves prophets or men inspired by God, and who used such inane claims to impose their beliefs upon mankind. Confucius, thus, was a philosophe, while Zoroaster, Hermes, and the original legislators of the ancient world, including Greece, were not. If the sages of ancient Greece had limited themselves to teaching moral truths, their names would be illustrious rather than mocked today, but many of them, in parts of their works, at least taught men real things about being just. Among the ancients, it is Cicero (who by himself, perhaps, was worth all the philosophers of Greece), Epictetus, the Antonine emperors, and Julian the Apostate who stand out most as genuine philosophes.

In France, for Voltaire, there have been few true philosophes throughout history, but, with the exception of Montaigne, they generally have been persecuted: Pierre Charron; Pierre Ramus; René Descartes; Pierre Gassendi, and "the immortal" Pierre Bayle. The fate of these true philosophes was to arouse, despite or because of their virtue, the hatred of religious fanatics. The enemies and would-be persecutors of the genuine philosophes today are "the religious hypocrites, the most cowardly and cruel species of all." Compare France and England, Voltaire concluded. In England, where religious toleration reigned, philosophers could live in honor and peace. Toleration was the medium in which philosophes were unmolested. The philosophes of France, thus, should know what "will make it easy for you to solve this problem."

In 1771, in a new edition of *Dictionnaire philosophique*, Voltaire added three further sections to his article on the "Philosophe," more than tripling it in length. In particular, he responded to charges that the Emperor Domitian and the satirist Lucian had persecuted or scorned, respectively, philosophical thinkers. What had drawn the enmity of the ancient world toward certain philosophers, Voltaire replied, was not any real status as philosophes, but their magic, their demonology, in short, their superstition. The ancient world respected its authentic philosophes, and, indeed, had emperors who were among their ranks. The recent history of France gave us the sad spectacle of nonphilosophical kings who oversaw religious persecutions and slaughters—Charles IX, Henry III, Louis XIII, for example—princes who were "ignorant, superstitious, cruel, and governed by their own passions." In contrast to those kings stood the philosophers, French and, as seen in the examples of John Locke, the third earl of Shaftesbury, and Herbert of Cherbury, English, by whom the world would have been far better governed.

In the world of contemporary letters, the struggle, as Voltaire portrayed it in the augmentation of his article, was between philosophes and fanatical theologians of all sects ("the starch-collared Lutheran, the savage Calvinist, the arrogant Anglican, the fanatical [Catholic] Jansenist, [and] the [Catholic] Jesuit who sees himself always in control"). In pursuit of satisfying their ambition, the theologians always war with each other, always corrupt philosophy with a "jumble" of theology, and always seek persecution for infidelity of the virtuous philosophes, as they now seek, in France, the silencing and persecution of the editors and authors of the *Encyclopédie*.

Voltaire concluded, in the expanded article, that "thinking people" now understood that the deepest benefit of authentic philosophy for humankind is its ability to destroy "religious rage," to disarm those who would slaughter in the name of religion. The mission of the philosophes was nothing less than to "soften" the morals of the people and to "instruct" the kings of the world.

Thus, in Voltaire's addition to his article, written without any inhibition or veiling whatsoever, we find the fullest self-image of the philosophe of the Enlightenment. There was a struggle between church and secular thinkers, between theologians and the philosophes, over who would form public opinion, shape ethics, and speak to power. The future was at stake.

From the 1750s to the 1780s, when France became much more politicized and focused on its immediate fiscal and political crises, there is a voluminous literary output from the philosophes. Every year, first scores, and then hundreds of works, large and small, major treatises and occasional brochures, became the rage of the reading public. Having defined themselves in contradistinction to the theologians and authorities of the French Catholic Church, the philosophes transformed the issue of religious toleration into their most powerful engine of intellectual and cultural warfare. By the 1760s, the church was on the defensive, and every act of censorship and religious denunciation of the scandal of published works of deistic or atheistic unbelief excited the interest of the reading public.

At the most obvious level, the mechanism of censorship broke down. Authors, except in the most striking and singular cases, were unmolested, and if, in rare instances, they faced minor punishment, their "martyrdom" only increased their public stature and renown. The theologians and antiphilosophes who denounced works succeeded only in piquing the curiosity of readers and, thus, in increasing the sales of works condemned or banned. Vast networks arose to publish and distribute works by the philosophes, most often involving Swiss and Dutch publishers. Occasionally, the church succeeded in rallying the authorities to more stringent policing of the book trade. In such instances, however, the goal of royal ministers and police officials—so many of whom were admirers and friends of the philosophes—was invariably just to drive up the cost of condemned books by prosecuting the final peddlers of such works. Even then, active efforts to suppress the circulation of philosophic works was always brief, ineffective, and intentionally porous.

At a deeper level, the belief in censorship and intolerance began to crumble in the reading public's mind. The philosophes succeeded in portraying a France divided between a fanatical and persecutorial "party of the devout," on the one hand, and a philosophical "party of humanity," on the other. There was a France of light and a France of darkness, between which the public had to choose. This rhetoric, widely shared and occurring in myriad forms, represented a sharp either/or that distinguishes the Enlightenment in France from that in any other European country.

For the philosophes, the issue of toleration became, both tactically and substantively, the battle cry of the Enlightenment, uniting its diverse tendencies and increasingly winning over first public opinion and then the state itself. The philosophes were able to transform the issue from the church's definition to their own. The church presented religious toleration—and the end of censorship that it entailed—as indifference, asking how a just person could be indifferent to the communication of God's truth and to the protection of his or her neighbor's soul. The philosophes, with stunning success, presented the issue as one of the rights that follow from responsibilities. They could say to their readers: You have responsibility for the consequences of your choices, and, thus, you have the right to know, to hear all voices, to reason, to judge, and to decide the great debates for yourselves.

Further, the philosophes used the issue of tolerance to drive a wedge between the church, which deemed intolerance a duty, and the crown, which judged the issue of tolerance—whatever decision it came to—to be a matter of royal discretion. From the perspective of the philosophes, all secular authority was obliged to work for the secular, public good. For the crown, determination of the public good was a royal prerogative. In a debate with the church that was prudently and effectively framed by the philosophes, the latter came to find improbable allies among the defenders of the rights of the king.

The scandal around the didactic historical novel *Bélisaire* (1767) by Jean-François Marmontel, crystallized these issues compellingly, and marked the turning point in the struggle of the philosophes for critical autonomy and public support in France. In chapter fifteen of *Bélisaire*, the

Roman general Belisarius lectured the emperor Justinian on ecclesiastical tolerance (the good of all creeds would be saved) and, above all, on civil tolerance. Marmontel argued, through his character, that a sovereign's duty was not to judge of truth or error, but to secure the happiness and tranquillity of his domains. A sovereign who sought to secure religious truth might arm either truth or error, a terrible danger, but the sovereign was not called upon to arm religion, because an omnipotent God did not depend upon the sovereign's assistance in the achievement of his designs. The only theoretical justification for civil intolerance would be secular and utilitarian, the view that coerced religious unity would be beneficial to a realm. History, however, taught us otherwise, and the sovereign should recognize that no good could come from educing the martyrdom of the most brave and sincere citizen, the violence of the most fanatical citizen, and the dishonesty of the average citizen. A king's authority rightfully extended over harmful public behavior, not private beliefs, and sovereign authority to maintain obedience to secular laws was weakened by involving it in matters beyond its concern. Eventually, without recourse to coercion, even the bitterest religious disputation becomes boring to its participants. Zeal without any possible support from political power dissipates quickly, and citizens turn from unproductive religious debate to more constructive routes to fame and position. Toleration and freedom of thought and expression were the allies, not the enemies, of royal authority, of peace, of prosperity, and of order.

Bélisaire evoked a storm of theological denunciation, outrage, and demands for prosecution. Marmontel, willing to compromise on issues of who was saved, nonetheless published a brochure, "Exposé of the Motives that Prevent Me from Subscribing to Civil Intolerance." As theologians sought to repress the work and the author, philosophes, led by Voltaire and Anne-Robert-Jacques Turgot, orchestrated a defense of *Bélisaire*. By agreeing to sign any profession involving dogma but refusing to recognize civil intolerance as a point of dogma, Marmontel had forced the church to fight him in precisely the area where the royal court was most interested, the prerogatives of the crown. The faculty of theology of the University of Paris (the Sorbonne) and the archbishop of Paris were preparing a condemnation of *Bélisaire*. For the king himself to declare his religious duties to the church was one thing; for the Sorbonne or the archbishop, in a censure of *Bélisaire*, to lecture the king publicly on those duties was quite another. A committee appointed by the king rejected any effort to specify royal obligations to intolerance, and when several firebrands at the Sorbonne objected, the king himself intervened, sending a letter ordering the theologians to accept a revised document.

By the time that *Bélisaire* was formally censured in 1768, almost a year had passed, in the course of which Marmontel had become a celebrity in France. Indeed, Voltaire seized upon the *Bélisaire* affair as an epochal opportunity for the philosophes. He himself defended Marmontel in immensely popular works, helped to oversee the mordant defense of *Bélisaire* by Turgot, and arranged for the stunning public vindication of Marmontel, in writing, by Catherine the Great, Frederick the Great, the king of Poland, and the crown prince of Sweden. *Bélisaire* was a runaway best-seller, and Marmontel was on his way to becoming not only royal historiographer at the court, but, by 1783, the sécrétaire-perpétuel of the French Academy, succeeding d'Alembert. For all practical purposes, the philosophes had triumphed.

Voltaire himself took the issue of toleration as his central cause, and his defenses of the victims of what he presented as religious persecution and judicial murder stirred the French reading public to the marrow of its being. Voltaire's occasional and major works on these topics led to the perpetual growth of his influence and prestige. Indeed, by 1778, the year of his death, Voltaire had achieved a virtual apotheosis upon his return to Paris, where he was celebrated by the centers of French intellectual, cultural, and political life. Well before the Revolution, which would marginalize and persecute so many surviving philosophes, drawn, as they were, to parties of moderation or of outright counterrevolution, the philosophes had achieved the moral conquest of France.

They had drawn the line of division: Who would advise and teach a nation, the clergy of the eighteenth-century French Catholic Church or the secular philosophes? For better or worse, posterity scarcely can name a single voice of that church. It still reads and teaches the philosophes.

[*See also* Alembert, Jean Le Rond d'; Diderot, Denis; Encyclopédie; Marmontel, Jean-François; Paris; Republic of Letters; Toleration; *and* Voltaire.]

BIBLIOGRAPHY

Dieckmann, Herbert. *Le Philosophe: Texts and Interpretations*. St. Louis, 1968. A major study of the *Encyclopédie* article "Philosophe," its publishing history, its various incarnations, and the critical responses that it has evoked.

Gay, Peter. *The Enlightenment: An Interpretation*. 2 vols. New York, 1966–1969. A provocative view of the philosophes that detaches them too much from their education and context, but that often captures interesting sides of their efforts to distinguish themselves from the Catholic world around them.

Kors, Alan Charles. *D'Holbach's Coterie: An Enlightenment in Paris*. Princeton, N.J., 1976. A close view, by the author of this article, of one circle of Enlightenment philosophes, examining their thought, but, especially, their ascent and place in the Old Regime.

Renwick, John. *Marmontel, Voltaire, and the Bélisaire Affair*. Oxford, 1974. Although the author perhaps misunderstands the theological dogmatic side of the *Bélisaire* affair, he provides the best study of the substance and cultural importance of this affair and of its place in the emergence of the philosophic party.

Roche, Daniel. *France in the Enlightenment*. Translated by Arthur Goldhammer. Cambridge, Mass., 1998. A rich and sweeping account of the France in which the philosophes flourished, by a historian attuned to the role and influence of the philosophes.

Voltaire. *Dictionnaire philosophique*. Edited by Raymond Naves, et al. Paris, 1967. An edition that offers both the original 1765 article and, in an appendix, the three sections that Voltaire added to the article in the edition of 1771.

ALAN CHARLES KORS

PHILOSOPHICAL DIALOGUE.

Throughout the eighteenth century, philosophical dialogue was a favored written form for the investigation of certain fundamental and vexed questions, including the following: whether the argument from design demonstrates the existence of the deity; the extent to which materialism or immaterialism most adequately accounts for phenomena; the proper understanding of what is natural; and whether the history of civilized society reveals a moral progress or a decline. These philosophical dialogues make no appeal to scriptural authority; they rely solely on reason and experience in addressing such issues. The two or three interlocutors in the dialogue express opposed alternatives, and the movement of the conversation supposedly captures the logical movement toward an authorized conclusion. Nevertheless, ironies also attend such a form, as in many ancient instances of the genre by Plato or Cicero: the dialogue may only ambiguously or indirectly indicate its position; issues may remain unresolved; or issues may be resolved in a way that defeats expectations or differs from the explicit conclusion.

The dialogues of George Berkeley—*Three Dialogues Between Hylas and Philonous* (1713) and *Alciphron* (1732)—perhaps most closely approximate a straightforward understanding of the form. In the first two of the *Three Dialogues*, Philonous leads Hylas to see the illogicalities entailed by the hypothesis of a material substance, and in the third, he answers all the objections Hylas can raise to the principle that to exist is to be perceived or to perceive. In *Alciphron*, Euphranor turns back the arguments of Bernard Mandeville and the earl of Shaftesbury [*see* Shaftesbury, Anthony Ashley Cooper], before he goes on to demonstrate the acceptability of Christianity because of its social utility, the plausibility of the historical record, and the reasonableness of its principal tenets. Yet, even these nonironic dialogues are qualified by paradoxes and contrary tendencies. The denial of material substance has struck most readers as absurd and far from the common sense that Philonous claims it to be. Moreover, Berkeley's attack on the freethinkers in *Alciphron* led him into an extensive use of irony and satire that seemed to adopt the weapons of his adversaries.

The philosophical dialogue in this period tends almost always to be mixed with irony, parody, and satire. Thus

Shaftesbury, in *The Moralists: A Philosophical Rhapsody* (1705), seeks through dialogue to move beyond his critique of enthusiasm as fanaticism: Theocles tries to bring a cool skeptic, Philocles, to appreciate the beauty and order of nature, but Theocles prevails primarily on the strength of a lay sermon expressing his elevated vision and converts Philocles, ironically, by means of a speech, rather than by reasoned argument in dialogue. By contrast, Mandeville constructs the second part of his *Fable of the Bees* (1729) so that it conforms closely to the classical form of the dialogue, unmixed with any of the rhapsodic sermons or letter writing that Shaftesbury included in his dialogue. Mandeville's spokesman Cleomenes, however, explicitly defends, over little or no opposition from his friend Horatio, the thesis of the essays in the first part of the *Fable*: those who claim that virtue, frugality, and temperance lead to prosperity, comfort, and earthly happiness are either deluded, ignorant, or hypocritical. He also offers an account of the origins of society to show that providence and virtue need not have played any role in the history of civilization. Thus, though classic in form, Mandeville's dialogue satirically overturns conventional and dominant associations of material progress with virtue and happiness.

The French encyclopedist Denis Diderot makes even more effective use of the unsettling potential of philosophical dialogue. His *Neveu de Rameau* (*Rameau's Nephew*) (written in 1761; published in 1805) leaves the conflict between "He" and "I"—between the spokesman for conventional virtues and everyday hypocrisies on the one hand, and the amoral embodiment of egoism, sensuality, and a brutal honesty on the other—entirely unsettled. The reader can find no middle ground between "He" and "I" on which to take a stand. In Diderot's series of dialogues that make up the *Supplement to Bougainville's "Voyage"* (written in 1772; published in 1796), his apparent spokesman, B., argues that civilized society multiplies hypocrisies, while moral ideas would imprison the natural man; in the process, B. undermines accepted sexual mores and ideas of property. Diderot articulates a comprehensive materialist philosophy in the three dialogues in *Le Rêve de d'Alembert* (*D'Alembert's Dream*) (written in 1769; published in 1830), again bringing into question conventional sexual mores, as well as ideas of individuality. Although the *Supplement* and the *Rêve* make fairly clear the position of the author, their arguments were so unconventional that, like *Le Neveu de Rameau*, they were not published until decades after Diderot's death.

David Hume's *Dialogues Concerning Natural Religion* (written in 1751; published in 1779) constitutes perhaps the most elaborate instance of the philosophical dialogue as a satiric form. The subversiveness of these dialogues results in part from Hume's giving the strongest arguments he could to each of the three interlocutors—the pessimistic fideist Demea, the optimistic deist Cleanthes, and the philosophical skeptic Philo. The work's principal satiric effect, however, results from its rigorous dismantling of the argument from design. Philo points out that according to an argument from analogy with human creation, this universe may be an early effort in a process of trial and error, or that the imperfections in the world we know may indicate its creation by an infantile or a senile deity. Moreover, we have experience of material reproduction creating intelligence, but not the reverse; by analogy with our experience, the creator might be a seed, an egg, or a spider spinning worlds out of its own entrails. Philo maintains that an a posteriori examination of the evils and sufferings in this world compels us to conclude that whatever force or being is responsible for its creation does not have a moral nature—at least not one accessible to human understanding. The young man who reports the dialogues to a friend professes himself convinced by his patron Cleanthes; yet despite this last word, Philo has the strongest and most striking arguments throughout the dialogue.

Thus, from Berkeley to Hume, philosophical dialogues exhibit wide variations in the positions they imply concerning the proper attitude toward materialism, the deity, nature, and civilization. Underlying all these divergences, however, the form exhibits throughout this period a pronounced tendency to serve unorthodox ideas, to multiply ironies and paradoxes, and to question its own conventions.

[*See also* Berkeley, George; Diderot, Denis; Hume, David; Satire *and* Shaftesbury, Anthony Ashley Cooper.]

BIBLIOGRAPHY

Davies, Hugh Sykes, and George Watson. *The English Mind: Studies in the English Moralists Presented to Basil Willey*. Cambridge, 1964. Includes essays on the use of dialogue by Shaftesbury, Berkeley, and Hume.

Hume, David. *Dialogues Concerning Natural Religion*, edited by Norman Kemp Smith. Indianapolis, Ind., 1947 [1935]. Contains an indispensable 100-page Introduction, which discusses the date of composition and the meaning of the *Dialogues*.

Hundert, E. J. *The Enlightenment's "Fable."* Cambridge, 1994. Chapter 1 discusses part two of Mandeville's *Fable*.

Klein, Lawrence. *Shaftesbury and the Culture of Politeness*. Cambridge, 1994. Philosophical conversation and civility in Shaftesbury.

Prince, Michael. *Philosophical Dialogue in the British Enlightenment*. Cambridge, 1996. Close analysis of the major dialogues in English; relates the decline of the dialogue to the rise of the novel.

FRANK PALMERI

PHILOSOPHY. Enlightenment philosophy took up a number of themes and debates from the late seventeenth century. There was no unanimity on these matters, of course, but there were discernible tendencies. There was a move toward materialism, determinism, and empiricism, and a move away from an uncritical acceptance of revealed providential Christianity, as well as from tradition, received authority, and undemocratic political power, from rationalistic metaphysical systems, and from any non-naturalistic conception of humanity.

Religion. The late seventeenth and the eighteenth centuries are replete with titles like *The Reasonableness of Christianity* (John Locke, 1695), *Christianity not Mysterious* (John Toland, 1696), *The Obligations of Natural Religion* (Samuel Clarke, 1705, 1706), *The Religion of Nature* (William Wollaston, 1722), *Essays on Natural Religion* (David Hume, 1751), and *Christianisme dévoilé* (baron d'Holbach, 1761). In books with titles like these, some sought to find a deistic kernel of natural or rational religion within an inessential shell of the miracles, revelations, and mysteries of traditional Christianity; some, more radically freethinking, sought actually to dispose of that shell and to retain only its kernel; yet others, totally atheistically, aimed to expose all religion as a completely empty sham of priestcraft and superstition.

Though the Cambridge Platonists, including Henry More and Ralph Cudworth, had emphasized the role of reason in religion, they did not elevate it above faith. Locke, however, argued that revelation and faith must be answerable to reason. Reason must judge whether a supposed revelation is genuinely such, just as reason may have something to say about what meaning should be attached to the words of the Bible. Moreover, even though those words may reveal things not directly discoverable by reason (for example, the promise of resurrection), nothing of this sort is essential for salvation. God has given us "sufficient a light of reason, that they to whom [the Bible] never came, could not (whenever they set themselves to search) either doubt the being of a God, or of the obedience due to Him." Locke, then, did not go so far as to hold that nothing should be a part of religion unless it was discoverable by reason—though others, such as Toland, did.

The dogmas and details of traditional revealed religion came under chidingly skeptical attack from Pierre Bayle in his *Dictionnaire historique et critique* (1697), a work much read and referred to by the French philosophes. He claimed that in unmasking unjustified pretenses to knowledge, his aim was to make room for faith, but this was often taken to be ironic evasiveness.

George Berkeley exhibited a reaction against the skepticism of Bayle and the general trend of freethinking deism. His *Principles of Human Knowledge* (1710), which argued for an immaterial world of God-dependent ideas, opposed him to the materialistic atheism that was typically located in Thomas Hobbes and Baruch de Spinoza, or found (as by Berkeley) implied by Locke. Similarly, Berkeley's

Alciphron (1732) defended traditional providential Christianity.

Along with the deists, Hume distinguished between "false" religion with its superstitions and rituals (discussed at some length in his *Natural History of Religion*, 1757) and "true" religion; however, his *Dialogues Concerning Natural Religion* (1779) did not offer much support to the natural theologian who wished, by appeal to reason and the methods of the natural sciences, to prove the existence of God and to construct a rational religion. It is not clear whether they offered support to anything that might still be called a religious belief in God, but they certainly lent none to beliefs meant to have consequences for how we should live.

In his attack on "true" religion, Hume is in contrast to a typical eighteenth-century deist, such as Voltaire. Voltaire, too, was hostile to Christianity, but he aimed to demonstrate the existence of a God benevolently disposed to mankind and provided a basis for morality—though the 1755 Lisbon earthquake and its horrors, described in *Candide* (1759), gave him considerable pause. In his attack on "false" religion, Hume was followed by Julien Offray de La Mettrie and baron d'Holbach, whose passionate anti-Christianity was associated with an out-and-out materialist atheism. In his *Système de la Nature* (1770), d'Holbach argued that organized religion is no more than a tyrannical system of social control, and that belief in God is produced by ignorance and weak timidity, and productive of fearful anxiety.

Toward the end of the century, Immanuel Kant's *Kritik der reinen Vernunft* (Critique of Pure Reason, 1781) argued systematically that no demonstration of God's existence could possibly succeed. Though Kant's arguments have been used in the interests of skeptical atheism or agnosticism, he himself had a role for God as a postulate or presupposition of moral thinking.

Freedom. Hobbes and Spinoza presented a picture according to which our actions are determined by prior causes, never by some uncaused act of will. Even though our own desires might be among these causes, this does not give us the "liberty of indifference," or complete absence of determinism, that some thinkers required for free will and human freedom. By contrast, Cambridge Platonists like More argued for our ability to overrule and set aside our desires. A similarly libertarian conception of freedom was perhaps advocated by Locke, who wrote of the "ability to suspend...desires," and certainly by Samuel Clarke in *Demonstration of the Being and Attributes of God* (1705) and in his correspondence with Leibniz (published in 1717). A definite trend in the eighteenth century is toward necessitarianism—often accompanied, as in d'Holbach and Diderot, by an underlying materialism. This trend can be seen

in Anthony Collins's *Concerning Human Liberty* (1717) and his *On Liberty and Necessity* (1729), David Hume's *Treatise of Human Nature* (1739) and *Enquiry Concerning Human Understanding* (1748), Diderot's *Encyclopédie* articles, Voltaire's *Dictionnaire philosophique* (1764), and d'Holbach's *Système de la nature* (1770).

Those who advocated a liberty of indifference and the ability to suspend and act outside our desires thought that freedom of this sort is a necessary condition of moral responsibility; without it, we can hardly be held accountable for what we do. This connection could be made even by those who thought we are *not* free in this sense, of course; it was made by Diderot, who, believing that we are determined in all we do, held that we are not responsible for it. A necessitarian, however, did not have to make this connection: Hume believed that we are causally determined in all that we do, but that in the case where those causes are internal, such as our own desires and wishes, we have "liberty of spontaneity." Moreover, he argued, not only is liberty of this sort sufficient for moral responsibility and the praise and blame that goes with it; it is required for them, quite contrary to the belief of those who think freedom and necessity are utterly incompatible. It is only because we are determined by desires and motives that might be changed that rewards and punishments for our actions make sense.

Kant argued for an accommodation between free will and necessity different from that constructed by Hume. Like Hume on the one side and the libertarians on the other, Kant thought that contra-causal freedom (such as "liberty of indifference") and a generally deterministic framework are as unmixable as oil and water. But whereas Hume found room within a deterministic framework for a different, non-contra-causal conception of freedom, Kant sought to reconcile the determinism of nature with the freedom of the subject, conceived as a moral agent, by making a distinction between a transcendent noumenal self able to make free choices in accordance with self-imposed universalizable rules of morality, and a phenomenal self determined by natural laws.

Empiricism and the Study of Mind. Although Locke's interest in the foundation of religion, rational and revealed, was the initial stimulus for his *Essay*, his influential masterpiece turned out to be much more: a classic statement of empiricism, an epistemological doctrine that goes back to Aristotle's dictum that there is nothing in the mind that was not first in the senses. According to Locke's "history of the soul" (as Voltaire called it), the human mind begins as "white paper, void of all characters." There are no innate ideas, as advocated earlier by Descartes and the Cambridge Platonists; Locke explains how the whole of human knowledge and thought uses only the materials given it by experience. Hume took up and developed Locke's basic project, discussing in detail the "associative" mechanisms and principles that he supposed to underlie the formation of beliefs. Perhaps because he was interested more in how certain important beliefs were formed than in their truth, he was taken to be somewhat skeptical. His discussion of causality, in particular, was attacked by Kant.

Locke's basic empiricism was carried on enthusiastically in Europe—for example, by Claude Helvétius's *De l'esprit* (1758), and, most famously, by Etienne Condillac's *Traité des sensations* (1754). In his account of the human understanding, Locke had taken for granted various operations in which the mind was supposed to engage concerning the ideas it had received from experience. Condillac saw that Locke's approach needed radicalizing and simplifying to show how those operations themselves could be seen as arising out of sensation.

Embodied in all these investigations into the human mind is a methodological approach that had its roots in Bacon and that bore the magnificent fruit of Newton's *Philosophiae naturalis principia mathematica* (1697). The impressive success of Newton's systematizing account of terrestrial and extraterrestrial motion suggested to the eighteenth century that other subjects besides natural philosophy should be studied in the same way—by beginning not with a priori principles, but rather with careful and considered observation, out of which generalizations may grow but to which they are always answerable.

Materialism. There was some tendency for the empiricist approach to human understanding to associate with materialism. This is manifested in Helvétius's *De l'esprit*, which combined the account of mental activities Condillac had given with a candid materialism that denied that the mind was anything other than a part of physical nature. The idea of an immaterial mind, as embodied in the canonical mid-seventeenth-century substance dualism (thinking mind/material body) of Descartes, was never without its supporters, such as More and the Cambridge Platonists, Berkeley, or Andrew Baxter (*Enquiry into the Nature of the Soul*, 1733). It was challenged, however, by those who rejected all immaterial, purely spiritual substances—including God—and by those, such as La Mettrie (*L'homme machine*, 1748), who extended to human beings the purely materialistic account Descartes had given of nonhuman animals.

Such challenges had been made even in Descartes's own time, by Hobbes and, less dogmatically, by Gassendi. Along with Spinoza (who, attributing both thought and extension to the same substance, was read as though that substance were basically material *rather than* immaterial), they continued to be cited as materialists. Yet equally prominent in the eighteenth century was a rather offhand suggestion that Locke made about the possibility of

thinking matter: "Since we know not wherein thinking consists...I see no contradiction...that the first eternal thinking being should, if he please, give to certain systems of created senseless matter, put together as he thinks fit, some degrees of sense, perception and thought." The suggestion was both referred to and taken up in various writings of Diderot, and its thrust was developed at length in La Mettrie's *Histoire naturelle de l'âme* (1745) and his *L'homme machine* (1748): feelings, sensation, and will are all properties of a material soul, and all of human behavior is the product of a physical organism. The materialist location of mental powers of thought and sensation in the body was helped by the development of a conception of matter as less passive and inert, and more active and forceful, than that typically entertained in the seventeenth century. Joseph Priestley's *Disquisitions Relating to Matter and Spirit* (1777), which argued that mental powers are the product of a particular physical organization, is a good example.

The reduction of the human soul to the body is characteristically associated with a rejection of God, human immortality, human freedom, and morality. The association is not inevitable, though; Locke is a clear illustration of this, despite his implication in the development of materialism. For one thing, he argued, thinking matter could be produced only by an immaterial God; and for another, "All the great ends of morality and religion, are well enough secured, without philosophical proofs of the soul's immateriality." The associations were there, however, both in those, such as Baxter, who clung to an immaterial soul, and those, such as Diderot, who finally relinquished it.

Ethics. The seventeenth century saw a number of views according to which ethics is like mathematics and geometry in consisting of truths that can be discovered by the use of pure reason. Toward the turn of the century, a trend began toward the assimilation of moral judgments to judgments of taste, even to feelings and sensations, rather than to objective truths.

More, one of the Cambridge Platonists, promulgated a doctrine of self-evident innate moral principles. Locke, too, though not thinking of morality as innate, held that, in principle, it was possible to place it "amongst the sciences capable of demonstration: wherein...from self-evident propositions, by necessary consequences, as incontestable as those in mathematics, the measures of right and wrong might be made out." Some of these "intellectualist" approaches to morality continued into the eighteenth century: examples include Samuel Clarke (*The Unchangeable Obligations of Natural Religion*, 1705), John Balguy (*The Foundation of Moral Goodness*, 1727, 1728), William Wollaston (*Religion of Nature Delineated*, 1722), and Richard Price (*Principal Questions and Difficulties in Morals*, 1757). However, with Anthony Ashley Cooper, third earl of Shaftesbury, there began a more "psycholog-ical," "naturalistic" approach to morality. We have, wrote Shaftesbury in his *Enquiry Concerning Virtue or Merit* (1711), a "sense of right and wrong," "a moral sense," based on a natural benevolence toward others.

Shaftesbury's claim that we are naturally unselfish and other-regarding met some resistance—for example, by Bernard Mandeville, whose *Fable of the Bees* (1714) is grounded in Hobbes's view of man as naturally selfish. It also precipitated discussion, as in Joseph Butler's *Analogy of Religion* (1736), on the relation between self- and other-interest. In contrast, Shaftesbury's underlying idea that morality is based on our natural psychological reactions was taken up with enthusiasm. Francis Hutcheson's *The Original of Our Ideas of Beauty and Virtue* (1725) developed the idea by comparing moral judgments with aesthetic reactions and judgments of taste; and the idea of morality as having to do with psychological reactions appeared most famously in Hume. In a reference to Clarke, Hume's *Treatise* attacks the idea that "virtue is nothing but a conformity to reason": morality is "more properly felt than judged of"; and an action "is virtuous or vicious . . . because its view causes a pleasure or uneasiness of a particular kind."

Politics. Besides having sound arguments for reject-ing the notion of innate ideas, Locke believed that this concept had been a device used by those in authority to reinforce established doctrines. As such, it was inconsis-tent with the individual responsibility that, Locke stressed, we have for our beliefs. This individualism, so congenial to Enlightenment thought in general, also shows itself in the account he gives of the origin of civil government and the basis of its authority. His *Treatises of Civil Gov-ernment* (1690) criticized Robert Filmer's earlier theories of absolute monarchy and the divine right of kings, and argued that rulers are not absolute. Locke built his the-ory on the idea of people living in a state of nature, in families and loose groups, without any political authority over them. In this state, they do have God-given rights and duties, but it does not follow that these are respected and fulfilled. As a consequence, the people agree to set up an authority to settle controversies and redress injuries, and so they leave the state of nature. Unlike the ruler of Hobbes's *Leviathan* (1651), who similarly comes to power through a "social contract," Locke's sovereign authority is not absolute but is always answerable to the will of the majority. Rulers themselves have duties to their subjects, and this means that resistance to them might be justified if their commands do not deserve obedience.

Hume's *Concerning the Original Contract* (1748) was targeted on Locke. He was far more sensitive to and laid far more stress on the actual facts of history, which, by and large, show that consent and contract had been merely one part, and then only seldom, of the basis for political authority. In fact, Locke had accepted the lack of historical evidence for his account of the creation of political authority, and he had also accepted that, in many cases, people are simply born into civil societies and come under laws and authority without choice. His response appealed to a distinction between tacit and explicit consent: however it was that one has come to be under a certain authority, by remaining there and not leaving the country, one gives tacit consent.

Hume also objected to the logic of basing allegiance on a contract or promise. As much explanation, or as little, is required of why a person should keep to his contract as it is of why he should obey the state: "We gain nothing by resolving the one into the other. The general interests or necessities of society are sufficient to establish both."

The individualism present in Locke was generally sup-posed to be present in Jean-Jacques Rousseau's defense of social contract theory. His *Contrat social* (1762) based political obligation on the voluntary submission of each individual. But, whereas Hobbes's citizens submit to an absolute monarch and Locke's to one whose rule is condi-tional on his ruling properly, Rousseau's submit to what he called "the general will." Though this can properly find expression only in a small state where citizens are not represented but vote directly, the "general will" is differ-ent from the "will of all." It is not a simple function of particular wills, but rather a will that is directed to the general good.

[*See also* Aesthetics; Economic Thought; Empiricism; Epistemology; Human Nature; Materialism; Moral Philos-ophy; Natural Philosophy and Science; Natural Religion; Political Philosophy; Revealed Religion; *and* Tradition.]

BIBLIOGRAPHY

Brown, Stuart, ed. *British Philosophy and the Age of Enlightenment.* (Routledge History of Philosophy, vol. 5.) London and New York, 1996. Its various chapters cover much of the material outlined here.

Cassirer, Ernst. *The Philosophy of the Enlightenment.* Translated by Fritz C. A. Koelln and James P. Pettegrove. Princeton, N.J., 1951. English translation of *Die Philosophie der Aufklärung* (1932), a good general study of Enlightenment thought.

Copleston, Frederick. *A History of Philosophy: Hobbes to Hume.* London, 1959. A sound general history of philosophy.

Copleston, Frederick. *A History of Philosophy: Wolff to Kant.* London, 1960. A sound general history of philosophy, including accounts of the French philosophes.

Gay, Peter. *The Enlightenment: An Interpretation.* 2 vols. London, 1970. Chaps. 3–7 of vol. 1 and chaps. 3–4 of vol. 2 of this excellent work are particularly relevant to the topics discussed here.

Gough, J. W. *The Social Contract: A Critical Study of Its Development.* 2d ed. Oxford, 1957.

Sorley, W. R. *A History of English Philosophy.* Cambridge, 1920. A bibliographically detailed history.

Stromberg, Roland M. *Religious Liberalism in Eighteenth-Century England.* Oxford, 1954.

White, R. J. *The Anti-Philosophers: A Study of the Philosophes in Eighteenth-Century France.* London, 1970.

Woolhouse, R. S. *The Empiricists*. Oxford, 1988. Covers Bacon, Hobbes, Gassendi, Locke, Berkeley, and Hume.

Yolton, John W. *Thinking Matter: Materialism in Eighteenth-Century Britain*. Minneapolis, 1984.

Yolton, John W. *Locke and French Materialism*. Oxford, 1991.

R. S. WOOLHOUSE

PHYSICO-THEOLOGY.

PHYSICO-THEOLOGY. Physico-theology was a particular form of natural theology that sought to give religious meaning and significance to the successes of the scientific revolution. Where, traditionally, natural theology had formed part of the deductive structure of scholastic philosophy, physico-theology sought to demonstrate the truth of the argument from design by a posteriori rather than a priori reasoning. Its emergence in the late seventeenth and eighteenth centuries reflects, then, the dissolution of the attempt to arrive at an integrated philosophical synthesis based on deductive reasoning that had informed not only the largely Aristotelian-based philosophy of the schools but also that of René Descartes.

As the name suggests, physico-theology sought to base theological apologetic quite directly on the findings of "physics" in its traditional sense of natural philosophy. It was to be particularly prominent in England where it meshed with the Baconian tradition that placed greater emphasis on firsthand observation than was customary in continental Europe, where the quest for an overarching philosophical synthesis lingered. For physico-theology depended for its force and public impact on direct illustrations of the design argument rather than a chain of philosophical reasoning. Such, for example, was the goal of the influential work of physico-theology by the naturalist John Ray, *The Wisdom of God Manifested in the Works of the Creation* (1691). Physico-theology therefore offered a way of integrating new scientific findings into a general culture largely shaped by theological concerns—a task that, as R. M. Young (1980) emphasizes, it continued to perform in Britain well into Victorian times.

Along with the empirical Baconian tradition, another stimulus to the development of physico-theology in seventeenth-century Britain was the desire to arrive at forms of theology that could unite all Protestants at a time when religious and political differences threatened to cause continual turmoil. Physico-theology offered a form of intellectual discourse that not only brought science and religion into a fruitful partnership but also directed attention to the essentials of Christian belief rather than points of doctrinal debate. Such considerations are reflected in the wording of Robert Boyle's bequest to found a series of lectures "for proving the Christian Religion, against notorious Infidels...not descending lower to any Controversies, that are among Christians themselves" (Jacob, 1976, 144).

These Boyle lectures, founded in 1691, were to serve as one of the most important vehicles for promoting physico-theology. In particular, some were used to promulgate the conclusions of Newton's *Principia* in a form that emphasized the extent to which the universe was dependent on the careful design and continuing providential care of a beneficent creator. Indeed, it was largely through the medium of physico-theology that Newton's major findings became known to an educated public that had limited mathematical competence but a well-developed taste for theological discussion. This fruitful alliance between Newton's work and Christian apologetic was first forged by the great classicist Richard Bentley in the first set of the Boyle lectures delivered in 1692. It was later further consolidated by other Boyle lecturers such as Samuel Clarke, William Whiston, and William Derham (whose lectures were published under the title *Physico-Theology: or, A Demonstration of the Being and Attributes of God, from the Works of Creation* [1713]).

Although the awesome achievement of Newton did help to create a particular association between physico-theology and the physical and astronomical sciences, natural history provided a simpler and more immediately accessible basis for physico-theology—as the earlier success of the writings of John Ray demonstrated. As the novelty of Newton's work faded so, too, there was an increasing tendency for physico-theologians to revert to examples drawn from natural history and medicine. This was particularly pronounced in the most influential of all works of physico-theology, William Paley's lucid *Natural Theology* (1802). Paley argued that astronomy was of limited utility in proving the existence of a creator-designer, although it could serve to promote a sense of awe at his works. But, for a general reader, he saw natural history and anatomy as providing much more immediate and striking illustrations of the hand of an intelligent designer.

In continental Europe, too, physico-theology was largely associated with the life sciences. The success of Abbé Noël-Antoine Pluche's eight-volume *Spectacle de la Nature* (1732) owed much to the way in which it demonstrated that creation was made for man as the image of the creator through illustrations drawn, as Paley was later to do, from anatomy and natural history. Within Germany the great naturalist Johann Fabricius (1668–1736) was one of the main proponents of physico-theology—a view of the world that also largely shaped the work of Carolus Linnaeus and his classificatory system.

Countries such as France, where there was considerable conflict between elements of the educated classes and the church, proved much less fertile grounds for the development of physico-theology than Britain, where there was a much greater inclination to turn scientific advance to the defense of the existing order in church and state. The French Revolution with its secularization of higher education further undercut the promotion of physico-theology within those parts of Europe under French control.

In Britain, however, the experience of the Revolution and the renewed emphasis on the alliance between church and state, which it promoted by reaction, served to reaffirm the worth of physico-theology. Paley's work strengthened the conviction that science and religion could be allies and an interest in physico-theology was further encouraged by the publication from 1833 to 1840 of the Bridgewater Treatises, which were intended to demonstrate "the power, wisdom, and goodness of God, as manifested in the Creation." However, even before Darwin's work challenged the basic assumptions of the design argument on which physico-theology was largely based, the growing complexity and diversity of scientific inquiry made this form of natural theology less attractive to an educated public that found recent scientific advances less and less accessible. Science and theology had, by the mid-nineteenth century, increasingly come to inhabit separate intellectual domains.

[*See also* Deism; Empiricism; Natural Philosophy and Science; *and* Natural Religion.]

BIBLIOGRAPHY

Brooke, J. *Science and Religion: Some Historical Perspectives.* Cambridge, 1991. Especially chapters 4–6.

Gascoigne, J. "From Bentley to the Victorians: The Rise and Fall of British Newtonian Natural Theology." *Science in Context* 2 (1988), 219–256.

Gillespie, N. C. "Natural History, Natural Theology, and Social Order: John Ray and the 'Newtonian Ideology.'" *Journal for the History of Biology* 20 (1987), 1–49.

Jacob, M. C. *The Newtonians and the English Revolution 1689–1720.* Hassocks, U.K., 1976. Especially chapters 4 and 5 on the Boyle lectures.

Kubrin, D. "Newton and the Cyclical Cosmos: Providence and the Mechanical Philosophy." In *Science and Religious Belief: A Selection of Recent Historical Studies*, edited by C. A. Russell, pp. 147–169. London, 1973.

Metzger, H. *Attraction universelle et religion naturelle chez quelques commentateurs anglais de Newton.* Paris, 1938. On the early development of Newtonian physico-theology.

Olson, R. *Science Deified and Science Defied: The Historical Significance of Science in Western Culture*, vol. 2, chapter 3. Berkeley, Calif., 1990.

Phillip, W. "Physicotheology in the Age of Enlightenment: Appearance and History." In *Studies on Voltaire and the Eighteenth Century*, vol. 57. Geneva, 1967. pages 1233–1297.

Westfall, R. S. *Science and Religion in Seventeenth-Century England.* New Haven, Conn., 1958.

Young, R. M. "Natural Theology, Victorian Periodicals, and the Fragmentation of a Common Context." In *Darwin to Einstein: Historical Studies on Science and Belief*, edited by C. Chant and J. Fauvel, pp. 69–106. London, 1980.

JOHN GASCOIGNE

PHYSICS. The meaning of the word "physics" changed dramatically during the course of the Enlightenment. The French academician and salonnier Jean Le Rond d'Alembert (1717–1783), in his *Discours préliminaire* (Preliminary Discourse to the *Encyclopédie*, 1751), divided the discipline into general physics (the metaphysics of bodies, or the general principles of material extension, motion, repulsion, and attraction) and particular physics (chemistry, mineralogy, botany, zoology, meteorology, physical astronomy, and cosmology). This Baconian division of knowledge, while admittedly old-fashioned even by mid-eighteenth-century standards, can be taken as a starting point for what constituted physics at the beginning of the Enlightenment. Noticeably absent are electricity, magnetism, and heat, which are discussed nowhere by d'Alembert, and mechanics, astronomy, optics, acoustics, and pneumatics, which are mentioned elsewhere under the rubric of mixed mathematics.

After Newton. Fifty or so years later, much had been removed from physics (chemistry, mineralogy, botany, and zoology in particular) and much added (electricity, magnetism, physical optics, heat, and the behavior of liquids and gases). Mixed mathematics still remained an independent discipline, but its methods of quantification and its central theory of mechanics were assiduously copied by physicists. There were several reasons why so many sub-disciplines left physics while so many others were added or created. The Cambridge University professor and government administrator Isaac Newton (1642–1727) provided successful exemplars of mathematical and experimental physics in his *Principia* (1687) and *Opticks* (1704), respectively. The *Principia* combined general physics (a universal theory of gravitation and a central force law), particular physics (physical astronomy and cosmology), and mixed mathematics (positional astronomy and mechanics) to correlate mathematical theory with existing physical observation, while the *Opticks* in general revealed a vast range of phenomena that were to be found in the laboratory and its Queries in particular hinted at the subtle forces and fluids that accounted for them. Some of these phenomena—most particularly electrical, magnetic, fluid, and caloric effects—later proved to be so extensive as to demand entire sub-disciplines within physics. Meanwhile, those parts of physics that stood no chance whatsoever of being mathematized—botany and zoology most obviously; chemistry more ambiguously—soon left behind the irksome and unproductive constrictions of mathematics to stand as independent and flourishing disciplines in their own right.

The Newtonian ideal of combining theory and praxis drove Enlightenment physics, and the successful examples, while rather few in actuality (and perhaps only fully realized in the case of astronomy), led to a tremendous optimism that the human command and understanding of nature was increasing everyday. Even if subjecting the phenomena of particular physics to the methods of mixed mathematics was a difficult and rarely accomplished feat, the enlightened could take satisfaction at the immense range of phenomena, never before witnessed by humans, that physics revealed. Sciences such as heat, electricity, and magnetism, which were underdeveloped at the beginning of the Enlightenment, by its end offered a cornucopia of novel effects created by experimentalists and demonstrators of great skill and imagination using devices and instruments that had never been thought of, let alone made, before. However, progress in theoretical understanding remained less satisfying: Once these phenomena had been demonstrated, their underlying entities remained invisible. Unlike Galilean inclined planes, or Cartesian tennis balls, or Huyghenian pendula, or Newtonian planets—objects whose mass, geometry, and motion were amenable to definition and measurement—the causes of heat, or electrical repulsion, or capillary action remained unknown. Even if, on pragmatic grounds, the question of causality was put to one side and the investigator tried to define a visible quantity, it was not clear what exactly such a quantity measured.

Theory and praxis were often separated, moreover, by substantial differences in social and intellectual interest between theoreticians and practitioners. For example, the Swiss academician Leonhard Euler (1707–1783) gained and kept his positions at the courts of Prussia and Russia because he produced mathematical theories and physical models of great brilliance that brought luster to the princes and monarchs who patronized him. His work had the potential to be (and occasionally was) useful, but he was not required by his patrons to cater to experimentalists or artisans, who found little practical application for his theories in their everyday work of producing experimental phenomena and making scientific instruments.

At times, these difficulties were overcome. The reclusive English aristocrat Henry Cavendish (1731–1810), the peripatetic Jesuit Ruggier Boscovich (1711–1787), and the Dutch professor Hermann Boerhaave (1668–1738) were all skilled at using scientific instruments to produce phenomena, make measurements, and test theories, to quite a high level of mathematical sophistication. It was Boerhaave who, along with his University of Leiden colleagues Willem Jacob 'sGravesande (1688–1742) and Petrus van Musschenbroek (1692–1761) and the English cleric and curator of experiments at the Royal Society of London John Desaguliers (1683–1744), popularized experimental physics, the style that came to dominate university and public lectures. These Anglo-Dutch Newtonians and those who followed them cultivated the first main branch of Enlightenment physics, which relied upon experiments and demonstrations to illuminate physical principles in an entertaining and pedagogically appealing manner without the use of difficult mathematics. They created a series of theoretical entities—subtle fluids—to bring some order to, if not actually to explain, the physical phenomena pertaining to light, magnetism, electricity, and heat, at the same time eliminating from physics or reducing to insignificance subjects such as botany, zoology, physiology, medicine, and chemistry. Meanwhile, those who were opposed to this relative indifference to mathematics—in the main, French- and German-speaking academicians like d'Alembert and Euler—tended to the other branch of Enlightenment physics, which sought to use the methods of mixed mathematics to quantify laboratory phenomena and create sophisticated mechanical models.

The Demonstration Experiment. The demonstration experiment formed an important and new part of the university curriculum, public lecture, and scientific textbook. In all three cases, students, auditors, and readers had little patience with or expertise in the niceties of mathematics or speculative theory. They wanted spectacular effects, intriguing puzzles, and simple answers; in short, they were looking to be both enlightened and entertained. Certain subjects filled these requirements very well, most particularly elementary mechanics and electricity. In 1717, after a trip to London to meet Newton and other distinguished members of the Royal Society, 'sGravesande was appointed professor of mathematics and astronomy at Leiden. Three years later, he converted his popular lecture courses into a textbook, *Physices Elementa Mathematica, Experimentis Confirmata* (Mathematical Elements of Physics Confirmed by Experiment), which established a style of science that still exists in today's elementary physics instruction. Newtonian mechanics lay at its heart, but it was a mechanics that, despite the first part of the book's title, relied on machines—levers, pulleys, gears, pendulums, suction and air pumps—rather than equations to illustrate principles of attraction; conservation of momentum; addition, multiplication, and transferral of force; and hydrostatic equilibrium.

The machines themselves, profusely illustrated in his book, were the personal property of 'sGravesande. Such working capital was expensive; upon his death, 'sGravesande's collection of demonstration instruments was bought by his university for 8,400 *livres*, about three times a comfortable professional annual salary. Lecturers and authors thus had to consider carefully whether the instruments they used would attract a fee-paying audience. Electrical instruments, because they demonstrated new and spectacular phenomena, did. The most important of these, a generator of electrical charge, was developed by the English instrument maker and curator of experiments at the Royal Society Francis

Hauksbee (c. 1666–1713), in the course of researches on the intriguing and beautiful glows of light that appear in the empty space above the mercury in barometers. Hauksbee's electrical machine was simple enough: a globe of glass spun by an inertial wheel that was turned by a human-powered handle. When touched by an appropriate object, the glass globe became electrified. It rapidly became fashionable for rapt onlookers to observe the weightless but powerful fluid, stored in specially constructed containers (Leyden jars), that could flow through conductors—to a shocking effect when those conductors were human—and attract or repel according to circumstances. Other physical experiments that delighted Enlightenment audiences included focusing light with gigantic concave mirrors to make enough heat to melt diamonds; re-creating the colors of the rainbow with Newton's prismatic experiments; illustrating the weight of the air as it pressed down on the piston of a model atmospheric (steam) engine; and demonstrating the immense amount of heat that could be poured into melting ice without changing its temperature.

The many phenomena of the demonstration lecture were qualitatively explained by the various subtle fluids of the Enlightenment, and if the oddities of those fluids are a little much for modern taste, it is important to realize that contemporaries mostly thought of them as convenient fictions whose explanatory power did not imply the actual existence of such substances. They became popular because the Newtonian alternative, action-at-a-distance microscopic force laws, faced profound problems. What were the size, mass, geometry, of the underlying particles? What were their laws of attraction and repulsion? How did microscopic particles account for the observed macroscopic forces, or vice versa? For example, the phenomenon of capillarity demonstrated that water was attracted to glass and could overcome the force of gravity to climb thin glass tubes to a measurable height. What microscopic glass and water entities, and what force laws, however, could account for this measurement? The analogue of the gravitational attraction between celestial bodies proved misleading, because the macroscopic particles (planets) were large, very few in number, and easily observable.

Instead, it was easier to imagine entities that carried with them a certain kind of force that varied with their number or density. In 1727, the English clergyman Stephen Hales (1677–1761) published the influential *Vegetable Staticks*, which demonstrated the capturing of a variety of airs in bottles inverted over water or mercury baths. These airs had formerly been confined in very small spaces (for example an apple), yet when released took up a great deal of space (a fermented apple released an air that filled a bottle roughly fifty times as large as the apple). Hales postulated that two different kinds of airs

accounted for such behavior: an elastic and unconfined air that repelled matter, and a sulfurous air that was attractive and confined the airs in solids. It was the former, repulsive air that Boerhaave, in his *Elementa Chemiae* of 1732, developed even further, positing an elementary fire that was, like air, weightless. Such a subtle fluid, Boerhaave argued, could account for the phenomena of heat, light, and electricity. His view remained popular for nearly two decades, until the increasing numbers of experimental phenomena could no longer be explained by a single immaterial entity.

By the end of the Enlightenment, matter had come to be divided into two kinds, subtle and ordinary. The former, more commonly known as the subtle fluids, weighed nothing and bore forces—electrical, magnetic, optical, caloric—that could be either attractive or repulsive. The latter, or ponderable, matter weighed something and bore only attractive forces: gravitational, cohesional, capillary, and chemical. These two kinds of matter were used to explain a wide variety of physical phenomena, including electricity, magnetism, light, and heat. Ordinary matter filled with electrical or magnetic subtle fluid could, depending upon circumstances, repel or attract. Light interacted with ordinary matter but not with itself: Rays of light did not interfere with each other, but were bent by transparent matter and could be brought to points of intensification (focused) by lenses and mirrors. Heat, or the caloric, repelled itself: caloric-rich ordinary matter did not cohere into one agglomeration, but could expand into a gas. The caloric flowed from hot to cold, and some substances (for example, water) had a huge capacity to absorb it, even at times without any temperature change. Not until the end of the eighteenth century did these qualitative concepts of flow, intensity, and capacity finally begin to be quantified.

Mixed Mathematical Sciences. Mixed mathematical sciences like astronomy, geodesy, navigation, and cartography developed in the Enlightenment by taking advantage of increasingly accurate measuring instruments, new mathematical techniques, and carefully organized fieldwork that made meticulous and extensive measurements on very large scales of time and space. These sciences had two effects on physics. Firstly, mixed mathematics helped answer many of the questions—What was the true shape of the globe? How far away was the sun from the earth?—that physics posed. Secondly, mixed mathematical techniques could be used to quantify many of the physical phenomena that demonstration experiments had created and subtle fluid theory had typified.

Enlightenment monarchs and princes liked to spend money on physics when the esoteric and the practical coincided. For instance, whether the earth was squashed like an onion (an oblate sphere) or squeezed like a lemon (a prolate sphere) was a nice question that had two opposing physical answers. Arguing for the oblate sphere were Newton and his followers, who reasoned that a spinning and not perfectly rigid earth must bulge at the equator. For the contrary position of the prolate sphere were the Cartesians, who inferred that the ether spinning the earth around must squeeze it at the equator. This would have remained an intriguing theoretical quarrel had it not made a real difference to mapmakers, who needed to know what the true shape of the earth was when they projected three-dimensional measurements of the earth's surface onto a two-dimensional representational flat map. Louis XV dispatched two well-equipped parties toward the North Pole (Lapland, 1736–1737) and the equator (Peru, 1735–1745) to resolve the issue using the standard techniques and instruments of surveying and astronomy. The arctic party returned home first and its leader, the French academician Pierre-Louis Moreaude Maupertuis (1698–1759), announced that the earth was squashed in the best Newtonian fashion. Maupertuis relied heavily on the accuracy of the mixed mathematical instruments—zenith sectors, theodolites, and pendulum clocks made by the English instrument maker George Graham (1673–1751)—to support his claims. The lesson, which was repeated throughout the Enlightenment, was clear. Physical questions could be answered by using the best instruments and mathematics available, provided it was clear what those tools actually measured.

In mixed mathematics, the quantities to be measured were already very well typified—the position of a planet in the sky corresponded to an angle, the height of a mountain to a distance, the swing of a pendulum to a unit of time—but the situation was often much more difficult in experimental physics. What, for example, did the angle of parting of two electrified leaves on an electroscope, or the length of mercury in a thermometer, correspond to; and how might those macroscopic entities, once defined robustly, be related to underlying microscopic entities? Theoretical entities such as the electrical charge (Q) accumulated on a conductor, or the capacity (C) of a Leyden jar to hold charge, or the tension (T) that existed between the two separated leaves of an electroscope that was attached to a charged conductor, emerged from the varied phenomena of the demonstration experiments of the first half of the eighteenth century and were related to actual measurements in laboratories. However, there was no simple, known relationship between, for instance, the number of times (N) that the handle of a particular electrical machine was turned, thereby generating charge on a conductor, and the angle (A) that the leaves of the electroscope indicated when attached to that conductor. Thus when the Italian professor of physics Alessandro Volta (1745–1827) developed in the 1780s a variable conductor whose capacity for holding charge increased linearly as the length (L) of the conductor increased, he could do little more than guess, on the basis of his own observations, that $N = LA$ and hence $Q = CT$. To prove that this latter equation was correct required a tremendous amount of work that could not be finished in the Enlightenment. First, the correct functional relationship between the angle of the leaves of the electroscope and the tension that caused it had to be determined. Second, standards had to be established between laboratories so that quantities that were specific to a given location could be related to quantities from other laboratories. For example, the number of turns of Volta's particular electrical machine (N) had to be calibrated with other machines, most conveniently, by establishing a common definition of the underlying actual charge (Q).

Throughout the Enlightenment, the ideal remained that mechanics ought to lie at the heart of physics. However, that ideal was rarely put into practice, primarily because the main practitioners of Enlightenment mechanics were not particularly interested in making their work applicable to physics or to the broader community of machine users. Instead, they concentrated on a rational mechanics that stripped out the messy variability of actual matter and created an idealized world of perfectly rigid spinning tops, elastic beams, vibrating strings, and nonturbulent fluids. Newton's mechanics provided a starting point, but it was a mechanics for two dimensions that took the conservation of momentum (a vector quantity, mass multiplied by velocity) as the primary unit of analysis. It was the great achievement of mathematicians from Daniel Bernoulli (1700–1782) to Euler that they created a mechanics of solid, three-dimensional, if admittedly ideal, objects and argued for the importance of the conservation of *vis viva* (a scalar quantity, mass multiplied by the square of velocity).

This school of rational mechanics reached its apotheosis with the brilliant work of the French academician and mathematician Joseph-Louis Lagrange (1736–1813), whose *Méchanique analytique* (Analytical Mechanics) of 1788 was purely algebraic and contained no references to the measured properties of actual matter. Thus Enlightenment physics, in one sense, ended as it had begun: Mathematical mechanics represented the ideal practice and stood at a very high level of sophistication but, outside of astronomy, it still had little real utility to physicists. Dramatic changes elsewhere, however—in the range and novelty of phenomena generated, the accuracy and utility of instruments, the difference in subjects covered, and the extent of quantification—meant that physics was a very different, and according to most observers, greatly improved discipline by the end of the Enlightenment. Thus the history of physics provided another piece of evidence for the enlightened that progress in human understanding was indeed possible.

[*See also* Alembert, Jean Le Rond d'; Buffon, Georges-Louis Leclerc de; Chemistry; Geography; Gravesande, Willem Jacob 's; Huygens, Christiaan; Leibniz, Gottfried Wilhelm von; Mapping; Medicine; Musschenbroek, Petrus van; Natural Philosophy and Science; Natural Religion; Newton, Isaac; Nieuwentijt, Bernard; Optics; Optimism, Philosophical; *and* Progress.]

BIBLIOGRAPHY

Anderson, R. G. W., J. A. Bennett, and W. F. Ryan, eds. *Making Instruments Count: Essays on Historical Scientific Instruments Presented to Gerard L'Estrange Turner*. Aldershot, U.K., 1993. A useful guide to more recent scholarship on the history of scientific instruments.

Daumas, Maurice. *Scientific Instruments of the 17th and 18th Centuries and Their Makers*. Translated by M. Holbrook. London, 1972. A classic and still unsurpassed account of the instruments of experimental physics and mixed mathematics and the men who made them.

Hankins, Thomas L. *Science and the Enlightenment*. Cambridge, 1985. A well-balanced, if rather brief, introduction.

Heilbron, J. L. *Elements of Early Modern Physics*. Berkeley, 1982. Intelligent, erudite, if a little quirky. Chapter 2, "The Physicists," gives a good account of their training and institutional location.

Heilbron, J. L. *Weighing Imponderables and Other Quantitative Science around 1800*. Berkeley, 1993. Difficult at times but very rewarding when read carefully.

Jacob, Margaret. *Scientific Culture and the Making of the Industrial West*. Oxford, 1997. Very good on the industrial context against which physics developed.

Jungnickel, Christa, and Russell McCormmach. *Cavendish, the Experimental Life*. Lewisburg, Pa., 1999. An exemplary scientific biography. Well worth buying and reading in full.

Morton, Alan Q., and Jane A. Wess. *Public and Private Science: The King George III Collection*. Oxford, 1993. Contains a superb collection of photographs of the machines and instruments that were used in Enlightenment physics demonstration lectures. If you cannot get to the London Science Museum or one of equivalent stature, turning the pages of this book is a fine substitute.

Olson, Richard. *Science Deified and Science Defied: The Historical Significance of Science in Western Culture*, vol. 2, *From the Early Modern Age Through the Early Romantic Era, c. 1640 to c. 1820*. Berkeley, 1982. A lively overview.

Rousseau, G. S., and Roy Porter, eds. *The Ferment of Knowledge: Studies in the Historiography of Eighteenth-Century Science*. Cambridge, 1980. A groundbreaking collection of essays. Chapters 2 (Simon Schaffer, "Natural Philosophy"), 8 (H. J. M. Bos, "Mathematics and Rational Philosophy"), 9 (J. L. Heilbron, "Experimental Natural Philosophy"), and 11 (Eric G. Forbes, "Cosmography") are all excellent.

Scholfield, Robert. *Mechanism and Materialism: British Natural Philosophy in the Age of Reason*. Princeton, N.J., 1970. An influential text.

Wolf, A. *A History of Science, Technology and Philosophy in the Eighteenth Century*. 2 vols. New York, 1939. Still the only large-scale work on eighteenth-century physics and very useful.

RICHARD J. SORRENSON

PHYSIOCRACY. An economic theory developed in France in the second half of the eighteenth century, the name Physiocracy comes from Greek *physis* "nature" and *Kratos* "power"; it first appeared in 1767 in the title of a collection of François Quesnay's writings edited by Pierre-Samuel Du Pont de Nemours, *Physiocratie, ou constitution naturelle du gouvernement le plus avantageux au genre humain*. The Physiocrats—called the *économistes* by their contemporaries—represent the first school of economists, which gathered around Quesnay, physician to the French king. The group consisted of Victor Riqueti, the marquis de Mirabeau, Dupont de Nemours, Pierre-Paul-François Le Mercier de La Rivière, Nicolas Baudeau, Guillaume-François Le Trosne, Charles Butré, Louis-Paul Abeille, Jean Saint Péravy, and Pierre Roubaud. Their fundamental assertion was the existence of a natural order that embodies the economic process. The physical world, they believed, is subject to immutable laws, and the social order is a part of this universal order. Knowledge of these laws represents the science of political economy. Proceeding from John Locke's perspective, property, liberty, and security were the underpinnings of their analysis of the origin and nature of civil society, in which the natural order reveals a harmony of interests among all social groups.

Economic Thought. From the beginning of the eighteenth century, a general movement developed in France advocating free trade against the protectionist practices of mercantilism. Pierre le Pesant de Boisguilbert's *Détail de la France* (1695) and *Dissertation sur la nature des richesses* (1707) emphasized the role of agriculture and depicted economic activities as a circular flow. Richard Cantillon's *Essai sur la nature du commerce en général*, published by Mirabeau in 1755, is a theoretical approach to economic process leading to a scientific model later adopted by the Physiocrats. In the same period, Vincent de Gournay's series of translations of foreign economic works familiarized French readers with economic thought. His argument for free trade captured in his slogan "laissez faire, laissez passer," shaped public opinion and influenced the campaign for economic liberty. Physiocracy belonged to this liberal movement, but it represented a turning point: its scientific analysis of the whole economic process and of the nature of society marked the origin of the science of political economy. Although lacking a clear definition, the physiocratic terms "net product" (*produit net*) and "advances" (*avances*) anticipated classical economics' principles of surplus and capital. Adam Smith's *An Inquiry into the Nature and Causes of the Wealth of Nations* (1776) moved away from Physiocracy, despite passing through its doctrines, and the relationship between Quesnay's and Smith's thought stirred discussions in economics until the beginning of the nineteenth century. Long after the decline of Physiocracy's political influence, Thomas Malthus, William Spence, James Maitland, earl of Lauderdale, John Stuart Mill, Antoine-Louis-Claude Destutt de Tracy, Germain Garnier, Charles Ganhil, and Jean-Baptiste Say continued to debate physiocratic principles.

In its scientific approach, Physiocracy represented the first organic attack against the mercantilism still largely accepted in France and universally practiced abroad. Its economic perspective was thoroughly new: output was given priority over money and exchange; wealth was not considered stationary in an economy, but subject to being generated and increased; war, consequently, was not considered the best means of growing to foreign countries' detriment; international free trade was recognized as universally and mutually profitable; the wealth of individuals rather than government power was the economy's aim; and technological improvement and increased productivity rather than population increase were a government's foremost concern.

Physiocracy belonged to the Enlightenment in its optimism, its belief in progress, and its exaltation of nature. Moreover, it represented an essential step in shaping individualism, in defining the social sciences, and in improving humankind through education.

Beyond their theoretical contribution to political economy, the Physiocrats were closely linked to the state of their own country. They shaped their theory in response to the financial problems of France at the beginning of the Seven Years' War (1757–1763), and their proposals stemmed from the reality of agrarian France and aimed at opposing the power of Great Britain. From this perspective, Physiocracy represents a system of economic policy based on a program of large investment in agriculture. In 1756 and 1757, Quesnay's articles on "Fermiers," "Grains," "Impôt," and "Hommes" (unpublished) for Diderot and d'Alembert's *Encyclopédie* presented the new idea that agriculture is the only productive economic activity, because land by its fruits is the sole source of wealth. In the physiocratic analysis, neither industry nor trade can create wealth; they only transform or move products and raw materials. For this reason, these activities are called "sterile," essential to agriculture but incapable of generating new wealth. In 1757, Quesnay met Mirabeau, a champion of the social role of the nobility who was celebrated for his *L'ami des hommes, ou Traité de la population*. Mirabeau became Quesnay's first disciple, and from their collaboration arose the corpus of physiocratic ideas. Quesnay published the *Tableau économique* (1758), Mirabeau the *Théorie de l'impôt* (1760) and (with Quesnay's help) the *Philosophie rurale, ou Économie générale et politique de l'agriculture* (1763). Two periodicals, the *Journal de l'agriculture, du commerce et des finances* and the *Éphémérides du citoyen*, became propaganda organs of the Physiocrats.

The *Tableau économique* is the first numerical representation of the economic process, considered as a circular flow of wealth. Quesnay analyzed, in a situation of economic liberty, the annual circulation of money of the gross national product among three social classes: proprietors, who receive land rent and hold the surplus, called *produit net*; cultivators, who oversee agricultural production; and the sterile class, comprising all other social groups. The *Tableau* analyses the expenses and circulation of commodities, by which the net product of agriculture returns at the end to the class of proprietors. Essential in this process is the class of cultivators (*fermiers*), who hold capital for investments, called advances: original advances (*avances primitives*), tools, seeds, and livestock to make the land profitable; and annual advances (*avances annuelles*) to meet operating costs. Land advances (*avances foncières*) were made by proprietors to reclaim land, and sovereign advances (*avances souveraines*) were all the expenses borne by the government.

Because proprietors receive from the *fermiers*, who rent their land, the part of income exceeding what is needed for the reconstruction of capital (the *produit net*), the only equitable form of taxation is a single, direct tax on land, called *impôt térritorial*, paid only by landowners. Through the land tax, the king becomes co-proprietor of the property of its subjects. This approach implied the abolition of indirect taxes and a profound change in the traditional system of taxation because it was a direct attack against the power of *fermiers généraux*, who contracted to collect taxes.

Physiocratic economic theory and fiscal proposals gave the nobility a new prominence in the ancien régime. The physiocratic landowner played a dynamic role in the management of great estates, a role inconsistent with that of the traditional aristocracy. The Physiocrats' call for economic liberty, technological improvements in agriculture, and centralized tax collection demanded the abolition of privileges and undermined the French corporate and mercantilist system. For short periods in 1763 and 1764, free circulation of wheat constituted a temporary success for the Physiocrats. In 1774, it seemed that Quesnay and his group had triumphed when Anne-Robert-Jacques Turgot became controller general. He was seen as a supporter of Physiocracy, even though his economic thought was less rigid and he did not accept its principle of the sole productivity of agriculture and its theory of legal despotism. His reformist program represented a victory of liberal ideas. Turgot restored free trade in wheat, but a rise in the price of bread brought about popular uprisings and, with them, the failure of Turgot, who was hated in traditional court circles. In any case, since the beginning of the 1770s the opposition of privileged groups and divisions among Enlightenment circles had also begun to erode the Physiocrats' influence.

Opposition. Opponents of Physiocracy came not only from the traditionalist elite but also stemmed from an important division among reformist groups that marked a turning point in the French Enlightenment. The physiocratic scientific perspective was judged too abstract an approach to reality, and the new economic principles were accused of being dogmatic and sectarian. For the *encyclopédistes*, the Physiocrats with their government links represented a group of experts rather than a ruling elite. Attacks against absolutism, religion, and traditional society and campaigns for civil rights were tested instruments for the philosophes, inconsistent with the technical and cautious reforms proposed by Quesnay, close to court circles. Gabriel Bonnot de Mably, in *Doutes proposés aux philosophes économistes sur l'ordre naturel et essentiel des sociétés politiques* (1768)—a reply to Le Mercier de La Rivière's *L'ordre naturel et essentiel des sociétés politiques* (1767), which summarized the economic and social discourse of the new economists—refuted the principles of evidence and of legal despotism; more significantly, he questioned the lawfulness of the right of property through a moralistic approach inconsistent with the Physiocrats' scientific economic perspective. Voltaire, in *L'homme aux quarante écus* (1768), ridiculed Quesnay's mathematical language and rejected his land tax theory. Coming from an economist and author of economic articles in the *Encyclopédie*, François Forbonnais's attacks were more specialized. In *Principes et observations économiques* (1767), he contested the claim for the exclusive productivity of agriculture, defending the productive role of commerce and industry. Furthermore, he rejected the physiocratic method as lacking adaptability to different situations.

Unconditional advocacy of free trade reinforced a growing sense of the inflexibility of Physiocracy, and popular riots caused by grain trade liberalization split the Enlightenment movement in France. Two different paths to reform stood out at that time: one was represented by the economic liberalism of Physiocracy, which promised long-term general improvement and increase in wealth, in spite of short-term costs for the weaker social groups; the other gave priority to the protection of the poor, which moved Diderot, Jacques Necker, and other reformers to criticize the Physiocrats' rigidity. The most lucid expression of this movement, and the strongest attack against Physiocracy, was Ferdinando Galiani's *Dialogues sur le commerce des bleds* (1770), a great success in France and abroad. Supported by Diderot, this Neapolitan cleric contested the superiority of agriculture, calling it the least reliable economic activity because it is vulnerable to weather. In brilliant prose, Galiani rejected the universal validity of Physiocracy and pointed out its insufficiency in the face of varying economic realities. The physiocratic scientific analysis symbolized for Galiani the abstract and deductive character of French thought. In the economic and political debates of the second half of the eighteenth century, the success of Galiani's attack represented the reassertion of the practical worth of mercantilist policies. Even after its political decline, however, Physiocracy in France continued to represent a strong voice for economic liberalism and tax reform, surviving in debates during the Revolution.

International Influence. At the same time, Physiocracy's explicitly scientific and universal character explains its influence outside France. Through personal links and collaboration, some Physiocrats played a role in foreign reforms. Le Mercier de La Rivière was consulted as legal expert by Empress Catherine II of Russia and by Bishop Massalski in Poland. For King Gustav III of Sweden, he wrote *De l'instruction publique* (1775), in which he proposed an educational system aimed at stabilizing the social order and characterized by a utilitarian approach. Mirabeau, Du Pont de Nemours, and Butré collaborated with the margrave Karl Frederick of Baden, a convert to Physiocracy, who tried to apply its ideas on land tax and education in his little state. Du Pont de Nemours became secretary of the Education Committee in Poland in 1774, when King Stanisław August Poniatowski proposed to modernize his country with a system of national schools after the expulsion of the Jesuits in 1773. Many years later, Dupont was enlisted by U.S. President Thomas Jefferson as an advisor in the creation of the University of Virginia. His *Sur l'éducation nationale dans les États-Unis*, sent to Jefferson in 1800, shows the evolution of Du Pont's ideas and his identification of education as a means to investigate and explain mass behavior in a democratic milieu.

Education. According to the physiocratic perspective, the science of economics discloses permanent laws of the natural order that the principle of evidence makes intelligible (Quesnay wrote the *Encyclopédie* article "Evidence," 1756). Therefore, knowledge of these laws was implicit in the appearance of economic science. The emphasis on education was one of the most important and original elements of physiocratic discourse, at once a propaganda instrument, a means of economic improvement, an element in the shaping of national culture, and a path of political influence. The pedagogical vocation of the Enlightenment placed education at the heart of eighteenth-century debates, and the Physiocrats stand out as the strongest voice advocating primary schools for peasants, essential to introducing improvements in agriculture and to shaping public opinion against arbitrary government. Although the movement as a whole shared this perspective, there were differences among individual approaches, since educational views reflect those of the relationship between culture and society.

Educational discourses reveal originality and dissimilarities among the Physiocrats, countering their image as a rigid sect. Paradoxically, Quesnay was the least original in this respect, having been engaged to define the group and its system. Education was for him the first of all positive laws, a necessity for peasants, and a means to stabilize the social order, but at the same time a guarantee against arbitrary power. In his early *Essai physique sur l'économie animale* (1736), he had defined liberty as the development of man's rational capacities. For Le Trosne, education was strictly a propaganda instrument of economic theory; for Le Mercier de La Rivière, interested mainly in political action, it was an essential element of the physiocratic natural order. Baudeau, who understood the importance of education even before his commitment to Physiocracy, perceived the relationship between education and social structure and outlined the role of education in securing social stability. As a philanthropic noble, Mirabeau advocated education for peasants and women, even in a traditional society, through his personal evolution from his moralistic pre-physiocratic perspective to his discovery of the socialization value of education. Dupont de Nemours, the youngest and most liberal of the group, viewed education as a way to influence public opinion and criticize absolutism; during the French Revolution, he saw the revolutionary implications of education, and later, as advisor to Jefferson, he understood its democratic value in a republican government.

Proceeding directly from the natural order, education for the Physiocrats meant not only establishing primary schools but also a wider cultural project with political implications: the formation of agricultural societies. Following the more general agronomic movement, which since the 1750s had been advocating the creation of agricultural societies to spread technical knowledge among peasants, the Physiocrats' proposals took a distinct approach, enlarging agronomic claims and stressing the cultural and political role of agricultural societies in directing government and implementing economic science. They succeeded temporarily in 1761, when the controller general Henri-Léonard Bertin, a supporter of economic reforms, created the first such society in Tours, followed by others in Paris, Lyon, Limoges, Orléans, Rouen, and Soissons. The attempt to transform these into propaganda instruments for Physiocracy failed early, however, owing to government opposition to political interference by the economists, who refused to limit their activities to educational and technical matters.

Political Thought. According to Physiocracy, political economy corresponds to social science, defined as the science that explains the workings of society. The natural order consequently concerns political organization as well, and the role of government. The political views of the Physiocrats were strongly attacked by their contemporaries and remain controversial for modern scholars. The Physiocrats believed that to function properly, the natural order, which corresponds to the economy, needs strong political power, which they called "legal despotism." "Despotism" meant for them a strong, unitary government; the adjective "legal" suggested resistance to arbitrary power. It implied a government that respected natural laws, limiting action to guaranteeing the working of economic laws to remove obstacles to free circulation and free trade; that is, government should be a tutelary power. Beyond the checks imposed by a public enlightened through education, the Physiocrats conceived an independent judiciary with authority to ensure that sovereign power acted in accordance with the natural order. Quesnay's articles *Le droit naturel* (1765) and *Le despotisme de la Chine* (1767), and Le Mercier de La Rivière's *L'ordre naturel et essentiel des sociétés politiques* are the main works developing the theory of legal despotism. Close to the court, the Physiocrats relied on the French king to revoke privileges and protectionist measures, and they tried to involve the government in reforms. The legal despotism theory was unfavorably received in Enlightenment circles, and the Physiocrats were called supporters of absolutism. Moreover, they refuted the system of counterbalancing forces that, from Montesquieu on, represented opposition to the monarchy in French political discourse. In rejecting the theory of checks and balances, the Physiocrats initiated the decline of French anglophilia, undermined still more by their opposition to the economic and political model represented by Great Britain.

Because of its attachment to the theory of legal despotism, Physiocracy has been seen as an attempt to join a market society to an authoritarian government and to place a modern economic system within a framework of traditional political power. Recent commentators have addressed this apparent contradiction, reconsidering its historical complexity. In fact, Physiocracy was the first attempt to integrate economics with social and political theory. The essential Physiocratic contradiction has been explained as the awareness of the difficulty of debating politics freely in France and of realizing economic change without upsetting the social order. Its acceptance of absolutism has been judged as a way of imposing conditions that would allow the realization of the natural order (Fox-Genovese). This authoritarian character of French liberal thought has been questioned by recent commentators investigating the implications of physiocratic political theory. This new approach is opening the way to reconsider, throughout the eighteenth century and the first years of the nineteenth, the relationship between the physiocratic tradition and the shaping of French liberalism.

In Physiocratic political theory, the role of provincial assemblies in the administration of the kingdom is an essential element in limiting absolutism. Mirabeau's unpublished *Traité de la monarchie* (Longhitano, 1999) and the relationship between Quesnay and Mirabeau in drafting this work (1757–1759) reveal a theory of representation within Physiocracy. This theory arose out of the call for restoration of the traditional provincial estates—assemblies of the three orders surviving in the provinces annexed late to the French kingdom—advanced by Mirabeau in 1750, before he met Quesnay. Collaboration with Quesnay led to replacing corporate assemblies of constituted orders with new forms of representation: provincial assemblies composed of property owners and aimed at administrative decentralization. The democratic evolution from participation in government by local elites to the idea of citizenship advanced at the Constituent Assembly in 1789 drew on Du Pont de Nemours's and Turgot's *Mémoires sur les municipalités* (1775), Le Trosne's *De l'administration provinciale et de la réforme de l'impôt* (1779), and Jean-Antoine-Nicolas de Caritat Condorcet's *Essai sur la constitution et les fonctions des assemblées provinciales* (1788). The Physiocratic perspective implied a social theory of representation opposite to the traditional idea of representation of constituted orders. This theory rests on the assumption that interest is the first bond of social order. Because interest is grounded in property, landowners best represent social interest, which joins men through economic links.

Even though the proposed provincial assemblies did not wield real political power, this proposal demands reconsideration of the Physiocrats' consent to absolutism and of the relationship between politics and economics in their thought. Physiocratic provincial assemblies represented a civil society that sought a part in the political life of France. Despite this, sovereign power was to remain unitary, though this does not imply absolutism or monarchy as the best form of government. The organization of civil power in society required a division of responsibilities that created forms of representation of the economic and social interests constituting the social order. The landowner was the best representative of the social interest because he held a genuinely political position in the struggle against corporate interests and privileged groups. For the Physiocrats, social order existed independently from any political government, monarchic or republican; its essential elements were unity of sovereignty and representation of economic interest. From this perspective, physiocratic political thought achieved a separation between economics and politics.

Physiocratic political discourse outlined a modern theory of representation that had great influence during the French Revolution and shaped the idea of republicanism as a representative system based on the priority of civil society over government, an idea expressed by Condorcet and the Girondists, the political group who opposed the Jacobin idea of the legal supremacy of revolutionary government.

Du Pont de Nemours's personal career, revolutionary experience, and interest in the United States exemplify the democratic evolution of the Physiocratic discourse on representation. The political importance of Physiocratic thought can be measured by its reception in the United States and its contribution to the shaping of American national identity. For Benjamin Franklin, Thomas Jefferson, and the Republican Party, aware that political economy strengthened the republican idea of links among economy, policy, and society, Physiocracy represented a scientific project of economic development, based on agriculture, that was different from the British commercial model and exalted the political importance of the landowner. This was essential for creating a democratic republic in such a huge country as the United States, where the landowners represented the general interest.

The legacy of Physiocracy—the characterization of political economy as a science, and the independence of civil society—shaped the content and character of French economic discourse. Attention to the social implications of economic theory characterized French economic thought from the Physiocrats to Jean-Baptiste Say and distinguished it from British economic theory, which conceived economics strictly as the science of the wealth of nations. This attitude consequently reveals important differences between French and British liberalism. The strong role of government in French political tradition made civil society more aware of its independence and of the distinction between civil and political rights. Grounded in this reality, Physiocracy undermined the universality of the British commercial model and outlined a different relationship between individual and government.

[*See also* Commerce and Trade; Economic Thought; Free Trade; Grain Trade; Mercantilism; *and* Quesnay, François.]

BIBLIOGRAPHY

Albertone, Manuela. *Fisiocrati, istruzione e cultura*. Turin, 1979.

Albertone, Manuela. "George Logan: un physiocrate américain." In *La diffusion internationale de la physiocratie (XVIIIᵉ–XIXᵉ)*, edited by Bernard Delmas, Thierry Demals, and Philippe Steiner, pp. 421–439. Grenoble, 1995.

Baker, Keith Michael. "Representation." In *The French Revolution and the Creation of Modern Political Culture: The Political Culture of the Old Regime*, edited by Keith Michael Baker, pp. 469–492. Oxford and New York, 1987. An important point of reference for the study of the representative theory in Physiocratic political thought.

Delmas, Bernard, Thierry Demals, and Philippe Steiner, eds. *La diffusion internationale de la Physiocratie (XVIIIᵉ–XIXᵉ)*. Grenoble, 1995.

Einaudi, Mario. *The Physiocratic Doctrine of Judicial Control*. Cambridge, Mass., 1938.

Fox-Genovese, Elizabeth. *The Origins of Physiocracy: Economic Revolution and Social Order in Eighteenth-Century France*. Ithaca, N.Y., 1976. The turning point in the reappraisal of the Physiocrats' political thought and its links with their economic theory.

Meek, Ronald Lindley. *The Economics of Physiocracy*. London, 1962.

Mirabeau, Victor Riqueti de, and François Quesnay. *Traité de la monarchie (1757–1759)*. Edited by Gino Longhitano. Paris, 1999. The long Preface by Longhitano thoroughly considers republican implications in Physiocratic political discourse.

Quesnay, François. *François Quesnay et la Physiocratie*. 2 vols. Paris, 1958.

Rosanvallon, Pierre. "Physiocrates." In *Dictionnaire critique de la Révolution française*, edited by François Furet and Mona Ozouf, pp. 359–371. Paris, 1988. Highlights the links between the Physiocrats' theory of provincial assemblies and the ideas of proprietor-citizen during the French Revolution.

Weulersse, Georges. *Le mouvement physiocratique en France (1756–1770)*. Paris, 1910. Weulersse's studies remain the high point in the investigation of Physiocracy.

Weulersse, Georges. *La physiocratie sous le ministère de Turgot et de Necker (1774–1781)*. Paris, 1950.

Weulersse, Georges. *La physiocratie à la fin du règne de Louis XV (1770–1774)*. Paris, 1959.

Weulersse, Georges. *La physiocratie à l'aube de la Révolution (1781–1792)*. Paris, 1985.

MANUELA ALBERTONE

PIETISM. The term Pietism is not easy to define. From the beginning it contained various meanings for different groups. In contrast to the term "piety," "Pietism" was coined to describe a reform movement within the Lutheran churches of Central Europe in the seventeenth and eighteenth centuries that stressed personal piety and personal religious devotion over religious formality and orthodoxy. In the early period of Pietism—from 1670, when Philipp Jakob Spener assembled the first conventicle in Frankfurt am Main, to the mid-1690s, when August Hermann Francke began to establish a series of educational and missionary institutions at Halle (soon to become the famous Franckesche Stiftungen)—the term was a pejorative characterization of a decidedly devout "reborn" Protestant not content with the ways of Lutheran orthodoxy. According to their opponents, Pietists were neglecting their civic duties while egoistically seeking salvation. In their own view, however, Spener, Francke, and their disciples were attempting to give new meaning to Christian values and virtues at a time when these were rapidly losing influence. During the first half of the eighteenth century, in both the Halle variety shaped by Francke and in the Herrnhut variety conceived by Nikolaus Ludwig Graf Zinzendorf, Pietism gained many new supporters from all walks of life, and the reform movement expanded into Scandinavia, the Baltic countries, Switzerland, and some British colonies in North America, such as Pennsylvania. During the second half of the eighteenth century, however, Pietism lost ground everywhere in Europe while the Enlightenment blossomed. In both these periods, the term Pietism no

Pietist Baptism. Moravians baptizing an infant. Engraving, 1757. (The Granger Collection, New York.)

longer had negative connotations; however, even then Pietists themselves preferred other terms to describe their groups and their activities. They used, for example, the term "children of God" to denote their chosenness, or "friends of truth," which meant that they alone understood the true meaning of biblical teachings.

As Pietism became an object of scholarly inquiry in the course of the nineteenth and twentieth centuries, the scope of the term's meaning changed once again. Heinrich Schmid, author of the first general history of Pietism (1863), included in his analysis the reform movement within Protestantism led by Spener and Francke, but not that of Zinzendorf and the Moravians. In his monumental three-volume *History of Pietism* (1880–1886), the Göttingen church historian Albrecht Ritschl used a much wider concept of Pietism. For him Zinzendorf and the *Herrnhuter* were an integral part of the movement.

Within traditional ecclesiastical historiography, Pietism had been viewed as a phenomenon of the late seventeenth century and, above all, the early eighteenth century, followed by the Enlightenment, by the *Erweckungsbewegung* (the German manifestation of the Second Great Awakening), by the later history of Protestantism under nationalism, liberalism, socialism, and totalitarianism, and, in particular, by domestic and foreign missions. In the late 1980s, the editors of the new *History of Pietism* decided that all of the later revival movements within Protestantism could best be understood if they were seen as a continuation and renewal of earlier Pietist efforts and achievements.

Theological, Cultural, and Social Ingredients of Pietism. Before the relationship of Pietism and the Enlightenment can be discussed, we must take a closer look at the theological, cultural, and social ingredients of Pietism. In its theological profile and program, Pietism possesses several distinct features.

First, Pietists believed in the idea of rebirth (*Wiedergeburt*). For them, God gives true-believing Christians the unique opportunity to overcome sinfulness, cleanse themselves from sin, and free themselves from the consequences of the Fall. With God's help, this process of remorse and atonement may lead to a new stage of Christian perfection, often termed "rebirth." Some Pietists believed that this stage of perfection, once achieved, cannot be lost and sets them apart from "children of the world" (*Weltkinder*) once and for all; others were convinced that Christian renewal is never completed, and that the status of rebirth entails a continuous struggle for salvation and a continuous effort to become ever more perfect as a Christian, and ever more deserving of God's grace. In this sense, rebirth was understood as a process of sanctification (*Heiligung*).

Second, Pietists held a strong belief in eschatology; from the time of Spener and Francke to the twentieth century, they have seen themselves as living in the "last times." Pietist conventicles are understood as communities of the remaining true children of God in the very last phase of salvation history before the return of Christ. While Satan rages, false prophets tempt true believers, and the antecedents of Antichrist and perhaps even Antichrist himself try to spoil God's creation and his plan for the salvation of humankind, the Pietists' unique task is to ensure that their souls will be saved at the Last Judgment. In this most dangerous journey, the book of Revelation is their guide. While some Pietists believed that Christ will return only in order to carry out the Last Judgment, others were convinced that before Judgment Day, Christ will reign for a glorious thousand years, together with his faithful children. Throughout the history of Pietism, the question of the validity of chiliasm (millenarian belief) remained controversial.

Third, from the beginning the Pietists were convinced that God had postponed the final judgment for a certain period, and that he expected them to use this extended period of grace to start building God's kingdom on earth. No one knew how long this period of grace would last, but all were sure that God's final verdict—whether they would be saved or doomed, whether they would live in eternal bliss in heaven or in internal agony in hell—would depend on their personal contribution to the establishment of God's kingdom in their own time. This conviction helps us to understand the innerworldly asceticism as well as the remarkable wordly activism typical of many Pietists. Even those who did not found special institutions or special organizations like those in Halle (for example eighteenth-century Württemberg Pietists) cannot be characterized as quietistic: they were very active in caring for the members of their conventicles, and many of them wrote edifying books or pious hymns.

A fourth characteristic of Pietism is scripturalism. For all Pietists, the Bible represented the main source of knowledge and the sole foundation of their faith. It contained everything that they had to know about history, nature, life, morals, and about the past, present, and future. Most Pietists also believed in miracles, convinced that God rules the world with the help of special revelations and special signs. Furthermore, they expected that God might intervene in their lives in a direct manner, through illness, death, and countless other ways. For Pietists, however, there were no signs more important, and more compelling, than the biblical message of the Old and New Testaments. It was their daily practice to read the Bible, either alone or with others. Throughout their lives, certain passages might be of special importance to them personally. They looked to the Bible to find answers when decisions had to be made. In short, reading the Bible was always more important for them than attending church service on Sundays.

Finally, Pietism is characterized by a firm commitment to missionary work, despite exceptions such as the eighteenth-century Württemberg Pietists, who believed that salvation history had reached its final stage, in which God no longer expected his children to engage in foreign missions. Württemberg Pietists believed that Luther and the Reformation had resurrected God's word from papal misuse, and that the sixteenth-century reformers had fulfilled God's command to spread his message to all peoples on all continents. Among eighteenth-century Pietists, however, such opinions were rare. By contrast, Francke and the Halle Pietists invested enormous effort in producing good cheap bibles and distributing these in foreign lands. The enthusiasm of Zinzendorf and his follower for foreign missionary work was even greater: many Moravians, or *Herrnhuter*, lost their lives as missionaries in Africa, Asia, and the Caribbean. By the early nineteenth century, Pietist involvement in missionary activities and in publishing Bibles grew even greater and included even the Württemberg Pietists. To be a Pietist was now almost the same as being active in (or actively supporting) foreign missionary work. According to Pietists, both these activities possessed special eschatological significance. Christ's second coming would occur only when all the peoples of the world had had a chance to hear or read God's word. Missionary work and Bible translation and distribution were means through which God's children attempted to fulfill the conditions for the return of Christ.

Religious Sociology. The religious sociology of Pietism has several notable features. In its early phases, Pietism was first and foremost a reform movement within the professional guild of Protestant pastors. More precisely, in the 1670s and 1680s, within the highly educated cohort of Protestant pastors, it expressed the wishes and expectations of a younger generation. When Spener published his programmatic pamphlet *Pia Desideria* in 1675, he was forty years old, and he soon became considered the patriarch of the new movement; many of his followers were much younger. Spener offered these younger reform-minded pastors advice and continued guidance. When Francke began his remarkable career at Halle in the 1690s, he was a pastor in his mid-twenties. When Zinzendorf assembled a congregation of reborn Christians at Herrnhut a generation later, it was his desire to be accepted as a pastor and bishop. Separatist Pietism was also led by young pastors, and it was only in the eighteenth century that separatism became strongly influenced by lay people. Well into the eighteenth century, Pietist conventicles were created only where pastors took the initiative, and, characteristically,

conventicles disappeared when Pietist pastors moved, or were moved, to other parishes. It was Pietist pastors who wrote almost all of the new edifying books, pamphlets, and hymns.

In addition, one must recognize the role of the conventicles, which were called the *ecclesiolae in ecclesia* ("little churches within the church"). According to Spener, founder of the first Pietist conventicle in 1670, these meetings offered to Christians who wanted to "grow" in their faith the opportunity to receive additional information, extra opportunities for prayer, and the sharing of religious experiences. Initially, therefore, Pietist conventicles were not designed to compete with Sunday services for the whole congregation, but, rather, as a supplement for devout members who formed a spiritual elite.

Spener's concept soon led to enormous tensions and many controversies. Time and again, in place after place, some members of a congregation attended the meetings of a conventicle, while others stayed away or felt excluded; these parishes would soon split into two groups, the "true believers" and the "children of the world." Resentment grew on both sides of the divide. Especially when eschatological matters were discussed intensively, many members of Pietist conventicles were inclined to separate from the established church completely. To officials of the state churches, the activities of conventicles often looked dangerous. They reacted by issuing *Pietistenedikte*, laws that restricted or forbade meetings of conventicles. The more they tried to control and supervise the conventicles, however, the more suspicious the members of these groups became of the official church, and the more fervent in their conviction. As early as the late seventeenth century, therefore, some separatist groups who had been outlawed decided to emigrate to the New World. There were, however, instances, in which Pietism survived and continued to grow without the special help of conventicles.

Spener was a prolific writer of edifying books and pamphlets. An important characteristic of Pietism, in fact, was the body of literature that the patriarchs of the movement accepted as conforming to their faith and enlarged with contributions of their own. Some early seventeenth-century works were included in this canon, such as those of Johann Arndt and even some of the early writings of Martin Luther, since the Pietists claimed to continue the work of the Reformation. Pietist authors produced an impressive number of literary works that they believed to be truly Christian—books, pamphlets, and hymns. Karl Heinrich von Bogatzky and Zinzendorf were prolific writers in the eighteenth century, Albert Knapp and Karl Gerok in the nineteenth. The ever-growing body of pious works, often stylistically simple, had a dual function. They were read in conventicles or in the homes of Pietist families, constantly reinforcing and internalizing the basic principles of Pietist belief. As a result, a common worldview, a common way of thinking, and even a common way of speaking developed. On the other hand, pious books and pamphlets were sold in special bookstores and distributed by itinerant Pietist booksellers in a missionary effort to nonbelievers, both at home and abroad.

As early as the late seventeenth century, networks were created by Pietist patriarchs, strengthened by a large number of "reborn" pastors and shaped by the common wish to produce and disseminate pious literature. Soon those who were part of them knew whom they could trust, with whom they could cooperate, and whom they should avoid. They kept in close contact by writing letters. When traveling, they visited each other, often stayed overnight, and used the meeting for prayer and Bible reading. Major themes of their letters and conversations were the growth of "God's kingdom," pastors who were reborn and supported the cause of Pietism, conventicles in other places, pious books and pamphlets worth reading; they wrote also about princes and magistrates and their attitudes toward Pietism, and about cities and territories where they were tolerated or persecuted. The archives at Halle and Herrnhut give ample testimony of the scope and intensity of these Pietist networks, and these are just the two most prominent examples of a much wider system of communication.

By the 1730s, Johann Jakob Moser and Johann Adam Steinmetz began to publish journals meant to intensify the exchange of information among Pietists. These journals, however, contain only part of the news being exchanged among believers; much of what was considered most important for God's true children was kept confidential. Pietists were convinced that these secrets were so precious that they should not be disseminated outside their circles. All these features are also characteristic of nineteenth- and twentieth-century Pietism. Up to the present time, Pietists have their own networks, share spiritual experience in an exclusive manner, and have their own special means through which they believe spiritual growth can be achieved and sustained.

Pietist institutions also played a critical role. The institution that Francke created at Halle served as a model for many later foundations, although none achieved the size or importance of the Franckesche Stiftungen. There were many kinds of Pietist institutions: educational ones with emphasis on the training of a Christian elite; charitable ones, many of them for handicapped people; homes for orphans; and, especially since the early nineteenth century, seminaries for the training of missionaries. In all these institutions, Pietists served as teachers; all had Pietist directors, or inspectors; and all soon became meeting places for the Pietists of the region in which they were located. As regards the sheer number of Pietist institutions, the nineteenth century offers even more examples than the eighteenth.

Pietism and the Enlightenment. The relationship of Pietism and the Enlightenment was complicated from the start and changed considerably over time. The beginning can best be described by looking at the University of Halle in the 1690s. Francke and Christian Thomasius were perhaps the two most impressive and influential figures in this newly founded university, where the Prussian ruler expected state servants to be trained according to the highest academic standards of the day. The Pietist leader Francke and the philosopher Thomasius, a key figure of the early Enlightenment, shared a number of convictions. Both were discontented with Lutheran orthodoxy. Both believed in the necessity of reform in society, and in higher education in particular. To achieve this, both were eager to introduce new subjects, new methods, and also new people into university teaching. They were convinced that the individual Christian was responsible for his or her own soul, and that God's gifts to each person—the unique combination of abilities—must be cultivated and given an outlet in work. In this sense, they both supported the growth of individualism.

Within a few years, however, the distance and also the rivalry between Francke and Thomasius increased. By 1720, the gulf between the supporters of Pietism and the supporters of Enlightenment at Halle University could no longer be bridged. To enlightened rationalists, human nature was not inherently corrupt as a result of original sin, and hence the development of a virtuous character did not require a "rebirth" through grace. Most striking was the widening gap between, on the one hand, Pietist biblicism and enlightened theology, which took a historical approach to the Bible. The proponents of Enlightenment believed that God had endowed all men with reason (*ratio*; *Vernunft*), and that it was their task to develop the rational capabilities through proper education and training. The proponents of Pietism, in contrast, were convinced that first and foremost they should save souls, because Judgment Day was approaching. For them, all kinds of knowledge, and the advancement of knowledge, were always secondary to true faith. Although they eagerly engaged in educational reforms and even emphasized the need for progress in the natural sciences (*Realien*), they never admitted biblical criticism, and they clung to the tenets of salvation history and to the special promise given to those who had experienced rebirth in faith.

In the 1720s and 1730s, a few incidents fostered mistrust between Pietism and the Enlightenment. When the enlightened philosopher Christian Wolff was expelled from Halle University in 1723 by the Prussian king, Francke played a significant role, and this did not remain a secret. In the 1730s, Johann Christoph Gottsched published a play, *Die Pietistery im Fischbeinrock* (Dietism in a Whalebone Garment) in which he ridiculed Pietist attitudes. When Frederick the Great came to power in 1740, one of his first decisions was to reinstate Wolff at Halle. Friend and foe alike took this as a sign that the period of Pietist influence at the Prussian court was over. By the 1750s, the Enlightenment even dominated at the Faculty of Theology of Halle University; by the 1770s, enlightened teaching principles were applied within the Franckesche Stiftungen.

By the early nineteenth century, Pietist distrust of the Enlightenment had deepened even further. The supporters of the *Erweckungsbewegung* were convinced that enlightened principles had led to rationalism, and that rationalistic positions had caused the French Revolution, which they considered a demonically inspired revolt of disbelief (*Unglauben*) and disobedience against God. Between the 1790s and the Congress of Vienna in 1815, many Pietists were sure that the Second Coming of Christ was imminent. Clearly, God demanded that his true children use the remaining time to save as many souls as possible. This meant even greater support for foreign missions, including the training of missionaries and the printing of inexpensive Bibles in many languages.

The triumph of liberalism and nationalism in the nineteenth century brought Pietists new challenges. Dealing with liberalism did not present great difficulties. German Pietists equated the principles of liberalism with the basic teachings of the Enlightenment, and so they supported conservative positions in politics, culture, and society. Coping with modern nationalism was more difficult. Some Pietists remained hostile to German unification under Prussian leadership and changed their views only after the Franco-Prussian war (1870–1871); others, among them Johann Hinrich Wichern and Friedrich von Bodelschwingh, cherished the idea of a collective national, social, and moral rebirth of the German people understood to be developing since 1848. Thus, they linked the question of German unification with the struggle against secularization and against social and moral ills. These Pietists were filled with joy and gratitude in 1870–1871, but since then, German Pietists have not been able to develop a more reflective, differentiated, and subtle view of the Enlightenment.

The story of the relationship of Pietism and the Enlightenment is one of estrangement, emerging in a series of controversies that led to disappointment and prejudice. In the first decade after the foundation of Halle University, Pietism and Enlightenment had much in common; areas of conflict seemed limited, if not minimal. By 1720, mutual misperceptions had gained ground, and so had mistrust. By the mid-eighteenth century, Pietists no longer attempted to understand the principles of enlightened thought, while Pietist resentment against enlightened projects and influence grew rapidly. Some of the leaders of the Enlightenment had grown up in a milieu shaped by Pietism and, as they emancipated themselves from their origins, they became very critical of that heritage. By 1800, under the impact of the French Revolution, the followers of Pietism and the followers of the Enlightenment seemed to live in two separate worlds, governed by different views, convictions, and practices. The leaders on both sides remained firmly rooted in their respective traditions and no longer saw it as their task to discuss, much less to overcome, theological differences—quite the contrary. Since the late eighteenth century, opposition to the positions of the Enlightenment has been an integral part of Pietism, certainly a unique development in the Western World. In Great Britain and the United States, reborn, reawakened Christians often supported progressive political causes and social reform, but not so in Germany.

After the unification of modern Germany in 1989, a new research center was created at the University of Halle to carry forward research on the Enlightenment and Pietism. After only a few years, however, the scholars in charge of this center concluded that the program was too controversial and could not be carried through successfully. After some discussion, two centers were established: one for research on Pietism, and another for research on the Enlightenment. It seems that the conflicts between the tradition of Pietism, and those interested in this tradition, and the field of Enlightenment, and those working in it, weighed heavier than interest in comparative studies or in a history of religion that would treat both. Perhaps this most recent Halle development is a fitting footnote to the troubled history of the relationship between Pietism and the Enlightenment since the 1690s.

[*See also* Aufklärung; Bible; Counter-Enlightenment; Education, *subentry on* Pedagogical Thought and Practice; Enthusiasm; Germany; Great Awakening, *subentries on* First Great Awakening *and* Second Great Awakening; Letters; Millenarianism; Reformed Churches, *subentry on* Lutheranism; Revealed Religion; Sermons, *subentries on* Evangelical Sermons *and* Protestant Sermons; Thomasius, Christian; *and* Universities.]

BIBLIOGRAPHY

Brecht, Martin, ed. *Geschichte des Pietismus*. Vol. 1. Göttingen, 1993. Part one of the new history of Pietism, dealing with the seventeenth and early eighteenth centuries.

Brecht, Martin, and Klaus Deppermann, eds. *Geschichte des Pietismus*. Vol. 2. Göttingen, 1995. Covers the eighteenth century, with special emphasis on the regional variants of Pietism.

Brecht, Martin. *Ausgewählte Aufsätze*. Vol. 2; *Pietismus*. Stuttgart, 1997. Essays by a leading scholar of Pietism.

Deppermann, Klaus. *Der hallesche Pietismus und der preussische Staat unter Friedrich III. (I.)*. Göttingen, 1961. Standard text on early Pietism in Prussia.

Fulbrook, Mary. *Piety and Politics*. Cambridge, 1983. Comparison of Pietism in Prussia and in Württemberg.

Hinrichs, Carl. *Preussentum und Pietismus*. Göttingen, 1971. In-depth analysis of Pietism in Prussia.

Lehmann, Hartmut. *Pietismus und weltliche Ordnung in Württemberg vom 17. bis zum 20. Jahrhundert*. Stuttgart, 1969. Detailed analysis of Pietism in Württemberg.

Lehmann, Hartmut. *Das Zeitalter des Absolutismus: Gottesgnadentum und Kriegsnot*. Stuttgart, 1980. Comprehensive description of religion in the seventeenth century, including Pietism.

Lehmann, Hartmut. *Religion und Religiosität in der Neuzeit*. Göttingen, 1996. Essays on the transformation of religion in modern Germany.

Ritschl, Albrecht. *Geschichte des Pietismus*. 3 vols. Bonn, 1880–1886. For a century, the master text on Pietism.

Wallmann, Johannes. *Philipp Jakob Spener und die Anfänge des Pietismus*. 2d ed. Tübingen, 1986. Best biography of the founder of Pietism.

Wallmann, Johannes. *Der Pietismus*. Göttingen, 1990. Concise, informative textbook.

Wallmann, Johannes. *Theologie und Frömmigkeit im Zeitalter des Barock*. Tübingen, 1995. Essays by a leading scholar of the history of Pietism.

HARTMUT LEHMANN

PICTURESQUE. *See* Aesthetics.

PILATI, CARLO ANTONIO (1733–1802), Italian philosopher, freethinker, and man of letters.

The life of Carlo Antonio Pilati fits ideally into the intellectual landscape of Italy during the second half of the eighteenth century. He was born in Tassullo, in the Trentino, an interesting crossroad between Italian and German culture. Pilati was a "self-taught cosmopolitan," as Franco Venturi described him, who divided his time between travel, teaching, changing residences, editorial activities, and attending Masonic meetings. In his formative years in Salzburg, he rejected the Catholic traditionalism of the German judicial world and developed an undying aversion toward the clergy. Reading Antonio Genovesi, Lodovico Antonio Muratori (whom he met in 1749), and especially Montesquieu set him on his chosen path. He also read jurists, historians, and theologians of the Leipzig and Göttingen schools, such as Christian Thomasius and Johann Lorenz Mosheim, who influenced the tenor of his studies and reflections. Between 1749 and 1758, the year he was named professor of civil law in Trento, he traveled in Germany, Holland, Denmark, and England. His restless desire to learn, together with writing his first work, led him to abandon teaching for two years in order to travel again through Italy and Europe.

The book that emerged from this experience was *L'esistenza della legge naturale impugnata e sostenuta da Carlantonio Pilati* (Existence of Natural Law Disputed and Defended by Carlantonio Pilati; Venice, 1764). Two years later, it was put on the Index of Prohibited Books because of Pilati's evident enthusiasm for Michel de Montaigne's ideas, as well as for those of the skeptics, Baruch de Spinoza, Claude-Adrien Helvétius, and Nicolas-Antoine Boulanger, and all those who denounced "the invention of religion." A German translation was published in 1767, edited by Wilhelm Heinrich Winning, a Protestant pastor in Coira, in the Grigioni mountains. This friendship helped him to start a publishing house in 1768 where he could freely publish works that certainly would not have seen the light in Trento: *Di una riforma d'Italia, ossia des mezzi di riformare i più cattivi costumi e le più perniciose leggi d'Italia* (On Reforming Italy, or Rather Ways to Reform the Worst Customs and Most Pernicious Laws of Italy, 1767); *Riflessioni di un italiano sopra la Chiesa in generale, sopra il clero sia regolare che secolare* (Reflections of an Italian Regarding the Church in General, and the Clergy, Both Regular and Secular, 1768); and his *Giornale Letterario* (Literary Journal, 1768), a periodical written in Italian for Italians.

All of his writing is imbued with extraordinary moral and polemical force. In the *Riforma*, he advanced a systematic proposal to confront the ills of Italy, "so burdensome and infinite in number," that articulated both an attack on religion and the requirements for legal and economic reform. His first objective was to reform the Roman Catholic Church, to reduce the clergy's excessive power, wealth, and domination of education in order to avoid the ruination of the state. He urged the abolition of the immunity that priests and ecclesiastical property enjoyed, insisting that church and clergy be subject to civil laws and should pay taxes. The ecclesiastic and temporal power of the pope should be confined to Rome. The first step needed to affirm these principles would be the abolition of the Inquisition, which would deprive the Roman Church of one of its most effective instruments of persecution and oppression.

An essential part of Pilati's reflections was the education of public opinion to reform not only laws but also customs. He envisioned new kinds of schools and academies, in order to make more effective use of information, and even using the theater for propaganda. The *Riforma* was a huge success also for the publisher, and the Amsterdam publisher Marc-Michel Rey published two editions in French in 1769. The work stirred the whole of philosophical Europe. Impressed by the fury of Pilati's passion, Voltaire considered contemporaneous French works on the same subject as cautious. He wrote, "there is no stronger or bolder work; it makes priests tremble and inspires courage in the laity" (letter to Charles Bordes of 17 December 1768).

Soon the orthodox began to wage a campaign against Pilati, who had just moved to Venice. In December 1769, the inquisitors had him arrested and expelled. He found support from his friends in Vienna and Milan, and in the spring of 1771, the margrave of Ansbach named him court adviser. Afterward, he went to Erlangen, thence to The Hague, and finally to London. Like other European intellectuals, he had high hopes for Frederick II of Prussia, but was soon disillusioned. In 1786–1787, during the height of Grand Duke Peter Leopold's reforms, he lived in Tuscany. By 1783 he may already have joined the Freemasons, as a member of the Order of the Illuminati of Weishaupt, which is not surprising, given Pilati's passionately radical existence. He was probably proposed by his friend Bassus, the founder of the publishing house in Poschiavo, from which, on the eve of 1789, many revolutionary ideas were spread throughout Italy.

[*See also* Freemasonry; Illuminati; *and* Italy.]

BIBLIOGRAPHY

Borelli, L., and Donati C. Di Secli, eds. *Atti della giornata di studi su Carlo Antonio Pilati, un illuminista trentino nell'Europa del '700.* Trento, 1985.

Deambrosis, M. "Filogiansenisti, anticuriali e giacobini nella seconda metà del Settecento nel Trentino." *Rassegna storica del Risorgimento* 48 (1961), 79–90.

Rigatti, M. *Un illuminista trentino del XVIII secolo: Carlo Antonio Pilati.* Florence, 1923.

Venturi, F. "Da illuminista a illuminato: Carlantonio Pilati." In *La cultural illuministica in Italia,* edited by Mario Fubini, pp. 233–243. Turin, 1957.

Venturi, F. *Settecento riformatore,* vol. 2, *La chiesa e la repubblica dentro i loro limiti.* Turin, 1976. See especially pages 250–325.

SILVIA BERTI

Translated from Italian by Joan B. Sax

PINTO, ISAAC DE (1717–1787), Dutch political economist.

De Pinto was born into one of the wealthiest Sephardic Jewish families of Amsterdam. Little is known about his youth until 1739, when he joined a mainly Jewish "friendly society" of enlightened conservatives. Two lectures he gave to this society, preserved in manuscript, make it clear that he rejected both materialism and skepticism, as is also evident from his *Précis des arguments contre les matérialistes* (1774; 2d ed., 1752).

In 1761, De Pinto settled in Paris, evidently in order to establish himself as a citizen of the Republic of Letters. He made the acquaintance of Denis Diderot and David Hume, both of whom he never ceased to admire. In 1762, he made his debut with *Réflexions critiques sur le premier chapitre du VIIe tome des oeuvres de monsieur de Voltaire au sujet des Juifs,* arguing that Voltaire had ignored the fundamental differences between civilized Jews from the Mediterranean and their eastern European coreligionists, whose moral deficiencies, he believed, could be accounted for by their social backwardness. Once this text was included in Antoine Guérée's *Lettres de quelques Juifs portugais et allemands à M. de Voltaire* (1769), De Pinto became a minor celebrity. His most important work, *Traité*

de la circulation et du crédit, published by the radicals Marc-Michel Rey and Charles Guillaume Frédéric Dumas in Amsterdam in 1771, was soon translated into English and German. By the time the work appeared, De Pinto had returned to Holland, where he settled in The Hague in 1765, cultivating friendships with such prominent Dutch Enlightenment figures as Frans Hemsterhuis and Rijklof Michael van Goens.

De Pinto first made his economic views known in *Essai sur le luxe* (1762), which offered a sophisticated analysis of the benefits of comfort and refinement and condemned only the quest for excessive luxury. His utilitarian relativism was purely secular, praising consumption as the engine of monetary circulation. Unlike most Dutch thinkers of the day, he also defended foreign investment as a legitimate economic strategy. De Pinto's work on the circulation of credit is one of the few Dutch eighteenth-century treatises on political economy of European renown. An ardent defender of the British system of raising public debt, he argued that such credit enhanced the circulation of money, which in turn had a beneficial effect on the general economy, being in fact its main principle of wealth. In De Pinto's view, therefore, the much-debated decline of the eighteenth-century Dutch Republic was not so much the result of moral decay as the outcome of general European economic developments. Economic crises, according to De Pinto, called for economic solutions, and the Dutch Republic had no other option than to continue its role as a center of financial services. His many critics, however, feared the ensuing neglect of indigenous manufacturing and trading industries. At the end of his life, he again supported British interests when, in his *Letters on the American Troubles* (1776), he took issue with the American Declaration of Independence, rejecting the concept of popular sovereignty and arguing that this act of rebellion was doomed to failure.

BIBLIOGRAPHY

Nijenhuis, I. J. A. "Een joodse philosophe: Isaac de Pinto (1717–1787) en de ontwikkeling van de politieke economie in de Europese Verlichting." Diss., Groningen, 1992.

Popkin, R. "Isaac de Pinto's Criticism of Mandeville and Hume on Luxury." In *Studies on Voltaire and the Eighteenth Century* 154, pp. 1705–1714. Oxford, 1976.

Wijler, J. S. *Isaac de Pinto: Sa vie et ses oeuvres.* Apeldoorn, 1923.

WIEP VAN BUNGE

PITY. See Sociability.

PIUS VII (1742–1823), pope (1800–1823).

Barnabà Chiaramonti, born to a patrician family in the Italian region of Romagna, was left fatherless at an early age; he entered the Benedictine order as an oblate at the age of nine, took his vows at sixteen, and assumed the name Gregorio. He resided at the convent of Santa Giustina in Padua from 1760 to 1763. Santa Giustina was linked to the intellectual French congregation of Saint-Maur, and Chiaramonti encountered Jansenist influence there. At the Benedictine abbey of San Giovanni Evangelista at Parma (1766–1775), he was exposed to the reforming efforts of the minister Du Tillot, who fought against Roman ecclesiology and the Roman Curia of Pope Clement XIII. He frequented learned circles in Parma that included Etienne Bonnot de Condillac, tutor of the young Ferdinand de Bourbon-Parma from 1758 to 1767, the Theatine Paciaudi, director of the Palatine Library in Parma, and professors of the Collegio Alberoni. For the abbey library, which was in his care, he procured the learned works of Dom Calmet, Jean Mabillon, Bernard de Montfaucon, and Lodovico Antonio Muratori. Shockingly, the name of the future pope appears among the twenty-seven individuals from Parma who subscribed to the Livorno edition of Diderot and d'Alembert's *Encyclopédie*, and he accepted the dedication of the 1784 Italian translation of Condillac *Essai sur les origines des connaissances humaines* (Essay on the Origins of Human Knowledge). Chiaramonti was apparently open at this time to the moderate trend of the Catholic Enlightenment.

Chiaramonti was summoned to Rome as professor of theology at the Collegio di San Anselmo (1775–1781). He was favored by his compatriot Gianangelo Braschi, who became Pope Pius VI in 1775, and he was named bishop of Tivoli (1781–1785), then of Imola (1785–1800). He was made a cardinal in 1785, at age forty-two. At Christmas 1797, with his diocese occupied by the French revolutionary armies and annexed to the Cisalpine Republic, he published a homily in which he maintained that "the democratic form of government...does not conflict with the Gospels." Following the death of Pius VI while a prisoner in France in summer 1799, the cardinals met in conclave at Venice under Austrian protection. After more than three months of confrontation between the *politicanti*, who favored a policy of accommodation, and the *zelanti*, who were intransigent on matters of religion and devoted to Austria, Chiaramonti was elected as a compromise candidate on 14 March 1800. He took the name Pius VII in homage to his predecessor and was crowned at San Giorgio Maggiore on 21 March.

Pius VII pursued a policy of prudent reform in the Papal States. On 15 July 1801, he agreed to a concordat with the French Republic that reestablished Catholicism as "the religion of the majority of French citizens" while omitting any reference to a "state religion," and he officiated at the crowning of Napoleon at Nôtre-Dame in Paris on 2 December 1804. He refused, however, to engage the Papal State in the continental blockade of England, and he defended the authority of the Holy See against attempts to make the church subservient to the interests of the French Empire. He was removed by force from the papal palace in Rome during the night of 5–6 July 1809, as the Papal State was being annexed to the Empire, and was imprisoned at Savona, near Genoa (August 1809–June 1812), and then at Fontainebleau near Paris (June 1812–January 1814). There he resisted persistent pressure from Napoleon to hand over the canonical investiture of bishops to the archbishops and to renounce Rome and the patrimony of Saint Peter.

Pius VII was taken back to Italy following the military collapse of the French Empire, entering Rome on 24 May 1814. The diplomatic skills of Cardinal Ercole Consalvi at the Congress of Vienna secured the reconstitution of almost the entire Papal States. The last years of Pius VII's pontificate were characterized by a policy of restoration, moderate on the whole, and by the pursuit of concordats with the states of Germany and Italy. The Company of Jesus (the Jesuits) was reinstituted by the constitution *Sollicitudo Omnium Ecclesiarum* (7 August 1814), and the pope condemned secret societies of liberal and nationalist inclination—the Carbonari and the Freemasons—in a bull of 21 September 1821. The pope of the revolutionary age had been formed by the Catholic Enlightenment of the second third of the eighteenth century; he had lived through the Napoleonic Empire and Metternich's Restoration, and he had survived five years of imprisonment guided by a faith in providence that implied steadfastness on matters of principle, attachment to the heritage of the past, and resignation before the will of God. Pius VII appears, in moments of both firmness and uncertainty, as the pope of the new age.

[*See also* Revealed Religion *and* Roman Catholicism.]

BIBLIOGRAPHY

Artaud de Montour, A. F. *Histoire de la vie et du pontificat du Pape Pie VII*. Paris, 1836.

Chadwick, Owen. *The Popes and European Revolution*. Oxford, 1981. A lively account of Roman Catholicism in the eighteenth century.

Koeppel, Philippe, ed. *Papes et papauté au XVIIIe siècle: VIe colloque franco-italien Société Française d'Étude du XVIIIe siècle*. Paris, 1999.

Leflon, J. *Pie VII*. Paris, 1958.

PHILIPPE BOUTRY

Translated from French by William McCuaig

PLUCHE, NOËL-ANTOINE

PLUCHE, NOËL-ANTOINE (1688–1761), French Catholic teacher and apologist.

Initially a teacher of humanities and then of rhetoric, Noël-Antoine Pluche eventually became a much-admired headmaster at the collège de Reims. Harassed for refusing to subscribe to the anti-Jansenist papal bull *Unigenitus*, he found refuge in Normandy, where he lived as a tutor.

Returning to Paris thanks to a reward for services rendered to the crown, he taught history and geography before devoting himself to the Scriptures and to pious exercises.

Pluche offers a representative example of the willingness of eighteenth-century French defenders of Christianity to adapt to their times. His eight-volume work, *Le spectacle de la nature, ou Entretiens sur les particularités de l'histoire naturelle qui ont paru les plus propres à rendre les jeunes gens curieux et à leur former l'esprit* (The Spectacle of Nature, or Conversations about the Particularities of Natural History That Have Appeared Most Apt to Make Young People Curious and Form Their Minds, 1732–1750), made use of his readers' infatuation with scientific subjects and put to it apologetical ends, judging that "the sight of nature is a popular theology in which all men can learn what it is in their interest to know." Joining the useful to the agreeable, the author, with the aid of illustrations, praised the beauties of creation and did so in the pleasing form of ordinary conversation. As the work unfolds, the young chevalier Du Breuil, on vacation in the country, is initiated into right-minded philosophy by his father's friend the count de Jonval, in the presence of the local parish priest and the countess. They carefully study in turn animals and plants (vol. 1), the earth's surface and its depths (vol. 2), the heavens and the various parts of the universe (vol. 3), man in and of himself (vol. 4), and man in relation to society (vols. 5–7). Volume 8, more overtly apologetical, considers man in his relations with God.

This encyclopedia of the theoretical and applied sciences for use by lay readers, in which nothing that might win over the reader is lacking—not even a gardener's manual or an essay on navigation—was highly successfully. Often reprinted, and translated into almost all the European languages, it constituted a "best-seller" in Enlightenment France. It was complemented in 1739 by *L'histoire du ciel, considérée selon les idées des poètes, des philosophes et de Moïse* (The History of Heaven, According to the Ideas of the Poets, the Philosophers, and Moses), which relied on Bishop William Warburton's system of explaining Greek mythology, and which strove to demonstrate the superiority of the biblical cosmogony, even independently of all Revelation. Pluche also contributed a treatise on the origin of languages, *La mécanique des langues et l'art de les assembler* (The Way Languages Work and the Art of Assembling Them, 1751), along with various works of education and sacred history.

If for Voltaire Pluche's *Histoire du ciel* was only a "bad novel," Nicolas-Antoine Boulanger, in the article "Déluge" in the *Encylopédie*, took into consideration the hypothesis, proposed in *Le spectacle de la nature*, of the existence of an antediluvian sea, and Jean-Jacques Rousseau, in his seventh "Promenade," borrowed from Pluche the idea that the depths of the earth were rich in mineral reserves for times to come. Pluche was frequently cited, moreover, in discussions of teaching (see, for example, the article "Inversion" in the *Encyclopédie*).

[*See also* Apologetics; Boulanger, Nicolas-Antoine; Physico-Theology; *and* Roman Catholicism.]

BIBLIOGRAPHY

Monod, Albert. *De Pascal à Chateaubriand: Les défenseurs français du christianisme de 1670 à 1802.* Paris, 1916; repr., Geneva, 1970, pp. 193–196.

SYLVIANE ALBERTAN-COPPOLA
Translated from French by Catherine Porter

PNEUMATICS. Pneumatics (the study of air) provided an important link between the scientific revolution and the chemical revolution. The emergence of pneumatic chemistry in the middle of the eighteenth century involved a conceptual transformation in which the idea of air as a chemically inert element gave way to the concept of the "aerial" (gaseous) state that encompassed a multiplicity of chemically distinct airs. This transformation started with the physical models of air constructed by Robert Boyle (1627–1691) and Isaac Newton (1642–1727); it involved new instruments of inquiry, theories of heat and electricity, and concerns about the disciplinary identity of chemistry and the utility of scientific knowledge.

In 1660, Boyle used the air pump to characterize quantitatively, in the form of Boyle's Law, the pressure, "elasticity," or "spring," of the air. Differentiating "perennial air" from ephemeral vapors and exhalations, Boyle treated elasticity as an essential and immutable property of the microscopic particles of air. Boyle's essentialist view of air reinforced the prevalent belief that air was a simple, immutable entity, incapable of entering into chemical combination with other substances. Newton challenged the essentialist view of air in 1687, when he derived the property of elasticity from a repulsive force that varied inversely with the distance between the particles of air. Newton argued that, at shorter distances, the repulsive force gave way to a short-range attractive force that was responsible for optical, magnetic, electrical, and chemical phenomena and that "fixed" air like any other chemical substance. By locating the property of elasticity between, rather than within, the particles of air, Newton removed the essentialist objection to the idea of air as a chemical entity and paved the way for the later development of pneumatic chemistry.

Newtonian natural philosophy shaped the physics of air. Newton's view of the all-pervasive ether as a more rarefied, subtler form of air encouraged natural philosophers to relate the phenomena of heat, light, and electricity to the action of imponderable elastic fluids. In 1727, Stephen Hales (1677–1761) used Newtonian principles to develop a two-substance theory of attractive matter and repulsive air that served as the model for subsequent fluid theories of heat, light, and electricity. In 1734, Hermann Boerhaave (1668–1738) combined the properties of Newton's ether and Hales's air in his view of "elementary fire," or "the matter of heat," as a subtle, elastic fluid, uniformly distributed throughout nature. William Cullen (1710–1790) questioned Boerhaave's doctrine of the uniform distribution of fire and rejected Hales's assumption that air was the only substance that could be made truly elastic; he traced elasticity to the presence of fire. Within this dualistic framework, Cullen and Joseph Black (1728–1799) linked thermal and chemical phenomena to changes in the state of matter, and Black and William Irvine (1743–1781) formulated the important doctrines of latent heat and heat capacities. From the early 1760s, Antoine Lavoisier (1743–1794) regarded elasticity as the result of the combination of ordinary matter with caloric ether, the matter of fire. Lavoisier's quest for an adequate theory of the gaseous state was a cornerstone of the chemical revolution.

The antihypothetical climate of late eighteenth-century science, shaped in part by the Newtonian desire to subject speculative discourse to the discipline of mathematical reasoning and experimental inquiry, encouraged the development of more accurate and reliable barometers and thermometers to measure the elasticity and heat content of air. Natural philosophers also used the air pump—an important icon of eighteenth-century science—as an instrument of demonstration and research. The deployment of the pneumatic trough, which consisted of a basin of liquid over which airs were collected and isolated in inverted jars, had an even greater impact on pneumatic chemists, who were not interested in the physical properties of air, but in the manipulation of chemically distinct airs.

Pneumatic chemistry began in 1727 when Hales identified the airs produced by the destructive distillation of various substances with common air, which he treated as a chemical principle. Black published the first account of an air different from common air in 1756, when he isolated and examined "fixed air" (carbon dioxide). While David MacBride (1723–1778) treated fixed air as a modification of the "universal aerial fluid," William Brownrigg (1711–1800) argued, in 1741, that airs could be as chemically distinct as solids and liquids. Henry Cavendish (1731–1810) and Joseph Priestley (1733–1804) gave empirical substance to Brownrigg's speculations, isolating and identifying over a dozen different airs, including hydrogen, oxygen, and the oxides of nitrogen. Cavendish incorporated the pneumatic domain into the phlogiston theory of chemistry, and Priestley developed an "aerial philosophy" of nature, shaped by his benevolent utilitarianism. Priestley's interest in the medicinal uses of airs

was part of the Enlightenment tradition of pneumatic medicine, which linked sanitary improvement and urban planning to social and political reform. This tradition reached its culmination in the Pneumatic Institution, founded by Thomas Beddoes (1760–1808) in 1797. The counter-Enlightenment backlash in the late eighteenth century closed the Institution, ruined Beddoes's reputation, and drove Priestley into political exile in America.

Before his untimely death in the French Revolution, Lavoisier engineered a revolution in chemistry by integrating the experimental results of British pneumatic chemistry into a theoretical framework shaped by Continental analytical chemistry and experimental philosophy. Lavoisier subsumed the chemistry of phlogiston and air, developed by Guillaume-François Rouelle (1703–1770) and the French disciples of Georg Ernst Stahl (1659–1734), under Boerhaave's physics of fire. Whereas the Stahlians held that, in its fixed form as phlogiston, the matter of fire could be deprived of its repulsive power and transformed into ordinary matter, subject to the laws of chemical combination, Lavoisier accorded caloric the role of an expansive or repulsive agent. Lavoisier's negotiation of this disciplinary boundary resulted in his

Pneumatics. Instrument used by Antoine Laurent Lavoisier (1743–1794) for the study of gas. (Conservatoire Nationale des Arts et Métiers, Paris/Lauros-Giraudon/Art Resource, NY.)

well-known claim that he had transferred the source of heat in combustion from the combustible (phlogiston) to the air (caloric), since fire was more abundant in the latter, repulsive form of matter. While the work of John Dalton (1766–1844) and Joseph-Louis Gay-Lussac (1778–1850) on the law of combining volumes completed the integration of pneumatic chemistry into normal chemistry, eighteenth-century pneumatics bequeathed to the nineteenth century the caloric theory of gases.

[*See also* Hales, Stephen; Lavoisier, Antoine-Laurent; Medicine, *subentry on* Practice of Medicine; Natural Philosophy and Science; Newton, Isaac; Physics; Popularization; Priestley, Joseph; Scientific Instruments; *and* Stahl, Georg Ernst.]

BIBLIOGRAPHY

Allan, D. G. C., and R. E. Schofield. *Stephen Hales, Scientist and Philanthropist*. London, 1980. A useful account of Hales's pioneering work in pneumatic chemistry and his place in the culture of Newtonian natural philosophy.

Donovan, A. L. *Philosophical Chemistry in the Scottish Enlightenment*. Edinburgh, 1975. Places Black's work on fixed air in the scientific and cultural context of the Scottish Enlightenment.

Fichman, Morris. "French Stahlism and Chemical Studies of Air." *Ambix* 18 (1971), 94–123. Explores links between the idea of air as a chemical element and Stahlian arguments for the irreducibility of chemistry to physics.

Fox, Robert. *The Caloric Theory of Gases: From Lavoisier to Regnault*. Oxford, 1971. Chapter 1 provides a seminal study of fluid theories of heat and air in the eighteenth century.

Jungnickel, Christa, and Russell McCormmach. *Cavendish: The Experimental Life*. Cranbury, N.J., 1999. Provides a valuable and detailed account of Cavendish's pneumatic chemistry, natural philosophy, and place in eighteenth-century science and society.

McEvoy, John G. "Joseph Priestley, 'Aerial Philosopher': Metaphysics and Methodology in Priestley's Chemical Thought, 1772–1781." *Ambix* 25 (1978), 1–55, 93–116, 153–175; 26 (1979), 16–38. Provides an account of Priestley's place in the tradition of British pneumatic chemistry and the philosophical foundations of his "aerial" philosophy.

Melhado, Morris. "Chemistry, Physics, and the Chemical Revolution." *Isis* 76 (1985), 195–211. Shows how Lavoisier's view of the gaseous state arose out of the complex intermingling of Stahlian chemistry and Boerhaave's physics.

Morris, Robert. "Lavoisier and the Caloric Theory." *British Journal for the History of Science* 6 (1972), 1–38. Shows how Lavoisier's concept of the gaseous state linked the study of heat to the science of chemistry.

Schofield, Robert E. *Mechanism and Materialism: British Natural Philosophy in the Age of Reason*. Princeton, N.J., 1970. An extended discussion of Newtonian theories of ethers, airs, and subtle fluids.

Shapin, Steven, and Simon Schaffer. *Leviathan and the Air-Pump: Hobbes, Boyle, and the Experimental Life*. Princeton, N.J., 1985. The definitive account of Boyle's work with the air pump and its reception by the scientific and philosophical community of the seventeenth century.

JOHN G. McEVOY

POETRY. Poetry in the century of the Enlightenment poses a philosophical problem and at the same time constitutes a major mode of expression and communication everywhere in the world. It is impossible, thus, to summarize in a few pages the richness of the international output, the diversity of the oeuvres of the various poets, the multiplicity of subjects and themes, and the episodes of literary life that make the history of poetry in the eighteenth century a drama with a thousand unexpected twists, and at times a sombre tragedy (which Alfred de Vigny would later stage in *Chatterton*). Apart from this abundance, however which is difficult to describe other than by compiling biographical notices and retelling a detailed history of each of the national literatures, the poetry of the eighteenth century strikes a modern observer by the distinctness and universality of its common traits, from one end of the century to the other and one end of the world to the other. These common traits throw into relief the close relation that exists between poetic creation and the philosophical movement of the Enlightenment; they define the difference between poetry then and what we call poetry today; they allow us to understand the prominent features of Romanticism as it quickens into life in the whole of Europe in the second half of the century and in France at the beginning of the century following.

The Legitimacy of Poetry. The legitimacy of poetry and the means it employed were under assault in numerous exchanges. Fraught with conventions, it seemed to elude the rules of reason and to flatter the least philosophic impulses of mankind: imagination, sensuality, the passions. Even its most reasonable and pedagogical forms, such as the fable, offended by obscurity and incoherence. One thinks of the ruthless critique of the *Fables* of Jean de La Fontaine (1621–1695) that Jean-Jacques Rousseau delivers in *Émile*. Antoine Houdar de La Motte proposed a logical conception of literature that excluded all poetic licence in principle; geometricians such as Jean Terrasson refused any role for inspiration, or for the fantasies of poetic language; English critics such as Joseph Addison, Richard Steele, and Alexander Pope, French ones such as Bernard Le Bovier de Fontenelle or Rémond de Saint-Mard emphasized the artificial character of pastoral poetry. In France especially, a radical calling into question of French poetic procedures, syllabic verse and rhyme, naturally led to the conclusion that prose was superior. Yet in practice the taste for poetry in verse did not decline at all, and even grew with the enlargement of the cultivated public educated in the elite institutions of secondary education known as collèges, reaching the point of a craze for verse, the "métromanie" that Piron made the subject of a very successful comedy (1738).

Though it was often viewed as a pointless detour, poetic language was at the same time exalted as the superior form of language, the more deeply pondered, dense, harmonious form, the one more capable of compelling assent or eliciting emotion from the reader. That explains why no domain could keep poetry out. To be set to verse constituted the more or less distant goal of every intellectual or literary effort; those that did not achieve this were modestly proffered as the results of an infirmity on the part of the author. Those who haughtily claimed superiority for prose were few. Poetry's prestige as a measured language, more worthy of attention and memory than prose, was based on rational reflections, rhetorical and linguistic in character, like those of J.-B. Du Bos in his *Réflexions critiques sur la poésie et la peinture* (Critical Reflections on Poetry and Painting, 1719). However, it was also, and primarily, based on the prestige acquired by the European literature of preceding centuries, the most highly regarded productions of which were in verse: the tragedies of Corneille, Racine, and Quinault, the great comedies of Molière, and the epics of John Milton, Torquato Tasso, and Ludovico Ariosto.

French Foundation, Latin Models, Biblical Influence. The pre-eminence of the French language at the beginning of the century, that "universality" that Rivarol has analyzed, evidently played an important role in the vogue for verse in all the European countries. France was the most populous country of Europe, and its political and military preponderance would be enough to account for the marked influence of its poetry in other countries. In addition, however the renown of the French "classics" had attracted admiration and imitation ever since the age that Voltaire called "the century of Louis XIV." The most resounding works among those classics, the most accessible as well to foreign readerships taken as a whole, were the ones in verse: those of Nicolas Boileau and La Fontaine, and also those of the dramatists. French theater was presented everywhere by traveling troupes or by amateurs.

It is well known that it was the prestige of French tragedy that sparked the national debate in Germany in the second half of the century. In Germany, Poland, and Italy the translations and adaptations did not always preserve the versified form, but the social and intellectual elite appreciated *Phèdre* or *Horace* in the original text, meaning they had access to all the effects that the versification of Racine or Pierre Corneille is capable of producing. Over the course of the century poetic syncreticism led to widespread utilization of foreign models in the national schools of poetry. Pope was inspired by Boileau, Louis Racine by Milton, Voltaire by John Dryden and Tasso. The practice of translation or adaptation in verse was one of the most highly esteemed and widely used literary modes in all countries.

Through it many an amateur experienced the difficulties and the joys of literary creation, and many a professional writer advanced through the preliminary phase toward a personal oeuvre. To compare attempts at poetic translation, read them in academies, publish them in periodicals, insert them into other works—all these were constant features of literary life in the eighteenth century everywhere in Europe. Voltaire scattered samples of verse translation throughout his *Lettres philosophiques* (1734) to give his French or francophone readers an idea of the riches of English poetry, and also to give them a flattering notion of his own talent. The practice of poetic translation is a testimonial to the mutual interest that poets and readers in each country had for the others; it shows that there existed a Europe of poetry, just as there existed a Europe of philosophy, and, in line with a tradition going back to the Renaissance, a European republic of letters.

Above all else, however, it reveals the common foundation on which all modern poetry was built in the eighteenth century: Latin poetry and the Bible. The century was marked, from north to south, by the expansion of teaching in the collèges: thanks to them a public grew up that had been formed, essentially, by the reading of the Latin poets, who were the basis of literary, and more generally, intellectual, training. This choice of learning material had been theorized from the end of the sixteenth century by the pedagogues of the Society of Jesus (Jesuits). The Latin prose writers, especially the historians, had their place in the curricula, but it was the poets who were made the object of the most thorough and richest study, with the help of ample commentaries that covered many different areas: history, mythology, rhetoric, philosophy, theology, political science, psychology, geography, physics, and astronomy. Verse appeared to be the receptacle that held the essential elements of thought and knowledge. The pupils were initiated into the making of verse in Latin and in their native languages.

Readers of poetry in the eighteenth century in all of Europe had not only a rich poetic culture to refer to, principally Latin but more and more, as the century progressed, modern too they also had a genuine technical competence that led them to take an interest in that "difficulty overcome" that verse represented, with its displays of bravura in handling the stanza, its essays in rhythm, and its innovations in vocabulary. Their approach to contemporary poetry was not only emotive, imaginative, and intellectual, it was also technical, almost professional. The familiarity of the public with the Latin poets had another consequence: poetic creation was often conceived as a dialogue with these old, but deathless, models, as the *Épître à Horace* (Letter to Horace, 1772) that Voltaire wrote in old age demonstrates. Voltaire's *La Henriade* (1723) too, however, can only be read in parallel with the *Aeneid* of Virgil, its model, and the case of Delille is yet clearer still, since he offered as a major poetic undertaking his complete verse translation of the *Georgics* of Virgil (1769).

If Latin culture crops up everywhere, in forms, themes, and language, it often went hand in glove with another influence, that flowing from familiarity with the poetic parts of the Bible. Even more pervasively than it was classical and philosophic, Europe was Christian by training, sensibility, and often conviction. Of course the historical and religious importance of the Bible was vigorously thrown into doubt, as in the *Dictionnaire philosophique* (1764) of Voltaire, in the name of a Deism that was shrugging off the contingencies of history. Yet the biblical text cast a spell, even with, or perhaps because of, its barbaric violence. The poetry of the primitive that Diderot called for, and that Europeans believed they had discovered in Ossian, was inspired by the Bible in the first place. One of the major sources of inspiration was the translation, or the paraphrase, of the psalms and the prophetic books. Through the selection of the excerpts translated, through personal commentary, through the application (based on practices deriving from figural language) of the biblical texts to the realities of contemporary history and their own destiny, poets like Jean-Baptiste Rousseau or Lefranc de Pompignan in France relied on the prestige of the word of God and on the familiarity of texts read or heard a thousand times.

Everywhere this strain of poetry drew sustenance from learned study of the Bible and its riches: in France at the Academy des Inscriptions, in England at Oxford, where Robert Lowth published *De sacra poesi Hebraeorum* (On the Sacred Poetry of the Hebrews, 1753), in Germany with Johann Gottfried Herder, who was inspired by Lowth (translated in 1751–1761) in his *Über den Geist der ebräische Poesie* (On the Spirit of Hebrew Poetry). His outlook, which emphasized the intrinsic poetic value of the Bible, in which one could supposedly discover language and sensibility in their primitive freshness, constitutes the point of arrival of a rediscovery of the biblical text to which the poetry of the eighteenth century owes a great deal, and which would go on to nourish major works of Romanticism.

Societal Influences. Another factor that unified the poetry of the Enlightenment was its links to social practices that, without being completely homogeneous, possessed numerous traits in common, at least in the higher strata of society. A great deal of the poetry produced in France especially, but also in Italy and Germany, was conceived in the interstices of society life and constituted one of the elements of sophistication. It was used to comment on, announce, or recount small occasions within a circle or a court. Poetic activity of this kind was closely linked to sociability, one of the virtues promoted by the philosophy of the Enlightenment as a whole, and to the ambition of the philosophes to play a role in the entourage of princes, into which poetry was a potent means of gaining admittance: it was thanks to his celebrity as a poet that Voltaire became an intimate of Frederick II (known as "the Great") of Prussia. The *Divertissements de Sceaux* published by Charles-Claude Genest, one of the familiars of the duchess of Maine, illustrate this vein, as do the *Oeuvres diverses* of Alexis Piron, a rival of Voltaire in the Parisian society of the first half of the century.

The category called in French *poésies fugitives* ("fugitive poems") contained much more than just occasional poetry, since "fugitive" signified merely that the poem in question "did not form part of a larger whole intended for publication," and so there are fugitive poems on religious, moral, narrative, and often polemic topics. Twentieth-century criticism has been content to use the word to connote poetic production fragile in nature and fleeting in its production and consumption, characteristics clearly evident in occasional pieces.

In fact, worldly poetry displays virtues of authenticity that monumental and elaborate forms, whether in poetry, the novel, or philosophy do not. This authenticity can disclose itself in texts that move the reader and that contain no trace of forced sociability, like the *Poésies érotiques* (Erotic Poems, 1778) of Évariste Parny, a collection of texts apparently written during the successive stages of a love affair actually experienced by the poet. Lived experience overrides the construct, and the personal accent masks the borrowings from tradition, even though many a reader took delight in detecting the rendition into French verse, and an exotic setting, of famous passages from Ovid or Propertius. Such an autobiographical transformation of the sublime topoi of the poetry of the past constituted one of the central ambitions of the poetry of the eighteenth century and converged with the notion, central to the philosophy of the Enlightenment, of the permanent and universal nature of mankind. So it is that occasional poetry, though fragile and superficial in certain respects and fated to wither rapidly, was able to constitute the heart of a renewed poetry that would flower with the romantic movement.

The theater exerted as much influence on the poetry of the Enlightenment as the life of society did. The word poetry itself implied theatrical poetry first and foremost, and there were few poets who did not try their luck on the stage. The most revered literary authors, Shakespeare, Racine, and Voltaire, were all dramatists. Further, poetry was principally conceived to be read or recited aloud: that is how the poets themselves presented their works in the circles in which poetic glory was conferred. Certain works of significant reputation and considerable length, like Pierre-Joseph Bernard's *L'art d'aimer* (Art of Loving, 1775) or Jean-François de Saint-Lambert's *Les saisons* (The Seasons, 1769) were only published decades after they became known to an elite audience through partial oral delivery.

The result was a very strong relish for effect, which artful modulation of the voice, such as a lingering pause, could heighten. Speeches delivered in verse were a flourishing genre in their own right, employed by Pope and Voltaire, and with several particularly prolific sub-genres. The *héroïde* was a poem in which a hero of history or mythology spoke in the first person; dialogues in verse amounted to sketches for comedies or philosophical treatises. The personal lyric itself was appreciated as a staged presentation, eloquent and moving, of the passions and predicaments of a central theatrical personage, the author himself. This "staging," with its deliberately adopted poses and its emphases, was to become one of the principal characteristics of romantic poetry. The interpenetration of poetry and theater led to the development of couplets in comedy, the comic opera, and opera itself—that fusion of poetry and music which Du Bos theorized and justified at the beginning of the century.

Poetry and the Philosophe. This international cultural backdrop to the poetry of the Enlightenment sustained many of its evolutions and phases. A concern to be inventive, the taste for surprise, obedience to the dictates of fashion (so powerful a force at this time, notably in the sophisticated, courtly, and journalistic circles that conferred success) brought about a series of renewals—always incomplete—of inspiration and form. If we consider the case of France, the point of departure is no doubt always a desire to complete the classic heritage. As Jean Le Rond d'Alembert asserted roundly in the preliminary discourse to the *Encyclopédie* (1746–1754), eighteenth-century people had the feeling that as far as literature went, there remained little for them to do after the brilliant triumphs of the preceding century, except in light poetry, in which taste was still being refined.

The end of the reign of Louis XIV and the years of the Regency (1715–1723) filled other gaps, however: Jean-Baptiste Rousseau experimented with the forms of an imposing lyricism that highlighted the figure of the poet of genius, misunderstood and banished, and the prophetic message of a poetry that judged and condemned the mediocrities and the injustices of modern civilization in the name of higher values. This was to be the stance of Vigny and Victor Hugo, who would follow Alphonse-Marie-Louis de Prat de Lamartine in taking up the very elaborate and impressive stanza schemes invented by J.-B. Rousseau, a poet read and admired in the nineteenth century. Fontenelle developed pastoral poetry, which had remained in the embryonic stage in France, by frankly applying the conventions of pastoral in a philosophic sense, as a means of representing an ideal of tranquillity and perfect sociability. Jean-Baptiste-Louis Gresset, in his

masterpiece, *Ver-Vert* (1734), the story in verse of a parrot in a convent of nuns, or Bernard in his *L'art d'aimer*, a pseudo-didactic poem inspired by Ovid that presents different aspects of hedonistic life in the refined setting of regency Paris, engaged in witty badinage in which nothing is too heavy or too solid, as the young Voltaire did in his early stories in verse or in *Le mondain* (The Mundane, 1736), and as Pope did in *The Rape of the Lock* (1712).

Bernard and Voltaire also put forward a bold philosophical position, from which the Christian expectation of salvation, and the sense of sin, were excluded. Poetry makes a contribution in its own way to the philosophe movement, as an indispensable means of gaining the interest of the requisite public (masculine, but feminine too) in the contemporary debate of ideas, and in presenting the practical consequences. Voltaire offered a genuine doctrinal exposition in his *Discours en vers sur l'homme* (Discourse in Verse on Mankind, 1738), in which he employs vivacity, anecdotes, and demonstrative dialogues to treat the questions of happiness, liberty, and the inequalities of social status. Louis Racine, son of the dramatist and a contemporary and ally of Voltaire, unfolds the whole of the religious debate that lay at the heart of intellectual and literary activity in the eighteenth century in his two great poems *La grâce* (1720) and *La religion* (1742).

Poetry became the vehicle of all the knowledge necessary in this grave debate, and at the same time it was animated by the passion and anguish that made the debate intimate and crucial. In a different yet comparable manner, Saint-Lambert, the friend of Voltaire and his rival for the affections of Mme. du Châtelet, presented a panorama of philosophic views on morality, marriage, the rural economy, urban development, mendicity, war, and nature at midcentury, and selected the traditional sequence of the seasons as the framework of his exposition. The poem that resulted, *Les Saisons* (The Seasons), was considered the masterpiece of the century by Voltaire, and remains the model of a large-scale philosophical poem. It includes descriptions, tales, tableaux, discussions, and is organized as an ensemble of eloquent and suggestive discourses, delivered by the poet himself or by his imaginary personages, all of them harmoniously interlinked. From Pope's *Essay on Man* (1733) to the major works of the poet of Sans-Souci, Frederick the Great, king of Prussia and poet in French, the intellectual vocation of poetry loomed large: the compression of meaning that verse imposes, the expressivity attained by variations in word order, the charm exerted by rhythm and sonority, amounted to powerful supports of thought in all languages. Before Johann Wolfgang von Goethe or Paul Valéry, the poet strode forth as sublime thinker.

In the eighteenth century, however, philosophy was not merely speculative: it had an encyclopedic character and brought together the areas of knowledge dominated by the critical spirit. That is why, especially after 1760, philosophic poetry largely took the path of description, often in the service of a didactic project: even more than Saint-Lambert's *Les Saisons*, it is Jacques Delille's *Les jardins* (The Gardens, 1782), an organized, explanatory guide to the great modern parks of Europe, that illustrates this trend, as does the agricultural compendium of Jean-Antoine Roucher, *Les mois* (The Months, 1779). Libertine and sentimental on the surface, poets like Parny and André-Marie de Chénier achieved, in their own way, the philosophic ambition that animated the whole of European poetry of the eighteenth century. We see this in Parny's great poem, *La guerre des dieux* (The War of the Gods, 1799), a fiercely anti-Christian work—as much so as Voltaire's whole philosophic oeuvre. Chénier's oeuvre was unfinished, but his plan for a poem on America (*L'Amérique*, 1794) also fitted into a philosophic outlook. Above all, in boldly celebrating the joys and torments of the purely earthly passions, in reviving themes of pagan poetry, these authors expressed their rejection of the expectations and scruples of Christians, as they rejected the moderate ideal of wisdom. Their lyrics proposed a pagan vision of the world and of life that constituted the natural prolongation of the critical effervescence of the Enlightenment.

Unity of Poetry: Passion and Reason. Despite the diversity of positions and genres, despite the dominant idea so well expressed by Fénelon in his *Lettre à l'Académie* (1715) that the success of any work lies in its conformity to the genre to which it belongs, despite the absence of an idea or doctrine unique to poetry, we can see that the works considered eminent by contemporaries are at bottom unified by a common ambition and a common search that we are entitled to describe as modern, and that is a contribution to the philosophic enterprise of the century. This unity of poetry was reinforced by a number of constants.

Enlightened conceptions of poetry inhabited a space of permanent tension between two ideal perspectives: in one, poetry is the perfection of language mastered by art, and so ornament is its defining characteristic (in France: rhyme, syllabic equality of the lines of verse; everywhere: the tropes, the rhythm chosen, the stanza form, the recourse to mythology); in the other, poetry is language stripped bare, closer to the natural cry, which can dispense with any ornament and overlap with expressive prose. This dilemma replicated the debate within the Enlightenment between partisans of technical, artistic, scientific progress, and the partisans of a return to nature. The forms that won the favor of poets and of the cultivated public were those that united these two tendencies and fulfilled the expectations of both. For example, the ode, which gained success in France beginning in the last years of the seventeenth century, and which, in the hands of J.-B. Rousseau in France, Mikhail Vasilyevich Lomonosov in Russia and Friedrich Gottlieb Klopstock in Germany won over all of Europe, is often constructed as a complex pattern of stanzas inspired by Pindar and Horace, and thus appears to be the peak of poetic art. The ode is also a primitive song, however, that gives voice to simple sentiments, primeval enthusiasm, the solidarity of a people, revolt or melancholy in the face of injustice and death.

Another example is the poem on the seasons, which gained distinction in the hands of Saint-Lambert, but also in those of François-Joachim de Pierre de Bernis, James Thomson, Heinrich von Kleist, Friedrich Hölderlin, Roucher, and William Blake. Overall, this genre is meant to express the elemental communion of man with nature, in accordance with a very ancient pattern and from a point of view that lessens the importance of civilization and history. Yet the poets have no hesitation in organizing this lyrical impulse into a methodical arrangement that lets them introduce moral, agricultural, and political lessons.

Yet another example is the epic, practiced in every language, whether by Voltaire in France or Klopstock in Germany. The close, prolonged attention to Homeric poetry generated by the debate between La Motte and Anne Dacier, and kept alive by learned works in England, Germany, Italy, and France, produced a tendency to see the epic as the simplest of poetic forms: a foundation narrative of a nation's destiny in which the elementary passions of men were expressed. This aspect may not be evident in *La Henriade*, because it is deeply influenced by the Virgilian model, but it is easy to discern in *Les Incas* (1777) by Jean-François Marmontel, since verse is there abandoned and prose adopted.

Thus the natural and spontaneous character of poetry manifested itself, in harmony with what the poem expressed: a religious sentiment founded on the contemplation of nature, love, family attachments, the wish for life to continue. At the same time, however, the epic was also a repository of the most complex techniques and effects of the art of poetry: pronouncements, highly staged scenes, descriptions, episodes, periphrasis, elevated vocabulary, and the intervention of allegorical figures. The epic was freighted with an entirely contemporary philosophic message: *La Henriade* develops the central theme of the evils, principally civil war, that the existence of organized religions entails; *Les Incas* illustrates one of the central tactics of the philosophy of the Enlightenment, the comparison of different civilizations and the simultaneous foregrounding of the relativity of beliefs and ethics, and its obverse: the nature, the sensibility, and the morality that all men share.

Poetry thus played different and important roles in the development and spread of the Enlightenment. It was used to present, in an agreeable manner, knowledge newly acquired, such as the discoveries of Newton in the *Discours* of Voltaire and the verse of Pope, Blake, and Cándido María Trigueros; or hygienic theories in Giuseppe Parini's poem *La salubrità dell'aria* (The Salubriousness of the Air). It served to expound the concatenation of ideas and materials in a doctrinal system, as in the poems of Louis Racine and Helvétius; but as it did so it expressed the experiences, the doubts, the antagonisms, and the fumblings of a particular individual not unlike the reader. Poetry added something existential to philosophical reflection by showing its links to everyone's lived experience. It was able to draw thought down from lofty realms by promoting polemical exchange. Passion and reason flowed together in the innumerable satires, epigrams, and songs that the philosophes exchanged among themselves and with their adversaries. Finally, poetry created a world of fantasy within which a philosophical lesson could be conveyed: we see this in the fables of Tomás Yriarte, John Gay, Christian Fürchtegott Gellert, Jean-Pierre Claris de Florian, Jacques Aubert, and many others, or in the tale told in verse as practiced by Voltaire.

The poetry of the Enlightenment did not develop alongside philosophy, for a different public. It expressed the qualities of the philosophe as they were defined in the article "Philosophe" in the *Encyclopédie*: sociability, the rejection of prejudice, the concern to make oneself useful, the aspiration for individual and collective happiness. It created a space in which very different men and women throughout the world could encounter one another: verse opened many doors, as evident in the triumphant voyage through Italy made by Mme. Du Boccage, one of the rare female poets to have attained celebrity in the eighteenth century. Poets were also princes like Frederick the Great, great lords like the Duke of Nivernois, professors like Gresset and Delille, journalists, actors, nobodies. Poetry brought together very different beings who shared a common passion; it created bonds among nations. Often looked at askance by the dominant rationalism as a collection of artifices and conventions, poetry won out as a higher language of reason and a more personal form of expression, in which the shadowy sides of the world and mankind also found their place.

[*See also* England; Germany; Goethe, Johann Wolfgang von; Literary Genres; Men and Women of Letters; Opera; Pope, Alexander; Romanticism; Sociability; Theater, *subentry on* Literary Genre; *and* Voltaire.]

BIBLIOGRAPHY

Arce, J. *La Poesia del siglo ilustrado.* Madrid, 1981.

Baldensperger, F. *Goethe en France.* Paris, 1904.

Brady, P. *Rococo Poetry in English, French, German, Italian.* Knoxville, Tenn., 1992.

Browning, R. M. *German Poetry in the Age of Enlightenment.* Pittsburgh, Pa., and London, 1978.

Cameron, M. *L'influence des Saisons de Thomson sur la poésie descriptive en France.* Paris, 1927.

Fabre, J. *Chénier.* Paris, 1965.

Fabre, J. *Lumières et romantisme.* Paris, 1980.

Finch, R. *The Sixth Sense: Individualism in French Poetry.* Toronto, 1966.

Griffin, D. *Regaining Paradise: Milton and the Eighteenth Century.* Cambridge, 1986.

Guitton, E. *Jacques Delille et le poème de la nature en France de 1750 à 1820.* Paris, 1974.

Knapp, R. G. *The Fortunes of Pope's Essay on Man in Eighteenth-Century France. Studies on Voltaire and the Eighteenth Century,* vol. 82. Geneva, 1971.

Menant, S. *La chute d'Icare: La crise de la poésie française (1700–1750).* Geneva, 1981.

Menant, S. *Esthétique de Voltaire.* Paris, 1995.

Munster, W. *La poétique du pittoresque en France de 1700 à 1830.* Geneva, 1991.

Pascal, J. N. *Les successeurs de La Fontaine au siècle des lumières.* New York, 1995.

Seth, C. "Poésie en Europe." In *Dictionnaire Européen des Lumières.* Paris, 1997.

Van Tieghem, P. *Ossian en France.* Paris, 1917.

SYLVAIN MENANT

Translated from French by William McCuaig

POIRET, PIERRE (1646–1719), French Reformed pastor, philosopher, and theologian.

Poiret was born in Metz. His father, an artisan, died young, and the orphaned youth received support for his studies from the parish. He studied theology in Basel and in Heidelberg. For a few years, he was a minister in Protestant French refugee parishes in the Palatinate. The Roman Catholic prophetess Antoinette Bourignon had considerable influence on his thought; Poiret became her disciple and oversaw the publication of her writings. After her death, he did not again hold a parish ministry, but he considered himself a pastor through his publications. Amid the Huguenots, he remained in the Netherlands, where all his own books were published, as well as those of various spiritual or mystical writers he edited. Poiret died in Rijnsburg, near Leiden.

At the outset, Poiret's thought was strongly marked by Descartes's rationalist philosophy and method. In the first edition of his major Latin treatise, *Cogitationes rationales* (1677), Poiret altered his stance on many philosophical and anthropological points. He affirmed the principle of a divine element in the human soul, created in the image of the Trinity. "Desire," the soul's main element, can never be fulfilled and quieted by the soul itself, but only by God. It is impossible to trust human reason, which is vainglorious and superficial. It cannot reach God himself, but only "God's idea," in Descartes's words; faith, however, can illumine the soul with God's presence. Poiret absolutely rejected predestination, insisting on freedom to accept or to refuse God's grace. He developed this system in his treatise *L'oeconomie divine* and in a pamphlet on children's Christian education. Those books, both translated into several languages, were widely circulated in Europe.

Poiret became a specialist on mystical theology. He explained its principles and identified families of mystical writers, attempting to convince Protestants that they might gain much from this common treasure of spirituality. He edited many texts: a Protestant adaptation of *The Imitation of Christ* (published in many editions), anthologies such as *La théologie du coeur*, the first collection of Mme. Guyon's writings, and other texts of so-called Quietist mysticism. He preached "peace for good souls" (the title of one of his books) and adopted an attitude of respecting others' convictions, similar to present-day ecumenicism. It is not necessary, in this view, to belong to a particular confession to be saved; to love God is the unique criterion. In the Eucharist, God gives to each faithful participant according to his faith.

Poiret was condemned by some prominent Protestants, including Pierre Jurieu and Pierre Bayle. The great Catholic archbishop and writer, Fénelon, condemned Poiret's refusal to convert to the Roman church. Poiret, who struggled for peace within Christianity, was very sensitive to criticism and replied strongly to his adversaries. His influence long persisted throughout Europe in circles of marginalized Protestants, notably those who called themselves "the internal souls." His movement from rationalism to mysticism reveals a powerful countercurrent of thought at the dawn of the Enlightenment.

[*See also* Cartesianism; Rationalism; *and* Reformed Churches.]

BIBLIOGRAPHY

Chevallier, Marjolaine. *Pierre Poiret.* (*Bibliotheca Dissidentium: Répertoire des non-conformistes religieux des seizième et dix-septième siècles*, vol. 5.) Baden-Baden, 1985. A complete bibliography of the books written or published by Poiret (content, different editions, translations).

Chevallier, Marjolaine. *Pierre Poiret (1646–1719): Du protestantisme à la Mystique.* Geneva, 1994.

Krieg, Gustav A. *Der mystische Kreis: Wesen und Werden der Theologie Pierre Poirets.* Göttingen, 1979.

Mori, Gianluca. *Tra Descartes e Bayle, Poiret e la teodicea.* Bologna, 1990. An interesting philosophical interpretation of the evolution of his thought.

Wieser, Max. *Peter Poiret, der Vater der romanischen Mystik in Deutschland.* Munich, 1932. The first, and valuable, study on this writer, with reproduction of some texts.

MARJOLAINE CHEVALLIER

POLAND. According to general opinion, the peak of the Polish Enlightenment was between 1788 and 1795, a brief period of effervescence, of intellectual and civic growth that did not prevent Poland's three powerful neighbors from erasing Poland from the map for 123 years, and indeed, that may have encouraged them to do so.

The Republic of the Two Nations. Geographically, politically, ethnically, and socially, what we call Poland encompassed, in the eighteenth century, a great variety of entities that gave this nation its unique character. This vast space extended from Poznan in the west to Vitebsk in the east, from the Baltic to the steppes near the Black Sea, from the Dnieper, and through the Carpathian mountains. It enclosed people and future nations that at the time led only a subterranean or parallel existence: Ruthenians (Byelorussians and Ukrainians), Jews (the great majority of the Jews of the world), and Lithuanians. All these groups passively resisted Polish assimilation by means of their religion, language, and customs. Only the Ukrainians resisted by numerous revolts. The Jews enjoyed an autonomy that kept them marginalized, while the other groups, more than 90 percent rural, were, like the Polish peasants themselves, kept out of civic existence in their heavy servitude.

Poland's political system was an exception among the absolutist and centralized states of Europe. Its designation as the Republic of the Two Nations was a reminder that it was formed in 1569, during the humanist fervor of the Polish Golden Age, by the fusion of the Lithuanian and Polish nobilities into a single parliament (the Diet). These nobles designated deputies who elected a king whose prerogatives were severely limited. Although both Lithuania and Poland preserved their own structures, after 1699 the official languages were Polish and Latin, and the Lithuanian and Ruthenian nobles, entirely under Polish influence, retained only a memory of their otherness. This "republican" regime, or more precisely a democracy of nobles, of a country not of the east, but of the north, provoked many misunderstandings among both philosophes and anti-philosophes.

Since the seventeenth century, the cultural climate accompanying the regime was known as Sarmatism, from the name of the hypothetical ancestors of the nobility, the Sarmats. This indicated a will to connect to a glorious chivalric past, in a happy rigidity, a favorable economic situation, and a naïve quietism based on a blissful and pacifist faith in providence, bathing in a prolonged baroque religiosity lasting since the Counter-Reformation, and maintained by a widespread Catholic clergy. Polish Catholicism was intolerant in regard to both the rare Protestants and the numerous Orthodox Christians of the east, scorned the Jews, and even desired to convert the Uniates, ancient Orthodox Christians who had, however, recognized the authority of the pope (in 1596) while conserving their Orthodox liturgical rites. The Jesuits, who played a predominant role in education during the first half of the century, maintained the intellectual level of the gentry on the basis of pious

Warsaw. View of the Plaza of the Iron Gate, Warsaw, painting (1779) by Bernardo Bellotto (1720–1780). (National Museum, Warsaw, Poland/Giraudon/Art Resource, NY.)

readings and baroque spiritual commentaries, fostering a spirit marked by litigiousness and a rather xenophobic inwardness. This "nation of nobles," conservative and cautious, exposed itself to the charge of what its neighbors called Polish "fanaticism."

All the royal elections of the eighteenth century unfolded under foreign "protection," that of Russia always being the most effective. In 1697, while France was backing Conti, it was Augustus II of Saxony whom the Russians caused to be elected. Dethroned by the Swedish, who established Stanislas Leszczyński in 1704, he returned in 1707. Augustus II's vague attempts at sovereignty were annulled in 1715, however, when Peter the Great, by a "silent Diet," imposed an almost total disarmament on Poland-Lithuania.

France did not abandon its "eastern barrier" (Sweden, Poland, and Turkey), and demonstrated this when the regent negotiated the marriage of the future Louis XV with Maria Leszczyńska, the daughter of the dethroned king, in 1725. His gold and his weak troops were unable to reinstate Leszczyński in 1733, however, at the death of Augustus II. A Diet, submissive to Russia, as always, instated Augustus III. Lorraine was given to Leszczyński, who established his court in Nancy and Luneville, assuring fertile artistic and intellectual ties between France and Poland.

Disarmed, the Republic became a Spanish refuge, crossed incessantly by the warring armies of its neighbors in war, but these passages did not greatly affect the prosperity of the great estates of the principal magnates who dominated the leading class. Residences, modeled after Versailles, flourished in Bialystok (Branicki family), in Puławy (the Czartoryski), in Tulczyn (the Potocki), in Lancut (the Lubomirski), in Koden (the Sapieha), in Nieśwież (the Radziwill), and so on. The luxury of these palaces introduced, more than in the seventeenth century, French influences, fashions, and refinements of style, of clothing, of the table, and especially of the boudoirs and salons, which were the centers of conversation. This conversation, after the middle of the century, gravitated toward serious subjects and a reflection on the means to escape powerlessness. Troupes of actors and musicians—Italian, French, and German—caused taste to evolve little by little among most nobility and the high clergy. The latter was even largely represented in the Masonic lodges, where the first partisans of an intellectual renewal met. In 1747, two bishops, the Zatuski brothers, opened their library to the public of Warsaw. The first projects of political reform started to circulate: those of Stanisław Poniatowski, father of the future king, in 1744, then those of Stanisław Konarski in 1763. The latter had created in 1740 a *collegium nobilium*, a school intended to change the nobility's mentality. In this spirit, he then developed a network of schools run by the Piarists, who were rivals of the Jesuits.

This timid awakening confirmed itself after the young Stanisław-Augustus Poniatowski, the former lover of

Catherine II, was elected to the throne in 1764. His vague desires for emancipation were bridled for twenty-five years before being fully realized, thus provoking the final catastrophe.

The king created a cadet school, in order eventually to restore military power; he founded a newspaper, the *Monitor*, in an attempt to fend off obscurantism; and he attempted to reestablish a public treasury by means of importation taxes. Poniatowski then ran up against the troublesomeness and duplicity of Frederick II and Catherine II, who used enlightened pretexts to satisfy their imperialism. Both rulers initially received support from the nobles opposed to the king (Confederation of Radom, 1767). However, when those same nobles discovered that Russia was not concerned about them, and only wished to maintain the anarchy that was so profitable to it, almost all of them rallied against their neighbor to the east (Confederation of Bar, 1768–1772).

The Confederation of Bar marked the first time the Polish nation pulled itself together before the insurrections of the nineteenth century. It also depended upon outraged Catholicism, the religious dimension being very significant. Catherine II's pretext of antifanaticism was shown to be false when the Orthodox serfs of the Ukraine believed they were authorized to massacre en masse Polish property owners and their Jewish allies at Human (1768). Fearing that this example would be contagious, the Russian army helped the weak Polish forces crush this rebellion and prevent it from spreading. Both sides of the conflict bribed Enlightened Europe in order to win its support. In 1771, Gabriel Bonnot de Mably (*Manifeste de la République confédérée de Pologne*) and Jean-Jacques Rousseau (*Considérations sur le gouvernement de Pologne*) aligned themselves with the Confederation of Bar, as did Étienne-François de Choiseul, while Voltaire wrote four opuscules and a tragedy supporting "Our Lady of Saint-Petersburg." The agitation of the confederates, who were feebly aided by a small French troop commanded by Charles-François du Périer Dumouriez, furnished the pretext for the first division of Poland, which was hastened by the intervention of Austria in 1773.

The Spread of Enlightenment. It was in the interest of Russia, whose influence remained dominant in what remained of the Republic of the Two Nations, to establish a minimum of order there. A permanent council, controlled by the empressarina's diplomatic resident in Warsaw, modernized the management of the country. Enlightened ideas, therefore, developed and spread, thanks to the commotion caused by the partition. This evolution was hindered by the lack of a large urban population, but fifteen years of peace and prosperity allowed some decisive achievements for the future.

The most remarkable of these achievements was, as a result of the abolition of the Jesuits by the pope, the recuperation of their academic network by the Commission of National Education. This resulted in the first European example of a global and centralized organization of education. A pyramidal hierarchy placed the two "major schools" (universities) of Kraków and Vilna at the head of secondary and primary schools. There were now lay teachers along with ecclesiastical ones. Academic programs were refounded, and new textbooks were edited with the help of foreign scholars such as Pierre-Samuel Du Pont de Nemours, Simon Lhuillier, and Étienne Bonnot de Condillac.

A new sociability appeared with the triumph of French customs and, often, the French language. Every aristocrat wanted to have his own private theater, and booksellers and publishers multiplied. The king set an example when during his "Thursday dinners" he would bring together the thinking elite and numerous artistic talents of his court. The Voltairian spirit even won over the high clergy, who ridiculed the monks (in works such as bishop Ignacy Krasicki's *Monachomachia* [1778]). The Freemasonry of the Grand Orient established itself in Poland and Lithuania after 1780. A new civic sense, stimulated by a reflection on the causes of decadence (Stanisław Staszic, *Remarques sur la vie de Jan Zamoyski*, 1785) signaled possible changes.

The opportunity for these changes presented itself in 1788, when Russia was fighting a war with Turkey while Prussia pretended to encourage the Polish reformers. The Diet, thus emboldened, carried on for four continuous years (and was therefore known as the "Great Diet"). With the support of the king, it initiated a profound revolution, which included the suppression of the *liberum veto*, the reconstitution of the army, the creation of an effective system of taxation, and the elaboration of a constitution. Despite the social discrepancies, these reforms were in harmony with the French Revolution. They were guided by bold thinkers such as Hugo Kołłątaj (*Prawo polityczne narodu polskiego* [Letters of an Anonymous Pole]) and Stanisław Staszic (*Przestrogi dla Polski* [Rights of the Poles]). They were not, however, influential or outspoken enough to change the attachment of the deputies (who, it must be recalled, were all nobles) to serfdom, nor their hostility to the integration of the Jews, nor their disdain for the urban population.

The constitution of 3 May 1791 thus remained timorous. Unlike the French constitution, which was promulgated three months later, it reinforced the royal power by rendering it hereditary and by adjoining five ministers to it. The empressarina, claiming that the "Jacobins" of Warsaw wanted to abolish serfdom, pretended to reply to a call for help from a small group of aristocrats that

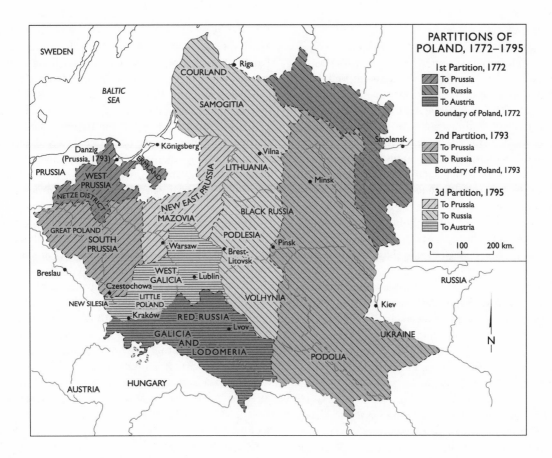

she herself had brought together, which was called the confederation of Targowica (1792), and had a large army brought into the Republic. Prussia withdrew its soldiers from the French front to take its part in Poland. Thus, in the same year (1793) that Louis XVI was decapitated due to the revolutionary triumph, Poland was divided a second time.

Galvanized by the example of the soldiers of Year II of the French Republic, some Polish troops, commanded by the general Tadeusz Kościuszko, revolted, hoping to drive away the partitioners. Their hope for French aid was in vain, however, and Kościuszko's appeal to the peasants, too late and too limited, collided with serfdom's opposition to change, due to the serfs' lack of a political and national conscience. The insurrection (1794) was limited to the cities of Warsaw, Kraków, and Vilna, where the urban violence, with its hangings and massacres of "traitors," recalled the Parisian Terror. These disorders terrified Poland's neighbors, who thereby found a motive to intervene again and seize what territory remained. The Prussians appeared the most hungry (the taking of Kraków, June 1795), so much so that Russia considered attacking them with the help of Austria. Finally, after the bloody siege of Warsaw by General Souvorov and the capture of Kościuszko in the battle of Maciejowice,

Poland's neighbors came to an agreement to totally divide the territory of the republic (October 1795).

Toward the last years of the eighteenth century, the "Polish cause" began to assume the major role that it would have in the nineteenth century. With the disappearance of their country, the patriots attempted to maintain in Europe the memory of the injustice they had suffered. Some put their energy into ensuring the influence of Polish cultural institutions in the divided territory, while others incessantly cultivated hope for national restoration.

Groups within the Polish Nation. Besides the masses of Polish peasants who were not integrated into the Republic, one must remember the four other groups whose national emergence took a long time to evolve. The Jews, who numbered 900,000 in 1791, comprising one tenth of the total population, had known the same rapid demographic growth—a tripling in one century—as the other groups, which made their almost exclusive presence in cities and small towns more and more problematic, leading to conflicts with the neighboring Poles, Ruthenians, and Lithuanians. This community underwent various forms of withdrawal and openness, all of which reinforced its identity. The development of Yiddish corresponded to a weakening of Talmudic dogma (which had been based on erudite knowledge of Hebrew), and was accompanied by a splitting into sects that were inspired by Islam or Christianity (such as Frankism, which developed after 1759), or into Hasidic circles, in which faith was much more popular and based on confidence in wise men (*saddiq*), the enemies of the rabbis. A fringe of this group adhered to a faith in progress and reason and adopted, as much in its customs as in its thought, ideas inspired by western Enlightenment. This movement, which willingly sought integration, was called the Haskalah. However, such integration was hardly possible because of the attachment of the Hasidic majority to a traditional way of life that was far removed from that of the Orthodox Slavs and the Catholics of the Republic, and also because of the latent hostility of the latter. During the Great Diet, diverse plans for assimilation, proposed by Polish Enlightenment thinkers (Mateusz Butrymowicz, Hugo Kołłątaj) and openly Jewish thinkers (Mendel Lewin of Satanów, known as Satanover), more or less pressed for integration. The majority of Jews who lived in the east were now located in the Russian Empire. Catherine II forbade them to move into the interior of the empire by creating a "zone of residence," which lasted until 1917.

What was called Lithuania in the political system of the Republic was only a historical souvenir of the once great duchy, maintained by nobles who were completely Polonized. The small core of Baltic peasants who perpetuated the primitive Lithuanian culture was still, in the eighteenth century, far from the resurrection it would undergo at the end of the nineteenth century. Still, it is necessary to point out this culture's survival, which was especially due to the activities of the Catholic clergy and certain scholars. The year 1718 saw the republication for the fifth time of the *Dictionarium trium linguarum* (in German, Latin, and Lithuanian), originally published in 1619 in Königsberg, and the *Rosary* by the Dominican Jerzy Kossakowski (originally published in 1681) existed in more than forty editions in the eighteenth century. Although in decline, the preaching of the Jesuits and the Dominicans was often in Lithuanian. The Polish Commission on National Education also recognized the need for an elementary reading book in Lithuanian (1775), a privilege that was not accorded to the Ruthenians or the Jews. In any case, the language was lively and rich enough to permit Kristijonas Donelaitis to create around 1775 the first literary work in Lithuanian, *Metai* (The Seasons), which, however, was not published until 1818.

The serfs of White Ruthenia and of Ruthenia proper (the Ukraine) were not included to the same degree within the Polish cultural orbit. The former, almost completely won over to Uniatism by the unceremonious liquidation of the Orthodox dioceses, better tolerated this acculturation than the latter, who continued to revolt in the eighteenth century as they did in the seventeenth. When the Great Diet finally examined, in 1791, the possibility of creating an autocephalous Orthodox Church reattached to the Patriarchate of Constantinople, it was too late. Too many inconsiderate gestures had deepened the gap between the Poles and the Ukrainians. In 1699, Ruthenian was rejected as an official language of the great duchy. In 1702, the Cossack troops of the Republic were dissolved. Catholicism, conquering, did not cease to discriminate against the "schismatics." And most significantly, the rigor of serfdom was more insupportable in Ruthenia than elsewhere, especially in the immense *starosties*, or lands of royal donation, accorded to the magnates. The violence of the revolts conducted by the *haïdamaks*, who were a kind of bandits of honor, was endemic, reaching its apogee in 1768 in Human. After fierce Polish and Russian-led repression, this zone remained, with the tacit agreement of the Russians, under the domination of Polish lords at least until 1863. The latter did not show their enlightenment in regard to their serfs, although their residences manifested a western refinement that was in shocking contrast with the backwardness that surrounded them.

The only part of Ruthenia where local identity was taken into account was the region that fell, after 1772, to Austria (consisting of 20 percent Ukrainians). Maria Theresa protected the Uniate Church, educating its priests separately and respecting their Slavonic language. In 1780 a seminary was established at Lvov, and from 1787 to 1809 there was a Studium Ruthenicum in the university of that city.

The deeper reasons for the disappearance of Poland—the degeneration of the humanist ideal brought about by a republic of nobles who were not numerous enough and a multicultural conglomeration that was not accepted—were completely misunderstood by contemporaries, both those who were directly concerned and those who were foreign observers. Only time, with gradual sociopolitical reflection and the upheaval of the geopolitical configuration of this part of Europe, would permit Poland's rebirth on an entirely new basis at the beginning of the twentieth century.

[*See also* Austria; France; Judaism; Roman Catholicism; *and* Russia.]

BIBLIOGRAPHY

Babicz, J. "Hugo Kołłątaj's Actualism and Its Position in the History of European Thought." *Charles Lyell Centenary Symposium*. London, 1975.

Beauvois, D. *Histoire de la Pologne*. Paris, 1995.

Fabre, J. *Stanislas-Auguste Poniatowski et l'Europe des lumières*. Paris, 1952, 1984.

Fedorowicz, J. K., M. Bogucka, and H. Samsonowicz. *A Republic of Nobles*. Cambridge, 1982.

Jedlicki, J. "Native Culture and Western Civilisation (Essay from the History of Polish Social Thought of the Years 1764–1863)." *Acta Poloniae Historica* 28 (1973).

Jobert, A. *La Commission d'Éducation Nationale en Pologne (1773–1794)*. Paris, 1941.

Leskiewicz, J. "Land Reforms in Poland (1764–1870)." *The Journal of European Economic History* 1 (1972).

Libiszowska, Z. "American Thought in Polish Political Writings of the Great Diet (1789–1792)." *Polish-American Studies* 1 (1976).

Rostworowski, E. *Historia powszechna, wiek XVIII (Universal History of the Eighteenth Century)*. Warsaw, 1977.

Topolski, J. "The Partitions of Poland in German and Polish Historiography." *Polish Western Affairs* 13 (1972).

DANIEL BEAUVOIS

Translated from French by Susan Romanosky

POLIGNAC, MELCHIOR DE (1661–1741), French cardinal, diplomat, and poet.

Born to a family of the oldest noble lineage, but not of great wealth, Melchior de Polignac was destined for the church from his youth. After a distinguished academic career in Paris and a stay in Rome, Polignac was named France's ambassador to Poland in 1693. At the death of John III Sobieski in 1696, he succeeded in having François-Louis, Prince de Conti, elected as king of Poland, but Frederick Augustus of Saxony claimed the crown and became king as Augustus II. Because of this diplomatic failure, upon his return to France Polignac was ordered to retire to his own abbey of Bonport. During this time, Polignac began to write a poem in Latin, *Anti-Lucretius*, which he continued to work on throughout his life. Reinstated at court in 1702, in 1704 Polignac was elected to the Académie Française.

As a result of his friendship with J.-B. Colbert, marquess de Torcy, secretary of foreign affairs, he became an auditor of the Papal Rota in Rome in 1706. Louis XIV employed him in the peace negotiations that put an end to the War of the Spanish Succession. When he was made cardinal (on 30 January 1713), he left the peace congress just before the signing of the treaties on which he had worked. He subsequently received many honors (he was elected to the Académie Royale des Sciences in 1715 and the Académie des Inscriptions in 1717) as well as ecclesiastical benefices (he was abbé of Bonport, Bégard, Corbie, and Anchin).

During the Regency (1715–1723), Polignac vigorously defended the memory of Louis XIV. Close to the duchess du Maine, he became involved in intrigues against the Regent. Ordained as a priest, he returned to Rome in 1724, where he remained as chargé d'affaires until 1732. He was especially known for the celebrations and feasts he gave, such as one honoring the birth of the dauphin in 1729. His penchant for pomp often strained his financial resources. He also built up a fine collection of paintings and ancient statuary. In 1725 Polignac became archbishop of Auch. After his death in 1741, Frederick II bought some of his collections.

In his *Mémoires*, Saint-Simon reproaches Polignac for being a sycophantic courtier. In reality, Polignac applied his charm, eloquence, and intelligence to the service of the king as well as to his own career as a negotiator. He did, however, become embroiled in scandals that brought disgrace upon him. However, his spirit, good humor, and network of friends made it easier for others to overlook his errors. Having a solid education and training as a theologian and jurist, he was interested in scientific experiments and knew how to reason subtly. His lengthy poem *Anti-Lucretius* was published posthumously in 1747. On behalf of a wholly orthodox Christian faith, Polignac wished to combat, through poetry, the ideas that Lucretius had advanced in that medium. After having publically praised Polignac as the "avenger of heaven and vanquisher of Lucretius," Voltaire, ultimately saw in this work only a "poem without poetry and philosophy without reason."

[*See also* Diplomacy; France; *and* Roman Catholicism.]

BIBLIOGRAPHY

Bély, Lucien. *Espions et ambassadeurs au temps de Louis XIV*. Paris, 1990.

Bély, Lucien. "Le cardinal de Polignac, courtisan ou négociateur?" *Cahiers Saint-Simon* 22 (1994), 7–16.

Paul, Pierre. *Le cardinal Melchior de Polignac (1661–1741)*. Paris, 1922.

LUCIEN BÉLY

Translated from French by Susan Romanosky

POLITENESS. The complex term *politeness* (French, *politesse*) helped to shape the social practices of the Enlightenment while articulating the Enlightenment's sense of itself. Long before the eighteenth century, in the tradition of writings about social courtesy, *politeness* designated norms of social interaction, especially conversation, a meaning it would retain. However, its prestige meant that polite conversation came to provide a general model for communication in the age of Enlightenment. At its broadest, *politeness* designated defining aspects of civilization and thus entered into attempts to conceptualize both the past evolution and the future direction of society.

Evolution of Politeness. Although a concept with an old pedigree, politeness was transformed in the later seventeenth century and the early eighteenth, receiving new meanings that proved distinctive for Enlightenment usage. Politeness began life as a norm of face-to-face social interaction, in the company of two other key ideas, courtesy and civility. One influential formulation of this complex of ideas has been Norbert Elias's thesis that civility, understood as a new regime of bodily and emotional control and comportment, was the specific product of the absolutist courts of early modern Europe, in particular the court of Louis XIV. Elias's thesis has been qualified by the recognition that the origins of

Politeness. "The End of Supper," engraving by Jean Michel Moreau the Younger. (Musée du Louvre, Paris/Réunion des Musées Nationaux/Art Resource, NY.)

European civility were both chronologically older (indeed, medieval) and geographically more diverse (arising in monasteries, schools, and academies as well as courts) than he proposed.

Nonetheless, developments in seventeenth-century French culture were crucial for the eighteenth-century usage of politeness. French writers wrote prodigiously on the topics of manners and politeness. More important, they developed a model of sociability that valued intelligence and cultivation while emphasizing self-effacement, reciprocity, and equality. In the seventeenth century, the French often referred to these values collectively as *honnêteté*, a concept distinct from *politesse*, which specified a more formal, hierarchical, and ceremonial approach to manners. While *politesse* was associated with the royal court, *honnêteté* developed in milieus of aristocratic sociability away from the court, notably in the salon.

The ideals and practices of the seventeenth-century French salon contributed to Parisian salon life in the high Enlightenment, but Enlightenment understandings of politeness were also crucially shaped by English ideas about polite interaction and its intellectual and cultural importance. One seventeenth-century English context for the development of polite norms of social interaction

was the culture of virtuosi pursuing historical, artistic, and scientific interests. Particularly after 1660, polite modes of exchange were elaborated in association with the development of a moderately skeptical and empirical approach to learning. Civil conversation offered itself as a tool to Robert Boyle and other scientists of the Royal Society in their campaign to rid inquiry of two menaces: one was intellectual dogmatism, associated with the Scholasticism still dominating the universities and, more currently, with Thomas Hobbes; the other was the distortion of religious understanding exemplified by enthusiasm and superstition.

Even more influential for the formation of an Enlightenment ideal of politeness was the contribution of Whig writers in England after the 1688 revolution, notably Joseph Addison, Richard Steele, and Anthony Ashley Cooper, third earl of Shaftesbury. As Whigs they supported the post-1688 regime, on behalf of which they advanced arguments of a cultural character. Shaftesbury in *Characteristics of Men, Manners, Opinions, Times* (1711), and Addison and Steele in their periodical publications (especially the *Tatler*, 1709–1711, and the *Spectator*, 1711–1712, 1714) sought to identify a cultural ideal suitable to the new political regime. Inspired by the French discourse of *honnêteté*, they mapped the contours of both exemplary and dysfunctional conversation. They also tapped the potential of the model of polite conversation for understanding the larger dynamics of communication and interaction in modern society. They began using the term to characterize a state of refinement in national cultures and the manners of advanced civilizations. This allowed them to transfer moral and cultural authority from such traditional institutions as royal courts and established churches to the more diffuse community of polite gentlemen.

Thus, the applicability of politeness spread from face-to-face sociability to more dispersed interactions in modern society, particularly those mediated by print. A wide range of Enlightenment writers used *politeness* to refer to the norms of interaction in a civil society and to the larger patterns of cultivation that civil society produced. Although the Whig politics of Addison, Steele, and Shaftesbury were specific to England, politeness as a norm of communication did imply an Enlightenment politics: it proposed a new model of communication which, removing authority from traditional institutions, transferred it to autonomous processes of conversation or, more generally, of public discourse.

Parameters of Politeness. In the courtesy tradition, politeness was commonly defined as the art of pleasing in company, especially in conversation, but the term was also used to characterize the substantive outcome of its own application. Thus, politeness as a norm of conversation was both means and end, technique and goal.

As an art, politeness was a discipline of the self, requiring that gentlemen and ladies, whose natural self-concern was intensified by the privileges of their social rank, curtail their own expressiveness. The theory of politeness proposed that pleasurable elite conversation was premised on a fundamental structural requirement: taking turns, talking and being talked to, listening and being listened to. Such reciprocity implied a striving toward egalitarianism, or at least an affectation of it. Hume, in *An Enquiry Concerning the Principles of Morals*, noted how, in polite conversation, "a mutual deference is affected; contempt of others disguised; authority concealed; attention given to each in his turn; and an easy stream of conversation maintained, without vehemence, without interruption, without eagerness for victory, and without any airs of superiority."

The polite requirement of modestly limiting the self was not, however, a demand for self-abnegation. Rather, at the heart of this art was the recognition, tinged with irony, that speakers who practiced a well-regulated self-effacement managed to please others while also showing off their own merits in the best light. By circumscribing the self, one gained others' respect and affection, which were put at risk by asserting the self too directly or conspicuously. Thus, polite conversation involved a mutual exchange of benefits; it was a collaboration, though hardly altruistic, in which individuals sought to please one another and gain mutual respect.

Though moderate self-effacement was an essential requirement, participants in polite conversation still had many opportunities to actualize a variety of talents and aptitudes. Polite conversibility became an arena for distinguished gentlemanly performance. It required mental abilities—wit, eloquence, intelligence, and imagination—and psychological capacities such as amiability and flexibility, as well as restraint. It also required information and knowledge. Since the topics of polite conversation had to be matters of common interest, its most eligible subject matter was the participants themselves and their affairs, the beau monde or "the World" in which sociable persons made their way. However, polite conversation was not restricted to social gossip. Its proponents argued that it should concern loftier matters: arts and letters, manners and morals, and sometimes even society, religion, and politics.

Indeed, the endorsement of politeness bespoke a deep concern to bring into closer proximity and perhaps even to amalgamate the elite of society and politics with that of learning, the arts, and reflection. Shaftesbury wrote:

> If the best of our modern Conversations are apt to run chiefly upon Trifles; if rational Discourses (especially those of a deeper Speculation) have lost their credit, and are in disgrace because of their *Formality*; there is reason for more Allowance in the way of *Humour* and *Gaiety*. An easier Method of treating these Subjects, will make 'em more agreeable and familiar. To dispute about 'em will be the same as about other Matters. They need not spoil good Company, or take from the Ease or Pleasure of a polite Conversation.

Similarly, in the tenth number of the *Spectator*, Addison defined the periodical's aim as integrating philosophy and society, bringing "Philosophy out of Closets and Libraries, Schools and Colleges, to dwell in Clubs and Assemblies, at Tea-Tables, and Coffee-Houses." (He made this idea concrete for his readers by organizing a good deal of the *Spectator*'s content around the depiction of a gentlemanly club.) A similar insight motivated Hume, in "Of Essay-Writing," to offer himself as an "ambassador from the dominions of learning to those of conversation," from the learned world to the conversible world. Thus, the norm of politeness promoted elite conversation as a favorable locale, and perhaps the most favored one, for engaging with the many topics that could be assigned to the notion of "philosophy."

Making polite conversation a paradigmatic site for edification and improvement implied remapping the organization of discourse in society and shifting moral, cultural, and even political authority within it. Such a politics of discourse was evident in the way that people distinguished polite conversation from alternative ideals and criteria. Since polite conversation assumed mixed company, it was contrasted with the more openly competitive and combative forms of homosocial discourse that dominated scholastic culture and the universities. In its way egalitarian, it served as a foil to the hierarchical principles reigning in princely courts. In its reciprocity and participatory character, it was contrasted with the more authoritarian practice of most churches. Polite conversation was often described as a zone of discursive freedom and play. It also offered space for questioning, doubt, and skepticism—hence its hostility to dogmatism, enthusiasm, and superstition. Its moderation made it the enemy of extremism and fanaticism. Its standards of accessibility and generality distanced it from specialist or technical discourse of any sort, whether religious or learned. Finally, its diversity and open-endedness distinguished it from speech or writing that aspired to be comprehensive, systematic, or conclusive. In many different ways, then, polite conversation could be mounted as a desirable alternative to inherited or traditional discursive practices.

Such claims on behalf of politeness became highly significant as writers used the parameters of polite conversation to give normative shape to spheres wider than the face-to-face interactions of the beau monde. Most immediately, the operations of print culture came to be informed by the model of polite conversation, which was said to govern the relations between writers and readers.

Equality, reciprocity, accessibility, and pleasingness were invoked to regulate the burgeoning world of print, now addressed not to select participants in face-to-face conversation but rather to a public. Polite conversation writ large was the public seeking information and edification so that it could assume responsibilities.

Politeness dictated distinct preferences among the genres of print communication. For example, Shaftesbury, following the manner of his mentor John Locke, conceived his early *Inquiry Concerning Virtue or Merit* as a work of demonstrative philosophy. When he later decided that "to philosophize, in a just signification, is but to carry good breeding a step higher," he designed the rest of his *Characteristicks* politely—that is, in the easy, conversible, and agreeable manner of polite conversation. Hume recapitulated this evolution when, after his *Treatise of Human Nature* attracted no public notice, he made a polite turn away from the demonstrative treatise and toward the informal essay and his more accessible *Enquiries*. Politeness aspersed the more formal, systematic, dogmatic, and comprehensive genres as vehicles for philosophy. It favored other forms: dialogues, said to be representations of conversations; letters, said to constitute conversational exchange in writing; and essays, to which were ascribed many of the discursive traits of conversation.

A periodical is not a genre, but the popularity of periodicals imitative of the *Tatler* and the *Spectator* registers the importance of politeness for the Enlightenment. These numerous imitators in cities across Europe were vehicles of enlightenment, and it is not surprising that essays on the nature of enlightenment by Moses Mendelssohn and Immanuel Kant were originally produced for this medium.

In the course of time, politeness came to be a model of discursive practice in general, which insisted that all subjects submit to its formal and sociable disciplines. The prestige of politeness tended to bring all modes of apprehension—spiritual, aesthetic, and cognitive—within the horizon of gentle conversibility, casting them as a species of elite accomplishment. Vast areas of European culture became saturated in their self-representation as polite domains, conversible, worldly, and genteel.

Not surprisingly, politeness transcended its original reference to face-to-face, upper-class social interaction and came to be used to describe refinement in the arts and, more generally, in the manners of a people: the condition of manners (French, *moeurs*; German, *Sitten*) that simultaneously conveyed interior moral dispositions and observable patterns of behavior, artifact, and institution. The ancient world, especially Greek civilization, was commonly said to epitomize politeness (for instance, by Saint-Évremond and Shaftesbury), but a competing view suggested that politeness was a modern development. Both Montesquieu and Hume associated politeness with the norms of modern monarchy as distinct from those of commercial republics. However, they also admitted, as did many others, that modern commerce and modern liberty had the effect of softening manners and encouraging politeness, both as a norm of interaction and as a general condition of refinement in society.

Practice of Politeness. Ideas of politeness had remarkable success in infiltrating many areas of discussion throughout the eighteenth century and informing many practices, routines, institutions, and organizations. Europeans imitated the Whig periodicals of Addison and Steele not just by publishing their own versions of them but also by re-creating the polite "clubbability" (eligibility for membership in a gentlemen's club) represented in them. Thus, the Whig moralist periodicals provided a blueprint for new ways to practice sociability.

An early illustration of this process is provided by the Gentleman's Society at Spalding, a market town in Lincolnshire, England. After the *Tatler* started appearing in 1709, a small group of local worthies subsidized its purchase by a coffeehouse where they met regularly to hear it read aloud. The reading was followed by a discussion among the members about the *Tatler*'s topics. These activities were soon supplemented by readings and discussion of recent poetry and prose and by presentations over a range of polite and learned topics, from antiquities to ornithology to taste. Over subsequent decades, the society added a more institutional dimension, formalizing its operations with rules and founding a library and a museum. As Maurice Johnson, one of its leading lights, wrote, the society was "a universal literary meeting for the sake of improvement in friendship and knowledge, without views of any other profit or pleasure."

All over Europe, such occasions combining edification and sociability proliferated. Indeed, this sort of association has become in recent interpretation an indicator, or even a defining attribute, of the Enlightenment. The forms and sites of such association were myriad. As in Spalding, the coffeehouse provided one convenient locale because it was an accessible, inexpensive, fairly democratic place, not just for drinking beverages but also for reading printed material and discussing all it suggested. Coffeehouses also provided a place for lectures, scientific demonstrations, concerts, exhibits, and auctions. Not all coffeehouses were polite, nor were all activities at any coffeehouse polite, but coffeehouses can be characterized as places for decorous conversation that refined the taste and polite capacities of those present.

At the other end of the institutional spectrum was the salon, which illustrates the way women participated in and shaped Enlightenment culture. The salon was an occasion for conversation convened regularly at the home of an elite woman, who, as *salonnière*, exercised an ordering and disciplining function. From the seventeenth century on, salons were sites for a redefinition of the French nobility according to the value of politeness. In the eighteenth century, the French tradition of *politesse* merged with Addisonian and Shaftesburian ideas, making salons occasions for the rich and bracing edificatory conversation that defined the Enlightenment in France.

Between the coffeehouse and the salon were many kinds of associations and societies all over Europe: language societies, learned academies, masonic lodges, reading circles, literary and all manner of other clubs. To be sure, these were not all polite in concept, let alone practice; however, many of them shared the basic parameters of politeness, seeking to combine sociability and edification in orderly conversation in an environment that mixed a range of people from different orders of society, including aristocrats.

Critique of Politeness. The significance of politeness for the Enlightenment is that, having arisen over a long period of time in various settings, it came to be used to conceptualize a new print-centered culture in which public discussion—that is, discussion by a public oriented toward public matters, whether the arts, morals, society or politics—now really mattered. Long before the eighteenth century, politeness was in tension with value systems that it challenged or displaced: it was always susceptible to critique from the standpoint of moral truth, sincerity, and authenticity. However, as the term itself became more ambitious in its application, so the critique became more embracing.

Acute analysts of the rise and consequences of commercial society, such as Adam Smith and Adam Ferguson, felt ambivalent about the price paid by humans for refinement and politeness. Immanuel Kant had his own reservations, which encouraged him to distinguish a deeper German *Kultur* from the polite—that is, superficial—civilization of the French; yet he still asserted, in *Anthropologie in Pragmatischer Hinsicht* (Anthropology from a Pragmatic Point of View), that "men are, one and all, actors—the more so the more civilized they are," admitting politeness "a very good thing." The most notorious and influential critic of politeness was Jean-Jacques Rousseau. In the *Discours sur les arts et sciences* (Discourse Concerning the Sciences and Arts, 1750), he followed the narrative that linked the rise of commerce to the softening of manners, the extension of sociability, and the rise of an ethos of mutual agreeability. However, his goal was to expose politeness for what, in his view, it really was: a malevolent simulacrum of virtue, a mode of ornamentation that obscured deformity. His attack on politeness served his goal of ridding the social world of theatricality and ornament in the name of genuineness and transparency. Rousseau therefore proposed the demise of the world of politeness, a suggestion taken up by those who wanted to carry Enlightenment ideals in radical directions.

[*See also* Salons *and* Sociability.]

BIBLIOGRAPHY

Becker, Marvin B. *The Emergence of Civil Society in the Eighteenth Century*. Bloomington, Ind., and Indianapolis, 1994. Abstract, sometimes turgid, but also stimulating, exploring ideas and practices of sociability in France and Britain.

Bödeker, Hans Erich. "Aufklärung als Kommunikationsprozess." *Aufklärung* 2 (1987), 89–111. An important examination of ideas about communication and their impact on intellectual and social practice in eighteenth-century Germany.

Carpanetto, Dino, and Giuseppe Ricuperati. *Italy in the Age of Reason, 1685–1789*. Translated by Caroline Higgitt. London and New York, 1987. A historical survey with chapters treating periodicals and associations in eighteenth-century Italy.

Currie, Pamela. "Moral Weeklies and the Reading Public in Germany, 1711–1750." *Oxford German Studies* 3 (1968), 69–86.

Elias, Norbert. *The Civilizing Process*. Translated by Edmund Jephcott. 2 vols. New York, 1978, 1982. English translation of *Über den Prozess der Zivilisation* (1939), a classic interpretation of the origins of politeness in court culture.

France, Peter. *Politeness and Its Discontents: Problems in French Classical Culture*. Cambridge, 1992. Essays on the prestige of politeness in eighteenth-century French literature and the tension of politeness with other norms.

Goldgar, Anne. *Impolite Learning: Conduct and Community in the Republic of Letters, 1680–1750*. New Haven, Conn., 1995. Discusses intellectual communication, both its normative principles and their transgression.

Goodman, Dena. *The Republic of Letters: A Cultural History of the French Enlightenment*. Ithaca, N.Y., 1994. An interpretation centering Enlightenment culture in the polite salon, with important implications for gender and Enlightenment.

Gordon, Daniel. *Citizens Without Sovereignty: Equality and Sociability in French Thought, 1670–1789*. Princeton, N.J., 1994. An intellectual history of sociability, with much attention to the related concepts of civility and politeness.

Habermas, Jürgen. *The Structural Transformation of the Public Sphere*. Translated by Thomas Burger with Frederick Lawrence. Cambridge, Mass., 1989. English translation of *Strukturwandel der Öffentlichkeit* (1962), the classic thesis of the expansion of public life and ideology in the eighteenth century.

Hirschman, Albert O. *The Passions and the Interests: Political Arguments for Capitalism before Its Triumph*. Princeton, N.J., 1977. A history of political discourse covering the legitimization of commerce by reference to its refining effects.

Im Hof, Ulrich. *Enlightenment*. Translated by William E. Yuill. Oxford, 1994. A survey with considerable treatment of the organs of Enlightenment sociability.

Klein, Lawrence E. *Shaftesbury and the Culture of Politeness: Moral Discourse and Cultural Politics in Early Eighteenth-Century England*. Cambridge, 1994. A study of the political implications of politeness in this influential writer.

Klein, Lawrence E. "Coffeehouse Civility, 1660–1714: An Aspect of Post-Courtly Culture in England." *Huntington Library Quarterly* 59 (1996), 30–51.

Pocock, J. G. A. *Virtue, Commerce, and History: Essays on Political Thought and History, Chiefly in the Eighteenth Century*. Cambridge, 1985. Contains several essays that explore the role of manners and politeness in eighteenth-century political and historical conceptualization.

Schochet, Gordon J., ed. *Politics, Politeness, and Patriotism* (Proceedings of the Folger Institute Center for the History of British Political Thought, vol. 5.) Washington, D.C., 1993. Contains essays on the use of politeness in the writings of several British writers.

Shapin, Steven. *A Social History of Truth: Civility and Science in Seventeenth-Century England*. Chicago, 1994. A comprehensive study of politeness as a tool of epistemological regulation.

Van Dülmen, Richard. *The Society of the Enlightenment: The Rise of the Middle Class and Enlightenment Culture in Germany*. Translated by Anthony Williams. New York, 1992. English translation of *Die Gesellschaft der Aufklärer: Zur bürgerlichen Emanzipation und aufklärischen Kultur in Deutschland* (1986), a useful survey of the expansion of association in eighteenth-century Germany.

LAWRENCE E. KLEIN

POLITICAL PHILOSOPHY. "All eyes are opened, or opening, to the rights of man," said Thomas Jefferson in his final exhortation to the Americans. "The general spread of the light of science has already laid open to every view the palpable truth, that the mass of mankind has not been born with saddles on their backs, nor a favored few booted and spurred, ready to ride them legitimately, by the grace of God." Here was the Enlightenment in its fondest expectation: a rational future of science, of popular government, and of triumph over human claims of divine authority. What caused this vast movement? If intellectuals such as Jefferson are to be believed, the decisive cause was the work of the enlightened philosopher-scientists. Before turning to contemporary views of Enlightenment political philosophy, then, let us first examine the self-history of such intellectuals.

When Jefferson commissioned a painting of his heroes, the subject was not statesmen or generals but John Locke, Francis Bacon, and Isaac Newton. The greatest trumpeting of eighteenth-century Enlightenment is Denis Diderot's comprehensive *Encyclopédie* (1751–1772); its *Discours préliminaire* traces the whole plan of reforming all the sciences and arts to Bacon's *Advancement of Learning* (1605). Medieval times had been "the most profound night," "the Renaissance was a restoration of ancient mistakes," and early scientists such as Galileo Galilei lifted merely "a corner" of the veil. It was Bacon, René Descartes, Locke, and Newton who "prepared from afar the light" that would gradually "illuminate the whole world."

If such indications are correct, the philosophic Enlightenment proper begins with Bacon's advocacy of a progressive scientific civilization, in the early 1600s, and ends with Jean-Jacques Rousseau's attacks, in the 1750s, on this "masterpiece of modern policy" (*Discourse on the Arts and Sciences*, 1750, and *Discourse on the Origin of Inequality*, 1755). The public triumphs arrived later: the French and American Revolutions, the Industrial Revolution, the technological revolution, the modern nation-state, and secularization.

It was this astonishing 150 years, seen as the philosophical flowering of the "illumination of the world," that encompassed the famous philosophic names and writings. Descartes's revision of the new science, the *Discourse on Method*, appeared in 1637. The new liberal political science flourished from Thomas Hobbes's *Leviathan* (1651) and Baruch de Spinoza's political-historical critique of the Bible, the *Theologico-Political Treatise* (1670), to Locke's *Letter Concerning Toleration* and *Two Treatises of Government* (1689, 1690). Pierre Bayle's *Historical and Critical Dictionary* and *Various Thoughts on the Occasion of a Comet* (1682) attacked the case for miracles and suggested the possibility of a humane society of atheists, severing the link between God and political order. Eventually, more wary and doubting versions appeared, such as David Hume's *Essays Moral and Political* (1741–1742) and, less than a decade before Rousseau's dissent, Montesquieu's comprehensive *L'esprit des lois* (Spirit of Laws, 1748). In short, in this view, the decisive founding of modern political philosophy was completed in a fertile burst. After that came the philosophic doubters, refounders, and synthesizers. Rousseau, Immanuel Kant, Georg Wilhelm Friedrich Hegel, John Stuart Mill, Friedrich Wilhelm Nietzsche, and Martin Heidegger—all are in different ways critics and reformers of their enlightened forbears.

Kant (1724–1804) might seem the quintessentially enlightened philosopher. He planned a worldwide rule of reason and of human autonomy through self-determining republics, a league of nations, and a universal cosmopolitanism. This turn to universal reason and moral law, however, represents a radical change. Kant would save reason and science from enlightened empiricism and morality from enlightened self-interest.

Still, the story is more complicated. Even during the great period of Enlightenment political philosophy, important philosophic critics arose, and after the flowering, enlightened premises retained much influence. The philosophic satirist Jonathan Swift had upheld ancient philosophers and scientists against the moderns in his "The Battle of the Books" (1704). His *Gulliver's Travels* (1726) suggested that scientific rationalism, in erasing common sense, turns the human world topsy-turvy. Earlier, after a similar diagnosis, the theologian and mathematician Blaise Pascal (1623–1662) urged not a return to ancient philosophy but a dependence upon faith in Christ. These critics, however, attested to the rising power of the new philosophy. Pascal accepted Cartesian physics, even if he found it irrelevant to the plight of mankind. It is also true that the Enlightenment's influence continued even in the later critics who would turn away from it. Rousseau indeed longed for the ancient city, Nietzsche (1844–1900) for ancient nobility and seriousness, Edmund Burke (1729–1797) for ancient prudence, and

Leviathan. Title page of Thomas Hobbes's *Leviathan* (London, 1651). [For a portrait of Hobbes, see the article "Hobbes, Thomas."] (New York Public Library, Astor, Lenox, and Tilden Foundations.)

Heidegger (1889–1976) for ancient tragedy. All retained suppositions from their enlightened predecessors, however, whether the belief that men are naturally equal and autonomous, or that their nature is decisively passion and will, or that they tend naturally to acquisitiveness and mastery without moral limit.

There is a yet graver problem with the preceding account. In fact, the scientific-technological project was inspired by a new critique of morality and a new political project. Enlightened philosophers share a novel "realism" about human needs and a new hope for mastering them, and these fundamentals appear first in the writings of Niccolò Machiavelli (1469–1527). "We are much beholden to Machiavelli and others that write what men do, and not what they ought to do," Bacon acknowledged in the *Advancement*. If so, the philosophic Enlightenment begins not with Bacon but with Machiavelli's advertisement, in the early 1500s, of a new continent for man and his thinking. This is not to deny, of course, the rich and often contradictory diversity of the innovators who follow, as they struggle to exploit and to tame the dramatic new possibilities of understanding and mastering the human condition.

The Beginning. Machiavelli proclaimed himself an innovator: he discovered "new modes and orders" by taking "a path as yet untrodden by anyone." The proclamation seems justified. His *The Prince* supplanted the traditional literature of instructing princes, and his *Discourses on Livy* overturned the traditional literature of Renaissance republicanism. He set forth new virtues—modes of acquiring goods for oneself and one's state—and new institutions, which manage the desires of others and thus enable the satisfaction of one's own. The result is the dynamic mix of liberated passions so visible in enlightened countries: leaders get domination and glory by supplying followers with security, wealth, and lesser glory. This unleashing of the passions has the surprising advantage of giving reason, now made instrumental to the passions, a new possibility of ascendancy in the world. This is the secret of Enlightenment's power in the face of religion's influence. Machiavelli was a partisan of both reason and human liberty, and he sought visibly to overthrow not only the authority of popes and churches but of religion and theology. He sought to allow human effort the satisfactions to which human nature was most strongly drawn. His raucous plays, *Mandragola* (1518) and *Clizia* (1525), show the comprehensiveness of the project. They aim to reform the family, to enlighten private life by showing an art of brokering mutual dealings in sex, security, and getting ahead.

Machiavelli also initiated the enlightened animus against the philosophic tradition. Since ancient political philosophy had imagined "republics and principalities" that had not existed "in truth," those old models, such as Aristotle's gentlemanly republic and Plato's philosopher-kings, were deemed utopian and misleading. Machiavelli sought instead "the effectual truth," the plans that were realizable in practice and could effectively benefit men. The ancients' mistake began at the beginning, with Socrates's turn to dialectical inquiry into men's opinions as to what is good and right. "For it is so far from how one

lives to how one should live that he who lets go of what is done for what should be done learns his ruin rather than his preservation." Machiavelli thought moral opinion too weak to rely upon. He began instead with the basic necessities of men. A leader must "learn to be able not to be good, and to use this and not use it according to necessity." Because men are good only by necessity, the true "modes and orders" are warlike attitudes (*virtu*) and a warlike state (*stato*), the "armored heart" and the public power needed for a world of acquisitive men lacking moral or religious restraint. Such a harsh outlook, however, is in its way humane. It arms princes and peoples to provide for themselves. Considering a rampaging river, Machiavelli reasons that if men would depend on themselves and concentrate on evils to come, they could provide "dikes and dams" for later floods; they could regulate "the impetus." Machiavelli's successors accepted his invitation to plan for control of nature.

Machiavelli himself focuses on a novel and foundational understanding of both virtue and politics. While he appeals to classical republicanism and civic virtue against otherworldly piety and humility, he revises classical republicanism. For example, he praises too the Roman emperors and especially the criminal Severus, who succeeded through deception, rapacity, and terror. In general, he recommends the attitudes needed for success, not the dispositions that go with good character and honorable patriotism. *The Prince* is especially concerned with refuting the sort of moral virtue praised in Aristotle's *Nicomachean Ethics*. Although everyone praises generosity, in practice the generous prince expends his resources, has to raise taxes, and becomes hated and endangered. Better to be stingy than generous. If to get followers you need to give, give what you take from others. Better to be unjust and win the people, say, by exploiting the rich. Although everyone praises honesty and keeping "faith," in practice the big gainers have been masters of deceit, who knew how to get around people's brains with feigned humanity and religion. Machiavelli's reformed virtue, in short, is an art of self-reliance needed to master a hostile world. The key ability is the dexterous mixture of intimidation and solicitude, "force and fraud," lion and fox, that enables one to acquire followers. "Ferocious" ambition needs to be mixed with a capacity for humane provision, all controlled by a versatile opportunism that adjusts to what "the times" allow and one's followers require. So the Italian adventurer Cesare Borgia first prosecuted exploitative warlords and set up a civil court and then executed spectacularly the hated prosecutor. The people were "stupefied and satisfied." Yet Severus, a would-be emperor, did the opposite and also succeeded. He allowed his soldiers "to inflict any kind of injury" on the people because he depended on not the people but the army. The people were quieted, being "astonished and stupefied" by terror, and the soldiers were "satisfied" and even "reverent." Machiavelli calls Severus a model of "a very fierce lion and a very astute fox."

Accordingly, Machiavelli revises also the most basic political notions. His enlightened "state" is an instrument of someone's gain: an imposed empire or domination (*imperio*) that serves the gain and security of some prince or people. Rule is mere domination, since all are out for themselves and there is no common good. It must be artificially constituted and imposed by terror, since man is not naturally political, nor is order divine. Machiavelli's is the seminal version of the modern revolutionary mentality, always prepared for extreme measures, and also of the artificially constituted but powerful modern state, centered on an executive with force for war and order. Intimidation must take priority over communal sharing in rule, since fear, which depends upon the ruler, is more reliable than love, which depends upon the ruled. Nevertheless, this is a policy for intimidation well used, not for indiscriminate cruelty. The prudent ruler should bring well-being and law-abidingness to his people, protecting lives, wives, children, honor, and property, especially property. Accordingly, Machiavelli recommends popular republics, which give men liberty to gain and joint power to protect themselves. Yet republics weaken and require correction by leaders, for the more free men are, the more they abandon restraints in favor of their own gain. Men being good only by necessity, the foundation in necessity must be continually renewed. A leader must restore the original terror, whether by prosecuting a grasping oligarch or by decimating an insolent mob.

It was Machiavelli who first achieved the Enlightenment's decisive simplification of the traditional sixfold classification of regimes: those for the common good (monarchy, aristocracy, popular republic) and against it (tyranny, oligarchy, democracy). For him there are only principalities and republics. Men cannot be relied upon to pursue a common good, and republics need both enterprising leaders (the new few) and followers of some spirit (the new people). The political problem is founding and keeping a state. Thus Machiavelli's division of states: princes found, while republics can keep. More to the point, princes are needed to lead, especially as generals, and the people are needed for their strength, especially in war. Machiavelli dwelled famously on the primacy of foreign affairs, and this too led him to reject the small and gentry republics commended by Aristotle or Plato. Since every state needs increasing military power (weakness invites attack, and other states will increase their power), a prince should favor the large, popular, and growing republics that can deploy big and willing armies. Besides, the imperial and grasping republic is more stable and safe domestically, for it can satisfy the desires of the few for glory and of the many for security and gain, while moderating their mutual hatred. Under the necessities of war, the few must attend to the wants of the many, whom they need as soldiers, and the many must defer to the few, whose abilities they need as officers. The determining force in this mixture is the reformed "great": chiefs who are "men of ability" rather than priests, lords, and leisured gentlemen. The people need power too, because the secret of a republic is not civic friendship but the managed rivalry of these two reformed and secularized parties, both of which are out for worldly gain. There should be assemblies and tribunes of the people, as well as a state of mind that does not disdain the people as sinful or vulgar.

Machiavelli's plans extended beyond ordinary states to the founding of a new state of mind, the "sect" (as he called it) that came to be called the Enlightenment. His animus was especially directed against the prevailing faith—the universal religion of the Bible—and his strategy exploited and undermined biblical otherworldliness to recommend his new modes and orders that can work in the world. He went so far as to reconceptualize legendary founders of religions as founders of states, in his sense; he included Moses among them. However shocking and blasphemous this first great modern transvaluation of traditional beliefs, one cannot deny that Machiavelli's philosophic followers appreciated not least his generalship in the war against religion.

The Project of Progress. Although Francis Bacon accepted Machiavelli's projects for a war of liberation from religion, for a this-worldly civilization, and for an ethics of getting ahead and a politics of imperial powers, he planned a sect that could rely more on hope and less on terror, war, and military empire. Bacon's essential innovations are a natural science that promises relief of human suffering and a civil politics of protective laws and a free economy. He thus devises a visionary worldly hope in progress, with which to battle otherworldly visions of salvation, and a more appealing practical politics. If men were more secure, comfortable, and free to gain and more dependent on scientists and experts, they would be more tractable, less inclined to war, and more easily managed.

Although Bacon reverts to utopianism, his is of a new kind. His *New Atlantis* is the first modern, future-oriented, science-fiction utopia. The old Atlantis, of Plato's *Critias* and *Timaeus*, deflated political hopes: even a much-diluted rule of the wise will not endure for long. The *New Atlantis* stokes a hopeful faith in the wise through an adventure story that promotes conversion. Christian Europeans, wandering, fearful, sick, and looking to God, are converted to modern Europeans, looking to enlightened caregivers and scientists. They find a people governed not by an image of God but of future welfare: a people cured by scientific medicine, dazzled by invented luxuries and conveniences, and made secure, orderly, comfortable, and sexually satisfied. In the background, a humane administrative "state" governs (the king is a figurehead). In the foreground are celebrated scientists and a laboratory for turning nature's powers to human use. Priests are for unenlightened immigrants. Under a veil of familiar-sounding customs for those not fully enlightened, Bacon mixes visionary hopes with effective powers and laws.

Bacon's practical politics twists Machiavellian fundamentals toward more economic empires. The *Essays or Counsels, Civil and Moral* (1625) develops an ethic of self-reliance with special attention to vocations and work, and a rather economic society that mixes hard-working ordinary folk with merchants, manufacturers, and financiers. Essays such as "Of Riches" and "Of Usury" were among the first writings advocating unlimited private acquisition and management of interest rates for the sake of growth and consumption. As to government itself, Bacon attends distinctively to administrators, counselors, and experts, as one sees in the *New Atlantis*, and to laws, judges, and jurisprudence. His *History of King Henry VII* (1622) shows both the enlightened despot who founds a state and the Parliament and laws that republicanize such a state. It fosters, especially, the laws of property that breed a middling class. Bacon's many writings on judges and jurisprudence undermine kingly courts and church law; they foster republican government and private rights. Judges are to be "lions under the throne." They respect sovereignty, but they reform laws to favor humane security for life and property. Bacon would mix economic and administrative men of ability with an industrious people, thus to produce the modern "great powers." These are the civil vehicles for the scientific movement that he chiefly recommends to the world.

The key to the new scientific civilization is conversion of the learned to a new method: a discipline that focuses the mind on what gives useful power over nature. In the *New Organon* (1622), Bacon corrects Aristotle's old "organon," a logic of the syllogism. Logic and philosophy, he contends, have hitherto produced no progress in knowledge or useful inventions; the claims of religion remain undefeated. But with a method assuring progress in truth and utility, one might have unity among philosophers, visible benevolence to men, and power over nature and men's opinions alike. The secret is a new end, power, and a corresponding new way of investigating, controlled experiment. Take utility or power as the truth to look for. Search then for moving causes, the processes producing effects. Look not by experience but by experiment (that is, by torturing nature to reveal the processes beneath the surface), and look especially for the most powerful processes, such as the forces involved in the atom. Then breed a scientific movement. Breed the cadre of industrious experimenters,

theorists, and technologists that will conduct the mass of experiments required, generalize the "laws of action" found, and apply the results. Thus one accumulates the sort of data, the "natural history" or formulas of production, that can "conquer nature in action." In the *New Atlantis*, the "end" of the scientific establishment is "knowledge of Causes, and secret motions of things; and the enlarging of the bounds of Human Empire, to the effecting of all things possible."

Bacon thus discovered a "cause" not only less repulsive than Machiavelli's wolf-like imperialism, but more universal in appeal, more appealing to the learned, and thus more suitable for spreading rationality. Whereas Machiavelli wrote in Italian, attacked the Latin of the church, and addressed political leaders, Bacon put his major works in "the universal language" and sought to make the learned guardians of the new science. The new scientists are to be enforcers of the methodical rules of reliable knowing and of the corresponding exclusion of pre-scientific intuitions, opinions, and divinations. Bacon's are the first "epistemological" writings in this modern sense. They develop Machiavelli's supposition that moral and religious intuitions are "imaginary," which he had not adequately argued, and they develop too Machiavelli's doubt of "primary notions," that is, all common-sense intuitions of what seem natural classes such as man, tree, opossum. It is man who "forms" the "matter" about him and must for his necessities reform and thus refound his political-religious world (*Prince*, 6). Bacon's epistemology codifies this disdain for nature and for intellect (the Socratics' peak of human nature). The "root of almost all evils in the sciences is the admiration of the mind," and what is needed is an "expurgation of the intellect." Hence the possibility of a complete "reconstruction" of the human outlook: we are "to try the whole thing anew upon a better plan, and to commence a total reconstruction of sciences, arts, and all human knowledge, raised upon the proper foundations." That is the radical enlightenment, armed with a universal razor and promising relief of the human condition.

René Descartes (1596–1650) made the scientific movement even more sweeping and confident, partly by radicalizing Bacon's skepticism as to the natural senses and mind and mathematizing the new science. Descartes too admired the method of experiment, expected "the mastery and possession of nature," and planned the overcoming of religion by the prospect of progress. He thought that critique and method alike needed a more certain foundation than particular experimental findings. Suppose God or some evil genius makes me doubt whether what I perceive is similar to what is there, or even whether any bodies exist? Precisely in that doubting Descartes found a formula for certainty. "I think, therefore I am." Descartes thus finds a solid foundation for science not in nature outside our control, or in our natural passions as such, but in the self's thinking made by the self. Made by us, we can rest assured of it. And if mathematics be simply the product of our definitions and calculations, it too can be excluded from doubt. Thus mathematics would give certainty to our interpretations or measurements of the outside world. In thus seeking to establish autonomous man and his autonomous science, Descartes established the thematic priority in modern philosophy of the self, consciousness, and the quantifying approach of a mathematical physics.

Still, there is also a moral or rather psychological teaching near the bottom of even these formulations. The ancient morals of virtue and contemplation may have been built on "sand and mud," even "quicksand and mud." Descartes, however, follows a certain pre-scientific "teaching of nature" propounded by the passions, and this sets the direction of science. The crucial passion is generosity, the passion of the strong; generosity is a resolution to execute what seems best for glory and security. Descartes's basic passion proves not much different from Machiavelli's (or Bacon's) basis in the passion for glory and domination. Still, the strong can obtain what they desire only by benefiting the weak in what they desire, that is, in life and comfort, health, affluence and security.

Descartes's masterwork, the *Discourse on Method*, is intended for broad appeal, being in the vernacular and in the form of a fetching autobiography: he popularized the new science as well as making its foundation clear and invulnerable. Accordingly, Descartes went beyond Bacon in advocating a society open to exchange of experiments, information, and ideas. Whatever the pervasive implications of the open society, Descartes restrained himself from much other counsel as to political and religious reform. For his discoveries, and his prudent restraint, he has been glorified as "the founder of modern philosophy."

Liberalism. It is liberalism that originates the famous doctrines of the rights of man, representative government, religious toleration, and free enterprise—the teachings of justice and free society that inspired the revolutionary triumph of enlightened principles in America and France and at times through much of the remaining world.

Although Thomas Hobbes (1588–1679) defended monarchy and criticized democracy and toleration, it is he who first discovered the modern doctrines of natural rights, representation, and the priority of peace. Hobbes too sought a realizable politics, based it on a reliable passion (fear of violent death), and looked to a science mathematically certain and guarded by an epistemology. But he focused on practical politics, forbearing Bacon's utopianism, and he recurred to justice as central, like Plato and unlike Machiavelli and Bacon. His major political works, *The Citizen* (1642), *Elements of Law* (1640), and *Leviathan* (1651), are different attempts to deduce political

science from his new beginning in a new-model natural justice, the right to life. He thus transforms traditional natural law, with its primacy of duty and its attention to conscience, higher inclinations, and God's directions. He replaces it with man-made theorems deduced from an individual claim; Hobbes's law of reason prescribes means of self-preservation, such as mutual agreements, peace, and inoffensiveness. In turn, the right to life is deduced from the passion of fear—since a man cannot help defending himself, it should be allowed him—or from a calculation that this is the effectual foundation of peace among men. He derives human equality similarly. "The weakest has strength enough to kill the strongest," or, given human selfishness, no one will be more prudent for your advantage than yourself. The result of this derivation of right from universal selfish want is a new-style universal idealism, which further simplifies his predecessors' picture of the moral world. Ambition itself is attacked. "Vainglory" is not bodily life, and the glory-seeking few are not to be relied on but indicted as dangerous to peace. One must take one's bearings from the condition of supposedly equal and endangered individuals whose preservation is endangered. This is the state of nature. Since each in his fears cannot trust another, and must build up power accordingly, the right of nature leads to a state of war. By nature, life is "solitary, poor, nasty, brutish, and short." But from fear of this natural condition of individuals Hobbes deduces the universal need for an artificial if absolute government: "the terror of some Power" that can bring the one thing needful, peace. Hobbes like Machiavelli finds terror at the foundation of government, but he holds that the necessity for such a power can be universally discerned if only men are enlightened as to their true necessities. Hobbes's strange pessimism about human nature coexists with a strange optimism as to the power of reason.

Hobbes advances many political innovations, including representative government, natural public law, and sovereign or absolute government. All liberal government begins in political self-denial: an agreement not to exercise power. Government governs. Yet government is itself an artificial institution that is the "representative" of the people. Hobbes begins both the science of impersonal government and representative government. Government bears and unites "wills," as Hobbes puts it. It thus "represents" the powers of individuals to provide rationally for the self-preservation they are presumed to desire but cannot obtain by nature. Hobbesian government, however, is also "sovereign." Its powers are absolute and unbounded, else it would not be certainly effective. Moreover, this representative and absolute artificial power must be everywhere instituted. Hence such a power is prescribed by natural public law, a doctrine that foreshadows the (very different) constitutionalism developed by Locke.

Since Hobbes himself would avoid separated powers, he recommends absolute monarchy and subjects church to state. He tries to show that Christian doctrine is compatible with his doctrine, even his sovereign's final word in interpreting God's word. One should add, finally, that Hobbes thought of himself as the first political scientist, the first to do with the rigor of quantitative reasoning what Plato and Aristotle had failed at. With the confidence born of political realism and scientific certainty, he thought that rational politics could not but follow if only his works replaced Scholasticism in the universities.

Spinoza made the most direct philosophic attacks hitherto on the Bible's claims, revised deterministically the enlightened philosophers' mixture of nature with human freedom, and was the first philosophic advocate of democracy and extensive freedom of speech. His *Theological-Political Treatise* (1670) set forth a barely concealed political and historical criticism of prophecy, miracles, and other Biblical claims. It scandalized the orthodox. It contributed to religious skepticism throughout Europe as well as to various forms of enlightened Judaism and enlightened Christianity. In his works, Spinoza praised the "ingenious Machiavelli," the *Leviathan*, Descartes's philosophy, and Bacon's method. Still, he displayed some misgivings about his enlightened predecessors. In his *Ethics* (1677, posthumous), he subordinated individual striving to the necessary order of nature and treated politics as necessarily guided by philosophers who are knowledgeable about that order. Moreover, he returned to the Socratic view that the philosophic life was unequivocally the best life. However, such ancient moral and philosophic themes were radically reformed to fit his enlightened foundations.

Politically speaking, Spinoza recommended a Hobbesian "state" that provides "peace and security" by mixing power with knowledge. Like Hobbes's theories, his ethics of freedom supposed that all men are moved by necessary passion. Unlike Hobbes, he supposed that men's freedom consists in their knowing: they are free insofar as they can understand and follow the leading passion, that of self-preservation or continuance. Freedom, then, is power, but requires knowledge, especially to avoid dangers from others in the state of war outside of society. Since human reason is natural (Hobbes had held it an invention) and seeks to know the rational order that protects human nature, this rational order, not mere want or desire, is naturally right. Natural right thus demands the security of all in freedom to reason. Given the equation of freedom and power, moreover, a state is most free and powerful when governed by the powers of all or of the majority; officials are representative agents of the people. On a rather Hobbesian basis, Spinoza thus rejected Hobbes's monarchism in favor of a democracy at once idealistic and power oriented. He recommends not only democracy

but also extensive freedom of speech. Yet Spinoza's democracy and freedom were to be guided by the knowing behind the scenes. Most men do not reason well and must be educated and trained for free citizenship. They need the philosopher's critique of ordinary religion and mistaken morals, his purified religion of love, his morals of freedom, and his politics of law, the state, and freedom of opinion. Still, this philosophic politics is secondary to the power of knowledge. The peak of rational power is the philosopher's inner freedom in knowing the order that ensures continuance of his being. Spinoza's recurrence to internal seriousness influenced Kant's idealistic reaction to the Enlightenment's focus on acquiring power.

John Locke is the essential philosopher-advocate of liberal freedom and government—and of the state of mind designed to protect and spread them. His *Second Treatise of Civil Government* (1690) became a bible of natural rights, free enterprise, popular government, constitutionalism, and rebellion against all regimes not popular and constitutional. The *Letter Concerning Toleration* (1689) outlined a new freedom of conscience, to seek salvation in one's own private way, and a new separation of state from church. The *Thoughts Concerning Education* (1693), while addressed to a gentleman, fostered education both private (not in church schools) and rather economic (not in gentlemanly arts and leisure). These books saw extraordinary sales, as did *The Reasonableness of Christianity* (1695) and even the epistemological *Essay Concerning Human Understanding* (1689). Locke was cautious, mixing his enlightened teachings with traditional-sounding appearances, and this helps account for the unprecedented appeal and the controversies as to what he believed. His liberalism has been called a reflection of capitalist market economy (C. P. Macpherson, *Political Theory of Possessive Individualism*, Oxford, 1962), and a variation on pious Protestantism (John Dunn, *The Political Thought of John Locke*, Cambridge, England, 1969), as well as a quintessentially enlightened doctrine.

Locke's major innovations are striking. He adds individual and popular self-reliance to Hobbes's effectual state. Society is made a civil society protecting "honest industry," and government is made chiefly a "legislative"—a national assembly constitutionally limited but representative of the majority.

If the watchwords of Hobbes are *peace* and *sovereignty*, those of Locke are *liberty* and *popular government*. He expanded Hobbes's natural right to life with rights to liberty and the acquisition of property, and trumpeted this doctrine of natural rights for societies everywhere. Locke attacks slavery, insists upon the religion of one's choice, and pays considerable attention to freeing women. He makes marriage contractual, allows divorce after the children are raised, and attacks paternal authority in favor of parental. In short, Locke tends to universalize self-reliance: he advocates bringing children up "to shift for themselves." Perhaps the crucial innovation is an economic liberty, the right to the fruits of one's labor, which both fosters enterprise and disciplines it. It is a right to acquire property, not chiefly to possess it, and to acquire it without effectual limit. While "as much" must be left for others, that constraint ends with crowding, and while one must not "waste," that constraint ends with durable money. Locke, however, does insist upon labor as title to property: rights of inheritance are undermined, and the "rational and industrious" given precedence to the querulous and idle. Locke popularizes both making one's fortune and the work ethic, and his free society of strivers is both the dynamic land of opportunity and the competitive system of anxious industry. Locke turns the Enlightenment economic; he is the first philosopher to provide independent writings on economics in the modern sense (not domestic economy) and to urge that interest rates vary with laws of supply and demand (*Some Considerations . . . of Interest and Money*, 1693).

Locke balances this economic society, which tends to oligarchy, with his popular government, which tends to democracy. His *Second Treatise* is a calculated lesson in the rules and beliefs that make government civil, that is, protector of the people. At the beginning and end he pricks up popular vigilance. The only title to lawful government is the people's consent; men are for political purposes free and equal; the people have the right to overthrow any government not liberal and constitutional. Throughout, he fosters popular government. Locke elevates "the *Majority*" to final authority in effect, a representative legislature to final authority in government, and a fixed constitution, embodying the people's consent, to a fundamental law over government. Nevertheless, he retains his predecessors' insistence on a powerful central government. While Locke's state of nature is not Hobbes's state of war, it tends to war. Government has to be a "mighty *Leviathan*." It needs an executive with power over foreign affairs and with powers beyond law in domestic affairs. Locke, however, democratizes and constitutionalizes the necessary powers. In wary circumlocutions he excludes monarchy as a legitimate government, demotes monarchs to at best chief executives, subordinates executives to the legislative (perhaps as "ministers" or a cabinet), and recommends a one-house legislature representing numbers and wealth (but not old families). Locke banishes from legitimate politics kingly power, aristocratic power, and ecclesiastical power. There is a radical edge to his insistence on a popular right of rebellion against any government that breaks the rational constitution that the people have established—or may be presumed to have established. The

paragon of enlightened politics is the patron of worldwide revolution.

Locke's less political works are designed to clear away the claims of traditional authorities—that is, of any authority other than the people, their rights, and reason. "The First Treatise of Government" discredits paternal authority in politics and thus anything like divine-right monarchy. At its center Locke deduces man's basic right to property from his "strong desire" for his own "preservation." The central truth is that man is free and not fundamentally subject to the righteousness of God the Father. *The Reasonableness of Christianity* (1695) develops accordingly an enlightened Christianity. And in the *Essay Concerning Human Understanding* (1689) Locke outlaws any claims to intuit moral ideas, "spirits," or species ("forms"). We receive only sensations from bodies without, and we finally use them according to abstract ideas, rational or imaginary, invented for our purposes. Locke would make a rational and protective human world.

The original philosophic Enlightenment closes with efforts by Montesquieu and Hume to dampen such confidence in reason. While neither doubted the fundamental direction (although Hume was a contemporary of Rousseau, who did), both feared doctrinal wars and revolutions not unlike the religious wars, and both feared also the undermining of tolerable governments. Hume, who entered into the modern theory of knowledge, discovered difficulties at the heart of liberal justice and of Enlightenment reason itself.

Montesquieu's first works showed his enlightened sympathies. Under cover of reporting erotic goings-on in a harem, *Lettres persanes* (*The Persian Letters*, 1721) satirized the despotic softness of European monarchies. *The Greatness of the Romans and Their Decline* (1734) followed Machiavelli's *Discourses* in blaming Rome's decline on pacific Christianity and on generals in far provinces of the empire. Nevertheless, it lacked Machiavelli's enthusiasm for princes and their glory. Montesquieu's masterwork is the *Spirit of Laws* (1748), a comprehensive inquiry into political orders rivaled only by Aristotle's *Politics*. Like Locke, Montesquieu would provide for the security of all; he would foster even the "tranquility" of mind that accompanies assured security. But he does not parade the rights of man or deduce institutions, and he favors in modern times balanced republics or moderate monarchies as circumstances permit. The important thing is a humane spirit of laws. The spirit of laws varies with the nature of a government (republic, monarchy, despotism) and with its principle (the supporting passion: such as virtue, honor, or fear). What is possible is also affected by circumstance, especially climate, geography, and the growth of population and commerce. Reacting against Lockean government by ideas, Montesquieu moves toward tracing laws to an equilibrium of forces that varies with the epoch. He discounts the political decisions and founding deeds so emphasized by Machiavelli and Hobbes.

The most important circumstance is the development of commerce. Commerce, with its sibling, luxury, softens manners and renders men sociable and dependent on one another. Earlier times allowed for simple despotisms, resting on fear, and simple republics, resting on virtue. But those times departed with the development of commerce, as well as big nations, feudalism, and the churches and priests of revealed religion. One model for Montesquieu's times is the complicated British commercial republic. Montesquieu interprets this as institutions of executive government and legislative opposition, balancing rich, poor, and monarchy. Government channels ambition, and economic society channels avarice. The model is less democratic than Locke's; if Locke was Jefferson's philosopher, Montesquieu was the American framers' philosopher. Montesquieu recommended a two-house legislative, with the Senate for the successful, wealthy, and distinguished, together with a single executive and a separate judiciary, including popular juries to protect the people's security from the executive's prosecutions. The British model, however, is not for every modern country; and it may have too much liberty. France will be better served by a monarchy moderated by church, the rich, customary law, and an enlightened judiciary.

The *Spirit of Laws* promotes laws of a humane spirit, laws to moderate any modern government, whatever its nature. Civil law should protect property and trade. Criminal law should provide strict safeguards for the accused, especially in treason trials. For similar reasons Montesquieu commended the power of unwritten law and of judicial revisions. Wary of enlightened doctrine and direct policy, he would transform customs and institutions by steps almost invisible. With his focus on the necessary causes behind laws and on the necessary development of commerce, Montesquieu came close to supposing a historical progress. He held back, however, from the sort of full philosophy of history that would appeal to those influenced by Rousseau.

Hume's political works included the *Essays Moral and Political* (1741–1742) and *History of England* (1754–1762). While these favor modern liberty and free government, they doubt the influence of plan, consent, and doctrine. Governments arose to serve man's interests, rather than by contract, and existed through habit and custom, rather than by decision and choice. Hume's doubts, however, went deeper. He called himself a "philosopher" and a "sceptic" and wrote a *Treatise on Human Nature* (1739) and *An Inquiry Concerning the Principles of Morals* (1751), as well as *Dialogues on Natural Religion* (1779, posthumous) and other works. Like his enlightened predecessors,

he sought to overthrow any revelation that opposed the promptings of nature and mind, but what distinguished Hume was his discovery of grave difficulties in enlightened philosophy itself. (Hume, Kant said, awoke him from dogmatic slumber). Because a man can't help fleeing death, Hobbes had argued, it ought to be allowed him. Hume questioned that move from an "is" to an "ought," however; a moral imperative does not follow from observation of a mere force. He found difficulties also with the induction of laws, and the account of causation, central to experimental and mechanistic science. From repeated observations one may infer a rule. But one can never know the rule to be certain or universal, given the dependence on future observations. From observing the effect of one thing striking another, one may infer a cause, but one can observe only the correlation and not the cause as such. It becomes a question whether experimental science gets at nature or merely at what we observe (and wish) in nature. Hume tried to remedy these cracks in the foundations of Enlightenment. He would restore inherent respect for judgments of good and bad by basing them upon pleasure or "sympathy." He thus fostered the (distinctly less calculating) Scottish Enlightenment. He would restore respect for scientific induction and knowledge of causes by relying on "habits" or "customs" of the mind. Still, Hume retained the enlightened premises: the primacy of security or "interests" for most moral and political purposes, and the possibility of knowing nature and thus of scientific truth. His skeptical questions, however, prefigured more radical doubts, doubts that swept away his makeshift remedies.

[*See also* Hobbes, Thomas; Hume, David; Jefferson, Thomas; Locke, John; Montesquieu, Charles-Louis de Secondat; Natural Philosophy and Science; Republicanism; *and* Rousseau, Jean-Jacques.]

BIBLIOGRAPHY

GENERAL WORKS

Blumenberg, Hans. *The Legitimacy of the Modern Age*. Cambridge and London, 1983. A provocative indictment of the enlightened philosophers for continuing a repressive moralism.

Gwyn, W. B. *The Meaning of the Separation of Powers*. New Orleans, 1965. An account of the major thinkers, such as Locke, in their political context.

Hiram, Caton. *The Politics of Progress: The Origins and the Development of the Commercial Republic, 1600–1835*. Gainesville, Tenn., 1988. A detailed study of the dissemination of the technological outlook and of enlightened political thought.

Manent, Pierre. *An Intellectual History of Liberalism*. Princeton, N.J., 1995. An elegant summary of the major figures.

Quentin, Skinner. *The Foundations of Modern Political Thought*. 2 vols. London and New York, 1978. A tracing of modern concepts to Lutheran, Thomistic, and Renaissance movements.

Rahe, Paul A. *Republics: Ancient and Modern*. Chapel Hill, N.C., and London, 1992. Book 2 is a useful survey of the modern developments, including those in political thought.

Tuck, Richard. *Natural Rights Theories*. Cambridge, 1979. A general introduction.

Vile, M. J. C. *Constitutionalism and the Separation of Powers*. Oxford, 1967. A survey of the changing doctrine in England, France, and the United States.

WORKS ON PARTICULAR PHILOSOPHERS

Faulkner, Robert K. *Francis Bacon and the Project of Progress*. Lanham, Md., 1993. A comprehensive account.

Gough, J. W. *John Locke's Political Philosophy*. Oxford, 1950. A useful brief account.

Mansfield, Harvey C., Jr. *Taming the Prince: The Ambivalence of Executive Power*. New York and London, 1989. An exacting study featuring Machiavelli, Hobbes, Locke, and Montesquieu.

Pangle, Thomas L. *Montesquieu's Philosophy of Liberalism: A Commentary on* The Spirit of the Laws. Chicago and London, 1973. The only such comprehensive commentary in English.

Seliger, Martin. *The Liberal Politics of John Locke*. London, 1968. A useful survey.

Strauss, Leo. *Natural Right and History*. Chicago, 1953. Chapter 5 is probably the most searching examination of the premises of Hobbes and Locke.

Strauss, Leo. *Spinoza's Critique of Religion*. New York, 1965. The authoritative examination, which concludes that the critique lacks adequate reasons.

ROBERT K. FAULKNER

POLYNESIA. *See* South Seas.

POMBAL, SEBASTIÃO JOSÉ DE CARVALHO E MELLO (1699–1782), Portuguese minister of state, conde de Oeiras (1759) and marques de Pombal (1769).

Pombal was born in Lisbon into a family of the untitled lesser nobility with a tradition of service to church and state. The family also had links with enlightened currents in contemporary Portugal. The Academia dos Ilustrados met at the house of Pombal's uncle in Lisbon, to whom Jacob de Castro Sarmento dedicated one of his works, and in 1733 the count of Ericeira sponsored Pombal's entry into the Royal Academy of History.

In 1739, Pombal was sent as Portuguese minister to London, where he remained until 1743. There he developed his understanding of commercial issues and of relations between England and Portugal, and he had contact with the Royal Society. Between 1745 and 1750, Pombal was Portuguese minister to Vienna. There he married the niece of marshal von Daun, gaining the favor of the Portuguese king's Austrian consort. In Vienna, Pombal also established contact with progressive thinkers such as Gerhard van Swieten and the Portuguese exile Antonio Nunes Ribeiro Sanches.

Pombal was recalled to Lisbon in 1750 and promoted to secretary of state for foreign affairs and war. His rise to the position of all-powerful chief minister of King Jose I was secured, first, by Pombal's brilliant handling of the rebuilding of Lisbon after the earthquake of 1755, and, second, by his equally determined (and cruel) treatment of the members of some of Portugal's leading noble families who were responsible for an unsuccessful attempt (1758) to assassinate the king. Pombal's regime was founded on the close collaboration of a relatively small number of Portuguese and some foreigners. The former included members of his own family—his brother Paulo was appointed inquisitor general—and various financiers and merchants. Pombal himself was very energetic. He contributed personally, for example, to the pamphlets that served his ferocious anti-Jesuit propaganda campaign, published and disseminated at home and abroad by the Portuguese government. Pombal's dismissal on the accession of Maria I was followed by attempts to have him tried for misuse of power, corruption, and fraud. However, it was difficult to condemn Pombal without condemning the king whom he had served, and the queen in effect abandoned the proceedings against him.

Pombal's development of his estate at Oeiras revealed both a determination to improve his property and a degree of refined taste that might be thought to confirm his credentials as an enlightened reformer. However, it is difficult to regard him as truly enlightened, particularly in view of his intolerance of opposition and his harsh treatment of his critics. Nevertheless, in his own day Pombal's character and regime affected not only Portugal but also a wider European public, and in some respects provided a model for reformers elsewhere. Subsequently, and particularly in Portugal itself, Pombal's attitude toward the Jesuits and the Roman Catholic Church made him a hero to liberals who sought primarily to reduce clerical power.

[*See also* Portugal.]

BIBLIOGRAPHY

Cheke, Marcus. *Dictator of Portugal: A Life of the Marquis of Pombal, 1699–1782*. London, 1938. Although rather old, still readable and useful.

Maxwell, Kenneth. *Pombal: Paradox of the Enlightenment*. Cambridge, 1995. Among the many excellent qualities of this recent study are the splendid illustrations.

Smith, John Athelstone. *The Marquis of Pombal*. 2 vols. London, 1843. Very old, but still very informative and highly readable.

CHRISTOPHER STORRS

POMPEII AND HERCULANEUM. The first discoveries took place at Herculaneum in 1709, and at Pompeii in 1738, but organized worksites were only set up in 1738 and 1760 respectively. The existence of the remains, however, had been known for a long time: the digging of the Sarno canal at the end of the sixteenth century, which cut across the site of Pompeii, brought to light expanses of wall and columns, but without arousing curiosity. Nor did the well-known letter of Pliny the Younger describing the eruption of Vesuvius in 79 CE prompt any attempt to discover the buried cities. Even when statues were uncovered, there was no immediate wave of excitement.

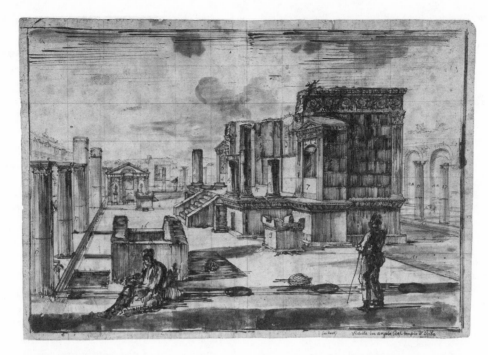

Ruins of Pompeii. The temple of Isis at Pompeii, drawing by Giovanni Battista Piranesi (1720–1778). (Pierpont Morgan Library, Gift of Mr. and Mrs. Eugene Victor Thaw/Art Resource, NY.)

Charles de Bourbon, *infante* of Spain, who received the Kingdom of the Two Sicilies (that is, Sicily and the Kingdom of Naples) in 1735 under the treaties that brought the war of the Polish Succession to an end, undertook the first important excavations and purchased the villa of Portici, the site of the theater of ancient Herculaneum, in order to do so. The underground exploration of the theater took place under difficult conditions: deep, badly ventilated tunnels had to be cut in the hardened lava flows, and then closed up when they threatened to collapse. In 1749 the edifice, stripped of its marble outer facing and its remaining statues, was measured, and a plan of it made. Tunnels dug in different directions made it possible to traverse the forum, where new statues of marble and bronze were discovered, as well as the first frescoes (1739: "Theseus and the minotaur," and "Achilles and Chiron"), which were immediately taken to shelter in the museum of Portici.

Individual villas were explored, notably the famous Villa of the Papyri (1751–1754), which was emptied of its treasures. At Herculaneum, visitors who went into these badly lit and dangerous tunnels deplored the random digging and the deteriorating state of the remains. At Pompeii the first probes were carried out in 1748, but the first "interesting" discoveries were made in the 1760s: these were the temple of Isis, the great theater, and the Odeum (1764). Behind these the "soldiers' camp," or barracks for the gladiators, was discovered in 1766. Several streets lined with shops were cleared, as were some houses, like the Surgeon's House, and the Villa of Diomedes outside the city (1771–1774). Systematic clearing was envisaged, but it only began in the nineteenth century.

From 1739 to 1765, travelers went only to Herculaneum and Portici. After 1765 a detour to Civita (Pompeii) was added, where the first monumental complex was cleared. Because visitors had to get permission, the modern state archives allow us to study the eighteenth-century pattern of their visits. In 1776 there were approximately one hundred requests for permission, of which twenty came from French travelers, about twenty from English ones, and about forty from Italians; to these we can add six Germans, one Albanian, and a handful of Spanish visitors.

The detached frescoes, statues, tools, pieces of furniture, and carbonized foodstuffs were on view at the Museum of Portici. Visitors were barely given time to observe them, much less to sketch them, or even take notes, especially when it came to the precious frescoes, because the king of Naples had reserved publication of the first descriptions and engravings of them for the series of volumes entitled *Antichità d'Ercolano* (Antiquities of Herculaneum), prepared under the supervision of the Accademia Ercolanense founded in 1755. The whole series comprises eight volumes in folio, of which the last emerged from the press in 1792. The ruins themselves had been drawn and engraved by artists (including Hubert Robert and Jean-Honoré Fragonard) working for the abbé de Saint-Non at a time (1777) when it was still forbidden to take measurements or survey the layout at the worksite (*Voyage pittoresque, ou Description du royaume de Naples et de Sicile* [Picturesque Voyage, or Description of the Kingdom of Naples and Sicily, 1781–1787]).

The inadequate conditions under which visits took place—at Herculaneum the tunnels were poorly buttressed and poorly lit, and at Portici the taking of notes was forbidden, for fear that a prolonged gaze might cause wear on the objects—caused discontent among travelers, who did not fail to criticize the methods of excavation, and even to belittle the discoveries, especially the French, who vented their disappointment at the paintings, which they judged unrefined, and the "petite" architecture of Pompeii. Johann Wolfgang von Goethe spoke of "small streets, small houses without windows; even the public buildings, the gate, the temple, an outlying villa, all of it seems more like little models made of cardboard than real buildings" (1787). The secrecy maintained around the collections at Portici caused exasperation, as did the enthusiastic publications of Italian antiquarians about the famous frescoes; these were reported in the English press, but the French press ignored them until around 1750, when news of the excavations began to spread.

Charles-Nicolas Cochin maintained a very severe attitude toward ancient painting (*Lettres sur les peintures d'Herculanum* [Letter on the Paintings of Herculaneum, 1751]), as did Johann Joachim Winckelmann, whose presence was judged unwelcome in the Kingdom of Naples following the publication of his *Sendschreiben von den Herculanischen Entdeckungen: An den Hochgebohrnen Herrn Heinrich Reichsgrafen von Brühl* (Letters to Count Heinrich von Brühl concerning the Discoveries at Herculaneum, 1762), which were also negative. In his *Geschichte der Kunst des Altertums* (History of the Art of Antiquity, 1764) Winckelmann developed his theories about the superiority of the Greeks over other peoples in the domain of the arts, provoking the wrath of Giambattista Piranesi, who defended the honor of the Romans.

In architecture a return to the antique is evident from 1750, but the discovery of the buried cities does not appear to have been the cause. The detailed study of the monuments, carried out on the basis of systematically gathered data, came later, in the first half of the nineteenth century. As for painting, the "bits of history" that were uncovered did not allow the partisans of the ancients to make their point of view prevail, and only the "little genres" like medallions, and small animal figurines, or ones based on fantasy, escaped criticism. These were given new life in the decorative arts, through the Pompeian style that was current at the turn of the nineteenth century.

Pompeii and Herculaneum helped Europeans to see beyond the monumental image of antiquity and discover daily life in the ancient world, in a way unfettered by the erudite knowledge found in books, and all the more vivid and moving because of the backdrop of tragedy. The houses became the subject of extended, and often quite personal, commentaries. The interest taken in volcanos, and in Vesuvius in particular, helped to heighten the emotional impact of a pilgrimage that novelists were later to put to their own uses. The science of archaeology, then in its infancy, took its first steps there: after the first overseer of the worksite, Joaquín de Alcubierre, pillaged the works of art that were uncovered, his associate Karl Weber worked out a plan for clearing Pompeii systematically, ceasing to think in terms of monuments and commencing to envision the city as a whole. New techniques were perfected, not without some damage, like the detaching of frescoes from their walls and the unrolling of carbonized manuscript scrolls. This was the domain—the science of archaeology—in which the discovery of the two cities had, without doubt, the most important consequences.

[*See also* Archaeology; Naples; Tradition; *and* Winckelmann, Johann Joachim.]

BIBLIOGRAPHY

Fiorelli, Giuseppe. *Pompeianarum antiquitatum historia.* 3 vols. Naples, 1860–1864. A description of the progress of the excavations based on the archives left by the first two supervisors of the worksite.

Fonti documentarie per la storia degli scavi di Pompei, Ercolano, e Stabia. Edited by the archivists of Naples. Archivio di Stato. Naples, 1979. An inventory of the available archival deposits.

Franchi dell'Orto, Luisa, ed. *Ercolano, 1738–1988: 250 anni di reicerca archeologica.* Rome, 1993. Includes a series of studies on the eighteenth century, the history of archaeology, and the reception of the excavations.

Grell, Chantal. *Herculanum et Pompéi dans les récits des voyageurs français du XVIIIe siècle.* Naples, 1982.

Michel, Christian. "Les peintures d'Herculanum et la querelle des Anciens et des Modernes." *Bulletin de la société d'histoire de l'Art Français, année 1984* (1986), 105–117.

Murga, Fernandez. *Los ingenieros españoles Roque Joaquín de Alcubierre y Francisco de la Vega, descubridores de Herculano, Pompeya y Estabia.* Madrid, 1962.

Pompéi: Travaux et envois des architectes français au XIXe siècle. Catalogue Paris-Rome. Rome, 1981. Contains a useful overview of the eighteenth century.

Pompeii as Source and Inspiration: Reflections on Eighteenth and Nineteenth-Century Art. Catalog. Ann Arbor, Mich., 1977.

CHANTAL GRELL
Translated from French by William McCuaig

PONTOPPIDAN, ERIK (1698–1764), Dano-Norwegian theologian and writer.

As a young village parson, Pontoppidan was strongly influenced by Pietism; in 1735, the Pietist Danish king Christian VI appointed him court chaplain in Copenhagen and a member of several clerical boards. After the death of

King Christian, Pontoppidan became bishop of Bergen See in Norway in 1747, and in 1755 accepted a newly created office as prochancellor of the University of Copenhagen. Both as a bishop and as a prochancellor, he showed great zeal in trying to implement comprehensive reforms. He proved to be an inflexible administrator, however, and, as a consequence, his efforts were opposed and mitigated by both the clergy of Bergen See and the professors at the University of Copenhagen. His most important contributions were his literary and scholarly activities, which were comprehensive and multifaceted.

Scholarly Career. In his early years as a theologian, Pontoppidan published Pietist-inspired devotional books and other works on religion. When confirmation was introduced as a ritual of the Danish state church in 1736, Pontoppidan was entrusted with writing an official explanation of the Lutheran Catechism. This was published and authorized in 1737, and introduced in the Dano-Norwegian state church the following year. Pontoppidan's explanation at first met with opposition in orthodox Lutheran circles, but by the end of the eighteenth century it was so well accepted that its replacement by a new and more enlightened explanation caused protest in Pietist circles. Between 1736 and 1740, he edited a hymnbook that was officially approved but never circulated. His *Everriculum fermenti veteris* (1736), used as a guide by vicars trying to eradicate superstition and reduce devotion to Catholic relics among the village population, is now a valuable folkloristic source. Between 1744 and 1752, he published the four-volume German language *Annales ecclesiae Danicae*, the most comprehensive history of the Danish church ever written. As a prochancellor, he taught pastoral theology for students of divinity; his lectures, *Collegium pastorale practicum*, were published in 1757.

Pontoppidan's interests covered a wider field than theology, however. He was also occupied with antiquarian and topographical studies, including transcriptions of inscriptions on tombstones. His topographical activities resulted in *Den Danske Atlas* (The Danish Atlas, 1763–1764), a detailed and ambitious description of Denmark based on information gathered above all from clergy around the country. In addition to history and geography, this work also includes physical and economic information and consideration of topical social problems such as the need for population growth.

In Norway, Pontoppidan's episcopal duties often required that he travel around the countryside of his see. *Norges Naturlige Historie* (Natural History of Norway, 1752–1753), was a description, based on his observations, of the Norwegian peasant population, their way of living and thinking, and of the Norwegian flora and fauna, inspired principally by the great Swedish naturalist Carolus Linnaeus.

As a young vicar in the duchy of Schleswig within the Danish monarchy, Pontoppidan had published a valuable work on the history of the Danish language, and while in Norway, he made similar studies of the Norwegian language. Between 1757 and 1764, he edited *Danmarks og Norges oeconomiske Magazin* (*Economic Magazine of Denmark and Norway*), in which the general public was invited to contribute useful studies on economic and physical matters. Many of these contributions anticipated the Danish agricultural reforms that took place later in the eighteenth century.

Contribution of Pontoppidan. Pontoppidan has traditionally been characterized as a Pietist. Certainly, Pietism was his original theological foundation, but his Pietism was moderate and loyal both to the Danish Lutheran state church and to the Danish absolutist government in general. Pontoppidan often stressed that there was no antagonism between human reason and Christianity. Furthermore, his Pietism was by no means merely contemplative and concentrated on devotional activities. It had a strong outward focus, evident in his scientific and scholarly writings comprising history, folklore, history of language, topography, geography, natural sciences, and economics. In 1742, Pontoppidan became a member of the newly founded Kongelige Danske Videnskabernes Selskab (Royal Danish Society of Sciences and Letters). As a prochancellor, he tried in vain to reform the study of divinity by including elements of natural science, and to strengthen the position of natural sciences at the university in general. His *Danmarks og Norges oeconomiske Magazin* marked the beginning of the systematic study of economics within the Danish monarchy and when, as a prochancellor, he met the new Enlightenment ideas, he met them with openness and tolerance.

As a scientist and a scholar, Pontoppidan was first and foremost a collector and a publisher; methodical criticism, analysis, systematization, and synthesis were not among his strengths. Despite their frequent transcriptional inaccuracies, Pontoppidan's works remain valuable and useful collections of source material that, like much folkloristic, linguistic, and natural scientific information, would otherwise have been lost.

When his interest in the natural and social sciences is taken into consideration, the term *Pietist* seems too one-sided and insufficient to apply to Pontoppidan. He should rather be seen as a transitional figure representative of the age between Pietism and the Enlightenment.

[*See also* Botany; Mapping; Pietism; Revealed Religion; *and* Scandinavia.]

BIBLIOGRAPHY

Bech, Svend Cedergreen. "Den danske atlas og værkets tilblivelseshistorie." In *Den danske Atlas* by Erik Pontoppidan, new ed. Copenhagen, 1968–1972. Addendum about the genesis of *Den danske Atlas*.

Horstbøll, Henril. "Civilisation og Nation." In *Danmarks historie,* edited by Søren Mørch, vol. 10. Copenhagen, 1992. Pontoppidan as a scholar and scientist, especially as a historian.

Jørgensen, Ellen. *Historieforskning og Historieskrivning i Danmark indtil Aar 1800.* Copenhagen, 1931. See pp. 196–202.

Kornerup, Bjørn. "Oplysningstiden 1746–1799." In *Den danske Kirkes Historie,* edited by Hal Koch and Bjørn Kornerup, vol. 5, pp. 251–255, 286–290. Copenhagen, 1951.

Løgstrup, Birgit. "Københavns Universitet 1732–1788." In *Københavns Universitet 1479–1979,* edited by Svend Ellehøj et al., vol. 1, pp. 363–367. Copenhagen, 1991. Pontoppidan as a prochancellor.

Neiiendam, Michael. *Erik Pontoppidan.* 2 vols. Copenhagen, 1930–1933. A comprehensive biography.

Pedersen, Johannes. "Pietismens Tid 1699–1746." In *Den danske Kirkes Historie,* edited by Hal Koch and Bjørn Kornerup, vol. 5, pp. 180–187. Copenhagen, 1951.

Michael Bregnsbo

POPE, ALEXANDER (1688–1744), English poet.

The son of a Catholic London linen draper, Pope suffered in his early teens from the symptoms of tuberculosis of the bone, which eventually caused severe curvature of his spine. As a boy, he read both classical and modern poetry voraciously, and the brilliance of his early *Pastorals* (1709) attracted much attention. Augustan literary production was a highly social and even political activity, and Pope's career was marked by a series of fierce skirmishes, but also by productive literary friendships. In 1711, the essayist Joseph Addison praised Pope's *Essay on Criticism* (1711) in his *Spectator,* and Pope was soon drawn into that periodical's circle of Whig wits. His *Windsor-Forest* (1713), which celebrated the Tory Peace of Utrecht, brought him to the attention of Jonathan Swift, with whom he soon formed the Scriblerus Club, which also included the poet and playwright John Gay. The Scriblerians wrote a number of learned satires collectively, which Pope polished and published. In 1713, Pope proposed a translation of Homer's *Iliad,* and with the help of powerful friends he secured a huge public subscription. Its publication between 1715 and 1720 established his reputation as England's national poet and made him financially independent. In 1719, he bought a house at Twickenham, near Windsor, where he was to live the rest of his life, landscaping its gardens and lovingly caring for his mother until her death in 1733. Pope did not cut much of a figure as a lover, but he did harbor at least one grand unrequited passion, for the married Orientalist Lady Mary Wortley Montagu; in the end, he found calmer affection and companionship in his Catholic neighbor, Martha Blount. Despite his illness, Pope's later career was highly productive: he published an edition of Shakespeare (1725), a translation of the *Odyssey* (1725–1726), *The Dunciad* (1728), a mock-epic satire of London literary life, *Imitations of Horace* (1733–1738), *Epistles to Several Persons* (1731–1735), and his great philosophical project,

Alexander Pope. Marble bust by Louis-François Roubillac (c. 1695 or 1705–1762). (©The Board of Trustees of the Victoria & Albert Museum, London/Art Resource, NY.)

An Essay on Man (1733–1734). Pope spent his final years securing his reputation; he published his heavily edited correspondence in 1737, and he reworked *The Dunciad* into the *Dunciad in Four Books* (1743), a final fusillade at enemies old and new.

Poetics and Design. Undoubtedly Pope's major contributions to his culture were his refining of an urbane poetic voice and his development of a particular set of virtuosic grammatical schemes within the strict discipline of the heroic couplet—schemes that were to be iterated many times over in the verse of poets until the end of the century. Much of Pope's stature as a stylist derives from his popular *Essay on Criticism,* an adaptation of Horace's *Ars poetica* that offers practical advice to modern critics and poets alike. For the latter in particular, he demonstrated, in lines that were universally admired, how sound should mirror sense in poetry. As a whole, the poem reproduces the major tenets of neoclassical aesthetics, though with (as Pope pointed out) less rigidity than such French theorists as Nicolas Boileau. The precepts of poetry are to be drawn from Homer, whose epics are treated as the source of all that is worthy in literature; even Virgil attained greatness only by a scrupulous modeling of his work on Homer. Pope balanced this emphasis on imitation, however, with a recognition of the need for license as well as rules. A felicitous departure from propriety and even "*brave Disorder*" (l. 152) were acceptable in Pope's eyes. In fact, when he turned to consider the task of the critic, he seemed to emphasize the need to treat the work of art as an organic whole. Moreover, the critic should not judge strictly by the standards of ancient poetry, but in accordance with the author's intention and with the work's affective impact on the reader. Such forgiveness, Pope implied, was demanded in an age and a culture so fallen from the grandeur of ancient Greece.

Pope's poetics describes how harmony can emerge from contraries; productive wit needs the restraint of judgment, and the poet's fertile genius needs the discipline of the critic's objective scrutiny. This conversation between opposites similarly informs the other aesthetic realm that obsessed Pope—landscape gardening. Pope dedicated himself to the design and ornamentation of his garden at Twickenham, which, despite its modest scale, became famous as embodying an emergent, distinctively modern approach to planting. Something of this approach had been adumbrated by Addison in *Spectator* no. 414, which attacked classical garden design with its open parterres and linear plantings. It was Pope's own *Epistle to Burlington* (1731), however, that was the most influential articulation of these principles, in its insistence that garden art should enhance rather than efface nature. Pope scorned equally the empty grandeur of sweeping lawns and vast artificial lakes and the showiness of fussy topiary and clusters of statues. Gardens, like houses, should be designed to divert and soothe, not to impress. The gardener should first "Consult the *Genius* of the *Place*" (l. 57), preserving the natural contours of the land and even enhancing its serpentine lines to create the effect of spontaneous beauty. Above all, the beauties of a garden should not be exposed all at once, but partly concealed behind natural landforms and irregular plantings to reward the questing visitor. In celebrating such "artful Wildeness" (l. 116), Pope captured in verse the key values of the picturesque movement that would come to dominate British landscape art in the latter half of the eighteenth century.

Philosophy. In many ways, Pope's career seemed designed as training to write an English epic to rival John Milton's *Paradise Lost* (1667). Over the years, he produced a series of parodic epics and even planned a heroic verse saga on Brutus, which never took flight. In the end,

Pope chose to mark the climax of his career not with an epic but with a philosophical poem with epic inflections, *An Essay on Man*. The *Essay* is, first and foremost, an exercise in theodicy—an attempt to account for God's allowing evil in the world—and it seems, from one angle, little more than a congeries of commonplaces about the relations between the human and the divine. Its attitudes are in many ways in tune with the easygoing latitudinarianism that had dominated Anglican theology since 1688. As a Catholic, Pope was always cagey about his religious beliefs, even with his closest friends, and he certainly went out of his way to appear orthodox in all matters. His argument was, moreover, less admired for its coherence than for its compressed and accessible articulation of time-honored truths.

Pope began his *Essay* by making a sustained case for epistemic humility in light of the obvious limits of our knowledge. Our views of the moral and material universes are inevitably partial; we are unfit to sit in judgment on a God who knows all and sees all. We can project, however, that a benign and rational God would not govern the universe by way of arbitrary, local interventions: "the first Almighty Cause / Acts not by partial, but by *gen'ral Laws*" (I: 145–146). Pope sustained this argument by invoking traditional notions of the chain of being, but he revivified this trope by mentioning modern scientific advances in cartography, anatomy, and astronomy to reinforce ideas of the regularity of God's plan. In this context, the most grievous human sin is pride; in laying claim to the places of the angels, we threaten, like Satan, to throw the universe into chaos. If we cannot judge of the whole, however, Pope felt that we are capable of knowing ourselves, and so he laid out a simple binarist psychology: "Two Principles in Human Nature reign; / *Self-Love*, to urge; and *Reason*, to restrain" (II: 53–54). From Montaigne, Pope developed the idea of a ruling passion that marks every character—a congenital propensity to a favorite vice and its allied virtue, such as the combination of avarice and prudence that marks the merchant. This potential chaos of desires is brought into harmony not by reason, but by a social love that is a natural outgrowth of the love of self. Pope finished the *Essay* with a discourse on ethics, arguing that happiness lies not with external goods but with the pleasures that attend the practice of charity. All happiness is thus social; the hermit and the tyrant can find no joy in their respective isolations.

If all these ideas were less than original, the poem as an apologetic text was both novel and distinctly modern in appealing to reason and experience alone, without reference to the revealed truths of Scripture. Pope dealt with atheistic doubt on its own terms, and so he ended up defending a deism that, though not at odds with Christianity, would seem radically incomplete to many of his contemporaries—so much so that he was even accused of being in sympathy with the thought of both Leibniz and Spinoza. Its bold, rationalist method also made the poem as attractive to subsequent generations of intellectuals—notably Immanuel Kant and Voltaire—as it was to lay Anglican readers.

[*See also* Addison, Joseph; Authorship; Deism; Landscape and Gardens; London; Neoclassicism; Poetry; Swift, Jonathan; *and* Translation.]

BIBLIOGRAPHY

WORKS BY POPE

The Twickenham Edition of the Poems of Alexander Pope. Edited by John Butt et al. 11 vols. New Haven, Conn., 1939–1969. A meticulous and fully annotated text of the poems, with all textual variants and full introductions to each poem.
The Correspondence of Alexander Pope. Edited by George Sherburn. 5 vols. Oxford, 1956.
The Poems of Alexander Pope. Edited by John Butt. London, 1963. A one-volume version of the *Twickenham Edition* above, without introductions and with much reduced annotation.
The Prose Works of Alexander Pope. Edited by Rosemary Cowler. Oxford, 1986. The major prose writings of 1725–1744.

STUDIES

Brown, Laura. *Alexander Pope.* Oxford, 1985. A critique of the ideologies of empire and capital at work in Pope's poetry.
Damrosch, Leopold, Jr. *The Imaginative World of Alexander Pope.* Berkeley, 1987. A reconstruction of Pope's mental, material, and social worlds.
Erskine-Hill, Howard. *The Social Milieu of Alexander Pope.* New Haven, Conn., 1975.
Jackson, Wallace, and R. Paul Yoder, eds. *Critical Essays on Alexander Pope.* New York, 1993. A useful collection offering selections from the work of major Pope scholars, representing a range of approaches.
Mack, Maynard. *Alexander Pope: A Life.* New Haven, Conn., 1985. The definitive biography, full of detail and engagingly written.
Nuttall, A. D. *Pope's "Essay on Man."* London, 1984. A close reading of the poem, taking Pope's philosophy and theology seriously.
Rumbold, Valerie. *Women's Place in Pope's World.* Cambridge, 1989.

PETER WALMSLEY

POPULARIZATION. To speak of the popularization of the Enlightenment implies first, the interlocking of sets of ideas, attitudes, and values that can be identified as characteristic of the Enlightenment, and then the diffusion of these ideas from the centers where they have been worked out and articulated, to a broader audience. Like most other intellectual movements, the Enlightenment was given form by philosophers, scientists, and writers, and then, over several generations, it spread more widely, so this model is broadly valid. For it to be of much use, however, it is necessary to define the core ideas and values that constitute the Enlightenment worldview, and then to determine both how far down the social scale these ideas and attitudes seem to have descended and the degree to which spokesmen of the movement hoped and thought it feasible to extend them.

An Elite Movement. The foundations of Enlightenment thought were laid at the end of the seventeenth century, primarily in England. Newton's celestial mechanics and the sensationalist psychology of John Locke explained the workings of the cosmos and of the human mind more convincingly than ever before. With the growing influence of the science of Newton's *Principia* (1687) and the conceptualization of man in Locke's *Essay Concerning Human Understanding* (1690), the mechanics of the world and of the human mind seemed exhilaratingly intelligible. In the expression of Peter Gay, Europeans—at least, upper-class Europeans—regained their nerve; but they did not regain too much nerve.

Unlike Descartes, who contributed significantly to demystifying the way the world was viewed, both Newton and Locke expressed doubts about the ability of philosophy and science to know all things, and both, modestly and wisely, restricted themselves, in the works for which they were best known, to things they could demonstrate. With their willingness to allow themselves to be limited by observable facts and their readiness to acknowledge that there were things whose natures they could not explain, there came a certain intellectual humility. The aversion of Enlightenment thinkers to metaphysics and to all-embracing systems, portrayed with savage humor in Voltaire's characterization of Pangloss in *Candide*, and more earnestly in the article "Philosophe" in the *Encyclopédie*, was rooted in the cautious empiricism that distinguished the founders of the movement.

The corollary of the philosophes' proposition that they could have no knowledge of things that extended beyond sensation and measurement was that such knowledge was equally unavailable to those who claimed it. Propositions of metaphysics and theology came to be regarded by adherents of the Enlightenment as unproven and unprovable. Where knowledge was unattainable, the appropriate response was not recourse to authority but toleration. Opposition to dogma, whether grounded in religion or in some other source, was characteristic of enlightened thinkers, and an expression of their liberalism. The key values of the Enlightenment were humanitarianism, in the utilitarian sense of maximizing the pleasures and minimizing the pains of the population at large; beneficence, or the obligation to do good to others, as part of a broader activist and reformist ethic; and finally, an assertion of the qualified equality of all human beings, which was less a call for leveling than a means of challenging privilege.

These ideas were worked out and articulated at the higher levels of society. The founders and main spokesmen of the movement tended to be academics, members of the liberal professions, clerics, and writers, with significant representation from the nobility. Denis Diderot and Jean-Jacques Rousseau, it is true, were born into families of skilled artisans, and rose in the social and cultural scales—not without difficulty—by their efforts and writings. These two men, however, were not read in the social milieu in which they originated. It was unusual for artisans to possess books, and when they did, such works were invariably religious or occupational. The dividing line between the enlightened and those who were not ran roughly and erratically through the upper levels of the artisanate. Culturally, at least for men, it divided those who had attended secondary schools, with their Latin-based curricula, from those who had not.

Progress and Diffusion. The leading figures of the Enlightenment have been described aptly as a mixed elite combining wealth, talent, and high social standing that cut across lines of class, occupation, and gender. They met in salons, academies, and masonic lodges, and less formally in cafés and private residences. Their works could be purchased from booksellers and were available directly for loan or consultation in reading rooms that charged modest fees; indirectly, they could be appropriated in the form of reviews or commentary in the periodical press. It is fair to designate the philosophes, their related publicists, and those who accepted their main assumptions and values as the enlightened community.

This community was restricted to the literate and educated upper levels of society, but it by no means included all those whose social, economic, or cultural standing potentially gave them access to it. Innumerable country gentlemen in the eighteenth century, like Squire Western in Fielding's *Tom Jones*, were interested in little more than their hounds and wine cellars, or the income from their lands. Most merchants were far more concerned with their ledgers than with the writings of Adam Smith and the Physiocrats. Many clerics and pious laymen saw no reason to interfere with a set of religious beliefs and practices that had offered hope and consolation, as well as material aid, for centuries to those who needed it, and whose contributions to social stability and the administration of the state were significant. Most did not, however, at least initially, think it unlikely that a constructive middle ground could be found where Enlightenment and Catholicism could meet.

There were many enlightened and reforming lawyers during the second half of the eighteenth century, but for every one of those there was a lawyer or judge prepared to enforce brutally a harsh and outdated legal code. Some of the most rigorous minds of the period were Jansenists who denied the basic premises of enlightened thought. Within the enlightened community, there was virtual unanimity that it was desirable and necessary to win over both the religious zealots and the merely indifferent

among their social equals, if not to their beliefs and values, then at least to their general worldview. Above the level of the artisanate, in what Jürgen Habermas has called the bourgeois public sphere, members of the enlightened community vigorously asserted the need and the desirability for the full popularization of their values and critical attitudes.

Most histories of the Enlightenment are cast as accounts of the conflict between enlightened elites and their usually equally well-educated and cultured opponents, whether clerics or devout laymen. In this struggle, spokesmen for church and state consistently lose ground, while advocates of enlightenment gain.

Probably the greatest account of the progress and diffusion of the Enlightenment is Daniel Mornet's *Les origines intellectuelles de la Révolution française* (1933). Mornet is particularly strong on the institutions and mechanisms—the academies, salons, various kinds of schools and classes, publication of books, pamphlets and periodicals—that spread Enlightenment values. He is also clear that these means of diffusion were directed at, and in fact hardly ever carried beyond, the comfortable world of the aristocracy and the middle classes. As Voltaire wrote of his *Dictionnaire philosophique*, one of the great works of popularization of the Enlightenment:

> This book will be read by enlightened persons alone; the common herd are not made for such knowledge; philosophy will never be their portion. Those who say there are truths that should be hidden from the people need not feel any alarm; the common people do not read; they work six days a week and go to the tavern on the seventh. In a word, the works of philosophy are made for philosophers alone, and every honest man should strive to be a philosopher without priding himself on being one.
>
> (Voltaire, 1962, vol. 1, 56)

If there was general agreement about the need to diffuse Enlightenment ideas and values among the cultural elites, the situation was far less clear with respect to the second level of popularization—that which concerned the working population and the poor.

In treating the cultural history of old-regime society, historians today distinguish between at least two broad cultural levels. Peter Burke, for example, has followed the cultural anthropologist Robert Redfield in calling them the "great" and "little" traditions. The great tradition, that of the elites, depended heavily on written or printed media, included all areas of formal learning, and was generally dominated by males. The battles between tradition-oriented clerics, lawyers, and intellectuals on one hand and philosophes on the other, forms a chapter in the history of the great tradition. The "little tradition" was that of the peasantry and most of the working population. Not impervious to print culture, it was nevertheless predominantly oral, relied on tradition and collective memory, varied regionally, and accorded a larger role to women. As Burke points out, these cultures were not mutually exclusive. At the beginning of the early modern period, the elites shared in popular culture, though the masses were largely excluded from that of the elites. From the sixteenth century through the eighteenth, the elites tended to distance themselves increasingly from popular culture.

For the men of the Enlightenment, the issue of whether or not to bring their culture to the people was contentious. In their eyes, the laboring population was deprived of anything that could properly be termed "culture." Peasants and workers were perceived to be ignorant, disorderly, superstitious, and limited by customs handed down from earlier generations and mindlessly accepted. Surely one way in which the social vision of the elites of the eighteenth century was deficient was in being unable to perceive the attitudes and customs of various strata of the common people as coherent wholes suited to the broad needs of the various communities in which they functioned. Having largely withdrawn from participation in popular culture themselves, the men and women of the Enlightenment, when idealizing the supposed simplicity and virtue of the common people, tended to see them as a cultural cipher. The question then became, should the ignorant, superstitious, and supposedly cultureless be enlightened? There was no unanimous response to this question, but a broad consensus did emerge during the last decades of the old regime. An examination of different views on popular education offers the most direct approach to the question of the popularization of the Enlightenment at lower cultural levels.

The Debate on Education. One indicator of the interests of members of the enlightened community is the themes for essay contests proposed by academies. On this score it appears that the question of how far Enlightenment should be made to extend was of considerable interest in the last decades of the Old Regime. In 1775, the Academy of Mantua set the topic of "A philosophical dissertation on the education of children, specifically: Which plan would best suit the children of the lower classes?" In 1779, the Academy of Châlons-sur-Marne asked, "Which would be the best plan of education for the people?" The following year, the Academy of Berlin posed the question "Is it useful to mislead the people?" for its essay contest—and received among the responses to it a strongly negative one from J.-A.-N. de Caritat Condorcet. Together with the many books and essays on this theme, these essay contests show how contemporaries felt about the prospect of extending enlightenment.

It is worth noting, first, that the debate on the education of the lower classes was framed in terms of broad social utility, so that instruction was taken as one factor among many, and one that had to be in harmony with the others. Within the enlightened community, there was a significant minority who would have denied literacy to the working population on the grounds that such knowledge was unnecessary for individual workers and might prove socially disruptive. It is worth emphasizing that such views were expressed by important and representative spokesmen of the Enlightenment and were not restricted to traditionalists. Louis René de Caradeuc de La Chalotais, an important magistrate in the parlement of Brittany, in his influential *Essay on National Education* of 1763, complained that the Brothers of Christian Schools were teaching the poor to read. Voltaire himself explicitly applauded and endorsed this passage. Both the magistrate and the philosophe viewed ignorance as pernicious, but both feared that providing peasants with the skills of literacy would cause them to become dissatisfied with their lot in life.

This view, although not unusual among the elites of French society toward the end of the old regime, was not the norm. The dominant opinion was that virtually all workers and peasants should learn to read and write at an elementary level, but not beyond this. Diderot, for example, favored making literacy generally available, but he warned against allowing the children of workers and peasants to attend secondary schools. Like most members of his community, Diderot did not regard the diffusion of Enlightenment thought evenly throughout society as an overriding imperative. Rather, he turned to the parameters set by economic and social utility to determine what kind of education should be given to children of different social standing.

Among the bearers of enlightened opinion, there was virtual unanimity that the working population should receive occupational instruction. How much proficiency was to be acquired in the skills of literacy was generally determined by economic or professional need. Peter Gay has argued rightly that, far from being doctrinaire and idealistic, Enlightenment thought on the whole was down to earth and pragmatic. In addressing the degree to which enlightened ideas and values could and should be disseminated, most spokesmen for the movement framed their views in the context of the economic realities of their time. They were aware of the harsh lot of most peasants and workers, and they expected that most laborers obviously would escape, if they could, a condition that demanded unremitting and exhausting labor without ensuring a regular and sufficient income.

Most social critics of the eighteenth century were acutely aware that their society provided relatively few positions for members of the liberal professions and for intellectuals. They knew that positions in teaching, the arts, and the liberal professions tended to be filled by children of established families, and they feared the consequences of working-class children achieving a degree of education that would qualify them for such positions. On the one hand, a surplus of well-educated young men unable to find work would create a dissatisfied intelligentsia (like that of Grub Street, described by Robert Darnton), which, it was feared, would contribute to social instability; on the other hand, young peasants and workers trained in the liberal arts would not willingly, as La Chalotais maintained, return to the plow or the workbench. Thus, the productive crafts would be deprived of the necessary manpower, while society would be burdened with impecunious and discontented layabouts. The widespread contemporary concern with depopulation, particularly of the countryside, as well as the Physiocrats' emphasis on the importance of agriculture and a plentiful rural labor supply, heightened concerns about too much education spreading too far down the social scale.

It is not accurate, however, to see the men and women of the Enlightenment as opposed to all education for the lower classes. Rather, they believed in an education suited to one's place in society. For the working population, this meant such occupational instruction as would be of immediate use, and a minimal level of competence in the skills of literacy. It was further recognized that the working population was part of civil society and thus needed a further dimension to its education—one that was referred to either as moral or as religious.

During the eighteenth century, education was overwhelmingly in the hands of the church, particularly in the case of the working population. In the French countryside, primary schools or *petites écoles* were common, and their masters were generally supervised by the curé. In practice, these schools ensured a rudimentary socialization of the peasantry in which religious instruction, often in the form of a catechism, was central, and the skills of literacy secondary.

For most members of the enlightened community, the predominance of the church in the field of education was problematic. For those who felt strongly that the state and society should be the first objects of allegiance, the Roman Catholic emphasis on transcendental values was unacceptable and needed to be replaced with training in citizenship. For others, Catholicism was far too tolerant of the irrationality and superstitions common among the working population and, indeed, itself fostered such superstitions. For most members of the elites who espoused Enlightenment values, it was necessary to reduce as much as possible false beliefs that tended to contribute to disorder or to inhibit economic productivity. This implied discountenancing superstitions and beliefs rooted in popular culture or in certain forms of

religious observance. It was more a matter of rooting out the pernicious than of providing a full, alternate enlightened view of the world. At least, workers and peasants might be offered some instruction in elementary physics so that, for example, having been taught the natural mechanism by which thunder is caused, they would lose their debilitating fear of it. Similarly, whatever reservations the educated might have about religion, they thought that the common people needed to be taught that there existed a just divine being who rewarded good deeds and punished bad ones. The truth of this doctrine was not at issue; rather, it was regarded as a safeguard of property, life, and social order appropriate for those who did not have the time or capability to find their way to the same conclusions philosophically.

Recognition of Limits. If this picture seems parsimonious and gloomy, one should bear in mind that it reflects the practicality of the men and women of the Enlightenment. In the economic conditions of the eighteenth century, the great majority of peasants and unskilled laborers were obliged to work from sunrise to sunset in order to earn a bare living. Without a radical redistribution of wealth or vastly improved methods of production—neither of which were regarded as practical possibilities during the Enlightenment—it was not feasible to suggest significantly broader or more generous programs of popular instruction. If it were part of a world in which social and economic realities had no weight, or if it were prepared to ignore those realities, the Enlightenment would no doubt have opted to endow all members of society with the same high cultural level. Recognizing the limitations that an underdeveloped economy imposed on their society, the enlightened community sought to encourage the economically self-sufficient levels of society to accept the full scope of Enlightenment culture, and to expose the peasantry and working population to such aspects of the Enlightenment program as seemed feasible under the harsh social and economical conditions of the time.

On a practical level, members of the enlightened community spent far more time and effort in attempting to convince people on their own cultural level to adopt their ideas and values. The working population was not a partner for debate, but rather an object of commiseration and beneficence. One of the rare attempts at this time to educate lower-class children outside established frameworks was undertaken by a provincial nobleman and former army officer, the count de Thélis, with the support of many enlightened and wealthy contemporaries. In the *écoles nationales militaires* that he organized and publicized, Thélis brought together the children of poor nobles with children of the rural poor in boarding schools whose goals blended education and military training with relief from poverty. To help make the schools economically self-sustaining, Thélis organized them around road-building, which the students were taught, and at which the poor commoners spent most of their time. The schools were organized along military lines, with both nobles and commoners receiving formal instruction. That of the nobles and officers-to-be was much more extensive than that of the commoners, which emphasized occupational and moral training, and preparation for military service. While potentially the stuff of a Dickens novel, Thélis's schools were a resourceful attempt at rural poverty relief and popular education, and received considerable support. A number of comparable institutions were established elsewhere in France. The charity schools in England run by the Society for the Promotion of Christian Knowledge were similarly concerned more with inculcating attitudes appropriate to those in positions of dependence than in ensuring mastery of the skills of literacy.

Little was done to bring the Enlightenment to the working population over the eighteenth century, but this is not necessarily to say that popular attitudes were not modified over this period, or that the cultural parameters of the masses remained fixed. Historians disagree on whether or not the popular romances, fairy tales, chapbooks, and almanacs show the influence of the Enlightenment or not, but if there is any indication of growing realism or rationalism in this escapist and sensationalist literature, published for profit and bought for its entertainment value, it is not immediately apparent. Nonetheless, there are indications of significant cultural shifts at this time.

In France, average male literacy rates increased from 29 percent of the population in 1686 to 47 percent in 1786, with great variations in region and with female rates lagging significantly behind, but still gaining ground. English male literacy rates increased from roughly 30 percent in the mid-seventeenth century to 60 percent by the late eighteenth, and in lowland Scotland, literacy was even more widespread, as indeed it was in certain other Protestant countries such as Sweden. Urban rates of literacy throughout Europe were significantly higher than rural ones, often reaching 80 or 90 percent for men and 60 or 70 percent for women. The increase in literacy and the growth of the print media in the eighteenth century were not without their impact on the working population.

Using findings from social history, Michel Vovelle has argued that a significant change in collective attitudes took place in the course of the eighteenth century. He notes the increase in literacy, the advent of contraception, the rise in the number of births out of wedlock, the decline in the number of requests for masses in wills, the secularization of formulas used in wills, the decline in the number of clerical vocations, and the shift away from penitent confraternities toward Freemasonry. Together these indicators suggest growing secularization and a crisis in the sense of community (Vovelle, 1990). The picture presented by Vovelle is, on the whole, one of disaggregation and loss. While it does not seem possible to link these changes in popular mentalities directly to the Enlightenment, it would appear that, while lagging behind those within the enlightened community, they are broadly parallel to them.

The popularization of the Enlightenment thus worked on at least two distinct levels. The educated and leisured elites were to be exposed to, and hopefully won over by, the whole panoply of Enlightenment ideas and values by means of full and open critical discussion. This debate, articulated through books, the periodical press, salons, academies, masonic lodges and other channels of communication, lies at the heart of most treatments of the Enlightenment. The second level of popularization is very different. Concerned with those strata of the population which were unable to acquire the cultural tools with which the Enlightenment was forged and articulated, it offered a set of ideas and values severely limited by considerations of utility. If the cultural equipment offered by the enlightened community to the working population is far from generous, it should be borne in mind that the economics of underdevelopment are unforgiving, and that social realism did not allow much more. The full and equal dissemination of enlightenment to all social levels remained at the time a utopian aspiration. That is, it remained an aspiration that could only be realized once social and economic conditions had been changed fundamentally.

[*See also* Education, *subentries on* Pedagogical Thought and Practice *and* Reform and Experiments; Enlightenment Studies; Literacy; People, The; Philosophes; *and* Print Culture.]

BIBLIOGRAPHY

Bollème, Geneviève. *Les almanachs populaires au XVIIᵉ et XVIIIᵉ siècles: Essai d'histoire sociale*. Paris and The Hague, 1969. A Key pioneering study of popular culture.

Brewer, John. *The Pleasures of the Imagination: English Culture in the Eighteenth Century*. New York, 1997. A fine conspectual work, examining art and music as well as literature, the provinces as well as London, popular culture as well as that of the elites and the contexts of culture as well as its achievements.

Burke, Peter. *Popular Culture in Early Modern Europe*. New York, 1978. The book in English that opened the field.

Chisick, Harvey. *The Limits of Reform in the Enlightenment: Attitudes toward the Education of the Lower Classes in Eighteenth-Century France*. Princeton, N.J., 1981.

Garnot, Benoît. *Le peuple au siècle des Lumières: Echec d'un dressage culturel*. Paris, 1990. Good on the cultural relations between elites and the masses.

Gay, Peter. *The Enlightenment: An Interpretation*. 2 vols. New York, 1966, 1969. The great liberal misinterpretation of the Enlightenment; indispensable.

La Chalotais, Louis Renè de Caradeuc de. *Essai d'éducation nationale, ou Plan d'études pour la jeunesse*. Paris, 1996. First published 1763.

Mandrou, Robert. *De la culture populaire aux 17ᵉ et 18ᵉ siècles: La Bibliothèque bleue de Troyes*. Paris, 1975.

Mornet, Daniel. *Les origines intellectuelles de la Révolution française, 1715–1787*. 6th ed. Paris, 1967. First Published in 1933; magisterial control of the literature and of channels of diffusion; probably the best and richest study of the Enlightenment ever made.

Muchembled, Robert. *Popular and Elite Culture in France, 1400–1750*. Translated by Lydia Cochrane. Baton Rouge, La., and London, 1985. English Translation of *Culture populaire et culture des élites dans la France moderne (XVᵉ–XVIIᵉ siècles)*, 1978.

Payne, Harry C. *The Philosophes and the People*. New Haven, Conn., and London, 1976.

Vovelle, Michel. "The Prerevolutionary Sensibility." In his *Ideologies and Mentalities*. Translated by Eamon O'Flaherty. Chicago, 1990.

HARVEY CHISICK

PORNOGRAPHY. The Enlightenment was the first age of mass-produced pornography, although the word "pornography" itself did not gain currency in European languages until the mid-nineteenth century. The Greek neologism *pornos graphos* materialized around 200 CE when Athenaeus, an obscure author, coined it to signify "the depiction of prostitutes" in words or in visual images. "Pornography" appears neither in Samuel Johnson's comprehensive *Dictionary of the English Language* (1755) nor in the *Encyclopédie* of Denis Diderot and Jean Le Rond d'Alembert, and in short entries on cognate topics, the *encyclopédistes* prove reticent. Whether discussing *érotique* (a genre of poetry; erotomania), *libertinage* (acceptable when maintained with the philosophy, good taste, and brio of the classical poets and their imitators), *libertins* (blasphemous Reformation fanatics), *obscénité* (inadmissible in polite society), *phallus* (a scandalous and primitive totem), or *le sexe* (those fine ladies who adorn society), contributors temper morality with an emollient decorum and an elusive wit. As such semantic niceties imply, individual differences in sexual imagination—differences that can be stimulated by a bewildering variety of representations in words and images—bedevil all commentary on pornography and the fantasies it engenders. Public morality and private fantasy often prove touchy bedfellows.

Not until the mid-1800s did the word "pornography" begin to acquire some of its twentieth-century meanings. Only then did the twin problems of displaying ancient erotica in museums and of classifying books in libraries—the cloistering of pornography from more humdrum collections in the British Library, the Bibliothèque Nationale, and elsewhere—prompt the emergence of "pornography" as a taxonomy under which immodest or provocative items could be catalogued. Nineteenth-century lexicographers began to define "pornography" both as "licentious painting employed to decorate the walls of rooms sacred to bacchanalian orgies [i.e., at Pompeii]" (*Webster's Dictionary*,

1864) and as "a treatise on prostitution," often in conjunction with "public hygiene" (*Littré's Dictionnaire Française*, 1866).

Enlightenment sex workers also challenged hygiene and public order in ways that differed from pornography itself. What developed during the Renaissance and Enlightenment were various genres of *pornos graphos*. In "whores' books," male authors wrote fictional accounts of all kinds of female sex workers. Pietro Aretino (1492–1556) inaugurated this popular genre with his *Ragionamenti* ("The Harlots' Dialogues," 1532–1534), in which he orchestrated the dialogues of fictional groups of women as an ex-courtesan discusses whether it is better for her daughter to become wife, nun, or sex worker. Satirical and saucy rather than libidinous, Aretino diverted his readers with sportive tales of clerical couplings. Another genre of *pornos graphos* addressed, discursively rather than fictively, the real-life problems of sex workers.

In *A Modest Defence of the Publick Stews* (1724), Bernard Mandeville (1670–1733), a Dutch physician and notorious freethinker who practiced in England, championed the civic benefits of red light districts, once they had been decriminalized and regulated; Mandeville's tone is bawdily sardonic. In 1769, Nicolas Restif de la Bretonne (1734–1806)—a French habitué of brothels and a compulsive scribbler of memoirs, plays, and best-selling salacious novels—published *Le Pornographe*, a jocose tract indicting social hypocrisy, subtitled "A Gentleman's Ideas on a Project for Regulating Prostitutes, Suitable for Preventing Misfortunes Occasioned by the Public Traffic in Women." Projects like Restif's enjoyed some Enlightenment currency: the French architect Claude-Nicolas Ledoux (1736–1806) sketched a phallic design (*Oikema*) for Restif's imagined pleasure palace. More whimsically utopian than Mandeville's brusque *Defence*, Restif's *Le Pornographe* offers a singular, inadvertent revival of Athenaeus's neologism.

At the beginning of a new millennium, we may define "pornography" as sexually explicit images and texts loosely customized to stimulate physical excitement, usually masturbation. But we can also share pornography with sexual partners; many cultures have such "pillow books," and they were used in Enlightenment brothels. During the Enlightenment, however, "pornography" constituted a much wider range of texts than our latter-day definition encompasses. John Cannon (1684–c. 1743), who became an excise officer and a schoolmaster, recorded how his mother once surprised him masturbating to a copy of Nicholas Culpeper's oft-reprinted *Directory for Midwives* (1651). Medical texts could function as dirty books. Indeed, the anonymous quack who scribbled *Onania* (c. 1716), a best-selling English tract that prompted a flood of Enlightenment works decrying masturbation, was all too aware of the potential pleasures of his text: this hack prefaced his work with admonitions against ejaculatory misinterpretation.

One detailed account, documentary rather than fictive, of the purchase and consumption of pornography survives from the Enlightenment. Samuel Pepys (1630–1703) recorded the full trajectory from bookshop to ejaculation. Theatergoer, bibliophile, civil servant, tireless commentator on politics, church business, and modern science—in short, a prototypical man of the Enlightenment—Pepys assiduously recorded all his doings in an extraordinarily candid *Diary* (1660–1669). On 13 January 1668, Pepys stopped at a London bookstore where he read *L'école des filles* (first ed., Paris, 1655; "The School of Girls, or the Philosophy of Women, Divided into Two Dialogues") which he described as "the most bawdy, lewd book that ever I saw, rather worse than *La putana errante* ["The Wandering Whore"; first ed., Venice 1585, one of Aretino's suppositious works]—so that I was ashamed of reading it." In the risqué dialogues that constitute its *Philosophy of Women*, conducted in the manner of a "whores' book," a knowledgeable woman instructs a virgin on how to give and take sexual pleasure; allusions to the coital position of "the woman on top" provide a leitmotif. On 8 February, Pepys plucked up the courage to buy *L'école des filles* and brought it home "in plain binding." On the next day, he retired to his study to read the book, purportedly "for information sake." To describe the emission it provoked, Pepys employed the same macaronic code in which he chronicled details of marital infidelity: "it did hazer my prick para stand all the while, and una vez to decharger; and after I had done it, I burned it, that it might not be among my books to my shame." This episode antedates Enlightenment hysteria about masturbation, but it already spotlights those dangers of imagination, of privacy, and of stimulation by fiction that were adduced by critics of novel-reading in the next century.

What made the Enlightenment the first great age of pornography was the technological revolution that had been ushered in more than two centuries earlier by the printing press. By 1660, pornography was becoming cheaper and more accessible. The spread of presses and of peddlers supported the clandestine distribution of dirty books and prints. Authors, publishers, booksellers, censors, and police played a mouse-and-cat game—prosecution and imprisonment routinely followed—but an international market boomed. Old chestnuts like *L'école des filles* were translated abroad, often under a false imprint, and reexported. Also swelling Enlightenment pornography were bawdy jest-books, obscene songs, and crude woodcuts, which remind us that class-based literacy was not the sole passport to erotic stimulation. In one jurisdiction or other, popular marriage manuals like *Aristotle's Masterpiece* (1684), prints of famous erotic paintings, political lampoons or scurrilous engravings, or scientific and antitheological tracts might also fall under the rubric of "forbidden books."

We can only speculate on women's recourse to pornography during the Enlightenment. The novelistic evidence that survives was disseminated by men—its raciness designed, presumably, for other men—and we have found but a single example of an English woman who maintained a manuscript collection of sexy poems. However, a remark by Jean-Jacques Rousseau (1671–1741)—who hovered, literally, over his own masturbation—about "those dangerous books that a fine lady finds inconvenient, because they can only be read with one hand," points either to an unrecorded female readership or to fresh elaborations of male fantasy. On the other hand, female readers may have discovered in "decent" novels about love and marriage (or in the more lurid Gothic romances) imaginative stimuli that most men could barely grasp.

What engaged the fantasies and anxieties of male writers of pornography were textual constructions of female sexuality. Female bodies became their locus for the expansion of female "knowledge," so that a woman's sense of self-awareness became inextricably linked to her sexual self-awareness. French writers especially dwelt on "the philosophy of women," most brilliantly (if anonymously) in *Thérèse philosophe* (1748), where concupiscent scenes are interspersed with an anticlericalism that endorses atheistic materialism. Thérèse's development as a "philosopher" coincides with her resort to masturbation. The novel, and presumably her "education," concludes when her keeper, the count, finally penetrates her. The fetishised female body could also serve a darker agenda. Marie-Antoinette's path to the guillotine was, sadly, littered with fantastical prints and stories of her vilely imagined couplings.

In the representation of sexual acts, fantasy and imaginative role-playing came into play. Did Pepys—a sexual harasser who beat his wife and servants—find himself fantasizing willy-nilly of women on top, and did he prove unable to control his responses to its representation? Might some heterosexual males who devoured John Cleland's *Memoirs of a Woman of Pleasure* (1748–1749; better known as *Fanny Hill*)—the greatest, sexiest, most unbuttoned, and most frequently reprinted and translated of the many "whores' books"—daydream of playing the female narrator's role, or that of the homosexuals on whom she spies? Flagellation, lesbianism, and hair-and-glove-fetishism pop up amid the heterosexual fornication in *Fanny Hill*, as they do in other Enlightenment pornography. Most readers neither reenacted nor, alas, tolerated such variations in the real world. "A man's thoughts shame hell," runs the old saw. "No man is a hypocrite in his pleasures," averred Samuel Johnson (1709–1784). But can hypocrisy pervade even fantasy? Scholars can only guess at pleasures in bedrooms past (or in other locations), but we can never know the fantasies that occupy those who consume their pornographic representation. Even the springs of Pepys's excitement remain murky.

Recently, historians have argued that dips in Enlightenment birthrates were attributable to a low incidence of sexual intercourse. Masturbation (whether joint or solitary) seems to have been widely practiced, despite the sudden spasm of medical texts like *Onania* and *Onanisme* (or "A Treatise upon the Disorder Produced by Masturbation," 1760) by the famous Swiss doctor Samuel-Auguste Tissot (1728–1797). Indeed, *Onanisme* informs a lengthy screed against manustrupration (a lexical variant of "masturbation") in the *Encylopédie* that endorses Tissot's shrill anxiety about its dire consequences. Between pornography as a guide to polymorphous fantasy and moralistic concerns about its upshot, Enlightenment conflict thus persisted.

For example, *The Harlot's Progress* (1732)—a series of six paintings that William Hogarth (1697–1764) speedily engraved as a set of best-selling prints—purports to be a cautionary tale about the misfortunes of Moll Hackabout as she degenerates from an innocent country lass newly arrived in London to a feckless courtesan,

cheap trick, jailbird, and syphilitic corpse. But Hogarth spiced moralism with sensationalism, titillating his audience with glimpses into Moll's client list and into her trade as dominatrix. In depicting Moll's degeneration, Hogarth thus accommodated a variety of responses, including a satirical indictment of his own purchasers for potential prurience, and hence of their hypocrisy about sex workers. Indeed, *The Harlot's Progress* proved both "pornographic"—a depiction of sex-workers, *pornos graphos*—and pornographically stimulating to sundry consumers, some doubtless "moral."

Images far lusher than Hogarth's burgeoned. In "Naked Woman Lying on a Sofa" (1752; Munich, Alte Pinakotek), François Boucher (1703–1770), most flamboyantly erotic of the French court painters, focused on the plump bottom of Louis XV's naked mistress as she sprawled carelessly. More salaciously inviting was the semi-clad variation of this pose in Boucher's "Brunette Odalisque" (1743; the Louvre), in which the model turns both her face and her bottom expectantly to the viewer's gaze. Privately commissioned, such paintings hung semi-publicly, but they were frequently reproduced in miniature for closeted scrutiny. Of Boucher's large canvases, Denis Diderot (1713–1784) growled that "they betray the imagination of a man who spends his time with prostitutes of the lowest grade." Yet Diderot had turned his own hand to

François Boucher, *Brunette Odalisque, 1743*. (Musée du Louvre, Paris/Eric Lessing/Art Resource, NY.)

writing pornography, certainly (but lugubriously) in *The Indiscreet Jewels* (1748), and allegedly (if exquisitely) in *Thérèse Philosophe*.

The involvement of the rich, the powerful, and the well-educated in its production and consumption indicates that pornography was not merely a perverse gymnasium for moral degenerates who belonged in prisons or asylums. Authors and artists solicited more than purely aesthetic responses from their audiences. Victor Riqueti, comte de Mirabeau (1749–1791), whose forays into pornography preceded his career as a revolutionary, hoped in the preface to *Ma Conversion, ou le libertin de qualité* (1783) that "the reading of this book will make the whole world masturbate." On Donatien-Alphonse-François de Sade (1740–1814), some comment seems inevitable. Despite the enduring fascination of his freakish life and works, we believe that Sade was a bad man and a boring writer who deserved his incarceration. The marquis viciously contravened the spirit of our contemporaneous mantra—"safe, sane, and consensual"—devised by "sado-masochists" who had become saddled with his sobriquet.

[*See also* Diderot, Denis; Human Nature; Literary Genres; Materialism; Painting; Print Culture; *and* Sade, Donatien-Alphonse-François de.]

BIBLIOGRAPHY

Cellard, Jacques. *Un Génie Dévergondé: Nicolas-Edme Rétif dit "de la Bretonne."* Paris, 2000. In this sparkling biography of the author of *Le Pornographe*, Cellard quotes splendidly from his many works.

Darnton, Robert. *The Forbidden Best-Sellers of Pre-Revolutionary France.* New York, 1996. In this wonderfully documented study of the illicit book trade, Darnton also analyzes "philosophical pornography" and provides a partial translation of *Thérèse Philosophe*.

Darnton, Robert. " 'Philosophical Sex': Pornography in Old Regime France." In *Sexualities in History: A Reader*, edited by Kim M. Phillips and Barry Reay, pp. 203–222. New York, 2002. A succinct yet panoramic survey by the leading scholar in an outstanding collection of essays.

Feher, Michel, ed. *The Libertine Reader: Eroticism and Enlightenment in Eighteenth-Century France.* New York, 1997. A very handy, yet substantial, paperback edition that includes translations of Diderot's *The Indiscreet Jewels* and de Sade's *Florville and Courval* but not, regrettably, a translation of *Thérèse Philosophe*.

Frappier-Mazur, Lucienne. *Writing the Orgy: Power and Parody in Sade.* Translated by Gillian C. Gill. Philadelphia, 1996. A readable and deft resuscitation of the marquis as a postmodern fabulist who transcends mere pornography.

Hitchcock, Tim. *English Sexualities, 1700–1800.* New York, 1997. Informative discussion of sex lives like John Cannon's. Excellent bibliography.

Hunt, Lynn, ed. *The Invention of Pornography: Obscenity and the Origins of Modernity.* New York, 1996. A germinal collection of essays that range across Enlightenment Europe.

Kraakman, Dorelies. "Reading Pornography Anew: A Critical History of Sexual Knowledge for Girls in French Erotic Fiction, 1750–1840." *Journal of the History of Sexuality* 4 (1994), 517–548. An important perspective on women from this indispensable journal.

Lasowski, Patrick Wald, ed. *Romanciers libertins du XVIIIe siècle.* Vol. 1. Paris, 2000. Already a gargantuan and learned, yet accessible and affordable, collection (which includes *Thérèse Philosophe*). Amazingly, and with impeccable commentary, Lasowski and his colleagues reprint the illustrations to many different editions. Here, sadly, these engravings too often demand a magnifying glass.

Mc Cormick, Ian, ed. *Secret Sexualities: A Sourcebook of 17th and 18th Century Writing.* New York, 1997. Instructive excerpts culled from a wide variety of English sources.

Moulton, Ian Frederick. *Before Pornography: Erotic Writing in Early Modern England.* New York, 2000. Essaying various definitions of pornography, Moulton skilfully links it to manuscript culture and to nationality.

Mudge, Bradford K. *The Whore's Story: Women, Pornography, and the British Novel, 1684–1830.* New York, 2000. An informative survey of fiction, publishers, masquerades, engravers, and painters.

Pettit, Alexander, and Patrick Spedding, eds. *Eighteenth-Century British Erotica.* 5 vols. Brookfield, Vt., 2001. Bumper crop of facsimile pornography: includes medical, criminological, and anthropological works as well as regular fare. With their scholarly apparatus, these volumes comprise a crucial research tool.

Porter, Roy. " 'The Secrets of Generation Display'd': *Aristotle's Masterpiece* in Eighteenth-Century England." In *Unauthorized Sexual Behavior During the Enlightenment*, edited by Robert P. Maccubbin, pp. 1–21. Cambridge, 1987. A leading historian of medicine and sexology examines a popular marital handbook in this wide-ranging collection of essays on Enlightenment sexuality and textuality.

Thompson, Roger. *Unfit for Modest Ears: A Study of Pornographic, Obscene and Bawdy Works Written or Published in England in the Second Half of the Seventeenth Century.* London, 1979. An excellent introduction, fully documented from texts that retained their popularity in the eighteenth century.

Turner, James Grantham. *Libertines and Radicals in Early Modern London: Sexuality, Politics and Literary Culture, 1630–1685.* Cambridge, 2002. A prolific, astute, and energetic commentator probes Samuel Pepys among many others.

Wagner, Peter. *Eros Revived: Erotica of the Enlightenment in England and America.* London, 1988. Although sloppily written and factually slipshod, this volume offers lavish illustrations and quotes copiously from pornographic texts.

H. J. ORMSBY-LENNON and
JOSEPH PAPPA

PORTHAN, HENRIK GABRIEL (1739–1804), Swedish-Finnish historian and folklorist.

Porthan spent almost his entire life in the sphere of the Royal Turku (Swedish Åbo) University (Regia Academia Aboensis), founded by Queen Christina of Sweden in 1640 and transferred to Helsinki in 1828 by Emperor Nicholas I of Russia, grand duke of Finland. Porthan carried on the tradition of his uncles, both professors at Turku University; one of them, Daniel Juslenius, later a bishop, was well-known for his work on the first comprehensive Finnish-Latin-Swedish lexicon (1745). Porthan's first theses (1758 and 1762) dealt with religious philosophy, but, probably due to his devotion to research and teaching he was never ordained to the priesthood, even though he was twice asked to propose his candidacy for bishop.

Inspired by Montesquieu, Jean-Jacques Rousseau, and the new Winkelmannian classics, Porthan eventually turned his attention toward history and literature. He became a lecturer in rhetoric and was appointed university librarian. Even after he had attained the position of professor of eloquence and poetics in 1777, he maintained his interest in and work on behalf of the library, which was transferred with the university to Helsinki in 1828 and is now the National Library of Finland.

Porthan worked as a professor until his death in 1804. He was the most influential teacher of his time in Finland, and he greatly contributed to the general level of knowledge and understanding of many generations of priests and civil servants.

Porthan's main field of interest was the classics; he lectured on Homer, Horace, and Ovid, and was the first in the realm to lecture on classical archeology. He also taught the theory of aesthetics and literary history. The new classical studies, the tradition of textual criticism developed by Johann David Michaelis, and August Ludwig Schlözer's anthropologically oriented view of history inspired him both in his teaching and his research. Schlözer, being a specialist in Nordic history and a pioneer of Russian history, inspired Porthan to prepare critical editions from Finnish (that is, Turku) diocesan sources, for which Porthan became known as the father of Finnish history. Porthan's methods were modern and his interests and learning wide; he used linguistics and ethnography, combining his reading of manuscripts (mainly in Stockholm and Uppsala) with observations made during his many trips around Finland and collected from his students and correspondents.

Porthan had in his youth undertaken an examination of the folkloric tradition of Finnish poetry, *De poësi fennica* (Finnish Poetry, published in five parts from 1766–1778). Ultimately, his ideas about Finnish folklore changed, and the work was left uncompleted. Initially influenced by his uncle's traditional view, Porthan moved toward a more anthropological orientation but never developed a clear idea of the chronology of Finnish folklore. He made no distinction between archaic-mythological, protohistorical, medieval, and contemporary popular poetry, because upon formal analysis they all manifested in Porthan's view a similar metric and poetic identity. The main merit of Porthan's work was to draw attention to Finnish folklore. It was only after his death, under the influence of the Romantic movement and the political situation in Europe—especially the creation of a separate Finnish state—that Finnish folklore attracted serious interest.

Porthan also studied the Finnish language, its dialects and its relation to the other Baltic Sea–region Finnic languages. He rejected the outmoded ideas of his uncle and others who believed Finnish to be a relative of Hebraic or other remote languages, and applied the critical approach of the Göttingen philologists and anthropologists, which led him to compare the inland Finns more with the newly discovered indigenous tribes of the new world. Porthan's Finnish studies attained new significance after the creation of the Finnish state in 1809, when the movement to shape a Finnish national identity became a reality.

[*See also* Scandinavia.]

MATTI KLINGE

PORTUGAL. In 1668, the kingdom of Portugal secured recognition of its independence from Spain, against which it had been fighting a war of "restoration" since 1640 under the leadership of the duke of Bragança, who became King John IV (1640–1656), and of his son and successor, Afonso VI (1656–1683). Portugal's success in this struggle owed a great deal to Spain's commitments elsewhere and to the aid given it by Spain's other enemies, notably the United Provinces, England, and France. Portugal had to pay for this help, however, by granting privileges to resident foreign merchants, although those merchants were still largely excluded from trading with Portugal's overseas empire, which (despite losses such as that of Ceylon to the Dutch) remained considerable. Portugal retained a presence in the East (notably at Goa and Macao), and its colonies or other outposts along the African coast were the basis for a lucrative slave trade with the Americas. Most important, however, the Portuguese recovered Brazil and its lucrative plantations from the Dutch. The discovery there in the 1690s of gold, and a generation later of diamonds, confirmed the enormous value of Brazil and underpinned much of the prosperity of early eighteenth century Portugal.

After 1668, however, Portugal continued to face the challenge of how to maintain its independence and its empire, particularly against Spain. One means of overcoming these difficulties was to exploit and develop its own economic resources, as was attempted by the third conde de Ericeira (1632–1690), the "Portuguese Colbert." However, Portugal continued to depend on the support of more powerful foreign states, including England, which valued Lisbon as an anchorage for its fleet and merchant shipping passing to and from the Mediterranean.

Foreign and particularly diplomatic contacts had a profound impact on some among Portugal's political, social, and cultural elite. The last, sometimes called *estrangeirados* by those who thought them too influenced by foreign attitudes and models, included dom Luis da Cunha, Portugal's minister at the Utrecht peace congress (1713), and his close friend, the fourth conde de Ericeira (1674–1743). Ericeira was a leading patron of new ideas and a member of various informal, private discussion groups—for example, the Academia dos Ilustrados—in Portugal. He was also director of the Lisbon Royal Academy of History, founded in 1720 by King John V

(1706–1750), and he was elected a member of the Royal Society of London in 1741. These men and their associates, always a small minority, contributed to the spread in Portugal of the ideas of Newton and other luminaries of the Enlightenment. Martinho de Mendonça de Pina Proença (1693–1743), a former governor of Minas Gerais in Brazil and an associate member of the Royal Academy of History who had met Christian Wolff on his travels, wrote a treatise on education, *Apontamentos para a educacao de um menino nobre* (1734), which revealed the influence of John Locke and François-Armand de Salignac de La Mothe Fénelon. Jacob de Castro Sarmento (1691–1762), a Jewish doctor who fled Portugal in 1721 but continued to concern himself with the spread of enlightened ideas in his native land, started work on a translation of Francis Bacon's *Novum Organum* as a contribution to the reform of the study of medicine in Portugal. He also dedicated to the heir to the Portuguese throne, the future King José I (1750–1777), a translation of a historical essay by Newton, *Cronologia Newtoniana epitomizada* (1737), and he translated Newton's theory on the tides in *Teorica verdadeira das mares conforme a filosofia do incomparavel cavalheiro Isaac Newton* (1737). Antonio Nunes Ribeiro Sanches (1699–1783) was another Jewish doctor who fled Portugal (in 1726) to escape the Inquisition; after studying at Leiden under Hermann Boerhaave and serving

as court physician in Russia, he settled in France, where he contributed an article on venereal illnesses to Diderot's *Encyclopédie*. He, too, continued to write and publish in Portuguese, including another treatise on education, *Cartas sobre a educação da mocidade* (1759). Newtonian ideas also reached Portugal through the works—notably *O Verdadero metodo de Estudar* (1746)—of Luis Antonio Vernei (1713–1792), a member of the anti-Jesuit Order of the Oratory, which had entrenched itself in Portugal after 1640. In Rome, where he was secretary to the Portuguese minister, Vernei had become acquainted with Ludovico Antonio Muratori.

Portugal's place in the Enlightenment, however, owes a great deal to the earthquake that struck on All Saints' Day (1 November) 1755. It killed about 15,000 people in Lisbon alone—about ten percent of its total population—and provoked diverse reactions in enlightened circles throughout Europe. In rebuilding the capital in the aftermath of this disaster, the first minister of José I, Sebastião José de Carvalho e Mello (1699–1782), marques de Pombal, consolidated his position. Pombal supervised the rebuilding of Lisbon along more modern and rational lines. As unrivaled chief minister, Pombal carried out major and wide-ranging reforms that in many respects echoes enlightened reform in other parts of contemporary Europe.

Portuguese Minister. Sebastião José de Carvalho e Mello, marquês de Pombal, foreign minister (1750–1756) and prime minister (1756–1777), overseeing the reconstruction of Lisbon after the earthquake of 1755. Portrait by Louis-Michel van Loo and J. Vernet, 1766. (Câmara Municipal de Oeiras, Portugal.)

In part prompted by an economic downturn from the 1750s on, Pombal sought to stimulate Portugal's economy—and to reduce its dependence on Britain—with the creation of a Board of Trade (1755) and the establishment of a number of monopolistic trading companies to carry on the trade with Brazil and to develop the colony's interior (1755), to control the production of port wine production and export (1756), to handle Brazil's sugar exports (1759), to carry on the trade of Mozambique, and to oversee and reactivate the fishing industry of the Algarve (1773).

Reform also affected the educational sphere. A business school (1755) and a college (1761) for the training of young nobles were set up, and the curriculum of Portugal's leading university at Coimbra was modernized (1772), a measure that attracted the interest of reformers abroad. Steps were also taken to make government more effective, including the establishment (1761) of a single central treasury. The army was reformed by the count of Schaumburg-Lippe, one of many foreigners who contributed to Enlightenment and reform in Portugal. Measures were taken to improve the effectiveness of government and Lisbon's control of its colonies, and (in 1774) to improve race relations and racial integration in Portuguese India. In Portugal itself, the prejudice against so-called New Christians, the descendants of Jews and Moors, was outlawed in 1768.

Pombal's fall after the accession of José's more conservative and orthodox daughter, Queen Maria I (1777–1816), meant the abandonment or reversal of some of his reforms. Nevertheless, this was not the end of schemes of enlightened progress. In 1779, the duke of Lafões promoted the foundation of the Royal Academy of Science, whose publication *Memorias Economicas* sought to stimulate agricultural and other improvement. Portugal's foreign trade continued to grow, as did its population. These developments, the continued growth of the press and of a reading public, and the spread of other Enlightenment institutions and values (including Freemasonry, from the 1760s) all contributed—particularly in the wake of the French invasion (1807) and the flight of the royal family to Brazil—to the weakening of Portugal's ancien régime and the spread of new liberal ideas, which played a part in the outbreak of revolution in Portugal in 1820.

[*See also* Pombal, Sebastião José de Carvalho e Mello *and* Spain.]

BIBLIOGRAPHY

Alden, Dauril. *Royal Government in Colonial Brazil, with Special Reference to the Administration of the Marques of Lavradio, Viceroy 1769–79.* Berkeley, 1968. An invaluable study of one key component of the Portuguese polity.

Alden, Dauril. *The Making of an Enterprise: The Society of Jesus in Portugal, Its Empire, and Beyond, 1540–1750.* Stanford, Calif., 1996. A vast general history of Portugal and its empire in the early modern era.

Birmingham, David. *A Concise History of Portugal.* Cambridge, 1993. Useful, if brief and very general.

Boxer, Charles. *The Portuguese Seaborne Empire, 1415–1825.* London, 1969. Useful both for Portugal and for the overseas dimension.

Ferreira Carrato, J. "The Enlightenment in Portugal and the Educational Reforms of the Marquis of Pombal." In *Studies on Voltaire and the Eighteenth Century*, vol. 167, *Facets of Education in the Eighteenth Century*, edited by J. A. Leith, pp. 359–393. Oxford, 1977. A useful study of a specific aspect of reform.

Fisher, H. E. S. *The Portugal Trade.* London, 1971. Good study of a key dimension, trade with Britain.

França, Jose-Augusto. *Une ville des lumières: La Lisbonne de Pombal.* Paris, 1965. Invaluable study of a key aspect of Pombal's achievement.

Godinho, Magalhaes. "Portugal and Her Empire, 1680–1720." In *The New Cambridge Modern History*, vol. 6, *The Rise of Great Britain and Russia 1688–1725*, edited by J. S. Bromley, pp. 509–540. Cambridge, 1971. A useful introduction, by the Portuguese doyen of early modern Portuguese studies.

Hansen, Carl. *Economy and Society in Baroque Portugal 1668–1703.* Minneapolis, 1981. Useful for the seventeenth-century background.

Hespanha, Manuel, ed. *O Antico Regime (1620–1807).* Vol. 4 of *Historia de Portugal*, directed by Jose Mattoso. Lisbon, 1998. An invaluable survey by modern Portuguese scholars, with useful tables and graphs.

Livermore, H. V. *A New History of Portugal.* London, 1966. A good general account.

Maxwell, Kenneth. "Pombal: the Paradox of Enlightenment and Despotism." In *Enlightened Absolutism: Reform and Reformers in Later Eighteenth Century Europe*, edited by Hamish Scott, pp. 75–118. London, 1990. A succinct, insightful survey, by the leading modern English-language authority.

Serrão, Joaquin Verissimo. *Historia de Portugal*, vols. 5 *(1640–1750)* and 6 *(1750–1807).* 2d ed. Lisbon, 1990. Well-founded, up-to-date general survey.

Shaw, L. M. E. *The Anglo-Portuguese Alliance and the English Merchants in Portugal, 1654–1810.* Aldershot, 1998. A useful study of one key aspect.

Venturi, Franco. *The End of the Old Regime in Europe, 1776–1789.* Translated by R. Burr Litchfield. Princeton, N.J., 1991. First published in 1984; deals with a relatively neglected subject in the non-Portuguese literature in the section "Portugal after Pombal."

CHRISTOPHER STORRS

POST, ELISABETH MARIA (1755–1812).

Post was the foremost female representative of sensibility in Dutch letters. When she was twelve, a reversal of fortune forced the family to move to the countryside. This period of penury and agricultural life left an indelible impression on Post's mind and writings.

Her first publication, *Het Land* (The Country, published anonymously in 1788), presents a correspondence between two female soulmates. Emilia, who has lost her fiancé and lives alone in the country, advocates the freedom of nature and its irregularity to her friend Eufrozyne. Nature testifies to God's benevolence and inspires the affections that generate moral and religious reflection, in contrast to the pernicious influence of city life. This novel is also a celebration of refined female feeling, and of tender friendship between women—one of the continuing themes in Post's life and letters. *Het Land* was widely praised and saw three impressions within a year.

Post followed *Het Land* with another epistolary fiction, *Reinhart: of Natuur en Godsdienst* (Pure-of-Heart: or Nature and Religion, three volumes, 1791–1792). This novel relates an episode from the life of a young man who attempts to establish a new life in the colony of Guyana. The text, the first Dutch fictional account of life in the Dutch West Indies, is dedicated to Post's brother Hermannus Hillebertus who had moved there to help his family financially. Although her brother's letters and narratives about Guyana may have provided indispensable factual detail, Post denied that this was a biographical account. The exotic setting offered an enhanced opportunity for the exercise of sensibility and for moralizing reflections on the eternal destiny of human beings and the certainty of the afterlife. The importance of *Reinhart* rests in the insight it provides into eighteenth-century Dutch thinking about slavery. Reinhart's accounts of the native Indians and the African slaves bear traces of his testing of Enlightenment notions of the "noble savage" against actual conditions. Life in the expatriate community puts constraints on Reinhart's ideals of fraternity and benevolence, and with a strong condemnation of the practice of slavery as he finds it, he withdraws from the community. Economic constraint forces him to continue as a slave-owning planter, but he founds a new community in which the slaves live better than the Dutch day laborers.

At the age of thirty-nine, Post fell in love with and married Justus L. Overdorp, eight years her junior, and a pastor in the seaside village of Noordwijk. Her *Gezangen der Liefde* (Songs of Love, 1794) were unusually direct in the candor with which they expressed her love for her husband, and Post was charged with a breach of decorum by the fairly tolerant Vaderlandsche Letter-oefeningen. A woman's public admission of love, however chaste, apparently constituted a transgression of contemporary convention. Post herself had characteristically noted that city-bred women who had "learned to pretend" would strongly disapprove of her freer and more natural stance. Her love of freedom and her autonomy have been compared to that of her friend Betje Wolff-Bekker.

Although well-known during her lifetime, Post's reputation has suffered from neglect. Feminist and colonial studies have contributed to a revival of interest in her work.

[*See also* Colonialism; Deken, Aagje; Men and Women of Letters; Novel; *and* Sensibility.]

BIBLIOGRAPHY

Brandt Corstius, J. C. *Idylle en Realiteit: Het Werk van Elisabeth Maria Post in Verband met de Ontwikkeling van de Europese Literatuur in de Tweede Helft van de Achttiende Eeuw.* Amsterdam, n.d. (1955). Places Post's style and ideas in a European context.

Paasman, A. N. *Elizabeth Maria Post (1755–1812): Een bio-bibliografisch onderzoek.* Amsterdam, 1974. Biographical and bibliographical documentation.

Paasman, A. N. *Reinhart: Nederlandse Literatuur en Slavernij Ten Tijde van de Verlichting.* Dissertation, University of Amsterdam, 1984. First study of *Reinhart* and Dutch colonial practice in the West Indies.

Prinsen J. L.zn., J. "Het Sentimenteele bij Feith, Wolff-Deken en Post." *De Gids* 79 (1915), 512–554. The first critical study of Post's work.

CHRISTINE VAN BOHEEMEN-SAAF

POST-STRUCTURALISM AND POST-MODERNISM.

The terms *post-modernism* and *post-structuralism* refer to schools of thought that have been influential in the humanities since the 1970s. Both schools call into question the claims of religion, philosophy, literature, and science to truth and transcendence. They are also characterized by a historical sense of discontinuity. The prefix *post* indicates that a period of moral and intellectual self-confidence has come to an end, and that a new period of self-doubting has begun. For both post-modernists and post-structuralists, "the Enlightenment" is a point of departure: the Enlightenment is the symbol of the "modern" that post-modernism criticizes as well as of the "structure" that post-structuralism "deconstructs." Both terms, post-modernism and post-structuralism, thus seem to acquire their meaning in binary opposition to a derogatory concept of the Enlightenment. One could say that "the Enlightenment" is to post-modernism and post-structuralism what the ancien régime was to the French Revolution. The Enlightenment is not just that which precedes post-modernism and post-structuralism, but that against which these movements define themselves as a positive new beginning.

Since post-modernism and post-structuralism present themselves as departures from the Enlightenment, critical references to the Enlightenment appear in nearly all the major works by post-modernist and post-structuralist theorists. The Enlightenment is, of course, not the only period these writers analyze. Scholars have energetically applied post-modernist and post-structuralist methods to every phase of European history, as well as to the study of non-European cultures. Yet the Enlightenment is the only historical reference point that is internal to the self-definition of post-modernism and post-structuralism. For this reason, it is important to look at some of the leading theorists of post-modernism and the place of the concept of the Enlightenment in their thought. The main goal of this article is to itemize the principal shortcomings of the Enlightenment as envisioned by post-modernist and post-structuralist thinkers. The discussion will begin, however, with an effort to be more precise about the very meaning of post-modernism and post-structuralism.

Definitions. It is hard to do justice to post-modernism and post-structuralism with brief definitions. A tendency to doubt all claims to truth is a salient feature of post-modernist and post-structuralist thought, but since epistemological skepticism even of the most radical kind has existed since ancient times, the inclination to doubt cannot be regarded as the very definition of these schools.

Definitional complexities also stem from the fact that *post-modernism* and *post-structuralism* are often linked together, like *socialism* and *communism*, to suggest that the terms are interchangeable, or that their meanings are very close. The terms are frequently paired so as to imply that anyone who is a post-modernist is also a post-structuralist, and vice versa; however, *post-modernism* and *post-structuralism* can also be used separately to represent different styles of analysis. Post-modernists are usually interested in institutions and patterns of social and political change; post-structuralists are more interested in the intensive analysis of particular literary and philosophical texts. A post-modernist writing about the Enlightenment is likely to use historical documents to claim that the Enlightenment is connected to colonialism, slavery, or the imprisonment (literal and figurative) of the domestic population. A post-structuralist is more likely to use the techniques of literary criticism to expose the contradictory arguments in a major Enlightenment text. It remains true, however, that post-modernists and post-structuralists are allies in a struggle against what they regard as an excessive confidence in reason that dates back to the Enlightenment. Because the Enlightenment can be studied either diachronically as a social and political movement or synchronically as a canon of texts, both post-modernists and post-structuralists find that the period can be treated in accordance with their distinctive methods. Any definition of these two schools must thus take into account that they have different approaches yet operate in a similar critical spirit and converge on the Enlightenment as a favorite target of reproach.

What is the constructive goal of this criticism? Perhaps the most serious obstacle to formulating a definition of post-modernism and post-structuralism is that the thinkers affiliated with these schools are more explicit about what they oppose than about what they support. The two movements are generally perceived as being on the left of the political spectrum, yet their thinkers do not theorize systematically about the kind of authority that they approve of, or the kind of society that they believe human beings should be working together to achieve. The preoccupation of post-modernists and post-structuralists with criticizing Western rationalism and ideals of progress has given them few options to fall back on for the definition of a positive program. In fact, before the rise of post-modernism and post-structuralism, the Left usually presupposed the power of reason to formulate blueprints for the reorganization of society. Marxism, for example, is a social science. The paradox is that post-modernists and post-structuralists have appropriated the anti-scientism that was characteristic of conservatism earlier in the twentieth century. As a result, it is difficult to connect post-modernism and post-structuralism to traditional leftist politics. One trenchant critic, Gerald Graff, has even suggested that post-modernists like to present themselves as social critics but are really purveyors of the relativistic spirit typical of capitalist ideology. According to Graff, post-modernism strikes against old intellectual standards while negating the possibility of institutionalizing new objective norms. It makes culture entirely a matter of individual interests and preferences—and this, Graff claims, is nothing other than the commercial attitude that capitalism supports.

Graff may have gone too far, but it is true that the definitions of post-modernism and post-structuralism given by post-modernist and post-structuralist thinkers themselves revolve more around negations than constructive ideals. "I define *postmodern* as incredulity toward metanarratives," wrote Jean-François Lyotard in *La condition postmoderne* (1979; Eng. tr., *The Postmodern Condition*). According to Lyotard, the two dominant metanarratives since the Enlightenment are the myth of the progressive liberation of humanity and the myth of the progressive increase of knowledge. Post-modernism, as he defines it, challenges the belief that freedom and science develop in a linear way. Post-modernism, however, does not clearly stand for a new mode of progressive action.

Research on the history of the word *post-modern* (for example, by Köhler and by Meier) shows that Arnold Toynbee, the English historian of comparative civilizations, employed it in the late 1940s to refer to the process of globalization that began in the late nineteenth century. For Toynbee, *modernity* referred to the formation of nation-states; *post-modernity* referred to the emergence of economic networks that made the world a place in which the nation was no longer the primary unity of affiliation for the individual. In the 1950s, American literary critics such as Irving Howe and Harry Levin used the term quite differently to describe postwar literature (such as the writings of John Updike and Thomas Pynchon) which they regarded as unduly informal and exhibitionist. They saw this new literature as lacking the courage and discipline of the modernists, exemplified by T. S. Eliot, James Joyce, and Ezra Pound.

These early usages suggest that the concept of the post-modern was originally a tool for reevaluating the way that Western history and thought is conventionally periodized in academic discourse. Throughout the nineteenth and early twentieth centuries, scholars had described the fifteenth and sixteenth centuries—the Renaissance and Reformation—as the beginning of modern individualism. They described the eighteenth century (the Enlightenment, the French Revolution of 1789, and the start of the Industrial Revolution in England) as the source of modern empiricism, egalitarianism, and prosperity. Finally, they described the early nineteenth century and Romanticism as the beginning of modern literature, with Eliot, W. B. Yeats, and Pound somehow representing the modernist variant of modernity. By the mid-twentieth century, this three- or four-tiered chronology of the modern was cumbersome, and it must have struck scholars like Toynbee, Howe, and Levin as out of touch with the most recent developments. To describe the postwar situation as yet another transition to the "modern" world probably struck these scholars as redundant and obscure. It therefore became convenient to refer to the latest round of perceived changes as "post-modern." It could thus be argued that post-modernism was, in the beginning, nothing more than a fascination with how to conceptualize recent change—an effort to dramatize the most important differences between past and present. This preoccupation with how to define the present in historical terms has remained a key feature of postmodernism.

There is, however, an important difference between the early usages of the term *post-modern* and the usages that have become popular since the late 1960s. Neither the historian Toynbee nor the literary scholars Howe and Levin set out to denigrate the modernity that came before post-modernity, nor do their ideas about the post-modern contain the assault on the Enlightenment and its legacy that is integral to post-modernism and post-structuralism today. It was in the late 1960s and early 1970s that literary critics in the United States, such as Leslie Fiedler, Ihab Hassan, and William Spanos, reversed the positions of Howe and Levin by praising the discontinuity between past and present and by affirming that postwar culture should not be judged by classic literary standards because those standards were outdated. It is unlikely, however, that this variant of post-modernism, which tended to denigrate the past, would have become as influential as it did were it not for the added force of the great French theorists Jean-François Lyotard, Jacques Derrida, and Michel Foucault. The French brought a deeper epistemological perspective, greater historical breadth, and a more intense style of writing to their criticism. It was also the French who made the Enlightenment a key reference point in postmodernist theory.

Why the French? France has been profoundly shaped by eighteenth-century conceptions of reason and nationality—conceptions that owe much to the Enlightenment but also reflect the country's even older Roman Catholic and absolutist traditions. The French political system is republican, grounded in the sovereignty of the people, yet it is the centralized state that speaks for the people. Local government is strictly subordinate to national government. Free enterprise and expression are more limited than in the United States, and the right to sue the government or to challenge laws through judicial review is more circumscribed. The French educational system is also highly centralized and hierarchical. It is no wonder, then, that France has produced many of the most acute analysts of the paradoxical relationships between the myths of freedom and the realities of power in democratic regimes.

There is more. French self-criticism, though explicable as a product of France's distinctive institutions, often assumes the form of an analysis of the entire Western world, not merely of France. Foucault's *Surveiller et punir: Naissance de la prison* (1975; Eng. tr., *Discipline and Punish: The Birth of the Prison*, 1977), for example, reads as an analysis of authority and repression in the West since the eighteenth century, even though most of the examples are French. This francocentric universalism is attributable to the fact that French intellectuals, even when revolting against their *patrie*, tend to go along with one of the old assumptions of French republican thought: that French history is equivalent to world history. Thus, even though much of the best post-modernist and post-structuralist thought is French in its genesis, it is not merely French in its reference. This helps to explain why recent French theory is easily transportable to other countries and has been received there with great interest. Yet the question remains as to why such criticism has found its warmest reception in the United States, a country that was, like France, founded in the eighteenth century, but that was not founded on the same state-centered conceptions of citizenship and rationality.

The answer may have something to do with what the historian Richard Hofstadter, in *Anti-Intellectualism in American Life* (1962), described as a tradition of "contempt for the past." In America, the ideal of democracy does not imply participation in a common high culture; it is connected instead to an image of individual independence and self-reliance. Americans have typically rejected the idea that the American soul, in order to be complete, requires an infusion of ideas borrowed from the past or from a foreign country. Post-modernism and post-structuralism, with their critique of European institutions and the canon of great books, appeal to this ingrained American attitude of cultural defiance. Simultaneously, they appeal to the need among students and professors for a special language, or jargon, that confers academic prestige on the knower. Thus, by confirming populism with an elite academic discourse, post-modernism and post-structuralism respond to two needs at once.

Debate continues as to the historical significance of post-modernism and post-structuralism; moreover, one should not confuse explanations for the popularity of these schools with explications of the best thinking within them. Criticism of post-modernism and post-structuralism cannot be effective if it considers merely the external reasons for their popularity. With this point in mind, we can look more closely at their approach to the concept of the Enlightenment.

Post-structuralism and the Enlightenment. Beginning in the 1950s, several academic disciplines in France developed the method known as structuralism. The movement was inspired by the linguistic theory of Ferdinand de Saussure, and its leading spokesman was the anthropologist Claude Lévi-Strauss. Saussure had argued that the meaning of a word or, more generally, a "signifier," is determined not by the intentions of the individual but by the signifier's binary relation to some other signifier within the language as a whole. Lévi-Strauss's cultural anthropology was a prime example of the application of Saussure's conception of language to the social sciences. He defined kinship relationships and myths as systems of representations, or, more precisely, as sets of sharply distinguished and complementary concepts, such as living/nonliving, male/female, raw/cooked, sun/moon, and so on.

Lévi-Strauss and other structuralists claimed that the system of signifiers is exhaustive. The dichotomies, in other words, effectively divide the world and cover all the phenomena that the group confronts in its daily life. In *De la grammatologie* (1967; Eng. tr., *Of Grammatology*, 1976), Derrida brilliantly challenged this supposition. He advocated the method of "deconstruction"—the process of showing, through close textual analysis, how definitions of fundamental concepts are undermined by the very effort to employ them. Deconstruction begins with the assumption that there is internal incoherence in even the most logical systems of thought. The role of the scholar is to show how a system of thought breaks down: how the key terms change their meaning in different situations, or how the system conceals those phenomena that its dichotomies cannot classify.

Derrida aimed his analysis directly at a conceptual distinction that was important in Lévi-Strauss's thought, the distinction between oral and text-based cultures, or between speech and writing. Lévi-Strauss, at least in Derrida's reading of him, naively saw speech as primitive and writing as modern, speech as natural and innocent and writing as artificial and alienating. Derrida's point was that all discourse is inherently problematic in its relationship to reality. Even primitive man is limited by language and has no direct route through the signifier to nature itself. More broadly, Derrida wished to emphasize that any effort to idealize one mode of language (whether primitive speech or formal logic) by condemning another mode of language constitutes a false dichotomy.

The concept of the Enlightenment enters into Derrida's work by way of Rousseau. Derrida noted that Lévi-Strauss admired and often quoted Rousseau—the Rousseau who had passionately defended nature against convention. Derrida's devastating analysis of Rousseau's thought on the degeneration of human language from a natural to an artificial condition, an analysis that takes up many pages in *Of Grammatology*, was one of his strategies for undermining Lévi-Strauss's tremendous authority in France. The emphasis on Rousseau also made it possible for Derrida to suggest that a long intellectual tradition, not just Lévi-Strauss's thought, was at stake. Derrida's polemic against one anthropologist thus became a critique of what he called, in his preface, the "age" of Rousseau. Elsewhere in the book, he refers to the eighteenth century as a period in which European thinkers became more aware than ever before of the contradictions that afflict language. He also claims, however, that the Enlightenment as a whole was a "reaction" against this awareness—an effort to explain away epistemological difficulties and to idealize the higher potential of human language. In yet other parts of the book, Derrida portrays this cult of language, which he calls "logocentrism," as if it were endemic in Western philosophy not just since the eighteenth century but from the beginning, since Plato. At other times, he appears to regard European philosophy from Leibniz to Hegel as the special period in which logocentrism became dominant.

Derrida's intensive analysis of Lévi-Strauss and Rousseau is thus accompanied by different frameworks of periodization, and so one cannot be sure of what he means by the "age" of Rousseau. In spite of this ambiguity, Derrida's suggestion that Rousseau was a typical thinker of the eighteenth century, and his claim that structuralism and its problems are a legacy of the "age" of Rousseau, threw the status of the Enlightenment radically into question. It also contributed to the tendency among Derrida's admirers to presume that the Enlightenment attitude toward knowledge and language was the opposite of their own critical attitude. One can see this in Paul de Man, who, like Derrida, treated Rousseau's linguistic theory as if it were a representative sample of Enlightenment epistemology. In *Allegories of Reading* (1979), de Man argues that Rousseau, and with him the entire Enlightenment, idealized the way in which individuals in the state of nature created concepts. He claims that Rousseau repressed the problem of the inherent discord between the universality of concepts and the diversity of reality. Since de Man pays special attention to Rousseau's discussion of how the concept of "man" arose in the state of nature, he implies that the Enlightenment idea of man led to the imposition of a false homogeneity on the vital differences among human beings.

Postmodernism and the Enlightenment. De Man's claim that Enlightenment texts affirm universality and negate diversity is a common theme not only of post-structuralists but also of post-modernists. Post-modernists, however, are particularly interested in how the Enlightenment authorized political and social institutions that were repressive and discriminatory in nature. In *Madness and Civilization: A History of Insanity in the Age of Reason* (1961), Michel Foucault argues that, in the seventeenth and eighteenth centuries, the concept of "madness" was opposed to the concept of "reason." This opposition made it possible to denigrate and incarcerate the insane. Foucault suggests that previously madness had been treated not as the absence of reason, but as an especially intense manifestation of spiritual understanding. In this way, he argues that the growth of modern rationalism displaced a more sensitive understanding of the fine line between insanity and reason and simultaneously created an unnecessary category of social exclusion. His argument in *Discipline and Punish* is similar: here, he claims that reformers in the eighteenth century, usually hailed as progressive and humanitarian, were more interested in social control than in justice. According to Foucault, the prison was one instance of a new kind of surveillance, not limited to criminality but implemented in schools and factories as well. While previous systems of discipline were corporal and based on terror, the new system was designed to affect the soul through the minute organization and supervision of daily life. The prison, school, and factory integrated individuals into highly structured routines and sought to produce a "docile" population.

It could well be argued that Foucault, who died in 1984, was the greatest post-modernist thinker. His methodological writings stress the need to appreciate radical discontinuity in history; and his thought as a whole constitutes a powerful critique of all notions of linear development derived from Hegel or Marx. Foucault was also the post-modernist thinker with the most profound understanding of institutions and ideas in the seventeenth and eighteenth centuries. His work never fails to be provocative, and it is essential reading for anyone interested in debates about the influence of the Enlightenment on modernity.

Yet there is also a curious gap in Foucault's scholarship. References to Rousseau, Voltaire, Montesquieu, Hume, Smith, and other thinkers traditionally regarded as central in the Enlightenment rarely occur in his works. He wrote nothing about the American and French revolutions. Readers of Foucault invariably sense that his thought is an indictment of the Enlightenment and its legacy. Yet he carries out this indictment not by refuting Ernst Cassirer's interpretation of Kant as a defender of individual autonomy (*Kants Leben und Lehre*, 1918; Eng. tr., *Kant's Life and Thought*, 1981), or Peter Gay's interpretation of Voltaire as a champion of minority rights (*Voltaire's Politics*, 1959), or Robert Palmer's account of the late eighteenth century as a breakthrough into democracy in several countries (*The Age of the Democratic Revolution*, 1959, 1964); instead, Foucault takes an entirely different perspective on the period, from which the standard reference points in eighteenth-century history no longer appear to be important. Foucault's method gives priority to the growth of new institutions of repression and to the ideas that underpinned these institutions. Occasionally he is able to work an Enlightenment thinker into his analysis of the ideologies of repression. *Discipline and Punish* contains some references to Cesare Beccaria, for example. Usually, however, he merely leaves it implicit that fuller analysis of Enlightenment thinkers would show that their ideas were vectors of exclusion and discipline.

The Foucauldian style of writing about something that is not the Enlightenment and implicitly criticizing the Enlightenment in the process has had a profound effect on scholarship. It has helped to engender a style of academic writing characterized by oblique reference to the Enlightenment. Post-modernist scholars often write about colonialism, racism, and other forms of chauvinism in modern Europe while referring to "the Enlightenment project" as a basic cause of these practices. The analysis of inequalities in such works is often perceptive, but the discussion of the Enlightenment is usually formulaic. Far from being intended to launch a serious discussion of eighteenth-century thought, such references to the Enlightenment are generally meant only to suggest that colonialism, racism, and other forms of prejudice are not exceptions to the democratic and scientific traditions in the West but rather are built into these traditions. Reference to the Enlightenment is thus a shorthand way of saying that progress and disaster are different sides of the same coin.

Post-modernists often take it for granted that Enlightenment thought amounts to the principle that reason can bring man in harmony with nature and thereby end all suffering. Some post-modernists regard this rationalism as historically important because it led Western thinkers to forget about the importance of myth and emotion in human life. These post-modernists argue that the effort to make culture entirely scientific in the long run led to the most irrational society that ever existed: the exploitative and alienating society of modern capitalism. This long-term process by which the Enlightenment unintentionally destroyed wisdom and community in the name of abstract knowledge is known as "the dialectic of Enlightenment," a term borrowed from the title of a 1947 book by Max Horkheimer and Theodor Adorno. (Horkheimer and Adorno themselves were more Marxist than post-modernist, but their book has provided post-modernism with some of its clichés about the Enlightenment.)

Other post-modernists see the evils of rationalism not as an unintended consequence of the Enlightenment but as a deliberate goal of it. In this case, the implication is that the philosophers of the Enlightenment intentionally set out to subjugate women and minorities and disguised their hegemonic pursuits with theories about "reason" and "nature." At least one of these two attitudes toward the Enlightenment (the Enlightenment as pernicious dialectic, and the Enlightenment as pernicious design) lies behind every reference to the Enlightenment in post-modernist thought, at least until very recently.

Scholars with both a strong interest in theory and a strong appreciation of the Enlightenment are in the process of reevaluating these biases. It has long been clear to specialists of eighteenth-century thought that many Enlightenment thinkers were not naive optimists and did not propagate a cult of abstract reason. The Enlightenment, as Ernst Cassirer showed so well in *The Philosophy of the Enlightenment* (1932), was largely a reaction against the systematic and deductive method of seventeenth-century philosophers such as Descartes and Leibniz. The greatest epistemologists of the Enlightenment, Hume and Kant, emphasized self-criticism and the limits of reason. The fact that much of Enlightenment thought assumes the form of stories and dialogues rather than abstract treatises also suggests that the thinkers of the period saw themselves as living in an age of post-rationalism. These realizations are leading scholars to reconsider the relationship between post-modernism and the Enlightenment. The Enlightenment, far from being the antithesis of post-modernism, may actually be one of its sources.

Whether this revisionism will end up producing a more refined version of post-modernism or a rejection of it remains to be seen. It will depend, no doubt, on how flexible the staunchest advocates of post-modernism are with respect to their historical assumptions. If post-modernism cannot exist, cannot constitute itself as a concept, without referring to the Enlightenment as its opposite, then it is destined to be outlived (one could even say deconstructed) by sound scholarship on the Enlightenment. But if post-modernists can accept it as a historical fact that the Enlightenment was not simply a matter of rationalism and sinister discipline, then they may gain strength by presenting their own school as a kind of neo-Enlightenment. Just as Voltaire railed against Pangloss, post-modernists can continue to challenge those who idealize democracy and capitalism; but to play the role of critics, they will have to know where criticism comes from. To be a pioneer, one must be an heir. It appears that the Enlightenment is the inheritance that post-modernists must accept if they wish to sustain their revolt against the present.

[*See also* Enlightenment Studies *and* Foucault, Michel.]

BIBLIOGRAPHY

POST-MODERNIST AND POST-STRUCTURALIST WORKS

De Man, Paul. *Allegories of Reading.* New Haven, Conn., 1979.

Derrida, Jacques. *Of Grammatology.* Baltimore, 1974.

Docherty, Thomas, ed. *Postmodernism: A Reader.* New York, 1993.

Foucault, Michel. *Discipline and Punish: The Birth of the Prison.* New York, 1977.

Foucault, Michel. *Madness and Civilization: A History of Insanity in the Age of Reason.* New York, 1965.

Lyotard, Jean-François. *The Postmodern Condition: A Report on Knowledge.* Minneapolis, 1984.

HISTORY OF THE CONCEPT

Köhler, Michael. "'Postmodernismus': Ein begriffsgeschichtlicher Überblick." *Amerikastudien* 22 (1977), 8–18.

Meier, S. "Postmoderne." In *Historisches Wörterbuch der Philosophie*, vol. 7, 1142–1145. Basel, 1990.

CRITICISM AND REEVALUATION

Gordon, Daniel, ed. *Postmodernism and the French Enlightenment.* New York, 2000. Most of the essays in this volume were published before in *Historical Reflections* 25, no. 2 (1999), with the same editor and title.

Graff, Gerald. "The Myth of the Postmodernist Breakthrough." *TriQuarterly* 26 (Winter 1973), 383–417.

Schmidt, James, ed. *What Is Enlightenment?: Eighteenth-Century Answers and Twentieth-Century Questions.* Berkeley, 1996. Contains readings from the German Enlightenment and extracts from recent German thinkers for and against the Enlightenment. Several of the readings raise the question of post-modernism's relationship to the Enlightenment.

DANIEL GORDON

POULLAIN DE LA BARRE, FRANÇOIS (1647–1723), French clergyman and philosopher.

While a student of theology at the Sorbonne, the University of Paris, Poullain adopted the new philosophy of the seventeenth-century French philosopher and scientist René Descartes (1596–1650); consequently, he discontinued his religious studies. A priest for eight years, he repudiated his vows, converted to Protestantism, and in 1688 fled to Geneva. (There, he married in 1690.) Poullain abandoned Scholasticism after attending a Cartesian lecture on the body. As a result, he reopened the century-long debate on woman's inferiority to men. The Scholastic theory of gender inequality was grounded in the circum-Mediterranean viewpoint of both Aristotle's philosophy and a literal, ahistorical interpretation of the Bible. The Aristotelian concept of matter, as compounded of four elements and four qualities, was used to explain the superiority of a man's temperament (hot and dry, like fire and air) and the inferiority of a woman's (cold and humid, like earth and water). Poullain undermined the scientific basis of the proponents of gender inequality by using the new Cartesian theory of nonqualitative matter. The religious arguments concerning the Book of Genesis and Eve's creation from Adam's rib, or from earth after Adam's creation, established women's nature as secondary to men's. Poullain questioned the authority of the common reading of scriptures by approaching the Bible rationally and sociologically. His truly radical thought can be explained from this double philosophical and religious shift.

Poullain further asserted the equality of races and classes, based on his rejection of the qualities within Aristotelian physics. Poullain's uncompromising acceptance of Descartes's *Discours de la méthode* (Discourse on Method, 1637), the first sentence of which states that *bon sens* ("good sense") is equally shared by all humankind, led him to conclude that "the mind does not have any gender" (or race, or class).

Poullain's rationalism was the key to his attitude toward the limitations of biblical authority. He refused to oppose scientific theory (based on experimental data and deductive analysis) and religious doctrine (grounded in given texts) but tried to reconcile them through a historical point of view, like the philosophers Thomas Hobbes (1588–1679) and Baruch de Spinoza (1632–1677). Poullain wrote three works on women—*De l'éducation des dames* (On the Education of Women, 1674); *De l'égalité des deux sexes* (On the Equality of the Two Genders, 1673); and *De l'excellence des hommes* (On the Excellence of Men, 1675). The end of the 1675 book contains a clear synthesis of the most radical biblical exegesis of his time. Also, views of his on natural law were more radical than those of his contemporaries; he approached it from a truly "common," that is, a nonelitist, point of view.

Poullain had the courage to carry the egalitarian premises of the Cartesian philosophy to their ultimate conclusion. The question of gender inequality, integrated into Poullain's complete subversion of "received ideas" (*idées recues*), functions both as an example of and as a metaphor for all inequalities—whether justified materially or religiously. His work constitutes the most coherent and daring synthesis of all the components of the new philosophy.

[*See also* Cartesianism.]

BIBLIOGRAPHY

WORKS BY POULLAIN
Poullain de la Barre, François. *The Woman as Good as the Man, or the Equality of Both Sexes.* Translated by A. L. London, 1688. English translation of *De l'egalité des deux sexes, Discours physique et moral.* Paris, 1673. The French version has been re-edited in Paris, 1984; the 1688 English translation in Detroit, 1988, with an introduction by Gerald M. MacLean. Another edition in English (with the French version on the facing page), entitled *The Equality of the Two Sexes*, has been translated, with a new introduction, by A. Daniel Frankforter and Paul J. Morman. Lewiston, N.Y., Lampeter, Wales, and Queenston, Ont., 1989.

Poullain de la Barre, François. *De l'éducation des dames pour la conduite de l'esprit dans les sciences et dans les mœurs. Entretiens.* Paris, 1674. Offset re-edition, with an introduction by Bernard Magné. Toulouse, 1980.

WORKS ABOUT POULLAIN
Alcover, Madeleine. *Poullain de la Barre: Une aventure philosophique.* Paris, Seattle, and Tübingen, 1981. First published monograph on Poullain, with a chapter on biography (completing Stock's 1961 Ph.D. dissertation), an updated bibliography, and a chapter devoted to the various editions, including the counterfeited. Extended discussion on Poullain's philosophical and religious ideas.
Stock, Marie Louise. "Poullain de la Barre: A Seventeenth-Century Feminist." Ph.D. diss., Columbia University, 1961. A pioneer work; first documented biography, with an excellent bibliography.
Stuurman, Siep. "Social Cartesianism: François Poulain de la Barre and the Origins of the Enlightenment." In *Journal of the History of Ideas* 58.4 (October 1997), 617–640. Interesting overview, with an updated bibliography and some new elements on the feminist debate in Poullain's time.

MADELEINE ALCOVER

POVERTY. The problem of poverty was visible and endemic in eighteenth-century Europe. In the cities, rich and poor were not as segregated as they are today. The prosperous might live on the lower floors of an apartment house, and the impoverished up under the eaves. Rich and poor rubbed shoulders constantly. In the countryside, almost everyone lived in fear of hunger, and only a few large-scale landowners and nobles escaped the threat of famine. Beggars were everywhere—outside churches, on the highways, in city streets, and near crossroads and bridges. Every parish had a poor widow, disabled worker, or orphan dependent on charity. The elite encountered a beggar or starving child every day.

Just how many destitute there were is hard to determine. Both contemporary estimates and historical analyses vary considerably. According to the Gregory King census, there were 30,000 vagabonds and 400,000 destitute families in England in 1688. In 1791, approximately 6 percent of the villagers in Burgundy were deemed too poor to pay taxes. Easier to weigh is urban poverty, for which we have relief rolls and hospital archives. In 1768 in Milan, vagabonds, beggars, and the unemployed accounted for 2,500 persons out of a total population of 125,000. In Angers, France, 10 percent of the population depended on municipal and church relief. Whether in Florence, Lyon, or Norwich, between 4 and 8 percent of the inhabitants had to depend on charity or municipal assistance to survive.

Contemporaries divided the poor into the deserving (primarily widows, orphans, and the aged) and the undeserving (vagrants, or so-called sturdy beggars). Historians divide the poor into the "conjunctural" and the "structural" poor. The conjunctural poor were individuals who occasionally fell on hard times and found themselves dependent on municipal relief. In Valladolid, Spain, this group included porters, water-carriers, and day laborers; in Mainz, porters, manual laborers, washerwomen, and seamstresses. In normal times, these individuals could feed themselves and their families, but their position was precarious. Chronically underemployed, they had no savings or reserves to tide them over, so when bad times occurred, they succumbed. High grain prices, rather than unemployment or layoffs, were the problem. Seventy percent of an urban worker's budget went to food, so a rise in bread prices could be disastrous. Subsistence crises or the combination of bad weather and high grain prices still occasionally rocked the European economy, especially in 1708–1709 and 1788–1789. Between 1795 and 1803, British harvests failed and destitution was widespread, aggravated by the Napoleonic Wars.

Alongside the occasional poor were the structural poor, or the chronically destitute. These individuals suffered not from occasional misfortune but from permanent ongoing disabilities of old age, injury, or illness. Anyone without a family was at risk, and the aged were likely to find themselves in that situation. So were widows, who constituted almost half of the individuals assisted in one Burgundian parish. Injury or debilitating disease could reduce even skilled craftsmen to the dole. Accidents in the workplace were not uncommon, and the poor hygiene of the period encouraged debilitating diseases. Also vulnerable were the very young. Child abandonment was common during the period. In 1772, the Paris Hospital-General admitted 7,676 infants, most of whom were quickly sent to wet-nurses in the surrounding countryside. Though the mortality rate was very high, these infants absorbed a substantial part of the hospital's budget, and the proportion increased as the century wore on. By 1790, the very old, the very young, the sick, and the disabled constituted the majority of individuals in French workhouses and on English parish relief rolls.

Poor Relief Measures. The institutions designed to cope with poverty had been born long before the Enlightenment, many in the sixteenth and seventeenth centuries. In the early 1500s, municipalities throughout Europe responded to poor harvests and an increase in the number of poor by abandoning medieval casual almsgiving in favor of more rational, selective means of relief. In England, bad harvests, urbanization, and the spread of husbandry increased vagrancy, causing the authorities to fear social unrest. The result was the so-called Elizabethan poor law, specifically the laws of 1531 and 1536 that made a parish responsible for its own poor folk. In 1589 and 1601, additional statutes established a tax—the parish rate—to provide funds for the parish. The Act of Settlement in 1660 established criteria for distinguishing between resident paupers and those whom a parish could expel. Parish overseers collected the poor rates and disbursed aid to impoverished families in both money and kind.

In the seventeenth century, beggars and vagrants were the target of most poor relief efforts. Punitive measures increased, and many European cities decided to imprison or confine beggars in workhouses. Michel Foucault has dubbed this movement "the great confinement" and has underscored the hodgepodge of individuals—the sick, the disabled, the insane, and the unemployed—who were thrown together in the new workhouses. Variously

Feeding the Hungry. Sisters of Charity distribute soup to the poor. Lithograph by C. de Last. (Bibliothèque Nationale de France, Paris.)

called workhouses, *spinhuis* or *Rasphuis* (Netherlands), *Tuchthuys* (Flanders), or hospitals-general (France), these large institutions sprang up all over northern Europe. By the late sixteenth century, Amsterdam had a workhouse, and similar institutions appeared in Brussels (1621), Paris (1656), Lübeck, Gdansk, Leipzig, and Vienna, and in almost all French cities of more than 20,000. Workhouses appeared later in Sweden (1724), Savoy (1717), and England (Bristol, 1796; Plymouth 1708; Norwich 1712). Among European countries, only Spain and Scotland failed to adopt the workhouse model. In Scotland, the Scottish church did not try to abolish begging; it preferred to regulate it by allowing certain licensed beggars, known as "blue cloaks" because of their distinctive dress, to solicit alms.

For most Europeans, the workhouse was primarily a place of labor, discipline, and religious instruction. All seventeenth-century Europeans regarded laziness as the cause of beggary and prescribed unremitting labor as an antidote. That many of the individuals eventually incarcerated were too old or injured to labor productively was of little concern. "The poor must be made to work as long and as hard as their strength and their place of detention permits," instructed the rules of the Paris Hospital-General. That the inmates' spinning or rope-making produced funds was largely beside the point. Work was not meant to be productive, but instructive: it inculcated discipline and therefore diminished the laziness and vice attributed to the poor.

The initiative in the movement to confine the poor came from several sources, but first from centralized authority. In France, a royal edict of 12 June 1663 called for the creation of hospitals-general or workhouses in every French town. In Savoy, Victor-Amadeus II issued a similar edict in 1717. Municipal governments too called for the confinement of the poor and provided the funds for workhouse construction or maintenance. Religious groups, however, proved the most zealous. In France, a secret ultra-devout confraternity, the Company of the Holy Sacrament, agitated for the incarceration of the "immoral"—madmen, beggars, prostitutes, and vagrants. In the past, historians identified workhouses and poor law reform with Protestantism, and in particular with Calvinism, but recent writers have argued that the two reforms, Protestant and Catholic, were more alike than different when it came to social welfare. The workhouse was as much a Catholic as a Protestant construction; in 1693, Pope Innocent XII called for the confinement of the beggars of Rome and transformed the Lateran Palace into a vast workhouse where paupers wove, spun, and made shoes.

The confining of the poor was the great innovation of the seventeenth century, but it was far from successful. Officials never succeeded in rounding up all the poor: beggars were too many, and workhouses too few to contain the sturdy poor. The structural poor—old, widowed, mad, or young—remained to be assisted or disciplined, or both. Alongside the workhouse, therefore, Catholics and Protestants donated money for the creation of orphanages, parish foundations, and maternity wards. Charity schools were particularly popular. In Italy, primary schools receiving children gratis had been in operation since the sixteenth century, and they were further promoted by the Company of Christian Doctrine. In France, "little schools" existed in Paris, Lyon, Rouen, and Reims, and more were created by the Christian Brothers, founded by Jean Baptiste de La Salle. In London, Christ's Hospital provided free primary education, and in Amsterdam, the Laurie-straat House extended basic education to poor orphans. Whether Catholic or Protestant, these institutions had religious goals. At the Christian Brothers' "little schools," religious literature provided the basis for education, and the children learned obedience and self-discipline as well as reading and writing.

The proliferation of charity schools around 1680 indicates that attitudes toward poverty were changing. In the years between 1680 and 1720, prolonged hardship caused by war and bad harvests prompted many French thinkers to criticize Louis XIV. Among the issues addressed were the crown's inability to eliminate begging or relieve poverty. For example, Pierre le Pesant de Boisguilbert (1694–1707) argued that heavy taxes, not laziness, created poverty. In the *Projet d'une dixme royale* (Royal Tithe, 1707), the military engineer Sébestien La Prestre de Vauban (1633–1707) criticized the monarchy's fiscal policy and attributed rural indebtedness to an oppressive and corrupt treasury. Begging and its elimination were the focus of a brief but influential brochure, "On Begging," written in 1724 by Charles Irené Castel, abbé de Saint Pierre (1658–1743). He advocated a central bureau to coordinate poor relief efforts and stipulated that it should be supported by earmarked taxes.

Centralized, state-administered poor relief was to become the rallying cry of poverty-related reforms during the Enlightenment. Another idea that appeared at the turn of the century was the notion that the poor should be investigated and, if possible, counted. In England, Gregory King drew up a census of the poor, the vagrant, and the disabled; the 1690s witnessed investigations of local poor-relief conditions by the Board of Trade. In France, Vauban suggested that beggars be counted and personally undertook such censuses. In 1697, the duke de Beauvilliers collected information on poverty from local officials, the intendants, in the great survey prepared for the heir to the throne, the duke of Burgundy. Additional inquiries into the state of the poor occurred in 1724, 1752–1753, 1764, and 1774. To count the poor came close to admitting they were a social category, not a religious one. Many of the ideas about poverty that emerged during the Enlightenment first materialized in the crucial years between 1680 and 1720.

As a Public Debate. During the mature Enlightenment, however, poverty was not a matter of concern just for officials and churchmen. It became a public issue, debated and written about by other learned people. In France, twenty books or essays on poverty were published between 1760 and 1780; in the 1780s, more than thirty such works were produced. Provincial academies commonly solicited essays on poverty and begging. In 1770, the academy at Chalons-sur-Marne offered a prize for the best essay on "the means of destroying begging in France" and received more than a hundred submissions. Academies in Nimes (1774), Amiens (1779), Besançon, Grenoble, and Metz also offered prizes for essays dealing with some aspect of poverty.

In this public debate, several themes predominated. One was old: the elimination of begging. Like their seventeenth-century predecessors, Enlightenment thinkers considered begging a scourge that could be eliminated only by forced labor, preferably in a prison. In the article "Begging" in the *Encyclopédie*, the chevalier de Jaucourt praised the workhouse and advised that recidivist beggars should be deported to the colonies. The hatred of begging was old, but Enlightenment thinkers did have some new remedies. First, the central government should undertake the punishment of beggars, and in a rational, orderly fashion. France led the way. In 1724, Louis XV banned begging and sentenced all vagrants to incarceration. Vagrancy did not disappear, however, so the king outlawed begging again in 1764. This time, a network of new institutions called *dépôts de mendicité*, or beggars' prisons, was created to receive vagrants arrested on the highways by the rural police. In 1783, there were thirty-three such institutions providing work and rudimentary medical care (especially treatment for venereal disease) to male and female vagrants. Enlightenment figures like Turgot and the Physiocrat Nicolas Baudeau (1730–1792) attacked the *dépôts* and suggested that they be replaced by more effective institutions, but they would persist into the nineteenth century.

Another major theme of Enlightenment thinking was the rejection of seventeenth-century institutions of public relief, especially the French hospitals-general. In the chapter on hospitals in *L'esprit des lois*, Montesquieu observed that pious foundations—the core support for many hospitals—encouraged rather than discouraged begging. Diderot echoed this belief in the entry "Hospital" in volume 8 of the *Encyclopédie*: he wrote that "it would be better to work for the prevention of poverty than multiply these institutions," and he condemned the old workhouses

for mixing the sick and the sound, the deserving and the undeserving poor. Turgot, in the *Encylopédie* entry "Foundations," attacked the hospital legacies and claimed they often did more harm than good by encouraging idleness and dependence. He then proposed that small institutions (*bureaux de charité*) that distributed bread to needy families should replace the old hospitals-general. As intendant in the Limousin and later as controller general, he encouraged the spread of *bureaux de charité*, which by the time of the Revolution existed in most urban parishes.

Having rejected the old-fashioned hospitals, Enlightenment thinkers preferred work—not as an end in itself, but as the only appropriate means of easing want. Here was the second major theme of the Enlightenment: work as a form of relief. In a much-quoted phrase, Montesquieu remarked that "a man is not poor because he lacks money, but because he does not work." In France, this formula received concrete realization in the *ateliers de charité*, or public works projects, promoted by the French monarchy in the second half of the eighteenth century. Established in 1770 in response to a bad harvest, the *ateliers* were of two kinds: one offered men work on roads; the other, known as *ateliers de filature* (spinning workshops), employed women and children in spinning, weaving, lacemaking, and knitting. During his ministry, Turgot expanded the number of *ateliers de charité* so that they existed in almost every province. By 1780, the *ateliers* were not only widespread but permanent; one in Normandy operated continuously from 1770 to 1789.

Reforms. Turgot's reforms embodied the third common theme in Enlightenment thinking about poverty: the conviction that the state bore responsibility for assisting the poor. Montesquieu maintained that "a few alms given to a naked man in the streets does not fulfill the obligations of the State, which owes all its citizens an assured subsistence, nourishment, appropriate clothing and work which does not damage their health." If French thinkers believed that welfare should flow from the state, it was because by 1770 it largely did. Some large urban hospitals-general persisted, but in 1764, rural hospices were abolished or brought under royal supervision. From that time on, Paris exercised authority over the hospitals through a commissioner or inspector general. Meanwhile, most experiments in poverty relief came from Paris, Vienna, or Florence.

In Austria, Joseph II in 1783 undertook a vast program for restructuring and reviving poor relief in Vienna and subsequently in all of Austria and Bohemia. The program was to be financed by the suppression of religious confraternities and the seizure of their endowments. Joseph II planned to create hospitals, maternity homes, and insane asylums, and to establish funds for home relief and public works projects. In 1781, he created the

Armenstitut, common funds for poor relief derived from local taxes.

In Prussia, too, the state undertook to organize poor relief. During the reign of Frederick William I, the first workhouses were erected there. Frederick II created more and established the Berlin workhouse, which could hold as many as a thousand individuals. Work—usually spinning and weaving wool—was the prescribed regime, and a schoolmaster taught orphans and foundlings residing in the hospital. Under the rubric of charity, Frederick II also offered special loans and incentives to paupers willing to colonize Prussian Poland and other rural areas.

In Italy, the rulers of Naples and Tuscany took the initiative in poor relief. In both kingdoms, the confiscated property of the Jesuits was designated for the poor. The king of Naples issued an edict in 1762, the "law of alms," which forced the clergy to earmark one-fifth of church revenues for poor relief. Throughout Mediterranean Europe, the Roman Catholic confraternities that had provided some relief both to members and to the poor were dissolved, and their income was reassigned to the state for distribution to the poor.

The notion that church property really belonged to the poor and should be confiscated on their behalf enjoyed considerable popularity in Catholic Europe. The Spanish philosopher Bernard Ward proposed that a secular national commission be established in Spain to coordinate all charitable endeavors. This commission would confiscate church property and then redistribute it to the poor. Diderot advocated a similar expropriation in his article "Hospital" in the *Encyclopédie*, suggesting that church lands be redistributed by the government to needy hospitals. Gradually, the notion that church lands belonged to the poor took hold, and expropriation was widely discussed on the eve of the Revolution of 1789.

Everywhere, the state advanced into the arena of poor relief—except in England. In neither content nor chronology does the history of English poor relief resemble that of the Continent. The Elizabethan statutes conferring responsibility for its poor on each parish remained in force with only minor amendments and changes until 1834. Localism was the rule, and Parliament stepped in only to regulate how the parish poor were to be defined. In 1660, the Act of Settlement decreed that any pauper resident more than twenty days had to be supported by the parish. Overseers did report their activities to Parliament, but otherwise they were left much to their own devices. At the same time, the workhouses that attracted criticism on the Continent were in high favor among English thinkers. In 1782, Parliament passed Gilbert's Act, which authorized parishes to set up workhouses. In contrast to the Continent, these institutions tended to proliferate, particularly in the industrializing north. But like their continental counterparts, the English workhouses tended to contain women, children, and the sick. Able-bodied males rarely found themselves in the workhouse or on the list of recipients of parish aid.

Although beggars remained the target of government policy, a new focus of concern appeared in the late eighteenth century: the young. Poverty led to the abandonment of children, and the number of foundlings skyrocketed during the century. Children found on public thoroughfares or abandoned outside hospitals were usually sent by hospital administrators to wet-nurses. In the countryside, the mortality rate of these children approached 70 percent. Rousseau suggested that mothers breast-feed their own children as a means of avoiding this terrible mortality. The abbé de Saint Pierre proposed the establishment of a common fund to supplement the income of poor but numerous families, thereby encouraging mothers to breast-feed their children rather than sending them to wet-nurses. In England, foundlings also stirred concern, leading to the creation of the London Foundling Hospital in 1745 by Thomas Coram.

Bienfaisance. Private gestures like Coram's had an important place in Enlightenment thinking about poverty. Personal acts of generosity were much appreciated, particularly in the last third of the century. Enlightenment thinkers did not call such acts charity; they invented a new word, *bienfaisance*. The term first appeared in the dictionary of the Académie Française of 1762, and the abbé de Saint Pierre (according to the entry "Construction" in the *Encyclopédie*) did much to popularize it. Roughly synonymous was another key phrase for Enlightenment thinkers: humanity. It too appeared in the 1760s and was popularized by Baudeau. The *Encyclopédie* defined the new philanthropy as "loving to oblige (others) and to do good." Enlightenment philanthropy differed from the old style of charity in that it was completely secular and gratuitous. No hope of heavenly reward motivated philanthropy; effectiveness—the relief of the material, not spiritual, circumstances of the poor—was its only concern.

Medical Care. This new secular outlook had profound effects on thinking about the poor. Now writers and officials could use the vocabulary and the tools of science to mitigate suffering. Around 1750, medicine and medical men became important in poor relief. The reforms of sanitary conditions in the Paris Hôtel-Dieu, suggested by the philanthropist Claude Humbert Piarron de Chamousset (1717–1773), were widely disseminated and popularized by both Voltaire and Diderot. Official concern for medical care was reflected in the appointment of Dr. Jean Colombier (1736–1789) to the post of inspector general of all France's prisons and workhouses in 1781. Colombier had done much to improve hygiene and medical facilities in Parisian jails and workhouses, and his reforms contributed to one of the important developments of the period: the birth of the hospital as a purely medical institution. Diderot, among others, suggested that the hodgepodge of individuals incarcerated in the hospitals-general be dispersed. Baudeau expressed the same idea in greater detail in *Idées d'un citoyen sur les besoins, les droits, et les devoirs des vrais pauvres* (Ideas of a Citizen on the Needs, Rights and Duties of the Authentic Poor, 1765). He argued that hospitals should treat only the sick, while the disabled, the old, and the orphaned should be taken care of at home. Gradually the work of the seventeenth-century "great confinement" was undone, and the hospital emerged as a true medical institution.

The new scientific view of the poor also led to the application of mathematics, specifically probability, to poverty. The first schemes for social insurance date from the late eighteenth century. Condorcet suggested that special *caisses de prévoyance*, or group savings accounts, be established throughout France that would allow workingmen to pool their resources and save enough money to live on in hard times. Though less sophisticated in construction, the charitable pawnshops (*prêts charitables*) created by royal officials and philanthropic individuals throughout France expressed the same desire not just to succor poverty but to prevent it.

A Different Perspective. The notion that poverty was not just preventable but undesirable can be traced to the Enlightenment. Seventeenth-century mercantilist thinkers had tended to regard want as a necessary evil. Low wages, they argued, were required to make the people work. If they were not hungry, laborers would have no incentive to labor, and production would grind to a halt. Eighteenth-century thinkers rejected this mercantilist notion. The French economists known as the Physiocrats argued against the utility of poverty and believed that prosperity, rather than misery, would lead to greater agricultural production. In the *Encyclopédie* article "Impôt," Jaucourt wrote that "those who argue that the peasant should not live at ease spout a maxim as false as it is contrary to humanity." Gradually a consensus emerged, and Adam Smith dealt the final blow to the argument for the utility of poverty. In the *Wealth of Nations* (1776), Smith rejected the notion that misery made workers productive and posited in its place the idea that higher wages benefited not just the laborer but society as a whole. The worker, Smith pointed out, was better fed and therefore more energetic. He was more content and more likely to reproduce (a growing population constituted an important measure of national welfare for all eighteenth-century thinkers). A happier worker would also be more productive, for he would work harder when he was assured of some benefit.

The Enlightenment did not eliminate poverty; it did not even successfully alleviate it. The political and international turmoil of the years after 1780 put poor relief on hold. At the same time, bad harvests and the disruptions of war aggravated the misery of the poor. Still, by creating a secular, materialistic outlook that sought the causes and remedies for poverty in the worldly realm of politics and economics, the Enlightenment created the conditions by which want might someday be eliminated.

BIBLIOGRAPHY

Adams, Thomas McStay. *Bureaucrats and Beggars: French Social Policy in the Age of the Enlightenment*. New York, 1990.

Fairchilds, Cissie. *Poverty and Charity in Aix-en-Provence, 1640–1789*. Baltimore, 1976.

Foucault, Michel. *Madness and Civilization: A History of Insanity in the Age of Reason*. Translated by Richard Howard. New York, 1965.

Gutton, Jean-Pierre. *La société et les pauvres en Europe (XVIe–XVIIIe siècles)*. Paris, 1974.

Hufton, Olwen. *The Poor in Eighteenth Century France*. Oxford, 1979.

Jones, Colin. *Charity and Bienfaisance: The Treatment of the Poor in the Montpellier Region, 1740–1815*. Cambridge, 1982.

Lindemann, Mary. *Patriots and Paupers: Hamburg, 1712–1830*. Oxford, 1990.

Marshal, Dorothy. *The English Poor in the Eighteenth Century*. London, 1926.

Norberg, Kathryn. *Rich and Poor in Grenoble: 1600–1814*. Berkeley, 1984.

Oxley, Geoffrey. *Poor Relief in England and Wales, 1601–1834*. London, 1974.

Payne, Harry C. *The Philosophes and the People*. New Haven, 1976.

Schwartz, Robert M. *Policing the Poor in Eighteenth-Century France*. Chapel Hill, N.C., 1988.

Webb, Sidney, and Beatrice Webb. *English Local Government: English Poor Law History*, Part 1; *The Old Poor Law*. London, 1927.

KATHRYN NORBERG

PRADES, JEAN-MARTIN DE (1724–1782), controversial French clergyman and onetime collaborator on the *Encyclopédie*.

Born in 1724 in Castelsarrasin, into an old noble family of southwestern France, Prades moved to Paris in 1741, where he received his doctorate in theology with high honors after presenting his thesis, *A la Jérusalem céleste* (To the Heavenly Jerusalem), at the Sorbonne in November 1751. Ordained a priest in 1749, he was nonetheless in contact with Denis Diderot and Jean Le Rond d'Alembert, and he became a contributor to the *Encyclopédie*. The compliments prefacing his article "Certitude" aroused the hostility of both the Jesuits and the Jansenists. Due to pressure from them and from the parlement de Paris, the Faculty of Theology revoked its decision and condemned the thesis that he had recently passed with honors. Taking refuge in the Netherlands to escape imprisonment, Prades wrote his *Apologie*. Voltaire, who was at the time the guest of Frederick II of Prussia (known as "the Great"), obtained for Prades the post of lecturer to the king in

1752. Although rehabilitated by the pope after making a retraction, initially valued by Frederick the Great, and both an archdeacon and academician in Prussia, Prades was nevertheless disgraced and incarcerated during the Seven Years' War (1756–1763). Freed in 1763, he was ordered to reside in Głogau. He died in 1782.

A Catholic cleric in the world of the Enlightenment, Prades chose to involve himself in the great debates of his time. Very early on, he had acquired a solid knowledge of the work of the new physicists and he resolutely embraced an empiricist anthropology and an "experimental metaphysics . . . as a Christian who does not fear for his religion" (*Apologie*).

An adversary of the innate ideas of René Descartes, Prades approved of John Locke's attempt to "examine Man rather than imagine him." However, he remained a dualist by affirming the existence of a mind that "deploys" an "active virtue" over the sensations (*Apologie*), thus prefiguring Immanuel Kant's a priori forms of consciousness.

Against what he saw as Thomas Hobbes's "barbarous law of inequality," he opposed "a right of equality that conformed to reason" (*A la Jérusalem céleste*). He conceded, however, that there were "inequalities" in "formed societies" owing to their being "civilized and political," and preventing a "war of all against all" (*Apologie*).

His religious thought included an "a posteriori demonstration" that employed the discovery of microscopic structures to obviate any explanation of the world by chance. The book of nature, "a revelation as old as the universe," speaks "in intelligible characters" to the "good sense of the mind." From this arises a theism, one that is, however, "insufficient," being without "the most fertile light of revelation" (*A la Jérusalem céleste*) of the Old and New Testaments.

Seen in the past as a Trojan horse of the Enlightenment within the church, Prades seems on the contrary to have been a *clericus in partibus infidelium* (a cleric in unbelieving regions). His "reasoned faith" fits into a long Catholic tradition of well-defined relations between open rationalism and the Christian faith.

[*See also* Encyclopédie; Frederick II; Philosophy; *and* Roman Catholicism.]

BIBLIOGRAPHY

WORKS BY PRADES

Jerusalem coelesti: A la Jérusalem céleste. Paris, 1752. His major thesis. In Latin and French.

Apologie de M. l'abbé de Prades. Amsterdam, 1752 and 1753. Including the thesis itself (in Latin and French), diverse letters about the controversy and condemnation, and the apology in three parts, the third of which is attributed to Diderot.

"Certitude." In *Encyclopédie* of d'Alembert and Diderot, with a preface and postface by Diderot.

Le tombeau de la Sorbonne. Constantinople, 1753. Voltaire gave his manner and tone to Prades's material.

Abrégé de l'histoire ecclésiastique de Fleury. 2 vols. Berne, 1767.

STUDIES ABOUT PRADES

Combes-Malavialle, Jean-François. "Vues nouvelles sur l'abbé de Prades." *Dix-huitième Siècle* 20 (1988), 377–397. Facts, aspects, and unknown documents on his life and character.

Combes-Malavialle, Jean-François. "L'incarcération de l'abbé de Prades à Magdebourg. *Dix-huitième Siècle* 25 (1993), 337–353. New discoveries about a previously unexplained event.

Gazier, A. "L'abbé de Prades, Voltaire et Frédéric II." In *Mélanges de littérature et d'histoire*, pp. 194–208. Paris, 1904.

Gundlach, Wilhelm. *Friedrich der Grosse und sein Vorleser Jean-Martin de Prades. Sammlung gemeinverständlicher Vorträge.* Hamburg, 1892. A very thorough study, but openly anti-French.

Monod, A. *De Pascal à Chateaubriand*. Paris, 1916. Pp. 331–338. This thesis addresses the fundamental theological and philosophical questions.

Noël, Denis. *Une figure énigmatique parmi les encyclopédistes: L'abbé Jean-Martin de Prades*. 2 vols. Strasbourg, 1973. This thesis, containing numerous archival and bibliographical references, is hostile to Prades, and accuses him of duplicity and complicity with the enemies of religion.

Spink, John S. "Un abbé philosophe: L'affaire Jean-Martin de Prades." *Dix-huitième Siècle* 3 (1971), 145–180. The most thoughtful and objective study.

Venturi, Franco. *Jeunesse de Diderot*. Geneva, 1967. Chapter 7, "L'affaire de Prades," pp. 192–236. Thoroughly documented chapter. Venturi believes in the complicity of Prades with the *encyclopédists*, and thus in his duplicity.

JEAN-FRANÇOIS COMBES DE PRADES

Translated from French by Susan Romanosky

PREJUDICE. In current American and English usage, the word "prejudice" denotes an irrational hatred of others based on their differences from oneself. During the Enlightenment, however, this definition was not among the meanings of the term "prejudice," which, outside the legal context, was used primarily in two contrasting senses that reflected opposing views of the roles of reason and the passions in epistemology, ethics, and politics. On the one hand, "prejudice" could denote any preconceived, inherited, or otherwise ill-thought-out opinion that inhibited the progress of knowledge. On the other, it could signify a time-honored and widely accepted or unquestioned assumption or practice that, as Edmund Burke put in his *Reflections on the Revolution in France* (1790), had come, by virtue of its inherent "reasonableness," to constitute a "model . . . and pattern . . . of approved utility" in moral and political life.

In the first sense then, "prejudice" is a source of error. Consider, for example, the following definition by Louis Jaucourt, author of the article "Préjugé" in volume 8 of Denis Diderot and Jean Le Rond d'Alembert's *Encyclopédie* (1765), the signature text of the French Enlightenment. A prejudice, he says, consistently with the literal meaning of Latin *praeiudicium*, is "a false judgment that the mind makes about the nature of things after an insufficient exercise of the intellectual faculties; this unfortunate fruit of ignorance hinders the understanding, blinds and imprisons it." Further, such aberrations of the mind are attributable to the unwarranted influence of the senses, the imagination, and especially the passions, all of which by turns enslave man's reason and in this manner "block forever the paths to truth." Thus, Jaucourt included among his collection of prejudices a whole series of obstacles to knowledge: the preference for errant certainty over productive doubt; the tendency to place slavish trust in general maxims even when they are challenged by the evidence of particular facts; the predisposition to defer to ancient authority, whether in the form of custom or of established philosophical or theological doctrine; uncritical reliance on the senses; the misuse of language; and the invasion of philosophy by theology. All generate faulty reasoning and betray the contamination of the understanding by the imagination and the passions, especially impatience, ambition, pride or false modesty, and self-love.

Whereas Jaucourt's primary concern was epistemological, Edmund Burke's perspective was ethical. He defined prejudices as "inbred sentiments which are the faithful guardians, the active monitors of our duty." In the realm of action, he contended, individual reason can only be impotent when unsupported by prejudice, which represents both the instinctive feelings of love and loyalty on which society depends, and the stock of communal reason that Burke calls "the general bank and capital of nations and of ages." That is because prejudice "is of ready application in the emergency; it previously engages the mind in a steady course of wisdom and virtue, and does not leave the man hesitating in the moment of decision, sceptical, puzzled, and unresolved." For Burke, prejudices—construed as established usages, customs, and habits of thought that embody the legacy of human wisdom and the fellow-feeling that preserves the race, and that enable individuals to translate ethical principles into actions—are indispensable to the moral education of the person and to the political health of any society.

It would be difficult to imagine two interpretations of the same concept more different in themselves and in their larger implications. Like Germaine Necker de Staël, for whom "enlightenment" meant "the ability to judge things on the basis of reason rather than habit," Jaucourt identified prejudice with reaction and made the progress of knowledge dependent on a continuing critique of accepted beliefs and of established institutions and authorities (though he was careful to warn against a mindless preference for innovation for its own sake). This criticism, in his view, ought properly to be an activity of individual minds, each of which wages its own struggle with the prejudices resulting from convention, one's own temperament and habits, or the generic human susceptibility to the passions. For Burke, in contrast, improvements in the moral and political condition of human beings cannot be the product of critique, given that there are "no discoveries... to be made in morality; nor many in the great principles of government, nor in the ideas of liberty." In these contexts, respect for habit and custom should take priority over the spirit of criticism, and the common fund of human wisdom over the activity of the individual reason. Moreover, insofar as Burke identified the prejudices with "inbred sentiments" that direct the mind in moral decision-making, they may be said to instruct reason rather than inhibit its activity. In sum, these opposing conceptions of prejudice reflect radically different anthropologies and epistemologies, and they appear to have radically different consequences for the practice of politics. In the remainder of this essay, we will examine some of the roots of these contrasting attitudes—both secular and religious—and attempt to evaluate their implications for our understanding of "Enlightenment."

In the early seventeenth century, when "new" philosophers sought to rebuild the foundations of reliable knowledge, and Catholic and Protestant controversialists debated their respective claims to truth, a pejorative notion of prejudice, conceived as an inchoate opinion inhibiting human progress towards knowledge or truth, played an important role in philosophical and religious polemic. This was both because it contributed to the urgent enterprise of explaining, and thus of avoiding error, and because it proved an effective means of criticizing opponents, whose arguments could conveniently be mustered as examples of ill-thought-out beliefs. In this climate, Francis Bacon (1561–1626), cited by Jaucourt as "the person who, more than any other, has meditated on the subject of prejudice," constructed a taxonomy of the causes of error that exercised a marked influence on the subsequent practitioners of the new philosophy. In his *Novum Organum* (1620), Bacon delineated the sources of false reasoning under the rubric "idols of the mind." Of these there are four types, all of which reappear as prejudices in Jaucourt's essay. The first, "idols of the tribe," or manifestations of an inherent tendency of the mind to be deceived that is characteristic of all human beings, includes, for example, the predisposition to rely uncritically on the senses, and the inclination to overgeneralize and jump to conclusions. The second, "idols of the cave," encompasses various examples of false judgment deriving from each individual's character and upbringing; the third, "idols of the market place," considered by Bacon "the most troublesome of all," includes those arising from faulty communication with others, from the ambiguity and misuse of language. Bacon's fourth category, the "idols of the theater"—so named because, like the stage, they offer us an illusory representation of the world—catalogs instances of faulty reasoning generated by comprehensive philosophical systems such as Aristotelianism or Platonism that attempt either to remake nature in their own image, or to mislead the understanding through an unwarranted "admixture of theology." During the seventeenth century, it became common practice among "new philosophers" of every stripe to elucidate the causes of error and to criticize the arguments of their opponents in a manner consistent with one or more of Bacon's categories.

Although Bacon's typology facilitated the identification of ill-considered judgments as the principal cause of error, it was René Descartes who, in the context of philosophy, most famously denominated them "prejudices," (*praeiudicia*) and made the process of overcoming them the cornerstone of his philosophical method. Prejudices acquired in childhood, inculcated by established philosophical authority, or generated by an uncritical reliance on the senses and never subjected to scrutiny, he wrote in *Principia philosophiae* (Principles of Philosophy, 1644), are the primary cause of all errors. It is crucial, therefore, for the philosopher who seeks true knowledge to doubt systematically both the evidence of the senses and the pronouncements of tradition and authority, and to pay attention instead "to the notions which we ourselves have in us." In other words, Descartes urged every inquirer after truth to rely on his own stock of reason, or "natural light." Only in this manner can knowledge be set on new and reliable foundations.

Enlighteners like Jaucourt thought of themselves as the heirs of seventeenth-century new philosophy, especially of Bacon and Descartes, at least insofar as these philosophers had made the activity of criticism the business of individual reason and had defined it as essential to the progress of knowledge. In other words, while the eighteenth-century philosophes had come to conceive of reason less as a collection of innate ideas or a body of sound knowledge than as a critical faculty of the mind, they did not just subscribe to the claim of their predecessors that "reason" may examine the claims of authority and tradition to legitimacy and truth. They extended it significantly to include a more thoroughgoing critique of established institutions and habits of thought. In the context of their project of systematic analysis and criticism, the concept of prejudice—employed to excellent polemical effect by the new philosophers in the war against Aristotle—again proved its rhetorical mettle, this time as an essential component of the idiom in which the anti-authoritarian dimension of Enlightenment expressed itself.

The understanding of prejudice so far outlined, however, was also rooted in older habits of thought whose persistence the French enlighteners were less inclined to acknowledge, given their ambivalent attitude toward antiquity and their commitment to an all-encompassing critique of traditional religion. For example, it is impossible to miss the classical and Christian influences at work in Jaucourt's account of how the passions enslave the reason. Here, Jaucourt relied not only on the negative account of the passions elaborated by ancient and early modern Stoicism, but also on a barely secularized Augustinian anthropology to construct his analysis of the natural defects of the understanding and of the passions as sources of prejudice. "Prejudice," he asserted, "is not always a sudden captivity of the judgment that occurs when it is plunged into darkness or seduced by will o' the wisps; it also arises from an unfortunate propensity of the mind to go astray, an inclination that plunges it into error despite its resistance." The effects of this congenital weakness of the mind are abetted by the passions, and especially by self-love, their "prime-mover," whose power to generate "prejudice" prevents the mind from appraising things "with a dry and indifferent eye," halts the understanding in its progress, and confounds its proper activity of judgment. In short, there exists an evident structural similarity between Jaucourt's dramatic conceptualization of the predicament of the mind as it attempts to resist its inherent weaknesses, and the ancient vision of the destructive power of the passions, transmitted to the early Christian world by the Stoics and communicated most effectively to the early modern period in christianized form by the writings of Augustine, who depicted the soul suffering from a taint of original sin that impairs the will's ability to desire the good.

Jaucourt's conception of prejudice as the result of epistemological concupiscence should not surprise us, for it had been characteristic of the new philosophy. For Jaucourt and other representatives of the French Enlightenment, however, the tendency to employ an Augustinian language that cohabited rather uncomfortably with a strident rhetoric of human perfectibility may also have been encouraged by events in French political culture. Throughout the 1750s, intense controversies related to Jansenism (a Catholic heresy whose proponents considered themselves the true followers of Augustine) preoccupied informed opinion and kept theological questions regarding the nature of the human will and its degree of freedom after the Fall before the public eye as objects of constant religious and political contestation. Given the prominence of these issues, as well as the centrality of Augustine in the related Jansenist–Jesuit debates, it is not surprising that a pronounced Augustinian coloring continued to characterize the idiom in which human weaknesses were discussed. Such examples of the persistence of Christian frameworks of thought in secular form are often evident in the writing of the French enlighteners, many of whom were trained in theology at university level and continued to think "with" it, despite their commitment to liberating philosophy from its chains. Consciously or unconsciously, they frequently exploited Christian categories and concepts in constructing new and anti-Christian interpretations of the world and of human experience.

Equally important in understanding the religious roots of the conception of prejudice as a source of error, however, is the legacy bequeathed to the Enlightenment by the interconfessional polemics of the sixteenth and seventeenth centuries. Since the early days of the Reformation, Protestant and Catholic controversialists in France and elsewhere had located the origins of "heresy" in a mindless and stubborn adherence to prejudice or habit; they claimed that this obstinacy was motivated not by reason but by passion, which blinds believers and prevents them from discerning truth. In choosing a religion, both sides argued, it is of the utmost importance to divest oneself of opinions fixed in childhood and to resist the passions that prevent us from examining whether that religion is true. This aspect of Protestant polemic has long been noted, and the Reformation principles of the necessity of examination and the independent interpretation of Scripture have often been ascribed a significant role in generating the broader critique of established institutions and authorities that reached its culmination in the eighteenth century, but equivalent Catholic strategies have not been similarly recognized. A close look at the Catholic controversial literature of the seventeenth century shows, however, that Roman proselytizers, despite their desire to strengthen the foundations of established religious authority, often engaged in polemic in the rationalistic mode, depicting their confessional opponents as ignorant and childish persons in thrall to their prejudices and passions, and urging potential converts to undertake a systematic investigation and independent evaluation of the legitimacy of Roman claims to absolute spiritual authority that depended on a progressive detachment from preconceived opinions. In short, on both sides of the confessional fence, prospective believers were urged to assure themselves of the truth or falsity of a religion—and thus to determine the nature of its authority over the individual—by using their reason to examine whether the proofs in its favor could be dismissed as mere prejudices. The heuristic model proposed here clearly resembles that put forward by Descartes for the search for true knowledge; in each case, the pursuit of truth, whether epistemological or religious, is identified with the activity of examination. By the end of the seventeenth century, then, both the high philosophical tradition and the hurly-burly of religious controversy offered educated publics in France and elsewhere a model of

thinking about established authorities that both reflected a progressive individualization of the sources of epistemological and religious certainty, and, to speak paradoxically, encouraged the habit of critique. By one of the many ironies of history, however, the controversialists may have been more influential in this development; the pamphlet literature of religious polemic probably reached a broader public than did formal philosophical texts, and the debates organized between polemicists of rival confessions came over time to constitute a form of entertainment, attracting increasingly large and passionate audiences who may have acquired the idiom of criticism more readily by oral than by written means.

When we return to Burke's definition of prejudice, we immediately notice a similar intertwining of secular and religious roots and of progressive and traditional elements. Insofar as Burke construes "prejudices" as "inbred sentiments...which monitor our duty," or as instinctive feelings of love and loyalty that strengthen social relations, his thinking appears to reflect two innovative and related features of eighteenth-century moral philosophy before Immanuel Kant: the claim that reason alone is not competent to guide the determinations of the will; and the corresponding rehabilitation of the passions, especially self-love, as powerful forces directing us toward benevolence. In his *Essay Concerning Human Understanding* (1690), John Locke had inaugurated the sensationalist psychology whose implications would preoccupy philosophers and reformers throughout the century and generate these new and distinctly un-Augustinian perspectives on the foundations of morality. He argued that ideas originated either directly in sense impressions, or in reflections of the mind on evidence the senses provided. Moral values arose from sensations of pleasure or pain, with the mind giving the name "good" to what experience showed to be pleasurable. Some moral philosophers of the next two generations boldly embraced the reductive and deterministic consequences of Locke's view, but others sought to avoid the self-interested account of moral behavior that his arguments appeared to entail. They either posited a unique moral faculty or "sense," as did the "sentimentalist" school and the philosophers of the Scottish Enlightenment; or they identified moral ideas, as Burke did, with emotions or "sentiments" that instruct the reason. The most cogent proponent of the latter view, and the closest to Burke in his understanding of the social origins of moral ideas, was David Hume (1711–1776), who contended that custom and habit, rather than reason, are the means whereby the mind orders the world of sense experience. Consistently with the limitations placed on reason by his epistemology, Hume argued in his *Treatise of Human Nature* (1739) that moral thought is the expression of sentiments that evolve because we must cooperate in society if we are to fulfill our natural needs. Taken together, all these lines of thought, including Burke's, depart from traditional conceptions of morality in that they not only insist on the nonrational foundations of moral behavior, but also acknowledge the malleability of human nature implicit in Locke's account.

Recall, however, that Burke (somewhat inconsistently) had identified prejudices, or forms of prejudgment, not only with sentiments but also with time-honored practices and unquestioned assumptions whose established status reflect their inherent "reasonableness." This argument—intended to demonstrate the limits of the sweeping critique of established institutions misguidedly indulged in by the French, according to Burke—reflects the persistence of an older mode of understanding morality, which, unlike the post-Lockean tradition, neither admitted that human moral nature could be altered nor denied that reason played a significant role in moral decision-making. As Joseph Levine has pointed out, it had been common in the seventeenth century, even among those who were most eager to jettison the authority of the ancients, to concede that, as Burke would argue, "there are no discoveries to be made in morality," and therefore that moral philosophy, like rhetoric, poetry, and oratory, had reached perfection in the hands of the Greeks and Romans. In other words, because they were thought to address the perennial questions posed by an unchanging human nature, these disciplines (unlike natural science, for example) were not considered susceptible to improvement. This early distinction between "the two cultures" was accepted even by Descartes, that most relentless of the moderns, who advised the philosopher to refrain—at least provisionally—from examining accepted morality or established religion, urging him instead to obey the laws and customs of his country, retain the religion in which he had been brought up, and rely on the opinions and practices of the most judicious part of the community to guide all his other actions. In the seventeenth century, then, there had been a general consensus that in moral inquiry the best arguments were ancient ones, and that in moral action the best authorities were time-honored and widely accepted assumptions and practices that embodied what is truly rational.

This sense of the "truly rational," employed by Burke to distinguish time-honored customs, usages, and institutions of English moral and political life from the radical innovations of the French revolutionaries, depended on a characteristic seventeenth-century distinction between "public" and "private" reason, which constituted an important part of the idiom in which religion and politics were then discussed. For example, the charge that Protestants had relied on "private reason" in daring to interpret the Bible for themselves and in questioning the authority of church tradition had long characterized Catholic polemic,

and accusations of political subversion were often linked by conservative theorists with a similar misuse of one's own personal stock of reason. It would be a mistake, however, to dismiss the attack on "private reason" as a mere demand for blind submission to established religious and political institutions, or as a repudiation of reason itself, without taking into account what was meant by "public reason," which, far from being conceived as antithetical to authority, was thought to reveal itself in the time-honored institutions and practices of daily life. This view had been characteristic of seventeenth-century English Catholic defenses of the authority of tradition, which had proven very effective in persuading conservative nobility and gentry to return to Rome. The clearest example of it, however, is in the writings of the early Stuart common lawyers, whose idiom the Catholics frequently adopted. In these jurists' view of the common law, as Glenn Burgess has explained, reason and custom or history were not seen as mutually exclusive alternatives; the common law, incorporating ancient custom and usage and the opinions and decisions of lawyers and law courts collected over time, was conceived simultaneously as the legacy of custom and the embodiment of reason. Reason, it was thought, expressed itself in customs, which represented rational solutions to human problems whose rationality was proven by their very longevity and degree of acceptance; in short, the more ancient and widespread a custom, the more it approached the status of a rational principle. As for the body of collected legal knowledge, it represented the communal reason refined to perfection. From these remarks, it is clear that the "reason" referred to by the common lawyers is not the "reason" of Jaucourt and the French enlighteners. For the latter, reason is an individual critical faculty. No longer confined to philosophy, it interrogates all established institutions and habits of thought on the basis of an appeal to abstract principle substantiated not by external authorities, but rather by the individual's own subjectivity. For the common lawyers—as for Burke, who praised the common law as "the collected reason of ages"—it is a body of collective wisdom enshrined in widely accepted customs and usages and sanctioned not by individual reasoning but by history and experience. This sense of reason as something public is crucial to understanding why Burke's case for prejudice made a rhetorically compelling, if not philosophically coherent, attack on the Enlightenment project of critique. By construing prejudices both as altruistic sentiments and as expressions of the collective reason, he could make the strong affective claim that, in contrast to the abstract principles produced by subjective reflection, prejudices contribute to the moral and political health of the community by reinforcing the sense of connectedness to others without which "the commonwealth itself would, in a few generations, crumble . . . into the dust and powder of individuality, and [be] at length dispersed to all the winds of heaven."

This brief exploration of an eighteenth-century term and its variant-meanings suggests that we need an intellectual history that takes heed of the paradoxes at the heart of the Enlightenment—one that can account, for example, for the persistence of old elements and the infusion of new ones in the construction of critique and counter-critique, as well as demonstrate the extent to which foundational concepts and concerns such as reason itself, the moral nature of the person, or the relation between individual and community were objects less of consensus than of contestation.

[*See also* Burke, Edmund; Cartesianism; Empiricism; Epistemology; Human Nature; Hume, David; Jaucourt, Louis; Locke, John; Reason; *and* Revealed Religion.]

BIBLIOGRAPHY

Ayers, Michael. "Theories of Knowledge and Belief." In *The Cambridge History of Seventeenth-Century Philosophy*, edited by Daniel Garber and Michael Ayers, vol. 2, pp. 1003–1061. Cambridge, 1998. Provides an excellent account of seventeenth-century analyses of the sources of error and of their polemical function.

Burgess, Glenn. *The Politics of the Ancient Constitution: An Introduction to English Political Thought, 1603–1642.* University Park, Pa., 1993. An excellent introduction to the language of the common law in the period before the civil war.

Burke, Edmund. *Reflections on the Revolution in France.* Edited by Conor Cruise O'Brien. Baltimore, 1969. Contains the account of prejudice that is essential to Burke's critique of the French revolutionaries.

Cassirer, Ernst. *The Philosophy of the Enlightenment.* Translated by Fritz C. Koelln and James P. Pettegrove. Princeton, N.J., 1979. Chapter 1 includes an excellent account of the changes in the meaning of "reason" from the seventeenth to the eighteenth century.

Descartes, René. *Principles of Philosophy.* Translated by Valentine Rodger Miller and Reese P. Miller. Dordrecht, 1991. Descartes's most ambitious work, in which he explains the method whereby philosophers can discover metaphysical truths and deduce scientific knowledge from them.

Dompnier, Bernard. *Le vénin de l'hérésie: Image du protestantisme et combat catholique au xviie siècle.* Paris, 1985. An overview of Catholic controversy in seventeenth-century France. Chapter 2 discusses the traditional association of heresy with passion and prejudice.

Gadamer, Hans-Georg. *Truth and Method.* Translated by Joel Weinsheimer and Donald G. Marshall. New York, 1989. Though he does not mention Burke, Gadamer draws a distinction similar to the one delineated here between the two Enlightenment understandings of prejudice. See pp. 271–285.

Hume, David. *A Treatise of Human Nature.* Vol. 3, *Of Morals.* London, 1740. Presents the argument that moral distinctions derive neither from reason, nor from a moral sense, but from sentiments that evolve in a social context, from our necessary cooperation with others.

Kors, Alan. *Atheism in France.* Vol. 1, *The Orthodox Sources of Disbelief.* Princeton, N.J., 1990. Chapter 3 contains an excellent discussion of the theological training of seventeenth- and eighteenth-century university students.

Levine, Joseph M. "Ancients and Moderns Reconsidered." *Eighteenth-Century Studies* 15 (1981), 72–89. An essential overview of the issues at stake in the seventeenth- and eighteenth-century "quarrel of the ancients and the moderns," by its most knowledgeable historian.

Locke, John. *An Essay Concerning Human Understanding.* London, 1997. Presents Locke's epistemology, and crucially, his seminal argument that human understanding is based on experience rather than innate ideas.

Pocock, J. G. A. *The Ancient Constitution and the Federal Law: A Study of English Historical Thought in the Seventeenth Century.* Cambridge, 1987. The essential work on the thought of seventeenth-century common lawyers.

Rex, Walter E. *Essays on Pierre Bayle and Religious Controversy.* The Hague, 1965. Chapter 1 contains an incisive discussion of the role of "prejudice" in the rhetoric of seventeenth-century Reformed polemicists.

Staël, Germaine de. *Considérations sur la révolution française.* Edited by Jacques Godechot. Paris, 1983. An early nineteenth century account of the cultural and political factors contributing to the French Revolution by a woman who had been close to the centers of power in France before 1789. In chapter 15, she delineates briefly her understanding of "Enlightenment."

Van Kley, Dale K. *The Religious Origins of the French Revolution: From Calvin to the Civil Constitution, 1560–1791.* New Haven, Conn., 1996. Argues that the French eighteenth century was as much a century of religious controversy as of Enlightenment; delineates the crucial role of theological conflict in pre-revolutionary political debates.

SUSAN ROSA

PRÉVOST D'EXILES, ANTOINE-FRANÇOIS

(1697–1763), novelist, translator, journalist, and encyclopedist.

Antoine-François Prévost was much more than the author of the justly acclaimed *Histoire du Chevalier Des Grieux et de Manon Lescaut* (1731). As a historian, moralist, and anthropologist—he once dreamed of writing a history of mankind—this gifted and prolific writer incarnates the tensions inherent in what the French literary historian Paul Hazard in 1935 called "the crisis of the European conscience." His numerous recantations, his equal attention to the sacred and to worldly pleasures, the inconstancy of his commitments, the sometimes confused abundance of his novels, in which digressions and theatrical coups abound—these multiple aspects of the man sum up the disquiet of a period on the cusp between tradition and modernity. There is a metaphysical pessimism in Prévost, a classicizing urge to turn back, a haunting nostalgia for a time of tranquil order. In this he is a man of the seventeenth century. There is also in him, however, a drive to know, to measure, to classify, a drive to understand everything and articulate it, matched by a focus on his own self and confidence in the prospect of progress and happiness flowing from the ascendancy of reason. As the compiler of a monumental *Histoire des voyages* (History of the Voyages, 1746–1759), Prévost shared the typical encyclopedist's wish to collect and make available the totality

The Abbé Prévost. (New York Public Library, Astor, Lenox, and Tilden Foundations.)

of knowledge. As one of the earliest journalists (he was editor of *Pour et Contre* [For and Against, 1733–1740] and the *Journal étranger* [Foreign Newspaper, 1755]) and a fervent polyglot, he was dedicated to spreading and sharing knowledge in a Republic of Letters that was growing ever more cosmopolitan. In these respects, he was a man of the Enlightenment.

The turbulent life of Prévost, a life of eager engagement and withdrawal, repentance and relapse, conversion and apostasy, resembles the raw material for one of his novels. After a youth marked by the painful loss, in the same year, of his mother and his sister Thérèse Claire (1711), Prévost set out into the world: he was by turns a pupil of the Jesuits, a soldier, a deserter (1712–1719), a novice with the Benedictines, then a monk (1720–1728). The *Aventures de Pomponius* (Adventures of Pomponius) of 1724, composed of libertine dialogues of the kind popular during the Regency and an imaginary voyage in imitation of Cyrano, were followed in 1728 by the first volumes of the *Mémoires et aventures d'un homme de qualité qui s'est retiré du monde* (Memoirs and Adventures of a Man of Quality Who Has Withdrawn from Society), a collection of sombre and pathetic tales narrated by the marquis de Renoncour. These works reveal Prévost's frustration at the austere rigor of cloistered monastic life. In the same year, the impatient abbé fled to Holland, where he converted to Protestantism. Arriving in England in November 1728, he converted to Anglicanism and obtained a post as a tutor, but after seducing the sister of his pupil he was forced to flee back to Holland in 1730, where he lived precariously by his pen. A tireless author, he worked simultaneously on the *Mémoires* and on *Le philosophe anglais, ou Histoire de Monsieur Cleveland* (The English Philosopher, or The Life of Mr. Cleveland), a fictitious account of the adventures of the natural son of Oliver Cromwell. These fictions are marked by a feeling of tragic disenchantment with the world that mirrors Prévost's own sense of defeat at this time. The author's cherished themes can all be found here, from the lost paradise of youth to the insoluble conflict between father and son, from the curse of love to the death of a beloved woman (sister or lover), from abduction to the descent into the grave.

The year 1731 marks a turning point in the life of Prévost, for at the Hague he met an adventuress, Lenki Eckhardt, with whom he engaged in a dangerous cycle of debt and crime for more than a decade. It was also the year in which the last volume of the *Mémoires, Manon Lescaut*, was published. Following a bankruptcy, Prévost fled to London accompanied by Eckhardt, and was there imprisoned for forgery and using false documents in 1733. The following year he returned secretly to France and successfully requested absolution from Pope Clement XII for his apostasy. Following a second novitiate and various altercations, Prévost became the almoner of the Prince de Conti in 1736. During this period he lived in grand style and frequented the salon of Émilie Le Tonnelier de Breteuil, marquise du Châtelet, as well as materialist and atheist circles and the Freemasons. But he did not break with the Catholic milieu and avoided compromising commitments; this cost him the support of the philosophes, beginning with Voltaire. Threatened with seizure for debt, incautiously caught up in polemics and scandals, criticized for the irreverent "libertinage" of works such as the *Mémoires pour servir à l'histoire de Malte* (Memories That Serve As the History of Malta, 1741), which roused the ire of the Knights of Malta, and the unflattering *Campagnes philosophiques, ou Mémoires de M. de Montcal . . .* (Philosophical Campaigns, or Memories of Mr. de Montcal, 1741), Prévost, during the years 1739–1741, was repeatedly forced to conceal his identity and flee. His reputation as a reprobate was at its peak. As in 1731, this new crisis corresponded to a period of intense productivity: from 1739 to 1742 there appeared the last part of *Cleveland* (vols. 7 and 8, 1739), volumes 2–6 of *Doyen de Killerine* (1739–1740), *Histoire de Marguerite d'Anjou* (1740), *Histoire d'une Grecque moderne* (1740), *Histoire de Guillaume le Conquérant* (1742). The publication of the "heroic" lives of Marguerite d'Anjou and William the Conqueror marked a turn in Prévost's work, as biographical novels gave way to historical biographies. Yet his concern was always to inscribe an individual destiny in a historical context: in the work of Prévost, fiction and history are indissoluble.

Back in Paris in 1742, Prévost began a new stage in his career, in which travel literature took the place of historical and fictional biography. In 1744 the *Voyages du capitaine Robert Lade*, a mixture of fiction and didactic narrative, appeared, followed in 1746 by the first two volumes (with thirteen more to follow) of the *Histoire générale des voyages*.

Yet as he wrote of travel and adventure, Prévost himself began to live more sagely. In 1746 he left Paris and took up residence at Chaillot (moving to Saint-Firmin near Chantilly at the beginning of the 1760s) in the company of Catherine Genty, the "governess" with whom he was to share the rest of his life. Though the 1750s were notable for the absence of any new novels by Prévost, his intense activity as a translator at this time should be seen as a continuation of his creative career. Through his choice of authors (Cicero, his model of wisdom) and of genres (the novel of manners, after Samuel Richardson and Thomas Sheridan, and historical narrative, after David Hume), Prévost was in effect pursuing his own authorial project, centered on the theme of the individual caught between "destiny" and liberty.

During one of the long walks he loved to take in his later years, Prévost died of apoplexy on 25 November 1763 at the age of sixty-six. A tireless explorer of the labyrinth of the passions, a veritable cartographer of the heart, Prévost participated in the great enterprise of the eighteenth century, which aimed to investigate both the natural world and human nature, and to grasp the complexity of their laws, their polymorphic disorder. Because his work reveals to us the tension between two orders of knowledge, because in reading it we come up against the unyielding opacity of the world, and finally because in it, fiction shows its power, Prévost may properly be considered an emblematic figure of the Enlightenment.

[*See also* Biography; Journals, Newspapers, and Gazettes, *subentry on* France; Literary Genres; *and* Republic of Letters.]

BIBLIOGRAPHY

Francis, Richard. *The Abbe Prévost's First-Person Narrators. Studies on Voltaire and the Eighteenth Century.* Oxford, 1992.
Sermain, Jean-Paul. *Rhétorique et roman au dix-huitième siècle: L'exemple de Prévost et de Marivaux (1728–1742).* Oxford, 1999.
Sgard, Jean. *Prévost romancier.* Paris, 1968.
Sgard, Jean. *L'abbé Prévost: Labyrinthes de la mémoire.* Paris, 1986.
Sgard, Jean. *Vingt études sur Prévost d'Exiles.* Grenoble, 1995.
Singerman, Alan. *L'abbé Prévost: l'amour et la morale.* Geneva, 1987.

THIERRY BELLEGUIC

Translated from French by William McCuaig

PRICE, RICHARD (1723–1791), Welsh Dissenting minister.

Price was born at Tynton, Llangeinor, Glamorgan, and was educated at various schools in South Wales and at Coward's Academy at Tenter Alley, Moorfields, London. His father, Rice Price (1673–1739) was also a dissenting minister. Richard Price made significant contributions in moral philosophy, theology, mathematics, actuarial science, demography, the development of insurance, national finance, and political pamphleteering. In his first publication, *A Review of the Principal Questions and Difficulties in Morals* (1758), he defended the objectivity of moral judgment against the subjectivism of Francis Hutcheson and David Hume. He held that moral judgment is an exercise of reason and as such makes accessible a body of moral principles that are immutable and universally true. Every man has a duty to follow his own moral judgment: although he may be mistaken, he will not be culpable if he does what he sincerely believes to be his duty, and if he has done all that he may be reasonably expected to do to inform his judgment. This principle of candor—the duty to seek the truth and to examine all one's beliefs in the light of reason—plays an important role in Price's theology (*Four Dissertations*, 1767; *Sermons on the Christian Doctrine*, 1787). Although there may be mysteries that are impenetrable to humans, we have the assurance that God has made accessible to reason all that one needs to live a virtuous life.

In 1764, Price edited and published Thomas Bayes's "An Essay towards Solving a Problem in the Doctrine of Chances," which appeared in the *Philosophical Transactions of the Royal Society*. The following year, he was elected a fellow of the Royal Society, one of his sponsors being Benjamin Franklin. Shortly afterward, Price was invited to advise the Society for Equitable Assurances on actuarial and demographic problems. A feverish burst of activity followed which led to the publication of *Observations on Reversionary Payments* (1771), a seminal work in the development of insurance. Price's interest was practical, in the sense that he wanted to make the conduct of business as efficient and as profitable as possible, but it also had a humanitarian motivation: he strove to avoid the misery that would be produced by fraudulent or incompetent management. Price also became well known for his advocacy of schemes for reducing the national debt by using sinking funds.

Price became widely known through his defense of the American rebels in his pamphlets *Observations on the Nature of Civil Liberty* (1776), *Additional Observations* (1777), *Two Tracts* (1778), and *Observations on the Importance of the American Revolution* (1784). His defense of the rebels and his advocacy of parliamentary reform were based on the principles of self-government. He proposed that every nation has the right to govern itself and not be subject to the alien will of another nation, and that every individual has the right to participate in some measure in the government of his own society. Price did not wish that America should become independent—he preferred the creation of a confederation in which the colonists and the home country could participate on equal terms—but he insisted that the Americans had the right to become independent if they so chose.

Toward the end of his career, Price became increasingly imbued with the optimism of the Enlightenment. His *The Evidence for a Future Period of Improvement in the State of Mankind* (1787) is a blend of millennialist expectations and the doctrine of progress. The principles on which he defended the Americans and the doctrine of natural rights formed the core of his defense of the French revolutionaries, whom he applauded enthusiastically in a famous sermon, *A Discourse on the Love of Our Country* (1789); it provoked the wrath of Edmund Burke in *Reflections on the Revolution in France* (1790). Burke sought to demolish Price's political philosophy. He anathematized Price's rationalism and the utopian optimism that sought to reconstruct social and political institutions on abstract, a priori principles, much to the peril of Christian civilization. Price replied briefly and effectively in a short preface to the fourth edition of his sermon, but his failing health precluded a more sustained reply.

[*See also* Burke, Edmund; Epistemology; Hume, David; Mathematics; Millenarianism; Moral Philosophy; Natural Rights; Reason; Reformed Churches; *and* Revolution.]

BIBLIOGRAPHY

Cone, Carl B. *Torchbearer of Freedom: The Influence of Richard Price on Eighteenth-Century Thought.* Lexington, Ky., 1952.

Peach, W. B. *The Ethical Foundations of the American Revolution.* Durham, N.C., 1979.

Price, Richard. *The Correspondence of Richard Price.* Edited by W. Bernard Peach and D. O. Thomas. 3 vols. Durham, N.C., and Cardiff, 1983–1994.

Price, Richard. *Political Writings.* Edited by D. O. Thomas. Cambridge, 1991.

Thomas, D. O. *The Honest Mind: The Thought and Work of Richard Price.* Oxford, 1977.

Thomas, D. O., John Stephens, and P. A. L. Jones, eds. *A Bibliography of the Works of Richard Price.* Aldershot, U.K., 1993.

D. O. THOMAS

PRIESTLEY, JOSEPH (1733–1804), English scientist, philosopher, and Dissenter.

Priestley was born on 24 March 1733 in Fairfield, six miles southwest of Leeds in the Calvinist stronghold of the West Riding of Yorkshire. In *Institutes of Natural and Revealed Religion*, published in three volumes between 1772 and 1774, he described his conversion from the Calvinist doctrines of predestination, the atonement, and the depravity of man, which emphasized God's arbitrary will, to an optimistic Unitarianism, which upheld the perfectibility of man living in an intelligible world created by a benevolent Deity. Priestley emphasized the rationality of his mature theism, which used the methods of science to discover God's will in nature and man's moral duties and religious expectations in Scripture. As a leading figure in the English Enlightenment, he sought to reform, rather than replace, religion with reason and useful knowledge.

The central doctrines of Priestley's Rational Christianity—necessity, materialism, and Socinianism (anti-Trinitarianism)—were enunciated in *Disquisition relating to Matter and Spirit* (1777) and *Letters to a Philosophical Unbeliever* (1787). In *History of the Corruptions of Christianity* (1782), he argued that these doctrines were compatible with a rational reading of the Bible, which showed that Christ was a mere man who preached the resurrection of the body, not the immortality of a nonexistent soul. In *Hartley's Theory of the Human Mind* (1775), he used the doctrine of the association of ideas, developed by the psychologist and liberal Anglican David Hartley, to argue that the perfectibility of man was the inevitable consequence of his increasing knowledge of a deterministic system of matter sustained and permeated by a benevolent Deity. Priestley linked scientific progress to the improvement of man's spiritual, social, and material circumstances, which was guaranteed by his millenarian Christianity.

The development of Priestley's thought was related to his complex identity as a minister, teacher, pamphleteer, and natural philosopher. He graduated from the Dissenting Academy at Daventry in 1755. After ministering in Suffolk and Cheshire, he joined the faculty at Warrington Academy in 1761, where he developed a philosophy of language, education, and history that was social, utilitarian, and associationistic. In *A Course of Lectures on the Theory of Universal Grammar* (1762), Priestley, in the manner of the English philosopher John Locke, linked correct linguistic usage to effective communication, which was grounded in the customary association of ideas and depended for its improvement on the scientific study of man, society, and history. The Enlightenment view of history as philosophy teaching by examples shaped the *History and Present State of Electricity with Original Experiments* that he published in 1767 with the help of the American scientist and statesman Benjamin Franklin. Priestley used his historical narrative to argue that scientific progress depended not on the theoretical insights of a few men of genius but on the patient and industrious observation of nature, which was open to all men. In *An Essay on a Course of Liberal Education for Civil and Active Life* (1765), he developed a pedagogy based on the experiences and associations of the individual and

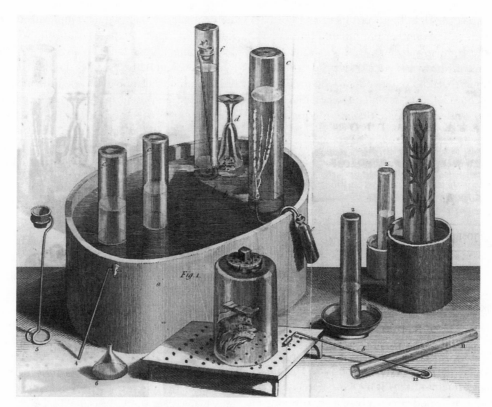

Priestley's Experiments. Frontispiece to *Experiments and Observations on Different Kinds of Air* (London, 1774). (Prints and Photographs Division, Library of Congress.)

outlined a curriculum designed to provide Dissenters with knowledge appropriate to their entrepreneurial and commercial interests. Influenced by the seventeenth-century philosopher and politician Francis Bacon, Priestley sought to improve society through the practical benefits of a science-based commerce.

Priestley returned to the ministry at Mill Hill Chapel, Leeds, in 1767, where he joined the national struggle of Dissenters to free themselves from the constraints placed on their civil, political, and economic liberties by the Test and Corporation Acts of 1761 and 1763 and the policies of George III toward the American colonies. Priestley championed the cause of civil liberty in *An Essay on the First Principles of Government* (1768). Influenced by Locke's doctrine of inalienable natural rights and by the hostility of the Commonwealthmen to absolute monarchy, arbitrary rule, and an established church, Priestley argued that the rational analysis of beliefs and opinions, which was essential to scientific progress and human perfectibility, required freedom of speech, worship, and education. Unlike his friend and fellow reformer Richard Price, who thought that political liberty, or participation in government, was essential to civil liberty, Priestley elevated civil liberty above political liberty and saw only a contingent relation between self-governance and the

liberties he cherished. As a proponent of laissez-faire economics, developed by the Scottish philosopher Adam Smith, Priestley favored a minimalist state that respected individual enterprise and accountability. He judged governments in terms of their contribution to the general happiness of mankind, thereby providing the founder of utilitarianism, Jeremy Bentham, with his initial inspiration. Any conflict between the rights of the individual and the utility of the whole was mitigated in Priestley's mind by his vision of a millenarian future of unbridled happiness, benevolence, and freedom.

Priestley moved to Calne, Wiltshire, in 1773, where he served as librarian and tutor for Lord Shelburne, who shared his opposition to the crown's policies toward the American colonies. Between 1781 and 1791, he ministered at the New Meetinghouse in Birmingham, where he enjoyed the company and support of the members of the Lunar Society, including the poet-physician Erasmus Darwin and the industrialist Josiah Wedgwood, the grandfathers of Charles Darwin. Wedgwood supplied him with apparatus for his research into the chemistry of gases, or pneumatic chemistry, which he began during his tenure at Leeds. Priestley fashioned a distinctive approach to pneumatic chemistry by fusing his Dissenting interest in piety, progress, and utility with the Lunar Society's program for linking science to an elite, provincial culture of rational politeness, urban civility, and refined amusement. He presented his chemical observations in the *Philosophical Transactions* of the Royal Society and in the six volumes of *Experiments and Observations on Different Kinds of Air* (three volumes) and *Experiments and Observations on Different Kinds of Air and Various Branches of Natural Philosophy* (three volumes), which were published between 1774 and 1786.

Influenced by the British pneumatic chemists Stephen Hales, Joseph Black, and Henry Cavendish, Priestley isolated and examined a dozen different gases, explored their medicinal virtues, and developed a test for the purity of the atmosphere—the eudiometer—that presupposed his Enlightenment interest in the role of the environment in urban planning and social reform. In accordance with his interest in utility, he maintained a strict distinction between facts and hypotheses in science, which he also used to emphasize his view of science as a cooperative experimental enterprise, free of speculation and prejudice of any sort. These Dissenting sensibilities shaped his opposition to the oxygen theory of chemistry developed by the French chemist Antoine-Laurent Lavoisier. Priestley detected in Lavoisier's attempt to impose a new theory on the chemical community a threat to the liberty of the individual mind that paralleled the usurped authority of the eighteenth-century religious state. He claimed that the correct nomenclature for chemistry would emerge from a consideration of experimental usage, not from the impositions of theoretical reason. While the fate of Faust awaited Lavoisier's intellectual hubris, Priestley insisted that, when approached with a just sense of the limits of our finite understanding, natural philosophy had no equal in its claim on man's interests and role in his perfection.

The peace of Priestley's laboratory was shattered by the turmoil of his public life, as the parliamentary struggle to repeal the Test and Corporation Acts intensified. In the sermon *The Importance and Extent of Free Inquiry in Matters of Religion*, which he preached on 5 November 1785, he used the notorious "gunpowder" metaphor to describe the explosive effect on the established church and state of the new forces of reason and criticism. This statement earned for him the nickname "Gunpowder Joe" that sealed in the popular imagination the link between Dissenting programs for religious reform and the seditious support of Price and Priestley for the American and French revolutions. The Tory press soon moved against the Dissenters and, on 14 July 1791, the church-and-king mob destroyed Priestley's house and laboratory. Priestley and his family retreated to the security of Price's congregation in Hackney, where he sought to defend himself in *Letters to the Right Honorable Edmund Burke, occasioned by his Reflections on the Revolution in France* (1791).

Priestley's defense fell on deaf ears, however, as the conservative reaction to the French Revolution intensified in England. Concerned for the safety of his family, he sailed for America in 1794, where he settled in Northumberland, Pennsylvania, and came to enjoy the benefits of a form of government he found relatively tolerable. This experience contributed to a significant shift in his political thought. His earlier emphasis on civil liberty gave way to an interest in political liberty, and his *Letters to the Inhabitants of Northumberland* (1799) became part of the Republican counterattack against the Federalists. When Priestley died on 6 February 1804, he was revered and mourned by that great republican Thomas Jefferson, the third president of the United States and a leading figure in the American Enlightenment.

[*See also* Chemistry; Darwin, Erasmus; Education, *subentry on* Pedagogical Thought and Practice; Lavoisier, Antoine-Laurent; Price, Richard; Reformed Churches; Revolution; Scottish Common Sense Philosophy; Socinianism; *and* Wedgwood, Josiah.]

BIBLIOGRAPHY

Anderson, R. G. W., and Christopher Lawrence, eds. *Science, Medicine and Dissent: Joseph Priestley (1733–1804)*. London, 1987. An edited collection of essays representing the most recent Priestley scholarship, valuable particularly for an understanding of Priestley's science, religion, and politics.

Conovan, Margaret. "The Un-Benthamite Utilitarianism of Joseph Priestley." *Journal of the History of Ideas* 45 (1984), 435–450.

Fitzpatrick, Martin, and D. O. Thomas, eds. *Enlightenment and Dissent*. Starting out as the *Price-Priestley Newsletter* (1–4, 1977–1980), this is the main journal for current Priestley scholarship.

Fruchtman, Jack. *The Apocalyptic Politics of Richard Price and Joseph Priestley: A Study in Late Eighteenth-Century Republican Millenarianism*. Philadelphia, 1983. Relates Priestley's political thought and action to his millenarian Christianity.

Gibbs, F. W. *Joseph Priestley: Adventurer in Science and Champion of Truth*. London, 1965. Best available complete biography of Priestley.

Golinski, Jan. *Science as Public Culture: Chemistry and Enlightenment in Britain, 1760–1820*. Chaps. 3, 4, and 5. Cambridge, 1992. Valuable account of Priestley's pneumatic chemistry and his relation with Lavoisier.

Graham, Jenny. *Revolutionary in Exile: The Emigration of Joseph Priestley to America, 1704–1804*. Philadelphia, 1995. Valuable account of the development of Priestley's political thought in the context of the important debate between Federalists and Antifederalists.

McEvoy, J. G., and J. E. McGuire. "God and Nature: Priestley's Way of Rational Dissent." In *Historical Studies in the Physical Sciences*, edited by Russell McCormmach, vol. 5, pp. 325–404. Princeton, N.J., 1975. A seminal work in Priestley scholarship, valuable for the synoptic unity it reveals in his variegated thought.

McEvoy, J. G. "Priestley Responds to Lavoisier's Nomenclature: Language, Liberty, and Politics in the English Enlightenment." In *Lavoisier in European Context: Negotiating a New Language for Chemistry*, edited by Bernadette Bensaude-Vincent and Ferdinando Abbri, pp. 123–142. Canton, Mass., 1995. Valuable for the close links it establishes between Priestley's chemistry and Enlightenment culture and philosophy.

Money, John. "Joseph Priestley in Cultural Context: Philosophic Spectacle, Popular Belief and Popular Politics in Eighteenth-century Birmingham, Part 1." *Enlightenment and Dissent* 7 (1988), 57–82; "Part 2." Ibid., 8 (1989), 68–89. A valuable study of the complex cultural forces that shaped the Birmingham riots.

Schaffer, Simon. "Priestley Questions: An Historiographical Survey." *History of Science* 22 (1984), 151–183. Valuable critical survey of the current state of Priestley scholarship, especially among historians of science.

Schofield, Robert E. *The Enlightenment of Joseph Priestley: A Study of His Life and Work from 1733 to 1773.* University Park, Pa., 1979. The first of the definitive two-volume biography of Priestley, valuable for an account of his life rather than for an analysis of his thought.

Schwartz, A. Truman, and John G. McEvoy. *Motion toward Perfection. The Achievement of Joseph Priestley.* Boston, 1990. An edited collection of papers, valuable for the scope of its scholarship.

JOHN G. MCEVOY

PRIMITIVISM. *See* Human Nature *and* Moral Philosophy.

PRINT CULTURE. In all countries of Enlightenment Europe, three markets for books constituted the world of "print culture": the market for new titles, that for *littérature du colportage* (chapbooks), and that for the works collected by bibliophiles. Each implied a particular form of book sales (the *librairie d'assortiment*, traveling peddlers, and public sales), specific repertories (the bookseller-publisher's selections and editions, "popular" collections, collector's books), and the differing expectations and potentials of the printed book.

The growth of market for new works faced the same constraints that regulated publishing activity in the age between Johannes Gutenberg's invention of movable type and the industrialization of printing. In its fundamental structure, the typographic workshop of the eighteenth century remained what it had been in the fifteenth. The work was still done using the same technology (movable type for composition, the hand press for printing), and printers faced the same problems: the supply of paper, the cost of which always constituted the greatest expense in publishing a book; hiring sufficient workers necessary for fluctuating labor needs; and coordination between the work of compositors and pressmen. The innovations that had changed the organization of composition in large printing houses—linking the work of the foreman, responsible for the final makeup of the page, with that of the compositors, who furnished him with rough pages—had not altered fundamentally either the division of labor or the processes of publication.

In contrast, publishing during the Enlightenment remained dependent on commercial capital. The publisher-booksellers and typographic societies ruled the game: they sought and usually obtained the protection of the authorities, who granted them privileges, monopolies, and patronage; they dominated the master printers who produced all or part of their editions; and they controlled the book market by developing the *librairie d'assortiment*, which allowed them to sell not only their own editions but also those of their colleagues, obtained through commercial exchange.

Unchanging technology and the capitalist domination of the bookshop led to limited print runs; a single edition was generally between 1,500 and 1,750 copies. Factors limiting press runs included the need to prevent type from being immobilized too long in composed forms; the fear of being unable to sell the printed copies quickly; and above all, the fact that the increase in a print run did not reduce the cost per sheet after the threshold of paying off fixed costs had been crossed.

For the most noted philosophical titles of the century, publishers overcame these constraints by issuing many new editions, authorized or pirated, and by increasing print runs. This was the case with Denis Diderot and Jean Le Rond d'Alembert's *Encyclopédie*. Between 1751 and 1782, its six editions (the Paris edition, two Italian pirated editions in Lucca and Livorno, the Geneva edition, the quarto edition of the Typographic Society of Neuchâtel, and the octavo edition of the typographic societies of Berne and Lausanne) put around 24,000 copies on the market, of which half were probably distributed within France and half elsewhere. This total reflects the fact that several of these editions had exceptional print runs: 4,225 copies for the Paris folio edition, 5,500 or 6,000 copies in Berne and Lausanne, and 8,000 copies from the Typographic Society of Neuchâtel, which (under the protection of the French authorities) had mobilized about twenty workshops in both Switzerland and France. By increasing the run and lowering the price per book through a change in format, the successive publishers of the *Encyclopédie* won a larger clientele made up of royal office-holders, administrators, clerks, and lawyers, and they facilitated the acquisition of the books by reading rooms and societies.

Beyond this work, emblematic of the Enlightenment, two genres dominated the enlightened market for printed books. The first was that of "philosophical books," a phrase that booksellers used to cover political lampoons, scandalous chronicles, materialist treatises, works of the popularizers of the Enlightenment, and pornographic texts. Published by enterprises operating around the borders of France, this critical and denunciatory literature circulated throughout Europe, but its public was primarily French. Banned pamphlets were introduced clandestinely into the kingdom, where they were pursued by the authorities. Their authors proclaimed that the monarchy had degenerated into despotism, and that the nobility and the court had fallen into degradation and debauchery. The most radical writings of the Enlightenment undermined the political and religious foundations of divine monarchy and of the traditional order. The printed book thus contributed powerfully to the erosion of former patterns of authority and deference.

The second major printed genre was that of periodicals. Throughout Europe, the number of printed journals increased, multiplying the types of periodicals: news gazettes, public notices, specialized titles, scholarly journals, and literary reviews. Their alliance with the Enlightenment was initially limited and cautious, but in offering opinions on published books they invited readers to practice criticism. Beneath their apparent neutrality, the reports and extracts that formed the bulk of journalistic writing habituated readers of periodicals to making use of their reason.

In its very exceptionality, the *Encyclopédie* bears witness to the confidence the Enlightenment placed in the circulation of printed matter. The philosophical spirit motivated all printed genres (dictionaries, treatises, compilations, anthologies, lampoons, pamphlets, gazettes) and enlisted traditional textual forms such as almanac, catechism, and treatises on civility. At the end of the century, Jean-Antoine-Nicolas de Caritat Condorcet marked strongly (and retrospectively) the link that tied the constitution of a new public space and the circulation of printed matter. In the eighth "epoch" of the *Esquisse des progrès de l'entendement humain*, he described three effects of printing, the invention that "multiplies indefinitely, and at little cost, the copies of a single work." First, printing opposed the coldness of reason, the critical examination of ideas, and the judgment of opinions formed in silence and solitude to the passions aroused and exalted by live speech exchanged among assembled people. Second, printing thus substituted demonstrations founded on reason for convictions elicited by rhetoric. Certitude and the irrefutability of the truth and thinking modeled on logical deduction and mathematical reasoning were thus fundamentally distinguished from groundless convictions based on the cleverness and enthusiasm of persuasive speech.

Finally, thanks to printing, rigorously argued truths could be displayed to all humanity. Whereas oral communication necessarily implied dividing up discussions and fields of knowledge, the circulation of printed texts allowed the universal exercise of reason. Thus, printing made it possible for public opinion to be formed, and this—unlike individual opinions, always changeable, doubting, and local—represented stability, certitude, and universality. By permitting exchange without the interlocutors' presence, Gutenberg's invention had established an invisible and immaterial tribunal whose judgments, based in reason, were to be imposed on all.

The importance given to Gutenberg's invention by the Enlightenment should not, however, mask the persistence in the eighteenth century of the circulation of manuscripts. There were several reasons for this. On one hand, the ethic of selflessness and reciprocity that was the basis for the Republic of Letters, the international community of scholars, privileged the manuscript in all its forms: epistolary exchange, memoirs, copied documents, and the distribution of works before printing. On the other hand, the wish to protect the circulation of philosophical manuscripts, dangerous for their authors and their readers, led to having them multiplied through hand copying and to transmitting them clandestinely. In both cases, it was a question of reducing the risks of corruption or of the destruction of texts held to be fundamental for the advancement of learning or for the critique of church or state. The continuing importance of *nouvelles à la main* (hand-copied newssheets)—collections of articles giving information on current events in chronological order—recalls that neither communication nor publication via manuscript had disappeared in the age of print. Born as private correspondences, handwritten gazettes could be addressed to a single consignee, often a prince, but more often they were copied in tens or hundreds and circulated widely among the literate public.

In *Was Ist Aufklärung?* (1784), Immanuel Kant did not separate manuscript communication from printed publication; he believed that only the exchange of writings could establish the public use of reason by private persons. Unlike the new forms of intellectual sociability (clubs, literary societies, lodges), which broke up the critical examination of ideas and institutions into multiple locations, the circulation of writing was constituting, at least potentially, the universal society of men. It designated an ideal public space for "the public use of our reason, that which we do as *scholar* for the entire *reading public*," and which authorizes each citizen "in his role as scholar, to make publicly, that is in writing," his remarks and criticisms, which could and should be deployed freely, without censure or exclusion. For Kant, it was when each individual could be in turn reader and scholar that humanity would have entered an enlightened age.

At the time Kant was writing, not all men had yet mastered writing, and the majority who bought books sought not new philosophical works but chapbooks. The existence of this market led publishers to print at the lowest cost, using second-hand fonts, mediocre paper, and reusable woodcuts, texts they had previously or simultaneously issued in more luxurious formats for a wealthier clientele. In France, this formula appeared in the second half of the sixteenth century; in the seventeenth century it became a specialty of certain book publishers and printers operating in Troyes and Rouen. These cumulatively established the collection of works that constituted the *Bibliothèque bleue*, so called because of the blue paper used to cover many of the books sold by hawkers (*colporteurs*) in town and country. The corpus of chapbooks was built up of series of titles that reflected certain popular genres (lives of the saints, novels of chivalry, fairy tales) along with instructive works (practices of piety, collections of recipes, manuals for apprentices) and recurrent themes (discourses on women, satires of the trades, accounts of villainy, the cries of Paris). The makeup of collections of new texts that repeated earlier formulas and titles already published was adjusted to suit the abilities of readers more interested in familiar forms than in original ones.

The French chapbook formula was neither isolated nor original. In all European countries and their colonies, there circulated print genres that shared the same characteristics: fabrication at the lowest possible cost, sale by hawkers, and publication of texts intended for the abilities and expectations of the majority of readers. There existed everywhere, therefore, tight links among an editorial formula, a specific body of texts, and a popular public—a public formed by the circles of artisans and shopowners in the towns and the most prosperous or best-educated villagers.

Depending on the time and the place, this association took different forms. In Spain, from the sixteenth century on, the usual book printed for the majority was the *pliego suelto*, a printed sheet folded twice, which produced a quarto booklet of eight pages, or multiples of that. Several genres were distributed in this format: verse romances drawn from the traditional poetic repertory or composed by anonymous authors but often attributed to the blind book-peddlers; *relaciones de sucesos*, which recounted in prose great political feats or extraordinary events; the texts of the *comedias* presented in the open-air theaters in large Spanish cities; and, from the eighteenth century on, abridged adaptations of fashionable novels and operas.

In England, from the beginning of the seventeenth century, the long-established publishers of ballad broadsheets invented and exploited the new market for chapbooks. The editorial formula was rigid, neatly distinguishing three categories of printed books: "small books," made up of twenty-four pages in octavo or duodecimo; "double books," composed of twenty-four pages formatted in quarto; and "histories" of thirty-two to seventy-two pages. The repertory of these "penny books" copied, adapted, and at times abridged older religious or secular texts of diverse genres and traditions that were quite similar to those that contemporary publishers and printers of Troyes were choosing for the *Bibliothèque bleue*. Distributed by hawkers to readers belonging to all levels of society, including the most humble, chapbooks went through numerous reeditions and very large print runs.

In the eighteenth century, the rigidity of the various formats relaxed, as shown by the variety of formats and lengths of the books in the *Bibliothèque bleue*, the diversification of the genres that made up the *literatura de cordel*, and innovative genres—for example, children's books—in chapbook format. Even before competition of new types of printed matter arose, the catalogs of chapbook publishers entered the eighteenth century in a state of diversity, thus loosening the tight links that had united formats and texts.

The third market for books was that for rare and precious works, objects of competition by collectors; their value depended on criteria of appreciation other than those of the usefulness or correctness of the text. Offered to connoisseurs at public sales and described in the catalogs of specialist booksellers, they were prized for the features such as condition, illustration, and binding, for their antiquity or provenance (as with Gothic, Aldean, or Elzevirian editions), their subjects (for example, heterodox writings were particularly sought in the eighteenth century), or their materials (e.g., editions on vellum). For a wealthy aristocratic European clientele of courtiers, nobility, and financiers; the passion for collecting books led to the construction of exclusive and curious reading rooms, quite different from the usual humanist and encyclopedic library, and to a relationship with the history of print culture that was not solely philological.

[*See also* Correspondence and Correspondents; Journals, Newspapers, and Gazettes; Publishing; *and* Reading and Reading Practices.]

BIBLIOGRAPHY

Braida, Lodovica. *Il comercio delle idee: Editoria e circolazione del libro nella Torino del Settecento*. Florence, 1995.

Chartier, Roger. *The Cultural Origins of the French Revolution*. Translated by Lydia C. Cochrane. Durham, N.C., and London, 1991. English translation of *Les origines culturelles de la Révolution française* (Paris, 1990).

Chartier, Roger, and Hans-Jürgen Lüsebrink, eds. *Colportage et lecture populaire: Imprimés de large circulation en Europe, XVIᵉ–XIXᵉ siècles*. Paris, 1996.

Darnton, Robert. *The Business of Enlightenment: A Publishing History of the Encyclopédie, 1775–1800*. Cambridge, Mass., 1979.

Darnton, Robert. *The Forbidden Best-Sellers of Pre-Revolutionary France*. New York, 1995.

Duval, Gilles. *Littérature de colportage et imaginaire collectif en Angleterre à l'époque des Dicey (1720–v. 1800)*. Bordeaux, 1991.

Goldgar, Ann. *Impolite Learning: Conduct and Community in the Republic of Letters 1680–1750*. New Haven, Conn., and London, 1994.

Goodman, Dena. *The Republic of Letters: A Cultural History of the French Enlightenment*. Ithaca, N.Y., and London, 1994.

Habermas, Jürgen. *The Structural Transformation of the Public Sphere: An Inquiry into a Category of Bourgeois Society*. Cambridge, 1989. English translation of *Strukturwandel der Öffentlichkeit: Untersuchungen zu einer Kategorie der bürgerlichen Gesellschaft* (Neuwied, 1962).

Kant, Immanuel. *Foundations of the Metaphysics of Morals and What Is Enlightenment*. Indianapolis, 1975.

Marco, Joaquín. *Literatura popular en España en los siglos XVIII y XIX: Una aproximación a los pliegos de cordel*. Madrid, 1977.

Maza, Sarah. *Private Lives and Public Affairs: The Causes Célèbres of Prerevolutionary France*. Berkeley, Calif., 1993.

Moureau, François, ed. *De bonne main: La communication manuscrite au XVIIIᵉ siècle*. Paris and Oxford, 1993.

Roche, Daniel. *Les Républicains des Lettres: Gens de culture et Lumières au XVIIIᵉ siècle*. Paris, 1988.

Spufford, Margaret. *Small Books and Pleasant Histories: Popular Fiction and Its Readership in Seventeenth-Century England*. London, 1981.

ROGER CHARTIER
Translated from French by Sylvia J. Cannizzaro

PROBABILITY. *See* Mathematics *and* Natural Philosophy and Science.

PROGRESS. Commentators on the Enlightenment have tended to assign special importance to its belief in progress, and to the historical optimism of the period generally, often identifying it as one of the Enlightenment's core ideas, a cornerstone of the entire movement's intellectual foundation, particularly in France. Since the 1950s, however, historians have given new emphasis to the philosophes' doubts and reservations about the likelihood of progress, and there is no longer consensus on the centrality of progress to the Enlightenment. Despite the numerous doubters, nevertheless, there can be no question that many, perhaps most, members of the eighteenth-century intellectual elite held broadly optimistic views about what had happened in the past or would happen in the future—although they formulated those views in diverse and frequently complicated terms.

The Idea of Progress. The most influential definition of *Progress* remains that of historian J. B. Bury, writing in 1920: "This idea means that civilisation has moved, is moving, and will move in a desirable direction." Many thinkers, however, consider historical change from perspectives other than that of civilization in its entirety, and only some see the present and the future as following a course that is uniform with that of the past. To be useful for historical generalization and analysis, the idea of progress needs to be treated more broadly. Here it is defined as the belief that there has been or will be change for the better in important aspects of social existence—a definition that has the special virtue of conforming fairly closely to the meanings of *progress* given in later eighteenth-century dictionaries.

Recognition of social change of this kind and magnitude comes most readily from a long-range historical sense. The Judeo-Christian tradition, with its linear view that history was aiming at something (redemption), offered one such

intellectual context, while the traditional Greco-Roman notion of a repeating cycle of golden, silver, bronze, and leaden ages offered another. Neither concept was monolithic, of course, and the two coexisted for many centuries after the fall of Rome. From the early Renaissance, humanists envisioned a history in which they themselves appeared as the worthy successors to classical antiquity, following a long period of decay and even darkness. The Protestants of the Reformation echoed this assessment in their criticism of medieval Roman Catholicism and their desire to restore essential elements of the early church. By the sixteenth century, the tripartite division of Western history into ancient, medieval, and modern eras was beginning to emerge.

The development of the idea of progress during the sixteenth and seventeenth centuries hinged on two closely related questions. First, did the arrival of the modern age represent the latest phase of a cyclical process or something new? Second, could and should classical antiquity, so revered by the humanists, be exceeded? A notable contribution to the answers came from the exploration of the non-European world and the discoveries of the Scientific Revolution, which called into question many beliefs of the ancients traditionally accepted as simple fact. Philosophers such as Francis Bacon and René Descartes emphasized new methods of intellectual investigation that challenged reliance on the authority of received opinions, including those from classical antiquity, promoting instead a burgeoning belief in the power of human reason, the importance of observation, and the advancement of knowledge. The doubts raised about the real stature of classical antiquity led to a long "Quarrel" or "battle" of Ancients and Moderns, over the supremacy of their respective achievements in literature, art, and other areas; an underlying question was the possible degeneration of human nature since ancient times. Meanwhile, the growth of commercial activity and urban life encouraged a concentration on quantitative precision which scientific investigation soon strongly reinforced. As they became known and accepted, the discoveries of the Scientific Revolution seemed to belie the theory of degeneration while reinforcing at least some of the claims of the moderns.

At the same time, the sense of uniqueness in history so central to Christianity was heightened by the deep Protestant interest in eschatology (the theology of the Last Things). Many believed that the split with Rome heralded a biblically prophesied strife between good and evil whose outcome would be a millennium of peace and happiness. Toward the end of the seventeenth century, a great Catholic theologian, Bishop Jacques-Bénigne Bossuet, reminded the wide audience of his work on universal history that all events since the Creation, profane as well as sacred, could be placed in a succession of epochs subject to a divine plan and to ongoing divine superintendence.

In all these ways, historical linearity, so deeply embedded in Christianity, was becoming ascendant for secular as well as religious reasons. Out of this complex climate emerged the progressivist thinking of the Enlightenment. Several patterns and diverse sources can be discerned among its wide array of forms, but it is important to know that the eighteenth century's historical optimism was often tempered or reduced by doubts and pessimism, frequently on the part of highly influential thinkers.

Varieties and Patterns. The belief in past or future progress, or both, was widespread among Enlightenment writers and, in all likelihood, their readers. The most common optimistic outlook involved knowledge-based disciplines among the arts and sciences, generally seen as cumulatively progressive in both short and long term, a viewpoint closely connected with the outcome of the quarrel of ancients and moderns.

For more than a century, the partisans of the ancients' achievements had retained the upper hand. By the 1690s, however, the cause of moderns came into its own, with such compelling supporters as Bernard le Bovier de Fontenelle, the longtime secretary of the French Académie Royale des Sciences, and William Wotton, an English classicist and clergyman. The scientific discoveries of recent decades, culminating in the path-breaking, synthetic accomplishment of Sir Isaac Newton in natural philosophy, made it much easier for the supporters of the moderns to argue their case. Fontenelle, Wotton, and their eighteenth-century followers contended that in certain fields—above all mathematics, the natural sciences, and philosophy—knowledge was cumulative. This was true, too, of most practical skills and techniques, such as navigation and printing. Given the cumulative achievements of these endeavors, it is hardly surprising that in all these areas the moderns found many supporters. For other disciplines, including literature and the fine arts, the proponents of the moderns acknowledged that final judgments were much less reliable because they usually involved opinion rather than criteria for analytical comparison. Nevertheless, even here there was a growing tendency to prefer Shakespeare, Racine, and Milton to Homer, Sophocles, and Virgil.

Although the Quarrel abated in intensity as the new century proceeded, it yielded a consistent Enlightenment belief in the tendency of knowledge to build on itself over time (and, thus, often an attitude of superiority toward classical antiquity). The progress of knowledge obviously was subject to discontinuities and even retrogressions from time to time, as the Middle Ages evidenced. Still, it seemed quite clear that the tide was coming in, and increasingly quickly. This view, expressed by both philosophes and their opponents all across Europe, undergirded that central project of the Enlightenment, the *Encyclopédie*, and appeared in key early statements by its editors, Denis Diderot and Jean Le Rond d'Alembert. It represented the most fundamental element of the idea of progress at the time.

Several less common eighteenth-century doctrines of progress also played important roles. In Britain and Germany, much more than in France, Christian writers frequently emphasized an improvement in religion itself. Among the English and the Scots, many clergymen saw not only secular but also religious knowledge as advancing cumulatively over time; some also believed that the true faith was spreading to more and more people around the globe, and some even expected a gradual improvement in religious institutions and the religious life of the faithful. Views of this kind appear among conservative and liberal Anglicans, English Dissenters, evangelicals such as John Wesley, and Scottish Presbyterians. They attributed religious progress both to divine providence and to human agency. This same combination underlay Gotthold Ephraim Lessing's celebrated *Education of the Human Race* (1780). In this work, the German philosopher and playwright posited a progressive divine revelation that guided human intellectual development toward the perfection of reason. Some historians have preferred to consider progress a purely secular idea, or at least one derived from providentialism through secularization, but these Protestant views reveal a more complicated story.

The relationship between providence and progress became most complex in the case of eighteenth-century eschatological conceptions, especially apocalypticism and millennialism. These appeared from time to time in France—with the Camisards around 1700, and in the early 1730s with the miracles and the convulsionaries of Saint-Médard in Paris (who included Voltaire's brother). For the most part, however, eschatology was a Protestant concern; in eighteenth-century Britain, many scholarly interpreters of biblical prophecies worked diligently to correlate past events with scriptural predictions, to assess the "signs of the times," and to determine the proximity of the millennium and other last things. Their efforts gave new intellectual impetus to the Christian hopes of thousands of readers and listeners, especially by suggesting that the millennium would begin in the not too distant future and would take place in an earthly setting similar to the present.

Least numerous but most influential in after years were the doctrines of general progress articulated from midcentury on, often by Enlightenment philosophes. These visions of broadly conceived improvement usually employed a long time-frame and were influenced substantially by the achievements of Western history since the later Middle Ages or the Renaissance. Among them were "stadial," four-stage theories that identified a progressive series of economic systems—hunting and gathering, pastoralism, agriculture, and finally commerce—as evolving over the ages in diverse civilizations. In this model, change in the means of subsistence was the organizing principle for understanding the development of society. In the more fully articulated instances of the stadial theory, each successive economic stage involved specific social, political, and intellectual forms. François Quesnay, the leader of the Physiocrats, Antoine Yves de Goguet, and Claude-Adrien Helvétius, all offered developed stadial theories that varied in complexity and emphasis.

Turgot. The first proponent of this approach in France was probably Anne-Robert-Jacques Turgot, writing in the early 1750s, long before he became comptroller general of finances. He saw strong evidence in the record of the past for the inevitability of future advances in science, technology, and moral behavior (though not in poetry or the fine arts). Based on the creative possibilities inherent in human genius and the potentialities for cumulative knowledge built into language, he thought indefinite progress was a central characteristic of life, and he considered the human species capable of perfectibility—not perfection itself, but an ever nearer approach to perfection. Turgot's outlook on progress, contained in unpublished lectures and an essay, was not widely known during his lifetime.

In England, very similar views appeared in print from the 1740s on. A diverse group of writers, ranging from Dissenters like the polymath Joseph Priestley to the Anglican bishop of Carlisle, Edmund Law, propounded the notion that there had been and would continue indefinitely to be progress on all fronts, from knowledge to happiness. Although they grounded this assessment on past human (and especially European) achievements, its warranty was a Christian vision of providential history. Their beliefs achieved a wide following and, apart from the theological underpinnings, paralleled the conceptions of more secular late-eighteenth-century English thinkers, from the great historian Edward Gibbon to the novelist and radical political writer William Godwin. The feminist author Mary Wollstonecraft, who was briefly Godwin's wife, held views about perfectibility similar to his; she believed that women eventually would achieve equality with men and begin to realize the power of improvement embodied in their capacity to reason. Influenced by these English views, Thomas Jefferson believed strongly in perfectibility and, like other Americans of the founding generation, felt certain that his own country would contribute much to the realization of the promise of indefinite progress.

Adam Smith. Meanwhile, Adam Smith constructed his own four-stage theory in Scotland at precisely the same time as Turgot in France, and it became part of both his lectures to university students and the *Wealth of Nations* (1776). Virtually all the leading lights of the Scottish intellectual elite—including the jurist Henry Home, Lord Kames, the philosopher and historian David Hume, the head of the Church of Scotland and Edinburgh University, William Robertson, and the professors Adam Ferguson and John Millar—devised stadial theses of some kind. To be sure, not all these Scots thought of the development of civilization in primarily economic terms. What they had in common was an understanding of history in which societies advanced from barbarism to refinement, and a conviction that there had been substantial progress in Europe toward a refined civilization, starting with the blossoming commerce of the late Middle Ages. Except for Ferguson, they differed from Turgot and the English in not sharing an ardent confidence about the future. They thought that the progress of recent centuries could continue, but they worried that the opulence of refined commercial life threatened morals. For most of the leading Scots, therefore, indefinite progress was possible but hardly guaranteed, and perfectibility was not a definitive human characteristic.

Condorcet. The most celebrated eighteenth-century doctrine of progress belonged to a man often called the last of the philosophes, the mathematician and reformer Jean-Antoine-Nicolas Caritat de Condorcet. While in hiding from the Jacobins in 1793–1794, he wrote a *Esquisse d'un tableau historique des progrès de l'esprit humain* that is often considered the epitome of Enlightenment belief in progress. It described ten epochs of history, linked by the advancement of rational intelligence along a path of indefinite progress, despite the great weight of priestcraft and other obstacles. Historical progress had occurred in all domains, had quickened recently, and was capable of further acceleration by knowledgeable human effort. Limitless perfectibility being a principal characteristic of the species, the coming tenth epoch held enormous promise. For example, Condorcet foresaw the end of warfare between nations and the development of international organizations to assure perpetual peace (as had a few others, from the little-known Charles-Irénée Castel, abbé de Saint-Pierre, who may have been the first to write about indefinite social progress, to the great philosopher Immanuel Kant, who thought the pursuit of progress and peace a moral obligation). The achievable goals of the tenth epoch also included equality for women, equality among nations, the spread of moral goodness and its application to politics, the end of disease, and the indefinite postponement of death. For Condorcet, a student of the optimistic views of Turgot and Priestley, progress led to a utopian future.

Sources of Optimism. With some regularity, historians have attributed the idea of progress to the secularization of Christian providentialism, thereby making Condorcet's utopia an earthly heaven. Not even a small set of influences, however, let alone a single factor such as secularization, adequately accounts for the abundance and diversity of beliefs in progress during the Enlightenment. In general, both intellectual and social considerations played important roles in the varied appeal of such notions. Certain intellectual traditions—especially the Christian vision of history, millennialism, themes concerning the advancement of learning, and the quarrel of ancients and moderns—contributed much to the context in which the idea of progress developed in the eighteenth century. At the same time, notable real-world changes also made essential contributions to the nature and appeal of the ideal of progress: the emergence of political stability in Britain, the agitation for reform in France, and the earliest stages of the Industrial Revolution. Nor is it possible to ignore the nurturing role played by local and national academies and learned societies in promoting belief in progress. Many of them existed precisely to make certain that improvements in the arts and sciences reached a wide audience, and to contribute to further advances by taking advantage of cooperative endeavor.

Among intellectual factors that were new, sensationalism was of particular significance. The concept that human beings are shaped largely by sensory experience, promulgated by John Locke in the late seventeenth century, soon became the standard view of most of the philosophes and their contemporaries. Works by David Hartley, Helvétius, and Étienne Bonnot de Condillac established a psychology according to which "malleability" or "pliability" was an essential human characteristic, with the implication that individuals, and by extension all of society, could be shaped for good (or ill) by experience. In building his conception of indefinite progress and perfectibility, Turgot relied heavily on this consideration, as did virtually all the British exponents of general progress and such American revolutionaries as Benjamin Rush. Rush emphasized education as the key to effecting improvement. Jeremy Bentham's utilitarian program to legislate for the greatest happiness of the greatest number rested heavily on similar considerations.

Of almost equal importance to the development of the idea of progress was the eighteenth century's historiographic revolution, led by such eminent figures as Voltaire, Robertson, Hume, and Gibbon. These and other writers of history broke away from the customary assemblage of facts and political chronology to provide broadly interpretive works in which habits, customs, and cultural and intellectual activities featured prominently. In addition, often under the influence of *L'esprit des lois* by Montesquieu, such historians tended to treat society as organically related in its various aspects, and mankind as

a social product. Montesquieu's ideas also stimulated the use of "conjectural" or "natural" history, used by many Scottish thinkers and others. Under this practice, what was known about Arab clans, American tribes, and ancient Mediterranean peoples became the basis for an imaginative reconstruction of the life and mores of early human society, for which documentary evidence did not exist. These innovations in historiography and early anthropology contributed greatly to seeing civilization as a whole and to envisioning its systemic alteration over time—vital elements of many doctrines of general progress. Furthermore, many of the leading historians and practitioners of conjectural history espoused in their own works a belief in progress.

Related to these historiographic changes were substantial adjustments in the perception of time itself. Thanks to contemporary geological and biological discoveries, the duration of existence expanded appreciably for many intellectuals and their readers. The eternal fixity of species came under scrutiny, and a proto-evolutionary point of view, "transformism," emerged. These developments called into question scriptural accounts and longstanding Christian traditions about the past, and, more important, they brought the idea of historical change to the center of an educated person's horizon. Likewise, the concept of the century entered the vernacular around 1700, furthering the division of time into quanta that had been initiated by the advent of mechanical clocks. Now it was possible to use specific labels (such as quattrocento) for specific periods, thereby capturing the historical essence of those eras. In general, uniformity and permanence were disappearing in favor of division and change. No wonder the English writer Samuel Johnson thought innovation omnipresent! The Western emphasis on *being* was giving way to ideas of *becoming*, and the belief in progress complemented and benefited from this transition.

Change and reform, including change in the general way of thinking, were central to the Enlightenment, of course. It was natural, therefore, for Bury to argue that, more than anything else, passionate desire for reform powered the spread of the idea of progress in France. Indeed, there can be no doubt that the quest of the French philosophes for dramatic changes in church and state went hand in hand with the argument made by many of them that progress was built into history. From this perspective, the idea of progress served as a hope, a utopia, or even a form of propaganda. But the experience of some change can readily produce expectations of still more, and this was true particularly for the British. Their achievement of a political system of comparative freedom and reliable functioning, the increasing prosperity associated with agricultural improvement and commercial prosperity, and the coming of an industrial economy all gave the British elite confidence—more confidence than was enjoyed by any other nation of the age. There, the growing sense of human capacity, renewed throughout the West with the Renaissance and propelled forward by Newtonian science, reached new heights. Little wonder that doubts and pessimism are harder to identify in England and even Scotland than elsewhere, until early nineteenth-century criticism of the Industrial Revolution.

Doubts and Alternatives. Throughout the Enlightenment, historical optimism was rarely unalloyed, and pessimism about history found frequent expression even among the greatest of the philosophes. For instance, Voltaire wrote much about progress, and sensationalism gave him a strongly optimistic outlook on the long-term possibilities for improvement through reason, yet grave doubts increasingly overtook him. He saw four high points in history (Periclean Athens, Rome under Caesar and Augustus, the Renaissance, and the age of Louis XIV), but these were like an oasis in a historical desert of cruelties, crimes, and follies. In his opinion, fanaticism posed an ongoing threat to the progress of true philosophy, and civilization was permanently vulnerable to degeneration; indefinite progress and perfectibility therefore seemed implausible. Diderot's views ran parallel; the progress of knowledge, insisted upon by the *Encyclopédie* as a chief characteristic of recent times, would eventually encounter an upper boundary, he thought. Likewise, happiness was limited by human biology and the evil inherent in human nature, while moral progress seemed to have gone almost as far as it could. Further, Diderot believed that decline inevitably followed growth, a theory of flux that also applied to his biological transformism. Montesquieu not only objected to perfectibility but also contended that eventual decadence was inherent in progress, with the spirit of any nation (and therefore its civilization) subject to decline in almost cyclical fashion. Both Montesquieu and Diderot knew about and may have read the work of Giambattista Vico, a Neapolitan professor and philosopher who early in the century had developed a cyclical theory of history. Vico believed that the cycle's continual pattern applied to every society, with each stage involving both gains and losses.

Substantial doubts of various kinds were hardly rare among the philosophes, therefore, and nonlinear alternatives to the idea of progress did exist. For their part, the orthodox Christian opponents of the French philosophes sometimes simply refused to accept progress as part of the divine dispensation and challenged the progressive implications of sensationalist psychology. Such a reaction was much less likely in Protestant countries, although Thomas Malthus's famous *Essay on the Principle of Population* (1798) constituted a response to the perfectibilism of Condorcet and Godwin by an Anglican clergyman who refused to accept the possibility of created beings perfecting themselves without divine assistance. Perfectibility elicited other hostile rejoinders, for example from John Adams, who thought it unrealistic, even though he was fundamentally optimistic about history and the future of his new country.

By contrast, the century's most provocative critic of progress, Jean-Jacques Rousseau, acknowledged the existence of a faculty of perfectibility as a unique human characteristic, responsible for the tremendous progress of the arts and sciences across the centuries. Unfortunately, he argued, it was precisely this progress that had ruined human morals; it subjected men and women, through their vanity, to the fulfillment of artificial needs, while suppressing the inborn human compassion for others. This process of degeneration had taken place in an increasingly civilized social setting and must be reversed there, not in a state of nature. Thus, Rousseau urged social, political, and educational reforms that would tap human virtues and promote dutiful citizenship in a moral society. This projected regeneration represented a vision of future progress, but the record of the past, so encouraging to other philosophes, was for Rousseau a history of disaster.

Rousseau marks the late Enlightenment transition to Romanticism, exemplified also by the German philosopher and clergyman Johann Gottfried von Herder, whose work emphasized the diversity of cultures and eras. He denied that there was a single standard by which all history could be judged, because each culture and each age had its own pattern of development. Consequently, it would not do to consider modern European civilization superior to that of the Middle Ages. Rather, the contribution of each nation or century was uniquely valuable; over long periods of time, rising and falling, they contributed to the collective education of humankind and thereby to the increase of true humanity. This was progress, surely, but hardly linear or celebratory of the accomplishments of the Enlightenment.

[*See also* Ancients and Moderns; Encyclopédie; Millenarianism; *and* Revealed Religion.]

BIBLIOGRAPHY

Becker, Carl L. *The Heavenly City of the Eighteenth-Century Philosophers*. New Haven, Conn., 1932. Classic statement of the theory that the philosophes adapted the idea of progress from providentialism, through secularization.

Berlin, Isaiah. *Vico and Herder: Two Studies in the History of Ideas*. New York, 1976. Conveniently reprints two essays on key figures offering alternatives to more typical eighteenth-century views on progress.

Blumenberg, Hans. *The Legitimacy of the Modern Age*. Translated by Robert M. Wallace. Cambridge, 1983. English translation of *Die Legitimität der Neuzeit*, first published in 1966. Sees the idea of progress as a uniquely modern concept and not as the result of secularization from Christian historical views.

Brumfitt, J. H. *Voltaire Historian*. Oxford, 1958; repr., Westport, Conn., 1985. Especially useful for understanding contemporary French historiography and the complexity of Voltaire's historical vision.

Bury, J. B. *The Idea of Progress: An Inquiry into Its Origin and Growth*. London, 1920. Still the standard work on the entire subject.

Frankel, Charles. *The Faith of Reason: The Idea of Progress in the French Enlightenment*. New York, 1948. Probably the best book ever written on a particular aspect of the history of this idea.

Gay, Peter. *The Enlightenment: An Interpretation*. 2 vols. New York, 1966, 1969. A classic, a lightning rod for criticism, and a work that popularized Enlightenment reservations about progress.

Green, F. C. *Rousseau and the Idea of Progress*. Oxford, 1950. Despite its brevity, the best account of Rousseau's outlook.

Hampson, Norman. *The Enlightenment*. Baltimore, 1968. Contains a stimulating chapter on time.

Kors, Alan Charles. *D'Holbach's Coterie: An Enlightenment in Paris*. Princeton, N.J., 1976. Illuminates the diverse historical outlook of this group, including Chastellux, Helvétius, and LeRoy.

Manuel, Frank. *The Prophets of Paris: Turgot, Condorcet, Saint-Simon, Fourier, and Comte*. Cambridge, Mass., 1962. Includes long, thoughtful chapters on Turgot and Condorcet.

Meek, Ronald. *Social Science and the Ignoble Savage*. Cambridge, 1976. First-rate chapters on Enlightenment versions of the four-stage theory.

Nisbet, Robert. *History of the Idea of Progress*. New York, 1980. Comprehensive, but highly opinionated, based largely on secondary accounts, and lacking references and bibliography.

Passmore, John. *The Perfectibility of Man*. New York, 1970. Brilliant introduction to the subject, with much Enlightenment material and insights into "malleability" as a result of sensationalism.

Pollard, Sidney. *The Idea of Progress: History and Society*. Harmondsworth, U.K., 1971. The best recent work on European versions of the idea since the seventeenth century; critics of the idea are considered, too.

Reill, Peter Hanns. *The German Enlightenment and the Rise of Historicism*. Berkeley, Calif., 1975. Includes a general assessment of the sources of the idea of progress in the *Aufklärung*.

Spadafora, David. *The Idea of Progress in Eighteenth-Century Britain*. New Haven, Conn., 1990. Covers both English and Scottish views and relates them to French thinking.

Vyverberg, Henry. *Historical Pessimism in the French Enlightenment*. Cambridge, Mass., 1958. Insightful, comprehensive account of French reservations and alternative views.

Wagar, W. Warren. "Modern Views of the Origins of the Idea of Progress." *Journal of the History of Ideas* 28 (1967), 55–70. The standard historiography of the topic.

DAVID SPADAFORA

PROPERTY. *See* Economic Thought.

PROTESTANTISM. *See* Reformed Churches *and* Revealed Religion.

PUBLISHING. The publishing and bookselling trades were essential to the diffusion of the ideas of the Enlightenment: without the technology of printing and the existence of a commercial network for the circulation of their works, the authors of the eighteenth century would have remained an isolated coterie without much influence on the world around them. Enlightenment authors regularly celebrated the contribution the "black art" had made to the progress of the human mind, and Benjamin Franklin achieved his status as an icon of the movement in part because he had been a printer and publisher as well as an author. "Hasn't printing liberated the enlightenment of peoples from all political and religious chains?" Condorcet asked in his *Esquisse d'un tableau historique des progès de l'esprit humain*. It is no accident that Diderot and d'Alembert's *Encyclopédie*, the collective intellectual project that symbolized the Enlightenment movement, was also one of the century's great publishing enterprises and one of its great best-sellers. Press freedom was one of the philosophes' characteristic demands, and a number of eighteenth-century authors, including Diderot and James Boswell, went beyond abstract considerations to write tracts about specific legislative issues involving the book trade. Conversely, a number of eighteenth-century publishers and booksellers actively engaged themselves on behalf of Enlightenment authors and their ideas. Although conflicts between writers and publishers were frequent, the payments they received from their publishers were a vital source of income for many of the period's authors, freeing them from dependence on patronage. Furthermore, publishers and booksellers, by pursuing their own interests, played a key role in the expansion of the reading public that was one of the movement's great aims.

Despite the strong connections between the book trade and the Enlightenment, both publishers and writers always remained conscious of the fact that the interests of the industry and those of the movement, though often parallel, were not identical. As long as readers would buy them, publishers were more than happy to print and sell books that had nothing to do with the Enlightenment, as well as the texts of the philosophes. Even Franklin, in his printing days, moved quickly to cash in on the religious enthusiasm of the Great Awakening in the American colonies. The same authors who hailed Gutenberg's invention also frequently lamented the role it played in circulating what they saw as superstitious, frivolous, or vulgar ideas. Enlightenment texts never dominated the eighteenth-century book market; indeed, the printing of books was just one part of the printing industry, coexisting with the printing and marketing of periodicals, almanacs, liturgical works, advertising, and job printing for governments and businesses of all kinds. Eager to protect their livelihood, printers and publishers were also generally less willing than authors to challenge government and religious authorities. Some authors, however, rejected the notion that ideas were commodities and opposed the protection of literary property on which publishers' profits depended. The relationship between publishing and bookselling and the project of Enlightenment was thus always a complicated one.

In the eighteenth century, the separation between publishing—the acquisition of manuscripts and the supervision of their printing—and bookselling was much less clear than it became later. Most publishers were also booksellers, and many also ran lending libraries and put out periodicals. Books were sold not only in shops devoted exclusively to that purpose but also by itinerant peddlers, or colporteurs, by *bouquinistes* operating from portable stands, and by merchants who dealt in a variety of other goods; eighteenth-century English provincial booksellers typically also handled stationery and patent medicines. The book trade had, of course, existed prior to the era of the Enlightenment. Gutenberg's invention had spread to most of Europe well before 1600, and there had long been bookstores in all major cities. Under Louis XIV, the French government had adopted a deliberate policy to restrict the number of printers, which remained limited until the French Revolution of 1789, but most other European rulers put no such obstacles in the way of the development of the trade. Booksellers were more numerous than printers. By the 1740s, there were at least 381 shops in England, spread among 174 towns. A directory of European booksellers published in 1778 lists 932 establishments in 236 French towns, with 129 shops in Paris alone. In the same year, there were at least 303 bookstores in the Dutch Republic—121 of them in Amsterdam, and the others distributed among forty other cities. The French book-trade almanac of 1778 also listed booksellers carrying French titles in other countries: such establishments existed in 104 German towns, 43 places in Italy, and in major cities in the British Isles, Poland, Russia, Sweden, Denmark, Spain, Portugal, Malta, and the American colonies. The number of shops selling works published in local languages was undoubtedly higher, especially in Germany, where data from the Napoleonic period show a network of small book-trade establishments reaching farther into the countryside than in any other part of Europe.

Although statistics on the number of books and periodicals published in the major European countries during the eighteenth century are all subject to a large margin of uncertainty, there is clear evidence of a consistent pattern of rising production, especially in the second half of the century. In France, the volume of books produced probably tripled between 1700 and 1770; in Germany, the number of new book titles published rose from around 750 a year in the early 1740s to as many as 5,000 in the 1780s and 1790s. The number of French-language periodicals published in Europe, forty-one in

1720, had climbed to 167 by 1780. The growth of the market for reading matter was due partly to population growth and a gradual rise in literacy rates, but the book-consuming public certainly did not grow as fast as the volume of publications. The increase in the sales of books and periodicals can probably be attributed mostly to the fact that the well-to-do minority of the population who accounted for most sales were buying and reading more printed matter than their ancestors. A shift from the "intensive" reading of a small number of books, mostly traditional religious texts, to "extensive" consumption of a constantly changing literary diet, which seems to have affected at least a significant part of the European reading public, stimulated the development of the book trade.

Changes in the book trade were partly responsible for this increased production. The period of the Enlightenment coincided with a growing commercialization of publishing, as individual entrepreneurs became more aggressive in their methods and their pursuit of profit and "enlightened" rulers adopted measures to favor greater competition. Although publishing had been a commercial, capitalist business from the outset, seventeenth-century publishers had often operated, voluntarily or involuntarily, in ways that put security ahead of innovation. In England, for example, the major booksellers had been grouped together in the Stationers' Company, which exercised a joint monopoly over most printed works and discouraged individual firms from seeking best-sellers or new markets—as John Locke complained. Members granted one another what were in effect perpetual copyrights for the books they published, ruling out competition and leaving authors with little bargaining power. The longstanding German practice by which booksellers exchanged printed works on a sheet-for-sheet basis meant that there was no reason to distinguish between works that were likely to appeal to the public and those with no market: the printer of a popular work had to trade copies to his colleagues for their less desirable publications, and he made no special profit. German booksellers were also able to return unsold copies to the publisher for full credit, which gave them no incentive to distinguish between titles in demand and others. The absence of effective copyright protection in all European countries made it difficult for the publisher of a successful book to keep his profits, and it discouraged generous payments to authors. Government-granted privileges provided publishers some protection for their properties, but at the price of submitting to censorship restrictions that limited their ability to respond to public interests.

England was a pioneer in moving toward institutional arrangements that made a more market-oriented form of publishing possible. After an unsuccessful attempt to impose rigid controls under the Stuart Restoration, the

A Print Shop. At left, a compositor picks letters from a typecase and makes up lines of text in a composing stick. At center, a typesetter puts the lines into a narrow tray called a galley. At right, a typesetter prepares two pages of type for printing. Illustration from the *Encyclopédie*.

Licensing Act, which had regulated printing, was allowed to lapse in 1695. This left publishing completely unregulated. Censorship was never restored, but in 1709, a Copyright Act, the first in any European country, set terms of twenty-one years for books already printed and fourteen years, renewable for an additional fourteen by the author, for new works. The dominant London publishers managed to prevent the development of a genuine free market for some decades, but in 1774, the House of Lords ruled explicitly that anyone could reprint a book after the legal term had expired. In France, a government edict of 1777 was intended to break up the Paris publishers' virtual monopoly over book publishing and encourage more competition. In Germany in the 1760s, the publisher Philipp Erasmus Reich organized the more entrepreneurially minded firms in his native Saxony, the center of the German book trade, to challenge the exchange system. Although booksellers in other parts of Germany resisted these reforms, the result was a marketing system that rewarded initiative on the part of publishers and encouraged larger payments to successful authors. Similar pressures from expansion-minded enterprises—like the Remondini firm in Bassano, which owned fifty presses

and employed more than one thousand workers and peddlers to print and sell its popular almanacs—led to the end of the Venetian book-exchange system after 1762.

Eighteenth-century publishers and booksellers did not just benefit from a growing market: they worked hard to promote interest in their products. Journals devoted to book reviews, a characteristic product of the earliest phases of the Enlightenment at the end of the seventeenth century, alerted readers to new publications and helped stimulate sales; organizing booksellers' catalogs more rationally made it easier for would-be purchasers to identify titles they wanted. During the eighteenth century, publishers made increasing use of publicity, circulating elaborate prospectuses and placing advertisements in the ever-growing number of periodicals. Authors contributed to this effort, reading selections from their works in Paris salons, for example, or—as in Voltaire's case—using their personal correspondence to drum up interest in their newest publications. Publishers also published books in smaller formats and sometimes sold them in sections to reduce prices and increase sales. Series such as Johnson's *Lives of the Poets* and Paulmy's *Bibliothèque universelle de romans* were meant to encourage purchasers to subscribe for a set of works rather than just a single book. The books sold thanks to these new practices of commercialization were not necessarily related to the Enlightenment, but the interest in reading and the enlargement of the potential audience for printed works that these tactics promoted served the philosophes' purposes.

The absence of any international recognition of copyright meant that even publishers in countries that had such legislation, like England, faced competition from printers in foreign countries. England's Copyright Act did not apply in Scotland or Ireland, where printers did a lively trade in cut-price editions of English authors, including Smollett, Goldsmith, and Gibbon, which were sold in England and especially in the North American colonies. When stricter legislation put an end to Scottish and Irish book piracy, many of its practitioners, such as the Dubliner Matthew Carey, migrated to the newly independent United States, where English copyrights could be ignored with impunity. Benjamin Franklin commented that "if books can be had much cheaper from Ireland . . . is this not an advantage, not to English booksellers, indeed, but to English readers, and to learning?" This reflected Enlightenment thinkers' divided loyalties on the issue: committed, on the one hand, to fair rewards for authors like themselves, they also wanted to see books and ideas circulated as widely as possible.

Extraterritorial firms played an even greater role in French-language publishing, and the contribution of publishers in the Netherlands, Avignon, Switzerland, Italy, and Germany to the French Enlightenment was essential. The expulsion of the Huguenots from France in 1685 had helped to implant a network of French-language printers and booksellers in the Netherlands. Pierre Bayle's *Dictionary*, the famous "arsenal of the Enlightenment," and his *Nouvelles de la République des lettres* were among the first important Enlightenment works put out on Dutch presses. Dutch publishers also produced the first editions of Montesquieu's *Persian Letters*, Rousseau's *Social Contract*, and innumerable other classics of the French Enlightenment. In Bayle's day, the Netherlands was at war with Louis XIV's France, and permitting the publication of subversive works was one way of striking back at the enemy. In the more stable conditions of the eighteenth century, extraterritorial publishing became largely a commercial affair, although some publishers eagerly embraced the ideas proposed in the Enlightenment texts they published. By putting out works that could not pass the censorship in France, foreign publishers tapped a lucrative market. As it became clear that the French government would not take serious retaliatory measures against neighboring states for tolerating such activities, similar enterprises were established in Switzerland (where Montesquieu's *De l'esprit des lois* [Spirit of the Laws] appeared in 1748),

in principalities along the Belgian and German borders (such as Bouillon, home to Pierre Rousseau's *Journal encyclopédique*), and in the papal enclave of Avignon. Some French-language books were also published in England, and two editions of the *Encyclopédie* were published in Italy.

The existence of this network of publishing enterprises had important consequences for the French Enlightenment. Despite the French censorship system, authors could be confident that almost anything they wrote, no matter how daring, would eventually be published and marketed, and that they would even be able to derive some income from their labors, although they might have to allow their creations to appear anonymously. Bans on the import of forbidden works served primarily to drive up prices and profits, rather than to keep such titles out of circulation. The success of these foreign editions provided a strong argument for broadening the boundaries of tolerance in France itself. Book-trade officials there were sympathetic to the complaint that excessively strict censorship let foreign publishers capture profits that should have been kept in the kingdom. The existence of the foreign presses therefore drove French censors to create an elaborate system of informal arrangements by which domestic publishers were allowed to put out works that were officially prohibited, often on condition that they appear with a false title page indicating that they had been printed abroad. The extraterritorial publishing network thus played an important role in broadening the space in which the French Enlightenment could operate.

The preservation of the business records of one Enlightenment-era extraterritorial publishing firm, the Société Typographique de Neuchâtel (STN), has allowed historians, most notably Robert Darnton, to explore in detail the way such enterprises operated. The STN published about 500 books in the twenty years from 1769 to 1789. At its height, the STN, which did its own printing, had six presses and employed as many as twenty compositors and pressmen. Enlightenment texts were only one part of its publishing program, which was dictated largely by considerations of marketing. The firm was willing to put out anything prohibited in France, including pornography, political tracts, and Protestant Bibles; it would also publish original works and pirate editions of titles that had been legitimately published in France if it thought there was enough demand for them. The STN dealt directly with some authors, including Louis-Sébastien Mercier and J.-P. Brissot, but more often it simply copied texts that were already in print and thereby avoided paying royalties. On some projects, such as the third edition of Diderot's *Encyclopédie*, the STN cooperated with other publishers, both in France and outside, indicating that the boundaries between French and foreign publishers were not absolute. For the diffusion of its products, the STN depended on local bookstores throughout Europe, with which it maintained an extensive correspondence and elaborate credit arrangements. Legal books could be shipped to vendors through normal channels, but the firm also had to have relations with smugglers who carried bundles over the Alps on their backs, and it had to be ready to resort to stratagems such as hiding the leaves of forbidden books between those of legal ones. Enterprises like the STN served the cause of the Enlightenment, not out of conviction, but because the conflict between the French censorship and the philosophes created a lucrative business opportunity.

The personal attitudes of individual publishers toward the new ideas circulating in the eighteenth century varied from hostility or indifference to deep commitment. Even in the latter case, however, publishers who lost sight of economic realities did not remain in business for long. Among the publishers for whom bookselling and propaganda were most closely linked were Prosper Marchand and Benjamin Franklin in the first half of the century, and Christoph Friedrich Nicolai and N.I. Novikov in the second. Marchand, who worked in Paris and later in the Netherlands, was the center of a network of international intellectual activity. A frequent intermediary for French authors looking for a Dutch publisher, he played an important role in circulating rationalist critiques of religion. Franklin helped create a network of printers and booksellers throughout the American colonies; the appeal of his own works, especially *Poor Richard's Almanac*, helped spread interest in reading. Nicolai, located in Berlin, took over his father's publishing firm in 1758. He had already associated himself with Lessing and Mendelssohn in putting out a journal, and in 1765 he founded the *Allgemeine Deutsche Bibliothek*, which became the most important book review in the German-speaking world and a powerful organ of Enlightenment propaganda. Nicolai also engaged himself as an author, taking on both the supporters of religious orthodoxy and new tendencies, such as the Sturm und Drang movement. Novikov, who leased the Moscow University press, also saw publishing as an opportunity to promote an ideological agenda but understood that he needed to be a good businessman as well as a man of ideas. He put out popular books unrelated to his real interests to earn money that would help finance projects to which he was personally committed.

More typical than Marchand, Franklin, Nicolai, or Novikov, however, were publishers who were primarily businessmen and who were interested in Enlightenment texts because they would sell, rather than because of any strong commitment to their content. In Amsterdam, Marc-Michel Rey won the confidence and friendship of a number of leading French authors, including Voltaire,

Rousseau, Diderot, and d'Holbach. His correspondence shows that he was genuinely affected by Rousseau's writings, especially his novels, but he did not necessarily share his authors' philosophical convictions. He published d'Holbach's atheist tracts in spite of the fact that he remained throughout his life a member in good standing of the Huguenot church. The Paris publisher Charles-Joseph Panckoucke had personal links to many leading authors; his sister Marie-Amélie had married J.-B. Suard, a well-connected man of letters, and a pilgrimage to Ferney to meet Voltaire was one of the high points of his life. Panckoucke certainly had no aversion to Enlightenment ideas; he took part in the publishing of the third edition of the *Encyclopédie*, negotiated about issuing a complete edition of Voltaire's work, and later undertook the *Encyclopédie methodique*, the largest of the era's encyclopedic projects. He also established the first great French periodical-publishing empire, acquiring the privileges for the country's official newspaper, the *Gazette de France*, its leading literary journal, the *Mercure de France*, and several other periodicals. His various projects gave him extensive patronage to distribute to needy writers and made him a great power in the country's literary life. The size and complexity of Panckoucke's undertakings, however, also made it imperative for him to keep on good terms with the authorities. Although he was unquestionably more sympathetic to the philosophes than to their opponents, his version of the Enlightenment was a very cautious one; the *Encyclopédie methodique*, for example, carefully avoided the controversies its predecessor had stirred up. In Leipzig, the Weidmann firm—run by Philipp Erasmus Reich, notable for his role in changing marketing procedures—was the leading publisher of Enlightenment texts, even though its director had none of Nicolai's intellectual ambitions.

The development of the publishing industry was important for Enlightenment authors not just because it made the circulation of their ideas possible but also because it provided many of them with crucial economic resources. Publishers freed authors from dependence on individual patrons, although many authors regarded their links with publishers and booksellers as a new form of exploitation. The relationships between Enlightenment authors and their publishers varied tremendously, depending on the character of the individuals involved and the nature of their contracts. Some of these collaborations satisfied both parties: Andrew Millar paid David Hume so well for his *History of England* that Hume declared, "I was become not only independent but opulent." In a few cases, celebrity authors like Klopstock were able to impose draconian terms on their publishers; more often, authors protested that they lost all control over their manuscripts to publishers who paid them only a flat sum, regardless of the work's success, and who considered themselves entitled to put out new editions without consulting the author. The Enlightenment era saw repeated attempts to organize authors so that they could bargain with or bypass commercial publishers—the Society for the Encouragement of Learning in England (1736), Klopstock's Deutsche Gelehrtenrepublik (1773–1774), the Buchhandlung der Gelehrten in Dessau (1781), and Beaumarchais's Société des Auteurs Dramatiques (1777)—but none had much success. The qualities that made for successful authorship were simply not the same as those needed for the successful production and marketing of books.

The relationship between the co-editor of the *Encyclopédie*, Diderot, and his publisher illustrates the complex nature of the relationship between the Enlightenment, the authors who embodied it, and the book trades. The initial idea for a French encyclopedia appears to have come from the publisher Le Breton, who continued to support the project even as it grew to a size that neither he nor Diderot—hired because of his record of success in completing earlier work efficiently—had imagined. Fired with enthusiasm for the enterprise, a number of prominent writers idealistically contributed articles for free, a degree of devotion the poverty-stricken Diderot could not afford. The salary he received for his work was an essential part of his income during the nearly thirty years from the project's inception to the publication of the final volume of illustrations, and it led him to remain loyal to the publisher even when the political difficulties that interrupted the work's appearance led some of its supporters, such as Voltaire, to urge that it be transferred abroad, regardless of the consequences for Le Breton. The publisher's ability to remind the authorities of the financial stakes involved in the project was crucial in ensuring the work's eventual appearance. Both Le Breton, through advertisements and prospectuses, and Diderot, through his network of intellectual connections, contributed effectively to the marketing of the work. Despite the very real cooperation between Diderot and Le Breton that made the project a success, there were also conflicts between them. Both profited from the venture, but on very unequal terms: Diderot earned about 80,000 livres for his editorial work, while the publishers' profit may have reached 2 million livres. As part of the agreement that allowed the distribution of the final volumes, Le Breton surreptitiously altered some of Diderot's more controversial articles; on the other hand, Diderot sometimes secretly supplied critics of the project with ammunition against his publisher. The final result was a contribution to the dissemination of Enlightenment ideas that would have been impossible without the financial and political resources of a well-connected publisher able to use the Europe-wide book-trade network effectively, but it was also an example of the way in which the workings of that industry favored the interests of publishers over those of authors.

The French Revolution's abolition of publishers' privileges put into practice the principles of free competition for which many Enlightenment authors had argued. The end of restrictions on publishing in France and the sudden shift in public demand ruined many traditional publishers, who were left with large stocks of unsalable works. Enterprising newcomers seized the opportunities offered by the situation to establish themselves, often by concentrating on newspapers and pamphlets. The enactment of a copyright law in 1793 changed the relationship between authors and publishers. The end of French censorship crippled the French-language publishers outside the country's borders: authors no longer needed their services. The Napoleonic regime reimposed some restrictions, such as a new but considerably higher limit on the number of licensed printers, but the country's expansion prevented the reestablishment of an extraterritorial industry. The development of power-driven printing machinery and cheap printing paper in the nineteenth century set in motion even greater changes in the book trades. By the middle of the century, many intellectuals had begun to see the book industry itself, with its devotion to the mass market, as an obstacle to the spread of new and original ideas. The idealistic identification of printing and Enlightenment characteristic of the eighteenth century was at an end.

[*See also* Almon, John; Authorship; Cabinets de Lecture; Censorship; Encyclopedias; Encyclopédie; Franklin, Benjamin; Journals, Newspapers, and Gazettes; Libraries; Literacy; Marchand, Prosper; Nicolai, Friedrich; Novikov, Nikolai Ivanovich; Panckoucke, Charles Joseph; Reading and Reading Practices; *and* Rey, Marc-Michel.]

BIBLIOGRAPHY

Amory, Hugh, and David D. Hall, eds. *A History of the Book in America*, vol. 1, *The Colonial Book in the Atlantic World*. Cambridge, 2000. A comprehensive history of the book trades in England's North American colonies up to 1790.

Barbier, Frédéric, et al., eds. *L'Europe et le livre: Réseaux et pratiques du négoce de librairie, XVIe-XIXe siècles*. Paris, 1996. A stimulating collection of recent articles by leading scholars, mostly but not exclusively dealing with the Enlightenment era.

Barbier, Frédéric, et al., eds. *Le livre et l'historien*. Geneva, 1997. This collection of articles in honor of book-history pioneer Henri-Jean Martin includes a number of important contributions dealing with the Enlightenment era.

Berkvens-Stevelinck, Christiane, et al., eds. *The* Magasin de l'Univers: *The Dutch Republic as the Centre of the European Book Trade*. Leiden, 1992. Studies of the role played by the Dutch publishing industry during the Enlightenment era.

Bödeker, Hans Erich, ed. *Histoires du livre: Nouvelles orientations*. Paris, 1995. A collective volume on publishing history, with a number of important articles on the eighteenth century.

Chartier, Roger, Henri-Jean Martin, and Jean-Pierre Vivet, eds. *Histoire de l'édition française*, vol. 2, *Le livre triomphant, 1660–1830*.

Paris, 1983. A massive collaborative volume summing up research on French-language publishing, including the activities of extra-territorial printers.

Cole, Richard Cargill. *Irish Booksellers and English Writers, 1740–1800.* London, 1986. A monograph documenting the role of Irish publishers in the dissemination of eighteenth-century English literature.

Darnton, Robert. *The Business of Enlightenment.* Cambridge, Mass., 1979. Darnton's detailed study of the publishing of the third edition of the *Encyclopédie* illustrates the complex workings of the international market for French-language books.

Darnton, Robert. *The Forbidden Best-Sellers of Pre-Revolutionary France.* New York, 1995. A synthesis of the author's extensive studies of the trade in prohibited books in France during the Enlightenment era.

Feather, John. *The Provincial Book Trade in Eighteenth-Century England.* Cambridge, 1985. An illuminating overview of the development of the bookselling network and the techniques by which books became an easily available commodity.

Hesse, Carla. *Publishing and Cultural Politics in Revolutionary Paris, 1789–1810.* Berkeley, Calif., 1991. An analysis of the French Revolution's impact on publishing and the book trade.

Kapp, Friedrich, and Johann Goldfriedrich. *Geschichte des deutschen Buchhandels.* 6 vols. Leipzig, 1970. The classic study of the German publishing industry, first published in 1908–1909. Vols. 2 (1648–1740) and 3 (1740–1804) cover the Enlightenment era.

Kiesel, Helmuth, and Paul Münch. *Gesellschaft und Literatur im 18. Jahrhundert.* Munich, 1977. A useful overview of publishing and reading in eighteenth-century Germany.

Marker, Gary. *Publishing, Printing, and the Origin of Intellectual Life in Russia, 1700–1800.* Princeton, N.J., 1985. Shows the role of the book trades in the development of the Russian Enlightenment.

Mumby, Frank A., and Ian Norrie. *Publishing and Bookselling.* 5th ed. London, 1974. Although dated, this is the best available brief overview of the history of publishing in eighteenth-century England.

Popkin, Jeremy. "The Book Trades in Western Europe during the Revolutionary Era." *Papers of the Bibliographical Society of America* 78 (1984), 403–445. Based on data from the Napoleonic period, documents differences between book-trade networks in the different regions of western Europe that probably existed earlier and shows how the book trades in France and neighboring territories were affected by the revolutionary upheaval.

Proust, Jacques. *Diderot et l'Encyclopédie.* Paris, 1995. First published in 1962, explains the relationship between Diderot and the work's publisher.

Selwyn, Pamela. *Everyday Life in the German Book Trade: Friedrich Nicolai as Bookseller and Publisher in the Age of Enlightenment, 1750–1810.* University Park, Pa., 2000. The life of the most important "enlightened" publisher in Germany.

Tucoo-Chala, Suzanne. *Charles-Joseph Panckoucke et la librairie française, 1736–1798.* Pau, 1977. The life and business strategies of the leading French publisher of the Enlightenment era.

Wittmann, Reinhard. *Geschichte des deutschen Buchhandels.* 2d ed. Munich, 1999. A succinct overview of the history of the book trades in Germany.

JEREMY D. POPKIN

PUFENDORF, SAMUEL (1632–1694), German natural law theorist, historian, and political philosopher.

Like many other figures of the German enlightenment, both early and late, Pufendorf came from a pious Lutheran background that emphasized moral religion and valued learning. Born a pastor's son at Dorfchemnitz in Saxony, he soon moved with his family to nearby Flöha, where they experienced some of the devastations of the politico-religious conflict known as the Thirty Years' War (1614–1648). After being tutored at home, Samuel followed his older brother, Esaias, to the Prinzenschule at Grimma near Leipzig, where he began to nourish the biblical, classical, and historical interests that persisted throughout his life. Between 1650 and 1658, he attended the University of Leipzig, except for a year (1657) at Jena, where he received his master's degree. At Leipzig, Pufendorf acquired his initial distaste for religious and scholastic dogmatism and developed an interest in jurisprudence and a respect for modern philosophers like Bacon and Descartes. Their works, along with those of Hugo Grotius and Thomas Hobbes, were taught by the eclectic polymath Erhard Weigel. Pufendorf shared Weigel's appreciation for the anti-authoritarianism of the moderns and their appeal to experience, and also his constructive ambition to reduce moral philosophy to a mathematical science—a notion clearly visible in Pufendorf's first work, the *Elementorum jurisprudentiae universalis libri octo* (Eight Books of the Elements of Universal Jurisprudence, 1660).

Samuel Pufendorf. Engraving by J. van Munnikhuysen after a portrait by D. Klocker Ehrenstrahl. (Prints and Photographs Division, Library of Congress.)

Contempt for the professorate (he refused the doctorate) and limited academic opportunities in Leipzig induced Pufendorf, in April 1658, to follow Esaias into the service of Sweden as tutor to the children of Peter Julius Coyet, the Swedish ambassador to Copenhagen. Here he was soon imprisoned because of his employer's complicity in Sweden's sudden resumption of hostilities with Denmark. When released about eight months later, Pufendorf was very ill, but he had also produced his first work, the so-called *Elementa*, which contains many elements of his later philosophy. Written without the benefit of library or notes and utilizing a quasi-mathematical form of organization, it aimed explicitly to reconcile the positions of Hobbes and Grotius.

Pufendorf next accompanied Coyet to the Netherlands, where he enrolled at Leiden University and edited several neo-Latin works. There he met the famous classicist Gronovius, as well as Grotius's son, Peter de Groot, who recommended him to the Elector Karl Ludwig, the tolerant Calvinist ruler of the Palatinate. This support, Pufendorf's strategic dedication of the *Elementa* to Karl Ludwig, and the latter's interest in a philosophical morality not based on sectarian theology led to Pufendorf's appointment to a chair in the philosophy faculty at Heidelberg. There he lectured on Grotius, deepened his knowledge of constitutional law, and gradually developed a new philosophical method more attentive to historical precedent and empirical evidence. This shift in method and Pufendorf's competence in German constitutional law became evident in his polemical, pseudonymous *De statu imperii Germanici* (On the Constitution of the German Empire, 1667), which exposed the functional weaknesses of the Empire as an irregular state lacking effective sovereignty. Here Pufendorf also began his lifelong criticism of the pernicious influence of religion (particularly Catholicism) on politics, using political and ecclesiastical history in the service of philosophical argument. He continued to elaborate his thoughts, including the *Elementa*, in a series of dissertations; and, by 1670, he had completed his magnum opus, *De jure naturae et gentium* (On the Law of Nature and of Nations), which was published in 1672. By this time, Pufendorf had relocated to the new university at Lund in Sweden.

The appearance of *De jure naturae* involved Pufendorf in a series of academic quarrels that reverberated well into the eighteenth century. The work's strict demarcation between natural, civil, and religious law seemed to its opponents to undermine all of these, and Pufendorf was accordingly accused of immorality, political subversion, and apostasy. Fortunately, he was both well connected and an excellent polemicist, besting most of his opponents in a series of sharp and entertaining exchanges that greatly clarified his views and gained him even more disciples

(e.g., Christian Thomasius). These essays were collected in 1686 as *Eris scandica* (The Scandinavian Quarrel). The success of *De jure naturae* also induced Pufendorf to issue a shorter student compendium of its main ideas entitled *De officio hominis et civis* (On the Duty of Man and Citizen, 1674). This work was equally popular and perhaps even more effective, especially during the eighteenth century, when it continued to be read extensively in both the original and other European languages.

After the Danish capture of Lund in 1677, Pufendorf moved to Stockholm, where he became privy councilor and state historian to Charles XI. In the latter capacity, he produced two long histories of Sweden (*Commentariorum de rebus Suecicis libri XXVI*, 1686; *De rebus a Carolo Gustavo Sueciae rege gestis commentariorum libri septem*, 1696), and an innovative survey of major European states told in terms of their respective national interests: *Einleitung zu der Historie der vornehmsten Reiche und Staaten, so itziger Zeit in Europa sich befinden* (An Introduction to the History of the Principal Kingdoms and States of Europe, 1682), which was enlarged in 1684 and eventually translated into many European languages. Indeed, its perceived utility was so great during the first half of the eighteenth century that it was often expanded and "continued" by others. Its realist concept of the state, regarded as a distinct, artificial persona with its own actions, history, and intentions, was rooted in Pufendorf's wider natural law philosophy; thus, it not only addressed the actual experiences of individual states but also offered them a theoretical standpoint from which to justify their respective policies.

In 1685, Louis XIV revoked the Edict of Nantes, formally ending religious toleration in France. Already under pressure in Sweden because of a recent wave of clerical fundamentalism, and incensed and worried by French and Catholic hegemonic pretensions, Pufendorf responded with *De habitu religionis christianae ad vitam civilem* (On the Relation of the Christian Religion to Civil Life, 1687), which contains his case for the state's separation from—and in the civil realm, precedence to—religion. Moreover, he accepted Elector Frederick William's invitation to come to Berlin, where many Huguenot refugees were being welcomed into what became known as The Refuge. Employed in Berlin as privy councilor and state historian, Pufendorf quickly produced two more massive histories: one of the Great Elector himself, *De rebus gestis Friderici Wilhelmi Magni* (1695), and the other a long fragment (not published until 1784) of his son's early years as ruler, *De rebus gestis Friderici Tertii*. The latter work is noteworthy because of its long and detailed account of the Glorious Revolution, which Pufendorf analyzed in terms of his theory of sovereignty and resistance.

The other important work of Pufendorf's final years is *Ius feciale divinum sive de consensu et dissensu protestantium* (The Divine Covenantal Law, or on Agreement and Disagreement among Protestants, 1695). It addressed the problem of religious diversity, elaborated the terms of political and ecclesiastical toleration, and proposed a minimalist theology for unifying Lutherans and Calvinists. Like *De habitu*, it appeared in several further editions, some in English.

Pufendorf's "modern" theory of natural law self-consciously eschewed the divisive epistemological pretensions of revealed theology and essentialist metaphysics; it proposed instead a common basis for ethics and politics in observed human nature. Its central sociality principle sought to mold Grotian social impulse, Hobbesian self-interest, and law-based obligation into an organized normative framework encompassing diverse human roles and institutions, including language, property, domestic relations, and, above all, the state. Its moral voluntarism, methodological empiricism, legal contractualism, and political realism—all illustrated with wide historical learning and applied to current events—supported a politics charged with managing social pluralism rather than instantiating truth or achieving perfection. This accounts for the theory's appeal to early modern rulers of emergent nation-states, who faced the concrete challenge of imposing order on their diverse territories, denominations, and peoples through a justifiable and judicious application of force.

Although he was a major intellectual influence throughout Europe for at least half a century after his death, Pufendorf's fate in the scholarly canon (where he is little known and less read) is vivid testimony to the power of historical reinterpretation. Though his works were reissued hundreds of times during the eighteenth century, and his version of natural law had many disciples, imitators, and popularizers, he nearly disappeared thereafter, effectively eclipsed by the strong, self-serving accounts of philosophy's past in German idealism. (This is particularly ironic in view of Pufendorf's own role in originating the history of moral philosophy as a genre.) There are at least two versions of this tale, and of Pufendorf's significance. J.B. Schneewind sees him as a pivotal figure on the way to Kantian autonomy, to which he indirectly contributed; this story follows Pufendorf's ideas through the British and French, as well as the German contexts. Another, mainly German account, detailed by Ian Hunter, regards him as the casualty of a revivified Christian metaphysics creatively reasserted by Leibniz and Kant; here he represents a fundamental alternative to the so-called religion of reason. That is, Pufendorf is either reinserted into the so-called mainstream that had lost track of him, or else presented as a road not taken. His perceived impact on the Enlightenment is clearly affected by these divergent readings, as is our own interpretation of that phenomenon and its relation to our theorizing.

[*See also* Natural Law; Scandinavia; *and* Toleration.]

BIBLIOGRAPHY

WORKS BY PUFENDORF

De jure naturae et gentium libri octo. Photographic reproduction of the edition of 1688, with a translation by C. H. and W. A. Oldfather. Carnegie Classics of International Law, no. 17. 2 vols. Vol. 2, translation. Oxford, 1934. Particularly useful for its organization of Pufendorf's many citations.

De officio hominis et civis juxta legem naturalem libri duo. Photographic reproduction of the edition of 1682, with a translation by Frank Gardner Moore. Carnegie Classics of International Law, no. 10. 2 vols. Vol. 2, translation. New York, 1927.

Elementorum jurisprudentiae universalis libri duo. Photographic reproduction of the edition of 1672, with a translation by William Abbott Oldfather. Carnegie Classics of International Law, no. 15. 2 vols. Vol. 2, translation. Oxford, 1931.

Gesammelte Werke. Edited by Wilhelm Schmidt-Biggemann. Berlin, 1996–. The first critical, comprehensive edition of Pufendorf's works. The following volumes have appeared to date: 1, *Briefwechsel* (1996), edited by Detlef Döring; 2, *De officio* (1997), edited by Gerald Hartung; 3, *Elementa jurisprudentiae universalis* (1999), edited by Thomas Behme; 4.1 and 4.2, *De jure naturae et gentium* (1998), edited by Frank Böhling; vol. 4.3 will contain the modern editor's notes for *De jure.*

Kleine Vorträge und Schriften. Edited and introduced by Detlef Döring. Frankfurt am Main, 1995. An important collection of incidental pieces by Pufendorf, with extensive and invaluable introductions by Döring.

On the Duty of Man and Citizen. Edited by James Tully, translated by Michael Silverthorne. Cambridge, 1991.

The Political Writings of Samuel Pufendorf. Edited by Craig L. Carr, translated by Michael J. Seidler. New York, 1994. New translations of important excerpts from *Elementa* and *De jure,* with a focus on the main doctrines and their supporting arguments.

STUDIES

Dufour, Alfred. "Pufendorf." In *The Cambridge History of Political Thought, 1450–1700.* Edited by J. H. Burns and Mark Goldie; chap. 19, pp. 561–588. Cambridge, 1991. Good treatment of Pufendorf's doctrine of the state, utilizing other works beside *De jure.*

Haakonssen, Knud. *Natural Law and Moral Philosophy: From Grotius to the Scottish Enlightenment.* Cambridge, 1996. Chap. 1, pp. 15–62. An expansive survey of the whole tradition, useful for seeing Pufendorf in relation to other major and minor figures. Particularly sensitive to contacts between the Continental and British contexts.

Hochstrasser, T. J. *Natural Law Theories in the Early Enlightenment.* Cambridge, 2000. Chaps. 2–3, pp. 40–110. Insightful study of the links between natural law and the early modern historiography of (moral) philosophy. Clarifies the evolution and eventual eclipse of natural law theories.

Hunter, Ian. *Rival Enlightenments: Civil and Metaphysical Philosophy in Early Modern Germany.* Cambridge, 2001. Chap. 4, pp. 148–196, offers a major new interpretation that perceptively contrasts Pufendorfian and Leibnizian natural law in the context of early modern German academic culture; the work also poses an important challenge to traditional readings of Kant, with implications for subsequent Kantians.

Krieger, Leonard. *The Politics of Discretion: Pufendorf and the Acceptance of Natural Law.* Chicago, 1965. One of the earliest studies of Pufendorf in English, still valuable for its biographical details; Krieger's strong interpretation works against its use as an entry to the subject, however.

Schneewind, J. B. *The Invention of Autonomy: A History of Modern Moral Philosophy.* Cambridge, 1998. Chap. 7, pp. 118–140, a magisterial survey, restores Pufendorf's stature as a pivotal moral philosopher in the early modern period, focusing on his voluntarism.

Seidler, Michael. "Introductory Essay." In *Samuel Pufendorf's 'On the Natural State of Men'*, edited and translated by Michael Seidler, pp. 1–69. New York, 1990. A broad introduction that also examines Pufendorf's constructive use of the state of nature.

Tuck, Richard. "The 'Modern' Theory of Natural Law." In *The Languages of Political Theory in Early-Modern Europe*, edited by Anthony Pagden, pp. 99–119. Cambridge, 1987. A seminal article characterizing modern (versus ancient and medieval) natural law—including Grotius, Hobbes, and Pufendorf—as a response to epistemological skepticism and cultural relativism.

Tully, James. "Editor's Introduction." In Samuel Pufendorf, *On the Duty of Man and Citizen*, edited by James Tully, translated by Michael Silverthorne, pp. xiv–xl. Cambridge, 1991. The best discussion of Pufendorf's demarcation of the realms of theology, philosophy, and civil law; also good on the relation between Pufendorf's moral and political philosophy.

MICHAEL J. SEIDLER

QUESNAY, FRANÇOIS (1694–1774), economic theorist.

For economic theorists and historians of economic thought, from Karl Marx to J. J. Schumpeter, Quesnay ranks among the great economists of all time, yet most people, including many intellectual historians, have never heard of him or of physiocracy, the economic school derived from his theories. His renown rests upon his having—shortly before Adam Smith—derived the first modern theory of the circular flow of the economy. His neglect results from the rapidity with which the development of capitalism and the attendant rise of modern economic theory bypassed his vision. For even as Quesnay provided the groundbreaking analysis of capitalist dynamics, he insisted that the land is the source of all wealth, thereby reducing commerce and manufacture to mere parasites upon agriculture.

Born of middling peasant stock, Quesnay began to read only after the age of eleven, but thereafter received instruction in Greek and Latin from a local priest or neighbor and was soon absorbing Plato, Aristotle, and Cicero. His father's death led him to undertake an apprenticeship with a Parisian engraver that brought him into contact with the world of medicine, and, while completing the apprenticeship, he enrolled in courses at the Faculté de Médicine and the surgeon's college in Paris. By 1717, he had completed his training in surgery and, in 1718, was accepted into the Paris Company of Surgeons.

From 1717 to 1723, Quesnay lived in Mantes-la-Jolie with his wife, but after her premature death at the birth of their fourth child, followed by the death of another of their children, he entered the personal service of the Duc de Villeroy, who introduced him into noble, military, and eventually royal circles. By 1744, these contacts had resulted in Quesnay's entry into and appointment as permanent secretary of the Parisian Academy of Surgery; his purchase of the position of first ordinary physician to the king; and his appointment as personal physician to Louis XV's mistress, Madame de Pompadour. In 1749, he moved to Versailles, where his position afforded him a privileged view of the myriad political, financial, and economic difficulties that confronted the monarchy of the ancien régime and increased his visibility among Parisian intellectuals.

Quesnay came to his interest in economics from a background in medicine, supplemented by extensive reading in metaphysics. Quests to explain his thought by the primary influence of any specific thinker, whether Sir Isaac Newton, René Descartes, Gottfried Wilhelm von Leibniz, Christian Wolff, the Dutch physician Hermann Boerhaave, or others, have always foundered on the eclecticism of his thought: He learned from all but followed none exclusively. An invitation to contribute to Denis Diderot's *Encyclopédie* probably prompted him to turn his attention to economics. Volume VI (1756) included his article "Fermiers" (Farmers), and volume VII (1757), his article "Grains." He also wrote "Hommes" (Mankind) and "Impôts" (Taxes), which never appeared because royal approval of the *Encyclopédie* had been withdrawn. In the articles, Quesnay embarked upon the development of his economic theories—a new conception of political economy itself. They especially manifest the emergence of his emphasis upon the importance of free trade in grain; of large-scale—or capitalist—agricultural production; and of substantial profits for farmers to permit them to reinvest.

Quesnay's economic speculations did not yet constitute a full-blown theory, but they attracted considerable attention, in part because they represented an attack on prevailing mercantilist doctrines, and in part because they resonated with the speculations of others. Initially, the most important response came from Victor de Riqueti, Marquis de Mirabeau and author of the wildly successful book, *L'ami des hommes, ou traité de la population* (The Friendship of Men, or a Treatise on Population, 1756). The traditionalist Mirabeau brought a different perspective than Quesnay's to the problem of the monarchy and the country, but he unhesitatingly embraced the essentials of Quesnay's doctrine of the primacy of agriculture in the creation of wealth, and over the ensuing decade, he would prove Quesnay's most fruitful and loyal collaborator. For Mirabeau decisively contributed to the development of physiocracy as a coherent and comprehensive theory of political economy. Together, apparently in 1758, they drafted a "Traité de la monarchie" (Treatise on Monarchy) in which they developed their view of the historical origins and current failures of the French monarchy. Their criticism of the monarchy ultimately precluded publication of the treatise, but elements of it informed both of their subsequent work, beginning with the "Tableau oeconomique avec ses explications" (Economic Table and Its Explanation), the first version of which Quesnay published in 1758.

In 1763, Quesnay and Mirabeau published *La philosophie rurale* (Rural Philosophy), containing the essence of Quesnay's mature political economy, which combined an insistence on the need for freedom of the grain trade (a radical and, to many, dangerous proposition in late-eighteenth-century France), with a call for a single tax (*l'impôt unique*) on land and a "despotism of the laws." By the early 1760s, calls for reform abounded in France, and Quesnay attracted a number of exceptionally able followers who were known as the economists or simply the sect. Through administrative positions, writings, and the editorship of a journal, they helped to disseminate his ideas, which also influenced the monarchy's experiment with freedom of the grain trade.

During the final decade of Quesnay's life, he continued to write, but at a declining rate, and his last book, *La physiocratie* (Physiocracy, 1767) comprised a two-volume collection of his articles, carefully edited by his disciple, Pierre Samuel Du Pont de Nemours. During the final decades of the eighteenth century, the rapid development of political economy, the emergence of industrial capitalism, and the upheavals of the French Revolution all combined to undermine interest in physiocracy, which nonetheless retained surprising influence in parts of eastern Europe and Latin America and which even attracted some followers in the United States. The failure of physiocracy to emerge as a leading branch of political economy should not obscure the startling originality and genius of Quesnay's economic vision, and his celebrated "Tableau"—a diagram of the flow of the economy—in its various forms long continued to fascinate and challenge the best economic minds.

[*See also* Economic Thought; Encyclopédie; *and* Physiocracy.]

BIBLIOGRAPHY

Fox-Genovese, Elizabeth. *The Origins of Physiocracy: Economic Revolution and Social Order in Eighteenth-Century France*. Ithaca, N.Y., 1976.

Hecht, Jacqueline. "La vie de François Quesnay." In Institut National d'Études Démographiques. *François Quesnay et la physiocratie*. 2 vols. Paris, 1958.

Herlitz, Lars. "Trends in the Development of Physiocratic Doctrine." *Scandinavian Economic History Review* IX (1961).

Kuczynski, Marguerite, and Ronald Meek. *Quesnay's* Tableau Économique, *with New Materials, Translations, and Notes*. London and New York, 1972.

Perrot, Jean-Claude. *Une histoire intellectuelle de l'économie politique (XVIIe–XVIIIe siècle)*. Paris, 1992.

Quesnay, François. *Oekonomische Schriften*. Edited by Marguerite Kuczynski. 2 vols. Berlin, 1972.

Weulersse, Georges. *Le mouvement physiocratique en France de 1756 à 1770*. 2 vols. Paris, 1910.

Weulersse, Georges. *Les manuscrits économiques de François Quesnay et du Marquis de Mirabeau aux Archives Nationals (M778 à 785), avec inventaire, extraits, et notes*. Paris, 1910.

ELIZABETH FOX-GENOVESE

R

RABAUT SAINT-ÉTIENNE, JEAN-PAUL (1743–1793), French pastor and political figure.

Born 14 November 1743, in Nîmes, Jean-Paul Rabaut was the eldest son of the Huguenot pastor Paul Rabaut, known as the Desert Preacher. At the age of six, he was sent by his father to school in Switzerland, where he was joined by his two brothers. To hide their identity from the agents of the French king, they were presented as cousins, and Jean-Paul took the name Saint-Étienne. After completing his studies in Geneva and Lausanne, he was certified as a preacher in 1764. He began his career in the ministry the following year in Nîmes, and quickly earned a following thanks to his learning, his religious fervor, and his qualities as a speaker. He worked to improve the fate of his fellow Protestants. In 1778, he wrote *Triomphe de l'intolérance* (Triumph of Intolerance), a novel published in London in 1779, better known as *Le Vieux Cévénol* (The Old Man of the Cévennes).

In 1785, on the initiative of the marquis de Lafayette, he left for Paris, where he wrote memoirs and report-letters on the situation of the Protestants; there he encountered the politically influential Chrétien-Guillaume Malesherbes. His fate was increasingly linked with political developments. He wrote several works on contemporary issues that were imbued with the Enlightenment spirit, including *Considérations sur les intérêts du tiers état* (Considerations on the Interests of the Third Estate).

On 27 March 1789, he was elected deputy of the Third Estate for the Sénéchaussée de Beaucaire. He was in favor of reforms in the kingdom—which had no chance of succeeding without the Third Estate—even though he remained attached to the monarchy.

During the year 1789, Rabaut Saint-Étienne often participated in the discussions of the Assembly and was a member of several committees. He took the initiative in the task of reorganizing the kingdom, and played an important role in drafting the *Déclaration des droits de l'homme* (Declaration of the Rights of Man). On behalf of Protestants he demanded not merely tolerance but also religious and political freedom. On 14 March 1790, he was elected president of the Assembly.

Rabaut Saint-Étienne was deeply disturbed by Louis XVI's flight and capture at Varennes; he blamed those around the king, but he nevertheless became a partisan of the republican regime. After the dissolution of the Constituent Assembly he remained in Paris and composed his *Précis de la Révolution française* (Précis of the French Revolution), in which he concluded that "the French Revolution was...the product of the Enlightenment, which had penetrated, more than was the case for other peoples, into all classes of citizens." In the same year, he also attended the meetings of the Jacobin Club.

In the elections for the Convention, he was elected deputy from the Aube department, and later was elected to serve as one of the secretaries of the Convention. Close to the Girondins and the moderates, and inspired by Jean-Jacques Rousseau's ideas, he prepared a national education plan.

In the king's trial, Rabaut Saint-Étienne spoke out against the Convention's abuses of power. On 23 January 1793, winning a victory over Georges Jacques Danton, he was elected president of the Convention. He also was a member of the Committee of Twelve that conducted an investigation into the Commune, and whose members were placed under indictment. On 2 June the Convention voted for the arrest of twenty-nine deputies from the Gironde, including Rabaut Saint-Étienne.

Rabaut Saint-Étienne hid in Versailles. On 25 July the Assembly determined that he resign his functions, then declared him (along with other Girondins) a traitor to the fatherland and pronounced him an outlaw.

With his brother, Rabaut-Pomier, Rabaut Saint-Étienne took refuge in Paris in the home of the Peyssacs, a Catholic family originally from Nîmes, but they were discovered during a search. He was sent before the revolutionary tribunal and, after a simple verification of identity, Antoine-Quentin Fouquier-Tinville signed the order for his execution.

[*See also* French Revolution; Political Philosophy; *and* Toleration.]

BIBLIOGRAPHY

Borrel, A. *Le pasteur Rabaut et ses trois fils*. Nîmes, France, 1854.

Collin de Plancy. *Oeuvres de Rabaut Saint-Étienne, précédées d'une notice sur sa vie*. 2 vols. Paris, 1826.

Dupont, André. *Rabaut Saint-Étienne, 1743–1793. Un protestant défenseur de la liberté religieuse*. Introduction by Jean Baubérot.

Geneva, 1989, new completed edition (1st ed. 1946). The basic work on Rabaut Saint-Étienne.

Dupont Auzas, Anne-Marie. "L'image de la Révolution française chez Rabaut Saint-Étienne." *Actes du Congrès mondial pour le bicentenaire de la Révolution*, vol. 2, pp. 1033–1041. Paris, 1990.

Les Rabaut: Du Désert à la Révolution. (Colloquium in Nîmes.) Montpellier, France, 1988. Contains several important communications on Rabaut Saint-Étienne's work and political activity.

MYRIAM YARDENI
Translated from French by Catherine Porter

RACE. The use of the French word *race* and its English equivalent in the early-modern period differed significantly from the modern concept that presents humanity as divided into broad categories defined by a fixed set of genetically derived physical traits. The term itself came into European languages in the early sixteenth century, probably derived from the Latin word *generatio* ("procreating") via late medieval Mediterranean dialects. Its principal meaning, when applied to humans, was that of lineage. In this context, *race* could refer to a specific family (the "races" of monarchs or, by extension, "noble races," royal or noble houses), to an entire national category, or even to all the descendants of Adam and Eve, as when the poet John Milton wrote of "the happy seat of some new Race call'd Man" (*Paradise Lost*, 1667).

Comte Henri de Boulainvilliers (1658–1722) is recognized as the major advocate of the notion of race in the early eighteenth century. For all his emphasis on blood and race, his approach owes more to the sixteenth-century concept than to the modern one. Not only did he see the nobility as subdivided into various "races" (i.e., extended families), but he also considered that the qualities of these races were transmitted principally through education rather than blood. As late as 1765, the *Encyclopédie*, which claimed to encompass the sum of French Enlightenment thought, continued to offer lineage, especially as applied to nobles, as the sole definition of *race* when applied to humans.

The first use of *race* in the modern sense dates from 1684. It is contained in an article published anonymously in the *Journal des Sçavans* (1684) by the physician François Bernier. Speaking on the basis of his travel experiences he stated "that there are mostly four or five species or races of men, which differ so much from one another that this difference can serve as a fair basis for a new division of the earth." Bernier claimed that a combination of physical features and skin color characterized each race. In order to be so considered, these features could not be "accidental," but "a part of [its] essence." Bernier's races differed somewhat from modern categories, and he did not explain how the physical traits he noted became fixed. The criteria he used, however, were truly modern, although he derived few value judgments from his observations.

The revival of polygenesis—the view that different human groups had separate origins—by the French literary figure Isaac de La Peyrère, in *Prae-Adamitae* (1655), was another testimony to the emergence of a new understanding of the term. Roundly condemned at the time, the idea was picked up in the eighteenth century, first by the British naval surgeon John Atkins (1685–1757), who applied it to "the black and white Race[s]" which, he argued, "have, *ab origine*, sprung from different-coloured first Parents" (*Voyage to Guinea, Brazil, and the West-Indies*, 1725). It was probably no accident that these theories came to the fore at a time when universalist religious explanations began to lose their power, and when a more secular view of history and a more scientific approach to nature began to emerge. Perhaps equally significant is the fact that the second half of the seventeenth century witnessed the increased use of African slaves in the American economy. At the same time, as Masarah Van Eyck has noted, initial attempts to incorporate some of the Natives into New France's European population, "so that, over time . . . [the two] become one people and one blood" (Colbert to Intendant Talon, 5 April 1667), were abandoned, and Native Americans began to be perceived as fundamentally different from colonists.

Natural scientists provided the next step in the construction of the modern concept of race. Adopting the model of the Great Chain of Being, in which nature progressed in one smooth process from the simplest forms to the most complex, along with the Aristotelian nomenclature of genus and species, the Swedish naturalist Carolus Linnaeus (1707–1778) proposed in *Systema Naturae* (1735) a classification that not only integrated humans within the animal kingdom but also subdivided mankind into several categories identified by physical traits, especially color, and by moral qualities. Thus, Europeans were deemed to be "ingenious, white, sanguine [and] governed by law," while Africans were described as "crafty, lazy, black, melancholy [and] governed by the arbitrary will of the master"; Americans were "governed by custom," and Asians "by opinion."

Even more influential was the work of Georges-Louis Leclerc de Buffon (1708–1788), who refined Linnaeus's classification in *Histoire naturelle* (1749–1788). Buffon clearly differentiated mankind from the rest of the animal kingdom on the basis of the common human ability to speak and therefore to think. He believed in the powerful influence of climate on organisms and posited that human varieties had degenerated from the original European norm (white and civilized) the farther north or south they had moved from the temperate zone; although not altogether fixed, these differences, both physical and moral, had become practically permanent. The Dutch naturalist Cornelius de Pauw (1739–1799)

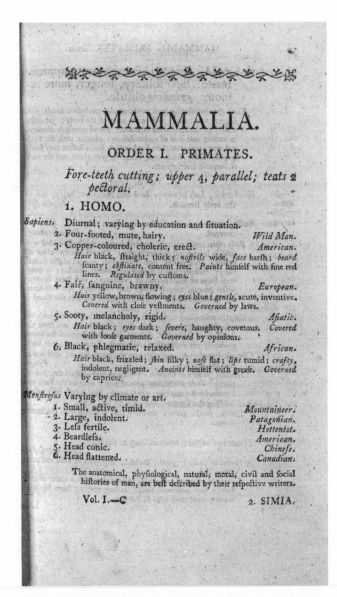

adopted Buffon's theories to conclude that the Inuit had so degenerated that they could be considered "brutish refuse" ("*avortons abrutis*") (*Recherches philosophiques sur les Américains*, 1770).

Johann Friedrich Blumenbach (1752–1840) completed the process of the development of race as a scientific concept. Basing his thesis on physical characteristics such as skin color and type of hair, but principally on cranial forms, Blumenbach proposed in *De generis humani varietate natura* (On the Natural Varieties of Mankind, 1775) a division that by its third edition (1795) would become five different *gentes* or races: Caucasian, Mongolian, Ethiopian, American, and Malay. However, he simply noted their physical differences and refused to provide a gradation of value among them.

From Race to Racism. Racism—which, unlike cultural prejudice, ascribes fixed, physically inscribed characteristics to real or imagined human groups—did not emerge only with the modern meaning of the term *race*. It is difficult to accept, for instance, that the discrimination the so-called New Christians suffered in Spain from the late fifteenth century to well beyond the eighteenth was purely the result of a suspicion that they remained crypto-Jews. Rather, the precept of "purity of the blood" (*limpieza de sangre*) marked a striking shift from medieval anti-Judaism, one objective of which had been to encourage conversion. Now a converted Jew remained a Jew by his very essence. Similarly, the English perception of the Irish as naturally inferior predated the development of the modern concept of race. It was, however, contact with non-European peoples, and their exploitation in a colonial context, that transformed racial theories derived from the natural sciences into a racist ideology focused especially on black Africans. The establishment of plantation economies in the Americas and the inability to use Native or European labor in them provided the key nexus for racial prejudice toward Africans. In effect, it made black slavery a material necessity, and a whole ideology was constructed to enforce its practice.

At the core of enlightened philosophy was universality, rejecting distinctions other than cultural among humans. Many of the philosophes condemned the treatment of blacks in the colonies. Montesquieu exemplified mainstream Enlightenment thought: *L'esprit des lois* (1748) denounced slavery and satirized belief in African inferiority on the basis of color. "It cannot be conceived," he mocked, "that God, who is a very wise being, placed a soul, and especially a good soul, in such a black body." Similarly, the *Encyclopédie* roundly condemned slavery, and enlightened thinkers from Guillaume-Thomas Raynal to Jean-Antoine-Nicolas de Caritat Condorcet and Henri Grégoire worked in the later eighteenth century for abolition of the slave trade.

This did not preclude eighteenth-century thinkers from believing in the superiority of Europeans. Arthur Hertzberg has argued that modern anti-Semitism was fully inscribed in the Enlightenment, which, on the basis of universal principles, rejected Jewish cultural particularism. For Claude-Adrien Helvétius, the "lazy" Africans and Caribs represented childish inertia, the Europeans maturity, and the Asians decadence and old age (*De l'homme*, 1774); Jean-Jacques Rousseau, who argued that humanity was so mixed as to render the concept of race meaningless, specifically excluded Africans from this observation (unpublished mss. cited in Poliakov, 1975). Even Montesquieu, Raynal, and Grégoire can be shown to have held disparaging views concerning blacks, though on cultural rather than racial bases, and Thomas Jefferson expressed a deep ambivalence about both their nature and the morality of slavery. Blacks may have been one's brothers, but they were not one's equals.

On occasion, color prejudice went beyond cultural rationale, the more significantly so since this involved major Enlightenment figures. In a note added in 1753 to his essay "Of National Character," David Hume questioned whether the inferiority of non-Europeans was not derived from nature and likened the works of a learned black to the copying of human speech by a parrot. As Richard H. Popkin has pointed out, "His view about non-whites cannot be dismissed as a fleeting observation." Voltaire, whose racial anti-Semitism is well documented, also subscribed to polygenesis, which led him to posit the existence of fixed races, possessed of distinct physical and moral qualities on the bases of which they could be hierarchically ranked. Whites were, he argued, "superior to . . . blacks, just as blacks are to monkeys, and monkeys to oysters and other animals of that kind" (*Traité de métaphysique*, 1734). He considered slavery to be the condition that "nature" had reserved for blacks (*Essai sur les moeurs*, 1753–1763). Similarly, for all the stress placed by thinkers of the *Aufklärung*, or German Enlightenment, on cultural and especially linguistic traits in differentiating national character, Immanuel Kant could argue that the superiority of Europeans (and especially Germans) was "innate, natural, in essence residing in the composition of the blood" (*Anthropology from a Pragmatic Point of View*, 1798). He considered cruelty a natural trait of the Spanish and ascribed it to the mixture of European and "Moorish" blood in Spain.

Such attitudes, like the theories advanced by natural scientists, comforted slave-owners and slave-traders when, toward the end of the century, they were challenged by abolitionists. Even before this, Edward Long, who had served in the West Indies, asked if blacks should not be considered "a different species of the same genus," closer to the orangutan than to their white masters. After all, he argued, blacks looked and smelled differently, carried black lice, were "void of genius" and possessed "no moral sense, no taste but for women . . . no wish but to be idle" (*History of Jamaica*, 1774). Thus, ideas developed in the colonies trickled back to Europe along with the wave of absentee planters and returning colonial officials, spreading to the noble and merchant aristocracies and to officialdom. This is evident in the government attitude toward black residents that developed in France from the 1760s onward. The duc de Choiseul, as Minister of the Marine, argued that the French character was being threatened by "a mixed blood, which increases daily" (Circular letter to the intendants, 30 April 1763). "If such an abuse is tolerated," the King's Attorney at the Paris

Admiralty Court warned, "we shall see the French nation disfigured" (Admiralty ordinances of 31 March and 5 April 1762). Such views led in the 1770s to legislation prohibiting nonwhites from entering France and forbidding those who were already there from marrying whites.

If it can be argued that the modern concept of race was fully developed by the mid-eighteenth century, the evidence applies only to the elite. Blacks were generally well received by members of the lower classes, who labored amicably by their sides and contracted marriages with them. Such social differentiations in attitudes, rather than the kind of qualitative distinction usually argued, may be what distinguishes eighteenth-century racism from the nineteenth-century brand, which spread to a more literate and secularized lower class through the popularization of the pseudosciences.

[*See also* Explorations and Contact; Human Nature; *and* Slavery.]

BIBLIOGRAPHY

Blakely, Allison. *Blacks in the Dutch World: The Evolution of Racial Imagery in a Modern Society*. Bloomington, Ind., 1993. A model study, which treats the representation of blacks in Dutch folklore, art, and literature from the Middle Ages onward.

Cohen, William B. *The French Encounter with Africans: White Response to Blacks, 1530–1880*. Bloomington, Ind., 1980. An attempt to replicate for France Jordan's analysis of English colonial attitudes and Walvin's study of blacks in England.

Davis, David Brion. *The Problem of Slavery in Western Culture*. Ithaca, N.Y., 1966. Seminal work on the subject.

Davis, David Brion, et al. "Constructing Race: Differentiating Peoples in the Early Modern World." Special issue of *William and Mary Quarterly*, 3d ser., 54.4 (January 1997), 3–252. The most recent collective volume on early modern race.

Duchet, Michèle. *Anthropologie et histoire au siècles des Lumières*. Paris, 1971. The best treatment of Enlightenment thought about the natural sciences.

Ellis, Harold A. "Genealogy, History, and the Aristocratic Reaction in Early Eighteenth-Century France: The Case of Henri de Boulainvilliers." *Journal of Modern History* 58 (1986), 414–451. Convincing revisionist treatment of a thinker usually identified as "one of the real ancestors of racism" (Poliakov, 1975).

Fredrickson, George M. *Racism: A Short History*. Princeton, N.J., 2002. Balanced treatment of the history of Western racism from the Middle Ages onward; includes essay on the historiography of the concept.

Hannaford, Ivan. *Race: The History of an Idea in the West*. Washington, D.C., and Baltimore, 1997. A recent treatment in the context of general European intellectual history.

Hertzberg, Arthur H. *The French Enlightenment and the Jews*. New York, 1968. Argues that the roots of modern anti-Semitism are found in the Enlightenment.

Jordan, Winthrop D. *White over Black: American Attitudes toward the Negro, 1550–1812*. Chapel Hill, N.C., 1968. The major work on the subject; contains an important chapter on Thomas Jefferson's views.

Poliakov, Léon. *The History of Anti-Semitism*. Vol. 3, *From Voltaire to Wagner*. Translated by Miriam Kochan. New York, 1975. English translation of vol. 3 of *Histoire de l'antisémitisme* (1968), the fundamental work by one of the most respected authors on the subject.

Poliakov, Léon. *Le Mythe aryen: Essai sur les sources du racisme et des nationalismes*. Paris, 1971. On the roots of twentieth-century racism.

Popkin, Richard H. "The Philosophical Basis of Eighteenth-Century Racism." In *Studies in Eighteenth-Century Culture* 3 (1973), 245–262. The most important article in a symposium on "Racism in the Eighteenth Century," edited by Harold E. Pagliaro.

Roger, Jacques. *Les Sciences de la vie dans la pensée française du XVIIIe siècle: La génération des animaux de Descartes à l'Encyclopédie*. 2d ed. Paris, 1971. Deals with the debates over what would later be understood as the biological sciences.

Van Eyck, Masarah. "'We Shall Be One People': Early Modern French Perceptions of the Amerindian Body" (Ph.D. diss., McGill University, 2001). Situates early modern perceptions of the "Others" in the context of humor theory.

Walvin, James. *Black and White: The Negro and English Society, 1555–1945*. London, 1973. A study of the nonwhite community residing in England; useful chapters on the eighteenth century.

PIERRE H. BOULLE

RADICATI DI PASSERANO, ALBERTO (1698–1737), Italian-born religious controversialist and author.

Alberto Radicati di Passerano, who was born in 1698 either at Passerano or Casalborgone, of an old Piedmontese noble family, did not pass through the world unnoticed. From Jean-Baptiste Argens to Pierre-Augustin Caron de Beaumarchais, from Voltaire to Johann Lorenz Mosheim, from Prosper Marchand to Johann Anton Trinius, a multitude of voices attested to the extent to which his troubled and desperate presence, and his radical and extreme reflections were vital to the panorama of Europe's cultural life.

Between 1719 and 1721, following bitter conflicts with his family and the death of his wife, he made a propitious visit to France, where he absorbed the critical cultural and political atmosphere of the Regency. His works reflected the influence of Pierre Bayle and Charles-Louis de Secondat Montesquieu, as well as contact with Huguenot circles. His second wife, Thérèse de la Villardière, with whom he returned to Piedmont, was suspected of being Huguenot. By 1725, Radicati thought the time right to propose to King Victor Amadeus II a program of political reform, at the center of which was the question of religion. He hoped to take advantage of the issues of sovereignty that had fed the controversy between the king and Rome, sharpening them radically and channeling them in a decidedly more anticlerical and antireligious direction. In rebelling against the clergy, Radicati hoped that Victor Amadeus would follow the example of Henry VIII, Louis XIV (in his Gallican phase), and Peter the Great, gaining control over ecclesiastical appointments and church property, and follow the courageous political and diplomatic actions of his youth, when, in a spirit of innovation and reform, he attempted to limit the church domination of schools and the power of the Inquisition. Those years were gone forever, however, and, by 1725,

Radicati began a voluntary exile, going first to London (1726–1734) and then to Holland (1735–1737). He never returned to Piedmont.

These other experiences provided the motives underlying his *Discours moraux, historiques et politiques* (Moral, Historical and Political Discourses) perhaps his most noted and important work, which he had already tried to publish in London in 1730. Only the first discourse appeared, with the title *Christianity Set in a True Light*, but the parts of the *Discours* began to circulate (the first complete edition of the work was published in English in 1734). Radicati's vigorously Erastian position, underlined by his rejection of the "priestly profession," had Protestant and Gallican undertones, and was inspired by other "rebels" in questions of religion, namely Jacques Basnage, Zeger Bernard van Espen, Paolo Sarpi, Richard Simon, Claude Fleury, Louis Élies Dupin, and others.

In his interpretation of the doctrine of Christ and the apostles, Radicati demonstrated the conflict between the evangelical principles and the practices of the Catholic Church, recalling the Protestant polemical tradition against Rome and the "papal" Church. The third discourse—quite radical in the English version—revealed to what degree Radicati had absorbed the most creative and highly critical part of the English deistic tradition, from Anthony Collins to John Toland, and Matthew Tindal to Thomas Woolston. Beginning with the title, he declares, as does Tindal in his *Christianity as Old as Creation*, that "the religion [of] Christ differs not from the religion of nature." Another work soon afterward had the significant title *Histoire abrégée de la profession sacerdotale ancienne et modern dédiée à la très illustre et très célèbre secte des Esprit-forts, par un Free-thinker chrétien* (Short History of the Ancient and Modern Priestly Profession, Dedicated to the Most Illustrious and Famous Freethinkers by a Christian Freethinker). Radicati paraphrased the titles of both Tindal and Collins, this time maliciously declaring himself convinced that free thought was as old as creation. It must be noted, however, that he defined himself as "a Christian freethinker." His attitude was therefore both violently anticlerical and, at the same time, religious. His religious sense revealed an admiration for Christ's morals and primitive Christianity, that in *Nazarenus et Lycurgos mis en parallèle* (The Nazarene and Lycurgus Compared), aspired to equality and communal property, while in the *Parallel between Muhamed and Sosem*, he mocked with erudite irony the facile "lies" of Muhammad and Moses.

The works described above (with the exception of *Parallel*) were published in 1736, in Rotterdam, in *Recueil de pièces curieuses sur les matières les plus intéressantes* (Collection of Curious Pieces on Most Interesting Subjects). Not included in this collection was his philosophically boldest and disturbing *A Philosophical Dissertation upon*

Death (1732), a courageous claim for the individual's right to self-determination, including the legal right to commit suicide. His main thesis was that every person is free to choose his death. This right to die is based on a fundamentally materialistic conception of nature and of man, and on an extreme form of moral relativism. The *Philosophical Dissertation* contained much more, but at its emotional heart lay this quasi-redemption of suicide, vindicated as the extreme choice of freedom, no matter the demands of state, religion, or nature.

In Radicati's *Dissertation*, however, we also see a more dramatic vision, which seems to be a projection of his personal discomfort; he eloquently described matter as dynamic, "compounded of a diversity of contraries, which, being intermingled, cannot in any wise be in repose." In his system, therefore, matter, considered identical with nature, reflects Spinoza's identification of God with substance, and also the Hobbesian idea that reality is composed of matter and movement. It is evident, however, that Radicati's materialism is not of the pantheistic rationalistic variety of Giordano Bruno's, as is that of Toland, for example. Nor is it the mechanistic view of Thomas Hobbes and René Descartes. He followed the atomist theory of the materialism of Democritus or Epicurus, but inspired by a form of Spinozist vitalism. "Nature" was precisely this matter, modified by the movement of an infinite variety of forms. Death, then, is only a "Dissolution of the Corporeal Parts, the which, separating from each other, do then assume other Forms, and receive other different Motions: Because Nature, ever busied in creating and destroying, makes Use of the Parts of one Body destroyed thence to form another Body which she is creating." This vision was completed by an element of vitalist naturalism, imbued with Newtonism: "Nature, being herself superlatively perfect, ever was and ever will be active; nor can she once cease from operating." The universe pictured in the *Philosophical Dissertation* is infinite and capable of incessant activity, in which every element lives in a constant process of generation and destruction. Matter alone remains unchanged, incorruptible, and eternally fertile.

Radicati died on 24 October 1737, alone, sick and miserable, drawing near to the Calvinist faith from which his moral and religious challenge had arisen.

[*See also* Calvinism; Death; Deism; Italy; *and* Materialism.]

BIBLIOGRAPHY
Ajello, Raffaele, et al., eds. *Dal Muratori al Cesarotti: Politici ed economisti del primo Settecento*, vol. 5: *Adalberto Radicati di Passerano*. Milan and Naples, 1978. A selected anthology of Radicati's works.
Alberti, Alberto. *Alberto Radicati di Passerano*. Turin, 1931.
Berman, David. *A History of Atheism in Britain from Hobbes to Russell*. London, 1988, pp. 93–95.
Berti, Silvia. "Radicali al margini: Materialismo, libero pensiero e diritto al suicidio in Radicati di Passerano. In *Anticristianesimo e libertà: Alle origini dell'Illuminismo*, pp. 180–205. Naples, 2002.
Gobetti, Piero. *Risorgimento senza eroi*. Turin, 1936, pp. 28–50. To this great liberal, antifascist intellectual we owe the first mature analysis of Radicati's thought.
Jacob, Margaret. *The Radical Enlightenment*. London, 1981, pp. 172–176.
Rivista Storica Italiana has sponsored important contributions on Radicati in 1963 (no. 2, edited by Franco Venturi), in 1984 (no. 2, edited by Silvia Berti, Edoardo Tottarolo, and Franco Venturi), and in 1991 (no. 2, edited by Edoardo Tortarolo).
Venturi, Franco. *Saggi sull'Europa illuminista*, vol. 1, *Alberto Radicati de Passerano*. Turin, 1954. This volume remains the fundamental study of Radicati, both for its biography and for the analysis of his thought and his place in contemporary culture.

SILVIA BERTI
Translated from Italian by Joan B. Sax

RADISHCHEV, ALEXANDER NIKOLAYEVICH

(1749–1802), Russian poet and reformist.

The founder of the Russian intelligentsia's radical tradition, Radishchev was a writer and poet whose "Ode to Liberty" inspired the Decembrists when they rose up against tsarist autocracy in 1825; his reputation as a revolutionary reached its peak, however, in the twentieth century. He was born into a cultivated gentry family. A tutor from France was engaged to teach him French when he was six; he went on to master Latin, German, Italian, English, and Church Slavonic. His connection with the St. Petersburg elite began when he entered the corps of pages in 1762, the year Catherine II seized power after a palace "revolution"—the term then used—in which the tsar, her estranged husband, was murdered. The new empress took a close interest in the education of her subjects, and it was at her behest that Radishchev, together with eleven other students, was sent abroad to the University of Leipzig. His five years in Saxony were not all happy: his best friend died; Radishchev himself often fell ill; the supervisor who accompanied the students beat and humiliated them, and they contemplated running away through England to North America.

Property and Serfdom. Radishchev returned to Russia in 1771. There he rose swiftly in the civil service, publishing his earliest work two years later—a translation of Mably's *Observations sur l'histoire de la Grèce*, which was remarkable for the notes added by the young author. The abbé Gabriel Bonnot de Mably was not a socialist *avant la lettre*, but like Rousseau in midcentury (whom Radishchev also read), Mably denounced private property as the principal source of all the evils of civilization; the rich were destined to get richer, while the poor sank into degradation. Radishchev's utopianism was influenced by French writers, but in examining the condition of the serfs in his own country, where they comprised two-thirds of the population, he brought to Russia a new way of thinking about the economic implications of ownership and productivity. In his *Journey from St. Petersburg to*

Moscow (1790), which he published anonymously on his own press, he warned his peers that failure to free the serfs would bring a revolution far more terrible than the rebellion of Emelian Pugachev, a Cossack who a few years earlier led a peasant insurrection of terrifying dimensions that brought the empress to the brink of flight.

Catherine was enraged by the book, although its form—modeled on Laurence Sterne's *Sentimental Journey* (1768)—is not inflammatory. The narrator travels from the imperial capital to Moscow and talks to ordinary people, but the author reflects with unprecedented audacity on the faults and misfortunes of a corrupt society based, as he sees it, on arbitrary power and oppression. The social issues he brings up Catherine was certainly aware of—she had, after all, discussed them during Diderot's visit to St. Petersburg—but the book's publication coincided with the French Revolution. Copies were destroyed; the author was sentenced to death, then reprieved and packed off to Siberia in a scandal that estranged the intellectuals the empress had earlier charmed. The *Journey* could only be published again inside the country with the abolition of censorship during the 1905 revolution, when both liberals and socialists claimed to be Radishchev's heirs.

Divided Legacy. The liberals of the early twentieth century maintained, correctly, that Radishchev's abolitionist argument ran counter to the commitment of Russia's Populists to communal forms of land tenure (such as the *mir*). Like Mably in his work on Greek history, Radishchev proposed that people are more productive when they enjoy all the fruits of their labor, an argument that the Russian government unfortunately did not accept when it legally freed the serfs in 1861 but left them tied to their communes. In contrast, socialists could think of Radishchev as a forerunner because of his faith in a future ideal society in which the sciences, arts, and crafts would reach perfection, property would be justly divided, violence would cease, and people would be brought together by fraternal love. Bolshevik ideologues extolled this part of Radishchev's Enlightenment thinking while ignoring his economics. They also ignored his deism and belief in an afterlife. Nor were they ever consistent in dealing with his individualism and his fierce defense of freedom of expression, which was inspired in part by Milton's *Areopagitica* (1643). Indeed, Milton, Shakespeare, and Voltaire—in that order—are proclaimed in the *Journey* as the three supremely great writers.

Radishchev was far from being the first to introduce Enlightenment ideas into Russian life and letters. Catherine herself had read the philosophes and seriously considered emancipating the serfs at the beginning of her reign, but the nobility on whom her illegitimate rule depended were overwhelmingly opposed. Radishchev was, however, the first to combine an intellectual's pre-Romantic

self-awareness with the notion of revolutionary transformation—if necessary, from below. With the collapse of the Soviet Union, his utopianism lost official support, as has that of Mably, Morelli, and Linguet, but his heroic status is still sustained by the mythopoeic way he chose to die, as well as by the idealization of his character begun by contemporaries. Sensitive and sentimental, honorable and naive, loyal to his friends and deeply attached to his family, Radishchev was also perceived as the neoclassical embodiment of aristocratic virtue at a time when the Russian nobility, thanks to a modicum of self-government granted by the empress, believed themselves to be free.

Catherine's persecution of Radishchev belied this, and several friends came to Radishchev's aid when his family followed him into Siberian exile. The public sympathy thus aroused made it expedient for Paul I, who succeeded Catherine, to permit him to return to his estate in 1797. He was granted full pardon by Alexander I in 1801, but in the very next year, while serving on a government committee set up to examine the prospect of introducing the English jury system to Russia, Radishchev committed suicide.

[*See also* Catherine II *and* Russia.]

BIBLIOGRAPHY

WORKS BY RADISHCHEV

Polnoe sobranie sochinenii. 3 vols. Moscow, 1938, 1941, 1952. Published by the USSR Academy of Sciences, this annotated edition of the collected writings was interrupted by the purges under Stalin and the war, so by the time the last volume appeared, the interpretation as reflected in the copious notes had much changed from that in the opening one.

Puteshestvie iz Peterburga v Moskvu. Moscow, 1935. A photomechanical printing of the original destroyed edition of 1790.

A Journey from St. Petersburg to Moscow. Edited with an introduction and notes by Roderick Page Thaler, translated by Leo Wiener. Cambridge, Mass., 1958. The only accurate English translation of the famous work.

Stikhotvoreniya. Edited by V. A. Zapadov. Moscow, 1975. In the *Biblioteka Poeta* series, annotated and containing the celebrated "Ode to Liberty" and Radishchev's other verse.

STUDIES

Lang, D. M. *The First Russian Radical: Alexander Radishchev, 1749–1802.* New York, 1960. The first English biography.

McConnell, Allen. *A Russian Philosophe: Alexander Radishchev, 1749–1802.* The Hague, 1964. Treats Radishchev's intellectual development more fully than does Lang.

Page, Tanya. "A Radishchev Monstrology: The *Journey from Petersburg to Moscow* and Later Writings in the Light of French Sources." In *American Contributions to the Eighth International Congress of Slavists*, pp. 605–629. Columbus, Ohio, 1978. The body of secondary literature on Radishchev is huge; many of the more interesting articles (such as this one) deal with the history of the writing of the *Journey* and its fate.

VALENTIN BOSS

RAMEAU, JEAN-PHILIPPE (1683–1764), French composer and music theorist.

No musician has been more closely identified with the eighteenth-century French Enlightenment, nor thought to have epitomized more fully its intellectual character, than Rameau. He was the most important opera composer of his day, and his many stage works became the touchstone for debate among the philosophes concerning problems of musical expression and poetics. Rameau's many writings as a music theorist likewise stirred intense interest and controversy among his contemporaries.

Rameau composed in various musical genres, but it was as a composer of opera that he was most renowned. Beginning with the premier of *Hippolyte et Aricie* in 1733 (adapted from Racine's classic tragedy *Phaedre*), Rameau produced another two dozen operas in a diversity of subgenres: *tragédie, opéra-ballet, comédie lyrique, pastorale héroïque*, and so on. Although he was initially criticized by the conservative defenders of Jean-Baptiste Lully for corrupting the tenets of the classical *tragédie en musique* through excesses of "spectacle" and musical opulence, by midcentury Rameau was acknowledged by almost all French critics as Lully's true heir. Writing work after work of unprecedented musical variety and dramatic scope, Rameau soon was able to attract distinguished librettists with whom to collaborate, including Voltaire, Jean-François Marmontel, and Louis de Cahusac. He quickly gained favor at court, being appointed by the king as *compositeur de la musique de la chambre du roy* in 1745.

It was perhaps inevitable that the preeminent composer of French opera would eventually be drawn into the quarrel ignited by Friedrich Melchior Grimm in 1751 concerning the respective merits of French and Italian music. Rameau was initially spared the most scathing criticism by partisans of the Bouffon troupe of Italian singers who visited Paris in 1751, but Jean-Jacques Rousseau's broadside attack on all French music in his notorious pamphlet *Lettre sur la musique française* (1753) could be read as nothing but a direct assault on Rameau's operas. For Rousseau, Rameau's music was far too emotionally stilted through reliance on harmonic artifice; it lacked the expressive freedom and natural lyricism of Italian music, which was rooted in melody. Rameau attempted to rebut Rousseau's arguments in his own petulant defense (*Observations sur notre instinct pour la musique* [Observations on Our Instinct for Music, 1754]), but he lacked the rhetorical skills of his adversaries. It must not be assumed, however, that Rameau was the obvious loser in the debate. Despite the ineptness of his prose, Rameau was able to offer profound insight into the role harmony may play in generating dramatic expression.

It was as a music theorist, in fact, that Rameau was perhaps most celebrated in the eighteenth century. Amid his prolific compositional output, he produced more than half a dozen major treatises concerning questions of music theory, as well as dozens of smaller works. In his last years, Rameau bemoaned the time he had lost composing music instead of contemplating more deeply the philosophical problems of "musical science" that came to absorb him. In his deep-seated intellectual ambitions, Rameau was a quintessential product of Enlightenment rationalism.

Seeking to understand scientifically the harmonic language of which he was an undisputed master, Rameau looked to natural philosophy for guidance. Influenced initially by Descartes's rational method (not to mention Descartes's own early musical writings), Rameau proposed a mechanistic model of harmonic syntax based on the generation and concatenation of chords using his system of the "fundamental bass" (*Traité de l'harmonie* [On Harmony, 1722]). Essentially, the fundamental bass is a succession of chord fundamentals ("roots") by which any harmonic succession can be tracked and reduced to a few fundamental cadential prototypes. If there were problems of empirical adequacy in Rameau's theory, it nonetheless offered an elegant simplification of musical harmony for pedagogical purposes. Its conceptual appeal was enhanced with Rameau's discovery in 1726 of the *corps sonore*—the ratios of resonating partials sounded in an ideal vibrating body. Because these ratios coincided with those by which most harmonies and their succession were composed (primarily perfect fifths and thirds), Rameau was convinced he had found the "natural" origin of music. In later works, Rameau further revised his theory of the fundamental bass, incorporating elements of Newtonian science to explain the tonal "attraction" of certain harmonic functions (*Génération harmonique* [Harmonic Generation, 1737]) and Lockean empiricism to understand the perceptual implications of the *corps sonore* (*Démonstration du principe de l'harmonie* [Demonstration of the Principle of Harmony, 1750]). In its broad trajectory from Cartesian mechanism through Newtonian cosmology and Lockean sensationalism, Rameau's music theory offers a surprisingly accurate barometer of evolving Enlightenment philosophy.

Although the details of Rameau's theory are often intricate, his basic claim to have discovered the founding principle of music was easily understandable. His discoveries were hailed by contemporary intellectuals as a stunning achievement on a par with Newton's in science; Rameau was dubbed the "Newton of harmony." The *encyclopédistes* were particularly drawn to Rameau's ideas, and a few such authors served in different capacities to help formulate and disseminate his writings. Diderot aided Rameau in the drafting of an important lecture read before the Paris Academy of Sciences in 1749 (published in 1750 as *Démonstration du principe de l'harmonie*), while Rousseau based many of his music articles for the *Encyclopédie* on Rameau's theories (despite that, Rameau would later take issue with these articles). Perhaps the greatest homage Rameau received, however, was from Jean Le

Rond d'Alembert, who, in the "Preliminary Discourse" to the *Encyclopédie*, praised the composer profusely as a "musician-philosophe." In 1752, d'Alembert further demonstrated his respect by issuing a short resumé of Rameau's music theory under the title *Elémens de musique théorique et pratique suivant les principes de M. Rameau* (Elements of Music Theoretical and Practical Following Rameau's Principles). Although the *Elémens* is not without its own distortions (partly owing to the differing epistemological presumptions of its author), it became an influential work, widely reprinted and consulted by musicians wishing to understand Rameau's writings.

In his last years, Rameau fell afoul of the *encyclopédistes*, although much of the blame must fall on the composer himself, who became increasingly obstinate and extravagant in his ontological claims on behalf of his beloved *corps sonore*. D'Alembert, in particular, came to reject forcefully what he perceived to be the unfounded scientific pretensions of Rameau's theory. Still, critics such as Diderot continued to acknowledge the value of Rameau's theory of the fundamental bass, and even at the end of the twentieth century, his music theory continues to form the foundation of most pedagogies of tonal music.

[*See also* Aesthetics; Encyclopédie; Music; *and* Opera.]

BIBLIOGRAPHY

Christensen, Thomas. *Rameau and Musical Thought in the Enlightenment*. Cambridge, 1993. A comprehensive intellectual biography of Rameau, with special attention to the scientific context of Rameau's music theories and the arguments they generated among his contemporaries.

Dill, Charles. *Monstrous Opera: Rameau and the Tragic Tradition*. Princeton, N.J., 1998. A brilliant study of the tensions facing the composer attempting dramatic innovations while hewing to the basic tenets of traditional operatic poetics.

Girdlestone, Cuthbert. *Jean-Philippe Rameau: His Life and Work*. Rev. ed. New York, 1969. An indispensable—if rather uncritical—source for any biography of Rameau, but Girdlestone's discussion of Rameau's music theories is unsympathetic and unreliable.

Kintzler, Catherine. *Jean-Philippe Rameau: Splendeur et naufrage de l'esthétique du plaisir à l'âge classique*. Paris, 1983. Provocative and entertaining, although Kintzler greatly overpolarizes the aesthetic arguments between Rousseau and Rameau.

Verba, Cynthia. *Music and the French Enlightenment: Reconstruction of a Dialogue*. New York, 1992. Valuable for its discussion of Rameau's relation with the *encyclopédistes*.

THOMAS CHRISTENSEN

RAMSAY, ANDREW MICHAEL (1686–1743), Scottish-born philosopher and religious mystic who flourished on the continent.

Born at Ayr, Scotland, on 9 July 1686, to a Presbyterian father and an Episcopalian mother, Andrew Ramsay was preoccupied with theological and metaphysical questions throughout his life. In an autobiography preserved in the Bibliothèque Méjanes, he recorded that his mother had early taught him the falsity of Calvinism "and above all of the frightful dogma of predestination." From an early age he studied the sciences and mathematics, before studying philosophy and theology, first at Glasgow, then at Edinburgh, where he completely lost his faith. He acknowledged being successively a disciple of Isaac Newton, Pierre Bayle, François-Armand Fénelon, and Nicolas Malebranche.

After studying mathematics in London with Newton's disciple Fatio de Duilliers, Ramsay traveled to Holland and came under the influence of the French Protestant mystic Pierre Poiret. Moving to France in 1710, Ramsay was converted to Roman Catholicism by Fénelon, the archbishop of Cambrai, whom he served first as secretary, then as editor and memorialist, publishing a *Discours de la poésie épique et de l'excellence du poème de* Télémaque (Discourse on Poetry and on the Excellence of the Poem *Télémaque*) as an introduction to the 1717 edition of Fénelon's utopian political novel *Aventures de Télémaque fils d'Ulysse* (The Adventures of Telemachus, Son of Ulysses); an *Essai de politique* (Essay on Politics) in 1719, based upon Fénelon's principles of tolerance and pure disinterested love, free from all hope of reward or fear of punishment; and *L'histoire de la vie de Fénelon* (Life of Fénelon) in 1723.

Well-connected at the exiled Jacobite court at Paris, and with French intellectuals and courtiers, Ramsay was a highly successful social-climber, and was given the title of chevalier of the Order of St. Lazare by the duc d'Orléans. He became a member of the Club de l'Entresol, to which he read portions of a manuscript that was published as *Les voyages de Cyrus* (Voyages of Cyrus) in 1727. This extremely popular, allegorical, and didactic novel was modeled on *Télémaque*, and the expanded edition of 1730 (in which he skillfully responded to his many critics) was translated into English by Alexander Pope's friend Nathaniel Hooke. Drawing upon Ralph Cudworth and many other sources, Ramsay artfully arranged the "lessons" of the young prince in such a way that readers would be drawn away from atheism and materialism in successive stages: the atheist becoming a deist, the deist becoming a Socinian, and the Socinian a Christian. Along the way there are lessons in physics, philosophy, and politics. The emphasis, however, is principally upon the theology of the pagans. The beliefs of the ancient Persians, Egyptians, Chaldeans, and Athenians are examined in order to prove that philosophers in all ages and places have had the idea of a supreme divinity, distinct and separate from matter.

Ramsay's philosophical heroes and villains are evident in *Cyrus*, but are explicitly discussed in a short article entitled "Psychomètre" in the Jesuit *Journal de Trévoux* of April 1735. Here pairs of thinkers are compared: the subtle Malebranche is to be preferred over the shallow John Locke. René Descartes and Newton are the greatest geniuses ever to have appeared in any century, and true physics results from the combination of their systems; the Scottish geometers are to be thanked for bringing about this reconciliation. Baruch de Spinoza is the chief villain. His system is a combination of Cabbalism, Cartesianism, and a badly misunderstood Thomism. By regarding thought and extension as two properties of the Supreme Being, Spinozism appears to be a gross materialism, but it is really the purest idealism. The best antidote to Spinoza is the English philosopher Henry More, who adopts the doctrine of Origen and embellishes it with doctrines drawn from Cabbalism and the Hebrew Mythology. For Ramsay, More's ideas—the free but eternal creation of the world; the immensity of the universe; the innumerable number of created intelligences and their preexistence, degradation, and redemption—all refute atheism and establish a general system of Providence that answers all of Pierre Bayle's objections arising from the origin and duration of evil.

Ramsay further developed and presented these ideas of More in his posthumously published *Philosophical Principles of Natural and Revealed Religion Unfolded in a Geometrical Order*, which appeared in two volumes in Glasgow in 1748–1749. This work is notable for its attempted refutation of Spinoza and for the anglicization of Ramsay's views. Ramsay's boyhood friend, Dr. John Stevenson, a medical doctor, and Francis Hutcheson, professor at Glasgow University, helped to edit the work for a British audience. Unlike his British contemporaries, Ramsay was impressed by the strength of Spinoza's ideas and by their influence upon French freethinkers and libertines. He also drew upon the Jesuit missionaries in China, the figurists, and he intended to publish his idiosyncratic theological views in a work entitled "Chinese Letters." He had befriended David Hume when the latter was in France in the mid-1730s, and he suggested Hume as a translator of this work, which never appeared. Most of Ramsay's other manuscripts were taken to Scotland after his death in 1743, and an inventory of them has been published in Henderson's biography. One of these manuscripts, on the ideas of the Scottish emigré economist John Law of Lauriston, is an imitation of Montesquieu's *Lettres persanes* (Persian Letters, 1721) and was published in an Amsterdam periodical edited by one of Ramsay's younger friends. This interesting piece has recently been attributed to Montesquieu, but it most likely was composed by Ramsay. The present location of Ramsay's manuscripts is unknown.

Though Ramsay had spent a brief period in Rome as tutor to the exiled James III's son, Charles Edward, he was permitted to travel in 1729 to England, where he received an honorary degree from Oxford University and was made a fellow of the Royal Society. He lived the remainder of his life in his adopted France, where his fame derived in great measure from his elegant French prose. Ramsay played a significant role in spreading Freemasonry in France, and in 1737 he delivered an important discourse to the order, in which he drew attention to the need for a "universal dictionary of the arts and sciences," a project which some have seen as brought to fruition by Diderot and d'Alembert.

[*See also* Bayle, Pierre; Fénelon, François-Armand de Salignac de La Mothe; Hume, David; Mysticism; Philosophy; *and* Poiret, Pierre.]

BIBLIOGRAPHY

Baldi, Marialuisa. *Verisimile, Non Vero: Filosofia e politica in Andrew Michael Ramsay*. Milan, 2002.

Carayol, Elizabeth. "*Le Démocrite français:* Un texte oublié du jeune Montesquieu?" *Dix-Huitième Siècle* 2 (1970), 3–12.

Childs, Nick. *A Political Academy in Paris, 1724–1731: The Entresol and Its Members*. Oxford, 2000.

Granderoute, Robert. "Quand l'auteur et le public collaborent: Les deux éditions des *Voyages de Cyrus*." *Dix-Huitième Siècle* 4 (1972), 255–270.

Henderson, G. D. *Chevalier Ramsay*. London, 1952.

Walker, D. P. *The Ancient Theology: Studies in Christian Platonism from the Fifteenth to the Eighteenth Century*. London, 1972.

Weil, Françoise. "Ramsay et la franc-maçonnerie." *Revue d'Histoire Littéraire de la France* 63 (1963), 272–278.

DAVID R. RAYNOR

RATIONALISM. The term "rationalism" has been used since the sixteenth century to describe those who emphasize reason over experience in the acquisition of knowledge. In standard taxonomies of the history of philosophy, the Rationalists (here, capitalized forms designate discrete "schools" of thinkers) are the seventeenth-century philosophers René Descartes, Baruch de Spinoza, Gottfried Wilhelm Leibniz, and Nicolas Malebranche. They are contrasted with the Empiricists, including the seventeenth- and eighteenth-century British philosophers Thomas Hobbes, John Locke, and David Hume. In the discourse of the Enlightenment, "rationalism" also denoted the attitude of those who would subject religious institutions, feudal privilege, and the social and political order to rational scrutiny and criticism. Such rationalist critics could be either Rationalists or Empiricists in the philosophical sense. Finally, "rationalism" was also used of those who subjected religion and theology to historical and critical investigation, leading to "higher criticism" of the Bible as a human document.

Philosophical Rationalism. The philosophical Rationalists agreed on one fundamental tenet: that reason—or, as they were more likely to say, "pure intellect"—can attain substantive metaphysical knowledge independently of the senses. Metaphysics was understood as the science of the basic structure of reality. In the seventeenth and eighteenth centuries, metaphysical knowledge purportedly included the essence and existence of God, the essences of mind and matter, and the basic principles of physics

("physics" as understood broadly, in its etymological sense, as the science of nature, including biology and psychology). Rationalists were optimists about metaphysics. That is, they believed that philosophers—or each Rationalist himself—could discover the basic principles of metaphysics. In their terms, they sought to establish a *science* of metaphysics, or a systematic body of metaphysical doctrine known with absolute certainty.

The definition of rationalism given here makes reference to reason or intellect as a cognitive faculty, or power of the human mind. Seventeenth-century philosophers were used to thinking of the mind as a knowing power or instrument, possessed of several subpowers or "faculties" of cognition. A standard list of such faculties included the senses, imagination, memory, and intellect or reason (reason sometimes was equated with intellect, and sometimes regarded as a further faculty, specialized in logical inference). Previous philosophers, including the various scholastic Aristotelians of the thirteenth to seventeenth centuries, accepted a similar list. Typical Aristotelians held that the intellect is necessary for genuine cognition, but they denied that it alone is sufficient. That is, they denied that the intellect can achieve knowledge on its own, without the senses. As they put it, "there is no thought without a phantasm," or sensory image. The Rationalists denied this claim. They contended that thought can occur without sensory images (or images in memory or imagination), and that such thoughts can provide knowledge of substantive truths about God, mind, and matter. Their theory of cognition was closer to Plato's than to Aristotle's.

Although the Rationalists agreed on this fundamental tenet, they disagreed over various metaphysical conclusions. In particular, they disagreed on the basic structure of the world (as revealed by intellect or reason), on the relation between mind and body, on the metaphysical theory of God, and on the extent to which humans must rely on sense perception to achieve knowledge of nature. They also disagreed on the ontology of the intellect. While affirming that the human mind "naturally" or "innately" has access to intellectual ideas of the essences of things, they disagreed on whether such ideas are found in minds as a separate, individual substance (one per person, as with Descartes and Leibniz), or are in the mind of God, who reveals them to humans (as Malebranche held), or are modes of mind that are actually identical with modes of matter (as two aspects of a single underlying substance, following Spinoza). None of the Rationalists accepted Plato's doctrine that the intellect perceives eternal Forms independent from God or the ideas in individual minds.

The Rationalists and their followers took interest in the new science of the seventeenth century. They believed that they could know, through the intellect alone, certain fundamental tenets of this science, such as (in Descartes's

and Malebranche's theories) that the essence of matter is extension and that the laws of motion depend on God's causal agency in preserving matter in motion. Their claim was not simply that "reasoning" or "intellection" must be applied to sensory experience—many Empiricists believed that—but that the intellect can discern substantive scientific truths in total independence from the senses. This did not mean that the Rationalists thought all natural science or "natural philosophy" could be known independently of sensory observation and experiment. In fact, none of the historical school of Rationalists adopted this extreme attitude. All accepted that human beings must depend on sensory experience in some of their knowledge of man and nature.

Early in the seventeenth century, prior to the writings of the paradigmatic Rationalists, Francis Bacon contrasted the "rationalist" with the "empiricist": "The Empiricists, in the manner of ants, collect their material and then use it; whereas the Rationalists, like spiders, spin their webs out of themselves" (1872–1876, 3:616). The historical Rationalists did believe that many truths could be "spun out" of reason or the intellect. None, however, felt that all knowledge could be produced in this fashion. Such extreme portrayals belong to the history of the interpretation of the

Francis Bacon. Engraving by R. Cooper, 1823. (New York Public Library, Astor, Lenox, and Tilden Foundations.)

Rationalists, a topic of interest in its own right, as indeed is the history of the eighteenth-century origin of the classification of philosophers into Rationalists and Empiricists, but these topics lie beyond the scope of this article.

Descartes. Descartes was a mathematical scientist before he was a rationalist metaphysician. In the 1620s, he achieved important results in mathematics and optics, including discovery of the sine law of refraction. Then, in 1629–1630, two things happened. First, he had a "metaphysical turn" in which he came to see the human mind as containing innate ideas that provide the first principles of physics. Second, he embarked on the project of developing a universal physics based on the view that the essence of matter is extension. In this physics, the basic explanatory principles are the size, shape, position, and motion of the small particles that compose the material universe, as well as the laws of motion established and regulated by God. Descartes's explanations of natural phenomena were known as "mechanical explanations" because he treated the small particles of things as interacting like components in a machine so as to produce characteristic effects. Thus, he held that the properties of water and oil (their differing viscosity and rates of evaporation) are explained by the fact that the particles of water are eel-like and so slide by one another easily, whereas particles of oil are bush-like, with twig-like appendages that become entangled with other particles of oil, or with the filaments in a piece of cloth.

Descartes held that the truth or likelihood of particular physical explanations, such as those for the properties of oil and water, can be determined only through observation and experiment. To that end, he spent much time in the early 1630s and mid-1640s dissecting animals with the aim of devising a mechanistic physiology to explain the vital processes and the behavior of human and animal bodies. At the same time, he believed he could show in his metaphysics that mechanical explanations were the right sort of explanation, thereby ruling out competing Aristotelian notions that material nature contains active principles and qualities instead of bare inert matter. He also thought his metaphysics showed that, although much of human and animal psychology can be explained in purely mechanistic terms, conscious experience and rational thought depend on an immaterial substance wholly distinct from matter. He ascribed minds to humans alone, believing that all the behaviors of nonhuman animals, including those depending on learning and memory, can be explained mechanistically. In his dualistic ontology of the human being, thought is the essence of an unextended and indivisible substance called "mind," and extension is the essence of a divisible substance called "matter," which is incapable of producing thought.

In 1641, Descartes published his main metaphysical results in the *Meditations on First Philosophy*. He republished his metaphysics in the first part of his *Principles of Philosophy* (1644), as a preamble to his physics. Other parts of his physics were published as essays prefaced by the *Discourse on the Method* (1637), and in the posthumous *World, or Treatise on Light* and *Treatise on Man* (1664). Although sometimes chastised in late-twentieth-century scholarship for denigrating the body and emotions, Descartes in fact held that human beings consist of embodied minds, and that sensation and emotion depend on embodiment. In 1649, the year before his death, he published an elaborate theory of the emotions or passions entitled *Passions of the Soul*.

Spinoza. Descartes had numerous followers, among whom the young Spinoza numbered himself. As his philosophical thought developed, Spinoza rejected both Cartesian mind-body dualism and the theory that God is separate from the created world. Instead, he identified God and nature. Accordingly, there is one infinite substance. It has infinite attributes, of which two are known to human beings: thought and extension. Thought and extension are two aspects of one substance, so that for every state of matter there is a corresponding mental state, or "idea," and every idea is related to matter. The states of both thought and extension succeed one another with unbroken necessity. Everything that happens is fully determined to happen by previous states. Neither God (nature) nor humans can do other than they do. The freedom of God and humans consists in their acting according to their natures. God does this automatically; human freedom varies according to the extent that the actions of a person are dominated by internal or external causes. Individual human beings are not substances but are merely locally organized bits of extended matter (the human body), along with the attendant idea of that organized matter (an idea that constitutes the human mind).

Spinoza conveyed these metaphysical thoughts most fully in his *Ethics*, published posthumously in 1677, the year of his death. He also produced a rationalist critique of religion, described below.

Malebranche. Malebranche was attracted to Cartesian philosophy when he read Descartes's *Treatise on Man* in 1664. He became interested in Cartesian philosophy and studied it assiduously. Ten years later, he published his *Search after Truth*. Theological in motivation, it presented a Cartesian picture of the universe, with some modifications. Malebranche accepted the basic elements of Descartes's physics, his doctrine that the essence of matter is extension, and his mind-body dualism. He argued, however, that individual minds do not contain the intellectual ideas that ground human knowledge, such as the idea of extension. Rather, such ideas exist in God, who allows human beings to "see" them in his divine mind when needed, or rather, reveals them to humans in a form they can grasp. Malebranche also developed a theme, hinted at in Descartes's *Correspondence* (published during the 1650s), that all causal agency resides with God. As espoused by Malebranche, this position is known as "occasionalism." It states that when bodies collide, God is responsible for redirecting their subsequent movement; one body does not directly cause the motion of another or impart force to it. Similarly, when the mind forms an intention to move the body, God effects the corresponding motion; and when the brain enters a certain state, God causes a corresponding sensation or emotion in the mind.

Other Cartesians. Descartes's philosophy was immensely popular during the second half of the seventeenth century and was widely taught, especially in England, Germany, and the Netherlands. His mechanistic physics was the most widely promulgated part of his work. Many textbook presentations of his physics and philosophy were written by Cartesians such as the Frenchmen Jacques Rohault and Pierre-Sylvain Régis, the Englishman Antoine Le Grand, and the Dutchman Adrian Heereboord. His mechanistic approach to physiology was adopted by numerous physicians, including the Dutchmen Cornelius ab Hogheland and Theodore Craanen. Rohault's presentation of Descartes's physics was translated into English by John Clarke, with annotations by his Newtonian brother, Samuel Clarke. In this form it was used to teach physics at Cambridge until around 1740. Le Grand's presentation of a full system of Cartesian philosophy, including logic, metaphysics, physics, and morals, was frequently reissued in the original Latin and was translated into English in 1694.

Cartesian textbooks in physics covered those aspects of the mind that pertain to mind-body union—including the operation of the senses and the formation of sensory experience—under the rubric of physics. The normal Aristotelian classification of psychology, or *De anima* studies ("animistics"), had placed it under physics on the grounds that the soul and its mental functions are part of nature. Some Cartesians, though not all, discussed the immaterial mind itself within physics (see Hatfield, 2000). The conception that an immaterial mind might nonetheless be considered part of nature had currency into the nineteenth century.

All the Cartesians, like Descartes himself, allowed that observation and experiment are needed in natural science. Some, such as Rohault and Le Grand, stressed this need. At the same time, all of the Cartesians named here, including Rohault and Le Grand, adopted the Cartesian view that some of the basic principles of physics—including the doctrine that the essence of matter is bare, inert extension—can be known through the intellect independently of experience. Descartes's mind-body dualism and his intellectualist epistemology were defining tenets for his followers, even those interested mainly in his mechanistic physics.

Leibniz. Leibniz also was attracted to Cartesianism early in life, but he subsequently rejected Descartes's doctrine that matter is purely inert, extended stuff. He objected to Descartes's laws of motion on empirical grounds, and he held that such laws can be known only through experience. He believed that force must be attributed to material substance as an intrinsic property. However, when Leibniz tried to conceive of individually existing entities, or substances, with an intrinsic force, his only models for active beings were minded entities such as humans and nonhuman animals (*Discourse on Metaphysics*, written 1686). He argued that the world, as created by God, consists of individual substances which he later called "monads" (*Monadology*, 1714). These monads are like little minds. Their inner states consist in perceptions, or representations of the world from a certain point of view. These perceptions follow one another according to fixed laws, described as "appetites." The monads do not interact causally with one another; rather, in creating them, God implants in each one a program or law entailing all its future states. He does this by envisioning the created world as whole and then creating each monad with a specific spatio-temporal point of view within that world. Some monads forever have the point of view of earth or rock; their inner states are very simple. Others have the point of view, for a time at least, of a living human being. In any case, each monad expresses the rest of the universe through its successive states of perception. Monads that constitute human souls also perceive, self-consciously, their own perceptual states.

Leibniz held that God, in creating the universe, surveys all possible worlds in a single intellectual act and then creates the best one. He also held that God, by his nature, acts in accordance with the principle of sufficient reason (according to which there must be a reason for everything), and that, being omniscient, he fully foresees the consequences of creating one or another possible world. Being all-good, God by nature chooses the best among the possible worlds. The notion of "bestness" is defined in terms of perfection or completeness; God creates the universe that contains the most being or reality, achieved by the least means. As Leibniz understood it, this meant achieving the most variety through the simplest means. Since Leibniz held that human beings are unable to grasp the infinitely complex logical problem of which world is best, a problem God solves without effort, he was of course unable to offer a complete reconstruction of the factors entering God's decision; however, he thought he could know that the best world would include simple laws of nature and beings with free will. From this mix, things that seem locally "bad" to humans will arise. Leibniz held that the bad things experienced by good or innocent humans are consistent with this world being, overall, the best one possible. His position was ridiculed by some eighteenth-century authors, including Voltaire in *Candide*. In Voltaire's novel, the steadfastly optimistic Pangloss is a mere parody of Leibniz; nowhere in all his talk of the "best possible world" does Pangloss engage the notion of creating the most through the least. Nonetheless, the satire does make the point that Leibniz's arguments are unlikely to convince anyone who does not already hold a specific theistic metaphysics and conception of divine providence.

Rationalism in eighteenth-century philosophers. The belief that reason or the intellect can attain substantive metaphysical knowledge was under attack throughout the eighteenth century. The attack was led by the British Empiricist philosophers Locke and Hume and the French Empiricist Condillac. Nonetheless, traditional rationalism, according to which the mind is able to prove God's existence and attributes and to discern the basic structure of the natural world, found some defenders.

Two notable defenders of reason's power were the German philosophers Christian August Crusius and Moses Mendelssohn. Crusius believed that the human understanding can discern the basic structure of the universe, or the possible things that can exist there. However, he limited the power of the human mind with respect to theology, allowing revelation to overturn the conclusions of our finite minds. Mendelssohn, in his prize-winning essay of 1763, *On Evidence in Metaphysical Sciences*, affirmed much of Descartes's epistemology, together with the basic metaphysics of Leibniz. He attributed innate ideas to the human mind and believed they serve as a basis for metaphysical tenets—though he allowed that the expression of such ideas is sometimes prompted by sensory experience. He affirmed Descartes's famous *cogito* argument, "I think, therefore I am," as a fundamental tenet on which an entire system of philosophy can be erected, independently of the senses. He also adopted Descartes's proof for the existence of God from an allegedly necessary connection between God's essence and existence (the so-called ontological argument). He also subscribed to Leibniz's doctrine that the world of extended matter is a well-founded set of appearances, grounded in the properties of underlying unextended substances. In addition, in his *Phaedo* (1767) Mendelssohn attempted to establish the immortality of the soul through purely metaphysical arguments that appealed to the soul's simplicity and, hence, its alleged indestructibility.

During the middle decades of the eighteenth century, Christian Wolff (1679–1754) was the preeminent philosopher in Germany. He is sometimes portrayed as a traditional Rationalist because he subscribed to the Leibnizian principle of sufficient reason. In fact, Wolff had no clear commitment to the notion that philosophy, or even metaphysics, is or can be based on pure intellect or reason, operating independently of the senses. He held instead that the intellect applies the principle of sufficient reason within experience and becomes convinced of its universal scope from considering cases of its application. He further argued that metaphysical and logical principles are derived from experience. For that reason, what he called "empirical psychology," or the empirical investigation of mental phenomena, is the foundation of both rational psychology and logic, just as empirical cosmology grounds rational cosmology. In the "rational" version of each science, principles derived from experience are accepted as universal and are then used in deductive explanations. Hence, Wolff is closer to the Aristotelian conception of the intellect as a power for finding truth in experience than to the Rationalist conception of a pure intellect operating independently of the senses.

Kant, although known as a defender of reason, was an opponent of traditional rationalism. His *Critique of Pure Reason* (1781) was written in order to assess the possibility of traditional metaphysics as an a priori science concerning God, the soul, and the substances underlying the natural world (the world "as it is in itself"). He concluded that human intellect or reason is incapable of achieving knowledge of such entities. He did allow a restricted metaphysics within the domain of possible experience, but he considered himself to have ended permanently what he termed "intellectualist" epistemology, a term he applied to Platonism and traditional rationalism alike.

Rationalism as Reasoned Criticism. During the seventeenth and eighteenth centuries, the term "rationalism" was applied to those who brought reasoned criticism to bear on social, political, and religious institutions and practices. In this connection, rationalists need not have appealed to reason as a sense-independent faculty of mind. Rather, they might contrast reason with revelation, or with political authority not founded on "rational" principles. The Empiricist philosopher David Hume subjected both religion and politics to rational scrutiny of this kind.

Seventeenth-century works by Hobbes and Spinoza provided paradigms for the rational criticism of religion. Both authors subjected allegedly revealed truths to reasoned scrutiny, but they differed in their conceptions of reason and, hence, in their results.

Fully half of Hobbes's *Leviathan* (published in 1651, reissued in 1670) was devoted to a criticism of the Bible as an independent source of religious doctrine. Hobbes questioned the purported authorship of various parts of the Bible, denied any rational basis for believing the Bible recorded the word of God, and rejected the purported grounds for positing immaterial spirits, angels, or devils.

He concluded that the doctrines contained in scripture can be accepted on either of two conditions: first, if they accord with the "Laws of Nature," which are laws for human conduct based on human nature and philosophical reasoning about human nature; or second, if such doctrines are promulgated by an appropriate ecclesiastical authority. Such an authority may be either a single church authority recognized by all Christian kings (there was no such authority in Hobbes's day, since the pope was not recognized by the English crown), or, failing that, by the various sovereigns of each Christian kingdom. In effect, he argued that religious doctrine should be accepted either by philosophical reasoning or from the governing authority of the political sovereign. Hobbes's notion of "reasoning" was logical reasoning about sensory evidence, not the sense-independent reason of the Rationalists.

Spinoza published his *Tractatus Theologico-Politicus* anonymously in 1670. In it, he challenged the independent authority of prophets and scripture and denied miracles. Like Hobbes, he discussed the authorship of the Bible and the historical circumstances of its composition. Unlike Hobbes, he affirmed that each human being had, in the intellect, an independent source of knowledge about the attributes of "God or nature," the nature of human beings, and the principles of human conduct. He concluded that "the supreme right of free thinking, even on religion, is in every man's power, and as it is inconceivable that such power could be alienated, it is also in every man's power to wield the supreme right and authority of free judgment in his behalf, and to explain and interpret religion for himself" (Spinoza, 1951, pp. 118–119). He used the word "man" advisedly here; although he held (by contrast with Hobbes) that democracy was the best form of government, he also contended it should be a democracy of male human beings. Had he been a Cartesian dualist, for whom the mind was a separate substance and thus the same regardless of gender, his political doctrine would have contradicted his Rationalism. As a dual-aspect monist (for whom the mind was the idea of the body, so that systematic bodily differences could be reflected in minds), however, Spinoza could consistently argue that women are not equal to men in character and ability. His argument was, however, of necessity an empirical argument based on the historical record of previous governments and social practices, in which men ruled. (Descartes also could allow empirically based differences in behavior according to gender, but only where mind-body interaction was involved.) In that regard, his monistic ontology distinguished his Rationalism from the Cartesian version, with its metaphysical basis for equality of intellect among all human beings.

[*See also* Cartesianism; Empiricism; Epistemology; Leibniz, Gottfried Wilhelm von; Malebranche, Nicolas; Mendelssohn, Moses; Philosophy; Reason; Spinoza, Baruch de; *and* Wolff, Christian.]

BIBLIOGRAPHY

SOURCES

Bacon, Francis. "Cogitata et visa" (Things Thought and Things Seen). In his *Works*, edited by James Spedding, Robert Leslie Ellis, and Douglas Denon Heath, new ed., vol. 3, pp. 591–620. London, 1872–1876.

Descartes, René. *Philosophical Writings*. Translated by John Cottingham, Robert Stoothoff, and Dugald Murdoch. 2 vols. Cambridge, 1984–1985. Includes Descartes's philosophical works and selections from his scientific writings.

Descartes, René. *Philosophical Writings*, vol. 3, *The Correspondence*. Translated by John Cottingham, Robert Stoothoff, Dugald Murdoch, and Anthony Kenny. Cambridge, 1991.

Hobbes, Thomas. *Leviathan*. Edited by Richard Tuck. Cambridge, 1991.

Le Grand, Antoine. *An Entire Body of Philosophy, According to the Principles of the Famous Renate des Cartes*. Translated by Richard Blome. New York, 1972. Reprint of the 1694 English translation of *Institutio philosophiae secundum principia D. Renati Descartes*, first published in 1672.

Leibniz, Gottfried Wilhelm. *Philosophical Essays*. Edited and translated by Roger Ariew and Daniel Garber. Indianapolis, 1989.

Malebranche, Nicolas. *The Search After Truth*. Translated by Thomas M. Lennon and Paul J. Olscamp. Columbus, 1980. English translation of *Recherche de la vérité*, originally published in 1674.

Mendelssohn, Moses. *Philosophical Writings*. Translated and edited by Daniel O. Dahlstrom. Cambridge, 1997. English translation of *Philosophische Schriften*, 2d ed., published in 1771.

Régis, Pierre-Sylvain. *Cours entier de philosophie: ou, Système général selon les principes de M. Descartes, contenant la logique, la métaphysique, la physique, et la morale*. New York, 1970. Reprint of 1691 edition.

Rohault, Jacques. *System of natural philosophy*. Translated by John Clarke, notes by Samuel Clarke. 2 vols. New York, 1987. Reprint of the second edition of the original English translation, London, 1728–1729. English translation of *Traité de physique*, originally published in 1671.

Spinoza, Baruch de. *Collected Works*. Edited and translated by Edwin Curley. Princeton, N.J., 1985. Thus far, only volume one has appeared; it includes the *Ethics*.

Spinoza, Baruch de. *A Theologico-Political Treatise and A Political Treatise*. Translated by R. H. M. Elwes. New York, 1951.

STUDIES

Beck, Lewis White. "From Leibniz to Kant." In *The Age of German Idealism*, edited by Robert C. Solomon and Kathleen M. Higgins, pp. 5–39. London, 1993. A summary account of major figures in German philosophy between Leibniz and Kant.

Cottingham, John. *The Rationalists*. Oxford, 1988. Introductory survey, with additional references.

Hatfield, Gary. "Descartes' Naturalism About the Mental." In *Descartes' Natural Philosophy*, edited by Stephen Gaukroger, John Schuster, and John Sutton, pp. 630–658. London, 2000. Discusses Descartes's theory of mind, and the theories of the late seventeenth century Cartesians Le Grand, Régis, and Rohault.

Parkinson, G. H. R., ed. *Routledge History of Philosophy*, vol. 4, *The Renaissance and Seventeenth-Century Rationalism*. London, 1993. Comprehensive survey, with additional references.

Robertson, J. M. *A Short History of Freethought, Ancient and Modern.* New York, 1972. Reprint of 1957 edition. Older survey of its topic.

Roehr, Sabine. *A Primer on German Enlightenment.* Columbia, Mo., 1995. Treatment of German Enlightenment philosophy in historical context, with a focus on German Rationalism and its opponents.

GARY HATFIELD

RAYNAL, GUILLAUME-THOMAS (1713–1796), French historian and man of letters.

Raynal's career mirrored the changing character of the French eighteenth century more faithfully than that of most of his contemporaries. With Jean-Antoine-Nicolas de Caritat Condorcet, he was the only notable figure of the French Enlightenment to live on into the Revolution, creating a rare direct link between the two great cultural and political movements of the period. His early career was marked by a change of comparable significance, from cleric to philosophe. While he was a pupil of the Jesuits in southwestern France, his intellectual bent had predisposed him to become a teacher with the order. By 1747, his critical intelligence and boundless appetite for knowledge no longer found satisfaction in the routine of a provincial pedagogue, and he set off to seek his fortune in Paris. In the parish of Saint-Sulpice, as a secular priest disaffected by ecclesiastical orthodoxy, he was drawn to the increasingly dissident literary and philosophical circles of the capital, where he found his intellectual home.

Raynal founded the journal *Nouvelles littéraires*, and edited the prestigious *Mercure de France*, gaining a reputation as a prodigiously industrious if not particularly gifted writer. He was more noteworthy for his compilations than for any original compositions. That assessment was borne out by a number of commissioned histories and compendia of historical anecdotes, in the main highly derivative, owing more to Raynal's ability to cut and paste from printed sources than to any ability to offer new insights into his chosen topics. These works are *Histoire du Stadhoudérat* (1747), *Histoire du Parlement d'Angleterre* (1748), *Anecdotes littéraires* (1750), *Anecdotes historiques, militaires et politiques* (1753) and *École militaire* (1762).

Histoire des deux Indes. His reputation as an ordinary journalist and historiographer changed, however, when he combined his journalistic and organizational skills with radical fervor as the chief author, editor, and prime mover of a history of European trade and colonialism, the *Histoire philosophique et politique des établissements et du commerce des Européens dans les deux Indes*, more commonly referred to as the *Histoire des deux Indes*. This work became one of the century's best-sellers.

The *Histoire des deux Indes*, whose title uses the contemporary geographical shorthand to refer to Asia and the Americas, first appeared in 1770 in an anonymous edition published without Raynal's approval. Its immediate success led to a revised and augmented second edition (1774), and a third edition (1780), yet further updated and augmented, that carried Raynal's name on the title page and his portrait as frontispiece of the first volume. His audacity in publicly admitting authorship of a work whose radical views had grown in intensity from edition to edition brought down the wrath of the authorities in the form of a public condemnation in 1781, which forced him into exile until 1784. Official irritation did nothing to slacken the enthusiasm of the reading public for the *Histoire des deux Indes*; indeed, it had the opposite effect. In Raynal's lifetime, more than forty official and pirated versions of the work were published, as well as numerous extracts and translations into all the major European languages. The English translations of the second and third editions were highly popular among readers from both the merchant classes and the Whig intelligentsia, who had greeted the original French edition with marked interest. During the French Revolution, the *Histoire* continued to be reprinted, its progressive views ensuring its status as a revolutionary vademecum, despite Raynal's own fall from grace in the eyes of the Jacobin ascendancy for preaching moderation as the Revolution was entering its most radical phase. Further updated in the posthumous edition of 1820, the *Histoire des deux Indes* maintained a readership well into the first half of the nineteenth century, no doubt less for its radical views—which, with the passage of time, had lost their edge—than for its continuing value as an informative and critical survey of European distant-water trade and the attendant growth of empire.

At a time when European commerce, settlement, and colonization were undergoing a huge expansion, and traditional authority was either in retreat in the face of progressive ideas or powerfully challenged by them, Raynal was able to bring to the public a well-informed history of trade that was both philosophical and political. This mix appealed to a wide readership, in France, across Europe, and in North America, which, while not homogenous, mostly believed that humanity's future well-being and prosperity lay in the increasing liberalization of every field of human activity, of trade, politics, religion, and morality. The kaleidoscopic mixture of historical narrative, anecdote, analysis, comment, and political harangue that combines with geographical, botanical, and anthropological descriptions to make up the *Histoire des deux Indes* left Raynal's reader free to draw on whatever aspects of the work reflected their own views and preoccupations.

Collaboration with Diderot. The heterogeneous character of the *Histoire des deux Indes* derives from the multiplicity of its sources, including a formidable range of published works, government papers, and the latest information garnered from carefully fostered contacts across Europe and North America, and from the team of writers

Raynal employed to assist him. Chief among these was Denis Diderot, whom he engaged to impart to his history the style and ideological weight of which he himself was incapable. Raynal's achievement was to draw together all these diverse strands into a whole whose polysemous character shocks us less today than it did some of his more fastidious contemporary critics. The encyclopedic range of the *Histoire*—diversity, discontinuity, and outright contradictions belie its orderly presentation of the activities of each trading nation with successive geographical areas—made it in some respects more closely related in spirit to the *Encyclopédie* of Diderot and D'Alembert than to the other great histories written during the Enlightenment.

In its radicalism, the *Histoire des deux Indes* went well beyond the *Encyclopédie*, benefiting from the greater atmosphere of public, if not official, tolerance that its predecessor had created. Whereas the *Encyclopédie* hid its more forthright attacks on religious orthodoxy, privilege, and the arbitrary exercise of power in obscure articles to which the reader was led through a network of cross-references, the *Histoire* exercised no such caution. It was overtly anticlerical; it frequently instructed the rulers of the world on their duties and castigated them for their tyrannical behavior; and it roundly condemned the rich and the wellborn for placing their interests before those of the nation or those over whom they had been given authority.

Admittedly, the author of most of these severe, far-reaching criticisms was Diderot, to whom can be attributed the chapters of the *Histoire* that condemn slavery and the cruel excesses of colonialism, and that voice enthusiastic support for the American Revolution. By the third edition, Raynal's work had become, as Diderot himself put it in his *Lettre apologétique de l'abbé Raynal*, "un livre qui fait naître des Brutus," a book that inspires men to slay tyrants. Diderot was concerned to defend by implication his own stake in Raynal's work as its most radical contributor, a role that—despite the absence of any reference on the title page to his participation—was an open secret. By contrast, Raynal's voice was more prudent in its radicalism, and as concerned with promoting the commercial advantages of colonialism as with denouncing its injustices. Nonetheless, Raynal showed considerable courage in granting Diderot a public and, largely uncensored forum for his subversive ideas, and it was Raynal rather than Diderot who was forced into exile as a consequence of their publication.

Legacy of Raynal. There is no need to question the sincerity of Diderot's praise when he asked elsewhere in his *Lettre apologétique*, "What other nation has its Raynal? None, not even England," and argued that posterity would be his best judge. As things turned out, posterity judged Raynal by consigning him to oblivion. The domestic and commercial agendas of the *Histoire des deux Indes* had been largely written into the manifestos of liberal politics of Europe and North America by the second half of the nineteenth century, while in the great age of European imperialism its anticolonialist rhetoric had lost its ability to persuade. By contrast, the twentieth century has seen a revival of Raynal's fortunes, as interest in the work that established his contemporary reputation has gathered pace with the development of postcolonialism. With the projected publication of a modern critical edition of the *Histoire des deux Indes*, by the Voltaire Foundation, Oxford, in 2003, Raynal's status as one of the most effective contemporary publicists of the French Enlightenment will no doubt fully regain the recognition it deserves.

[*See also* Colonialism; Commerce and Trade; Diderot, Denis; *and* Encyclopédie.]

BIBLIOGRAPHY

Feugère, Anatole. *Un précurseur de la Révolution: L'abbé Raynal (1713–1796)*. Angoulême, 1922; repr., Geneva, 1970. A full and reliable account of Raynal's life and work on which recent research continues to build.
Goggi, Gianluigi, and Gilles Bancarel. *Raynal, de la polémique à l'histoire*. Oxford, 2000. Studies of Raynal's life and intellectual career.
Lüsebrink, Hans-Jürgen, and Anthony Strugnell, eds. *L'histoire des deux Indes: Réécriture et polygraphie*. Oxford, 1995. Textual studies of the *Histoire des deux Indes*.
Lüsebrink, Hans-Jürgen, and Manfred Tietz, eds. *Lectures de Raynal: L'histoire des deux Indes en Europe et en Amérique au XVIIIe siècle*. Oxford, 1991. Studies of the contemporary reception of the *Histoire des deux Indes*.
Wolpe, Hans. *Raynal et sa machine de guerre: L'histoire des deux Indes et ses perfectionnements*. Paris, 1956.

ANTHONY STRUGNELL

READING AND READING PRACTICES. Can the age of Enlightenment be characterized as that of a revolution in reading? Contemporaries would doubtless have responded affirmatively, so strong was their awareness of the mutations that had transformed both print production and reading practices. From midcentury on, in particular, the number of discourses expressing a sharp perception of such a transformation multiplied.

Travel accounts and descriptions of everyday life stressed the new universality of reading, present in all social circles under a variety of circumstances. A veritable "reading mania," also described as a "reading fever" and a "reading fury" (German texts refer to *Lesesucht*, *Lesefieber*, and *Lesewut*) took hold of the population. In medical discourse, this phenomenon took the form of a diagnosis emphasizing the destructive effects of excessive reading, perceived both as an individual disturbance and a collective epidemic. In such a diagnosis, reading, because it allied immobility of the body and excitement of the imagination, led to physical exhaustion, the rejection of reality, and a preference for the chimerical. Hence the closeness to other solitary practices, and the relationships drawn, in medical treatises, as in erotic novels, between reading and onanism. The reading of lascivious works was often described as the prelude to less intellectual pursuits. The two practices led, furthermore, to the same symptoms: paleness, anxiety, indifference, and prostration. The danger was greatest when the reading material was a novel and the reader a woman in the solitude of a retreat, removed from the regard of others. Excess threatened all readers, however, in particular the most avid, since the physical symptoms (the engorgement of the stomach and the intestines associated with the disturbance of the nerves) were also those that characterized hypochondria—the malady par excellence of people of letters. This theory of the overheated imagination, part of the period's sensualist psychology, thus gave a new, more radical formulation to the ancient denunciations of the perils of fiction, such as those based in the Christian condemnation of bad examples and the Platonic theme of the expulsion of poets from the Republic. Philosophical discourse also passed a negative judgment on excessive reading. It denounced reading for distraction and to pass time as a veritable "narcotic" (Johann Gottlieb Fichte's term) or as an "act of high treason toward humanity because it belittles a means of attaining superior ends" (according to Theodor Bergk).

Painters, designers, and engravers certainly provided other representations of reading, whether in the decoration of earthenware or porcelain vessels, oilcloths, and fob watches, or in the form of silhouettes and figurines. This proliferating imagery drew attention to new readers (women, children, artisans, peasants) and new habits: reading outdoors, in the garden or in nature, reading while walking, reading in bed (as preparation for or substitute for erotic encounters), and reading aloud in social situations, such as salons or domestic gatherings. All these representations indicated, in their own way, that reading practices had changed, that readers were more numerous, and that readers were mad about reading.

We can match these perceptions with the pair of notions constructed by Rolf Engelsing, who contrasted a traditional, so-called "intensive" reading and a modern "extensive" reading—a practice described and condemned by contemporaries. According to this dichotomy, the "intensive" reader was limited to a closed body of texts that were read and reread, memorized and recited, heard and learned by heart, and transmitted from generation to generation. Such a manner of reading bore a strong imprint of sacredness, subjecting the reader to the authority of the text. The "extensive" reader was completely different: he or she consumed numerous, new, and ephemeral printed works; read them quickly and avidly; and approached them with a distanced and critical regard. A relationship

with texts that was communal and respectful would thus have been succeeded by a free, casual, and irreverent reading.

Many criticisms can be made of this chronology of a "before" and an "after" of reading separated by a veritable "revolution." In effect, "extensive" readers were numerous in the time of supposedly "intensive" reading. Think of the erudite humanists. The two objects emblematic of their manner of reading were the book wheel, which allowed them to read several books at once, and the commonplace book, in the columns of which the reader could record citations, examples, and information. Both indicate a practice that relied on an accumulation of readings that proceeded by extracts, compilations, and comparisons, and that implied the exercise of criticism, philological in this case.

Inversely, it was at the very moment of the "extensive" reading revolution that, with Samuel Richardson, Jean-Jacques Rousseau, Jacques-Henri Bernardin de Saint-Pierre, and Johann Wolfgang von Goethe, the most "intensive" style of reading was created, through which the novel takes hold of the reader, binds him to the text, and governs his thoughts and actions. The reading of *Pamela* or *Clarissa*, *La nouvelle Héloïse*, *Paul et Virginie*, or *Die Leiden des jungen Werthers* (The Sorrows of Young Werther) displaced practices of sacralized reading onto a new (or renewed) literary form. The novel was read and reread, learned by heart, cited, and recited. Readers were invaded by a text that they inhabited; they identified with the hero of the story, and deciphered their own lives through the fictions of the plot. In this new type of "intensive" reading, the entire sensibility was engaged. The reader (often a woman) could hold back neither emotions nor tears. Turned upside down, the reader would sometimes take up a pen, become an author in turn, and even more often, write to the author who, through his work, had become a veritable director of conscience and existence.

Readers of novels were not, furthermore, the only "intensive" readers at the time of the reading revolution. The reading of the majority, and of the most humble, fed by titles from the publishing houses of colportage, remained controlled by traditional habits. The reading of chapbooks, of the *Bibliothèque bleue*, and of the *literatura de cordel*, enduringly conserved the characteristics of a rare and difficult practice, which presupposed listening and memorization. The texts that made up these collections were thus the object of an appropriation that played on recognition (of genres, themes, and motifs) more than on the discovery of new works, and that remained foreign to the expectations and manners of hurried, insatiable, and skeptical readers.

These observations lead us to call into doubt the validity of a clear-cut opposition between two styles of reading, held to be incompatible and successive. For all that, is it necessary to abandon the very idea of a reading revolution in the eighteenth century? Perhaps not, if we take into account the objective changes that transformed the connection to texts throughout western Europe. The first stemmed from the growth and diversification of print production. Everywhere the range of books increased: in England, according to inventories of editions conserved, 65,000 titles were published in the 1790s, compared with 21,000 in the 1710s; in Germany, the catalog of works put up for sale at the fair of Frankfurt offered 1,384 titles in 1765; 1,892 in 1775; 2,713 in 1785; 3,257 in 1795; and 3,906 in 1800. Greatly augmented, the production of the book was likewise profoundly transformed. The religious book, which dominated production in the seventeenth century and at the beginning of the eighteenth century, lost ground to belles lettres (this was the case at the fair of Frankfurt, where literature increased from 6 percent in 1740 to 21.5 percent in 1800) or the sciences and practical works (this was the case in France, where the rise of that category in the requests for permission was in inverse proportion to the collapse on the part of religious titles, which still constituted a third of the production in the 1720s but accounted for no more than a quarter at the beginning of the 1750s, and only a tenth in the 1780s).

To this authorized production was added the circulation on a large scale of all the books that the booksellers called "philosophical." From 1770 on, these vendors distributed clandestinely—and above all in the kingdom of France—pornographic or modern literature, the most radical works of the Enlightenment, and an entire ensemble of satires, lampoons, and chronicles of scandals that denounced the despotism of the prince and the corruption of the nobility. Published by typographic societies established in Switzerland, the Netherlands, or the German principalities; prohibited but nevertheless introduced in large number into the kingdom; sometimes confiscated upon entry into Paris or in the shops of the publishers—these "philosophical books," the catalog of which is made up of many hundreds of titles, constituted a dangerous but much sought-after merchandise.

The most spectacular of the transformations that affected print production was, without any doubt, the multiplication and mutation of journals. The increased number of new enterprises (some lasting, others ephemeral) was impressive, let alone the comparative curves of new periodicals in German and in French. In the first decade of the 1700s, 64 titles appeared in German, compared with 40 in the French language, published either within or outside of the kingdom. In the course of the century, the disparity between the two bodies of periodicals grew: in the 1720s, the numbers of new productions were respectively 133 and 53; in the 1740s, 260 and 98; in the 1760s,

410 and 137; in the 1770s, 718 and 188; and, finally, in the last decade of the century, 1,225 and 277 (but this number does not take into account the journalistic explosion of the years 1789 and 1790 in Paris and France). The growth in the number of titles was marked by the appearance of new types of journals. In Germany, for example, scholarly and literary periodicals gave way to moral weeklies ("Moralischen Wochenschriften"), preoccupied with usefulness and the common good, and to historical and political journals that, after 1770, offered to the enlightened public discussions of affairs of state. The press thus became the main basis for a political sociability that involved debates about recent events, state reforms, and basic concepts of political philosophy.

The book, for its part, became more accessible. The triumph of the small formats made the book a constant companion. Louis-Sébastien Mercier noted, "The mania for small formats succeeded that for large pages...These little books had the advantage of being able to be pocketed, to add to the diversion of a promenade, and to overcome the boredom of travel," while the German poet Jean-Paul stated, "When one remembers the former volumes in folio which weighed several pounds, bound in wood, in copper, with hinges of brass wire...and when one holds in the hand a little pocket book ("Taschenbuch"): one can think himself happy." With the small formats, reading had become more free. The book no longer had to be set down in order to be read, and the reader no longer had to be seated in order to read it: a new, more casual and immediate connection to reading matter came into being.

More manageable, the book was likewise more easily acquired and consulted. Certainly, its price increased: in Germany, the price of novels in their original edition increased eight or nine times in the last third of the eighteenth century. At the same time, a double corrective limited or obviated the effects of this increased cost. First of all, the practice on a large scale of counterfeiting (that is, the publication of a title in violation of the privilege of the editor who possesses the property or the copyright of the work) necessarily lowered the sale price of books since their counterfeit editor dispensed with the purchase of the manuscript from its author and with the fees necessary for obtaining a privilege. Counterfeiting was a major part of publishing activity. It was practiced by provincial publishers and foreign typographic societies at the expense of Parisian editors, who monopolized privileges granted by the monarchy and the market for new works; by Scottish and provincial publishers at the expense of members of the Stationers' Company of London, dispossessed in 1710 through the Statute of Queen Anne of the perpetual ownership of their copyrights; and by bookseller-editors of the different German and Italian states at the expense of their confrères in other states, since in the empire as in Italy the fragmentation of political sovereignties tightly limited the enforcement zone for privileges conceded by a particular authority. In these commercial struggles between booksellers in search of a clientele, the reader was the principal beneficiary.

On the other hand, institutions where reading did not necessarily imply the purchase of a book multiplied throughout Europe. A first possibility was provided by booksellers. Under diverse names (circulating libraries, rental libraries, *Leihbibliotheken*, *cabinets littéraires*), the service offered was the same: for an annual or monthly rental fee, readers could read in the shop or carry home with them works that the bookseller's catalog offered for rent. The formula was very successful in England. Perhaps inspired by the coffeehouses that put journals and pamphlets at the disposal of their clients, it appeared from the first decades of the century and developed rapidly after 1740. An inventory (without doubt incomplete) records the existence, more or less enduring, of 380 circulating libraries during the eighteenth century: 112 in London and 268 in the counties, dispersed among 119 different locations. The phenomenon thus extended far beyond only the large cities. The same was true in France, but on a lesser scale. The first literary reading room was opened in Lyon in 1759, and a survey, also surely incomplete, was able to identify the presence of thirteen reading rooms in Paris and thirty-six in the provinces between that date and 1789.

A second formula was that of the voluntary association, endowed with collectively approved statutes. Its members, for an annual subscription, could borrow works acquired collectively, which were either sold by auction at the end of each year (as was the case for book clubs), or conserved in the library of the society (as with subscription libraries). In England, book clubs flourished beginning in the 1720s, and the first subscription library was founded in 1758 in Liverpool. In Germany, the movement to create these *Lesegesellschaften* grew strongly from 1770 on: if there were only 17 foundings before that date, there were 50 between 1770 and 1779, 170 between 1780 and 1789, and 200 between 1790 and 1800. The diffusion followed a double route: from north of the Rhine, reformed and enlightened, to the southern regions, first Protestant then, from 1780 forward, Catholic; and from the largest cities to the small towns, indeed even to certain rural communities. Reading societies participated fully in three processes essential to the age of Enlightenment: they furthered the initiation of a democratic sociability, since any decision made therein was subject to the principle of a majority vote that ignored differences of profession and background; they constituted one of the instruments of the process of civilization, since their statutes censored rude behavior; and finally, they contributed (along with literary societies and Masonic lodges) to the construction of a social and intellectual network that made up the reality of the new public sphere where, at a distance from the authority of the sovereign, private persons debated affairs of state and the actions of the prince. By permitting more readers to read more books and by offering a large market for periodicals and large editorial undertakings (dictionaries, encyclopedias, and *bibliothèques*), the reading societies profoundly changed the practices of reading and contributed to the fashioning of a new type of reader.

These developments furnished a favorable environment for a more pervasive presence of print, a rapid development of new genres, both literary and editorial, and for new

Reading the Newspapers. Drawing by L. L. Boilly, 1795. (Bibliothèque Nationale, Paris/Giraudon/Art Resource, NY.)

manners of reading. They were the implied reverse side of the image, so often evoked at the end of the century by painters (Jean-Baptiste Greuze) and writers (Nicolas Restif de la Bretonne) of a peasant and patriarchal practice, in which the head of the family would read out loud for his assembled household in the evening. This ideal representation expressed the nostalgia for a lost way of life, for a world in which the book was revered and authority was respected. This mythologized ideal of communal reading was an implied rebuke to what had evidently become the ordinary gestures of a way of reading that was completely contrary: urban, careless, and casual.

Does this ensemble of mutations and of representations constitute a reading revolution? For those in doubt, there are strong arguments stemming from the permanence of the same conditions of printed production. In the eighteenth century, the fabrication of the book remained, in effect, what it had been since the time of Johannes Gutenberg, without major changes in techniques, labor, or print runs (generally limited to 1,250 or 1,500 copies per edition). Furthermore, publishing activity remained subject (except in England after 1695) to preliminary censorship by political authorities, who accorded privileges and permissions. Publishers were also threatened by condemnations pronounced after publication by civil and religious authorities, and were held back, throughout Mediterranean Europe (Portugal, Spain, and Italy), by the prohibitions of the church's Index of Prohibited Books and the prosecutions of the Inquisition (which did not, however, manifest the extreme rigor that is often supposed).

Nevertheless, within this stability of technique and of censorship, print production had modified its foundation, and readers had transformed their practices—this, at least, is expressed by all the representations of reading that, for better and more often for worse, opposed the present ways of reading to those of a bygone past.

Does this allow us to speak of a "revolution?" Perhaps, but under two conditions. The first is to recognize that this "revolution" was only one reading revolution—not *the* reading revolution. Others had preceded it, tied to the invention of the codex, to the origination of reading silently, and to passage from the monastic model of writing to the scholastic model of reading. Others also followed it: in the nineteenth century, with the democratization of the audience of the printed work, and in the twentieth century, with the advent of the electronic text. Thus, the innovations of the eighteenth century must be situated in their correct place, within a long history of the changing contexts and practices of reading. The second condition is to take into account and to specify the disparities, gaps, and limits that characterized the reading revolution of the Enlightenment. It was more marked in certain places (European countries long familiar with written culture) and in certain social circles (the bourgeoisies of the intellectual trades and the liberal professions).

In the eighteenth century, for the best-educated readers, the range of possible readings seems to have grown and to have offered a repertory of possibilities previously unknown. Such an articulation of diverse reading practices, available to a single community or a single reader, is another reason to reject simplistic oppositions. Each reader was, at different times, an "intensive" and an "extensive" reader, who read for himself and for others, in solitude and in society.

A letter written in 1784 by Luise Meyer, who was a lady's companion in the home of Countess Stolberg, bears witness to this. It shows, in effect, how different readings punctuated the progress of her days:

> We have breakfast at ten o clock. Then Stolberg reads a chapter of the Bible and a song from the *Lieder* of Klopstock to us. Everyone returns to their rooms. I read passages from the *Spectator*, from the *Physiognomik*, and from several other books the countess gave me. She comes down to find me, during this time Lotte [the daughter of the count and countess] translates, and I read to her, for an hour, the *Pontius Pilatus* of Lavater. While she takes her Latin course, I copy something for her, or I read for myself, until mealtime. After lunch and coffee, Fritz [the countess's brother-in-law] reads passages taken from biographies, then Lotte comes to find me and I read Milton to her for an hour. Next, we go upstairs and I read Plutarch to the count and countess until nine o clock at night, tea time. After tea, Stolberg reads a chapter of the Bible and a song of Klopstock, and then good night.

During the day, which opened and closed with the biblical and the poetic word, Luise Meyer practiced different types of reading: silent and private reading for herself in the retreat of her room, didactic readings required by the education of her student, and reading out loud to those for whom she worked.

Why not conclude that the reading revolution of the eighteenth century lay precisely in this capacity to manipulate the manners of reading? Hence its limits, since such a competence was not given to all—far from it—but primarily to the most expert and the most affluent readers. Hence likewise, its complex nature, since it is necessary to recognize it not in the imposition of a new style, but in the increased diversity of practices.

[*See also* Cabinets de Lecture; Libraries; Literary Genres; *and* Print Culture.]

BIBLIOGRAPHY

Benedict, Barbara M. *Making the Modern Reader: Cultural Mediation in Early Modern Literary Anthologies*. Princeton, N.J., 1996.

Braida, Lodovica. *Il commercio delle idee: Editoria e circolazione del libro nella Torino del Settecento*. Edited by Leo S. Olschki. Florence, 1995.

Chartier, Roger. *The Cultural Uses of Print in Early Modern France*. Princeton, N.J., 1987.

Dann, Otto, ed. *Lesegesellschaften und bürgerliche Emanzipation: Ein europäischer Vergleich*. Munich, 1981.

Darnton, Robert. "Readers Respond to Rousseau: The Fabrication of Romantic Sensitivity." In his *The Great Cat Massacre and Other Episodes in French Cultural History*. New York, 1984.

Darnton, Robert. *The Forbidden Best-Sellers of Pre-Revolutionary France*. New York and London, 1995.

Engelsing, Rolf. *Der Bürger als Leser: Lesergeschichte in Deutschland, 1500–1800*. Stuttgart, 1974.

Engelsing, Rolf. "Die Perioden der Lesergeschichte in der Neuzeit: Das statistische Ausmass und die soziokulturelle Bedeutung der Lektüre." *Archiv für Geschichte des Buchwesens* 10 (1970), 944–1002.

Raven, James, et al., eds. *The Practice and Representation of Reading in England*. Cambridge, 1996.

Schön, Erich. *Der Verlust der Sinnlichkeit oder Die Verwandlung des Lesers: Mentalitätswandel um 1800*. Stuttgart, 1987.

Wittmann, Reinhard. *Buchmarkt und Lektüre im 18. und 19. Jahrhundert: Beiträge zum literarischen Leben, 1750–1850*. Tübingen, 1982.

Wittmann, Reinhard. "Was There a Reading Revolution at the End of the Eighteenth Century?" In *A History of Writing in the West*, edited by Guglielmo Cavallo and Roger Chartier, pp. 284–312. Cambridge, 1999.

ROGER CHARTIER
Translated from French by Sylvia J. Cannizzaro

REASON. The term "reason" and its cognates in other languages (Latin *ratio*, French *raison*, German *Vernunft*) were used in a variety of ways in the seventeenth and eighteenth centuries. In its basic meaning, "reason" denoted a faculty or capacity of the mind. The faculty of reason was contrasted with the other cognitive faculties—the senses, imagination, and memory—and with the will or faculty of volition. Generically, reason was equated with intellect or understanding; however, writings in psychology and metaphysics distinguished between reason and intellect: intellect was the faculty of making individual judgments, and reason was the faculty of connecting judgments in a logical sequence. In this sense, to reason is to form syllogistic arguments, or to engage in mathematical proofs or demonstrations, or perhaps simply to draw sound conclusions from the available evidence.

In a related meaning, to reason implied to think in an orderly manner. Some thinkers transferred this meaning to nature, regarding the order found in nature as the expression of reason. At first, the rational order of nature was seen as something implanted in nature by divine reason—that is, by God in creating nature. Accordingly, to discover the laws of nature was to find a rational pattern set down by God. Some philosophers (notably, the Cambridge Platonist Henry More) argued that God created a "world soul," which infused the entire material world and directed all natural events in an orderly manner. The seventeenth-century Dutch philosopher Baruch de Spinoza held a more radical view that equates God with nature as a whole. Accordingly, the rational order of nature is the same thing as divine reason; or, conversely, divine reason is nothing more than the laws of nature as a whole. The eighteenth-century French materialist baron d'Holbach ascribed intrinsic order to nature, without an immanent intellect. The Scottish philosopher David Hume also hypothesized that order could exist in nature without being injected by divine reason or produced by thought of any kind. He explained that the apparent "wisdom and contrivance" found in the bodies of living things could arise through natural processes, on the assumption that living things could arise from matter randomly taking on various forms, and that any living thing thus arising would not survive unless its parts were "adjusted" to one another and to the surrounding world. (Hume here sketched a principle of natural selection, a forerunner to the theory developed by Charles Darwin.)

Some philosophers contrasted reason with sensory experience. Accordingly, to appeal to reason was to forsake sensory experience in favor of pure thought. In technical philosophical language, the faculty of pure thought was more usually labeled with the equivalent terms "pure intellect" or "pure understanding." Reason was also contrasted with faith or revelation. In this context, to reason meant to rely on the natural powers of the human mind rather than on religious faith or authority. The contrast between reason and faith did not presuppose that reason could operate independently of sensory experience. That is, one could be an empiricist in epistemology and nonetheless appeal to reason (based on sensory evidence) by contrast with faith.

Reason was understood as the faculty that distinguishes human beings from other animals, enabling distinctly human cognition and behavior. Most philosophers of the period (save Descartes and his followers) attributed some cognition to animals, albeit based entirely in the senses and appetites; dogs can recognize their masters and can learn to anticipate the actions of the hare. Humans, however, can develop scientific knowledge and can regulate their actions beyond the momentary pursuit of food or the satisfaction of other appetitive needs. Some philosophers held that moral conduct arises from following reason rather than the passions. The passions included body-based emotions and sense-based inclinations to act. Even philosophers who denied sense-independent content to reason could propose that human conduct should be regulated by rational principles, which would simply be principles aimed at better outcomes in the long run as opposed to the inclinations of the moment.

Especially in the eighteenth century, the term "reason" was invoked to imply an independent, critical spirit of inquiry. Human reasoning or critical assessment was to be applied to all topics, including religion, politics, and morals. In this regard, the Enlightenment has been called the "Age of Reason." There is a slight irony here, because the prototypical Enlightenment thinkers—including John Locke in the early English Enlightenment; Voltaire, Denis Diderot, Condillac, Claude-Adrien Helvétius, and d'Holbach in the French; and Hume in the Scottish—did not grant reason the ability to achieve knowledge on its own, independently of the senses. The major figures of the eighteenth-century Enlightenment were not philosophical Rationalists (the capitalized form designates a discrete "school"). When they appealed to reason, they were simply invoking a spirit of objective, unbiased inquiry. The paradigmatic example of this use of reason was Isaac Newton's success in natural science. Many Enlightenment thinkers, including especially Diderot, d'Holbach, and Hume, hoped that the Newtonian spirit of rational, empirically based inquiry could be extended to all areas of belief, including religion, and to the study of humankind itself. A "science of man" might then be used as the basis for moral and political theory. In this way, rational knowledge might support political reform and human progress. (Jean-Jacques Rousseau dissented, contending that science and civilization had in fact reduced man's freedom and distorted his natural moral goodness.)

Reason in Rationalist Philosophy. The early French Rationalist René Descartes, in his first published work, *Discourse on the Method of Rightly Conducting One's Reason and Seeking the Truth in the Sciences*, published anonymously in 1637, described "reason" as the cognitive faculty that distinguishes human beings from other animals. He also spoke of intellect or understanding as a faculty for perceiving or representing truth and goodness. In his first serious philosophical work, the *Meditations on First Philosophy* (1641), he referred more often to intellect (*intellectus*) than to reason (*ratio*). Subsequent Rationalist philosophers, including Spinoza and Gottfried Wilhelm von Leibniz, typically favored the term "intellect" over "reason" when speaking of the rational power of the human mind.

The Rationalists held that human desire and conduct are guided by the intellect. All of them except Spinoza distinguished intellect from will. (Spinoza identified will with intellect, as the inclination to affirm or deny the content of a thought, an inclination we follow of necessity.) They all ascribed freedom to the will (or to the whole human being), while allowing that freedom is compatible with being determined in one's thoughts and actions. Descartes and Leibniz held that the will naturally (i.e., by its nature) affirms whatever the intellect perceives to be true and good. The extent to which our conduct follows the good thus depends on how accurately we perceive the good. Someone who follows the passions is caught up in sensory goods, real or apparent; someone who follows reason uses the intellect to achieve a clear and distinct perception of the good, as it applies to himself or herself, or

to the community or polity. On this view, the bad is never knowingly chosen: bad behavior results from a confused or mistaken perception of the good.

Reason in Empiricist Philosophy. The early Empiricist philosopher Thomas Hobbes denied that humans have a faculty of intellect or reason separate from the senses and imagination. In his objections to Descartes's *Meditations* (published by Descartes, together with his own replies), Hobbes argued that all human thought depends on images. He described two levels of understanding or reasoning, both dependent on imagination. First, humans and other animals can make one sensory image the sign for another, as when a cat learns to come at the sound of its food bowl touching the floor. Second, humans are able to "reason" using names and logical relations, and hence to achieve greater subtlety and generality than other animals. According to Hobbes, reasoning is simply "reckoning," using words and connecting them together correctly. When individuals apply such reasoning to their self-preservation, they discover the "laws of nature" that underlie morals and politics. In Hobbes's view, individuals who reason correctly from these laws will enter a social contract granting authority to an absolute sovereign.

Locke also adopted the Empiricist stance that all knowledge comes from the senses, but he did not follow Hobbes in reducing reason to imagination. Rather, he held that the mind has certain powers for comparing ideas and forming judgments. These include the power of abstraction, or of using one particular idea to stand for a whole group of particular ideas, as when the word "triangle" or an image of a particular triangle comes to stand for all manner of triangles. (Locke did not actually hold that a single abstract idea of a triangle must simultaneously *be* both acute and obtuse, though subsequent readers attributed that position to him.) Locke argued that the human understanding is capable of achieving only probable opinion about the natural world, not certainty, but he allowed demonstrative certainty in mathematics and morals. In those areas, he contended, human beings are free to assume precise definitions, since those definitions are not constrained by independently existing things. Thinkers can settle on definitions of geometrical figures and reason demonstratively using those definitions. They can decide how to define political notions such as property, and then reason from those definitions to laws concerning property. The definition stipulatively settles what it is for something to be property. By contrast, humans are not free to decide what gold is or what a rabbit is, because these things exist in nature independently of human definition.

Hume also affirmed that all the content of human cognition depends on the senses. He characterized reason or understanding as the perception of relations among ideas. Perceptions of such relations underlie pure mathematics.

Although the content of mathematical ideas must derive from experience, Hume held that the relations among ideas can be considered abstractly—that is, independently of whether such relations actually exist in the empirical world. (He considered it an empirical question whether geometry describes physical objects or not.) According to Hume, all other knowledge is of two sorts. It is either (1) the perception of current sensory impressions or ideas derived from memory and imagination, or (2) inferences concerning "matters of fact" that go beyond current ideas. However, he argued, all inferences concerning matters of fact depend on reasoning about cause and effect, and such "reasoning" is mediated by nothing other than "the general and more establish'd properties of the imagination." Reason or the understanding is reduced to imagination. The established properties of the imagination are the psychological laws of association. In forming beliefs about relations between the flame on the stove and the heating of food, the wind and the swaying of grass, or the hammer and the nail, we rely only on associations built up through previous experience. We associate one hammer with another through the principle of resemblance; we associate the flame with the stove through the principle of spatio-temporal contiguity; and we associate the wind with the swaying grass through the associative principle of cause and effect, which says that our causal reasoning is based entirely on the fact that in past experience, A and B have been constantly conjoined, so that B has usually or always followed upon A. The regular sequence of B following A, and our associatively induced expectation of seeing B next when we see A, is all we can mean in saying that A causes B.

Hume denied the Rationalist claim that humans have access to purely intellectual perceptions of the essences of things. He argued that if we possessed such intellectual perceptions, we would be able to perceive "necessary connections" between causes and effects. We would be able to see that flame *must* heat what is near it, that the hammer *must* drive the nail. However, he contended, we are never able to foresee such effects by pure intellect or reason, nor can we find any impossibility in the thought that the flame would not heat the food, or the hammer not drive the nail. We simply have very strong expectations that they will do so, based on past experience with fires and hammers. However—and here is Hume's clincher—past experience itself provides no absolute basis for such expectations because we cannot *prove* that the future must be like the past. (Any proof appealing to the fact that, in the past, events have resembled those of the past would beg the question about the future from the present point onward.) We are left with mere habit, not rational insight or demonstrative evidence, to guide our factual reasoning.

It was an Enlightenment theme that reason, or empirical reasoning, should guide and restrain the passions. Hume is often seen as an exception to the trend. In fact, his position on the relation between reason and the passions is subtle and interesting. Although he first seems to subjugate reason to the passions, he ends up attributing the formation of important classes of passions to judgment and reasoning.

Famously, Hume asserted, "Reason is, and ought only to be the slave of the passions." To support this claim, he argued that reason cannot provide the motive for action. Thus far, his position was consistent with that of Descartes, who held that will induces action while the intellect simply passively perceives the good. Hume, however, did not allow purely intellectual perception of the good: for him, all good and evil are based on pain and pleasure, which attend external or internal sensations. Pain and pleasure are natural motivators; other natural motivators include instincts toward "benevolence and resentment, the love of life, and kindness to children." However, although by instinct we seek pleasure and avoid pain, not all pains and pleasures arise from instinct or innate constitution. We are trained through education and human convention to feel pain at injustice and pleasure when justice is served. This training is guided by artificial principles arrived at through experience during the formation of society. In the case of property rights, for instance, Hume held that individual members become "sensible" of the advantage of forming a society in which property rights are enforced. The agreement to enforce such rights is not natural in human beings, but artificial and cultivated. The decision to cultivate such attitudes depends on "judgment and understanding," which means it arises through reflection on experience, including experience of what happens when property rights are not protected by societal sanction. Thus, though reason is, as regards motivation, "slave" to the passions, the passions are trained as a result of rational reflection. The cultivation of moral passions thus falls under the purview of Humean understanding or reason.

The eighteenth-century English psychologist David Hartley adopted an even more radical stance than Hume toward human understanding and reason. Like Hobbes, Locke, and Hume, he grounded all cognition in sensory ideas. Although not a materialist, he held that all sensation, and hence all thought, occurs only when the fibers of the brain vibrate a certain way. As a result of experience, the vibrations of the brain become associated so that when one set of vibrations occurs, a corresponding set is produced in nearby regions of the brain. Hartley explained that all human thoughts and actions that go beyond bare sensation and instinct result from such association. He was a complete determinist, holding that every human action is wholly determined by a person's current sensory state and past history of association, which determines the current vibrational and associational state.

Hartley developed his theory using traditional psychological terms, reinterpreted in light of his account of human thought and behavior. He divided ideas into sensory and intellectual, but he defined intellectual ideas as those arising through mere associative combination of sensory ideas. He spoke of the faculties of memory, imagination, understanding, affection, and will. Understanding is "that Faculty, by which we contemplate mere Sensations and Ideas, pursue Truth, and assent to, or dissent from, Propositions." He defined truth as nothing more than a word we learn to apply by association with other words or signs; thus, we learn to associate the word "true" with the signs "12 × 12 = 144." Some actions he dubbed "voluntary," meaning only that they follow immediately from a previous state of mind, such as desire or aversion. Desire and aversion are the natural consequences of pleasure and pain. All pleasures and pains are constructed out of sensory pleasure and pain. Human motives reduce to the pursuit of sensory pleasure and the avoidance of sensory pain.

Hartley's theory is encapsulated in his accounts of rational and practical assent. He defined rational assent and dissent as follows:

> Rational assent then to any Proposition may be defined a Readiness to affirm it to be true, proceeding from a close Association of the Ideas suggested by the Proposition, with the Idea, or internal Feeling, belonging to the Word Truth; or of the Terms of the Proposition with the Word Truth. Rational Dissent is the Opposite of this. This Assent might be called verbal; but as every Person Supposes himself always to have a sufficient Reason for such Readiness to affirm or deny, I rather choose to call it Rational.
>
> (1966, 1:324)

Practical assent is just a readiness to act in a manner that follows from rational assent. To suppose one "has a reason" for a belief is simply to associate those particular words with a felt disposition for one thought (called the reason) to be followed by another thought (the conclusion or assertion). All such transitions are mediated by sense-induced brain vibrations and the mechanisms by which they become interconnected and conjoined. We come to say that milk is white and gold is yellow because of the associations formed among the words and ideas; we hear the word "milk" when a white, liquid, potable substance is before us. Hartley gave no account of how error or falsehood arises from associative processes, or how it is recognized when it does. The most he could say is that a feeling of falsehood arises when one set of associations comes into conflict with another, and that we are taught, when we feel the conflict, to say that one of the associative connections (presumably the weaker) is false.

Reason in the Enlightenment. The twentieth-century German neo-Kantian philosopher Ernst Cassirer offered the following assessment of the place of reason in Enlightenment philosophy: "The eighteenth century is imbued with a belief in the unity and immutability of reason. Reason is the same for all thinking subjects, all nations, all epochs, all cultures" (1951, p. 6). The elevation of reason was an Enlightenment theme, but the "reason" so elevated was variously conceived, and some mainstream thinkers denied all or many of the tenets cited by Cassirer.

Although the seventeenth-century Rationalists held a notion of reason like that Cassirer describes, the Rationalist movement faded in the eighteenth century. A moderate Empiricist such as Locke would have agreed that reason, or the human understanding, exhibits similarities in all humans, but he had no grounds for positing an absolute unity of reason. According to Hume and Hartley, the extent to which reason is a unity must rely on the degree of similarity among psychological laws and brain structures in all human beings, together with commonness of experience among all individuals, but such similarities and commonalities are not absolute.

The canonical French Enlightenment philosophes, including Voltaire, Condillac, Diderot, and d'Alembert, were empiricists. For them, reason depended on sense and feeling. With no innate ideas to give structure to thought, human rationality was viewed as something that grows organically with experience. The French social thinker Charles de Secondat Montesquieu was especially insistent about the disunity of opinion across time and place, with multiple perspectives arising from multiple experiential milieux. The various radical empiricisms had to allow the possibility of radically divergent belief systems because they posited no fixed intellectual structure to guarantee commonality of thought. Yet Montesquieu himself retained belief in a universal human intellect, which simply manifests itself differently in differing geographical and social circumstances. He further contended that the order of the universe is a manifestation of the divine reason of its creator.

For the French thinkers, an invocation to proceed on the basis of reason was a call to think for oneself, to decide what to believe independently of religious and political authority, and to adopt an empirical and scientific approach to the basis of politics and morals. D'Holbach, the only genuine materialist besides Diderot among the French thinkers named here, expressed this independence of thought:

> The *enlightened man*, is man in his maturity, in his perfection; who is capable of pursuing his own happiness; because he has learned to examine, to think for himself, and not to take that for truth upon the authority of others, which experience has taught him examination will frequently prove erroneous.
>
> (1970, p. 12)

Still, among the French philosophes and other radical empiricists, independent thought could lead to the notion of a supreme being, or even to belief in the truth of Christianity. Voltaire argued for deism. Hartley offered natural theological arguments that God exists, and he engaged in scriptural criticism to show that the Bible is the word of God. The independence of Enlightenment thought included the freedom to arrive at traditional beliefs.

Reason in Kant and Hegel. Immanuel Kant upheld the autonomy of reason in relation to experience, but he took a middle path between empiricism and rationalism. He was convinced that traditional Rationalist metaphysics could not achieve its goals. He therefore agreed with Empiricist critics such as Hume that there can be no rational proof for the existence of God or the simplicity (and immortality) of the soul. However, he allowed a limited sphere of rational doctrine in metaphysics and morals. In theoretical metaphysics, or the metaphysics of nature, he defended the mind's ability to know a priori—that is, independently of experience—certain fundamental principles such as the causal law (that every event in nature has a natural cause); but such principles can be known to hold only within the domain of experience. This means that the causal law could not be used to infer a first cause or a creator of the universe. Its use is limited to the world of the senses, the natural world. In practical metaphysics, or the metaphysics of morals, Kant argued that reason can establish a moral law as the basis of a systematic ethics. He thus denied that ethics can or need be limited to considerations of mere pleasure, pain, and natural appetite. Rather, he argued that human beings are able to act from purely rational principles, independent of sensual inclination.

Georg Wilhelm Friedrich Hegel (1770–1831) criticized the Enlightenment conception of reason for being overly narrow. His indictment included the universal reason of the Rationalists, the sense-based reasoning of the Empiricists, the scientifically inspired empiricism of the eighteenth century, and Kant's retrenched moral reason. He rejected the reduction of thought to feeling and of reason to calculating utility, as well as any strict opposition between reason and passion or emotion. (In the twentieth century, the Frankfurt school—e.g., Horkheimer and Adorno, 1972—argued that the Enlightenment transformed reason into mere utilitarian means-end reasoning, but Hegel was aware of the wider field of Enlightenment thought.)

Hegel argued that reason is immanent in nature, in the very order of the natural world. It is expressed in the laws of motion and the organization of living matter. In human beings, reason at first finds expression in conscious thinking, then becomes self-consciously aware of itself. However, human reason is not fully open to itself in single acts of reflection or rational insight, nor can its structure be discovered directly in the speech and behavior of a given period of history. Rather, reason develops throughout history. Hegel's famous "march of the world spirit" is the unfolding of immanent reason through historical events. Previous philosophical systems are instances or moments of reason, but not complete specimens. The structure of reason includes the dialectical movement of thought from one system to another, each stage bringing reason to fuller self-consciousness than the last.

Reason lurks in the historically significant actions of human beings. Hegel held that passions or emotions contain latent expressions of reason. Through the "cunning of reason," individuals who act to further their own interests are tacitly led—by their own unanalyzed and passionately felt insight into "what needs to be done"—to further the ends of universal reason. Emotions naturally tie one to one's family and friends. Such emotions involve a concern for other human beings. Perception of what needs to be done for their good naturally leads, through the impersonal character of even latent reason, to actions that tend toward the betterment of society as a whole.

For Hegel, philosophy was only one of reason's cultural manifestations; reason is also expressed in art, religion, politics, and social structure. Hegel treated human culture as the expression of minded reason in the world. Reason appears not only in the Enlightenment's paradigms of logic, mathematics, and natural science, but also in the organization of human life, the production of artifacts, and the belief systems of various peoples. Hegel's broadened conception of reason's expression remains of interest today, despite evidence from twentieth-century political history that the world spirit marches on a bumpy road.

[*See also* Cassirer, Ernst; Empiricism; Epistemology; Hartley, David; Human Nature; Hume, David; Kant, Immanuel; Locke, John; Philosophy; Prejudice; Reason; Rationalism; *and* Skepticism.]

BIBLIOGRAPHY

SOURCES

Descartes, René. *Philosophical Writings.* Translated by John Cottingham, Robert Stoothoff, and Dugald Murdoch. 2 vols. Cambridge, 1984–1985. Includes Descartes's philosophical works and selections from his scientific writings.

Hartley, David. *Observations on Man, His Frame, His Duty, and His Expectations.* Gainesville, Fla., 1966. Reprint of the original London edition of 1749.

Hegel, Georg Wilhelm Friedrich. *Introduction to the Philosophy of History.* Translated by Leo Rauch. Indianapolis, 1988. This work, based on student notes, is the most accessible introduction to Hegel's writings.

Hegel, Georg Wilhelm Friedrich. *Phenomenology of Spirit.* Translated by A. V. Miller. Oxford, 1977. English translation of *Die Phänomenologie des Geistes,* first published in Bamberg und Würzburg, 1807. Hegel's criticisms of "the Enlightenment" appear in the section on "spirit," as part of the subsection on "culture."

Hobbes, Thomas. *Leviathan.* Edited by Richard Tuck. Cambridge, 1991. Originally published in 1651.

Holbach, Paul Henri Thiry. *System of Nature, or, The Laws of the Moral and Physical World.* Translated by H. D. Robinson. New York, 1970.

Reprint of 1868 edition; English translation of *Système de la nature*, first published in London, 1770.

Hume, David. *Principal Writings on Religion*. Edited by J. C. A. Gaskin. Oxford, 1993. Includes the *Dialogues Concerning Natural Religion* (1779) and the *Natural History of Religion* (1757). The *Dialogues*, Part VIII, contains the speculation that living things could arise naturally, on the assumption that matter would naturally take many forms, and that any ill-formed being would not survive.

Hume, David. *A Treatise of Human Nature*. Edited by Peter H. Nidditch. 2d ed. Oxford, 1978. Originally published 1739–1740, with the subtitle "Being an Attempt to Introduce the Experimental Method of Reasoning into Moral Subjects."

Locke, John. *An Essay Concerning Human Understanding*. Edited by Peter H. Nidditch. Oxford, 1975. Originally published in 1690, and issued in several revised editions during Locke's lifetime, with the changes shown in the Nidditch edition.

Montesquieu, Charles de Secondat. *The Spirit of the Laws*. Translated by Anne M. Cohler, Basia Carolyn Miller, and Harold Samuel Stone. Cambridge, 1989. English translation of *De l'Esprit des lois*, originally published in Geneva in 1748.

STUDIES

Beiser, Frederick C. *The Fate of Reason: German Philosophy from Kant to Fichte*. Cambridge, Mass., 1987.

Beiser, Frederick C. *The Sovereignty of Reason: The Defense of Rationality in the Early English Enlightenment*. Princeton, N.J., 1996.

Cassirer, Ernst. *Philosophy of the Enlightenment*. Translated by Fritz C. A. Koelln and James P. Pettegrove. Princeton, N.J., 1951. English translation of *Philosophie der Aufklärung* (1932), a good general study of Enlightenment philosophy.

Hinchman, Lewis P. *Hegel's Critique of the Enlightenment*. Tampa, 1984. Good in-depth treatment focusing on political philosophy, with a concluding chapter on present-day applications.

Horkheimer, Max. *Eclipse of Reason*. New York, 1947. A critique of Enlightenment reason, narrowly equated with the utilitarian stream in Enlightenment thought.

Horkheimer, Max, and Theodor W. Adorno. *Dialectic of Enlightenment*. Translated by John Cumming. New York, 1972. English translation of *Philosophische Fragmente* (New York, 1944).

Pinkard, Terry P. *Hegel's Dialectic: The Explanation of Possibility*. Philadelphia, 1988. An excellent introduction to Hegel's epistemology.

Saine, Thomas P. *The Problem of Being Modern, or, The German Pursuit of Enlightenment from Leibniz to the French Revolution*. Detroit, Mich., 1997. Good historical treatment of German philosophy and letters of the period.

GARY HATFIELD

REFORM. *See* Political Philosophy *and* Utilitarianism.

REFORMED CHURCHES. [*This entry contains four subentries, on* Lutheranism, *the* Swiss Reformed Church, *the* Dutch Reformed Church, *and* Presbyterianism.]

Lutheranism

German Lutheranism proved singularly susceptible to the influence of Enlightenment ideas. There was no conflict between the new philosophy and the dominant theological trends. Indeed, for much of the eighteenth century, Aufklärung and enlightened Lutheran Protestantism were all but synonymous. In view of the integration of the German territorial church into the state, this symbiotic relationship of Aufklärung and Lutheran thinking also had important practical consequences. Protestant churchmen engaged enthusiastically in the cause of practical reform and improvement. Their strong commitment to a "Christian" reform of society under the direction of the state has led some to argue that they fostered inherently quietist and conformist traditions in German society. They were, however, by no means uncritical of authority, and their commitment to reform rather than revolution mirrored attitudes in the German lands generally.

The most important indigenous source of attitudes that predisposed Lutheran thinkers to enlightened ideas was Pietism. Initiated by Philipp Jakob Spener (1635–1705) in the 1660s, Pietism attacked the dogmatic certainties of orthodox Lutheranism, which it regarded as ossified and institutionalized. A new emphasis on personal piety and practical Christianity aimed to revitalize the church by mobilizing the laity. Although leading Pietists such as Spener and August Hermann Francke (1663–1727) also bitterly opposed any form of rationalism, they paved the way for the new theology. Their ideas undermined the hegemony of orthodoxy, and they preached a general priesthood that implied a diminution of the authority of the clergy over the laity.

Other significant influences were John Locke, Pierre Bayle, English deism, physico-theology, and Baruch de Spinoza. However, though the discussion of natural religion was central to the emergence of a new theological consensus, its most radical forms found few open converts in the German lands. Most German Lutheran thinkers, both clerical and lay, formulated their views in opposition to what were perceived as the atheistical tendencies of these imported ideas.

This perception was due primarily to the development of philosophical rationalism, first in the Protestant German universities in the late seventeenth and early eighteenth centuries, then in the periodical literature that emerged in the 1720s. In different ways, the leading thinkers of this movement, such as Gottfried Wilhelm von Leibniz (1646–1716), Christian Thomasius (1655–1728), and Christian Wolff (1679–1754), all sought to reconcile reason with revelation and faith, and to harmonize the findings of new scientific discoveries and speculation with traditional Christianity. None of them rejected the established Lutheran church or challenged its role in society. All of them, however, insisted that religion must turn away from the destructive confessional polemics and conflicts of the past. Like the Pietists, though opposed by them, they were concerned with practical religion. They insisted that God intended that religion be useful to man and society (arguing from an optimistic view of the potential of human reason rather than, like the Pietists, from the need of individual atonement). Philosophical rationalism achieved its most systematic elaboration and final establishment as the dominant university and popular philosophy in the 1720s in the writings of Christian Wolff, whose students and disciples dominated the Aufklärung until the 1780s.

The new direction in theology was initiated early in the eighteenth century by Johann Franz Buddeus (1667–1729) and Christoph Matthäus Pfaff (1686–1760). Each combined elements of traditional orthodoxy with new Pietist attitudes. While Buddeus openly opposed Wolff, Pfaff remained neutral; their main aim was to combat any form of atheism. Their "rational" or "enlightened" orthodoxy was translated into a wholehearted embrace of systematizing Wolffianism by Siegmund Jakob Baumgarten (1706–1757), a man praised by Voltaire as the "crown of German scholars" and by others as the "oracle of the German theologians." As professor of theology in Halle after 1734, he transformed the center of North German Pietism into the fount of the Protestant Aufklärung that dominated Lutheran theology for the next half-century.

This movement came to be known as Neologism. Its dominant figures were Baumgarten's pupils Johann Salomon Semler (1725–1791) and Johann Gottlieb Tellner (1724–1774), together with Johann Friedrich Jerusalem (1709–1789) and Johann Joachim Spalding (1717–1804). The bookseller, journalist, and novelist Friedrich Nicolai (1733–1810) also played an important role in popularizing the works and ideas of the Neologians, especially through his influential review, the *Allgemeine Deutsche Bibliothek* (1765–1805). Their theological writings were complemented by the work of ecclesiastical and biblical historians like Johann Lorenz von Mosheim (1694–1755), Johann August Ernesti (1708–1781), and Johann David Michaelis (1717–1791).

In general, the Neologians measured everything against reason. They did not reject revelation, but they viewed anything in Scripture that did not conform to reason as an accidental historical addition or as plain deception. They did not deny the divinity of Christ; however, they tended to view him not as the son of God or as the savior, but as a noble teacher of mankind, like Socrates. As exponents of philosophical theology, they saw themselves in the tradition of Philipp Melanchthon (1497–1560). While they did not challenge traditional dogma, they accorded it less weight than did the orthodox tradition. Combined with a strongly historical approach, this generated a strong commitment to religious toleration and a renewed interest in the reunification of the Christian churches. A practical understanding of Scripture, which sought by

textual analysis to distinguish between the word of God and the historical descriptions of human actions, was matched with a practical concern for the Christian in society and an emphasis on social ethics. These principles, when translated into teaching in the pulpits, inspired a range of interests that later prompted the charge that the Neologians had all but destroyed religion and deprived theology of its meaning and content. Frequent sermons on subjects such as inoculation, eating habits, or even prudent coppice management and animal husbandry seem to justify the derision subsequently poured on the worldly concerns of the Neologians. On the other hand, sermons against slavery, dueling, torture, capital punishment, or simple bad government confound the argument that the enlightened clergy were just servile conformists.

Though dominant until the 1790s, the Neologians were constantly attacked by both Pietists and orthodox theologians and provoked periodically by isolated naturalists, deists, and materialists. Their rebuttals of these critics served to elucidate many of their ideas on specific points. However, they failed to rise to the major challenge posed to them by Lessing's posthumous publication of Hermann Samuel Reimarus's (1694–1768) Spinozist writings as *Fragmente des Wolfenbütteler Ungenannten* (1774–1775). Lessing's attempt to force the Neologians to answer the charge that they had confused theology with philosophy merely provoked the orthodox Johann Melchior Goeze (1718–1786) in what became the most bitter German theological controversy of the century.

Neologism was finally undermined in the 1790s. In Prussia, the reaction began with Johann Christoph Woellner's Religious Edict (1788). More generally, the movement fell victim to the suspicion and growing hostility to which all Aufklärung ideals were subjected by German governments in the wake of the French Revolution. In theological terms, they were also challenged by the rationalism of Kant and his followers, who destroyed the link between reason and revelation by limiting reason exclusively to the realm of experience, and by supranaturalists who drew on the Pietist tradition. Although Aufklärung ideals continued to remain influential at the pastoral level and in historical-critical theology well into the nineteenth century, Idealism and Romanticism increasingly set the tone of theological writing in the postrevolutionary era.

[See also Aufklärung; Germany; Pietism; Revealed Religion; and Scandinavia.]

BIBLIOGRAPHY

Aner, Karl. *Die Theologie der Lessingzeit.* Halle, Germ., 1929. Still the most comprehensive survey of Protestant Enlightenment theology.
Barth, Karl. *Die protestantische Theologie im 19. Jahrhundert: Ihre Vorgeschichte und ihre Geschichte.* Zurich, 1947. Contains an excellent, if highly critical, survey of the eighteenth century; particularly scathing about Aner's enthusiasm for the Neologians.

Fulbrook, Mary. *Piety and Politics: Religion and the Rise of Absolutism in England, Württemberg and Prussia.* Cambridge, 1983. A stimulating comparative account of Protestantism and the development of the state.

Saine, Thomas P. *The Problem of Being Modern, or the German Pursuit of Enlightenment from Leibniz to the French Revolution.* Detroit, Mich., 1997. One of the few works in English that presents an overview, albeit unsystematic, of the interaction between science and religion in German thought.

Stroup, John. *The Struggle for Identity in the Clerical Estate: Northwest German Protestant Opposition to Absolutist Policy in the Eighteenth Century.* Leiden, 1984. An examination of the political situation and attitudes of the Lutheran clergy in the Enlightenment.

JOACHIM WHALEY

Swiss Reformed Church

Two major intellectual currents informed eighteenth-century Swiss Calvinism. One was the Enlightenment, with its reformist optimism and its emphasis on reason and critical inquiry. The other was the religious movement called Pietism. What historians alternatively call "liberal," "reasonable," or "Enlightened" orthodoxy evolved in large part as a response to these two somewhat contradictory impulses.

The seventeenth century had seen the consolidation of Calvinist doctrine in the shape of reformed scholasticism. The effort to systematize, elaborate, and defend right dogma had led to a certain doctrinal hardening illustrated by the *Formula Consensus* (1675). Prospective ministers of the Swiss Reformed Church were obliged to sign this strict formula of orthodoxy, which included the statement that, due to original sin, man is "subject to the wrath and malediction of God; and this from the first moment of his birth and before he has committed any Actual Sin. . . . He inherits this Corruption at the very time of his conception, and it makes him totally depraved."

By the end of the seventeenth century, however, a growing number of Swiss Calvinists were recoiling from this kind of doctrinal rigor. They came to believe that too much time and energy were being spent on relatively obscure matters of dogma such as predestination and original sin at the expense of what they regarded as more important ethical concerns. They thought that a rigid and overly pessimistic theology was counterproductive: it led to schism among the Protestant churches and moral despondency among the faithful. Moreover, traditional Calvinist theology was proving ineffectual in countering the alarming growth in popularity of deism and even atheism. Such concerns were only amplified by the ominous rise of Pietism in various parts of Switzerland as elsewhere in Europe. Reacting against what they also saw as the cold dogmatism and rigidity of reformed scholasticism, Pietists emphasized the necessity of an individually experienced spiritual rebirth and a greater concern for personal and social ethics. Proclaiming the need for a second Reformation, some Pietists found it necessary to withdraw from established churches and organized their own conventicles and communion services in their private homes.

In other words, at the same time that the *Formula Consensus* was being drawn up and enforced in Switzerland, such a statement of orthodoxy was becoming increasingly outdated and even irrelevant. The Swiss Reformed Church now faced greater dangers and more radical adversaries than the *Formula* had been designed to combat. In view of the changed historical circumstances, it seemed imperative for orthodox Calvinists to adopt a new approach. It is one of the distinguishing characteristics of eighteenth-century Swiss Calvinism that, in order better to defend and propagate their religion, its spokespersons adopted the language and tools of the Enlightenment.

The three individuals most responsible for ushering in a new kind of Reformed orthodoxy were Samuel Werenfels (1657–1740) of Basel, Jean-Frédéric Ostervald (1663–1747) of Neuchâtel, and Jean-Alphonse Turrettini (1671–1737) of Geneva. Often called the "Helvetic triumvirate," these friends and colleagues agreed that traditional Calvinist theology needed to be reformed in order better to confront the challenges of the eighteenth century. In his *Traité des sources de la corruption* (Treatise on the Sources of Corruption, 1700), Ostervald went so far as to identify the current state of Calvinist orthodoxy as one of the main sources of human corruption.

The most important of the three men was undoubtedly Turrettini, whose engaging teaching style and clarity of exposition made him an ideal popularizer of "enlightened orthodoxy." The son of a highly respected and staunchly orthodox theologian, Turrettini wanted, above all, to uphold and defend the "pure doctrine of Christ." In so doing, however, he worried less about doctrinal integrity than about apologetics, adopting a surprisingly eclectic mix of arguments drawn liberally from the intellectual culture of his times. Anxious to prove the essential harmony of reason and revelation, Turrettini argued that the "pure doctrine of Christ" could not contradict reason, even if it did, at times, surpass it. "Reason is even more necessary in theology than in human jurisprudence," he claimed, "because it is possible that men make unreasonable laws that contradict one another, but it is not possible that God teaches us things that make no sense, or things that are contradictory." Like Werenfels and Ostervald, Turrettini believed that not all dogmas were equally important and that the Church would do well to concentrate on Christianity's "fundamental articles" or "essential truths." It was hoped that such an approach would help to reunite Protestants and, moreover, would demonstrate the "reasonableness" of Christianity. The existence of God, the immortality of the soul, and Christianity's essential moral rules could all be grasped and proved by natural reason.

Worried that his religion was losing ground because it had become "too dry," Turrettini stressed its moral and practical aspects. In his teachings, the doctrines of predestination and original sin were considerably attenuated. It was under his guidance that Geneva abrogated the *Formula Consensus*; the city's pastors now agreed that the contested matters "were not very important," and in any case "not essential for salvation." Perhaps even more significantly, Geneva's pastoral corps felt that the disputed doctrines had "no influence on morals." Geneva's liturgical texts and psalm book were also modified, as was its French text of the Bible. Ostervald's catechism, published in Geneva in 1702, began to compete successfully with Calvin's, eventually becoming a veritable best-seller in its abbreviated and revised versions. These rationalizing and moralizing tendencies, instigated by Turrettini, were furthered by his disciple and successor in Geneva, Jacob Vernet (1698–1789). Following the efforts of these men, sermons of the eighteenth century emphasized moral instruction and Christian behavior, significantly deemphasizing the doctrines of original sin and predestination and, indeed, depreciating the value of doctrinal explication.

In short, by the mid-eighteenth century, the Swiss Reformed Church had undergone an Enlightenment of its own: it now embraced a relatively tolerant and optimistic theology, which granted a large space to natural theology. Its advocates celebrated not only Christianity's "reasonableness," but its "usefulness" to society as well. Those areas of Switzerland under the control of the Bernese government took a bit longer openly to embrace this new theology. Anxious to repress what it held to be Arminian tendencies in Lausanne, Bern imposed the *Formula Consensus* on the city as late as 1722. An oath of "association" was also required with the express aim of extirpating the heresies of Pietism, Arminianism, and Socinianism. Historians agree, however, that these actions by Bern had little more than symbolic effect. Elsewhere in Calvinist Switzerland, theology in the territories of Bern became increasingly rational, liberal, and undogmatic over time. The Calvinism that Jean-Jacques Rousseau found in Geneva and that Edward Gibbon encountered in Lausanne had in fact evolved into something very close to Arminianism or even Socinianism, a form of Calvinism that the eminent Swiss historian Henri Vuilleumier later would deem "not very orthodox" at all.

[*See also* Arminianism; Bible; Pietism; Rationalism; Revealed Religion; Sermons; *and* Switzerland.]

BIBLIOGRAPHY

Barthel, Pierre. "La 'Religion de Neuchâtel' au petit matin du XVIIIᵉ siècle, un phénomène unique en Europe!" *Musée neuchâtelois* (1987), 41–80.

Pitassi, Maria-Cristina. *De l'orthodoxie aux Lumières: Genève, 1670–1737*. Geneva, 1992. A clear and concise introduction by a recognized expert in the field.

Pitassi, Maria-Cristina. "Evolution de la théologie de la Réforme à l'aube du XVIIIᵉ siècle." In *Histoire de la littérature en Suisse romande: Du Moyen Âge à 1815*, edited by Roger Francillon. Lausanne, Switzerland, 1996.

Röllin, Stefan. "L'influence du piétisme et des Lumières sur les confessions au XVIIIᵉ siècle." In *Histoire du christianisme en Suisse: Une perspective oecuménique*, edited by Lukas Vischer, Lukas Schenker, Rudolf Dellsperger, and Oliver Fatio. Geneva, 1995.

Vuilleumier, Henri. *Histoire de l'Église Réformée du Pays de Vaud sous le régime bernois*. 4 vols. Lausanne, Switzerland, 1927–1933. A somewhat out-dated but still useful general history of the Reformed Church in the French-speaking part of Switzerland.

HELENA ROSENBLATT

Dutch Reformed Church

The mainstream Protestant Dutch Enlightenment was marked by pro-Christian, moderate features and aspired to a harmonious relationship between reason and revelation. Dutch Protestant dissenters such as Lutherans, Mennonites, and Remonstrants were receptive to Enlightenment ideas. A more radical version of enlightenment was present among freethinking exiles from England, France, and Germany, as well as in circles of Freemasons.

The national and international Enlightenment—in the successive forms of Cartesianism, Spinozism, Anglo-American and French deism, and German Rationalism—evoked a variety of reactions among the Dutch Reformed, leading to a series of polemical debates from the 1650s to the 1790s. The overall conclusion that emerges from these debates is that the Dutch Reformed Church strove for a middle-of-the-road religious liberalism. Various prominent Reformed theologians propagated a mild rationalism, pleading for moderation and toleration and preferring a middle way between unbelief and enthusiasm. Thus, in the course of the eighteenth century, a new climate was manifest within the Reformed Church.

Despite this, the vehemence of the polemics testifies to the persistence within the Reformed Church of both Calvinist orthodoxy and Pietism. Major issues included biblical exegesis, the status of philosophy, new methods of preaching, the ideal of the reunion of Protestant churches, attitudes toward non-Christian religions, the relationship between church and state, and natural rights.

Cartesianism and Its Critics. The clash between traditional and enlightened beliefs started about 1650, when a mixture of Cartesianism, Copernicanism, and Reformed theology led to the formulation of a Cartesian theology. The battle about this kind of enlightened theology was fought by two major parties: the traditional, strictly Pietistic Voetians, disciples of Gisbertus Voetius (1589–1676), and the more liberal-minded Cocceians, disciples of

Johannes Cocceius (1603–1669). This feud dominated the religio-political scene in the Dutch Republic for many decades. While the Voetians fiercely opposed any kind of Cartesian theology, clinging to scholastic-Aristotelian theology, the Cocceians propagated moderately Cartesian notions, which they combined with their biblical theology. Lodewijk Meijer's *Philosophia S. Scripturae Interpres* ([Cartesian] Philosophy the Interpreter of Scripture, 1666) acted as a catalyst and led to a fundamental change in the traditional relationship between theology and philosophy, in which theology lost its primary position.

Other writings, such as Baruch de Spinoza's *Tractatus Theologico-Politicus* (1670), proved to orthodox Calvinists that deism and atheism had found a foothold not merely in the United Provinces in general, but also within the Dutch Reformed Church itself. The result was an ongoing battle between orthodox and liberal Reformed. In the 1690s, a major controversy broke out when the Amsterdam minister Balthasar Bekker, inspired by Cartesian dualism, denied, in his widely reprinted *De betoverde weereld* (The World Bewitched) the impact of the devil on human actions. Spinozism also acquired adherents among Cocceian theologians, such as the Zwolle minister Frederik van Leenhof (1647–1715). Cartesianism and Spinozism occasioned the first debate on atheism in the early modern Dutch Republic, both schools of thought being accused of it.

In reaction to radical Cartesianism, Cocceian theologians formulated a moderately liberal Reformed theology, paving the way for the moderate version of the Dutch Protestant Enlightenment. Being experts in philology and attracted to Cartesian tenets, liberal Cocceians deviated from orthodox interpretations of various biblical passages. Academic theologians and Orientalists played an important role here, including Campegius Vitringa the elder, Joan Alberti, Herman Venema, Albert Schultens, and Jan Jacob Schultens. The debate on Cocceian-Cartesian theology thus helped to liberate exegesis from dogmatic constraint and stimulated the beginnings of modern Bible criticism.

Around 1720, the controversy on Cartesianism gave way to debates about British and French deism. It is difficult to assess the impact of deism on Dutch religion. Dutch deists seem to have been rare, but deism elicited a stream of apologetic works in the Dutch Republic, of both national and external origin. Apologists waged war on John Toland, Lord Bolingbroke, Voltaire, and others, employing two major instruments: physico-theology and prophetic theology. Liberal Reformed intellectuals propagated a mixture of empiricism and Newtonianism, advancing their optimistic physico-theology as an apologetic instrument in order to prove the existence of a benevolent creator and his providential government in creation. Physico-theological works by Bernard Nieuwentijt and

Johannes Florentinus Martinet enjoyed an international audience. Like the "argument from design," the "argument from prophecy" enjoyed great popularity in the United Provinces. "Prophetic theology," a biblico-historical genre, was employed mainly by Cocceian theologians.

Toleration. The great apologetic effort by Reformed authors in the eighteenth century testifies to a deeply felt threat from the influx of radical enlightened ideas in the United Provinces. This did not, however, hinder many of these Reformed apologists from developing moderately enlightened ideas that gained a steadily growing popularity in the course of the century. There was a gradual shift in religious attitudes within the Dutch Reformed Church, largely inspired by enlightened notions about religious toleration. Orthodox opposition to the new mood persisted, however, as can be inferred from the intensive polemics on the issue of the salvation of virtuous pagans (the so-called Socratic War), which was occasioned by the Dutch translation of Jean-François Marmontel's *Bélisaire* in the 1770s and the upheaval over German rationalist theology in the 1780s and 1790s.

From about 1740 on, the battle over toleration dominated the religious scene. Drawing on arguments advanced by John Locke and Pierre Bayle, Dutch thinkers also turned to their national history to plead the cause of toleration. In the 1770s and 1780s, the Dutch Revolt and the Golden Age propagated a new national consciousness. Conservative Calvinists regarded the ideals of the liberal Reformed in terms of Arminianism, deism, Pelagianism, Arianism, hypothetical universalism, and indifferentism, which all threatened the traditional Calvinist orthodoxy defined in the Belgic Confession, the Heidelberg Catechism, and the canons of Dort.

From time to time, the question of book censorship was raised by orthodox Calvinists hoping to stem the enlightened tide. Works by Voltaire and Rousseau were forbidden in the 1760s, but, owing to the decentralized political structure of the United Provinces, such measures had only local or regional impact. Defenders of Calvinist orthodoxy were particularly shocked by the fact that the attacks on the Christian faith were no longer confined to an intellectual elite but now extended to other strata of society. They felt uneasy about the fact that journals, pamphlets, and broadsheets available to any interested reader were spreading enlightened ideas freely. This process of enlightenment of the common people changed the religious atmosphere significantly, and the general populace was addressed increasingly in both enlightened and anti enlightened publications in the last decades of the eighteenth century.

From about 1780 on, a novel enlightened force made itself felt in the Dutch Republic: German rationalist theology (Neology) formulated by liberal Protestant theologians who strove to purify theology by reducing dogma to a few essentials. If the message of these "new Reformers" was not particularly new by the end of the eighteenth century, the fact that it was propagated by prominent divines and leaders of the church shocked traditionalist believers in the Dutch Republic, especially since many of these innovative publications were translated into Dutch. In Rotterdam, a series of lectures was organized by the Reformed to ward off this threat. Protestant dissenters showed themselves to be greatly interested in the new modern German theology and applauded its religious minimalism. It also met with opposition among conservative members. Within the Amsterdam Lutheran Church, a controversy over German theological minimalism resulted in a schism in the early 1790s.

The Church and Society. Organized sociability was considered an important instrument for influencing public opinion, so the counteroffensive against freethinking and alleged atheism was enhanced by apologetic societies such as the Haagsche Genootschap (The Hague Society), the foundation of which (1785) was occasioned by both German theology and Anglo-American Deism. Joseph Priestley's *History of the Corruptions of Christianity* (1782) was seen as the epitome of unbelief by the founding members of the Haagsche Genootschap. Interestingly enough, Priestley, like Richard Price and Thomas Paine, appears to have found avid readers among Protestant dissenters in the Dutch Republic. Through essay contests, religious societies succeeded in putting controversial issues high on the national agenda. The prize essay list of Teyler's Godgeleerd Genootschap (Theological Society), founded in 1778 by the rich Mennonite merchant Pieter Teyler van der Hulst of Haarlem, reflects interest in such topics as biblical exegesis, toleration, and human rights.

For most of the eighteenth century, the Dutch Reformed Church remained the established church of the United Provinces, although, as the century progressed, its political and ecclesiastical privileges were called into question. Political and religious motives were closely intertwined, as the battle between Patriots and Orangists in the 1780s showed. The liberal Reformed wing, which shared the growing dislike of theological controversies and pleaded for wider toleration, often joined other Protestant denominations in their struggle against the civil and ecclesiastical privileges of the established church.

Eventually, the enlightened toleration party would triumph: in 1795, all religio-political privileges were abolished in the Netherlands. In the wake of the Batavian Revolution, separation between church and state was officially proclaimed (August 1796) in a decree stating that "the principles of liberty, equality and fraternity do not allow for a privileged church," and that "all placards and resolutions of the former States General, born of the late

union of church and state, should be abolished." The separation of church and state implied the equality of all Protestant and Roman Catholic citizens in the United Provinces. Jews were granted civil rights shortly afterward, in September 1796. In the wake of these decisions, the Remonstrants made an attempt at uniting the Protestant churches, but their irenic project failed. To both orthodox and enlightened Reformed and non-Reformed, it appeared that by 1800 the Enlightenment had made an indelible mark on Dutch religion; the next century, however, would prove them at least partially wrong.

[*See also* Arminianism; Bayle, Pierre; Bekker, Balthasar; Bible; Cartesianism; Deism; Locke, John; Marmontel, Jean-François; Meijer, Lodewijk; Netherlands; Newtonianism; Nieuwentijt, Bernard; Physico-Theology; Rationalism; Revealed Religion; Sermons; *and* Toleration.]

BIBLIOGRAPHY

Bosma, Jelle. *Woorden van een gezond verstand: De invloed van de Verlichting op de in het Nederlands uitgegeven preken van 1750 tot 1800* (with English summary). Nieuwkoop, Neth., 1997. This study deals with the gradual shift in Dutch religious thinking and feeling by analyzing Protestant sermons published in Dutch, delivered by Dutch Reformed and Dissenters alike, showing cultural change between 1750 and 1800 from a comparative perspective.

Buisman, J. W. *Tussen vroomheid en Verlichting: Een cultuurhistorisch en–sociologisch onderzoek naar enkele aspecten van de Verlichting in Nederland (1755–1810)* (with French summary). 2 vols. Zwolle, Neth., 1992. A highly interesting insight into susceptibility to Enlightenment notions through a discussion of various reactions to disasters (such as the Lisbon earthquake) and analyzing debates on such topics as criminal law, slavery, and the position of women.

Bunge, L. van. "Balthasar Bekker's Cartesian Hermeneutics and the Challenge of Spinozism." *British Journal for the History of Philosophy* 1 (1993), 55–79.

Eijnatten, Joris van. *Mutua Christianorum Tolerantia: Irenicism and Toleration in the Netherlands: The Stinstra Affair, 1740–1745.* Florence, 1998. Analysis of the important debate on toleration occasioned by the deposition of the Mennonite minister Johannes Stinstra.

Gestel, Paul van. "Dutch Reactions to Thomas Paine's 'Age of Reason.'" In *Studies on Voltaire and the Eighteenth Century* 378, pp. 271–301. Oxford, 1999.

Israel, Jonathan I. *The Dutch Republic: Its Rise, Greatness, and Fall 1477–1806.* Oxford, 1995.

Israel, Jonathan I. *Radical Enlightenment: Philosophy and the Making of Modernity 1650–1750.* Oxford, 2001.

Jacob, Margaret C. *The Radical Enlightenment: Pantheists, Freemasons and Republicans.* London, 1981.

Jacob, Margaret C. "Radicalism in the Dutch Enlightenment." In *The Dutch Republic in the Eighteenth Century: Decline, Enlightenment, and Revolution*, edited by Margaret C. Jacob and Wijnand W. Mijnhardt, pp. 224–240. Ithaca, N.Y., and London, 1992.

Mijnhardt, Wijnand W. "The Dutch Enlightenment: Humanism, Nationalism, and Decline." In *The Dutch Republic in the Eighteenth Century: Decline, Enlightenment, and Revolution*, edited by Margaret C. Jacob and Wijnand W. Mijnhardt, pp. 197–223. Ithaca, N.Y., and London, 1992.

Vuyk, Simon. *De verdraagzame gemeente van vrije christenen: Remonstranten op de bres voor de Bataafse Republiek, 1780–1800* (with English summary). Amsterdam, 1995. Offers a discussion of the political and social activities of the Remonstrants in the last decades of the eighteenth century, their ideas on church and state, and their attempt to unite the Protestant churches in the young Batavian Republic.

Wall, Ernestine van der. "Orthodoxy and Scepticism in the Early Dutch Enlightenment." In *Scepticism and Irreligion in the Seventeenth and Eighteenth Centuries*, edited by Richard H. Popkin and Arjo Vanderjagt, pp. 121–141. Leiden, Neth., 1993.

Wall, Ernestine van der. "Toleration and Enlightenment in the Dutch Republic." In *Toleration in Enlightenment Europe*, edited by Ole Peter Grell and Roy Porter, pp. 114–132. Cambridge, 2000.

Wall, Ernestine van der. *Socrates in de hemel? Een achttiende-eeuwse polemiek over deugd, verdraagzaamheid en vaderland*. Hilversum, Neth., 2000. Discussion of the controversy, occasioned by Marmontel's *Bélisaire*, between traditional and moderately enlightened intellectuals on deism, toleration, and national feeling in the 1760s and 1770s.

ERNESTINE VAN DER WALL

Presbyterianism

For a brief period in the revolutionary decade of the 1640s, Presbyterianism had seemed poised to become the established church in Britain and Ireland. With the Solemn League and Covenant of 1643, the English and Scottish Parliaments had pledged to establish a common Presbyterian Church order. The predominantly English Assembly of Divines had by 1646 drafted the Westminster Confession of Faith, a systematic expression of Calvinist teaching, and in 1647 the Church of Scotland adopted the Westminster Confession as its standard of faith. However, the dream of a Presbyterian settlement in Britain and Ireland died amid the warfare after 1648. Following the Restoration in 1660, the crown, with Anglican support, moved to suppress Presbyterianism. In England and Wales, Presbyterian clergy were ejected from their livings in the established church, and repression reduced Presbyterians to a remnant. Repression was less successful in Scotland, where, despite ejections of Presbyterian clergy and brutal military action against the Presbyterian covenanters, Presbyterianism retained broad popular support. It also survived in Ireland, especially among the Scottish settlers in Ulster.

The revolution of 1688 brought relief to the Presbyterians. In England and Wales, the Toleration Act of 1689 granted Dissenters, including Presbyterians, a degree of legal protection. More significantly, in 1690 William III reluctantly agreed to reestablish Presbyterianism within the Church of Scotland in order to placate his Scottish supporters. In Ireland, William III granted the Presbyterian clergy an annual royal grant as a reward for their support. By 1700, Presbyterianism was again a significant religious force—the established church in Scotland, a privileged minority church in Ireland, and a tolerated church in England and Wales. The act for parliamentary union of England and Scotland in 1707 guaranteed the preservation of the Presbyterian settlement in Scotland. At the same time, however, the state made it clear that it expected the Presbyterians to be moderate in their politics and piety. There must be no return to the ambitions of the seventeenth century.

From the early eighteenth century, Presbyterians in the three kingdoms moved away from dogmatic zeal and covenanting fervor and embraced a more rational and restrained faith, with emphasis on simple and dignified worship, a disciplined life, and a learned ministry. In England, Presbyterian academies promoted the epistemology of John Locke, the study of the laws of natural science, a broadminded approach to Scripture, and toleration of differences in belief. This openness led some Presbyterians to reject the predestinarian doctrines of the Westminster Confession in favor of Arminian teachings on the freedom of the will. Others were drawn to Arianism, the belief that Christ was a created being and not one with God the Father. Those attracted to Arianism tended to reject the reformed teachings on the total depravity of human nature and the need for a mediator between the righteous God and a sinful humanity. They embraced an optimistic view of the human capacity for improvement. In 1719, a national assembly of Presbyterians held at Salters Hall in London considered charges brought against two ministers for holding Arian views. By a narrow majority, the assembly refused to condemn the Arian ministers and instead called for openness and toleration on the question. Following the Salters Hall decision, Arian views gradually spread through English Presbyterianism. By the 1770s, some were moving from Arianism to Unitarianism; however, the spread of Arian and Unitarian views also brought a steady decline in English Presbyterian numbers.

In 1719, the same year as the Salters Hall decision, a group of Irish Presbyterians in the synod of Ulster called for an end to the synod's requirement that ministers must subscribe to the Westminster Confession of Faith. These "New Light" nonsubscribers insisted on freedom of conscience and argued that the church should not define terms of communion beyond those given by Christ in Scripture. Orthodox Calvinists resisted the calls to relax the terms of subscription, and a controversy raged until 1726, when New Light nonsubscribers withdrew from the synod to form the separate Presbytery of Antrim. New Light principles continued to spread; by the end of the century, probably the majority of Irish Presbyterians had quietly embraced New Light views on subscription. Many New Light ministers were also drawn to Arian views and to an emphasis on reason, natural laws, and a belief in progress; some also embraced republican political ideas.

In Scotland, religious moderatism gradually gained ground within the established Presbyterian Church. To foster moderation, the British Parliament imposed the

Patronage Act on the Church of Scotland in 1712. This restored to lay patrons, the large majority of whom were landowners, the right to present ministers in the parish churches. The patrons tended to present men of liberal sentiments and polished manners whose sermons emphasized practical morality. The Scottish universities promoted freedom of inquiry and moral philosophy. In the towns, Presbyterian clergymen increasingly engaged the thought of the Enlightenment and participated in debating and literary societies such as the Select Society of Edinburgh or the Glasgow Literary Society. Presbyterian clergymen made significant contributions in history, philosophy, rhetoric, and natural science. After about 1760, a moderate party under the leadership of William Robertson—an Edinburgh minister, historian, and, after 1762, principal of Edinburgh University—gained ascendancy in the Church of Scotland and promoted toleration, freedom of conscience, and a culture of improvement. Moderate leaders, however, resisted attempts to loosen the terms of subscription to the Westminster Confession, fearing that this might weaken Scotland's Presbyterian establishment. After 1733, many dogmatic Calvinists withdrew from the established church in protest against both patronage and the influence of moderatism. By the end of the eighteenth century, however, most Presbyterian seceders were themselves embracing liberal views and experiencing what they themselves termed "New Light" on certain aspects of the Westminster Confession.

Presbyterianism was carried to the North Atlantic colonies, especially New Jersey and the Carolinas, by eighteenth-century Scottish and Irish settlers. Colonial Presbyterianism also experienced controversies over subscription to the Westminster Confession. Some were drawn to the rationalism and moderation of the New Light (in America, called "Old Light") mood in British and Irish Presbyterianism. Others, however—such as the Tennent clerical family, associated with the "Log College" opened in 1726 at Neshaminy, Pennsylvania—held firmly to the Westminster doctrines of election and salvation by grace, and they played a leading role in the Great Awakening of the 1740s, which in America was associated with the term "New Light."

[See also Clubs and Societies; Deism; Edinburgh; Edwards, Jonathan; England; Enthusiasm; Great Awakening; Ireland; Revealed Religion; Robertson, William; Scotland; Skepticism; and Witherspoon, John.]

BIBLIOGRAPHY

Bolam, C. Gordon, Jeremy Goring, H. L. Short, and Roger Thomas. *The English Presbyterians from Elizabethan Puritanism to Modern Unitarianism.* London, 1968. A sound general survey, especially good on Unitarian developments.

Brooke, Peter. *Ulster Presbyterianism: The Historical Perspective 1610–1970.* Belfast, 1994. A revised second edition of the 1986 work, better on the political than the religious context.

Griffiths, Olive M. *Religion and Learning: A Study in English Presbyterian Thought from the Bartholomew Ejections (1662) to the Foundation of the Unitarian Movement.* Cambridge, 1935. Remains a valuable study, especially strong on eighteenth-century theological controversies.

Haakonssen, Knud, ed. *Enlightenment and Religion: Rational Dissent in Eighteenth-Century Britain.* Cambridge, 1996. A carefully edited volume of innovative essays on British Dissent.

McBride, Ian R. *Scripture Politics: Ulster Presbyterians and Irish Radicalism in the Late Eighteenth Century.* Oxford, 1998. A fine study of Presbyterian popular piety in Ulster, with emphasis on the background of the Rising of 1798.

McIntosh, John R. *Church and Theology in Enlightenment Scotland: The Popular Party, 1740–1800.* Edinburgh, 1998. An exploration of Scottish Presbyterian evangelicalism.

Sher, Richard B. *Church and University in the Scottish Enlightenment: The Moderate Literati of Edinburgh.* Princeton, N.J., 1985. The best account of the moderate movement within eighteenth-century Scottish Presbyterianism.

Westerkamp, Marilyn J. *Triumph of the Laity: Scots-Irish Piety and the Great Awakening 1625–1760.* New York, 1988. An authoritative study of popular piety and theological developments within Scottish, Irish, and North American Presbyterianism.

STEWART J. BROWN

REGENCY. *See* France.

REGISTER OF GRIEVANCES (*Cahier de doléances*). *See* French Revolution *and* Political Philosophy.

REIMARUS, HERMANN SAMUEL (1694–1768), North German philologist, Orientalist, and philosopher.

Reimarus is remembered principally for his criticism of the Bible, Christian origins, and theology in the "Wolfenbüttel Fragments," excerpts from a 4,000-page manuscript that were posthumously and anonymously published in part by Gotthold Ephraim Lessing in 1777–1778. The controversy that followed led to serious challenges to the reliability of Scripture in matters of fact and the possibility of establishing religion on the basis of historical events, whatever their attestation (e.g., the Resurrection). Reimarus and his promoter, Lessing, thus attained canonical status as associated founders of the German Enlightenment, or Aufklärung, and as courageous inaugurators of rigorous scrutiny of early Christianity.

It was thus in contrast to the moderately enlightened German revision of Christianity that Reimarus found his historical place. Reimarus had studied both classical and Hebrew philology at Jena and Wittenberg and had abandoned theological study for philology and other erudite pursuits. He visited England and the Netherlands and then became a distinguished teacher in the Academic Gymnasium in his native Hamburg. There he appeared outwardly as a defender of Christianity in the tradition of physico-theology; for historians, however, he looms as a figure so radical that he could have no immediate successors. A storm of conservative clerical reaction broke once the excerpts from Reimarus's manuscript saw print, and Lessing was obliged by his ducal patron to break off publication of the excerpts, which his privileged position as ducal librarian had allowed him to print without prior censorship.

For later historians of biblical criticism, philosophy, and theology, Reimarus and Lessing have come to occupy a position rather like that which Marxism assigned to the Peasants' War of 1525: a revolutionary explosion doomed to immediate failure, but at the same time a token of the coming victory of the historically inevitable. Under the influence of English deism and of a radical reading of Christian Wolff, Reimarus in his secret treatise—known in English as *Apology or Defense for the Rational Worshipers of God*—rejected his public stance of defending an easy transition from the religion of reason to that of biblical revelation and affirmed the opposite. In the words of Christoph Bultmann, Reimarus concluded: "First, the biblical traditions showed no marks of a divine revelation...they exhibited an image of God irreconcilable with the natural knowledge of God. Second, the connection between the Old and New Testament...did not support any proof of Christian principles of faith on the basis of Old Testament promises. Third, the essentially political character of the activity of Jesus had been covered over and falsified by the formation of primitive Christian tradition and by the Gospels and the letters of the Apostle Paul, making it the point of departure for a religion of salvation" (1998, vol. 8, pp. 210–211; translation by John Stroup).

Four points should be mentioned on the larger significance of Reimarus. First, it is striking that Reimarus could reach such extreme conclusions under the influence of Wolff, given the conservative nature of his milieu and the tendency of the age to mold all rationalism in the direction of ultimately supporting a remodeled version of official Christianity; this provides support for reading Wolff as more radical than has often been supposed. Second, Reimarus could have a positive impact in Germany only after his negative critique was taken by Lessing as the occasion for a basic positive reorientation of Protestant religiosity, in ways pointing ahead to the historical dynamism and inward religiosity of later Idealism and Romanticism. Third, Reimarus's underlying motive of shoring up the doctrine of the immortality of the soul (and his repudiation of the Old Testament specifically because he found that it rejected this doctrine) needs careful attention, pointing as it does to later attacks on both the Old Testament in Christian use and the eventual questioning of any survival of human identity after death. Finally, the customary praise of Reimarus as a neglected pioneer in emphasizing the eschatological or apocalyptic theme in the preaching of Jesus needs to be rethought from a

perspective looking back on two centuries of European cultural and religious criticism. From this perspective, Reimarus anticipated both the general devaluation of the special status of conventional Christian faith and the secularizing reapplication of selected themes from Judaeo-Christian apocalyptic thought. The latter legitimates a cultural criticism founded on philosophical pessimism and seeking authority by pointing to the alleged confluence of themes in Gnosticism, Hinduism, and Buddhism with the world-denying mentality implicit in Judeo-Christian apocalyptic thought. The vogue of Arthur Schopenhauer and those influenced by the very broad cultural diffusion of his themes brought these approaches to a remarkable series of fruitions in the century after 1848.

[*See also* Aufklärung; Bible; Lessing, Gotthold Ephraim; *and* Revealed Religion.]

BIBLIOGRAPHY

PRIMARY SOURCES

Lessing, Gotthold Ephraim. *Lessing's Theological Writings*. Edited by Henry Chadwick. Stanford, Calif., 1957.

Reimarus, Hermann Samuel. *Apologie oder Schutzschrift für die vernünftigen Verehrer Gottes*. 2 vols. Frankfurt, 1972.

Reimarus, Hermann Samuel. *Fragments*. Edited by Charles H. Talbert, translated by Ralph S. Fraser. Philadelphia, 1970. Excellent front matter includes an 1877 overview by David Friedrich Strauss.

Reimarus, Hermann Samuel. *The Goal of Jesus and His Disciples*. Edited and translated by George Wesley Buchanan. Leiden, 1970.

SECONDARY WORKS

Boehart, William. *Politik und Religion: Studien zum Fragmentenstreit (Reimarus, Goeze, Lessing)*. Scharzenbek, Germany, 1988.

Bultmann, Christoph. "Reimarus, Hermann Samuel." In *Deutsche Biographische Enzyklopädie*. Edited by Walther Killy and Rudolf Vierhaus, vol. 8, pp. 210–211. Munich, 1998. Masterful treatment in brief compass.

Frei, Hans W. *The Eclipse of Biblical Narrative: A Study in Eighteenth and Nineteenth Century Hermeneutics*. New Haven, Conn., 1974.

Hermann Samuel Reimarus: Ein "bekannter Unbekannter" der Aufklärung in Hamburg. Göttingen, Germany, 1973.

Lötzsch, Frieder. *Was Ist "Ökologie"? Hermann Samuel Reimarus: Ein Beitrag zur Geistesgeschichte des 18. Jahrhunderts*. Cologne and Vienna, 1987.

Schultze, Harald. "Reimarus, Hermann Samuel (1694–1768)." In *Theologische Realenzyklopädie*, edited by Gerhard Müller et al., vol. 28, pp. 470–473. Berlin and New York, 1997. Excellent bibliography.

Stemmer, Peter. *Weissagung und Kritik: Eine Studie zur Hermeneutik bei Hermann Samuel Reimarus*. Göttingen, Germany, 1983.

Walter, Wolfgang, ed. *Hermann Samuel Reimarus 1694–1768: Beiträge zur Reimarus-Renaissance in der Gegenwart*. Göttingen, Germany, 1998.

Walter, Wolfgang, and Ludwig Borinski, eds. *Logik im Zeitalter der Aufklärung: Studien zur "Vernunftlehre" von Hermann Samuel Reimarus*. Göttingen, Germany, 1980.

JOHN STROUP

REINHOLD, KARL LEONHARD

REINHOLD, KARL LEONHARD (1758–1823), one of the first followers of Kant and an important precursor of German Idealism.

After his education in Vienna at the colleges of the Jesuits and the Regular Clerics of St. Paul, Reinhold taught philosophy there between 1778 and 1783. Having become disillusioned, under the influence of Enlightenment thought, about the church, he left his community and fled to Weimar. In Weimar he became acquainted with Christoph Martin Wieland, whose daughter he married. In 1785, he became the editor of Wieland's *Teutscher Merkur*. Reinhold eventually published his "Letters on Kantian Philosophy" between 1786 and 1787 in this journal, which made him famous. Arthur Schopenhauer called him the "first apostle" of Kant. This is not exactly true, but his *Letters* did much to popularize Kant. Soon people spoke of "the Kant-Reinholdian Philosophy." In 1787 he became a professor in Jena on the basis of his *Letters* and a recommendation from Kant. From 1793 until his death he taught at the University of Kiel.

Reinhold did not remain a follower of Kant, however. His so-called "Philosophy of the Elements," as developed in the *Essay towards a New Theory of the Faculty of Representation* and *The Foundation of Philosophical Knowledge* (1794), was an attempt to give a foundation to Kant's theory and to answer David Hume, whom he understood as a radical skeptic, who had raised the problem of the possibility of "objective truth" (or whether we can know things in themselves). Since any answer to Hume must consist in proof that we possess such objective truth, and since Kant had not provided a complete answer, Reinhold meant to do so. He tried to show that an account of the original constitution of the faculty of cognition would fill this gap. This involved his infamous "principle of consciousness," which states, "representation is distinguished in consciousness by the subject from both the subject and object, and is referred to both." It means, among other things, that we can distinguish between consciousness and its objects. Reinhold argued that, because this distinction is possible only if we know the "in-itself," we must possess "objective truth."

This rather obscure modification or defense of Kant soon made Reinhold the target of criticism. Thus, Gottlob Ernst Schulze criticized him severely in his anonymous book *Aenesidemus, or On the Foundations of the Philosophy of Elements, as Delivered by Professor Reinhold in Jena Together with a Defense of Skepticism against the Presumptions of the Criticism of Reason*. This work is a sustained argument intended to prove that Kantian philosophy had neither answered skepticism in general nor Hume in particular. Schulze's critique had a deep influence on the young Fichte and the early development of German Idealism. Reinhold himself gave up his "elementary philosophy" as a result of reading it, became first a follower of Fichte, then an ally of Jacobi, and finally an advocate of a "rational realism" that was in some ways close to the philosophy of Thomas Reid.

[*See also* Aufklärung *and* Kant, Immanuel.]

BIBLIOGRAPHY

Between Kant and Hegel: Texts in the Development of Post-Kantian Idealism. Translated and edited by George di Giovanni and H. S. Harris. Albany, N.Y., 1985.

Breazeale, Daniel. "Fichte's Aenesidemus Review and the Transformation of German Idealism." *Review of Metaphysics* 34 (1980–1981), 545–568.

Breazeale, Daniel. "Between Kant and Fichte: Karl Leonhard Reinhold's 'Elementary Philosophy.'" *Review of Metaphysics* 35 (1981–1982), 785–821.

Reinhold, Karl Leonhard. "Philosophy of the Elements." In *Essay towards a New Theory of the Faculty of Representation*. Jena, 1789; 2d ed., 1795.

MANFRED KUEHN

RELIGIOUS CONVERSION. During the seventeenth century in Europe, accounts of religious conversion by both Catholics and Protestants came to constitute a primary genre of the literature of confessional controversy. Composed sometimes by articulate converts or, perhaps more frequently, by the clergymen who advised them, these records of "motives and reasons" for leaving one Christian denomination and joining another were intended to persuade by example. Converts recorded the process whereby they had become convinced of the superior claims to truth of the religion they had chosen to embrace. As a result, such accounts were often presented publicly (in the context of a religious service celebrating the event) or printed, and when the convert was a person of consequence, they circulated widely.

For various reasons, Protestant conversions to Catholicism were more numerous everywhere in Europe during this period than the reverse, and accounts of them were more frequently recorded. Protestants of the time lacked any official conversion program, while the Roman Catholic Church set out to make good the losses of the Reformation. Catholics engaged in an organized campaign of evangelization, often supported, as in France and the Empire, by secular governments, and dependent on rhetorical strategies self-consciously tailored to the differing capacities of elite and popular audiences. In keeping with early church tradition, which advised converting important people so that they in turn could influence others, Catholic proselytizers made a special effort to convert members of the educated classes, especially Protestant aristocrats, and they were more systematic than their confessional opponents in publicizing the conversions they obtained.

The Catholic campaign to reclaim eminent individuals for the faith thus generated a large body of literature. It included not only the conversion accounts themselves, but also treatises on how to obtain conversions, polemical texts aimed at potential converts, and records of disputations organized for their benefit. Like interconfessional polemic, generally, this literature, while not monolithic, was often marked by strategies of rhetoric and argumentation that, despite the intentions of their framers, helped to foster the rationalized discourse about religion that we have come to identify with the Enlightenment.

First and most important to consider in this context is the rhetoric of rationalism that frequently characterized both the conversion accounts and the polemical treatises addressed to potential converts. Catholic proselytizers took special care to distinguish eminent converts from their counterparts among the lower orders, from whom a pious submission to the conclusions of their betters, instilled by appeals to the senses, was thought to be all that was properly required. Thus, they often acknowledged the exalted intellectual capacities of their elite targets and encouraged them to examine the religions with independence of mind. In similar fashion, such converts frequently asserted the intellectual respectability of their change of faith by representing themselves as disinterested seekers after truth who had read, studied, traveled, conversed with learned men, or otherwise engaged in a prolonged independent investigation of Roman claims in order to reach a reasoned acceptance of Catholic authority; their acceptance was marked by a notable paucity of references to God and especially to Christ, who appeared in these texts far less frequently as redeemer than as founder of a church. Returning Protestant accusations of Catholic "superstition" and "idolatry" in kind, converts tarred their former coreligionists with the brush of unreason, chastising them for their ignorance and dismissing them as childish persons in thrall to their prejudices and incapable of logical argument, who nevertheless insisted on blind submission to an inconsistent theology and a disordered ecclesiology. From a rhetorical point of view, then, this literature sought to persuade an educated audience—in a manner consistent with their dignity and social preeminence—that Catholicism was a reasonable religion. Unlike the pretensions of the Reformers, this rhetoric suggests, Rome's claim to be the church founded by Christ could be verified by independent historical investigation and rational argument, and its authority in spiritual matters therefore proved infallible and hence *entitled* to submission.

Crucially, the substance of Catholic doctrine played little role in this literature. Rather, for converts and polemicists alike, the church's claims to absolute spiritual authority became the central concern, as revelation yielded pride of place to arguments drawn from reason and history supporting the credentials of the institution. From the perspective of Enlightenment critiques of traditional religion, two implications of this shift in emphasis are important. Most obvious is the suggestion, often implicit

in the rhetoric of the conversion accounts, that naturalistic inquiry, independent investigation, and rational judgment exclusively determine the truth or falsity of a religion. Supporting this rhetoric was a time-honored apologetic strategy that aimed, following Aquinas, to lay the groundwork for faith in arguments addressed to reason; these included the claim that the church was the means God had chosen to impart his revelation to human beings. In traditional apologetics, such arguments had been confined to a certain moment in the act of faith, preparing the way for a subsequent assent to the Christian mysteries that could not be entirely rational. In seventeenth-century Catholic polemics, however, arguments supporting the credentials of the Roman Church were often severed from their original apologetic context, in a manner that appeared to reduce the act of faith to its natural and rational component. This process was especially evident in many Catholic conversion accounts, where references to the Christian mysteries are often minimal, and converts are shown embracing the faith with no further ado once they have become convinced that Rome is the true church.

Second, in elaborating the polemic supporting Rome's credentials, Catholic controversialists were making a case for its absolute spiritual authority, to which they hoped that potential converts would wholeheartedly submit. Ironically, however, they offered a model of conversion that may have subverted their aim, insofar as it encouraged systematic examination of the foundations of that authority. In this last respect, the Catholic literature of conversion reflects the concern to define legitimate authority and the conditions for submission to it that marked all areas of human inquiry in the seventeenth century, and that helped set the stage for the more thoroughgoing critique of institutions and traditions that characterized the century of the Enlightenment.

[*See also* Apologetics; Revealed Religion; *and* Roman Catholicism.]

BIBLIOGRAPHY

Christ, Günter. "Fürst, Dynastie, Territorium und Konfession: Beobachtungen zu Fürstenkonversionen des ausgehenden 17 und beginnenden 18. Jahrhunderts." *Saeculum* 24 (1973), 367–388. An overview of the Catholic campaign to convert the German nobility; good analysis of the political and social contexts of these conversions.

La conversion au XVIIe siècle: Actes du XIIe collogue de Marseille. Marseilles, 1983. Includes valuable studies of Catholic polemical strategies based on close readings of the literature directed at an educated public in France.

Dompnier, Bernard. *Le vénin de l'hérésie: Image du protestantisme et combat catholique au XVIIe siècle.* Paris, 1985. An overview of Catholic controversy in seventeenth-century France; also provides good examples of how controversialists tailored conversion strategies to elite and popular audiences.

Garstein, Oskar. *Rome and the Counter-Reformation in Scandinavia.* 3 vols. Oslo, 1961, 1980; Leiden, 1992. Offers the last word on the campaign to recatholicize Scandinavia.

Parker, Geoffrey. *Europe in Crisis, 1598–1648.* Ithaca, N.Y., 1979. Chap. 2 offers a brief overview of Catholic efforts to reclaim the nobility of Europe.

Questier, Michael C. *Conversion, Politics and Religion in England, 1580–1625.* Cambridge, 1996. Discusses conversion from the perspective of what Catholicism and Protestantism meant to individual converts; also includes an excellent discussion of the Catholic polemical theology of the church.

Rosa, Susan. "Seventeenth-Century Catholic Polemic and the Rise of Cultural Rationalism: An Example from the Empire." *Journal of the History of Ideas* 57 (1996), 87–107. Analyzes one text that illustrates the rationalistic strain in seventeenth-century Catholic polemic and discusses its implications.

SUSAN ROSA

RELIGIOUS ORDERS. *See* Benedictines of Saint-Maur; Jesuits; Oratorians; Revealed Religion; *and* Roman Catholicism.

REPRESENTATIONS OF READING. In the *Encyclopédie* of Denis Diderot and Jean le Rond d'Alembert, two entries by Louis Jaucourt define the reader and reading. The article "Lecteur," after a neutral definition of a reader as "any person who reads a book, a piece of writing, a work," is devoted entirely to a severe criticism of the readers of the time, who are said to judge everything without knowing or understanding anything: "Almost all of us want to have the glory of pronouncing judgment, and almost all of us flee from the attention, the examination, the work, and the means of acquiring knowledge." Going back to the remarks of "an able man of the century of Louis XIV" (presumably La Bruyère), Jaucourt enumerates the causes that spoil judgment: self-satisfaction or complacency, which makes the reader love any book in which he recognizes himself; partiality, which leads him to hate books by authors whom he dislikes; jealousy, which makes him disparage work of which he is incapable; and, finally, the pretense of intellect and borrowed taste, which condemn good works and praise the mediocre. This denunciation depicts weaknesses of spirit and character without really describing the practices themselves. In the form and the tone of a moral discourse in the old style, it finishes by calling on authors to turn away from false glory: "Let authors be less keen on the approval of the majority than of the most intelligent part of the public."

The article "Lecture" ("Reading"), on an entirely different level, sketches a typology of the manners of reading and a theory of their effects. Jaucourt constructs a strong opposition between reading only with the eyes and reading out loud:

> The first requires only the knowledge of letters, of their sound, and of how they go together; it becomes rapid through practice, and suffices for a man in a study. The other manner demands, in order to please the ears of the auditors, much more knowledge

of reading for itself; it requires, to please those who listen, perfect understanding of the things read to them, harmonious sound, clear pronunciation, and felicitous flexibility in the organs of the voice, as much for the changing of tone as for necessary pauses.

More demanding, reading out loud is dangerously seductive and blurs judgment:

> The work that one hears read agreeably seduces more than the work read to oneself dispassionately in one's study. It is also in this last manner that reading is most useful; for in order to harvest the full fruit of the work, silence, rest, and meditation are necessary.

Reading done in silence and seclusion is the primary condition of the critical exercise: "That which is heard passes quickly, that which is read is digested thoroughly."

In "digests thoroughly," Jaucourt revived a phrase used by humanists to contrast studious reading, applied and silent, with two other practices: reading done in common, in a small, friendly, select group: and, implicitly, the hurried and casual reading condemned in the article "Lecteur." Unlike the neo-Platonic texts of the Renaissance, which called silent reading much more able to capture the reader than reading out loud, Jaucourt, like Condorcet later, situated in the voice a power of seduction capable of captivating the imagination and subjugating judgment.

For Jaucourt, only reading done in silence and in solitude could really be called reading—that which allowed one to "adorn the intellect and form judgment." It was against such a practice that he measured the weaknesses of bad readers, sketched in a series of portraits that satirize the professions:

> Nevertheless, reading is an effort for most men; military officers who neglected it in their youth are unable to enjoy it in their maturity. Gamblers want the deal of the cards and the throw of the dice that occupy their soul, with no need for sustained attention. Financiers, always moved by the love of interest, are insensitive to the cultivation of their minds. Government ministers, and people in charge of business, have no time to read; or if they read at times, it is, to use an image from Plato, only as fugitive slaves who fear their masters.

To this observation can be compared the representation of the reading required or imposed, as Diderot described it in the "Éloge, de Richardson" (1762), by Samuel Richardson's novels. Four traits characterize the modes and effects of this reading. First, it is seen as a "rereading," as though the work had always been there. Injunctions urged readers to "read Richardson, read him ceaselessly." The novel had to be frequented, like the Bible. Constant rereadings made the book a companion of works and days, instilled in memory, a guide for life.

Second, although reading Richardson could be done in common, with each member of an assembled company reading to the others in turn; or several could read it separately, for the purpose of discussing it in common. However, the true reading that the novels expect and merit demands that the reader be removed from the urgencies of the world. Diderot wrote:

> Richardson's details are displeasing to and should displease a frivolous and dissipated man; but it is not for that man that he wrote; it is for the tranquil and solitary man, who has known the vanity of noise and worldly amusements, and who likes to inhabit the obscurity of a retreat, and to be moved in a useful way in silence.

The vocabulary—"solitary," "retreat," "silence"—marks the transfer of the old model of devotional reading to the novelistic text. It indicates also that such a text can only fully touch a minority: "Richardson's works will more or less please most people, in most times and places; but the number of readers who will feel the full effect of his work will never be large."

Solitary or communal, reading Richardson mobilized all the reader's sensibility, agitated the heart and the body, and provoked cries and tears. Diderot transformed his reader into a spectator of the effects produced by the most moving passages of *Clarissa*:

> I was with a friend when they delivered the [serial installment containing] the burial and testament of Clarissa.... He took hold of the pages, retired to a corner, and read. I watched him closely: at first I saw tears falling; soon he interrupted himself, and was sobbing; suddenly he got up, walked without knowing where he was going, let out cries like a desolate man, and addressed the most bitter reproaches to the entire Harlowe family.

The increasingly violent movements of body and soul emphasize the irrepressible disturbance that invaded the reader: tears, sobs, agitation, shouts and, finally, curses. Further on in the "Éloge," the emotion provoked by reading (in this case, of a scene from Richardson's *Pamela*) culminate in "the most violent tremors."

The final trait that characterized the relationship with Richardson's novels was the abolition of all distinctions between the world of the book and the world of the reader. The reader, often a woman, was projected into the account, and the fictional heroes became the reader's fellows. For some, novels even produced a belief in the real existence of the protagonists:

> One day a woman of taste and of uncommon sensitivity, greatly preoccupied by the story of Grandisson which she had just read, said to one of her friends who was leaving for London: Will you please visit on my account Miss Emily, Mr. Belfort, and above all Miss Howe, if she is still living?

What gave the novel such a sense of reality was its universality. As Diderot explained, unlike a historical account, which "embraces only a portion of history, only one point on the surface of the globe," Richardson's works, because they allow humanity to be seen in its very essence, unveil a superior truth, valid for all places and all times: "The human heart which was, is, and always will be the same, is the model from which you copy." This resolves the contradiction between the infinite variety of the novel's characters and its exposure of the constants of the human heart, which permits the flesh-and-blood readers to identify with the heroes of fiction. The community of readers produced by Richardson's novels was founded on shared gestures, emotions, and engagements.

These representations indicate clearly the polarization of the discourses devoted to reading during the Enlightenment. These discourses oscillated constantly between contradictory characterizations: on the one hand, distance from the written work, the exercise of judgment, and lucid reasoning; on the other, "absorption" into the text, emotional sharing, and the engagement of sensibility. Painters during the eighteenth century produced many portraits of readers, male and female, and made this tension apparent. For some, reading was a critical practice, the basis for scholarly work, the exchange of ideas, and the enlightened administration of territories and populations. Men of letters, erudite men, and powerful men were the privileged subjects of representations that tied the progress of human understanding to that of society. Other subjects (sometimes portrayed by the same painters) were seen reading in a context of abandonment to the seductions of the imagination, the strength of sentiments, and the pleasures of the senses.

In many French eighteenth-century paintings, a woman reading in secret or in solitude is discovered in an emotional response, either restrained or reckless. Fragonard's *Jeune Fille Lisant* (National Gallery, Washington), comfortably settled, reads with wise and applied attention a book held elegantly in her right hand. Behind the perfect immobility of the reader, withdrawn from the world, the spectator perceives the absorption and the tension within her. A little earlier in the century, two paintings—Jeaurat's *Scène Intérieur* (private collection) and Baudoin's *La Lecture* (Musée des Arts Décoratifs, Paris)—similarly situate the act of reading in private space. In opulent interiors signs of feminine intimacy are accumulated: the little family dog, comfortable furniture for everyday use, the armchair where the body relaxes, and disorder, discreet or intrusive. In both paintings, the reader, a young woman in everyday dress, is surprised at the instant when her thoughts escape from the book she is reading, now laid aside. Troubled, she lets herself go, her head resting on a cushion, her expression perturbed, her body languid. Obviously, her book is one that moves the senses and excites the imagination. The painter thus invites the spectator to enter an intimate feminine world. Even more daring artists cast feminine readers of novels (sentimental or erotic) as protagonists in paintings playing on the ambivalence of condemnation and voyeurism.

Even when neither feminine nor romantic, the reading represented in the eighteenth century was a private pursuit. The book in masculine portraits, formerly a sign of the subject's background or profession, became a companion of solitude. Traditionally, books were the sign of knowledge, often a source of power, as in the portrait of Mirabeau painted by Aved and shown in the Salon of 1743 (Musée du Louvre, Paris). For this inherited iconography the eighteenth-century portrait tended to substitute another: that of the act of reading itself, which presupposed an intimate connection between the reader and the book. Innovative variations depicted reading outdoors, seated under an arbor; reading in a field, frequent in portraits of English aristocratic families; and reading while walking, as in the cut-out silhouettes of Goethe in the 1780s.

In the painting *Camille Desmoulins en Prison* by Hubert Robert (Wadsworth Atheneum, Hartford, Connecticut), the representation of solitary reading changes meaning. In the enforced isolation of imprisonment, the book becomes a companion of distress, much like familiar objects or the portrait of a loved one. It introduces into the prison enclosure the memory of the outside world, fortifying the soul against a cruel fate. In secularized form, this representation from the end of the century invests new meaning in ancient images of devotional reading in which a reader (often, Saint Jerome or Saint Paul) in a voluntary retreat nourished or experienced his faith in a solitary relationship with Scripture.

In counterpoint to solitary readers, other paintings attested to the ongoing practice of reading in society. The *Lecture de Molière* by Jean-François de Troy (1728, Collection of the marquess of Cholmondeley; see the cover illustration of volume 3 of this encyclopedia) depicts an opulent salon where an aristocratic company of two men and five women listen to Molière being read by one of the men. The women, dressed informally, are comfortably settled in their armchairs; one leans toward the reader to watch the text he is reading. In the back of the room is a low bookshelf surmounted by a clock that reads half past three. The reader has stopped; his listeners catch or avoid one another's gaze, as if listening has sent each back to his or her own thoughts or desires.

The aesthetic that governs Troy's painting presupposes the presence of the spectator, arrested by the glances that the subjects address to him. Other painters might represent people who are unconscious of being observed—readers, the engrossed, the sleeping, or the blind. Diderot was the theoretician of this paradoxical aesthetic, which made the effect of the work depend on the negation of the place of the spectator or, as in the case of Richardson's novels, of the reader. For him, the production of this absence, by and through the work itself, was the condition of its power. It founded simultaneously its theatrical or romantic aesthetic, which privileged the transformation of intrigue in paintings, and its strongly dramatic concept of painting. Like all representations, those the authors and painters of the eighteenth century gave of reading are not to be read, or seen, as a direct reflection of social practices but, first, as the expression of the intentions and codes that dictated them.

[*See also* Diderot, Denis; Encyclopédie; Jaucourt, Louis; Novel; Painting; Print Culture; Reading and Reading Practices; *and* Richardson, Samuel.]

BIBLIOGRAPHY

Chartier, Roger. "Diderot, Richardson, et la lectrice impatiente." *MLN* 114 (1999), 647–666.

Fried, Michael. *Absorption and Theatricality: Painting and Beholder in the Age of Diderot*. Berkeley, Los Angeles, and London, 1980.

Goulemot, Jean Marie. *Forbidden Texts: Erotic Literature and its Readers in Eighteenth-Century France*. Philadelphia, 1994.

Nies, Fritz. *Bahn und Bett und Blütenduft: Eine Reise durch die Welt der Leserbilder*. Darmstadt, Germany, 1991.

Schön, Erich. *Der Verlust der Sinnlichkeit oder Die Verwandlung des Lesers: Mentalitätswandel um 1800*. Stuttgart, Germany, 1987.

Wittmann, Reinhard. *Buchmarkt und Lektüre im 18. und 19. Jahrhundert: Beiträge zum literarischen Leben, 1750–1850*. Tübingen, 1982.

ROGER CHARTIER

Translated from French by Sylvia J. Cannizzaro

REPUBLICANISM. [*This entry contains six subentries, an overview and discussions of republicanism in* Great Britain, The United States, France, The Netherlands, *and* Latin America.]

An Overview

Republicanism, the school of thought advocating government by free citizens and their representatives rather than by hereditary nobles or monarchs, is one of the central but most contested ideas of the Enlightenment. From the late seventeenth to the early nineteenth centuries in Europe, North America, and other lands influenced by the ferment of the Age of Reason, the two-thousand-year tradition of republican thinking was a central arena of writing and debate. Modern versions of republicanism arose in Britain, the Continent, and America, invoking the classical Greek and Roman republics and the medieval and Renaissance city-states. The new republicans had to confront, however, the philosophical claims of liberalism, which prized individual liberty and rights over traditional republican concerns with communal liberty and civic participation. Scholars continue to debate the relationship between classical republicanism, liberalism, and modern republicanism in the chief writings and events of the two great revolutions of the period in America and France. While liberalism dominated political theory in the West during the late twentieth century, various forms of republicanism reappeared as an influential criticism of liberal individualism and materialism.

The Republican Tradition, Constitutional Monarchy, and Machiavelli's Legacy. Republicanism arose in classical Greece and Rome with the argument that politics and government were "the common affair" (in Latin, *res publica*), not the private reserve of hereditary monarchs or oligarchs. Republican government was to be conducted by citizens, or by their elected representatives, with citizenship limited to free males and often further restricted by wealth and place of birth. Aristotle argued in his account of "polity" that republican government was distinct from democracy—rule by the popular masses—and most classical and medieval theorists agreed. Republics thus took more aristocratic or more democratic forms, always emphasizing some degree of citizen participation and, in particular, military service to defend the regime. The classical republican theory of Plato, Aristotle, Cicero, and Polybius therefore emphasizes civic virtue and the cultivation of character traits required to repel threats from kings, tyrants, and hereditary rule generally. The aim of a republic was the common weal and the liberty of the citizenry, a life of religious, martial, and civic virtue defined by communal understanding. Republics thus were related to, but distinct from, the "mixed regime" hailed by Aristotle and Polybius as the key to stable, secure, and equitable political rule, since the latter combined the claims to rule and the distinctive institutions of monarchs, aristocrats, and democrats alike.

Republicanism declined in the face of the Alexandrian and Roman Empires and did not resurface with their demise. A revival began with the small communes and complex monarchies of medieval Europe, which coincided with the rediscovery of Aristotle by the Latin West in the twelfth and thirteenth centuries. The scholastic theologian Thomas Aquinas argued that politics and political prudence were worthy of human concern and not exclusively the church's domain, and anticipated modern constitutionalism by reformulating the argument for a mixed regime. The constitutional monarchies of late medieval and early-modern Europe limited royal power through complicated laws and institutions, defining the claims of nobles, the church, and eventually the common people through parliaments or assemblies. The medieval Italian city-states emphasized civic participation and military defense, with citizenship largely the preserve of patrician families and wealthy merchants. Niccolò Machiavelli's *Discorsi sopra la prima deca di Tito Livio* (Discourses on Livy, c. 1517) has been hailed as the masterwork of Renaissance republican theory, and Enlightenment authors cite the fundamental strains of both modern liberalism and modern republicanism it contains. There is significant debate about Machiavelli's influence upon republicanism in the modern period and upon the Enlightenment generally, with some finding his "civic humanism" a development of the classical republicanism of Aristotle and Cicero (see J. G. A. Pocock, *The Machiavellian Moment*, 1975; and Quentin Skinner, *The Foundations of Modern Political Thought*, 1978). Others find his ruthless concern with political and material success, his criticisms of Christianity, and his equal advice to republics and tyrants evident both in the *Discourses* and *Il principe* (The Prince, c. 1513) as the source of a fundamental break with classical republicanism and with classical and medieval philosophy generally (see Leo Strauss, *Thoughts on Machiavelli*, Chicago, 1958; and Harvey Mansfield, *Machiavelli's Virtue*, 1996). At the cusp of the Enlightenment period the versions of republican thinking advanced in England by James Harrington (1611–1677) and Algernon Sidney (1622–1683) criticized absolute monarchy in the name of liberty. Meanwhile, the foundations of liberalism laid by Thomas Hobbes (1588–1679) and Baruch de Spinoza (1632–1677) challenged the established order of throne and church from another direction.

Liberalism and Modern Republicanism. The most influential theorist of Enlightenment liberalism, and of what might be called liberal republicanism, was the English philosopher John Locke (1632–1704). His *Two Treatises of Government* (1689) justified Parliament's establishment of a new monarch in the Glorious Revolution of 1688, but also laid the foundations for subsequent liberal democratic thinking. Locke's *First Treatise* attacked the theory of divine right of kings in the classic manner of Enlightenment philosophy, trusting to human reason over any received tradition, whether Scripture, inherited political forms, or the patriarchal family. He developed this philosophy, seemingly sympathetic to republicanism, in the *Second Treatise*, by advancing doctrines about human nature, natural rights, and the aims of government that favored modern liberalism over traditional republican concerns. Locke adapted Hobbes's state of nature theory about the original social contract to emphasize not just the original consent of individuals to government but continual consent. The aim of all just, reasonable government is protection of individual rights to life, liberty, and property. Locke was associated with the radical Whigs and Levelers and thus with republican politics in late-seventeenth-century England, and the tenor of his political philosophy favors ruling popular majorities. Still, his constitutionalism emphasized an institutional separation of powers and individual security more than republican concerns with participation, civic virtue, and the common weal. His endorsement of the rule of law but also of a right of revolution echoed republicanism, but his emphasis on acquisition of personal wealth and a continual executive prerogative successfully pulled antimonarchical thinking toward modern concerns with utility and commerce. The emphasis on individual autonomy in the *Two Treatises* is elaborated in his *Letter Concerning Toleration* (1689) and *Reasonableness of Christianity* (1695), works that transformed republican liberty toward the Enlightenment distinction between state and society and advanced the trend toward modern secularism.

Classical republicanism seems to have fared better in France than in Lockean England, but here, too, debate arises as to whether criticisms of monarchy and of early-modern European politics were informed more by liberal modernity or the republican tradition. Montesquieu (1689–1755) echoed Machiavelli's celebration of the Roman republic in his *Considérations sur les causes de la grandeur des romains* (Considerations on the Causes of the Greatness of the Romans, 1734), but as with Machiavelli there is novel praise for the factionalism of the republic and an endorsement of imperial greatness. Montesquieu thought that Roman factionalism generated the energy and military expansion that secured greater power, thereby challenging an Aristotelian political science that sought to avoid conflict through legally balanced claims to rule and proper civic character. Montesquieu's complicated relationship with classical republicanism continues in his influential *L'esprit des lois* (The Spirit of Laws, 1748), a work not studied as widely today as Locke's *Second Treatise*, even though it was more directly important to the framers of the most successful modern constitution, the American Constitution of 1787, than was Locke's text. Early in his massive work Montesquieu seems to praise small republics for their emphasis on political virtue and civic liberty. His further inquiries into the proper spirit of laws for any given people and place fully reveal, however, his doubts about the suitability of republicanism in light of modern views about liberty, security, and commerce. His ideal regime would approximate the complicated institutions and party politics developing in eighteenth-century England, where the relevant remnants of republicanism—a concern for liberty and participation—were blended with the modern imperatives of a large territory, wealth, and protection of individual conscience and property. Montesquieu's criticisms and adaptations of republicanism were both anticipated and elaborated by David Hume (1711–1776), then by such other thinkers of the Scottish Enlightenment as Adam Smith (1723–1790). Along with the English jurist William Blackstone (1723–1780), this Montesquieuian strain in the Enlightenment developed the ideas of institutional separation, federalism, political economy, property law, and interest-based politics fundamental to modern liberal democracy. Their own thinking, and that of the American framers who studied them, sought to some degree to accommodate traditional concerns with individual moral virtue, religious belief, and public-spiritedness. Still, the liberal elements in this synthesis have weakened the republican elements over time, eventually giving rise to the globalized phenomenon of liberal, commercial society predominant today.

These philosophical and intellectual developments are interwoven with particular political events and criticisms of church and throne. For example, the oligarchic republics of Venice and Genoa remained powerful well into the Enlightenment, although their demise in the Napoleonic wars seemed to confirm Montesquieu's view that commerce and political power are viable in modernity only given the large territory available in federalized republics or liberalized monarchies. The Swiss federation maintained a vibrant participatory republicanism throughout the modern period in part due to its secure mountain location, and to the greater respect for material success evident in Protestantism. Events in Geneva and in Poland in the latter half of the eighteenth century, however, led to consideration of the striking revival of classical republicanism attempted by Rousseau.

Rousseau, Kant, and the Dilemmas of Modern Republicanism. Rousseau (1712–1778) criticized modern liberal philosophy—and any accommodations with it made by republicans—in the name of the nobler politics of Sparta and Rome. His two *Discourses* (1750, 1755) reveal both a son of the Enlightenment and a severe critic of human reason and progress. He repudiated modern commerce, science, and technology, while defining humans as radically historical beings who developed reason only through the happenstance of social proximity. His *Du contract social* (The Social Contract, 1762) sought to salvage Enlightenment concerns with individual rights and rational self-governance despite the fact that the *Discourses* had undermined their foundations in nature. Claiming inspiration from his birthplace, the Calvinist republic of Geneva, he argued that all other regimes were illegitimate and tried to revive the collective politics of classical republicanism on radically modern foundations. The common weal became "the general will," the great founder became "the great legislator," and the concern with civic character and revealed religion became a modern civil religion that openly replaced the City of God with the City of Man. Representation was repudiated in favor of direct citizen participation, but he accepted the necessity of administering a large state through a modern executive and civil service that implemented the general will.

When the Confederation of Bar in Poland (1768–1772) commissioned his advice for establishing a republic free of the intrigues of Europe's dynasties, Rousseau's

Considerations sur le gouvernement de Pologne (Considerations on Poland, 1762) surprisingly accommodated many traditional aristocratic dimensions of Polish republicanism. While the early leaders of the French Revolution adopted a similar stance, the eventual leaders insisted upon the purer, radical aspects of Rousseau's doctrines. Even as those principles produced a new Roman militarism and paved the way for a new Roman dictator, the German philosopher Immanuel Kant (1724–1804) envisioned more moderate consequences of modern popular revolution. His *Zum ewigen Frieden* (Perpetual Peace, 1795) suggested that democracies committed to moral egalitarianism would not wage war upon each other, and that thus, a league of republics could build historical momentum toward world peace and security. One criticism of this "democratic peace" theory, and of the collective security efforts of the League of Nations (1919) and United Nations (1946), is that individualistic, tranquillity-loving liberal republics fail to support the military preparations or tough diplomacy that, given a particular enemy, might achieve peace more readily than statements of peaceful intentions. The recent school of communitarianism or civic republicanism in political theory similarly criticizes the loss of civic purpose and political dignity under Enlightenment liberalism, and debates the relative presence of republican and liberal ideas in the eighteenth century. Still, few civic republicans today advocate restoration of the more inegalitarian aspects of republicanism. The practical and theoretical efficacy of recent criticisms of liberalism and globalization may rest upon how seriously we are willing to examine the fundamental tenets of modern republicanism and liberalism, and to consider alternative views.

[*See also* Bill of Rights; Constitution of the United States; Democracy; French Revolution; Hume, David; Jefferson, Thomas; Kant, Immanuel; Locke, John; Montesquieu, Charles de Secondat; Natural Rights; Political Philosophy; Republicanism, *subentry on* The United States; *and* Rousseau, Jean-Jacques.]

BIBLIOGRAPHY

PRIMARY SOURCES

Hume, David. *Essays: Moral, Political, and Literary.* Edited by Eugene Miller. Indianapolis, 1985.

Kant, Immanuel. *Kant's Political Writings.* 2d ed. Edited by Hans Reiss and translated by H. B. Nisbet. Cambridge, 1991.

Locke, John. *Two Treatises of Government.* Edited by Peter Laslett. Cambridge, 1988.

Montesquieu, Baron de. *The Spirit of the Laws.* Edited by Anne Cohler, Basia Miller, and Harold Stone. Cambridge, 1989.

Rousseau, Jean-Jacques. *The Social Contract, with Geneva Manuscript and Political Economy.* Edited by Roger Masters. New York, 1978.

SECONDARY SOURCES

Ashcraft, Richard. *Revolutionary Politics and Locke's Two Treatises of Government.* Princeton, N.J., 1986. Examines Locke's political philosophy in the historical context of late-eighteenth-century England, with particular attention to his radical Whig and republican activities.

The Invention of the Modern Republic. Edited by Biancamaria Fontana. Cambridge, 1994. Scholars examine the political thought of modern republicanism in historical context, generally suggesting that modern innovations are recognizable developments of the republican tradition.

Kant and Political Philosophy: The Contemporary Legacy. Edited by Ronald Beiner and William James Booth. New Haven, Conn., 1993. Diverse scholars examine the connection between Kant's philosophical writings, practical issues of his day, and enduring issues in political thought and international relations.

The Legacy of Rousseau. Edited by Clifford Orwin and Nathan Tarcov. Chicago, 1997. American and French scholars examine Rousseau's political and moral philosophy, and his relation to the French Revolution and subsequent international relations theory.

Machiavelli and Republicanism. Edited by Gisela Bock, Quentin Skinner, and Maurizio Viroli. Cambridge, 1990. Elaborates the view of Pocock and Skinner that, when Machiavelli and the thinkers he influenced are understood in historical context, modern republicanism can be seen as a development of classical republicanism.

Pangle, Thomas. *The Spirit of Modern Republicanism: The Moral Vision of the American Founders and the Philosophy of Locke.* Chicago, 1988. Argues, in the vein of Leo Strauss, that modern republicanism is fundamentally indebted to modern liberalism and thus marks a decisive break with the classical tradition.

Rahe, Paul. *Republics Ancient and Modern.* Volume 2, *New Modes and Order in Early Modern Political Thought.* Volume 3, *Inventions of Prudence: Constituting the American Regime.* Chapel Hill, N.C., 1992–1994. The final two volumes of a compendious study of both political philosophy and history, arguing that modern republicanism breaks with the classical tradition but that the American founding synthesized liberalism, modern republicanism, and classical republican ideas.

Riesenberg, Peter. *Citizenship in the Western Tradition: Plato to Rousseau.* Chapel Hill, N.C., 1992. An historical study of citizenship and republicanism in classical Greece and Rome, the medieval and Renaissance Italian cities, and the eighteenth century and French revolutionary eras in Europe.

PAUL O. CARRESE

Great Britain

During the 1640s, a series of arguments were put forward that supported the establishment of a republic in Great Britain—among them, that no defense against a tyrannical king existed other than civil war and that the nation's constitutional structure placed the natural executive authority in the hands of Parliament. One of the most significant groups that called for a republic during this period was the Levellers; it maintained that inasmuch as all political power ultimately rested in the hands of the people, then a constitutional structure that provided the king and lords veto power over legislation was ultimately flawed. The religious sympathies of many antiroyalists, particularly their opposition to the power of episcopacy, suggested that they also opposed monarchical authority. In addition, Calvinist doctrine was interpreted as conferring on the people a right of resistance against a monarch who violated God's ordinances. Finally, support for a republic was often linked to the concepts of consent and of rights, as was the case with John Milton and Marchamont Nedham. This was particularly true in republican writing after 1660. Apprehensions about centralized power were regularly couched in terms of the prescriptive rights of Englishmen, as well as of the need for a vigilant electorate to act as guardians of English liberty.

The most important republican theorist of the period was James Harrington (1611–1677), author of *The Commonwealth of Oceana* (1656), whose political philosophy was couched in the language of civil religion. A great admirer of ancient Israel, Harrington fashioned his own commonwealth along similar lines, wherein religion served to make better citizens. Its stability and health, he concluded, rested on a clear separation of public and private interests, as well as on laws that ensured a balance of property, which would restrain men from pursuing their selfish interests. Only when private concerns were effectively subordinated to the public good could the polity flourish. The health of the republic and the well-being of its subjects lay not in the pursuit of individual gain, but rather, in an electorate that had effectively identified its own welfare with that of the commonwealth. Harrington was preoccupied with preserving a virtuous freeholding citizenry, independent of government patronage, who actively participated in public life. As a consequence, he regarded commerce and the marketplace as corrupting forces. Harrington said nothing about abstract rights and liberties; he did not find the locus of oppression in the state but in corruption. These views bear the indelible imprint of Italian political philosopher Niccolò Machiavelli (1469–1527), to whom Harrington and the civic humanist writers who followed him were deeply indebted. Harrington's views were to give shape and direction to the writings of his contemporary Henry Neville and to a host of Augustan writers, among them Andrew Fletcher of Saltoun and Henry St. John, Viscount Bolingbroke. All displayed a preference for landed wealth and agrarian values and were preoccupied with questions of political morality and corruption.

Although the Interregnum and the Restoration muted explicit calls for the establishment of a republic in Great Britain, they did not mark an end to republican sentiments. In fact, the term *republic*, as it was often understood in Great Britain from the sixteenth century through the eighteenth, referred to any form of government in which power was widely shared and the public interest was given priority over private concerns. In this broader sense, the principles of republicanism were regarded as perfectly compatible with constitutional monarchy, and most republican theorists writing after 1660 were quite prepared to accept monarchical government provided it were constrained by suitable safeguards against royal tyranny. Even Algernon Sidney, one of the foremost Whig radicals and a zealous republican, at one point was prepared to support the restored monarchy. Sidney's *Discourses Concerning Government*, published in 1698, some fifteen years after the author's execution for sedition, blends discussions of the traditional rights of Englishmen against oppressive government, the right of resistance, and political authority's sole reliance on the consent of the governed, with more classic civic humanist concerns, such as the need for a vigilant landowning electorate and the identification of liberty with a virtuous citizenry.

Although republican sentiments continued to be voiced after the Glorious Revolution, they were partially eclipsed by the theory of inalienable rights and limited government that was put forward by John Locke in his *Second Treatise of Government* (1690). Locke's essay was to have the effect of recasting mainstream political theory in Britain and providing a new set of political principles that were to dominate eighteenth-century political discourse: All men in the state of nature are equal; the basis of all legitimate government is the consent of the governed; all men possess certain inviolable rights; and the civil magistrate is bound by the terms of the original contract by which he holds authority to respect these rights. Should the civil magistrate violate this contract, people have a right to resist him. While the Lockean paradigm greatly weakened the concerns of civic humanism, it did not entirely replace them. In fact, Locke was deeply concerned with the moral dimensions of productive labor and with man as a social and political being.

Possibly the best example of the political language of post-Lockean Whig thought appears in John Trenchard's and Thomas Gordon's *Cato's Letters*, originally published between 1720 and 1723. The letters are a preeminent instance of the literature of political opposition during the Augustan Age and for the next fifty years were to serve as exceptionally important revolutionary tracts in the American colonial struggle against the crown (1763–1783). While *Cato's Letters* embraced a Lockean conception of rights and individual liberty and spoke favorably of commerce and trade, they had strong elements of classical republicanism, particularly an emphasis on corruption and a fear of the gratification of private passion at the public expense. Although earlier republicanism had misgivings about commerce and trade in all its manifestations, this had been transmuted during the late seventeenth century and early eighteenth into a distrust of commercial activity solely when it was linked to government. Only when the public expense was subordinated to private concerns, that is, only when the government was manipulated to advance the special interests of a few at the expense of the many did self-interest clash with the duties of a citizen. British republicanism's legacy to the American colonies was, in the main, of this type. To the extent that

Thomas Jefferson and James Madison, among others, were sympathetic to classical republicanism, it was in this sense, that the danger to society lay in the intrusion of government into the marketplace, thus magnifying the effects of private passion to the detriment of the people. Their misgivings centered not on commerce, but on the marriage of commerce and the state.

In this attenuated sense, republicanism had its greatest impact on the founding of the United States of America. Jefferson's admiration for those engaged in agrarian pursuits rested their self-reliant character, neither dependent on the largesse of government nor obligated to its functionaries. The coupling of trade and industry with government would, he felt, corrupt the polity and lead inexorably to tyranny. For that reason, American citizens were enjoined to be eternally vigilant of their liberties, a theme that was again voiced during and after the French Revolution, in the closing years of the eighteenth century.

[*See also* American Revolution; Democracy; Glorious Revolution; Locke, John; *and* Political Philosophy.]

BIBLIOGRAPHY

Appleby, Joyce. *Liberalism and Republicanism in the Historical Imagination*. Cambridge, Mass., 1992. Traces the development of liberal and republican ideas from seventeenth-century England to late eighteenth-century United States of America.

Barber, Sarah. *Regicide and Republicanism: Politics and Ethics in the English Revolution, 1646–1659*. Edinburgh, 1998. An excellent account of arguments put forward in support of regicide and for the establishment of a republic during England's Civil War.

Brugger, Bill. *Republican Theory in Political Thought: Virtuous or Virtual?* New York, 1999. An overview of republican principles as they were manifested in political writing, from the mid-seventeenth century to the present. Brugger's attempt to schematize differing aspects of republicanism tends to slight the complexities associated with the term and does an injustice to the writers he cites.

Huyler, Jerome. *Locke in America: The Moral Philosophy of the Founding Era*. Lawrence, Kan., 1995. A thorough exploration of Locke's role in shaping eighteenth-century U.S. political thought; contributes to the understanding of republicanism in the New World.

Kramnick, Isaac. *Republicanism and Bourgeois Radicalism: Political Ideology in Late Eighteenth-Century England and America*. Ithaca, N.Y., 1990.

Pangle, Thomas L. *The Spirit of Modern Republicanism: The Moral Vision of the American Founders and the Philosophy of Locke*. Chicago, 1988. Offers the view that republicanism, as it was understood by the American founders, was a fusion of classical republican and Lockean ideas.

Peltonen, Markku. *Classical Humanism and Republicanism in English Political Thought, 1570–1640*. Cambridge, 1995.

Pocock, J. G. A. *The Machiavellian Moment: Florentine Political Thought and the Atlantic Tradition*. Princeton, N.J., 1975. By far the most important work tracing eighteenth-century political thought to the civic humanist tradition Niccolò Machiavelli and James Harrington.

Wootton, David, ed., *Republicanism, Liberty, and Commercial Society, 1649–1776*. Stanford, Calif., 1994. The best overall study of republicanism, spanning the period from England's Civil War to the American Revolution.

Zuckert, Michael. *Natural Rights and the New Republicanism*. Princeton, N.J., 1994. An important monograph on the link between the theory of natural rights and radical Whig thought, including its republican manifestations.

RONALD HAMOWY

The United States

When royal authority was tightly fastened around the American colonies in 1763, Americans rapidly turned to republicanism as the ideological basis for their opposition to monarchy and as an imperative for their social and political arrangements. If republicanism was almost universally accepted by eighteenth-century Americans, however, its meaning was a source of constant disputation. In an oft-quoted remark, John Adams once complained that "there is not a more unintelligible word in the English language than republicanism." More recently, scholars of the American founding have traced out a number of varieties of republicanism, including civic republicanism, liberal republicanism, agrarian republicanism, and labor republicanism, and have debated the character of Anglo-American republicanism.

Commonwealth Ideology, Lockean Natural Rights, and the American Revolution. The distinctively American variation of republicanism that accompanied the American Revolution was opposed to monarchical absolutism, to all hereditary, class, and party privilege, and to "democracy," which was still thought of as the turbulent rule of the many. American republicanism was grounded in a commitment to popular government and to the rule of law rather than of men. In constructing an American republicanism to justify independence from the British monarchy, American colonists doubtlessly drew upon and synthesized ideas from many sources, including common law, British constitutionalism, Roman republicanism, classical literature, and Protestant Christianity. Two sets of ideas, however, were most important in the formation of early American republicanism and thus central to its initial meaning. These were commonwealth or Country Party ideology and Lockean natural rights philosophy.

Brought to the American colonists through the writings of seventeenth- and eighteenth-century English "coffeehouse radicals," including John Trenchard and Thomas Gordon, Algernon Sidney, and Benjamin Hoadly, Country Party ideology was an extreme form of libertarianism rooted in a profound suspicion that liberty was perpetually threatened by the exercise of governmental power. Country Party radicals opposed not only standing armies but ministerial corruption, which they believed was fostered by the king's use of placemen and patronage. Conversely, they favored mixed and balanced constitutional forms, glorified the independent proprietor, and emphasized the fragility of republican governments and the necessity within them of the exercise of self-denying virtue.

Although relatively unimportant in seventeenth- and eighteenth-century Britain, this constellation of ideas was, according to its leading student, "devoured" by the American colonists because it provided them with a logic for opposing the reimposition of British rule in the colonies after the Seven Years' War ended in 1763 (Bailyn, 1967, 43). When, for example, the colonists decried the Sugar Act, Stamp Act, and eventually the Tea Act and Boston Port Act, they increasingly voiced the belief that the English government had become unbalanced and "corrupt."

While commonwealth ideology provided American colonists with a framework for identifying the conspiracy against their liberties and for opposing British rule as a threat to their virtue, Lockean natural rights philosophy provided them with a justification for rebellion that could be presented to the impartial opinion of the world and that was based on the threat that an arbitrary and tyrannical monarch posed to inalienable rights. Exemplified in the Declaration of Independence, Lockean natural rights philosophy rested on the proposition that "all men are created equal" or, differently put, that all men are independent and equal before the formation of civil society because no one is by nature subject to the authority of others. This proposition suggested to Thomas Jefferson and other Americans that governments are artifices created and given legitimacy by the consent of the governed. Most importantly however, it also suggested that legitimate governments are instituted to protect the unalienable or nontransferable, God-given rights of the citizenry and that when they systematically violate these rights, rebellion is justified.

Forms of American Republicanism. If the American amalgam of commonwealth ideology and Lockean natural rights philosophy provided a widely shared vocabulary upon which the American Revolution was perceived and justified, the founders nevertheless soon disagreed fundamentally among themselves about how "popular" their republican governments should be and how they should be structured. Inspired by opposition ideology and written immediately following independence, the first state constitutions were designed to prevent executive usurpation of power and to ensure that public officials were under the immediate control of the people. Many of these constitutions gave the lion's share of power to the legislative branch, provided for the election of numerous representatives from relatively circumscribed districts, required annual elections of these representatives, and established provisions by which the people could petition and instruct their representatives. Meanwhile, the Articles of Confederation created a unicameral national government empowered primarily to conduct external defense. Not ratified until 1781, the articles created a government that was modeled after ancient confederations, as each state retained all power not expressly enumerated in the document and exercised equal influence through its one vote in Congress.

As is well known, however, the men who eventually framed the United States Constitution believed that the national government created by the Articles of Confederation was not strong enough to command respect at home or abroad and that the republican state governments were excessively democratic. The impotence of the national government, James Madison argued in his famous essay "Vices of the Political System of the United States," was evident in its inability to collect requisitions and to prevent the states from encroaching on national prerogatives, from engaging in commercial warfare with each other, and from violating treaties. The problems of the state governments, Madison continued, were visible in the "multiplicity," "mutability," and "injustices" of their laws. Problems such as those experienced by the states, Madison maintained in *The Federalist Papers*, "have in truth been the mortal diseases under which popular governments have every where perished."

The task set in Philadelphia for the framers of the American Constitution of 1788 was to address both of these sets of problems while working within the imperatives of a revolutionary ideology that demanded that any government fit for the American people must be "strictly republican." They thus developed a new form of republican government based upon a "new science of government." The government created by the American Constitution of 1788 was grounded in popular sovereignty and thus could be said to be "strictly republican." Nevertheless, the framers also believed that extent of territory, staggered and indirect schemes of election, the election of representatives from large legislative districts, six-year terms for senators and life appointments for federal judges, and a system of checks designed to give independence to the Senate, and Executive would not only protect liberty, but also promote energy, stability, and wisdom.

The Antifederalists countered that the government proposed in 1788 would result in an aristocracy or oligarchy. Drawing heavily upon the republicanism of 1776, the Antifederalists raised fears of unlimited taxation, corrupted representation, standing armies, and, in general, violations of the natural rights of the people. They also argued that the proposed Constitution would lead to the abolishment of the state governments and to the uncontrollable expansion of judicial and executive power within the national government.

In general, disagreements over whether republican government required direct popular influence or only popular control continued long after the ratification of the Constitution. On one side of the political spectrum, John Adams and Alexander Hamilton both stressed the stability that was gained by long and even lifetime appointments for public officials. This position made them vulnerable to the charge that they were "monarchists" or "aristocrats," not true champions of republican government. On the other side of this spectrum, Jefferson came to believe that "action by the citizens in person, in affairs within their reach and competence, and in all others by representatives, chosen immediately, and removable by themselves, constitutes the essence of a republic." As a result of such statements, Jefferson and many other members of his party were often accused of being radical democrats or Jacobins.

Character of American Republicanism. When ratification of the Constitution was completed, Americans entered into a new stage of political development and began to address a different set of questions. In this stage, Americans confronted questions about how they wished to define themselves as a people and to be viewed by the world, about what kind of relationship they wanted with their mother country, about how their economic life would be organized, and in general about the moral character of their nation. These issues—especially questions about political economy—divided the nation into its first political parties, which in turn articulated contrasting visions of American republicanism.

Hoping to replicate in America the economic plan that had led to Great Britain's emergence as a world power, Hamilton developed his systematic, highly structured, and integrated program of public finance and plan for industrialization. Hamilton's system included the generous funding of both the continental debt and state debts incurred during the Revolution. Thus concentrated and liquidated, the debt could become a "public blessing" because it would act as a capital fund to be used by merchants in building businesses and expanding American commerce and industry. It would also, Hamilton believed, create a consolidated national elite composed of creditors, military officers, merchants, and bankers.

In Hamilton's vision of America's future, this program for funding and assumption of the national debt was to be linked with the creation of a national bank to provide a stable currency and a source of credit for the merchant elite. Hamilton's economic program also provided for government encouragement of manufactures for those industries that would promote the most widespread prosperity. The ability of the United States to achieve these goals, Hamilton and the Federalists realized, depended upon an extensive view of the powers of the national government and thus broad construction of the Constitution and also on sound and stable commercial relations with Great Britain.

In contrast to this vision of "commercial republicanism," the Jeffersonian Republicans believed that the United States should remain primarily an agrarian nation. This would best be done, Madison and Jefferson argued, by combining commercial discrimination against nations that refused to negotiate favorable trade policies with the United States with land expansion to perpetuate an agrarian society and to forestall the development of large-scale public manufacturing in the United States. Tonnage discrimination against British ships, the Jeffersonians fully understood, might create commercial warfare with Great Britain, but it was necessary, they believed, to help secure economic independence from Great Britain. In the eyes of the Jeffersonian Republicans, the Constitution had been written—and indeed the Revolution had been fought, in part at least—to ensure independence and reciprocity for American shipping and to defend America's national honor.

Furthermore, the Jeffersonians believed that, when combined with westward expansion, the exportation of America's agricultural products would allow the ever-increasing population of the United States to remain occupied as farmers and prevent them from being reduced to wage labor or government dependency. An agrarian citizenry, both Madison and Jefferson believed, was uniquely capable of exercising the independent virtue necessary for republican self-government. In direct opposition to Hamilton's financial system, this vision of American republicanism was biased toward the South and agricultural interests, and it was premised on a healthy respect for constitutional limits on the powers of the national government, a corresponding respect for the residual powers of the states, and a commitment to the meaning of the Constitution as it was understood at ratification.

Republicanism and American Political Identity. Finally, in all of its forms, American republicanism was initially important in the formation of American political identity and has had a strong, recurring role in American political development. Most obviously, the tension within America's natural rights republicanism between the liberal strain emphasizing the protection of individual rights and the republican strain emphasizing political participation and popular rule has been one of the most constant sources of political conflict in United States history. Throughout U.S. history, Americans have fought over the extent of the majority's power, the recognition and limitations of rights, and over whether the protection of these rights unduly impedes the realization of broad public purposes.

In addition, American republicanism was initially linked to justifications for excluding African Americans, Native Americans, and women from political participation. In particular, the idea of federalism within American republicanism reflected a residue of the classical republican belief that the republican form of government could exist only within a small geographical area with a homogeneous and martial citizenry. Acting upon the desire to promote homogeneity, states often passed laws excluding nonwhite males from political participation. Meanwhile, women were excluded from political participation on the beliefs that they would be corrupted by politics, could not meet the republican requirements of economic independence and martial virtue, and were naturally suited as "republican mothers" who could best serve the nation by preparing their male children for political participation.

More commonly, though, strains within the unique amalgam of America's republicanism have also provided an inspiration for democratic reform and a perfectionistic impulse within American political thought. The Lockean liberal strain within American republicanism has forced repeated confrontations between Americans' professed beliefs in natural equality and the equal rights of all and its exclusionary policies. Meanwhile, Country Party ideology has reenforced Americans' suspicions about governmental corruption and their beliefs in the necessity of virtue and vigilance in both public officials and the citizenry.

[*See also* Adams, John; American Revolution; Bill of Rights; Constitution of the United States; Declaration of Independence; Democracy; Federalist, The; Federalists and Antifederalists; Jefferson, Thomas; Natural Rights; *and* Political Philosophy.]

BIBLIOGRAPHY

Appleby, Joyce. "Republicanism in Old and New Contexts." *William and Mary Quarterly* 42 (1982), 20–34. Here, and in her other writings, Appleby has called for the interpretation of Jeffersonian political and economic ideas as a species of Lockean liberalism.

Bailyn, Bernard. *The Ideological Origins of the American Revolution.* Cambridge, Mass., 1967; repr., 1992. Bailyn's pathbreaking study traced out the importance of "commonwealth ideology" to American Revolutionaries and launched a historiographical revolution.

Banning, Lance. *The Jeffersonian Persuasion: Evolution of a Party Ideology.* Ithaca, N.Y., 1978. Challenging Gordon Wood's contention that the formation of the American Constitution of 1787 marked the "end of classical politics," Banning contends that commonwealth ideology continued to be an important dimension of Jeffersonian opposition ideology even as the Jeffersonians modernized and adapted the ideas that they inherited.

Banning, Lance. "Jeffersonian Ideology Revisited: Liberal and Classical Ideas in the New American Republic." *William and Mary Quarterly* 39 (1982), 3–19. Banning counters Appleby's liberal interpretation by urging scholars to understand Jeffersonian ideas as a complex blend of modern liberalism and classical republicanism.

Cornell, Saul. *The Other Founders: Anti-Federalism and the Dissenting Tradition in America, 1788–1828.* Chapel Hill, N.C., 1999. Excellent study of Antifederalist thought in general and in particular of the Antifederalists' legacy of the suspicion of centralized power.

Elkins, Stanley, and Eric McKitrick. *The Age of Federalism: The Early American Republic, 1788–1800.* New York, 1993. The definitive historical narrative of the 1790s, this work is especially important for its exploration of the conflicting understandings of the character of American republicanism held by the Jeffersonian Republicans and the Federalists.

Gibson, Alan. "Ancients, Moderns, and Americans: The Republicanism-Liberalism Debate Revisited." *History of Political Thought* 21 (2000), 261–307. This essay examines the scholarly consensus that has emerged in the last decade over the question of whether the political thought of the American founders is best described as a species of liberalism or republicanism.

Kerber, Linda. *Women of the Republic.* Chapel Hill, N.C., 1980. Documents the ideology of "republican motherhood" and the legal and social status of women in the early republic.

Lutz, Donald S. *Popular Consent and Popular Control: Whig Political Theory in the Early State Constitutions.* Baton Rouge, La., 1980. Lutz establishes the differences between the understandings of consent embodied in the state constitutions written from 1776 to 1787 and the Federalist conception of consent written into the U.S. Constitution of 1788.

McCoy, Drew. *The Elusive Republic: Political Economy in Jeffersonian America.* Chapel Hill, N.C., 1980. Definitive study of the political economy of the American founders and their understandings of the social and economic conditions necessary for the maintenance of republican governments.

Pocock, J. G. A. *The Machiavellian Moment: Florentine Political Thought and the Atlantic Republic Tradition.* Princeton, N.J., 1975. Along with the studies of Bailyn and Wood, one of the masterworks of the "republican synthesis."

Rahe, Paul. *Republics: Ancient and Modern: Classical Republicanism and the American Revolution.* Chapel Hill, N.C., 1992. Encyclopedic analysis of the history of republicanism from the ancients to the American Revolution, stressing the fundamental differences between ancient and American republicanism.

Rodgers, Daniel T. "Republicanism: The Career of a Concept." *Journal of American History* 79 (June 1992), 11–38. A definitive historiographical essay on the emergence of the republican interpretation, the methodological assumptions underlying it, and its transformation.

Shalhope, Robert. "Toward a Republican Synthesis: The Emergence of an Understanding of Republicanism in American Historiography." *William and Mary Quarterly* 29 (1972), 49–80.

Shalhope, Robert. "Republicanism and Early American Historiography." *William and Mary Quarterly* 39 (1982), 334–356. In these two essays, Shalhope analyzes the body of scholarship that created the "republican synthesis."

Smith, Rogers. *Civic Ideals: Conflicting Visions of Citizenship in U.S. History.* New Haven, Conn., 1997. A magisterial work that charts the importance of inegalitarian and ascriptive ideologies in American history and examines their relationship to America's liberal republicanism.

Wood, Gordon S. *The Creation of the American Republic, 1776–1787.* Chapel Hill, N.C., 1969; repr., 1998. Wood's classic study of the transformation of American political thought from the republicanism of the American Revolution to the formation of a "new science of politics" based upon self-interest at the framing of the Constitution. Wood's study is particularly strong in its analysis of the formation of state constitutions in the period between the Revolution and the formation of the Constitution.

Wood, Gordon S. *The Radicalism of the American Revolution.* New York, 1992. This Pulitzer prize–winning study examines the democratization of American politics during the age of revolution. Wood argues that the "monarchical" culture of colonial society was republicanized as a result of the American Revolution and that this unintentionally led to the formation of a modern, democratic, capitalistic America.

Zuckert, Michael. *The Natural Rights Republic: Studies in the Foundation of the American Political Tradition.* Notre Dame, Ind., 1996. One of the best interpretations in print of the Declaration of

Independence, the Lockean natural rights philosophy embedded in it, and the interactions within the founders' political thought of Lockean natural rights philosophy with other strains of American political thought.

Zuckert, Michael. *Natural Rights and the New Republicanism*. Princeton, N.J., 1994. This study criticizes proponents of the republican synthesis for misunderstanding the character of commonwealth ideology and proposes that the seventeenth- and eighteenth-century English radicals (and subsequently the American founders) combined Locke's understanding of the ends of government with a republican science of politics.

ALAN GIBSON

France

Early in July 1791, just weeks after Louis XVI's failed flight to Varennes, the marquis de Condorcet gave a speech to the Cercle Social, a Parisian political club, advocating the creation of a republic in France. This speech, in the words of Pierre Nora, "marked the conversion of the Enlightenment to the republican ideal." This trenchant observation suggests a number of themes to explore. The first and most obvious is that the declaration of the first French Republic in September 1792 was not a logical outgrowth of Enlightenment philosophy. Indeed, for most thinkers of the French Enlightenment, republicanism was not an ideal at all, but rather a discredited form of government that had been shown historically to lead either to mob rule and anarchy or to tyranny. Second, among the revolutionaries themselves, there were still very few committed republicans as late as the summer of 1791. Even in the midst of the crisis triggered by the king's flight, a number of revolutionaries whom we would today consider radicals publicly disavowed the idea of a republic, and the deputies of the Constituent Assembly presented to the French people the fiction that the king had been kidnapped, in an effort to preserve public confidence in the monarchy. At least some of the people of Paris refused to accept that fiction, but when they gathered on the Champ de Mars on 17 July 1791 to sign petitions calling for the king's abdication, the marquis de Lafayette ordered the National Guard to open fire on the crowd. In the aftermath of this massacre, those who had most actively rallied the people against the king were forced into hiding, and the idea of a republic became once again disreputable. It was another year until a popular insurrection toppled the monarchy (10 August 1792), leading to the declaration of the first French Republic on 22 September 1792, despite the best efforts of the revolutionary leadership to preserve the constitutional monarchy. This first French Republic was short-lived (though Napoleon preserved the name even after declaring himself emperor), and this suggests a final theme: the difficulty that the deputies encountered in reaching consensus on a republican constitution, and their inability to put into practice a workable republican system of government. Given the excesses of the Terror, which seemed to confirm in the minds of its critics their skepticism about republican government, it is remarkable that the ideal of a republic has remained so enduring ever since, not only among French men and women but for much of the rest of the world as well.

The Idea of Republicanism before the Revolution. Enlightenment thinkers and French revolutionaries may have been skeptical about republicanism, but that is not to say that they never discussed it. Before the eighteenth century, however, Catholic political theorists in France made reference to republicanism chiefly to castigate the Huguenot (Protestant) minority for their alleged disloyalty to the monarchy. Across the Channel, the English Civil War, the execution of Charles I, and the eventual emergence of Oliver Cromwell as a despotic ruler did much to confirm the impression among French thinkers that republics were not a stable form of government.

Out of that political instability, however, came the writings of political theorists such as Locke, Shaftesbury, and Bolingbroke, and these drew the attention of French intellectuals in the eighteenth century. The new century also brought a revival of interest in the Greek and Roman classics. These influences are apparent in the works of Montesquieu, most notably in *L'esprit des lois* (1748). A nobleman himself and a member of the parlement of Bordeaux, Montesquieu ultimately came to be seen in France principally as an advocate of aristocratic restraint on the despotic tendencies of monarchical power. In his theoretical discussion of different forms of government, however, he devoted considerable attention to republicanism, describing at length its "ideal type"—the participatory republic exemplified by the ancient Greek polis—as well as the modern liberal republic that he had observed at first hand while living in England. Montesquieu contrasted the virtue that he viewed as an essential attribute of the populace of a republic to the honor among subjects of a monarchy and the fear that prevailed under despotism. Although Montesquieu concluded that a republican form of government was ill suited to a country like France, his emphasis on civic virtue stands as an important contribution to the French republican tradition.

The figure who looms largest in the eighteenth-century development of republican ideas in France is Jean-Jacques Rousseau. In his *Discours sur l'origine et les fondemens de l'inégalite parmi les hommes* (Discourse on the Origins of Inequality, 1755) and *Du contract social* (The Social Contract, 1762), Rousseau called into question the divine right of monarchs and presented a theoretical argument that all legitimate government must derive from popular sovereignty, as expressed through the general will. Rousseau idealized the Greek city-states, particularly Sparta, but he joined Montesquieu in doubting the applicability of the republican forms of the ancient world to the modern French state. Specifically, Rousseau insisted on the incompatibility between popular sovereignty and representation. In a country of twenty million people, a participatory republic was a virtual impossibility, and in Rousseau's view, the general will could not be expressed through representatives. Unlike Montesquieu, Rousseau scorned the English system, asserting that the English were truly free only at the moment when they participated in elections.

Some historians have questioned the influence of Rousseau on the eve of the Revolution, pointing out that, between 1762 and 1789, only two editions of *Du contract social* were published. It is worth noting, however, that his novels *La nouvelle Heloïse* and *Émile* were enormously popular during those years and contained many of his political ideas. Moreover, between 1789 and 1799, *Du contract social* was republished thirty-two times, ample evidence of an extensive reading public, and Rousseau became a virtual patron saint of the influential Jacobin clubs.

Rousseau's vision of the ideal republic placed more demands on its citizens than did Montesquieu's, calling on them to sacrifice individual interests to the civic community of virtue, the *res publica* of the ancient city-states. It was for this same reason, in part, that Denis Diderot, coeditor of the *Encyclopédie*, considered the republic unsuited to the modern nation-state. Human psychology had changed, in his view; modern men desired happiness and self-fulfillment and were no longer willing to devote themselves entirely to the common good. It is not surprising that the entry "Republic" in the *Encyclopédie*, written by Louis Jaucourt, focused almost entirely on the ancient republics and described the form as historically outmoded.

Religion and Republicanism. We must look not only to political philosophy for traces of republicanism in eighteenth-century France. Some important recent scholarship, in particular the work of Dale Van Kley, has pointed to the Jansenist controversy within the French Catholic Church as an important source of progressive political ideas critical of the excesses of absolutist monarchy. Beginning with the papal bull *Unigenitus* (1713) and culminating with an order of the archbishop of Paris in the 1750s denying them the sacraments, Jansenists found themselves the targets of concerted royal persecution. The response of the Jansenist minority to that persecution focused criticism not only on the hierarchy of the Catholic Church (by appealing to the conciliar tradition within the church), but also on the sacred character of the monarchy itself. Many Jansenists were prominent members of the parlement of Paris, the high court (largely aristocratic) responsible for registering royal edicts. When Louis XV's chancellor, Maupeou, imposed reforms in 1770 that effectively stripped the parlements of much of their authority

by creating new royal courts, the religious controversy that had simmered for twenty years became an open political controversy, with Jansenist *parlementaires* taking the lead in the pamphlet war against the Maupeou reforms.

Notable among these pamphlets was one published in Bordeaux by Guillaume-Joseph Saige, a young lawyer whose cousin sat on the parlement of Bordeaux. In his pamphlet, *Catechisme du Citoyen*, Saige combined Jansenist and Rousseauist ideas, arguing, on the one hand, that the conciliarist tradition within the French Catholic Church represented a kind of republicanism, and, on the other, that the many communes of rural France represented "so many little republics within the great republic of the French nation." So incendiary was this pamphlet, with its direct challenge to monarchical despotism and its insistence that sovereignty was embodied not in the king but in the nation, that the parlement of Bordeaux itself ordered it to be burned.

The Estates-General. A vast array of pamphlets and remonstrances defended the parlements as the legitimate constitutional restraint on royal power at the end of the ancien régime, but not all political theorists looked to those institutions for the solution to France's political woes. Two works by Gabriel Bonnot de Mably—*Observations sur l'histoire de France* (1765, 1788) and *Des Devoirs et des droits du citoyen* (Duties and Rights of the Citizen, 1789)—were published at the very moment of the ancien régime's final constitutional crisis and championed the Estates-General as the only legitimate embodiment of the nation's sovereignty. Like most of the other works cited here, Mably's writings were couched in the language of classical republicanism.

The Estates-General, convened by Louis XVI in late 1788, was a traditional institution, but it had not met since 1614. This lengthy adjournment, coinciding with the consolidation of royal absolutism, left much room for debate about both the composition of the Estates-General and the procedures for its deliberations. Six weeks of stalemate between aristocratic and commoner delegates followed the opening session on 5 May 1789; then the Estates-General underwent a revolutionary transformation. On 17 June, the majority of delegates declared themselves to be a National Assembly, no longer meeting at the pleasure of the king but rather as representatives of the nation itself. Faced with a financial crisis and popular mobilization throughout France, Louis XVI had no choice but to accept this declaration. France now became a constitutional monarchy.

The Role of the King. What was the place of the king to be in the new French polity? The preamble to the Declaration of the Rights of Man and the Citizen, adopted by the National Assembly in late August 1789, made no mention of the king, and Article III stated quite plainly that "the principle of all sovereignty rests essentially in the nation." While sovereignty had now shifted from the king to the people, the deputies had no intention of abolishing the monarchy. In September, the Assembly drafted articles vesting legislative authority in a unicameral legislature, while granting a suspensive veto to the king. In doing so, the deputies created an inherently unstable situation, which Robespierre would later term a "republic with a monarch at its head." The constitution of 1791 clearly paid heed to Rousseau—the unicameral legislature was to be the embodiment of the general will—but it seemingly granted the king the power to thwart the general will, and it ignored Rousseau's injunction that the general will could not practically be represented. Those unresolved tensions would ultimately bring down the constitutional monarchy.

That Louis XVI proved unwilling to accept his limited role as constitutional monarch should hardly be surprising, but the deputies of the Constituent Assembly, and the Legislative Assembly that followed, also were unwilling to exercise decisively the national sovereignty that they claimed to represent by deposing the recalcitrant monarch. It was the people of Paris, joined by several battalions of Marseillais and other provincials, who toppled the monarchy in a violent insurrection on 10 August 1792.

The Remains of Republicanism. One year earlier, even as he called for the creation of a republic, Condorcet had expressed his concern that the people would need to be taught what a republic was. But who was to teach them? Under the republican regime, even the most radical of the deputies, the Jacobins, remained profoundly skeptical of the ideal of popular sovereignty. Each government whittled away at it, first in the name of emergency wartime government under the Terror, and then in the name of stability and order under the Directory. If the mobilization of popular politics was responsible, almost by accident, for the creation of the French Republic, the suppression of popular politics led, almost unwittingly, to the rise of Napoleon Bonaparte. The consensus of Enlightenment thinkers that a republic was not suited to a country like France seemed to have been confirmed.

[*See also* French Revolution; Jansenism; Political Philosophy; *and* Rousseau, Jean-Jacques.]

BIBLIOGRAPHY

Baker, Keith M. *Inventing the French Revolution*. Cambridge, 1990. See especially chaps. 4, 6, 9, 10, and 11 for discussion of thinkers and intellectual currents related to the emergence of republican ideas.

Baker, Keith M., ed. *The Political Culture of the Old Regime*. Oxford, 1987. Essays by an international array of leading scholars, delivered first as papers at a conference in conjunction with the Bicentennial of the French Revolution.

Bell, David A. *Lawyers and Citizens: The Making of a Political Elite in Old Regime France*. Oxford, 1994. An examination of the impact of the legal profession on the political culture of 18th-century France.

Chartier, Roger. *The Cultural Origins of the French Revolution*. Translated by Lydia G. Cochrane. Durham, N.C., 1991. A reflective study by one of France's leading cultural historians.

Fontana, Biancamaria, ed. *The Invention of the Modern Republic*. Cambridge, 1994. A stimulating collection of essays by an international array of scholars of history and political theory.

Hignonnet, Patrice. *Sister Republics: The Origins of French and American Republicanism*. Cambridge, Mass., 1988. Focuses principally on the social and cultural contexts in which republican ideas emerged in the two countries.

Hunt, Lynn A., David Lansky, and Paul Hanson. "The Failure of the Liberal Republic in France, 1795–1799: The Road to Brumaire." *Journal of Modern History* 51 (1979) 734–759.

Lucas, Colin, ed. *The Political Culture of the French Revolution*. Oxford, 1988. Essays by an international array of leading scholars, delivered first as papers at a conference in conjunction with the Bicentennial of the French Revolution.

Nicolet, Claude. *L'idée républicaine en France, 1789–1924*. Paris, 1982. Focuses principally on the nineteenth century, but begins with an overview of eighteenth-century currents.

Nora, Pierre. "Republic." In *A Critical Dictionary of the French Revolution*, pp. 792–805, edited by François Furet and Mona Ozouf. Cambridge, Mass., 1989. An excellent short essay on the idea of the republic as it developed during the course of the Revolution.

Van Kley, Dale K. *The Religious Origins of the French Revolution: From Calvin to the Civil Constitution, 1560–1791*. New Haven, Conn., 1996. A pathbreaking study that explores in detail the complicated influence of Jansenism on eighteenth-century political culture in France.

Van Kley, Dale K., ed. *The French Idea of Freedom: The Old Regime and the Declaration of Rights of 1789*. Stanford, Calif., 1994. A collection of essays by various scholars focusing on one aspect of the republican ideal.

Vincent, K. Steven. *Pierre-Joseph Proudhon and the Rise of French Republican Socialism*. Oxford, 1984. See especially pp. 34–41 for a remarkably concise and insightful discussion of republicanism in the thought of Montesquieu and Rousseau.

Wright, Johnson Kent. *A Classical Republican in Eighteenth-Century France: The Political Thought of Mably*. Cambridge, 1999.

PAUL R. HANSON

The Netherlands

Historians long believed that Dutch political thought of the eighteenth century was not worthy of a place in the history of republicanism. Until the 1980s, there was a consensus in the historiography of republican thought that, in the Netherlands, serious theorizing about the republican state developed relatively late—from about 1650—and disappeared rather early, just before 1700. The "Golden Age" of the Dutch was not only a flowering of achievements in trade, sciences, and arts, but also their finest hour in respect to republicanism, with contributions from Baruch de Spinoza, Pieter de la Court, and Johan de la Court. After that time, however, the political Enlightenment in the Netherlands was perceived as no more than a flickering lamp.

In the 1980s and 1990s, however, interest in the Dutch Enlightenment intensified, with new research by Lynn Hunt, Margaret Jacob, Keith Baker, Robert Darnton,

François Furet, and Franco Venturi, and this has led to a serious reappraisal of the period's particular characteristics. One concern of this research is the Anglo-American debate on the nature of republicanism and its relevance for understanding the Dutch revolutionary period between 1780 and 1800. Although the Patriot revolution has almost faded from Dutch collective memory, specialists in the field were inspired by its bicentenary in 1987 to reinterpret the period. Studies by Bernard Bailyn, Gordon Wood, and especially John Pocock raised the question of whether republicanism on the margins of the North Sea was entirely different from its manifestations in the Atlantic world, or instead participated in them. In terms of method, this debate was also fueled by the conceptual approach (*Begriffsgeschichte*) of Reinhardt Koselleck and his colleagues.

By 2001, a consensus had emerged from scholarly debate on the Patriot movement of 1780–1787 on the following points. Opposition to the stadholder (monarch) William V of Orange-Nassau and his political clients in all the country's seven provinces grew from 1780 on as the fourth Anglo-Dutch war did painful damage to the economy and precipitated a loss of self-respect. Under the banner of Patriotism, a socially diverse coalition of city regents and burghers voiced their grievances and ambitions. In the beginning, the movement drew mainly on the seventeenth-century republicanism associated with the Grand Pensionary, Johan de Witt, and defended by Pieter de la Court. In their view, true liberty would exist when commerce could flourish under a political system in which the state assembly of the province of Holland was sovereign, and the power of the stadholderate was abolished or at least curtailed. Within a few years, however, a much more radical republican agenda was put forward by a second group, a coalition of a few noblemen, some city regents, and many burghers. Upholding the new concept of popular sovereignty, they sought to neutralize the stadholderate and to transfer power to an enlarged electorate. The Patriots proposed to democratize city government and to install institutions of popular control in order to restore ancient liberties, at the same time preserving the confederal framework of the Union of Utrecht (1579). Mutual dislike of royalty in the stadholderate initially created a bridge between the two groups of Patriots, but the radicalism of the second group became manifest in their use of a free political press to appeal to public opinion and in their demand for a citizen militia as a counterforce to the standing army commanded by William V. In 1787, with the country in a state of civil war, Frederick II of Prussia intervened and crushed the republicans' dreams after armed Patriots had blocked his sister, William V's wife Wilhelmina, on her way to Holland.

Despite this consensus among historians, they differ on the issue of the continuity of republicanism in the Netherlands. In the 1970s, a new orthodoxy argued that Patriotism should be considered as the beginning of a process that was interrupted between 1787 and 1795 and then completed from 1796 onward in the new Batavian Republic, with the support of the French army. Simon Schama (1977) views Patriot and Batavian ideas as nearly identical. De Wit (1965, 1978), a founder of this new orthodoxy, went so far as to suggest a line of continuity to the revised Dutch constitution of 1848, making the Patriots into liberals *avant la lettre*. This interpretation has been much revised subsequently. Some specialists argue that Patriotism was strongly rooted in the ancien régime. For some of these, Patriotism, though not unresponsive to Enlightenment ideals, was caught in its own history, to such an extent that it must be reinterpreted as an unsuccessful or even nonrevolutionary movement (Leeb, 1973). Others emphasize that the Patriot movement operated within the old social and political distribution of power in local communities, and thus it should be placed within a tradition of city republicanism based on corporate institutions that had emerged during the Middle Ages. Nevertheless, these latter also recognize the innovative ideas and actions of the Patriots (Te Brake, 1989; Israel, 1995; Prak, 1999).

A third approach, developed in the 1980s, claims that Patriotism in the 1780s broke away from the ancien régime in many ways. It succeeded in creating a modern political culture and constructed its own variety of republicanism. N. C. F. van Sas has demonstrated that a strong national feeling emerged, stimulated by new political periodicals that were read in new types of reading societies whose members learned to handle weapons and engaged in military exercises—sometimes in public—in order to communicate their message of democratic republicanism. Innovations appeared in political concepts as well, to be noted with dismay by the enlightened defenders of the stadholderate (Velema, 1993). Patriot republicanism, this view argues, was based on principles derived from classical sources and Enlightenment literature (by authors such as Andrew Fletcher, Thomas Gordon, John Trenchard, Richard Price, Joseph Priestley, and Charles de Secondat Montesquieu), and the American constitutions; this learning was applied to Dutch history with a view toward "restoring" the country's ancient constitution, a process far from complete in 1787. The innovative character of Patriot republicanism is demonstrated by the fact that restoration did not stop at the city walls. A radical current of opinion existed around 1787 that questioned, on the basis of popular sovereignty, the legitimacy of a system in which cities and territories lacked representation in the state assemblies; this entailed attacks on the position of the nobility. The abolition of the stadholderate was not an issue, historians of this tendency argue, because the office could be redefined in a modern way as a position in the executive branch of government, without any of the prerogatives of a sovereign monarch (Klein, 1995).

Most historians agree that several lines of continuity can be drawn from the Patriot republicanism of the 1780s to the Batavian debates of the 1790s. However, it is also recognized that a declaration of individual rights, the separation of church and state, the abolition of the stadholderate, and the establishment of a unitary state (1798)—entailing the dissolution of the corporate structures and the confederal framework of the Union of Utrecht—became possible only after the upheaval of 1787, and with the support of foreign military force from France, the largest unitary republic in western Europe.

[*See also* Netherlands; Political Philosophy; *and* Spinoza, Baruch de.]

BIBLIOGRAPHY

Bots, H., and W. W. Mijnhardt, eds. *De Droom van de Revolutie: Nieuwe Benaderingen van het Patriottisme*. Amsterdam, 1988. Contains some interesting essays on political innovation (Van Sas) and conservative response (Velema). Result of a conference on the Patriot and Brabant revolution under the auspices of the Dutch/Belgian Society for Eighteenth-Century Studies.

Grijzenhout, F., W. W. Mijnhardt, and N. C. F. van Sas, eds. *Voor Vaderland en Vryheid: De Revolutie van de Patriotten*. Amsterdam, 1987. Essays dealing with such themes as the Dutch Enlightenment (Mijnhardt), the political press (Van Sas), and political art (Grijzenhout) in the 1780s.

Israel, Jonathan. *The Dutch Republic: Its Rise, Greatness and Fall 1477–1806*. Oxford, 1995.

Jacob, Margaret C., and Wijnand Mijnhardt, eds. *The Dutch Republic in the Eighteenth Century: Decline, Enlightenment and Revolution*. Ithaca, N.Y., and London, 1992. An excellent collection of essays by leading specialists on Dutch politics and culture, with attention to the Patriot movement and republicanism (Van Sas, Te Brake, Pocock, Velema).

Klein, S. R. E. *Patriots Republikanisme: Politieke Cultuur in Nederland 1766–1787*. Amsterdam, 1995.

Kossmann, E. H. "Dutch Republicanism." In *Politieke Theorie en Geschiedenis: Verspreide Opstellen en Voordrachten*, pp. 211–233. Amsterdam, 1987. Reprint of earlier, rather skeptical reply (1985) to Pocock's thesis of an Atlantic republican tradition and its value for Dutch history.

Leeb, I. L. *The Ideological Origins of the Batavian Revolution: History and Politics in the Dutch Republic 1747–1800*. The Hague, 1973.

Prak, Maarten. *Republikeinse Veelheid, Democratisch Enkelvoud. Sociale Verandering in het Revolutietijdvak: 's-Hertogenbosch 1770–1820*. Nijmegen, Netherlands, 1999.

Sas, N. C. F. van. "Vaderlandsliefde, nationalisme en vaderlands gevoel in Nederland, 1770–1813." *Tijdschrift voor Geschiedenis* 3–4 (1989), 471–495.

Schama, Simon. *Patriots and Liberators: Revolution in the Netherlands 1780–1813*. New York, 1977. Still a readable account of the revolutionary period, but has been criticized on several issues and contains inaccuracies.

Te Brake, Wayne. *Regents and Rebels: the Revolutionary World of an Eighteenth-Century Dutch City*. Cambridge, Mass., and Oxford, 1989. Socio-political analysis of revolutionary process in Deventer, compared to other cities in the province of Overijssel.

Velema, Wyger R. E. *Enlightenment and Conservatism in the Dutch Republic: The Political Thought of Elie Luzac (1721–1796)*. Assen and Maastricht, Neth., 1993. Analysis of one of the defenders of a commercial republic combined with a strong stadholderate. Discusses Luzac as fierce opponent of Patriot republicanism, taking into account the problem of enlightenment and modernity.

Wit, C. H. E. de. *De Strijd tussen Aristocratie en Democratie in Nederland, 1780–1848: Kritisch Onderzoek van een Historisch Beeld en Herwaardering van een Periode*. Heerlen, Neth., 1965.

Wit, C. H. E. de. *Het Ontstaan van het Moderne Nederland en zijn Geschiedschrijving*. Oirsbeek, Neth., 1978.

Zee, Th. S. M. van der, J. G. M. M. Rosendaal, and P. G. B. Thissen, eds. *1787: De Nederlandse Revolutie?* Amsterdam, 1988. Seventeen essays on various topics of the Patriot movement.

STEPHAN KLEIN

Latin America

Enlightenment thought and republicanism first emerged in Latin America under a colonial regime. New institutions and ideas led to questions about the colonial regime's legitimacy. Examples of republicanism in the United States and France provided hope for Latin American intellectuals. Then, war in Europe provided Latin Americans with the opportunity to pursue republicanism. While they successfully obtained independence, republican government was short-lived because of the inability to achieve stability, legitimacy, and popular government.

Enlightenment ideas of rationalization and free trade led to substantial and successful reform of the Spanish colonial system under the Bourbon monarchs, but also created new tensions within the Latin American elite. The reign of Charles III (1759–1788), in particular, created a more efficient economic system through institutional reform. In the New World, this entailed greater centralization with the goal of providing greater profit for the home country, Spain. The primary means was by instituting the intendant system, characterized by increased oversight by Spanish-born (*peninsulares*) bureaucrats and by the increasing exclusion of Creoles (those of Spanish descent born in the colonies) from government offices. The Bourbon reforms further enriched Spain, but they heightened Creole dissatisfaction with the *peninsulares* and eventually with the colonial system itself.

Latin American Creoles, also influenced by Enlightenment ideas, began to question the legitimacy of the colonial system. Prior to the Bourbon reforms, legitimacy had been based on religion. The Bourbons established new bases of legitimacy—rationality and material progress—which led many Creoles to doubt whether the system was rational for them. At first, Creole patriots sought reforms within the colonial system that would eliminate many of the preferences for *peninsulares*, thus allowing the Latin American elites a greater role. Eventually, however, these failed efforts at reform gave rise to Creole republicanism—an effort to abolish the colonial system entirely. Creole elites divided between the patriots who desired reform of the colonial system and the republicans who desired to establish their own government based on Enlightenment ideals.

The reforms and ideas that were transmitted through the colonial system were key to the development of Latin American republicanism. They not only created new conflicts within the colonies between the Creoles and *peninsulares*, but also established a new manner in which to assess the legitimacy of the regime. As Creoles increasingly questioned that legitimacy, external events provided additional impetus toward revolt. First, the American and French Revolutions provided important alternative models. Then, the Napoleonic Wars created an opportunity for Latin America to achieve independence and pursue its own notions of republicanism.

The American and French Revolutions provided quite different models for Creole republicans. The American Revolution raised the hopes that the chains of Europe could be cast aside and that a stable, representative government could be achieved. The French Revolution also raised the hopes for successful revolt—while also raising fears about the aftermath. The majority of the Latin American population was indigenous, mixed, or African and held a lower position in the social hierarchy. If the old system were abolished, then these peoples might desire revenge—and eventually take it out on the white elites. Creole republicans were conflicted because they desired an outcome like the American Revolution, yet feared that their circumstances were even more precarious than those of the French Revolution. In Latin America, not only were class distinctions important, but they were reinforced by racial distinctions.

Partially due to these circumstances and fears, the republican movement was much weaker and slower to develop in Latin America. Francisco Miranda was an early advocate of republicanism, but he found little support for his ventures. He did, however, participate in the French and American movements. In 1806 he made his first attempt in Latin America, but failed miserably. Only after Napoleon conquered Spain and Portugal in 1807 did the republican movement successfully lead to independence. The Napoleonic wars created the opportunity for republicanism to succeed, because a power vacuum left Latin America relatively isolated while European war raged. These factors raised possibilities for success, but it was the republican leaders who truly fulfilled it. Most notable among these leaders was Simón Bolívar.

Known as the Liberator, Bolívar was the most important military and intellectual leader of independence. He was educated in Enlightenment ideas in childhood by his tutor as well as a tour of Europe. At an early age, he devoted himself to the cause of republicanism and independence.

Despite many setbacks, he managed to win Latin American independence—but he was unable to make republicanism thrive. His writings provide an insightful application of Enlightenment ideas combined with an understanding of the American and French experiences, yet reveal an astute awareness of the problematic differences in Latin America.

Like many Creoles, Bolívar had doubts about the ability of most Latin Americans to exercise self-governance. After an early setback at the hands of the *llaneros* (black, mestizo, and Indian "roughnecks"), he had even greater reason to fear "mob rule" by nonwhites. His "Letter from Jamaica," written in exile, questions whether Latin Americans had the knowledge and character for representative government. Because in his view Latin Americans lacked the virtues of the citizens of the United States, Bolívar gradually came to believe that autocracy was necessary, and the constitutions he wrote reflected it. The popular will would best be expressed through centralized authority and a strong leader who acted for the people's benefit. Jean-Jacques Rousseau's "general will" became the Latin American model rather than the checks and balances of Locke and Montesquieu. This inauspicious beginning is often pointed to as a major reason that Latin American constitutions continue to vest power in a strong executive surrounded by weak competing institutions.

Bolívar believed that a strong leader, perhaps even a dictator, was necessary, yet he refused to become one himself. Thus, the one individual who might have been able to provide unity and stability was unable to compromise his republican principles in practice. Instead, he witnessed the disintegration of stable governments and a descent into chaos ruled by local, corrupt caudillos (strongmen).

[*See also* Bolívar, Simón; Miranda, Francisco; *and* Spain.]

BIBLIOGRAPHY

Brading, D. A. *Classical Republicanism and Creole Patriotism: Simon Bolivar (1783–1830) and the Spanish American Revolution*. Cambridge, 1983.

Brading, D. A. *The First America: The Spanish Monarchy, Creole Patriots and the Liberal State, 1492–1867*. Cambridge, 1991.

Harvey, Robert. *Liberators: Latin America's Struggle for Independence, 1810–1830*. New York, 2000.

Jorrín, Miguel, and John D. Martz. *Latin American Political Thought and Ideology*. Chapel Hill, N.C., 1970.

MacLachlan, Colin M. *Spain's Empire in the New World: The Role of Ideas in Institutional and Social Change*. Berkeley, Calif., 1988.

Wiarda, Howard J. *The Soul of Latin America: The Cultural and Political Tradition*. New Haven, Conn., 2001.

ROGER D. REYNOLDS

REPUBLIC OF LETTERS. A defining commonplace of European and, later, American intellectual culture from the sixteenth to the eighteenth centuries, the idea of the Republic of Letters symbolized and helped to shape the social and discursive practices of intellectual life, institutions, and sociability, and it was, in turn, modified by them as they evolved. In 1752, when Voltaire wrote about the "literary republic" that had gradually been established throughout Europe in the age of Louis XIV (*Siècle de Louis XIV*, chap. 34), he was drawing on a notion that had existed in the cultural imaginary of Europeans for hundreds of years. The term appears to have emerged in the Latin form, *respublica litteraria*, in the early fifteenth century. The two words *res* and *publica* mean, respectively, "matter" or "object," and "public" or "common"; *litteraria* denotes learning or knowledge, including scientific knowledge, rather than literature in the narrower sense of our own time. The expression was used, then, to refer to the shared pursuit of knowledge for the common good, and it never lost this primary meaning, although it was invested over time with other meanings and symbolic powers of representation. Such was the case at the time of the Renaissance.

A paradigm shift occurred in the worldview of Europeans in the sixteenth century following the invention of the printing press, which brought about an increased circulation of knowledge and books, the discovery of the New World, and the rediscovery of classical texts from Greek and Roman antiquity. According to the French author Jean Bodin, writing in *Les six livres de la République* (1576), all peoples were now interconnected and "marvelously involved in the universal Republic, as if they were part of one and the same city." Of course, Bodin was using the concept of the republic in a political, albeit ideal, sense. Scholars such as Erasmus also thought in these terms, seeing themselves as citizens of the world (*cives mundi*) and members of the *respublica litteraria*, which united all like-minded people everywhere, past, present, and future. The Republic of Letters was, then, a conceptual space defined in terms of cosmopolitanism and universality, although in reality its membership was limited to the educated elite and was, therefore, almost exclusively male, university-educated, and European.

It was, however, also an actual space defined by a common language, Latin (the language of education in this period), networks of communication, and cooperative enterprise. Although scholars did travel between different centers of learning and acted as vectors of information, communication was for the most part by correspondence. Those involved in scientific investigation or the task of editing biblical and classical texts wrote to one another with requests for help. Books and samples were exchanged; research was undertaken on behalf of others, in the form of visits to libraries, deciphering of manuscripts, or consultations with specialists, and the results were conveyed by letter, or in packages carried by travelers and mutual friends. In other words, learning was based on collaborative interconnection and cooperative networks of intellectual exchange, which were practical expressions of the ideal of the *respublica litteraria*; these were to receive further elaboration in the seventeenth century.

The picture of the solitary thinker reinventing knowledge by deduction from first principles, promoted by Descartes's philosophy, tends to predominate in our image of the seventeenth century, but the reality was very different. Francis Bacon's utopian image in *New Atlantis* (1627) of what he called "Solomon's House"—a vast powerhouse of research into all branches of knowledge, based on induction and experiment, exploratory voyages, collaboration, and intellectual exchange—is a more meaningful, albeit ideal, representation of the contemporary world of learning. This is the period that witnessed the creation throughout Europe of what we designate as the institutions of the Republic of Letters: academies, book fairs, clubs, salons, societies, libraries, gazettes, newspapers, and periodicals. All of these were designed to facilitate the circulation of information and the pursuit of knowledge—which was becoming increasingly specialized—to help people keep up with the latest developments, to create networks of exchange, and to provide places, means, and occasions of sociability. In few of these was Latin still used as the language of exchange, having been replaced by the vernacular languages or, toward the end of the century, by French.

As a result of these developments, there was a notable expansion in the cultural elites, which now included people who had not received a university education, such as many members of the bourgeoisie and also many more women. Women prodigies had always been a part of the *respublica litteraria*, but in both the seventeenth and the eighteenth centuries, more conventionally educated women became the driving force behind the salon movement, although they still remained in the minority overall. From the outset, as Jürgen Habermas has written, these new cultural elites were an educated, critical, reading public who played an increasingly central role in the formation of opinion. Whether this critical public was constituted, at least in part, by the ideal of the Republic of Letters, or whether in fact it gave rise to further elaboration of that ideal is impossible to say. What is clear is that, at the end of the seventeenth century and the beginning of the eighteenth, lexicographers and scholars attempted to define and codify the evolving notion of the *respublica litteraria*.

Significantly, the three French language dictionaries that appeared between 1680 and 1694 all agree in defining the Republic of Letters as a corporate body of learned people, a definition that formalized its existence as never before. In 1684, Pierre Bayle, a Huguenot refugee, launched the *Nouvelles de la République des Lettres* (News of the Republic of Letters) in Amsterdam; in the preface, he outlined the values it would exemplify. In his view, the Republic of Letters was a "fraternity" where scholars were to be judged not on their social standing but on learning alone. He undertook to exclude all causes of division from his periodical, specifically mentioning religious differences, and he urged his readers to concentrate on what united them: the shared pursuit of knowledge. He also invited them to send him books and information, which they did, and he created a vast network of correspondence with them that kept him informed of the latest publications and news. In other words, although Bayle wrote the vast majority of the articles himself, his periodical in fact embodied a community of discourse, which he defined as a meritocracy based on principles of fraternity, equality, reciprocal communication, and tolerance.

In the first edition of the *Dictionnaire historique et critique* (1697), Bayle gave another influential and frequently quoted definition of the Republic of Letters (art. "Catius," footnote D). It was a "state," he wrote, presided over by truth and reason, where discursive interaction was typified by reciprocal criticism and intellectual independence, since no authority—familial, social, or political—could prohibit the inhabitants from exercising their natural right to make war on error and ignorance. Other thinkers produced similar definitions: Vigneul-Marville in 1700 stressed the diversity (of age, gender, religion, ethnic or social origin, language or culture) of the members of the Republic of Letters; Pierre Desmaizeaux in 1729 insisted on their freedom and independence of judgment. Jean Le Clerc in 1706 wrote about it as an alternative state that took no part in the wars between nations, but instead provided a conceptual space where scholars could engage collaboratively in the pursuit of learning, although this might result in learned battles and the spilling of ink. In 1708, Christian Loeber observed that it was a "universal society" engaged in transmitting "true knowledge" to posterity (Bots and Waquet, 18–21, 39). Thus, by the turn of the century, the concept of the Republic of Letters had been transformed into a self-conscious alternative community of rational, critical discourse that sought to embody certain values, including collaborative learning, impartiality, and the right to pursue the truth without interference from the authorities.

In the eighteenth century, then, when the philosophes and others—for example, Gisbert Cuper, Gottfried Wilhelm von Leibniz, Friedrich Gottlieb Klopstock, or Gotthold Ephraim Lessing—referred to the Republic of Letters, they were not innovating, but rather situating themselves in a great cultural tradition that they sought to develop. The most outstanding example of the ideals, values, and practices associated with that tradition is the *Encyclopédie* of Denis Diderot and Jean le Rond d'Alembert, which, as its title page proclaims, was the work of a "society of learned people" engaged in rational investigation. Its objective, like that of Solomon's House in Bacon's utopia—the collection of all the scattered knowledge of the globe—could be realized only by the collaboration on a grand scale of people from all walks of life, as Diderot reminded readers. While the *Encyclopédie* may be outstanding, however, it is not untypical of intellectual sociability in this period, when people of lesser repute, including those of both genders whose names are often lost to us, expanded their cultural world, conceptualizing it as the Republic of Letters. Academies, clubs, salons, and societies were founded throughout Europe, especially in provincial towns, and also in the American colonies. Periodicals, journals, and newspapers were launched (and sometimes lost), and correspondence networks widened to include the American colonies to the west and Russia to the east. Freemasonry offered yet another opportunity for intellectual sociability and collaborative interaction; and reading clubs, commercial lending libraries, and coffeehouses became centers for formal and informal discussion. As a result of these developments, ideas, information, books, and learning were diffused to a far wider public, made up of both genders and of social strata from outside the participating elites of the previous century. In their different ways, these institutions exemplified one or other of the ideals of the Republic of Letters as already defined.

Learned periodicals and newspapers, for example, not only drew information from correspondents, as Bayle had done; they also began to publish their letters and views, thereby making their readers members of a discursive community and participants in a body of opinion that had been shaped collaboratively. Academies, salons, and societies had corresponding members, both at home and abroad, and meetings were often held to fit in with the arrival of the post from foreign correspondents. By the 1750s, the academies of science in Europe were in regular contact, and they occasionally collaborated on projects that required the involvement of observers from all over the world. Although French continued to be the principal language of intellectual exchange (it was the language used by Leibniz to write to the majority of his four hundred correspondents, many of them German), the increased use of other vernaculars drove journals and academies to engage translators to maintain international communication. Collaboration and communication across national boundaries were also encouraged by the prizes offered by academies and societies, such as the one advertised by the Dijon Academy in 1749, which stimulated Jean-Jacques Rousseau to present his famous essay on the relationship between learning and morality. Greater opportunities for travel, including the Grand Tour and journeys undertaken to universities and other centers of learning (the *peregrinatio academica* or *voyage littéraire*) made for increased contact between people engaged in the common pursuit of knowledge.

Eighteenth-century intellectual sociability seems to exemplify, then, the values of the Republic of Letters that had been nourished by cultured people over the centuries, but in fact, a radical shift had occurred since the Renaissance. The Republic of Letters had always been an alternative community driven by the ideals of reason, truth, tolerance, reciprocal service, equality, universality, criticism, intellectual independence, and impartiality. It was not an apolitical community, as some historians have claimed. On the contrary, individuals and groups, often motivated by these or similar ideals, engaged actively and critically with social, political, and religious institutions. They did not act as a corporate body, however. By the 1750s in France (earlier in England), the gradual expansion of the participating elites had created what Habermas calls a "public sphere." This was a space no longer limited to scholars, but shared by all who were "adept in the public use of reason" and the free exchange of opinions and ideas (Habermas, 1992, 105). Public opinion, which continued to be conceptualized in accordance with the values of the Republic of Letters as rational, critical, universal, and impartial, had become "a new political space with a legitimacy and authority apart from that of the crown" (Baker, 1990, 199). It was to play an important part in the elaboration of a new kind of politics in which authority was subject to its scrutiny and public policy the result of its deliberations.

If we stand back in conclusion from what the Republic of Letters became, and from the ideals and values that inspired it, certain limitations and shortcomings become obvious. Because its membership was more exclusive than inclusive in nature, its claim to universality is clearly more formal than real. Its egalitarianism is suspect for similar reasons. Although it established reciprocity between elite social groups, women and others less fortunate were mostly excluded. Certain places, institutions, and people were more important than others: cities had priority over rural centers, and Paris over all other cities; academies located in capital cities claimed precedence over those in the provinces; and outstanding individuals—Erasmus, for example, who was known as the prince of the Republic of Letters—carried more weight than the run-of-the-mill. Its members claimed to act in accordance with reason and to be motivated by tolerance, but they were all too often driven by envy, bitterness, and the will to power when they engaged in debate and reciprocal criticism. Their intellectual independence was frequently compromised by patronage, state controls, or censorship; and their

pursuit of impartiality ultimately alienated knowing and knowledge from embodiment and all the diversity and enrichment that implies. The cosmopolitan ideal was increasingly limited by communication problems created by the use of vernacular languages, misunderstandings arising out of national rivalries, and chauvinistic impulses generated by war. Yet, for all its limitations, the Republic of Letters was a set of social and discursive practices that functioned as a motivating and transforming ideal in the construction of what we designate as modernity.

[*See also* Academies; Bayle, Pierre; Cabinets de Lecture; Cartesianism; Censorship; Clubs and Societies; Coffeehouses and Cafes; Correspondence and Correspondents; Diderot, Denis; Encyclopédie; England; Freemasonry; Grand Tour; Habermas, Jürgen; Journals, Newspapers, and Gazettes; Language Theories; Le Clerc, Jean; Learned Societies; Libraries; Men and Women of Letters; Netherlands; Paris; Patronage; Politeness; Republicanism; Rousseau, Jean-Jacques; Salons; Scientific Journals; Sociability; Toleration; Translation; *and* Voltaire.]

BIBLIOGRAPHY

Baker, K. M. *Inventing the French Revolution: Essays on French Political Culture in the Eighteenth Century*. Cambridge, 1990. Some useful chapters on ideology and the notion of public opinion.

Bordo, S. *The Flight to Objectivity: Essays on Cartesianism and Culture*. Albany, N.Y., 1987.

Bots, H. "Le *Dictionnaire* de Pierre Bayle: Magasin et protocole de la République des Lettres." In *Critique, savoir et érudition à la veille des Lumières*, edited by H. Bots, pp. 205–215. Amsterdam and Maarssen, 1998.

Bots, H., and F. Waquet. *La république des lettres*. Brussels, 1997. Thorough survey of the notion of the Republic of Letters, particularly good on the sixteenth and seventeenth centuries.

Daston, L. "The Ideal and Reality of the Republic of Letters in the Enlightenment." *Science in Context* 4/2 (1991), 367–386. Insightful on the evolution of the scientific community.

Goldgar, A. *Impolite Learning, Conduct and Community in the Republic of Letters 1680–1750*. New Haven, Conn., and London, 1995. A study of the practices and value systems of the scholarly community with an almost exclusive attention on male scholars, writers, and journalists.

Goodman, D. *The Republic of Letters: A Cultural History of the French Enlightenment*. Ithaca, N.Y., and London, 1994. Interesting thesis, heavily influenced by Habermas, about the transformation of the Republic of Letters into a political public sphere and the corresponding yet gradual exclusion of women.

Habermas, J. *The Structural Transformation of the Public Sphere*. Translated by T. Burger. Oxford, 1992. Provides the theoretical framework for much recent work on the Enlightenment, although it is often questionable both as to gender analysis and detail.

Labalme, P. H., ed. *Beyond Their Sex: Learned Women of the European Past*. New York and London, 1980.

Lloyd, G. *The Man of Reason: "Male" and "Female" in Western Philosophy*. London, 1984.

Roche, D. *Le siècle des lumières en province: Académies et académiciens provinciaux, 1680–1789*. Paris, 1978. The last two chapters consider the institutions and culture of the Republic of Letters; many incidental examples throughout of the way it functions as a motivating ideal.

and the emerging hypothesis of the existence of other inhabited worlds—contributed to the weakening of biblical history from the Creation to Christ's incarnation and redemption. The tales of travelers in remote countries inhabited by peoples untouched by European culture revealed that there were beliefs and superstitions shared by numerous religious traditions, and this too raised doubts about the supremacy of the Christian religion. Finally, the use of historical and philological tools showed the shaky basis of the *pia philosophia*. This led to a reappraisal of ancient history outside the providential frame proposed by the Christian tradition, which placed Christ's revelation at the center of human history. As a result, Christianity was gradually relegated to a status equal with other revealed religions, and it assumed the semblance of a product of interested legislators and clergy.

Spinoza's Analysis of the Old Testament. The doubts and allegations raised against revealed religion, however,

Revealed Religions. Judaism and Christianity are two among the many religions represented in the frontispiece to *L'origine de tous les cultes, ou Religion universelle* (1794) by Charles-François Dupuis (1742–1809). Etching by L. Pauquet after a drawing by Ducoudray. (British Library, London.)

also reignited interest in the study of its foundations in the light of increasing scientific knowledge, new philosophical concepts, and new and more sophisticated methodologies of historical and philological research. In critically tackling revealed religion, thinkers reconsidered a number of problems connected with its being "revealed." These went beyond more general issues such as the existence and nature of God, the position of mankind in the universe, the possibility of a reciprocal relationship between God and mankind, or the ability of human reason to know religious truths. They now included also the very possibility and existence of divine revelation and the conditions of its identification; divine inspiration; prophecy; the authority of God's alleged messengers and of the miracles invoked as warrants of their mission; the trustworthy transmission of the revealed word; the addressees of this word; and the authentic comprehension of its content.

One source that profoundly influenced reflection on these topics was Spinoza's *Tractatus theologico-politicus* (1670). Spinoza's analysis of Old Testament tradition portrayed prophecy or alleged divine revelation as deriving solely from the sphere of human imagination, which has as its object not the knowledge of religious truth, but solely the persuasion to obedience. True divine law was to be found in the natural order of things. In this way, divine legislative intervention in the history of the Jews should be read as the "defective intelligence of Adam and his descendants." The fact that "God was represented as a governor, a legislator, a merciful and just king" was the result of their ignorance, because "these are attributes of human nature alone and are completely extraneous to divine nature." The institutions and ceremonies of the Old Testament, moreover, could not be charged with special, universal, soteriological value (relating to salvation); they had merely political value, related solely to the temporal sphere, the prosperity of the Jewish kingdom, and the well-being of the Jewish nation. Moses was seen as an astute political figure, able to present his own law as divine law, so that "the people would comply with its duties out of devotion, rather than out of fear."

Spinoza's criticism of miracles sought to destroy any remaining illusion that might grant the seal of divine origin to revealed religion. The immutable order of nature proved the impossibility of miracles: "Nothing happens against nature and nature keeps a fixed and immutable order." Purported miracles should be regarded simply as "unusual natural things, the causes of which are unknown." The pages that sacred scripture dedicated to the narration of miracles confirmed for Spinoza that "Scripture does not teach anything by means of its immediate causes, but it only narrates, and [does so] in that order and with those expressions which have the greatest power of moving mankind in general and the common people especially toward devotion." Recourse to sacred scripture—the essential foundation of revealed religion in the Judeo-Christian tradition—thus lost any value for knowing and establishing true religion. Furthermore, for Spinoza, the corrupted state in which scripture has been handed down showed the untrustworthiness of the sacred text for any fixed and certain comprehension of the revealed word. The rift between faith and reason became unbridgeable. As reason was unable to compel adherence to revealed religion, so revelation could not illuminate rational knowledge. The foundation of an individual's adherence to a revealed religion could be only a choice of faith, which demanded "piety rather than truth" and which "is pious and availing to salvation only in virtue of obedience." Truth, including religious truth, was alien to revelation; it belonged only to philosophy.

Spinoza's close criticism of revealed religion and his appeal to reason and philosophy as the only guides to knowing the truth paved the way for two main developments. First, ethics could be based solely on an analysis of human nature and of the interplay of the passions, quite independent of the precepts of revealed religion. Second, as Spinoza argued in the *Ethica*, religious truth could be seen as founded solely in the knowledge of the mind "which proceeds from the adequate idea of certain of God's attributes to the adequate knowledge of the essence of things," and knowledge of the causes of the necessary and eternal order led in turn to the "intellectual love of God."

Spinoza's work had a limited audience, but popularizers, although they were a restricted number, soon disseminated similar arguments in pamphlets targeted at broader audiences and written in an incisive style that briefly and synthetically reformulated the suggestions and arguments of ancient and recent philosophers against revealed religion, and proposed with almost catechetic concision the features of a purely rational religion.

Charles Blount and *Religio Laici*. The work of Charles Blount, one of the most prominent authors of pre-Lockean deism, repeated the critical remarks—of the libertines, Hobbes, and Spinoza—that aimed to show the impossibility of revealed religion and the necessity of professing the *religio laici* of which Herbert of Cherbury had spoken at the beginning in *De veritate* (On Truth, 1624). In the controversial *Miracles, No Violations of the Law of Nature* (1683), Blount reiterated Spinoza's and Hobbes's objections against miracles with the intention of depriving this fundamental argument of any possible apologetic force. The reformulation of the five universal articles of natural religion, drawn from the formulation of Herbert of Cherbury, went hand in glove in his work with the explicit rejection of all revealed religions, none of which was able to prove unequivocally its divine origin (*Religio laici*, 1683). How can certainty be based on imagination, on a

voice, on a vision, or on ecstasy? Do not all revelations, both pagan and Christian, rest on these weak foundations? It is not reasonable to base assent on uncertain visions and apparitions, unverifiable witnesses, tales of prodigious events that could be the work of impostors or the effect of natural forces, or prophecies at best obscure. On the contrary, we need to build a rigorous foundation of religion and an a priori formulation of universally valid rational principles to inform the true and unique religious relationship, and to constitute the absolute parameters of judgment of the contents of revealed religions. The foundation of these principles can only be reason, Blount concluded, which "being the first Revelation of God, is first to be believed, not depending on doubtful Fact without us, but full of its own Light shining always in us" (*Summary Account of the Deist Religion*, 1686).

Blount's account of natural religion stressed the importance of reason in the knowledge of religious truth and vindicated the positive abilities of "unassist'd reason," which should be liberated from an inferior status as an "imperfect Light" waiting to be perfected by revelation. He also tried strongly to deny the value of any revealed religion, as clearly indicated by the subtitle of Blount's brief *Essay on Natural Religion* which identified it as a treatment *Of Natural Religion, as opposed to Divine Revelation*. Blount's opposition to revealed religion subsequently tended in an increasingly specific way against the Christian religion. With the denial of Christ's redemption and of his role of mediator, the affirmation of the self-sufficiency of human virtue for salvation, and the vindication of the adequacy of our natural concept of God, Blount had already drawn precise lines of attack against the doctrines of Christianity. He advanced his attack in *The Oracles of Reason* (1693), where he claimed that even the birth of Christianity was due to a "Temporal Interest" (158), since it was only the result of millennarian expectations of an oppressed Jewish people.

The Defense of Religion by Grotius and Others. The objections raised in the seventeenth and eighteenth centuries against revealed religion, and in particular against Christianity, stimulated the interest not only of philosophers and theologians, but also more generally of educated people. Antireligious essays targeted at a general audience, such as Blount's, called for clear and comprehensible answers for people unable to tackle the study of long apologetic treatises or to follow sophisticated critical analysis of texts. It is, therefore, not surprising that Hugo Grotius's *De veritate religionis Christianae* (On the Truth of the Christian Religion, 1627), remained one of the most widely read books until the end of the eighteenth century. Its dozens of editions in various languages testify to the persistence of interest in the reasons and foundations of the Christian revealed religion.

Written in plain, direct language, this short treatise aimed to show those who came into contact with heathens in China and Guinea, Muslims in the Middle East, and Jews, that Christianity was the true revealed religion. Grotius stressed the superiority of Christian doctrine and morality, together with the perfect conformity of Christian teaching with that of the most enlightened reason. He also emphasized, however, that Christianity was the true religion because it was truly revealed: Christ, who preached this religion, was God's messenger, who proved his mission with miracles and, in particular, with his resurrection: "Christ himself revealed a new dogma as a divine mandate, as both his own [disciples] and the others confess, sure it follows for certain, that the dogma is true."

The defenders of the Christian religion could not rest content with republishing Grotius. As François Lamy wrote in his *Réfutation du sistème de Spinosa* (1696), answers to the attack on revealed religion should embrace all the objections raised and therefore should follow the same lines traced by those who had delivered it. This was a task reserved, on the one hand, for learned philologists and historians, and on the other, for philosophers.

In answer to the criticisms raised by Spinoza against the sacred text and the Judeo-Christian tradition, many Catholic and Protestant writers attempted to demonstrate that these criticisms lacked a solid foundation. In his *Demonstratio evangelica* (1679), Pierre-Daniel Huet claimed that all the doctrines of the *Tractatus theologico-politicus* had to be radically rejected because they lacked scientific foundation, and in a letter to Christoph Sand, he also called them impious, licentious, and absurd.

Measured Criticism of Spinoza. Other scholars intervened in the debate, convinced that the historical and critical theses of the *Tractatus* should not be condemned without qualification and that certain critical remarks of Spinoza, such as those relating to corruption of the sacred text or to the identification of the authors of single books, should not lead to the denial of revealed religion but to the restoration of scripture's purity and true meaning. The Oratorian priest Richard Simon recognized in his *Histoire critique du Vieux Testament* (1678) the state of corruption of the text of the sacred scripture, but he undertook to mend this by providing a critical history of both the text of the Bible from Moses to the present and of the principal versions of it. The goal of his exegetical and critical work was to restore sacred scripture to the veneration of his contemporaries as a faithful expression of a revealed inheritance entrusted not to the dead letter but to the tradition of the church.

The young Protestant scholar Jean Le Clerc also felt the urgency of moving against Spinozism, despite his opposition to the concept of inspiration proposed by Simon—in his view, too dependent on tradition—and to many other

theses of the Oratorian, as he explained in his *Sentimens de quelques théologiens d'Hollande* (1685). In a letter of December 1681, he asserted the necessity that a refutation of the *Tractatus theologico-politicus* be conducted with intelligent measure. His answer to Spinoza did not limit itself to a few brief essays; it was expressed in great critical and exegetical works on the Old and New Testaments.

The Place of Cartesianism. Some thinkers saw the impious philosophical theses of Spinoza as the logical development of Cartesian philosophy. They proposed, as a remedy, the rejection of Cartesianism itself. This opinion was shared by Gottfried Wilhelm von Leibniz, who in a letter of 1697 reiterated "that Spinoza did nothing else than to cultivate certain seeds of the Philosophy of Mr. Descartes, so that I believe it to be really important for Religion, and for piety, that this Philosophy be corrected by the elimination of the mistakes which are mixed with truth." Did Cartesian philosophy really contain the seeds of a negation of the Christian revelation? René Descartes presented his *Meditations* (1647) as a defense of the Christian religion. Moreover, he attempted to elaborate an explanation of the eucharistic mystery, and he declared in clear terms against Henricus Regius: "I have never seen anybody affirming that the nature of things admits that something could go differently from what it is taught by the sacred Scripture, unless he wanted indirectly to show that he did not have faith in Scripture. In fact, since we are born as human beings and only subsequently we have became Christians, it is not plausible that one should seriously embrace opinions that he regards as contrary to right reason, which is constitutive of man, in order to embrace faith, in virtue of which he is a Christian."

Among the voices raised in defense of Cartesian philosophy against charges such as Leibniz's was that of François Lamy, who claimed that the most rigorous metaphysics (in particular Cartesian metaphysics) could convince human reason of the necessity and the truth of revealed religion. In his *Réfutation du sistême de Spinosa*, he reaffirmed the profound connection between revealed religion and philosophy. He remarked "that religion and certainty of faith depend themselves in a certain way on metaphysics, insofar as this latter has to prove to them at least that there is a God, that this God is not a deceiver and that his testimony is infallible." At the same time, "it is good to join reason to faith and to move from faith to understanding." Finally, "religion needs Metaphysics to defend itself against its enemies." Having demonstrated the great distance of Spinoza's metaphysics from that of Descartes, Lamy repeatedly spoke, in a direct echo of Cartesian thinking, of the "evident truth of the Christian religion." He showed that the alleged absurdity of the Incarnation or of miracles arose from "chimeras" and "extravagant ideas" of the oneness of substance and of the necessity of the whole, maintained by Spinoza but extraneous to Descartes's teaching.

François Fénelon agreed with this profound trust in the role of philosophy. In the *Lettres sur divers sujets concernant la religion et la métaphysique* (1718), he set out to show "how much the simple principles of metaphysics are fertile and decisive in order to lead by a shorter way to the perfect knowledge of religion," and how precisely the consequences drawn from these principles are able to demonstrate "the truth of the Jewish religion until the advent of Jesus Christ, the truth of Christianity which succeeded to Moses's law, and finally the truth of the Catholic church against all the sects which separated themselves from it."

Many philosophers outside the speculative lines directly inspired by Descartes continued to maintain the rational conformity of the teaching and precepts of the revealed Christian religion and to assert a strong link between reason and divine revelation. The chief example is Leibniz, whose *Essais de Théodicée* (1710) represented the outcome of a continuous and profound, if fragmented, meditation on topics related to revelation and to the principal dogmas of the Christian religion—a train of thought Leibniz began to move toward a systematic formulation as early as the *Confessio philosophi* (1673). Answering the challenges of Pierre Bayle, who reduced religious allegiance to a fideistic choice carried out despite the presence of evident contradictions, Leibniz never tired of highlighting the perfect conformity to reason of Christ's teaching and the sublime continuity between the order of nature and the order of grace. Jesus, he wrote, "teaches with all the force of a legislator that the immortal souls move on to another life where they have to receive the wages of their actions," and "only he does what so many philosophers tried in vain to do." There cannot be a true piety to which knowledge is extraneous, as there cannot be true religion without or (even worse) against reason. In fact "one could not love God, without knowing his perfections, and this knowledge contains the principles of true piety." True piety indeed consists in the love of God, but it is "an enlightened love, where fervour is paired with light." Human reason is certainly limited, and it should not delude itself by claiming to be able to comprehend, by virtue of revelation, the whole divine truth, or to prove the mysteries contained in it. Despite this limitation, human reason is nevertheless able to receive revealed doctrines and to support them against objections. To claim that there is a space inside revealed religion for something contradictory or irrational would in fact coincide with a negation of revealed religion itself.

The Corruption by Metaphysics. The attempts of these thinkers to show the rational conformity of Christianity, seen as true revealed religion, sometimes risked undue superimposition of concerns pertaining to particular philosophical systems, or a transposition of the divine message into interpretive categories extraneous to it. Once the revealed word became entangled in debates between philosophical and theological schools, the risk of corrupting it was high. This danger had been already emphasized in the *Entretiens sur diverses matières de théologie* (1685) by Jean Le Clerc, who had become worried by the results of Cartesian scholasticism and, in particular, by the developments proposed by Nicolas Malebranche. He expressed the conviction that "modern metaphysics, just like that of the scholastics, is good only for troubling the spirit, and even for corrupting theology," and he invited his contemporaries to study scripture free from the preoccupations of metaphysicians, but armed instead with solid philological and historical erudition. According to Le Clerc, God has in fact given to us "the lights of reason and Revelation" not in order to satisfy our metaphysical curiosities or to build theological systems but "to comprehend his will properly and to ensure us of the truth of the religion he gave to us. This is the use which should be made of reason within Religion."

Locke and Religion. John Locke—the philosopher regarded by the whole Enlightenment as a trustworthy point of reference and seen, as Voltaire put it, as the person "who has developed human reason for man" (*Lettres philosophiques*, 13)—handed down to eighteenth-century philosophers an equable and lucid critical meditation on the foundations of religion and Christian revelation. The study of the foundations of ethics and revealed religion, the verification of the possibilities and extension of our knowledge in these spheres, the criticism both of popular beliefs and of dogmatic systems, and the attempt to resolve ethical and religious issues remained constant points of reference for Locke. Summarizing a twenty-year-long meditation, in the *Essay Concerning Human Understanding* (1689, book 4, chap. 18) Locke ascertained clearly the respective spheres of competence of reason and faith and defined their reciprocal relations, which assigned revelation its proper space. This was a concern already expressed as early as 1676 in the pages of his diary written in Montpellier. There, following the indications offered by his friend Robert Boyle in his volume on the *Reconcileableness of Reason and Religion* (1675), his intention was to come to a definition of the boundaries between faith and reason: "If the distinct provinces of faith and reason are not to be set out by these boundaries, I believe, in matters of religion, that there will be no use, no room, for reason at all; and those extravagant opinions and ceremonies that are to be found in the several religions of the world will not deserve to be blamed. For to this crying up of faith in opposition to reason, we may, I think, in good measure ascribe those absurdities that fill almost all the religions which possess and divide mankind" (Ms. Locke f. 1, p. 420).

Acknowledging the possibility of divine revelation, however, was to lead Locke to an even more profound inquiry concerning the nature and extent of revelation. His aim was both to identify the true revealed religion and to avoid religious fanaticism. A manuscript of 1687 sums up Locke's thought on the value of internal inspiration. Under the title *An Inward Inspiration or Revelation*, he anticipates remarks later repeated in the chapter on enthusiasm he added to the fourth edition of the *Essay* (book 4, Chap. 19). Locke was seeking, as a guarantee of authentic divine inspiration, "some other rule either of reason or revelation, which must distinguish those emotions of the minde as proceeding from several causes else the most extravagant boundless enthusiasme must pass for revelation." Internal inspiration on its own cannot be considered a sufficient warranty of divine inspiration. The Bible itself suggests miraculous signs of divine intervention as an external criterion: "For as there were need of signes to convince those they were sent to, that the prophets were messengers sent from God, soe there was need also of some signe some way of distinction whereby the messenger was from God. This God spoke to Moses not by a bare influence in his minde, but out of a bush all on fire that consumed not" (*ibid.* f. 74, and *Essay*, 4.19.15). The argument of miracles as proofs of the divine origin of revelation was thus forcefully reiterated; later still, Locke reaffirmed the validity of this argument and studied its conditions in his *Discourse of Miracles* (1702, published in 1706).

Locke's inquiry did not stop at this important phase of critical clarification, however. Having defined in the *Essay* the relationship between faith and reason and having investigated the criteria by which it is possible to identify a revelation as coming from God, he wanted to study the revealed word and to listen to it. The result was his *The Reasonableness of Christianity, as Delivered in the Scriptures* (1695), in which the image of the Christian revelation is that of a religion that perfectly conforms to the most profound expectations of human beings, even the most humble. In his preaching of the Gospel to the poor (Matt. 11:5), Jesus brought a message of salvation rather than complex treatises of doctrinal truths. He clearly promised to those who would believe in him and acknowledge him as the Messiah the gifts of salvation, of eternal life, and of the Holy Spirit. Although the authority of Jesus' teaching depended solely on his being God's representative, as proved by miracles, Locke claimed that it was never opposed to the most profound requirements of human rationality. Where probability and uncertainty open room for error, there Christ's teaching enters; where vice or superstition mislead human beings, there his work of teacher and guide intervenes; where the limitation of human reason appears in things concerning our salvation, there divine revelation comes to our rescue. Jesus led humanity back to monotheism and called people to a morality they had never before attained. Worship was reformed by Jesus into an internal, spiritual worship, far removed from the outward pomp of ceremonies.

Criticism of Locke. It was not long, however, before Locke's theses—in particular, those expressed in the *Reasonableness*—were read as premises of a negation of revealed religion. This anti-Christian interpretation of Locke did not take into account the fact that in this work—as in his later *Paraphrases and Notes on the Epistles of St. Paul* (1705–1707)—Locke was concerned with interpreting scripture by means of scripture itself. Moreover, he proposed these allegedly suspect theses not because they conformed to reason, but because they were clearly taught by scripture. Among these theses was that of a distinction between fundamental and nonfundamental articles of faith—a thesis which, although it had already been maintained by numerous reformed theologians who were above suspicion, some people wrongly interpreted as an attempt to reduce the revealed message to the narrowest boundaries of natural religion.

Locke's doctrines became suspect above all because they were readily utilized by deistic authors to destroy the foundations of any revealed religion, in particular the Christian. John Toland, in his *Christianity Not Mysterious* (1696), set about eliminating from revealed religion everything supernatural and mysterious. His intention was to deny credibility to the specific content of revelation (that is, what is "above Reason") by equating it with the irrational and contradictory ("contrary to Reason") and therefore finding it incomprehensible. Starting from Locke's explanation of knowledge as "the Perception of the Agreement or Disagreement of our Ideas," Toland excluded the possibility of a reasonable assent in the absence of evidence deriving from clear and distinct ideas. Divine revelation ceases to be "a necessitating Motive of Assent" and is reduced to a mere "Means of Information." The evidence of the content became the criterion of assent: "I believe nothing purely upon his word without evidence in the things themselves." The Gospels, once liberated from mystery and from every supernatural element ("there is nothing mysterious or above Reason in the Gospel"), is presented as the announcement of pure natural religion: Jesus "fully and clearly preach'd the purest Morals, he taught that reasonable Worship, and those just Conceptions of Heaven and Heavenly Things, which were more obscurely signifi'd or design'd by the Legal Observations. So having stripp'd the truth of all those external Types and Ceremonies which made it difficult before, he render'd it easy and obvious to the meanest Capacities."

Locke also had to exert himself against the erudite bishop of Worcester, Edward Stillingfleet, in order to distance his doctrines from those of Toland. In the *Letter to the Right Reverend Edward Lord Bishop of Worcester* (1697), he adamantly refused to be associated with deistic authors, and with Toland in particular. He defended his philosophical system, showing that far from being opposed to the doctrines of the Gospels, it gave heed to the divine doctrine. He never maintained that certainty was based only on clear and distinct ideas, as Toland claimed. This had misled Stillingfleet into an unjustified association of the two thinkers. Locke remarked, "I do say, That all our Knowledge is founded in simple Ideas; but I do not say, it is all deduced from clear Ideas; much less that we cannot have any certain Knowledge of the Existence of any thing, whereof we have not a clear, distinct, complex Idea." Locke acknowledged a space for certainty outside the circle of simple clear and distinct ideas, whereas Toland denied the specific mysteries of Christianity.

Deism. A new and important step toward the use of Locke's epistemological doctrine in advancing deism was made in 1707 by Anthony Collins in *An Essay Concerning the Use of Reason in Propositions, the Evidence Thereof Depends upon Human Testimony*. This work, devoted to the study of religious knowledge based on testimony, focused on the witness of the prophets, Christ, and the apostles. In order reasonably to give assent to propositions of faith, Collins maintained, the credibility of the witness is not enough; the things reported must also be credible. This credibility of "things" involves not only the comprehensibility of single ideas and the exclusion of everything irrational and contradictory; it also requires the exclusion of everything that is "above Reason." If reason is identified with human reason, there is no difference between what is superior to it and what is contrary to it. Robert Boyle's and Locke's tripartite distinction among propositions that are either agreeable, above reason, or contrary to reason no longer holds, since "all Propositions considered as Objects of Assent or Dissent, are adequately divided into Propositions agreeable or contrary to Reason. And there remains no third Idea under which to rank them." Human reason remains the only criterion of truth, and its task is to judge the truth of any doctrine, including revealed ones.

The work of Toland, Collins, and the English deists was not limited to bending certain epistemological theses of Locke to the task of denying the possibility of a revelation of truths that are above reason. It also directly tackled the criticism of traditional arguments in support of an alleged "divine testimony." Prophecies and miracles were indicated as external signs of this divine intervention. Against prophecies and their probative value, Collins wrote once again in his *Discourse of the Grounds and Reasons of the Christian Religion* (1724) and his *Scheme of Literal Prophecy Considered* (1726). In direct polemic against Whiston, he claimed a purely symbolic and allegorical sense of scriptural prophecies. In the absence of a clear literal reference to events of the New Testament and in the presence of equivocal and arbitrary reciprocal connections, prophecies were reduced to symbols and allegories, deprived of any probative value. The argument regarding miracles suffered an identical fate in the writings of Thomas Woolston, who in his six *Discourses on the Miracles of Our Saviour* (1727–1729) applied the criterion of allegorical interpretation to the miracles narrated in the Gospels, showing how "they, in whole or in part, were never wrought, but are only related as parabolic Narratives of what would be mysteriously and more wonderfully done by him."

Natural religion thus became, for these deistic philosophers, the only true religion, based purely on reason, or more precisely on human reason, which is the only means bestowed by God on all men for this purpose. Matthew Tindal forcefully expressed this opinion in *Christianity as Old as Creation* (1730): "What God requires us to know, believe, profess, and practise, must be in itself a reasonable service; but whether what is offer'd to us as such, be really so, 'tis Reason alone which must judge; as the Eye is the sole Judge of what is visible, the Ear of what is audible, so Reason of what is reasonable." Religion must always and only conform to the rational human order, and natural light is the only means to establish the truth of religion. Tindal no longer spoke of a perfecting of natural religion through revelation. The former is in fact already a perfect religion, based on the nature of things, on the immutable relationship among beings, from which arises the one fundamental precept: the fear of God and the good of mankind.

The Boyle Lectures. The most famous English theologians preached in defense of revealed religion from the pulpit of Saint Paul's Cathedral in London in a series of sermons established as the Boyle Lectures. Against the atheists and deists, many of them—especially during the first years—preferred to insist on the profound rationality of Christian religion by showing how revealed religion was the perfection of rational religion. In 1697, Francis Gastrell spoke on *The Certainty and Necessity of Religion in General: Or the First Grounds and Principles of Humane Duty Establis'd*; in 1699, the bishop of Rochester, Samuel Bradford, claimed *The Credibility of the Christian Revelation, from it's Intrinsick Evidence*; George Stanhope stressed *The Wisdom of the Christian Religion* in his sermons of 1701–1702 to show "The Truth and Excellence of the Christian Religion." Samuel Clarke, in sermons preached in 1704–1705 and published in *A Demonstration of the Being and Attributes of God* and *A Discourse Concerning* *the Unchangeable Obligations of Natural Religion, and the Truth and Certainty of the Christian Revelation*, presented the Christian revelation as the completion of truths already acquired or reachable by means of purely rational powers and as a further guarantee of religious truth. The norm of moral conduct and the certainty of a future state of reward or punishment are truths within the reach of human reason; the contribution of revelation is reduced to a further assurance and to authoritative confirmation.

Some voices, however, arose against this revalorization of reason in support of revealed religion. Joseph Butler, in his *Fifteen Sermons* (1726), pointed out the ignorance, blindness, and obscurity of mankind, resulting from the impossibility for our reason to sound out the divine action. Therefore, "the wisest and most knowing cannot comprehend the works of God, the methods and designs of his providence in the creation and government of the world." Acknowledgment of the limitation of human reason, however, did not lead Butler to passive resignation or fideistic choices. In the deistic dilemma between perfect comprehension of the divine order and its absolute incomprehensibility, he sought a middle way through an appeal to analogy. In his *Analogy of Religion Natural and Revealed to the Constitution and the Course of Nature* (1736), he maintained that by analogy it is possible to refind the link between the natural and supernatural orders. The homogeneity between these two orders, both products of the divine will, allows us to refer them to the same general laws and principles of divine conduct. Within this perspective, revelation receives its full legitimization as a trustworthy guide for our limited reason. Only God, the author of both creation and revelation, has complete comprehension of the reason and scheme of things.

More radical was William Law's opposition to rationalistic defenses of revealed religion. Law was influenced by mystical writings (such as the anonymous *Fides et ratio collatae ac suo utroque loco redditae*) in which reason—the light of a corrupted nature unable to rise to the knowledge of the divine—was replaced by faith, conceived as the "live and substantial light of God in us." Law's aim was the liberation of the space of revelation from the subjection to human reason championed by Tindal. In *The Case of Reason, or Natural Religion* (1731), he showed that revelation, which is the work of God, precedes and surpasses every purely human judgment. Since no human judgment precedes or bonds divine action and revelation, "a revelation is to be receiv'd as coming from God, not because of its internal excellence, or because we judge it to be worthy of God; but because God has declar'd it to be his, in as plain and undeniable a manner, as he has declar'd creation and providence to be his.... And as we can only know what is worthy of God in creation, by knowing what he has created; so we can no otherway possibly know what

is worthy of God to be reveal'd, but by a revelation." It is not conformity with the dictates of human reason, but only miracles and what is above reason that can give us a guarantee of divine action. It is in fact precisely by means of miracles and mysteries that God manifests himself. These can only be above the ordinary course of things, and therefore above our comprehension, which is limited to the ordinary.

Hume and Natural Religion. To stress the incapacity of reason could have very negative consequences for revealed religion, however, as is manifest in David Hume's *Dialogues Concerning Natural Religion* (1779) and *Natural History of Religion* (1757). In *An Enquiry Concerning Human Understanding* (1758), Hume had shown not only that our aesthetic and moral judgments are rooted in instinct, but also that all our intellectual persuasions are of identical origin. Our ideas arise from impressions, and sensation allows their connection and association. Therefore, "all the philosophy in the world, and all the religion, which is nothing but a species of philosophy, will never be able to carry us beyond the usual course of experience." No rational discourse has ever led mankind to confess God, nor had recourse to miracles been able to convince reason of the truth of revelation. It is rather concern for the events of life—hope and fear—that created the gods. Religion is founded on "irrational and superstitious principles"; and when "any immediate communication with the deity" is claimed, the "inflamed imagination" cannot restrain itself and descends into "madness, fury, rage." The pairing of religion with morality is torn asunder: the history of the religions of mankind shows how the believer "will still seek the divine favour, not by virtue and good morals, which alone can be acceptable to a perfect being, but either by frivolous observances, by intemperate zeal, by rapturous extasies, or by the belief of mysterious and absurd opinions."

Opposition from Philosophes. The philosophes of the Continent drew freely from the doctrines of the seventeenth-century libertines and other scholars in order to develop criticisms of revealed religion and Christianity and spread them among an even broader audience. Voltaire, who had encountered deistic literature during his youthful stay in England, broadcast with caustic irony the most biting accusations against any alleged revealed religion, in particular against the biblical tradition of the Old and New Testaments, against the figures of Moses, Christ, the apostles, and the prophets, and against the apologetical arguments of prophecies, miracles, and martyrdom. This criticism was carried out in a systematic way in the entries of his *Dictionnaire philosophique* (1764) and in his *Examen important de Milord Bolingbroke ou le Tombeau du fanatisme* (1767); and in every one of his works—even those of a historical or fictional nature—we encounter this purposeful demolition of the Christian religion. In his view, Christian revelation, once reduced to its original purity, would contain nothing other than a message of brotherhood directed to all men and women, especially the poorest. He accepted Jesus of Nazareth as a "rustic Socrates," but certainly not as God's messenger or as the redeemer, and even less as God become man.

Revealed religion encountered its most radical opposition from the *coterie holbachique*. The materialistic and atheistic opinions shared by Paul-Henri Thiry d'Holbach and the philosophes who frequented his salon—including Denis Diderot, Jacques-André Naigeon, and Claude-Adrien Helvétius—left no space whatever for religion. Precisely in order to fight against religion—any kind of religion—d'Holbach oversaw the publication and circulation of clandestine antireligious manuscripts composed between the end of the seventeenth century and the beginning of the eighteenth, as well as the publication of French translations of the writings of the most important English deists, usually in atheized form.

During the seventeenth century, scholars, philosophers, and apologists continued to deepen the study of issues related to revelation and Christianity, and they carried forward their battle against the objections raised by libertines, deists, and atheists. Their efforts did not succeed, however, in counteracting the spread of antireligious thought. Their long trains of reasoning could not match the effects of the lively pamphlets and biting words of the opposition. Voltaire was well aware of this distinction when he decided to do battle with the weapons of irony, but he suggested another explanation in 1778. Among the defenders of revealed religion, men of genius, such as Pascal, had been lacking in recent years: "Of so many eternal polemists, only Pascal remained, because he alone was a man of genius; he is still on his feet above the ruins of his century."

[*See also* Apologetics; Deism; Enthusiasm; Judaism; Natural Religion; Philosophes; Prejudice; Reformed Churches; Roman Catholicism; *and* Toleration.]

BIBLIOGRAPHY

SOURCES

Blount, Charles. *Religio laici*. London, 1683; facsimile repr., New York, 1975.

Blount, Charles. *The Oracles of Reason*. London, 1693; facsimile repr., London, 1995.

Boyle, Robert. *Some Considerations about the Reconcileableness of Reason and Religion*. London, 1675; edited in *The Works of the Honourable Robert Boyle*, edited by Thomas Birch, vol. 4, pp. 151–191. London, 1772; facsimile repr., Hildesheim, 1965–1966.

Butler, Joseph. *Fifteen Sermons Preached at Rolls Chappel*. London, 1726. Edited by W. R. Matthews. London, 1969.

Butler, Joseph. *The Analogy of Religion, Natural and Revealed, to the Constitution and Course of Nature*. London, 1736; New York, 1961.

Clarke, Samuel. *A Demonstration of the Being and Attributes of God, and A Discourse Concerning the Unchangeable Obligations of Natural Religion, and the Truth and Certainty of the Christian Revelation*. London, 1705–1706; facsimile repr., Stuttgart and Bad Cannstatt, 1964.

Collins, Anthony. *A Discourse of the Grounds and Reasons of the Christian Religion*. London, 1724.

Fénelon, François. *Oeuvres*. Edited by Jacques Le Brun. 2 vols. Paris, 1983–1997.

Grotius, Hugo. *De veritate religionis Christianae*. Leiden, 1627. English translation, *True Religion Explained, and Defended against the Archenemies Thereof in These Times*. London, 1632; facsimile repr., Amsterdam and New York, 1971.

Hume, David. *Principal Writings on Religion Including Dialogues Concerning Natural Religion, and The Natural History of Religion*. Edited by J. C. A. Gaskin. Oxford, 1993.

Lamy, François. *Le nouvel athéisme renversé, ou Réfutation du sistème de Spinosa*. Paris, 1696.

Law, William. *The Case of Reason or Natural Religion, Fairly and Fully Stated, in Answer to a Book Entitul'd "Christianity as Old as the Creation."* London, 1731.

Le Clerc, Jean. *Epistolario*. Edited by Mario Sina and Maria Grazia Sina. 4 vols. Florence, 1987–1997.

Le Clerc, Jean. *Sentimens de quelques théologiens d'Hollande sur l'Histoire critique du Vieux Testament, composée par le P. Richard Simon de l'Oratoire*. Amsterdam, 1685; facsimile in Bibliothèque Nationale de France, *Gallica*.

Leibniz, Gottfried Wilhelm von. *Essais de theodicée sur la bonté de Dieu, la liberté de l'homme, et l'origine du mal*. Amsterdam, 1710. English translation, *Theodicy: Essays on the Goodness of God, the Freedom of Man, and the Origin of Evil*. Edited by Austin Farrer. London, 1951.

Locke, John. *The Reasonableness of Christianity: as Delivered in Scriptures*. London, 1695. Edited by John C. Higgins Biddle. Oxford, 2000.

Locke, John. *A Paraphrase and Notes on the Epistles of St. Paul*. London, 1705–1707. Edited by A. W. Wainwright. 2 vols. Oxford, 1987.

Simon, Richard. *Histoire critique du Vieux Testament*. Paris, 1678; Rotterdam, 1685; facsimile repr., Geneva, 1971.

Spinoza, Baruch de. *Tractatus theologico-politicus*. Hamburg [Amsterdam], 1670. English translation by Samuel Shirley. Leiden, 1989.

Toland, John. *Christianity Not Mysterious: or a treatise shewing that there is Nothing in the Gospel contrary to reason, nor above it: and that no christian doctrine can be properly call'd a mystery*. London, 1696; facsimile repr., Stuttgart and Bad Cannstatt, Germany, 1964.

STUDIES

Byrne, Peter. *Natural Religion and the Nature of Religion: The Legacy of Deism*. London and New York, 1989.

Cragg, G. R. *From Puritanism to the Age of Reason: A Study of Changes in Religious Thought within the Church of England, 1660 to 1700*. Cambridge, 1950.

Downey, J. *The Eighteenth-Century Pulpit: A Study of the Sermons of Butler, Berkeley, Seker, Sterne, Whitefield, and Wesley*. Oxford, 1969.

Everdell, W. *Christian Apologetics in France, 1730–1789*. New York, 1987.

Lund, Roger D., ed. *The Margins of Orthodoxy: Heterodox Writing and Cultural Response, 1660–1750*. Cambridge, 1995.

McKenna, Antony. *De Pascal à Voltaire: Le rôle des Pensées de Pascal dans l'histoire des idées entre 1670 et 1734*. 2 vols. Oxford, 1990.

Morton, R. E., and J. D. Browning, eds. *Religion in the Eighteenth Century*. New York and London, 1979.

Pitassi, Maria Cristina. *De l'orthodoxie aux Lumières: Genève 1670–1737*. Geneva, 1992.

Sina, Mario. *L'avvento della ragione: "Reason" e "above Reason" dal razionalismo teologico inglese al deismo.* Milan, 1976.

Vernière, Paul. *Spinoza et la pensée française avant la Révolution.* 2 vols. Paris, 1954.

Young, Brian W. *Religion and Enlightenment in Eighteenth-Century England: Theological Debate from Locke to Burke.* Oxford, 1998.

MARIO SINA

Translated from Italian by Maria Rosa Antognazza

REVELATION. *See* Revealed Religion.

REVOLUTION. Hannah Arendt famously argued that it was with the French Revolution that the ancient notion of revolution, hitherto understood as implying a cycle of return, took on its modern signification as an act of transformation oriented toward the future. The shift was a more complicated and extended one than this claim might suggest. By the time of the Enlightenment, *revolution* had already shed as its primary meaning the astronomically inspired idea of a cycle bringing things back to their point of departure. That use of the term certainly remained in the dictionaries, but from the late seventeenth century on it was more common to cast revolutions—usually negatively, and in the plural rather than the singular—as vicissitudes of fortune, mutations and disorders erupting within the flow of human affairs. Revolution in this sense was an ex post facto category of historical understanding: It was recognized retrospectively as a fact; it did not open up the horizon of an act. As late as 1798, the fifth edition of the dictionary of the French Academy offered this conventional meaning—and harked back to a substantial body of eighteenth-century historiography that had described revolutions occurring throughout political history—by observing that "one says, the Roman revolutions, the revolutions of Sweden, the revolutions of England for the memorable and violent changes which have agitated these countries." Strikingly, though, a supplement to that same edition added new forms of the word. *Revolutionary* was offered as a descriptor of a particular moment or act of transformation, as of the persons and deeds devoted to producing it; *revolutionize* became the term for what these latter did. Revolution itself had been revolutionized; transformed into a domain of lived experience, it had become an act of transformation carried out by self-conscious agents.

Perhaps the most fundamental condition of possibility for this dramatic shift in meaning was the invention of civil society as an ontological frame of human existence. Enlightenment thinkers offered a vision of human life as grounded in an autonomous order endowed with a mechanism producing stability through the very process of constant change. Society understood in this sense had to have a history far different from the endless vicissitudes of historical time implied in the conventional use of the term *revolution*. Against the conventional succession of revolutions introducing abrupt changes or political disruptions, Enlightenment philosophy, therefore, set other revolutions taking form as longer-term social and cultural transformations, at once more profound and more beneficent. Increasingly, it became possible to talk about a "happy" revolution, the most exemplary of which became the succession of events soon characterized and celebrated as the "American Revolution." Franco Venturi has described well the impact of this conceptualization of events on European political consciousness as transatlantic observers followed the American journey from "the right to change one's government" to "the duty to create a government that would no longer need to be torn down and remade" (Venturi, 129–130).

To the extent that Enlightenment historiography took as its object world history—the history of human civilization as a whole—the revolutions it identified as dynamic processes of transformation also had universal implications: They were not merely local events but phenomena of world-historical significance. Fundamental to the mechanism of human progress, they were (in Voltaire's remarkable phrase) the "wheels in the machine of the universe." Condorcet's *Esquisse d'un tableau historique des progrès de l'esprit humain* (1795) was to give canonical expression to this conception of universal human history as a succession of transformations in the human spirit.

In the idiom and terms of the Enlightenment, therefore, the meaning of *revolution* as the disorder of events in the flow of human time, a consequence of the instability of all things human, began to give way to "revolution" as dynamic transformational process, an expression of the historical rhythm of the progress of society. The philosophes not only expanded the concept of revolution to universal significance, but began to shift the chronological inflection of the term. Extended chronologically as process, it constituted a domain of lived experience and offered a new horizon of expectation. In this sense, the Enlightenment itself was a profound revolution already underway, a process of cultural transformation that was already separating past from present and reorienting expectations toward the future. Condorcet caught this view precisely when he recalled his age as marking the stage in human history as one in which the influence of "the progress of philosophy and the dissemination of enlightenment...upon public opinion, of public opinion upon nations or their leaders, suddenly ceases to be a slow, imperceptible affair, and produces a revolution in the whole order of several nations, a certain earnest of the revolution that must one day include in its scope the whole of the human race" (*Sketch for a Historical Picture of the Progress of the Human Mind*, 1955, 127–128). The notion of revolution was thus both universalized and reoriented from past to future, taking on an entirely new set of meanings as it came to designate a process of transformation within modern society.

There was, of course, an alternative to this view of social transformation through the progress of Enlightenment. A different note was struck by Jean-Jacques Rousseau in a celebrated passage of *Émile* (1762) announcing the approach of "a state of crisis and the age of revolutions." There was more to this formulation than a reiteration of the conventional meaning of revolution as vicissitude and change, the inevitable play of fortune in all human affairs. Rousseau's reference to a "state of crisis" points to a link between "revolution" and "crisis" that is worth emphasizing, especially in relationship to the classical republicanism that informed so much of his thinking. It need hardly be pointed out after the research of J. G. A. Pocock that in the language of classical republicanism the essential problem of politics was that of sustaining civic virtue, and with it the life of the political body through time. Hence the centrality in this idiom of organic metaphors: images of vigor and weakness, health and sickness, life and death. Hence the weight of the metaphor of crisis, understood as the moment in which the very existence of the body politic hangs in the balance, in which either its health and vigor will be recovered or it will fall into an irreversible, fatal sickness. As classical republicanism increasingly took the form of a critique of the growth of modern commercial society, so then the notion of crisis was extended to describe the effects of the destructive forces within that society as wealth and luxury fed the despotism sustained in its turn by courts, ministers, and standing armies. "I hold it to be impossible that the great monarchies of Europe still have long to last," Rousseau added as a footnote to his prediction of an age of revolutions in *Émile*. "All have shined, and every state which shines is on the decline. I have reasons more particular than this maxim for my opinion, but it is unseasonable to tell them, and everyone sees them only too well" (194).

There was thus a new prophetic tone in Rousseau's warning. Revolution as extended crisis here became the negative image of the philosophes' conception of revolution as transformational process. The prognosis of such a crisis was taken up nowhere more passionately than in Simon-Nicolas-Henri Linguet's *Annales politiques*, perhaps the most compelling French-language journal of the entire prerevolutionary period. Linguet offered a diagnosis of the "singular revolution threatening Europe," a revolution radically different from the peaceful transformation promised by philosophes and administrative reformers. With that warning he offered a conception of revolution as the decisive turning point at which a society, like a sick patient, will live or die. Beneath the appearances of cultural and social progress that seemed to many of his contemporaries to make this age the happiest and most peaceful in the annals of European civilization, Linguet saw a more malignant process of exploitation and emiseration of the masses. In his view, modern society had reached the point where a terrible crisis was inevitable: Either the oppressed would expire in silent misery, stifling the European economy for lack of a workforce, or they would be emboldened by despair to rise up and establish a new liberty. On the eve of the French Revolution, this radical journalist, famous for his memoir of imprisonment in the Bastille, purveyed a powerful sense that time itself was quickening as society hurtled toward that moment in which an entire way of life would hang in the balance between extinction and regeneration.

Three principal notions of revolution can therefore be seen in play on the eve of the French Revolution. The term still evoked its most conventional meaning of a moment of disorder, a dramatic change, usually for the worse, but it also connoted an extended process of social and cultural transformation, or a particular event (observed or anticipated) that served that process in advancing the universal progress of humankind. Conversely, it could also be appropriated to redescribe the same process of social transformation in negative terms, as issuing in an extended crisis of life and death in the social body. Reordered and recombined, these connotations were to give resonance to the events of 1789 as contemporaries struggled to give these events their meaning. In the process, the "French Revolution" was invented, and with it the modern concept of revolution.

The dynamic of this development is very well seen in the pages of *Révolutions de Paris*, the most widely read of the new journals that sprang into being in the summer of 1789. Starting as a series of pamphlets relating the "revolutions of the capital," it quickly became a periodical announcing "the astonishing revolution that has just taken place." From chronicling "that revolution for ever memorable in the annals of our history," its editor soon found himself in competition with other journalists (and other political actors) to shape the ongoing course of events that had become "the French Revolution." In this understanding of the term, revolution was no longer recalled as a fact; experienced (and continually extended) as a moment of profound existential uncertainty, it was opened up indefinitely as a domain of intense political action that would shape the future of the French and of all humanity.

As portrayed in *Révolutions de Paris*, this French Revolution was a crisis in which, "all remedies having been exhausted," the social body was poised between life and death. It had been produced by the action of a bitter and oppressed people rising up from its misery, but it would be continued as the work of philosophy. "Only excessive misery and the progress of enlightenment can bring about a revolution in a people that has grown old in the degradation of servitude," the journal explained. The formulation was a crucial one: It meant that only in combination with "the peaceful operation of philosophy" could the "severe vengeance" of the people secure a salutary outcome. Anxieties of profound disruption could thus be alleviated by the promise of reason. It was easier, however, to open up the moment of revolution in this way than it was to close it again. The Revolution, it was to turn out, could not be assured by philosophy until humanity itself had been transformed. Nor could it be brought to a close until all those standing in the way of this transformation had been destroyed. To end the Revolution, moreover, was necessarily to see it as an outcome, which was to see it from outside—which was to cease to be "revolutionary." It followed that the Revolution could never be ended, but only defeated. A powerful ideological dynamic had been set in motion, destined for a long history.

[*See also* American Revolution; Democracy; French Revolution; Political Philosophy; *and* Republicanism, *subentries on* Great Britain, The United States, France, The Netherlands, *and* Latin America.]

BIBLIOGRAPHY
Arendt, Hannah. *On Revolution.* New York, 1963.
Baker, Keith Michael. *Inventing the French Revolution: Essays on French Political Culture in the Eighteenth Century.* Cambridge, 1990. Offers (pp. 203–223) a fuller account (with more detailed references) of much of the analysis presented here.
Baker, Keith Michael. "Transformations of Classical Republicanism in Eighteenth-Century France." *Journal of Modern History* (2001), 32–53. Develops some themes mentioned here.
Condorcet, Jean-Antoine-Nicolas de Caritat. *Sketch for a Historical Picture of the Historical Progress of the Human Mind.* Translated by June Barraclough. London, 1955.
Goulemot, Jean. *Le règne de l'histoire: Discours historiques et révolutions, XVII–XVIIIᵉ siècle.* Paris, 1996. A fundamental analysis of the conventional eighteenth-century notion of "revolutions" as political vicissitudes. Still awaiting an English translation.
Koselleck, Reinhart. *Futures Past: On the Semantics of Historical Time.* Translated by Keith Tribe. Cambridge, Mass., 1985. The best introduction in English to this historian's fundamental work on the reorientation of time in the period of the Enlightenment.
Pocock, J. G. A. *The Machiavellian Moment.* Princeton, N.J., 1975.
Rey, Alain. *"Révolution": Histoire d'un mot.* Paris, 1989. The most comprehensive account of French uses in the eighteenth century. Not available in English.
Rousseau, Jean-Jacques. *Émile.* Translated by Allan Bloom. New York, 1979.
Venturi, Francisco. *The End of the Old Regime in Europe, 1776–1789,* vol. 1, *The Great States of the West.* Princeton, N.J., 1991. See especially pages 3–143.

KEITH MICHAEL BAKER

REVOLUTION, AMERICAN. *See* American Revolution.

REVOLUTION, FRENCH. *See* French Revolution.

REVOLUTIONARY CULTS. The French Revolution maintained a troubled relationship with religion. It represented one of the most anti-Christian and anticlerical moments in history, directly battling the Roman Catholic Church on the field of temporal power by insisting on the nationalization of the clergy's property, the swearing of the constitutional oath by priests, and the secularization of the civil state, a process culminating in the "dechristianization" of the Year II. The revolutionaries wanted, nevertheless, to form their own religion with the regeneration, baptism, and proclamation of a new world. Their desire gave rise to revolutionary cults with their own martyrs, rites, beliefs, festivals, goddesses, and even a "supreme being." The deputy Armand-Gaston Camus threw out this phrase of defiance and challenge to the church: "Surely we have the power to change religions." Mona Ozouf has asked, "Should we take him at his word and believe that there was a revolutionary religion other than that in the wish, or illusion, of the men of the Revolution?"

In the beginning, the Revolution had no need for such defiance, since it began with the consent and support of the traditional religion. The series of festivals of federation, which reached a high point with the Parisian Federation of 14 July 1790, displayed a potential for fusion between religious and revolutionary fervor. The *Te Deum* merged with the civic oath, the tricolor flags of the national guard were blessed, and the patriotic cockade and the new revolutionary Credo were adopted. The French Church, willingly Gallican, supported by the positive image of the "good priest" and enlightened by a hierarchy in part won over to the new ideas, wanted to keep a central role in the ceremonies of the Revolution, celebrating the links between the revolutionary gospel and that of the New Testament and exalting the mysticism of a "patriot Jesus." In the churches, they preached adherence to the regeneration of a country reconciled with its origins, political and religious, and prayed for the "holy equality of God's children." Claude Fauchet, close to the Girondins, extolled in lengthy sermons, discourses, and catechisms "the accord of religion and liberty." As the historian of French Catholicism, André Latreille, has pointed out, this moment has to be seen as marking a "quasi-messianic" alliance between the Catholic religion and the Revolution.

This alliance was weakened little by little, then violently shattered, by the effects of the Civil Constitution of the Clergy, and especially by the constitutional oath that all members of the clergy had to take from the fall of 1790 on. The flight of the king and the denunciation of the Revolution by Pope Pius VI solved nothing, and the situation was exacerbated by the "pantheonization" of Voltaire in July

1791. The Revolution now took a resolutely anticlerical turn, as the decisions of September 1792 confirmed. The republic, in effect, made a frontal attack on the power of the church by secularizing registration of births, marriages, and deaths, which had been the traditional function of the clergy, and by legalizing divorce, which appeared to many priests as a provocation. The constitutional clergy began to desert the revolutionary camp. Further, anticlericalism became militant and willful with the wave of dechristianization that swept over all of France following the activism of certain deputies "on mission," many of them former clerics. The winter of 1793–1794 was thus the only moment in French history when the public practice of Catholic worship was totally interrupted, at times finding refuge in the private sphere of personal belief and clandestine ceremonies. Officially, the churches were forbidden to Catholicism; the priests, having abdicated, were reduced to silence or pursued as suspects; and ceremonies of worship were repressed. The exterior signs of Christianity were vandalized: crosses, wayside crucifixes, statues of the saints and of Christ, and religious ornaments were overturned, destroyed, or pillaged. These iconoclastic scenes—the holy vial shattered in Reims, for example—accompanied burlesque processions displaying the relics of the downcast religion; on 7 November 1793, the Convention received treasures torn from the churches of Nièvre. These actions were loudly approved by some radical revolutionaries, such as Jacques-René Hébert, Pierre-Gaspard Chaumette, and Joseph Fouché, a group for whom anticlericalism served as a political tool in the struggle for power that split the Montagnard factions of the Convention.

From these dechristianizing practices was born a kind of substitute religion that tried to take over the role played by Catholicism in public life at the beginning of the Revolution. In this sense, we can speak of the intention to establish a revolutionary religion. The elite republicans, who were deists, clearly understood the need to borrow from Christianity the principles and forms of belief in order to arouse the masses to spiritual and ritual commitment to the Revolution. The void left by the disappearance of Catholicism could not be filled without this transfer of sacredness. This made the revolutionary religion a veritable form of worship, though one composed of somewhat heterogeneous elements: the dedication of the churches to Reason, offerings of silver, abjurations by priests, dechristianizing processions, festivals of Reason, victory celebrations, and ceremonies dedicated to "martyrs of liberty" such as Louis-Michel Lepeletier de Saint-Fargeau, Jean-Paul Marat, Joseph Chalier, and Joseph Bara. Each rededication featured a liturgy derived from Catholic worship—with revolutionary priests in charge—its setting (the altar of the homeland), its hymns and patriotic choirs, its sacred texts (the constitution, the oath, and the republican catechism), its processions, and its sociability (the fraternal banquet). Jacobin discourse itself was not insensitive to religious or mystical influences, as can be seen in the effort to confer a kind of sainthood on the Mountain, on the key values of equality, fraternity, and liberty, and on the instruments of the law—the Convention and the guillotine. In certain parts of the west where civil war was raging, saintly republican women were credited with quasi-miraculous powers; for example, after Perrine Dugué, a nineteen-year-old republican from Thorigné, was murdered by three Chouans in March 1796, witnesses said they had seen her "rising to heaven with tricolor wings"; Marie Martin, another young woman slain by Chouans in Ille-et-Vilaine, was dubbed Sainte Pataude ("Saint Clumsy"), and her tomb was covered with votive offerings.

Even more than the goddesses of Reason personified by very young women, and more than these tricolor saints, the cult of Marat fulfilled this spontaneous need for revolutionary religion. After the assassination of the "friend of the people" on 13 July 1793, his body was displayed to the sans-culottes in a violently emotional funeral. Jacques-Louis David's painting depicting his death, a magnificent republican *pietà* derived from a *Deposition from the Cross* by Caravaggio, was presented to the Convention and hung beside *Lepeletier sur Son Lit de Mort* above the tribune of orators, like altarpieces offered to the faithful in a church. From that moment, a national religion took form. Marat's blood was venerated like that of Jesus, as a mystical sacrifice; his mortal remains became the body of a sublime victim. His relics were soon displayed from district to district: the bathtub, the dagger, and the sheet in which his murdered body had rested. An intense diffusion of his image through engravings and busts reinforced the growing legend of Marat, who ended up personifying in his body the martyred body in the flesh, representing in many ways the whole of the republican community. Surrounded by other martyrs of liberty, he was at the center of republican festivals, discourses, and civic ceremonies. He was a hero, not a god, one might say; he was, above all, a martyr whose blood sacrifice consecrated the new revolutionary community, whose beliefs and ceremonies were unified by the concept of the Terror.

The cult of Reason and that of Marat were succeeded by another variation on the project of revolutionary religion: the cult of the Supreme Being, devised with the avowed goal of sorting out the religious and moral ideas of the Revolution. Maximilien Robespierre said that it was a matter of ending the Revolution by instituting a religion of the state. This cult was intimately tied to the destiny of "L'Incorruptible," as Robespierre was called. He put an end to dechristianization with his speech to the Jacobins on 1 Frimaire (21 November) of the Year II

Revolutionary Martyr. *The Death of Marat*, painting (1793) by Jacques-Louis David (1748–1825). Marat was stabbed to death by Charlotte Corday on 13 July 1793. (Musées Royaux des Beaux-Arts de Belgique, Brussels/Giraudon/Art Resource, NY.)

of the Revolution, denouncing Hébert and Chaumette as "new fanatics" suspected of "aristocratic atheism"; he then announced the festival of the Supreme Being in his report of 18 Floreal (7 May), when he established, according to republican principles, the calendar of civic ceremonies appropriate for a "regenerated people." Robespierre presided over the Parisian festival on 20 Prairial (8 June), called by some the "pontiff" of the festival. In the end, the cult was abolished with the fall of Robespierre.

These festivals, in the provinces as well as in Paris, were much like those of the church. An allegory of atheism was burned at the stake, allowing symbols of eternity and signs of immortality to appear. Then began a procession of the elderly, housewives, young girls, and children, with pauses for hymns, bouquets thrown to the skies in homage to the "Great Organizer," and prayers of gratitude to the Supreme Being. This outdoor rite, with its aim of keeping both atheism and superstition at a distance, was a working drawing of a religion. It enjoyed a certain success, according to witnesses of the day and the numerous addresses that celebrated it before the Convention. Without doubt, this was because it actualized

and gave religious finality to the festive ideal of the Enlightenment, and because it benefited from effective means of massive propagation: public notices, hymns, engravings, sculptures, civic almanacs, and the personal authority of Robespierre. Though ephemeral, the cult of the Supreme Being thus experienced the same spectacular success, among elite republicans as among the common people, as had the cult of the martyrs of liberty.

The Directory likewise had its revolutionary cults, theophilanthropic and "decadal." In this case, an ensemble of official, semiofficial, and private festivals were organized, generally to challenge the resurgence of Catholicism. These projects attempted to found the republic on several symbolic signs and shared ceremonial rites: the republican calendar and the celebration of the tenth day of the *decade* (the new ten-day week), familial virtue, the harmony of the new society with nature, and commemorations of great republican events. In spite of several successes (notably the decadal festivals), these cults excluded the masses through particular rituals (theophilanthropy was largely inspired by masonic rituals), their abstraction of the celebrated values, and a direction at times too rigid and stilted. A small core of militants, defrocked priests, journalists, booksellers, and political personnel ensured these cults a certain persistence, but they lacked a strong local establishment and the fervor that surrounded, for example, the cult of Marat or the processions of the Supreme Being.

The diversity of the revolutionary cults, and their fate, always rather ephemeral, should not lead us to disregard them. They disclose a fundamental truth of the revolutionary adventure: the shared belief that a religion was indispensable to the very existence—harmonious and dynamic, structured and consensual—of the new social and political community. The new religion would first be made of morality, and ordered by certain rites, precepts, and symbols, the very respect for which formed the morals of the people. Ernest Renan saw in the space depicted by these revolutionary cults an "Eden of happy bourgeois, enjoying themselves in groups, believing by decree." This widespread and decreed happiness, even if soon set aside, nevertheless proved the permanence of an ideal of the Revolution: to found on the ruins of Catholic "superstition" an ensemble of cults that would allow republican values, symbols, sensibilities, and gestures to clothe themselves in spirituality. In this, they represent one of the most significant transfers of sacredness in Western history.

[*See also* Citizenship; French Revolution; Natural Religion; Republicanism, *subentry on* France; Revolution; Revolutionary Theater; *and* Spectacles.]

BIBLIOGRAPHY

Aulard, Alphonse. *Le culte de la raison et le culte de l'Être Suprême (1793–1794).* Paris, 1892.

Bianchi, Serge. "Cultes révolutionnaires." In *Dictionnaire historique de la Révolution française*, edited by A. Soboul. Paris, 1989.

Bowman, Franck-Paul. *Le Christ romantique, 1789: Le sans-culotte de Nazareth*. Geneva, 1973.

Mathiez, Albert. *Les origines des cultes révolutionnaires (1789–1792)*. Paris, 1904.

Mathiez, Albert. *La Théophilanthropie et le culte décadaire (1796–1801): Essai sur l'histoire religieuse de la Révolution*. Paris, 1904.

Ozouf, Mona. "Religion révolutionnaire." In *Dictionnaire critique de la Révolution française*, edited by F. Furet and M. Ozouf. Paris, 1988.

Vovelle, Michel. *La Révolution contre l'Église: De la Raison à l'Être Suprême*. Paris, 1988.

Antoine de Baecque
Translated from French by Sylvia J. Cannizzaro

REVOLUTIONARY THEATER. No play written and produced during the French Revolution has found its way into the canon, but the period from 1789 to 1799 is, by almost any measure, the most vital moment in the history of theater in the West: at least a thousand new plays were written and performed. With the law of 13 January 1791 abolishing the privileged status of the Comédie Française, the Comédie Italienne, and the Opéra, and declaring the freedom of theatrical performance, approximately fifty new theaters opened in Paris alone, and there were roughly twenty-five theatrical performances every day in Paris. Major newspapers such as the *Moniteur*, *Chronique de Paris*, and *Journal de Paris* ran daily theater columns; several newspapers were devoted solely to covering the theater and opera; and tracts commenting on and offering reforms of the theater abounded. Theater remained France's single most prestigious form of artistic production during the Revolutionary decade just as it had been throughout the eighteenth-century, and a successful play was the quickest way for an ambitious young writer to establish a reputation. It was also the most potentially lucrative form of writing. Many of the era's most notable playwrights were also deeply involved in Revolutionary political life: Marie-Joseph Chénier, deputy to the national convention and the period's most important tragic playwright; François de Neufchâteau, deputy and minister of the interior and author of, among other works, a notorious stage adaptation of Samuel Richardson's *Pamela*; and Olympe de Gouges, political activist, author of the now celebrated *Déclaration des droits de la femme et de la citoyenne* (Declaration of the Rights of Women and Citizens), and of four plays written and performed during the Revolution that treated issues ranging from the inhumanity of monastic vows (*Le couvent, ou Les voeux forces* [The Convent, or The Forced Vows]), to the cruelty of slavery (*L'esclavage des noirs, ou L'heureux naufrage* [Black Slavery, or The Fortunate Shipwreck]), to the glorious victories of the Revolutionary armies (*L'entrée de Dumouriez à Bruxelles* [The Entry of Dumouriez into Brussels]).

Throughout the Revolution, the theater remained a primary crucible of public opinion. Although scholars of

Revolutionary Theater. Interior of the Théâtre de la République, Paris, revolutionary period. (Bibliothèque Nationale, Paris/Giraudon/Art Resource, NY.)

Revolutionary political culture have focused overwhelmingly on the contributions of print culture to the formation of public opinion, there is no doubt that for the hundreds or thousands of spectators who crowded into the public theaters, attending plays offered an opportunity not only to learn and to be moved, but also to ratify and express their views in concert with a larger assembly: Participating as a member of a theater audience was a particularly significant and meaningful crowd experience. Many revolutionary politicians hoped to make the theaters into "schools of the Revolution," but indeed actors, authors, theater directors, and even government officials were often on the receiving end of lessons dealt by audiences. Audience disturbances and riots often forced theater companies to perform plays that had been forbidden by the government, or obstructed the performance of plays that audiences considered objectionable or counterrevolutionary.

Many commentators have remarked that Revolutionary theater made no fundamental formal break with the past: Tragedy and high comedy were still written as five-act plays in verse. The proliferation of new theaters and the end of special privileges for the established theaters however, did, lead to a breakdown in generic absolutism and to the invention of a host of new types of plays such as parades and *faits historiques*. Vaudeville and melodrama, two relatively new and previously marginal forms, flourished.

The affair over *Charles IX, ou L'école des rois* (Charles IX, or The School for Kings) by Marie-Joseph Chénier, first performed on 4 November 1789, arguably brought an end to the crown's administration of the theater. The play recounts Cardinal de Lorraine's conspiracy with Catherine de Médicis to commit the Saint Bartholemew's Day massacre. It presents the weakness of Charles IX and shows his ultimately criminal acquiescence in his advisers' plots. The tragedy was understood as a blow to the monarchy that sought to suppress it; only persistent and potentially violent action on the part of audiences won its performance. Chénier's inspiration for the play was Voltaire. It was Voltaire who had hoped to establish a truly national tragedy based on France's modern history (a subject previously banned from the stage) and who had remarked that staging the story of the Saint Bartholomew's Day massacre would be a crucial step in the creation of such a theater.

While Voltaire was the Revolution's tragic muse, Jean-Jacques Rousseau was its unlikely inspiration for comedy, at least in the case of Philippe-François Fabre d'Eglantine. In his famous antitheatrical screed, *Lettre à M. d'Alembert sur les spectacles* (Letter to Mr. d'Alembert on Plays, 1758), Rousseau argued that comedy was structurally incapable of fulfilling its traditional task of holding up a corrective mirror to society because it had to please an audience that liked to see its manners and morals celebrated, not

challenged. For example, in Molière's *Le misanthrope*, Rousseau argues, the sincere Alceste who challenges society's hypocrisy is ridiculed while the cynical wisdom of the conventional man-about-town Philinte is validated. In Fabre's enormously successful *Le Philinte de Molière, ou la Suite du misanthrope* (Sequel to *The Misanthrope*, 1790), the fanatically sincere Alceste becomes the model for the new citizen and the conventionally hypocritical Philinte stands not only for the bankruptcy of Old Regime society but also for that of Old Regime comedy.

Perhaps the most surprising continuity between the theatrical aesthetics of the Enlightenment and those of the Revolution is the persistent interest in *drame*. Denis Diderot was not drama's inventor but he was certainly its primary proponent and theoretician. In works such as *Entretiens sur Le fils naturel* (Discussion of the *Fils Naturel*, 1757), Diderot made the case for this new mixed genre—serious plays about the personal lives of ordinary people—on the basis of the powerful emotional and moral effects it produced on spectators. Dramas were an important part of the revolutionary repertoire, recounting family crises such as adultery or parental neglect, tyranny, and obstruction of marriages in the context of revolutionary culture. A cheating husband was not only a bad spouse but also a bad citizen, since he ruined the life not only of his wife but also that of a girl who might otherwise find a good husband and create a stable patriotic household.

Revolutionary theater grew out of the dramatic traditions of the Enlightenment, but it also freely adapted those traditions to its own new and ever-changing circumstances. This novel flexibility ensured theater's continued cultural relevance and prominence.

[*See also* Aesthetics; Diderot, Denis; French Revolution; Rousseau, Jean-Jacques; Theater; *and* Voltaire.]

BIBLIOGRAPHY

Carlson, Marvin. *The Theater of the French Revolution*. Ithaca, N.Y., 1966. Narrative of the effects of the French Revolution on the major Parisian theaters.

Étienne, C. G., and A. Martainville. *Histoire du théâtre français depuis le commencement de la Revolution jusqu'à la Réunion Général*. 4 vols. Paris, 1802. Near-contemporary narrative account that covers the entire Revolutionary decade. The authors were themselves both playwrights and theater critics.

Huet, Marie-Hélèlne. *Rehearsing the Revolution: Staging Marat's Death, 1793–1797*. Translated by Robert Hurley. Berkeley, Calif., 1982. Analyzes the role of spectacle in Revolutionary political culture. Argues for an analogy between the structure of the stage and the structure of Revolutionary political institutions, especially the Revolutionary tribunal.

Kennedy, Emmet, Marie-Laurence Netter, James P. McGregor, and Mark V. Olsen. *Theater, Opera, and Audiences in Revolutionary Paris*. Westport, Conn., 1996. Provides statistical data on theater repertories, receipts, and performances. Essays offer interpretations of the data collected.

Ravel, Jeffrey. *The Contested Parterre: Public Theater and French Political Culture, 1680–1791.* Ithaca, N.Y., 1999. Locates the importance of the theater as a public institution from its zenith in the seventeenth century through the early years of the French Revolution.

SUSAN A. MASLAN

REY, MARC-MICHEL (1720–1780), Dutch printer and bookseller.

The son of French Huguenot expatriates, Rey was born in Geneva. His father, Isaac Rey, was a packager for the bookseller Marc-Michel Bousquet. Little is known of his mother, Marguerite Duseigneur Rey. The boy received no formal education and went to work for Bousquet at the age of seventeen. He quit after seven years and in 1744 moved to Amsterdam. On 31 January 1746, Amsterdam's guild of booksellers and printers admitted Rey into its ranks. In 1747, he married Elisabeth Bernard, daughter of the printer and author Jean-Frédéric Bernard. By his death in 1780, Rey had become one of Europe's wealthiest and most influential printers.

Over the course of his thirty-year career, Rey was intimately connected with the Enlightenment. He printed the works of many authors, most notably Jean-Jacques Rousseau, the baron d'Holbach, and Voltaire. Beginning in December 1749, Rey reproduced one of Europe's leading scientific reviews, the *Journal des sçavans*. After 1754, he joined his reprints of the *Journal des sçavans* with the *Journal de Trévoux* and added his own *Additions d'Hollande*. When Denis Diderot considered printing his many unpublished writings during the last years of his life, he wrote to Rey. Ultimately, Diderot confirmed Rey's place in the firmament of Enlightenment figures; in his correspondence with Rey, he insisted that without the printer, the philosophes would have "preached in the desert."

Working just outside France and within easy reach of the remainder of enlightened Europe, Rey was able to serve the large French-language market. France itself accounted for three-quarters of his sales. Because of Amsterdam's proximity and relative freedom, the city was an attractive place to print dangerous works. In addition to the standard fare of religious treatises, secular histories, novels, and almanacs, Rey produced a wide variety of works prohibited just across the border. These ranged from the merely titillating, like Diderot's *Les bijoux indiscrets* (1748), to bold anticlerical tracts like the baron d'Holbach's *Le Christianisme dévoilé* (1766) and *Le système de la nature* (1770). Rey kept this work secret by using false imprints that listed Geneva or London as the place of publication.

It was Rey's privileged relations with Rousseau that brought him to the attention of nineteenth- and twentieth-century historians. The two first met in 1754. In the next ten years, Rey produced most of the first editions of the Genevan philosopher's works, including the *Discours sur l'origine de l'inégalité* (1755), the *Lettre à d'Alembert sur les spectacles* (1758), *La nouvelle Héloïse* (1761), *Du contrat social* (1762), the so-called *Lettre à Christophe de Beaumont* (1763), and the *Lettres écrites de la montagne* (1764). After Rousseau's flight into exile in 1762, Rey offered the beleaguered philosopher asylum.

During the negotiations over *La nouvelle Héloïse*, Rousseau began to resist the constraints Rey placed on his "copyright." In the eighteenth-century world of publishing, Continental authors lost the rights to manuscripts once they had appeared in print. Rousseau sought to retain his by packaging the novel with a proposal to reprint his collected works in a general edition. Rey objected to these tactics, and the ensuing quarrel drove the prickly Rousseau away temporarily; he ultimately settled on the Dutch printer Jean Néaulme to print *Émile, ou de l'éducation* (1762). Nevertheless, before the printing of *Émile* was complete, Rousseau offered a portion of the project to Rey.

In part because of his relations with Rousseau, and certainly because of the danger involved, Rey kept his business dealings with Voltaire hidden. Their association began in mid-1752. The financial incentives were too great for Rey to ignore—Voltaire's works sold very well. By the time Rousseau had all but given up writing for his contemporaries, Rey was printing for Voltaire in earnest. One work in particular marked a turning point in their relations. In July 1764, Voltaire issued his *Dictionnaire philosophique*. Appropriating the format and the critical spirit of Diderot and d'Alembert's *Encyclopédie* and containing innumerable scandalous statements, it was designed to arouse controversy. Voltaire chose Rey to print the second edition of the work, though both publicly denied any connection with either edition.

Over the next ten years, Voltaire tapped Rey to print the largest portion of his works, either in the original edition or as reprints. In 1766, the same year that Rey printed the *Lettres secrètes de M. de Voltaire à ses amis du Parnasse*, he reissued *Le philosophe ignorant* and the *Lettres sur les miracles*; in 1768, Rey printed Voltaire's *Relation du bannissement des Jésuites de la Chine*. Their association continued without any significant break until 1773. Nevertheless, Voltaire publicly appeared to betray his compatriot. He consistently blamed Europe's printers, and Rey in particular, for "falsely" attributing his own works to him. In 1765, for example, he publicly denied having written the *Dictionnaire philosophique* and *L'évangile de la raison*. In this instance, Rey was willing to play along by printing Voltaire's statements and then insisting that his objections did not actually amount to a denial of authorship. Thanks to the drawn-out public controversy, both works sold vigorously.

Rey's flirtation with controversial ideas and authors had few substantial consequences in his lifetime. Only his standing in the church was affected. On his arrival in Amsterdam in 1744, Rey had joined the Walloon community. Though Mme. Rey was scrupulous about religious matters, Rey appears to have adhered to the Protestant faith only out of convention. As his printing shop became more prosperous, he increasingly adopted the anticlerical and antireligious sentiments found within the many works he printed. In May 1766, six pastors denounced him before the Consistory of the Church for printing statements "filled with impieties" in his *Additions d'Hollande*. Rey was ordered to appear before the Consistory, where he renounced his membership in the Walloon Church. When he died, he was buried not on consecrated ground but just outside the city of Amsterdam.

[*See also* Amsterdam; Censorship; Publishing; Rousseau, Jean-Jacques; *and* Voltaire.]

BIBLIOGRAPHY

Birn, Raymond. "[Marc-]Michel's Enlightenment." In *Le Magasin de l'Univers: The Dutch Republic as the Centre of the European Book Trade*, edited by C. Berkvens-Stevelinck et al., pp. 23–31. Leiden, 1992. Contains a complete bibliography as of 1992.

Fajn, Max. "Marc-Michel Rey: Boekhandelaar op de Bloemmark." *Proceedings of the American Philosophical Society* 118 (1974), 260–268. A brief English-language biographical treatment of Rey.

Françon, Marcel. "La condamnation de 'l'Émile.'" *Annales de la Société Jean-Jacques Rousseau* 31 (1946–1949), 209–245.

Gallas, K.-R. "Autour de Marc-Michel Rey et de Rousseau." *Annales de la Société Jean-Jacques Rousseau* 17 (1926), 73–90. A response to Schinz's article.

Schinz, Albert. "Jean-Jacques Rousseau et le libraire-imprimeur Marc-Michel Rey." *Annales de la Société Jean-Jacques Rousseau* 10 (1914–1915), 1–134. The first substantial treatment of Rousseau's relations with Rey.

Vercruysse, Jeroom. *Voltaire et la Hollande*. In *Studies on Voltaire and the Eighteenth Century* 46. Geneva, 1966.

Vercruysse, Jeroom. *Voltaire et Marc Michel Rey*. In *Studies on Voltaire and the Eighteenth Century* 58, pp. 1707–1763. Geneva, 1967. Part of a four-volume publication covering the International Congress on the Enlightenment, Saint Andrews, Scotland.

SEAN C. GOODLETT

RHETORIC. It has often been observed that *Enlightenment* and *eighteenth century* are not interchangeable expressions. This is perhaps nowhere more true than in the teaching and practice of rhetoric, which, if anything, looked more frequently to classical antiquity than to the "modern" for both structure and substance. A hint of this can be found in a manifesto regarding university reform published in midcentury, *Plan de l'enseignement de la rhétorique présenté par les professeurs de rhétorique de l'Université de Paris, en exécution de l'arrêt du Parlement du 3 Septembre 1762*. There we find the professors reiterating the "reforms" of 1598 that prescribed a long list of Greek and Latin authors to be studied in the rhetoric course, emphasizing Cicero and Quintilian supplemented by study and imitation of sundry church fathers and weekly explications of passages from Psalms. The only "modern" work mentioned is Charles Rollin's *Traité des études: De la manière d'enseigner et d'étudier les belles-lettres par rapport à l'esprit et au coeur* (1726–1728).

Publication demographics establish the point even more firmly. The eighteenth century saw countless editions of the rhetorical works of Cicero, editions and abridgments of the *Institutio oratoria* of Quintilian, and perhaps most striking, dozens of editions of Longinus's *Peri hypsous* (On the Sublime), not to mention numerous reprints of Nicolas Boileau's 1674 text and translation, *L'art poétique*, and other translations of Longinus into English, German, Italian, Dutch, and Portuguese. Add to the volume of "primary" texts in circulation the long line of rhetoric textbooks from the abbé Breton's *De la rhétorique selon les preceptes d'Aristote, de Cicéron et de Quintilian* (1703) through Edmé Mallet's *Principes pour la lecture des Orateurs* (1753) to Johann Georg Sulzer's observations in his *Allgemeine Theorie der schönen Künste* (1774) and the enormous number of rhetoric textbooks printed for Jesuit schools across all of Europe, from Coimbra, Portugal, to as far east as Vilnius, Lithuania, during the eighteenth century, and it is clear that the classical Greco-Roman tradition more than held its own in this "modern" era. Even the Russian Mikhail Vasilievich Lomonosov (1711–1765), who was influenced by Johan Christoph Gottsched, built his *Kratkoie roukovodstvo k krasnoretchiu* (A Short [at 300 pages in length] Introduction to Eloquence, 1748) around the traditional *inventio, dispositio, elocutio* pattern.

The Rhetoric Curriculum. Consistent with the continuing vitality of the classics, the rhetoric curriculum in colleges and universities—at worst, a set of empty formulas; at best, a solid grounding in the humanities—remained largely unchanged. Students were trained in the traditional parts of the art (invention, arrangement, style, and delivery, with memory left to "natural" ability); the standard parts of a speech (exordium, narration, proof, and peroration); the standard "genres" of oratory (forensic, deliberative, epideictic); and in composing and delivering declamations on prescribed themes. Although rhetorical training was seen as good preparation for careers in law or in the pulpit, common to the vast majority of treatises on rhetoric published in the eighteenth century was the aim of producing *honnêtes hommes* ("gentlemen") capable of mixing in polite company and making a good impression in the effort to improve their station in life. This "adjustment" in the curriculum's agenda (hardly peculiar to the eighteenth century) accounts for the broadening of the scope of instruction from public speaking to speaking and writing of all sorts; and for the corresponding assimilation of "rhetoric" to the study of belles lettres, which in turn was aimed at the cultivation and refinement of aesthetic taste.

Those innovations that we do see in the teaching of rhetoric were due to changes in the student populations—increasingly, the sons of the emerging bourgeoisie aspiring to upward social mobility—and pedagogical reforms designed to cater to that population. For instance, while Latin continued to be the primary language of instruction well into the eighteenth century, we see also various efforts to adjust to conditions imposed by the various vernaculars, including debates over what qualifies as "good" French, German, Spanish, or English. Such concerns are evident in, for instance, Gottsched's *Ausführliche Redekunst* (1728, with several subsequent expanded editions), Gregorio Mayans y Siscar's *Retórica* (1757, 1786), and George Campbell's *Philosophy of Rhetoric* (1776). The pedagogical reforms, for their part, stemmed in part from a shift from inculcation to cultivation as the aim of the teacher and in part from the philosophical rationale for that shift, as articulated chiefly by John Locke in his enormously influential *Some Thoughts Concerning Education* (1693).

One of the most influential spokesmen for educational reform was Charles Rollin (1661–1741), whose *Traité* went into thirteen French editions before 1800 and was translated into German (1750), four times into Italian, and into Russian (1789); it went into ten English editions in England and Ireland before the century was over. The *Traité* is not only about rhetoric, but moves from general considerations about the aims of education (cultivating *le bon goût* and *la capacité pour les affaires*) through treatments of grammar, poetry, rhetoric, history, philosophy, and principles of school administration. In his discussion of educational theory, Rollin follows both Quintilian and Locke in his belief that children are born tabula rasa, the "blank slate" that can be inscribed by the parent or teacher; and in the belief that children are inherently good, since human nature, even if outside conditions may distort or corrupt it, is itself good. Thus, it is that Rollin's educational philosophy prefigures (although it is by no means the same as) works such as Jean-Jacques Rousseau's *Émile* (1762); and, with particular regard to the teaching of *l'éloquence*, relies more on exposing students only to "the best" in order to cultivate and improve their inborn capacity to recognize and appreciate that which is elegantly and artistically expressed. These themes persist in conceptions of taste and eloquence (and its devices) throughout the century, appearing even in the entries in the *Encyclopédie* on *goût* (7.761, Voltaire and d'Alembert), *éloquence* and *style* (5.529–531 and 15.551–554, Jaucourt), and *trope* (16.697–703, Beauzée); and Rollin's influence spread as far abroad as Scotland, where we see it in the rhetorics of George Campbell and Hugh Blair late in the century.

Improvement. Keeping in mind the social-mobility aspect of the teaching of rhetoric and the continuing grip held on eighteenth-century rhetorics by the classical past (there are few greater admirers of Cicero than Voltaire, for instance), some additional intersections of rhetorical doctrine with themes more generally philosophical and matters of virtual consensus on the Continent and in the British Isles can be detected. One such theme is that of improvement: individuals can be molded into cultivated members of polite society (a social reality, not a philosophical construct); and as more individuals are so molded, society as a whole is improved.

Such improvement is viewed by writers as varied as Denis Diderot, Charles-Irénée Castel, Adam Smith, and George Campbell within the larger framework of the doctrine of progress. Humanity, almost everyone seems to have agreed, had evolved, by way of several stages of development (most often, four), from a primitive barbarism to a more refined and civilized state. This is a belief that appears in many areas of inquiry—Henry Home, Lord Kames adopts it in his treatises on law, natural history, and in his *Elements of Criticism* (1762). Three- and four-stage accounts appear on the development of language itself in Rousseau's "Essai sur l'origine des langues," which greatly influenced Beauzée's article on *langue* in the *Encyclopédie* (9.249–266), which in turn influenced Blair's observations in his *Lectures on Rhetoric and Belles-Lettres* (nos. 6–9).

It appears as well in "histories" of rhetoric, as in Campbell's account in the introduction to his *Philosophy of Rhetoric*, which delineates (1) an initial stage in which orators simply spoke, without "the aid of any previous and formal instruction"; (2) the next stage, in which classifications of modes of argument or forms of speech were produced; (3) another advance to the stage at which the effect of oratory are investigated; and (4), the stage at which one seeks to account for those effects according to the principles of human nature—"that knowledge of human nature which, besides its other advantage, adds both weight and evidence to all precedent discoveries and rules." It is, of course, at this last stage that Campbell sees himself operating. Based as it is on *science* (in the broader eighteenth-century sense of the term), the study of rhetoric is transformed into the effort to produce a "theory" of the art.

Expression and Communication. Another apparent matter of consensus is that rhetoric is useful only for expressing or communicating, not for discovering or establishing, "facts." The discovery of facts, everyone from Francis Bacon on seems to agree, is achieved only in the empirical disciplines, the sciences, history, and so on. This seems to account for the relatively atrophied state of rhetorical "invention" in many eighteenth-century texts and its replacement by Baconian "recollection," as in Joseph Priestley's *Lectures on Oratory and Criticism* (1776). Mayans's *Retórica* and Gottsched's *Ausführliche Redekunst* are exceptions, in this respect, due probably to the deeply conservative climates in which they wrote in Valencia and Leipzig, for they both import into their courses the whole apparatus of Ciceronian *inventio*. The notion that rhetoric appeals not to the intellect, but to imagination and will, whether it is deployed in the interests of communicating information or arousing an audience to action, also seems to be a matter of common consent. The only difference is in the degree to which a speaker (or writer) is able to impress the imagination and how strong an emotional response those impressions are able to provoke. There is a strong tie to, if not a reduction to, emotion when it comes to persuasive speaking and writing, however, even in authors as diverse as Balthasar Gibert (*La rhétorique, ou les règles de l'éloquence*, 1730) and Campbell in 1776.

This, of course, is the kind of rhetoric the philosophes mistrusted and attacked (usually using quite vivid images and usually quite passionately), as philosophers had done going all the way back to Plato. Indeed, it is a notion of how rhetoric works that even writers of rhetorics are quick to qualify or hedge. At this point, we are brought back to the "cultivation" agenda—students must be exposed to nothing but the best not only to improve their taste but to add to their moral formation, which, it is assumed, will prevent them from misusing their skills in life after school. To these ends, students were exposed to the best of Greek and Latin prose and poetry (including expurgated works of Ovid and Catullus); and, as interests in vernaculars intensified, versions of, for example, Cicero in French or German, and eventually "classics" such as Jean Racine or even Miguel de Cervantes. In the course of the eighteenth century, exemplary texts occupy an increasingly large part of European rhetorics, both "traditional" and "modern." Evidently sensitive to the appetite for such examples for imitation and edification, Gottsched included more in each successive edition of his *Redekunst*, to the point that he provides more than three hundred pages of them in the 1759 edition. A third of Blair's *Lectures on Rhetoric and Belles-Lettres* is given over to a lengthy list of recommended reading—which, no doubt, he expected his students to do.

The primary rhetorical devices for impressing the imagination are tropes and figures, with prose rhythm and artful composition close behind. On these subjects, we find intersections with the dominant psychophysiological models of the time. César Chesneau Du Marsais (1676–1756), strongly influenced by his predecessors at Port-Royal, succeeded in his *Des tropes* (1730) (not, strictly speaking, a rhetoric text) in organizing figures by attaching them to the several mental operations established by philosophical psychology. David Hartley, in his *Observations on Man* (1749), rationalized the process by which physical impulses connected up with "psychological" states. The latter's theories about the "association of ideas" (hardly

original, save for their physiological reductionism) were assimilated by Joseph Priestley in his *Lectures*.

Taste and the Sublime. Two themes often characterized as belonging to the Enlightenment were matters of far less consensus than the others we have seen: taste and the sublime, on both of which there was considerable, and sometimes acrimonious, debate. "Taste," a word on everyone's lips in the eighteenth century, usually in the sense of "in good taste," was not a matter merely of aesthetics. It had psychological, epistemological, and political dimensions as well. Cultivation of taste is in many rhetorics from the beginning to the end of the eighteenth century a keynote and leading theme: it is central to Rollin's aims, is discussed early in Gottsched (1.21, pp. 64–73), and is treated at some length in Blair's lectures two through five. The same set of questions frames most discussions of the subject: Is taste an innate capacity or an acquired one? Is it an independent faculty, what Jean-Baptiste DuBos called a "sixth sense," or is it derived from the mind's other faculties? To what extent, if any, can it be cultivated or improved? Is taste merely a matter of subjective preference, or is there an objective standard? The answers given vary greatly—indeed, the variety is evident in the article on the subject in the 1778 edition of the *Encyclopédie* (16.339–357), which embraces the differing views of Montesquieu, Voltaire, and d'Alembert—and sometimes we find writers (Rollin, Home, Blair, among others) who attempt to come down on both sides of the argument. Joseph Addison, for instance, observed in 1712 that while the faculty of taste "must in some degree be born with us ... there are several methods for cultivating and improving it" (*Spectator*, no. 409). Some writers want to restrict taste to questions of appreciation; others to see taste as crucial in both the reception and production of eloquence: These are two sides of the same coin. Sometimes, when we think we see agreement, we find that it has been reached on the basis of what turn out to be incompatible grounds or different understandings of the terms of the discussion. What all seem to share, however, is a keen awareness of the link between *le bon goût* and perceived social standing.

As for "the sublime," there is comparable debate and disagreement. On the one hand, we have writers such as Jean-François Marmontel and Silvain who locate the sublime in objects—and not just discursive artifacts—that impress us mightily. Opposed to this position are those who locate it in affect, *sentiment* (combining the cognitive and the affective), *"un mouvement du coeur."* There is also disagreement over the role played by reasoning or judgment in apprehending sublimity: for some, "reasoning can never be sublime" (Jaucourt in the 1778 edition of the *Encyclopédie*, 31.835), for sublimity is something that strikes us immediately; and for others (Bouhours,

Immanuel Kant), it cannot be completely detached from rational operations. Interestingly, both of these issues in contention are consequences of the liberties Boileau took with the text of Longinus, adding phrases not found in the original Greek but according to Boileau's own sense of what was truly "poetic." A third division of opinion is evident in disagreements about what we might call "magnitude." On the one hand, we see Silvain and Jaucourt, who state that the sublime *élève l'âme, la ravit, et lui donne une haute idée d'elle même* ("elevates the soul, enraptures it, and gives it a lofty idea of itself"); and on the other, we see Edmund Burke stressing the sense of limitation imposed by experiencing the truly sublime. It is perhaps not a coincidence that the former view prefigures the rhetorical excesses of the Revolution and the latter Burke's eloquent rejection of it.

It is, in short, not possible to isolate a rhetoric that is peculiarly that of the Enlightenment. This is true not only because of the persistence of differing and often incompatible views on the subject, but also because even proponents of enlightened thought found much in the classical tradition to admire and learn from. A keen interest is evident from the vast number of publications dedicated to the study of ancient history, philosophy, politics, and of course rhetoric that appear between 1760 and 1789. As has been noted, even those philosophes who condemned rhetoric found themselves using it and using it well. Moreover, it should be evident that the leading ideas of the rhetoricians in the present brief survey are not eighteenth-century ideas but seventeenth-century ideas—and ideals, at least up until the initial stirrings of Revolutionary fervor. Aside from Cicero, Quintilian, and Longinus, it is such thinkers as Bernard Lamy, Antoine Arnauld, and Locke, not to mention, for example, Gerrit Vos and Sanctius, who dominate the study of the verbal arts. "Rhetoric," in short, does not fit the stereotypes associated with the Enlightenment.

[*See also* Aesthetics; Classicism; Education; Epistemology; Imagination; Language Theories; Neoclassicism; *and* Tradition.]

BIBLIOGRAPHY

There is no comprehensive bibliography for rhetoric or the classical tradition in the eighteenth century. An extensive list can be found in Dieter Breuer and Günther Kopsch's "Rhetoriklehrbücher" in *Rhetorik: Beiträge zu ihrer Geschichte in Deutschland vom 16–20, Jahrhundert*, edited by Helmut Schanze (Frankfurt, 1974), pp. 222–337; for France, Alexander Cioranescu, *Bibliographie de la littérature française du dix-huitième siècle* (Paris, 1969), I, pp. 210–212. Editions of classical authors published in the eighteenth century are listed in *Bibliotheca Scriptorum Classicorum*, 2 vols., edited by Wilhelm Engelmann and Eduard Pruess (Leipzig, 1880). Books on the classical tradition published in France are listed in Chantal Grell, *Le Dix-huitième siècle et l'antiquité en France: 1680–1789*, 2 vols. (Oxford, 1995) (*Studies on Voltaire and the Eighteenth Century*, nos. 330 and 331), vol. 2, pp. 1205–1256.

Abbott, Don Paul. "Mayans' *Retórica* and the Search for a Spanish Rhetoric." *Rhetorica* 11 (1993), 157–180.
Brody, Jules. *Boileau and Longinus*. Geneva, 1958.
Conley, Thomas M. "Eighteenth-Century Rhetorics." In *Rhetoric in the European Tradition*, pp. 188–234. Chicago, 1992.
France, Peter. *Rhetoric and Truth in France: Descartes to Diderot*. Oxford, 1972. Still a book to be highly recommended.
France, Peter. "Quintilian and Rousseau: Oratory and Education." *Rhetorica* 13 (1995), 301–321.
France, Peter. "Lumière, politesse et énergie (1750–1776)." In *Histoire de la rhétorique dans l'Europe moderne: 1450–1950*, edited by Marc Fumaroli, pp. 945–999. Paris, 1999.
Howell, Wilbur Samuel. *Eighteenth-Century British Logic and Rhetoric*. Princeton, N.J., 1972. Long a standard reference, but not as informative as it ought to be.
Liard, Louis. *L'enseignement supérieur en France: 1789–1889*. Paris, 1888. Among the appended *"pièces justificatives"* is the 1762 *"Plan,"* pp. 330–340.
Sermain, Jean-Paul. "Le code du bon goût (1725–1750)." In *Histoire de la rhétorique dans l'Europe moderne*, edited by Marc Fumaroli, pp. 879–943.
Warnick, Barbara. "Charles Rollin's *Traité* and the Rhetorical Theories of Smith, Campbell, and Blair." *Rhetorica* 3 (1985), 45–65.

THOMAS M. CONLEY

RICCI, SCIPIONE DE' (1741–1810), bishop of Pistoia and Prato (1780–1791).

Born in Florence into an aristocratic family, Ricci studied in Rome at the Jesuit college under the protection of a relative, Lorenzo Ricci, who was the superior of the order. He graduated in law at Pisa in 1762 and became a priest in 1766. As vicar-general to the archbishop of Florence, F. G. Incontri, Ricci soon came into contact with many important exponents of Italian and European Jansenism. His reputation for austerity and religious learning induced grand duke Pietro Leopoldo to propose him, in 1780, to Pope Pius VI as bishop of the united diocese of Pistoia and Prato. Here Ricci, with the agreement of the grand duke, made great religious reforms, inspired by Jansenist ideas and the guidance of an "enlightened piety" already manifest in Habsburg reforms in Austria and Lombardy.

Aspects of the Jansenist Enlightenment are particularly striking in many of his pastoral letters. In these, he insists on the contrast between the "venerable, enlightened antiquity" of the church and the "clouded truths" of his own time; the "useful" role the parish clergy could take on in society; the importance of knowledge of Christian truth by the faithful; and the need for a greater autonomy of individual religious awareness. The combative bishop enthusiastically sided with Pietro Leopoldo's reforms of ecclesiastical institutions. The suppression of numerous convents and monasteries, lay confraternities, and many benefices without pastoral responsibility allowed the foundation of the "ecclesiastical patrimony" of Pistoia and Prato, whose administration was entrusted to Ricci. The income from this was used for the reorganization of parishes and for improvement of the economic conditions of priests. Most notably, however, following autonomous tendencies of eighteenth-century episcopalism against Rome, Ricci initiated headstrong struggle against traditional religious conformity and cultural models inherited from the Counter-Reformation.

Driven by strong enlightened fervor and the ideal of restoring the forms of the primitive Christian church, Ricci bitterly criticized the new devotions of the *Via Crucis* (Way of the Cross) and the Sacred Heart. He was also strongly opposed to the widespread practice of indulgences, which were even applicable to the dead, and to the excessive and, in his opinion, superstitious practices of the cult of relics and images of saints and the Virgin Mary. Simplicity and clarity characterized Ricci's reforms of the liturgy and of public expressions of the divine service to encourage the "reasonable" participation of the faithful in rites and ceremonies, such as the introduction of little missals with texts in Italian instead of Latin.

Ricci devoted particular attention to the training of the secular clergy. Legends of saints and apocryphal episodes were eliminated from the Roman Breviary on the basis of the progress of historical criticism. Above all, however, seminary curricula were reformed, replacing old scholastic programs with the reading of Scripture and of the Church Fathers such as St. Augustine, and strengthening advanced studies of theology and morals by the founding of an ecclesiastic academy. The diocesan synod of Pistoia in 1786, in which following Jansenist suggestions, parish priests were given a deliberative vote and no longer only a consultative one, represented the culmination of this reform. The Pistoia synod was requested by the grand duke himself as part of a total reform, in both the Jansenist and Enlightenment sense, of the church in the grand duchy, and was closely watched by European Jansenists. Strong opposition by an assembly of Tuscan archbishops and bishops in 1787, the hostility of ministers of the grand duchy toward Ricci because of his privileged links with the grand duke, violent popular reaction to the reforms, and the departure of Pietro Leopoldo from Tuscany to ascend the imperial throne forced Ricci, in 1791, to abandon running the diocese and withdraw from public life. The Pistoia synod was condemned by Rome in the 1794 bull *Auctorem fidei*, but Ricci gave his formal submission only in 1805. The last years of Ricci's life were devoted to drafting his *Memoirs*, an essential document for the self-defense of his work as a reforming bishop.

[*See also* Jansenism; Josephinism; National Churches; *and* Roman Catholicism.]

BIBLIOGRAPHY

Bocchini Camaiani, Bruna, and Marcello Verga, eds. *Lettere di Scipione de' Ricci a Pietro Leopoldo.* 3 vols. Florence, 1990–1992.

Fantappiè, Carlo. *Riforme ecclesiastiche e resistenze sociali: La sperimentazione istituzionale nella diocesi di Prato alla fine dell'antico regime.* Bologna, 1986.

Gelli, Agenore, ed. *Memorie di Scipione de' Ricci vescovo di Prato e Pistoia scritte da lui medesimo.* 2 vols. Florence, 1865; repr., Pistoia, Italy, 1980.

Lamioni, Claudio, ed. *Lettere di vescovi e cardinali a Scipione de' Ricci (1780–1793).* Pistoia, Italy, 1988.

Lamioni, Claudio, ed. *Il Sinodo di Pistoia del 1786: Atti del Convegno internazionale per il secondo centenario, Pistoia-Prato, 25–27 settembre 1986.* Rome, 1991. Essential reading.

Stella, Pietco, ed. *Atti e decreti del Concilio diocesano di Pistoia dell'gnno 1786.* 2 vols. Florence, 1986.

MARIO ROSA

RICHARDSON, SAMUEL (1689–1761), English printer and man of letters.

Richardson was one of nine children of a provincial carpenter; he had a poor education, although it was his good fortune to be apprenticed at age seventeen to a printer. He taught himself much and by sheer determination overcame personal hardships in a life marked by domestic tragedy. He buried eight children and his first wife. By 1733, he had risen in his profession to be printer to the House of Commons and was later to print works such as the *Philosophical Transactions* of the Royal Society of London.

Other publishers and friends encouraged him to use his talents to become an author himself. His novels began as a series of letter-writing exercises that were published in 1741 and date from the time in which he was composing, with some help from an admiring coterie of London women, *Pamela, or Virtue Rewarded* (1740). This was successful, and a second part was printed in the following year. Henry Fielding found this story of character development foolish and in 1743 parodied it in *Shamela*. Richardson's second revolutionary novel, the seven-volume *Clarissa Harlowe* (1747–1748), was a disturbing psychological drama revolving around lust, love, shame, and family ties and obligations. Its twenty-six characters and 585 letters and postscripts produced a kaleidoscopic array of realistic situations, emotional inconsistencies, deviance from and conformity to social codes, while setting new levels for self-revelation and repartee. Richardson had exploded the parameters of the epistolary novel as it had been known and replaced it with a mode of fiction that defied stereotypes and emphasized the complexity of the human situation. He was particularly interested in his characters' responses to an environment that seemed to ordain one set of behaviors and norms while they saw these as obstacles to be overcome. That is the dominant theme of his fiction.

His third great book, *Sir Charles Grandison* (1753–1754), attempted to create a Protestant epic hero much as Clarissa was a sort of Christian martyr. Here too his technique is extraordinarily modern in its ability to anticipate readers' viewpoints and reactions and to incorporate these into the letters exchanged by the characters. Richardson, for all his innovations, remained, however, squarely within the context of Protestant didactic literature. That is attested to by his 1756 children's book, *The Paths of Virtue Delineated*. Still, he had to defend himself against critics who saw his novels as prurient, disordered, and morbid. They thought then, and sometimes still think, that his writing was less moral and Christian than it should have been, and accused him of deliberately exploiting dubious materials in sensationalist ways. This is unlikely, but few had then ventured where he went.

These novels were translated into the major European languages by writers such as the abbé Prévost, who translated the three novels mentioned above into French, often with changes that startle modern readers. They had profound influence upon European writers who imitated Richardson's works or wrote criticisms of them, as did Diderot. Rousseau and Goethe were galvanized by the novels and were among the many who imitated Richardson's scrupulous, almost scientific, gathering of data about human consciousness, including the narcissism of suffering and the unlimited potential for self-discovery. In short, in Britain and abroad, his work was a harbinger of romanticism.

[*See also* Novel *and* Romanticism.]

BIBLIOGRAPHY

Brophy, Elizabeth Bergen. *Samuel Richardson*. Boston, 1987. A careful review of Richardson's career in light of his artistic precepts and one that deals with the scholarly debate surrounding interpretations of Richardson in the 1980s.

Doody, Margaret Anne. *A Natural Passion: A Study of the Novels of Samuel Richardson*. Oxford, 1974. This analysis of the coherence of Richardson's vision as a novelist anticipates later studies by her related to the depth and intricacies of Richardson's psychological portraits.

Eaves, T. C. Duncan, and Ben D. Kimpel. *Samuel Richardson: A Biography*. Oxford, 1971. Arguably the richest source available connecting Richardson's life, novels, and correspondence to the synchronic reception of his work.

Flynn, Carol Houlihan. *Samuel Richardson: A Man of Letters*. Princeton, N.J., 1982. Explores the manner by which Richardson liberated the novel from conventions—and perhaps liberated himself in the process—by creating characters who defy archetypal limitations.

Harris, Jocelyn. *Samuel Richardson*. Cambridge, 1987. A lively, well-balanced introduction to Richardson's novels with sufficient critical interpretation to attract the attention of those familiar with the subject.

ROBERT J. FRAIL

RIGHTS. *See* Political Philosophy.

RITTENHOUSE, DAVID (1732–1796), American instrument-maker, astronomer, and second president of the American Philosophical Society (1791–1796).

Rittenhouse, "second to no astronomer living," in Thomas Jefferson's words, embodied for his contemporaries the native "mechanical genius" of American science. Born to a Germantown, Pennsylvania, farming family in 1732, Rittenhouse was a self-taught Newtonian. He became an instrument-maker with a penchant for natural philosophy. In 1763, he participated in the survey of the boundary between Maryland and Pennsylvania conducted by English surveyors Charles Mason and Jeremiah Dixon, and he later did similar work for the state of Pennsylvania. It was Rittenhouse's passion for astronomy that earned him the greatest measure of fame. At his Norriton farm outside Philadelphia, he constructed an observatory from which he joined astronomers across the American colonies in observing the transit of Venus in 1769. The observations were published in the Royal Society's *Philosophical Transactions*, earning Rittenhouse a solid reputation among European astronomers.

In 1767, Rittenhouse began his work on the first of two complicated orreries, one for the College of New Jersey at Princeton and one for the College of Philadelphia. The orreries were intricate working scale models of the solar system, calibrated for accurate astronomical calculations, but they were also beautiful—"curiously polished, silvered and painted in proper places, and otherwise ornamented"—and were designed to play "music of the spheres" when the winch was turned to set the planets in motion, appropriately blending an aesthetic appreciation for the created order of things with usefulness.

Rittenhouse's 1775 oration to the American Philosophical Society cemented his reputation as a leading colonial astronomer and demonstrated that he, like many other Philadelphians, was eager to bend scientific interests to patriotic purposes. During the American Revolution, he served as engineer for the city's Committee of Safety, worked to fortify harbor defenses, and consulted on the manufacture of munitions. His political career included serving as a delegate to the state constitutional convention (1776), as a member of the Pennsylvania Assembly, and as state treasurer. The admiration of Rittenhouse's scientific contemporaries brought him the presidency of the American Philosophical Society and was deepened by his election to membership in the British Royal Society in 1795. Jefferson succeeded him as president of the Philosophical Society.

Like the Philadelphia botanist John Bartram, Rittenhouse moved without formal training through an enlightened world inhabited by educated men, but in the context of revolutionary and republican Philadelphia, this was viewed as his greatest virtue. To Thomas Jefferson, for instance, Rittenhouse's Princeton orrery was a wondrous artifact that demonstrated America's salutary climate, both natural and intellectual. To the Edinburgh-educated Philadelphia physician Benjamin Rush, Rittenhouse's self-initiation in the mysteries of astronomy and Newtonian mathematics supported the view that the study of classical languages was a waste of time for the plain but enlightened scholars of the new republic. Even though the solitary path to education chosen by the clockmaker-astronomer made him an unusual rather than a typical figure in Philadelphia's Enlightenment, Rittenhouse has served historians of American science as a symbol of its practical foundations.

[*See also* American Philosophical Society; Astronomy; Philadelphia; *and* Scientific Instruments.]

BIBLIOGRAPHY

Greene, John C. *American Science in the Age of Jefferson*. Ames, Iowa, 1984. Includes brief treatment of Rittenhouse's contributions to astronomy, and his influence on later American astronomers.

Hindle, Brooke. *David Rittenhouse*. Princeton, N.J., 1964. Places Rittenhouse in the context of wider developments in revolutionary Philadelphia's community of science.

Rittenhouse, David. "A Description of a New Orrery." In *Early Transactions of the American Philosophical Society, published in the American Magazine, during 1769*, pp. 10–13. Facsimile reprint, Philadelphia, 1969. One of the earliest descriptions of the Princeton orrery, published by the Society "to give pleasure to persons of a curious and philosophical turn."

Stearns, Raymond Phineas. *Science in the British Colonies of America*. Chicago, 1970. Contains a helpful comparative account of Rittenhouse's work during the colonial period.

NINA REID-MARONEY

ROBERTSON, WILLIAM (1721–1793), Scottish historian, clergyman, and educator.

Born in the parish manse of Borthwick, Midlothian, Robertson was educated at the parish school in Borthwick and, later, at the grammar school in nearby Dalkeith. In 1735, he entered the University of Edinburgh, completing courses in philosophy, rhetoric, and history, but he did not obtain a degree. In 1740–1741, he studied divinity at the university and was ordained a Church of Scotland minister. In 1744, he became pastor of the rural parish of Gladsmuir, approximately twelve miles (7 kilometers) southeast of Edinburgh. In 1758, he was moved to Lady Yester's Chapel in Edinburgh and, in 1761, to Old Greyfriars. On 10 March 1762, he was appointed principal of the University of Edinburgh, a post he held for his lifetime. During his career, he received honorary doctoral degrees from the University of Glasgow (1758) and of Aberdeen (1764); he also held the sinecure posts of chaplain of Stirling Castle (1759) and chaplain-in-ordinary for Scotland (1761); he was named historiographer royal for Scotland in 1763. He was also recognized in other countries and received membership in the Academy of History, Madrid (1777), the Academy of Sciences, Padua (1781), and the Saint Petersburg Academy of Sciences (1783). At his death, he was one of the most widely known intellectuals in Europe.

Works. Robertson is most remembered for his historical writing in the English language. He began working on Scottish history during his years in Gladsmuir and,

shortly after his move to Edinburgh, published his first book, *The History of Scotland during the Reigns of Queen Mary and King James VI* (2 vols., 1759). The book was a huge success because Robertson appeared to his readers to move Scotland into the mainstream of polite Enlightenment culture. He was the first to write a history in English with consistent stylistic polish. In his treatment of the volatile sixteenth-century Scottish events, Robertson deftly contained the antigovernment Jacobite sentiment that remained in Scotland, left from the Rebellion of 1745; the result was a strong yet balanced endorsement of the progress, made possible by the union of England and Scotland, that occurred in the seventeenth and eighteenth centuries.

Robertson followed his success with another, even larger triumph, publishing *The History of the Reign of the Emperor Charles V* (3 vols., 1769), with its immediately famous introductory volume that was subtitled *A View of the Progress of Society in Europe, from the Subversion of the Roman Empire, to the Beginning of the Sixteenth Century*. In it, Robertson traced both the evolution of laws and manners that gave rise to the European state system and the concept of the balance of power that formed the European context for his Scottish history. The first volume is a sweeping survey of twelve centuries; the other two are a detailed analysis of the politics of Habsburg rule in the sixteenth century. Unable to include treatment of the sixteenth-century Spanish discoveries in the New World, Robertson immediately began work on his third major work, *The History of America* (2 vols., 1777). With its dramatic narrative sweep and its provocative confrontation between the Spanish and the Native Americans, not to mention a prose style more flexible and evocative than that used in his earlier books, the *History of America* is often regarded as his most interesting, original, and even Romantic work.

Robertson's last published history was the comparatively brief *Historical Disquisition Concerning the Knowledge Which the Ancients Had of India* (1791), where he extended his longstanding interest in the interaction of cultures to the ancient world and to the easterly direction of European expansion. The first two-thirds is a narrative of the commercial contacts that the Indian subcontinent had with the outside world, from ancient times to the sixteenth century; the last third is a long appendix that describes broad patterns of India's culture, demonstrating both Robertson's wide historical interests and his liberal humanism.

Career. Although Robertson's historical writing is perhaps his most visible contribution to Enlightenment culture, his role in the church and in the university were very important. During the 1750s, Robertson gained influence in the General Assembly of the Church of Scotland, along with a small group of ministers who formed the core of the

Moderate party. His election as moderator in 1763 (though a position he held only for one year) was an indication of his rise to prominence; and his appointment as principal of the university guaranteed his annual place in the church's most important deliberative body. The 1760s and 1770s were then the period of his greatest influence in the church, although the Moderates' policies of patronage and toleration, as well as their efforts to create a more cultured ministry, were often controversial. Robertson resigned as Moderate leader in 1780, but he held his clerical appointment at Old Greyfriars until his death. Robertson's contributions to the University of Edinburgh as principal were substantial: he improved the library, developed a museum, and made faculty appointments to strengthen science and medicine. In 1768, he launched an ambitious subscription scheme of rebuilding; although his initial effort failed, and rebuilding did not begin until 1789, his continuing efforts ultimately made a new building possible.

In an important sense, then, Robertson is best appreciated not simply as a historian but as a practitioner of Enlightenment—someone for whom religious and educational practices, as well as the writing of history, were equally important ways to bring Enlightenment values to his society.

[*See also* Academies; Edinburgh; Scotland; *and* Universities.]

BIBLIOGRAPHY

Brown, Stewart J., ed. *William Robertson and the Expansion of Empire*. Cambridge, 1997. Essays focused on his work as a historian, with a bibliography of writing about Robertson from 1755 to 1996.

Carlyle, Alexander. *Anecdotes and Characters of the Times*. Edited by James Kinsley. London, 1973. Contains observations of Robertson's character and behavior, based on Carlyle's intimate friendship with him.

Clark, Ian D. L. "From Protest to Reaction: The Moderate Regime in the Church of Scotland, 1752–1805." In *Scotland in the Age of Improvement: Essays in Scottish History in the Eighteenth Century*, edited by Nicholas T. Phillipson and Rosalind Mitchison, pp. 200–224. Edinburgh, 1970. The best brief introduction to the politics of the Moderate party, based on Clark's doctoral dissertation (Cambridge, 1964).

Fraser, Andrew G. *The Building of Old College: Adam, Playfair and the University of Edinburgh*. Edinburgh, 1989. The most specific account of Robertson's role in the rebuilding of the university.

O'Brien, Karen. *Narratives of Enlightenment: Cosmopolitan History from Voltaire to Gibbon*. Cambridge, 1997. Chapters 5 and 6, on Robertson, are an up-to-date survey of his historical work.

Robertson, William. *The Works of William Robertson*. Edited by Richard B. Sher et al. 12 vols. London, 1996. The best edition and the only one that presents all Robertson's miscellaneous works (see vol. 12, edited and introduced by Jeffrey Smitten); also the important early lives by John Erskine, Dugald Stewart, and Henry Brougham, plus an introduction to Robertson as a historian by Nicholas Phillipson.

Sher, Richard B. *Church and University in the Scottish Enlightenment: The Moderate Literati of Edinburgh*. Princeton, N.J., 1985. Outstanding study of Robertson and his colleagues, from the point of view of the social history of ideas.

Smitten, Jeffrey. "Selected Bibliography: William Robertson." Website at http://www.c18.org/biblio. Secondary bibliography, updated at least once each year.

JEFFREY SMITTEN

ROCOCO. Stylistic label, period designation, or epithet of derision, the term *rococo* has proven as unstable and provocative as the art it describes. That art includes interior decoration—such as the Parisian salons of the Hôtel de Soubise, completed by Germain Boffrand in 1732—snuffbox designs by Justin-Aurèle Meissonier, paintings by Antoine Watteau and William Hogarth, writings by Jonathan Swift and Denis Diderot, and stage sets by Jacques Lajoue. Although rococo art works were produced throughout Europe and in the Americas, the style was centered on France and is often associated with both the Regency (1715–1730) and the reign of Louis XV (1730–1774). In his landmark study of the rococo style (1949), Fiske Kimball located its origin in Pierre Lepautre's 1699 design for a chimney panel, but he found its full articulation in Meissonier's *Livre d'ornemens* (Book of Ornaments, 1734). Meissonier improvised on the cartouche form, dissolving the boundary between frame and filling with decorative arabesques.

Characteristics. Subsequent writers have defined the rococo more generally. Objects and texts are categorized as rococo for their delicacy, lightness, variety, fantasy, sensuality, mobility, wit, and fragmentation. Rococo art is an art of self-conscious illusion that encourages spectators to be both involved in the image and aware of the artifice. This aspect is evident in the decoration of interiors like those by François de Cuvilliés for the Amalienberg in Munich (1734–1739), where mirrors fragment and reflect the room in cycles of repetition. Mirrors produce a fragmentation of attention, a flickering between illusion and awareness. In a similar way, rococo paintings like François Boucher's 1756 portrait of Mme. de Pompadour (Munich, Alte Pinakotek) invite reading as both depth and surface; they present the viewer with an illusion of three-dimensional space, but, through a technique called *papillotage*, they constantly draw the eye to the painted surface with deft brush work that distracts from the illusion. These strategies can be compared with techniques of interruption in narrative, such as those Diderot used in the novel *Jacques le fataliste et son maître* (written c. 1773). Analogously, the reader of rococo poetry oscillates between the superficial, seemingly haphazard surface and the underlying metrical structure. It is important to note, however, that there was not in the eighteenth century an expressly defined poetic of the rococo. The style's adversaries first articulated its characteristics negatively and retrospectively, and those who appreciate the rococo have wrestled with their definition ever since.

Rococo Theater. The Residenztheater, Munich, by François Cuvilliés. (Foto Marburg/Art Resource, NY.)

"Rococo" is related etymologically to *rocaille*, ornamental shellwork in grottoes and gardens. In 1772, the French architect Jacques-François Blondel used *rocaille* to name the style of interior decoration we now call Rococo; contemporaries referred to it as *style moderne*, *genre pittoresque*, *goût nouveau*, or *goût de ce siècle*. The *style rocaille*, by century's end, would derisively be called *rococo*. Étienne Delécluze, a biographer of the neoclassical painter Jacques-Louis David, wrote that the artist Maurice Quai in 1796 first used the expressions *Pompadour* and *rococo* to defame the art produced under Louis XV. By 1836, "rococo" had appeared in English usage; *Frazer's Magazine* noted it as studio slang, a new *mot d'argot*. *rococo* combines *rocaille* with *barocco*, an adjective meaning misshapen, malformed, and convoluted, which was used to denigrate works of seventeenth-century Italian artists like Borromini and Bernini. The easy move from *barocco* to *rococo* was duplicated in the first critical studies of the style, which considered rococo a late phase of the baroque. In the hands of Jacob Burckhardt, rococo became generally synonymous with the dissolution that marked late phases of all styles.

Expression of the Ancien Régime. Two of the most enduring aspects of the rococo are its associations with aristocracy and femininity, summed up in its connection with Mme. de Pompadour, mistress to Louis XV. Although Maurice Quai used the connection to ridicule the rococo, others—like the Goncourt brothers, writing in the nineteenth century—articulated a more positive alliance consonant with their nostalgia for the ancien régime. Largely responsible for promoting a rococo revival, the Goncourts called Pompadour "a patron of luxury goods and of the rocaille . . . the godmother and the queen of the rococo." More recent commentators, such as Rémy Saisselin, have viewed Pompadour as emblematic of the rococo because her style of patronage treated art as a luxury good and spending as necessary to her social station. Connecting money, luxury, art, and women as integral parts of the rococo restates the views of eighteenth-century critics who, with moral condemnation, identified elite culture and rococo luxury products as feminine. Montesquieu, and later Rousseau, viewed aristocratic *politesse* and luxury as both profligate and feminizing, and throughout the revolutionary period, critics attributed a lack of manliness to the ancien régime's corrupt and decadent social order. Today, rococo art is often associated with the refined sensuality and *volupté* that marked French aristocratic taste.

A Feminine Style. Later writers have often labeled the rococo feminine, based on characteristics such as charm, curvilinear form, delicacy, grace, and frivolity. Mario Praz further associated the rococo with female sexuality, since he takes the central motif of the shell, with its "cozy concavity," to be symbolic of the female genitals. The shell was long a token of Venus, and in defining the rococo, Hans Sedlmayr and Hermann Bauer identify Venus as a central figure of its iconography, and lovemaking as one of its most persistent themes—particularly evident in French painting, as in Watteau's *fête galante*, *The Pilgrimage to Cythera* (1717). More recently, Norman Bryson has argued further that rococo principally defines not a style but an erotics, basing his analysis on paintings such as Boucher's *The Setting of the Sun* (1752; London: Wallace Collection). By breaking with Renaissance conventions of perspective, such works push the viewer closer to the bodies they depict and encourage him to consume the image with the least possible resistance. In the psychoanalytic model Bryson employs, to be consumed by the gaze of another is to be placed in a feminine position, so the erotics of rococo painting again depend on its alleged femininity.

The easy association of the rococo with the feminine and the aristocratic is rendered problematic in some social histories of art. Thus, Arnold Hauser saw in the rococo two polarities in a dialectical opposition that corresponds to the antagonisms within the society of its period, since rococo art could be found both at court and in the bourgeois circles opposed to the court. Perhaps most significant, Hauser found rococo art subversive in its parody or travesty of traditional elements. Some recent accounts of the rococo (Crown, Park, and Howells) have also noted its subversive elements, associating the style with Carnival, the grotesque, the comic, or the mixing of high and low genres. These aspects are represented in the comic works of English artists like William Hogarth or Thomas Rowlandson, the arabesques and decorative panels of Antoine Watteau, and the ornamental designs of Meissonier and Lajoue. In analyzing the subversive character of rococo forms, Sedlmayr and Bauer cast the style as an artistic revolution that might have been especially dangerous because it "came playfully on little velvet paws."

[*See also* Aesthetics; Architecture; Feminist Theory; Novel; Painting; *and* Poetry.]

BIBLIOGRAPHY

Bryson, Norman. *Word and Image: French Painting of the Ancien Regime*. Cambridge, 1981.

Crown, Patricia. "British Rococo as Social and Political Style." *Eighteenth-Century Studies* 23 (1990), 269–282.

Hauser, Arnold. *The Social History of Art*. New York, 1958.

Hobson, Marion. *The Object of Art: The Theory of Illusion in Eighteenth-Century France*. Cambridge, 1982. A compelling analysis of Rococo form related to ideas about illusionism, considering literature, theater, and the visual arts.

Howells, Robin. "Rococo and Carnival." In *Studies on Voltaire and the Eighteenth Century*, vol. 308, pp. 185–218. Oxford, 1993.

Kimball, Fiske. *The Creation of the Rococo*. Philadelphia, 1943. The classic text on the Rococo style, focused on French decorative interiors.

Park, William. *The Idea of the Rococo*. Newark, Del., 1992. Identifies and analyzes characteristics of the Rococo style in the literature and visual arts of several national traditions.

Praz, Mario. *Mnemosyne: The Parallel between Literature and the Visual Arts*. Princeton, N.J., 1970.

Saisselin, Rémy. *The Enlightenment against the Baroque: Economics and Aesthetics in the Eighteenth Century*. Berkeley, Calif., 1992. A useful book that considers the relation between Rococo arts and patterns of aristocratic spending.

Scott, Katie. *The Rococo Interior*. New Haven, Conn., 1995. An account of French architecture and interior design emphasizing the social and political issues surrounding the Rococo style.

Sedlmayr, Hans, and Hermann Bauer. "Rococo." In *Encyclopedia of World Art*, vol. 12, p. 258. New York, 1966.

MARY SHERIFF

ROLAND, MARIE-JEANNE (Manon Phlipon) (1754–1793), French writer and political figure.

Although born into relative obscurity, Manon Phlipon played an important role both in revolutionary politics and in French letters. The only child of a Parisian engraver, she was given an education well beyond that customary for her sex and social rank. She read widely and was especially drawn to the writings of Jean-Jacques Rousseau, Tacitus, and Plutarch. The development of her republican and pre-Romantic sensibilities can be traced in her memoirs and in her voluminous correspondence. Greatly admired by Stendhal and other nineteenth-century writers for their literary qualities and historical significance, these works provide a vivid chronicle of life in the late Enlightenment and early revolutionary period.

In her mid-twenties, Manon married Jean-Marie Roland, an erudite, austere man twenty years her senior. On his family estate near Lyon, she devoted herself to educating their daughter and to overseeing the farm while her husband was away on his tours as regional inspector of manufactures. During this period, she collaborated with her husband on numerous technical and scholarly works, including a three-volume *Dictionnaire des manufactures, arts et métiers* for the revised edition of Denis Diderot's *Encyclopédie*.

Fervent republicans, the Rolands greeted the Revolution with unbounded enthusiasm. Under the pressure of events, Mme. Roland's life and writings underwent a radical politicization. To serve the revolutionary cause, she became a regular, albeit anonymous, contributor to republican journals. In 1790, her husband represented Lyon in the Constitutional Convention in Paris, where he became a member of the Jacobin Society. When he was appointed secretary of the club's correspondence committee, Mme. Roland eagerly shared his work. Convinced that shaping public opinion could play a vital role in the success of the Revolution, she put all her skill into answering the many letters from provincial correspondents. By 1791, however, the Rolands broke with the Jacobins, becoming central figures in the Girondin faction.

After her husband's unexpected appointment as Louis XVI's minister of the interior in March 1792, her collaboration became even more crucial to his success. She was the moving force behind his propaganda bureau and served as his secret political advisor and ghostwriter. She composed a number of the key documents of his ministry, including his letter of protest to Louis XVI. Published by the Assembly (at her urging), Roland's letter to the king played a significant role in turning the tide of public opinion against the monarchy, which was abolished on 10 August 1792.

Mme. Roland's role as the Egeria of the Girondins seemed to offer an ideal opportunity to fulfill her political aspirations. In the intimacy of the Girondin circle, her opinions carried increasing weight, although she remained behind the scenes. In response to charges that she had secretly run her husband's ministry, she insisted that she merely served as his secretary. From the testimony of her memoirs, however, it is clear that she was much more than a mere scribe, and that charges she was the hidden power behind her husband's ministry were not unfounded. Her subtle transgression of traditional gender barriers did not go unperceived and was capitalized on by the Rolands' political enemies in the campaign of slander and persecution that eventually led her to the guillotine.

As the Girondists' popularity declined, Jacobin politicians and journalists multiplied their attacks against the Rolands. It was repeatedly charged that, under his wife's influence, Roland had plotted with enemy forces and had misappropriated public funds to spread counterrevolutionary propaganda. The viciousness and frequency of these attacks reflect the degree of power and influence attributed to her. Imprisoned in June 1793 on charges of treason, Mme. Roland was executed on 8 November. During this five-month imprisonment, she wrote her memoirs in order to escape the gloom of prison and to defend herself against the charges of her political enemies. Recounting her life's story and the political events she had witnessed proved not only a way to justify herself in the eyes of posterity, but also a means of fulfilling her talents and ambitions as a writer.

[*See also* French Revolution.]

BIBLIOGRAPHY

WORKS BY ROLAND

Roland, Marie-Jeanne. *Lettres de Madame Roland.* Edited by Claude Perroud and Marthe Conor. 4 vols. Paris, 1900–1915. The first two volumes were published as vol. 112, parts 1 and 2, in the series *Collection de documents inédits sur l'histoire de la France*, in 1913 and 1915 respectively; the third and fourth volumes were published earlier in the same series as vol. 104, parts 1 and 2, in 1900 and 1902.

Roland, Marie-Jeanne. *Un Voyage en Suisse* [1787]. Edited by G. R. de Beer. Neuchâtel, Switzerland, 1937.

Roland, Marie-Jeanne. *Mémoires de Madame Roland* [1793]. Edited by Paul de Roux. Paris, 1986.

WORKS ABOUT ROLAND

Chaussinand-Nogaret, Guy. *Madame Roland: Une femme en Révolution.* Paris, 1985.

Gelfand, Elissa D. "Madame Roland." In *Imagination in Confinement: Women's Writings from French Prisons*, pp. 130–152. Ithaca, N.Y., 1983.

May, Gita. *De Jean-Jacques Rousseau à Madame Roland.* Geneva, 1964.

May, Gita. *Madame Roland and the Age of Revolution.* New York, 1970.

Outram, Dorinda. "Words and Flesh: Mme. Roland, the Female Body and the Search for Power." In *The Body and the French Revolution: Sex, Class, and Political Culture*, pp. 124–152. New Haven, Conn., 1989.

Trouille, Mary. "Revolution in the Boudoir: Madame Roland's Subversion of Rousseau's Feminine Ideals." In *Sexual Politics in the Enlightenment: Women Writers Read Rousseau*, pp. 163–192. Albany, N.Y., 1997.

MARY SEIDMAN TROUILLE

ROMAN CATHOLICISM. The momentous cultural and political changes that occurred in Europe between the end of the seventeenth century and the beginning of the eighteenth set the stage for the transformation of Catholic religious practice and institutions during the Enlightenment.

The Embrace of New Concepts. In contrast to the late Counter-Reformation, the historical erudition of the Benedictines of the Congregation of Saint-Maur and the diffusion of Locke's and Newton's philosophic-scientific thinking made possible a novel critical awareness of the past, and led to the elaboration of more advanced epistemological and conceptual paths. Two of the greatest exemplars of eighteenth-century Italian culture are the Modenese intellectual Ludovico Antonio Muratori (1672–1750) and the Neapolitan illuminist Antonio Genovesi (1713–1769).

Muratori, a historian, also laid the foundations for an enlightened concept of religion (*Della regolata devozione dei cristiani*, 1747); for the analysis of social evils and injustices (*Della carità cristiana*, 1723); for fostering trust in the government of European sovereigns (*Della pubblica felicità*, 1749); and for the evangelistic mission of the Roman Catholic Church in the New World (*Il Cristianesimo felice*, 1743). His reforming project was discussed and welcomed not only in Italy but also in Spain in the 1740s and 1750s; in the 1780s in Austria, it influenced many aspects of Maria Theresa's and Joseph II's reforms.

Genovesi advocated an internal rebirth of traditional Catholic culture influenced by Newtonian natural theology and Anglo-Dutch thinking, and based on a close link between science and religion (*Elementa metaphysicae*, 1743). Although Genovesi's reforms, faced with difficult obstacles, were destined to fail at the beginning of the 1750s, they would bear fruit in the economic and political sectors.

The difficult convergences between Catholicism and the Enlightenment were weakened by Rome's condemnation of Locke's "reasonable Christianity" (1737) and of latitudinarian religious tendencies, from the first condemnation of Freemasonry (1738; a second condemnation followed in 1751) to the prohibition of important works of the early Enlightenment (Montesquieu in 1751, Voltaire in 1753–1757). All attempts to reconcile the two broke down definitively after the deaths of Muratori (1750) and Pope Benedict XIV (1758). The apprehension of Rome and the ecclesiastical hierarchy was further heightened by the reforms of enlightened sovereigns and the continuing offensive of the Enlightenment against Christianity, and against Catholicism in particular. The church's counterattack under the papacy of Clement XIII reached its zenith in the solemn condemnation of Helvétius's *De l'esprit* (On the Mind, 1758) and of the *Encyclopédie* (1759), marking the by now unbridgeable gap between Christian belief and that of the philosophes. This assertiveness continued under Clement XIV and Pius VI, with severe repressive measures against the materialistic writings of La Mettrie and d'Holbach and the works of the mature Enlightenment, from Voltaire to Diderot.

Catholic Aufklärung. Despite these definitive actions by Rome, there developed within Catholicism, especially in the 1770s and 1780s, a rich movement of thought now identified by historians as the Catholic or Christian Aufklärung (German, "Enlightenment"). Recent scholars view this as a composite and also a contradictory movement characterized by a dual tension: cultural dynamism and a commitment to apologetics, or defense of the faith.

On one hand, the Catholic Aufklärung is depicted as a moment of Christian religious consciousness that accepted reason as an instrument but not an end, and that was often spurred on—in accordance with Jansenism on the religious level and with reforming governments on the political level—to a revision of the structures and methods of the church after the Council of Trent. In its struggle against baroque Catholicism (i.e., characterized by a strong devotion toward saints and the Virgin Mary), papal prerogatives, and the Society of Jesus (which it considered the epitome of current historical degeneration), the reformers took action for a return to the clarity and simplicity of an idealized primitive church—a return that scholars of ancient scriptural and patristic sources joined with a return, in the Enlightenment sense, to "origins."

On the other hand, worry over the impetuous development of "philosophic incredulity" stimulated an apologetic effort. The Catholic Aufklärung, reflecting on the relationship between religion and society and the fundamental sociability of Christianity, tried to work out a "Christian philosophy" in opposition to the Enlightenment. It tried—though without fully welcoming the great themes of the century, from tolerance to natural rights—to build the image of a church at the service of Christian people, the bearer of a reasonable, intelligent faith for everyone, open to dialogue with the world and with contemporary science.

The Catholic Aufklärung was, therefore, a reform movement within the church that was linked, though in discordant harmony, with the Enlightenment reform movement and with interventions by reforming sovereigns who were inclined to welcome the collaboration of religious forces with the state in a more general process of cultural and social transformation. In the first half of the eighteenth century, especially during the papacy of Benedict XIV, relations between the Holy See and political powers were organized around a series of concordats with the Kingdom of Naples, Sardinia, and Austrian Lombardy in the Italian peninsula, and with Portugal and Spain beyond Italy. In the 1760s and 1770s, however, there were decisive changes in the context of ecclesiastic institutions and in the very life of the Catholic Church. The laws then promulgated to block the continuous increase of ecclesiastic property and provisions to curb the increase of both the secular and the regular ecclesiastic population were preludes to the still more drastic interventions of the 1780s. In the Habsburg hereditary dominions and Austrian Lombardy,

in Habsburg-Lorraine Tuscany, in the Bourbon Italian territories of Naples and Sicily and Parma, and in Bourbon Spain, and in Portugal, this trend of intervention included the suppression of the Society of Jesus (1773), the suppression of the right of asylum in churches, and the revocation of personal immunity of the clergy.

Other repressive measures included the suppression of monasteries, convents, and confraternities, and also of institutions—for example, the courts of the Roman Inquisition, the state Inquisition in Sicily, and the episcopal and inquisitorial offices for ecclesiastical censure—that since the mid-sixteenth century had been instruments of religious, cultural, and moral control on the part of the Tridentine church, especially in Italian territory. These negative measures were counterbalanced by a series of positive reforms such as the reorganization of the secular clergy, especially for the care of souls, the reordering and improving of the network of ecclesiastic benefices, and intervention in clerical education. These reforms were intended better to balance the ecclesiastic and religious needs of the church with the political and social needs of the state. Through reform of the seminaries—where thanks to the commitment of many bishops new philosophical-scientific disciplines were taught and the teaching of theology and morals renewed—and through the founding of ecclesiastic academies, as was done in Tuscany under the government of Grand Duke Peter Leopold, or of general seminaries like those set up by Emperor Joseph II, the figure of the "good parish priest" was placed at the center of the ideals and practices of political power and of the most sensitive sectors of the ecclesiastic world.

Enlightened Piety. As for the religious education of the faithful, after attempts at spreading Muratori's idea of temperate devotion under Benedict XIV, the concept of an enlightened piety, purified in rites and devotions, was introduced on the fundamental level of collective religious practice during the ecclesiastic reforms of the 1780s. Temperate devotion had aimed at reducing the uncontrolled excesses of Counter-Reformation and baroque religiosity, found in the worldly pomp of religious ceremonies and the cult of the Virgin and saints, practiced especially in the confraternities. It also aimed at imprinting on devotions substantial christocentric orientation, and at exalting the value of sacrifice and the communal sense of the Mass, instead of focusing on posthumous benefits for the faithful tied to indulgences for the dead and devotion offered for souls in Purgatory. The concept of enlightened piety was much more radical in its proposals. The state, rather than the church, guided its reforms, especially through the efforts of Joseph II in Austria and Peter Leopold in Habsburg Italy. The confraternities were abolished, replaced by a single parish confraternity for charity. The role of the religious orders was reduced. It was in the parishes that worship was to find its most authentic and "enlightened" expression, through the parish priest, devoted to teaching his flock sound moral doctrine and the connected duties of the faithful in family and social life. There was a new simplicity of the rites, stripped of sumptuous trappings; they were made more understandable by the substitution of national languages for Latin in some public prayers and certain moments of the sacramental liturgy.

Faced with these reforms, the official response of the Church of Rome was to move in the opposite direction, with the development of popular missions and the broad diffusion of tender, sentimental devotions such as the Sacred Heart of Jesus and the Way of the Cross. Especially popular were pious booklets inspired by this type of religious practice; its greatest interpreter was Saint Alfonso Maria de Liguori, author of *L'amore delle anime cioè riflessioni ed affetti sulla passione di Gesù Cristo* (1751), *Massime eterne* (1758), *Novena del Santo Natale* (1758), and *Pratica d'amare Gesù Cristo* (1768), one of the most widespread ascetic books in the eighteenth century. In religious art, a preference developed for simple, familiar subjects (the life of the Virgin, the Holy Family, the adoration of the Shepherds, the infancy of Jesus), and artists turned from great figurative compositions to series of engravings and small reproductions. In this climate, especially at the end of the century, there occurred a "feminization" of religious practice; increasing participation of women in the daily aspects of worship and devotion, and more attention to women's religious life by confessors, spiritual directors, authors of devotional writings, and creators of religious iconography.

Regional Differences of Catholic Aufklärung. Even the shared elements of the Catholic Aufklärung took on different aspects in various European regions. In Portugal, the movement mixed rationalist philosophy (Christian Wolff and John Locke) with French Jansenist episcopalianism, and, especially under the government of the marquis of Pombal, it was predominantly anti-Jesuit. The Spanish *Ilustración*, with the works of Benito Jeronimo de Feijoo and Gregorio Mayans y Siscar, influenced by Muratori, privileged historical criticism, liturgical and patristic studies, and, in the framework of a strong pastoral commitment, preaching and catechesis, inspired by the call for a "return" to the Bible. The exercise of state power, however, remained balanced between novelty and tradition, tending toward the latter, not only because of resentment toward the French Enlightenment but also because of the persistent control of the Inquisition.

In German Catholic regions, opening to the Enlightenment took on uncertain outlines. The Rhineland appeared more enlightened, in part because of support by the high and low clergy for Freemasonry—a phenomenon that was, in fact, widespread among Catholic ecclesiastics in Europe

of the ancien régime. In general, there was an ecumenical and unionist spirit and openness toward the Protestant confession, following the pressure for ecclesiastical tolerance expressed by Justinus Febronius (pseudonym of Johann Nikolaus von Hontheim, the auxiliary bishop of Trier) in *De statu ecclesiae* (1763). In the Austrian Low Countries, theological and ecclesiological interests represented in the University of Louvain contributed to forming—thanks to the writings of the canonist Zeger Bernhard van Espen—the ideological underpinning of Joseph II's reforms; the goal was to insert the church, as van Espen wrote, "into the natural order of the state." However, national resistance to the reforms, together with strong anti-Jansenist and philo-Jesuit currents, exploded in the violent reactions of the "Revolution" in Brabant (1789–1790).

More than in the Low Countries, however, it was the hereditary Habsburg territories and Austrian Lombardy that hosted the most organic and radical realization of the Catholic Aufklärung, undoubtedly inspired by the general movement but bolstered by the agenda of Joseph II. This policy, known as Josephinism, was aimed at transforming a collection of territories into a homogeneous state; it was characterized, from the religious point of view, by the conquests of the Counter-Reformation. Religious tolerance toward non-Catholic minorities was guaranteed by the 1781 edict of toleration, in which the German Catholic episcopate, strongly autonomous in regard to Rome, assumed official responsibility toward the state, and the secular clergy, especially the parish priests, were considered as "useful" to society in forming their flocks as subjects faithful to the church and obedient to the sovereign.

In the Habsburg Italian territories, after Lombardy, Tuscany was the most active center of ecclesiastic and religious reform. In contrast to Joseph II's forceful attempt to achieve a national church, reform in Tuscany proceeded gradually, according to a model both enlightened and Jansenist; the latter element was absent from more state-controlled imperial reformism. The Tuscan model assigned an essential role to local churches in an attempt to loosen the bonds of hierarchical order and Roman centralism. This attempt begun by Grand Duke Peter Leopold with the bishop of Pistoia and Prato, Scipione dé Ricci, through the 1786 synod of Pistoia, failed because of the general pulling back from reforms at the end of the 1780s, with the election of Grand Duke Peter Leopold as emperor and the beginning of the French Revolution.

The French church was not diminished by such reforms, although the Commission of the Regular Clergy (from 1766) frequently initiated suppression of ancient abbeys and wealthy monasteries, by now without monks, and tried to limit mendicant orders. The church in France was divided between a high clergy that was aristocratic and often worldly, but not beyond the rule of the dioceses, and a low clergy imbued with Jansenist sympathies and attracted to Enlightenment reforms, as became clear at the time of the Revolution. The French church's main preoccupation in the eighteenth century was the need to stand up to the ever more threatening offensive of the Enlightenment through preaching and apologetic writings, which were for the most part different from the kind inspired by the Catholic Aufklärung—although Mme. de Genlis's celebrated *La religion considérée comme l'unique base du bonheur* (1787) could be considered an example of such inspiration. This apologetic effort intensified in the 1770s, after the *Avertissement sur les effets pernicieux de l'incrédulité* was published by the Assembly of the Clergy of France (1775), and after the encyclical *Inscrutabile Divinae Sapientiae* was issued in the same year by Pius VI against the culture and ideology of the Enlightenment. This document resumed and developed Clement XIII's anti-Enlightenment encyclical *Christianae Reipublicae salus* (1766) and the direction taken in various condemnations issued from Rome against individual Enlightenment authors.

Early in the eighteenth century, French Catholic apologetics eagerly engaged unbelief on issues of empirical fact and history. Because of the growing intensity of the Catholic-Enlightenment dispute in France, historical apologetics like C. F. Houtteville's *La religion chrétienne prouvée par les faits* (1722, often reprinted) fell out of fashion. Empirical apologetics had already been affected by scathing enlightened criticism, and scientific apologetics (e.g., the abbé Pluche's *Le spectacle de la nature*, 1722) was not taken up again, despite its success in the first half of the century. The 1750s and 1760s saw a "spiritualistic" and Jansenist apologetics typified by the works of the Oratorian Le Large de Lignac, with his call to conscience and interior conviction against determinism (*Le témoignage du sens intime et de l'expérience opposé à la foi profane et ridicule des fatalistes modernes*, 1760), Louis-Antoine Caraccioli's *La religion de l'honnête homme* (1766) against Rousseau, and Louis Racine's *La religion* (1742, 1747, 1752), which celebrated tolerant religion and urged meeting human needs.

The attack by the philosophes was answered, in the second half of the century, both by the moderate criticism of the Jesuit *Mémoires de Trévoux* (until the suppression of the order) and at greater length by the violent polemics of the Jansenist *Nouvelles Ecclésiastiques*. Jesuits or ex-Jesuits and Jansenists, in different ways, formed a united front against a common adversary. The Jesuits were more compliant, able cleverly to exploit even the boldest Enlightenment achievements, like the *Encyclopédie*, but also to prepare significant arguments of conservative and reactionary inspiration, first against reforming policy and then against revolutionary thinking. The Jansenist response was more rigid and hostile; its tragic religious vision contrasted strongly with Enlightenment optimism.

Now leading the defense of the church, however, were the exponents of the episcopate and their pastoral letters. Among them were Malvin de Montazet, archbishop of Lyon, author of the famous "Sur les sources de l'incrédulité" ("On the sources of unbelief," 1776), and César Guillaume de La Luzerne, bishop of Langres, whose "Sur l'excellence de la religion chrétienne" (1786) was reprinted into the nineteenth century. Numerous other apologists emerged: Nicolas-Sylvestre Bergier, for example, attacked Rousseau in *Le déisme réfuté par lui-même* (1765), Boulanger in *Apologie de la religion chrétienne* (1769), and d'Holbach in *L'examen du matérialisme* (1771), and offered a general anti-Enlightenment polemic in *Certitude des preuves du Christianisme* (1763). Other examples of this trend were G. Gauchat's *Lettres critiques, ou Analyse et réfutation de divers écrits modernes contre la religion* (1755–1763) and C. Nonotte's *Dictionnaire philosophique de la religion* (1763) and his resentful, diffuse attacks against Voltaire. The Savoyard Barnabite, and later cardinal, Hyacinth Sigismond Gerdil, exhibited keener philosophical ability in his confutation of Locke (*L'immatérialité de l'âme contre M. Locke*, 1747), and of Rousseau (*Discours philosophique sur l'homme considéré relativement à l'état de nature et à l'état de société*, 1769).

Because these Catholic apologetic writers thought that unbelief derived from "corruption of the heart"—from the proud refusal to believe—they emphasized the social usefulness and fundamental goodness of religion—as a guarantee of an earthly happiness before the celestial—more than its truth. Their considerable achievement could not conceal, however, a substantially defensive attitude toward "the certainties of faith," or the weakness of their mode of intellectual argument, which was often tautological in its call to a "sacrifice of the mind" as necessary for Christian piety in the face of unfathomable mysteries and dogma.

Catholic Aufklärung in a New Light. The responses to the great crisis of Roman Catholicism in the eighteenth century were therefore varied, and its relationships with the Enlightenment oscillated between rapprochement and violent combat. The historiographical identification of a Catholic and Christian Aufklärung was useful to German Catholic scholars of the late nineteenth and the twentieth centuries, such as Sebastian Merkle, as a reaction to the *Kulturkampf* (battle of civilization), in order to emphasize the nonreactionary characteristics of Catholic culture in the century of the Enlightenment. This concept was particularly fruitful in the area of research into the cultural and political-religious history of the German and Austrian territories in the eighteenth century, especially with reference to Hapsburg reformism. It was effectively used in the late twentieth century by cultural historians, and it stimulated new research into the religious aspects of the century of Enlightenment, alongside research already dedicated to the reforming versus the radical Enlightenment, or to the political-ecclesiastic and religious disputes with Jansenism. This new historical attitude contributed to form a more complex and clear picture of the interlacing of politics, religion, and culture in the age between the Reformation and the Revolution.

Beginning in the last thirty years of the eighteenth century, another response arose from the Catholic hierarchy, the papacy and Roman Curia, and the majority of bishops in various countries—indeed, among large sectors of Catholic culture. Each developed, according to its own dynamic but within an ever more coherent and unified political-religious orientation, its reaction both to the Enlightenment and to the reforming interventions of European sovereigns. There was strong opposition to reforms believed to threaten the church, despite some yielding, as in the suppression of the Jesuits. If this opposition did not succeed in blocking the process of secularization in society, it at least stimulated reaction to the reforms themselves well before the events of the French Revolution.

Ironically, the willingness to engage with modern thinking urged by the Catholic Aufklärung corresponded to an ever more rigid conservatism in doctrine and ecclesiastical teaching as the church recoiled from the French Revolution. Condemnation of Jansenism (of the Synod of Pistoia) in 1794 or of French Revolutionary principles (of the Civil Constitution of the Clergy) in 1791, together with the diffusion of conservative and traditionalist thinking (Joseph de Maistre and Louis de Bonald), strengthened authority and papal teaching in the Catholic Church, and the definition of a "Christian society" under the guidance of the Roman pontiff. In reaction to widespread dechristianization and distancing of urban elites from religion, a conscious orientation gradually spread through church institutions and general European Catholic society, which was aimed at creating a new social and religious consensus and stronger links between the church and the popular masses, in particular the rural ones.

This was the strong nucleus and predominant legacy of eighteenth-century Catholicism. The transformation that had occurred in religious life, the confrontation of Catholicism with a changing world, and the new thought and pluralistic choices that matured within the Catholic Aufklärung had replaced Counter-Reformation uniformity with new bases for the relationship between religion and politics in the transition between the modern and contemporary eras.

[*See also* Benedict XIV; Clement XIV; Genovesi, Antonio; Italy; Jansenism; Jesuits; Josephism; *and* Muratori, Lodovico Antonio.]

BIBLIOGRAPHY

Châtellier, Louis, ed. *Religions en transition dans la seconde moitié du XVIIIe siècle.* Oxford, 2000.

Cragg, Gerald R. *The Church and the Age of Reason, 1648–1789.* (Pelican History of the Church.) Harmondsworth, U.K., 1972.

Les courants chrétiens de l'Aufklärung en Europe de la fin du XVIIe siècle jusque vers 1830. Congrès de Varsovie, 25 juin–1 juillet 1978, sect. II. (Bibliothèque de la *Revue d'histoire ecclésiastique*, fasc. 68; Miscellanea Historiae Ecclesiasticae 6.) Wrocław, Poland, and Brussels, 1987.

Levillain, Philippe, ed. *The Papacy: An Encyclopedia.* 3 vols. New York and London, 2002. See especially the entry "Enlightenment," vol. 1, pp. 527–531.

Monod, Albert. *De Pascal à Chateaubriand: Les défenseurs français du christianisme de 1670 à 1802.* Paris, 1916; repr. New York, 1971.

Palmer, Robert R. *Catholics and Unbelievers in Eighteenth-Century France.* Princeton, N.J., 1939.

Rosa, Mario. *Settecento religioso: Politica della ragione e religione del cuore.* Venice, 1999.

Schneider, B. "'Katholische Aufklärung': Zum Werden und Wert eines Forschungsbegriffs." *Revue d'Histoire Ecclésiastique* 93 (1998), 354–397.

MARIO ROSA

ROMANTICISM. It was once a commonplace of literary and intellectual history that Romanticism was the antithesis of the Enlightenment. More recently, there was a consensus that Romanticism grew out of the Enlightenment and was in a fundamental sense its continuation. In the contradictory spirit of Romanticism itself, it now seems clear that both assertions are true, and that a dialectical approach is necessary to understand Romanticism's complex relationship to its predecessor.

This is, however, a difficult notion to articulate. It is possible to cite many examples of hostile Romantic utterances about the Enlightenment on one side (William Blake's "Mock on, Mock on, Voltaire, Rousseau"), and on the other, examples of direct Romantic filiation with various Enlightenment positions, but such a balance sheet is not a very useful approach. The countereffort to relate a synthetic "Romanticism" to a synthetic "Enlightenment," however, runs the risk of relying on oversimplified, easily contested definitions of both. Yet finally only such an approach seems to offer any hope of producing more than a list of unrelated continuities and differences. One check on excessively facile ideal-typical constructions can be provided by paying attention to what—and who—constituted the Enlightenment in the consciousness of the Romantics themselves.

German Romanticism. To the first generation of German Romantics, the Aufklärung (the German Enlightenment) was simultaneously inspiration and inhibition, to be assimilated and then surpassed. In the forms of the neoclassical aesthetics of Johann Joachim Winckelmann, Gotthold Ephraim Lessing, and Friedrich Schiller and in the philosophy of Immanuel Kant, the Aufklärung represented the ideals of rational autonomy and the harmonious integration of all the various aspects of personality. It was as proponents of these Enlightenment ideals that early Romantics initially became enthusiastic supporters of the French Revolution. Developing an idea proposed by Winckelmann, the literary critic Friedrich Schlegel argued concerning Greek poetry that the synthesis of radical individual freedom and morality represented in Athenian comedy and drama could only have been founded on Athens's republican constitution. He drew the appropriate contemporary political inference in an essay on modern republicanism, criticizing the cautious definition that Kant had advanced in *Zum ewigen Frieden* (1795) and insisting, in a revolutionary extension of both Kant and Rousseau, that in practical terms, the general will could mean only the will of a majority; republicanism was necessarily democratic.

Romanticism proper came into being, however, only when Schlegel and his colleagues went beyond Kant's idea of a rationally bounded autonomy to Johann Gottlieb Fichte's notion of the self as an infinitely striving subjectivity that in principle knows no boundaries except those of its own finitude. The dangerous implications of this idea, both for their personal lives and for their politics, caused most of them (the poet Friedrich Hölderlin was a notable but complex exception) to back away from political activism. In this first phase, however, early Romanticism represented a further radicalization of Enlightenment notions of freedom in both aesthetics and intimate relationships, even as it represented a retrenchment in politics. Autonomy now meant the absolute freedom of Romantic art, which, as Schlegel famously wrote in the Athenaeum Fragment 116, "recognizes as its first commandment that the will of the poet can tolerate no law above itself." Form (including moral order) is not imposed by external rules, not even by the inner law of Kant's Categorical Imperative, but is the organic creation of the integrated personality, whose harmonious totality is guaranteed by the experience of ideal love.

The idea of political freedom did not disappear completely from early Romanticism. Though the Romantics turned increasingly to the idea of monarchy as the only feasible political integrating principle for radical individuality, they attempted to retain the ideal of individual political freedom within that framework. The idiosyncratic politics of the treatise *Glauben und Leibe* (Faith and Life, 1798) by Novalis, which argued for the integration of monarchy and republic as the necessary elements of a truly universal state, was the most audaciously paradoxical of the early German Romantic formulations. Novalis attempted to fuse radical individuality with an entity representing totality—one that is simultaneously external to the individual yet an extension of him, thus making his aspirations to infinite freedom safe. As inherently free egos, all men, Novalis claimed, were in principle worthy of the throne. The legitimacy of the Prussian monarch derived from that fact that he was both the incarnation and the model of the absolute ego; the purpose of his rule was ultimately to cancel out his own authority by preparing all men, through his example, for freedom in a polity of self-governing equals.

The early Romantics themselves could not, however, sustain this tenuous synthesis. As Frederick Beiser (1992) points out, what separates early from later German Romanticism is the distinction between the former's relatively egalitarian idea of community and the latter's more authoritarian and paternalistic idea of the state. The dangers of self-aggrandizing Romantic desire, whose political counterpart seemed to be the social chaos caused by the French Revolution and later by advancing capitalism, pushed German Romanticism in an ever more conservative direction. Even at its most conservative, though, it never wholly surrendered its vision of an extended Enlightenment individualism. Partly in response to the humiliations inflicted by Napoleonic France, second-generation German Romantics devised a putatively unique German version of individuality that displaced it from the person onto the nation or state. True individuality was thus not incompatible with social solidarity, as was merely "French" or self-interested individualism; rather, it was the salutary effect of identifying with the unique spirit of one's collectivity. Much of second-generation German Romanticism involved the construction of a unique "personality" for Germany out of its history, language, and folk culture—for example, the folk songs collected (and composed) by Aachim von Arnim in *Des Knaben Wunderhorn* (1805–1808), or the folk tales assembled (and often revised) by the brothers Grimm (1812). These celebrants of folk culture recognized the "higher reality" of magic and the supernatural, the very things the Enlightenment abhorred, yet they too were in the service of an ideal of individuality that grew out of the Enlightenment. Friedrich Schlegel's compromise with conservatism involved the idealization of the Habsburg Empire's universal monarchy, whose unity under the aegis of the Roman Catholic Church made safely possible the harmonious flourishing of plural national individualities. The Enlightenment ideal of cosmopolitanism lived on in the heart of Romantic reaction.

French Romanticism. The course of French Romanticism showed that it was not inevitable that the political individualism fostered by Enlightenment ideology during the French Revolution would be surrendered in the first generation. However, the trajectory of the initially most influential first-generation French Romantic, the young Breton aristocrat François-René de Chateaubriand, followed that of the early German Romantics. At the outbreak of the Revolution, he was part of a group of thinkers and writers (including Delisle de Sales, Jean François La Harpe, Pierre-Louis Guingené, Ponce Denise Édouard Le Brun, and Sebastian R. N. de Chamfort) who comprised the last generation of the philosophes. Though of second rank themselves, they had introduced Chateaubriand to the work of Rousseau and Montesquieu, which, like that of the abbés Mably and Raynal with whom he was already familiar, argued the superior virtue of ancient republics over modern commercial monarchies. Despite the doubts of Enlightenment elders about the viability of republicanism in large modern states, Chateaubriand became a convinced republican in theory, though in the early stages of the Revolution he favored a constitutional monarchy and the end of aristocratic privilege. The Revolution would have carried him away, he later said, if not for its violence. Repulsed by it, but not disillusioned about its ideals, he left for the United States to investigate modern republicanism in action. It was not, however, the American political experiment that most drew him; under the spell of the "noble savage" of Enlightenment writers such as Rousseau, Marmontel, and La Bruyère, Chateaubriand hoped to find unspoiled freedom and sociability among the Indians of the American wilderness.

What he found instead was a new, heady, and dangerous idea of freedom in himself. More than the life of the Indians, the endless wilderness itself represented for him the possibility of a radical extension of the idea of authenticity that Rousseau had described in *Discours sur l'origine de l'inégalité* (1755). It was an experience of infinite freedom—the fulfillment of what Chateaubriand called *le vague des passions*, his virtually untranslatable expression for a passion for the indeterminate. It was the exact counterpart of the young German Romantics' idea of absolute freedom and totality, and it met the same fate within Chateaubriand. Made aware of its psychological and interpersonal dangers almost as suddenly as he had been intoxicated by it, he drew back, then recoiled from what he understood in retrospect to have been a politics deformed by it. The capture of Louis XVI at Varennes moved him to return to France to fight in the royalist cause.

Chateaubriand's earliest Romantic writings, the short stories "Atala" and "René," both included in *Le génie du christianisme* (The Genius of Christianity, 1802), are cautionary tales about the dangers of *le vague des passions* in its most exalted secular and interpersonal form, sexual love. Only religion provided an adequate and safe venue for it. In religious yearning, expressed in such earthly creations as the Gothic cathedral and in the heavenly vision of the fulfillment of Christ's love in the afterlife, passion had an adequate object that would never disappoint, and for which the quest would never be destructive. Religious fervor is often taken to be the main difference between the Enlightenment and Romanticism, but Chateaubriand's romantic religiosity, like that of his close German Protestant counterpart Friedrich Schleiermacher, was quite untraditional. It represents the realization of longings for infinite individual fulfillment. The love of Christ was not the ascetic negation of erotic desire but its actualization, and the "genius" of religion lay not in its dogmatic truth but in the inspiration it offered to human creativity. The same powerful residue of individuality is to be found in Chateaubriand's politics. His conservatism was a brand of politics that tried to preserve individual liberty while serving as a bulwark against the injection of *le vague des passions* into public life, a phenomenon he identified with the politics of Jacobinism. In practical terms, this meant a defense of the freely granted charter under which the restored Louis XVIII ruled, a delicate compromise that instituted checks on absolute rule without formally installing the principle of popular sovereignty that had led to despotism. As Chateaubriand succinctly put it, his whole system entailed the political goals of the Revolution, but not the political men of the Revolution; a royalist out of reason, he claimed to remain a republican—and a radical individualist—by taste.

The fact that the Romantic writers Benjamin Constant and Germaine de Staël did not follow Chateaubriand's path to conservatism is attributable, in part, to their somewhat different Enlightenment roots. Schooled in the modernizing ideas of the Scottish Enlightenment thinkers as much as in the classical republican tradition, Constant believed in the superiority of modern to ancient liberty. The modern private sphere gave more scope for individual freedom and variety than did the demands of republican citizenship. With the French Revolution, Constant came to believe that the only reliable guarantor of the right and the opportunity to enjoy that freedom was representative government based on the sovereignty of the people. At the same time, he was deeply suspicious of the individual self-interest that drove the private sphere, not only on political grounds but also on emotional and spiritual grounds. Self-interest deflected people from political participation, but worse, it was an arid and corrosive sentiment that drained life of color by drying up the emotions. In particular, it prevented people from forgetting themselves and giving themselves up to "enthusiasm," a term he took from Staël. Enthusiasm meant to her a passion for the infinite that was best expressed in the reverie of the heart and the vastness of thought, as opposed to a passion and fanaticism fixed on a single idea or object. In one sense the exact counterpart of the German Romantic yearning for the Absolute, it differed precisely in this last qualification, which prevented Constant from projecting the infinite onto either the object of love or the polity. He saw no need to back away from the Revolution and its individualistic ideals because of its turn to violence.

Constant had been for a brief time a defender of the regime of the Terror because he initially saw it as a necessary measure to protect the gains of the Revolution against its many enemies, but he had quickly come to see the danger in the fusion of virtue and enthusiasm. There was no greater threat to individual liberty than sanctifying one view of the good life and enforcing it by governmental coercion. On the other hand, the same awareness of the danger of identifying the infinite with a single object made him wary of trying to realize the yearning for it in romantic love. His novel *Adolphe* (1816) documents the conflicts and disappointments of the quest for love that knows both the limitations of the object and its own narcissism, corrupted by the self-interest that has invaded even the most intimate emotions. The Romantic desire for infinity had to be reserved largely to the spheres of religion and art, where it could be imaginatively indulged without the error of reifying it in the concrete and finite. Unlike Chateaubriand, however, Constant did not believe that the needs of Romantic individuality could be confined to the inner sphere of faith and imagination; they had to be engaged in the interpersonal, yet without compromising individual freedom. Thus, the idea of modern political participation and service to society had more than the instrumental value of protecting individual rights; it gave the individual the opportunity to rise above purely individual concerns and strive for moral and spiritual wholeness. In this way, Constant was able to unite Romanticism with political individualism.

Under Chateaubriand's influence, French Romanticism was largely royalist and Catholic during the Restoration, but there was a significant liberal coterie, under the leadership of Stendhal, that recruited former royalists like Victor Hugo and Alphonse Lamartine when the ultraconservatives threatened to revoke even the modest gains of the Revolution. It was Hugo, in the preface to his play *Hernani* (1829), who argued that Romanticism meant the absolute freedom of the creative artist, and that liberty in art demanded liberty in politics—indeed, that liberty in literature was the offspring of political liberty. What was wrong with Enlightenment neoclassicism was not its fundamental aim of reconciling autonomy and morality, but the restrictive way it went about it. By trying to eliminate the idiosyncratic, the grotesque, and the ugly, it short-circuited the problem of creating genuine human wholeness. The challenge to art was to create a harmony that would include all aspects of life.

Enlightenment ideals lived on in other ways as well in second-generation French Romanticism. One of the major inspirations of Stendhal's hero Julien Sorel in *Le rouge et le noir* (1830) was the *Confessions* of Rousseau, whose ideals of authenticity and sincerity guide him, however fitfully, through the corrupting temptations of falseness demanded by success in an era of hierarchy and hypocrisy. The Enlightenment spirit of criticism and skepticism breathes in the author's deft satire of the church and the aristocracy, with their irrational pretensions to authority, and also of the contradictions and confusions of his own hero, who in the throes of ambition violates his own ideals of truthfulness, rationality, and sincerity.

English Romanticism. One of the most eminent modern critics of English Romanticism, Geoffrey Hartmann, remarks in passing that it did not abrogate but "revised" the Enlightenment. Certainly its relationship to the Enlightenment is not adequately, or even accurately, defined by two conventional claims: on the one hand, that William Wordsworth's and the early Samuel Taylor Coleridge's psychological and aesthetic theories were rooted in Enlightenment associationist epistemology; and on the other, that their major break with the Enlightenment was with its religious skepticism. The problem of assessing continuity and change in this piecemeal way is illustrated by the fact that when Coleridge broke with Enlightenment empiricism, he moved to the no less "enlightened" Idealist epistemology of Kant. The appeal of Idealism for Coleridge was that it assigned an active and creative role to the mind in the formation of knowledge. The autonomous creative self, the heir of Enlightenment autonomy, is also at the heart of English Romanticism, though uniquely transformed, as is evident in the poetic trajectory of Wordsworth.

Wordsworth's initial poetic project was rooted in the picturesque ideal of eighteenth-century loco-descriptive poetry: reflecting the world as a plenitude that created its harmony by reconciling all of the oppositions within reality, epitomized in the polarity of autonomous man and lawlike nature. That project failed even before the French Revolution, because Wordsworth could find no way to accommodate, in his vision, the lone individual, the sublime imagination, and the alienated outcast. The challenge to his project became even greater when, under the influence of the French Revolution and the radical individualism of William Godwin, he expanded the idea of the individual to encompass a freedom so radical that it knew no restraints from nature or history, not even those of "general laws"; instead, it was guided only by the "light of circumstance, flashed / Upon an independent intellect." In this formulation the Enlightenment ideal of the autonomous mind reached its apogee and was simultaneously exploded; even reason was no longer a constraint on the freedom of the independent intellect. How could an individual with such freedom relate to the rest of humanity and the world?

Wordsworth's recoil at this extreme claim for the self, which quickly plunged him into an abyss of relativistic despair, did not involve the total surrender of radical freedom. It did mean, as in the case of the early German Romantics, a retreat from the activism of revolutionary politics, where unbounded freedom could lead to great crimes. His recoil also led him to temper the mind's absolute independence theoretically by reconnecting it with nature. This renewed relationship, however, was a paradoxical one in which the mind was at once dependent on nature, safely harbored in its sheltering matrix, and its partner and co-creator in the vision of the unity of all things. Indeed, nature's infinite power—as Wordsworth wrote in *The Prelude* (1805)—was the "genuine counterpart / And brother" of the "glorious faculty / Which higher minds bear with them as their own." This was hardly a traditional religious position; indeed, from a traditional point of view, it was virtually blasphemy. Such a "higher" mind, Wordsworth claimed, senses in itself the "underpresence" of God, "or whatsoe'er is dim / Or vast in its own being"; God and the human mind are one. If Romanticism meant a sense of awe before the infinite, it was not an attitude of submission to an external law. It is true that, for Wordsworth as for all the Romantics, nature was to be grasped as an infinite whole. Newtonian science and analytic reason in general, which took nature apart in mechanical laws of cause and effect, destroyed its mystery and beauty. "Our meddling intellect / Mis-shapes the beauteous form of things," Wordsworth lamented. "We murder to dissect"—a complaint, unthinkable in the Enlightenment, echoed over and over again, as by John Keats in *Lamia* (1819): "Philosophy will clip an Angel's wings / Conquer all mysteries by rule and line, / Empty the haunted air, and gnomed mine, / Unweave a rainbow." For the Romantics, nature's mystical wholeness was not a limitation on the autonomous mind, but an invitation to the mind to find itself. This is the essence of Coleridge's famous definition of the poetic imagination as the repetition in the finite mind of the eternal act of creation in the infinite "I am." It was only later in Wordsworth's poetry that the idea of the mind's tenuous—because contradictory—balance of reciprocity with and dependence on nature hardened into a more orthodox religious belief, with the self subordinated once again to a traditional divinity. Yet in the unpublished *Prelude*, however much it was revised in the light of Wordsworth's increasingly orthodox beliefs, the vision of the infinite autonomous mind partnered with nature lived on as the radical legacy of his early years.

The second generation of Romantics, particularly Lord Byron and Percy Bysshe Shelley, regarded Wordsworth as an apostate from the cause of liberty. They believed that he had surrendered to reaction out of both fear and opportunism, and they reaffirmed the value of autonomy, including its political dimension, which he had once espoused. This meant for both of them a continuing radical skepticism concerning established institutions, especially those of religion, that demanded the sacrifice of human freedom and joy. Byron and Shelley are in a direct line of Enlightenment opposition to superstition and authoritarian faith. Both poets were also aware that if freedom had gone wrong during the Revolution, it was for internal reasons as much as for external ones. The inner temptations of both submission to authority and tyrannical narcissistic grandiosity had to be explored in order to prepare for freedom a humanity unused to self-rule. In his dramatic poems *Manfred* (1816–1817) and *Cain* (1821), Byron wrestled with the problems of guilt over the misuse of freedom and of the religious temptations of forgiveness and consolation at the cost of submission to authority, ultimately rejecting them for an affirmation of individual agency and moral responsibility: "The mind which is immortal makes *itself* / Requital for its good or evil thoughts / Is its own origin of ill and end / And its own time and place." In *Prometheus Unbound* (1820), Shelley identified the tyrannical Zeus, who had punished the rebellious Prometheus, as an emblem of humanity's own worst potential, the corruption of freedom and love into self-love and the lust for domination. Only when freedom recognizes its own temptations to omnipotence and controls them is it capable of the mutuality on which both true love and a free polity are based. Yet at the same time, for Shelley, it is only through union with the whole that humanity is truly free; that union is symbolized at the end of the poem by the marriage of Prometheus and Asia, and more generally in his Romanticized version of religion. The Romantic hope and project of fusing what Hegel called subjective, or individual, freedom with objective, or infinite, freedom, which derived from the Enlightenment project of reconciling individual freedom with community, is beautifully rendered by Shelley's lines from *Epipsychidion*: "I know / That Love makes all things equal; I have heard / By mine own heart this joyous truth averred: / The spirit of the *worm* beneath the sod / In love and worship, blends itself with God."

Conclusion. Ultimately, the complex relationship of Romanticism to the Enlightenment is perhaps best caught in Friedrich Schleiermacher's paradoxical delineation of the basic human drives that comprise the self. On the one hand, he claimed in the first edition of *On Religion: Addresses to Its Cultivated Despisers* (1799), the self longs "to expand . . . outwards into the world, and so to permeate everything with itself, to share of itself with everything . . . . It wants to penetrate everything and fill everything with reason and freedom." On the other hand, as he wrote in the second edition of 1806, "The opposing drive is the dread fear of standing as a single individual alone against the whole; it is the longing to surrender and be completely absorbed in it, to feel taken hold of and determined by it." Schleiermacher's characterization of the first drive is an authentic Enlightenment attitude. His characterization of the second is the negation of the Enlightenment. Both attitudes are at the heart of Romanticism.

[*See also* Aufklärung; Chateaubriand, François-René de; Kant, Immanuel; Rousseau, Jean-Jacques; Schiller, Friedrich; *and* Staël, Germaine Necker de.]

BIBLIOGRAPHY

Abrams, M. H. *Natural Supernaturalism: Tradition and Revolution in Romantic Literature.* New York, 1971. The classic interpretation of Romanticism as the secularization of Christian and Neo-Platonic concepts of individuation in reaction to the French Revolution.

Beiser, Frederick C. *Enlightenment, Revolution, and Romanticism: The Genesis of Modern German Political Thought, 1790–1800.* Cambridge, Mass., 1992. The best available discussion of the relationship of the first-generation German Romantics to the Enlightenment and the later changes within German Romanticism.

Berlin, Isaiah. *The Roots of Romanticism.* (A. W. Mellon Lectures in the Fine Arts.) Princeton, N.J., 1999. An eloquent but problematic exposition of the old idea of a fundamental opposition between Romanticism and the Enlightenment.

Bewell, Alan. *Wordsworth and the Enlightenment: Nature, Man, and Society in the Experimental Poetry.* New Haven, Conn., 1989.

Brown, Marshall. "Romanticism and Enlightenment." In his *Turning Points: Essays in the History of Cultural Expressions.* Stanford, Calif., 1997. An interpretation of Romanticism as a continuation of Enlightenment.

Hartmann, Geoffrey. "Was it for this . . .?": Wordsworth and the Birth of the Gods." In *Romantic Revolutions: Criticism and Theory,* edited by Kenneth R. Johnston et al. Bloomington, Ind., 1990. An important comment on the relation of Romanticism and Enlightenment by one of the century's most important Wordsworth interpreters.

Holmes, Stephen. *Benjamin Constant and the Making of Modern Liberalism.* New Haven, Conn., 1984. An indispensable interpretation of Constant's political thought and its origins.

Isbell, John Claiborne. *The Birth of Romanticism: Truth and Propaganda in Staël's "De l'Allemagne," 1810–1813.* Cambridge, 1994. Includes useful references to de Staël's relationship to Enlightenment thinkers.

Izenberg, Gerald N. *Impossible Individuality: Romanticism, Revolution, and the Origins of Modern Selfhood, 1787–1802.* Princeton, N.J., 1992. An interpretation of the Romantic project of radical individuality and its Enlightenment origins.

Kitson, Peter J. "Beyond the Enlightenment: The Philosophical, Scientific and Religious Inheritance." In *A Companion to Romanticism,* edited by Duncan Wu. Oxford, 1998. A succinct statement of a traditional position.

Orel, Harold. *English Romantic Poets and the Enlightenment: Nine Essays on a Literary Relationship.* Banbury, U.K., 1973. The most complete discussion of English Romantic continuities with and breaks from the Enlightenment.

Vietta, Silvio. "Frühromantik und Aufklärung." In *Die literarische Frühromantik,* edited by Silvio Vietta. Göttingen, Germany, 1983. An important discussion of the relationship of early German Romanticism and the Enlightenment.

GERALD N. IZENBERG

ROME, ANCIENT. *See* Ancient Rome.

ROUSSEAU, JEAN-JACQUES (1712–1778), Swiss-French author, philosopher, and theorist.

Born in Geneva in 1712 to Suzanne Bernard and Isaac Rousseau, a clockmaker, Jean-Jacques Rousseau left his native city at fifteen to seek his fame, if not his fortune, elsewhere. Although he never returned to Geneva for any significant length of time, Rousseau sometimes signed his writings "Citizen of Geneva." He remembered fondly Geneva's republican origins, simplicity, and small size, all of which he felt contributed to its special status as a virtuous community. When Jean le Rond d'Alembert, in his *Encyclopédie* article "Genève," proposed that the city should have a national theater, Rousseau responded with his *Lettre à d'Alembert sur les spectacles* (1758), contending that theater's corrupting influence should be kept out of his native country.

Rousseau thus lived a life of exile, self-imposed from an early age but later imposed on him, as it was on other contemporary writers such as Voltaire. The inflammatory nature of their writings often disturbed religious or political sensibilities. Condemnation of works by the censor could mean the arrest of authors, who sometimes had to flee the authorities or face imprisonment. Denis Diderot's incarceration at Vincennes for his *Lettres sur les aveugles* (1749) was a constant reminder to the period's authors of the very real consequences of their audacious writings. Rousseau himself later had to flee France in 1762 after the publication of *Émile*, condemned for its heretical support of natural over revealed religion.

Early Works. After a fourteen-month stay in Turin (1728–1729), Rousseau returned to the Savoy region of France and the household of Mme. de Warens, from which he had originally set out. She offered the young man, by turns, maternal support and amorous adventure. Rousseau spent about twelve years, on and off, with her at Annecy and Chambéry, reading and writing. He left for Lyons in 1740 to become a tutor for the Mably family, a position he kept for little more than a year. Sometime during this long formative period, he developed the passion for music that persisted throughout his life. After he arrived in Paris in 1742, his first serious intellectual work was in this area. Having developed an original system of musical notation, he was solicited by Diderot

Jean-Jacques Rousseau. Bronze bust by Jean-Antoine Houdon (1741–1828). (Musée du Louvre, Paris/Alinari/Art Resource, NY.)

and d'Alembert to contribute numerous articles on music to the *Encyclopédie*, which they were just beginning to edit.

Rousseau's first fame, however, came from his award-winning reply to a question posed by the Academy of Dijon in 1750 about the moral effects of the arts and sciences on society. Rousseau's first two discourses, the *Discours sur les sciences et les arts* (1750) and the *Discours sur l'origine et les fondements de l'inégalité parmi les hommes* (1755), established his reputation as a moral thinker, but the publication of his *Du contrat social* in 1762 revealed the deeply political character of his ideas. To appreciate fully the complexity of Rousseau's thinking, however, one must also consider his innovative contributions in other domains: as a moralist, a political thinker, an educational theorist, a novelist, and a writer of autobiography.

Moral Philosophy. As a moralist, Rousseau's originality lay in taking what turned out to be the position counter to the *encyclopédistes*. Voltaire, soon joined by the contributors to the *Encyclopédie*, had launched an attack on the perceived prejudices, fanaticism, and superstition of the ancien régime, but however much they criticized the old culture, Voltaire and the *encyclopédistes* accepted many of its fundamental principles, such as the belief in the basic soundness of artistic and scientific

advances. Rousseau, by contrast, took a radical approach in condemning society itself as the source of all contemporary ills. He believed that human beings are innately good and that the arts and sciences serve only to corrupt men and women. Like the seventeenth-century philosopher and mathematician Blaise Pascal, Rousseau considered the powers of the human heart, or feeling, superior to reason. Against the evil influence of society and culture, Rousseau set the primordial goodness of nature. In the first and second *Discours*, he developed his thesis of society's corruption and nature's goodness. It is important to understand, however, what Rousseau meant by nature, or the state of nature. He associated it not merely with the physical state and its purity, but also with many positive abstract qualities—including, among others, freedom, sentiment and spontaneity, openness or truth, and clarity. These contrast respectively with the inequality, reason and reflection, hypocrisy, and confusion Rousseau saw in the culture of his time.

According to Rousseau, society cannot return to the natural state of goodness or to any golden age, but a wise legislator can steer the culture toward an enhanced sense of virtue, because human beings are essentially perfectible creatures. Rousseau denounced the degeneration of morals he witnessed around him, and a certain pessimism emerges from his works. Nonetheless, he sought positively to rescue humanity from the quagmire into which he believed it had fallen. So long as one can still detect human feeling, which Rousseau found in pity, there is hope for the species. In his political writings (beginning with the two *Discours* and followed by *Economie politique*, *Du contrat social*, *Projet de constitution pour la Corse*, and *Considérations sur le gouvernement de Pologne*, among others), Rousseau thus attempted to fashion virtuous citizens. Presumably, these citizens would be capable of submitting their own individual wills (*volonté particulière*) to the corporate will of the society (*volonté générale*), and of subordinating selfish love (*amour-propre*) to the love of self that coalesces with that of the species and the community (*amour de soi*).

Morality and politics work hand in hand, but Rousseau believed in the crucial centrality of politics for effecting needed changes for the well-being of the state. A revolutionary thinker at heart, he devised political solutions that would help solve moral, economic, and other problems. The power Rousseau invested in the state, for instance, serves to diminish the power of individuals to dominate others; ideally, no one should be or feel dependent on anyone else. Rousseau saw the pitfalls of dependence for both the rulers and the ruled. A ruling class can develop an artificial need for the rest of society to depend on it, just as the ruled indeed can become overly dependent. Political disequilibrium can engender an inflated sense of worth, leading to the extremes of despotism and slavery.

In all events, Rousseau wanted to safeguard human freedom, which he viewed as an inalienable birthright, above all other political considerations. Consequently, his thinking on other questions, such as the right to property, could be less radical. Although Rousseau condemned the original division of property as the beginning of inequality, he took a conservative, practical stance on the protection of property rights, once established by the social compact. He understood physical inequalities as natural and inevitable, and he could countenance a limited number of inequalities so long as they did not impinge on everyone's basic right to live freely and did not create any humiliating dependence on other people. He deplored extreme inequalities, however—especially those arising from the unbridled pursuit of luxury and power. His insistence on freedom was his way of cultivating humans' innate goodness through virtue in an otherwise corrupt society.

Émile. With *Émile* (1762), Rousseau presented his educational theory in almost novelistic form. Instead of devising ways to promote a child's social and cultural development, Rousseau viewed his task as preventing the pernicious forces of society from taking hold of young Émile's life. Using sensationist theory as both a philosophy and a psychology, as it was formulated by his friend Étienne Bonnot de Condillac, Rousseau urged an attempt to inculcate a sense of the child's freedom from his earliest days. Contemporary childrearing practices—such as swaddling, with its severe restriction of the child's movement—were condemned; if humans are born free, Rousseau argued, we should not put them immediately into tightly wrapped clothing that might give them the wrong idea about their existence and become a lesson in servitude. From their sensory experiences, children should form their own ideas and be allowed to grow in self-confidence and in the authority of their own decisions.

Although Rousseau subscribed somewhat to sensationist principles, he differed from Condillac and, especially, from Claude-Adrien Helvétius, whose *De l'esprit* (1758) he criticized. For Rousseau, the mind is an active mechanism, not a passive one, as it tended to be for Condillac and as it certainly was for Helvétius, who traced all of the mind's faculties to physical sensibility. That Rousseau never wrote his projected *La Morale sensitive, ou le Matérialisme du sage* reflects his belief in a conscience and in an immaterial soul. He wanted to keep his distance from those materialists who would deny any human spirituality. To allow the young Émile enough time to develop sound ideas through feelings and sensation, the age of reason is delayed as long as possible; we should not create "young doctors," as Rousseau put it.

Émile is also important for its words on breastfeeding, and it has gained a certain notoriety for its depiction of the role of women. Rousseau encouraged mothers to keep close physical and emotional contact with their own children through breastfeeding, a practice that the upper classes had relegated to nursemaids. Because these hired nurses often had too many babies to feed, many children suffered from malnutrition and eventually died. Rousseau's suggestion clearly saved lives, even if it also brought some women back into the confined domestic sphere that Rousseau considered their natural place. He viewed with alarm his period's rising libertine tendencies, which no doubt made some women prefer passionate affairs to maternal obligations. His thoughts on the complementarity of the sexes in *Émile*, coupled with his reduction of women to the domestic sphere, were severely repudiated by Mary Wollstonecraft at the end of the century, and she has been joined by many later feminists. For many women in Rousseau's day, however, his ideas were received as liberating insofar as they put mothers in touch with their children and with their maternal identity, a revolution for the nuclear family.

La nouvelle Héloïse. Although *Émile* did not elicit unanimous approval of its pages on religion or the role of women, his novel *Julie, ou La nouvelle Héloïse* certainly appealed to a wide readership. It became the best-seller of the century in France and is today considered one of the first full-fledged novels in the French language to have attained stability of form and respect from the public. Mme. de La Fayette's *La princesse de Clèves* typically passes as the first novel in French, but between its appearance in 1678 and the publication of *La nouvelle Héloïse* in 1761, the French novel underwent major transformations in content and form. The epistolary format for fiction, borrowed by Rousseau, was hardly new: Montesquieu had used it successfully for social critique in his *Lettres persanes* (1721), as had Françoise de Graffigny in her best-selling *Lettres d'une Péruvienne* (1747).

Masterfully employing the period's language of sensibility, Rousseau managed to create fictional characters with whom one ideally felt a spiritual identification. Julie and Saint-Preux embody not only the century's highest aspirations for intensity of feeling, but also its hopes for democratization. Julie's elevated social status and Saint-Preux's modest origins do not keep them from being on a par emotionally or morally. In fact, Rousseau described a moral elite at Clarens, the Swiss setting for the novel, that does not discriminate on the basis of social class. Its members communicate transparently with one another, tête-à-tête in private chambers. The contrast with the libertine novel (Crébillon's *Egarements du coeur et de l'esprit*, 1736, for example) could hardly be more striking. Private chambers such as the boudoir, in libertine literature, had come to represent scenes of moral decay and debauchery; for Rousseau, however, they elicit a sense of friendship and intimacy. Rousseau's novel is not without its own moral ambiguities, though. Saint-Preux's passion for Julie does not diminish as the novel progresses. Although the heroine's death puts an end to her sexual temptations, this novel, like many others of its day, is sustained dramatically by the dialectic of desire.

Confessions. As a writer of autobiography, Rousseau achieved with many readers the complicity he had aroused for his fictional characters. In this case, however, he himself was the main character. Rousseau's *Confessions*, published posthumously in 1782, broke new ground in literature in many ways. The work is generally considered the first autobiography in French. The *Essais* of the French Renaissance humanist Michel de Montaigne are sometimes cited as autobiographical in tone, insofar as Montaigne spoke of his inner self, but not nearly in the same self-conscious manner as did Rousseau. Rousseau invited his reader to come to know him intimately—under the skin, as the epigraph to his *Confessions* ("intùs et in cute") suggested. Such an understanding required Rousseau to lay bare for his reader his very soul, and all the events of his life, lofty as well as sordid. It has been difficult for any reader, either in Rousseau's time or our own, to forget the references to his abandoning all his five children to orphanages, despite the protestations of his female partner and later wife, Thérèse Levasseur. Nor can one underestimate the effect that references to his masturbation (*péché solitaire*) must have had on contemporary readers' acute sensitivity. Bald-faced allusions to erotic activities were usually reserved for clandestine pornographic or "philosophical" texts, and not set into literature in the generally accepted sense. Just as he had mixed social classes in *La nouvelle Héloïse*, Rousseau mixed high and low sentiments in his *Confessions*, challenging conventional notions of literature.

Above all, it was Rousseau's search for truth in representing himself that drove him to new limits. He followed the writing of the *Confessions* with *Rousseau juge de Jean-Jacques, Dialogues*. Not content with the portrait he had left of himself in the *Confessions*, and increasingly anxious about misrepresentations of his life, Rousseau here conducted a kind of self-trial in which a fictional "Rousseau" judges the life of the real Jean-Jacques. In the process, Rousseau the author points out the shortcomings of others' disfiguring and partial portraits of him, while making a supreme effort to convince the reader of the truth and unity of his own self-portrait.

Later Life. Working in solitude between 1756 and 1760, Rousseau began to break off his relations with those in the *encyclopédiste* movement (notably, Grimm and Diderot) and with Louise Tardieu d'Esclavelles Épinay, one of his benefactors. Shortly after the publication of *Émile* in 1762, he adopted a simple form of "Armenian" dress, partly as a way of marking his difference from those in fashionable society circles and partly as a disguise. He feared, rightly in some cases, pursuit by the authorities and reprisal by his enemies, or even by former friends such as Diderot or Voltaire. His four *Lettres à Malesherbes* (1762) are some of the first concrete signs of his mounting concern about the way he was being portrayed in public. Late in his life, Rousseau became increasingly obsessed with leaving a truthful image of himself for posterity, and he wrote prodigiously to correct the record with his *Confessions* and *Dialogues*.

Two years before his death, Rousseau began composing his *Rêveries du promeneur solitaire*. Although one senses that he was still trying to come to terms with his deep anxiety about misrepresentations of himself, this last work exudes an unmistakable peace of mind. Rousseau recorded the ecstasy he felt on rare occasions in his life and attempted to recapture the bliss of these privileged moments. Botanizing and assembling herbaria in Switzerland emerge as special earlier pastimes that had restored tranquillity to his sometimes tortured spirit. This work suggests a return to nature as a lasting way to achieve personal happiness. Taken together with his exalted descriptions of alpine scenery in *La nouvelle Héloïse* and his words about the pleasure of country living in the *Confessions*, the *Rêveries du promeneur solitaire* reinforce the image of Rousseau as a contemplative admirer of nature. Nature was not just a mental construct for his theoretical writings about morality, politics, and education; it also served as a kind of psychotherapeutic and practical cure for Rousseau in his bleakest moments of despair. When he died at Ermenonville in 1778, he was buried on the Île des Peupliers there, surrounded by water and the garden of the marquis de Girardin—a fitting final resting place for this lover of nature—but he was not to remain there for long.

Rousseau's legacy, like Voltaire's, was immediately obvious during the French Revolution; both writers were considered as having contributed substantially to the overthrow of the Old Regime. Consequently, their remains were transferred to the Pantheon in Paris—Voltaire's in 1791, and Rousseau's in 1794. Although the *Du contrat social* had not been widely read before the Revolution, it was hailed as one of the movement's premier texts. What made Rousseau a champion of the downtrodden was the example of his own life. He identified with the poor and oppressed, and he created a radically new sense of individualism that allowed others to identify emotionally with him. Although Rousseau's moral authority may be challenged by his abandonment of his children, he clearly had an important message that inspired revolutionaries to attempt building a republic of virtue. Moreover, his

Rousseau and Revolution. Revolutionary allegory with a portrait of Rousseau, by Nicolas H. Jeurat de Bertry, 1794. (Musée de la Ville de Paris, Musée Carnavalet, Paris/Giraudon/Art Resource, NY.)

BIBLIOGRAPHY

Blum, Carol. *Rousseau and the Republic of Virtue: The Language of Politics in the French Revolution*. Ithaca, N.Y., 1986. Rightly underscores the identification that the revolutionaries, and especially Robespierre, had with Rousseau as a person.

Burgelin, Pierre. *La Philosophie de l'existence de J.-J. Rousseau*. Paris, 1973.

Darnton, Robert. *The Great Cat Massacre and Other Episodes in French Cultural History*. New York, 1984. Chapter 6 provides a valuable glimpse of the acute sensibility of eighteenth-century readers and their tearful responses to Rousseau's works.

Derathé, Robert. *Jean-Jacques Rousseau et la science politique de son temps*. Paris, 1979. Gives the natural law background to Rousseau's political writings and cites his major contributions to democratic government.

Jouvenal, Bertrand de. "Rousseau the Pessimistic Evolutionist." *Yale French Studies* 28 (1962), 83–96.

Kelly, Christopher. *Rousseau's Exemplary Life: The Confessions as Political Philosophy*. Ithaca, N.Y., 1987.

Masters, Roger D. *The Political Philosophy of Rousseau*. Princeton, N.J., 1968. Good sections on Rousseau's notion of inequality.

May, Georges. *Le Dilemme du roman au XVIIIᵉ siècle: Étude sur les rapports du roman et de la critique (1715–1761)*. New Haven, Conn., 1963.

May, Gita. "Rousseau's 'Antifeminism' Reconsidered." In *French Women and the Age of Enlightenment*. Edited by Samia I. Spencer. Bloomington, Ind., 1984, pp. 309–317. A brief but balanced view of women's reactions to Rousseau in the eighteenth century.

O'Neal, John C. *Seeing and Observing: Rousseau's Rhetoric of Perception. Stanford French and Italian Studies*, vol. 41. Saratoga, Calif., 1985. For Rousseau's notion of public and private morality, see pp. 19–31; a discussion of Rousseau's narrative strategies for readers of his autobiographical works can be found on pp. 96–111.

O'Neal, John C. "Rousseau's Theory of Wealth." *History of European Ideas* 7 (1986), 453–467.

O'Neal, John C. *The Authority of Experience: Sensationist Theory in the French Enlightenment*. University Park, Pa., 1996. Chapter 7 discusses the sensationist underpinnings of Rousseau's educational theory.

Rousseau, Jean-Jacques. *Oeuvres complètes*. Edited by Bernard Gagnebin and Marcel Raymond. 5 vols. Paris, 1959–1995. The standard French edition of Rousseau's complete works; the introductions and notes to the various works are very useful.

Shklar, Judith N. *Men and Citizens: A Study of Rousseau's Social Theory*. Cambridge, 1969.

Starobinski, Jean. *Jean-Jacques Rousseau: Transparency and Obstruction*. Translated by Arthur Goldhammer. Chicago, 1988. One of the established reference works for Rousseau; an insightful presentation of the binary oppositions operative in Rousseau's writings.

Trouille, Mary Seidman. *Sexual Politics in the Enlightenment: Women Writers Read Rousseau*. Albany, N.Y., 1997. Reviews critical responses to Rousseau's views on women by Mme. d'Épinay, Mme. Roland, Mme. de Staël, Mary Wollstonecraft, Stéphanie de Genlis, and Olympe de Gouges.

JOHN C. O'NEAL

message still has resonance for any society that has lost touch with its foundations for public and private morality. His investment of political sovereignty in the people remains one of the fundamental concepts of democracy today. With their emphasis on discovery learning and the steps of cognitive development, child psychologists and educational theorists in the twentieth century have no doubt been affected by Rousseau's approach to gradual learning by children, who ideally grow by stages from their own experience. Finally, his contributions to the novel of sensibility or feeling and to autobiography make him a precursor of Romanticism and one of the major influences on modern contemporary literature, with its emphasis on the self. In sum, today's Western culture has been profoundly shaped in numerous ways by this seminal Enlightenment thinker.

[*See also* Autobiography; Education; Encyclopédie; French Revolution; Literary Genres; Men and Women of Letters; Moral Philosophy; Music; Natural Law; Natural Religion; Novel; *and* Political Philosophy.]

ROWSON, SUSANNA (1762–1824), English-American actress, writer, and educator.

Susanna Haswell was born in Portsmouth, England, the daughter of an officer in the Royal Navy, but she spent her childhood in what is now Hull, Massachusetts, and was educated at home. The American Revolution brought the family back to London, where Susanna married William Rowson, who had some affiliation with Covent Garden Theatre. The couple remained childless, but Susanna Rowson raised her husband's illegitimate son.

Rowson began her career in England as an actress and writer of poetry and fiction. Underlying the seduction plots of her early novels is the Enlightenment belief in universal reason. Rowson's fiction extols middle-class ideals and shows how a woman could rise above the limitations of birth to achieve independence and self-interest without seeking a wealthy husband or social position. The stories of her heroines, including her best-known novel, *Charlotte Temple* (1791), urge women not to succumb to the corrupting influence of a man's looks, money, and aristocratic rank, but to appreciate instead the measured moderation of honest, humane men. In *Victoria* (1786), *Mary, or the Test of Honour* (1789), and *Rebecca, or the Fille de Chambre* (1792), Rowson's heroines forgive the "fallen woman" not from Christian charity, but because all women need communal support, and even the socially disgraced may have something to offer other women. *Mentoria; or the Young Lady's Friend* (1791) urges readers to seek guidance and friendship from older, wiser women, as well as to obey their parents and be cautious with men. *Mentoria* also suggests that education can help a woman rise above the limitations of birth and lead to prosperity and upward mobility. Rowson thus became one of a number of women writers who urged literacy for both men and women as the foundation of civic responsibility and virtue.

When she moved permanently to the new United States in 1793, Rowson was quick to apply her democratic values to the American Enlightenment. Since postwar audiences responded favorably to notions of liberty in any form, her popular stage play *Slaves in Algiers* (1794) conjoined political liberty with sexual liberty in an outspoken rejection of tyranny based on sex and of the use of women as sexual commodities.

In 1797, at age thirty-five, Rowson abandoned the stage to open the first "female academy" in Boston. She devoted the rest of her life to the formal education of the daughters of upper-class Boston families and to the writing of textbooks and histories as well as poetry and fiction. Her later works demonstrate Rowson's republican patriotism and belief in universal reason. Like much eighteenth-century poetry, Rowson's verse was intended to further a moral or a political position rather than to express personal emotion. *Reuben and Rachel; or, Tales of Old Times* (1798), a history disguised as fiction, derives from Rowson's sense of Enlightenment republicanism; Rachel, the heroine, demonstrates intellectual parity with men. Rowson's 1822 textbook, *Exercises in History*, with its biographies of women warriors, queens, and political leaders, exemplifies the Enlightenment concept of the mind as genderless.

Her readers and students, the women of the new republic, would serve their nation if they properly developed their minds.

[*See also* Education; Men and Women of Letters; *and* Novel.]

BIBLIOGRAPHY

Parker, Patricia L. *Susanna Rowson*. Boston, 1986. Biography, critical description of Rowson's works, and annotated bibliography of secondary sources.

Vail, Robert W. G. *Susanna Haswell Rowson, The Author of Charlotte Temple: A Bibliographic Study*. Worcester, Mass., 1933. Lists editions of Rowson's publications.

PATRICIA L. PARKER

ROYAL COURTS AND DYNASTIES. The critical, disrespectful spirit of the Enlightenment might seem hard to reconcile with the principles of hereditary right and dynastic glory inseparable from most royal polities, or with the etiquette-obsessed courts that encased them. In fact, the majority of European monarchs (some eagerly, others constrained by the emergence of public opinion)—including the Bourbons in France, Spain, and Naples; the Hohenzollerns in Prussia; the Romanovs in Russia; and the Vasas in Sweden—associated their regimes with a range of policy initiatives favored by Enlightenment protagonists, because they gauged that state and dynastic power could only be strengthened thereby. In many European states, Enlightenment agendas (the variations were considerable) so merged with royal policy that nineteenth-century historians coined the term "enlightened despotism"; modified as "enlightened absolutism," this term of historical art has found new favor with scholars since the 1980s.

There was no inherent incompatibility between dynastic monarchy and the modernization and renovation of state institutions favored by the advocates of Enlightenment reform. The chaos endemic in elective monarchies such as Poland-Lithuania was a reminder of the stability that hereditary kingship could confer and the benefits of inducing a crowned head to impose "enlightened" policies on reluctant leading subjects or powerful corporate interests such as the Roman Catholic Church. One should not underestimate the protean dimension of the eighteenth-century states system, which encouraged many princes to pursue change out of self-interest and familial interest. Several eighteenth-century monarchies—including Britain (1707), Prussia (1701), and Savoy (1713)—were new creations whose rulers proved capable of marrying tradition with Enlightenment in varying degrees of intelligent synthesis. Some dynasties, like the English and Scottish Stuarts, were monarchs without a crown after 1714; others—like the House of Savoy, the cadet branch of the Habsburgs, in Tuscany; and the House of Hanover—found that international treaties could shift the territories allotted to their scepters. Elsewhere, as in Poland and the Holy Roman Empire, the elective principle was a reality and was still capable of causing disputed successions and diplomatic ruptures. In these varying circumstances, Enlightenment initiatives could have much to commend them. It often suited royalist apologetics to present the monarch as the first servant of the state, at the service of his people rather than imposed on them by descent and sanctified by the church in a coronation ceremony. Acceptance by monarchs of the final supremacy of the rule of law in a given state was not an innovation of the Enlightenment, but it was given new currency in the eighteenth century. It was not necessarily incompatible with absolutist tendencies within the state, for much depended on how the law was created in an individual polity. Where royal policy—as in the reforms of the triumvirate in France in the last years of Louis XV's reign (1771–1774)—seemed to "philosophical" opinion to fly in the face of those conventions, the chorus of criticism could be deafening.

Court Society in Eighteenth-Century Europe. The political thrust of the Enlightenment toward the creation of rationalized legal codes, the diminution of corporate privileges, and the limited extension of religious toleration were all desirable policy objectives for dynasts, in principle. They had to be measured against the practical considerations of enactment, which might delay, modify, or cancel them, depending on local circumstances. Absolutism was really viable only in the smaller states, such as Piedmont and Portugal; even there, eliciting elite cooperation was of paramount importance. Successful government in eighteenth-century Europe remained essentially a partnership between aristocracy and king, and monarchy, as the fountain of honor, could not dispense with a court into which that fountain would flow first. Advancement in noble rank, a court office conferred, or a pension extracted were all means of achieving the acceptance of contentious policies. The fact was that patronage and clientage mattered as much as they had in previous centuries; the privileged orders expected the state to be run in a way that suited their interests, and monarchs generally accepted that presumption. For the ambitious noble careerist, the court still essentially resembled the honey-pot it had been for his ancestors, with attendance an opportunity as well as an obligation. It could also function as a playground or consolation prize for highborn aristocrats who were no longer admitted into administration. Thus, the Spanish court under the Bourbons offered the grandees a splendid substitute for participation in the real decision-making process of the country. If power was slowly ebbing from court society, material rewards could still be high: the maréchal de Belle-Isle, Louis XV's minister of war, received 133,000 livres

annually from the treasury. Such perquisites reduced the chances of destabilization that could ensue when there was a collapse of mutual regard between Enlightenment dynast and court nobility.

Courts did more than survive down into the Napoleonic era and beyond: they flourished in most states as centers of power, as well as of intrigue, at least until 1750, and then experienced only a very gradual decline in the four decades up to the French Revolution of 1789, as bureaucracy ceased to be rudimentary. Government and court still overlapped. The prominence of ministers like George III's Lord Bute or Carlos IV's Godoy was due essentially to their status as royal favorites, an unofficial position that many historians find hard to admit survived into the Enlightenment. The female favorites of queens with a taste for politics could also be serious power brokers, as the activities of Marie-Antoinette's intimate, Diane, duchesse de Polignac, frequently revealed. Marie-Antoinette herself was a major force in French court politics of the 1780s, but such influence was by no means unusual for a queen consort. For instance, in line with Rousseauian precepts, Frederick the Great's sister Lovisa Ulrica, queen of Sweden (1751–1771), an enlightened francophile, took a special care over the education of her son, the future Gustav III.

The employment of expert advisers assisted both policy formulation and implementation. By the 1770s, most European regimes were drawing on the professional services of men like Anne-Robert-Jacques Turgot and François Quesnay in France, the conde de Aranda in Spain, Joseph Banks and William Eden in Britain, and even Johann Wolfgang von Goethe in Saxe-Weimar; their presence in government both enhanced dynastic prestige and contributed to public efficiency. Such enlightened officialdom added a new dimension to the older patronage pattern of recruiting librarians, chaplains, and royal tutors into the court circle—the new men could be conduits of Enlightenment, especially in smaller states. In Weimar, Goethe filled the office of librarian to Duke Karl August but acted as de facto chief minister, a combination exactly comparable to that of Johann Bernhard Basedow in the tiny enclave of Anhalt-Dassau. The presence of talented individuals around the sovereign showed the court acting as a center of science and learning as well as of sound government, and it tended to win favorable notice from opinion-formers—the men of letters, as the French *Encyclopédie* called them—whose status reached its zenith by the mid-eighteenth century, and who mostly felt at home in royal Europe. The physical proximity for consultative purposes of an international celebrity like Voltaire (with Frederick II of Prussia at Sans-Souci, 1751–1755) or Denis Diderot (the guest of Catherine II of Russia, 1773–1774) could be flattering to both parties.

Archetypal "enlightened absolutists" such as Frederick II or Joseph II, who could barely be said to have had a court at all, were the exception, not the rule. Enlightenment thinking did not advocate the outright abolition of courts, but it was concerned to slim down elaborate hierarchies that added nothing to the welfare of the public. Sovereigns more concerned with the useful than with the decorative were broadly in agreement with this hardheaded approach, and court establishments were usually one of the first targets of an incoming reform-minded minister. Household reform, however, had been a recurrent preoccupation of kings before the eighteenth century; the Enlightenment merely gave it contemporary justification. Reformist initiatives were tempered by the tactical desirability for kings of not shutting down too many valuable patronage networks or alienating the elite by depriving their families of the hereditary opportunity to serve the monarch. It could result in political ill will and factional rivalry that might militate against the success of Enlightenment policy objectives in the realm at large. Thus, from a combination of royal pragmatism and the ready availability of more compelling targets (like the Jesuits), court life was by no means a casualty of the Enlightenment.

Monarchies and Reform Politics: A Variety of Experiences. Versailles in the eighteenth century was no longer the cynosure of a monarchical polity that it had been in Louis XIV's long reign. The tardiness of Louis XV (r. 1715–1774) to embrace the policy preferences of the philosophes made his an embarrassing central presence in the French *siècle des lumières*; this omission was compounded by an unsavory dissoluteness and dramatic foreign policy failure in the Seven Years' War (1756–1763). Neither Louis XV nor Louis XVI (r. 1774–1792) found the ritual elements of court life much to his taste, but, down to the Revolution, courtiers retained an influence on the workings of power at the center in France that was reflected in the physical proximity of government apartments and state rooms in the palace of Versailles. The influence and intrigues of courtiers intensified factional bickering: the most successful players tended to be those who combined the role of minister and courtier, such as René Nicolas Charles Augustin de Maupeou (served 1774–1781), or a strong minister like Étienne François, duc de Choiseul (served 1759–1770) backed by a strong royal mistress like Mme. de Pompadour. "Enlightened" ministers such as Turgot or Jacques Necker, with distinctive reform programs, could easily find themselves undone by whispering campaigns in court society.

Louis XVI was well disposed in principle toward Enlightenment values such as religious toleration (limited civil recognition was granted to Huguenots in 1787) and the undesirability of war as an instrument of policy, but he lacked the febrile energy of his brother-in-law,

the Austrian emperor Joseph II (joint ruler from 1765, sole ruler 1780–1790). The latter rapidly imposed a comprehensive reform program across his diverse monarchy in the 1780s. However, what appeared enlightened to the emperor appeared arbitrary to his many critics in Hungary and the Austrian Netherlands, who rejected uniformity and saw privilege (whether corporate or individual) as the best guarantee of public liberties. Rulers of more compact states and much tinier courts in the German *Reich*—for example, Joseph's youngest brother, Max Franz, archbishop-elector of Cologne—found it easier to implement what is often called the "state Enlightenment." As products of the pre-Enlightenment cameralist tradition, German intellectuals did not doubt the power of the state for good; when acting as officials, they rarely found courtiers powerful enough to obstruct them—indeed, they often doubled as courtiers themselves. Both Protestant and Catholic principalities in Germany were open to Enlightenment influences, even Bavaria, a Counter-Reformation bastion. The popular Elector

Imperial Brothers. Joseph II of Austria, Holy Roman Emperor, and Leopold, grand duke of Tuscany. Portrait by Giovanni Panealbo (fl. 1770–1782). Leopold succeeded his brother Joseph as Holy Roman Emperor in 1790. (Galleria Sabauda, Turin, Italy/Alinari/Art Resource, NY.)

Maximilian III (1727–1777) implemented important legal and administrative reforms despite resistance from the clergy and some courtiers.

These regressive forces were almost as strong in the kingdom of Savoy-Piedmont, whose monarchs—perhaps because they already possessed an efficient, absolutist-style authority after the reign of Victor Amadeus II (abdicated 1730)—saw little benefit in embracing specifically Enlightenment prescriptions. The Savoyard nobility was relatively open and tied to the monarchy; here courtliness was less valued than administrative competence. In Naples (an independent kingdom from 1734), the Bourbons employed a series of reforming ministers, notably Bernardo di Tanucci (prime minister from 1759 to 1776), a sign of the willingness of the enlightened intelligentsia to work closely with the crown. Despite royal sponsorship, Tanucci's reforms were held up by the clergy and lawyers, whose privileges they appeared to jeopardize. His downfall was eventually brought about by the young Austrian queen Maria Carolina in 1776. Putting her husband, Ferdinand IV, in the shadows, she was the chief patron at court of the Franco-English minister John Acton, head of the finance and commercial ministries after 1782. He attempted to confirm the power of the Neapolitan monarchy and put reformers into place on his new Supreme Council of Finances. It was in Habsburg Italy, in Lombardy and Tuscany, that enlightened rulers were most keenly committed to achieving efficient reforms. Assisted by his ministers Pompeo Neri and Francesco Maria Gianni, Grand Duke Peter Leopold of Tuscany (r. 1765–1790) brought in free trade in grain and a new courts structure and criminal code. He became a leading sponsor of Jansenist-inspired changes aimed at restoring the Roman Catholic Church to a primitive state of excellence; its high point was the synod of Pistoia in 1786, after which the grand duke lost his nerve in the face of popular antagonism.

Peter Leopold's wish to turn Tuscany into the model of an enlightened polity was entertained by a sovereign who was not technically a dynast at all: Stanisław August Poniatowski of Poland-Lithuania, the ex-lover of Catherine the Great of Russia, who took up his throne in 1764. He had to face three obstacles that were close to insuperable: his genuinely elective status in a "commonwealth," the reluctance of the numerous nobles to accept any erosion of their legal privileges, and the determination of the neighboring great powers not to permit him any policy initiative that might obstruct their own interests. The anglophile king's determination to make his kingship meaningful led to contestation with the Confederation of Bar between 1768 and 1772, and to the first partition of his kingdom in 1772. Stanislaw tried again after Russia's attention was engrossed by war, and the "Four Years' Diet" (1788–1792) produced the 3 May 1791 Constitution, a settlement that many commentators (including Edmund Burke) compared favorably to the French constitution of the same year. It gave Russia the excuse for armed intervention, another partition in 1793, and the elimination of the commonwealth altogether from the map of Europe in 1795.

Stanislaw had hoped to tempt Voltaire to Warsaw, and he tried in vain to win the amity of Diderot and Friedrich Melchior Grimm. They confined their plaudits to Catherine II of Russia (r. 1762–1796), the archetypal female enlightened sovereign, who returned the compliment during the first half of her reign; d'Alembert declined an offer to act as tutor to her son, the future Tsar Paul I, but Jean François La Harpe came out to teach her grandson, Alexander. Catherine's intellectual dedication to the Enlightenment values of Montesquieu (she called his *Esprit des lois* her "prayer book") and of Cesare Beccaria was apparent in her *Great Instruction*, or *Nakaz*, of 1767. There was cameralist-style legislation like the Provincial Statute (1775), Police Ordinance (1782), Charter to the Nobles and the Towns (1785), and National Schools Statute (1786). However, policy initiatives were constrained by Catherine's sense of what realistically could be achieved in the government of her vast state—and, after Yemelyan Ivanovich Pugachev's rebellion of 1773–1775, that amounted to less and less. As her disillusionment with the French Enlightenment increased, she began to refer contemptuously to her former mentors as "liars" and heaped praise on legal pragmatists such as Sir William Blackstone. Born a German, and a convert to Orthodoxy, she gloried in her adopted Romanov identity and threw all her authority into extending Russia's territorial ascendancy at the expense of the Ottoman Empire, Sweden, and Poland. She carried the aristocracy with her in this policy choice. Peter the Great's Table of Ranks (1722) had made service to the state the basis of noble privilege; though this condition was relaxed by Peter III in the Manifesto of Freedom (1762), most aristocrats continued to serve because of the prestige, honors, and grants of land that proximity to the imperial throne often secured. The 1785 Charter to the Nobles, a fundamental law of the realm recognizing their corporate rights, confirmed the end of compulsory noble service. The promotion of Catherine's lovers (and often their families and dependents) within the nobility gave an edge to factional jockeying for patronage and policy influence among the magnates. Court society revived under the empress's aegis, elite manners improved, and the humiliations visited on its members by Peter and the empresses Anna and Elisabeth were forgotten.

The power enjoyed by Catherine was almost matched by her keenest royal rival, Gustav III of Sweden (r. 1771–1792). His bloodless military coup of 1772 revived the power of the monarchy after over half a century of constitutional restraint known as the "age of liberty" (1719–1772). A new constitution made the king uncontestable head of the executive while retaining the Diet for legislative purposes. Gustav quickly consolidated and extended his personal authority, and the trend was formally recognized by the Act of Union and Security (1789). In technical terms, Sweden was not an absolutist regime, but Gustav tended to behave as if it were; not for nothing had he read the French physiocrats on the desirability of a strong royal power. Torture was discarded, the stranglehold of the Lutheran Church relaxed, and the currency reformed. He was a stylish monarch, as anxious to make government work efficiently as any of his crowned contemporaries, but with a late Enlightenment interest in masonic societies, Swedenborgianism, and Mesmerism that reflected his theatrical personality and unstable temperament. Though the court and its spectacles mattered greatly to him, his populist policies gradually alienated the nobility, who had been the dominant political class in the "age of liberty." Its members were directly affected after 1789 by Gustav's opening up of most public offices to commoners and giving peasants the chance to buy land. Their disaffection resulted in his assassination in March 1792 by an aristocratic conspiracy.

In Spain, the new Bourbon dynasty brought its own distinctive brand of absolutism from across the Pyrenees at the turn of the eighteenth century, and this bore fruit with the development of a more professional bureaucracy and army. Royal control over the church was confirmed by the regalian policies of Carlos III (r. 1759–1788) and the expulsion of the Jesuits from both Spain and Spanish America in 1767. The social order, however, remained little affected by Enlightenment critiques, and the crown well knew that the price of administrative improvement was keeping the nobility content in terms of patronage and court preferment. Carlos, who had twenty-four years' experience as ruler of Naples before he inherited Spain, managed this fine balance and commanded respect for his dedication to his monarchical metier, even if he was never as enlightened as progressive thinkers or ministers like Pedro Rodriguez Campomanes wished. This reflected the continuing power of the provincial elites, who, for instance, thwarted agricultural reforms sponsored by the crown in southern Spain. In Portugal, the Braganza dynasty produced no sovereign who matched Carlos's competence, but they patronized a minister, Sebastião José de Carvalho e Mello de Pombal (José I's chief minister, 1750–1777), whose destruction of the Jesuits and ruthless suppression of his opponents showed that enlightened absolutism and arbitrary power could not always be disentangled in a state without a representative legislature; Portugal's main representative institution, the Cortes, did not sit between 1698 and 1820. Pombal's reform of the educational system, secularization of the Inquisition, antiracial legislation, and encouragement of trade produced social change on a scale that probably exceeded that in any contemporary European state.

Survival and Revival of the Court in the Late Eighteenth Century. Dynasts could not easily discard the trappings of court life without risking the visible dignity of hereditary monarchy, which could never be disassociated from its public legitimacy. Court ceremonial did not cease to be a means of bolstering royal authority in the eighteenth century, although the level of informality increased. In Russia, the Table of Ranks (1722) accorded lower precedence to court positions and reflected the decreased importance of court rituals in Peter's polity. As long as there were royal households, however, there would be courtiers, and as long as there were courtiers, there would be intrigue close to the throne. Petty power struggles for precedence and preferment might be distractions or worse, but the court offered scope for patronage that few kings could find elsewhere. Significantly, the elective ruler Stanislaw of Poland recognized that his pretensions to active kingship were inseparable from a court society. Having acquired a castle at Ujazdów, he soon established his own royal household of about six hundred (including the Royal Guards), and he hoped to create a service nobility by such measures as forming a body of royal pages drawn from the poorest noble families. In establishing the Order of St. Stanislaw in 1765, he became one of several sovereigns to found new orders of chivalry as a means of increasing the patronage at their disposal. In Britain, the revived Order of the Bath (1725) and the new Order of St. Patrick (1783) had far more aspirants than places; in Spain, the Order of Carlos III (1771) was intended to reward political, administrative, and military service for a wider range of service noblemen than those who had been eligible for membership in the old military orders.

In most states, dynasts and courtiers alike realized, when confronted by the republican revolution in France, that they stood or fell together: a monarchical crusade needed spectacle and color to arouse popular enthusiasm. Although royal household expenditures fell in the 1790s, this was attributed to the exigencies of war rather than to any enlightened commitment to shift public revenues to more useful centers of state life. It was a remarkable reversal that conspicuous consumption at court was no longer perceived as parasitism. For two or three decades, courtiers had been under threat from ministers (usually noblemen themselves) bent on economies of scale and convinced that a lavish court was an expensive incongruity in an efficient state. In France, where Louis XVI's brothers had households that duplicated in microcosm the king's own, those princes were the constant target of reforming ministers. This was part of the general trend toward creating a service nobility, but it was often hard to discern because, as in Russia and Prussia, French military and bureaucratic functions tended to overlap with court positions.

Late eighteenth-century courts were dominated by wealthy noblemen whose interest in mainstream Enlightenment values had been awakened by their education and confirmed by the socializing process. They worked with progressive monarchs, or tried to do so until the outright attack on privileges launched by Emperor Joseph II in the early 1780s and by the French National Assembly a decade later; these reforms entailed further reduction in court places and the demotion to mere decorativeness of the courtiers who remained. However, the deaths of Frederick II of Prussia (1786) and Joseph II of Austria (1790) and the outbreak of the French Revolutionary War in 1792 terminated the heroic era of Enlightenment monarchy and rekindled a sense of common purpose between kings and courtiers. That meant returning to an earlier dispensation in which reform policies were not the hallmark of enlightened rule, but part of a range of policy options available to any monarch for the well-being of the state. Courts and colorful rituals emphasizing the ceremonial and symbolic facets of kingship would be rediscovered by old and new dynasts in Napoleonic Europe, not least in multiethnic, multinational, multilingual state structures such as the Austro-Hungarian Empire, where they became means of holding disparate regions together, however irrational that might be.

[*See also* Austria; Catherine II; England; Enlightened Despotism; France; Germany; Hungary; Italy; Josephinism; Russia; *and* Scandinavia.]

BIBLIOGRAPHY

Adamson, John, ed. *The Princely Courts of Europe, 1500–1750.* London, 1998. The successor volume to Dickens (1977).

Alexander, John T. *Catherine the Great: Life and Legend.* New York, 1989.

Blanning, T. C. W. *Reform and Revolution in Mainz, 1743–1803.* Cambridge, 1974. Exhaustive and readable study of the last decades of an imperial electorate.

Bucholz, R. O. *The Augustan Court: Queen Anne and the Decline of Court Culture.* Cambridge, 1993. The only serious study of the post-1700 British court to date.

Butterwick, Richard. *Poland's Last King and English Culture: Stanislaw August Poniatowski, 1732–1798.* Oxford, 1998.

Clark, S. *State and Status: The Rise of the State and Aristocratic Power in Western Europe.* Cardiff, Wales, 1995.

Dickens, A. G., ed. *The Courts of Europe: Politics, Patronage and Royalty, 1400–1800.* London, 1977. Pioneering comparative survey.

Elias, Norbert. *The Court Society.* Translated by Edmund Jephcott. New York, 1983. Vol. 3 of *The Civilizing Process*; sociological in its emphasis and highly influential.

Herr, Richard. *The Eighteenth-Century Revolution in Spain.* Princeton, N.J., 1958.

Ingrao, Charles. *The Hessian Mercenary State: Ideas, Institutions and Reforms under Frederick II, 1760–1785.* New York and Cambridge, 1987.

Lukowski, J. T. *Liberty's Folly: The Polish-Lithuanian Commonwealth in the Eighteenth Century.* London, 1991.

Lynch, John. *Bourbon Spain, 1700–1808.* Oxford, 1989.

Madariaga, Isabel de. *Russia in the Age of Catherine the Great.* London, 1981. A detailed overall survey by a world authority on the empress.

Maxwell, Kenneth R. *Pombal: An Enlightenment Paradox.* Cambridge, 1994.

Nicolas, Jean. *La Savoie au XVIIIᵉ siècle: Noblesse et bourgeoisie.* 2 vols. Paris, 1978.

Nordmann, C. *Gustave III.* Lille, France, 1986.

Oresko, Robert, G. C. Gibbs, and H. M. Scott, eds. *Royal and Republican Sovereignty in Early Modern Europe: Essays in Memory of Ragnhild Hatton.* Cambridge, 1997. Illustrated collection of essays representing the latest research.

Porter, Roy, and Mikulás Teich, eds. *The Enlightenment in National Context.* Cambridge, 1981.

Raeff, Marc. *The Well-Ordered Police State: Social and Institutional Change through Law in the Germanies and Russia, 1600–1820.* New Haven, Conn., 1983.

Rodríguez, Laura. *Reforma e Ilustración en la Espana del siglo XVIII.* Madrid, 1975.

Scheider, Theodor. *Frederick the Great.* Edited and translated by Sabina Berkeley and H. M. Scott. Cambridge, 2000. First published in the 1980s by the leading German authority on Frederick of the postwar era.

Scott, H. M. *Enlightened Absolutism: Reforms and Reformers in Late Eighteenth-Century Europe.* Basingstoke, U.K., 1990.

Scott, H. M., ed. *The European Nobilities in the Seventeenth and Eighteenth Centuries.* Harlow, U.K., 1995. An edited collection documenting the nobility in various nations and covering most of eastern Europe.

Symcox, Geoffrey. *Victor Amadeus II: Absolutism in the Savoyard State, 1675–1730.* London, 1983. A rare English-language study of this kingdom.

Venturi, Franco. *Italy and the Enlightenment: Studies in a Cosmopolitan Century.* Edited by Stuart Woolf, translated by Susan Corsi. London, 1972.

Zamoyski, Adam. *The Last King of Poland.* London, 1992.

NIGEL ASTON

ROYAL SOCIETY OF LONDON.

The Royal Society, founded in 1662 and still flourishing today, was an important London club with many features that made it very different from modern scientific societies: it had no state-sanctioned power to direct the production of science or technology in England; its members (called "fellows") were not selected or paid (with very few exceptions) by the state; and it was not an institution with specialized intellectual aims. Like most modern scientific societies, however, it selected its own members and conferred scientific credibility on them as long as they behaved in a gentlemanly fashion and freely shared the fruits of their labors. The fellows showered one another, their peers abroad, and their society with gifts of specimens, demonstrations, engravings, accounts, observations, models, instruments, theorems, journals, manuscripts, books, letters, papers, administrative services—and, of course, talk. Indeed, it was the main business of the society to decide what to do with the gifts and to judge which contributions were suitable to publish or describe in the society's journal, the *Philosophical Transactions*, which has been published almost without interruption from 1665 to the present.

Many fellows did little more than adorn the Society with their eminence and patronage, but without their two pounds twelve shillings a year (or twenty-seven pounds six shillings for life membership), the society would have disappeared; unlike continental European scientific institutions, it received no regular revenue from the monarch. More active fellows were listened to and lauded not because of any social prominence but because of their professional and craft capabilities and their devotion to science. The Royal Society was a club where a variety of men (women were explicitly excluded) learned of scientific developments that stimulated them to further activity. This is not to say, however, that anybody could belong to the Royal Society. Men of high social status joined easily, those of middling status less so, and those of low social class not at all. Over the eighteenth century, two-fifths of the (non-foreign) fellows were either peers or gentlemen by virtue of their social position alone; another two-fifths belonged to established genteel professions such as military officers, lawyers, physicians, and clerics; and the remaining members pursued a variety of occupations.

Their studies sprouted from the two great branches of Enlightenment knowledge: the natural and the artificial. The first is what people made of the world through perception or ratiocination, using their heads; the second is what they made in the world, through intervention with technical devices or symbolic manipulation, using their hands. This bifurcation of knowledge and activities corresponded very roughly to eighteenth-century social divisions. The fellows who pursued natural knowledge were mostly genteel, university-trained, and prosperous. They were independently wealthy gentlemen (Sir Joseph Banks, the Honorable Henry Cavendish, Thomas Young), university dons with endowed chairs (Sir Isaac Newton, James Bradley), successful physicians (Sir Hans Sloane), and clerics with ample livings (Stephen Hales). Those who pursued technical knowledge, in contrast, usually gained part of their income by their manual skill. They practiced chemistry (the teacher and preacher Joseph Priestley, the Royal Institution lecturer Sir Humphry Davy), electricity (the colonial printer, author, and politician Benjamin Franklin), architecture (Robert Hooke, Robert Adam), instrument making (the telescope makers John Dollond and William Herschel, the watchmaker George Graham, and the sextant maker Jesse Ramsden), engineering (the military engineer Benjamin Robins, the civil engineer John Smeaton, the mechanical engineer James Watt), navigation (the naval officer Captain James Cook), and surgery (John Hunter, William Cheselden). The Royal Society thus contained men from both sides of this basic division of knowledge, although not without conflict.

Royal Society. Frontispiece to Thomas Sprat's *History of the Royal Society* (1667) by Wenceslaus Hollar. Fame crowns the bust of King Charles I, which is flanked by the first president of the Society, William Viscount Brouncker (*left*), and Francis Bacon. (New York Public Library, Astor, Lenox, and Tilden Foundations.)

The society did not claim to take all of knowledge into its purview: metaphysics, religion, logic, and poetry were absent. Perhaps more surprising, given the founding rhetoric of the society and the practices of its most famous fellow, Sir Isaac Newton, is the almost complete absence of pure mathematics and speculative natural philosophy, and the rather infrequent focus on experimentation (electricity or chemistry). The dominant areas of investigation, each accounting for between one-third and one-fifth of all activities reported, were natural history (zoology, botany, geology, meteorology, and anthropology); medicine, surgery, and anatomy; and "mixed" or applied mathematics (astronomy, geography, optics, mechanics, astronomy, and engineering).

Topics that seized the imagination of the fellows and a wider public included analyzing sunlight (Newton, 1700s; Young, 1800s), transmitting and storing electricity (the dyer Stephen Gray, 1730s; Franklin, 1740s, 1750s), detecting the aberration of starlight (Bradley, 1720s) and a new planet (Herschel, 1770s), measuring the shape of the earth (Graham, 1730s) and the size of the solar system (the Astronomer Royal, Nevil Maskelyne, 1760s), mapping new lands (Cook, 1760s, 1770s), describing new peoples (the naturalist Johann Forster, 1770s), capturing and analyzing exotic airs and gases (Hales, 1720s; Priestley and Cavendish, 1760s, 1770s), creating new chemical elements with batteries (Davy, 1800s), and investigating muscular and nervous action (Hunter, 1780s; Everard Home, 1790s, 1800s). Its members, if not the Royal Society itself, were involved in every important scientific endeavor in eighteenth-century Britain. As a body, the society collaborated with other learned societies to organize observations worldwide of the transits of Venus in 1761 and 1769, and to collect and publish the results.

[*See also* Academies; Banks, Joseph; Clubs and Societies; Franklin, Benjamin; Hales, Stephen; Learned Societies; Natural Philosophy and Science; Newton, Isaac; *and* Priestley, Joseph.]

BIBLIOGRAPHY

Boas Hall, Marie. *Promoting Experimental Learning: Experiment and the Royal Society, 1660–1727*. Cambridge, 1992. A sensitive and well-written account.

Hunter, Michael. *Establishing the New Science: The Experience of the Early Royal Society, 1660–1727*. Woodbridge, U.K., 1989. A useful collection of essays on the Society's early years.

Lyons, Henry. *The Royal Society: 1660–1940*. London, 1944. Some important archival work, but unreliable in its historical judgments.

McClellan, James E. I. *Science Reorganized: Scientific Societies in the Eighteenth Century*. New York, 1985. Deservedly the standard account.

Sorrenson, Richard. "Towards a History of the Royal Society in the Eighteenth Century." *Notes and Records of the Royal Society of London* 50 (1996), 29–46.

Weld, Charles. *A History of the Royal Society*. 2 vols. London, 1848, 1858. Astonishingly, still the best book-length work on the Society's eighteenth-century history.

RICHARD J. SORRENSON

RUMFORD, COUNT (Benjamin Thompson) (1753–1814), social reformer, inventor, and physicist.

Thompson was born in Woburn, Massachusetts. The early death of his parents limited his educational opportunities, and while he became conversant with many of the fundamental themes in the physical sciences of his era, he was essentially self-educated in these fields. In 1771, he began a career as a schoolteacher in Concord, New Hampshire. Committed not only to self-advancement, but also to social climbing, in 1772 he married Sarah Rolfe, a wealthy widow. He separated from his wife in 1775.

Throughout most of his life, he held military rank of some nature and became devoted to developing efficient ways of organizing and utilizing armies in both war and peace. A strong supporter of Great Britain, Thompson prepared for British forces in America a detailed assessment of the strength and nature of colonial forces in the "State of the Rebel Army." From the spring of 1776 to the fall of 1781, he served the British crown as an adviser on American affairs. From 1781 to 1783, he fought in the Revolutionary War as a lieutenant colonel in the king's American Dragoons. With the end of the war, he believed that he could find greater opportunities for advancement on the Continent. In 1783, he became a colonel and aide-de-camp to Charles Theodore, elector of Bavaria. During his fourteen years of service in Bavaria, Thompson had the opportunity to develop his thoughts not only on the application of science and technology to the theoretical nature of heat and light, but also to the advancement of human society.

Through his essays and policies, he attempted to put his ideas into operation. Acknowledging the expense of an army in peacetime and the low level of a soldier's education and training, he introduced schools of industry that prepared them for useful careers after military service. In Bavaria, he utilized the army in a variety of paramilitary functions, rebuilding riverbanks, repairing highways, draining marshes, planting gardens to provide fresh food for themselves and their families, and waging war against those conditions that created impoverishment. Always a systematic thinker, he sought to eradicate poverty in Munich in 1790 by developing social welfare teams composed of priests, surgeons, physicians, apothecaries, and distinguished citizens to attack the underlying causes of poverty among the aged, infirm, disadvantaged, and impoverished. For his service to Bavaria, Thompson was made a count of the Holy Roman Empire in 1792.

Thompson's *Essays, Political, Economical and Philosophical*, published in 1796, presented his thoughts on the methods by which the practical application of science could improve society and satisfy human needs. Much of his thought and activity is focused upon the application of science to practical issues. His practical studies led to many innovations, including designs for the construction of coffee percolators, double boilers, cooking roasters, oil lamps, and more efficient chimneys, fireplaces, and stoves. He believed that technology was science's gift to society. Rumford was also a gifted theoretical scientist who contemplated and investigated the transmission of light through glass and the convection of heat and radiation. To encourage the investigation of heat or light, he established in 1796 the Rumford Medals to be awarded annually by the Royal Society of London and the American Academy of Arts and Sciences for original work in this area. In 1799, he became one of the founders and early financial supporters of the Royal Institution of Great Britain. While living in Paris, he married in 1805 the widow of the distinguished French chemist Antoine Lavoisier. He died at Auteuil near Paris in 1814.

[*See also* American Revolution; Education; *and* War and Military Theory.]

BIBLIOGRAPHY

Count Rumford's correspondence and personal papers may be found in collections held by the British Museum, the Public Record Office, the Library of the Royal Society, the Royal Institution of Great Britain, the New Hampshire Historical Society, Harvard University Library, the William L. Clements Library, and the American Academy of Arts and Sciences. He published more than sixty papers in English, German, and French, as well as four volumes of *Essays*, which appeared in both English and American editions. The earliest American edition of his works is *The Complete Works of Count Rumford*, 4 vols. Boston, 1870–1875.

Sanborn C. Brown has prepared a modern edition of these works and addressed many of the confusing questions surrounding their publication: *The Nature of Heat* (Cambridge, 1968), *Practical Applications of Heat* (Cambridge, 1969), *Devices and Techniques* (Cambridge, 1969), *Light and Armament* (Cambridge, 1970), and *Public Institutions* (Cambridge, 1970). The first substantive examination of Thompson's life was prepared by George E. Ellis, *Memoir of Sir Benjamin Thompson, Count Rumford, With Notices of His Daughter* (Boston, 1871).

G. I. Brown, *Count Rumford: The Extraordinary Life of a Scientific Genius* (New York, 2000); Sanborn Brown, *Count Rumford, Physicist Extraordinary* (Garden City, N.Y., 1962); Egon Larsen, *An American in Europe* (New York, 1953); W. J. Sparrow, *Knight of the White Eagle* (London, 1964); and James Alden Thompson, *Count Rumford of Massachusetts* (New York, 1935) all provide solid introductions to his life and bibliographies that indicate additional works that can be consulted for details of his life and career.

PHILLIP DRENNON THOMAS

RUSH, BENJAMIN (1746–1813), physician, medical educator, social reformer, and political activist.

Rush was born in Byberry Township, Pennsylvania, just northeast of Philadelphia, to John Rush, a gunsmith and farmer, and Susannah Hall Harvey. The family moved to Philadelphia when Rush was two; his father died three years later, and his mother thereafter supported the family by operating a grocery store. At age eight, Rush went to live and to school with his uncle, the Rev. Dr. Samuel Finley, who operated Nottingham Academy in Maryland. Sufficiently prepared to enter the College of New Jersey (now Princeton University) at thirteen, he received his A.B. the following year, 1760. From Finley and from Princeton's president, the Rev. Samuel Davies, Rush imbibed a solid education in the liberal arts, an American patriotism, and a commitment to evangelical Calvinism that he never abandoned.

Rush's medical training began with an apprenticeship under Dr. John Redman in Philadelphia from 1761 to 1766 and attendance at the lectures of Drs. John Morgan and William Shippen at the newly founded College of Philadelphia. At Redman's urging, Rush continued his education at the University of Edinburgh from 1766 to 1768, where he earned an M.D., followed with observation at London hospitals and a trip to France, where he met with physicians and philosophes. The experiences of this period did much to shape Rush's subsequent attitudes and interests. He learned the chemistry he would teach for many years from Edinburgh's Joseph Black, and his ideas on the grouping and causes of disease derived from the lectures

of the eminent William Cullen and conversation with his fellow student John Brown. Cullen's lectures and his observations at London hospitals contributed to the way that Rush practiced medicine. The cosmopolitan and materialistic air of the European capitals softened somewhat his rigid Calvinism, but not his evangelicalism. He adopted the Scottish Common Sense philosophy from one of its more conservative proponents, James Beattie, while also absorbing materialist and environmentalist ideas from the English Christian philosopher David Hartley. Exposure to the radical Whig ideology of Scottish thinkers and English dissenters confirmed and intensified his American patriotism and introduced him to republicanism. Out of all this, Rush fashioned a unified intellectual foundation by which he could combine rationalistic science, revealed religion, and republicanism, all dependent upon the constant active support of a loving God whose gifts to this world were to endow mankind with a moral faculty, the capacity to reason, and simple laws that underlay all realms of human endeavor.

Upon his return to Philadelphia in 1769, Rush began a career that put his philosophy to work and that illustrates two of the characteristics most often attributed to the American Enlightenment: its focus on application as well as ideation; and its eclectic nature. Rush became America's most eminent physician, but he was also a noted political activist, a religious evangelical, a promoter of enlightened education, and a social reformer supportive of a variety of causes. Throughout his career he wrote prolifically about everything he did.

Embracing republicanism because he believed that its simple scheme for locating political sovereignty in the people was favored by God, Rush defended American opposition to Great Britain's colonial policies while in Europe, and after his return to Philadelphia became a supporter of independence. He found a publisher for Thomas Paine's great 1776 pamphlet and suggested its title, *Common Sense*. He helped bring about Pennsylvania's 1776 constitutional convention, and represented it in the Second Continental Congress where he signed the Declaration of Independence. Becoming disillusioned with governmental policies under Pennsylvania's 1776 constitution, he campaigned constantly for its reform until a new convention met in 1790. He also ardently supported the new United States Constitution both in print and in the state ratifying convention in 1787.

Rush reconciled his Christian evangelicalism with Enlightenment thinking by arguing that atonement and salvation were the simplest of religious doctrines. By the early 1780s, he believed that God wished for the universal salvation of mankind. Uncomfortable both as a Presbyterian and later as an Episcopalian, he argued for denominational pluralism and for the separation of church and state.

Rush both taught and practiced medicine for over forty years. From 1769 on, he taught first chemistry, then the theory and practice of medicine at the institution that was, successively, the College of Philadelphia, the University of the State of Pennsylvania, and finally the University of Pennsylvania. He also trained hundreds of apprentices, who worked for him two or three at a time. From 1784 on, Rush was a surgeon at the Pennsylvania Hospital and after 1787, he took charge of the insane patients, humanely arguing for better treatment. In 1786, he set up the Philadelphia Dispensary, modeled after the London dispensaries that ministered to the poor. The following year he helped start the College of Physicians of Philadelphia to help ensure high standards for medical practitioners. Always willing to treat the poor as well as the affluent, he became a hero to Philadelphians for being one of the few doctors who stayed in the city to treat patients during the yellow fever outbreak of 1793.

As part of his philosophical predilection toward simplicity, Rush by the 1790s, had reduced his mentor Cullen's categorization of disease from more than seventeen hundred varieties to one: a morbid excitation of the usually tranquil nervous system, stemming from convulsive action in the blood vessels. Whatever the symptoms, successful treatment required rebalancing the nervous system through depletion of blood or bile or both. Rush acted on his theory during the yellow fever outbreak, achieving great success, but also drawing criticism for the rigors of his treatments.

Rush's environmentalism, republicanism, and Christian optimism engaged him in a variety of reforms, the most significant of which was education for civic virtue. Toward this end, he advocated plans of education for Pennsylvania, for women, and for a national university, while helping to found two colleges: Dickinson; and Franklin and Marshall. He also advocated temperance, penal reform, and the abolition of slavery.

[See also American Revolution and Medicine.]

BIBLIOGRAPHY

WORKS BY RUSH

Essays, Literary, Moral & Philosophical. Philadelphia, 1798; reprint edition, Schenectady, N.Y., 1988. Rush's commentary on education, religion, politics, and reform.

The Letters of Benjamin Rush. Edited by Lyman Butterfield. 2 vols. Princeton, N.J., 1951. Provides insight into Rush's personality, ideas, and varied activities.

The Selected Writings of Benjamin Rush. Edited by Dagobert D. Runes. New York, 1947. Rush's essays on many subjects, including politics, education, temperance, and abolition.

Sixteen Introductory Lectures, to Courses of Lectures Upon the Institutes and Practice of Medicine, with a Syllabus of the Latter . . . . Philadelphia, 1811; Shaw and Shoemaker, Early American Imprints, 2d

series, 1801–1819, microtext # 23846. Rush's views on the medical profession, offering insight into his character.

WORKS ABOUT RUSH

Binger, Carl Alfred Lanning. Revolutionary Doctor: Benjamin Rush, 1746–1813. New York, 1966. The most comprehensive biography.

D'Elia, Donald J. Benjamin Rush, Philosopher of the American Revolution. American Philosophical Society Transactions n.s. 64 (1974), 1–113. The most insightful examination of Rush's intellectual makeup and the sources of his thought.

Fox, Claire G., Gordon L. Miller, and Jacqueline C. Miller. Benjamin Rush, M.D.: A Bibliographic Guide. Westport, Conn., 1996. A chronological listing of all works by and about Rush, with some annotation.

Hawke, David F. Benjamin Rush, Revolutionary Gadfly. Indianapolis, Ind., and New York, 1971. A lively biography with a political focus.

DAVID W. ROBSON

RUSSIA. In 1682, the ten-year-old Peter I (1672–1725) ascended the tsar's throne, together with his handicapped elder half-brother, Ivan V, who died in 1696. In 1689, Peter overthrew the regency of his sister and, leaving Ivan to carry out the religious duties of a tsar, he frequented the foreign quarter in Moscow, played at soldiers with his friends—the kernel of the future Guards Regiments—and developed interests in shipbuilding, mechanical devices, and the European way of life. The search for an ally in a war against the Ottoman Empire, together with curiosity about the Western world, led him in 1697 to embark incognito on the "Great Embassy" to European courts. Having failed to secure support in the West, Peter abandoned plans for expansion on the Black Sea and turned to the alternative policy of obtaining an outlet on the Baltic by declaring war on Sweden, in alliance with the elector of Saxony, Augustus II the Strong, recently elected king of Poland.

Defeat by the army of Charles XII of Sweden at Narva (1700) led Peter to embark on military and domestic reforms, which he pursued erratically at first, but more systematically after the great victory of Poltava (1709). He modernized the organization and supply of the army, built a fleet on the Baltic after he acquired the mouth of the Neva in 1703, and created an armaments industry. Many of Peter's administrative reforms were borrowed from Sweden. He had allowed the Muscovite Duma to fade away; he replaced it in 1711 with a Governing Senate, which presided over a number of functional "colleges" in Swedish style and was itself supervised by a procurator general responsible directly to the tsar. The reformed administration was enshrined in a number of codes (Military Code, 1716; Naval Code, 1720; General Regulations for the civil administration, 1720), again largely based on Swedish models. The taxation system was remodeled as a "poll tax" of seventy-five kopeks levied on all males over the age of sixteen, except for nobles, priests,

Moscow. View from the Kremlin. Anonymous engraving (1799). (Historical Museum, Moscow/ Scala/Art Resource, NY.)

and common soldiers. The new poll tax necessitated the registration of everyone liable to it in his village or town: this swept previous categories of peasants and town-dwellers into a harsher form of bondage to their place of residence, or, in the case of serfs, to their landowners.

The nobility did not escape Peter's reforming zeal. In 1721, he introduced an elaborate "table of ranks," or precedence, to replace the Muscovite system of *mestnichestvo* ("placing"), abolished in 1682. Borrowed in large part from usage in Prussia, Denmark, and Sweden, it placed all officers and officials in fourteen hierarchically graded ranks, from field marshal in rank one to palace cooks and barbers in rank fourteen. Nonnobles acquired hereditary nobility on becoming officers in rank fourteen, or on reaching rank eight in the civil branch. Aristocracy was not however replaced by meritocracy, as has often been assumed, but the intermittent compulsory service hitherto performed by nobles turned into continuous lifelong service. The Russian Orthodox Church also came under state control. No new patriarch, who might rival the tsar in charismatic authority, was appointed after 1700, and the church was placed under a form of collegial government, the Holy Synod, supervised by a lay procurator. The country remained deeply religious, but the state became largely secular. The final victory over Sweden and the annexation of the Baltic provinces of Livonia and Estonia in 1710 were confirmed by the Treaty of Nystad in 1721, when Peter changed his title from tsar to "imperator," in a straightforward challenge to the Holy Roman Emperor of the West as Roman Emperor of the East.

Peter's regime was imposed by violence and was replete with surveillance, denunciations, and brutal punishments. Inevitably, his reforming frenzy and the human costs of projects such as the building of the new capital, St. Petersburg (founded in 1703), led to a groundswell of opposition against him, manifested in popular risings, large-scale flight among the peasantry and Old Believers (those who had rejected the ecclesiastical reforms of Patriarch Nikon in the seventeenth century and now regarded Peter as Antichrist), and among some circles around the heir to the throne, Aleksey Petrovich. After a successful flight abroad, Aleksey was lured back, tortured, tried for treason, sentenced to death, and died before the sentence could be carried out. Peter, left without a male heir, enacted a law of succession (22 February 1722) that authorized a reigning tsar to appoint an heir of his choice. The law was subsequently justified and explained in one of the major Russian expositions of the absolutist nature of Russian government, *The Justice of the Monarch's Will*, usually attributed to Archbishop Feofan Prokopovich (1677?–1736), which drew largely on contemporary Western political theory and reconciled absolute power with natural law. Peter's death in 1725 without naming an heir inaugurated the series of coups d'état in favor of female rulers that punctuated the eighteenth century. A law of succession was finally enacted in 1797 by the Emperor Paul I (1754–1801); it excluded women unless all male heirs had died out.

The death of Peter led to a loss of momentum in the assimilation of change. In the period 1725–1762, the country suffered from the absence of clear and forceful direction. An attempt in 1730 by a group of higher-ranking nobles influenced by foreign (Swedish, and, to a lesser extent, English) political systems to limit the powers of the ruler failed dismally. Russian armies were, however, successful in war against the Turks and in the Seven Years' War.

Catherine II. The accession of Catherine II in 1762 injected new life into the Russian polity. Born Sophia of Anhalt Zerbst (1729–1796), she had been brought to Russia at the age of fourteen to marry the heir to the throne, Peter I's grandson, Duke Peter of Holstein Gottorp (1728–1762). He succeeded in alienating the most powerful social forces in the country and was overthrown and killed in June 1762 in a coup d'état by his wife and her supporters in the Guards regiments. Exceptionally well read in the classics of the French Enlightenment and of German cameralism, Catherine intended to rule as well as reign. She believed in strengthening the authority of the state, but at the same time in enlarging and clearly defining the space in which civil society could develop. In 1767, she summoned an assembly, the Legislative Commission, of some 540 elected representatives of the free estates; it excluded only those peasants who were serfs of private landowners, the priesthood (as distinct from the Holy Synod, which sent one deputy), and privates in the armed forces. It was a codifying, not a constitutional assembly, and was not intended to consider the political structure of the Russian Empire. Though it drafted no law code, the Legislative Commission collected an enormous amount of information on the state of Russia, and the draft codes prepared in its various subcommissions were used in subsequent legislation. It was prorogued in 1768 on the outbreak of war with the Ottomans, which ended with the victorious Peace of Kutschuk Kainardzhi (1774), by which Catherine acquired a stretch of Black Sea coast from the mouth of the Dnieper to the Bug River. This was enlarged in 1783 by the unopposed annexation of the Crimea and, as a result of the second Turkish war (1787–1792), of the coast between the Bug and the Dniester. The three partitions of Poland-Lithuania (1772, 1793, and 1795) greatly enlarged Russian territory in the West.

The financial strains of the war of 1768–1774, the burden of conscription, and the fear of being forced into regular army service sparked a serious uprising in 1773–1774 among the free Yaik and Dnieper Cossacks, led by the Don Cossack Yemelyan Pugachov. The revolt was widely supported by serfs, state peasants, peasants in industrial enterprises, and Bashkir tribesmen in the territory between the Yaik River and the Volga, in the Urals, and in Western Siberia; it lasted until September 1774. Catherine had secularized the estates of the church in 1764, thus freeing about 800,000 peasants from personal dependence, but the Pugachev revolt rendered any attempt to improve the condition of the serfs hazardous in the eyes of the government and the nobility.

More and better local administration now became Catherine's first priority. In 1775, she introduced a new division of the provinces into smaller units and elected participation on an "estate basis" in a network of local law courts and administrative bodies. The Charters to the Nobles and to the Towns (1785) spelled out the personal and corporate rights of both social groups. The Charters confirmed the freedom from service of the nobles, already granted in 1762, their right to own serf villages, and the abolition of corporal punishment for nobles and the top classes of townsmen. The use of torture was de facto phased out, and religious toleration was quietly introduced. In 1786, a national system of free but not compulsory primary and secondary schools was set up in towns and cities throughout the empire, coeducational, totally secular, and open even to serfs with the permission of their owners.

Culture and the Enlightenment. When Peter opened Russia to the West, much of what he borrowed belonged to the Western way of life, and not specifically to the Enlightenment. Moreover, it is necessary to distinguish between ideas and ideals that were promoted by the state on the one hand, and those that gradually penetrated into Russian society and flourished as a result of private initiative and cultural assimilation on the other. In Peter's reign, state direction of cultural life was marked. From architecture to furnishing, from clothes to manners, Russian society was forced into a new mold.

At the end of the seventeenth century, Russian culture had briefly been oriented toward Latin Poland, but Peter's contacts in the foreign quarter aroused his interest in northern European Protestant culture. He was influenced by the program put forward by the German philosopher Gottfried Wilhelm von Leibniz (1646–1716), who advised him to recruit foreigners, to allow Russians to travel abroad, to establish an academy of sciences, and to study the geography, natural history, resources, and history of Russia. Peter followed all these suggestions, and the Academy of Sciences, finally founded in 1726, eventually became the center from which radiated Russian contacts with the intellectual world outside. Recognizing the importance of communicating with his subjects, Peter imported printing presses and recruited printers. In 1707, a new "civil script," much easier to read, replaced the Old Church Slavonic script, now to be used only for religious works. By far the greatest number of works published in his reign consisted of laws, manifestos, regulations, and other official documents, such as treaties. *Vedomosti* ("News") was published from 1702 to 1727, the first Russian periodical intended for public consumption and providing information from home and abroad. Technical books were translated (leaving out the purple patches), and moral guidance was offered by Samuel Pufendorf's *De jure naturae et gentium* (On the Duties of Man and Citizen) and information in his *Historie der vornehmsten Reiche und Staaten* (History of the Major European Powers). Peter found in Pufendorf's version of natural law the approach to philosophy most easily assimilated by those unfamiliar with its vocabulary.

In this early period of Russian cultural westernization, the dominant influence was that of the German *Frühaufklärung* (early Enlightenment), mediated by the massive presence of German scholars, many of them educated in the pietism of A. H. Francke and Christian Wolff in Halle, which combined the study of natural law with respect for religion and secular authority. German was a much more accessible language than French to Russians at this stage, thanks to the many Baltic Germans who entered Russian service, the Lutheran church in St. Petersburg, and German merchants, schools, and tutors. Wolff, recommended to Peter by Leibniz, in turn recommended many other Germans to work in Russia, and most Russians who studied abroad at this time went to Halle or Marburg.

Feofan Prokopovich, archbishop of Pskov and later metropolitan of Moscow, had spent some time as a Uniate in a Jesuit college in Rome; on his return, he reconverted to Orthodoxy and became the outstanding Russian writer, poet, theologian, and philosopher; the most forceful exponent of the Petrine ideology; and the center of the most influential literary circle. The emphasis on German scientific thought at this stage hindered the penetration of Newtonianism, and preference was given to the philosophy of Descartes. Fontenelle's *Entretiens sur la pluralité des mondes* (Conversations on the Plurality of Worlds, 1686) was translated as early as 1740 by the poet Antiokh Kantemir (1709–1744), but the most popular physics textbook was by Christian Wolff (1679–1754), translated by the Russian polymath of peasant origin, Mikhail Vasilievich Lomonosov (1711–1765). Educated in Marburg, Lomonosov later became an academician, chemist, mineralogist, poet, historian—and a noble and a serf-owner. The emphasis in the Academy was on scientific thought; it was dominated by the Swiss mathematician Leonhard Euler, who maintained Russian links with the Academy of Berlin.

Surveying and mapping Russia formed part of the duties of academicians, in accordance with Leibniz's recommendation, and Russian expeditions to Siberia and Kamchatka, which continued throughout the century, collected a vast amount of ethnographic, botanical, and geographical information, much of which soon became available outside Russia. Academicians, notably Gerhard Müller (1705–1783), promoted the scientific study of natural history, language, and history. Knowledge of the Russian past was furthered by the collection and publication of chronicles and other documents, and the increasing interest in the origins and evolution of Russia contributed to a debate on national self-definition in relation to western Europe, as well as to an intensification of national feeling among the educated elite. Müller edited the historical journal *Sammlung Russischer Geschichte* for a number of years, providing reliable historical information about Russia to academicians and scholars abroad.

Education was central to Peter's vision, and he was successful in the professional schools he established—for instance, the School of Navigation—but the "cipher schools" he attempted to set up throughout the country gradually disappeared. The Infantry Cadet Corps was founded in 1731 in response to the demand for educational facilities to enable nobles to fulfill service requirements. Its curriculum and the teaching methods changed over time, but noble cadets combined a professional with a general education and were taught to be gentlemen as well as soldiers. The Cadet Corps published a literary journal in the 1750s in which many future poets and dramatists cut their teeth, and the idea of the noble *Kulturträger* ("upholder of civilization") was born. The University of Moscow was founded in 1755 as the result of behind-the-scenes pressure from Ivan Ivanovich Shuvalov (1727–1797), the favorite of Empress Elizabeth (1741–1762), and from Lomonosov. The majority of the teachers were German, including all the teachers of jurisprudence until 1768, when the first Russian, the Scottish-trained Simeon E. Desnitsky, was appointed. By midcentury, the French language had joined though not superseded German, and French literature and political thought in the original language became familiar to educated Russians. Few people read English yet.

Personal contact with the French philosophes was encouraged by Catherine's private correspondence with Voltaire, Jean Le Rond d'Alembert, Denis Diderot, and Friedrich Melchior Grimm, and though Diderot's visit to Russia in 1773–1774 was disappointing for both the philosophe and the empress. The range of interests among the budding Russian intelligentsia is reflected in the number of works published in Russian, which rose from 1,482 titles in 1755–1775 to 7,845 from 1775 to 1800. Selections from the *Encyclopédie*, Montesquieu's *L'esprit des lois* and Rousseau's *La nouvelle Héloïse* were translated by men of letters, either on their own initiative or at the request of a society to commission translations that was set up by Catherine in 1768. Rousseau's *Émile* suffered a transient official ban, but excerpts were published in subsequent years, including the daring *Profession de foi du vicaire savoyard* ("Profession of faith of the Savoyard vicar," 1770); most of his works were eventually translated into Russian, while the *Du contrat social* appeared in German in Riga, again by private initiative.

By midcentury, Russia had also acquired public spaces in which intellectual and cultural life could take place—clubs, lecture rooms in the Academy, theaters, salons, and masonic lodges. The Free Economic Society was founded in 1765 to discuss Physiocratic principles and the improvement of agriculture; there were public lectures in the Academy of Sciences (its library was open twice a week to the general reader) and in Moscow University. The Academy of Arts, founded in 1757, sent many students abroad to study. Travel to the West became more frequent; indeed, the Grand Tour became fashionable, thanks to the establishment by Peter I of permanent diplomatic posts in many countries. Just as stimulating were the visits to the Mediterranean of several naval squadrons sent to take part in the war against the Turks in 1768–1774; Russian officers brought home impressions from Renaissance and classical Italy, and from classical Greece.

Contacts with the West stimulated the development of Freemasonry, first introduced into Russia in the 1740s. By the 1770s, a large number of officers and officials belonged to one or another branch. Masonic activity provided a spiritual outlet to many who were disillusioned with the Orthodox Church, and the publishing activity of the leader of the Rosicrucians, Nikolai I. Novikov, was vast.

To galvanize the Academy of Sciences into renewed activity, Catherine appointed the renowned Princess Dashkova as director in 1782. A cultivated woman with a wide circle of friends in France, England, and Scotland, she was the first and only woman ever to head such an institution. She was subsequently appointed to direct a newly established Russian Academy of Letters, which set about producing a dictionary and a grammar. The Academy of Science was also the center for a number of people actively concerned with Russian history, both with correcting the many errors made by foreign historians about Russia (such as the abbé Chappe d'Auteroche in his *Voyage en Sibérie*, 1768) and with publishing new materials, such as the medieval ballad, the *Lay of Prince Igor*. History served two purposes in Russia: it was a moral example to teach statesmen how to act, and it was a means of arousing patriotism and pride in the fatherland. The principles of historical criticism and historical research were still in their infancy, however; an academician such as Lomonosov could be reluctant to publish a historical document because of the tradition of state secrecy. There had been considerable controversy in the 1750s over whether the Russian state owed its origins to Scandinavian conquest (the "Normanist theory") or to the native Slav population. Controversy flared again in the 1790s over the systematically negative portrayal of Russian history in French historiography, which led to a well-mounted counterattack by Russian amateur historians (there were no professional ones) who gravitated around Catherine; she herself was very interested in the history of Russia, on which she had written *Notes* for her grandchildren.

State-directed activity was effective in Catherine's reign in two ways. She actively promoted intellectual initiatives by her patronage (often financial), her interest, and her example, and she personally initiated many policies that reflected the ideas of eighteenth-century cameralist writers who used the language of the Enlightenment.

The *Instruction*, or *Nakaz*, that Catherine wrote for the Legislative Commission in 1767 drew largely on Montesquieu's *L'esprit des lois* and Cesare Beccaria's *Dei delitte e delle pene* (On Crimes and Punishments, 1765), which Catherine read in French, as well as on Baron Bielfeld's *Institutions Politiques* (1760; Russian translation, 1768–1775). It put into circulation their ideas and those of many other writers. The *Instruction* and the debates in the Commission familiarized educated public opinion with concepts of natural law, and thus rendered political discussion respectable—and even publishable, as long as it did not offend against religion, decency, or the sovereign. Catherine financed a program of translations of ancient Greek and Latin, as well as English and French, political, literary, and historical works; she herself started a satirical weekly, *Vsyakaya Vsyachina* (loosely, "all sorts of things"), modeled on the English *The Rambler* and *The Spectator*, and it inspired many imitators and rivals. New subjects for discussion arose, partly as a result of the stimulus of the Legislative Commission. Serfdom, which had hitherto been largely taken for granted, was first publicly discussed in an essay competition organized by the Free Economic Society in 1765, on the theme of whether the peasant should possess property in land or only movable property. Catherine experimented with changes in land tenure on some court estates, and the satirical journals, notably *Truten'* (The Drone), published by Novikov, launched biting attacks on serfdom. Prince Dmitri A. Golitsyn, longtime Russian ambassador to Paris and The Hague, was interested in physics and was a close personal friend of many French intellectuals; he produced several proposals for official action to limit serfdom. The historian Prince M. M. Shcherbatov appeared as its defender in the Legislative Commission. Alexander Nikolayevich Radishchev's criticism of serfdom and of the absolutist government of Russia in *The Journey from Petersburg to Moscow* (1790, influenced by Raynal) was judged so subversive that he was condemned to ten years' exile in Siberia.

Some important Enlightenment ideas were reflected in actual government measures in the second half of the century. The influence of the English jurist William Blackstone is conspicuous in the provincial reform of 1775, with its attempt at the separation of the judiciary and the executive, and the introduction of equity courts. English influence can also be detected in the definition of civil rights as set out in the Charters to the Nobles and Townspeople of 1785, possibly deriving from the lawyer Simeon E. Desnitsky, who had studied with Adam Smith at Glasgow University. Catherine sponsored a translation of Blackstone into Russian (1780), and her interest in English political and juridical thought is manifest in the large number of constitutional documents of English history, such as Magna Carta and the Bill of Rights, that were translated for her private study.

Finally, the empress's interest in both the range and the quality of education was remarkable. John Amos Comenius (1592–1670), François de Salignac de La Mothe Fénelon (1651–1715), and possibly John Locke (whose *Education of Children* was first translated in 1759) influenced her main educational adviser, I. I. Betskoy, who in 1764 published the *General Plan for the Education of Young People of Both Sexes*, approved by her. Based on Rousseauist principles in general, its object was to create a new kind of people, and, Catherine hoped, a Third Estate. She favored education by precept and moral persuasion, learning by play, and the complete elimination of corporal punishment. These principles were, in theory, put into effect in her early educational foundations, such as the Foundling Home in Moscow and the Smol'nyy Institute for Noble Girls and a parallel institute for middle-class girls. The General Plan was translated into French and published in The Hague in 1774, under the supervision of Diderot on his return from Russia. At one time, Catherine was very taken with the educational theories of the German pedagogue Johann Basedow (1723–1790), which he put into practice in his Philanthropin in Dessau. In the end, however, she realized that a national school system could not be founded on the lavish Rousseauian system, so she adopted the methods introduced in the Austrian school reform of Maria Theresa in 1774, based on the pedagogical conceptions of Johann Ignaz von Felbiger (1724–1788). The education was totally secular—priests were not even allowed to teach the catechism; children were brought up to be obedient subjects in the estate to which they had been called, and corporal punishment was forbidden, though in vain.

The French Revolution acted as a brake on the public expression of ideas in Russia, and the previously tolerated Freemasons began to be viewed as seditious. Novikov's publishing enterprise was closed down, and he was arrested and sentenced in 1792 to ten years' imprisonment in the fortress of Schlüsselburg for reasons that may have involved his alleged masonic contacts with the Grand Duke Paul. In 1796, the relative freedom of the printed word, introduced in 1783 when anyone was authorized to own a printing press, disappeared when private presses were closed and censorship of imported books was introduced.

It must be admitted that western European culture in general, and the Enlightenment in particular, affected only a very small elite in the Russian population. At midcentury, many of the older nobles were still illiterate, and the mass of poorer nobles had few cultural opportunities. Cultural life was concentrated mainly in the two capitals and in some provincial capitals, notably in Siberia, where energetic governors (often Freemasons) led the way. The merchant class enjoyed a higher degree of literacy than has generally been supposed, but it was also deeply religious. Meanwhile, a new class was emerging: the so-called *raznochintsy* or people who belonged to no class, a category that included the embryonic professional classes, university graduates, architects, painters, writers, and teachers, who were to underpin the intelligentsia in the nineteenth century.

[*See also* Academies, *subentry on* Russia; Catherine II; Education; Enlightened Despotism; *and* Saint Petersburg Academy.]

BIBLIOGRAPHY

Anisimov, Evgenii. V. *Vremya petrovskikh reform*. Leningrad, 1989. Abridged English translation by John T. Alexander, *Reforms of Peter the Great: Progress through Coercion in Russia*. New York, 1993. Challenges the hitherto dominant Soviet interpretation.

Bartlett, Roger P., Anthony G. Cross, and Karen Rasmussen. *Russia and the World of the Eighteenth Century*. (Proceedings of the Third International Conference of the Study Group on Eighteenth Century Russia, Bloomington, Ind., 1984.) Columbus, Ohio, 1986.

Boss, Valentin. *Newton and Russia: The Early Influence, 1698–1796*. Cambridge, Mass., 1972.

De Madariaga, Isabel. *Russia in the Age of Catherine the Great*. New Haven, Conn., 1981. The standard work on Catherine II; see also de Madariaga's *Politics and Culture in Eighteenth Century Russia: Collected Essays* (London and New York, 1998) and "The Russian Nobility in the Seventeenth and Eighteenth Centuries," in *The European Nobilities in the Seventeenth and Eighteenth Centuries*, vol. 2, edited by H. M. Scott, pp. 223–273 (London and New York, 1995).

Dixon, S. *The Modernisation of Russia, 1676–1825*. Cambridge, 1999. Gives a very penetrating analysis of political and intellectual trends.

Eydel'man, N. *Gran' vekov: Politicheskaya bor'ba v Rossii konets XVIII nachalo XIX stoletiia*. (The Turn of the Century: The Political Struggle in Russia between the Eighteenth and Nineteenth Centuries.) Moscow, 1982. A perceptive account of the overthrow of Paul I.

Garrard, John G., ed. *The Eighteenth Century in Russia*. Oxford, 1973. A useful collection of articles on the Enlightenment in Russia.

Hartley, Janet M. *A Social History of the Russian Empire, 1650–1825*. New York and London, 1999. A balanced account.

Hubner, E., J. Kusber, and Peter Nitsche. *Russland zur Zeit Katharinas: Absolutismus, Aufklärung, Pragmatismus*. Cologne, 1998. One of the best collections of articles to celebrate the bicentennial of the death of Catherine II.

Hughes, Lindsey. *Russia in the Age of Peter the Great*. New Haven, Conn., 1998. An up-to-date, scholarly, and wide-ranging treatment.

Kamensky, Aleksandr B. *Ot Petra I do Pavla I*. Moscow, 1999.

Karamzin, Nikolay M. *Memoir on Ancient and Modern Russia*. Translated and edited by Richard Pipes. Cambridge, Mass., 1952.

Lentin, A. *Peter the Great: The Law on the Imperial Succession*. Oxford, 1996. Reproduces the original Russian version of *The Justice of the Monarch's Will*, with translation and useful commentary.

Lopatin, V. S. *Ekaterina II; G. A. Potemkin: Lichnaia perepiska, 1769–1791*. Moscow, 1997. An outstanding contribution to the study of Russia in the age of Catherine II.

MacGrew, R. *Paul I of Russia, 1754–1801*. New York and Oxford, 1992. The only satisfactory treatment in English.

Marker, Gary. *Publishing, Printing and the Origins of Intellectual Life in Russia, 1700–1800*. Princeton, N.J., 1985. A thorough and scholarly treatment.

Martin, Alexander M. *Romantics, Reformers, Reactionaries: Russian Conservative Thought and Politics in the Reign of Alexander I.* DeKalb, Ill., 1997.

Omel'chenko, O. *Zakonnaya monarkhiya.* (Lawful Monarchy.) Moscow, 1993. Pursues the influence of the English constitution on Catherine II's political thought in an innovative way.

Scharf, Claus. *Katharina II: Deutschland, und die Deutschen.* Mainz, Germany, 1995. Discusses German influence on political life and on educational policy and literature.

Scharf, Claus, ed. *Katharina II, Russland und Europa: Beiträge zur internationalen Forschung.* Mainz, Germany, 2001. A major contribution on the bicentenary of Catherine's death.

Sebag Montefiore, Simon. *Prince of Princes: The Life of Potemkin.* London, 2000.

ISABEL DE MADARIAGA

RUYSCH, FREDERIK (1638–1731), Dutch anatomist.

The son of a secretary in the service of the state, Ruysch was born in The Hague (Netherlands) and as a boy was apprenticed to an apothecary's shop. By 1661, he had taken his examinations in pharmacy and was managing an apothecary's shop in his native city. In the same year, he married Marie Post. His daughter, Rachel (1664–1750), helped her father in his old age in making anatomical preparations.

Soon after his marriage, Ruysch began his medical studies at the University of Leiden, although he continued to live in The Hague. When he received his doctorate in medicine in 1664, Ruysch established a medical practice in his native city. In 1665, Ruysch succeeded in demonstrating the presence of valves in the lymphatic vessels. At the end of 1666, Ruysch was nominated *praelector* of anatomy for the surgeon's guild in Amsterdam, a position which he held until his death. He attended the session of the guild on 12 January, and thereafter moved to that city. The position of *praelector* included the teaching of anatomy to apprentice-surgeons in the guild and public anatomical demonstrations. From 1672 to 1712, Ruysch was also city obstetrician; in 1679, he was appointed physician to the Court of Justice and, in 1685, he became professor of botany at the Athenaeum Illustre, thereby becoming the supervisor of the botanical garden. Ruysch was elected a Fellow of the Royal Society of London in 1720, and a member of the Parisian Académie Royale des Sciences in 1727.

Ruysch's main occupation was in the field of anatomy, and he gave private lessons in that field to Dutch and foreign students. He devoted himself to making anatomical preparations, as a master in the technique of preservation; he became famous for his conservation of organs and entire corpses by injecting preserving fluids. His anatomical and zoological cabinet was soon a major attraction for foreign visitors. In 1691, Ruysch edited a catalog of his cabinet in both Dutch and Latin: *Musaeum anatomicum Ruyschianum, sive catalogus rariorum quae in authoris aedibus asservantur*, which had two more printings, in 1721 and in 1737. He described his preparations and findings extensively in a series of ten volumes, *Thesaurus Anatomicus* (1701–1715). In 1717, Peter the Great of Russia bought Ruysch's collection, containing 935 items for 3,000 Dutch *guilders*, and it is still almost intact in the Museum of Anthropology and Ethnography of the Academy of Sciences in Saint Petersburg. By 1727, Ruysch had established another collection, which after his death was sold by public auction. The greater part was bought for August II of Poland, who donated it to the University of Wittenberg.

Ruysch's collection consisted not only of curiosities with medical and scientific significance but also had artistic and, above all, moralistic value. Ruysch was guided by the biblical idea that "all is vanity": he arranged his skeletons with symbols of mortality in their hands, provided with suitable texts. As a result of his observations, and his expertise in the area of organic preservation, Ruysch was one of the founders of eighteenth-century anatomy.

[*See also* Academies; Amsterdam; Botany; Medicine; Midwifery; Natural History; Netherlands; Royal Society of London; Saint Petersburg Academy; *and* Scientific Instruments.]

BIBLIOGRAPHY

Hendrik Engel's Alphabetical List of Dutch Zoological Cabinets and Menageries. 2d enl. edited by Pieter Smit. Amsterdam, 1986. See pages 234–236.

Lindeboom, Gerrit A. "Ruysch, Frederik." In *Dictionary of Scientific Biography*, edited by Charles Coulston Gillispie, vol. 12, pp. 39–42. New York, 1975.

Luyendijk-Elshout, Antoni M. "Death Enlightened. A Study of Frederik Ruysch." *Journal of the American Medical Association* 212 (1970), 121–126.

H. A. M. SNELDERS